- BLOOMSBURY
  CONCISE DICTIONARY
  of QUOTATIONS

• BLOOMSBURY CONCISE DICTIONARY of QUOTATIONS

Anne Stibbs
John Daintith

BLOOMSBURY

First published 1992
This paperback edition first published 1993

Copyright © 1992 by Bloomsbury Publishing
Limited
Bloomsbury Publishing Limited, 2 Soho Square,
London W1V 5DE

Extracts from the Authorized King James
Version of the Bible, which is Crown Copyright,
are reproduced by permission of Eyre and
Spottiswoode, Her Majesty's Printers

A CIP catalogue record for this book is available
from the British Library

ISBN 0-7475 1459 3

Designed by Fielding Rowinski
Compiled by
Market House Books Ltd, Aylesbury
Typeset by
Market House Books Ltd, Aylesbury and
Florencetype Ltd, Kewstoke, Avon
Printed and bound in Great Britain by
Cox & Wyman Ltd, Reading, Berkshire

Contents

• Acknowledgments

Editors

Ruth Salomon
Rosalind Fergusson

Contributors

Fran Alexander
Elizabeth Bonham
Eve Daintith
Alan Isaacs
Amanda Isaacs
Sandra McQueen
Elizabeth Martin
Kate Newman
David Pickering
Kathy Rooney
Jessica Scholes
Gwynneth Shaw
Tracey Smith
Brenda Tomkins
Linda Wells

• Introduction

A quotation is a short passage or phrase from a book, play, poem, speech, etc., especially one that is remembered and repeated because it is particularly perceptive or simply because it is amusing. As Samuel Johnson said in his *Dictionary*

> *Every quotation contributes something to the stability or enlargement of the language.*

Quotations may also tell us something about particular events. We have it on the authority of the Duke of Wellington that the Battle of Waterloo was

> *... a damned nice thing – the nearest run thing you ever saw in your life ...*

And they may tell us something about the author or speaker. The comedian Kenneth Williams has pointed out that quotes

> *...give us a nodding acquaintance with the originator which is often socially impressive.*

In this book we have selected about 6500 quotations that we hope will be useful. The main arrangement is under thematic categories – Absence, Abstinence, Academics, etc. These contain quotations that are about particular topics. A few categories contain quotations that are examples of a theme – for example Epitaphs and Last Words.

In addition we have included about 115 biographical entries, alphabetized according to the surname of the author or speaker. Typically, these entries consist of a short biography followed by a few quotations about the author. These are then followed by a representative selection of quotations by the author. In choosing biographical entries we have been guided solely by how quotable the author is, irrespective of literary or other merit.

Throughout the book a network of cross references directs the user to related entries. A full list of themes is given in the front the book.

Under a given thematic heading the quotations are arranged in alphabetical order of speaker or writer (by surname). Where the same author has more than one quotation, they are arranged in alphabetical order of the references. In the case of biographical entries, the quotations **about** the author are ordered according to the name of the person making the remark. Quotations **by** the author are arranged according to the references. First come the author's own works in alphabetical order (but ignoring the 'A' or 'The'). Then follow works by other people in which the subject is quoted, again in alpha order. Finally, we give extracts from speeches, letters, etc., which are generally arranged in date order.

Every effort has been made to find reliable references for all the quotations in the book, although there are a few cases in which this has not been possible. Some quotations are widely attributed to an author, in which case the reference is given as 'Attrib'. In fact, there are examples, as in the case of Samuel Goldwyn, in which the remarks were almost certainly never made by the person to whom they are attributed. Nevertheless, we decided to include these, if only because they are too good to leave out. Some quotations are attributed to two or more people. In these cases, we have added explanatory notes to the reference. Another problem is exemplified by Mae West. Many of her sayings are lines from films and, strictly, the author is the screenwriter. However, they are so closely associated with her that we have included them under her name.

The book contains two indexes:

A **Keyword index** contains phrases listed under key words in the quotation. It enables the user to locate a half-remembered quotation to find the exact wording or the author or reference.

A **Names index** lists all the pople quoted in the book. Names printed in bold type are of authors who have biographical entries.

In both indexes, reference is to the headword and to the quotation number under that headword (not to the page number).

The arrangement of the book and the indexes are designed to make this dictionary a useful reference and source of quotations. As Dorothy Parker once said

> *I might repeat to myself...a list of quotations from minds profound – if I can remember any of the damn things.*

We hope that this book will help jog the memory as well as providing an informative and enjoyable selection through which to browse.

AS, JD

• List of Subjects

ABSENCE
ABSTINENCE
ACADEMICS
ACCIDENTS
ACCUSATION
ACHIEVEMENT
ACTING
ACTION
ACTORS
ADAPTABILITY
ADDICTION
ADMIRATION
ADULTERY
ADVERTISING
ADVICE
AFTERLIFE
AGE
AGREEMENT
AIDS
ALCOHOL
AMBITION
AMERICA
AMERICANS
ANCESTRY
ANGER
ANIMALISM
ANIMALS
APOLOGIES
APPEARANCE
APPEARANCES
ARCHITECTURE
ARGUMENTS
ARISTOCRACY
ARMY
ART
ARTISTS
ARTS
ASSASSINATION
ASTRONOMY
ATHEISM
AUTHORITARIAN-
ISM
AUTUMN
BABIES
BEAUTY
BED
BEGINNING

BELIEF
BEQUESTS
BETRAYAL
BIBLE
BIOGRAPHY
BIRTH
BITTERNESS
BLESSING
BLINDNESS
BOATS
BOOKS
BOREDOM
BORES
BORROWING
BREVITY
BRIBERY
BRITAIN
BRITISH
BRITISH EMPIRE
BUREAUCRACY
BUSINESS
CAMBRIDGE
CANNIBALISM
CAPITALISM
CATHOLICISM
CATS
CAUTION
CENSORSHIP
CERTAINTY
CHANGE
CHARACTER
CHARITY
CHARM
CHILDREN
CHIVALRY
CHOICE
CHRISTIANITY
CHRISTMAS
CHURCH
CINEMA
CIVILIZATION
CLASS
CLASSICS
CLASSIFICATION
CLEANNESS
CLERGY
CLOTHES

COLD WAR
COMFORT
COMMITMENT
COMMUNISM
COMPLAINTS
COMPLIMENTS
COMPROMISE
CONCEIT
CONFLICT
CONFORMITY
CONFUSION
CONSCIENCE
CONSERVATION
CONSERVATISM
CONSTANCY
CONTENTMENT
CONTRACEPTION
CONVERSATION
CORRUPTION
COUNTRYSIDE
COURAGE
COURTESY
COWARDICE
CREATION
CRICKET
CRIME
CRITICISM
CRITICS
CRUELTY
CULTURE
CURIOSITY
CURSES
CUSTOM
CYNICISM
DAMNATION
DANGER
DAY
DEATH
DEBAUCHERY
DECEPTION
DECISION
DECLINE
DEFEAT
DELUSION
DEMOCRACY
DEPARTURE
DESIGN

DESIRE
DESPAIR
DESTINY
DETERMINATION
DEVIL
DIARIES
DIPLOMACY
DISAPPOINT-
MENT
DISASTER
DISCONTENT
DISCOVERY
DISEASE
DISILLUSION
DISMISSAL
DOCTORS
DOGS
DOOMSDAY
DOUBT
DREAMS
DRINKS
DROWNING
DRUGS
DRUNKENNESS
DUTY
ECOLOGY
ECONOMICS
EDITORS
EDUCATION
EFFORT
EGOTISM
EMBARRASS-
MENT
EMOTION
ENDING
ENDURANCE
ENEMIES
ENGLAND
ENGLISH
ENTHUSIASM
ENVIRONMENT
ENVY
EPITAPHS
EQUALITY
ETERNITY
ETIQUETTE
EUROPE

x

A

□ABSENCE□

See also separation

1 Absence makes the heart grow fonder,
Isle of Beauty, Fare thee well!
Thomas Haynes Bayly (1797–1839) British writer.
Isle of Beauty

2 Absence is to love what wind is to fire; it extinguishes the small, it inflames the great.
Bussy-Rabutin (Roger de Rabutin, Comte de Bussy; 1618–93)
French soldier and writer.
Histoire amoureuse des Gaules

3 Why art thou silent! Is thy love a plant
Of such weak fibre that the treacherous air
Of absence withers what was once so fair?
William Wordsworth (1770–1850) British poet.
Miscellaneous Sonnets, III

□ABSTINENCE□

See also alcohol, self-denial, sex, smoking

1 He neither drank, smoked, nor rode a bicycle.
Living frugally, saving his money, he died early,
surrounded by greedy relatives. It was a great
lesson to me.
John Barrymore (1882–1942) US actor.
The Stage, Jan 1941 (J. P. McEvoy)

2 If someone asks for a soft drink at a party, we no
longer think he is a wimp.
Edwina Currie (1946–) British politician.
Speech, Dec 1988

3 Teetotallers lack the sympathy and generosity of
men that drink.
W. H. Davies (1871–1940) British poet.
Shorter Lyrics of the 20th Century, Introduction

4 It was a brilliant affair; water flowed like champagne.
William M. Evarts (1818–1901) US lawyer and statesman.
Describing a dinner given by US President Rutherford B. Hayes
(1877–81), an advocate of temperance
Attrib.

5 If you resolve to give up smoking, drinking and
loving, you don't actually live longer; it just
seems longer.
Clement Freud (1924–) British Liberal politician and
broadcaster.
The Observer, 27 Dec 1964

6 Mr Mercaptan went on to preach a brilliant sermon on that melancholy sexual perversion
known as continence.
Aldous Huxley (1894–1964) British novelist.
Antic Hay, Ch. 18

7 My experience through life has convinced
me that, while moderation and temperance in
all things are commendable and beneficial,
abstinence from spirituous liquors is the best
safeguard of morals and health.
Robert E. Lee (1807–70) US general.
Letter, 9 Dec 1869

8 The few bad poems which occasionally are created during abstinence are of no great interest.
Wilhelm Reich (1897–1957) Austrian-born US psychiatrist.
The Sexual Revolution

9 The people who are regarded as moral luminaries are those who forego ordinary pleasures
themselves and find compensation in interfering
with the pleasures of others.
Bertrand Russell (1872–1970) British philosopher.
Sceptical Essays

10 Lastly (and this is, perhaps, the golden rule), no
woman should marry a teetotaller, or a man who
does not smoke.
Robert Louis Stevenson (1850–94) Scottish writer.
Virginibus Puerisque

11 Though in silence, with blighted affection, I pine,
Yet the lips that touch liquor must never touch
mine!
G. W. Young (19th century) British writer.
The Lips That Touch Liquor

□ACADEMICS□

See also education, intellectuals

1 A professor is one who talks in someone else's
sleep.
W. H. Auden (1907–73) British poet.
Attrib.

2 First come I; my name is Jowett.
There's no knowledge but I know it.
I am Master of this college:
What I don't know isn't knowledge.
H. C. Beeching (1859–1919) British academic.
Referring to Benjamin Jowett, master of Balliol College, Oxford
The Masque of Balliol

3 It's no use trying to be *clever* – we are all clever
here; just try to be *kind* – a little kind.
F. J. Foakes Jackson (1855–1941) British academic.
Advice given to a new don at Jesus College, Cambridge
Noted in A. C. Benson's Commonplace Book

4 Like so many ageing college people, Pnin had
long ceased to notice the existence of students
on the campus.
Vladimir Nabokov (1899–1977) Russian-born US novelist.
Pnin, Ch. 3

5 I am the Dean of Christ Church, Sir:
There's my wife; look well at her.

She's the Broad and I'm the High;
We are the University.
Cecil Arthur Spring-Rice (1859–1918) British diplomat.
The Masque of Balliol

□ACCIDENTS□

See also disaster, misfortune

1 The Act of God designation on all insurance poli-
cies; which means, roughly, that you cannot be
insured for the accidents that are most likely to
happen to you.
Alan Coren (1938–   ) British humorist and writer.
The Lady from Stalingrad Mansions, 'A Short History of
Insurance'

2 Accidents will occur in the best-regulated fami-
lies.
Charles Dickens (1812–70) British novelist.
David Copperfield, Ch. 28

3 O Diamond! Diamond! thou little knowest the
mischief done!
Isaac Newton (1642–1727) British scientist.
Said to a dog that set fire to some papers, representing several
years' work, by knocking over a candle
Wensley-Dale…a Poem (Thomas Maude)

4 The chapter of accidents is the longest chapter in
the book.
John Wilkes (1725–97) British politician.
Attrib. in *The Doctor* (Southey), Vol. IV

□ACCUSATION□

See also responsibility

1 I do not know the method of drawing up an indict-
ment against an whole people.
Edmund Burke (1729–97) British politician.
Speech on Conciliation with America (House of Commons, 22
Mar 1775)

2 *J'accuse.*
I accuse.
Émile Zola (1840–1902) French novelist.
Title of an open letter to the French President, denouncing the
French army's conduct in the Dreyfus affair
L'Aurore, 13 Jan 1898

□ACHIEVEMENT□

See also effort, success

1 Our greatest glory is not in never falling, but in
rising every time we fall.
Confucius (K'ung Fu-tzu; 551–479 BC) Chinese philosopher.
Analects

2 One never notices what has been done; one can
only see what remains to be done.
Marie Curie (1867–1934) Polish chemist.
Letter to her brother, 18 Mar 1894

3 We never do anything well till we cease to think
about the manner of doing it.
William Hazlitt (1778–1830) British essayist.
On Prejudice

4 For, as I suppose, no man in this world hath lived
better than I have done, to achieve that I have
done.
Thomas Malory (1400–71) English writer.
Morte d'Arthur, Bk. XVII, Ch. 16

5 Log-cabin to White House.
W. M. Thayer (1820–98) US writer.
The title of his biography of James Garfield, US president

6 To achieve great things we must live as though
we were never going to die.
Marquis de Vauvenargues (1715–47) French soldier and
writer.
Réflexions et maximes

□ACTING□

See also action, actors, cinema, criticism, plays, theatre

1 Theatre director: a person engaged by the management to conceal the fact that the players cannot act.
James Agate (1877–1947) British theatre critic.
Attrib.

2 It's not whether you really cry. It's whether the
audience thinks you are crying.
Ingrid Bergman (1915–1982) Swedish film and stage actress.
Halliwell's Filmgoer's and Video Viewer's Companion

3 Pray to God and say the lines.
Bette Davis (Ruth Elizabeth Davis; 1908–89) US film star.
Advice to the actress Celeste Holm
Attrib.

4 It is. But not as hard as farce.
Edmund Gwenn (1875–1959) British actor.
On his deathbed, in reply to the comment 'It must be very hard'
Time, 30 Jan 1984

5 Acting is therefore the lowest of the arts, if it is an
art at all.
George Moore (1852–1933) Irish writer and art critic.
Mummer-Worship

6 The art of acting consists in keeping people from
coughing.
Ralph Richardson (1902–83) British actor.
The Observer

7 Imagination! imagination! I put it first years ago,
when I was asked what qualities I thought necessary for success upon the stage.
Ellen Terry (1847–1928) British actress.
The Story of My Life, Ch. 2

8 Ladies, just a little more virginity, if you don't
mind.
Herbert Beerbohm Tree (1853–1917) British actor and
theatre manager.
Directing a group of sophisticated actresses
Smart Aleck (H. Teichmann)

□ ACTION □

See also acting

1 Footprints on the sands of time are not made by sitting down.
   Proverb

2 Let's meet, and either do, or die.
   Francis Beaumont (1584–1616) English dramatist
   The Island Princess, II:2

3 Deliberation is the work of many men. Action, of one alone.
   Charles De Gaulle (1890–1970) French general and statesman.
   War Memoirs, Vol. 2

4 Suit the action to the word, the word to the action; with this special observance, that you o'erstep not the modesty of nature.
   William Shakespeare (1564–1616) English dramatist.
   Hamlet, III:2

5 So many worlds, so much to do,
   So little done, such things to be.
   Alfred, Lord Tennyson (1809–92) British poet.
   In Memoriam A.H.H., LXXIII

□ ACTORS □

See also acting, cinema, criticism, plays, theatre

1 An actor's a guy who, if you ain't talking about him, ain't listening.
   Marlon Brando (1924–) US film star.
   The Observer, 'Sayings of the Year', Jan 1956

2 An actor is something less than a man, while an actress is something more than a woman.
   Richard Burton (Richard Jenkins; 1925–84) British actor.
   Halliwell's Filmgoer's and Video Viewer's Companion

3 Never meddle with play-actors, for they're a favoured race.
   Miguel de Cervantes (1547–1616) Spanish novelist.
   Don Quixote, Pt. II, Ch. 11

4 Remember you are a star. Never go across the alley even to dump garbage unless you are dressed to the teeth.
   Cecil B. de Mille (1881–1959) US film producer and director.
   Halliwell's Filmgoer's and Video Viewer's Companion

5 Actors should be treated like cattle.
   Alfred Hitchcock (1889–1980) British film director.
   Said in clarification of a remark attributed to him, 'Actors are like cattle'
   Quote, Unquote (N. Rees)

6 At one time I thought he wanted to be an actor. He had certain qualifications, including no money and a total lack of responsibility.
   Hedda Hopper (1890–1966) US writer.
   From Under My Hat

7 They didn't act like people and they didn't act like actors. It's hard to explain. They acted more like they knew they were celebrities and all. I mean they were good, but they were *too* good.
   J. D. Salinger (1919–) US novelist.
   The Catcher in the Rye, Ch. 17

□ ADAPTABILITY □

See also change

1 Remember that to change your mind and follow him who sets you right is to be none the less free than you were before.
   Marcus Aurelius (121–180 AD) Roman emperor.
   Meditations, Bk. VIII, Ch. 16

2 Mahomet made the people believe that he would call a hill to him…when the hill stood still, he was never a whit abashed, but said, 'If the hill will not come to Mahomet, Mahomet will go to the hill.'
   Francis Bacon (1561–1626) English philosopher.
   Often misquoted as 'If the mountain will not come to Mohammed'
   Essays, 'Of Boldness'

3 President Robbins was so well adjusted to his environment that sometimes you could not tell which was the environment and which was President Robbins.
   Randall Jarrell (1914–65) US author.
   Pictures from an Institution, Pt. I, Ch. 4

4 As time requireth, a man of marvellous mirth and pastimes, and sometimes of as sad gravity, as who say: a man for all seasons.
   Robert Whittington (16th century) English writer.
   Referring to Sir Thomas More, after Erasmus
   Vulgaria, Pt. II, 'De constructione nominum'

□ ADDICTION □

1 Cocaine isn't habit-forming. I should know – I've been using it for years.
   Tallulah Bankhead (1903–68) US actress.
   Pentimento (Lillian Hellman), 'Theatre'

2 Every form of addiction is bad, no matter whether the narcotic be alcohol or morphine or idealism.
   Carl Gustav Jung (1875–1961) Swiss psychoanalyst.
   Memories, Dreams, Reflections, Ch. 12

□ ADDISON □
Joseph

(1672–1719) British essayist. A Whig politician, he entered parliament in 1708. Addison contributed numerous essays to the *Tatler* and was cofounder (with Richard Steele) of *The Spectator* (1711).

QUOTATIONS ABOUT ADDISON

1 Whoever wishes to attain an English style, familiar but not coarse and elegant but not ostentatious, must give his days and nights to the volumes of Addison.
   Samuel Johnson (1709–84) British lexicographer.
   Lives of the Poets

2 'Tis not in mortals to command success,
But we'll do more, Sempronius; we'll deserve it.
Cato, I:2

3 The woman that deliberates is lost.
Cato, IV:1

4 What pity is it
That we can die but once to serve our country!
Cato, IV:4

5 *Sir Roger* told them, with the air of a man who
would not give his judgment rashly, that 'much
might be said on both sides'.
Sir Roger de Coverley was a fictional archetype of the old-fashioned and eccentric country squire.
The Spectator, 122

6 We are always doing something for posterity, but
I would fain see posterity do something for us.
The Spectator, 583

7 See in what peace a Christian can die.
Last words

□ADMIRATION□

1 A fool always finds a greater fool to admire him.
Nicolas Boileau (1636–1711) French writer.
L'Art poétique, I

2 I do think better of womankind than to suppose
they care whether Mister John Keats five feet
high likes them or not.
John Keats (1795–1821) British poet.
Letter to Benjamin Bailey, 18 July 1818

3 Many a man has been a wonder to the world,
whose wife and valet have seen nothing in him
that was even remarkable. Few men have been
admired by their servants.
Michel de Montaigne (1533–92) French essayist.
Essais, III

4 Not to admire, is all the art I know
To make men happy, and to keep them so.
Alexander Pope (1688–1744) British poet.
Imitations of Horace, 'To Mr. Murray'

5 Age cannot wither her, nor custom stale
Her infinite variety. Other women cloy
The appetites they feed, but she makes hungry
Where most she satisfies.
William Shakespeare (1564–1616) English dramatist.
Antony and Cleopatra, II:2

6 'A was a man, take him for all in all,
I shall not look upon his like again.
William Shakespeare
Hamlet, I:2

7 He was a great patriot, a humanitarian, a loyal
friend – provided, of course, that he really is
dead.
Voltaire (François-Marie Arouet; 1694–1778) French writer.
Giving a funeral oration
Attrib.

8 The sweetest thing that ever grew
Beside a human door!
William Wordsworth (1770–1850) British poet.
Lucy Gray

□ADULTERY□

See also marriage, sex, unfaithfulness

1 What men call gallantry, and gods adultery,
Is much more common where the climate's sultry.
Lord Byron (1788–1824) British poet.
Don Juan, I

2 I have looked on a lot of women with lust. I've
committed adultery in my heart many times.
God recognises I will do this and forgives me.
Jimmy Carter (1924–) US statesman and president.
Remark

3 Sara could commit adultery at one end and weep
for her sins at the other, and enjoy both operations at once.
Joyce Cary (1888–1957) British novelist.
The Horse's Mouth, Ch. 8

4 I say I don't sleep with married men, but what I
mean is that I don't sleep with happily married
men.
Britt Ekland (1942–) Swedish film actress.
Attrib.

5 You know, of course, that the Tasmanians, who
never committed adultery, are now extinct.
W. Somerset Maugham (1874–1965) British novelist.
The Bread-Winner

6 Madame, you must really be more careful. Suppose it had been someone else who found you
like this.
Duc de Richelieu (1766–1822) French statesman.
Discovering his wife with her lover
The Book of Lists (D. Wallechinsky)

7 With all my heart. Whose wife shall it be?
John Horne Tooke (1736–1812) British clergyman, politician,
and etymologist.
Replying to the suggestion that he take a wife
Attrib.

□ADVERTISING□

1 It pays to advertise.
Anonymous
Already current by c. 1912 when Cole Porter used it as the title of
an early song

2 Advertising is the most fun you can have with your clothes on.
Jerry Della Femina (1936-) Advertising executive.
From those wonderful folks who gave you Pearl Harbor

3 Half the money I spend on advertising is wasted, and the trouble is I don't know which half.
Viscount Leverhulme (1851–1925) British industrialist.
Confessions of an Advertising Man (D. Ogilvy)

4 The consumer isn't a moron; she is your wife. You insult her intelligence if you assume that a mere slogan and a few vapid adjectives will persuade her to buy anything.
David Ogilvy (1911-) British businessman.
Confessions of an Advertising Man, Ch. 5

5 Freedom of the press in Britain is freedom to print such of the proprietor's prejudices as the advertisers don't object to.
Hannen Swaffer (1879–1962) British journalist.
Attrib.

□ADVICE□

1 Advice is seldom welcome; and those who want it the most always like it the least.
Earl of Chesterfield (1694–1773) English statesman.
Letter to his son, 29 Jan 1748

2 I intended to give you some advice but now I remember how much is left over from last year unused.
George Harris (1844–1922) US congressman.
Said when addressing students at the start of a new academic year
Braude's Second Encyclopedia (J. Braude)

3 On my twenty-first birthday my father said, 'Son, here's a million dollars. Don't lose it.'
Larry Niven (1938-) US science-fiction writer.
When asked 'What is the best advice you have ever been given?'
Attrib.

4 One gives nothing so freely as advice.
Duc de la Rochefoucauld (1613–80) French writer.
Maximes, 110

5 Don't tell your friends their social faults, they will cure the fault and never forgive you.
Logan Pearsall Smith (1865–1946) US writer.
Afterthoughts

6 No one wants advice – only corroboration.
John Steinbeck (1902–68) US novelist.

7 It's queer how ready people always are with advice in any real or imaginary emergency, and no matter how many times experience has shown them to be wrong, they continue to set forth their opinions, as if they had received them from the Almighty!
Annie Sullivan (1866–1936) US teacher of the handicapped.
Letter, 12 June 1887

8 I have lived some thirty years on this planet, and I have yet to hear the first syllable of valuable or even earnest advice from my seniors.
Henry David Thoreau (1817–62) US writer.
Walden, 'Economy'

9 Are you in trouble? Do you need advice? Write to Miss Lonelyhearts and she will help.
Nathaniel West (Nathan Weinstein; 1903–40) US novelist.
Miss Lonelyhearts

□AFTERLIFE□
See also death, heaven

1 CLOV. Do you believe in the life to come?
HAMM. Mine was always that.
Samuel Beckett (1906–89) Irish novelist and dramatist.
Endgame

2 That which is the foundation of all our hopes and of all our fears; all our hopes and fears which are of any consideration: I mean a Future Life.
Joseph Butler (1692–1752) British churchman.
The Analogy of Religion, Introduction

3 We have no reliable guarantee that the afterlife will be any less exasperating than this one, have we?
Noël Coward (1899–1973) British dramatist.
Blithe Spirit, I

4 We sometimes congratulate ourselves at the moment of waking from a troubled dream; it may be so the moment after death.
Nathaniel Hawthorne (1804–64) US novelist and writer.
American Notebooks

5 Is there another life? Shall I awake and find all this a dream? There must be, we cannot be created for this sort of suffering.
John Keats (1795–1821) British poet.
Letter, 1820

6 My doctrine is: Live that thou mayest desire to live again – that is thy duty – for in any case thou wilt live again!
Friedrich Wilhelm Nietzsche (1844–1900) German philosopher.
Eternal Recurrence

7 After your death you will be what you were before your birth.
Arthur Schopenhauer (1788–1860) German philosopher.
Parerga and Paralipomena

8 The dread of something after death –
The undiscover'd country, from whose bourn
No traveller returns.
William Shakespeare (1564–1616) English dramatist.
Hamlet, III:1

9 I am going a long way
With these thou seest – if indeed I go
(For all my mind is clouded with a doubt) –
To the island-valley of Avilion;

Where falls not hail, or rain, or any snow,
Nor ever wind blows loudly; but it lies
Deep-meadow'd, happy, fair with orchard lawns
And bowery hollows crown'd with summer sea,
Where I will heal me of my grievous wound.
Alfred, Lord Tennyson (1809–92) British poet.
Idylls of the King, 'The Passing of Arthur'

10 One world at a time.
Henry David Thoreau (1817–62) US writer.
On being asked his opinion of the hereafter
Attrib.

□ AGE □

See also longevity, old age, youth

1 I am past thirty, and three parts iced over.
Matthew Arnold (1822–88) British poet and critic.
Letter to A. H. Clough, 12 Feb 1853

2 A man that is young in years may be old in hours,
if he have lost no time.
Francis Bacon (1561–1626) English philosopher.
Essays, 'Of Youth and Age'

3 The only thing I regret about my past life is the
length of it. If I had my past life over again I'd
make all the same mistakes – only sooner.
Tallulah Bankhead (1903–68) US actress.
The Times, 28 July 1981

4 What is an adult? A child blown up by age.
Simone de Beauvoir (1908–86) French writer.
La Femme rompue

5 If thou hast gathered nothing in thy youth, how
canst thou find any thing in thine age?
Bible: Ecclesiasticus
25:3

6 No man also having drunk old wine straightway
desireth new: for he saith, The old is better.
Bible: Luke
5:39

7 Old age is … a lot of crossed off names in an
address book.
Ronald Blythe (1922–   ) British author.
The View in Winter

8 Being now come to the years of discretion.
The Book of Common Prayer
Order of Confirmation

9 Therefore I summon age
To grant youth's heritage.
Robert Browning (1812–89) British poet.
Rabbi ben Ezra, XIII

10 Ah well, perhaps one has to be very old before
one learns how to be amused rather than
shocked.
Pearl Buck (1892–1973) US novelist.
China, Past and Present, Ch. 6

11 A lady of a 'certain age', which means
Certainly aged.
Lord Byron (1788–1824) British poet.
Don Juan, VI

12 A man is as old as he's feeling,
A woman as old as she looks.
Mortimer Collins (1827–76) British writer.
The Unknown Quantity

13 Youth is a blunder; manhood a struggle; old age
a regret.
Benjamin Disraeli (1804–81) British statesman.
Coningsby, Bk. III, Ch. 1

14 I am resolved to grow fat and look young till
forty, and then slip out of the world with the first
wrinkle and the reputation of five-and-twenty.
John Dryden (1631–1700) British poet and dramatist.
The Maiden Queen, III

15 Men are but children of a larger growth;
Our appetites as apt to change as theirs,
And full as craving too, and full as vain.
John Dryden
All for Love, IV

16 The years between fifty and seventy are the hardest. You are always being asked to do things, and
you are not yet decrepit enough to turn them
down.
T. S. Eliot (1888–1965) US-born British poet and dramatist.
Time, 23 Oct 1950

17 Here I am, an old man in a dry month,
Being read to by a boy, waiting for rain.
T. S. Eliot
Gerontion

18 *Si jeunesse savait; si vieillesse pouvait.*
If only youth knew, if only age could.
Henri Estienne (1528–98) French scholar.
Les Prémices

19 At sixteen I was stupid, confused, insecure
and indecisive. At twenty-five I was wise, self-
confident, prepossessing and assertive. At forty-
five I am stupid, confused, insecure and indecisive. Who would have supposed that maturity is
only a short break in adolescence?
Jules Feiffer (1929–   ) US writer, cartoonist, and humorist.
The Observer, 3 Feb 1974

20 At twenty years of age, the will reigns; at thirty,
the wit; and at forty, the judgement.
Benjamin Franklin (1706–90) US scientist and statesman.
Poor Richard's Almanack

21 A diplomat is a man who always remembers a
woman's birthday but never remembers her age.
Robert Frost (1875–1963) US poet.
Attrib.

22 She may very well pass for forty-three
In the dusk, with a light behind her!
W. S. Gilbert (1836–1911) British dramatist.
Trial by Jury

23 You will recognize, my boy, the first sign of old
age: it is when you go out into the streets of London and realize for the first time how young the
policemen look.
Seymour Hicks (1871–1949) British actor-manager.
They Were Singing (C. Pulling)

24 Whenever a man's friends begin to compliment
him about looking young, he may be sure that
they think he is growing old.
Washington Irving (1783–1859) US writer.
Bracebridge Hall, 'Bachelors'

25 I am just turning forty and taking my time about
it.
Harold Lloyd (1893–1971) US silent-film comedian.
Reply when, aged 77, he was asked his age
The Times, 23 Sept 1970

26 But at my back I always hear
Time's winged chariot hurrying near;
And yonder all before us lie
Deserts of vast eternity.
Andrew Marvell (1621–78) English poet.
To His Coy Mistress

27 A man is only as old as the woman he feels.
Groucho Marx (Julius Marx; 1895–1977) US comedian.
Attrib.

28 How soon hath Time, the subtle thief of youth,
Stolen on his wing my three-and-twentieth year!
John Milton (1608–74) English poet.
Sonnet: 'On Being Arrived at the Age of Twenty-three'

29 Do you think my mind is maturing late,
Or simply rotted early?
Ogden Nash (1902–71) US poet.
Lines on Facing Forty

30 At 50, everyone has the face he deserves.
George Orwell (Eric Blair; 1903–50) British novelist.
Last words in his manuscript notebook, 17 Apr 1949

31 Each generation imagines itself to be more intelligent than the one that went before it, and wiser
than the one that comes after it.
George Orwell
Book Review

32 One of the pleasures of middle age is to *find out*
that one WAS right, and that one was much
righter than one knew at say 17 or 23.
Ezra Pound (1885–1972) US poet.
ABC of Reading, Ch. 1

33 You know, by the time you reach my age, you've
made plenty of mistakes if you've lived your life
properly
Ronald Reagan (1911–) US politician and president.
The Observer, 'Sayings of the Week', 8 Mar 1987

34 The young have aspirations that never come to
pass, the old have reminiscences of what never
happened.
Saki (Hector Hugh Munro; 1870–1916) British writer.
Reginald at the Carlton

35 When I was young, I was told: 'You'll see, when
you're fifty. I am fifty and I haven't seen a thing.
Erik Satie (1866–1925) French composer.
From a letter to his brother
Erik Satie (Pierre-Daniel Templier), Ch. 1

36 Doth not the appetite alter? A man loves the meat
in his youth that he cannot endure in his age.
William Shakespeare (1564–1616) English dramatist.
Much Ado About Nothing, II:3

37 Crabbed age and youth cannot live together:
Youth is full of pleasure, age is full of care;
Youth like summer morn, age like winter
weather;
Youth like summer brave, age like winter bare.
William Shakespeare
The Passionate Pilgrim, XII

38 All that the young can do for the old is to shock
them and keep them up to date.
George Bernard Shaw (1856–1950) Irish dramatist and critic.
Fanny's First Play

39 It's a funny thing about that bust. As time goes on
it seems to get younger and younger.
George Bernard Shaw
Referring to a portrait bust sculpted for him by Rodin
More Things I Wish I'd Said (K. Edwards)

40 One's prime is elusive. You little girls, when you
grow up, must be on the alert to recognize your
prime at whatever time of your life it may occur.
You must then live it to the full.
Muriel Spark (1918–) British novelist.
The Prime of Miss Jean Brodie, Ch. 1

41 I was born old and get younger every day. At
present I am sixty years young.
Herbert Beerbohm Tree (1853–1917) British actor and
theatre manager.
Beerbohm Tree (Hesketh Pearson)

42 Life begins at forty.
Sophie Tucker (Sophia Abuza; 1884–1966) Russian-born US
singer.
Attrib.

43 From birth to age eighteen, a girl needs good parents. From eighteen to thirty-five, she needs
good looks. From thirty-five to fifty-five, she

needs a good personality. From fifty-five on, she needs good cash.
Sophie Tucker
Attrib.

44 One should never trust a woman who tells one her real age. A woman who would tell one that, would tell one anything.
Oscar Wilde (1854–1900) British dramatist.
A Woman of No Importance, I

45 My heart leaps up when I behold
A rainbow in the sky:
So was it when my life began;
So is it now I am a man;
So be it when I shall grow old,
Or let me die!
The Child is Father of the Man;
And I could wish my days to be
Bound each to each by natural piety.
William Wordsworth (1770–1850) British poet.
My Heart Leaps Up

46 Be wise with speed,
A fool at forty is a fool indeed.
Edward Young (1683–1765) British poet.
Love of Fame, II

☐ AGREEMENT ☐

1 I am always of the opinion with the learned, if they speak first.
William Congreve (1670–1729) British Restoration dramatist.
Incognita

2 We seldom attribute common sense except to those who agree with us.
Duc de la Rochefoucauld (1613–80) French writer.
Maximes, 347

3 Our agenda is now exhausted. The secretary general is exhausted. All of you are exhausted. I find it comforting that, beginning with our very first day, we find ourselves in such complete unanimity.
Paul Henri Spaak (1899–1972) Belgian statesman.
Concluding the first General Assembly meeting of the United Nations

4 Ah! don't say you agree with me. When people agree with me I always feel that I must be wrong.
Oscar Wilde (1854–1900) Irish-born British dramatist.
The Critic as Artist, Pt. 2

5 If two men on the same job agree all the time, then one is useless. If they disagree all the time, then both are useless.
Darryl F. Zanuck (1902–79) US film producer.
The Observer, 'Sayings of the Week', 23 Oct 1949

☐ AIDS ☐

1 Everywhere I go I see increasing evidence of people swirling about in a human cesspit of their own making.
James Anderton (1932–) British Chief Constable of Greater Manchester.
Referring to AIDS

2 It could be said that the Aids pandemic is a classic own-goal scored by the human race against itself.
Princess Anne (1950–) The Princess Royal, only daughter of Elizabeth II.
Remark, Jan 1988

3 My message to the businessman of this country when they go abroad on business is that there is one thing above all they can take with them to stop them catching AIDS, and that is the wife.
Edwina Currie (1946–) British politician.
The Observer, 15 Feb 1987

4 Every time you sleep with a boy you sleep with all his old girlfriends.
Government-sponsored AIDS advertisement, 1987

5 Sex is on the up. All this hooplah about Aids is rubbish. People I know rarely wear condoms. If it was true that Aids was a threat, swingers would be dropping like flies.
Robert McGinley US president of North America Swing Clubs Association.
The Sunday Times, 14 June 1992

☐ ALCOHOL ☐

See also abstinence, drinks, drunkenness, public houses

1 If all be true that I do think,
There are five reasons we should drink;
Good wine – a friend – or being dry –
Or lest we should be by and by –
Or any other reason why.
Dean Aldrich (1647–1710) English poet.
Reasons for Drinking

2 So who's in a hurry?
Robert Benchley (1889–1945) US humorist.
When asked whether he knew that drinking was a slow death
Attrib.

3 Woe unto them that rise up early in the morning, that they may follow strong drink; that continue until night, till wine inflame them!
Bible: Isaiah
5:11

4 Drink no longer water, but use a little wine for thy stomach's sake and thine often infirmities.
Bible: I Timothy
5:23

5 No man also having drunk old wine straightway desireth new: for he saith, The old is better.
Bible: Luke
5:39

6 Look not thou upon the wine when it is red, when it giveth his colour in the cup, when it moveth itself aright.
At the last it biteth like a serpent, and stingeth like an adder.
Bible: Proverbs
23:31–32

7 If we heard it said of Orientals that they habitually drank a liquor which went to their heads, deprived them of reason and made them vomit, we should say: 'How very barbarous!'
Jean de La Bruyère (1645–96) French satirist.
Les Caractères

8 The heart which grief hath cankered
Hath one unfailing remedy – the Tankard.
C. S. Calverley (1831–84) British poet.
Beer

9 Alcohol is like love: the first kiss is magic, the second is intimate, the third is routine. After that you just take the girl's clothes off.
Raymond Chandler (1888–1959) US novelist.
The Long Good-bye

10 So was hir joly whistle wel y-wet.
Geoffrey Chaucer (c. 1342–1400) English poet.
The Canterbury Tales, 'The Reve's Tale'

11 First you take a drink, then the drink takes a drink, then the drink takes you.
F. Scott Fitzgerald (1896–1940) US novelist.
Ackroyd (Jules Feiffer), '1964, May 7'

12 Best while you have it use your breath,
There is no drinking after death.
John Fletcher (1579–1625) English dramatist.
With Jonson and others
The Bloody Brother, II:2

13 And he that will go to bed sober,
Falls with the leaf still in October.
John Fletcher
The Bloody Brother, II:2

14 Let schoolmasters puzzle their brain,
With grammar, and nonsense, and learning,
Good liquor, I stoutly maintain,
Gives genius a better discerning.
Oliver Goldsmith (1728–74) Irish-born British writer.
She Stoops to Conquer, I

15 He that goes to bed thirsty rises healthy.
George Herbert (1593–1633) English poet.
Jacula Prudentum

16 Malt does more than Milton can
To justify God's ways to man.
A. E. Housman (1859–1936) British scholar and poet.
A Shropshire Lad, 'The Welsh Marches'

17 Claret is the liquor for boys; port for men; but he who aspires to be a hero must drink brandy.
Samuel Johnson (1709–84) British lexicographer.
Life of Johnson (J. Boswell), Vol. III

18 Come, let me know what it is that makes a Scotchman happy!
Samuel Johnson
Ordering for himself a glass of whisky
Tour to the Hebrides (J. Boswell)

19 O, for a draught of vintage! that hath been
Cool'd a long age in the deep-delved earth.
John Keats (1795–1821) British poet.
Ode to a Nightingale

20 O for a beaker full of the warm South,
Full of the true, the blushful Hippocrene,
With beaded bubbles winking at the brim,
And purple-stained mouth.
John Keats
Ode to a Nightingale

21 Even though a number of people have tried, no one has yet found a way to drink for a living.
Jean Kerr (1923–) US dramatist.
Poor Richard

22 The tranquilizer of greatest value since the early history of man, and which may never become outdated, is alcohol, when administered in moderation. It possesses the distinct advantage of being especially pleasant to the taste buds.
Nathan Masor (1913–)
Attrib.

23 No man is genuinely happy, married, who has to drink worse gin than he used to drink when he was single.
H. L. Mencken (1880–1956) US journalist.
Prejudices, 'Reflections on Monogamy'

24 Then to the spicy nut-brown ale.
John Milton (1608–74) English poet.
L'Allegro

25 A torchlight procession marching down your throat.
John L. O'Sullivan (1813–95) US writer.
Referring to whisky
Collections and Recollections (G. W. E. Russell), Ch. 19

26 *In vino veritas*.
Truth comes out in wine.
Pliny the Elder (Gaius Plinius Secundus; 23–79 AD) Roman scholar.
Natural History, XIV

27 It is the unbroken testimony of all history that alcoholic liquors have been used by the strong-

est, wisest, handsomest, and in every way best
races of all times.
George Edward Bateman Saintsbury (1845–1933) British
writer and critic.
Notes on a Cellar-Book

28 People may say what they like about the decay of
Christianity; the religious system that produced
green Chartreuse can never really die.
Saki (Hector Hugh Munro; 1870–1916) British writer.
Reginald on Christmas Presents

29 By insisting on having your bottle pointing to the
north when the cork is being drawn, and calling
the waiter Max, you may induce an impression
on your guests which hours of laboured boasting
might be powerless to achieve. For this purpose,
however, the guests must be chosen as carefully
as the wine.
Saki
The Chaplet

30 It provokes the desire, but it takes away the performance. Therefore much drink may be said to
be an equivocator with lechery.
William Shakespeare (1564–1616) English dramatist.
Macbeth, II:3

31 Alcohol is a very necessary article…It enables
Parliament to do things at eleven at night that no
sane person would do at eleven in the morning.
George Bernard Shaw (1856–1950) Irish dramatist and critic.
Major Barbara, II

32 Fifteen men on the dead man's chest
Yo ho ho, and a bottle of rum!
Drink and the devil had done for the rest –
Yo-ho-ho, and a bottle of rum!
Robert Louis Stevenson (1850–94) Scottish writer.
Treasure Island, Ch. 1

33 There are two things that will be believed of any
man whatsoever, and one of them is that he has
taken to drink.
Booth Tarkington (1869–1946) US novelist.
Penrod, Ch. 10

34 It's a Naive Domestic Burgundy, Without Any
Breeding. But I think you'll be Amused by its Pre-
sumption.
James Thurber (1894–1961) US humorist.
Men, Women and Dogs

□ ALLEN □
Woody
(Allen Stewart Konigsberg; 1935–) US film actor and director.
His films include *Play It Again, Sam* (1972), *Annie Hall* (1977),
and *The Purple Rose of Cairo* (1985).

1 Is sex dirty? Only if it's done right.
All You've Ever Wanted to Know About Sex

2 It was the most fun I ever had without laughing.
Referring to sex.
Annie Hall

3 Don't knock it, it's sex with someone you love.
Referring to masturbation.
Annie Hall

4 I'm really a timid person – I was beaten up by
Quakers.
Sleeper

5 My brain: it's my second favorite organ.
Sleeper

6 It's not that I'm afraid to die. I just don't want to
be there when it happens.
Without Feathers, 'Death (A Play)'

7 I don't want to achieve immortality through my
work…I want to achieve it through not dying.
Woody Allen and His Comedy (E. Lax)

□ AMBITION □
See also desire

1 *Per ardua ad astra.*
Hard and high to the stars!
Anonymous
Motto of the Royal Air Force

2 Ah, but a man's reach should exceed his grasp,
Or what's a heaven for?
Robert Browning (1812–89) British poet.
Andrea del Sarto

3 Man partly is and wholly hopes to be.
Robert Browning
A Death in the Desert

4 A slave has but one master; an ambitious man
has as many masters as there are people who
may be useful in bettering his position.
Jean de La Bruyère (1645–96) French satirist.
Les Caractères

5 The shades of night were falling fast,
As through an Alpine village passed
A youth, who bore, 'mid snow and ice,
A banner with the strange device,
Excelsior!
Henry Wadsworth Longfellow (1807–82) US poet.
Opening of a poem best known as a Victorian drawing-room
ballad, and the butt of many music-hall jokes. Excelsior means
'higher' (Latin)
Excelsior

6 If you would hit the mark, you must aim a little
above it;
Every arrow that flies feels the attraction of
earth.
Henry Wadsworth Longfellow
Elegiac Verse

7 Ambition should be made of sterner stuff.
William Shakespeare (1564–1616) English dramatist.
Julius Caesar, III:2

8 I have no spur
To prick the sides of my intent, but only
Vaulting ambition, which o'er-leaps itself,
And falls on th' other.
William Shakespeare
Macbeth, I:7

9 And he that strives to touch the stars,
Oft stumbles at a straw.
Edmund Spenser (1552–99) English poet.
The Shepherd's Calendar, 'July'

□ **AMERICA** □

See also Americans

1 Our society distributes itself into Barbarians, Philistines, and Populace; and America is just ourselves, with the Barbarians quite left out, and the Populace nearly.
Matthew Arnold (1822–88) British poet and critic.
Culture and Anarchy, Preface

2 God bless the USA, so large,
So friendly, and so rich.
W. H. Auden (1907–73) British poet.
On the Circuit

3 Yankee Doodle came to town
Riding on a pony;
Stuck a feather in his cap
And called it Macaroni.
Edward Bangs (fl. 1775) US songwriter.
Yankee Doodle; or Father's Return to Camp

4 O beautiful for spacious skies,
For amber waves of grain,
For purple mountain majesties
Above the fruited plain!
America! America!
God shed His grace on thee
And crown thy good with brotherhood
From sea to shining sea!
Katharine Lee Bates (1859–1929) US writer and poet.
America the Beautiful

5 I called the New World into existence to redress the balance of the Old.
George Canning (1770–1827) British statesman.
Speech, 12 Dec 1826

6 America is the only nation in history which miraculously has gone directly from barbarism to degeneration without the usual interval of civilization.
Georges Clemenceau (1841–1929) French statesman.
Attrib.

7 Patriotism is easy to understand in America; it means looking out for yourself while looking out for your country.
Calvin Coolidge (1872–1933) US president.
Attrib.

8 The business of America is business.
Calvin Coolidge
Speech, Washington, 17 Jan 1925

9 America is a country of young men.
Ralph Waldo Emerson (1803–82) US poet and essayist.
Society and Solitude, 'Old Age'

10 The United States is like a gigantic boiler. Once the fire is lighted under it there is no limit to the power it can generate.
Lord Grey (1862–1933) British statesman.
Their Finest Hour (Winston S. Churchill), Ch. 32

11 The United States, I believe, are under the impression that they are twenty years in advance of this country; whilst, as a matter of actual verifiable fact, of course, they are just about six hours behind it.
Harold Hobson (1904–) British theatre critic and writer.
The Devil in Woodford Wells, Ch. 8

12 The American system of rugged individualism.
Herbert Clark Hoover (1874–1964) US statesman.
Speech, New York, 22 Oct 1928

13 The United States has to move very fast to even stand still.
John Fitzgerald Kennedy (1917–63) US statesman.
The Observer, 'Sayings of the Week', 21 July 1963

14 'Tis the star-spangled banner; O long may it wave
O'er the land of the free, and the home of the brave!
Francis Scott Key (1779–1843) US lawyer.
The Star-Spangled Banner

15 Give me your tired, your poor,
Your huddled masses yearning to breathe free,
The wretched refuse of your teeming shore,
Send these, the homeless, tempest-tossed to me,
I lift my lamp beside the golden door!
Emma Lazarus (1849–87) US poet and philanthropist.
Used as an inscription on the Statue of Liberty
The New Colossus

16 In other countries, art and literature are left to a lot of shabby bums living in attics and feeding on booze and spaghetti, but in America the successful writer or picture-painter is indistinguishable from any other decent business man.
Sinclair Lewis (1885–1951) US novelist.
Babbitt, Ch. 14

17 The immense popularity of American movies abroad demonstrates that Europe is the unfinished negative of which America is the proof.
Mary McCarthy (1912–89) US novelist.
On the Contrary

18 America...where law and customs alike are based on the dreams of spinsters.
Bertrand Russell (1872–1970) British philosopher.
Marriage and Morals

19 In the United States there is more space where nobody is than where anybody is. That is what makes America what it is.
Gertrude Stein (1874–1946) US writer.
The Geographical History of America

20 America is a large, friendly dog in a very small room. Every time it wags its tail it knocks over a chair.
Arnold Toynbee (1889–1975) British historian.
Broadcast news summary, 14 July 1954

21 Sometimes people call me an idealist. Well, that is the way I know I am an American. America is the only idealistic nation in the world.
Woodrow Wilson (1856–1925) US statesman.
Speech, Sioux Falls, 8 Sept 1919

22 America…is the prize amateur nation of the world. Germany is the prize professional nation.
Woodrow Wilson
Speech, Aug 1917
Mr Wilson's War (John Dos Passos), Pt. III, Ch. 13

23 America is God's Crucible, the great Melting-Pot where all the races of Europe are melting and re-forming!
Israel Zangwill (1864–1926) British writer.
The Melting Pot, I

☐ AMERICANS ☐

1 Good Americans, when they die, go to Paris.
Thomas Gold Appleton (1812–84) US writer.
Autocrat of the Breakfast Table (O. W. Holmes), Ch. 6

2 There is nothing the matter with Americans except their ideals. The real American is all right; it is the ideal American who is all wrong.
G. K. Chesterton (1874–1936) British writer.
New York Times, 1 Feb 1931

3 Scratch an American and you get a Seventh Day Adventist every time.
Lord Hailsham (1907–) British Conservative politician.
The Observer, 'Sayings of the Week', 1 June 1969

4 There won't be any revolution in America…The people are too clean. They spend all their time changing their shirts and washing themselves. You can't feel fierce and revolutionary in a bathroom.
Eric Linklater (1899–1974) Scottish novelist.
Juan in America, Pt. V, Ch. 3

5 No one can kill Americans and brag about it. No one.
Ronald Reagan (1911–) US politician and president.
The Observer, 'Sayings of the Week', 27 Apr 1986

6 An American is either a Jew, or an anti-Semite, unless he is both at the same time.
Jean-Paul Sartre (1905–80) French writer.
Altona

7 That strange blend of the commercial traveller, the missionary, and the barbarian conqueror, which was the American abroad.
Olaf Stapledon (1886–1950) British philosopher and science-fiction writer.
Last and First Men, Ch. 3

8 Americans have been conditioned to respect newness, whatever it costs them.
John Updike (1932–) US novelist.
A Month of Sundays, Ch. 18

9 MRS ALLONBY. They say, Lady Hunstanton, that when good Americans die they go to Paris.
LADY HUNSTANTON. Indeed? And when bad Americans die, where do they go to?
LORD ILLINGWORTH. Oh, they go to America.
Oscar Wilde (1854–1900) Irish-born British dramatist.
See Thomas Gold APPLETON
A Woman of No Importance, I

10 Like so many substantial Americans, he had married young and kept on marrying, springing from blonde to blonde like the chamois of the Alps leaping from crag to crag.
P. G. Wodehouse (1881–1975) British humorous novelist.
Wodehouse at Work to the End (Richard Usborne), Ch. 2

☐ ANCESTRY ☐

See also aristocracy, family

1 I can trace my ancestry back to a protoplasmal primordial atomic globule. Consequently, my family pride is something in-conceivable. I can't help it. I was born sneering.
W. S. Gilbert (1836–1911) British dramatist.
The Mikado, I

2 The difference between us is that my family begins with me, whereas yours ends with you.
Iphicrates (d. 353 BC) Athenian general.
Reply to a descendant of Harmodius (an Athenian hero), who had derided Iphicrates for being the son of a cobbler
Attrib.

3 Being Southerners, it was a source of shame to some members of the family that we had no recorded ancestors on either side of the Battle of Hastings.
Harper Lee (1926–) US writer.
To Kill a Mockingbird, Pt. I, Ch. 1

☐ ANGER ☐

1 The man who gets angry at the right things and with the right people, and in the right way and at the right time and for the right length of time, is commended.
Aristotle (384–322 BC) Greek philosopher.
Nicomachean Ethics, Bk. IV

2 When they heard these things, they were cut to the heart, and they gnashed on him with their teeth.
Bible: Acts
7:54

3 Never go to bed mad. Stay up and fight.
Phyllis Diller (1917–) US writer and comedienne.
Phyllis Diller's Housekeeping Hints

4 Anger is one of the sinews of the soul.
Thomas Fuller (1608–61) English historian.
The Holy State and the Profane State

5 Spleen can subsist on any kind of food.
William Hazlitt (1778–1830) British essayist.
On Wit and Humour

6 Anger supplies the arms.
Virgil (Publius Vergilius Maro; 70–19 BC) Roman poet.
Aeneid, Bk. I

□ ANIMALISM □

See also evolution, lust, mankind, sex

1 But oh, the farmyard world of sex!
Harley Granville-Barker (1877–1946) British actor and dramatist.
The Madras House, IV

2 Be a good animal, true to your animal instincts.
D. H. Lawrence (1885–1930) British novelist.
The White Peacock, Pt. II, Ch. 2

3 – 'Do you come here often?'
'Only in the mating season.'
Spike Milligan (1918–) British comic actor and author.
The Goon Show

4 The wren goes to't, and the small gilded fly
Does lecher in my sight.
William Shakespeare (1564–1616) English dramatist.
King Lear, IV:6

□ ANIMALS □

See also cats, dogs, horses, rabbits

1 And God said, Let the earth bring forth the living creature after his kind, cattle, and creeping thing, and beast of the earth after his kind: and it was so.
Bible: Genesis
1:24

2 Whenever you observe an animal closely, you feel as if a human being sitting inside were making fun of you.
Elias Canetti (1905–) Bulgarian-born novelist.
The Human Province

3 Animals are such agreeable friends – they ask no questions, they pass no criticisms.
George Eliot (Mary Ann Evans; 1819–80) British novelist.
Scenes of Clerical Life, 'Mr Gilfil's Love Story', Ch. 7

4 Nothing can be more obvious than that all animals were created solely and exclusively for the use of man.
Thomas Love Peacock (1785–1866) British novelist.
Headlong Hall, Ch. 2

5 There are two things for which animals are to be envied: they know nothing of future evils, or of what people say about them.
Voltaire (François-Marie Arouet; 1694–1778) French writer.
Letter, 1739

6 I think I could turn and live with animals, they're so placid and self-contained,
I stand and look at them long and long.
Walt Whitman (1819–92) US poet.
Song of Myself, 32

□ ANTHONY □
Susan B(rownell)

(1820–1906) US editor and campaigner for women's suffrage. From 1850 she collaborated with Elizabeth Stanton in compiling *The Revolution*, a women's rights newspaper, and with Mathilda Gage on *The History of Woman Suffrage*. She was president (1892–1900) of the National American Woman Suffrage Association.

QUOTATIONS ABOUT ANTHONY

1 We touch our caps, and place to night
The visitor's wreath upon her,
The woman who outranks us all
In courage and honor.
Ida Husted Harper *Life and Work of Susan B. Anthony*, Vol. I

QUOTATIONS BY ANTHONY

2 There never will be complete equality until women themselves help to make laws and elect lawmakers.
The Arena, 'The Status of Women, Past, Present and Future', May 1897

3 And yet, in the schoolroom more than any other place, does the difference of sex, if there is any, need to be forgotten.
Elizabeth Cady Stanton, Vol. II (ed. Theodore Stanton and Harriot Stanton Blatch)

4 Men their rights and nothing more; women their rights and nothing less.
The Revolution, Motto

□ APOLOGIES □

See also regret

1 Love means never having to say you're sorry.
Erich Segal (1937–) US writer.
Love Story

2 Mr. Speaker, I said the honorable member was a liar it is true and I am sorry for it. The honourable member may place the punctuation where he pleases.

Richard Brinsley Sheridan (1751–1816) British dramatist. On being asked to apologize for calling a fellow MP a liar Attrib.

3 It is a good rule in life never to apologize. The right sort of people do not want apologies, and the wrong sort take a mean advantage of them.

P. G. Wodehouse (1881–1975) British humorous novelist. *The Man Upstairs and Other Stories*

☐ APPEARANCE ☐

See also appearances, beauty, clothes

1 A homely face and no figure have aided many women heavenward.

Minna Antrim (1861–?) US writer. *Naked Truth and Veiled Allusions*

2 But if a woman have long hair, it is a glory to her: for her hair is given her for a covering.

Bible: I Corinthians 11:15

3 Unnecessary dieting is because everything from television and fashion ads have made it seem wicked to cast a shadow. This wild, emaciated look appeals to some women, though not to many men, who are seldom seen pinning up a *Vogue* illustration in a machine shop.

Peg Bracken (1918–) US writer and humorist. *The I Hate to Cook Book*

4 Remember Mary Archer in the witness box. Your vision of her will probably never disappear. Has she elegance? Has she fragrance? Would she have – without the strain of this trial – a radiance?

Bernard Caulfield (1914–) British judge. Summing up the court case between Jeffrey Archer and the *News of the World*, July 1987 *The Times*, 24 July 1987

5 Alas, after a certain age every man is responsible for his face.

Albert Camus (1913–60) French existentialist writer. *The Fall*

6 Sunburn is very becoming – but only when it is even – one must be careful not to look like a mixed grill.

Noël Coward (1899–1973) British dramatist. *The Lido Beach*

7 There is a great difference between painting a face and not washing it.

Thomas Fuller (1608–61) English historian. *Church History*, Bk. VII

8 Where's the cheek that doth not fade, Too much gaz'd at? Where's the maid Whose lip mature is ever new?

John Keats (1795–1821) British poet. *Fancy*, I

9 It always seemed to me that men wore their beards, like they wear their neckties, for show. I shall always remember Lewis for saying his beard was part of him.

D. H. Lawrence (1885–1930) British novelist. *St Mawr*

10 The Lord prefers common-looking people. That is why he makes so many of them.

Abraham Lincoln (1809–65) US statesman. *Our President* (James Morgan), Ch. 6

11 He looks as if he had been weaned on a pickle.

Alice Roosevelt Longworth (1884–1980) US hostess. Referring to John Calvin Coolidge, US president 1923–29 *Crowded Hours*

12 Gentlemen always seem to remember blondes.

Anita Loos (1891–1981) US novelist. *Gentlemen Prefer Blondes*, Ch. 1

13 Men seldom make passes At girls who wear glasses.

Dorothy Parker (1893–1967) US writer. Attrib.

14 Had Cleopatra's nose been shorter, the whole face of the world would have changed.

Blaise Pascal (1623–62) French philosopher and mathematician. *Pensées*, II

15 Why not be oneself? That is the whole secret of a successful appearance. If one is a greyhound why try to look like a Pekinese?

Edith Sitwell (1887–1964) British poet and writer. *Why I Look As I Do*

16 A short neck denotes a good mind…You see, the messages go quicker to the brain because they've shorter to go.

Muriel Spark (1918–) British novelist. *The Ballad of Peckham Rye*, Ch. 7

17 Enclosing every thin man, there's a fat man demanding elbow-room.

Evelyn Waugh (1903–66) British novelist. *Officers and Gentlemen*, Interlude

☐ APPEARANCES ☐

See also deception, hypocrisy

1 The lamb that belonged to the sheep whose skin the wolf was wearing began to follow the wolf in the sheep's clothing.

Aesop (6th century BC) Reputed Greek writer of fables. *Fables*, 'The Wolf in Sheep's Clothing'

2 The French are wiser than they seem, and the Spaniards seem wiser than they are.

Francis Bacon (1561–1626) English philosopher. *Essays*, 'Of Seeming Wise'

3 Keep up appearances; there lies the test
The world will give thee credit for the rest.
Charles Churchill (1731–64) British poet.
Night

4 I may not hope from outward forms to win
The passion and the life, whose fountains are
within.
Samuel Taylor Coleridge (1772–1834) British poet.
Dejection: An Ode

5 Appearances are not held to be a clue to the
truth. But we seem to have no other.
Ivy Compton-Burnett (1892–1969) British novelist.
Manservant and Maidservant

6 No man could be so wise as Thurlow looked.
Charles James Fox (1749–1806) British Whig politician.
Lives of the Lord Chancellors (Campbell), Vol. V

7 Strip the phoney tinsel off Hollywood and you'll
find the real tinsel underneath.
Oscar Levant (1906–72) US pianist and actor.
Attrib.

8 Things are entirely what they appear to be and
behind them…there is nothing.
Jean-Paul Sartre (1905–80) French writer.
Nausea

9 Care I for the limb, the thews, the stature, bulk,
and big assemblance of a man! Give me the spirit.
William Shakespeare (1564–1616) English dramatist.
Henry IV, Part Two, III:2

10 Through tatter'd clothes small vices do appear;
Robes and furr'd gowns hide all.
William Shakespeare
King Lear, IV:6

11 Our purses shall be proud, our garments poor;
For 'tis the mind that makes the body rich;
And as the sun breaks through the darkest
clouds,
So honour peereth in the meanest habit.
William Shakespeare
The Taming of the Shrew, IV:3

12 It is only shallow people who do not judge by
appearances.
Oscar Wilde (1854–1900) Irish-born British dramatist.
The Picture of Dorian Gray, Ch. 2

□ ARCHITECTURE □

See also houses, stately homes

1 You have to give this much to the Luftwaffe –
when it knocked down our buildings it did not
replace them with anything more offensive than
rubble. We did that.
Charles, Prince of Wales (1948–) Eldest son of
Elizabeth II.
See also SITWELL
The Observer, 'Sayings of the Week', 6 Dec 1987

2 Like a carbuncle on the face of an old and valued
friend.
Charles, Prince of Wales
Referring to a proposed modern extension to the National Gallery
Speech, 1986

3 'Fan vaulting'…an architectural device which
arouses enormous enthusiasm on account of the
difficulties it has all too obviously involved but
which from an aesthetic standpoint frequently
belongs to the 'Last-supper-carved-on-a-peach-
stone' class of masterpiece.
Osbert Lancaster (1908–86) British cartoonist.
Pillar to Post, 'Perpendicular'

4 What has happened to architecture since the second world war that the only passers-by who can
contemplate it without pain are those equipped
with a white stick and a dog?
Bernard Levin (1928–) British journalist.
The Times, 1983

5 No person who is not a great sculptor or painter
can be an architect. If he is not a sculptor or
painter, he can only be a *builder*.
John Ruskin (1819–1900) British art critic and writer.
Lectures on Architecture and Painting

6 When we build let us think that we build for ever.
John Ruskin
The Seven Lamps of Architecture, Ch. 6, 'The Lamp of Memory'

7 Architecture in general is frozen music.
Friedrich Wilhelm Joseph von Schelling (1775–1854)
German philosopher.
Philosophie der Kunst

8 How simple-minded of the Germans to imagine
that we British could be cowed by the destruction of our ancient monuments! As though any
havoc of the German bombs could possibly
equal the things we have done ourselves!
Osbert Sitwell (1892–1969) British writer.
See also CHARLES, PRINCE OF WALES
The Collected Essays, Journalism and Letters of George Orwell,
Vol. III

9 In *Architecture* as in all other *Operative* Arts, the
end must direct the *Operation*. The *end* is to build
well. Well building hath three Conditions. *Commodity, Firmness*, and *Delight*.
Henry Wotton (1568–1639) English poet and diplomat.
Elements of Architecture, Pt. I

□ ARGUMENTS □

1 There is only one way under high heaven to get
the best of an argument – and that is to avoid it.
Dale Carnegie (1888–1955) US lecturer and writer.
Dale Carnegie's Scrapbook

2 It takes in reality only one to make a quarrel. It is
useless for the sheep to pass resolutions in

favour of vegetarianism while the wolf remains of a different opinion.
Dean Inge (1860–1954) British churchman.
Outspoken Essays

3 Though a quarrel in the streets is a thing to be hated, the energies displayed in it are fine; the commonest man shows a grace in his quarrel.
John Keats (1795–1821) British poet.
Letter

4 When men understand what each other mean, they see, for the most part, that controversy is either superfluous or hopeless.
Cardinal Newman (1801–90) British theologian.
Sermon, Oxford, Epiphany 1839

5 Quarrels would not last so long if the fault were on only one side.
Duc de la Rochefoucauld (1613–80) French writer.
Maximes, 496

6 The most savage controversies are those about matters as to which there is no good evidence either way.
Bertrand Russell (1872–1970) British philosopher.
Unpopular Essays

7 I love argument, I love debate. I don't expect anyone just to sit there and agree with me, that's not their job.
Margaret Thatcher (1925–) British politician and prime minister.
The Times, 1980

□ ARISTOCRACY □

See also ancestry, class, Houses of Parliament, nobility, stately homes, titles

1 One has often wondered whether upon the whole earth there is anything so unintelligent, so unapt to perceive how the world is really going, as an ordinary young Englishman of our upper class.
Matthew Arnold (1822–88) British poet and critic.
Culture and Anarchy, Ch. 2

2 Like many of the upper class
He liked the sound of broken glass.
Hilaire Belloc (1870–1953) French-born British poet.
New Cautionary Tales, 'About John'

3 The nobility of England, my lord, would have snored through the Sermon on the Mount.
Robert Bolt (1924–) British playwright.
A Man for All Seasons

4 We, my lords, may thank heaven that we have something better than our brains to depend upon.
Earl of Chesterfield (1694–1773) English statesman.
Speech, House of Lords
The Story of Civilization (W. Durant), Vol. 9

5 Democracy means government by the uneducated, while aristocracy means government by the badly educated.
G. K. Chesterton (1874–1936) British writer.
New York Times, 1 Feb 1931

6 The Stately Homes of England
How beautiful they stand,
To prove the upper classes
Have still the upper hand.
Noël Coward (1899–1973) British dramatist.
Operette, 'The Stately Homes of England'

7 If human beings could be propagated by cutting, like apple trees, aristocracy would be biologically sound.
J. B. S. Haldane (1892–1964) British geneticist.
The Inequality of Man, title essay

8 There are no credentials They do not even need a medical certificate. They need not be sound either in body or mind. They only require a certificate of birth – just to prove that they are first of the litter. You would not choose a spaniel on these principles.
David Lloyd George (1863–1945) British Liberal statesman.
Budget Speech, 1909

9 An aristocracy in a republic is like a chicken whose head has been cut off: it may run about in a lively way, but in fact it is dead.
Nancy Mitford (1904–73) British writer.
Noblesse Oblige

10 Kind hearts are more than coronets,
And simple faith than Norman blood.
Alfred, Lord Tennyson (1809–92) British poet.
Lady Clara Vere de Vere, VI

11 If the French noblesse had been capable of playing cricket with their peasants, their chateaux would never have been burnt.
George Macaulay Trevelyan (1876–1962) British historian.
English Social History, Ch. XIII

12 Unlike the male codfish which, suddenly finding itself the parent of three million five hundred thousand little codfish, cheerfully resolves to love them all, the British aristocracy is apt to look with a somewhat jaundiced eye on its younger sons.
P. G. Wodehouse (1881–1975) British humorous novelist.
Wodehouse at Work to the End (Richard Usborne), Ch. 5

□ ARMY □

See also officers, soldiers, war, weapons

1 Oh! the grand old Duke of York
He had ten thousand men;
He marched them up to the top of the hill,
And he marched them down again.
And when they were up they were up,
And when they were down they were down,

And when they were only half way up,
They were neither up nor down.
Anonymous
Traditional

2 Conduct...to the prejudice of good order and
military discipline.
Anonymous
Army Act, 40

3 An army is a nation within a nation; it is one of the
vices of our age.
Alfred de Vigny (1797–1863) French writer.
Servitude et grandeur militaire, 1

4 Ours is composed of the scum of the earth.
Duke of Wellington (1769–1852) British general and
statesman.
Of the British army
Remark, 4 Nov 1831

5 The army ages men sooner than the law and philosophy; it exposes them more freely to germs,
which undermine and destroy, and it shelters
them more completely from thought, which
stimulates and preserves.
H. G. Wells (1866–1946) British writer.
Bealby, Pt. VIII, Ch. 1

☐ ARNOLD ☐
Matthew

(1822–88) British poet and critic, who served for 35 years as
inspector of schools.

QUOTATIONS ABOUT ARNOLD

1 He is not as handsome as his photographs – or
his poetry.
Henry James (1843–1916) US novelist.
Letter to Charles Eliot Norton, 31 Mar 1873

2 Arnold is a dandy Isaiah, a poet without pas-
sion...
George Meredith (1829–1909) British novelist.
Fortnightly Review, July 1909

QUOTATIONS BY ARNOLD

3 One has often wondered whether upon the
whole earth there is anything so unintelligent, so
unapt to perceive how the world is really going,
as an ordinary young Englishman of our upper
class.
Culture and Anarchy, Ch. 2

4 I often, therefore, when I want to distinguish
clearly the aristocratic class from the Philistines
proper, or middle class, name the former, in my
own mind *the Barbarians*.
Culture and Anarchy, Ch. 3

5 But that vast portion, lastly, of the working-class
which, raw and half-developed, has long lain half-
hidden amidst its poverty and squalor, and is
now issuing from its hiding-place to assert an
Englishman's heaven-born privilege of doing as
he likes, and is beginning to perplex us by marching where it likes, meeting where it likes, bawl-
ing what it likes, breaking what it likes – to this
vast residuum we may with great propriety give
the name of Populace.
Culture and Anarchy, Ch. 3

6 Is it so small a thing
To have enjoy'd the sun,
To have lived light in the spring,
To have loved, to have thought, to have done?
Empedocles on Etna

7 Home of lost causes, and forsaken beliefs, and
unpopular names, and impossible loyalties!
Referring to Oxford.
Essays in Criticism, First Series, Preface

8 A wanderer is man from his birth.
He was born in a ship
On the breast of the river of Time.
The Future

9 Wandering between two worlds, one dead,
The other powerless to be born.
The Grande Chartreuse

10 Culture, the acquainting ourselves with the best
that has been known and said in the world, and
thus with the history of the human spirit.
Literature and Dogma, Preface

11 Time may restore us in his course
Goethe's sage mind and Byron's force:
But where will Europe's latter hour
Again find Wordsworth's healing power?
Memorial Verses

12 He will find one English book and one only,
where, as in the *Iliad* itself, perfect plainness of
speech is allied with perfect nobleness; and that
book is the Bible.
On Translating Homer

13 Cruel, but composed and bland,
Dumb, inscrutable and grand,
So Tiberius might have sat,
Had Tiberius been a cat.
Poor Matthias

14 Before this strange disease of modern life,
With its sick hurry, its divided aims.
The Scholar Gipsy

15 Resolve to be thyself: and know, that he
Who finds himself, loses his misery.
Self-Dependence

16 Truth sits upon the lips of dying men.
Sohrab and Rustum

17 And see all sights from pole to pole,
And glance, and nod, and bustle by;
And never once possess our soul
Before we die.
A Southern Night

18 And sigh that one thing only has been lent
To youth and age in common – discontent.
Youth's Agitations

19 I am past thirty, and three parts iced over.
Letter to A. H. Clough, 12 Feb 1853

□ ART □

See also artists, arts, design, painting

1 The object of art is to give life a shape.
Jean Anouilh (1910–87) French dramatist.
The Rehearsal

2 The lower one's vitality, the more sensitive one is
to great art.
Max Beerbohm (1872–1956) British writer.
Seven Men, 'Enoch Soames'

3 Art for art's sake.
Victor Cousin (1792–1867) French philosopher.
Lecture, Sorbonne, 1818

4 Art is a jealous mistress.
Ralph Waldo Emerson (1803–82) US poet and essayist.
Conduct of Life, 'Wealth'

5 Art has to move you and design does not, unless
it's a good design for a bus.
David Hockney (1937–) British painter, draughtsman and
printmaker.
Remark, Oct 1988

6 In free society art is not a weapon…Artists are
not engineers of the soul.
John Fitzgerald Kennedy (1917–63) US statesman.
Address at Dedication of the Robert Frost Library, 26 Oct 1963

7 But the Devil whoops, as he whooped of old:
'It's clever, but is it art?'
Rudyard Kipling (1865–1936) Indian-born British writer.
The Conundrum of the Workshops

8 I do not know whether he draws a line himself.
But I assume that his is the direction…It makes
Disney the most significant figure in graphic art
since Leonardo.
David Low (1871–1963) New-Zealand-born newspaper
cartoonist.
Walt Disney (R. Schickel), Ch. 20

9 Art is not a mirror to reflect the world, but a ham-
mer with which to shape it.
Vladimir Mayakovsky (1893–1930) Soviet poet.
The Guardian, 11 Dec 1974

10 Nothing unites the English like war. Nothing
divides them like Picasso.
Hugh Mills (1913–71) British screenwriter.
Prudence and the Pill

11 Abstract Expressionism was invented by New
York drunks.
Joni Mitchell (1943–) US singer and songwriter.
Interview, BBC television, 1985

12 All art constantly aspires towards the condition
of music.
Walter Pater (1839–94) British critic.
The Renaissance, 'The School of Giorgione'

13 On the floor I am more at ease, I feel nearer,
more a part of the painting, since this way I can
walk around it, work from the four sides and literally be 'in' the painting.
Jackson Pollock (1912–56) US artist.
Pollock (Tomassoni)

14 Burnings of people and (what was more valu-
able) works of art.
A. L. Rowse (1903–) British historian and critic.
Historical Essays (H. R. Trevor-Roper)

15 Life without industry is guilt, and industry with-
out art is brutality.
John Ruskin (1819–1900) British art critic and writer.
Lectures on Art, 3, 'The Relation of Art to Morals', 23 Feb 1870

16 Fine art is that in which the hand, the head, and
the heart of man go together.
John Ruskin
The Two Paths, Lecture II

17 Skill without imagination is craftsmanship and
gives us many useful objects such as wicker work
picnic baskets. Imagination without skill gives us
modern art.
Tom Stoppard (1937–) Czech-born British dramatist.
Artist Descending a Staircase

18 Art is not a handicraft, it is the transmission of
feeling the artist has experienced.
Leo Tolstoy (1828–1910) Russian writer.
What is Art?, Ch. 19

19 Any authentic work of art must start an argument between the artist and his audience.
Rebecca West (Cicely Isabel Fairfield; 1892–1983) British
novelist and journalist.
The Court and the Castle, Pt. I, Ch. 1

20 All Art is quite useless.
Oscar Wilde (1854–1900) Irish-born British dramatist.
The Picture of Dorian Gray, Preface

21 Art is the most intense mode of individualism
that the world has known.
Oscar Wilde
The Soul of Man Under Socialism

☐ARTISTS☐
See also art, painting

1 Poets and painters are outside the class system, or rather they constitute a special class of their own, like the circus people and the gipsies.
Gerald Brenan (Edward Fitzgerald Brenan; 1894–1987) British writer.
Thoughts in a Dry Season, 'Writing'

2 Beware of the artist who's an intellectual also. The artist who doesn't fit.
F. Scott Fitzgerald (1896–1940) US novelist.
This Side of Paradise, Bk. II, Ch. 5

3 An amateur is an artist who supports himself with outside jobs which enable him to paint. A professional is someone whose wife works to enable him to paint.
Ben Shahn (1898–1969) US artist.
Attrib.

4 What is an artist? For every thousand people there's nine hundred doing the work, ninety doing well, nine doing good, and one lucky bastard who's the artist.
Tom Stoppard (1937–   ) Czech-born British dramatist.
Travesties, I

5 A painter should not paint what he sees, but what will be seen.
Paul Valéry (1871–1945) French poet and writer.
Mauvaises Pensées et Autres

6 An artist is someone who produces things that people don't need to have but that he – for *some* reason – thinks it would be a good idea to give them.
Andy Warhol (Andrew Warhola; 1926–87) US pop artist.
From A to B and Back Again, 'Atmosphere'

7 A living is made, Mr Kemper, by selling something that everybody needs at least once a year. Yes, sir! And a million is made by producing something that everybody needs every day. You artists produce something that nobody needs at any time.
Thornton Wilder (1897–1975) US novelist and dramatist.
The Matchmaker, II

☐ARTS☐

1 The excellence of every art is its intensity, capable of making all disagreeables evaporate, from their being in close relationship with beauty and truth.
John Keats (1795–1821) British poet.
Letter to G. and T. Keats, 21 Dec 1817

2 The whole of art is an appeal to a reality which is not without us but in our minds.
Desmond MacCarthy (1877–1952) British writer and theatre critic.
Theatre, 'Modern Drama'

3 Music begins to atrophy when it departs too far from the dance...poetry begins to atrophy when it gets too far from music.
Ezra Pound (1885–1972) US poet.
ABC of Reading, 'Warning'

4 The secret of the arts is to correct nature.
Voltaire (François-Marie Arouet; 1694–1778) French writer.
Épitres, 'À M. de Verrière'

☐ASSASSINATION☐
See also killing, murder

1 They really are bad shots.
Charles De Gaulle (1890–1970) French general and statesman.
Remark after narrowly escaping death in an assassination attempt
Ten First Ladies of the World (Pauline Frederick)

2 Assassination has never changed the history of the world.
Benjamin Disraeli (1804–81) British statesman.
Speech, House of Commons, 1 May 1865

3 Will no one rid me of this turbulent priest?
Henry II (1133–89) King of England.
Referring to Thomas Becket, Archbishop of Canterbury; four of Henry's household knights took these words literally, hurried to Canterbury, and killed Becket in the cathedral (Dec 1170)
Attrib.

4 Assassination is the extreme form of censorship.
George Bernard Shaw (1856–1950) Irish dramatist and critic.
The Shewing-Up of Blanco Posnet, 'The Limits of Toleration'

☐ASTRONOMY☐
See also moon, space, stars, sun, universe

1 ...in my studies of astronomy and philosophy I hold this opinion about the universe, that the Sun remains fixed in the centre of the circle of heavenly bodies, without changing its place; and the Earth, turning upon itself, moves round the Sun.
Galileo Galilei (1564–1642) Italian scientist.
Letter to Cristina di Lorena, 1615

2 *Eppur si muove.*
Yet it moves.
Galileo Galilei
Referring to the Earth. Remark supposedly made after his recantation (1632) of belief in the Copernican system
Attrib.

3 Astronomy teaches the correct use of the sun and the planets.
Stephen Leacock (1869–1944) English-born Canadian economist and humorist.
Literary Lapses, 'A Manual of Education'

☐ATHEISM☐
See also God, religion

1 God never wrought miracle to convince atheism, because his ordinary works convince it.
Francis Bacon (1561–1626) English philosopher.
Essays, 'Of Atheism'

2 For none deny there is a God, but those for whom it maketh that there were no God.
Francis Bacon
Essays, 'Of Atheism'

3 An atheist is a man who has no invisible means of support.
Harry Emerson Fosdick (1878–1969) US baptist minister.
Attrib.

4 He was an embittered atheist (the sort of atheist who does not so much disbelieve in God as personally dislike Him).
George Orwell (Eric Blair; 1903–50) British novelist.
Down and Out in Paris and London, Ch. 30

5 It has been said that the highest praise of God consists in the denial of Him by the atheist, who finds creation so perfect that he can dispense with a creator.
Marcel Proust (1871–1922) French novelist.
À la recherche du temps perdu: Le Côté de Guermantes

☐ AUDEN ☐
W(ystan) H(ugh)
(1907–73) British poet; professor of poetry at Oxford University (1956–61). Auden made his name in the 1930s.

QUOTATIONS ABOUT AUDEN

1 We have one poet of genius in Auden who is able to write prolifically, carelessly and exquisitely, nor does he seem to have to pay any price for his inspiration.
Cyril Connolly (1903–74) British journalist.
Enemies of Promise

2 The high watermark, so to speak, of Socialist literature is W. H. Auden, a sort of gutless Kipling.
George Orwell (Eric Blair; 1903–50) British novelist.
The Road to Wigan Pier

QUOTATIONS BY AUDEN

3 Political history is far too criminal and pathological to be a fit subject of study for the young. Children should acquire their heroes and villains from fiction.
A Certain World

4 All sin tends to be addictive, and the terminal point of addiction is what is called damnation.
A Certain World

5 Happy the hare at morning, for she cannot read The Hunter's waking thoughts.
The Dog Beneath the Skin (with Christopher Isherwood)

6 Man is a history-making creature who can neither repeat his past nor leave it behind.
The Dyer's Hand, 'D. H. Lawrence'

7 Some books are undeservedly forgotten; none are undeservedly remembered.
The Dyer's Hand, 'Reading'

8 To save your world you asked this man to die: Would this man, could he see you now, ask why?
Epitaph for an Unknown Soldier

9 To us he is no more a person Now but a climate of opinion
In Memory of Sigmund Freud

10 Now Ireland has her madness and her weather still, For poetry makes nothing happen.
In Memory of W. B. Yeats, II

11 To the man-in-the-street, who, I'm sorry to say Is a keen observer of life, The word Intellectual suggests straight away A man who's untrue to his wife.
Note on Intellectuals

12 When it comes, will it come without warning Just as I'm picking my nose? Will it knock on my door in the morning, Or tread in the bus on my toes? Will it come like a change in the weather? Will its greeting be courteous or rough? Will it alter my life altogether? O tell me the truth about love.
Twelve Songs, XII

13 Our researchers into Public Opinion are content That he held the proper opinions for the time of year; When there was peace, he was for peace; when there was war, he went.
The Unknown Citizen

14 If there are any of you at the back who do not hear me, please don't raise your hands because I am also nearsighted.
Starting a lecture in a large hall.
In *Book of the Month Club News*, Dec 1946

15 A professor is one who talks in someone else's sleep.
Attrib.

☐ AUSTEN ☐
Jane
(1775–1817) British novelist. Her novels of middle-class life combine humour with perceptive characterization.

QUOTATIONS ABOUT AUSTEN

1 More can be learnt from Miss Austen about the nature of the novel than from almost any other writer.
Walter Allen (1911–) British author and literary journalist.
The English Novel

2 That young lady has a talent for describing the involvements and feelings and characters of ordinary life which is to me the most wonderful thing I ever met with.
Walter Scott (1771–1832) Scottish novelist.
Journals, 14 Mar 1826

QUOTATIONS BY AUSTEN

3 One half of the world cannot understand the pleasures of the other.
Emma, Ch. 9

4 Nobody is healthy in London, nobody can be.
Emma, Ch. 12

5 A man...must have a very good opinion of himself when he asks people to leave their own fireside, and encounter such a day as this, for the sake of coming to see him. He must think himself a most agreeable fellow.
Emma, Ch. 13

6 Human nature is so well disposed towards those who are in interesting situations, that a young person, who either marries or dies, is sure to be kindly spoken of.
Emma, Ch. 22

7 She was nothing more than a mere goodtempered, civil and obliging young woman; as such we could scarcely dislike her – she was only an Object of Contempt.
Love and Friendship

8 A woman, especially if she have the misfortune of knowing anything, should conceal it as well as she can.
Northanger Abbey, Ch. 14

9 One does not love a place the less for having suffered in it unless it has all been suffering, nothing but suffering.
Persuasion, Ch. 20

10 It is a truth universally acknowledged, that a single man in possession of a good fortune must be in want of a wife.
The opening words of the book.
Pride and Prejudice, Ch. 1

11 A lady's imagination is very rapid; it jumps from admiration to love, from love to matrimony in a moment.
Pride and Prejudice, Ch. 6

12 Happiness in marriage is entirely a matter of chance.
Pride and Prejudice, Ch. 6

13 One cannot be always laughing at a man without now and then stumbling on something witty.
Pride and Prejudice, Ch. 40

14 For what do we live, but to make sport for our neighbours, and laugh at them in our turn?
Pride and Prejudice, Ch. 57

15 I have been a selfish being all my life, in practice, though not in principle.
Pride and Prejudice, Ch. 58

16 Mrs Hall of Sherbourne was brought to bed yesterday of a dead child, some weeks before she expected, owing to a fright. I suppose she happened unawares to look at her husband.
Letter, 27 Oct 1798

17 I do not want people to be very agreeable, as it saves me the trouble of liking them a great deal.
Letter, 24 Dec 1798

18 We met...Dr Hall in such very deep mourning that either his mother, his wife, or himself must be dead.
Letter to Cassandra Austen, 17 May 1799

□ **AUTHORITARIANISM** □

See also tyranny

1 *Roma locuta est; causa finita est.*
Rome has spoken; the case is concluded.
St Augustine of Hippo (354–430) Bishop of Hippo.
Sermons, Bk. I

2 Then cometh the end, when he shall have delivered up the kingdom to God, even the Father; when he shall have put down all rule and all authority and power.
For he must reign, till he hath put all enemies under his feet.
The last enemy that shall be destroyed is death.
Bible: I Corinthians
15:24–26

3 Dictators ride to and fro upon tigers which they dare not dismount. And the tigers are getting hungry.
Winston Churchill (1874–1965) British statesman.
While England Slept

4 I will have this done, so I order it done; let my will replace reasoned judgement.
Juvenal (Decimus Junius Juvenalis; 60–130 AD) Roman satirist.
Satires, VI

5 Big Brother is watching you.
George Orwell (Eric Blair; 1903–50) British novelist.
Nineteen Eighty-Four

6 I don't mind how much my ministers talk – as long as they do what I say.
Margaret Thatcher (1925–) British politician and prime minister.
The Times, 1987

□ **AUTUMN** □

See months, seasons

B

☐ BABIES ☐

See also birth, children

1 Every baby born into the world is a finer one than the last.
Charles Dickens (1812–70) British novelist.
Nicholas Nickleby, Ch. 36

2 These wretched babies don't come until they are ready.
Queen Elizabeth II (1926–) Queen of the United Kingdom.
Remark, Aug 1988

3 Other people's babies –
That's my life!
Mother to dozens,
And nobody's wife.
A. P. Herbert (1890–1971) British writer and politician.
A Book of Ballads, 'Other People's Babies'

4 A loud noise at one end and no sense of responsibility at the other.
Ronald Knox (1888–1957) British Roman Catholic priest.
Attrib.

☐ BEAUTY ☐

See also admiration, appearance, compliments

1 You know, you can only perceive real beauty in a person as they get older.
Anouk Aimee (1932–) French actress.
Remark, Aug 1988

2 There is no excellent beauty that hath not some strangeness in the proportion.
Francis Bacon (1561–1626) English philosopher.
Essays, 'Of Beauty'

3 Beauty and the lust for learning have yet to be allied.
Max Beerbohm (1872–1956) British writer.
Zuleika Dobson, Ch. 7

4 Exuberance is Beauty.
William Blake (1757–1827) British poet.
The Marriage of Heaven and Hell, 'Proverbs of Hell'

5 For beauty being the best of all we know
Sums up the unsearchable and secret aims
Of nature.
Robert Bridges (1844–1930) British poet.
The Growth of Love

6 Beauty in distress is much the most affecting beauty.
Edmund Burke (1729–97) British politician.
On the Sublime and Beautiful, Pt. III

7 She walks in beauty, like the night
Of cloudless climes and starry skies;

And all that's best of dark and bright
Meet in her aspect and her eyes.
Lord Byron (1788–1824) British poet.
She Walks in Beauty

8 There is nothing ugly; *I never saw an ugly thing in my life:* for let the form of an object be what it may, – light, shade, and perspective will always make it beautiful.
John Constable (1776–1837) British landscape painter.
Letter to John Fisher, 23 Oct 1821

9 Love built on beauty, soon as beauty, dies.
John Donne (1573–1631) English poet.
Elegies, 2, 'The Anagram'

10 Beauty in things exists in the mind which contemplates them.
David Hume (1711–76) Scottish philosopher.
Essays, 'Of Tragedy'

11 Beauty is altogether in the eye of the beholder.
Margaret Wolfe Hungerford (c. 1855–97) Irish novelist.
Also attributed to the US soldier and writer Lew Wallace (1827–1905)
Molly Bawn

12 A thing of beauty is a joy for ever:
Its loveliness increases; it will never
Pass into nothingness; but still will keep
A bower quiet for us, and a sleep
Full of sweet dreams, and health, and quiet breathing.
John Keats (1795–1821) British poet.
Endymion, I

13 'Beauty is truth, truth beauty,' – that is all
Ye know on earth, and all ye need to know.
John Keats
Ode on a Grecian Urn

14 Was this the face that launch'd a thousand ships
And burnt the topless towers of Ilium?
Sweet Helen, make me immortal with a kiss.
Christopher Marlowe (1564–93) English dramatist.
Doctor Faustus, V:1

15 Beauty stands
In the admiration only of weak minds
Led captive.
John Milton (1608–74) English poet.
Paradise Regained, Bk. II

16 There are no ugly women, only lazy ones.
Helena Rubinstein (1882–1965) Polish-born US cosmetics manufacturer.
My Life for Beauty, Pt. II, Ch. 1

17 Remember that the most beautiful things in the world are the most useless, peacocks and lilies for instance.
John Ruskin (1819–1900) British art critic and writer.
The Stones of Venice, Vol. I, Ch. 2

18 I always say beauty is only sin deep.
Saki (Hector Hugh Munro; 1870–1916) British writer.
Reginald's Choir Treat

19 Beauty itself doth of itself persuade
The eyes of men without an orator.
William Shakespeare (1564–1616) English dramatist.
The Rape of Lucrece, I

20 For she was beautiful – her beauty made
The bright world dim, and everything beside
Seemed like the fleeting image of a shade.
Percy Bysshe Shelley (1792–1822) British poet.
The Witch of Atlas, XII

21 The beauty myth of the present is more insidious
than any mystique of femininity yet: A century
ago, Nora slammed the door of the doll's house;
a generation ago, women turned their backs on
the consumer heaven of the isolated multi-
applianced home; but where women are trapped
today, there is no door to slam. The contemporary ravages of the beauty backlash are destroying women physically and depleting us
psychologically. If we are to free ourselves from
the dead weight that has once again been made
out of femaleness, it is not ballots or lobbyists or
placards that women will need first; it is a new
way to see.
Naomi Wolf US writer.
The Beauty Myth

22 All changed, changed utterly:
A terrible beauty is born.
W. B. Yeats (1865–1939) Irish poet.
Easter 1916

☐ BEAUVOIR ☐
Simone de
(1908–86) French writer and feminist. A powerful writer and philosopher, she has written a number of novels reflecting various
aspects of existentialist thought, including *Le Sang des autres* (*The
Blood of Others*; 1944) and *Tous les hommes sont mortels* (*All Men
are Mortal*; 1946). Her most influential work is *Le Deuxième Sexe*
(*The Second Sex*; 1949).

1 A man would never get the notion of writing a
book on the peculiar situation of the human male.
Le Deuxième Sexe (*The Second Sex*)

2 One is not born a woman, one becomes one.
Le Deuxième Sexe (*The Second Sex*)

3 If you live long enough, you'll see that every victory turns into a defeat.
Tous les hommes sont mortels

4 If you haven't been happy very young, you can
still be happy later on, but it's much harder. You
need more luck.
Observer, 'Sayings of the Week', 19 May 1975

☐ BED ☐
See also idleness, rest, sleep

1 Early to bed and early to rise, makes a man
healthy, wealthy and wise.
Proverb

2 O! it's nice to get up in the mornin',
But it's nicer to stay in bed.
Harry Lauder (Hugh MacLennon; 1870–1950) Scottish
music-hall artist.
Song

3 And so to bed.
Samuel Pepys (1633–1703) English diarist.
Diary, 6 May 1660 and *passim*

4 Not to be abed after midnight is to be up betimes.
William Shakespeare (1564–1616) English dramatist.
Twelfth Night, II:3

5 Early to rise and early to bed makes a male
healthy and wealthy and dead.
James Thurber (1894–1961) US humorist.
Fables for Our Time, 'The Shrike and the Chipmunks'

☐ BEERBOHM ☐
Sir Max
(1872–1936) British writer and caricaturist. His only novel,
Zuleika Dobson (1911), is set in Oxford.

QUOTATIONS ABOUT BEERBOHM

1 The Incomparable Max.
George Bernard Shaw (1856–1950) Irish dramatist and critic.
Dramatic Opinions and Essays, Vol. II

2 He has the most remarkable and seductive
genius – and I should say about the smallest in
the world.
Lytton Strachey (1880–1932) British writer.
Letter to Clive Bell, 4 Dec 1917

QUOTATIONS BY BEERBOHM

3 There is always something rather absurd about
the past.
1880

4 Great men are but life-sized. Most of them,
indeed, are rather short.
And Even Now

5 I believe the twenty-four hour day has come to
stay.
A Christmas Garland, 'Perkins and Mankind'

6 Most women are not so young as they are
painted.
A Defence of Cosmetics

7 Anything that is worth doing has been done frequently. Things hitherto undone should be
given, I suspect, a wide berth.
Mainly on the Air

8 It needs no dictionary of quotations to remind me that the eyes are the windows of the soul.
Zuleika Dobson, Ch. 4

9 Women who love the same man have a kind of bitter freemasonry.
Zuleika Dobson, Ch. 4

10 You will think me lamentably crude; my experience of life has been drawn from life itself.
Zuleika Dobson, Ch. 7

11 You cannot make a man by standing a sheep on its hind legs. But by standing a flock of sheep in that position you can make a crowd of men.
Zuleika Dobson, Ch. 9

12 She was one of the people who say, 'I don't know anything about music really, but I know what I like'.
Zuleika Dobson, Ch. 16

13 They were a tense and peculiar family, the Oedipuses, weren't they?
Max: A Biography (D. Cecil)

☐ BEGINNING ☐

See also prophecy

1 No task is a long one but the task on which one dare not start. It becomes a nightmare.
Charles Baudelaire (1821–67) French poet.
My Heart Laid Bare

2 The distance doesn't matter; it is only the first step that is difficult.
Marquise du Deffand (Marie de Vichy-Chamrond; 1697–1780) French noblewoman.
Referring to the legend of St Denis, who is traditionally believed to have carried his severed head for six miles after his execution
Letter to d'Alembert, 7 July 1763

3 From today and from this place there begins a new epoch in the history of the world.
Goethe (1749–1832) German poet and dramatist.
On witnessing the victory of the French at the battle of Valmy
The Story of Civilization (W. Durant), Vol. II

4 'Tis always morning somewhere in the world.
Richard Henry Horne (1803–84) English writer.
Orion, Bk III, Ch. 2

5 We stand today on the edge of a new frontier.
John Fitzgerald Kennedy (1917–63) US statesman.
Said on his nomination as Presidential candidate
Speech, Democratic Party Convention, 15 July 1960

☐ BEHN ☐
Aphra

(1640–89) English novelist and dramatist. She had 17 plays performed in London, the most notable of which was *The Rover* (1678). She is chiefly remembered for her exotic novel *Oronooko* (1688), containing the first attack on slavery in English literature.

QUOTATIONS ABOUT BEHN

1 Mrs Behn is still to be found here and there in the dusty worm eaten libraries of old country houses, but as a rule we imagine she has been ejected from all *decent* society for more than a generation or two.
Anonymous *Saturday Review*, 'Literary Garbage', 27 Jan 1862

2 Mrs Behn was the first woman in history to earn her living as an author and her remains were appropriately entombed in the cloisters of Westminster Abbey.
Frank Muir (1920–) British writer and broadcaster. *The Frank Muir Book*

QUOTATIONS BY BEHN

3 Since Man with that inconstancy was born,
To love the absent, and the present scorn,
Why do we deck, why do we dress
For a short-liv'd happiness?
Poems on Several Occasions, 'To Alexis'

4 Love ceases to be a pleasure, when it ceases to be a secret.
The Lover's Watch, 'Four o'clock'

☐ BELIEF ☐

See also faith, religion

1 Vain are the thousand creeds
That move men's hearts: unutterably vain;
Worthless as wither'd weeds.
Emily Brontë (1818–48) British novelist.
Last Lines

2 *Action will furnish belief,* – but will that belief be the true one?
This is the point, you know.
Arthur Hugh Clough (1819–61) British poet.
Amours de voyage, V

3 Believe it or not.
R. L. Ripley (1893–1949) US writer.
Title of newspaper column

4 I believe because it is impossible.
Tertullian (c. 160–225 AD) Carthaginian father of the church.
The usual misquotation of 'It is certain because it is impossible.'
De Carne Christi, V

5 If there were a verb meaning 'to believe falsely', it would not have any significant first person, present indicative.
Ludwig Wittgenstein (1889–1951) Austrian philosopher.
A Certain World (W. H. Auden)

☐ BELLOC ☐
(Joseph) Hilaire (Pierre)

(1870–1953) French-born British poet, essayist, and historian; Liberal MP for Salford (1906–10). Publications include *Cautionary Tales* (1907) and biographies of major historical figures. He was an ardent Roman Catholic.

QUOTATIONS ABOUT BELLOC

1 He is conscious of being decrepit and forgetful, but not of being a bore.
Evelyn Waugh (1903–66) British novelist.
Diary, 1 May 1945

QUOTATIONS BY BELLOC

2 Child! do not throw this book about;
Refrain from the unholy pleasure
Of cutting all the pictures out!
Preserve it as your chiefest treasure.
The Bad Child's Book of Beasts, 'Dedication'

3 The Chief Defect of Henry King
Was chewing little bits of String.
Cautionary Tales, 'Henry King'

4 A trick that everyone abhors
In little girls is slamming doors.
Cautionary Tales, 'Rebecca'

5 They died to save their country and they only saved the world.
The English Graves

6 When I am dead, I hope it may be said:
'His sins were scarlet, but his books were read.'
Epigrams, 'On His Books'

7 I'm tired of Love: I'm still more tired of Rhyme.
But Money gives me pleasure all the Time.
Fatigue

8 Whatever happens, we have got
The Maxim Gun, and they have not.
Referring to African natives.
The Modern Traveller

9 The Microbe is so very small
You cannot make him out at all.
More Beasts for Worse Children, 'The Microbe'

10 I always like to associate with a lot of priests because it makes me understand anti-clerical things so well.
Letter to E. S. P. Haynes, 9 Nov 1909

11 I am a Catholic. As far as possible I go to Mass every day. As far as possible I kneel down and tell these beads every day. If you reject me on account of my religion, I shall thank God that he has spared me the indignity of being your representative.
Said in his first election campaign.
Speech, Salford, 1906

12 Candidates should not attempt more than six of these.
Suggested addition to the Ten Commandments.
Attrib.

□ BENNETT □
(Enoch) Arnold
(1867–1931) British novelist. His novels, set in his native Staffordshire, include *Anna of the Five Towns* (1902) and *Clayhanger* (1910).

QUOTATIONS ABOUT BENNETT

1 Bennett – a sort of pig in clover.
D. H. Lawrence (1885–1930) British novelist.
Letter to Aldous Huxley, 27 Mar 1928

QUOTATIONS BY BENNETT

2 The people who live in the past must yield to the people who live in the future. Otherwise the world would begin to turn the other way round.
Milestones

3 Pessimism, when you get used to it, is just as agreeable as optimism.
Things that have Interested Me, 'The Slump in Pessimism'

4 Being a husband is a whole-time job. That is why so many husbands fail. They cannot give their entire attention to it.
The Title, I

5 Journalists say a thing that they know isn't true, in the hope that if they keep on saying it long enough it will be true.
The Title, II

6 Good taste is better than bad taste, but bad taste is better than no taste.
The Observer, 'Sayings of the Week', 24 Aug 1930

□ BEQUESTS □

1 When you have told anyone you have left him a legacy the only decent thing to do is to die at once.
Samuel Butler (1835–1902) British writer.
Samuel Butler: A Memoir (Festing Jones), Vol. 2

2 The man who leaves money to charity in his will is only giving away what no longer belongs to him.
Voltaire (François-Marie Arouet; 1694–1778) French writer.
Letter, 1769

□ BETJEMAN □
Sir John
(1906–84) British poet; poet laureate (1972–84). Publications include *Collected Poems* (1958), *High and Low* (1976), and a verse autobiography, *Summoned by Bells* (1960).

QUOTATIONS ABOUT BETJEMAN

1 By appointment: Teddy Bear to the Nation.
Alan Bell
The Times, 20 Sept 1982

2 You've no idea how original it was to write like Tennyson in the 1930s, rather than Eliot or Auden.
Lord David Cecil (1902–86) British writer and critic.
Remark

3 We invite people like that to tea, but we don't marry them.
Lady Chetwode
Lady Chetwode later became Betjeman's mother-in-law.
Remark

QUOTATIONS BY BETJEMAN

4 You ask me what it is I do. Well actually, you know,
I'm partly a liaison man and partly P.R.O.
Essentially I integrate the current export drive
And basically I'm viable from ten o'clock till five.
Executive

5 Phone for the fish knives Norman,
As Cook is a little unnerved;
You kiddies have crumpled the serviettes
And I must have things daintily served.
How to get on in Society

6 Come, friendly bombs, and fall on Slough
It isn't fit for humans now.
There isn't grass to graze a cow
Swarm over, Death!
...
Come, friendly bombs, and fall on Slough
To get it ready for the plough.
The cabbages are coming now:
The earth exhales.
Slough

□BETRAYAL□

See also treason

1 And forthwith he came to Jesus, and said, Hail, master; and kissed him.
And Jesus said unto him, Friend, wherefore art thou come? Then came they, and laid hands on Jesus, and took him.
Bible: Matthew
26:49–50

2 I hate the idea of causes, and if I had to choose between betraying my country and betraying my friend, I hope I should have the guts to betray my country.
E. M. Forster (1879–1970) British novelist.
Two Cheers for Democracy, 'What I Believe'.

3 *Et tu, Brute?*
You too, Brutus?
William Shakespeare (1564–1616) English dramatist.
Said by Julius Caesar
Julius Caesar, III:1

□BIBLE□

See also religion

1 He will find one English book and one only, where, as in the *Iliad* itself, perfect plainness of speech is allied with perfect nobleness; and that book is the Bible.
Matthew Arnold (1822–88) British poet and critic.
On Translating Homer

2 It's just called 'The Bible' now. We dropped the word 'Holy' to give it a more mass-market appeal.
Editor, Hodder & Stoughton
The Daily Telegraph, 30 Dec 1989

3 I have spent a lot of time searching through the Bible for loopholes.
W. C. Fields (1880–1946) US actor.
Said during his last illness
Attrib.

4 We have used the Bible as if it was a constable's handbook – an opium-dose for keeping beasts of burden patient while they are being overloaded.
Charles Kingsley (1819–75) British writer.
Letters to the Chartists, 2

5 The English Bible, a book which, if everything else in our language should perish, would alone suffice to show the whole extent of its beauty and power.
Lord Macaulay (1800–59) British historian.
Essays and Biographies, 'John Dryden'. *Edinburgh Review*

6 The number one book of the ages was written by a committee, and it was called The Bible.
Louis B. Mayer (1885–1957) Russian-born US film producer.
Comment to writers who had objected to changes in their work
The Filmgoer's Book of Quotes (Leslie Halliwell)

7 There's a Bible on that shelf there. But I keep it next to Voltaire – poison and antidote.
Bertrand Russell (1872–1970) British philosopher.
Kenneth Harris Talking To: 'Bertrand Russell' (Kenneth Harris)

8 The Bible is literature, not dogma.
George Santayana (1863–1952) US philosopher.
Introduction to the Ethics of Spinoza

□BIOGRAPHY□

1 The Art of Biography
Is different from Geography.
Geography is about Maps,
But Biography is about Chaps.
Edmund Clerihew Bentley (1875–1956) British writer.
Biography for Beginners

2 History is the essence of innumerable biographies.
Thomas Carlyle (1795–1881) Scottish historian and essayist.
Critical and Miscellaneous Essays, 'History'

3 There is properly no history; only biography.
Ralph Waldo Emerson (1803–82) US poet and essayist.
Essays, 'History'

4 Just how difficult it is to write biography can be reckoned by anybody who sits down and considers just how many people know the real truth about his or her love affairs.
Rebecca West (Cicely Isabel Fairfield; 1892–1983) British novelist and journalist.
Vogue magazine

□BIRTH□

See also babies, life and death

1 A woman when she is in travail hath sorrow, because her hour is come: but as soon as she is delivered of the child, she remembereth no more the anguish, for joy that a man is born into the world.
Bible: John
16:21

2 For man's greatest crime is to have been born.
Pedro Calderón de la Barca (1600–81) Spanish dramatist.
La Vida es Sueño, I

3 The history of man for the nine months preceding his birth would, probably, be far more interesting and contain events of greater moment than all the three-score and ten years that follow it.
Samuel Taylor Coleridge (1772–1834) British poet.
Miscellanies, Aesthetic and Literary

4 If men had to have babies they would only ever have one each.
Diana, Princess of Wales (1961–) Wife of Prince Charles.
The Observer, 'Sayings of the Week', 29 July 1984

5 Birth may be a matter of a moment. But it is a unique one.
Frédérick Leboyer (1918–) French obstetrician.
Birth Without Violence

6 MACBETH. I bear a charmed life, which must not yield
To one of woman born.
MACDUFF. Despair thy charm;
And let the angel whom thou still hast serv'd
Tell thee Macduff was from his mother's womb
Untimely ripp'd.
William Shakespeare (1564–1616) English dramatist.
Macbeth, V:8

□BITTERNESS□

1 The dupe of friendship, and the fool of love; have I not reason to hate and to despise myself? Indeed I do; and chiefly for not having hated and despised the world enough.
William Hazlitt (1778–1830) British essayist.
On the Pleasure of Hating

2 It is very difficult to get up resentment towards persons whom one has never seen.
Cardinal Newman (1801–90) British theologian.
Apologia pro Vita Sua (1864), 'Mr Kingsley's Method of Disputation'

3 He gave a deep sigh – I saw the iron enter into his soul!
Laurence Sterne (1713–68) Irish-born British writer.
A Sentimental Journey, 'The Captive. Paris'

□BLAKE□
William

(1757–1827) British poet, painter, engraver, and visionary. Blake's mystical engravings and watercolours illustrate such works as *Songs of Innocence* (1789) and the poem *Jerusalem* (1804–20).

QUOTATIONS ABOUT BLAKE

1 …William Blake's insanity was worth more than the sanity of any number of artistic mediocrities.
Gerald Abraham
Radio Times, 10 Dec 1937

2 Where other poets use reality as a springboard into space, he uses it as a foothold when he returns from flight.
Arthur Symons (1865–1945) British poet.
William Blake

QUOTATIONS BY BLAKE

3 For everything that lives is holy, life delights in life.
America

4 Every wolf's and lion's howl
Raises from Hell a human soul.
Auguries of Innocence

5 A truth that's told with bad intent
Beats all the lies you can invent.
Auguries of Innocence

6 He who shall teach the child to doubt
The rotting grave shall ne'er get out.
Auguries of Innocence

7 To see a World in a grain of sand,
And a Heaven in a wild flower,
Hold Infinity in the palm of your hand,
And Eternity in an hour.
Auguries of Innocence

8 Humility is only doubt,
And does the sun and moon blot out.
The Everlasting Gospel

9 Great things are done when men and mountains meet;
This is not done by jostling in the street.
Gnomic Verses

10 He who would do good to another must do it in Minute Particulars.
General Good is the plea of the scoundrel, hypocrite, and flatterer.
Jerusalem

11 I care not whether a man is Good or Evil; all that I care
Is whether he is a Wise Man or a Fool. Go! put off Holiness,
And put on Intellect.
Jerusalem

12 Without Contraries is no progression. Attraction and Repulsion, Reason and Energy, Love and Hate, are necessary to Human existence.
The Marriage of Heaven and Hell, 'The Argument'

13 If the doors of perception were cleansed everything would appear to man as it is, infinite.
The Marriage of Heaven and Hell, 'A Memorable Fancy'

14 Prisons are built with stones of Law, brothels with bricks of Religion.
The Marriage of Heaven and Hell, 'Proverbs of Hell'

15 Sooner murder an infant in its cradle than nurse unacted desires.
The Marriage of Heaven and Hell, 'Proverbs of Hell'

16 The road of excess leads to the palace of Wisdom.
The Marriage of Heaven and Hell, 'Proverbs of Hell'

17 A fool sees not the same tree that a wise man sees.
The Marriage of Heaven and Hell, 'Proverbs of Hell'

18 Love seeketh not itself to please,
Nor for itself hath any care,
But for another gives its ease,
And builds a Heaven in Hell's despair.
Songs of Experience, 'The Clod and the Pebble'

19 Love seeketh only Self to please,
To bind another to its delight,
Joys in another's loss of ease,
And builds a Hell in Heaven's despite.
Songs of Experience, 'The Clod and the Pebble'

20 Tiger! Tiger! burning bright
In the forests of the night,
What immortal hand or eye
Could frame thy fearful symmetry?
Songs of Experience, 'The Tiger'

21 When the stars threw down their spears,
And watered heaven with their tears,
Did he smile his work to see?
Did he who made the Lamb make thee?
Songs of Experience, 'The Tiger'

22 Piping down the valleys wild,
Piping songs of pleasant glee,
On a cloud I saw a child.
Songs of Innocence, Introduction

23 'Pipe a song about a Lamb!'
So I piped with merry cheer.
Songs of Innocence, Introduction

24 To Mercy, Pity, Peace, and Love
All pray in their distress.
Songs of Innocence, 'The Divine Image'

25 Man's Desires are limited by his Perceptions; none can desire what he has not perceived.
There is no Natural Religion

26 To generalize is to be an idiot.
Life of Blake (Gilchrist)

□ BLESSING □

See also prayer

1 Matthew, Mark, Luke and John,
The bed be blest that I lie on.
Thomas Ady (17th century) English poet.
A Candle in the Dark

2 I see the moon,
And the moon sees me;
God bless the moon,
And God bless me.
Anonymous
Gammer Gurton's Garland

3 The Lord bless thee, and keep thee:
The Lord make his face shine upon thee, and be gracious unto thee:
The Lord lift up his countenance upon thee, and give thee peace.
Bible: Numbers
6:24–26

4 'God bless us every one!' said Tiny Tim, the last of all.
Charles Dickens (1812–70) British novelist.
A Christmas Carol

□ BLINDNESS □

1 How reconcile this world of fact with the bright world of my imagining? My darkness has been filled with the light of intelligence, and behold, the outer day-light world was stumbling and groping in social blindness.
Helen Keller (1880–1968) US writer and lecturer.
The Cry for Justice (ed. Upton Sinclair)

2 Ask for this great deliverer now, and find him Eyeless in Gaza at the mill with slaves.
John Milton (1608–74) English poet.
Samson Agonistes

3 O dark, dark, dark, amid the blaze of noon,
Irrecoverably dark, total eclipse,
Without all hope of day!
John Milton
Samson Agonistes

4 He clapped the glass to his sightless eye,
And 'I'm damned if I see it', he said.
Henry John Newbolt (1862–1938) British poet.
Referring to Lord Nelson at the Battle of Copenhagen
Admirals All

5 And so I betake myself to that course, which is
almost as much as to see myself go into my grave
– for which, and all the discomforts that will
accompany my being blind, the good God prepare me!
Samuel Pepys (1633–1703) English diarist.
The closing words of Pepys's *Diary*; he lived another 34 years and
did not go blind
Diary, 31 May 1669

☐ BOATS ☐

See also navy, sea

1 There's something wrong with our bloody ships
today.
Earl Beatty (1871–1936) British admiral.
Remark during Battle of Jutland, 30 May 1916
Attrib.

2 As idle as a painted ship
Upon a painted ocean.
Samuel Taylor Coleridge (1772–1834) British poet.
The Rime of the Ancient Mariner, I

3 Jolly boating weather,
And a hay harvest breeze,
Blade on the feather,
Shade off the trees
Swing, swing together
With your body between your knees.
William Johnson Cory (1823–92) British schoolmaster and
poet.
Eton Boating Song

4 Fair stood the wind for France
When we our sails advance.
Michael Drayton (1563–1631) English poet.
Agincourt

5 There is nothing – absolutely nothing – half so
much worth doing as simply messing about in
boats.
Kenneth Grahame (1859–1932) Scottish writer.
The Wind in the Willows, Ch. 1

6 The little ships, the unforgotten Homeric cata-
logue of *Mary Jane* and *Peggy IV*, of *Folkestone
Belle*, *Boy Billy*, and *Ethel Maud*, of *Lady Haig*
and *Skylark*... the little ships of England brought
the Army home.
Philip Guedalla (1889–1944) British writer.
Referring to the evacuation of Dunkirk
Mr. Churchill

7 Quinquireme of Nineveh from distant Ophir
Rowing home to haven in sunny Palestine,
With a cargo of ivory,
And apes and peacocks,
Sandalwood, cedarwood, and sweet white wine.
John Masefield (1878–1967) British poet.
Cargoes

8 Dirty British coaster with a salt-caked smoke
stack,
Butting through the Channel in the mad March
days,
With a cargo of Tyne coal,
Road-rail, pig-lead,
Firewood, iron-ware, and cheap tin trays.
John Masefield
Cargoes

9 Now the sunset breezes shiver,
And she's fading down the river,
But in England's song for ever
She's the Fighting Téméraire.
Henry John Newbolt (1862–1938) British poet.
The Fighting Téméraire

☐ BOOKS ☐

See also criticism, fiction, literature, novels, publishing, reading,
writing

1 Some books are undeservedly forgotten; none
are undeservedly remembered.
W. H. Auden (1907–73) British poet.
The Dyer's Hand, 'Reading'

2 Some books are to be tasted, others to be swal-
lowed, and some few to be chewed and digested.
Francis Bacon (1561–1626) English philosopher.
Essays, 'Of Studies'

3 And further, by these, my son, be admonished: of
making many books there is no end; and much
study is a weariness of the flesh.
Bible: Ecclesiastes
12:12

4 A good book is the purest essence of a human
soul.
Thomas Carlyle (1795–1881) Scottish historian and essayist.
Speech made in support of the London Library
Carlyle and the London Library (F. Harrison)

5 'What is the use of a book,' thought Alice, 'without pictures or conversation?'
Lewis Carroll (Charles Lutwidge Dodgson; 1832–98) British
writer.
Alice's Adventures in Wonderland, Ch. 1

6 Go, litel book, go litel myn tragedie.
O moral Gower, this book I directe To thee.
Geoffrey Chaucer (c. 1342–1400) English poet.
Troilus and Criseyde, 5

7 Due attention to the inside of books, and due contempt for the outside, is the proper relation between a man of sense and his books.
Earl of Chesterfield (1694–1773) English statesman.
Letter to his son, 10 Jan 1749

8 Books cannot always please, however good; Minds are not ever craving for their food.
George Crabbe (1754–1832) British poet.
The Borough, 'Schools'

9 Books, we are told, propose to *instruct* or to *amuse*. indeed!…The true antithesis to knowledge, in this case, is not *pleasure*, but *power*. All that is literature seeks to communicate power; all that is not literature, to communicate knowledge.
Thomas De Quincey (1785–1859) British writer.
Letters to a Young Man

10 A book is not harmless merely because no one is consciously offended by it.
T. S. Eliot (1888–1965) US-born British poet and dramatist.
Religion and Literature

11 Books are made not like children but like pyramids…and they're just as useless! and they stay in the desert!…Jackals piss at their foot and the bourgeois climb up on them.
Gustave Flaubert (1821–80) French novelist.
Letter to Ernest Feydeau, 1857

12 Learning hath gained most by those books by which the printers have lost.
Thomas Fuller (1608–61) English historian.
The Holy State and the Profane State

13 A book may be amusing with numerous errors, or it may be very dull without a single absurdity.
Oliver Goldsmith (1728–74) Irish-born British writer.
The Vicar of Wakefield, Advertisement

14 Get stewed:
Books are a load of crap.
Philip Larkin (1922–85) British poet.
A Study of Reading Habits

15 There can hardly be a stranger commodity in the world than books. Printed by people who don't understand them; sold by people who don't understand them; bound, criticized and read by people who don't understand them; and now even written by people who don't understand them.
Georg Christoph Lichtenberg (1742–99) German physicist and writer.
Aphorisms

16 In recommending a book to a friend the less said the better. The moment you praise a book too highly you awaken resistance in your listener.
Henry Miller (1891–1980) US novelist.
The Books In My Life

17 Who kills a man kills a reasonable creature, God's image; but he who destroys a good book,

kills reason itself, kills the image of God, as it were in the eye.
John Milton (1608–74) English poet.
Areopagitica

18 A good book is the precious life-blood of a master spirit, embalmed and treasured up on purpose to a life beyond life.
John Milton
Areopagitica

19 The books one reads in childhood, and perhaps most of all the bad and good bad books, create in one's mind a sort of false map of the world, a series of fabulous countries into which one can retreat at odd moments throughout the rest of life, and which in some cases can even survive a visit to the real countries which they are supposed to represent.
George Orwell (Eric Blair; 1903–50) British novelist.
Riding Down from Bangor

20 At last, an unprintable book that is readable.
Ezra Pound (1885–1972) US poet.
Referring to *Tropic of Cancer* by Henry Miller

21 When a new book is published, read an old one.
Samuel Rogers (1763–1855) British poet.
Attrib.

22 We all know that books burn – yet we have the greater knowledge that books cannot be killed by fire. People die, but books never die. No man and no force can abolish memory…In this war, we know, books are weapons.
Franklin D. Roosevelt (1882–1945) US Democratic president.
Message to American Booksellers Association, 23 Apr 1942

23 If a book is worth reading, it is worth buying.
John Ruskin (1819–1900) British art critic and writer.
Sesame and Lilies, 'Of Kings' Treasuries'

24 All books are divisible into two classes, the books of the hour, and the books of all time.
John Ruskin
Sesame and Lilies, 'Of Kings' Treasuries'

25 How long most people would look at the best book before they would give the price of a large turbot for it!
John Ruskin
Sesame and Lilies, 'Of Kings' Treasuries'

26 Books are good enough in their own way, but they are a mighty bloodless substitute for life.
Robert Louis Stevenson (1850–94) Scottish writer.
Virginibus Puerisque

27 A good book is the best of friends, the same today and for ever.
Martin Farquhar Tupper (1810–89) British writer.
Proverbial Philosophy, 'Of Reading'

28 Books, I don't know what you see in them...I can understand a person reading them, but I can't for the life of me see why people have to write them.
Peter Ustinov (1921–) British actor.
Photo-Finish

29 There is no such thing as a moral or an immoral book. Books are well written, or badly written.
Oscar Wilde (1854–1900) Irish-born British dramatist.
The Picture of Dorian Gray, Preface

□ BOREDOM □

See also bores

1 I wanted to be bored to death, as good a way to go as any.
Peter De Vries (1910–) US novelist.
Comfort me with Apples, Ch. 17

2 You ought not to be ashamed of being bored. What you ought to be ashamed of is being boring.
Lord Hailsham (1907–) British Conservative politician.
The Observer, 'Sayings of the Week', 12 Oct 1975

3 Symmetry is tedious, and tedium is the very basis of mourning. Despair yawns.
Victor Hugo (1802–85) French writer.
Les Misérables, Vol. II, Bk. IV, Ch. 1

4 The effect of boredom on a large scale in history is underestimated. It is a main cause of revolutions, and would soon bring to an end all the static Utopias and the farmyard civilization of the Fabians.
Dean Inge (1860–1954) British churchman.
The End of an Age, Ch. 6

5 Is not life a hundred times too short for us to bore ourselves?
Friedrich Wilhelm Nietzsche (1844–1900) German philosopher.
Jenseits von Gut und Böse

6 When you're bored with yourself, marry and be bored with someone else.
David Pryce-Jones (1936–) British author and critic.
Owls and Satyrs

□ BORES □

See also boredom

1 *Bore,* n. A person who talks when you wish him to listen.
Ambrose Bierce (1842–?1914) US writer and journalist.
The Devil's Dictionary

2 Society is now one polish'd horde,
Form'd of two mighty tribes, the *Bores* and *Bored*.
Lord Byron (1788–1824) British poet.
Don Juan, XIII

3 A bore is a man who, when you ask him how he is, tells you.
Bert Leston Taylor (1866–1921) US journalist.
Attrib.

4 Somebody's boring me, I think it's me.
Dylan Thomas (1914–53) Welsh poet.
Remark made after he had been talking continuously for some time
Four Absentees (Rayner Heppenstall)

5 A healthy male adult bore consumes each year one and a half times his own weight in other people's patience.
John Updike (1932–) US novelist.
Assorted Prose, 'Confessions of a Wild Bore'

□ BORROWING □

1 Be not made a beggar by banqueting upon borrowing, when thou hast nothing in thy purse: for thou shalt lie in wait for thine own life, and be talked on.
Bible: Ecclesiasticus
18:33

2 The human species, according to the best theory I can form of it, is composed of two distinct races, the men who borrow, and the men who lend.
Charles Lamb (1775–1834) British essayist.
Essays of Elia, 'The Two Races of Men'

3 Borrowers of books – those mutilators of collections, spoilers of the symmetry of shelves, and creators of odd volumes.
Charles Lamb
Essays of Elia, 'The Two Races of Men'

4 Neither a borrower nor a lender be;
For loan oft loses both itself and friend,
And borrowing dulls the edge of husbandry.
This above all: to thine own self be true,
And it must follow, as the night the day,
Thou canst not then be false to any man.
William Shakespeare (1564–1616) English dramatist.
Hamlet, I:3

5 Let us all be happy, and live within our means, even if we have to borrer the money to do it with.
Artemus Ward (Charles Farrar Browne; 1834–67) US humorous writer.
Science and Natural History

□ BREVITY □

See also sermons, speeches, verbosity

1 Good things, when short, are twice as good.
Baltasar Gracián (1601–58) Spanish writer.
The Art of Worldly Wisdom

2 But the shortest works are always the best.
Jean de La Fontaine (1621–95) French poet.
Fables, X, 'Les Lapins'

3 Brevity is the soul of lingerie.
Dorothy Parker (1893–1967) US writer.
While Rome Burns (Alexander Woollcott)

4 Trust the man who hesitates in his speech and is quick and steady in action, but beware of long arguments and long beards.
George Santayana (1863–1952) US philosopher.
Soliloquies in England, 'The British Character'

5 Brevity is the soul of wit.
William Shakespeare (1564–1616) English dramatist.
Hamlet, II:2

6 Men of few words are the best men.
William Shakespeare
Henry V, III:2

☐ **BRIBERY** ☐

See also corruption

1 To a shower of gold most things are penetrable.
Thomas Carlyle (1795–1881) Scottish historian and essayist.
History of the French Revolution, Pt. I, Bk. III, Ch. 7

2 I have often noticed that a bribe...has that effect – it changes a relation. The man who offers a bribe gives away a little of his own importance; the bribe once accepted, he becomes the inferior, like a man who has paid for a woman.
Graham Greene (1904–91) British novelist.
The Comedians, Pt. I, Ch. 4

3 Though authority be a stubborn bear, yet he is oft led by the nose with gold.
William Shakespeare (1564–1616) English dramatist.
The Winter's Tale, IV:3

☐ **BRITAIN** ☐

See also British, British Empire, England, Ireland, patriotism, Scotland, Wales

1 You must not miss Whitehall. At one end you will find a statue of one of our kings who was beheaded; at the other the monument to the man who did it. This is just an example of our attempts to be fair to everybody.
Edward Appleton (1892–1965) British physicist.
Referring to Charles I and Cromwell
Speech, Stockholm, 1 Jan 1948

2 Land of Hope and Glory, Mother of the Free, How shall we extol thee, who are born of thee? Wider still and wider shall thy bounds be set; God who made thee mighty, make thee mightier yet.
A. C. Benson (1862–1925) British writer.
Land of Hope and Glory

3 God save our Gracious King,
Long live our noble King,
God save the King.
Send him victorious,
Happy and glorious.
Henry Carey (c. 1690–1743) English poet and musician.
God Save the King

4 Britain is not a country that is easily rocked by revolution...In Britain our institutions evolve. We are a Fabian Society writ large.
William Hamilton (1917–) Scottish MP.
My Queen and I, Ch. 9

5 We may be a small island, but we are not a small people.
Edward Heath (1916–) British politician and prime minister.
The Observer, 'Sayings of the Week', 21 June 1970

6 Once, when a British Prime Minister sneezed, men half a world away would blow their noses. Now when a British Prime Minister sneezes nobody else will even say 'Bless You'.
Bernard Levin (1928–) British journalist.
The Times, 1976

7 When Britain first, at heaven's command,
Arose from out the azure main,
This was the charter of the land,
And guardian angels sung this strain:
'Rule, Britannia, rule the waves;
Britons never will be slaves.'
James Thomson (1700–48) British poet.
Alfred: a Masque, Act II

☐ **BRITISH** ☐

See also Britain, English, Irish, Scots, Welsh

1 The British love permanence more than they love beauty.
Hugh Casson (1910–) British architect.
The Observer, 'Sayings of the Week', 14 June 1964

2 The maxim of the British people is 'Business as usual'.
Winston Churchill (1874–1965) British statesman.
Speech, Guildhall, 9 Nov 1914

3 They are the only people who like to be told how bad things are – who like to be told the worst.
Winston Churchill
Speech, 1921

4 It is beginning to be hinted that we are a nation of amateurs.
Lord Rosebery (1847–1929) British statesman.
Rectorial Address, Glasgow, 16 Nov 1900

5 Other nations use 'force'; we Britons alone use 'Might'.
Evelyn Waugh (1903–66) British novelist.
Scoop, Bk. II, Ch. 5

☐ **BRITISH EMPIRE** ☐

1 The loss of India would mark and consummate the downfall of the British Empire. That great organism would pass at a stroke out of life into history. From such a catastrophe there could be no recovery.
Winston Churchill (1874–1965) British statesman.
Speech to Indian Empire Society, London, 12 Dec 1930

2 I have not become the King's First Minister in order to preside over the liquidation of the British Empire.
Winston Churchill
Speech, Mansion House, 10 Nov 1942

3 'Can't' will be the epitaph of the British Empire – unless we wake up in time.
Oswald Mosley (1896–1980) British politician.
Speech, Manchester, 9 Dec 1937

4 His Majesty's dominions, on which the sun never sets.
Christopher North (John Wilson; 1785–1854) Scottish writer.
Noctes Ambrosianae, 20 Apr 1829

5 The Empire is a Commonwealth of Nations.
Lord Rosebery (1847–1929) British statesman.
Speech, Adelaide, 18 Jan 1884

□ BRONTË □
Anne
(1820–49) British novelist. Youngest of the three Brontë sisters and daughter of Patrick Brontë, the rector of Haworth, Yorkshire. Her best known works, *Agnes Grey* (1847) and *The Tenant of Wildfell Hall* (1948), were published under the pseudonym Acton Bell.

QUOTATIONS ABOUT ANNE BRONTË

1 A sort of literary Cinderella.
George Moore (1852–1933) Irish writer and art critic. *Conversations in Ebury Street*

QUOTATIONS BY ANNE BRONTË

2 What is it that constitutes virtue, Mrs. Graham? Is it the circumstance of being able and willing to resist temptation; or that of having no temptations to resist?
The Tenant of Wildfell Hall, Ch. 3

3 Keep a guard over your eyes and ears as the inlets of your heart, and over your lips as the outlet, lest they betray you in a moment of unwariness.
The Tenant of Wildfell Hall, Ch. 16

□ BRONTË □
Charlotte
(1816–55) British novelist. Eldest daughter of Patrick Brontë, the rector of Haworth, Yorkshire. Her best known works, *Jane Eyre* (1847), *Shirley* (1849), and *Villette* (1853), were published under the pseudonym Currer Bell.

QUOTATIONS ABOUT CHARLOTTE BRONTË

1 If these remarkable works are the productions of a woman we shall only say she must be a woman pretty nearly unsexed; and Jane Eyre strikes us as a personage much more likely to have sprung ready-armed from the head of a man and that head a pretty hard one, than to have experienced, in any shape, the softening influence of a female creation.
James Lorimer (1818–90) British jurist and philosopher. *North British Review*, Aug 1849

QUOTATIONS BY CHARLOTTE BRONTË

2 Vain favour! coming, like most other favours long deferred and often wished for, too late!
Jane Eyre, Ch. 3

3 The soul fortunately, has an interpreter – often an unconscious, but still a truthful interpreter – in the eye.
Jane Eyre, Ch. 28

4 Reader, I married him.
Jane Eyre, Ch. 38

5 An abundant shower of curates has fallen upon the north of England.
Shirley, Ch. 1

□ BRONTË □
Emily
(1818–48) British novelist. Daughter of Patrick Brontë, the rector of Haworth, Yorkshire she was educated mostly at home. She spent much time on the wild moors surrounding Haworth, which are portrayed so vividly in her major work *Wuthering Heights* (1847), published under the pseudonym Ellis Bell.

QUOTATIONS ABOUT EMILY BRONTË

1 Emily Brontë remains the sphinx of literature.
W. Robertson Nicoll (1851–1923) British writer. *Chambers Encyclopedia of English Literature*

QUOTATIONS BY EMILY BRONTË

2 No coward soul is mine,
No trembler in the world's storm-troubled sphere:
I see Heaven's glories shine,
And faith shines equal, arming me from fear.
Last Lines

3 Once drinking deep of that divinest anguish, How could I seek the empty world again?
Remembrance

4 A good heart will help you to a bonny face, my lad...and a bad one will turn the bonniest into something worse than ugly.
Wuthering Heights, Ch. 7

□ BROWNING □
Elizabeth Barrett
(1806–61) British poet. Her works include *Sonnets from the Portuguese* (1850), *Aurora Leigh* (1857), *The Seraphim and Other Poems* (1838), *Poems Before Congress* (1860), and *Last Poems* (1862).

QUOTATIONS ABOUT ELIZABETH BROWNING

1 Fate has not been kind to Mrs Browning. Nobody reads her, nobody discusses her, nobody troubles to put her in her place.
Virginia Woolf (1882–1941) British novelist. *Second Common Reader*

QUOTATIONS BY ELIZABETH BROWNING

2 Since when was genius found respectable?
Aurora Leigh, Bk VI

3 Do you hear the children weeping, O my brothers,
Ere the sorrow comes with years?
The Cry of the Children

4 God's gifts put man's best gifts to shame.
Sonnets from the Portuguese, XXVI

5 I love thee with a love I seemed to lose
With my lost saints – I love thee with the breath,
Smiles, tears, of all my life! – and, if God choose,
I shall but love thee better after death.
Sonnets from the Portuguese, XLIII

☐ BROWNING ☐
Robert

(1812–89) British poet. *Men and Women* (1855), *Dramatis Personae* (1864), and *The Ring and the Book* (1868–69), were written after his marriage to the poet Elizabeth Barrett, with whom he eloped to Italy in 1846.

QUOTATIONS ABOUT ROBERT BROWNING

1 Browning used words with the violence of a
horse-breaker, giving out the scent of a he-goat.
But he got them to do their work.
Ford Madox Ford (1873–1939) British novelist.
The March of Literature

2 He might have passed for a politician, or a financier, or a diplomatist or, indeed, for anything but
a poet.
George William Russell (1867–1965) Irish poet and
dramatist.
Portraits of the Seventies

QUOTATIONS BY ROBERT BROWNING

3 So free we seem, so fettered fast we are!
Andrea del Sarto

4 Ah, but a man's reach should exceed his grasp,
Or what's a heaven for?
Andrea del Sarto

5 Why need the other women know so much?
Any Wife to any Husband

6 I never saw a brute I hated so;
He must be wicked to deserve such pain.
Childe Roland to the Dark Tower Came, XIV

7 How very hard it is
To be a Christian!
Easter-Day, I

8 At last awake
From life, that insane dream we take
For waking now.
Easter-Day, XIV

9 That's the wise thrush; he sings each song twice
over,
Lest you should think he never could recapture
The first fine careless rapture!
Home Thoughts from Abroad

10 She had
A heart – how shall I say? – too soon made glad,
Too easily impressed.
My Last Duchess

11 Suddenly, as rare things will, it vanished.
One Word More, IV

12 Rats!
They fought the dogs and killed the cats,
And bit the babies in the cradles.
The Pied Piper of Hamelin

13 And the muttering grew to a grumbling;
And the grumbling grew to a mighty rumbling;
And out of the houses the rats came tumbling.
The Pied Piper of Hamelin

14 The year's at the spring,
And day's at the morn;
Morning's at seven;
The hill-side's dew-pearled;
The lark's on the wing;
The snail's on the thorn;
God's in His heaven –
All's right with the world.
Pippa Passes, Pt. I

15 Therefore I summon age
To grant youth's heritage.
Rabbi ben Ezra, XIII

16 What of soul was left, I wonder, when the kissing
had to stop?
A Toccata of Galuppi's

☐ BUREAUCRACY ☐

1 I'm surprised that a government organization
could do it that quickly.
Jimmy Carter (1924–) US statesman and president.
Visiting Egypt, when told that it took twenty years to build the
Great Pyramid
Presidential Anecdotes (P. Boller)

2 A committee is a cul-de-sac down which ideas are
lured and then quietly strangled.
Barnett Cocks (1907–) British political writer.
New Scientist, 1973

3 Whatever was required to be done, the Circumlocution Office was beforehand with all the public
departments in the art of perceiving – HOW NOT
TO DO IT.
Charles Dickens (1812–70) British novelist.
Little Dorrit, Bk. I, Ch. 10

4 A Royal Commission is a broody hen sitting on a china egg.
Michael Foot (1913–) British Labour politician and journalist.
Speech, House of Commons, 1964

5 A difficulty for every solution.
Herbert Samuel (1870–1963) British Liberal statesman.
Referring to the Civil Service
Attrib.

6 The working of great institutions is mainly the result of a vast mass of routine, petty malice, self interest, carelessness, and sheer mistake. Only a residual fraction is thought.
George Santayana (1863–1952) US philosopher.
The Crime of Galileo

7 My life's been a meeting, Dad, one long meeting. Even in the few committees I don't yet belong to, the agenda winks at me when I pass.
Gwyn Thomas (1913–81) British writer.
The Keep, I

8 The British civil service…is a beautifully designed and effective braking mechanism.
Shirley Williams (1930–) British politician.
Speech, Royal Institute of Public Administration, 11 Feb 1980

☐ BURKE ☐
Edmund
(1729–97) British politician and political philosopher. He entered parliament as a Whig in 1765. In *Reflections on the Revolution in France* (1790) he condemned the French Revolution.

QUOTATIONS ABOUT BURKE

1 Burke was a damned wrong-headed fellow, through his whole life jealous and obstinate.
Charles James Fox (1749–1806) British Whig politician.
Attrib.

QUOTATIONS BY BURKE

2 The only infallible criterion of wisdom to vulgar minds – success.
Letter to a Member of the National Assembly

3 There is, however, a limit at which forbearance ceases to be a virtue.
Observations on a Publication, 'The Present State of the Nation'

4 I am convinced that we have a degree of delight, and that no small one, in the real misfortunes and pains of others.
On the Sublime and Beautiful, Pt. I

5 Beauty in distress is much the most affecting beauty.
On the Sublime and Beautiful, Pt. III

6 Man is by his constitution a religious animal.
Reflections on the Revolution in France

7 Superstition is the religion of feeble minds.
Reflections on the Revolution in France

8 All government, indeed every human benefit and enjoyment, every virtue, and every prudent act, is founded on compromise and barter.
Speech on Conciliation with America (House of Commons, 22 Mar 1775)

9 The use of force alone is but *temporary*. It may subdue for a moment; but it does not remove the necessity of subduing again: and a nation is not governed, which is perpetually to be conquered.
Speech on Conciliation with America (House of Commons, 22 Mar 1775)

10 Kings are naturally lovers of low company.
Speech on the Economical Reform (House of Commons, 11 Feb 1780)

11 The people are the masters.
Speech on the Economical Reform (House of Commons, 11 Feb 1780)

12 And having looked to government for bread, on the very first scarcity they will turn and bite the hand that fed them.
Thoughts and Details on Scarcity

13 Liberty, too, must be limited in order to be possessed.
Letter to the Sherriffs of Bristol, 1777

14 Nothing is so fatal to religion as indifference, which is, at least, half infidelity.
Letter to William Smith, 29 Jan 1795

15 The greater the power, the more dangerous the abuse.
Speech, House of Commons, 7 Feb 1771

☐ BURNS ☐
Robert
(1759–96) Scottish poet. A farmer's son, Burns established his reputation with *Poems, Chiefly in the Scottish Dialect* (1786). He subsequently wrote many songs, notably *Auld Lang Syne*, and the narrative poem *Tam o' Shanter*, all of which made him the national poet of Scotland.

QUOTATIONS ABOUT BURNS

1 The largest soul of all the British lands came among us in the shape of a hard-handed Scottish peasant.
Thomas Carlyle (1795–1881) Scottish historian and poet.
On Heroes, Hero-Worship and the Heroic in History, Lecture V

QUOTATIONS BY BURNS

2 O Thou! Whatever title suit thee –
Auld Hornie, Satan, Nick, or Clootie.
Address to the Devil

3 Should auld acquaintance be forgot,
And never brought to min'?
Auld Lang Syne

4 Gin a body meet a body
Coming through the rye;
Gin a body kiss a body,
Need a body cry?
Coming through the Rye

5 On ev'ry hand it will allow'd be,
He's just – nae better than he should be.
A Dedication to Gavin Hamilton

6 Here lie Willie Michie's banes;
O Satan, when ye tak him,
Gie him the schoolin' of your weans,
For clever deils he'll mak them!
Epitaph on a Schoolmaster

7 Green grow the rashes O,
Green grow the rashes O,
The sweetest hours that e'er I spend,
Are spent amang the lasses O!
Green Grow the Rashes

8 Man's inhumanity to man
Makes countless thousands mourn!
Man was Made to Mourn

9 My heart's in the Highlands, my heart is not
here;
My heart's in the Highlands a-chasing the deer;
Chasing the wild deer, and following the roe,
My heart's in the Highlands, wherever I go.
My Heart's in the Highlands

10 My love is like a red red rose
That's newly sprung in June:
My love is like the melodie
That's sweetly play'd in tune.
A Red, Red Rose

11 Wee, sleekit, cow'rin', tim'rous beastie,
O what a panic's in thy breastie!
To a Mouse

12 The best laid schemes o' mice an' men
Gang aft a-gley,
An' lea'e us nought but grief an' pain
For promis'd joy.
To a Mouse

13 But yet the light that led astray
Was light from Heaven.
The Vision

☐ BUSINESS ☐

See also capitalism

1 Here's the rule for bargains: 'Do other men, for
they would do you.' That's the true business precept.
Charles Dickens (1812–70) British novelist.
Martin Chuzzlewit, Ch. 11

2 Whenever you see a successful business, someone once made a courageous decision.
Peter F. Drucker

3 A business that makes nothing but money is a
poor kind of business.
Henry Ford (1863–1947) US car manufacturer.
Interview

4 No nation was ever ruined by trade.
Benjamin Franklin (1706–90) US scientist and statesman.
Essays, 'Thoughts on Commercial Subjects'

5 Remember that time is money.
Benjamin Franklin
Advice to a Young Tradesman

6 Where wealth and freedom reign, contentment
fails,
And honour sinks where commerce long pre-
vails.
Oliver Goldsmith (1728–74) Irish-born British writer.
The Traveller

7 He's a businessman...I'll make him an offer he
can't refuse.
Mario Puzo (1920–) US writer.
The Godfather, Ch. 1

8 A friendship founded on business is better than a
business founded on friendship.
John D. Rockefeller (1839–1937) US industrialist.

9 A dinner lubricates business.
William Scott (1745–1836) British jurist.
Life of Johnson (J. Boswell), 1791

10 The customer is always right.
H. Gordon Selfridge (1857–1947) US-born businessman.
Slogan adopted at his shops

11 The big print giveth and the fine print taketh
away.
J. Fulton Sheen (1895–1979) US Roman Catholic archbishop.
Referring to his contract for a television appearance
Attrib.

12 All business sagacity reduces itself in the last
analysis to a judicious use of sabotage.
Thorstein Bunde Veblen (1857–1929) US social scientist.
The Nature of Peace

13 Being good in business is the most fascinating
kind of art.
Andy Warhol (Andrew Warhola; 1926–87) US pop artist.
Observer, 1 Mar 1987

14 Business underlies everything in our national life, including our spiritual life. Witness the fact that in the Lord's Prayer the first petition is for daily bread. No one can worship God or love his neighbour on an empty stomach.
Woodrow Wilson (1856–1925) US statesman.
Speech, New York, 1912

☐ BUTLER ☐
Samuel
(1612–80) English satirist, secretary to George Villiers, 2nd Duke of Buckingham. The satirical poem *Hudibras* (1663–78), a mock romance, is his most famous work.

1 When civil fury first grew high,
And men fell out they knew not why.
Hudibras, Pt. I

2 To swallow gudgeons ere they're catched,
And count their chickens ere they're hatched.
Hudibras, Pt. II

3 Love is a boy, by poets styl'd,
Then spare the rod, and spoil the child.
Hudibras, Pt. II

4 Oaths are but words, and words but wind.
Hudibras, Pt. II

5 What makes all doctrines plain and clear?
About two hundred pounds a year.
Hudibras, Pt. III

6 The souls of women are so small,
That some believe they've none at all.
Miscellaneous Thoughts

☐ BYRON ☐
George Gordon, 6th Baron
(1788–1824) British poet. The melancholy *Childe Harold's Pilgrimage* (1812) brought him to the attention of literary society. After scandalizing London with his sexual exploits he lived abroad, largely in Italy; his later works include the poetic drama *Manfred* (1817) and the epic satire *Don Juan* (1819–24).

QUOTATIONS ABOUT BYRON

1 When Byron's eyes were shut in death,
We bow'd our head and held our breath.
He taught us little: but our soul
Had *felt* him like the thunder's roll.
Matthew Arnold (1822–88) British poet and critic.
Memorial Verses

2 Mad, bad, and dangerous to know.
Lady Caroline Lamb (1785–1828) The wife of William Lamb.
Journal

QUOTATIONS BY BYRON

3 The land self-interest groans from shore to shore,
For fear that plenty should attain the poor.
The Age of Bronze, XIV

4 I like the weather, when it is not rainy,
That is, I like two months of every year.
Beppo

5 While stands the Coliseum, Rome shall stand;
When falls the Coliseum, Rome shall fall;
And when Rome falls – the World.
Childe Harold's Pilgrimage, IV

6 The spirit burning but unbent,
May writhe, rebel – the weak alone repent!
The Corsair, II

7 What men call gallantry, and gods adultery,
Is much more common where the climate's sultry.
Don Juan, I

8 Man, being reasonable, must get drunk;
The best of life is but intoxication.
Don Juan, II

9 All tragedies are finish'd by a death,
All comedies are ended by a marriage.
Don Juan, III

10 Cost his enemies a long repentance,
And made him a good friend, but bad acquaintance.
Don Juan, III

11 Though sages may pour out their wisdom's treasure,
There is no sterner moralist than Pleasure.
Don Juan, III

12 There is a tide in the affairs of women,
Which, taken at the flood, leads – God knows where.
Don Juan, VI

13 A lady of a 'certain age', which means
Certainly aged.
Don Juan, VI

14 Now hatred is by far the longest pleasure;
Men love in haste, but they detest at leisure.
Don Juan, XIII

15 'Tis pleasant, sure, to see one's name in print;
A book's a book, although there's nothing in't.
English Bards and Scotch Reviewers

16 If I should meet thee
After long years,
How should I greet thee? –
With silence and tears.
When we two parted

17 I awoke one morning and found myself famous.
Remark made after the publication of *Childe Harold's Pilgrimage* (1812).
Entry in Memoranda

C

□ CAMBRIDGE □

See also England, Oxford

1 Oxford is on the whole more attractive than Cambridge to the ordinary visitor; and the traveller is therefore recommended to visit Cambridge first, or to omit it altogether if he cannot visit both.
Karl Baedeker (1801–59) German publisher.
Baedeker's Great Britain, 'From London to Oxford'

2 For Cambridge people rarely smile,
Being urban, squat, and packed with guile.
Rupert Brooke (1887–1915) British poet.
The Old Vicarage, Grantchester

3 The King to Oxford sent a troop of horse,
For Tories own no argument but force:
With equal skill to Cambridge books he sent,
For Whigs admit no force but argument.
William Browne (1692–1774) English physician.
A reply to TRAPP
Literary Anecdotes (Nichols), Vol. III

4 This is the city of perspiring dreams.
Frederic Raphael (1931–) British author.
The Glittering Prizes: An Early Life, III

5 The King, observing with judicious eyes
The state of both his universities,
To Oxford sent a troop of horse, and why?
That learned body wanted loyalty;
To Cambridge books, as very well discerning
How much that loyal body wanted learning.
Joseph Trapp (1679–1747) English churchman and academic.
Written after George I donated the Bishop of Ely's library to Cambridge; for a reply see BROWNE
Literary Anecdotes (Nichols), Vol. III

□ CANNIBALISM □

1 Eating people is wrong.
Michael Flanders (1922–75) British comedian and songwriter.
The Reluctant Cannibal

2 The better sort of Ishmaelites have been Christian for many centuries and will not publicly eat human flesh uncooked in Lent, without special and costly dispensation from their bishop.
Evelyn Waugh (1903–66) British novelist.
Scoop, Bk. II, Ch. 1

□ CAPITALISM □

See also business

1 Property has its duties as well as its rights.
Thomas Drummond (1797–1840) British engineer and statesman.
Letter to the Earl of Donoughmore, 22 May 1838

2 If I had to give a definition of capitalism I would say: the process whereby American girls turn into American women.
Christopher Hampton (1946–) British writer and dramatist.
Savages, Sc. 16

3 It is the unpleasant and unacceptable face of capitalism but one should not suggest that the whole of British industry consists of practices of this kind.
Edward Heath (1916–) British politician and prime minister.
Referring to the Lonrho Affair
Speech, House of Commons, 15 May 1973

4 Militarism…is one of the chief bulwarks of capitalism, and the day that militarism is undermined, capitalism will fail.
Helen Keller (1880–1968) US writer and lecturer.
The Story of My Life

5 We cannot remove the evils of capitalism without taking its source of power: ownership.
Neil Kinnock (1942–) British politician.
Tribune, 1975

6 Under capitalism we have a state in the proper sense of the word, that is, a special machine for the suppression of one class by another.
Lenin (Vladimir Ilich Ulyanov; 1870–1924) Russian revolutionary leader.
The State and Revolution, Ch. 5

7 Capitalist production begets, with the inexorability of a law of nature, its own negation.
Karl Marx (1818–83) German philosopher and revolutionary.
Das Kapital, Ch. 15

8 I have gone to war too…I am going to fight capitalism even if it kills me. It is wrong that people like you should be comfortable and well fed while all around you people are starving.
Sylvia Pankhurst (1882–1960) British suffragette.
The Fighting Pankhursts (David Mitchell)

9 Property is theft.
Pierre Joseph Proudhon (1809–65) French socialist.
Qu'est-ce que la Propriété?, Ch. 1

□ CARLYLE □
Thomas

(1795–1881) Scottish historian and essayist. *Sartor Resartus,* a philosophical work, appeared in 1836; his subsequent writings include *The French Revolution* (1837) and *Heroes, Hero-Worship and the Heroic in History* (1841).

QUOTATIONS ABOUT CARLYLE

1 It was very good of God to let Carlyle and Mrs Carlyle marry one another and so make only two people miserable instead of four.
Samuel Butler (1835–1902) British writer.
Attrib.

2 Carlyle is a poet to whom nature has denied the faculty of verse.
Alfred, Lord Tennyson (1809–92) British poet.
Letter to W. E. Gladstone

3 A poet without love were a physical and metaphysical impossibility.
Critical and Miscellaneous Essays, 'Burns'

4 A witty statesman said, you might prove anything by figures.
Critical and Miscellaneous Essays, 'Chartism'

5 History is the essence of innumerable biographies.
Critical and Miscellaneous Essays, 'History'

6 A well-written Life is almost as rare as a well-spent one.
Critical and Miscellaneous Essays, 'Richter'

7 The three great elements of modern civilization, Gunpowder, Printing, and the Protestant Religion.
Critical and Miscellaneous Essays, 'The State of German Literature'

8 The true University of these days is a collection of books.
Heroes and Hero-Worship, 'The Hero as Man of Letters'

9 France was a long despotism tempered by epigrams.
History of the French Revolution, Pt. I, Bk. I, Ch. 1

10 No man who has once heartily and wholly laughed can be altogether irreclaimably bad.
Sartor Resartus, Bk. I, Ch. 4

☐ CARROLL ☐
Lewis

(Charles Lutwidge Dodgson; 1832–98) British writer and mathematician; author of the children's classics *Alice's Adventures in Wonderland* (1865) and *Through the Looking-Glass* (1872).

1 'What is the use of a book,' thought Alice, 'without pictures or conversation?'
Alice's Adventures in Wonderland, Ch. 1

2 'You are old, Father William,' the young man said,
'And your hair has become very white;
And yet you incessantly stand on your head –
Do you think at your age, it is right?'
Alice's Adventures in Wonderland, Ch. 5

3 This time it vanished quite slowly, beginning with the end of the tail, and ending with the grin, which remained some time after the rest of it had gone.
Describing the Cheshire Cat.
Alice's Adventures in Wonderland, Ch. 6

4 'Then you should say what you mean,' the March Hare went on. 'I do,' Alice hastily replied; 'at least – at least I mean what I say – that's the same thing, you know.'
'Not the same thing a bit!' said the Hatter. 'Why, you might just as well say that "I see what I eat" is the same thing as "I eat what I see!"'
Alice's Adventures in Wonderland, Ch. 7

5 'Take some more tea,' the March Hare said to Alice, very earnestly.
'I've had nothing yet,' Alice replied in an offended tone, 'so I can't take more.'
'You mean you can't take *less*,' said the Hatter: 'it's very easy to take *more* than nothing.'
Alice's Adventures in Wonderland, Ch. 7

6 Take care of the sense, and the sounds will take care of themselves.
Alice's Adventures in Wonderland, Ch. 9

7 'Reeling and Writhing, of course, to begin with,' the Mock Turtle replied; 'and then the different branches of Arithmetic – Ambition, Distraction, Uglification, and Derision.'
Alice's Adventures in Wonderland, Ch. 9

8 'Where shall I begin, please your Majesty?' he asked.
'Begin at the beginning' the King said, gravely, 'and go on till you come to the end: then stop.'
Alice's Adventures in Wonderland, Ch. 11

9 'No, no!' said the Queen. 'Sentence first – verdict afterwards.'
Alice's Adventures in Wonderland, Ch. 12

10 'The time has come,' the Walrus said,
'To talk of many things:
Of shoes – and ships – and sealing-wax –
Of cabbages – and kings –
And why the sea is boiling hot –
And whether pigs have wings.'
Through the Looking-Glass, Ch. 4

11 The rule is, jam tomorrow and jam yesterday – but never jam today.
Through the Looking-Glass, Ch. 5

12 'When *I* use a word,' Humpty Dumpty said in rather a scornful tone, 'it means just what I choose it to mean – neither more nor less.'
Through the Looking-Glass, Ch. 6

☐ CATHOLICISM ☐
See also Christianity, Protestantism, religion

1 *Ad majorem Dei gloriam.*
To the greater glory of God.
Anonymous
Motto of the Jesuits

2 The Papacy is not other than the Ghost of the deceased Roman Empire, sitting crowned upon the grave thereof.
Thomas Hobbes (1588–1679) English philosopher.
Leviathan, Pt. IV, Ch. 37

3 There is no idolatry in the Mass. They believe God to be there, and they adore him.
Samuel Johnson (1709–84) British lexicographer.
Life of Johnson (J. Boswell), Vol. II

4 Since God has given us the papacy, let us enjoy it.
Leo X (Giovanni de' Medici; 1475–1521) Pope (1513–21).
Men of Art (T. Craven)

5 Becoming an Anglo-Catholic must surely be a sad business – rather like becoming an amateur conjurer.
John St Loe Strachey (1901–63) British politician.
The Coming Struggle for Power, Pt. III, Ch. 11

6 'God knows how you Protestants can be expected to have any sense of direction,' she said. 'It's different with us. I haven't been to mass for years, I've got every mortal sin on my conscience, but I know when I'm doing wrong. I'm still a Catholic.
Angus Wilson (1913–91) British novelist.
The Wrong Set, 'Significant Experience'

□CATS□

See also animals

1 Cruel, but composed and bland,
Dumb, inscrutable and grand,
So Tiberius might have sat,
Had Tiberius been a cat.
Matthew Arnold (1822–88) British poet and critic.
Poor Matthias

2 Macavity, Macavity, there's no one like Macavity,
There never was a Cat of such deceitfulness and suavity.
He always has an alibi, and one or two to spare:
At whatever time the deed took place – MACAVITY WASN'T THERE!
T. S. Eliot (1888–1965) US-born British poet and dramatist.
Macavity: The Mystery Cat

3 I have noticed that what cats most appreciate in a human being is not the ability to produce food which they take for granted – but his or her entertainment value.
Geoffrey Household (1900–88) British writer.
Rogue Male

4 If a fish is the movement of water embodied, given shape, then cat is a diagram and pattern of subtle air.
Doris Lessing (1919–) British novelist.
Particularly Cats, Ch. 2

5 When I play with my cat, who knows whether she is not amusing herself with me more than I with her?
Michel de Montaigne (1533–92) French essayist.
Essais, II

6 If a dog jumps onto your lap it is because he is fond of you; but if a cat does the same thing it is because your lap is warmer.
A. N. Whitehead (1861–1947) British philosopher.
Dialogues

□CAUTION□

See also prudence

1 And all should cry, Beware! Beware!
His flashing eyes, his floating hair!
Weave a circle round him thrice,
And close your eyes with holy dread,
For he on honey-dew hath fed,
And drunk the milk of Paradise.
Samuel Taylor Coleridge (1772–1834) British poet.
Kubla Khan

2 Chi Wen Tzu always thought three times before taking action. Twice would have been quite enough.
Confucius (K'ung Fu-tzu; 551–479 BC) Chinese philosopher.
Analects

3 The only way to be absolutely safe is never to try anything for the first time.
Magnus Pyke (1908–) British scientist, television personality, and writer.
BBC radio programme

□CENSORSHIP□

See also pornography, prudery

1 Whenever books are burned men also in the end are burned.
Heinrich Heine (1797–1856) German poet and writer.
Almansor

2 Censorship is more depraving and corrupting than anything pornography can produce.
Tony Smythe (1938–) Chairman of the National Council for Civil Liberties, Great Britain.
The Observer, 'Sayings of the Week', 18 Sept 1972

3 God forbid that any book should be banned. The practice is as indefensible as infanticide.
Rebecca West (Cicely Isabel Fairfield; 1892–1983) British novelist and journalist.
The Strange Necessity, 'The Tosh Horse'

□CERTAINTY□

See also self-confidence

1 If a man will begin with certainties, he shall end in doubts, but if he will be content to begin with doubts, he shall end in certainties.
Francis Bacon (1561–1626) English philosopher.
The Advancement of Learning, Bk. I, Ch. 5

2 Of that there is no manner of doubt –
No probable, possible shadow of doubt –
No possible doubt whatever.
W. S. Gilbert (1836–1911) British dramatist.
The Gondoliers, I

□ CERVANTES □
Miguel de
(1547–1616) Spanish novelist and dramatist; creator of *Don Quixote* (1605; 1615), a satirical romance of chivalry.

QUOTATIONS ABOUT CERVANTES

1 Cervantes laughed chivalry out of fashion.
Horace Walpole (1717–97) British writer.
Letter to Sir Horace Mann, 19 July 1774

QUOTATIONS BY CERVANTES

2 A silly remark can be made in Latin as well as in Spanish.
The Dialogue of the Dogs

3 Take care, your worship, those things over there are not giants but windmills.
Don Quixote, Pt. I, Ch. 8

4 Didn't I tell you, Don Quixote, sir, to turn back, for they were not armies you were going to attack, but flocks of sheep?
Don Quixote, Pt. I, Ch. 18

5 Fear has many eyes and can see things underground.
Don Quixote, Pt. I, Ch. 20

6 In me the need to talk is a primary impulse, and I can't help saying right off what comes to my tongue.
Don Quixote, Pt. I, Ch. 30

7 Every man is as Heaven made him, and sometimes a great deal worse.
Don Quixote, Pt. II, Ch. 4

8 Well, now, there's a remedy for everything except death.
Don Quixote, Pt. II, Ch. 10

9 There are only two families in the world, my old grandmother used to say, The *Haves* and the *Have-Nots*.
Don Quixote, Pt. II, Ch. 20

10 A private sin is not so prejudicial in the world as a public indecency.
Don Quixote, Pt. II, Ch. 22

11 Tell me what company thou keepest, and I'll tell thee what thou art.
Don Quixote, Pt. II, Ch. 23

□ CHANDLER □
Raymond
(1888–1959) US novelist, famous for his detective stories and thrillers. His detective, Philip Marlowe, first appeared in *The Big Sleep* (1939).

1 It was a blonde. A blonde to make a bishop kick a hole in a stained-glass window.
Farewell, My Lovely, Ch. 13

2 She gave me a smile I could feel in my hip pocket.
Farewell, My Lovely, Ch. 18

3 If my books had been any worse I should not have been invited to Hollywood, and if they had been any better I should not have come.
The Life of Raymond Chandler (F. MacShane)

4 When I split an infinitive, god damn it, I split it so it stays split.
Letter to his English publisher

□ CHANGE □
See also conservatism, constancy, progress, transience

1 Can the Ethiopian change his skin, or the leopard his spots? then may ye also do good, that are accustomed to do evil.
Bible: Jeremiah
13:23

2 All reform except a moral one will prove unavailing.
Thomas Carlyle (1795–1881) Scottish historian and essayist.
Critical and Miscellaneous Essays, 'Corn Law Rhymes'

3 Variety's the very spice of life
That gives it all its flavour.
William Cowper (1731–1800) British poet.
The Task

4 Most women set out to try to change a man, and when they have changed him they do not like him.
Marlene Dietrich (Maria Magdalene von Losch; 1904–92) German-born film star.
Attrib.

5 Come mothers and fathers
Throughout the land
And don't criticize
What you can't understand.
Bob Dylan (Robert Allen Zimmerman; 1941–) US popular singer.
The Times They Are A-Changin'

6 One must never lose time in vainly regretting the past nor in complaining about the changes which cause us discomfort, for change is the very essence of life.
Anatole France (Jacques Anatole François Thibault; 1844–1924) French writer.
Attrib.

7 Everything flows and nothing stays.

Heraclitus (c. 535–c. 475 BC) Greek philosopher.
Cratylus (Plato), 402a

8 Change is not made without inconvenience, even from worse to better.

Richard Hooker (c. 1554–1600) English theologian.
English Dictionary (Johnson), Preface

9 There is a certain relief in change, even though it be from bad to worse; as I have found in travelling in a stage-coach, that it is often a comfort to shift one's position and be bruised in a new place.

Washington Irving (1783–1859) US writer.
Tales of a Traveller, 'To the Reader'

10 Well, I find that a change of nuisances is as good as a vacation.

David Lloyd George (1863–1945) British Liberal statesman.
On being asked how he maintained his cheerfulness when beset by numerous political obstacles
Attrib.

11 The wind of change is blowing through the continent. Whether we like it or not, this growth of national consciousness is a political fact.

Harold Macmillan (1894–1986) British politician and prime minister.
Speech, South African Parliament, 3 Feb 1960

12 At last he rose, and twitched his mantle blue:
To-morrow to fresh woods, and pastures new.

John Milton (1608–74) English poet.
Lycidas

13 Through all the changing scenes of life.

Nahum Tate (1652–1715) Irish-born English poet.
New Version of the Psalms, 'Through all the Changing'

14 And slowly answer'd Arthur from the barge:
'The old order changeth, yielding place to new,
And God fulfils himself in many ways.'

Alfred, Lord Tennyson (1809–92) British poet.
Idylls of the King, 'The Passing of Arthur'

☐ CHARACTER ☐

1 A patronizing disposition always has its meaner side.

George Eliot (Mary Ann Evans; 1819–80) British novelist.
Adam Bede

2 Talent develops in quiet places, character in the full current of human life.

Goethe (1749–1832) German poet and dramatist.
Torquato Tasso, I

3 A tart temper never mellows with age, and a sharp tongue is the only edged tool that grows keener with constant use.

Washington Irving (1783–1859) US writer.
The Sketch Book, 'Rip Van Winkle'

4 What is character but the determination of incident? What is incident but the illustration of character?

Henry James (1843–1916) US novelist.
Partial Portraits, 'The Art of Fiction'

5 It is with narrow-souled people as with narrow-necked bottles: the less they have in them, the more noise they make in pouring it out.

Alexander Pope (1688–1744) British poet.
Thoughts on Various Subjects

6 There is no such thing as psychological. Let us say that one can improve the biography of the person.

Jean-Paul Sartre (1905–80) French writer.
The Divided Self (R. D. Laing), Ch. 8

☐ CHARITY ☐

See also generosity, parasites

1 The living need charity more than the dead.

George Arnold (1834–65) US poet and humorist.
The Jolly Old Pedagogue

2 In charity there is no excess.

Francis Bacon (1561–1626) English philosopher.
Essays, 'Of Goodness, and Goodness of Nature'

3 Feed the World
Let them know it's Christmas.

Band Aid
Song written to raise money for the relief of famine in Ethiopia
Do They Know It's Christmas?

4 Though I speak with the tongues of men and of angels, and have not charity, I am become as sounding brass, or a tinkling cymbal.
And though I have the gift of prophecy, and understand all mysteries, and all knowledge; and though I have all faith, so that I could remove mountains, and have not charity, I am nothing.
And though I bestow all my goods to feed the poor, and though I give my body to be burned, and have not charity, it profiteth me nothing.
Charity suffereth long, and is kind; charity envieth not; charity vaunteth not itself, is not puffed up,
Doth not behave itself unseemly, seeketh not her own, is not easily provoked, thinketh no evil;
Rejoiceth not in iniquity, but rejoiceth in the truth;
Beareth all things, believeth all things, hopeth all things, endureth all things.
Charity never faileth: but whether there be prophecies, they shall fail; whether there be tongues, they shall cease; whether there be knowledge, it shall vanish away.
For we know in part, and we prophesy in part.
But when that which is perfect is come, then that which is in part shall be done away.
When I was a child, I spake as a child, I understood as a child, I thought as a child: but when I became a man, I put away childish things.

For now we see through a glass, darkly; but then
face to face: now I know in part; but then shall I
know even as also I am known.
And now abideth faith, hope, charity, these three;
but the greatest of these is charity.
Bible: I Corinthians
13:1–13

5 But a certain Samaritan, as he journeyed, came
where he was: and when he saw him, he had compassion on him,
And went to him, and bound up his wounds, pouring in oil and wine, and set him on his own beast,
and brought him to an inn, and took care of him.
And on the morrow when he departed, he took
out two pence, and gave them to the host, and
said unto him, Take care of him; and whatsoever
thou spendest more, when I come again, I will
repay thee.
Bible: Luke
10:33–35

6 All our doings without charity are nothing worth.
The Book of Common Prayer
Collect, Quinquagesima Sunday

7 Charity begins at home, is the voice of the world.
Thomas Browne (1605–82) English physician and writer.
Religio Medici, Pt. II

8 Charity is the power of defending that which we
know to be indefensible. Hope is the power of
being cheerful in circumstances which we know
to be desperate.
G. K. Chesterton (1874–1936) British writer.
Heretics, Ch. 12

9 No people do so much harm as those who go
about doing good.
Mandell Creighton (1843–1901) British churchman.
Life

10 I'm not interested in the bloody system! Why has
he no food? Why is he starving to death?
Bob Geldof (1952–) Irish rock musician.
The Observer, 'Sayings of the Week', 27 Oct 1985

11 To keep a lamp burning we have to keep putting
oil in it.
Mother Teresa (Agnes Gonxha Bojaxhui; 1910–)
Yugoslavian missionary in Calcutta.
Time, 'Saints Among Us', 29 Dec 1975

□ CHARM □

1 All charming people have something to conceal,
usually their total dependence on the appreciation of others.
Cyril Connolly (1903–74) British journalist.
Enemies of Promise, Ch. 16

2 Oozing charm from every pore,
He oiled his way around the floor.
Alan Jay Lerner (1918–86) US songwriter.
My Fair Lady, II:1

3 It is absurd to divide people into good and bad.
People are either charming or tedious.
Oscar Wilde (1854–1900) Irish-born British dramatist.
Lady Windermere's Fan, I

□ CHAUCER □
Geoffrey
(c. 1342–1400) English poet. *The Canterbury Tales* is a collection
of stories told by pilgrims on their way to Canterbury. His other
works include the poem *The Book of the Duchess* and *Troilus and
Criseyde*.

QUOTATIONS ABOUT CHAUCER

1 Chaucer, notwithstanding the praises bestowed
on him, I think obscene and contemptible; he
owes his celebrity merely to his antiquity.
Lord Byron (1788–1824) British poet.
Attrib.

2 I read Chaucer still with as much pleasure as any
of our poets. He is a master of manners and of
description and the first tale-teller in the true
enlivened, natural way.
Alexander Pope (1688–1744) British poet.
Attrib.

QUOTATIONS BY CHAUCER

3 A Clerk ther was of Oxenford also,
That un-to logik hadde longe y-go.
The Canterbury Tales, Prologue

4 She was a worthy womman al hir lyve,
Housbondes at chirche-dore she hadde fyve,
Withouten other companye in youthe.
Referring to the wife of Bath.
The Canterbury Tales, Prologue

5 The smyler with the knyf under the cloke.
The Canterbury Tales, 'The Knight's Tale'

6 For of fortunes sharp adversitee
The worst kinde of infortune is this,
A man to have ben in prosperitee,
And it remembren, what is passed is.
Troilus and Criseyde, 3

□ CHESTERFIELD □
Philip Dormer Stanhope, 4th Earl of
(1694–1773) English statesman and diplomat; author of the
famous *Letters* (1774) to his illegitimate son. Appointed ambassador to The Hague in 1728, he subsequently served in Ireland and
as secretary of state (1746–48).

QUOTATIONS ABOUT CHESTERFIELD

1 The only Englishman who ever maintained that
the art of pleasing was the first duty in life.
Voltaire (François-Marie Arouet; 1694–1778) French writer.
Letter to Frederick the Great, 16 Aug 1774

2 Be wiser than other people if you can, but do not tell them so.
Letter to his son, 19 Nov 1745

3 Whatever is worth doing at all is worth doing well.
Letter to his son, 10 Mar 1746

4 An injury is much sooner forgotten than an insult.
Letter to his son, 9 Oct 1746

5 Do as you would be done by is the surest method that I know of pleasing.
Letter to his son, 16 Oct 1747

6 I knew once a very covetous, sordid fellow, who used to say, 'Take care of the pence, for the pounds will take care of themselves.'
Possibly referring to William Lowndes.
Letter to his son, 6 Nov 1747

7 I recommend you to take care of the minutes: for hours will take care of themselves.
Letter to his son, 6 Nov 1747

8 Advice is seldom welcome; and those who want it the most always like it the least.
Letter to his son, 29 Jan 1748

9 Due attention to the inside of books, and due contempt for the outside, is the proper relation between a man of sense and his books.
Letter to his son, 10 Jan 1749

10 Idleness is only the refuge of weak minds.
Letter to his son, 20 July 1749

11 Women are much more like each other than men: they have, in truth, but two passions, vanity and love; these are their universal characteristics.
Letter to his son, 19 Dec 1749

12 Religion is by no means a proper subject of conversation in a mixed company.
Letter to his godson

13 Make him a bishop, and you will silence him at once.
When asked what steps might be taken to control the evangelical preacher George Whitefield.
Attrib.

14 Give Dayrolles a chair.
Said on his deathbed when visited by his godson, Solomon Dayrolles.
Last words

☐ CHESTERTON ☐
G(ilbert) K(eith)
(1874–1936) British essayist, novelist, and poet. His detective stories feature the priest Father Brown and his novels include *The Napoleon of Notting Hill* (1904). After conversion to Roman Catholicism (1933) much of his writing was religious.

1 A great deal of contemporary criticism reads to me like a man saying: 'Of course I do not like green cheese: I am very fond of brown sherry.'
All I Survey

2 The modern world...has no notion except that of simplifying something by destroying nearly everything.
All I Survey

3 There is a road from the eye to the heart that does not go through the intellect.
The Defendant

4 All slang is metaphor, and all metaphor is poetry.
The Defendant

5 The rich are the scum of the earth in every country.
The Flying Inn

6 One sees great things from the valley; only small things from the peak.
The Hammer of God
Heretics, Ch. 1

7 There is no such thing on earth as an uninteresting subject; the only thing that can exist is an uninterested person.
Heretics, Ch. 1

8 We ought to see far enough into a hypocrite to see even his sincerity.
Heretics, Ch. 5

9 Carlyle said that men were mostly fools. Christianity, with a surer and more reverend realism, says that they are all fools.
Heretics, Ch. 12

10 A good novel tells us the truth about its hero; but a bad novel tells us the truth about its author.
Heretics, Ch. 15

11 The artistic temperament is a disease that afflicts amateurs.
Heretics, Ch. 17

12 To be clever enough to get all that money, one must be stupid enough to want it.
The Innocence of Father Brown

13 You can only find truth with logic if you have already found truth without it.
The Man who was Orthodox

14 The human race, to which so many of my readers belong.
The Napoleon of Notting Hill, Vol. I, Ch. 1

15 The madman is not the man who has lost his reason. The madman is the man who has lost everything except his reason.
Orthodoxy, Ch. 1

16 The cosmos is about the smallest hole that a man can hide his head in.
Orthodoxy, Ch. 1

17 Before the Roman came to Rye or out to Severn strode,
The rolling English drunkard made the rolling English road.
The Rolling English Road

18 Is ditchwater dull? Naturalists with microscopes have told me that it teems with quiet fun.
The Spice of Life

19 Compromise used to mean that half a loaf was better than no bread. Among modern statesmen it really seems to mean that half a loaf is better than a whole loaf.
What's Wrong with the World

20 Just the other day in the Underground I enjoyed the pleasure of offering my seat to three ladies.
Suggesting that fatness had its consolations.
Das Buch des Lachens (W. Scholz)

21 Democracy means government by the uneducated, while aristocracy means government by the badly educated.
New York Times, 1 Feb 1931

22 Education is simply the soul of a society as it passes from one generation to another.
The Observer, 'Sayings of the Week', 6 July 1924

23 The only way to be sure of catching a train is to miss the one before it.
Vacances à tous prix, 'Le Supplice de l'heure' (P. Daninos)

24 A puritan's a person who pours righteous indignation into the wrong things.
Attrib.

□ CHILDREN □

See also babies, family, youth

1 It was no wonder that people were so horrible when they started life as children.
Kingsley Amis (1922–) British novelist.
One Fat Englishman, Ch. 14

2 Children sweeten labours, but they make misfortunes more bitter.
Francis Bacon (1561–1626) English philosopher.
Essays, 'Of Parents and Children'

3 Children have never been very good at listening to their elders, but they have never failed to imitate them.
James Baldwin (1924–87) US writer.
Esquire, 1960

4 But when Jesus saw it, he was much displeased, and said unto them. Suffer the little children to come unto me, and forbid them not: for of such is the kingdom of God.
Bible: Mark
10:14

5 Verily I say unto you, Except ye be converted, and become as little children, ye shall not enter into the kingdom of heaven.
Bible: Matthew
18:3

6 He that spareth his rod hateth his son: but he that loveth him chasteneth him betimes.
Bible: Proverbs
13:24

7 You can do anything with children if you only play with them.
Bismarck (1815–98) German statesman.
Attrib.

8 It is only rarely that one can see in a little boy the promise of a man, but one can almost always see in a little girl the threat of a woman.
Alexandre Dumas, fils (1824–95) French writer.
Attrib.

9 Anybody who hates children and dogs can't be all bad.
W. C. Fields (1880–1946) US actor.
Attrib.

10 To bear many children is considered not only a religious blessing but also an investment. The greater their number, some Indians reason, the more alms they can beg.
Indira Gandhi (1917–84) Indian stateswoman.
New York Review of Books, 'Indira's Coup' (Oriana Fallaci)

11 The business of being a child interests a child not at all. Children very rarely play at being other children.
David Holloway (1924–) Literary editor.
The Daily Telegraph, 15 December 1966

12 At every step the child should be allowed to meet the real experiences of life; the thorns should never be plucked from his roses.
Ellen Key (Karolina Sofia Key; 1849–1926) Swedish writer.
The Century of the Child, Ch. 3

13 A child's a plaything for an hour.
Mary Lamb (1764–1847) Sister of Charles Lamb.
Parental Recollections

14 Where are the children I might have had? You may suppose I might have wanted them.

Drowned to the accompaniment of the rattling of a thousand douche bags.
Malcolm Lowry (1909–57) British novelist.
Under the Volcano, Ch. 10

15 The nice thing about having relatives' kids around is that they go home.
Cliff Richard (1940–) British pop singer.
Remark, Nov 1988

16 Parents learn a lot from their children about coping with life.
Muriel Spark (1918–) British novelist.
The Comforters, Ch. 6

17 Never have children, only grandchildren.
Gore Vidal (1925–) US novelist.
Two Sisters

18 The English are growing demented about children. When I was a boy the classroom had icicles inside every window in this time of year. We were savagely beaten three times a week…
Auberon Waugh (1939–) British novelist.
The Diaries of Auberon Waugh 1976–1985, 'January 25, 1979'

☐ CHIVALRY ☐

See also courtesy

1 A gentleman is any man who wouldn't hit a woman with his hat on.
Fred Allen (1894–1956) US comedian.
Attrib.

2 Even nowadays a man can't step up and kill a woman without feeling just a bit unchivalrous.
Robert Benchley (1889–1945) US humorist.
Chips off the Old Benchley, 'Down in Front'

3 Somebody has said, that a king may make a nobleman, but he cannot make a gentleman.
Edmund Burke (1729–97) British politician.
Letter to William Smith, 29 Jan 1795

4 He was a verray parfit gentil knight.
Geoffrey Chaucer (c. 1342–1400) English poet.
Referring to the knight
The Canterbury Tales, Prologue

5 Some say that the age of chivalry is past, that the spirit of romance is dead. The age of chivalry is never past, so long as there is a wrong left unredressed on earth.
Charles Kingsley (1819–75) British writer.
Life (Mrs C. Kingsley), Vol. II, Ch. 28

6 It is almost a definition of a gentleman to say that he is one who never inflicts pain.
Cardinal Newman (1801–90) British theologian.
The Idea of a University, 'Knowledge and Religious Duty'

☐ CHOICE ☐

1 Any colour, so long as it's black.
Henry Ford (1863–1947) US car manufacturer.
Referring to the colour options offered for the Model-T Ford car
Attrib.

2 Two roads diverged in a wood, and I –
I took the one less traveled by,
And that has made all the difference.
Robert Frost (1875–1963) US poet.
The Road Not Taken

3 We have to believe in free will. We've got no choice.
Isaac Bashevis Singer (1904–91) Polish-born US writer.
The Times, 21 June 1982

☐ CHRISTIANITY ☐

See also Catholicism, Protestantism, religion

1 'Christianity, of course but why journalism?'
Arthur Balfour (1848–1930) British statesman.
In reply to Frank Harris's remark, '…all the faults of the age come from Christianity and journalism'
Autobiography (Margot Asquith), Ch. 10

2 Onward, Christian soldiers,
Marching as to war,
With the Cross of Jesus
Going on before.
Sabine Baring-Gould (1834–1924) British author and hymn writer.
Onward Christian Soldiers

3 Therefore the Lord himself shall give you a sign;
Behold, a virgin shall conceive, and bear a son, and shall call his name Immanuel.
Butter and honey shall he eat, that he may know to refuse the evil, and choose the good.
Bible: Isaiah
7:14–15

4 He it is, who coming after me is preferred before me, whose shoe's latchet I am not worthy to unloose.
Bible: John
1:27

5 The next day John seeth Jesus coming unto him, and saith, Behold the Lamb of God, which taketh away the sin of the world.
Bible: John
1:29

6 For God so loved the world, that he gave his only begotten Son, that whosoever believeth in him should not perish, but have everlasting life.
Bible: John
3:16

7 Then spake Jesus again unto them, saying, I am the light of the world: he that followeth me shall

not walk in darkness, but shall have the light of
life.
Bible: John
8:12

8 I am the good shepherd: the good shepherd
giveth his life for the sheep.
Bible: John
10:11

9 Jesus saith unto him, I am the way, the truth, and
the life: no man cometh unto the Father, but by
me.
Bible: John
14:6

10 Then said Jesus unto his disciples, If any man
will come after me, let him deny himself, and
take up his cross, and follow me.
Bible: Matthew
16:24

11 How very hard it is
To be a Christian!
Robert Browning (1812–89) British poet.
Easter-Day, I

12 Christianity has done a great deal for love by
making a sin of it.
Anatole France (Jacques Anatole François Thibault;
1844–1924) French writer.
The Garden of Epicurus

13 Christianity is part of the Common Law of
England.
Matthew Hale (1609–76) English judge.
Historia Placitorum Coronae (ed. Sollom Emlyn)

14 Tell me the old, old story
Of unseen things above,
Of Jesus and His glory
Of Jesus and His love.
Katherine Hankey (1834–1911) British hymn writer.
Tell Me the Old, Old Story

15 A local cult called Christianity.
Thomas Hardy (1840–1928) British novelist.
The Dynasts, I:6

16 The Christian religion not only was at first
attended with miracles, but even at this day cannot be believed by any reasonable person without one. Mere reason is insufficient to convince
us of its veracity: and whoever is moved by faith
to assent to it, is conscious of a continued miracle
in his own person, which subverts all the principles of his understanding, and gives him a determination to believe what is most contrary to
custom and experience.
David Hume (1711–76) Scottish philosopher.
Essays, 'Of Miracles'

17 Christianity accepted as given a metaphysical
system derived from several already existing and
mutually incompatible systems.
Aldous Huxley (1894–1964) British novelist.
Grey Eminence, Ch. 3

18 Fight the good fight with all thy might,
Christ is thy strength and Christ thy right,
Lay hold on life, and it shall be
Thy joy and crown eternally.
John Monsell (1811–75) British hymn writer.
Hymn

19 No kingdom has ever had as many civil wars as
the kingdom of Christ.
Baron de Montesquieu (1689–1755) French writer.
Lettres persanes

20 I call Christianity the one great curse, the one
enormous and innermost perversion, the one
great instinct of revenge, for which no means are
too venomous, too underhand, too underground
and too petty – I call it the one immortal blemish
of mankind.
Friedrich Wilhelm Nietzsche (1844–1900) German
philosopher.
The Antichrist

21 Christianity has made of death a terror which
was unknown to the gay calmness of the Pagan.
Ouida (Marie Louise de la Ramée; 1839–1908) British novelist.
The Failure of Christianity

22 Christianity is the most materialistic of all great
religions.
William Temple (1881–1944) British churchman.
Reading in St John's Gospel, Vol. I, Introduction

☐ **CHRISTINE DE PISAN** ☐

(1364–1430) French poet, author, and scholar, who took up writing to support herself and her three children after the death of her
husband. Her works include *La Cité des Dames* (*The City of
Ladies*; 1405), which tells of women who were famous for their
heroism and virtue and *Livre des trois vertus* (1406), which is a
treatise on women's education.

1 You ask whether woman possesses any natural
intelligence. Yes. It can be developed to become
wisdom, and then it is most beautiful.
La Cité des Dames, Prologue

2 If it were customary to send little girls to school
and to teach them the same subjects as are
taught to boys, they would learn just as fully and
would understand the subtleties of all arts and
sciences. Indeed, maybe they would understand
them better...for just as women's bodies are
softer than men's, so their understanding is
sharper.
La Cité des Dames, Prologue

3 Honour to Womankind. It needs must be That
God loves Woman, since He fashioned Thee.
Of Six Medieval Women (Alice Kemp-Welch)

□CHRISTMAS□

See also Christianity

1 I have often thought, says Sir Roger, it happens very well that Christmas should fall out in the Middle of Winter.
Joseph Addison (1672–1719) British essayist.
The Spectator, 269

2 Once in royal David's city
Stood a lowly cattle shed,
Where a Mother laid her Baby
In a manger for His bed:
Mary was that Mother mild,
Jesus Christ her little Child.
C. F. Alexander (1818–95) British hymn writer.
Once in Royal David's City

3 As I sat on a sunny bank,
On Christmas Day in the morning,
I spied three ships come sailing by.
Anonymous
As I sat on a Sunny Bank

4 The holly and the ivy,
When they are both full grown,
Of all the trees that are in the wood,
The holly bears the crown.
The rising of the sun
And the running of the deer,
The playing of the merry organ,
Sweet singing in the choir.
Anonymous
The Holly and the Ivy

5 And she brought forth her firstborn son, and wrapped him in swaddling clothes, and laid him in a manger; because there was no room for them in the inn.
Bible: Luke
2:7

6 And there were in the same country shepherds abiding in the field, keeping watch over their flock by night.
And, lo, the angel of the Lord came upon them, and the glory of the Lord shone round about them: and they were sore afraid.
And the angel said unto them, Fear not: for, behold, I bring you good tidings of great joy, which shall be to all people.
Bible: Luke
2:8–10

7 And when they were come into the house, they saw the young child with Mary his mother, and fell down, and worshipped him: and when they had opened their treasures, they presented unto him gifts; gold, and frankincense, and myrrh.
And being warned of God in a dream that they should not return to Herod, they departed into their own country another way.
Bible: Matthew
2:11–12

8 O little town of Bethlehem,
How still we see thee lie;
Above thy deep and dreamless sleep
The silent stars go by.
Phillips Brooks (1835–93) US Episcopal bishop.
O Little Town of Bethlehem

9 Christians awake, salute the happy morn,
Whereon the Saviour of the world was born.
John Byrom (1692–1763) British poet and hymn writer.
Hymn for Christmas Day

10 Fortified in their front parlours, at Yuletide men are the more murderous. Drunk, they defy battle-axes, bellow of whale-bone and dung.
Geoffrey Hill (1932–   ) British poet.
Mercian Hymns, XXVI, 'Offa's Bestiary'

11 'Twas the night before Christmas, when all through the house
Not a creature was stirring, not even a mouse;
The stockings were hung by the chimney with care,
In hopes that St Nicholas soon would be there.
Clement Clarke Moore (1779–1863) US writer.
In *Troy Sentinel*, 23 Dec 1823, 'A Visit from St. Nicholas'

12 Good King Wenceslas looked out,
On the Feast of Stephen;
When the snow lay round about,
Deep and crisp and even.
John Mason Neale (1818–66) British churchman.
Good King Wenceslas

13 It came upon the midnight clear,
That glorious song of old,
From Angels bending near the earth
To touch their harps of gold;
'Peace on the earth; good will to man
From Heaven's all gracious King.'
The world in solemn stillness lay
To hear the angels sing.
E. H. Sears (1810–76) US clergyman.
That Glorious Song of Old

14 At Christmas play and make good cheer,
For Christmas comes but once a year.
Thomas Tusser (1524–80) English farmer.
Five Hundred Points of Good Husbandry, 'The Farmer's Daily Diet'

15 To perceive Christmas through its wrapping becomes more difficult with every year.
Elwyn Brooks White (1899–1985) US journalist and humorist.
The Second Tree from the Corner

□CHURCH□

See also clergy, religion

1 And I say also unto thee, That thou art Peter, and upon this rock I will build my church; and the gates of hell shall not prevail against it.
And I will give unto thee the keys of the kingdom of heaven: and whatsoever thou shalt bind on

earth shall be bound in heaven: and whatsoever thou shalt loose on earth shall be loosed in heaven.
Bible: Matthew
16:18–19

2 For where two or three are gathered together in my name, there am I in the midst of them.
Bible: Matthew
18:20

3 The Church exists for the sake of those outside it.
William Temple (1881–1944) British churchman.
Attrib.

□ CHURCHILL □
Sir Winston Leonard Spencer
(1874–1965) British statesman and writer, prime minister 1940–45, 1951–55. After service as a war correspondent in the Boer War, he became first Lord of the Admiralty in World War I and led a coalition government in World War II. He was celebrated for his skill as an orator and was the author of several historical books.

QUOTATIONS ABOUT CHURCHILL

1 I thought he was a young man of promise; but it appears he was a young man of promises.
Arthur Balfour (1848–1930) British statesman.
Said of Winston Churchill on his entry into politics, 1899.
Winston Churchill (Randolph Churchill), Vol. I

2 The first time you meet Winston you see all his faults and the rest of your life you spend in discovering his virtues.
Lady Constance Lytton (1869–1923) British suffragette.
Edward Marsh (Christopher Hassall), Ch. 7

3 Winston has devoted the best years of his life to preparing his impromptu speeches.
F. E. Smith (1872–1930) British lawyer and politician.
Attrib.

4 Simply a radio personality who outlived his prime.
Evelyn Waugh (1903–66) British novelist.
Evelyn Waugh (Christopher Sykes)

QUOTATIONS BY CHURCHILL

5 Well, the principle seems the same. The water still keeps falling over.
When asked whether the Niagara Falls looked the same as when he first saw them.
Closing the Ring, Ch. 5

6 Headmasters have powers at their disposal with which Prime Ministers have never yet been invested.
My Early Life, Ch. 2

7 So they told me how Mr Gladstone read Homer for fun, which I thought served him right.
My Early Life, Ch. 2

8 Which brings me to my conclusion upon Free Will and Predestination, namely – let the reader mark it – that they are identical.
My Early Life, Ch. 3

9 It is a good thing for an uneducated man to read books of quotations.
My Early Life, Ch. 9

10 Those who can win a war well can rarely make a good peace and those who could make a good peace would never have won the war.
My Early Life, Ch. 26

11 I must point out that my rule of life prescribed as an absolutely sacred rite smoking cigars and also the drinking of alcohol before, after, and if need be during all meals and in the intervals between them.
Said during a lunch with the Arab leader Ibn Saud, when he heard that the king's religion forbade smoking and alcohol.
The Second World War

12 In war, resolution; in defeat, defiance; in victory, magnanimity; in peace, goodwill.
Epigram used by Sir Edward Marsh after World War II; used as 'a moral of the work' in Churchill's book.
The Second World War

13 Wars are not won by evacuations.
Referring to Dunkirk.
Their Finest Hour

14 Don't talk to me about naval tradition. It's nothing but rum, sodomy, and the lash.
Former Naval Person (Sir Peter Gretton), Ch. 1

15 Everybody has a right to pronounce foreign names as he chooses.
The Observer, 'Sayings of the Week', 5 Aug 1951

16 This is the sort of English up with which I will not put.
The story is that Churchill wrote the comment in the margin of a report in which a Civil Servant had used an awkward construction to avoid ending a sentence with a preposition. An alternative version substitutes 'bloody nonsense' for 'English'.
Plain Words (E. Gowers), Ch. 9

17 *The Times* is speechless and takes three columns to express its speechlessness.
Referring to Irish Home Rule.
Speech, Dundee, 14 May 1908

18 The maxim of the British people is 'Business as usual'.
Speech, Guildhall, 9 Nov 1914

19 Labour is not fit to govern.
Election speech, 1920

20 I cannot forecast to you the action of Russia. It is a riddle wrapped in a mystery inside an enigma.
Broadcast talk, 1 Oct 1939

21 Victory at all costs, victory in spite of all terror, victory however long and hard the road may be; for without victory there is no survival.
Speech, House of Commons, 13 May 1940

22 We shall not flag or fail. We shall fight in France, we shall fight on the seas and oceans, we shall fight with growing confidence and growing strength in the air, we shall defend our island, whatever the cost may be, we shall fight on the beaches, we shall fight on the landing grounds, we shall fight in the fields and in the streets, we shall fight in the hills; we shall never surrender.
Speech, House of Commons, 4 June 1940

23 The battle of Britain is about to begin.
Speech, House of Commons, 1 July 1940

24 Never in the field of human conflict was so much owed by so many to so few.
Referring to the Battle of Britain pilots.
Speech, House of Commons, 20 Aug 1940

25 Give us the tools, and we will finish the job.
Referring to Lend-lease, which was being legislated in the USA.
Radio Broadcast, 9 Feb 1941

26 Do not let us speak of darker days; let us rather speak of sterner days. These are not dark days: these are great days – the greatest days our country has ever lived.
Address, Harrow School, 29 Oct 1941

27 When I warned them that Britain would fight on alone whatever they did, their Generals told their Prime Minister and his divided Cabinet: 'In three weeks England will have her neck wrung like a chicken.'
Some chicken! Some neck!
Referring to the French Government.
Speech, Canadian Parliament, 30 Dec 1941

28 The Almighty in His infinite wisdom did not see fit to create Frenchmen in the image of Englishmen.
Speech, House of Commons, 10 Dec 1942

29 There are few virtues which the Poles do not possess and there are few errors they have ever avoided.
Speech, House of Commons, 1945

30 An iron curtain has descended across the Continent.
Address, Westminster College, Fulton, USA, 5 Mar 1946

31 We must build a kind of United States of Europe.
Speech, Zurich, 19 Sept 1946

32 Perhaps it is better to be irresponsible and right than to be responsible and wrong.
Party Political Broadcast, London, 26 Aug 1950

33 To jaw-jaw is better than to war-war.
Speech, Washington, 26 June 1954

34 The nation had the lion's heart. I had the luck to give the roar.
Said on his 80th birthday

□ CINEMA □

See also Goldwynisms

1 I like a film to have a beginning, a middle and an end, but not necessarily in that order.
Jean-Luc Godard (1930–) French film director.
Attrib.

2 Photography is truth. And cinema is truth twenty-four times a second.
Jean-Luc Godard
Le Petit Soldat

3 Why should people go out and pay money to see bad films when they can stay at home and see bad television for nothing?
Samuel Goldwyn (Samuel Goldfish; 1882–1974) Polish-born US film producer.
The Observer, 'Sayings of the Week', 9 Sept 1956

4 A wide screen just makes a bad film twice as bad.
Samuel Goldwyn
Attrib.

5 The very meaninglessness of life forces man to create his own meaning. If it can be written or thought, it can be filmed.
Stanley Kubrick (1928–) US film director.
Halliwell's Filmgoer's and Video Viewer's Companion

□ CIVILIZATION □

See also culture

1 Civilization is a method of living, an attitude of equal respect for all men.
Jane Addams (1860–1935) US social worker.
Speech, Honolulu, 1933

2 I wish I could bring Stonehenge to Nyasaland to show there was a time when Britain had a savage culture.
Hastings Banda (1906–) Malawi statesman.
The Observer, 'Sayings of the Week', 10 Mar 1963

3 The three great elements of modern civilization, Gunpowder, Printing, and the Protestant Religion.
Thomas Carlyle (1795–1881) Scottish historian and essayist.
Critical and Miscellaneous Essays, 'The State of German Literature'

4 I think it would be a good idea.
Mahatma Gandhi (Mohandas Karamchand Gandhi; 1869–1948) Indian national leader.
On being asked for his view on Western civilization
Attrib.

5 There is precious little in civilization to appeal to a Yeti.
Edmund Hillary (1919–) New Zealand mountaineer.
The Observer, 'Sayings of the Week', 3 June 1960

6 The degree of a nation's civilization is marked by its disregard for the necessities of existence.
W. Somerset Maugham (1874–1965) British novelist.
Our Betters, I

☐ CLASS ☐

See also aristocracy, equality, public, snobbery

1 You can measure the social caste of a person by the distance between the husband's and wife's apartments.
Alfonso XIII (1886–1941) Spanish monarch.
Attrib.

2 I often, therefore, when I want to distinguish clearly the aristocratic class from the Philistines proper, or middle class, name the former, in my own mind *the Barbarians*.
Matthew Arnold (1822–88) British poet and critic.
Culture and Anarchy, Ch. 3

3 O let us love our occupations,
Bless the squire and his relations,
Live upon our daily rations,
And always know our proper stations.
Charles Dickens (1812–70) British novelist.
The Chimes, '2nd Quarter'

4 All shall equal be.
The Earl, the Marquis, and the Dook,
The Groom, the Butler, and the Cook,
The Aristocrat who banks with Coutts,
The Aristocrat who cleans the boots.
W. S. Gilbert (1836–1911) British dramatist.
The Gondoliers, I

5 Bow, bow, ye lower middle classes!
Bow, bow, ye tradesmen, bow, ye masses!
W. S. Gilbert
Iolanthe, I

6 All the world over, I will back the masses against the classes.
William Ewart Gladstone (1809–98) British statesman.
Speech, Liverpool, 28 June 1886

7 Dialect words – those terrible marks of the beast to the truly genteel.
Thomas Hardy (1840–1928) British novelist.
The Mayor of Casterbridge, Ch. 20

8 '*Bourgeois*,' I observed, 'is an epithet which the riff-raff apply to what is respectable, and the aristocracy to what is decent'.
Anthony Hope (Sir Anthony Hope Hawkins; 1863–1933) British novelist.
The Dolly Dialogues

9 You may be the most liberal Liberal Englishman, and yet you cannot fail to see the categorical difference between the responsible and the irresponsible classes.
D. H. Lawrence (1885–1930) British novelist.
Kangaroo, Ch. 1

10 An Englishman's way of speaking absolutely classifies him
The moment he talks he makes some other Englishman despise him.
Alan Jay Lerner (1918–86) US songwriter.
My Fair Lady, I:1

11 I'm not interested in classes...Far be it from me to foster inferiority complexes among the workers by trying to make them think they belong to some special class. That has happened in Europe but it hasn't happened here yet.
John Llewellyn Lewis (1880–1969) US labour leader.
The Coming of the New Deal (A. M. Schlesinger, Jnr), Pt. 7, Ch. 25

12 Said Marx: 'Don't be snobbish, we seek to abolish
The 3rd Class, not the 1st.'
Christopher Logue (1926–) British poet and dramatist.
Christopher Logue's ABC, 'M'

13 The history of all hitherto existing society is the history of class struggles.
Karl Marx (1818–83) German philosopher and revolutionary.
The Communist Manifesto, 1

14 The one class you do *not* belong to and are not proud of at all is the lower-middle class. No one ever describes himself as belonging to the lower-middle class.
George Mikes (1912–87) Hungarian-born British writer.
How to be Inimitable

15 I don't think one 'comes down' from Jimmy's university. According to him, it's not even red brick, but white tile.
John Osborne (1929–) British dramatist.
Look Back in Anger, II:1

16 There are two classes in good society in England. The equestrian classes and the neurotic classes.
George Bernard Shaw (1856–1950) Irish dramatist and critic.
Heartbreak House

17 I am a gentleman. I live by robbing the poor.
George Bernard Shaw
Man and Superman

18 It is impossible for one class to appreciate the wrongs of another.
Elizabeth Stanton (1815–1902) US suffragette.
History of Woman Suffrage (with Susan B. Anthony and Mathilda Gage), Vol. I

19 The ship follows Soviet custom: it is riddled with class distinctions so subtle, it takes a trained Marxist to appreciate them.
Paul Theroux (1941–) US-born writer.
The Great Railway Bazaar, Ch. 30

20 No writer before the middle of the 19th century wrote about the working classes other than as grotesque or as pastoral decoration. Then when they were given the vote certain writers started to suck up to them.
Evelyn Waugh (1903–66) British novelist.
Interview
Paris Review, 1963

21 The constitution does not provide for first and second class citizens.
Wendell Lewis Willkie (1892–1944) US lawyer and businessman.
An American Programme, Ch. 2

☐ CLASSICS ☐

1 They were a tense and peculiar family, the Oedipuses, weren't they?
Max Beerbohm (1872–1956) British writer.
Max: A Biography (D. Cecil)

2 So they told me how Mr Gladstone read Homer for fun, which I thought served him right.
Winston Churchill (1874–1965) British statesman.
My Early Life, Ch. 2

3 Nor can I do better, in conclusion, than impress upon you the study of Greek literature which not only elevates above the vulgar herd, but leads not infrequently to positions of considerable emolument.
Thomas Gaisford (1799–1855) British classicist.
Christmas Day Sermon at Oxford
Reminiscences of Oxford (Revd W. Tuckwell)

4 To the Greeks the Muse gave native wit, to the Greeks the gift of graceful eloquence.
Horace (Quintus Horatius Flaccus; 65–8 BC) Roman poet.
Ars Poetica

5 The classics are only primitive literature. They belong in the same class as primitive machinery and primitive music and primitive medicine.
Stephen Leacock (1869–1944) English-born Canadian economist and humorist.
Homer and Humbug

6 Every man with a belly full of the classics is an enemy of the human race.
Henry Miller (1891–1980) US novelist.
Tropic of Cancer, 'Dijon'

☐ CLASSIFICATION ☐
See also generalizations

1 One of the unpardonable sins, in the eyes of most people, is for a man to go about unlabelled. The world regards such a person as the police do an unmuzzled dog, not under proper control.
T. H. Huxley (1825–95) British biologist.
Evolution and Ethics

2 Decades have a delusive edge to them. They are not, of course, really periods at all, except as any

other ten years would be. But we, looking at them, are caught by the different name each bears, and give them different attributes, and tie labels on them, as if they were flowers in a border.
Rose Macaulay (1889–1958) British writer.
Told by an Idiot, Pt. II, Ch. 1

☐ CLEANNESS ☐

1 Bath twice a day to be really clean, once a day to be passably clean, once a week to avoid being a public menace.
Anthony Burgess (John Burgess Wilson; 1917–) British novelist.
Mr Enderby, Pt. I, Ch. 2

2 MR PRITCHARD. I must dust the blinds and then I must raise them.
MRS OGMORE-PRITCHARD. And before you let the sun in, mind it wipes its shoes.
Dylan Thomas (1914–53) Welsh poet.
Under Milk Wood

3 Have you ever taken anything out of the clothes basket because it had become, relatively, the cleaner thing?
Katherine Whitehorn (1926–) British journalist.
The Observer, 'On Shirts', 1964

☐ CLERGY ☐
See also Church, religion

1 This is a true saying, If a man desire the office of a bishop, he desireth a good work.
A bishop then must be blameless, the husband of one wife, vigilant, sober, of good behaviour, given to hospitality, apt to teach;
Not given to wine, no striker, not greedy of filthy lucre; but patient, not a brawler, not covetous.
Bible: I Timothy
3:1–3

2 It is no accident that the symbol of a bishop is a crook, and the sign of an archbishop is a double-cross.
Dom Gregory Dix (1901–52) British monk.
Letter to *The Times*, 3 Dec 1977 (Francis Bown)

3 For clergy are men as well as other folks.
Henry Fielding (1707–54) British novelist.
Joseph Andrews, Bk II, Ch. 6

4 In old time we had treen chalices and golden priests, but now we have treen priests and golden chalices.
John Jewel (1522–71) English bishop.
Certain Sermons Preached Before the Queen's Majesty

5 A man who is good enough to go to heaven, is good enough to be a clergyman.
Samuel Johnson (1709–84) British lexicographer.
Life of Johnson (J. Boswell), Vol. II

6 How can a bishop marry? How can he flirt? The most he can say is, 'I will see you in the vestry after service.'

Sydney Smith (1771–1845) British clergyman and essayist.
Memoir (Lady Holland)

7 I never saw, heard, nor read, that the clergy were beloved in any nation where Christianity was the religion of the country. Nothing can render them popular, but some degree of persecution.

Jonathan Swift (1667–1745) Irish-born Anglican priest and writer.
Thoughts on Religion

8 There is a certain class of clergyman whose mendicity is only equalled by their mendacity.

Frederick Temple (1821–1902) British churchman.
Remark at a meeting of the Ecclesiastical Commissioners
Years of Endeavour (Sir George Leveson Gower)

☐ CLOTHES ☐

See also appearance, beauty, fashion, nakedness

1 I go to a better tailor than any of you and pay more for my clothes. The only difference is that you probably don't sleep in yours.

Clarence Seward Darrow (1857–1938) US lawyer.
Reply when teased by reporters about his appearance
2500 Anecdotes (E. Fuller)

2 She had on a little black cocktail number and the baddest suede, pointy, red shoes you ever saw.

Ben Elton (1959–) British writer and comedian.
Stark

3 'Good heavens!' said he, 'if it be our clothes alone which fit us for society, how highly we should esteem those who make them.'

Marie Ebner von Eschenbach (1830–1916) Austrian writer.
The Two Countesses

4 The sense of being well-dressed gives a feeling of inward tranquillity which religion is powerless to bestow.

C. F. Forbes (1817–1911) British writer.
Social Aims (Emerson)

5 Those who make their dress a principal part of themselves, will, in general, become of no more value than their dress.

William Hazlitt (1778–1830) British essayist.
On the Clerical Character

6 Fine clothes are good only as they supply the want of other means of procuring respect.

Samuel Johnson (1709–84) British lexicographer.
Life of Johnson (J. Boswell), Vol. II

7 Brevity is the soul of lingerie.

Dorothy Parker (1893–1967) US writer.
While Rome Burns (Alexander Woollcott)

8 Costly thy habit as thy purse can buy,
But not express'd in fancy; rich, not gaudy;
For the apparel oft proclaims the man.

William Shakespeare (1564–1616) English dramatist.
Hamlet, I:3

9 The only man who really needs a tail coat is a man with a hole in his trousers.

John Taylor (20th century) The editor of the *Tailor and Cutter*.
The Observer, 'Shouts and Murmurs'

10 You can say what you like about long dresses, but they cover a multitude of shins.

Mae West (1892–1980) US actress.
Peel Me a Grape (J. Weintraub)

☐ COLD WAR ☐

1 Let us not be deceived – we are today in the midst of a cold war.

Bernard Baruch (1870–1965) US financier and presidential adviser.
Speech, South Carolina Legislature, 16 Apr 1947

2 An iron curtain has descended across the Continent.

Winston Churchill (1874–1965) British statesman.
The phrase 'iron curtain' was originally coined by Joseph Goebbels
Address, Westminster College, Fulton, USA, 5 Mar 1946

☐ COLERIDGE ☐
Samuel Taylor

(1772–1834) British poet, chiefly remembered for such works as *Kubla Khan* (composed in 1797, under the influence of opium) and *The Rime of the Ancient Mariner* (1798). His *Lyrical Ballads* (1798), written with William Wordsworth, was extremely influential.

QUOTATIONS ABOUT COLERIDGE

1 A weak, diffusive, weltering, ineffectual man.

Thomas Carlyle (1795–1881) Scottish historian and essayist.
Attrib.

QUOTATIONS BY COLERIDGE

2 Nothing can permanently please, which does not contain in itself the reason why it is so, and not otherwise.

Biographia Literaria, Ch. 14

3 That willing suspension of disbelief for the moment, which constitutes poetic faith.

Biographia Literaria, Ch. 14

4 Swans sing before they die – 'twere no bad thing,
Did certain persons die before they sing.

Epigram on a Volunteer Singer

5 On awaking he…instantly and eagerly wrote down the lines that are here preserved. At this moment he was unfortunately called out by a person on business from Porlock.

Kubla Khan (preliminary note)

6 In Xanadu did Kubla Khan
A stately pleasure-dome decree:
Where Alph, the sacred river, ran
Through caverns measureless to man
Down to a sunless sea.
Kubla Khan

7 It was a miracle of rare device,
A sunny pleasure-dome with caves of ice!
Kubla Khan

8 Reviewers are usually people who would have
been poets, historians, biographers,...if they
could; they have tried their talents at one or at
the other, and have failed; therefore they turn
critics.
Lectures on Shakespeare and Milton, I

9 The faults of great authors are generally excellences carried to an excess.
Miscellanies, 149

10 If men could learn from history, what lessons it
might teach us! But passion and party blind our
eyes and the light which experience gives is a lan-
tern on the stern, which shines only on the
waves behind us!
Recollections (Alsop)

11 As idle as a painted ship
Upon a painted ocean.
The Rime of the Ancient Mariner, I

12 Water, water, every where,
And all the boards did shrink;
Water, water, every where,
Nor any drop to drink.
The Rime of the Ancient Mariner, II

13 Like one, that on a lonesome road
Doth walk in fear and dread,
And having once turned round walks on,
And turns no more his head;
Because he knows, a frightful fiend
Doth close behind him tread.
The Rime of the Ancient Mariner, VI

14 A sadder and a wiser man,
He rose the morrow morn.
The Rime of the Ancient Mariner, VII

15 I wish our clever young poets would remember
my homely definitions of prose and poetry; that
is, prose = words in their best order; – poetry =
the best words in the best order.
Table Talk

16 What comes from the heart, goes to the heart.
Table Talk

17 I believe the souls of five hundred Sir Isaac New-
tons would go to the making up of a Shakespeare
or a Milton.
Letter to Thomas Poole, 23 Mar 1801

☐ COMFORT ☐
See also endurance, sympathy

1 I beg cold comfort.
William Shakespeare
King John, V:7

2 Like a bridge over troubled water,
I will ease your mind.
Paul Simon (1942–) US singer.
Bridge Over Troubled Water

☐ COMMITMENT ☐

1 One cannot be a part-time nihilist.
Albert Camus (1913–60) French existentialist writer.
The Rebel

2 Catholics and Communists have committed
great crimes, but at least they have not stood
aside, like an established society, and been indifferent. I would rather have blood on my hands
than water like Pilate.
Graham Greene (1904–91) British novelist.
The Comedians, Pt. III, Ch. 4

3 I love being at the centre of things.
Margaret Thatcher (1925–) British politician and prime
minister.
Reader's Digest, 1984

☐ COMMUNISM ☐
See also Marxism, Russia, socialism

1 Socialism with a human face.
Alexander Dubček (1921–) Czechoslovak statesman.
A resolution by the party group in the Ministry of Foreign Affairs,
in 1968, referred to Czechoslovak foreign policy acquiring 'its
own defined face'
Attrib.

2 Communism is Soviet power plus the electrification of the whole country.
Lenin (Vladimir Ilich Ulyanov; 1870–1924) Russian
revolutionary leader.
Political slogan of 1920, promoting the programme of electrification

3 Communism is like prohibition, it's a good idea
but it won't work.
Will Rogers (1879–1935) US actor and humorist.
Autobiography, Nov 1927

4 For us in Russia communism is a dead dog,
while, for many people in the West, it is still a living lion.
Alexander Solzhenitsyn (1918–) Soviet novelist.
The Listener, 15 Feb 1979

5 Communism continued to haunt Europe as a spectre – a name men gave to their own fears and blunders. But the crusade against Communism was even more imaginary than the spectre of Communism.
A. J. P. Taylor (1906–90) British historian.
The Origins of the Second World War, Ch. 2

6 Lenin's method leads to this: the party organization at first substitutes itself for the party as a whole. Then the central committee substitutes itself for the party organization, and finally a single dictator substitutes himself for the central committee.
Leon Trotsky (Lev Davidovich Bronstein; 1879–1940) Russian revolutionary.
The Communist Parties of Western Europe (N. McInnes), Ch. 3

□COMPLAINTS□

1 We have first raised a dust and then complain we cannot see.
Bishop Berkeley (1685–1753) Irish churchman and philosopher.
Principles of Human Knowledge, Introduction

2 The world is disgracefully managed, one hardly knows to whom to complain.
Ronald Firbank (1886–1926) British novelist.
Vainglory

3 If you are foolish enough to be contented, don't show it, but grumble with the rest.
Jerome K. Jerome (1859–1927) British humorist.
Idle Thoughts of an Idle Fellow

□COMPLIMENTS□

See also admiration, beauty, flattery, love, praise

1 She isn't a bad bit of goods, the Queen! I wish all the fleas in my bed were as good.
Miguel de Cervantes (1547–1616) Spanish novelist.
Don Quixote, Pt. I, Ch. 30

2 She is Venus when she smiles;
But she's Juno when she walks,
And Minerva when she talks.
Ben Jonson (1573–1637) English dramatist.
The Underwood, 'Celebration of Charis, V. His Discourse with Cupid'

3 Shall I compare thee to a summer's day?
Thou art more lovely and more temperate.
Rough winds do shake the darling buds of May,
And summer's lease hath all too short a date.
William Shakespeare (1564–1616) English dramatist.
Sonnet 18

4 Won't you come into the garden? I would like my roses to see you.
Richard Brinsley Sheridan (1751–1816) British dramatist.
Said to a young lady
Attrib. in *The Perfect Hostess*

5 Roses are flowering in Picardy,
But there's never a rose like you.
Frederic Edward Weatherly (1848–1929) British lawyer and songwriter.
Roses of Picardy

□COMPROMISE□

1 We know what happens to people who stay in the middle of the road. They get run over.
Aneurin Bevan (1897–1960) British Labour politician.
The Observer, 9 Dec 1953

2 All government, indeed every human benefit and enjoyment, every virtue, and every prudent act, is founded on compromise and barter.
Edmund Burke (1729–97) British politician.
Speech on Conciliation with America (House of Commons, 22 Mar 1775)

3 Compromise used to mean that half a loaf was better than no bread. Among modern statesmen it really seems to mean that half a loaf is better than a whole loaf.
G. K. Chesterton (1874–1936) British writer.
What's Wrong with the World

□CONCEIT□

See also egotism, pride

1 It was prettily devised of Aesop, 'The fly sat upon the axletree of the chariot-wheel and said, what a dust do I raise.'
Francis Bacon (1561–1626) English philosopher.
Essays, 'Of Vain Glory'

2 If ever he went to school without any boots it was because he was too big for them.
Ivor Bulmer-Thomas (1905–) British writer and politician.
Referring to Harold Wilson
Remark, Conservative Party Conference, 1949

3 Vanity plays lurid tricks with our memory.
Joseph Conrad (Teodor Josef Konrad Korzeniowski; 1857–1924) Polish-born British novelist.
Lord Jim

4 We are so vain that we even care for the opinion of those we don't care for.
Marie Ebner von Eschenbach (1830–1916) Austrian writer.
Aphorism

5 Conceit is the finest armour a man can wear.
Jerome K. Jerome (1859–1927) British humorist.
Idle Thoughts of an Idle Fellow

6 Self-love is the greatest of all flatterers.
Duc de la Rochefoucauld (1613–80) French writer.
Maximes, 2

7 Vanity dies hard; in some obstinate cases it outlives the man.
Robert Louis Stevenson (1850–94) Scottish writer.
Prince Otto

8 I think, historically, the term 'Thatcherism' will be seen as a compliment.
Margaret Thatcher (1925–) British politician and prime minister.
Remark, Oct 1985

9 I think I have become a bit of an institution – you know, the sort of thing people expect to see around the place.
Margaret Thatcher
Remark, July 1987

☐ CONFLICT ☐

See also opposites

1 Without Contraries is no progression. Attraction and Repulsion, Reason and Energy, Love and Hate, are necessary to Human existence.
William Blake (1757–1827) British poet.
The Marriage of Heaven and Hell, 'The Argument'

2 No, when the fight begins within himself, A man's worth something.
Robert Browning (1812–89) British poet.
Bishop Blougram's Apology

3 Two souls dwell, alas! in my breast.
Goethe (1749–1832) German poet and dramatist.
Faust, Pt. I

4 Two loves I have, of comfort and despair, Which like two spirits do suggest me still; The better angel is a man right fair, The worser spirit a woman colour'd ill.
William Shakespeare (1564–1616) English dramatist.
Sonnet 144

☐ CONFORMITY ☐

See also orthodoxy

1 When in Rome, live as the Romans do: when elsewhere, live as they live elsewhere.
St Ambrose (c. 339–397) Bishop of Milan.
Advice to St Augustine

2 Take the tone of the company you are in.
Earl of Chesterfield (1694–1773) English statesman.
Letter to his son, 9 Oct 1747

3 Whoso would be a man must be a nonconformist.
Ralph Waldo Emerson (1803–82) US poet and essayist.
Essays, 'Self-Reliance'

4 Why do you have to be a nonconformist like everybody else?
James Thurber (1894–1961) US humorist.
Attrib. Actually a cartoon caption by Stan Hunt in the *New Yorker*

☐ CONFUSION ☐

1 I can't say I was ever lost, but I was bewildered once for three days.
Daniel Boone (1734–1820) US pioneeer.
Reply when asked if he had ever been lost
Attrib.

2 'Curiouser and curiouser!' cried Alice.
Lewis Carroll (Charles Lutwidge Dodgson; 1832–98) British writer.
Alice's Adventures in Wonderland, Ch. 2

3 Bewitched, Bothered and Bewildered.
Lorenz Hart (1895–1943) US songwriter.
From the musical *Babes in Arms*
Song title

4 I had nothing to offer anybody except my own confusion.
Jack Kerouac (1922–69) US novelist.
On the Road, Pt. II

☐ CONGREVE ☐
William

(1670–1729) British Restoration dramatist, whose comedies include *Love for Love* (1695) and *The Way of the World* (1700). He also wrote a tragedy, *The Mourning Bride* (1697).

QUOTATIONS ABOUT CONGREVE

1 William Congreve is the only sophisticated playwright England has produced; and like Shaw, Sheridan, and Wilde, his nearest rivals, he was brought up in Ireland.
Kenneth Tynan (1927–80) British theater critic.
Curtains, 'The Way of the World'

2 He spoke of his works as trifles that were beneath him.
Voltaire (François-Marie Arouet; 1694–1778) French writer.
Letters concerning the English nation

QUOTATIONS BY CONGREVE

3 See how love and murder will out.
The Double Dealer, IV:6

4 O fie miss, you must not kiss and tell.
Love for Love, II:10

5 I know that's a secret, for it's whispered every where.
Love for Love, III:3

6 Music has charms to soothe a savage breast.
The Mourning Bride, I

7 Heaven has no rage like love to hatred turned, Nor hell a fury like a woman scorned.
The Mourning Bride, III

8 SHARPER. Thus grief still treads upon the heels of pleasure:
Marry'd in haste, we may repent at leisure.
SETTER. Some by experience find those words mis-plac'd:
At leisure marry'd, they repent in haste.
The Old Bachelor, V:8

9 Say what you will, 'tis better to be left than never to have been loved.
The Way of the World, II:1

10 I nauseate walking; 'tis a country diversion, I loathe the country and everything that relates to it.

The Way of the World, IV:4

□ CONNOLLY □
Cyril (Vernon)

(1903–74) British journalist and writer. A contributor to the *New Statesman*, the *Sunday Times*, and other papers, he published several collections of essays, such as *Enemies of Promise* (1938).

QUOTATIONS ABOUT CONNOLLY

1 Writers like Connolly gave pleasure a bad name.

E. M. Forster (1879–1970) British novelist.
Attrib.

QUOTATIONS BY CONNOLLY

2 The ape-like virtues without which no one can enjoy a public school.

Enemies of Promise, Ch. 1

3 Literature is the art of writing something that will be read twice; journalism what will be grasped at once.

Enemies of Promise, Ch. 3

4 As repressed sadists are supposed to become policemen or butchers so those with irrational fear of life become publishers.

Enemies of Promise, Ch. 3

5 I have always disliked myself at any given moment; the total of such moments is my life.

Enemies of Promise, Ch. 18

6 Life is a maze in which we take the wrong turning before we have learnt to walk.

The Unquiet Grave

7 In the sex-war thoughtlessness is the weapon of the male, vindictiveness of the female.

The Unquiet Grave

8 There is no fury like an ex-wife searching for a new lover.

The Unquiet Grave

9 Better to write for yourself and have no public, than write for the public and have no self.

Turnstile One (ed. V. S. Pritchett)

10 The man who is master of his passions is Reason's slave.

Turnstile One (ed. V. S. Pritchett)

□ CONSCIENCE □
See also integrity

1 Conscience, I say, not thine own, but of the other: for why is my liberty judged of another man's conscience?

Bible: I Corinthians
10:29

2 Conscience is the internal perception of the rejection of a particular wish operating within us.

Sigmund Freud (1856–1939) Austrian psychoanalyst.
Totem and Taboo

3 Conscience is the inner voice that warns us somebody may be looking.

H. L. Mencken (1880–1956) US journalist.
A Mencken Chrestomathy

4 Thus conscience does make cowards of us all;
And thus the native hue of resolution
Is sicklied o'er with the pale cast of thought.

William Shakespeare (1564–1616) English dramatist.
Hamlet, III:1

□ CONSERVATION □
See also ecology, environment

1 Contrary to popular mythology, it is not my Department's mission in life to tarmac over the whole of England.

Paul Channon (1935–) British politician.
Speech, Sept 1988

2 Population growth is the primary source of environmental damage.

Jacques Cousteau (1910–) French naval officer and underwater explorer.
Remark, Jan 1989

3 Trees are poems that the earth writes upon the sky. We fell them down and turn them into paper that we may record our emptiness.

Kahil Gibran (1883–1931) Lebanese mystic and poet.
Sand and Foam

4 Green politics is not about being far left or far right, but far-sighted.

David Icke (1952–) Green Party spokesman.
Speech, Green Party conference, Sept 1989

5 The biggest waste of water in the country by far is when you spend half a pint and flush two gallons.

Prince Philip (1921–) The consort of Queen Elizabeth II.
Speech, 1965

6 Simply having a convention which says you must not make species extinct does not make a blind bit of difference.

Prince Philip
Referring to the UN treaty on world conservation, Mar 1989
The Sunday Correspondent, 31 Dec, 1989

□CONSERVATISM□
See also change

1 All conservatism is based upon the idea that if
you leave things alone you leave them as they
are. But you do not. If you leave a thing alone you
leave it to a torrent of change.
G. K. Chesterton (1874–1936) British writer.
Orthodoxy, Ch. 7

2 I do not know which makes a man more conservative – to know nothing but the present, or nothing but the past.
John Maynard Keynes (1883–1946) British economist.
The End of Laisser-Faire, I

3 What is conservatism? Is it not adherence to the
old and tried, against the new and untried?
Abraham Lincoln (1809–65) US statesman.
Speech, 27 Feb 1860

4 You can't teach an old dogma new tricks.
Dorothy Parker (1893–1967) US writer.
Wit's End (R. E. Drennan)

5 The radical invents the views. When he has worn
them out, the conservative adopts them.
Mark Twain (Samuel Langhorne Clemens; 1835–1910) US
writer.
Notebooks

□CONSTANCY□
See also change, conservatism

1 Consistency is contrary to nature, contrary to
life. The only completely consistent people are
the dead.
Aldous Huxley (1894–1964) British novelist.
Do What you Will

2 *Plus ça change, plus c'est la même chose.*
The more things change, the more they stay the
same.
Alphonse Karr (1808–90) French writer.
Les Guêpes, Jan 1849

3 For men may come and men may go
But I go on for ever.
Alfred, Lord Tennyson (1809–92) British poet.
The Brook

4 Still glides the Stream, and shall for ever glide;
The Form remains, the Function never dies.
William Wordsworth (1770–1850) British poet.
The River Duddon, 'After-Thought'

□CONTENTMENT□
See also happiness, satisfaction

1 Live with the gods. And he does so who constantly shows them that his soul is satisfied with
what is assigned to him.
Marcus Aurelius (121–180 AD) Roman emperor.
Meditations, Bk. V, Ch. 27

2 Here with a Loaf of Bread beneath the Bough,
A Flask of Wine, a Book of Verse – and Thou
Beside me singing in the Wilderness –
And Wilderness is Paradise enow.
Edward Fitzgerald (1809–83) British poet.
The Rubáiyát of Omar Khayyám

3 Nought's had, all's spent,
Where our desire is got without content.
'Tis safer to be that which we destroy,
Than by destruction dwell in doubtful joy.
William Shakespeare (1564–1616) English dramatist.
Macbeth, III:2

□CONTRACEPTION□
See also sex

1 Vasectomy means not ever having to say you're
sorry.
Larry Adler (1914–) US harmonica player and entertainer.
Attrib.

2 I want to tell you a terrific story about oral contraception. I asked this girl to sleep with me and she
said 'no'.
Woody Allen (Allen Stewart Konigsberg; 1935–) US film
actor.
Woody Allen: Clown Prince of American Humor (Adler and
Feinman), Ch. 2

3 He no play-a da game. He no make-a da rules!
Earl Butz (1909–) US politician.
Referring to the Pope's strictures against contraception
Remark, 1974

4 The command 'Be fruitful and multiply' was
promulgated according to our authorities,
when the population of the world consisted of
two people.
Dean Inge (1860–1954) British churchman.
More Lay Thoughts of a Dean

5 It is now quite lawful for a Catholic woman to
avoid pregnancy by a resort to mathematics,
though she is still forbidden to resort to physics
and chemistry.
H. L. Mencken (1880–1956) US journalist.
Notebooks, 'Minority Report'

6 Contraceptives should be used on every conceiv-
able occasion.
Spike Milligan (1918–) British comic actor and author.
The Last Goon Show of All

□CONVERSATION□
See also speech

1 Questioning is not the mode of conversation
among gentlemen.
Samuel Johnson (1709–84) British lexicographer.
Life of Johnson (J. Boswell), Vol. II

2 That is the happiest conversation where there is no competition, no vanity but a calm quiet interchange of sentiments.
Samuel Johnson
Life of Johnson (J. Boswell), Vol. II

3 Beware of the conversationalist who adds 'in other words'. He is merely starting afresh.
Robert Morley (1908–92) British actor.
The Observer, 'Sayings of the Week', 6 Dec 1964

4 Ideal conversation must be an exchange of thought, and not, as many of those who worry most about their shortcomings believe, an eloquent exhibition of wit or oratory.
Emily Post (1873–1960) US writer.
Etiquette, Ch. 6

5 Conversation has a kind of charm about it, an insinuating and insidious something that elicits secrets from us just like love or liquor.
Seneca (c. 4 BC–65 AD) Roman author.
Epistles

6 There is no such thing as conversation. It is an illusion. There are intersecting monologues, that is all.
Rebecca West (Cicely Isabel Fairfield; 1892–1983) British novelist and journalist.
There Is No Conversation, Ch. 1

☐ CORRUPTION ☐
See also bribery, decline

1 Among a people generally corrupt, liberty cannot long exist.
Edmund Burke (1729–97) British politician.
Letter to the Sheriffs of Bristol, 1777

2 Corruption, the most infallible symptom of constitutional liberty.
Edward Gibbon (1737–94) British historian.
Decline and Fall of the Roman Empire, Ch. 21

3 As killing as the canker to the rose.
John Milton (1608–74) English poet.
Lycidas

4 All things can corrupt perverted minds.
Ovid (Publius Ovidius Naso; 43 BC–17 AD) Roman poet.
Tristia, Bk. II

5 Any institution which does not suppose the people good, and the magistrate corruptible is evil.
Robespierre (1758–94) French lawyer and revolutionary.
Déclaration des Droits de l'homme, 24 Apr 1793

6 Something is rotten in the state of Denmark.
William Shakespeare (1564–1616) English dramatist.
Hamlet, I:4

7 For sweetest things turn sourest by their deeds:
Lilies that fester smell far worse than weeds.
William Shakespeare
Sonnet 94

☐ COUNTRYSIDE ☐
See also ecology, flowers, Nature, trees

1 God made the country, and man made the town.
William Cowper (1731–1800) British poet.
The Task

2 Ever charming, ever new,
When will the landscape tire the view?
John Dyer (1700–58) British poet.
Grongar Hill

3 When I am in the country I wish to vegetate like the country.
William Hazlitt (1778–1830) British essayist.
On Going a Journey

4 Here of a Sunday morning
My love and I would lie,
And see the coloured counties,
And hear the larks so high
About us in the sky.
A. E. Housman (1859–1936) British scholar and poet.
A Shropshire Lad, 'Bredon Hill'

5 Under the greenwood tree
Who loves to lie with me,
And turn his merry note
Unto the sweet bird's throat,
Come hither, come hither, come hither.
Here shall he see
No enemy
But winter and rough weather.
William Shakespeare (1564–1616) English dramatist.
As You Like It, II:5

☐ COURAGE ☐
See also endurance, heroism, patriotism

1 Because of my title, I was the first to enter here. I shall be the last to go out.
Duchesse d'Alençon (d. 1897) Bavarian-born duchess.
Refusing help during a fire, 4 May 1897, at a charity bazaar in Paris. She died along with 120 others
Attrib.

2 Perhaps your fear in passing judgement is greater than mine in receiving it.
Giordano Bruno (1548–1600) Italian philosopher.
Said to the cardinals who excommunicated him, 8 Feb 1600
Attrib.

3 Boldness, and again boldness, and always boldness!
Georges Jacques Danton (1759–94) French political activist.
Speech, French Legislative Committee, 2 Sept 1792

4 Courage is the price that Life exacts for granting peace.
Amelia Earhart (1898–1937) US flyer.
Courage

5 The boy stood on the burning deck
Whence all but he had fled;

The flame that lit the battle's wreck
Shone round him o'er the dead.
Felicia Dorothea Hemans (1793–1835) British poet.
Casabianca

6 It is better to be the widow of a hero than the wife of a coward.
Dolores Ibarruri (1895–1989) Spanish politician.
Speech, Valencia, 1936

7 We dip our colours in honour of you, dear women comrades, who march into battle together with the men.
Dolores Ibarruri (1895–) Spanish-born Russian revolutionary and editor.
Speeches and Articles, 1936–1938

8 Then out spake brave Horatius,
The Captain of the Gate:
'To every man upon this earth
Death cometh soon or late.
And how can man die better
Than facing fearful odds,
For the ashes of his fathers,
And the temples of his Gods?'
Lord Macaulay (1800–59) British historian.
Lays of Ancient Rome, 'Horatius', 27

9 The stubborn spear-men still made good
Their dark impenetrable wood,
Each stepping where his comrade stood,
The instant that he fell.
Walter Scott (1771–1832) Scottish novelist.
Marmion, VI

10 Nature gave me the form of a woman; my actions have raised me to the level of the most valiant of men.
Semiramis (8th century BC) Assyrian queen.
Women of Beauty and Heroism (Frank B. Goodrich)

11 Once more unto the breach, dear friends, once more;
Or close the wall up with our English dead.
William Shakespeare (1564–1616) English dramatist.
Henry V, III:1

12 Half a league, half a league,
Half a league onward,
All in the valley of Death
Rode the six hundred.
Alfred, Lord Tennyson (1809–92) British poet.
The Charge of the Light Brigade

13 Into the jaws of Death,
Into the mouth of Hell.
Alfred, Lord Tennyson
The Charge of the Light Brigade

14 Fortune favours the brave.
Terence (Publius Terentius Afer; c. 190–159 BC) Roman poet.
Phormio

15 The three-o'-clock in the morning courage, which Bonaparte thought was the rarest.
Henry David Thoreau (1817–62) US writer.
Walden, 'Sounds'

☐ COURTESY ☐
See also chivalry, etiquette, manners, respect

1 If a man be gracious and courteous to strangers, it shews he is a citizen of the world.
Francis Bacon (1561–1626) English philosopher.
Essays, 'Of Goodness and Goodness of Nature'

2 Courtesy is not dead – it has merely taken refuge in Great Britain.
Georges Duhamel (1884–1966) French writer.
The Observer, 'Sayings of Our Times', 31 May 1953

☐ COWARD ☐
Sir Noël
(1899–1973) British actor, dramatist, and songwriter. After his first success, *The Vortex* (1924), he wrote a number of comedies, including *Blithe Spirit* (1941) and *Brief Encounter* (1946), both made into films. His songs include *Mad Dogs and Englishmen*.

QUOTATIONS ABOUT COWARD

1 He was his own greatest invention.
John Osborne (1929–) British dramatist.
Attrib.

2 He was once Slightly in *Peter Pan*, and has been wholly in Peter Pan ever since.
Kenneth Tynan (1927–80) British theater critic.
Attrib.

QUOTATIONS BY COWARD

3 We have no reliable guarantee that the afterlife will be any less exasperating than this one, have we?
Blithe Spirit, I

4 There's always something fishy about the French.
Conversation Piece, I:6

5 Everybody was up to something, especially, of course, those who were up to nothing.
Future Indefinite

6 The Stately Homes of England
How beautiful they stand,
To prove the upper classes
Have still the upper hand.
Operette, 'The Stately Homes of England'

7 Strange how potent cheap music is.
Private Lives

8 Don't put your daughter on the stage, Mrs Worthington.
Song title

9 Mad dogs and Englishmen go out in the mid-day sun.
Song title

10 I've over-educated myself in all the things I shouldn't have known at all.
Wild Oats

11 Work is much more fun than fun.
The Observer, 'Sayings of the Week', 21 June 1963

12 Dear 338171 (May I call you 338?).
Starting a letter to T. E. Lawrence, who had retired from public life to become Aircraftsman Ross, 338171.
Letters to T. E. Lawrence

13 I never realized before that Albert married beneath him.
After seeing a certain actress in the role of Queen Victoria.
Tynan on Theatre (K. Tynan)

□ COWARDICE □
See also self-preservation

1 None but a coward dares to boast that he has never known fear.
Marshal Foch (1851–1929) French soldier.
Attrib.

2 To a surprising extent the war-lords in shining armour, the apostles of the martial virtues, tend not to die fighting when the time comes. History is full of ignominious getaways by the great and famous.
George Orwell (Eric Blair; 1903–50) British novelist.
Who Are the War Criminals?

3 Cowards die many times before their deaths: The valiant never taste of death but once.
William Shakespeare (1564–1616) English dramatist.
Julius Caesar, II:2

□ COWPER □
William
(1731–1800) British poet. A lawyer and commissioner of bankrupts, his life was dogged by depression, bouts of insanity, and suicide attempts. His ballad *John Gilpin's Ride* (1783) and the long poem *The Task* (1785) established his reputation; he also translated Homer.

QUOTATIONS ABOUT COWPER

1 That maniacal Calvinist and coddled poet.
Lord Byron (1788–1824) British poet.
Attrib.

QUOTATIONS BY COWPER

2 Rome shall perish – write that word In the blood that she has spilt.
Boadicea

3 He found it inconvenient to be poor.
Charity

4 Absence from whom we love is worse than death.
'Hope, like the Short-lived Ray'

5 Says John, It is my wedding-day, And all the world would stare, If wife should dine at Edmonton, And I should dine at Ware.
John Gilpin

6 God moves in a mysterious way His wonders to perform; He plants his footsteps in the sea, And rides upon the storm.
Olney Hymns, 35

7 The bud may have a bitter taste, But sweet will be the flower.
Olney Hymns, 35

8 For 'tis a truth well known to most, That whatsoever thing is lost – We seek it, ere it come to light, In every cranny but the right.
The Retired Cat

9 God made the country, and man made the town.
The Task

10 Variety's the very spice of life That gives it all its flavour.
The Task

11 Nature is but a name for an effect Whose cause is God.
The Task

12 Mountains interposed Make enemies of nations, who had else, Like kindred drops, been mingled into one.
The Task

13 Slaves cannot breathe in England; if their lungs Receive our air, that moment they are free; They touch our country, and their shackles fall.
A situation resulting from a judicial decision in 1772.
The Task

14 Knowledge dwells In heads replete with thoughts of other men; Wisdom in minds attentive to their own.
The Task

□ CREATION □

1 In the beginning God created the heaven and the earth.
And the earth was without form, and void; and darkness was upon the face of the deep. And the Spirit of God moved upon the face of the waters. And God said, Let there be light: and there was light.
And God saw the light, that it was good: and God divided the light from the darkness.

And God called the light Day, and the darkness he called Night. And the evening and the morning were the first day.
Bible: Genesis
1:1–5

2 And God called the dry land Earth; and the gathering together of the waters called he Seas: and God saw that it was good.
And God said, Let the earth bring forth grass, the herb yielding seed, and the fruit tree yielding fruit after his kind, whose seed is in itself, upon the earth: and it was so.
Bible: Genesis
1:10–11

3 And God made two great lights: the greater light to rule the day, and the lesser light to rule the night: he made the stars also.
Bible: Genesis
1:16

4 And God said, Let the earth bring forth the living creature after his kind, cattle, and creeping thing, and beast of the earth after his kind: and it was so.
Bible: Genesis
1:24

5 And God said, Let us make man in our image, after our likeness: and let them have dominion over the fish of the sea, and over the fowl of the air, and over the cattle, and over all the earth, and over every creeping thing that creepeth upon the earth.
So God created man in his own image, in the image of God created he him; male and female created he them.
And God blessed them, and God said unto them, Be fruitful, and multiply, and replenish the earth, and subdue it: and have dominion over the fish of the sea, and over the fowl of the air, and over every living thing that moveth upon the earth.
Bible: Genesis
1:26–28

6 When the stars threw down their spears,
And watered heaven with their tears,
Did he smile his work to see?
Did he who made the Lamb make thee?
William Blake (1757–1827) British poet.
Songs of Experience, 'The Tiger'

7 Little Lamb, who made thee?
Dost thou know who made thee?
William Blake
Songs of Innocence, 'The Lamb'

8 Whan that the month in which the world bigan,
That highte March, whan God first maked man.
Geoffrey Chaucer (c. 1342–1400) English poet.
The Canterbury Tales, 'The Nun's Priest's Tale'

9 'Who is the Potter, pray, and who the Pot?'
Edward Fitzgerald (1809–83) British poet.
The Rubáiyát of Omar Khayyám

10 I cannot forgive Descartes; in all his philosophy he did his best to dispense with God. But he could not avoid making Him set the world in motion with a flip of His thumb; after that he had no more use for God.
Blaise Pascal (1623–62) French philosopher and mathematician.
Pensées, II

□ CRICKET □

See also sport and games

1 I do love cricket – it's so very English.
Sarah Bernhardt (Sarah Henriette Rosine Bernard; 1844–1923) French actress.
On seeing a game of football
Nijinsky (R. Buckle)

2 It's more than a game. It's an institution.
Thomas Hughes (1822–96) British novelist.
Referring to cricket
Tom Brown's Schooldays, Pt. II, Ch. 7

3 There's a breathless hush in the Close tonight –
Ten to make and the match to win –
A bumping pitch and a blinding light,
An hour to play and the last man in.
Henry John Newbolt (1862–1938) British poet.
Vitaï Lampada

4 I tend to believe that cricket is the greatest thing that God ever created on earth…certainly greater than sex, although sex isn't too bad either.
Harold Pinter (1930–) British dramatist.
The Observer, 5 Oct 1980

5 I have always looked upon cricket as organised loafing.
William Temple (1881–1944) British churchman.
Address to parents when headmaster of Repton School

6 If the French noblesse had been capable of playing cricket with their peasants, their chateaux would never have been burnt.
George Macaulay Trevelyan (1876–1962) British historian.
English Social History, Ch. XIII

□ CRIME □

See also murder, theft

1 And surely your blood of your lives will I require; at the hand of every beast will I require it, and at the hand of man; at the hand of every man's brother will I require the life of man.
Whoso sheddeth man's blood, by man shall his blood be shed: for in the image of God made he man.
Bible: Genesis
9:5–6

2 If poverty is the mother of crime, stupidity is its father.
Jean de La Bruyère (1645–96) French satirist.
Les Caractères

3 Crime, like virtue, has its degrees.
Jean Racine (1639–99) French dramatist.
Phèdre, IV:2

□ CRITICISM □

See also actors, compliments, insults, poets, writers

1 I am bound by my own definition of criticism: a disinterested endeavour to learn and propagate the best that is known and thought in the world.
Matthew Arnold (1822–88) British poet and critic.
Essays in Criticism, First Series, 'Functions of Criticism at the Present Time'

2 Of all fatiguing, futile, empty trades, the worst, I suppose, is writing about writing.
Hilaire Belloc (1870–1953) French-born British poet.
The Silence of the Sea

3 And why beholdest thou the mote that is in thy brother's eye, but considerest not the beam that is in thine own eye?
Bible: Matthew
7:3

4 He who discommendeth others obliquely commendeth himself.
Thomas Browne (1605–82) English physician and writer.
Christian Morals, Pt. I

5 A great deal of contemporary criticism reads to me like a man saying: 'Of course I do not like green cheese: I am very fond of brown sherry.'
G. K. Chesterton (1874–1936) British writer.
All I Survey

6 If you hear that someone is speaking ill of you, instead of trying to defend yourself you should say: 'He obviously does not know me very well, since there are so many other faults he could have mentioned'.
Epictetus (c. 60–110 AD) Stoic philosopher.
Enchiridion

7 There are two things which I am confident I can do very well: one is an introduction to any literary work, stating what it is to contain, and how it should be executed in the most perfect manner; the other is a conclusion, shewing from various causes why the execution has not been equal to what the author promised to himself and to the public.
Samuel Johnson (1709–84) British lexicographer.
Life of Johnson (J. Boswell), Vol. I

8 You *may* abuse a tragedy, though you cannot write one. You may scold a carpenter who has made you a bad table, though you cannot make a table. It is not your trade to make tables.
Samuel Johnson
Referring to the qualifications needed to indulge in literary criticism
Life of Johnson (J. Boswell), Vol. I

9 The pleasure of criticizing robs us of the pleasure of being moved by some very fine things.
Jean de La Bruyère (1645–96) French satirist.
Les Caractères

10 People ask you for criticism, but they only want praise.
W. Somerset Maugham (1874–1965) British novelist.
Of Human Bondage, Ch. 50

11 Prolonged, indiscriminate reviewing of books involves constantly *inventing* reactions towards books about which one has no spontaneous feelings whatever.
George Orwell (Eric Blair; 1903–50) British novelist.
Confessions of a Book Reviewer

12 'Tis hard to say, if greater want of skill
Appear in writing or in judging ill.
Alexander Pope (1688–1744) British poet.
An Essay on Criticism

13 Damn with faint praise, assent with civil leer,
And, without sneering, teach the rest to sneer.
Alexander Pope
Epistle to Dr. Arbuthnot

14 The Stealthy School of Criticism.
Dante Gabriel Rossetti (1828–82) British painter and poet.
Letter to the *Athenaeum*, 1871

15 For I am nothing if not critical.
William Shakespeare (1564–1616) English dramatist.
Othello, II:1

16 As far as criticism is concerned, we don't resent that unless it is absolutely biased, as it is in most cases.
John Vorster (Balthazar Johannes Vorster; 1915–83) South African politician.
The Observer, 'Sayings of the Week', 9 Nov 1969

17 You have riches and freedom here but I feel no sense of faith or direction. You have so many computers, why don't you use them in the search for love?
Lech Walesa (1943–) Polish trade unionist.
Speech, Dec 1988

□ CRITICS □

1 I will try to account for the degree of my aesthetic emotion. That, I conceive, is the function of the critic.
Clive Bell (1881–1964) British art critic.
Art, Pt. II, Ch. 3

2 A man must serve his time to every trade
Save censure – critics all are ready made.
Lord Byron (1788–1824) British poet.
English Bards and Scotch Reviewers

3 Reviewers are usually people who would have
been poets, historians, biographers,…if they
could; they have tried their talents at one or at
the other, and have failed; therefore they turn
critics.
Samuel Taylor Coleridge (1772–1834) British poet.
Lectures on Shakespeare and Milton, I

4 A good critic is one who narrates the adventures
of his mind among masterpieces.
Anatole France (Jacques Anatole François Thibault;
1844–1924) French writer.
The Literary Life, Preface

5 I sometimes think
His critical judgement is so exquisite
It leaves us nothing to admire except his opinion.
Christopher Fry (1907–) British dramatist.
The Dark is Light Enough, II

6 Asking a working writer what he thinks about
critics is like asking a lamp-post how it feels
about dogs.
Christopher Hampton (1946–) British writer and
dramatist.
The Sunday Times Magazine, 16 Oct 1977

7 What is a modern poet's fate?
To write his thoughts upon a slate;
The critic spits on what is done,
Gives it a wipe – and all is gone.
Thomas Hood (1799–1845) British poet.
Alfred Lord Tennyson, A Memoir (Hallam Tennyson), Vol. II, Ch. 3

8 Critics are more malicious about poetry than
about other books – maybe because so many
manqué poets write reviews.
Elizabeth Jennings (1926–) British poet.
Remark, Dec 1987

9 A fly, Sir, may sting a stately horse and make him
wince; but one is but an insect, and the other is a
horse still.
Samuel Johnson (1709–84) British lexicographer.
Life of Johnson (J. Boswell), Vol. I

10 Insects sting, not from malice, but because they
want to live. It is the same with critics – they
desire our blood, not our pain.
Friedrich Wilhelm Nietzsche (1844–1900) German
philosopher.
Miscellaneous Maxims and Reflections

11 Nor in the critic let the man be lost.
Alexander Pope (1688–1744) British poet.
An Essay on Criticism

12 The greater part of critics are parasites, who, if
nothing had been written, would find nothing to
write.
J. B. Priestley (1894–1984) British novelist.
Outcries and Asides

13 A critic is a man who knows the way but can't
drive the car.
Kenneth Tynan (1927–80) British theatre critic.
New York Times Magazine, 9 Jan 1966

14 A good drama critic is one who perceives
what is happening in the theatre of his time.
A great drama critic also perceives what is not
happening.
Kenneth Tynan
Tynan Right and Left, Foreword

□CRUELTY□
See also hurt, nastiness, violence

1 The wish to hurt, the momentary intoxication
with pain, is the loophole through which the pervert climbs into the minds of ordinary men.
Jacob Bronowski (1908–74) British scientist and writer.
The Face of Violence, Ch. 5

2 Man's inhumanity to man
Makes countless thousands mourn!
Robert Burns (1759–96) Scottish poet.
Man was Made to Mourn

3 Fear is the parent of cruelty.
J. A. Froude (1818–94) British historian.
Short Studies on Great Subjects, 'Party Politics'

4 A cruel story runs on wheels, and every hand
oils the wheels as they run.
Ouida (Marie Louise de la Ramée; 1839–1908) British novelist.
Wisdom, Wit and Pathos, 'Moths'

5 The infliction of cruelty with a good conscience
is a delight to moralists. That is why they
invented Hell.
Bertrand Russell (1872–1970) British philosopher.
Sceptical Essays 'On the Value of Scepticism'

□CULTURE□
See also civilization, philistinism

1 Culture, the acquainting ourselves with the best
that has been known and said in the world, and
thus with the history of the human spirit.
Matthew Arnold (1822–88) British poet and critic.
Literature and Dogma, Preface

2 Culture is the passion for sweetness and light,
and (what is more) the passion for making them
prevail.
Matthew Arnold
Literature and Dogma, Preface

3 Whenever I hear the word 'culture'...I reach for my gun.

Hans Johst German dramatist.
Schlageter, I:1

□ CURIE □
Marie Sklodowska

(1867–1934) Polish chemist, who emigrated to France in 1891 and pioneered research into radioactivity. In 1895 she married Pierre Curie (1859–1906), a French physicist. In 1903 she shared the Nobel prize for physics with Pierre Curie and Henri Becquerel, for their work on radioactivity, and was awarded the 1911 Nobel prize for chemistry for her discovery of polonium and radium.

QUOTATIONS ABOUT CURIE

1 Women cannot be part of the Institute of France.

Emile Hilaire Amagat (1841–1915) French physicist. Comment following the rejection of Marie Curie by the Académie des Sciences, for which she had been nominated in 1910. She was rejected by one vote, and refused to allow her name to be submitted again or, for ten years, to allow her work to be published by the Académie.

2 Marie Curie is, of all celebrated beings, the only one whom fame has not corrupted.

Albert Einstein (1879–1955) German-born US physicist. *Madame Curie* (Eve Curie)

QUOTATIONS BY CURIE

3 After all, science is essentially international, and it is only through lack of the historical sense that national qualities have been attributed to it.

Memorandum, 'Intellectual Co-operation'

4 All my life through, the new sights of Nature made me rejoice like a child.

Pierre Curie

5 I have no dress except the one I wear every day. If you are going to be kind enough to give me one, please let it be practical and dark so that I can put it on afterwards to go to the laboratory.

Referring to a wedding dress.
Letter to a friend, 1849

6 One never notices what has been done; one can only see what remains to be done.

Letter to her brother, 18 Mar 1894

□ CURIOSITY □

See also wonder

1 Be not curious in unnecessary matters: for more things are shewed unto thee than men understand

Bible: Ecclesiasticus
3:23

2 'If everybody minded their own business,' the Duchess said in a hoarse growl, 'the world would go round a deal faster than it does.'

Lewis Carroll (Charles Lutwidge Dodgson; 1832–98) British writer.
Alice's Adventures in Wonderland, Ch. 6

3 The world is but a school of inquiry.

Michel de Montaigne (1533–92) French essayist.
Essais, III

4 Curiosity will conquer fear even more than bravery will.

James Stephens (1882–1950) Irish novelist.
The Crock of Gold

5 Disinterested intellectual curiosity is the life blood of real civilisation.

George Macaulay Trevelyan (1876–1962) British historian.
English Social History, Preface

□ CURSES □

1 A plague o' both your houses!
They have made worms' meat of me.

William Shakespeare (1564–1616) English dramatist.
Romeo and Juliet, III:1

2 Curses are like young chickens, they always come home to roost.

Robert Southey (1774–1843) British poet.
The Curse of Kehama, Motto

3 'The curse is come upon me,' cried
The Lady of Shalott.

Alfred, Lord Tennyson (1809–92) British poet.
The Lady of Shalott, Pt. III

4 She has heard a whisper say,
A curse is on her if she stay
To look down to Camelot.

Alfred, Lord Tennyson
The Lady of Shalott, Pt. II

□ CUSTOM □

See also habit

1 *O tempora! O mores!*
What times! What customs!

Cicero (106–43 BC) Roman orator and statesman.
In Catilinam, I

2 Custom, then, is the great guide of human life.

David Hume (1711–76) Scottish philosopher.
An Enquiry Concerning Human Understanding

3 Custom calls me to't.
What custom wills, in all things should we do't,
The dust on antique time would lie unswept,
And mountainous error be too highly heap'd
For truth to o'erpeer.

William Shakespeare (1564–1616) English dramatist.
Coriolanus, II:3

☐CYNICISM☐

1 Cynicism is an unpleasant way of saying the truth.

Lillian Hellman (1905–84) US dramatist.
The Little Foxes, I

2 God is love, but get it in writing.

Gypsy Rose Lee (1914–70) US striptease artist.
Attrib.

3 A cynic is a man who, when he smells flowers, looks around for a coffin.

H. L. Mencken (1880–1956) US journalist.
Attrib.

4 A man who knows the price of everything and the value of nothing.

Oscar Wilde (1854–1900) Irish-born British dramatist.
A cynic
Lady Windermere's Fan, III

D

☐DAMNATION☐

See also devil, hell

1 You will be damned if you do – And you will be damned if you don't.
Lorenzo Dow (1777–1834) British churchman.
Speaking of Calvinism
Reflections on the Love of God

2 Ugly hell, gape not! come not, Lucifer!
I'll burn my books!
Christopher Marlowe (1564–93) English dramatist.
Doctor Faustus, V:2

☐DANGER☐

1 Defend us from all perils and dangers of this night.
The Book of Common Prayer
Morning Prayer, Prayer of St Chrysostom

2 Dangers by being despised grow great.
Edmund Burke (1729–97) British politician.
Speech, House of Commons, 11 May 1792

3 Of course I realized there was a measure of danger. Obviously I faced the possibility of not returning when first I considered going. Once faced and settled there really wasn't any good reason to refer to it.
Amelia Earhart (1898–1937) US flyer.
Referring to her flight in the 'Friendship'
20 Hours: 40 Minutes – Our Flight in the Friendship, Ch. 5

4 Believe me! The secret of reaping the greatest fruitfulness and the greatest enjoyment from life is to *live dangerously!*
Friedrich Wilhelm Nietzsche (1844–1900) German philosopher.
Die Fröhliche Wissenschaft, Bk. IV

☐DAY☐

1 Now the day is over,
Night is drawing nigh,
Shadows of the evening
Steal across the sky.
Sabine Baring-Gould (1834–1924) British author and hymn writer.
The Evening Hymn

2 The day begins to droop –
Its course is done:
But nothing tells the place
Of the setting sun.
Robert Bridges (1844–1930) British poet.
Winter Nightfall

3 The day Thou gavest, Lord, is ended,
The darkness falls at Thy behest.
John Ellerton (1826–93) British churchman.
A Liturgy for Missionary Meetings

4 The Curfew tolls the knell of parting day,
The lowing herd winds slowly o'er the lea,
The plowman homeward plods his weary way,
And leaves the world to darkness and to me.
Thomas Gray (1716–71) British poet.
Elegy Written in a Country Churchyard

5 Sweet day, so cool, so calm, so bright,
The bridal of the earth and sky.
George Herbert (1593–1633) English poet.
Virtue

6 The candles burn their sockets,
The blinds let through the day,
The young man feels his pockets
And wonders what's to pay.
A. E. Housman (1859–1936) British scholar and poet.
Last Poems, 'Eight O'Clock'

☐DEATH☐

See also afterlife, assassination, drowning, epitaphs, equality in death, execution, funerals, killing, last words, life and death, love and death, memorials, mortality, mourning, murder, obituaries, posterity, suicide

1 God grants an easy death only to the just.
Svetlana Alliluyeva (1926–) Russian writer; daughter of Joseph Stalin.
Twenty Letters to a Friend

2 As Amr lay on his death-bed a friend said to him: 'You have often remarked that you would like to find an intelligent man at the point of death, and to ask him what his feelings were. Now I ask *you* that question. Amr replied, 'I feel as if heaven lay close upon the earth and I between the two, breathing through the eye of a needle.'
Amr Ibn Al-As (d. 664) Arab conqueror of Egypt.
The Harvest of a Quiet Eye (Alan L. Mackay)

3 O Death, where is thy sting-a-ling-a-ling,
O Grave, thy victoree?
The bells of hell go ting-a-ling-a-ling
For you but not for me.
Anonymous
Song of World War I

4 Swing low sweet chariot,
Comin' for to carry me home,
I looked over Jordan an' what did I see?
A band of Angels coming after me,
Comin' for to carry me home.
Anonymous
Swing Low, Sweet Chariot

5 I have often thought upon death, and I find it the least of all evils.
Francis Bacon (1561–1626) English philosopher.
An Essay on Death

6 I do not believe that any man fears to be dead, but
only the stroke of death.
Francis Bacon
An Essay on Death

7 Men fear death, as children fear to go in the dark;
and as that natural fear in children is increased
with tales, so is the other.
Francis Bacon
Essays, 'Of Death'

8 It is natural to die as to be born; and to a little
infant, perhaps, the one is as painful as the other.
Francis Bacon
Essays, 'Of Death'

9 To die will be an awfully big adventure.
J. M. Barrie (1860–1937) British novelist and dramatist.
Peter Pan, III

10 Graveyards have a morbid reputation. Many peo-
ple associate them with death.
Bishop of Bath and Wells (1935–) British churchman.
Remark, Apr 1988

11 The physician cutteth off a long disease; and he
that is today a king tomorrow shall die.
Bible: Ecclesiasticus
10:10

12 Behold, I shew you a mystery; We shall not all
sleep, but we shall all be changed,
In a moment, in the twinkling of an eye, at the last
trump: for the trumpet shall sound, and the dead
shall be raised incorruptible, and we shall be
changed.
For this corruptible must put on incorruption,
and this mortal must put on immortality.
So when this corruptible shall have put on incorruption, and this mortal shall have put on
immortality, then shall be brought to pass the
saying that is written, Death is swallowed up in
victory.
O death, where is thy sting? O grave, where is
thy victory?
Bible: I Corinthians
15:51–55

13 And I looked, and behold a pale horse: and his
name that sat on him was Death, and Hell followed with him. And power was given unto them
over the fourth part of the earth, to kill with
sword, and with hunger, and with death, and with
the beasts of the earth.
Bible: Revelations
6:8

14 In the hour of death, and in the day of judgement.
The Book of Common Prayer
Morning Prayer, Prayer of St Chrysostom

15 For I say, this is death, and the sole death,
When a man's loss comes to him from his gain,

Darkness from light, from knowledge ignorance,
And lack of love from love made manifest.
Robert Browning (1812–89) British poet.
A Death in the Desert

16 Days and moments quickly flying,
Blend the living with the dead;
Soon will you and I be lying
Each within our narrow bed.
Edward Caswall (1814–78) British hymn writer.
Hymn

17 Alack he's gone the way of all flesh.
William Congreve (1670–1729) British Restoration dramatist.
Squire Bickerstaff Detected, attrib.

18 He'd make a lovely corpse.
Charles Dickens (1812–70) British novelist.
Martin Chuzzlewit, Ch. 25

19 Because I could not stop for Death,
He kindly stopped for me;
The carriage held but just ourselves
And Immortality.
Emily Dickinson (1830–86) US poet.
The Chariot

20 Death be not proud, though some have called
thee
Mighty and dreadful, for, thou art not so.
John Donne (1573–1631) English poet.
Holy Sonnets, 10

21 Any man's death diminishes me, because I am
involved in Mankind; And therefore never send
to know for whom the bell tolls; it tolls for thee.
John Donne
Devotions, 17

22 Sin brought death, and death will disappear with
the disappearance of sin.
Mary Baker Eddy (1821–1910) US religious leader.
Science and Health, with Key to the Scriptures

23 So death, the most terrifying of ills, is nothing to
us, since so long as we exist, death is not with us;
but when death comes, then we do not exist. It
does not then concern either the living or the
dead, since for the former it is not, and the latter
are no more.
Epicurus (341–270 BC) Greek philosopher.
Letter to Menoeceus

24 It hath been often said, that it is not death, but
dying, which is terrible.
Henry Fielding (1707–54) British novelist.
Amelia, Bk. III, Ch. 4

25 Strange, is it not? that of the myriads who
Before us pass'd the door of Darkness through,
Not one returns to tell us of the Road,
Which to discover we must travel too.
Edward Fitzgerald (1809–83) British poet.
The Rubáiyát of Omar Khayyám

26 Death destroys a man, the idea of Death saves him.
E. M. Forster (1879–1970) British novelist.
Howards End, Ch. 27

27 Can storied urn or animated bust
Back to its mansion call the fleeting breath?
Can honour's voice provoke the silent dust,
Or flatt'ry soothe the dull cold ear of death?
Thomas Gray (1716–71) British poet.
Elegy Written in a Country Churchyard

28 Death is still working like a mole,
And digs my grave at each remove.
George Herbert (1593–1633) English poet.
Grace

29 Death...It's the only thing we haven't succeeded in completely vulgarizing.
Aldous Huxley (1894–1964) British novelist.
Eyeless in Gaza, Ch. 31

30 Who doesn't regret Lazarus was not
Questioned about after-lives? Of course
He only reached death's threshold. I fear what
Dark exercises may with cunning powers
Do when I am brought
To my conclusion
Elizabeth Jennings (1926–) British poet and writer.
The Fear of Death

31 I die because I do not die.
St John of the Cross (Juan de Yepes y Alvarez; 1542–91) Spanish churchman and poet.
Coplas del alma que pena por ver a dios

32 It matters not how a man dies, but how he lives. The act of dying is not of importance, it lasts so short a time.
Samuel Johnson (1709–84) British lexicographer.
Life of Johnson (J. Boswell), Vol. II

33 I am able to follow my own death step by step.
Now I move softly towards the end.
Pope John XXIII (Angelo Roncalli; 1881–1963) Italian churchman.
Remark made two days before he died
The Guardian, 3 June 1963

34 Darkling I listen; and, for many a time
I have been half in love with easeful Death,
Call'd him soft names in many a mused rhyme,
To take into the air my quiet breath;
Now more than ever seems it rich to die,
To cease upon the midnight with no pain,
While thou art pouring forth thy soul abroad
In such an ecstasy!
John Keats (1795–1821) British poet.
Ode to a Nightingale

35 I shall soon be laid in the quiet grave – thank God for the quiet grave – O! I can feel the cold earth upon me – the daisies growing over me – O for this quiet – it will be my first.
John Keats
In a letter to John Taylor by Joseph Severn, 6 Mar 1821

36 Teach me to live, that I may dread
The grave as little as my bed.
Thomas Ken (1637–1711) English bishop.
An Evening Hymn

37 In the long run we are all dead.
John Maynard Keynes (1883–1946) British economist.
Collected Writings, 'A Tract on Monetary Reform'

38 That is the road we all have to take – over the Bridge of Sighs into eternity.
Søren Kierkegaard (1813–55) Danish philosopher.
Kierkegaard Anthology (Auden)

39 O pity the dead that are dead, but cannot make the journey, still they moan and beat against the silvery adamant walls of life's exclusive city.
D. H. Lawrence (1885–1930) British novelist.
The Houseless Dead

40 There is a Reaper whose name is Death,
And, with his sickle keen,
He reaps the bearded grain at a breath,
And the flowers that grow between.
Henry Wadsworth Longfellow (1807–82) US poet.
The Reaper and the Flowers

41 It is the only disease you don't look forward to being cured of.
Herman J. Mankiewicz (1897–1953) US journalist and screenwriter.
Referring to death
Citizen Kane

42 Whom the gods love dies young.
Menander (c. 341–c. 290 BC) Greek dramatist.
Dis Exapaton

43 One dies only once, and it's for such a long time!
Molière (Jean Baptiste Poquelin; 1622–73) French dramatist.
Le Dépit amoureux, V:3

44 Oh well, no matter what happens, there's always death.
Napoleon I (Napoleon Bonaparte; 1769–1821) French emperor.
Attrib.

45 And in the happy no-time of his sleeping
Death took him by the heart.
Wilfred Owen (1893–1918) British poet.
Asleep

46 She closed her eyes; and in sweet slumber lying
her spirit tiptoed from its lodging-place.
It's folly to shrink in fear, if this is dying;
for death looked lovely in her lovely face.
Petrarch (Francesco Petrarca; 1304–74) Italian poet.
Triumphs

47 The surgeon is quiet, he does not speak.
He has seen too much death, his hands are full
of it.
Sylvia Plath (1932–63) US poet and writer.
Winter Trees, 'The Courage of Shutting-Up'

48 I mount! I fly!
O grave! where is thy victory?
O death! where is thy sting?
Alexander Pope (1688–1744) British poet.
The Dying Christian to his Soul

49 He who pretends to look on death without fear
lies. All men are afraid of dying, this is the great
law of sentient beings, without which the entire
human species would soon be destroyed.
Jean Jacques Rousseau (1712–78) French philosopher.
Julie, or the New Eloise

50 I have a rendezvous with Death
At some disputed barricade.
Alan Seeger (1888–1916) US poet.
I Have a Rendezvous with Death

51 Why, he that cuts off twenty years of life
Cuts off so many years of fearing death.
William Shakespeare (1564–1616) English dramatist.
Julius Caesar, III:1

52 O mighty Caesar! dost thou lie so low?
Are all thy conquests, glories, triumphs, spoils,
Shrunk to this little measure?
William Shakespeare
Julius Caesar, III:1

53 He that dies pays all debts.
William Shakespeare
The Tempest, III:2

54 Nothing in his life
Became him like the leaving it: he died
As one that had been studied in his death
To throw away the dearest thing he ow'd
As 'twere a careless trifle.
William Shakespeare
Macbeth, I:4

55 I care not; a man can die but once; we owe God a
death.
William Shakespeare
Henry IV, Part Two, III:2

56 Death is the veil which those who live call life:
They sleep, and it is lifted.
Percy Bysshe Shelley (1792–1822) British poet.
Prometheus Unbound, III

57 It is a modest creed, and yet
Pleasant if one considers it,
To own that death itself must be,
Like all the rest, a mockery.
Percy Bysshe Shelley
The Sensitive Plant, III

58 I do really think that death will be marvellous…If
there wasn't death, I think you couldn't go on.
Stevie Smith (Florence Margaret Smith; 1902–71) British poet.
The Observer, 9 Nov 1969

59 Sleep after toil, port after stormy seas,
Ease after war, death after life does greatly
please.
Edmund Spenser (1552–99) English poet.
The Faerie Queene, I:9

60 Under the wide and starry sky
Dig the grave and let me lie.
Glad did I live and gladly die,
– And I laid me down with a will.
This is the verse you grave for me:
'Here he lies where he longed to be;
Home is the sailor, home from sea,
And the hunter home from the hill.'
Robert Louis Stevenson (1850–94) Scottish writer.
Underwoods, Bk. I, 'Requiem'

61 Even so, in death the same unknown will appear
as ever known to me. And because I love this life,
I know I shall love death as well.
The child cries out when from the right breast
the mother takes it away, in the very next
moment to find in the left one its consolation.
Rabindranath Tagore (1861–1941) Indian poet and
philosopher.
Gitanjali

62 I, born of flesh and ghost, was neither
A ghost nor man, but mortal ghost.
And I was struck down by death's feather.
Dylan Thomas (1914–53) Welsh poet.
Before I knocked

63 After the first death, there is no other.
Dylan Thomas
A Refusal to Mourn the Death, by Fire, of a Child in London

64 Go and try to disprove death. Death will disprove
you, and that's all!
Ivan Turgenev (1818–83) Russian novelist.
Fathers and Sons, Ch. 27

65 There's no repentance in the grave.
Isaac Watts (1674–1748) English theologian and hymn writer.
Divine Songs for Children, 'Solemn Thoughts of God and Death'

66 We are laid asleep
In body, and become a living soul:
While with an eye made quiet by the power
Of harmony, and the deep power of joy,
We see into the life of things.
William Wordsworth (1770–1850) British poet.
Lines composed a few miles above Tintern Abbey

□DEBAUCHERY□

See also animalism, lust, pleasure, sex

1   *Debauchee*, n. One who has so earnestly pursued pleasure that he has had the misfortune to overtake it.
    Ambrose Bierce (1842–?1914) US writer and journalist.
    The Devil's Dictionary

2   No one ever suddenly became depraved.
    Juvenal (Decimus Junius Juvenalis; 60–130 AD) Roman satirist.
    Satires, II

3   We're poor little lambs who've lost our way,
    Baa! Baa! Baa!
    We're little black sheep who've gone astray,
    Baa-aa-aa!
    Gentleman-rankers out on the spree,
    Damned from here to Eternity,
    God ha' mercy on such as we,
    Baa! Yah! Bah!
    Rudyard Kipling (1865–1936) Indian-born British writer.
    Gentleman-Rankers

4   Home is heaven and orgies are vile
    But you need an orgy, once in a while.
    Ogden Nash (1902–71) US poet.
    Home, 99.44 100% Sweet Home

5   Once: a philosopher; twice: a pervert!
    Voltaire (François-Marie Arouet; 1694–1778) French writer.
    Turning down an invitation to an orgy, having attended one the previous night for the first time
    Attrib.

□DECEPTION□

See also appearances, hypocrisy, insincerity, lying

1   Beware of false prophets, which come to you in sheep's clothing, but inwardly they are ravening wolves.
    Bible: Matthew
    7:15

2   You can fool some of the people all the time and all the people some of the time; but you can't fool all the people all the time.
    Abraham Lincoln (1809–65) US statesman.
    Attrib.

3   False face must hide what the false heart doth know.
    William Shakespeare (1564–1616) English dramatist.
    Macbeth, I:7

4   You can fool too many of the people too much of the time.
    James Thurber (1894–1961) US humorist.
    Fables for Our Time, 'The Owl Who Was God'

□DECISION□

See also determination

1   Tender-handed stroke a nettle,
    And it stings you for your pains;

Grasp it like a man of mettle,
And it soft as silk remains.
Aaron Hill (1685–1750) British poet and dramatist.
Verses Written on Window

2   If someone tells you he is going to make 'a realistic decision', you immediately understand that he has resolved to do something bad.
    Mary McCarthy (1912–89) US novelist.
    On the Contrary

□DECLINE□

1   And though the Van Dycks have to go
    And we pawn the Bechstein grand,
    We'll stand by the Stately Homes of England.
    Noël Coward (1899–1973) British dramatist.
    Operette, The Stately Homes of England

2   It is only a step from the sublime to the ridiculous.
    Napoleon I (Napoleon Bonaparte; 1769–1821) French emperor.
    Remark following the retreat from Moscow, 1812
    Attrib.

3   Now there are fields where Troy once was.
    Ovid (Publius Ovidius Naso; 43 BC–17 AD) Roman poet.
    Heroides, Bk. I

4   There may have been disillusionments in the lives of the medieval saints, but they would scarcely have been better pleased if they could have foreseen that their names would be associated nowadays chiefly with racehorses and the cheaper clarets.
    Saki (Hector Hugh Munro; 1870–1916) British writer.
    Reginald at the Carlton

5   The difference between our decadence and the Russians' is that while theirs is brutal, ours is apathetic.
    James Thurber (1894–1961) US humorist.
    The Observer, 'Sayings of the Week', 5 Feb 1961

6   Plain living and high thinking are no more.
    William Wordsworth (1770–1850) British poet.
    Sonnets, 'O friend! I know not'

7   Milton! thou shouldst be living at this hour:
    England hath need of thee; she is a fen
    Of stagnant waters: altar, sword, and pen,
    Fireside, the heroic wealth of hall and bower,
    Have forfeited their ancient English dower
    Of inward happiness.
    William Wordsworth
    Sonnets, 'Milton! thou shouldst'

□DEFEAT□

See also loss

1   'Tis better to have fought and lost,
    Than never to have fought at all.
    Arthur Hugh Clough (1819–61) British poet.
    Peschiera

2 Of all I had, only honour and life have been
spared.
Francis I (1494–1547) King of France.
Referring to his defeat at the Battle of Pavia, 24 Feb 1525; usually
misquoted as 'All is lost save honour.'
Letter to Louise of Savoy (his mother), 1525

3 A man can be destroyed but not defeated.
Ernest Hemingway (1899–1961) US novelist.
The Old Man and the Sea

4 Woe to the vanquished.
Livy (Titus Livius; 59 BC–17 AD) Roman historian.
History, V:48

5 Every man meets his Waterloo at last.
Wendell Phillips (1811–84) US reformer.
Speech, Brooklyn, 1 Nov 1859

6 Another year! – another deadly blow!
Another mighty empire overthrown!
And we are left, or shall be left, alone.
William Wordsworth (1770–1850) British poet.
Napoleon defeated Prussia at the Battles of Jena and Anerstädt,
14 Oct 1806
Sonnets, 'Another year!'

☐ DELUSION ☐

1 But yet the light that led astray
Was light from Heaven.
Robert Burns (1759–96) Scottish poet.
The Vision

2 Take care, your worship, those things over there
are not giants but windmills.
Miguel de Cervantes (1547–1616) Spanish novelist.
Don Quixote, Pt. I, Ch. 8

3 Take the life-lie away from the average man and
straight away you take away his happiness.
Henrik Ibsen (1828–1906) Norwegian dramatist.
The Wild Duck, V

☐ DEMOCRACY ☐

See also class, government, majority, public, republic

1 One man shall have one vote.
John Cartwright (1740–1824) British writer.
People's Barrier Against Undue Influence

2 Some comrades apparently find it hard to under-
stand that democracy is just a slogan.
Mikhail Gorbachov (1931–) Soviet statesman.
The Observer, 'Sayings of the Week', 1 Feb 1987

3 Democracy is only an experiment in government, and it has the obvious disadvantage of
merely counting votes instead of weighing them.
Dean Inge (1860–1954) British churchman.
Possible Recovery?

4 The ballot is stronger than the bullet.
Abraham Lincoln (1809–65) US statesman.
Speech, 19 May 1856

5 This country, with its institutions, belongs to the
people who inhabit it. Whenever they shall grow
weary of the existing government, they can exercise their constitutional right of amending it, or
their revolutionary right to dismember or over-
throw it.
Abraham Lincoln
First Inaugural Address, 4 Mar 1861

6 Man's capacity for evil makes democracy necessary and man's capacity for good makes democracy possible.
Reinhold Niebuhr (1892–1971) US churchman.
Quoted by Anthony Wedgwood Benn in *The Times*, 18 Jul 1977

7 Democracy passes into despotism.
Plato (429–347 BC) Greek philosopher.
Republic, Bk. 8

8 Democracy means simply the bludgeoning of
the people by the people for the people.
Oscar Wilde (1854–1900) Irish-born British dramatist.
The Soul of Man under Socialism

9 The world must be made safe for democracy.
Woodrow Wilson (1856–1925) US statesman.
Address to Congress, asking for a declaration of war 2 Apr 1917

☐ DEPARTURE ☐

See also dismissal, parting

1 Come, dear children, let us away;
Down and away below.
Matthew Arnold (1822–88) British poet and critic.
The Forsaken Merman

2 She left lonely for ever
The kings of the sea.
Matthew Arnold
The Forsaken Merman

3 Once I leave, I leave. I am not going to speak to
the man on the bridge, and I am not going to spit
on the deck.
Stanley Baldwin (1867–1947) British statesman.
Statement to the Cabinet, 28 May 1937

4 Adieu, adieu! my native shore
Fades o'er the waters blue.
Lord Byron (1788–1824) British poet.
Childe Harold's Pilgrimage, I

5 And they are gone: aye, ages long ago
These lovers fled away into the storm.
John Keats (1795–1821) British poet.
The Eve of Saint Agnes, XLII

6 She's leaving home after living alone for so many
years.
John Lennon (1940–80) British rock musician.
She's Leaving Home (with Paul McCartney)

☐DESIGN☐

See also art

1   A machine for living in.
    Le Corbusier (Charles-Édouard Jeanneret; 1887–1965)
    French architect.
    Referring to a house
    Towards a New Architecture

2   Art will make our streets as beautiful as the
    woods, as elevating as the mountain-side: it will
    be a pleasure and a rest, and not a weight upon
    the spirits to come from the open country into a
    town. Every man's house will be fair and decent,
    soothing to his mind and helpful to his work.
    William Morris (1834–96) British designer, artist, and poet.

3   Today industrial design has put murder on a
    mass-production basis.
    Victor Papanek
    Design for the Real World

4   It will be a great day when cutlery and furniture
    designs (to name but two) swing like the
    Supremes.
    Michael Wolff

5   The tall modern office building is the machine
    pure and simple…the engine, the motor and the
    battleship the works of the century.
    Frank Lloyd Wright (1869–1959) US architect.

☐DESIRE☐

See also hunger, lust

1   Those who restrain Desire, do so because theirs
    is weak enough to be restrained.
    William Blake (1757–1827) British poet.
    The Marriage of Heaven and Hell, 'Those who restrain Desire…'

2   Sooner murder an infant in its cradle than nurse
    unacted desires.
    William Blake
    The Marriage of Heaven and Hell, 'Proverbs of Hell'

3   Man's Desires are limited by his Perceptions;
    none can desire what he has not perceived.
    William Blake
    There is no Natural Religion

4   O, she is the antidote to desire.
    William Congreve (1670–1729) British Restoration dramatist.
    The Way of the World, IV:14

5   There is nothing like desire for preventing the
    thing one says from bearing any resemblance to
    what one has in mind.
    Marcel Proust (1871–1922) French novelist.
    À la recherche du temps perdu: Le Côté de Guermantes

6   There are two tragedies in life. One is to lose
    your heart's desire. The other is to gain it.
    George Bernard Shaw (1856–1950) Irish dramatist and critic.
    Man and Superman, IV

7   Desire is the very essence of man.
    Benedict Spinoza (Baruch de Spinoza; 1632–77) Dutch
    philosopher.
    Ethics

☐DESPAIR☐

See also sorrow

1   A castle called Doubting Castle, the owner
    whereof was Giant Despair.
    John Bunyan (1628–88) English writer.
    The Pilgrim's Progress, Pt. I

2   Not, I'll not, carrion comfort, Despair, not feast
    on thee;
    Not untwist – slack they may be – these last
    strands of man
    In me or, most weary, cry *I can no more.* I can;
    Can something, hope, wish day come, not
    choose not to be.
    Gerard Manley Hopkins (1844–99) British Jesuit and poet.
    Carrion Comfort

3   Don't despair, not even over the fact that you
    don't despair.
    Franz Kafka (1883–1924) Czech novelist.
    Diary

4   The mass of men lead lives of quiet desperation.
    Henry David Thoreau (1817–62) US writer.
    Walden, 'Economy'

☐DESTINY☐

See also purpose

1   I felt as if I were walking with destiny, and that all
    my past life had been but a preparation for this
    hour and this trial.
    Winston Churchill (1874–1965) British statesman.
    The Gathering Storm, Ch. 38

2   Which brings me to my conclusion upon Free
    Will and Predestination, namely – let the reader
    mark it – that they are identical.
    Winston Churchill
    My Early Life, Ch. 3

3   'Tis all a Chequer-board of Nights and Days
    Where Destiny with Men for Pieces plays:
    Hither and thither moves, and mates, and slays,
    And one by one back in the Closet lays.
    Edward Fitzgerald (1809–83) British poet.
    The Rubáiyát of Omar Khayyám, XLIX

4   The Moving Finger writes; and, having writ,
    Moves on: nor all thy Piety nor Wit
    Shall lure it back to cancel half a Line,
    Nor all thy Tears wash out a Word of it.
    Edward Fitzgerald
    The Rubáiyát of Omar Khayyám, LI

5 I go the way that Providence dictates with the assurance of a sleepwalker.
Adolf Hitler (1889–1945) German dictator.
Referring to his successful re-occupation of the Rhineland, despite advice against the attempt
Speech, Munich, 15 Mar 1936

6 Do not try to find out – we're forbidden to know – what end the gods have in store for me, or for you.
Horace (Quintus Horatius Flaccus; 65–8 BC) Roman poet.
Odes, I

7 And yet the order of the acts is planned,
The way's end destinate and unconcealed.
Alone. Now is the time of Pharisees.
To live is not like walking through a field.
Boris Pasternak (1890–1960) Russian Jewish poet and novelist.
Hamlet (trans. Henry Kamen)

8 Man never found the deities so kindly
As to assure him that he'd live tomorrow.
François Rabelais (1483–1553) French satirist.
Pantagruel, Bk. III, Ch. 2

9 Fate sits on these dark battlements, and frowns;
And as the portals open to receive me,
Her voice, in sullen echoes, through the courts,
Tells of a nameless deed.
Ann Radcliffe (1764–1823) British novelist.
The Mysteries of Udolpho

10 There's a divinity that shapes our ends,
Rough-hew them how we will.
William Shakespeare (1564–1616) English dramatist.
Hamlet, V:2

11 The ancient saying is no heresy:
Hanging and wiving goes by destiny.
William Shakespeare
The Merchant of Venice, II:9

12 I embrace the purpose of God and the doom assigned.
Alfred, Lord Tennyson (1809–92) British poet.
Maud, III

13 Every bullet has its billet.
William III (1650–1702) King of England.
Journal (John Wesley), 6 June 1765

□ DETERMINATION □

See also decision, endurance, inflexibility, persistence, stubbornness

1 Don't listen to anyone who tells you that you can't do this or that. That's nonsense. Make up your mind, you'll never use crutches or a stick, then have a go at everything. Go to school, join in all the games you can. Go anywhere you want to.
But never, never let them persuade you that things are too difficult or impossible.
Douglas Bader (1910–82) British fighter pilot.
Speaking to a fourteen-year-old boy who had had a leg amputated after a road accident
Flying Colours (Laddie Lucas)

2 There is no such thing as a great talent without great will-power.
Honoré de Balzac (1799–1850) French novelist.
La Muse du département

3 The spirit burning but unbent,
May writhe, rebel – the weak alone repent!
Lord Byron (1788–1824) British poet.
The Corsair, II

4 What though the field be lost?
All is not lost – the unconquerable will,
And study of revenge, immortal hate,
And courage never to submit or yield:
And what is else not to be overcome?
John Milton (1608–74) English poet.
Paradise Lost, Bk. I

5 Look for me by moonlight;
Watch for me by moonlight;
I'll come to thee by moonlight, though hell should bar the way!
Alfred Noyes (1880–1958) British poet.
The Highwayman

6 We are not now that strength which in old days
Moved earth and heaven; that which we are, we are;
One equal temper of heroic hearts,
Made weak by time and fate, but strong in will
To strive, to seek, to find, and not to yield.
Alfred, Lord Tennyson (1809–92) British poet.
Ulysses

□ DEVIL □

See also damnation, hell

1 And he said unto them, I beheld Satan as lightning fall from heaven.
Bible: Luke
10:18

2 And there was war in heaven: Michael and his angels fought against the dragon; and the dragon fought and his angels,
And prevailed not; neither was their place found any more in heaven.
And the great dragon was cast out, that old serpent, called the Devil, and Satan, which deceiveth the whole world: he was cast out into the earth, and his angels were cast out with him.
Bible: Revelations
12:7–9

3 And that no man might buy or sell, save he that had the mark, or the name of the beast, or the number of his name.
Here is wisdom. Let him that hath understanding

count the number of the beast: for it is the number of a man; and his number is Six hundred threescore and six.

Bible: Revelations
13:17–18

4 O Thou! Whatever title suit thee –
Auld Hornie, Satan, Nick, or Clootie.

Robert Burns (1759–96) Scottish poet.
Address to the Devil

5 Wherever God erects a house of prayer,
The Devil always builds a chapel there;
And 'twill be found, upon examination,
The latter has the largest congregation.

Daniel Defoe (1660–1731) British journalist and writer
The True-Born Englishman, Pt. I

6 It is so stupid of modern civilization to have given up believing in the devil when he is the only explanation of it.

Ronald Knox (1888–1957) British Roman Catholic priest.
Let Dons Delight

7 Sometimes
The Devil is a gentleman.

Percy Bysshe Shelley (1792–1822) British poet.
Peter Bell the Third

☐ DIARIES ☐

1 Let diaries, therefore, be brought in use.

Francis Bacon (1561–1626) English philosopher.
Essays, 'Of Travel'

2 Only good girls keep diaries. Bad girls don't have the time.

Tallulah Bankhead (1903–68) US actress.
Attrib.

3 I do not keep a diary. Never have. To write a diary every day is like returning to one's own vomit.

Enoch Powell (1912–   ) British politician.
Sunday Times, 6 Nov 1977

4 What is a diary as a rule? A document useful to the person who keeps it, dull to the contemporary who reads it, invaluable to the student, centuries afterwards, who treasures it!

Ellen Terry (1847–1928) British actress.
The Story of My Life, Ch. 14

☐ DICKENS ☐
Charles

(1812–70) British novelist. His career began with contributions to magazines using the pen name Boz, *Pickwick Papers* (1837) bringing him sudden fame. His many subsequent novels, all appearing in monthly instalments and depicting the poverty of the working classes in Victorian England, have remained immensely popular.

QUOTATIONS ABOUT DICKENS

1 One would have to have a heart of stone to read the death of Little Nell without laughing.

Oscar Wilde (1854–1900) Irish-born British dramatist.
Lecturing upon Dickens.
Lives of the Wits (H. Pearson)

QUOTATIONS BY DICKENS

2 'There are strings', said Mr Tappertit, 'in the human heart that had better not be wibrated.'

Barnaby Rudge, Ch. 22

3 It is a melancholy truth that even great men have their poor relations.

Bleak House, Ch. 28

4 Annual income twenty pounds, annual expenditure nineteen nineteen six, result happiness. Annual income twenty pounds, annual expenditure twenty pounds ought and six, result misery.

David Copperfield, Ch. 12

5 Accidents will occur in the best-regulated families.

David Copperfield, Ch. 28

6 As she frequently remarked when she made any such mistake, it would be all the same a hundred years hence.

Said by Mrs Squeers.
Nicholas Nickleby

7 Here's the rule for bargains: 'Do other men, for they would do you.' That's the true business precept.

Martin Chuzzlewit, Ch. 11

8 He'd make a lovely corpse.

Martin Chuzzlewit, Ch. 25

9 He had but one eye, and the popular prejudice runs in favour of two.

Said by Mr Squeers.
Nicholas Nickleby, Ch. 4

10 When he has learnt that bottinney means a knowledge of plants, he goes and knows 'em. That's our system, Nickleby; what do you think of it?

Said by Mr Squeers.
Nicholas Nickleby, Ch. 8

11 Every baby born into the world is a finer one than the last.

Nicholas Nickleby, Ch. 36

12 'If the law supposes that,' said Mr Bumble…'the law is a ass – a idiot.'

Oliver Twist, Ch. 51

13 I think...that it is the best club in London.
Mr Tremlow describing the House of Commons.
Our Mutual Friend, Bk. II, Ch. 3

14 'It's always best on these occasions to do what
the mob do.'
'But suppose there are two mobs?' suggested Mr
Snodgrass.
'Shout with the largest,' replied Mr Pickwick.
Pickwick Papers, Ch. 13

15 Wery glad to see you indeed, and hope our
acquaintance may be a long 'un, as the gen'l'm'n
said to the fi' pun' note.
Pickwick Papers, Ch. 25

16 Anythin' for a quiet life, as the man said wen he
took the sitivation at the lighthouse.
Pickwick Papers, Ch. 43

17 A smattering of everything, and a knowledge of
nothing.
Sketches by Boz, 'Tales', Ch. 3

18 It was the best of times, it was the worst of times,
it was the age of wisdom, it was the age of foolishness, it was the epoch of belief, it was the epoch
of incredulity, it was the season of Light, it was
the season of Darkness, it was the spring of hope,
it was the winter of despair, we had everything
before us, we had nothing before us, we were all
going direct to Heaven, we were all going direct
the other way.
The opening words of the book.
A Tale of Two Cities, Bk. I, Ch. 1

☐ DICKINSON ☐
Emily
(1830–86) US poet who has been called 'the New England
mystic'. She wrote over 1700 poems on themes of love, death,
nature, and religion of which only seven were published in her
lifetime. Posthumous collections include *Poems by Emily
Dickinson* (1890), *The Single Hound: Poems of a Lifetime* (1914),
and *Bolts of Melody: New Poems of Emily Dickinson* (1945).

1 Because I could not stop for Death,
He kindly stopped for me;
The carriage held but just ourselves
And Immortality.
The Chariot

2 Parting is all we know of heaven,
And all we need of hell.
My Life Closed Twice Before its Close

3 Pain – has an Element of Blank –
It cannot recollect
When it begun – or if there were
A time when it was not –.
Pain

4 Success is counted sweetest
By those who ne'er succeed.
Success is Counted Sweetest

☐ DIPLOMACY ☐
See also tact

1 It is better for aged diplomats to be bored than
for young men to die.
Warren Austin (1877–1962) US politician and diplomat.
When asked if he got tired during long debates at the UN
Attrib.

2 There are three groups that no British Prime
Minister should provoke: the Vatican, the Treas-
ury and the miners.
Stanley Baldwin (1867–1947) British statesman.
A similar remark is often attributed to Harold Macmillan
Attrib.

3 To jaw-jaw is better than to war-war.
Winston Churchill (1874–1965) British statesman.
Speech, Washington, 26 June 1954

4 An appeaser is one who feeds a crocodile –
hoping that it will eat him last.
Winston Churchill
Attrib.

5 When you have to kill a man it costs nothing to
be polite.
Winston Churchill
Justifying the fact that the declaration of war against Japan was
made in the usual diplomatic language
The Grand Alliance

6 Treaties are like roses and young girls – they last
while they last.
Charles De Gaulle (1890–1970) French general and
statesman.
Attrib.

7 All diplomacy is a continuation of war by other
means.
Chou En Lai (1898–1976) Chinese statesman.

8 *La cordiale entente qui existe entre mon gouverne-
ment et le sien.*
The friendly understanding that exists between
my government and hers.
Louis Philippe (1773–1850) King of France.
Referring to an informal understanding reached between Britain
and France in 1843. The more familiar phrase, 'entente cordiale',
was first used in 1844
Speech, 27 Dec 1843

9 A diplomat these days is nothing but a head-
waiter who's allowed to sit down occasionally.
Peter Ustinov (1921–) British actor.
Romanoff and Juliet, I

10 No nation is fit to sit in judgement upon any other
nation.
Woodrow Wilson (1856–1925) US statesman.
Address, Apr 1915

11 An ambassador is an honest man sent to lie
abroad for the good of his country.
Henry Wotton (1568–1639) English poet and diplomat.
Life (Izaak Walton)

☐DISAPPOINTMENT☐

See also disillusion, expectation

1 Unhappiness is best defined as the difference between our talents and our expectations.

Edward de Bono (1933–) British physician and writer.
The Observer, 'Sayings of the Week', 12 June 1977

2 The best laid schemes o' mice an' men
Gang aft a-gley,
An' lea'e us nought but grief an' pain
For promis'd joy.

Robert Burns (1759–96) Scottish poet.
To a Mouse

3 Mountains will heave in childbirth, and a silly little mouse will be born.

Horace (Quintus Horatius Flaccus; 65–8 BC) Roman poet.
Ars Poetica

4 Look in my face; my name is Might-have-been.
I am also called No-more, Too-late, Farewell.

Dante Gabriel Rossetti (1828–82) British painter and poet.
The House of Life, 'A Superscription'

5 Oh, I wish that God had not given me what I prayed for! It was not so good as I thought.

Johanna Spyri (1827–1901) Swiss writer.
Heidi, Ch. 11

6 He said that he was too old to cry, but it hurt too much to laugh.

Adlai Stevenson (1900–65) US statesman.
Said after losing an election, quoting a story told by Abraham Lincoln
Speech, 5 Nov 1952

☐DISASTER☐

See also accidents

1 Let us hope…that a kind of Providence will put a speedy end to the acts of God under which we have been labouring.

Peter De Vries (1910–) US novelist.
The Mackerel Plaza, Ch. 3

2 An Act of God was defined as *something which no reasonable man could have expected.*

A. P. Herbert (1890–1971) British writer and politician.
Uncommon Law

3 Beautiful Railway Bridge of the Silv'ry Tay!
Alas, I am very sorry to say
That ninety lives have been taken away
On the last Sabbath day of 1879,
Which will be remember'd for a very long time.

William McGonagall (1830–1902) Scottish poet.
The Tay Bridge Disaster

☐DISCONTENT☐

See also envy

1 And sigh that one thing only has been lent
To youth and age in common – discontent.

Matthew Arnold (1822–88) British poet and critic.
Youth's Agitations

2 The idiot who praises, with enthusiastic tone,
All centuries but this, and every country but his own.

W. S. Gilbert (1836–1911) British dramatist.
The Mikado, I

3 How is it, Maecenas, that no one lives contented with his lot, whether he has planned it for himself or fate has flung him into it, but yet he praises those who follow different paths?

Horace (Quintus Horatius Flaccus; 65–8 BC) Roman poet.
Satires, I

4 I am sick o' wastin' leather on these gritty pavin'-stones,
An' the blasted English drizzle wakes the fever in my bones;
Tho' I walks with fifty 'ousemaids outer Chelsea to the Strand,
An' they talks a lot o' lovin', but wot do they understand?
Beefy face an' grubby 'and –
Law! Wot do they understand?
I've a neater, sweeter maiden in a cleaner, greener land!

Rudyard Kipling (1865–1936) Indian-born British writer.
The Road to Mandalay

5 He disdains all things above his reach, and pre-ferreth all countries before his own.

Thomas Overbury (1581–1613) English poet.
Miscellaneous Works, 'An Affectate Traveller'

6 While not exactly disgruntled, he was far from feeling gruntled.

P. G. Wodehouse (1881–1975) British humorous novelist.
The Code of the Woosters

☐DISCOVERY☐

See also exploration, science, space

1 *Eureka!*
I have found it!

Archimedes (c. 287–212 BC) Greek mathematician.
An exclamation of joy supposedly uttered as, stepping into a bath and noticing the water overflowing, he saw the answer to a problem and began the train of thought that led to his principle of buoyancy
Attrib.

2 Look, stranger, at this island now
The leaping light for your delight discovers.

W. H. Auden (1907–73) British poet.
Look, Stranger

3 God could cause us considerable embarrass-ment by revealing all the secrets of nature to us;

we should not know what to do for sheer apathy and boredom.

Goethe (1749–1832) German poet and dramatist.
Memoirs (Riemer)

4 Discovery consists of seeing what everybody has seen and thinking what nobody has thought.

Albert Szent-Györgyi (1893–1986) Hungarian-born US biochemist.
The Scientist Speculates (I. J. Good)

☐DISEASE☐

1 We are led to think of diseases as isolated disturbances in a healthy body, not as the phases of certain periods of bodily development.

Sir Clifford Allbutt (1836–1925)
Bulletin of the New York Academy of Medicine, 4:1000, 1928 (F. H. Garrison)

2 Once I am sure a patient has terminal cancer I tell them straight, I say, 'Its time to go visit with the grand-children.' They seem to appreciate it.

Anonymous
Said by a doctor from New Mexico
The Encyclopedia of Alternative Medicine and Self-Help (ed. Malcolm Hulke)

3 Before this strange disease of modern life, With its sick hurry, its divided aims.

Matthew Arnold (1822–88) British poet and critic.
The Scholar Gipsy

4 Cure the disease and kill the patient.

Francis Bacon (1561–1626) English philosopher.
Essays, 'Of Friendship'

5 The remedy is worse than the disease.

Francis Bacon
Essays, 'Of Seditions and troubles'

6 GOUT, n. A physician's name for the rheumatism of a rich patient.

Ambrose Bierce (1842–c. 1914) US writer and journalist.
The Devil's Dictionary

7 Diseases crucify the soul of man, attenuate our bodies, dry them, wither them, shrivel them up like old apples make them so many anatomies.

Robert Burton (1577–1640) English scholar and churchman.
The Anatomy of Melancholy, 1

8 Evil comes at leisure like the disease; good comes in a hurry like the doctor.

G. K. Chesterton (1874–1936) British writer.
The Man who was Orthodox

9 Life is an incurable disease.

Abraham Cowley (1618–67) English poet.
To Dr Scarborough

10 There is a dread disease which so prepares its victim, as it were, for death...a disease in which death and life are so strangely blended, that death takes a glow and hue of life, and life the

gaunt and grisly form of death – a disease which medicine never cured, wealth warded off, or poverty could boast exemption from – which sometimes moves in giant strides, and sometimes at a tardy sluggish pace, but, slow or quick, is ever sure and certain.

Charles Dickens (1812–70) British novelist.
Nicholas Nickleby, Ch. 49

11 Epidemics have often been more influential than statesman and soldiers in shaping the course of political history, and diseases may also colour the moods of civilizations.

René and Jean Dubos (1901– ; 1918–)
The White Plague, Ch. 5

12 Disease is an experience of mortal mind. It is fear made manifest on the body.

Mary Baker Eddy (1821–1910) US religious reader and scientist.
Science and Health, Ch. 14

13 We're all going to go crazy, living this epidemic every minute, while the rest of the world goes on out there, all around us, as if nothing is happening, going on with their own lives and not knowing what it's like, what we're going through. We're living through war, but where they're living it's peacetime, and we're all in the same country.

Larry Kramer (1935–) US dramatist and novelist.
The Normal Heart

14 It is the only disease you don't look forward to being cured of.

Herman J. Mankiewicz (1897–1953) US journalist and screenwriter.
Referring to death
Citizen Kane

15 While there are several chronic diseases more destructive to life than cancer, none is more feared.

Charles H. Mayo (1865–1939) US physician.
Annals of Surgery, 83:357, 1926

16 The Muse but serv'd to ease some friend, not Wife,
To help me through this long disease, my life.

Alexander Pope (1688–1744) British poet.
Epistle to Dr. Arbuthnot

17 Cur'd yesterday of my disease,
I died last night of my physician.

Matthew Prior (1664–1721) British poet.
The Remedy Worse than the Disease

18 Diseases are the tax on pleasures.

John Ray (1627–1705) English naturalist.
English Proverbs

19 The diseases which destroy a man are no less natural than the instincts which preserve him.
George Santayana (1863–1952) Spanish-born US philosopher, poet, and critic.
Dialogues in Limbo, 3

20 Disease is not of the body but of the place.
Seneca (c. 4 BC–65 AD) Roman writer.
Epistulae ad Lucilium

21 Not even remedies can master incurable diseases.
Seneca
Epistulae ad Lucilium

22 The development of industry has created many new sources of danger. Occupational diseases are socially different from other diseases, but not biologically.
Henry E. Sigerist (1891–1957)
Journal of the History of Medicine and Allied Sciences, 13:214, 1958

23 Decay and disease are often beautiful, like the pearly tear of the shellfish and the hectic glow of consumption.
Henry David Thoreau (1817–62) US writer.
Journal, 11 June 1852

24 The art of medicine consists of amusing the patient while Nature cures the disease.
Voltaire (1694–1788) French writer.
Attrib.

☐ DISILLUSION ☐

See also disappointment

1 The price one pays for pursuing any profession or calling is an intimate knowledge of its ugly side.
James Baldwin (1924–87) US writer.
Nobody Knows My Name

2 If you live long enough, you'll see that every victory turns into a defeat.
Simone de Beauvoir (1908–86) French writer.
Tous les hommes sont mortels

3 A new generation grown to find all Gods dead, all wars fought, all faiths in man shaken.
F. Scott Fitzgerald (1896–1940) US novelist.
Tales of the Jazz Age

4 One stops being a child when one realizes that telling one's trouble does not make it better.
Cesare Pavese (1908–50) Italian novelist and poet.
The Business of Living: Diaries 1935–50

☐ DISMISSAL

1 You have sat too long here for any good you have been doing. Depart, I say, and let us have done with you. In the name of God, *go!*
Leopold Amery (1873–1955) British statesman.
Said to Neville Chamberlain using Cromwell's words
Speech, House of Commons. May 1940

2 It is not fit that you should sit here any longer!...you shall now give place to better men.
Oliver Cromwell (1599–1658) English soldier and statesman.
Speech to the Rump Parliament, 22 Jan 1655

3 Go, and never darken my towels again!
Groucho Marx (Julius Marx; 1895–1977) US comedian.
Duck Soup

4 There comes a time in every man's life when he must make way for an older man.
Reginald Maudling (1917–77) British politician.
Remark made on being replaced in the shadow cabinet by John Davies, his elder by four years
The Guardian, 20 Nov 1976

5 Stand not upon the order of your going,
But go at once.
William Shakespeare (1564–1616) English dramatist.
Macbeth, III:4

☐ DISRAELI ☐
Benjamin, 1st Earl of Beaconsfield

(1804–81) British statesman of Italian-Jewish descent, who became Conservative prime minister (1868; 1874–80). He was supported by Queen Victoria, whom he made Empress of India. He also wrote novels, including *Coningsby* (1844) and *Sybil* (1845).

QUOTATIONS ABOUT DISRAELI

1 He was without any rival whatever, the first comic genius whoever installed himself in Downing Street.
Michael Foot (1913–) British Labour politician and journalist.
Debts of Honour

2 Disraeli lacked two qualities, failing which true eloquence is impossible. He was never quite in earnest, and he was not troubled by dominating conviction.
Henry Lucy (1843–1924) British journalist.
Sixty Years In The Wilderness

QUOTATIONS BY DISRAELI

3 Youth is a blunder; manhood a struggle; old age a regret.
Coningsby, Bk. III, Ch. 1

4 Almost everything that is great has been done by youth.
Coningsby, Bk. III, Ch. 1

5 'Sensible men are all of the same religion.' 'And pray what is that?' inquired the prince. 'Sensible men never tell.'
Endymion, Bk. I, Ch. 81

6 'My idea of an agreeable person,' said Hugo Bohun, 'is a person who agrees with me.'
Lothair, Ch. 35

7 'Two nations; between whom there is no intercourse and no sympathy; who are as ignorant of

each other's habits, thoughts, and feelings, as if they were dwellers in different zones, or inhabitants of different planets; who are formed by a different breeding, are fed by a different food, are ordered by different manners, and are not governed by the same laws.'
'You speak of–' said Egremont, hesitatingly. 'THE RICH AND THE POOR.'
Sybil, Bk. II, Ch. 5

8 A majority is always the best repartee.
Tancred, Bk. II, Ch. 14

9 It destroys one's nerves to be amiable every day to the same human being.
The Young Duke

10 I will not go down to posterity talking bad grammar.
Remark made when correcting proofs of his last parliamentary speech, 31 Mar 1881.
Disraeli (Blake), Ch. 32

11 I know he is, and he adores his maker.
Replying to a remark made in defense of John Bright that he was a self-made man.
The Fine Art of Political Wit (L. Harris)

12 A Conservative government is an organized hypocrisy.
Speech, 17 Mar 1845

13 He has to learn that petulance is not sarcasm, and that insolence is not invective.
Said of Sir C. Wood.
Speech, House of Commons, 16 Dec 1852

14 Assassination has never changed the history of the world.
Speech, House of Commons, 1 May 1865

15 Lord Salisbury and myself have brought you back peace – but a peace I hope with honour.
Speech, House of Commons, 16 July 1878
Speech, 27 July 1878

16 If a traveller were informed that such a man was leader of the House of Commons, he may well begin to comprehend how the Egyptians worshipped an insect.
Referring to Lord John Russell.
Attrib.

17 Nobody is forgotten when it is convenient to remember him.
Attrib.

18 Her Majesty is not a subject.
Responding to Gladstone's taunt that Disraeli could make a joke out of any subject, including Queen Victoria.
Attrib.

19 She is an excellent creature, but she never can remember which came first, the Greeks or the Romans.
Referring to his wife.
Attrib.

20 When I want to read a novel I write one.
Attrib.

21 I am dead: dead, but in the Elysian fields.
Said on his move to the House of Lords.
Attrib.

22 No, it is better not. She will only ask me to take a message to Albert.
On his deathbed, declining an offer of a visit from Queen Victoria.
Attrib.

☐ DOCTORS ☐

See also disease, drugs, health and healthy living, illness, medicine, remedies

1 I am dying with the help of too many physicians.
Alexander the Great (356–323 BC) King of Macedon.
Attrib.

2 And he said unto them, Ye will surely say unto me this proverb, Physician, heal thyself: whatsoever we have heard done in Capernaum, do also here in thy country.
Bible: Luke
4:23

3 I suppose one has a greater sense of intellectual degradation after an interview with a doctor than from any human experience.
Alice James (1848–92) US diarist.
The Diary of Alice James (ed. Leon Edel), 27 Sept 1890

4 Who shall decide when doctors disagree?
Alexander Pope (1688–1744) British poet.
Moral Essays, III

5 Cur'd yesterday of my disease,
I died last night of my physician.
Matthew Prior (1664–1721) British poet.
The Remedy Worse than the Disease

☐ DOGS ☐

See also animals

1 A huge dog, tied by a chain, was painted on the wall and over it was written in capital letters 'Beware of the dog.'
Petronius Arbiter (1st century AD) Roman satirist.
Latin, *Cave canem*
Satyricon: Cena Trimalchionis, 29

2 The great pleasure of a dog is that you may make a fool of yourself with him and not only will he not scold you, he will make a fool of himself too.
Samuel Butler (1835–1902) British writer.
Notebooks

3 'Tis sweet to hear the watch-dog's honest bark
Bay deep-mouthed welcome as we draw near
home;
'Tis sweet to know there is an eye will mark
Our coming, and look brighter when we come.
Lord Byron (1788–1824) British poet.
Don Juan, I

4 Anybody who hates children and dogs can't be
all bad.
W. C. Fields (1880–1946) US actor.
Attrib.

5 That indefatigable and unsavoury engine of pollu-
tion, the dog.
John Sparrow (1906–) British lawyer and academic.
Letter to *The Times*, 30 Sep 1975

6 I loathe people who keep dogs. They are cowards who haven't got the guts to bite people themselves.
August Strindberg (1849–1912) Swedish dramatist.
A Madman's Diary

7 Daddy wouldn't buy me a bow-wow, bow-wow.
I've got a little cat
And I'm very fond of that.
Joseph Tabrar (20th century) US songwriter.
Daddy Wouldn't Buy Me A Bow-wow (song)

□ DONNE □
John
(1573–1631) English poet of the metaphysical school. He was
ordained at the age of 43 and was appointed Dean of St Pauls
(1621). His verse includes *Divine Poems* (1607) and *Epithala-
mium* (1613).

QUOTATIONS ABOUT DONNE

1 With Donne, whose muse on dromedary trots,
Wreathe iron pokers into true-love knots.
Samuel Taylor Coleridge (1772–1834) British poet.
On Donne's Poetry

2 Dr Donne's verses are like the peace of God; they
pass all understanding.
James I (1566–1625) King of England.

QUOTATIONS BY DONNE

3 Come live with me, and be my love,
And we will some new pleasures prove
Of golden sands, and crystal brooks,
With silken lines, and silver hooks.
The Bait

4 But I do nothing upon myself, and yet I am mine
own Executioner.
Devotions, 12

5 No man is an Island, entire of itself; every man is
a piece of the Continent, a part of the main.
Devotions, 17

6 Any man's death diminishes me, because I am
involved in Mankind; And therefore never send
to know for whom the bell tolls; it tolls for thee.
Devotions, 17

7 Love built on beauty, soon as beauty, dies.
Elegies, 2, 'The Anagram'

8 Death be not proud, though some have called
thee
Mighty and dreadful, for, thou art not so.
Holy Sonnets, 10

□ DOOMSDAY □

1 Immediately after the tribulation of those days
shall the sun be darkened, and the moon shall
not give her light, and the stars shall fall from
heaven, and the powers of the heavens shall be
shaken:
And then shall appear the sign of the Son of man
in heaven: and then shall all the tribes of the
earth mourn, and they shall see the Son of man
coming in the clouds of heaven with power and
great glory.
And he shall send his angels with a great sound
of a trumpet, and they shall gather together his
elect from the four winds, from one end of
heaven to the other.
Bible: Matthew
24:29–31

2 'Tis the Last Judgment's fire must cure this place,
Calcine its clods and set my prisoners free.
Robert Browning (1812–89) British poet.
Childe Roland to the Dark Tower Came, XI

3 Don't wait for the Last Judgement. It takes place
every day.
Albert Camus (1913–60) French existentialist writer.
The Fall

4 When all the world dissolves,
And every creature shall be purified,
All place shall be hell that is not heaven.
Christopher Marlowe (1564–93) English dramatist.
Doctor Faustus, II:1

□ DOUBT □
See also indecision, scepticism

1 If a man will begin with certainties, he shall end
in doubts, but if he will be content to begin with
doubts, he shall end in certainties.
Francis Bacon (1561–1626) English philosopher.
The Advancement of Learning, Bk. I, Ch. 5

2 And immediately Jesus stretched forth his hand,
and caught him, and said unto him, O thou of little faith, wherefore didst thou doubt?
Bible: Matthew
14:31

3 He who shall teach the child to doubt
The rotting grave shall ne'er get out.
William Blake (1757–1827) British poet.
Auguries of Innocence

4 The trouble with the world is that the stupid are
cocksure and the intelligent full of doubt.
Bertrand Russell (1872–1970) British philosopher.
Autobiography

☐DOYLE☐
Sir Arthur Conan

(1856–1930) British writer and creator of the detective Sherlock
Holmes. Originally a doctor, he ceased to practise in 1890,
devoting himself entirely to his writing. He also wrote books on
spiritualism.

1 It is an old maxim of mine that when you have
excluded the impossible, whatever remains, however improbable, must be the truth.
The Beryl Coronet

2 You know my method. It is founded upon the
observance of trifles.
The Boscombe Valley Mystery

3 Depend upon it, there is nothing so unnatural as
the commonplace.
A Case of Identity

4 It is my belief, Watson, founded upon my experience, that the lowest and vilest alleys of London
do not present a more dreadful record of sin than
does the smiling and beautiful countryside.
Copper Beeches

5 'It is my duty to warn you that it will be used
against you,' cried the Inspector, with the magnificent fair play of the British criminal law.
The Dancing Men

6 It is quite a three-pipe problem.
The Red-Headed League

7 'Is there any point to which you would wish to
draw my attention?'
'To the curious incident of the dog in the night-
time.'
'The dog did nothing in the night-time.'
'That was the curious incident,' remarked
Sherlock Holmes.
The Silver Blaze

8 London, that great cesspool into which all the
loungers of the Empire are irresistibly drained.
A Study in Scarlet

9 Mediocrity knows nothing higher than itself, but
talent instantly recognizes genius.
The Valley of Fear

☐DREAMS☐

1 Dreams and predictions ought to serve but for
winter talk by the fireside.
Francis Bacon (1561–1626) English philosopher.
Essays, 'Of Prophecies'

2 So I awoke, and behold it was a dream.
John Bunyan (1628–88) English writer.
The Pilgrim's Progress, Pt. I

3 The people's prayer, the glad diviner's theme,
The young men's vision, and the old men's
dream!
John Dryden (1631–1700) British poet and dramatist.
Absalom and Achitophel, I

4 Last night I dreamt I went to Manderley again.
Daphne Du Maurier (1907–89) British novelist.
Rebecca, Ch. 1

5 Underneath the arches
We dream our dreams away.
Bud Flanagan (Robert Winthrop; 1896–1968) British
comedian.
Underneath the Arches

6 All men dream: but not equally. Those who
dream by night in the dusty recesses of their
minds wake in the day to find that it was vanity:
but the dreamers of the day are dangerous men,
for they may act their dream with open eyes, to
make it possible.
T. E. Lawrence (1888–1935) British soldier and writer.
Seven Pillars of Wisdom, Ch. 1

7 Dreams are true while they last, and do we not
live in dreams?
Alfred, Lord Tennyson (1809–92) British poet.
The Higher Pantheism

8 I have spread my dreams under your feet.
Tread softly because you tread on my dreams.
W. B. Yeats (1865–1939) Irish poet.
He wishes For The Cloths of Heaven

☐DRINKS☐
See also alcohol, drunkenness, water

1 I the Trinity illustrate,
Drinking watered orange-pulp –
In three sips the Arian frustrate;
While he drains his at one gulp.
Robert Browning (1812–89) British poet.
Soliloquy of the Spanish Cloister

2 I am willing to taste any drink once.
James Cabell (1879–1958) US novelist and journalist.
Jurgen, Ch. 1

3 Coffee which makes the politician wise,
And see through all things with his half-shut
eyes.
Alexander Pope (1688–1744) British poet.
The Rape of the Lock, III

4 Here thou great Anna! whom three realms obey,
Dost sometimes counsel take – and sometimes
Tea.
Alexander Pope
The Rape of the Lock, III

☐DROWNING☐

See also death

1 O Lord, methought what pain it was to drown,
What dreadful noise of waters in my ears,
What sights of ugly death within my eyes!
William Shakespeare (1564–1616) English dramatist.
Richard III, I:4

2 Nobody heard him, the dead man,
But still he lay moaning:
I was much further out than you thought
And not waving but drowning.
Stevie Smith (Florence Margaret Smith; 1902–71) British poet.
Not Waving But Drowning

☐DRUGS☐

1 A drug is that substance which, when injected
into a rat, will produce a scientific report.
Anonymous

2 A man who cannot work without his hypodermic
needle is a poor doctor. The amount of narcotic
you use is inversely proportional to your skill.
Martin H. Fischer (1879–1962)
Fischerisms (Howard Fabing and Ray Marr)

3 Half the modern drugs could well be thrown out
the window except that the birds might eat them.
Martin H. Fischer
Fischerisms (Howard Fabing and Ray Marr)

4 A hundred doses of happiness are not enough:
send to the drug-store for another bottle – and,
when that is finished, for another…There can be
no doubt that, if tranquillizers could be bought as
easily and cheaply as aspirin they would be con-
sumed, not by the billions, as they are at present,
but by the scores and hundreds of billions. And a
good, cheap stimulant would be almost as popular.
Aldous Huxley (1894–1963) British writer.
Brave New World Revisited, Ch. 8

5 What is dangerous about the tranquillizer is that
whatever peace of mind they bring is a packaged
peace of mind. Where you buy a pill and buy
peace with it, you get conditioned to cheap solu-
tions instead of deep ones.
Max Lerner (1902–) Russian-born US teacher, editor, and
journalist.
The Unfinished Country, 'The Assault on the Mind'

6 Two great European narcotics, alcohol and
Christianity.
Friedrich Wilhelm Nietzsche (1844–1900) German
philosopher.
The Twilight of the Idols, 'Things the Germans Lack'

7 Imperative drugging – the ordering of medicine
in any and every malady – is no longer regarded
as the chief function of the doctor.
William Osler (1849–1919) Canadian physician.
Aequanimitas, with Other Addresses, 'Medicine in the Nineteenth
Century'

☐DRUNKENNESS☐

See also alcohol

1 Come landlord, fill the flowing bowl,
Until it doth run over…
For tonight we'll merry, merry be,
Tomorrow we'll be sober.
Anonymous
Come, Landlord, Fill the Flowing Bowl

2 What shall we do with the drunken sailor
Early in the morning?
Hoo-ray and up she rises
Early in the morning.
Anonymous
What shall we do with the Drunken Sailor?

3 For when the wine is in, the wit is out.
Thomas Becon (1512–67) English Protestant churchman.
Catechism, 375

4 Others mocking said, These men are full of new
wine.
Bible: Acts
2:13

5 Wine is a mocker, strong drink is raging: and
whosoever is deceived thereby is not wise.
Bible: Proverbs
20:1

6 Man, being reasonable, must get drunk;
The best of life is but intoxication.
Lord Byron (1788–1824) British poet.
Don Juan, II

7 If merely 'feeling good' could decide, drunkenness would be the supremely valid human experience.
William James (1842–1910) US psychologist and philosopher.
Varieties of Religious Experience

8 A man who exposes himself when he is intoxi-
cated, has not the art of getting drunk.
Samuel Johnson (1709–84) British lexicographer.
Life of Johnson (J. Boswell), Vol. III

9 Better sleep with a sober cannibal than a
drunken Christian.
Herman Melville (1819–91) US novelist.
Moby Dick, Ch. 3

☐DRYDEN☐
John

(1631–1700) British poet and dramatist. His play *Marriage à la
Mode* (1673) and the verse satire *Absalom and Achitophel* (1681)
were highly regarded. He was made poet laureate by Charles II in
1668, but having become a Catholic in 1685, he was deprived of
the office by William of Orange on his accession.

QUOTATIONS ABOUT DRYDEN

1 He never heartily and sincerely praised any human being, or felt any real enthusiasm for any subject he took up.
John Keble (1792–1866) British poet and clergyman.
Lectures on Poetry

QUOTATIONS BY DRYDEN

2 In pious times, e'r Priest-craft did begin, Before Polygamy was made a Sin.
Absalom and Achitophel, I

3 Great Wits are sure to Madness near alli'd And thin Partitions do their Bounds divide.
Absalom and Achitophel, I

4 Bankrupt of Life, yet Prodigal of Ease.
Absalom and Achitophel, I

5 For Politicians neither love nor hate.
Absalom and Achitophel, I

6 Nor is the Peoples Judgment always true: The Most may err as grosly as the Few.
Absalom and Achitophel, I

7 Beware the Fury of a Patient Man.
Absalom and Achitophel, I

8 To die for faction is a common evil, But to be hanged for nonsense is the Devil.
Absalom and Achitophel, II

9 None but the Brave deserves the Fair.
Alexander's Feast

10 Errors, like Straws, upon the surface flow; He who would search for Pearls must dive below.
All for Love, Prologue

11 By viewing Nature, Nature's handmaid, art, Makes mighty things from small beginnings grow.
Annus Mirabilis

12 He was naturally learned; he needed not the spectacles of books to read nature; he looked inwards, and found her there.
Referring to Shakespeare.
Essay of Dramatic Poesy

13 For, Heaven be thanked, we live in such an age, When no man dies for love, but on the stage.
Mithridates, Epilogue

14 Happy the Man, and happy he alone, He who can call today his own:

He who, secure within, can say, Tomorrow do thy worst, for I have liv'd today.
Translation of Horace, III

☐ DUTY ☐

See also obligation

1 From a very early age, I had imbibed the opinion, that it was every man's duty to do all that lay in his power to leave his country as good as he had found it.
William Cobbett (1763–1835) British journalist and writer.
Political Register, 22 Dec 1832

2 Do your duty and leave the rest to the Gods.
Pierre Corneille (1606–84) French dramatist.
Horace, II:8

3 England expects every man will do his duty.
Lord Nelson (1758–1805) British admiral.
Signal hoisted prior to the Battle of Trafalgar, 1805

4 When a stupid man is doing something he is ashamed of, he always declares that it is his duty.
George Bernard Shaw (1856–1950) Irish dramatist and critic.
Caesar and Cleopatra, III

☐ DYLAN ☐
Bob

(Robert Allen Zimmerman; 1941–) US popular singer and songwriter. Originally a member of the 1960s protest movement, producing such albums as *The Times They Are A-changin'* (1964), in the late 1970s his conversion to Christianity led to such religious albums as *Saved* (1980).

1 How many roads must a man walk down Before you call him a man?
Blowin' in the Wind

2 How does it feel To be without a home Like a complete unknown Like a rolling stone?
Like a Rolling Stone

3 She knows there's no success like failure And that failure's no success at all.
Love Minus Zero No Limit

4 Come mothers and fathers Throughout the land And don't criticize What you can't understand
The Times They Are A-Changin'

5 Yeah, some of them are about ten minutes long, others five or six.
On being asked, during an interview, if he would say something about his songs

E

☐ECOLOGY

See also conservation, environment

1 As cruel a weapon as the cave man's club, the chemical barrage has been hurled against the fabric of life.
Rachel Carson (1907–64) US biologist.
The Silent Spring

2 Man has been endowed with reason, with the power to create, so that he can add to what he's been given. But up to now he hasn't been a creator, only a destroyer. Forests keep disappearing, rivers dry up, wild life's become extinct, the climate's ruined and the land grows poorer and uglier every day.
Anton Chekhov (1860–1904) Russian dramatist.
Uncle Vanya, I

3 It will be said of this generation that it found England a land of beauty and left it a land of beauty spots.
Cyril Joad (1891–1953) British writer and broadcaster.
The Observer, 'Sayings of Our Times', 31 May 1953

4 We are living beyond our means. As a people we have developed a life-style that is draining the earth of its priceless and irreplaceable resources without regard for the future of our children and people all around the world.
Margaret Mead (1901–78) US anthropologist.
Redbook, 'The Energy Crisis – Why Our World Will Never Again Be the Same.'

5 The Irish Sea is naturally radioactive, the Sellafield discharges are less radioactive than the sea they are discharged into.
Cecil Parkinson (1931–) British politician.
Speech, Nov 1987

6 We are wealthy and wasteful but this can't go on. If we don't eat dog biscuits, we could end up eating our dog instead.
Magnus Pyke (1908–) British scientist, television personality, and writer.
The Observer, 'Sayings of the Week', 12 Jan 1975

7 Had we gone the way of France and got 60 per cent of our electricity from nuclear power, we should not have environmental problems.
Margaret Thatcher (1925–) British politician and prime minister.
Speech, Oct 1988

8 To the average British farmer, organic farming is about as relevant as caviar and a flight on Concorde.
Oliver Walston (1941–)
Speech, Jan 1989

☐ECONOMICS☐

1 A budget is a method of worrying before you spend instead of afterwards.
Anonymous

2 Provided that the City of London remains as at present, the Clearing-house of the World.
Joseph Chamberlain (1836–1914) British politician.
Speech, Guildhall, London, 19 Jan 1904

3 Annual income twenty pounds, annual expenditure nineteen nineteen six, result happiness. Annual income twenty pounds, annual expenditure twenty pounds ought and six, result misery.
Charles Dickens (1812–70) British novelist.
David Copperfield, Ch. 12

4 If freedom were not so economically efficient it certainly wouldn't stand a chance.
Milton Friedman (1912–) US economist.
Remark, Mar 1987

5 Having a little inflation is like being a little pregnant.
Leon Henderson (1895–1986) US economist.
Attrib.

6 Economics is a subject that does not greatly respect one's wishes.
Nikita Khrushchev (1894–1971) Soviet statesman.
Attrib.

7 Population, when unchecked, increases in a geometrical ratio. Subsistence only increases in an arithmetical ratio.
Thomas Robert Malthus (1766–1834) British clergyman and economist.
Essays on the Principle of Population

8 A nation is not in danger of financial disaster merely because it owes itself money.
Andrew William Mellon (1855–1937) US financier.
Attrib.

9 In the days when the nation depended on agriculture for its wealth it made the Lord Chancellor sit on a woolsack to remind him where the wealth came from. I would like to suggest we remove that now and make him sit on a crate of machine tools.
Prince Philip (1921–) The consort of Queen Elizabeth II.
Speech, Aug 1986

10 Recession is when a neighbour loses his job; depression is when you lose yours.
Ronald Reagan (1911–) US politician and president.
The Observer, 'Sayings of the Week', 26 Oct 1980

11 One man's wage rise is another man's price increase.

Harold Wilson (1916–) British politician and prime minister.
The Observer, 'Sayings of the Week', 11 Jan 1970

☐ EDITORS ☐

See also books, journalism, newspapers, publishing

1 Where were you fellows when the paper was blank?

Fred Allen (1894–1956) US comedian.
Said to writers who heavily edited one of his scripts
Attrib.

2 An editor is one who separates the wheat from the chaff and prints the chaff.

Adlai Stevenson (1900–65) US statesman.
The Stevenson Wit

☐ EDUCATION ☐

See also academics, classics, examinations, learning, punishment

1 What we must look for here is, first, religious and moral principles; secondly, gentlemanly conduct; thirdly, intellectual ability.

Thomas Arnold (1795–1842) British educator.
Address to the Scholars at Rugby

2 Studies serve for delight, for ornament, and for ability.

Francis Bacon (1561–1626) English philosopher.
Essays, 'Of Studies'

3 The true University of these days is a collection of books.

Thomas Carlyle (1795–1881) Scottish historian and essayist.
Heroes and Hero-Worship, 'The Hero as Man of Letters'

4 His English education at one of the great public schools had preserved his intellect perfectly and permanently at the stage of boyhood.

G. K. Chesterton (1874–1936) British writer.
The Man Who Knew Too Much

5 Education is simply the soul of a society as it passes from one generation to another.

G. K. Chesterton
The Observer, 'Sayings of the Week', 6 July 1924

6 I pay the schoolmaster, but 'tis the schoolboys that educate my son.

Ralph Waldo Emerson (1803–82) US poet and essayist.
Journal

7 It is not that the Englishman can't feel – it is that he is afraid to feel. He has been taught at his public school that feeling is bad form. He must not express great joy or sorrow, or even open his mouth too wide when he talks – his pipe might fall out if he did.

E. M. Forster (1879–1970) British novelist.
Abinger Harvest, 'Notes on the English character'

8 They go forth into it with well-developed bodies, fairly developed minds, and undeveloped hearts.

E. M. Forster
Referring to public schoolboys going into the world
Abinger Harvest, 'Notes on the English Character'

9 Education made us what we are.

Claude-Adrien Helvétius (1715–71) French philosopher.
Discours XXX, Ch. 30

10 And seek for truth in the groves of Academe.

Horace (Quintus Horatius Flaccus; 65–8 BC) Roman poet.
Epistles, II

11 You sought the last resort of feeble minds with classical educations. You became a schoolmaster.

Aldous Huxley (1894–1964) British novelist.
Antic Hay

12 Some experience of popular lecturing had convinced me that the necessity of making things plain to uninstructed people was one of the very best means of clearing up the obscure corners in one's own mind.

T. H. Huxley (1825–95) British biologist.
Man's Place in Nature, Preface

13 There is now less flogging in our great schools than formerly, but then less is learned there; so that what the boys get at one end they lose at the other.

Samuel Johnson (1709–84) British lexicographer.
Life of Johnson (J. Boswell), Vol. II

14 Nothing would more effectively further the development of education than for all flogging pedagogues to learn to educate with the head instead of with the hand.

Ellen Key (Karolina Sofia Key; 1849–1926) Swedish writer.
The Century of the Child, Ch. 3

15 Four times, under our educational rules, the human pack is shuffled and cut – at eleven-plus, sixteen-plus, eighteen-plus and twenty-plus – and happy is he who comes top of the deck on each occasion, but especially the last. This is called Finals, the very name of which implies that nothing of importance can happen after it. The British postgraduate student is a lonely forlorn soul...for whom nothing has been real since the Big Push.

David Lodge (1935–) British author.
Changing Places, Ch. 1

16 Universities are the cathedrals of the modern age. They shouldn't have to justify their existence by utilitarian criteria.

David Lodge
Nice Work IV

17 If you educate a man you educate a person, but if you educate a woman you educate a family.

Ruby Manikan (20th century) Indian Church leader.
The Observer, 'Sayings of the Week', 30 Mar 1947

18 A whale ship was my Yale College and my Harvard.
Herman Melville (1819–91) US novelist.
Moby Dick, Ch. 24

19 And if education is always to be conceived along the same antiquated lines of a mere transmission of knowledge, there is little to be hoped from it in the bettering of man's future. For what is the use of transmitting knowledge if the individual's total development lags behind?
Maria Montessori (1870–1952) Italian doctor and educationalist.
The Absorbent Mind

20 We teachers can only help the work going on, as servants wait upon a master.
Maria Montessori
The Absorbent Mind

21 School yourself to demureness and patience.
Learn to inure yourself to drudgery in science.
Learn, compare, collect the facts.
Ivan Pavlov (1849–1936) Russian physiologist.
Bequest to the Academic Youth of Soviet Russia, 27 Feb 1936

22 'Tis education forms the common mind,
Just as the twig is bent, the tree's inclined.
Alexander Pope (1688–1744) British poet.
Moral Essays, I

23 A man who has never gone to school may steal from a freight car, but if he has a university education he may steal the whole railroad.
Franklin D. Roosevelt (1882–1945) US Democratic president.
Attrib.

24 But, good gracious, you've got to educate him first.
You can't expect a boy to be vicious till he's been to a good school.
Saki (Hector Hugh Munro; 1870–1916) British writer.
Reginald in Russia

25 For every person wishing to teach there are thirty not wanting to be taught.
W. C. Sellar (1898–1951) British humorous writer.
And Now All This

26 No profit grows where is no pleasure ta'en;
In brief, sir, study what you most affect.
William Shakespeare (1564–1616) English dramatist.
The Taming of the Shrew, I:1

27 He who can, does. He who cannot, teaches.
George Bernard Shaw (1856–1950) Irish dramatist and critic.
Man and Superman, 'Maxims for Revolutionists'

28 Indeed one of the ultimate advantages of an education is simply coming to the end of it.
B. F. Skinner (1904–90) US psychologist.
The Technology of Teaching.

29 Education is what survives when what has been learnt has been forgotten.
B. F. Skinner
New Scientist, 21 May 1964, 'Education in 1984'

30 To me education is a leading out of what is already there in the pupil's soul. To Miss Mackay it is a putting in of something that is not there, and that is not what I call education, I call it intrusion....
Muriel Spark (1918–) British novelist.
The Prime of Miss Jean Brodie, Ch. 2

31 Soap and education are not as sudden as a massacre, but they are more deadly in the long run.
Mark Twain (Samuel Langhorne Clemens; 1835–1910) US writer.
The Facts concerning the Recent Resignation

32 That's the public-school system all over. They may kick you out, but they never let you down.
Evelyn Waugh (1903–66) British novelist.
Decline and Fall, Pt. I, Ch. 3

33 The battle of Waterloo was won on the playing fields of Eton.
Duke of Wellington (1769–1852) British general and statesman.
Attrib.

34 A very large part of English middle-class education is devoted to the training of servants...In so far as it is, by definition, the training of upper servants, it includes, of course, the instilling of that kind of confidence which will enable the upper servants to supervise and direct the lower servants.
Raymond Henry Williams (1921–88) British academic and writer.
Culture and Society, Ch. 3

☐EFFORT☐

See also work

1 I have nothing to offer but blood, toil, tears and sweat.
Winston Churchill (1874–1965) British statesman.
On becoming prime minister
Speech, House of Commons, 13 May 1940

2 A world where nothing is had for nothing.
Arthur Hugh Clough (1819–61) British poet.
The Bothie of Tober-na-Vuolich, Bk. VIII, Ch. 5

3 The world is divided into people who do things and people who get the credit. Try, if you can, to belong to the first class. There's far less competition.
Dwight Morrow (1873–1931) US statesman.
Dwight Morrow (Harold Nicolson)

4 As is the case in all branches of art, success depends in a very large measure upon individual

initiative and exertion, and cannot be achieved except by dint of hard work.
Anna Pavlova (1881–1931) Russian ballet dancer.
Pavlova: A Biography (ed. A. H. Franks), 'Pages of My Life'

☐ EGOTISM ☐

See also conceit, pride, selfishness

1 No poet or novelist wishes he were the only one who ever lived, but most of them wish they were the only one alive, and quite a number fondly believe their wish has been granted.
W. H. Auden (1907–73) British poet.
The Dyer's Hand, 'Writing'

2 *Egotist*, n. A person of low taste, more interested in himself than in me.
Ambrose Bierce (1842–?1914) US writer and journalist.
The Devil's Dictionary

3 An author who speaks about his own books is almost as bad as a mother who talks about her own children.
Benjamin Disraeli (1804–81) British statesman.
Speech in Glasgow, 19 Nov 1873

4 No man thinks there is much ado about nothing when the ado is about himself.
Anthony Trollope (1815–82) British novelist.
The Bertrams, Ch. 27

☐ EINSTEIN ☐
Albert

(1879–1955) German physicist who became a Swiss citizen (1901) and later a US citizen (1940). His theory of relativity revolutionized scientific thought. He was persuaded to write to President Roosevelt to warn him that Germany could possibly make an atomic bomb.

QUOTATIONS ABOUT EINSTEIN

1 The genius of Einstein leads to Hiroshima.
Pablo Picasso (1881–1973) Spanish painter.
Life with Picasso (Françoise Gilot and Carlton Lake)

QUOTATIONS BY EINSTEIN

2 Science without religion is lame, religion without science is blind.
Out of My Later Years

3 God does not play dice.
Einstein's objection to the quantum theory, in which physical events can only be known in terms of probabilities. It is sometimes quoted as 'God does not play dice with the Universe'.
Albert Einstein, Creator and Rebel (B. Hoffman), Ch. 10

4 If only I had known, I should have become a watchmaker.
Reflecting on his role in the development of the atom bomb.
New Statesman, 16 Apr 1965

5 Common sense is the collection of prejudices acquired by age eighteen.
Scientific American, Feb 1976

6 A theory can be proved by experiment; but no path leads from experiment to the birth of a theory.
The Sunday Times, 18 July 1976

7 As far as the laws of mathematics refer to reality, they are not certain, and as far as they are certain, they do not refer to reality.
The Tao of Physics (F. Capra), Ch. 2

☐ ELIOT ☐
George

(Mary Ann Evans; 1819–80) British writer. Her major works include *Adam Bede* (1859), *The Mill on the Floss* (1860), *Silas Marner* (1861), *Middlemarch* (1871–72), and *Daniel Deronda* (1876).

1 It's but little good you'll do a-watering the last year's crop.
Adam Bede

2 He was like a cock who thought the sun had risen to hear him crow.
Adam Bede

3 A different taste in jokes is a great strain on the affections.
Daniel Deronda

4 I should like to know what is the proper function of women, if it is not to make reasons for husbands to stay at home, and still stronger reasons for bachelors to go out.
The Mill on the Floss, Ch. 6

☐ ELIOT ☐
T(homas) S(tearns)

(1888–1965) US-born British poet and dramatist. He worked as a bank clerk before publication of his *Prufrock and Other Observations* (1917). *The Waste Land* (1922) established his reputation, which was confirmed by his *Four Quartets* (1935–41). His verse dramas include *Murder in the Cathedral* (1935) and *The Cocktail Party* (1949).

QUOTATIONS ABOUT ELIOT

1 He is very yellow and glum. Perfect manners. Dyspeptic, ascetic, eclectic. Inhibitions. Yet obviously a nice man and a great poet.
Harold Nicolson (1886–1968) British writer.
Diary, 2 May 1932

QUOTATIONS BY ELIOT

2 Hell is oneself;
Hell is alone, the other figures in it
Merely projections. There is nothing to escape from
And nothing to escape to. One is always alone.
The Cocktail Party, I:3

3 Time present and time past
Are both perhaps present in time future,
And time future contained in time past.
Four Quartets, 'Burnt Norton'

4 Human kind
Cannot bear very much reality.
Four Quartets, 'Burnt Norton'

5 This is the way the world ends
Not with a bang but a whimper.
The Hollow Men

6 Macavity, Macavity, there's no one like Macavity,
There never was a Cat of such deceitfulness and
suavity.
He always has an alibi, and one or two to spare:
At whatever time the deed took place –
MACAVITY WASN'T THERE!
Macavity: The Mystery Cat

7 The last temptation is the greatest treason:
To do the right deed for the wrong reason.
Murder in the Cathedral, I

8 Birth, and copulation, and death.
That's all the facts when you come to brass tacks.
Sweeney Agonistes, 'Fragment of an Agon'

9 And I will show you something different from
either
Your shadow at morning striding behind you,
Or your shadow at evening rising to meet you
I will show you fear in a handful of dust.
The Waste Land, 'The Burial of the Dead'

□ELIZABETH I□
(1533–1603) Queen of England. The daughter of Henry VIII and
Anne Boleyn, she established the Protestant Church in England
and had her Catholic cousin, Mary, Queen of Scots, beheaded.
The Elizabethan age was one of greatness for England.

QUOTATIONS ABOUT ELIZABETH I

1 The queen did fish for men's souls, and had so
sweet a bait that no one could escape her network.
Christopher Hatton
Attrib.

2 As just and merciful as Nero and as good a Chris-
tian as Mahomet.
John Wesley (1703–91) British religious leader.
Journal, 29 Apr 1768

QUOTATIONS BY ELIZABETH I

3 Though God hath raised me high, yet this I
count the glory of my crown: that I have reigned
with your loves.
The Golden Speech, 1601

4 Madam I may not call you; mistress I am
ashamed to call you; and so I know not what to
call you; but howsoever, I thank you.
Writing to the wife of the Archbishop of Canterbury, expressing
her disapproval of married clergy.
Brief View of the State of the Church (Harington)

5 God may pardon you, but I never can.
To the Countess of Nottingham.
History of England under the House of Tudor (Hume), Vol. II, Ch. 7

6 I will make you shorter by a head.
Sayings of Queen Elizabeth (Chamberlin)

7 I know I have the body of a weak and feeble
woman, but I have the heart and stomach of a
King, and of a King of England too.
Speech at Tilbury on the approach of the Spanish Armada

8 All my possessions for a moment of time.
Last words

□EMBARRASSMENT□

1 The question about everything was, would it
bring a blush to the cheek of a young person?
Charles Dickens (1812–70) British novelist.
Pondered by Mr Podsnap
Our Mutual Friend, Bk. I, Ch. 11

2 Man is the only animal that blushes. Or needs to.
Mark Twain (Samuel Langhorne Clemens; 1835–1910) US
writer.
Following the Equator, heading of Ch. 27

□EMOTION□
See also passion, sentimentality

1 There is a road from the eye to the heart that
does not go through the intellect.
G. K. Chesterton (1874–1936) British writer.
The Defendant

2 The intellect is always fooled by the heart.
Duc de la Rochefoucauld (1613–80) French writer.
Maximes, 102

3 Light breaks where no sun shines;
Where no sea runs, the waters of the heart
Push in their tides.
Dylan Thomas (1914–53) Welsh poet.
Light breaks where no sun shines

4 Pure and complete sorrow is as impossible as
pure and complete joy.
Leo Tolstoy (1828–1910) Russian writer.
War and Peace, Bk. XV, Ch. 1

□ENDING□

1 This is the way the world ends
Not with a bang but a whimper.
T. S. Eliot (1888–1965) US-born British poet and dramatist.
The Hollow Men

2 We'll to the woods no more,
The laurels all are cut.
A. E. Housman (1859–1936) British scholar and poet.
Last Poems, Introductory

3 The bright day is done,
And we are for the dark.
William Shakespeare (1564–1616) English dramatist.
Antony and Cleopatra, V:2

☐ENDURANCE☐

See also comfort, courage, determination, misfortune, suffering

1 Nothing happens to any man that he is not
formed by nature to bear.
Marcus Aurelius (121–180 AD) Roman emperor.
Meditations, Bk. V, Ch. 18

2 Through the night of doubt and sorrow
Onward goes the pilgrim band,
Singing songs of expectation,
Marching to the Promised Land.
Sabine Baring-Gould (1834–1924) British author and hymn
writer.
Through the Night of Doubt and Sorrow

3 ...we could never learn to be brave and patient, if
there were only joy in the world.
Helen Keller (1880–1968) US writer and lecturer.
Atlantic Monthly (May 1890)

4 Sorrow and silence are strong, and patient endur-
ance is godlike.
Henry Wadsworth Longfellow (1807–82) US poet.
Evangeline

5 Know how sublime a thing it is
To suffer and be strong.
Henry Wadsworth Longfellow
The Light of Stars

6 No pain, no palm; no thorns, no throne; no gall,
no glory; no cross, no crown.
William Penn (1644–1718) English preacher.
No Cross, No Crown

7 Had we lived, I should have had a tale to tell of
the hardihood, endurance, and courage of my
companions which would have stirred the heart
of every Englishman. These rough notes and our
dead bodies must tell the tale.
Captain Robert Falcon Scott (1868–1912) British explorer.
Message to the Public

8 Men must endure
Their going hence, even as their coming hither:
Ripeness is all.
William Shakespeare (1564–1616) English dramatist.
King Lear, V:2

9 If you can't stand the heat, get out of the kitchen.
Harry S. Truman (1884–1972) US statesman.
Perhaps proverbial in origin, possibly echoes the expression
'kitchen cabinet'
Mr Citizen, Ch. 15

10 O you who have borne even heavier things, God
will grant an end to these too.
Virgil (Publius Vergilius Maro; 70–19 BC) Roman poet.
Aeneid, Bk. I

11 Maybe one day we shall be glad to remember
even these hardships.
Virgil
Aeneid, Bk. I

12 I sing of arms and the man who first from the
shores
of Troy came destined an exile to Italy and the
Lavinian beaches, much buffeted he on land and
on
the deep by force of the gods because of fierce
Juno's never-forgetting anger.
Virgil
Referring to Aeneas
Aeneid, Bk. I

13 Much in sorrow, oft in woe,
Onward, Christians, onward go.
Henry Kirke White (1785–1806) British poet.
A hymn, better known in its later form, 'Oft in danger, oft in woe'

☐ENEMIES☐

1 But I say unto you, Love your enemies, bless
them that curse you, do good to them that hate
you, and pray for them which despitefully use
you, and persecute you;
That ye may be the children of your Father
which is in heaven: for he maketh his sun to rise
on the evil and on the good, and sendeth rain on
the just and on the unjust.
For if ye love them which love you, what reward
have ye? do not even the publicans the same?
Bible: Matthew
5:44–46

2 Even a paranoid can have enemies.
Henry Kissinger (1923–) German-born US politician and
diplomat.
Time, 24 Jan 1977

3 They made peace between us; we embraced, and
we have been mortal enemies ever since.
Alain-René Lesage (1668–1747) French writer.
Le Diable boiteux, Ch. 3

4 He makes no friend who never made a foe.
Alfred, Lord Tennyson (1809–92) British poet.
Idylls of the King, 'Lancelot and Elaine'

☐ENGLAND☐

See also Britain, Cambridge, English, London, Oxford,
patriotism

1 And did those feet in ancient time
Walk upon England's mountains green?
And was the holy lamb of God
On England's pleasant pastures seen?
...
I will not cease from mental fight,
Nor shall my sword sleep in my hand,

Till we have built Jerusalem
In England's green and pleasant land.
William Blake (1757–1827) British poet.
Better known as the hymn 'Jerusalem', with music by Sir Hubert
Parry; not to be confused with Blake's longer poem *Jerusalem*
Milton, Preface

2 England is the mother of parliaments.
John Bright (1811–89) British radical politician.
Speech, Birmingham, 18 Jan 1865

3 For England's the one land, I know,
Where men with Splendid Hearts may go;
And Cambridgeshire, of all England,
The shire for Men who Understand.
Rupert Brooke (1887–1915) British poet.
The Old Vicarage, Grantchester

4 Oh, to be in England
Now that April's there.
Robert Browning (1812–89) British poet.
Home Thoughts from Abroad

5 In England there are sixty different religions,
and only one sauce.
Domenico Caracciolo (1715–89) Governor of Sicily.
Attrib.

6 There are many things in life more worthwhile
than money. One is to be brought up in this our
England which is still the envy of less happy
lands.
Lord Denning (1899–) British judge.
The Observer, 'Sayings of the Week', 4 Aug 1968

7 The Continent will not suffer England to be the
workshop of the world.
Benjamin Disraeli (1804–81) British statesman.
Speech, House of Commons, 15 Mar 1838

8 England is the paradise of women, the purgatory
of men, and the hell of horses.
John Florio (c. 1553–1625) English lexicographer.
Second Fruits

9 Living in England, provincial England, must be
like being married to a stupid but exquisitely
beautiful wife.
Margaret Halsey (1910–) US writer.
With Malice Toward Some

10 Pass a law to give every single wingeing bloody
Pommie his fare home to England. Back to the
smoke and the sun shining ten days a year and
shit in the streets. Yer can have it.
Thomas Keneally (1935–) Australian novelist.
The Chant of Jimmy Blacksmith

11 It was one of those places where the spirit of
aboriginal England still lingers, the old savage
England, whose last blood flows still in a few
Englishmen, Welshmen, Cornishmen.
D. H. Lawrence (1885–1930) British novelist.
St Mawr

12 In an English ship, they say, it is poor grub, poor
pay, and easy work; in an American ship, good
grub, good pay, and hard work. And this is appli-
cable to the working populations of both countries.
Jack London (1876–1916) US novelist.
The People of the Abyss, Ch. 20

13 In no country, I believe, are the marriage laws so
iniquitous as in England, and the conjugal relation, in consequence, so impaired.
Harriet Martineau (1802–76) British writer.
Society in America, Vol. III, 'Marriage'

14 In England there is only silence or scandal.
André Maurois (Émile Herzog; 1885–1967) French writer.
Attrib.

15 When people say England, they sometimes
mean Great Britain, sometimes the United King-
dom, sometimes the British Isles, – but never
England.
George Mikes (1912–87) Hungarian-born British writer.
How to be an Alien

16 England is not the jewelled isle of Shakespeare's
much-quoted passage, nor is it the inferno
depicted by Dr Goebbels. More than either it
resembles a family, a rather stuffy Victorian
family, with not many black sheep in it but with
all its cupboards bursting with skeletons...A
family with the wrong members in control – that,
perhaps, is as near as one can come to describing
England in a phrase.
George Orwell (Eric Blair; 1903–50) British novelist.
The Lion and the Unicorn, 'England Your England'

17 Damn you, England. You're rotting now, and
quite soon you'll disappear.
John Osborne (1929–) British dramatist.
Letter in *Tribune*, Aug 1961

18 There'll always be an England
While there's a country lane,
Wherever there's a cottage small
Beside a field of grain.
Clarke Ross Parker (1914–74) British songwriter.
There'll Always Be an England

19 England is the paradise of individuality, eccen-
tricity, heresy, anomalies, hobbies, and humours.
George Santayana (1863–1952) US philosopher.
Soliloquies in England, 'The British Character'

20 This royal throne of kings, this sceptred isle,
This earth of majesty, this seat of Mars,
This other Eden, demi-paradise,
This fortress built by Nature for herself
Against infection and the hand of war,
This happy breed of men, this little world,
This precious stone set in the silver sea,
Which serves it in the office of a wall,
Or as a moat defensive to a house,
Against the envy of less happier lands;

This blessed plot, this earth, this realm, this England,
This nurse, this teeming womb of royal kings,
Fear'd by their breed, and famous by their birth.
William Shakespeare (1564–1616) English dramatist.
Richard II, II:1

21 Well, I cannot last ever; but it was always yet the trick of our English nation, if they have a good thing, to make it too common.
William Shakespeare
Henry IV, Part Two, I:2

☐ ENGLISH ☐

See also British, nationality

1 That typically English characteristic for which there is no English name – *esprit de corps.*
Frank Ezra Adcock (1886–1968) British classicist.
Presidential address

2 I like the English. They have the most rigid code of immorality in the world.
Malcolm Bradbury (1932–) British academic and novelist.
Eating People is Wrong, Ch. 5

3 The wish to spread those opinions that we hold conducive to our own welfare is so deeply rooted in the English character that few of us can escape its influence.
Samuel Butler (1835–1902) British writer.
Erewhon, Ch. 20

4 All the faces here this evening seem to be bloody Poms.
Charles, Prince of Wales (1948–) Eldest son of Elizabeth II.
Remark at Australia Day dinner, 1973

5 *Non Angli sed Angeli*
Not Angles, but angels.
Gregory I (540–604) Pope and saint.
Attrib.

6 …it takes a great deal to produce ennui in an Englishman and if you do, he only takes it as convincing proof that you are well-bred.
Margaret Halsey (1910–) US writer.
With Malice Toward Some

7 …the English think of an opinion as something which a decent person, if he has the misfortune to have one, does all he can to hide.
Margaret Halsey
With Malice Toward Some

8 The English (it must be owned) are rather a foul-mouthed nation.
William Hazlitt (1778–1830) British essayist.
On Criticism

9 The Englishman never enjoys himself except for a noble purpose.
A. P. Herbert (1890–1971) British writer and politician.
Uncommon Law

10 When two Englishmen meet, their first talk is of the weather.
Samuel Johnson (1709–84) British lexicographer.
The Idler

11 An Englishman, even if he is alone, forms an orderly queue of one.
George Mikes (1912–87) Hungarian-born British writer.
How to be an Alien

12 Continental people have sex life; the English have hot-water bottles.
George Mikes
How to be an Alien

13 England is a nation of shopkeepers.
Napoleon I (Napoleon Bonaparte; 1769–1821) French emperor.
Attrib.

14 But Lord! to see the absurd nature of Englishmen, that cannot forbear laughing and jeering at everything that looks strange.
Samuel Pepys (1633–1703) English diarist.
Diary, 27 Nov 1662

15 Remember that you are an Englishman, and have consequently won first prize in the lottery of life.
Cecil Rhodes (1853–1902) South African statesman.
Dear Me (Peter Ustinov), Ch. 4

16 The English have no respect for their language, and will not teach their children to speak it…It is impossible for an Englishman to open his mouth, without making some other Englishman despise him.
George Bernard Shaw (1856–1950) Irish dramatist and critic.
Pygmalion, Preface

☐ ENTHUSIASM ☐

1 Nothing is so contagious as enthusiasm.…It is the genius of sincerity and truth accomplishes no victories without it.
Edward Bulwer-Lytton (1803–73) British novelist and politician.
Dale Carnegie's Scrapbook

2 Nothing great was ever achieved without enthusiasm.
Ralph Waldo Emerson (1803–82) US poet and essayist.
Essays, 'Circles'

3 The love of life is necessary to the vigorous prosecution of any undertaking.
Samuel Johnson (1709–84) British lexicographer.
The Rambler

4 To business that we love we rise betime,
And go to't with delight.
William Shakespeare (1564–1616) English dramatist.
Antony and Cleopatra, IV:4

☐ENVIRONMENT☐

See also conservation, ecology

1 They improvidentially piped growing volumes of sewage into the sea, the healing virtues of which were advertised on every railway station.
Robert Cecil (1913–) British writer.
Referring to seaside resorts
Life in Edwardian England

2 If sunbeams were weapons of war, we would have had solar energy long ago.
George Porter (1920–) British chemist.
The Observer, 'Sayings of the Week', 26 Aug 1973

3 The emergence of intelligence, I am convinced, tends to unbalance the ecology. In other words, intelligence is the great polluter. It is not until a creature begins to manage its environment that nature is thrown into disorder.
Clifford D. Simak (1904–) US journalist.
Shakespeare's Planet

☐ENVY☐

See also discontent, jealousy

1 Yet though my lamp burns low and dim, Though I must slave for livelihood – Think you that I would change with him? You bet I would!
F. P. Adams
The Rich Man

2 I am sure the grapes are sour.
Aesop (6th century BC) Reputed Greek writer of fables.
Fables, 'The Fox and the Grapes'

3 Nearly every man in the city wants a farm until he gets it.
Jacob M. Braude

4 Fools may our scorn, not envy raise, For envy is a kind of praise.
John Gay (1685–1732) English poet and dramatist.
Fables

5 The man with toothache thinks everyone happy whose teeth are sound.
George Bernard Shaw (1856–1950) Irish dramatist and critic.
Man and Superman

6 Never having been able to succeed in the world, he took his revenge by speaking ill of it.
Voltaire (François-Marie Arouet; 1694–1778) French writer.
Zadig, Ch. 4

☐EPITAPHS☐

See also memorials, obituaries

1 She sleeps alone at last.
Robert Benchley (1889–1945) US humorist.
Suggested epitaph for an actress
Attrib.

2 Their name, their year, spelt by the unlettered muse,
The place of fame and elegy supply:
On many a holy text around she strews,
That teach the rustic moralist to die.
Thomas Gray (1716–71) British poet.
Elegy Written in a Country Churchyard

3 In lapidary inscriptions a man is not upon oath.
Samuel Johnson (1709–84) British lexicographer.
Life of Johnson (J. Boswell), Vol. II

4 Nowhere probably is there more true feeling, and nowhere worse taste, than in a churchyard – both as regards the monuments and the inscriptions. Scarcely a word of true poetry anywhere.
Benjamin Jowett (1817–93) British theologian.
Letters of B. Jowett (Abbott and Campbell)

5 Alas, poor Yorick! I knew him, Horatio: a fellow of infinite jest, of most excellent fancy.
William Shakespeare (1564–1616) English dramatist.
Hamlet, V:1

☐EQUALITY☐

See also class, feminism, human rights

1 Equality may perhaps be a right, but no power on earth can ever turn it into a fact.
Honoré de Balzac (1799–1850) French novelist.
La Duchesse de Langeais

2 From the point of view of sexual morality the aeroplane is valuable in war in that it destroys men and women in equal numbers.
Ernest William Barnes (1874–1953) British clergyman and mathematician.
Rise of Christianity

3 What makes equality such a difficult business is that we only want it with our superiors.
Henry Becque (1837–99) French dramatist.
Querelles littéraires

4 All service ranks the same with God –
With God, whose puppets, best and worst,
Are we: there is no last or first.
Robert Browning (1812–89) British poet.
Pippa Passes, Pt. I

5 It is the effeminate man – when it is not the prejudiced and jealous male – who dislikes woman and fears her emancipation. It is the abnormal woman whose conception of the movement after freedom is one of antagonism to the 'stronger sex'...A vast amount of energy is wasted in futile argument as to the relative superiority of men and women.
Elizabeth Chesser
Woman, Marriage and Motherhood

6 I thought a woman was a free agent, as well as a man, and was born free, and could she manage herself suitably, might enjoy that liberty to as much purpose as the men do; that the laws of

matrimony were indeed otherwise...and those such that a woman gave herself entirely away from herself, in marriage, and capitulated only to be, at best, but an upper servant.
Daniel Defoe (1660–1731) British journalist and writer.
Roxana

7 I am not belittling the brave pioneer men, but the sunbonnet as well as the sombrero has helped to settle this glorious land of ours.
Edna Ferber (1887–1968) US writer and scenarist.
Cimarron, Ch. 23

8 The majestic egalitarianism of the law, which forbids rich and poor alike to sleep under bridges, to beg in the streets, and to steal bread.
Anatole France (Jacques Anatole François Thibault; 1844–1924) French writer.
The Red Lily, Ch. 7

9 Men are made by nature unequal. It is vain, therefore, to treat them as if they were equal.
J. A. Froude (1818–94) British historian.
Short Studies on Great Subjects, 'Party Politics'

10 A just society would be one in which liberty for one person is constrained only by the demands created by equal liberty for another.
Ivan Illich (1926–) Austrian sociologist.
Tools for Conviviality

11 His foreparents came to America in immigrant ships. My foreparents came to America in slave ships. But whatever the original ships, we are both in the same boat tonight.
Jesse Jackson (1941–) US Black statesman.
Speech, July 1988

12 Your levellers wish to level *down* as far as themselves; but they cannot bear levelling *up* to themselves.
Samuel Johnson (1709–84) British lexicographer.
Life of Johnson (J. Boswell), Vol. I

13 I have a dream that one day this nation will rise up, live out the true meaning of its creed: we hold these truths to be self-evident, that all men are created equal.
Martin Luther King (1929–68) US Black civil-rights leader.
He used the words 'I have a dream' in a number of speeches
Speech, Washington, 27 Aug 1963

14 All animals are equal but some animals are more equal than others.
George Orwell (Eric Blair; 1903–50) British novelist.
Animal Farm, Ch. 10

15 EQUALITY...is the thing. It is the only true and central premise from which constructive ideas can radiate freely and be operated without prejudice.
Mervyn Peake (1911–68) British novelist.
Titus Groan, 'The Sun goes down'

16 I think the King is but a man as I am: the violet smells to him as it doth to me.
William Shakespeare (1564–1616) English dramatist.
Henry V, IV:1

17 Hath not a Jew eyes? Hath not a Jew hands, organs, dimensions, senses, affections, passions, fed with the same food, hurt with the same weapons, subject to the same diseases, healed by the same means, warmed and cooled by the same winter and summer, as a Christian is? If you prick us, do we not bleed? If you tickle us, do we not laugh? If you poison us, do we not die? And if you wrong us, shall we not revenge?
William Shakespeare
The Merchant of Venice, III:1

18 Whatever women do, they must do it twice as well as men to be thought half as good. Luckily, this is not difficult.
Charlotte Witton
Attrib.

19 Pale Death kicks his way equally into the cottages of the poor and the castles of kings.
Horace (Quintus Horatius Flaccus; 65–8 BC) Roman poet.
Odes, I

20 A heap of dust alone remains of thee;
'Tis all thou art, and all the proud shall be!
Alexander Pope (1688–1744) British poet.
Elegy to the Memory of an Unfortunate Lady

□ ETERNITY □
See also immortality, time

1 Kiss till the cow comes home.
Francis Beaumont (1584–1616) English dramatist.
Scornful Lady, II:2

2 As it was in the beginning, is now, and ever shall be: world without end.
The Book of Common Prayer
Morning Prayer, Gloria

3 Thou, silent form, dost tease us out of thought
As doth eternity: Cold Pastoral!
John Keats (1795–1821) British poet.
Ode on a Grecian Urn

4 Eternity's a terrible thought. I mean, where's it going to end?
Tom Stoppard (1937–) Czech-born British dramatist.
Rosencrantz and Guildenstern Are Dead, II

□ ETIQUETTE □
See also manners

1 It is necessary to clean the teeth frequently, more especially after meals, but not on any account with a pin, or the point of a penknife, and it must never be done at table.
St Jean Baptiste de la Salle (1651–1719)
The Rules of Christian Manners and Civility, I

2 We could not lead a pleasant life,
And 'twould be finished soon,
If peas were eaten with the knife,
And gravy with the spoon.
Eat slowly: only men in rags
And gluttons old in sin
Mistake themselves for carpet bags
And tumble victuals in.
Walter Raleigh (1861–1922) British scholar.
Laughter from a Cloud, 'Stans puer ad mensam'

3 I think she must have been very strictly brought
up, she's so desperately anxious to do the wrong
thing correctly.
Saki (Hector Hugh Munro; 1870–1916) British writer.
Reginald on Worries

□EUROPE□

See also Britain, England, France, Germany, Ireland, Russia,
Scotland, Switzerland, Venice, Wales

1 But the age of chivalry is gone. That of
sophisters, economists, and calculators, has succeeded; and the glory of Europe is extinguished
for ever.
Edmund Burke (1729–97) British politician.
Reflections on the Revolution in France

2 We must build a kind of United States of Europe.
Winston Churchill (1874–1965) British statesman.
Speech, Zurich, 19 Sept 1946

3 In Western Europe there are now only small
countries – those that know it and those that
don't know it yet.
Théo Lefèvre (1914–73) Belgian prime minister.
The Observer, 'Sayings of the Year', 1963

4 We are part of the community of Europe and we
must do our duty as such.
Marquess of Salisbury (1830–1903) British statesman.
Speech, Caernarvon, 11 Apr 1888

5 This going into Europe will not turn out to be the
thrilling mutual exchange supposed. It is more
like nine middle-aged couples with failing marriages meeting in a darkened bedroom in a Brussels hotel for a Group Grope.
E. P. Thompson (1924–) British historian.
On the Europe debate, *Sunday Times*, 27 Apr 1975

6 That Europe's nothin' on earth but a great big
auction, that's all it is.
Tennessee Williams (1911–83) US dramatist.
Cat on a Hot Tin Roof, I

□EVIL□

See also good and evil, sin, vice

1 *Honi soit qui mal y pense.*
Evil be to him who evil thinks.
Anonymous
Motto for the Order of the Garter

2 It takes a certain courage and a certain greatness
even to be truly base.
Jean Anouilh (1910–87) French dramatist.
Ardèle

3 Wherefore I praised the dead which are already
dead more than the living which are yet alive.
Yea, better is he than both they, which hath not
yet been, who hath not seen the evil work that is
done under the sun.
Bible: Ecclesiastes
4:2–3

4 But evil men and seducers shall wax worse and
worse, deceiving, and being deceived.
Bible: II Timothy
3:13

5 And this is the condemnation, that light is come
into the world, and men loved darkness rather
than light, because their deeds were evil.
Bible: John
3:19

6 The belief in a supernatural source of evil is not
necessary; men alone are quite capable of every
wickedness.
Joseph Conrad (Teodor Josef Konrad Korzeniowski;
1857–1924) Polish-born British novelist.
Under Western Eyes, Part 2

7 But evil is wrought by want of thought,
As well as want of heart!
Thomas Hood (1799–1845) British poet.
The Lady's Dream

8 He who passively accepts evil is as much
involved in it as he who helps to perpetrate it.
Martin Luther King (1929–68) US Black civil-rights leader.
Stride Towards Freedom

9 Farewell remorse! All good to me is lost;
Evil, be thou my Good.
John Milton (1608–74) English poet.
Paradise Lost, Bk. IV

10 There is scarcely a single man sufficiently aware
to know all the evil he does.
Duc de la Rochefoucauld (1613–80) French writer.
Maximes, 269

11 Friends, Romans, countrymen, lend me your
ears
I come to bury Caesar, not to praise him.
The evil that men do lives after them;
The good is oft interred with their bones.
William Shakespeare (1564–1616) English dramatist.
Julius Caesar, III:2

□ EVOLUTION □

See also survival

1 From an evolutionary point of view, man has stopped moving, if he ever did move.
Pierre Teilhard de Chardin (1881–1955) French Jesuit and palaeontologist.
The Phenomenon of Man, Postscript

2 Man is developed from an ovule, about the 125th of an inch in diameter, which differs in no respect from the ovules of other animals.
Charles Darwin (1809–82) British life scientist.
The Descent of Man, Ch. 1

3 We must, however, acknowledge, as it seems to me, that man with all his noble qualities, still bears in his bodily frame the indelible stamp of his lowly origin.
Charles Darwin
Closing words
Descent of Man, Ch. 21

4 I have called this principle, by which each slight variation, if useful, is preserved, by the term of Natural Selection.
Charles Darwin
Origin of Species, Ch. 3

5 The expression often used by Mr Herbert Spencer of the Survival of the Fittest is more accurate, and is sometimes equally convenient.
Charles Darwin
Origin of Species, Ch. 3

6 I asserted – and I repeat – that a man has no reason to be ashamed of having an ape for his grandfather. If there were an ancestor whom I should feel shame in recalling it would rather be a *man* – a man of restless and versatile intellect – who, not content with an equivocal success in his own sphere of activity, plunges into scientific questions with which he has no real acquaintance, only to obscure them by an aimless rhetoric, and distract the attention of his hearers from the real point at issue by eloquent digressions and skilled appeals to religious prejudice.
T. H. Huxley (1825–95) British biologist.
Replying to Bishop WILBERFORCE in the debate on Darwin's theory of evolution at the meeting of the British Association at Oxford. No transcript was taken at the time; the version above is commonly quoted. After hearing Wilberforce's speech, and before rising himself, Huxley is said to have remarked, 'The Lord has delivered him into my hands!'
Speech, 30 June 1860

7 And, in conclusion, I would like to ask the gentleman…whether the ape from which he is descended was on his grandmother's or his grandfather's side of the family.
Samuel Wilberforce (1805–73) British churchman.
See T. H. HUXLEY
Speech, 30 June 1860

□ EXAMINATIONS □

See also education

1 Examinations are formidable even to the best prepared, for the greatest fool may ask more than the wisest man can answer.
Charles Caleb Colton (?1780–1832) British clergyman and writer.
Lacon, Vol. II

2 Do not on any account attempt to write on both sides of the paper at once.
W. C. Sellar (1898–1951) British humorous writer.
1066 And All That, Test Paper 5

□ EXAMPLE □

1 Example is the school of mankind, and they will learn at no other.
Edmund Burke (1729–97) British politician.
Letters on a Regicide Peace, letter 1

2 What you do not want done to yourself, do not do to others.
Confucius (K'ung Fu-tzu; 551–479 BC) Chinese philosopher.
Analects

3 Men are not hanged for stealing horses, but that horses may not be stolen.
George Saville (1633–95) English statesman.
Political, Moral and Miscellaneous Thoughts and Reflections

4 A precedent embalms a principle.
William Scott (1745–1836) British jurist.
An opinion given while Advocate-General
Attrib.; also quoted by Benjamin Disraeli (1848)

5 Do not, as some ungracious pastors do,
Show me the steep and thorny way to heaven,
Whiles, like a puff'd and reckless libertine,
Himself the primrose path of dalliance treads
And recks not his own rede.
William Shakespeare (1564–1616) English dramatist.
Hamlet, I:3

□ EXCELLENCE □

See also superiority

1 Whatever is worth doing at all is worth doing well.
Earl of Chesterfield (1694–1773) English statesman.
Letter to his son, 10 Mar 1746

2 The danger chiefly lies in acting well,
No crime's so great as daring to excel.
Charles Churchill (1731–64) British poet.
Epistle to William Hogarth

3 The best is the enemy of the good.
Voltaire (François-Marie Arouet; 1694–1778) French writer.
Dictionnaire philosophique, 'Art dramatique'

☐EXCESS☐

See also extravagance, moderation

1 *L'embarras des richesses.*
A superfluity of good things.
Abbé Lénor Jean d'Allainval (1700–53) French dramatist.
Play title

2 What fun it would be to be poor, as long as one
was *excessively* poor! Anything in excess is most
exhilarating.
Jean Anouilh (1910–87) French dramatist.
Ring Round the Moon

3 The road of excess leads to the palace of
Wisdom.
William Blake (1757–1827) British poet.
The Marriage of Heaven and Hell, 'Proverbs of Hell'

4 I would remind you that extremism in the
defence of liberty is no vice. And let me remind
you also that moderation in the pursuit of justice
is no virtue!
Barry Goldwater (1909–) US politician.
Speech, San Francisco, 17 July 1964

5 'Tis not the drinking that is to be blamed, but the
excess.
John Selden (1584–1654) English historian.
Table Talk

6 The lady doth protest too much, methinks.
William Shakespeare (1564–1616) English dramatist.
Hamlet, III:2

7 To gild refined gold, to paint the lily,
To throw a perfume on the violet,
To smooth the ice, or add another hue
Unto the rainbow, or with taper-light
To seek the beauteous eye of heaven to garnish,
Is wasteful and ridiculous excess.
William Shakespeare
King John, IV:2

8 Moderation is a fatal thing, Lady Hunstanton.
Nothing succeeds like excess.
Oscar Wilde (1854–1900) Irish-born British dramatist.
A Woman of No Importance, III

☐EXECUTION☐

See also last words, martyrdom, punishment

1 And almost all things are by the law purged with
blood; and without shedding of blood is no remission.
Bible: Hebrews
9:22

2 And when they were come to the place, which is
called Calvary, there they crucified him, and the
malefactors, one on the right hand, and the other
on the left.
Bible: Luke
23:33

3 I die a Christian, according to the Profession of
the Church of England, as I found it left me by
my Father.
Charles I (1600–49) King of England.
Speech on the scaffold, 30 Jan 1649

4 It is a far, far, better thing that I do, than I have
ever done; it is a far, far, better rest that I go to,
than I have ever known.
Charles Dickens (1812–70) British novelist.
Said by Sydney Carton
A Tale of Two Cities, Bk. II, Ch. 15

5 Depend upon it, Sir, when a man knows he is to
be hanged in a fortnight, it concentrates his mind
wonderfully.
Samuel Johnson (1709–84) British lexicographer.
Life of Johnson (J. Boswell), Vol. III

6 If we are to abolish the death penalty, I should
like to see the first step taken by our friends the
murderers.
Alphonse Karr (1808–90) French writer.
Les Guêpes, Jan 1849

7 Be of good comfort, Master Ridley, and play the
man; we shall this day light such a candle, by
God's grace, in England as I trust shall never be
put out.
Hugh Latimer (1485–1555) English churchman.
Said to Nicholas Ridley as they were about to be burnt at the
stake for heresy
Famous Last Words (B. Conrad)

8 He nothing common did or mean
Upon that memorable scene,
But with his keener eye
The axe's edge did try.
Andrew Marvell (1621–78) English poet.
Referring to the execution of Charles I
An Horatian Ode upon Cromwell's Return from Ireland

9 The world itself is but a large prison, out of which
some are daily led to execution.
Walter Raleigh (1554–1618) English explorer.
Said after his trial for treason, 1603
Attrib.

10 'Tis a sharp remedy, but a sure one for all ills.
Walter Raleigh
Referring to the executioner's axe just before he was beheaded
Attrib.

11 If you give me six lines written by the most hon-
est man, I will find something in them to hang
him.
Cardinal Richelieu (1585–1642) French statesman.
Exact wording uncertain
Attrib.

12 '*O liberté! O liberté! Que de crimes on commet en
ton nom!'*

Oh liberty! Oh liberty! What crimes are commit-
ted in thy name!
Madame Roland (1754–93) French revolutionary.
Said as she mounted the steps of the guillotine
Attrib.

□ EXISTENCE □

1 Dear Sir, Your astonishment's odd:
I am always about in the Quad.
And that's why the tree
Will continue to be,
Since observed by Yours faithfully, God.
Anonymous
The response to KNOX's limerick

2 Let us be moral. Let us contemplate existence.
Charles Dickens (1812–70) British novelist.
Martin Chuzzlewit, Ch. 10

3 As far as we can discern, the sole purpose of
human existence is to kindle a light in the darkness of mere being.
Carl Gustav Jung (1875–1961) Swiss psychoanalyst.
Memories, Dreams, Reflections, Ch. 11

4 There once was a man who said 'God
Must think it exceedingly odd
If he find that this tree
Continues to be
When there's no one about in the Quad.'
Ronald Knox (1888–1957) British Roman Catholic priest.
For a reply, *see* ANONYMOUS
Attrib.

5 I know perfectly well that I don't want to do anything; to do something is to create existence –
and there's quite enough existence as it is.
Jean-Paul Sartre (1905–80) French writer.
Nausea

□ EXPECTATION □

See also disappointment, hope

1 As I know more of mankind I expect less of them,
and am ready now to call a man *a good man*, upon
easier terms than I was formerly.
Samuel Johnson (1709–84) British lexicographer.
Life of Johnson (J. Boswell), Vol. IV

2 'Blessed is the man who expects nothing, for he
shall never be disappointed' was the ninth beati-
tude.
Alexander Pope (1688–1744) British poet.
Letter to Fortescue, 23 Sept 1725

□ EXPEDIENCY □

1 And my parents finally realize that I'm kidnapped
and they snap into action immediately: they rent
out my room.
Woody Allen (Allen Stewart Konigsberg; 1935–) US film
actor.
Woody Allen and His Comedy (E. Lax)

2 I would rather be an opportunist and float than
go to the bottom with my principles round my
neck.
Stanley Baldwin (1867–1947) British statesman.
Attrib.

3 You can't learn too soon that the most useful
thing about a principle is that it can always be sacrificed to expediency.
W. Somerset Maugham (1874–1965) British novelist.
The Circle, III

4 No man is justified in doing evil on the ground of
expediency.
Theodore Roosevelt (1858–1919) US Republican president.
The Strenuous Life

□ EXPERIENCE □

See also history, past

1 Experience is a good teacher, but she sends in
terrific bills.
Minna Antrim (1861–?) US writer.
Naked Truth and Veiled Allusions

2 You will think me lamentably crude: my experi-
ence of life has been drawn from life itself.
Max Beerbohm (1872–1956) British writer.
Zuleika Dobson, Ch. 7

3 Experience isn't interesting till it begins to repeat
itself – in fact, till it does that, it hardly *is* experience.
Elizabeth Bowen (1899–1973) Irish novelist.
The Death of the Heart, Pt. I, Ch. 1

4 If men could learn from history, what lessons it
might teach us! But passion and party blind our
eyes and the light which experience gives is a lan-
tern on the stern, which shines only on the
waves behind us!
Samuel Taylor Coleridge (1772–1834) British poet.
Recollections (Allsop)

5 How many roads must a man walk down
Before you call him a man?
Bob Dylan (Robert Allen Zimmerman; 1941–) US popular
singer.
Blowin' in the Wind

6 What experience and history teach is this – that
people and governments never have learned anything from history, or acted on principles
deduced from it.
Hegel (1770–1831) German philosopher.
Philosophy of History, Introduction

7 A moment's insight is sometimes worth a life's
experience.
Oliver Wendell Holmes (1809–94) US writer.
The Professor at the Breakfast Table, Ch. 10

8 Nothing ever becomes real till it is experienced –
even a proverb is no proverb to you till your life
has illustrated it.
John Keats (1795–1821) British poet.
Letter to George and Georgiana Keats, 19 Mar 1819

9 All experience is an arch wherethro'
Gleams that untravelled world, whose margin
fades
For ever and for ever when I move.
Alfred, Lord Tennyson (1809–92) British poet.
Ulysses

□ EXPERTS □

1 An expert is a man who has made all the mis-
takes, which can be made, in a very narrow field.
Niels Bohr (1885–1962) Danish physicist.
Attrib.

2 An expert is someone who knows some of the
worst mistakes that can be made in his subject,
and how to avoid them.
Werner Heisenberg (1901–76) German physicist.
Physics and Beyond

3 Specialist – A man who knows more and more
about less and less.
William James Mayo (1861–1934) US surgeon.
Also attributed to Nicholas Butler

□ EXPLANATIONS □

1 I am one of those unfortunates to whom death is
less hideous than explanations.
Wyndham Lewis (1891–1969) British journalist and writer.
Welcome to All This

2 There is occasions and causes why and where-
fore in all things.
William Shakespeare (1564–1616) English dramatist.
Henry V, V:1

□ EXPLOITATION □

1 Thus the devil played at chess with me, and yielding a pawn, thought to gain a queen of me, taking
advantage of my honest endeavours.
Thomas Browne (1605–82) English physician and writer.
Religio Medici, Pt. I

2 Mortals, whose pleasures are their only care,
First wish to be imposed on, and then are.
William Cowper (1731–1800) British poet.
The Progress of Error

□ EXPLORATION □
See also discovery

1 The fair breeze blew, the white foam flew,
The furrow followed free;
We were the first that ever burst
Into that silent sea.
Samuel Taylor Coleridge (1772–1834) British poet.
The Rime of the Ancient Mariner, II

2 Go West, young man, and grow up with the coun-
try.
Horace Greeley (1811–72) US politician and journalist.
Also attributed to the US writer John Soule (1815–91), *Terre
Haute* (Indiana) *Express*, 1851
Hints toward Reform

□ EXTRAVAGANCE □
See also excess, luxury, money, ostentation, thrift

1 Riches are for spending.
Francis Bacon (1561–1626) English philosopher.
Essays, 'Of Expense'

2 All progress is based upon a universal innate
desire on the part of every organism to live
beyond its income.
Samuel Butler (1835–1902) British writer.
Notebooks

3 All decent people live beyond their incomes
nowadays, and those who aren't respectable live
beyond other people's. A few gifted individuals
manage to do both.
Saki (Hector Hugh Munro; 1870–1916) British writer.
The Match-Maker

F

□ FACTS □
See also truth

1 Facts do not cease to exist because they are ignored.
Aldous Huxley (1894–1964) British novelist.
Proper Studies

2 Facts speak louder than statistics.
Geoffrey Streatfield (1897–1978) British lawyer.
The Observer, 'Sayings of the Week', 19 Mar 1950

□ FAILURE □
See also success

1 She knows there's no success like failure
And that failure's no success at all.
Bob Dylan (Robert Allen Zimmerman; 1941–) US popular singer.
Love Minus Zero No Limit

2 Show me a good and gracious loser and I'll show you a failure.
Knute Rockne (1888–1931) US football coach.
Attrib.

3 Like a dull actor now
I have forgot my part and I am out,
Even to a full disgrace.
William Shakespeare (1564–1616) English dramatist.
Coriolanus, V:3

□ FAIRIES □
See also supernatural

1 Every time a child says 'I don't believe in fairies' there is a little fairy somewhere that falls down dead.
J. M. Barrie (1860–1937) British novelist and dramatist.
Peter Pan, I

2 When the first baby laughed for the first time, the laugh broke into a thousand pieces and they all went skipping about, and that was the beginning of fairies.
J. M. Barrie

3 There are fairies at the bottom of our garden.
Rose Fyleman (1877–1957) British writer.
Fairies and Chimneys

□ FAITH □
See also belief, faithfulness, God, religion, trust

1 Now faith is the substance of things hoped for, the evidence of things not seen.
Bible: Hebrews
11:1

2 These all died in faith, not having received the promises, but having seen them afar off, and were persuaded of them, and embraced them, and confessed that they were strangers and pilgrims on the earth.
Bible: Hebrews
11:13

3 For we walk by faith, not by sight.
Bible: II Corinthians
5:7

4 Even so faith, if it hath not works, is dead, being alone.
Bible: James
2:17

5 The prayer that reforms the sinner and heals the sick is an absolute faith that all things are possible to God – a spiritual understanding of Him, an unselfed love.
Mary Baker Eddy (1821–1910) US religious leader.
Science and Health, with Key to the Scriptures

6 And I said to the man who stood at the gate of the year: 'Give me a light that I may tread safely into the unknown'. And he replied: 'Go out into the darkness and put your hand into the hand of God. That shall be to you better than light and safer than a known way.'
Minnie Louise Haskins (1875–1957) US writer.
Remembered because it was quoted by George VI in his Christmas broadcast, 1939
The Desert, Introduction

7 Faith may be defined briefly as an illogical belief in the occurrence of the improbable.
H. L. Mencken (1880–1956) US journalist.
Prejudices, 'Types of Men'

8 Even such is Time, that takes in trust
Our youth, our joys, our all we have,
And pays us but with age and dust;
Who in the dark and silent grave,
When we have wandered all our ways,
Shuts up the story of our days;
But from this earth, this grave, this dust,
My God shall raise me up, I trust.
Walter Raleigh (1554–1618) English explorer.
Written on the night before his execution
Attrib.

9 'Tis not the dying for a faith that's so hard, Master Harry – every man of every nation has done that – 'tis the living up to it that is difficult.
William Makepeace Thackeray (1811–63) British novelist.
Henry Esmond, Ch. 6

10 Faith consists in believing when it is beyond the power of reason to believe. It is not enough that a thing be possible for it to be believed.
Voltaire (François-Marie Arouet; 1694–1778) French writer.
Questions sur l'encyclopédie

□FAITHFULNESS□

See also loyalty

1 It is better to be unfaithful than faithful without wanting to be.
Brigitte Bardot (1934–) French film actress.
The Observer, 'Sayings of the Week', 18 Feb 1968

2 Through perils both of wind and limb,
Through thick and thin she follow'd him.
Samuel Butler (1612–80) English satirist.
Hudibras, Pt. II

3 I have been faithful to thee, Cynara! in my fashion.
Ernest Dowson (1867–1900) British lyric poet.
Non Sum Qualis Eram Bonae Sub Regno Cynarae

4 We only part to meet again.
Change, as ye list, ye winds; my heart shall be
The faithful compass that still points to thee.
John Gay (1685–1732) English poet and dramatist.
Sweet William's Farewell

□FAME□

See also popularity, posterity, reputation

1 A celebrity is a person who works hard all his life to become known, then wears dark glasses to avoid being recognized.
Fred Allen (1894–1956) US comedian.
Treadmill to Oblivion

2 Fame is like a river, that beareth up things light and swollen, and drowns things weighty and solid.
Francis Bacon (1561–1626) English philosopher.
Essays, 'Of Praise'

3 Fame is sometimes like unto a kind of mushroom, which Pliny recounts to be the greatest miracle in nature, because growing and having no root.
Thomas Fuller (1608–61) English historian.
The Holy State and the Profane State

4 Fame is a powerful aphrodisiac.
Graham Greene (1904–91) British novelist.
Radio Times, 10 Sept 1964

5 Every man has a lurking wish to appear considerable in his native place.
Samuel Johnson (1709–84) British lexicographer.
Letter to Sir Joshua Reynolds
Life of Johnson (J. Boswell), Vol. II

6 One of the drawbacks of Fame is that one can never escape from it.
Nellie Melba (Helen Porter Mitchell; 1861–1931) Australian soprano.
Melodies and Memories

7 Fame is the spur that the clear spirit doth raise
(That last infirmity of noble mind)
To scorn delights, and live laborious days.
John Milton (1608–74) English poet.
Lycidas

8 'What are you famous *for*?'
'For nothing. I am just famous.'
Iris Murdoch (1919–) Irish-born British novelist.
The Flight from the Enchanter

9 The more you are talked about, the more you will wish to be talked about. The condemned murderer who is allowed to see the account of his trial in the Press is indignant if he finds a newspaper which has reported it inadequately....Politicians and literary men are in the same case.
Bertrand Russell (1872–1970) British philosopher.
Human Society in Ethics and Politics

10 Love of fame is the last thing even learned men can bear to be parted from.
Tacitus (c. 55–c. 120 AD) Roman historian.
Histories, IV, 6

11 To famous men all the earth is a sepulchre.
Thucydides (c. 460–c. 400 BC) Greek historian and general.
History of the Peloponnesian War, Bk. II, Ch. 43

12 In the future, everyone will be famous for 15 minutes.
Andy Warhol (Andrew Warhola; 1926–87) US pop artist.
Attrib.

13 It's the place where my prediction from the sixties finally came true: 'In the future everyone will be famous for fifteen minutes.' I'm bored with that line. I never use it anymore. My new line is, 'In fifteen minutes everybody will be famous.'
Andy Warhol
Andy Warhol's Exposures

□FAMILIARITY□

1 No man is a hero to his valet.
Andy Warhol (Andrew Warhola; 1926–87) US pop artist.
Andy Warhol's Exposures
Anne-Marie Bigot de Cornuel (1605–94) French society hostess.
Lettres de Mlle Aïssé, 13 Aug 1728

2 I like familiarity. In me it does not breed contempt. Only more familiarity.
Gertrude Stein (1874–1946) US writer.
Dale Carnegie's Scrapbook

3 He began to think the tramp a fine, brotherly, generous fellow. He was also growing accustomed to something – shall I call it an olfactory bar – that had hitherto kept them apart.
H. G. Wells (1866–1946) British writer.
Bealby, Pt. VI, Ch. 3

☐FAMILY☐

See also ancestry, children, marriage

1 He that hath wife and children hath given hostages to fortune; for they are impediments to great enterprises, either of virtue or mischief.
Francis Bacon (1561–1626) English philosopher.
See also LUCAN
Essays, 'Of Marriage and Single Life'

2 The joys of parents are secret, and so are their griefs and fears.
Francis Bacon
Essays, 'Of Parents and Children'

3 Fathers, provoke not your children to anger, lest they be discouraged.
Bible: Colossians
3:21

4 Behold, every one that useth proverbs shall use this proverb against thee, saying, As is the mother, so is her daughter.
Bible: Ezekiel
16:44–45

5 If one is not going to take the necessary precautions to avoid having parents one must undertake to bring them up.
Quentin Crisp (?1910–) Model, publicist, and writer.
The Naked Civil Servant

6 Fate chooses your relations, you choose your friends.
Jacques Delille (1738–1813) French abbé and poet.
Malheur et pitié, I

7 It is a melancholy truth that even great men have their poor relations.
Charles Dickens (1812–70) British novelist.
Bleak House, Ch. 28

8 The mother-child relationship is paradoxical and, in a sense, tragic. It requires the most intense love on the mother's side, yet this very love must help the child grow away from the mother and to become fully independent.
Erich Fromm (1900–80) US psychologist and philosopher.

9 Good families are generally worse than any others.
Anthony Hope (Sir Anthony Hope Hawkins; 1863–1933) British novelist.
The Prisoner of Zenda, Ch. 1

10 A poor relation – is the most irrelevant thing in nature.
Charles Lamb (1775–1834) British essayist.
Last Essays of Elia, 'Poor Relations'

11 They fuck you up, your mum and dad.
They may not mean to, but they do.
They fill you with the faults they had
And add some extra, just for you.
Philip Larkin (1922–85) British poet.
This be the Verse

12 Far from being the basis of the good society, the family, with its narrow privacy and tawdry secrets, is the source of all our discontents.
Edmund Leach (1910–) British social anthropologist.
In the BBC Reith Lectures for 1967. Lecture reprinted in *The Listener*

13 I have a wife, I have sons: all of them hostages given to fate.
Lucan (Marcus Annaeus Lucanus; 39–65 AD) Roman poet.
See also BACON
Works, VII

14 A group of closely related persons living under one roof; it is a convenience, often a necessity, sometimes a pleasure, sometimes the reverse; but who first exalted it as admirable, an almost religious ideal?
Rose Macaulay (1889–1958) British writer.
The World My Wilderness, Ch. 20

15 The sink is the great symbol of the bloodiness of family life. All life is bad, but family life is worse.
Julian Mitchell (1935–) British writer.
As Far as You Can Go, Pt. I, Ch. 1

16 Children aren't happy with nothing to ignore,
And that's what parents were created for.
Ogden Nash (1902–71) US poet.
The Parents

17 Parents are sometimes a bit of a disappointment to their children. They don't fulfil the promise of their early years.
Anthony Powell (1905–) British novelist.
A Buyer's Market

18 For there is no friend like a sister
In calm or stormy weather;
To cheer one on the tedious way,
To fetch one if one goes astray,
To lift one if one totters down,
To strengthen whilst one stands.
Christina Rossetti (1830–74) British poet.
Goblin Market

19 It is a wise father that knows his own child.
William Shakespeare (1564–1616) English dramatist.
The Merchant of Venice, II:2

20 All happy families resemble one another, each unhappy family is unhappy in its own way.
Leo Tolstoy (1828–1910) Russian writer.
Anna Karenina, Pt. I, Ch. 1

21 No man is responsible for his father. That is entirely his mother's affair.
Margaret Turnbull (fl. 1920s–1942) US writer.
Alabaster Lamps

22 Don't hold your parents up to contempt. After all, you are their son, and it is just possible that you may take after them.
Evelyn Waugh (1903–66) British novelist.
The Tablet, 9 May 1951

☐ FANATICISM ☐

1 Defined in psychological terms, a fanatic is a man who consciously over-compensates a secret doubt.
Aldous Huxley (1894–1964) British novelist.
Vulgarity in Literature, Ch. 4

2 Fanatics have their dreams, wherewith they weave
A paradise for a sect.
John Keats (1795–1821) British poet.
The Fall of Hyperion, I

3 You are never dedicated to something you have complete confidence in. No one is fanatically shouting that the sun is going to rise tomorrow. They *know* it's going to rise tomorrow. When people are fanatically dedicated to political or religious faiths or any other kind of dogmas or goals, it's always because these dogmas or goals are in doubt.
Robert T. Pirsig (1928–) US writer.
Zen and the Art of Motorcycle Maintenance, Pt. II, Ch. 13

☐ FASCISM ☐
See also Hitler, Nazism

1 Fascism is a religion; the twentieth century will be known in history as the century of Fascism.
Benito Mussolini (1883–1945) Italian dictator.
On Hitler's seizing power
Sawdust Caesar (George Seldes), Ch. 24

2 Fascism is not an article for export.
Benito Mussolini
Report in the German press, 1932

3 Every communist has a fascist frown, every fascist a communist smile.
Muriel Spark (1918–) British novelist.
The Girls of Slender Means, Ch. 4

4 Fascism means war.
John St Loe Strachey (1901–63) British politician.
Slogan, 1930s

☐ FASHION ☐
See also clothes

1 Fashion is architecture: it is a matter of proportions.
Coco Chanel (1883–1971) French dress designer.
Coco Chanel, Her Life, Her Secrets (Marcel Haedrich)

2 One had as good be out of the world, as out of the fashion.
Colley Cibber (1671–1757) British actor and dramatist.
Love's Last Shift, II

3 One week he's in polka dots, the next week he's in stripes.
Cos he's a dedicated follower of fashion.
Ray Davies British pop musician.
Dedicated Follower of Fashion

4 In olden days, a glimpse of stocking
Was looked on as something shocking,
But now, Heaven knows,
Anything goes.
Cole Porter (1893–1964) US songwriter.
Anything Goes

5 For an idea ever to be fashionable is ominous, since it must afterwards be always old-fashioned.
George Santayana (1863–1952) US philosopher.
Winds of Doctrine, 'Modernism and Christianity'

6 Fashions, after all, are only induced epidemics.
George Bernard Shaw (1856–1950) Irish dramatist and critic.
Doctor's Dilemma, Preface

7 A love of fashion makes the economy go round.
Liz Tilberis (1947–) Editor of Vogue.
Remark, Aug 1987

☐ FEAR ☐

1 It is a miserable state of mind to have few things to desire and many things to fear.
Francis Bacon (1561–1626) English philosopher.
Essays, 'Of Empire'

2 For God hath not given us the spirit of fear; but of power, and of love, and of a sound mind.
Bible: II Timothy
1:7

3 There is no fear in love; but perfect love casteth out fear: because fear hath torment. He that feareth is not made perfect in love.
Bible: I John
4:18

4 Fear has many eyes and can see things underground.
Miguel de Cervantes (1547–1616) Spanish novelist.
Don Quixote, Pt. I, Ch. 20

5 Like one, that on a lonesome road
Doth walk in fear and dread,
And having once turned round walks on,
And turns no more his head;
Because he knows, a frightful fiend
Doth close behind him tread.
Samuel Taylor Coleridge (1772–1834) British poet.
The Rime of the Ancient Mariner, VI

6 Let me assert my firm belief that the only thing we have to fear is fear itself.
Franklin D. Roosevelt (1882–1945) US Democratic president.
First Inaugural Address, 4 Mar 1933

7 Fear lent wings to his feet.
Virgil (Publius Vergilius Maro; 70–19 BC) Roman poet.
Aeneid, Bk. VIII

□FEMINISM□

See also equality, sexes, woman's role, women

THOSE IN FAVOUR

1 Men their rights and nothing more; women their rights and nothing less.
Susan B. Anthony (1820–1906) US editor.
The Revolution, Motto

2 ...there never will be complete equality until women themselves help to make laws and elect lawmakers.
Susan B. Anthony
In *The Arena*, (May 1897) 'The Status of Women, Past, Present and Future'

3 The extension of women's rights is the basic principle of all social progress.
Charles Fourier (1772–1837) French social reformer.
Théorie des Quatre Mouvements

4 Where young boys plan for what they will achieve and attain, young girls plan for whom they will achieve and attain.
Charlotte Perkins Gilman (1860–1935) US writer.
Women and Economics, Ch. 5

5 Merely external emancipation has made of the modern woman an artificial being...Now, woman is confronted with the necessity of emancipating herself from emancipation, if she really desires to be free.
Emma Goldman (1869–1940) Russian-born US anarchist, political agitator and organizer, lecturer, and editor.
'The Tragedy of Women's Emancipation', *Anarchism and Other Essays*

6 A woman needs a man like a fish needs a bicycle.
Graffiti

7 I know you do not make the laws but I also know that you are the wives and mothers, the sisters and daughters of those who do.
Angelina Grimké (1805–79) US writer and reformer.
The Anti-Slavery Examiner (Sep 1836), 'Appeal to the Christian Women of the South'

8 ...the emancipation of women is practically the greatest egoistic movement of the nineteenth century, and the most intense affirmation of the right of the self that history has yet seen...
Ellen Key (Karolina Sofia Key; 1849–1926) Swedish writer.
The Century of the Child, Ch. 2

9 ...is it to be understood that the principles of the Declaration of Independence bear no relation to half of the human race?
Harriet Martineau (1802–76) British writer.
Society in America, Vol. III, 'Marriage'

10 The most important thing women have to do is to stir up the zeal of women themselves.
John Stuart Mill (1806–73) British philosopher.
Letter to Alexander Bain, 14 July 1869

11 ...the rumblings of women's liberation are only one pointer to the fact that you already have a discontented work force. And if conditions continue to lag so far behind the industrial norm and the discomfort increases, you will find...that you will end up with an inferior product.
Elaine Morgan (1920–) British writer.
The Descent of Woman, Ch. 11

12 No *man*, not even a doctor, ever gives any other definition of what a nurse should be than this– "devoted and obedient." This definition would do just as well for a porter. It might even do for a horse. It would not do for a policeman.
Florence Nightingale (1820–1910) British nurse.
Notes on Nursing

13 The vote, I thought, means nothing to women. We should be armed.
Edna O'Brien (1936–) Irish novelist.
Quoted as epigraph to *Fear of Flying* (Erica Jong), Ch. 16

14 Women had always fought for men, and for their children. Now they were ready to fight for their own human rights. Our militant movement was established.
Emmeline Pankhurst (1858–1928) British suffragette.
My Own Story

15 We have taken this action, because as women...we realize that the condition of our sex is so deplorable that it is our duty even to break the law in order to call attention to the reasons why we do so.
Emmeline Pankhurst
Speech in court, 21 Oct 1908
Shoulder to Shoulder (ed. Midge Mackenzie)

16 Women have been emancipated on condition that they don't upset men, or interfere too much with men's way of life.
Constance Rover (1910–) British lecturer and feminist.
There's Always been a Women's Movement this Century (Dale Spender)

17 The Bible and Church have been the greatest stumbling block in the way of woman's emancipation.
Elizabeth Cady Stanton (1815–1902) US suffragette and abolitionist.
Free Thought Magazine, Sept 1896

18 The prolonged slavery of women is the darkest page in human history.
Elizabeth Stanton
History of Woman Suffrage (with Susan B. Anthony and Mathilda Gage), Vol. I

19 *Declaration of Sentiments:*...We hold these truths to be self-evident: that all men and women are created equal...
Elizabeth Stanton
History of Woman Suffrage (with Susan B. Anthony and Mathilda Gage), Vol. I

20 If we had left it to the men *toilets* would have been the greatest obstacle to human progress. *Toilets* was always the reason women couldn't become engineers, or pilots, or even members of parliament. They didn't have women's toilets.
Rebecca West (Cicely Isabel Fairfield; 1892–1983) British novelist and journalist.
There's Always been a Women's Movement this Century (Dale Spender)

21 People call me a feminist whenever I express sentiments that differentiate me from a doormat or a prostitute.
Rebecca West
Attrib.

22 Women have always been the guardians of wisdom and humanity which makes them natural, but usually secret, rulers. The time has come for them to rule openly, but together with and not against men.
Charlotte Wolff (1904–86) German-born British writer.
Bisexuality: A Study, Ch. 2

23 Women have served all these centuries as looking-glasses possessing the magic and delicious power of reflecting the figure of man at twice its natural size.
Virginia Woolf (1882–1941) British novelist.
A Room of One's Own

24 The *divine right* of husbands, like the divine right of kings, may, it is hoped, in this enlightened age, be contested without danger.
Mary Wollstonecraft 1759–97) British writer.
A Vindication of the Rights of Woman, Ch. 3

25 I do not wish them to have power over men; but over themselves.
Mary Wollstonecraft
Referring to women
A Vindication of the Rights of Woman, Ch. 4

THOSE AGAINST

26 There is a tide in the affairs of women, Which, taken at the flood, leads – God knows where.
Lord Byron (1788–1824) British poet.
Don Juan, VI

27 The First Blast of the Trumpet Against the Monstrous Regiment of Women.
John Knox (c. 1514–72) Scottish religious reformer.
Title of Pamphlet, 1558

28 Women's Liberation is just a lot of foolishness. It's the men who are discriminated against. They can't bear children. And no one's likely to do anything about that.
Golda Meir (1898–1978) Russian-born Israeli stateswoman.
Attrib.

29 The Queen is most anxious to enlist every one who can speak or write to join in checking this mad, wicked folly of 'Woman's Rights', with all its attendant horrors, on which her poor feeble sex is bent, forgetting every sense of womanly feeling and propriety.
Victoria (1819–1901) Queen of the United Kingdom.
Letter to Sir Theodore Martin, 29 May 1870

30 The thought could not be avoided that the best home for a feminist was in another person's lab.
James Dewey Watson (1928–) US geneticist.
The Double Helix, Ch. 2

...AND A FINAL WORD

31 The battle for women's rights has been largely won.
Margaret Thatcher (1925–) British politician and prime minister.
The Guardian, 1982

32 WOMEN'S RIGHTS NOW!!
Followed by
Yes Dear
Exchange of graffiti

□ FICTION □

See also books, literature, novels, writing

1 Science fiction is no more written for scientists than ghost stories are written for ghosts.
Brian Aldiss (1925–) British science-fiction writer.
Penguin Science Fiction, Introduction

2 There are many reasons why novelists write, but they all have one thing in common – a need to create an alternative world.
John Fowles (1926–) British novelist.
The Sunday Times Magazine, 2 Oct 1977

3 Casting my mind's eye over the whole of fiction, the only absolutely original creation I can think of is Don Quixote.
W. Somerset Maugham (1874–1965) British novelist.
10 Novels and Their Authors, Ch. 1

□ FIRST IMPRESSIONS □

1 First feelings are always the most natural.
Louis XIV (1638–1715) French king.
Repeated by Mme de Sévigné

2 Who ever loved, that loved not at first sight?
Christopher Marlowe (1564–93) English dramatist.
Hero and Leander, I

3 Mistrust first impulses; they are nearly always good.
Talleyrand (Charles Maurice de Talleyrand-Périgord; 1754–1838) French politician.
Sometimes attrib. to Count Montrond
Attrib.

☐ FISHING ☐

See also sport and games

1 Fly fishing may be a very pleasant amusement; but angling or float fishing I can only compare to a stick and a string, with a worm at one end and a fool at the other.
Samuel Johnson (1709–84) British lexicographer.
Attrib. in *Instructions to Young Sportsmen* (Hawker)

2 Angling is somewhat like poetry, men are to be born so.
Izaak Walton
The Compleat Angler, Ch. 1

3 Angling may be said to be so like the mathematics, that it can never be fully learnt.
Izaak Walton
The Compleat Angler, Epistle to the Reader

☐ FITZGERALD ☐
F(rancis) Scott (Key)
(1896–1940) US novelist. His first successful novel was the autobiographical *This Side of Paradise* (1920). This was followed by *The Great Gatsby* (1925) and *Tender is the Night* (1934) before he declined into alcoholism.

QUOTATIONS ABOUT FITZGERALD

1 Fitzgerald was an alcoholic, a spendthrift and a superstar playboy possessed of a beauty and a glamour that only a Byron could support without artistic ruination.
Anthony Burgess (1917–) British novelist and critic.
The Observer, 7 Feb 1982

2 The poor son-of-a-bitch!
Dorothy Parker (1893–1967) US writer.
Quoting from *The Great Gatsby* on paying her last respects to Fitzgerald.
Thalberg: Life and Legend (B. Thomas)

QUOTATIONS BY FITZGERALD

3 In the real dark night of the soul it is always three o'clock in the morning.
See ST JOHN OF THE CROSS.
The Crack-Up

4 I entertained on a cruising trip that was so much fun that I had to sink my yacht to make my guests go home.
The Crack-Up, 'Notebooks, K'

5 Beware of the artist who's an intellectual also. The artist who doesn't fit.
This Side of Paradise, Bk. II, Ch. 5

6 A big man has no time really to do anything but just sit and be big.
This Side of Paradise, Bk. III, Ch. 2

7 First you take a drink, then the drink takes a drink, then the drink takes you.
Ackroyd (Jules Feiffer), '1964, May 7'

8 All good writing is *swimming under water* and holding your breath.
Letter to Frances Scott Fitzgerald

☐ FLATTERY ☐

See also compliments, insincerity, praise, servility

1 It is happy for you that you possess the talent of flattering with delicacy. May I ask whether these pleasing attentions proceed from the impulse of the moment, or are the result of previous study?
Jane Austen (1775–1817) British novelist.
Pride and Prejudice, Ch. 14

2 Every woman is infallibly to be gained by every sort of flattery, and every man by one sort or other.
Earl of Chesterfield (1694–1773) English statesman.
Letter to his son, 16 Mar 1752

3 Be advised that all flatterers live at the expense of those who listen to them.
Jean de La Fontaine (1621–95) French poet.
Fables, I, 'Le Corbeau et le Renard'

4 Flattery is all right so long as you don't inhale.
Adlai Stevenson (1900–65) US statesman.
Attrib.

☐ FLOWERS ☐

See also gardens

1 She wore a wreath of roses,
The night that first we met.
Thomas Haynes Bayly (1797–1839) British writer.
She Wore a Wreath of Roses

2 Just now the lilac is in bloom
All before my little room.
Rupert Brooke (1887–1915) British poet.
The Old Vicarage, Grantchester

3 I sometimes think that never blows so red
The Rose as where some buried Caesar bled;
That every Hyacinth the Garden wears
Dropt in her Lap from some once lovely Head.
Edward Fitzgerald (1809–83) British poet.
The Rubáiyát of Omar Khayyám (1st edn.), XVIII

4 And I will make thee beds of roses
And a thousand fragrant posies.
Christopher Marlowe (1564–93) English dramatist.
The Passionate Shepherd to his Love

5 Gather the flowers, but spare the buds.
Andrew Marvell (1621–78) English poet.
The Picture of Little T.C. in a Prospect of Flowers

6 'Tis the last rose of summer
Left blooming alone;
All her lovely companions
Are faded and gone.
Thomas Moore (1779–1852) Irish poet.
Irish Melodies, ''Tis the Last Rose'

7 Say it with flowers.
Patrick O'Keefe (1872–1934) US advertising agent.
Slogan for Society of American Florists

8 But as we went along there were more and yet more and there at last under the boughs of the trees, we saw that there was a long belt of them along the shore, about the breadth of a country turnpike road. I never saw daffodils so beautiful they grew among the mossy stones about and about them, some rested their heads upon these stones as on pillow for weariness and the rest tossed and reeled and danced and seemed as if they verily laughed with the wind that blew upon them over the lake.
Dorothy Wordsworth (1771–1855) British diarist and sister of William Wordsworth.
The Grasmere Journals, 15 Apr 1802

9 I wandered lonely as a cloud
That floats on high o'er vales and hills,
When all at once I saw a crowd,
A host, of golden daffodils.
William Wordsworth
I Wandered Lonely as a Cloud

□ FLYING □
See also travel

1 Had I been a man I might have explored the Poles or climbed Mount Everest, but as it was my spirit found outlet in the air....
Amy Johnson (1903–41) British flyer.
Myself When Young (ed. Margot Asquith)

2 I feel about airplanes the way I feel about diets. It seems to me that they are wonderful things for other people to go on.
Jean Kerr (1923–) US dramatist.
The Snake Has All the Lines, 'Mirror, Mirror, on the Wall'

3 There are only two emotions in a plane: boredom and terror.
Orson Welles (1915–85) US film actor.
The Observer, 'Sayings of the Week', 12 May 1985

4 Nor law, nor duty bade me fight,
Nor public men, nor cheering crowds,
A lonely impulse of delight
Drove to this tumult in the clouds;
I balanced all, brought all to mind,
The years to come seemed waste of breath,

A waste of breath the years behind
In balance with this life, this death.
W. B. Yeats (1865–1939) Irish poet.
An Irish Airman Foresees his Death

□ FOOD □
See also etiquette, greed, obesity

1 I always eat peas with honey
I've done it all my life,
They do taste kind of funny,
But it keeps them on the knife.
Anonymous
Peas

2 I'm a man
More dined against than dining.
Maurice Bowra (1898–1971) British scholar.
Summoned by Bells (J. Betjeman)

3 Some hae meat, and canna eat,
And some wad eat that want it,
But we hae meat and we can eat,
And sae the Lord be thankit.
Robert Burns (1759–96) Scottish poet.
The Selkirk Grace

4 The Queen of Hearts, she made some tarts,
All on a summer day:
The Knave of Hearts, he stole those tarts,
And took them quite away!
Lewis Carroll (Charles Lutwidge Dodgson; 1832–98) British writer.
Alice's Adventures in Wonderland, Ch. 11

5 Soup of the evening, beautiful Soup!
Lewis Carroll
Said by the Mock Turtle
Alice's Adventures in Wonderland, Ch. 10

6 The right diet directs sexual energy into the parts that matter.
Barbara Cartland (1902–) British romantic novelist.
Remark, Jan 1981

7 Don't eat too many almonds; they add weight to the breasts
Colette (1873–1954) French novelist.
Gigi

8 Bouillabaisse is only good because cooked by the French, who, if they cared to try, could produce an excellent and nutritious substitute out of cigar stumps and empty matchboxes.
Norman Douglas (1868–1952) British novelist.
Siren Land, 'Rain on the Hills'

9 The way to a man's heart is through his stomach.
Fanny Fern (1811–72) US writer.
Willis Parton

10 Take your hare when it is cased...
Hannah Glasse (18th century) English writer.
Often misquoted as, 'First catch your hare'
The Art of Cookery Made Plain and Easy, Ch. 1

11 The British hamburger thus symbolised, with savage neatness, the country's failure to provide its ordinary people with food which did anything more for them than sustain life.
Clive James (1939–) Writer and broadcaster, born in Australia.
Falling Towards England, Ch.17

12 They dined on mince, and slices of quince,
Which they ate with a runcible spoon;
And hand in hand, on the edge of the sand,
They danced by the light of the moon.
Edward Lear (1812–88) British artist and writer.
The Owl and the Pussy-Cat

13 Food is an important part of a balanced diet.
Fran Lebowitz (1950–) US writer.
Metropolitan Life, 'Food for Thought and Vice Versa'

14 Many children are suffering from muesli-belt malnutrition.
Professor Vincent Marks British nutritionist.
Remark, June 1986

15 To eat well in England you should have breakfast three times a day.
W. Somerset Maugham (1874–1965) British novelist.
Attrib.

16 Kissing don't last: cookery do!
George Meredith (1828–1909) British novelist.
The Ordeal of Richard Feverel, Ch. 28

17 One should eat to live, not live to eat.
Molière (Jean Baptiste Poquelin; 1622–73) French dramatist.
L'Avare, III:2

18 Some breakfast food manufacturer hit upon the simple notion of emptying out the leavings of carthorse nosebags, adding a few other things like unconsumed portions of chicken layer's mash, and the sweepings of racing stables, packing the mixture in little bags and selling them in health food shops.
Frank Muir (1920–) British writer and broadcaster.
Upon My Word!

19 An army marches on its stomach.
Napoleon I (Napoleon Bonaparte; 1769–1821) French emperor.
Attrib.

20 The vulgar boil, the learned roast an egg.
Alexander Pope (1688–1744) British poet.
Satires and Epistles of Horace Imitated, Bk II

21 To the old saying that man built the house but woman made of it a 'home' might be added the modern supplement that woman accepted cooking as a chore but man has made of it a recreation.
Emily Post (1873–1960) US writer.
Etiquette, Ch. 34

22 Great restaurants are, of course, nothing but mouth-brothels. There is no point in going to them if one intends to keep one's belt buckled.
Frederic Raphael (1931–) British author.
The Sunday Times Magazine, 25 Sep 1977

23 Yes, cider and tinned salmon are the staple diet of the agricultural classes.
Evelyn Waugh (1903–66) British novelist.
Scoop, Bk. 1, Ch. 1

24 You breed babies and you eat chips with everything.
Arnold Wesker (1932–) British dramatist.
Chips with Everything, I:2

☐ FOOLISHNESS ☐

See also ignorance, stupidity, wisdom and foolishness

1 Give not that which is holy unto the dogs, neither cast ye your pearls before swine, lest they trample them under their feet, and turn again and rend you.
Bible: Matthew
7:6

2 Answer a fool according to his folly, lest he be wise in his own conceit.
Bible: Proverbs
26:5

3 The world is made up for the most part of fools and knaves.
Duke of Buckingham (1628–87) English politician.
To Mr Clifford, on his Humane Reason

4 The wisest fool in Christendom.
Henri IV (1553–1610) King of France.
Referring to James I of England
Attrib.

5 Mix a little foolishness with your serious plans: it's lovely to be silly at the right moment.
Horace (Quintus Horatius Flaccus; 65–8 BC) Roman poet.
Odes, IV

6 You cannot fashion a wit out of two half-wits.
Neil Kinnock (1942–) British politician.
The Times, 1983

7 Lord, what fools these mortals be!
William Shakespeare (1564–1616) English dramatist.
A Midsummer Night's Dream, III:2

☐ FOOTBALL ☐

See also sport and games

1 Professional football is no longer a game. It's a war. And it brings out the same primitive instincts that go back thousands of years.
Malcolm Allison British football manager.
The Observer, 'Sayings of the Week', 14 Mar 1973

2 I loathed the game…it was very difficult for me to show courage at it. Football, it seemed to me,

is not really played for the pleasure of kicking a ball about, but is a species of fighting.
George Orwell (Eric Blair; 1903–50) British novelist.
Such, Such Were The Joys

3 Football isn't a matter of life and death – it's much more important than that.
Bill Shankly (1914–81) British football manager.
Attrib.

4 Footeball…causeth fighting, brawling, contention, quarrel picking, murder, homicide and great effusion of bloode, as daily experience teacheth.
Philip Stubbes (fl. 1583–91) English puritan pamphleteer.
Anatomie of Abuses

□FORCE□

See also oppression, power politics, violence

1 Force is not a remedy.
John Bright (1811–89) British radical politician.
Speech, Birmingham, 16 Nov 1880

2 The use of force alone is but *temporary*. It may subdue for a moment; but it does not remove the necessity of subduing again: and a nation is not governed, which is perpetually to be conquered.
Edmund Burke (1729–97) British politician.
Speech on Conciliation with America (House of Commons, 22 Mar 1775)

□FORGIVENESS□

1 Then said Jesus, Father, forgive them; for they know not what they do. And they parted his raiment, and cast lots.
Bible: Luke
23:34

2 Then came Peter to him, and said, Lord, how oft shall my brother sin against me, and I forgive him? till seven times?
Jesus saith unto him, I say not unto thee, Until seven times: but, Until seventy times seven.
Bible: Matthew
18:21–22

3 The cut worm forgives the plough.
William Blake (1757–1827) British poet.
The Marriage of Heaven and Hell, 'Proverbs of Hell'

4 Once a woman has forgiven her man, she must not reheat his sins for breakfast.
Marlene Dietrich (Maria Magdalene von Losch; 1904–92) German-born film star.
Marlene Dietrich's ABC

5 To err is human, to forgive, divine.
Alexander Pope (1688–1744) British poet.
An Essay on Criticism

6 Beware of the man who does not return your blow: he neither forgives you nor allows you to forgive yourself.
George Bernard Shaw (1856–1950) Irish dramatist and critic.
Man and Superman, 'Maxims for Revolutionists'

7 The stupid neither forgive nor forget; the naive forgive and forget; the wise forgive but do not forget.
Thomas Szasz (1920–) US psychiatrist.
The Second Sin

□FRANCE□

See also Europe, French Revolution, Paris

1 All Gaul is divided into three parts.
Julius Caesar (100–44 BC) Roman general and statesman.
De Bello Gallico, Vol. I, Ch. 1

2 France was a long despotism tempered by epigrams.
Thomas Carlyle (1795–1881) Scottish historian and essayist.
History of the French Revolution, Pt. I, Bk. I, Ch. 1

3 The French will only be united under the threat of danger. Nobody can simply bring together a country that has 265 kinds of cheese.
Charles De Gaulle (1890–1970) French general and statesman.
Speech, 1951

4 A Frenchman must be always talking, whether he knows anything of the matter or not; an Englishman is content to say nothing, when he has nothing to say.
Samuel Johnson (1709–84) British lexicographer.
Life of Johnson (J. Boswell), Vol. IV

5 *Allons, enfants, de la patrie,*
Le jour de gloire est arrivé.
Come, children of our native land,
The day of glory has arrived.
Rouget de Lisle (Claude Joseph Rouget de Lisle; 1760–1836) French military engineer and composer.
La Marseillaise (French national anthem)

6 Yet, who can help loving the land that has taught us
Six hundred and eighty-five ways to dress eggs?
Thomas Moore (1779–1852) Irish poet.
The Fudge Family in Paris

7 A mademoiselle from Armenteers,
She hasn't been kissed for forty years,
Hinky, dinky, par-lee-voo.
Edward Rowland (20th century) British songwriter.
Armentières was completely destroyed (1918) in World War I
Mademoiselle from Armentières (song)

8 They are a loyal, a gallant, a generous, an ingenious, and good-temper'd people as is under heaven – if they have a fault, they are too *serious*.
Laurence Sterne (1713–68) Irish-born British writer.
A Sentimental Journey, 'The Character. Versailles'

9 France is a country where the money falls apart in your hands and you can't tear the toilet paper.
Billy Wilder (Samuel Wilder; 1906–) Austrian-born US film director.
Attrib.

□FRANKNESS□

See also honesty, sincerity, truth

1 But of all plagues, good Heaven, thy wrath can send,
Save me, oh, save me, from the candid friend.
George Canning (1770–1827) British statesman.
New Morality

2 The great consolation in life is to say what one thinks.
Voltaire (François-Marie Arouet; 1694–1778) French writer.
Letter, 1765

□FREEDOM□

See also human rights, imprisonment

1 So free we seem, so fettered fast we are!
Robert Browning (1812–89) British poet.
Andrea del Sarto

2 Liberty, too, must be limited in order to be possessed.
Edmund Burke (1729–97) British politician.
Letter to the Sheriffs of Bristol, 1777

3 England may as well dam up the waters from the Nile with bulrushes as to fetter the step of Freedom, more proud and firm in this youthful land.
Lydia M. Child (1802–80) US abolitionist campaigner.
The Rebels, Ch. 4

4 But what is Freedom? Rightly understood,
A universal licence to be good.
Hartley Coleridge (1796–1849) British poet.
Liberty

5 The condition upon which God hath given liberty to man is eternal vigilance.
John Philpot Curran (1750–1817) Irish judge.
Speech on the Right of Election of Lord Mayor of Dublin, 10 July 1790

6 Yes, 'n' how many years can some people exist
Before they're allowed to be free?
Yes, 'n' how many times can a man turn his head,
Pretending he just doesn't see?
The answer, my friend, is blowin' in the wind.
Bob Dylan (Robert Allen Zimmerman; 1941–) US popular singer.
Blowin' in the Wind

7 *Laissez faire, laissez passer.*
Liberty of action, liberty of movement.
Jean Claude Vincent de Gournay (1712–59) French economist.
Speech, Sept 1758

8 The love of liberty is the love of others; the love of power is the love of ourselves.
William Hazlitt (1778–1830) British essayist.
The Times, 1819

9 I know not what course others may take; but as for me, give me liberty or give me death.
Patrick Henry (1736–99) US statesman.
Speech, Virginia Convention, 23 Mar 1775

10 *Nullius addictus iurare in verba magistri,*
Quo me cumque rapit tempestas, deferor hospes.
Not bound to swear allegiance to any master,
wherever the wind takes me I travel as a visitor.
Horace (Quintus Horatius Flaccus; 65–8 BC) Roman poet.
Nullius in verba is the motto of the Royal Society
Epistles, I

11 The tree of liberty must be refreshed from time to time with the blood of patriots and tyrants. It is its natural manure.
Thomas Jefferson (1743–1826) US statesman.
Letter to W. S. Smith, 13 Nov 1787

12 I have got no further than this: Every man has a right to utter what he thinks truth, and every other man has a right to knock him down for it. Martyrdom is the test.
Samuel Johnson (1709–84) British lexicographer.
Life of Johnson (J. Boswell), Vol. IV

13 The Liberty of the press is the *Palladium* of all the civil, political and religious rights of an Englishman.
Junius An unidentified writer of letters (1769–72) to the *London Public Advertiser*.
Letters, 'Dedication'

14 It is true that liberty is precious – so precious that it must be rationed.
Lenin (Vladimir Ilich Ulyanov; 1870–1924) Russian revolutionary leader.
Attrib.

15 Those who deny freedom to others, deserve it not for themselves.
Abraham Lincoln (1809–65) US statesman.
Speech, 19 May 1856

16 Many politicians of our time are in the habit of laying it down as a self-evident proposition, that no people ought to be free till they are fit to use their freedom. The maxim is worthy of the fool in the old story, who resolved not to go into the water till he had learnt to swim. If men are to wait for liberty till they become wise and good in slavery, they may indeed wait for ever.
Lord Macaulay (1800–59) British historian.
Literary Essays Contributed to the 'Edinburgh Review', 'Milton',

17 The liberty of the individual must be thus far limited; he must not make himself a nuisance to other people.
John Stuart Mill (1806–73) British philosopher.
On Liberty, Ch. 3

18 None can love freedom heartily, but good men;
the rest love not freedom, but licence.
John Milton (1608–74) English poet.
Tenure of Kings and Magistrates

19 Liberty is the right to do everything which the
laws allow.
Baron de Montesquieu (1689–1755) French writer.
L'Esprit des lois

20 My government will protect all liberties but one
– the liberty to do away with other liberties.
Gustavo Diaz Ordaz (1911–) President of Mexico
(1964–1970).
Inaugural speech

21 *Laissez faire, laissez passer.*
Let it be, let it pass.
François Quesnay (1694–1774) French economist.
Attrib.

22 '*O liberté! O liberté! Que de crimes on commet en
ton nom!*'
Oh liberty! Oh liberty! What crimes are commit-
ted in thy name!
Madame Roland (1754–93) French revolutionary.
Said as she mounted the steps of the guillotine at her execution
Attrib.

23 Man was born free and everywhere he is in
chains.
Jean Jacques Rousseau (1712–78) French philosopher.
Du contrat social, Ch. 1

24 No human being, however great, or powerful,
was ever so free as a fish.
John Ruskin (1819–1900) British art critic and writer.
The Two Paths, Lecture V

25 Man is condemned to be free.
Jean-Paul Sartre (1905–80) French writer.
Existentialism is a Humanism

26 You took my freedom away a long time ago and
you can't give it back because you haven't got it
yourself.
Alexander Solzhenitsyn (1918–) Soviet novelist.
The First Circle, Ch. 17

27 It is by the goodness of God that in our country
we have those three unspeakably precious
things: freedom of speech, freedom of conscience, and the prudence never to practise
either of them.
Mark Twain (Samuel Langhorne Clemens; 1835–1910) US
writer.
Following the Equator, heading of Ch. 20

28 I disapprove of what you say, but I will defend to
the death your right to say it.
Voltaire (François-Marie Arouet; 1694–1778) French writer.
Attrib.

29 Two voices are there; one is of the sea,
One of the mountains; each a mighty voice:

In both from age to age thou didst rejoice,
They were thy chosen music, Liberty!
William Wordsworth (1770–1850) British poet.
Sonnets, 'Two voices are there'

☐ FRENCH REVOLUTION ☐

See also France, revolution

1 It was the best of times, it was the worst of times,
it was the age of wisdom, it was the age of foolishness, it was the epoch of belief, it was the epoch
of incredulity, it was the season of Light, it was
the season of Darkness, it was the spring of hope,
it was the winter of despair, we had everything
before us, we had nothing before us, we were all
going direct to Heaven, we were all going direct
the other way.
Charles Dickens (1812–70) British novelist.
The opening words of the book
A Tale of Two Cities, Bk. I, Ch. 1

2 How much the greatest event it is that ever hap-
pened in the world! and how much the best!
Charles James Fox (1749–1806) British Whig politician.
Referring to the fall of the Bastille, 14 July 1789
Letter to Fitzpatrick, 30 July 1789

3 Bliss was it in that dawn to be alive,
But to be young was very heaven!
William Wordsworth (1770–1850) British poet.
The Prelude, XI

☐ FRIENDS ☐

See also enemies, friendship

1 Forsake not an old friend; for the new is not com-
parable to him: a new friend is as new wine; when
it is old, thou shalt drink it with pleasure.
Bible: Ecclesiasticus
9:10

2 Cost his enemies a long repentance,
And made him a good friend, but bad acquaint-
ance.
Lord Byron (1788–1824) British poet.
Don Juan, III

3 Tell me what company thou keepest, and I'll tell
thee what thou art.
Miguel de Cervantes (1547–1616) Spanish novelist.
Don Quixote, Pt. II, Ch. 23

4 Have no friends not equal to yourself.
Confucius (K'ung Fu-tzu; 551–479 BC) Chinese philosopher.
Analects

5 Fate chooses your relations, you choose your
friends.
Jacques Delille (1738–1813) French abbé and poet.
Malheur et pitié, I

6 A Friend may well be reckoned the masterpiece
of Nature.
Ralph Waldo Emerson (1803–82) US poet and essayist.
Essays, 'Friendship'

7 I get by with a little help from my friends.
John Lennon (1940–80) British rock musician.
With a Little Help from My Friends (with Paul McCartney)

8 It is more shameful to distrust one's friends than to be deceived by them.
Duc de la Rochefoucauld (1613–80) French writer.
Maximes, 84

9 A friend should bear his friend's infirmities,
But Brutus makes mine greater than they are.
William Shakespeare (1564–1616) English dramatist.
Julius Caesar, IV:3

10 Associate yourself with men of good quality if you esteem your own reputation; for 'tis better to be alone than in bad company.
George Washington (1732–99) US statesman.
Rules of Civility

☐FRIENDSHIP☐

See also friends, love and friendship

1 Two are better than one; because they have a good reward for their labour.
For if they fall, the one will lift up his fellow: but woe to him that is alone when he falleth; for he hath not another to help him up.
Bible: Ecclesiastes
4:9–10

2 I've noticed your hostility towards him…I ought to have guessed you were friends.
Malcolm Bradbury (1932–) British academic and novelist.
The History Man, Ch. 7

3 Should auld acquaintance be forgot,
And never brought to min'?
Robert Burns (1759–96) Scottish poet.
Auld Lang Syne

4 We'll tak a cup o' kindness yet,
For auld lang syne.
Robert Burns
Auld Lang Syne

5 Two may talk together under the same roof for many years, yet never really meet; and two others at first speech are old friends.
Mary Catherwood (1847–1901) US writer.
Mackinac and Lake Stories, 'Marianson'

6 It is not so much our friends' help that helps us as the confident knowledge that they will help us.
Epicurus (341–270 BC) Greek philosopher.

7 These are called the pious frauds of friendship.
Henry Fielding (1707–54) British novelist.
Amelia, Bk. III, Ch. 4

8 Always, Sir, set a high value on spontaneous kindness. He whose inclination prompts him to cultivate your friendship of his own accord, will love

you more than one whom you have been at pains to attach to you.
Samuel Johnson (1709–84) British lexicographer.
Life of Johnson (J. Boswell), Vol. IV

9 Friendship is unnecessary, like philosophy, like art.… It has no survival value; rather it is one of those things that give value to survival.
C. S. Lewis (1898–1963) British academic and writer.
The Four Loves, Friendship

10 A true bond of friendship is usually only possible between people of roughly equal status. This equality is demonstrated in many indirect ways, but it is reinforced in face-to-face encounters by a matching of the posture of relaxation or alertness.
Desmond Morris (1928–) British biologist.
Manwatching, 'Postural Echo'

11 To like and dislike the same things, that is indeed true friendship.
Sallust (Gaius Sallustius Crispus; c. 86–c. 34 BC) Roman historian and politician.
Bellum Catilinae

☐FUNERALS☐

See also death

1 Most of the people who will walk after me will be children, so make the beat keep time with short steps.
Hans Christian Andersen (1805–75) Danish writer.
Planning the music for his funeral
Hans Christian Andersen (R. Godden)

2 When we attend the funerals of our friends we grieve for them, but when we go to those of other people it is chiefly our own deaths that we mourn for.
Gerald Brenan (Edward Fitzgerald Brenan; 1894–1987) British writer.
Thoughts in a Dry Season, 'Death'

3 'If you don't go to other men's funerals,' he told Father stiffly, 'they won't go to yours.'
Clarence Shepard Day (1874–1935) US writer.
Life With Father, 'Father plans'

4 Not a drum was heard, not a funeral note,
As his corse to the rampart we hurried.
Charles Wolfe (1791–1823) Irish poet.
The Burial of Sir John Moore at Corunna, I

☐FUTURE☐

See also past, present, promises, prophecy, time

1 Years hence, perhaps, may dawn an age,
More fortunate, alas! than we,
Which without hardness will be sage,
And gay without frivolity.
Matthew Arnold (1822–88) British poet and critic.
The Grande Chartreuse

2 I have a vision of the future, chum.
The workers' flats in fields of soya beans
Tower up like silver pencils.
John Betjeman (1906–84) British poet.

3 Boast not thyself of tomorrow; for thou knowest
not what a day may bring forth.
Bible: Proverbs
27:1

4 *Future*, n That period of time in which our affairs
prosper, our friends are true and our happiness is
assured.
Ambrose Bierce (1842–?1914) US writer and journalist.
The Devil's Dictionary

5 I never think of the future. It comes soon enough.
Albert Einstein (1879–1955) German-born US physicist.
Interview, 1930

6 I have seen the future and it works.
Lincoln Steffens (1866–1936) US journalist.
Speaking to Bernard Baruch after visitng the Soviet Union, 1919
Autobiography, Ch. 18

7 The future is made of the same stuff as the
present.
Simone Weil (1909–43) French philosopher.
On Science, Necessity, and the Love of God (ed. Richard Rees),
'Some Thoughts on the Love of God'

G

□ GARDENS □

See also flowers

1 Mary, Mary, quite contrary,
How does your garden grow?
With silver bells and cockle shells,
And pretty maids all in a row.
Anonymous
Tommy Thumb's Pretty Song Book

2 God Almighty first planted a garden. And indeed
it is the purest of human pleasures.
Francis Bacon (1561–1626) English philosopher.
Essays, 'Of Gardens'

3 But there went up a mist from the earth, and
watered the whole face of the ground.
And the Lord God formed man of the dust of the
ground, and breathed into his nostrils the breath
of life; and man became a living soul.
And the Lord God planted a garden eastward in
Eden; and there he put the man whom he had
formed.
And out of the ground made the Lord God to
grow every tree that is pleasant to the sight, and
good for food; the tree of life also in the midst of
the garden, and the tree of knowledge of good
and evil.
And a river went out of Eden to water the garden.
Bible: Genesis
2:6–10

4 A garden is a lovesome thing, God wot!
Thomas Edward Brown (1830–97) British poet.
My Garden

5 To get the best results you must talk to your veg-
etables.
Charles, Prince of Wales (1948–) Eldest son of Elizabeth
II.
The Observer, 'Sayings of the Week', 28 Sept 1986

6 God the first garden made, and the first city Cain.
Abraham Cowley (1618–67) English poet.
The Garden

□ GENERALIZATIONS □

See also classification

1 To generalize is to be an idiot.
William Blake (1757–1827) British poet.
Life of Blake (Gilchrist)

2 All generalizations are dangerous, even this one.
Alexandre Dumas, fils (1824–95) French writer.
Attrib.

3 Any general statement is like a cheque drawn on
a bank. Its value depends on what is there to
meet it.
Ezra Pound (1885–1972) US poet.
ABC of Reading, Ch. 2

□ GENEROSITY □

See also charity, gifts, kindness, parasites

1 Every man according as he purposeth in his
heart, so let him give; not grudgingly, or of necessity: for God loveth a cheerful giver.
Bible: II Corinthians
9:7

2 Heal the sick, cleanse the lepers, raise the dead,
cast out devils: freely ye have received, freely
give.
Bible: Matthew
10:8

3 Experience was to be taken as showing that one
might get a five-pound note as one got a light for
a cigarette; but one had to check the friendly
impulse to ask for it in the same way.
Henry James (1843–1916) US novelist.
The Awkward Age

□ GENIUS □

See also talent, talent and genius

1 Genius is one per cent inspiration and ninety-
nine per cent perspiration.
Thomas Edison (1847–1931) US inventor.
Attrib.

2 True genius walks along a line, and, perhaps, our
greatest pleasure is in seeing it so often near falling, without being ever actually down.
Oliver Goldsmith (1728–74) Irish-born British writer.
The Bee, 'The Characteristics of Greatness'

3 The true genius is a mind of large general powers, accidentally determined to some particular
direction.
Samuel Johnson (1709–84) British lexicographer.
Lives of the English Poets, 'Cowley'

4 When a true genius appears in the world, you
may know him by this sign, that the dunces are
all in confederacy against him.
Jonathan Swift (1667–1745) Irish-born Anglican priest and
writer.
Thoughts on Various Subjects

□ GERMANY □

See also Europe, Hitler, Nazism, World War II

1 *Deutschland, Deutschland über alles.*
Germany, Germany before all else.
Heinrich Hoffmann von Fallersleben (1798–1876)
German poet.
German national anthem

2 Germany will be either a world power or will not
be at all.
Adolf Hitler (1889–1945) German dictator.
Mein Kampf, Ch. 14

3 Only peace will emanate from German soil in future.
Helmut Kohl (1930–) German statesman; chancellor of Germany (1990–).
Following the unification of Germany
The Daily Telegraph, 29 Dec 1990

4 America…is the prize amateur nation of the world. Germany is the prize professional nation.
Woodrow Wilson (1856–1925) US statesman.
Speech, Aug 1917
Mr Wilson's War (John Dos Passos), Pt. III, Ch. 13

□ GIBBON □
Edward
(1737–94) British historian whose monumental *The History of the Decline and Fall of the Roman Empire* (1776–88) caused considerable controversy for its treatment of Christianity.

QUOTATIONS ABOUT GIBBON

1 Gibbon is an ugly, affected, disgusting fellow, and poisons our literary club for me. I class him among infidel wasps and venomous insects.
James Boswell (1740–95) Scottish lawyer and writer.
Diary, 1779

QUOTATIONS BY GIBBON

2 To the University of Oxford I acknowledge no obligation; and she will as cheerfully renounce me for a son, as I am willing to disclaim her for a mother. I spent fourteen months at Magdalen College: they proved the fourteen months the most idle and unprofitable of my whole life.
Autobiography

3 The romance of *Tom Jones*, that exquisite picture of human manners, will outlive the palace of the Escurial and the imperial eagle of the house of Austria.
Autobiography

4 The various modes of worship, which prevailed in the Roman world, were all considered by the people as equally true; by the philosopher, as equally false; and by the magistrate, as equally useful. And thus toleration produced not only mutual indulgence, but even religious concord.
Decline and Fall of the Roman Empire, Ch. 2

5 Corruption, the most infallible symptom of constitutional liberty.
Decline and Fall of the Roman Empire, Ch. 21

6 All that is human must retrograde if it does not advance.
Decline and Fall of the Roman Empire, Ch. 71

□ GIFTS □
See also generosity, materialism

1 Every good gift and every perfect gift is from above, and cometh down from the Father of lights, with whom is no variableness, neither shadow of turning.
Bible: James
1:17

2 Heal the sick, cleanse the lepers, raise the dead, cast out devils: freely ye have received, freely give.
Bible: Matthew
10:8

3 The manner of giving is worth more than the gift.
Pierre Corneille (1606–84) French dramatist.
Le Menteur, I:1

□ GILBERT □
Sir William Schwenk
(1836–1911) British dramatist and comic writer. His comic verse published as *Bab Ballads* (1896) preceded his libretti for 14 comic operas written for Arthur Sullivan's music.

1 I always voted at my party's call,
And I never thought of thinking for myself at all.
HMS Pinafore, I

2 Stick close to your desks and never go to sea,
And you all may be Rulers of the Queen's Navee!
HMS Pinafore, I

3 I see no objection to stoutness, in moderation.
Iolanthe, I

4 I often think it's comical
How Nature always does contrive
That every boy and every gal
That's born into the world alive
Is either a little Liberal
Or else a little Conservative!
Iolanthe, II

5 The House of Peers, throughout the war,
Did nothing in particular,
And did it very well.
Iolanthe, II

6 I am the very model of a modern Major-General,
I've information vegetable, animal and mineral,
I know the kings of England, and I quote the fights historical,
From Marathon to Waterloo, in order categorical.
The Pirates of Penzance, I

7 When constabulary duty's to be done –
A policeman's lot is not a happy one.
The Pirates of Penzance, II

8 He combines the manners of a Marquis with the morals of a Methodist.
Ruddigore, I

9 Sir, I view the proposal to hold an international exhibition at San Francisco with an equanimity bordering on indifference.
Gilbert, His Life and Strife (Hesketh Pearson)

10 My dear chap! Good isn't the word!
Speaking to an actor after he had given a poor performance.
Attrib.

☐ GLORY ☐

1 May God deny you peace but give you glory!
Miguel de Unamuno y Jugo (1864–1936) Spanish writer.
Closing words
The Tragic Sense of Life

2 *Sic transit gloria mundi.*
Thus the glory of the world passes away.
Thomas à Kempis (Thomas Hemmerken; c. 1380–1471)
German monk.
The Imitation of Christ, I

☐ GOD ☐

See also atheism, creation, faith, prayer, religion

1 God be in my head,
And in my understanding;
God be in my eyes,
And in my looking;
God be in my mouth,
And in my speaking;
God be in my heart,
And in my thinking;
God be at my end,
And at my departing.
Anonymous
Sarum Missal

2 Every man thinks God is on his side. The rich
and powerful know that he is.
Jean Anouilh (1910–87) French dramatist.
The Lark

3 It were better to have no opinion of God at all,
than such an opinion as is unworthy of him.
Francis Bacon (1561–1626) English philosopher.
Essays, 'Of Superstition'

4 Then Peter opened his mouth, and said, Of a
truth I perceive that God is no respecter of
persons.
Bible: Acts
10:34

5 Be strong and of a good courage, fear not, nor be
afraid of them: for the Lord thy God, he it is that
doth go with thee; he will not fail thee, nor forsake thee.
Bible: Deuteronomy
31:6

6 I am the Lord thy God, which have brought thee
out of the land of Egypt, out of the house of bondage.
Thou shalt have no other gods before me.
Thou shalt not make unto thee any graven
image, or any likeness of any thing that is in
heaven above, or that is in the earth beneath, or
that is in the water under the earth:

Thou shalt not bow down thyself to them, nor
serve them: for Lord thy God am a jealous God,
visiting the iniquity of the fathers upon the children unto the third and fourth generation of
them that hate me;
And shewing mercy unto thousands of them that
love me, and keep my commandments.
Thou shalt not take the name of the Lord thy God
in vain; for the Lord will not hold him guiltless
that taketh his name in vain.
Remember the sabbath day, to keep it holy.
Six days shalt thou labour, and do all thy work:
But the seventh day is the sabbath of the Lord
thy God: in it thou shalt not do any work, thou,
nor thy son, nor thy daughter, thy manservant,
nor thy maidservant, nor thy cattle, nor thy
stranger that is within thy gates:
For in six days the Lord made heaven and earth,
the sea, and all that in them is, and rested the seventh day: wherefore the Lord blessed the sabbath day, and hallowed it.
Honour thy father and thy mother: that thy days
may be long upon the land which the Lord thy
God giveth thee.
Thou shalt not kill.
Thou shalt not commit adultery.
Thou shalt not steal.
Thou shalt not bear false witness against thy
neighbour.
Thou shalt not covet thy neighbour's house, thou
shalt not covet thy neighbour's wife, nor his manservant, nor his maidservant, nor his ox, nor his
ass, nor any thing that is thy neighbour's.
Bible: Exodus
20:2–17

7 And he said, Thou canst not see my face: for
there shall no man see me, and live.
Bible: Exodus
33:20

8 For the kingdom of God is not in word, but in
power.
Bible: I Corinthians
4:20

9 Man has learned to cope with all questions of
importance without recourse to God as a working hypothesis.
Dietrich Bonhoeffer (1906–45) German theologian.
Letters and Papers from Prison, 8 June 1944

10 A God who let us prove his existence would be an
idol.
Dietrich Bonhoeffer
No Rusty Swords

11 God's gifts put man's best gifts to shame.
Elizabeth Barrett Browning (1806–61) British poet.
Sonnets from the Portuguese, XXVI

12 Thou shalt have one God only; who
Would be at the expense of two?
Arthur Hugh Clough (1819–61) British poet.
The Latest Decalogue, 1

13 God moves in a mysterious way
His wonders to perform;
He plants his footsteps in the sea,
And rides upon the storm.
William Cowper (1731–1800) British poet.
Olney Hymns, 35

14 It is the final proof of God's omnipotence that he
need not exist in order to save us.
Peter De Vries (1910–   ) US novelist.
The Mackerel Plaza, Ch. 2

15 What sort of God are we portraying and believing in if we insist on what I will nickname 'the
divine laser beam' type of miracle as the heart
and basis of the Incarnation and Resurrection?
Bishop of Durham (1925–   ) British churchman.
Speech, July 1986

16 God is subtle but he is not malicious.
Albert Einstein (1879–1955) German-born US physicist.
Inscribed over the fireplace in the Mathematical Institute,
Princeton. It refers to Einstein's objection to the quantum theory
Albert Einstein (Carl Seelig), Ch. 8

17 At bottom God is nothing more than an exalted
father.
Sigmund Freud (1856–1939) Austrian psychoanalyst.
Totem and Taboo

18 O worship the King, all glorious above!
O gratefully sing his power and his love!
Our Shield and Defender – the Ancient of Days,
Pavilioned in splendour, and girded with praise.
Robert Grant (1779–1838) British hymn writer.
Hymn

19 Holy, holy, holy, Lord God Almighty!
Early in the morning our song shall rise to thee.
Reginald Heber (1783–1826) British bishop and hymn writer.
Holy, Holy, Holy

20 The world is charged with the grandeur of God.
Gerard Manley Hopkins (1844–99) British Jesuit and poet.
God's Grandeur

21 Mine eyes have seen the glory of the coming of
the Lord:
He is trampling out the vintage where the grapes
of wrath are stored.
Julia Ward Howe (1819–1910) US writer.
Battle Hymn of the American Republic

22 An honest God is the noblest work of man.
Robert G. Ingersoll (1833–99) US lawyer and agnostic.
Gods

23 A man with God is always in the majority.
John Knox (c. 1514–72) Scottish religious reformer.
Inscription, Reformation Monument, Geneva, Switzerland

24 What God does, He does well.
Jean de La Fontaine (1621–95) French poet.
Fables, IX, 'Le Gland et la Citrouille'

25 God is the immemorial refuge of the incompetent, the helpless, the miserable. They find not
only sanctuary in His arms, but also a kind of
superiority, soothing to their macerated egos; He
will set them above their betters.
H. L. Mencken (1880–1956) US journalist.
Notebooks, 'Minority Report'

26 Let us with a gladsome mind
Praise the Lord, for he is kind,
For his mercies ay endure,
Ever faithful, ever sure.
John Milton (1608–74) English poet.
Psalm

27 One on God's side is a majority.
Wendell Phillips (1811–84) US reformer.
Speech, Brooklyn, 1 Nov 1859

28 God is really only another artist. He invented the
giraffe, the elephant, and the cat. He has no real
style, He just goes on trying other things.
Pablo Picasso (1881–1973) Spanish painter.
Life with Picasso Ch. 1 (Françoise Gilot and Carlton Lake),

29 Write down that they hope they serve God; and
write God first; for God defend but God should
go before such villains!
William Shakespeare (1564–1616) English dramatist.
Much Ado About Nothing, IV:2

30 In the days of my youth I remembered my God!
And He hath not forgotten my age.
Robert Southey (1774–1843) British poet.
The Old Man's Comforts, and how he Gained them

31 Yet her conception of God was certainly not
orthodox. She felt towards Him as she might
have felt towards a glorified sanitary engineer;
and in some of her speculations she seems
hardly to distinguish between the Deity and the
Drains.
Lytton Strachey (1880–1932) British writer.
Eminent Victorians, 'Florence Nightingale'

32 It is a mistake to assume that God is interested
only, or even chiefly, in religion.
William Temple (1881–1944) British churchman.
Attrib.

33 If God did not exist, it would be necessary to
invent Him.
Voltaire (François-Marie Arouet; 1694–1778) French writer.
Épîtres, 'À l'auteur du livre des trois Imposteurs'

34 If God made us in His image, we have certainly
returned the compliment.
Voltaire
Le Sottisier

□**GOLDSMITH**□
Oliver

(1728–74) Irish-born British writer, dramatist, and poet. He is remembered for his novel *The Vicar of Wakefield* (1776) and the play *She Stoops to Conquer* (1773) in addition to a considerable amount of verse.

QUOTATIONS ABOUT GOLDSMITH

1 No man was more foolish when he had not a pen in his hand, or more wise when he had.
Samuel Johnson (1709–84) British lexicographer.
The Life of Johnson (J. Boswell)

2 An inspired idiot.
Horace Walpole (1717–97) British writer.
Attrib.

QUOTATIONS BY GOLDSMITH

3 True genius walks along a line, and, perhaps, our greatest pleasure is in seeing it so often near falling, without being ever actually down.
The Bee, 'The Characteristics of Greatness'

4 As writers become more numerous, it is natural for readers to become more indolent.
The Bee, 'Upon Unfortunate Merit'

5 Ill fares the land, to hast'ning ills a prey,
Where wealth accumulates, and men decay;
Princes and lords may flourish, or may fade;
A breath can make them, as a breath has made;
But a bold peasantry, their country's pride,
When once destroy'd, can never be supplied.
The Deserted Village

6 The doctor found, when she was dead,
Her last disorder mortal.
Elegy on Mrs. Mary Blaize

7 The dog, to gain some private ends,
Went mad and bit the man.
Elegy on the Death of a Mad Dog

8 The man recovered of the bite,
The dog it was that died.
Elegy on the Death of a Mad Dog

9 The true use of speech is not so much to express our wants as to conceal them.
Essays, 'The Use of Language'

10 Friendship is a disinterested commerce between equals; love, an abject intercourse between tyrants and slaves.
The Good-Natured Man, I

11 Let schoolmasters puzzle their brain,
With grammar, and nonsense, and learning,
Good liquor, I stoutly maintain,
Gives genius a better discerning.
She Stoops to Conquer, I

12 Laws grind the poor, and rich men rule the law.
The Traveller

13 Conscience is a coward, and those faults it has not strength enough to prevent it seldom has justice enough to accuse.
The Vicar of Wakefield, Ch. 13

□**GOLDWYNISMS**□

Sayings attributed to Samuel Goldwyn (Samuel Goldfish; 1882–1974), the Polish-born US film producer. Most are apocryphal. *See also* cinema, mixed metaphors

QUOTATIONS ABOUT GOLDWYN

1 You always knew where you were with Goldwyn – nowhere.
F. Scott Fitzgerald (1896–1940) US novelist.
Some Sort of Epic Grandeur

2 The trouble, Mr. Goldwyn, is that you are only interested in art and I am only interested in money.
George Bernard Shaw (1856–1950) Irish dramatist and critic.
Turning down Goldwyn's offer to buy the screen rights of his plays.
The Movie Moguls (Philip French), Ch. 4

QUOTATIONS BY GOLDWYN

3 Let's have some new clichés.
The Observer, 'Sayings of the Week', 24 Oct 1948

4 Too caustic? To hell with cost; we'll make the picture anyway.

5 We're overpaying him but he's worth it.

6 What we want is a story that starts with an earthquake and works its way up to a climax.

7 I am willing to admit that I may not always be right, but I am never wrong.

8 I don't care if it doesn't make a nickel, I just want every man, woman, and child in America to see it!
Referring to his film *The Best Years of Our Lives*.

9 A wide screen just makes a bad film twice as bad.

10 For years I have been known for saying 'Include me out'; but today I am giving it up for ever.
Address, Balliol College, Oxford, 1 Mar 1945

11 In two words: im - possible.
Attrib.

12 Anybody who goes to see a psychiatrist ought to have his head examined.

13 Every director bites the hand that lays the golden egg.

14 I'll give you a definite maybe.

15 A verbal contract isn't worth the paper it's written on.

16 You ought to take the bull between the teeth.

17 We have all passed a lot of water since then.

18 I read part of it all the way through.

19 If Roosevelt were alive he'd turn in his grave.

20 It's more than magnificent – it's mediocre.

21 'Why only twelve?' 'That's the original number.' 'Well, go out and get thousands.'
Referring to the number of disciples while filming a scene for *The Last Supper.*

22 Yes, I'm going to have a bust made of them.
Replying to an admiring comment about his wife's hands.

23 Tell me, how did you love my picture?

24 The trouble with this business is the dearth of bad pictures.

25 Why should people go out and pay money to see bad films when they can stay at home and see bad television for nothing?

OTHER EXAMPLES

Not all Goldwynisms were said by Goldwyn. Here is a selection of remarks that could have been by him, but were, in fact, said by others.

26 The Jews and Arabs should sit down and settle their differences like good Christians.
Warren Austin (1877–1962) US politician and diplomat.
Attrib.

27 All my shows are great. Some of them are bad. But they are all great.
Lew Grade (Lewis Winogradsky; 1906–   ) British film and TV producer.
The Observer, 'Sayings of the Week', 14 Sept 1975

28 What about it? Do you want to crucify the boy?
Lew Grade
Referring to the revelation that an actor portraying Christ on television was living with a woman to whom he was not married.
Attrib.

29 Once you're dead, you're made for life.
Jimi Hendrix (1942–70) US rock musician.
Attrib.

30 We have to believe in free will. We've got no choice.
Isaac Bashevis Singer (1904–91) Polish-born US writer.
The Times, 21 June 1982

☐ **GOLF** ☐

See also sport and games

1 It's not in support of cricket but as an earnest protest against golf.
Max Beerbohm (1872–1956) British writer.
Said when giving a shilling towards W. G. Grace's testimonial
Carr's Dictionary of Extraordinary English Cricketers

2 Golf may be played on Sunday, not being a game within the view of the law, but being a form of moral effort.
Stephen Leacock (1869–1944) English-born Canadian economist and humorist.
Other Fancies, 'Why I refuse to play Golf'

☐ **GOOD** ☐

See also good and evil, righteousness, virtue

1 *Summum bonum.*
The greatest good.
Cicero (106–43 BC) Roman orator and statesman.
De Officiis, I

2 Goodness does not more certainly make men happy than happiness makes them good.
Walter Savage Landor (1775–1864) British poet and writer.
Imaginary Conversations, 'Lord Brooke and Sir Philip Sidney'

3 Abashed the devil stood,
And felt how awful goodness is.
John Milton (1608–74) English poet.
Paradise Lost, Bk. IV

4 The good is the beautiful.
Plato (429–347 BC) Greek philosopher.
Lysis

5 Do good by stealth, and blush to find it fame.
Alexander Pope (1688–1744) British poet.
Epilogue to the Satires, Dialogue I

6 How far that little candle throws his beams!
So shines a good deed in a naughty world.
William Shakespeare (1564–1616) English dramatist.
The Merchant of Venice, V:1

7 Nothing can harm a good man, either in life or after death.
Socrates (469–399 BC) Athenian philosopher.
Apology (Plato)

8 – My goodness those diamonds are lovely!
Goodness had nothing whatever to do with it.
Mae West (1892–1980) US actress.
Used in 1959 as the title of the first volume of her autobiography
Diamond Lil, film 1932

☐GOOD AND EVIL☐

See also evil, good, virtue and vice

1 There is so much good in the worst of us,
And so much bad in the best of us,
That it hardly becomes any of us
To talk about the rest of us.
Anonymous
Good and Bad

2 The good die early, and the bad die late.
Daniel Defoe (1660–1731) British journalist and writer.
Character of the late Dr. Annesley

3 The web of our life is of a mingled yarn, good and
ill together.
William Shakespeare (1564–1616) English dramatist.
All's Well that Ends Well, IV:3

☐GOSSIP☐

See also secrecy

1 No one gossips about other people's secret vir-
tues.
Bertrand Russell (1872–1970) British philosopher.
On Education

2 I remember that a wise friend of mine did usually
say, 'that which is everybody's business is
nobody's business'.
Izaak Walton (1593–1683) English writer.
The Compleat Angler, Ch. 2

☐GOVERNMENT☐

*See also democracy, Houses of Parliament, monarchy, opposi-
tion, politicians, politics*

1 The danger is not that a particular class is unfit to
govern. Every class is unfit to govern.
Lord Acton (1834–1902) British historian.
Letter to Mary Gladstone, 1881

2 Where some people are very wealthy and others
have nothing, the result will be either extreme
democracy or absolute oligarchy, or despotism
will come from either of those excesses.
Aristotle (384–322 BC) Greek philosopher.
Politics, Bk. IV

3 The object of government in peace and in war is
not the glory of rulers or of races, but the happiness of the common man.
Lord Beveridge (1879–1963) British economist.
Social Insurance

4 Too bad all the people who know how to run the
country are busy driving cabs and cutting hair.
George Burns (1896–) US comedian.

5 A small acquaintance with history shows that all
Governments are selfish and the French Govern-
ments more selfish than most.
David Eccles (1904–) British politician.
The Observer, 'Sayings of the Year', 29 Dec 1962

6 The principles of a free constitution are irrecoverably lost, when the legislative power is nominated by the executive.
Edward Gibbon (1737–94) British historian.
Decline and Fall of the Roman Empire, Ch. 3

7 A government that is big enough to give you all
you want is big enough to take it all away.
Barry Goldwater (1909–) US politician.
Bachman's Book of Freedom Quotations (M. Ivens and
R. Dunstan)

8 They that are discontented under *monarchy*, call
it *tyranny*; and they that are displeased with *aristocracy*, call it *oligarchy*: so also, they which find
themselves grieved under a *democracy*, call it
anarchy, which signifies the want of government;
and yet I think no man believes, that want of government, is any new kind of government.
Thomas Hobbes (1588–1679) English philosopher.
Leviathan, Pt. II, Ch. 19

9 Every country has the government it deserves.
Joseph de Maistre (1753–1821) French monarchist.
Lettres et Opuscules Inédits, 15 Aug 1811

10 The worst government is the most moral. One
composed of cynics is often very tolerant and
human. But when fanatics are on top there is no
limit to oppression.
H. L. Mencken (1880–1956) US journalist.
Notebooks, 'Minority Report'

11 Government, even in its best state, is but a neces-
sary evil; in its worst state, an intolerable one.
Thomas Paine (1737–1809) British writer.
Common Sense, Ch. 1

12 Parliament is the longest running farce in the
West End.
Cyril Smith (1928–) British Liberal politician.
The Times, 23 Sept 1977

13 It would be desirable if every government, when
it comes to power, should have its old speeches
burned.
Philip Snowden (1864–1937) British politician.
Biography (C. E. Bechofer Roberts)

14 Governments needs to have both shepherds and
butchers.
Voltaire (François-Marie Arouet; 1694–1778) French writer.
Notebooks

15 Many people consider the things which government does for them to be social progress, but
they consider the things government does for
others as socialism.
Earl Warren (1891–1971) US lawyer.
Peter's Quotations (Laurence J. Peter)

16 The people's government, made for the people, made by the people, and answerable to the people.
Daniel Webster (1782–1852) US statesman.
Second speech on Foote's resolution, 26 Jan 1830

17 If people behaved in the way nations do they would all be put in straitjackets.
Tennessee Williams (1911–83) US dramatist.
BBC interview

☐ GRAMMAR ☐

See also language, words

1 'Whom are you?' said he, for he had been to night school.
George Ade (1866–1944) US dramatist and humorist.
Bang! Bang!: The Steel Box

2 When I split an infinitive, god damn it, I split it so it stays split.
Raymond Chandler (1888–1959) US novelist.
Letter to his English publisher

3 This is the sort of English up with which I will not put.
Winston Churchill (1874–1965) British statesman.
The story is that Churchill wrote the comment in the margin of a report in which a Civil Servant had used an awkward construction to avoid ending a sentence with a preposition. An alternative version substitutes 'bloody nonsense' for 'English'
Plain Words (E. Gowers), Ch. 9

4 Grammar, which can govern even kings.
Molière (Jean Baptiste Poquelin; 1622–73) French dramatist.
Les Femmes savantes, II:6

5 Why care for grammar as long as we are good?
Artemus Ward (Charles Farrar Browne; 1834–67) US humorous writer.
Pyrotechny

☐ GRATITUDE ☐

1 There are minds so impatient of inferiority that their gratitude is a species of revenge, and they return benefits, not because recompense is a pleasure, but because obligation is a pain.
Samuel Johnson (1709–84) British lexicographer.
The Rambler

2 Thank me no thankings, nor proud me no prouds.
William Shakespeare (1564–1616) English dramatist.
Romeo and Juliet, III:5

☐ GREATNESS ☐

1 The dullard's envy of brilliant men is always assuaged by the suspicion that they will come to a bad end.
Max Beerbohm (1872–1956) British writer.
Zuleika Dobson

2 Great things are done when men and mountains meet;
This is not done by jostling in the street.
William Blake (1757–1827) British poet.
Gnomic Verses

3 Nothing grows well in the shade of a big tree.
Constantin Brancusi (1876–1957) Romanian sculptor.
Refusing Rodin's invitation to work in his studio
Compton's Encyclopedia

4 No great man lives in vain. The history of the world is but the biography of great men.
Thomas Carlyle (1795–1881) Scottish historian and essayist.
Heroes and Hero-Worship, 'The Hero as Divinity'

5 The world's great men have not commonly been great scholars, nor great scholars great men.
Oliver Wendell Holmes (1809–94) US writer.
The Autocrat of the Breakfast Table, Ch. 6

6 To be alone is the fate of all great minds – a fate deplored at times, but still always chosen as the less grievous of two evils.
Arthur Schopenhauer (1788–1860) German philosopher.
Aphorismen zur Lebensweisheit

7 Some are born great, some achieve greatness, and some have greatness thrust upon 'em.
William Shakespeare (1564–1616) English dramatist.
Twelfth Night, II:5

8 'My name is Ozymandias, king of kings:
Look on my works, ye Mighty, and despair!'
Percy Bysshe Shelley (1792–1822) British poet.
Ozymandias

☐ GREED ☐

See also food, materialism, obesity

1 Beware that you do not lose the substance by grasping at the shadow.
Aesop (6th century BC) Reputed Greek writer of fables.
Fables, 'The Dog and the Shadow'

2 Gluttony is an emotional escape, a sign something is eating us.
Peter De Vries (1910–) US novelist.
Comfort me with Apples, Ch. 7

3 The mountain sheep are sweeter,
But the valley sheep are fatter;
We therefore deemed it meeter
To carry off the latter.
Thomas Love Peacock (1785–1866) British novelist.
The Misfortunes of Elphin, Ch. 11, 'The War-Song of Dinas Vawr'

4 Wealth is like sea-water; the more we drink, the thirstier we become; and the same is true of fame.
Arthur Schopenhauer (1788–1860) German philosopher.
Parerga and Paralipomena

5   People will swim through shit if you put a few
    bob in it.
    Peter Sellers (1925–80) British comic actor.
    Halliwell's Filmgoer's and Video Viewer's Companion

□ GREER □
Germaine

(1939–) Australian writer and feminist. Her books include *The
Female Eunuch* (1970), *Sex and Destiny* (1984), *Daddy, We Hardly
Knew You* (1989), and *The Change* (1991).

1   Probably the only place where a man can feel
    really secure is in a maximum security prison,
    except for the imminent threat of release.
    The Female Eunuch

2   Mother is the dead heart of the family, spending
    father's earnings on consumer goods to enhance
    the environment in which he eats, sleeps and
    watches the television.
    The Female Eunuch

3   Buttock fetishism is comparatively rare in our
    culture...Girls are often self-conscious about
    their behinds, draping themselves in long capes
    and tunics, but it is more often because they are
    too abundant in that region than otherwise.
    The Female Eunuch

□ GREETINGS □

1   *Atque in perpetuum, frater, ave atque vale.*
    And for ever, brother, hail and farewell!
    Catullus (c. 84–c. 54 BC) Roman poet.
    Carmina, CI

2   Dr Livingstone, I presume?
    Henry Morton Stanley (1841–1904) British explorer.
    On finding David Livingstone at Ujiji on Lake Tanganyika,
    Nov 1871
    How I found Livingstone, Ch. 11

□ GUIDANCE □
See also leadership

1   Everyman, I will go with thee, and be thy guide.
    In thy most need to go by thy side.
    Anonymous
    Everyman Pt. 1

2   A little onward lend thy guiding hand
    To these dark steps, a little further on.
    John Milton (1608–74) English poet.
    Samson Agonistes

□ GUILT □
See also conscience, regret

1   It is quite gratifying to feel guilty if you haven't
    done anything wrong: how noble! Whereas it is
    rather hard and certainly depressing to admit
    guilt and to repent.
    Hannah Arendt (1906–75) German-born US philosopher and
    historian.
    Eichmann in Jerusalem, Ch. 15

2   When Pilate saw that he could prevail nothing,
    but that rather a tumult was made, he took water,
    and washed his hands before the multitude, say-
    ing, I am innocent of the blood of this just person:
    see ye to it.
    Then answered all the people, and said, His
    blood be on us, and on our children.
    Bible: Matthew
    27:24–25

3   Love bade me welcome; yet my soul drew back,
    Guilty of dust and sin.
    George Herbert (1593–1633) English poet.
    Love

4   You will put on a dress of guilt
    and shoes with broken high ideals.
    Roger McGough (1937–) British poet.
    Comeclose and Sleepnow

5   Out, damned spot! out, I say!
    William Shakespeare (1564–1616) English dramatist.
    Macbeth, V:1

H

□HABIT□

See also custom

1 Curious things, habits. People themselves never knew they had them.
Agatha Christie (1891–1976) British detective-story writer.
Witness for the Prosecution

2 Men's natures are alike; it is their habits that carry them far apart.
Confucius (K'ung Fu-tzu; 551–479 BC) Chinese philosopher.
Analects

3 Cultivate only the habits that you are willing should master you.
Elbert Hubbard (1856–1915) US writer.
Attrib.

□HALF MEASURES□

1 Two half-truths do not make a truth, and two half-cultures do not make a culture.
Arthur Koestler (1905–83) Hungarian-born British writer.
The Ghost in the Machine, Preface

2 I'm not really a Jew; just Jew-ish, not the whole hog.
Jonathan Miller (1934–) British doctor and television and stage director.
Beyond the Fringe

□HAPPINESS□

See also contentment, laughter, pleasure

1 The greatest happiness of the greatest number is the foundation of morals and legislation.
Jeremy Bentham (1748–1832) British philosopher.
The Commonplace Book

2 Happiness is a mystery like religion, and should never be rationalized.
G. K. Chesterton (1874–1936) British writer.
Heretics, Ch. 7

3 That action is best, which procures the greatest happiness for the greatest numbers.
Francis Hutcheson (1694–1746) Scottish philosopher.
Inquiry into the Original of our Ideas of Beauty and Virtue, Treatise II, 'Concerning Moral Good and Evil'

4 That all who are happy, are equally happy, is not true. A peasant and a philosopher may be equally *satisfied*, but not equally *happy*. Happiness consists in the multiplicity of agreeable consciousness.
Samuel Johnson (1709–84) British lexicographer.
Life of Johnson (J. Boswell), Vol. II

5 …because happiness is not an ideal of reason but of imagination.
Immanuel Kant (1724–1804) German philosopher.
Grundlegung zur Metaphysik der Sitten, II

6 When a small child…I thought that success spelled happiness. I was wrong. Happiness is like a butterfly which appears and delights us for one brief moment, but soon flits away.
Anna Pavlova (1881–1931) Russian ballet dancer.
Pavlova: A Biography (ed. A. H. Franks), 'Pages of My Life'

7 Happiness: a good bank account, a good cook, a good digestion.
Jean Jacques Rousseau (1712–1778) French philosopher.
Attrib.

8 Happiness is not best achieved by those who seek it directly.
Bertrand Russell (1872–1970) British philosopher.
Mysticism and Logic

9 Every time I talk to a savant I feel quite sure that happiness is no longer a possibility. Yet when I talk with my gardener, I'm convinced of the opposite.
Bertrand Russell
Attrib.

10 To be without some of the things you want is an indispensable part of happiness.
Bertrand Russell
Attrib.

11 One is happy as a result of one's own efforts, once one knows the necessary ingredients of happiness – simple tastes, a certain degree of courage, self denial to a point, love of work, and, above all, a clear conscience. Happiness is no vague dream, of that I now feel certain.
George Sand (Aurore Dupin, Baronne Dudevant; 1804–76) French novelist.
Correspondence, Vol. V

12 Happiness is the only sanction of life; where happiness fails, existence remains a mad and lamentable experiment.
George Santayana (1863–1952) US philosopher.
The Life of Reason

13 Happiness? That's nothing more than health and a poor memory.
Albert Schweitzer (1875–1965) French Protestant theologian, philosopher, physician and musician.
Attrib.

14 A lifetime of happiness: no man alive could bear it: it would be hell on earth.
George Bernard Shaw (1856–1950) Irish dramatist and critic.
Man and Superman, I

15 Happiness is an imaginary condition, formerly often attributed by the living to the dead, now usually attributed by adults to children, and by children to adults.
Thomas Szasz (1920–) US psychiatrist.
The Second Sin

16 Happiness is no laughing matter.
Richard Whately (1787–1863) British churchman.
Apothegms

17 The hell with it. Who never knew the price of happiness will not be happy.
Yevgeny Yevtushenko (1933–) Soviet poet.
Lies

□HASTE□
See also impetuosity

1 'Will you walk a little faster?' said a whiting to a snail,
'There's a porpoise close behind us, and he's treading on my tail.'
Lewis Carroll (Charles Lutwidge Dodgson; 1832–98) British writer.
Alice's Adventures in Wonderland, Ch. 10

2 In skating over thin ice, our safety is in our speed.
Ralph Waldo Emerson (1803–82) US poet and essayist.
Essays, 'Prudence'

3 Slow and steady wins the race.
Robert Lloyd (1733–64) British poet.
The Hare and the Tortoise

4 For fools rush in where angels fear to tread.
Alexander Pope (1688–1744) British poet.
An Essay on Criticism

5 If it were done when 'tis done, then 'twere well
It were done quickly.
William Shakespeare (1564–1616) English dramatist.
Macbeth, I:7

□HATE□
See also bitterness, love and hate

1 We can scarcely hate any one that we know.
William Hazlitt (1778–1830) British essayist.
On Criticism

2 If you hate a person, you hate something in him that is part of yourself. What isn't part of ourselves doesn't disturb us.
Hermann Hesse (1877–1962) German novelist and poet.
Demian, Ch. 6

3 Few people can be happy unless they hate some other person, nation or creed.
Bertrand Russell (1872–1970) British philosopher.
Attrib.

4 An intellectual hatred is the worst.
W. B. Yeats (1865–1939) Irish poet.
A Prayer for My Daughter

□HAZLITT□
William
(1778–1830) British essayist and journalist. His collections of writings include *Lectures on the English Poets* (1818) and *The Spirit of the Age* (1825).

1 He is your only good damner, and if I am ever damned I should like to be damned by him.
John Keats (1795–1821) British poet.
Attrib.

2 The least pain in our little finger gives us more concern and uneasiness than the destruction of millions of our fellow-beings.
American Literature, 'Dr Channing'

3 Man is an intellectual animal, and therefore an everlasting contradiction to himself. His senses centre in himself, his ideas reach to the ends of the universe; so that he is torn in pieces between the two, without a possibility of its ever being otherwise.
Characteristics

4 His worst is better than any other person's best.
English Literature, Ch. XIV, 'Sir Walter Scott'

5 You will hear more good things on the outside of a stagecoach from London to Oxford than if you were to pass a twelvemonth with the undergraduates, or heads of colleges, of that famous university.
The Ignorance of the Learned

6 Those who make their dress a principal part of themselves, will, in general, become of no more value than their dress.
On the Clerical Character

7 We can scarcely hate any one that we know.
On Criticism

8 No young man believes he shall ever die.
On the Feeling of Immortality in Youth

9 There is not a more mean, stupid, dastardly, pitiful, selfish, spiteful, envious, ungrateful animal than the public. It is the greatest of cowards, for it is afraid of itself.
On Living to Oneself

10 The art of pleasing consists in being pleased.
On Manner

11 We never do anything well till we cease to think about the manner of doing it.
On Prejudice

12 The love of liberty is the love of others; the love of power is the love of ourselves.
The Times, 1819

13 Well, I've had a happy life.
Last words

☐HEALTH AND HEALTHY LIVING☐

See also doctors, illness, medicine, remedies

1 Young ladies should take care of themselves. Young ladies are delicate plants. They should take care of their health and their complexion. My dear, did you change your stockings?
Jane Austen (1775–1817) British novelist.
Emma, Ch. 34

2 The strongest possible piece of advice I would give to any young woman is: Don't screw around, and don't smoke.
Edwina Currie (1946–) British politician.
The Observer, 'Sayings of the Week', 3 Apr 1988

3 Nutritional research, like a modern star of Bethlehem, brings hope that sickness need not be a part of life.
Adelle Davis (1904–74) US nutritionist and writer.
The New York Times Magazine, 'The Great Adelle Davis Controversy', 20 May 1973

4 Our body is a magnificently devised, living, breathing mechanism, yet we do almost nothing to insure its optimal development and use…The human organism needs an ample supply of good building material to repair the effects of daily wear and tear.
Indra Devi (1899–) Russian-born US yogini and writer.
Renewing Your Life Through Yoga, Ch. 2

5 A wise man ought to realize that health is his most valuable possession.
Hippocrates (c. 460 –c. 377 BC) Greek physician.
A Regimen for Health, 9

6 Vegetarianism is harmless enough, though it is apt to fill a man with wind and self righteousness.
Robert Hutchison (1871–1960)
Attrib.

7 Other books have been written by men physicians…One would suppose in reading them that women possess but one class of physical organs, and that these are always diseased. Such teaching is pestiferous, and tends to cause and perpetuate the very evils it professes to remedy.
Mary Ashton Livermore (c. 1820–1905) US writer.
What Shall We Do with Our Daughters?, Ch. 2

8 Some breakfast food manufacturer hit upon the simple notion of emptying out the leavings of carthorse nosebags, adding a few other things like unconsumed portions of chicken layer's mash, and the sweepings of racing stables, packing the mixture in little bags and selling them in health food shops.
Frank Muir (1920–) British writer and broadcaster.
Upon My Word!

9 Look to your health: and if you have it, praise God, and value it next to a good conscience; for health is the second blessing that we mortals are capable of; a blessing that money cannot buy.
Izaak Walton (1593–1683) English writer.
The Compleat Angler, Pt. I, Ch. 21

☐HEAVEN☐

See also afterlife

1 And he dreamed, and behold a ladder set up on the earth, and the top of it reached to heaven: and behold the angels of God ascending and descending on it.
Bible: Genesis
28:12

2 And Jacob awaked out of his sleep, and he said, Surely the Lord is in this place; and I knew it not. And he was afraid, and said, How dreadful is this place! this is none other but the house of God, and this is the gate of heaven.
Bible: Genesis
28:16–17

3 In my Father's house are many mansions: if it were not so, I would have told you. I go to prepare a place for you.
Bible: John
14:2

4 Then let him receive the new knowledge and wait us,
Pardoned in heaven, the first by the throne!
Robert Browning (1812–89) British poet.
The Lost Leader

5 Probably no invention came more easily to man than Heaven.
Georg Christoph Lichtenberg (1742–99) German physicist and writer.
Aphorisms

6 A heav'n on earth.
John Milton (1608–74) English poet.
Paradise Lost, Bk. IV

7 Glorious things of thee are spoken,
Zion, city of our God.
John Newton (1725–1807) British hymn writer.
Glorious Things

8 It may be only glory that we seek here, but I persuade myself that, as long as we remain here, that is right. Another glory awaits us in heaven and he who reaches there will not wish even to think of earthly fame.
Petrarch (Francesco Petrarca; 1304–74) Italian poet.
Secretum

9 Heaven, as conventionally conceived, is a place so inane, so dull, so useless, so miserable, that nobody has ever ventured to describe a whole day in heaven, though plenty of people have described a day at the seaside.
George Bernard Shaw (1856–1950) Irish dramatist and critic.
Misalliance, Preface

☐ HELL ☐

See also damnation, devil

1 Every wolf's and lion's howl
Raises from Hell a human soul.
William Blake (1757–1827) British poet.
Auguries of Innocence

2 Abandon hope, all ye who enter here.
Dante (1265–1321) Italian poet.
The inscription at the entrance to Hell
Divine Comedy, Inferno, III

3 Long is the way
And hard, that out of hell leads up to light.
John Milton (1608–74) English poet.
Paradise Lost, Bk. II

4 The way down to Hell is easy.
Virgil (Publius Vergilius Maro; 70–19 BC) Roman poet.
Aeneid, Bk. VI

☐ HEMINGWAY ☐
Ernest

(1898–1961) US novelist, who lived for much of his life in Paris.
His first successful novel was *The Sun Also Rises* (1926); subsequent novels include *A Farewell to Arms* (1929) and *For Whom the
Bell Tolls* (1940). He was a keen sportsman and admirer of
bullfighting.

QUOTATIONS ABOUT HEMINGWAY

1 He has a capacity for enjoyment so vast that he
gives away great chunks to those about him, and
never even misses them.... He can take you to a
bicycle race and make it raise your hair.
Dorothy Parker (1893–1967) US writer.
New Yorker, 30 Nov 1929

QUOTATIONS BY HEMINGWAY

2 If you are lucky enough to have lived in Paris as a
young man, then wherever you go for the rest of
your life, it stays with you, for Paris is a moveable
feast.
A Moveable Feast, Epigraph

3 A man can be destroyed but not defeated.
The Old Man and the Sea

4 Because I am a bastard.
When asked why he had deserted his wife for another woman.
Americans in Paris (B. Morton)

☐ HEROISM ☐

See also courage, endurance, patriotism, war

1 They died to save their country and they only
saved the world.
Hilaire Belloc (1870–1953) French-born British poet.
The English Graves

2 ANDREA. Unhappy the land that has no heroes.
GALILEO. No, unhappy the land that needs heroes.
Bertolt Brecht (1898–1956) German dramatist.
Galileo, 13

3 In short, he was a perfect cavaliero,
And to his very valet seem'd a hero.
Lord Byron (1788–1824) British poet.
Beppo

4 Women, wronged in one way or another, are
given the overwhelming beauty of endurance,
the capacity for high or low suffering, for violent
feeling absorbed, finally tranquilized, for the radiance of humility, for silence, secrecy, impressive
acceptance. Heroines are, then, heroic.
Elizabeth Hardwick (1916–   ) US writer, educator, drama
and literary critic.
Seduction and Betrayal: Women in Literature

5 Being a hero is about the shortest-lived profes-
sion on earth.
Will Rogers (1879–1935) US actor and humorist.
Saturday Review, 'A Rogers Thesaurus', 25 Aug 1962

☐ HISTORIANS ☐

See also history

1 A good historian is timeless; although he is a
patriot, he will never flatter his country in any
respect.
François Fénelon (1651–1715) French writer and prelate.
Letter to M. Dacier

2 The historian must have...some conception of
how men who are not historians behave. Otherwise he will move in a world of the dead.
E. M. Forster (1879–1970) British novelist.
Abinger Harvest, 'Captain Edward Gibbon'

3 Great abilities are not requisite for an Historian... Imagination is not required in any high
degree.
Samuel Johnson (1709–84) British lexicographer.
Life of Johnson (J. Boswell), Vol. I

4 History is too serious to be left to historians.
Iain Macleod (1913–70) British politician.
The Observer, 'Sayings of the Week', 16 July 1961

5 A historian is a prophet in reverse.
Friedrich von Schlegel (1772–1829) German diplomat,
writer, and critic.
Das Athenäum

☐ HISTORY ☐

See also experience, historians, past

1 History is the sum total of the things that could
have been avoided.
Konrad Adenauer (1876–1967) German statesman.

2 Political history is far too criminal and pathological to be a fit subject of study for the young. Chil-

dren should acquire their heroes and villains from fiction.
W. H. Auden (1907–73) British poet.
A Certain World

3 Man is a history-making creature who can neither repeat his past nor leave it behind.
W. H. Auden
The Dyer's Hand, 'D. H. Lawrence'

4 History is the essence of innumerable biographies.
Thomas Carlyle (1795–1881) Scottish historian and essayist.
Critical and Miscellaneous Essays, 'History'

5 History is philosophy teaching by examples.
Dionysius of Halicarnassus (40–8 BC) Greek historian.
Ars rhetorica, XI:2

6 History is an endless repetition of the wrong way of living.
Lawrence Durrell (1912–90) British novelist.
The Listener, 1978

7 History is more or less bunk. It's tradition. We don't want tradition. We want to live in the present and the only history that is worth a tinker's damn is the history we make today.
Henry Ford (1863–1947) US car manufacturer.
Chicago Tribune, 25 May 1916

8 History never looks like history when you are living through it. It always looks confusing and messy, and it always feels uncomfortable.
John W. Gardner (1912–) US writer.
No Easy Victories

9 His reign is marked by the rare advantage of furnishing very few materials for history; which is, indeed, little more than the register of the crimes, follies, and misfortunes of mankind.
Edward Gibbon (1737–94) British historian.
Referring to the reign of Antoninus Pius
Decline and Fall of the Roman Empire, Ch. 3

10 It takes a great deal of history to produce a little literature.
Henry James (1843–1916) US novelist.
Life of Nathaniel Hawthorne, Ch. 1

11 It is impossible to write ancient history because we do not have enough sources, and impossible to write modern history because we have far too many.
Charles Pierre Péguy (1873–1914) French writer.
Clio

12 There is no history of mankind, there are only many histories of all kinds of aspects of human life. And one of these is the history of political power. This is elevated into the history of the world.
Karl Popper (1902–) Austrian-born British philosopher.
The Open Society and Its Enemies

13 Progress, far from consisting in change, depends on retentiveness. Those who cannot remember the past are condemned to repeat it.
George Santayana (1863–1952) US philosopher.
The Life of Reason

14 History is past politics, and politics present history.
John Robert Seeley (1834–95) British historian.
Quoting the historian E. A. Freeman
The Growth of British Policy

15 All our ancient history, as one of our wits remarked, is no more than accepted fiction.
Voltaire (François-Marie Arouet; 1694–1778) French writer.
Jeannot et Colin

16 Indeed, history is nothing more than a tableau of crimes and misfortunes.
Voltaire
L'Ingénu, Ch. 10

17 Anything but history, for history must be false.
Robert Walpole (1676–1745) British statesman.
Walpoliana

18 The greater part of what passes for diplomatic history is little more than the record of what one clerk said to another clerk.
George Malcolm Young (1882–1959) British historian.
Victorian England: Portrait of an Age

☐ HITLER ☐
Adolf

(1889–1945) German dictator, who became president of the Nazi party in 1921 and chancellor of Germany in 1933. His campaign of world conquest led to World War II, defeat and disgrace for Germany, and his own suicide.

QUOTATIONS ABOUT HITLER

1 The people Hitler never understood, and whose actions continued to exasperate him to the end of his life, were the British.
Alan Bullock (1914–) British academic and historian.
Hitler, A Study in Tyranny, Ch. 8

2 I have only one purpose, the destruction of Hitler, and my life is much simplified thereby. If Hitler invaded Hell I would make at least a favourable reference to the Devil in the House of Commons.
Winston Churchill (1874–1965) British statesman.
The Grand Alliance

3 That garrulous monk
Benito Mussolini
Referring to Hitler.
The Second World War (W. Churchill)

4 I wouldn't believe Hitler was dead, even if he told me so himself.
Hjalmar Schacht (1877–1970) German banker.
Attrib.

5 All those who are not racially pure are mere chaff.
Mein Kampf, Ch. 2

6 Only constant repetition will finally succeed in imprinting an idea on the memory of the crowd.
Mein Kampf, Ch. 6

7 The broad mass of a nation...will more easily fall victim to a big lie than to a small one.
Mein Kampf, Ch. 10

8 In starting and waging a war it is not right that matters, but victory.
The Rise and Fall of the Third Reich (W. L. Shirer), Ch. 16

9 The essential thing is the formation of the political will of the nation: that is the starting point for political action.
Speech, Düsseldorf, 27 Jan 1932

10 I go the way that Providence dictates with the assurance of a sleepwalker.
Referring to his successful re-occupation of the Rhineland, despite advice against the attempt.
Speech, Munich, 15 Mar 1936

☐ HOME ☐

See also homesickness, travel

1 Home is the place where, when you have to go there,
They have to take you in.
Robert Frost (1875–1963) US poet.
The Death of the Hired Man

2 A man travels the world over in search of what he needs and returns home to find it.
George Moore (1852–1933) Irish writer and art critic.
The Brook Kerith, Ch. 11

3 Mid pleasures and palaces though we may roam,
Be it ever so humble, there's no place like home;
...
Home, home, sweet, sweet home!
There's no place like home! there's no place like home!
John Howard Payne (1791–1852) US actor and dramatist.
Clari, or the Maid of Milan

4 Seek home for rest,
For home is best.
Thomas Tusser (1524–80) English farmer.
Five Hundred Points of Good Husbandry, 'Instructions to Housewifery'

☐ HOMESICKNESS ☐

See also home, nostalgia

1 Oh give me a home where the buffalo roam,
Where the deer and the antelope play,

Where seldom is heard a discouraging word
And the skies are not cloudy all day.
Brewster Higley (19th century) US songwriter.
Home on the Range

2 The accent of one's birthplace lingers in the mind and in the heart as it does in one's speech.
Duc de la Rochefoucauld (1613–80) French writer.
Maximes, 342

3 Breathes there the man, with soul so dead,
Who never to himself hath said,
This is my own, my native land!
Whose heart hath ne'er within him burn'd,
As home his footsteps he hath turn'd
From wandering on a foreign strand!
Walter Scott (1771–1832) Scottish novelist.
The Lay of the Last Minstrel, VI

4 In home-sickness you must keep moving – it is the only disease that does not require rest.
H. de Vere Stacpoole (1863–1931) Irish-born novelist.
The Bourgeois

5 Good-bye Piccadilly, Farewell Leicester Square;
It's a long, long way to Tipperary, but my heart's right there!
Harry Williams (1874–1924) British songwriter.
Written with Jack Judge (1878–1938)
It's a Long Way to Tipperary

6 I travelled among unknown men
In lands beyond the sea;
Nor, England! did I know till then
What love I bore to thee.
William Wordsworth (1770–1850) British poet.
I Travelled among Unknown Men

☐ HOMOSEXUALITY ☐

See also sex

1 But the men of Sodom were wicked and sinners before the Lord exceedingly.
Bible: Genesis
13:13

2 The...problem which confronts homosexuals is that they set out to win the love of a 'real' man. If they succeed, they fail. A man who 'goes with' other men is not what they would call a real man.
Quentin Crisp (?1910–) Model, publicist, and writer.
The Naked Civil Servant

3 I am the Love that dare not speak its name.
Lord Alfred Douglas (1870–1945) British writer and poet.
Two Loves

4 This sort of thing may be tolerated by the French, but we are British – thank God.
Lord Montgomery (1887–1976) British field marshal.
Comment on a bill to relax the laws against homosexuals
Daily Mail, 27 May 1965

5 I have no doubt that lesbianism makes a woman virile and open to *any* sexual stimulation, and

that she is more often than not a more adequate and lively partner in bed than a 'normal' woman.
Charlotte Wolff (1904–) German-born British psychiatrist and writer.
Love Between Women

6 Lesbianism is not a matter of sexual preference, but rather one of political choice which every woman must make if she is to become woman-identified and thereby end male supremacy.
Lesbianism and the Women's Movement (ed. N. Myron and C. Burch)

□ HONESTY □

See also frankness, integrity, sincerity, truth

1 Though I be poor, I'm honest.
Thomas Middleton (1580–1627) English dramatist.
The Witch, III:2

2 To be honest, as this world goes, is to be one man pick'd out of ten thousand.
William Shakespeare (1564–1616) English dramatist.
Hamlet, II:2

3 I thank God I am as honest as any man living that is an old man and no honester than I.
William Shakespeare
Much Ado About Nothing, III:5

4 Though I am not naturally honest, I am so sometimes by chance.
William Shakespeare
The Winter's Tale, IV:3

5 Father, I cannot tell a lie. I did it with my little hatchet.
George Washington (1732–99) US statesman.
Attrib.

6 Honesty is the best policy; but he who is governed by that maxim is not an honest man.
Richard Whately (1787–1863) British churchman
Apophthegms

□ HONOUR □

See also titles

1 And they were offended in him. But Jesus said unto them, A prophet is not without honour, save in his own country, and in his own house.
Bible: Matthew
13:57

2 That chastity of honour, that felt a stain like a wound.
Edmund Burke (1729–97) British politician.
Reflections on the Revolution in France

3 Remember, men, we're fighting for this woman's honour; which is probably more than she ever did.
Groucho Marx (Julius Marx; 1895–1977) US comedian.
Duck Soup

4 Honour pricks me on. Yea, but how if honour prick me off when I come on? How then? Can honour set to a leg? No. Or an arm? No. Or take away the grief of a wound? No. Honour hath no skill in surgery, then? No. What is honour? A word. What is in that word? Honour. What is that honour? Air.
William Shakespeare (1564–1616) English dramatist.
Henry IV, Part One, V:1

5 Brothers all
In honour, as in one community,
Scholars and gentlemen.
William Wordsworth (1770–1850) British poet.
The Prelude, IX

□ HOPE □

See also ambition, desire, expectation, optimism

1 Still nursing the unconquerable hope,
Still clutching the inviolable shade.
Matthew Arnold (1822–88) British poet and critic.
The Scholar Gipsy

2 While there is life, there's hope,' he cried;
'Then why such haste?' so groaned and died.
John Gay (1685–1732) English poet and dramatist.
Fables

3 After all, tomorrow is another day.
Margaret Mitchell (1909–49) US novelist.
The closing words of the book
Gone with the Wind

4 Hope springs eternal in the human breast;
Man never is, but always to be blest.
Alexander Pope (1688–1744) British poet.
An Essay on Man, I

□ HORACE □

(Quintus Horatius Flaccus; 65–8 BC) Roman poet. His *Odes* and *Epistles* portray Roman life in considerable detail.

1 'Painters and poets alike have always had licence to dare anything.' We know that, and we both claim and allow to others in their turn this indulgence.
Ars Poetica

2 I strive to be brief, and I become obscure.
Ars Poetica

3 Not gods, nor men, nor even booksellers have put up with poets' being second-rate.
Ars Poetica

4 To save a man's life against his will is the same as killing him.
Ars Poetica

5 If possible honestly, if not, somehow, make money.
Epistles, I

6 We are just statistics, born to consume resources.
Epistles, I

7 You may drive out nature with a pitchfork, yet she'll be constantly running back.
Epistles, I

8 Pale Death kicks his way equally into the cottages of the poor and the castles of kings.
Odes, I

9 Drop the question what tomorrow may bring, and count as profit every day that Fate allows you.
Odes, I

10 *Carpe diem*
Seize the day.
Odes, I

11 When things are steep, remember to stay level-headed.
Odes, II

12 *Dulce et decorum est pro patria mori.*
It is a sweet and seemly thing to die for one's country.
Odes, III

13 Undeservedly you will atone for the sins of your fathers.
Odes, III

14 What do the ravages of time not injure? Our parents' age (worse than our grandparents') has produced us, more worthless still, who will soon give rise to a yet more vicious generation.
Odes, III

15 Not to hope for things to last for ever, is what the year teaches and even the hour which snatches a nice day away.
Odes, IV

16 Mix a little foolishness with your serious plans: it's lovely to be silly at the right moment.
Odes, IV

☐ HORSES ☐

See also animals, hunting, sport and games

1 When I appear in public people expect me to neigh, grind my teeth, paw the ground and swish my tail – none of which is easy.
Princess Anne (1950–) The Princess Royal, only daughter of Elizabeth II.
The Observer, 'Sayings of the Week', 22 May 1977

2 As lene was his hors as is a rake.
Geoffrey Chaucer (c. 1342–1400) English poet.
The Canterbury Tales, Prologue

3 They say princes learn no art truly, but the art of horsemanship. The reason is, the brave beast is no flatterer. He will throw a prince as soon as his groom.
Ben Jonson (1573–1637) English dramatist.
Timber, or Discoveries made upon Men and Matter

4 It takes a good deal of physical courage to ride a horse. This, however, I have. I get it at about forty cents a flask, and take it as required.
Stephen Leacock (1869–1944) English-born Canadian economist and humorist.
Literary Lapses, 'Reflections on Riding'

5 To confess that you are totally Ignorant about the Horse, is social suicide: you will be despised by everybody, especially the horse.
W. C. Sellar (1898–1951) British humorous writer.
Horse Nonsense

6 A horse! a horse ! my kingdom for a horse.
William Shakespeare (1564–1616) English dramatist.
Richard III, V:4

☐ HOSPITALITY ☐

1 I'd rather be a host than a guest. As Beerbohm wonderfully observed, a happy host makes a sad guest.
Harold Acton (1904–) British writer.
The Times, 18 Apr 1970

2 Let brotherly love continue.
Be not forgetful to entertain strangers: for thereby some have entertained angels unawares.
Bible: Hebrews
13:1–2

☐ HOUSES ☐

See also architecture, home, stately homes

1 Houses are built to live in and not to look on; therefore let use be preferred before uniformity, except where both may be had.
Francis Bacon (1561–1626) English philosopher.
Essays, 'Of Building'

2 A house is a machine for living in.
Le Corbusier (Charles-Édouard Jeanneret; 1887–1965) Swiss-born French architect.
Towards an Architecture

3 It's 'aving 'ouses built by men, I believe, makes all the work and trouble.
H. G. Wells (1866–1946) British writer.
Kipps, Bk. III, Ch. 1

☐ HOUSES OF PARLIAMENT ☐

See also aristocracy, government, politics

1 This is a rotten argument, but it should be good enough for their lordships on a hot summer afternoon.
Anonymous
A note on a ministerial brief read out by mistake in the House of Lords
The Way the Wind Blows (Lord Home), 1976

2 The House of Lords is like a glass of champagne that has stood for five days.
Clement Attlee (1883–1967) British statesman and Labour prime minister.
Attrib.

3 A severe though not unfriendly critic of our institutions said that 'the cure for admiring the House of Lords was to go and look at it.'
Walter Bagehot (1826–77) British economist and journalist.
The English Constitution, 'The House of Lords'

4 The House of Lords is the British Outer Mongolia for retired politicians.
Tony Benn (1925–   ) British politician.
Speech, 11 Feb 1962

5 The House of Peers, throughout the war,
Did nothing in particular,
And did it very well.
W. S. Gilbert (1836–1911) British dramatist.
Iolanthe, II

6 Every man has a House of Lords in his own head. Fears, prejudices, misconceptions – those are the peers, and they are hereditary.
David Lloyd George (1863–1945) British Liberal statesman.
Speech, Cambridge, 1927

7 The British, being brought up on team games, enter their House of Commons in the spirit of those who would rather be doing something else. If they cannot be playing golf or tennis, they can at least pretend that politics is a game with very similar rules.
Cyril Northcote Parkinson (1919–   ) British historian and writer.
Parkinson's Law, Ch. 2

8 The House of Lords must be the only institution in the world which is kept efficient by the persistent absenteeism of most of its members.
Herbert Samuel (1870–1963) British Liberal statesman.
News Review, 5 Feb 1948

9 The quality of debate is pretty high – and it is, I think, good evidence of life after death.
Donald Soper (1903–   ) British Methodist Minister.
Listener, 17 Aug 1978

10 The House of Lords, an illusion to which I have never been able to subscribe – responsibility without power, the prerogative of the eunuch throughout the ages.
Tom Stoppard (1937–   ) Czech-born British dramatist.
Lord Malquist and Mr Moon, Pt. VI, Ch. 1

11 You must build your House of Parliament upon the river: so…that the populace cannot exact their demands by sitting down round you.
Duke of Wellington (1769–1852) British general and statesman.
Words on Wellington (Sir William Fraser)

☐ HOUSEWORK ☐

See also woman's role

1 Housekeeping ain't no joke.
Louisa May Alcott (1832–88) US novelist.
Little Women, Pt. 1

2 Our motto: Life is too short to stuff a mushroom.
Shirley Conran (1932–   ) British designer and journalist.
Superwoman, Epigraph

3 There was no need to do any housework at all. After the first four years the dirt doesn't get any worse.
Quentin Crisp (?1910–   ) Model, publicist, and writer.
The Naked Civil Servant

4 Cleaning your house while your kids are still growing
Is like shoveling the walk before it stops snowing.
Phyllis Diller (1917–   ) US writer and comedienne.
Phyllis Diller's Housekeeping Hints

☐ HOUSMAN ☐
A(lfred) E(dward)

(1859–1936) British scholar and poet. His own verse collections include *A Shropshire Lad* (1896) and *Last Poems* (1922).

QUOTATIONS ABOUT HOUSMAN

1 A prim, old-maidish, rather second-rate, rather tired, rather querulous person.
A. C. Benson (1862–1925) British writer.
Diaries

QUOTATIONS BY HOUSMAN

2 The candles burn their sockets,
The blinds let through the day,
The young man feels his pockets
And wonders what's to pay.
Last Poems, 'Eight O'Clock'

3 Even when poetry has a meaning, as it usually has, it may be inadvisable to draw it out…Perfect understanding will sometimes almost extinguish pleasure.
The Name and Nature of Poetry

4 Look not in my eyes, for fear
They mirror true the sight I see,

And there you find your face too clear
And love it and be lost like me.
A Shropshire Lad, 'March'

5 Malt does more than Milton can
To justify God's ways to man.
A Shropshire Lad, 'The Welsh Marches'

□ HUMAN CONDITION □

See also human nature, life, mankind

1 Man that is born of a woman is of few days, and full of trouble.
Bible: Job
14:1

2 If God were suddenly condemned to live the life which he has inflicted on men, He would kill Himself.
Alexandre Dumas, fils (1824–95) French writer.
Pensées d'album

3 The world is a beautiful place
to be born into
if you don't mind some people dying
all the time
or maybe only starving
some of the time
which isn't half so bad
if it isn't you.
Laurence Ferlinghetti (1919–) US poet.
Pictures of the Gone World

4 Oh wearisome condition of humanity!
Born under one law, to another bound.
Fulke Greville (1554–1628) English poet and politician.
Mustapha, V:6

5 The condition of man…is a condition of war of everyone against everyone.
Thomas Hobbes (1588–1679) English philosopher.
Leviathan, Pt. I, Ch. 4

6 You come into the world alone, you go out alone. In between it's nice to know a few people, but being alone is a fundamental quality of human life, depressing as that is.
Helen Mirren (1945–) British actress.
Remark, Jan 1989

7 Brief and powerless is Man's life; on him and all his race the slow, sure doom falls pitiless and dark.
Bertrand Russell (1872–1970) British philosopher.
Mysticism and Logic, 'A Free Man's Worship'

8 All the world's a stage,
And all the men and women merely players;
They have their exits and their entrances;
And one man in his time plays many parts,
His acts being seven ages.
William Shakespeare (1564–1616) English dramatist.
As You Like It, II:7

9 When we are born, we cry that we are come
To this great stage of fools.
William Shakespeare
King Lear, IV:6

10 We have to believe in free-will. We've got no choice.
Isaac Bashevis Singer (1904–91) Polish-born US writer.
The Times, 21 June 1982

11 All men should strive to learn before they die
What they are running from, and to, and why.
James Thurber (1894–1961) American humorist.
Attrib.

12 For what human ill does not dawn seem to be an alternative?
Thornton Wilder (1897–1975) US novelist and dramatist.
The Bridge of San Luis Rey

□ HUMAN NATURE □

See also mankind

1 Human nature is so well disposed towards those who are in interesting situations, that a young person, who either marries or dies, is sure to be kindly spoken of.
Jane Austen (1775–1817) British novelist.
Emma, Ch. 22

2 A man's nature runs either to herbs, or to weeds; therefore let him seasonably water the one, and destroy the other.
Francis Bacon (1561–1626) English philosopher.
Essays, 'Of Nature in Men'

3 There is in human nature generally more of the fool than of the wise.
Francis Bacon
Essays, 'Of Boldness'

4 Nature is often hidden, sometimes overcome, seldom extinguished.
Francis Bacon
Essays, 'Of Nature in Men'

5 Nature, to be commanded, must be obeyed.
Francis Bacon
Novum Organum

6 You may drive out nature with a pitchfork, yet she'll be constantly running back.
Horace (Quintus Horatius Flaccus; 65–8 BC) Roman poet.
Epistles, I

7 We need more understanding of human nature, because the only real danger that exists is man himself…We know nothing of man, far too little. His psyche should be studied because we are the origin of all coming evil.
Carl Gustav Jung (1875–1961) Swiss psychoanalyst.
BBC television interview

8 Out of the crooked timber of humanity no straight thing can ever be made.

Immanuel Kant (1724–1804) German philosopher.
Idee zu einer allgemeinen Geschichte in weltbürgerlicher Absicht

9 Scenery is fine – but human nature is finer.

John Keats (1795–1821) British poet.
Letter to Benjamin Bailey, 13 Mar 1818

10 'Tis the way of all flesh.

Thomas Shadwell (1642–92) English dramatist.
The Sullen Lovers, V:2

11 It is part of human nature to hate the man you have hurt.

Tacitus (c. 55–c. 120 AD) Roman historian.
Agricola, 42

□ HUMAN RIGHTS □

See also equality, freedom, racism

1 All human beings are born free and equal in dignity and rights.

Anonymous
Universal Declaration of Human Rights (1948), Article 1

2 *Liberté! Égalité! Fraternité!*
Freedom! Equality! Brotherhood!

Anonymous
Motto for French Revolutionaries

3 We hold these truths to be self-evident: that all men are created equal; that they are endowed by their Creator with certain unalienable rights; that among these are life, liberty, and the pursuit of happiness.

Thomas Jefferson (1743–1826) US statesman.
Declaration of American Independence, 4 July 1776

4 We look forward to a world founded upon four essential human freedoms. The first is freedom of speech and expression – everywhere in the world. The second is freedom of every person to worship God in his own way – everywhere in the world. The third is freedom from want…everywhere in the world. The fourth is freedom from fear…anywhere in the world.

Franklin D. Roosevelt (1882–1945) US Democratic president.
Speech to Congress, 6 Jan 1941

5 Freedom is an indivisible word. If we want to enjoy it, and fight for it, we must be prepared to extend it to everyone, whether they are rich or poor, whether they agree with us or not, no matter what their race or the colour of their skin.

Wendell Lewis Willkie (1892–1944) US lawyer and businessman.
One World, Ch. 13

□ HUMILITY □

See also service, servility

1 Blessed are the meek: for they shall inherit the earth.

Bible: Matthew
5:5

2 Humility is only doubt,
And does the sun and moon blot out.

William Blake (1757–1827) British poet.
The Everlasting Gospel

3 It is difficult to be humble. Even if you aim at humility, there is no guarantee that when you have attained the state you will not be proud of the feat.

Bonamy Dobrée (1891–1974) British scholar and writer.
John Wesley

4 The humble and meek are thirsting for blood.

Joe Orton (1933–67) British dramatist.
Funeral Games, I

5 Take physic, pomp;
Expose thyself to feel what wretches feel.

William Shakespeare (1564–1616) English dramatist.
King Lear, III:4

6 When I survey the wondrous Cross,
On which the Prince of Glory died,
My richest gain I count but loss
And pour contempt on all my pride.

Isaac Watts (1674–1748) English theologian and hymn writer.
When I Survey the Wondrous Cross

7 Gentle Jesus, meek and mild,
Look upon a little child;
Pity my simplicity,
Suffer me to come to thee.

Charles Wesley (1707–88) British religious leader.
Hymns and Sacred Poems

□ HUMOUR □

See also laughter, nonsense, puns

1 The marvellous thing about a joke with a double meaning is that it can only mean one thing.

Ronnie Barker (1929–) British comedian.
Sauce, 'Daddie's Sauce'

2 The world would not be in such a snarl, had Marx been Groucho instead of Karl.

Irving Berlin (Israel Baline; 1888–1989) US composer.
Telegram to Groucho Marx on his seventy-first birthday

3 It's a good deed to forget a poor joke.

Brendan Bracken (1901–58) British newspaper publisher and politician.
The Observer, 'Sayings of the Week', 17 Oct 1943

4 I remain just one thing, and one thing only – and that is a clown.

It places me on a far higher plane than any politician.
Charlie Chaplin (Sir Charles Spencer C.; 1889–1977) British film actor.
The Observer, 'Sayings of the Week', 17 June 1960

5 A joke's a very serious thing.
Charles Churchill (1731–64) British poet.
The Ghost, Bk. IV

6 Men will confess to treason, murder, arson, false teeth, or a wig. How many of them will own up to a lack of humour?
Frank More Colby (1865–1925) US editor.
Essays, I

7 No mind is thoroughly well organized that is deficient in a sense of humour.
Samuel Taylor Coleridge (1772–1834) British poet.
Table Talk

8 Total absence of humour renders life impossible.
Colette (1873–1954) French novelist.
Chance Acquaintances

9 As for the Freudian, it is a very low, Central European sort of humour.
Robert Graves (1895–1985) British poet and novelist.
Occupation: Writer

10 His foe was folly and his weapon wit.
Anthony Hope (Sir Anthony Hope Hawkins; 1863–1933) British novelist.
Written for the inscription on the memorial to W. S. Gilbert, Victoria Embankment, London

11 The coarse joke proclaims that we have here an animal which finds its own animality either objectionable or funny.
C. S. Lewis (1898–1963) British academic and writer.
Miracles

12 Impropriety is the soul of wit.
W. Somerset Maugham (1874–1965) British novelist.
The Moon and Sixpence, Ch. 4

13 True wit is nature to advantage dress'd;
What oft was thought, but ne'er so well express'd.
Alexander Pope (1688–1744) British poet.
An Essay on Criticism

14 Comedy, we may say, is society protecting itself – with a smile.
J. B. Priestley (1894–1984) British novelist.
George Meredith

15 A comedian can only last till he either takes himself serious or his audience takes him serious.
Will Rogers (1879–1935) US actor and humorist.
Newspaper article, 1931

16 Everything is funny, as long as it's happening to somebody else.
Will Rogers
The Illiterate Digest

17 A jest's prosperity lies in the ear
Of him that hears it, never in the tongue
Of him that makes it.
William Shakespeare (1564–1616) English dramatist.
Love's Labour's Lost, V:2

18 It's hard to be funny when you have to be clean.
Mae West (1892–1980) US actress.
The Wit and Wisdom of Mae West (ed. J. Weintraub)

☐ HUNGER ☐
See also desire, food

1 The best sauce in the world is hunger.
Miguel de Cervantes (1547–1616) Spanish novelist.
Don Quixote, Pt. II, Ch. 5

2 If only it were as easy to banish hunger by rubbing the belly as it is to masturbate.
Diogenes (412–322 BC) Greek philosopher.
Lives and Opinions of Eminent Philosophers (Diogenes Laertius)

3 They that die by famine die by inches.
Matthew Henry (1662–1714) English nonconformist minister.
Exposition of the Old and New Testaments

4 The war against hunger is truly mankind's war of liberation.
John Fitzgerald Kennedy (1917–63) US statesman.
Speech, World Food Congress, 4 June 1963

5 A hungry stomach has no ears.
Jean de La Fontaine (1621–95) French poet.
Fables, IX, 'Le Milan et le Rossignol'

6 Let them eat cake.
Marie-Antoinette (1755–93) Queen of France.
On being told that the people had no bread to eat; in fact she was repeating a much older saying
Attrib.

☐ HUNTING ☐
See also sport and games

1 Detested sport,
That owes its pleasures to another's pain.
William Cowper (1731–1800) British poet.
The Task

2 Wild animals never kill for sport. Man is the only one to whom the torture and death of his fellow-creatures is amusing in itself.
J. A. Froude (1818–94) British historian.
Oceana, Ch. 5

3 D'ye ken John Peel with his coat so gay?
D'ye ken John Peel at the break of the day?
D'ye ken John Peel when he's far far away
With his hounds and his horn in the morning?
'Twas the sound of his horn called me from my bed,
And the cry of his hounds has me oft-times led;

For Peel's view-hollo would waken the dead,
Or a fox from his lair in the morning.
John Woodcock Graves (1795–1886) British poet, huntsman, and songwriter.
John Peel

4 It is very strange, and very melancholy, that the paucity of human pleasures should persuade us ever to call hunting one of them.
Samuel Johnson (1709–84) British lexicographer.
Johnsonian Miscellanies (ed. G. B. Hill), Vol. I

5 The English country gentleman galloping after a fox – the unspeakable in full pursuit of the uneatable.
Oscar Wilde (1854–1900) Irish-born British dramatist.
A Woman of No Importance, I

□HURT□
See also cruelty, insensitivity, nastiness, suffering

1 Those have most power to hurt us that we love.
Francis Beaumont (1584–1616) English dramatist.
The Maid's Tragedy, V:6

2 We flatter those we scarcely know,
We please the fleeting guest,
And deal full many a thoughtless blow
To those who love us best.
Ella Wheeler Wilcox (1850–1919) US poet.
Life's Scars

□HUXLEY□
Aldous
(1894–1964) British novelist and essayist. His novels include *Antic Hay* (1923), *Point Counter Point* (1928), *Brave New World* (1932), and *Eyeless in Gaza* (1936). His non-fiction includes *The Doors of Perception* (1954).

QUOTATIONS ABOUT HUXLEY

1 Mr. Huxley is perhaps one of those people who have to perpetrate thirty bad novels before producing a good one.
T. S. Eliot (1888–1965) US-born British poet and dramatist.
Attrib.

2 Like a piece of litmus paper he has always been quick to take the colour of his times.
Anonymous
The Observer, Profile, 27 Feb 1949

QUOTATIONS BY HUXLEY

3 Thanks to words, we have been able to rise above the brutes; and thanks to words, we have often sunk to the level of the demons.
Adonis and the Alphabet

4 There are few who would not rather be taken in adultery than in provincialism.
Antic Hay, Ch. 10

5 Official dignity tends to increase in inverse ratio to the importance of the country in which the office is held.
Beyond the Mexique Bay

6 The time of our Ford.
Brave New World, Ch. 3

7 The proper study of mankind is books.
Chrome Yellow

8 We participate in a tragedy; at a comedy we only look.
The Devils of Loudon, Ch. 11

9 Consistency is contrary to nature, contrary to life. The only completely consistent people are the dead.
Do What you Will

10 The quality of moral behaviour varies in inverse ratio to the number of human beings involved.
Grey Eminence, Ch. 10

11 I can sympathize with people's pains, but not with their pleasures. There is something curiously boring about somebody else's happiness.
Limbo, 'Cynthia'

12 Most of one's life…is one prolonged effort to prevent oneself thinking.
Mortal Coils, 'Green Tunnels'

13 She was one of those indispensables of whom one makes the discovery, when they are gone, that one can get on quite as well without them.
Mortal Coils, 'Nuns at Luncheon'

14 There is no substitute for talent. Industry and all the virtues are of no avail.
Point Counter Point

15 That all men are equal is a proposition to which, at ordinary times, no sane individual has ever given his assent.
Proper Studies

16 Those who believe that they are exclusively in the right are generally those who achieve something.
Proper Studies

17 Facts do not cease to exist because they are ignored.
Proper Studies

18 Most human beings have an almost infinite capacity for taking things for granted.
Themes and Variations

19 Defined in psychological terms, a fanatic is a man who consciously over-compensates a secret doubt.
Vulgarity in Literature, Ch. 4

☐ HYPATIA ☐

(c. 370–415) Egyptian Neoplatonist philosopher and mathematician who became head of the Neoplatonist school of philosophy at Alexandria.

QUOTATIONS ABOUT HYPATIA

1 Donning the philosopher's cloak, and making her way through the midst of the city, she explained publicly the writings of Plato, or Aristotle, or any other philosopher, to all who wished to hear.
Hesychius *Critic*, 1903 (Joseph McCabe)

QUOTATIONS BY HYPATIA

2 Men will fight for a superstition quite as quickly as for a living truth – often more so, since a superstition is so intangible you cannot get at it to refute it, but truth is a point of view, and so is changeable.
Little Journeys to the Homes of Great Teachers (Elbert Hubbard), 'Hypatia'

3 He who influences the thought of his times, influences all the times that follow. He has made his impress on eternity.
Little Journeys to the Homes of Great Teachers (Elbert Hubbard), 'Hypatia'

4 To rule by fettering the mind through fear of punishment in another world, is just as base as to use force.
Little Journeys to the Homes of Great Teachers (Elbert Hubbard), 'Hypatia'

☐ HYPOCHONDRIA ☐

1 People who are always taking care of their health are like misers, who are hoarding a treasure which they have never spirit enough to enjoy.
Laurence Sterne (1713–68) Irish-born British writer.
Attrib.

2 The imaginary complaints of indestructible old ladies.
Elwyn Brooks White (1899–1985) US journalist and humorist.
Harper's Magazine, Nov 1941

☐ HYPOCRISY ☐

See also example, insincerity

1 Woe unto you, scribes and Pharisees, hypocrites! for ye are like unto whited sepulchres, which indeed appear beautiful outward, but are within full of dead men's bones, and of all uncleanness.
Bible: Matthew
23:27

2 The smyler with the knyf under the cloke.
Geoffrey Chaucer (c. 1342–1400) English poet.
The Canterbury Tales, 'The Knight's Tale'

3 We ought to see far enough into a hypocrite to see even his sincerity.
G. K. Chesterton (1874–1936) British writer.
Heretics, Ch. 5

4 Man is the only animal that learns by being hypocritical. He pretends to be polite and then, eventually, he *becomes* polite.
Jean Kerr (1923–) US dramatist.
Finishing Touches

5 Hypocrisy is the most difficult and nerve-racking vice that any man can pursue; it needs an unceasing vigilance and a rare detachment of spirit. It cannot, like adultery or gluttony, be practised at spare moments; it is a whole-time job.
W. Somerset Maugham (1874–1965) British novelist.
Cakes and Ale, Ch. 1

6 For neither man nor angel can discern
Hypocrisy, the only evil that walks
Invisible, except to God alone.
John Milton (1608–74) English poet.
Paradise Lost, Bk. III

7 Hypocrisy is the homage paid by vice to virtue.
Duc de la Rochefoucauld (1613–80) French writer.
Maximes, 218

8 Well, whiles I am a beggar, I will rail
And say there is no sin but to be rich;
And being rich, my virtue then shall be
To say there is no vice but beggary.
William Shakespeare (1564–1616) English dramatist.
King John, II:1

9 Come not, when I am dead,
To drop thy foolish tears upon my grave,
To trample round my fallen head,
And vex the unhappy dust thou wouldst not save.
Alfred, Lord Tennyson (1809–92) British poet.
Come Not, When I Am Dead

10 I hope you have not been leading a double life, pretending to be wicked and being really good all the time. That would be hypocrisy.
Oscar Wilde (1854–1900) Irish-born British dramatist.
The Importance of Being Earnest, II

11 A Christian is a man who feels
Repentance on a Sunday
For what he did on Saturday
And is going to do on Monday.
Thomas Russell Ybarra (b. 1880) Venezuelan-born US writer.
The Christian

I

☐ IDEALISM ☐

1 If you can talk with crowds and keep your virtue,
Or walk with Kings – nor lose the common touch,
If neither foes nor loving friends can hurt you,
If all men count with you, but none too much;
If you can fill the unforgiving minute
With sixty seconds' worth of distance run,
Yours is the Earth and everything that's in it,
And – which is more – you'll be a Man my son!
Rudyard Kipling (1865–1936) Indian-born British writer.
If

2 Ideal mankind would abolish death, multiply
itself million upon million, rear up city upon city,
save every parasite alive, until the accumulation
of mere existence is swollen to a horror.
D. H. Lawrence (1885–1930) British novelist.
St Mawr

3 An idealist is one who, on noticing that a rose
smells better than a cabbage, concludes that it
will also make better soup.
H. L. Mencken (1880–1956) US journalist.
Sententiae

4 If a woman like Eva Peron with no ideals can get
that far, think how far I can go with all the ideals
that I have.
Margaret Thatcher (1925–   ) British politician and prime
minister.
The Sunday Times, 1980

☐ IDEAS ☐

See also opinions, theory

1 A stand can be made against invasion by an
army; no stand can be made against invasion by
an idea.
Victor Hugo (1802–85) French writer.
Histoire d'un Crime, 'La Chute'

2 Many ideas grow better when transplanted into
another mind than in the one where they sprang
up.
Oliver Wendell Holmes Jnr (1841–1935) US jurist.

3 Society goes on and on and on. It is the same with
ideas.
Ramsey MacDonald (1866–1937) British statesman and
prime minister.
Speech, 1935

4 An idea isn't responsible for the people who
believe in it.
Don Marquis (1878–1937) US journalist.
New York Sun

☐ IDLENESS ☐

See also bed, laziness, leisure, unemployment

1 Idleness is only the refuge of weak minds.
Earl of Chesterfield (1694–1773) English statesman.
Letter to his son, 20 July 1749

2 It is impossible to enjoy idling thoroughly unless
one has plenty of work to do.
Jerome K. Jerome (1859–1927) British humorist.
Idle Thoughts of an Idle Fellow

3 I like work; it fascinates me. I can sit and look at it
for hours. I love to keep it by me; the idea of getting rid of it nearly breaks my heart.
Jerome K. Jerome
Three Men in a Boat, Ch. 15

4 We would all be idle if we could.
Samuel Johnson (1709–84) British lexicographer.
Life of Johnson (J. Boswell), Vol. III

5 Young people ought not to be idle. It is very bad
for them.
Margaret Thatcher (1925–   ) British politician and prime
minister.
The Times, 1984

6 For Satan finds some mischief still
For idle hands to do.
Isaac Watts (1674–1748) English theologian and hymn writer.
Divine Songs for Children, 'Against Idleness and Mischief'

☐ IGNORANCE ☐

See also foolishness, innocence, stupidity

1 To each his suff'rings, all are men,
Condemn'd alike to groan;
The tender for another's pain,
Th' unfeeling for his own.
Yet ah! why should they know their fate?
Since sorrow never comes too late,
And happiness too swiftly flies.
Thought would destroy their paradise.
No more; where ignorance is bliss,
'Tis folly to be wise.
Thomas Gray (1716–71) British poet.
Ode on a Distant Prospect of Eton College

2 The ignorant man always adores what he cannot
understand.
Cesare Lombroso (1853–1909) Italian criminologist.
The Man of Genius, Pt. III, Ch. 3

3 I count religion but a childish toy,
And hold there is no sin but ignorance.
Christopher Marlowe (1564–93) English dramatist.
The Jew of Malta, Prologue

4 From ignorance our comfort flows,
The only wretched are the wise.
Matthew Prior (1664–1721) British poet.
To the Hon. Charles Montague

5 Somebody else's ignorance is bliss.
Jack Vance (1916–) US writer.
Star King

6 Ignorance is like a delicate exotic fruit; touch it,
and the bloom is gone.
Oscar Wilde (1854–1900) Irish-born British dramatist.
The Importance of Being Earnest, I

□ ILLNESS □

See also disease, doctors, drugs, health and healthy living, medicine, remedies

1 My message to the businessmen of this country
when they go abroad on business is that there is
one thing above all they can take with them to
stop them catching Aids, and that is the wife.
Edwina Currie (1946–) British politician.
The Observer, 'Sayings of the Week', 15 Feb 1987

2 Much of the world's work, it has been said, is
done by men who do not feel quite well. Marx is a
case in point.
John Kenneth Galbraith (1908–) US economist.
The Age of Uncertainty, Ch. 3

3 Every time you sleep with a boy you sleep with
all his old girlfriends.
Government-sponsored AIDS advertisement, 1987

4 Hungry Joe collected lists of fatal diseases and
arranged them in alphabetical order so that he
could put his finger without delay on any one he
wanted to worry about.
Joseph Heller (1923–) US novelist.
Catch-22, Ch. 17

5 How few of his friends' houses would a man
choose to be at when he is sick.
Samuel Johnson (1709–84) British lexicographer.
Life of Johnson (J. Boswell), Vol. IV

6 Oh what can ail thee, knight at arms
Alone and palely loitering;
The sedge has wither'd from the lake,
And no birds sing.
John Keats (1795–1821) British poet.
La Belle Dame Sans Merci

7 How sickness enlarges the dimensions of a
man's self to himself.
Charles Lamb (1775–1834) British essayist.
Last Essays of Elia, 'The Convalescent'

8 Only do always in health what you have often
promised to do when you are sick.
Sigismund (1368–1437) Holy Roman Emperor.
His advice on achieving happiness
Biographiana, Vol. I

9 Most of the time we think we're sick, it's all in the
mind.
Thomas Wolfe (1900–38) US novelist.
Look Homeward, Angel, Pt. I, Ch. 1

□ IMAGINATION □

1 Art is ruled uniquely by the imagination.
Benedetto Croce (1866–1952) Italian philosopher.
Esthetic, Ch. 1

2 She has no imagination and that means no
compassion.
Michael Foot (1913–) British Labour politician and
journalist.
Referring to Margaret Thatcher
Attrib.

3 Were it not for imagination, Sir, a man would be
as happy in the arms of a chambermaid as of a
Duchess.
Samuel Johnson (1709–84) British lexicographer.
Life of Johnson (J. Boswell), Vol. III

4 I am certain of nothing but the holiness of the
heart's affections and the truth of imagination –
what the imagination seizes as beauty must be
truth – whether it existed before or not.
John Keats (1795–1821) British poet.
Letter to Benjamin Bailey, 22 Nov 1817

5 Imagination and fiction make up more than three
quarters of our real life.
Simone Weil (1909–43) French philosopher.
Gravity and Grace

□ IMITATION □

See also originality

1 Imitation is the sincerest form of flattery.
Charles Caleb Colton (?1780–1832) British clergyman and
writer.
Lacon, Vol. I

2 When people are free to do as they please, they
usually imitate each other.
Eric Hoffer (1902–83) US writer.
The Passionate State of Mind

3 You will, Oscar, you will.
James Whistler (1834–1903) US painter.
Replying to Oscar Wilde's exclamation 'I wish I had said that!'
Attrib.

□ IMMORTALITY □

See also eternity, mortality, posterity

1 I don't want to achieve immortality through my
work...I want to achieve it through not dying.
Woody Allen (Allen Stewart Konigsberg; 1935–) US film
actor.
Woody Allen and His Comedy (E. Lax)

2 No young man believes he shall ever die.
William Hazlitt (1778–1830) British essayist.
On the Feeling of Immortality in Youth

3 He had decided to live for ever or die in the
attempt.
Joseph Heller (1923–) US novelist.
Catch-22, Ch. 3

4 We feel and know that we are eternal.
Benedict Spinoza (Baruch de Spinoza; 1632–77) Dutch
philosopher.
Ethics

5 A slumber did my spirit seal;
I had no human fears:
She seemed a thing that could not feel
The touch of earthly years.
No motion has she now, no force;
She neither hears nor sees;
Rolled round in earth's diurnal course,
With rocks, and stones, and trees.
William Wordsworth (1770–1850) British poet.
A Slumber did my Spirit seal

□ IMPERFECTION □

See also mistakes, perfection, weakness

1 Watch and pray, that ye enter not into temptation:
the spirit indeed is willing, but the flesh is weak.
Bible: Matthew
26:41

2 When you have faults, do not fear to abandon
them.
Confucius (K'ung Fu-tzu; 551–479 BC) Chinese philosopher.
Analects

3 Even imperfection itself may have its ideal or per-
fect state.
Thomas De Quincey (1785–1859) British writer.
Murder Considered as one of the Fine Arts

4 We must touch his weaknesses with a delicate
hand. There are some faults so nearly allied to
excellence, that we can scarce weed out the fault
without eradicating the virtue.
Oliver Goldsmith (1728–74) Irish-born British writer.
The Good-Natured Man, I

5 We only confess our little faults to persuade peo-
ple that we have no large ones.
Duc de la Rochefoucauld (1613–80) French writer.
Maximes, 327

6 If we had no faults of our own, we would not take
so much pleasure in noticing those of others.
Duc de la Rochefoucauld (1613–80) French writer.
Maximes, 31

7 Oh. I have got lots of human weaknesses, who
hasn't?
Margaret Thatcher (1925–) British politician and prime
minister.
The Times, 1983

8 We are none of us infallible – not even the young-
est of us.
William Hepworth Thompson (1810–86) British academic.
Referring to G. W. Balfour, who was a junior fellow of Trinity Col-
lege at the time
Collections and Recollections (G. W. E. Russell), Ch. 18

□ IMPETUOSITY □

See also haste, spontaneity

1 There are some who speak one moment before
they think.
Jean de La Bruyère (1645–96) French satirist.
Les Caractères

2 Celerity is never more admir'd
Than by the negligent.
William Shakespeare (1564–1616) English dramatist.
Antony and Cleopatra, III:7

3 A youth to whom was given
So much of earth – so much of heaven,
And such impetuous blood.
William Wordsworth (1770–1850) British poet.
Ruth

□ IMPORTANCE □

See also triviality

1 In heaven an angel is nobody in particular.
George Bernard Shaw (1856–1950) Irish dramatist and critic.
Man and Superman, 'Maxims for Revolutionists'

2 Art and religion first; then philosophy; lastly
science. That is the order of the great subjects
of life, that's their order of importance.
Muriel Spark (1918–) British novelist.
The Prime of Miss Jean Brodie, Ch. 2

□ IMPRESSIONABILITY □

1 She had
A heart – how shall I say? – too soon made glad,
Too easily impressed.
Robert Browning (1812–89) British poet.
My Last Duchess

2 Give me a girl at an impressionable age, and she
is mine for life.
Muriel Spark (1918–) British novelist.
The Prime of Miss Jean Brodie, Ch. 1

□ IMPRISONMENT □

See also freedom, oppression, slavery

1 A robin redbreast in a cage
Puts all Heaven in a rage.
William Blake (1757–1827) British poet.
Auguries of Innocence

2 O! dreadful is the check – intense the agony
When the ear begins to hear, and the eye begins
to see;
When the pulse begins to throb – the brain to
think again –

The soul to feel the flesh, and the flesh to feel the chain.
Emily Brontë (1818–48) British novelist.
The Prisoner

3 Stone walls do not a prison make,
Nor iron bars a cage.
Richard Lovelace (1618–58) English poet.
To Althea, from Prison

4 We think caged birds sing, when indeed they cry.
John Webster (1580–1625) English dramatist.
The White Devil, V:4

5 I never saw a man who looked
With such a wistful eye
Upon that little tent of blue
Which prisoners call the sky.
Oscar Wilde (1854–1900) Irish-born British dramatist.
The Ballad of Reading Gaol, I:3

6 I know not whether Laws be right,
Or whether Laws be wrong;
All that we know who lie in gaol
Is that the wall is strong;
And that each day is like a year,
A year whose days are long.
Oscar Wilde
The Ballad of Reading Gaol, V:1

□ IMPROVEMENT □

See also progress

1 He so improved the city that he justly boasted that he found it brick and left it marble.
Augustus (63 BC–14 AD) Roman emperor.
Referring to Rome
The Lives of the Caesars (Suetonius), 'Augustus'

2 I've got to admit it's getting better.
It's a little better all the time.
John Lennon (1940–80) British rock musician.
Getting Better (with Paul McCartney)

□ INCOMPETENCE □

1 This island is almost made of coal and surrounded by fish. Only an organizing genius could produce a shortage of coal and fish in Great Britain at the same time.
Aneurin Bevan (1897–1960) British Labour politician.
Speech, Blackpool, 18 May 1945

2 The grotesque chaos of a Labour council – a *Labour* council – hiring taxis to scuttle around a city handing out redundancy notices to its own workers.
Neil Kinnock (1942–) British politician.
Attacking militant members in Liverpool
Speech, Labour Party Conference, Bournemouth, 1985

3 He really deserves some sort of decoration…a medal inscribed 'For Vaguery in the Field'.
John Osborne (1929–) British dramatist.
Look Back in Anger, I

4 Work is accomplished by those employees who have not yet reached their level of incompetence.
Laurence J. Peter (1919–90) Canadian writer.
The Peter Principle

5 Madame, there you sit with that magnificent instrument between your legs, and all you can do is *scratch* it!
Arturo Toscanini (1867–1957) Italian conductor.
Rebuking an incompetent woman cellist
Attrib.

□ INDECISION □

1 I will have nothing to do with a man who can blow hot and cold with the same breath.
Aesop (6th century BC) Reputed Greek writer of fables.
Fables, 'The Man and the Satyr'

2 Nothing is so exhausting as indecision, and nothing is so futile.
Bertrand Russell (1872–1970) British philosopher.
Attrib.

3 I must have a prodigious quantity of mind; it takes me as much as a week, sometimes, to make it up.
Mark Twain (Samuel Langhorne Clemens; 1835–1910) US writer.
The Innocents Abroad, Ch. 7

□ INDEPENDENCE □

See also self-reliance, society

1 When in the course of human events, it becomes necessary for one people to dissolve the political bonds which have connected them with another, and to assume among the powers of the earth the separate and equal station to which the laws of nature and of Nature's God entitle them, a decent respect to the opinions of mankind requires that they should declare the causes which impel them to the separation.
Thomas Jefferson (1743–1826) US statesman.
Declaration of Independence, Preamble

2 I think it much better that…every man paddle his own canoe.
Captain Frederick Marryat (1792–1848) British novelist.
Settlers in Canada, Ch. 8

□ INDIFFERENCE □

See also insensitivity

1 But what is past my help is past my care.
Francis Beaumont (1584–1616) English dramatist.
With John Fletcher
The Double Marriage, I:1

2 Nothing is so fatal to religion as indifference, which is, at least, half infidelity.
Edmund Burke (1729–97) British politician.
Letter to William Smith, 29 Jan 1795

3 At length the morn and cold indifference came.
Nicholas Rowe (1674–1718) English dramatist.
The Fair Penitent, I:1

□ INDIVIDUALITY □

See also opinions, taste

1 Here's tae us wha's like us?
Gey few, and they're a' deid.
Anonymous
Scottish toast

2 Nature made him, and then broke the mould.
Ludovico Ariosto (1474–1533) Italian poet.
Referring to Charlemagne's paladin, Roland
Orlando furioso

3 It is the common wonder of all men, how among
so many million of faces, there should be none
alike.
Thomas Browne (1605–82) English physician and writer.
Religio Medici, Pt. II

□ INDULGENCE □

1 Love is a boy, by poets styl'd,
Then spare the rod, and spoil the child.
Samuel Butler (1612–80) English satirist.
Hudibras, Pt. II

2 Every luxury was lavished on you – atheism,
breast-feeding, circumcision. I had to make my
own way.
Joe Orton (1933–67) British dramatist.
Loot, I

□ INDUSTRIAL RELATIONS □

See also diplomacy, strikes

1 British management doesn't seem to understand
the importance of the human factor.
Charles, Prince of Wales (1948–) Eldest son of
Elizabeth II.
Speech, Parliamentary and Scientific Committee lunch, 21 Feb
1979

2 Industrial relations are like sexual relations. It's
better between two consenting parties.
Vic Feather (1908–76) British trade-union leader.
Guardian Weekly, 8 Aug 1976

3 It might be said that it is the ideal of the employer
to have production without employees and the
ideal of the employee is to have income without
work.
E. F. Schumacher (1911–77) German-born economist.
The Observer, 'Sayings of the Week', 4 May 1975

□ INFERIORITY □

See also equality, mediocrity

1 Wherever an inferiority complex exists, there is
a good reason for it. There is always something

inferior there, although not just where we per-
suade ourselves that it is.
Carl Gustav Jung (1875–1961) Swiss psychoanalyst.
Interview, 1943

2 It is an infallible sign of the second-rate in nature
and intellect to make use of everything and
everyone.
Ada Beddington Leverson (1862–1933) British writer.
The Limit

3 No one can make you feel inferior without your
consent.
Eleanor Roosevelt (1884–1962) US writer and lecturer.
This is My Story

□ INFINITY □

1 The Desire of Man being Infinite, the possession
is Infinite, and himself Infinite.
William Blake (1757–1827) British poet.
There is no Natural Religion

2 I cannot help it; – in spite of myself, infinity tor-
ments me.
Alfred de Musset (1810–57) French dramatist and poet.
L'Espoir en Dieu

□ INFLEXIBILITY □

See also determination, stubbornness

1 You cannot shake hands with a clenched fist.
Indira Gandhi (1917–84) Indian stateswoman.
Remark at a press conference, New Delhi, 19 Oct 1971

2 U-turn if you want to. The lady's not for turning.
Margaret Thatcher (1925–) British politician and prime
minister.
Speech, Conservative Conference, 1980

3 Minds like beds always made up,
(more stony than a shore)
unwilling or unable.
William Carlos Williams (1883–1963) US poet.
Paterson, I, Preface

□ INFLUENCE □

See also inspiration, power

1 How to Win Friends and Influence People.
Dale Carnegie (1888–1955) US lecturer and writer.
Book title

2 Practical men, who believe themselves to be
quite exempt from any intellectual influences,
are usually the slaves of some defunct economist. Madmen in authority, who hear voices in
the air, are distilling their frenzy from some academic scribbler of a few years back.
John Maynard Keynes (1883–1946) British economist.
The General Theory of Employment, Interest and Money, Bk. VI,
Ch. 24

3 Athens holds sway over all Greece; I dominate Athens; my wife dominates me; our newborn son dominates her.
Themistocles (c. 528–462 BC) Athenian statesman.
Explaining an earlier remark to the effect that his young son ruled all Greece
Attrib.

4 The hand that rocks the cradle
Is the hand that rules the world.
William Ross Wallace (1819–81) US poet and songwriter.
John o'London's Treasure Trove

□ INGRATITUDE □

1 And having looked to government for bread, on the very first scarcity they will turn and bite the hand that fed them.
Edmund Burke (1729–97) British politician.
Thoughts and Details on Scarcity

2 Our gratitude to most benefactors is the same as our feeling for dentists who have pulled our teeth. We acknowledge the good they have done and the evil from which they have delivered us, but we remember the pain they occasioned and do not love them very much.
Nicolas Chamfort (1741–94) French writer.
Maximes et pensées

3 Blow, blow, thou winter wind,
Thou art not so unkind
As man's ingratitude.
William Shakespeare (1564–1616) English dramatist.
As You Like It, II:7

4 Ingratitude, thou marble-hearted fiend,
More hideous when thou show'st thee in a child
Than the sea-monster!
William Shakespeare
King Lear I:4

5 I hate ingratitude more in a man
Than lying, vainness, babbling drunkenness,
Or any taint of vice whose strong corruption
Inhabits our frail blood.
William Shakespeare
Twelfth Night, III:4

□ INJUSTICE □

1 Those who have had no share in the good fortunes of the mighty often have a share in their misfortunes.
Bertolt Brecht (1898–1956) German dramatist.
The Caucasian Chalk Circle

2 When one has been threatened with a great injustice, one accepts a smaller as a favour.
Jane Welsh Carlyle (1801–66) The wife of Thomas Carlyle.
Journal, 21 Nov 1855

3 To disarm the strong and arm the weak would be to change the social order which it's my job to preserve. Justice is the means by which established injustices are sanctioned.
Anatole France (Jacques Anatole François Thibault; 1844–1924) French writer.
Crainquebille

4 Undeservedly you will atone for the sins of your fathers.
Horace (Quintus Horatius Flaccus; 65–8 BC) Roman poet.
Odes, III

5 We was robbed!
Joe Jacobs (1896–1940) US boxing manager.
Complaining to the audience when the heavyweight title of Max Schmeling, whom he managed, was passed to Jack Sharkey
Attrib.

6 The government burns down whole cities while the people are forbidden to light lamps.
Mao Tse-Tung (1893–1976) Chinese communist leader.
Attrib.

7 I am a man
More sinn'd against than sinning.
William Shakespeare (1564–1616) English dramatist.
King Lear, III:2

□ INNOCENCE □

See also conscience, ignorance

1 Now I am ashamed of confessing that I have nothing to confess.
Fanny Burney (Frances Burney D'Arblay; 1752–1840) British novelist.
Evelina, Letter 59

2 Now my innocence begins to weigh me down.
Jean Racine (1639–99) French dramatist.
Andromaque, III:1

3 'But the Emperor has nothing on at all!' cried a little child.
Hans Christian Andersen (1805–75) Danish writer.
The Emperor's New Clothes

4 No, it is not only our fate but our business to lose innocence, and once we have lost that, it is futile to attempt a picnic in Eden.
Elizabeth Bowen (1899–1973) Irish novelist.
In *Orion III*, 'Out of a Book'

5 Ralph wept for the end of innocence, the darkness of man's heart, and the fall through the air of the true, wise friend called Piggy.
William Golding (1911–) British novelist.
Lord of the Flies, Ch. 12

6 And the wild boys innocent as strawberries.
Dylan Thomas (1914–53) Welsh poet.
The hunchback in the park

□INNOVATION□

See also conservatism, novelty, originality, progress

1 He that will not apply new remedies must expect
new evils: for time is the greatest innovator.
Francis Bacon (1561–1626) English philosopher.
Essays, 'Of Innovations'

2 I once knew a chap who had a system of just
hanging the baby on the clothes line to dry and
he was greatly admired by his fellow citizens for
having discovered a wonderful innovation on
changing a diaper.
Damon Runyon (1884–1946) US writer.
Short Takes, 'Diaper Dexterity'

□INNUENDO□

See also meaning

1 There was an old man of Boulogne
Who sang a most topical song.
It wasn't the words
That frightened the birds,
But the horrible double-entendre.
Anonymous

2 Where more is meant than meets the ear.
John Milton (1608–74) English poet.
Il Penseroso

□INSENSITIVITY□

See also hurt, indifference

1 Miss Buss and Miss Beale
Cupid's darts do not feel.
How different from us,
Miss Beale and Miss Buss.
Anonymous
Written about the headmistresses of North London Collegiate
School and Cheltenham Ladies' College, respectively

2 Just as the meanest and most vicious deeds
require spirit and talent, so even the greatest
deeds require a certain insensitiveness which on
other occasions is called stupidity.
Georg Christoph Lichtenberg (1742–99) German physicist
and writer.
Aphorisms

□INSIGNIFICANCE□

See also triviality

1 There are some people who leave impressions
not so lasting as the imprint of an oar upon the
water.
Kate Chopin (1851–1904) US writer.
The Awakening, Ch. 34

2 She was one of those indispensables of whom
one makes the discovery, when they are gone,
that one can get on quite as well without them.
Aldous Huxley (1894–1964) British novelist.
Mortal Coils, 'Nuns at Luncheon'

□INSINCERITY□

See also hypocrisy

1 Experience teaches you that the man who looks
you straight in the eye, particularly if he adds a
firm handshake, is hiding something.
Clifton Fadiman (1904–) US writer.
Enter, Conversing

2 He who praises everybody praises nobody.
Samuel Johnson (1709–84) British lexicographer.
Life of Johnson (J. Boswell), Vol. III

3 Most friendship is feigning, most loving mere
folly.
William Shakespeare (1564–1616) English dramatist.
As You Like It, II:7

□INSPIRATION□

1 That I make poetry and give pleasure (if I give
pleasure) are because of you.
Horace (Quintus Horatius Flaccus; 65–8 BC) Roman poet.
Odes, IV

2 Biting my truant pen, beating myself for spite:
'Fool!' said my Muse to me, 'look in thy heart and
write.'
Philip Sidney (1554–86) English poet and courtier.
Sonnet, Astrophel and Stella

3 I did not write it. God wrote it. I merely did his
dictation.
Harriet Beecher Stowe (1811–96) US novelist.
Referring to *Uncle Tom's Cabin*
Attrib.

4 The true God, the mighty God, is the God of
ideas.
Alfred de Vigny (1797–1863) French writer.
La Bouteille à la mer

□INSULTS□

See also actors, criticism, politicians

1 I don't want you here – now sod off!
Princess Anne (1950–) The Princess Royal, only daughter
of Elizabeth II.
Remark, Jan 1987

2 Come in, you Anglo-Saxon swine
And drink of my Algerian wine.
'Twill turn your eyeballs black and blue,
And damn well good enough for you.
Brendan Behan (1923–64) Irish playwright.
Painted as an advert on the window of a Paris café (the owner of
which could not speak English)
My Life with Brendan (B. Behan)

3 If there is anyone here whom I have not insulted,
I beg his pardon.
Johannes Brahms (1833–97) German composer.
Said on leaving a gathering of friends
Brahms (P. Latham)

4 An injury is much sooner forgotten than an insult.
Earl of Chesterfield (1694–1773) English statesman.
Letter to his son, 9 Oct 1746

5 The Cat, the Rat, and Lovell our dog
Rule all England under a hog.
William Collingbourne (d. 1484) English landowner.
The cat was Sir William Catesby; the rat Sir Richard Ratcliffe; the dog Lord Lovell, who had a dog on his crest. The wild boar refers to the emblem of Richard III
Chronicles (R. Holinshed), III

6 Good-morning, gentlemen both.
Elizabeth I (1533–1603) Queen of England.
When addressing a group of eighteen tailors
Sayings of Queen Elizabeth (Chamberlin)

7 A semi-house-trained polecat.
Michael Foot (1913–) British Labour politician and journalist.
Referring to Norman Tebbitt
Speech, House of Commons

8 Like being savaged by a dead sheep.
Denis Healey (1917–) British Labour politician.
Referring to the attack launched by Geoffrey Howe upon his Budget proposals
The Listener, 21 Dec 1978

9 In a disastrous fire in President Reagan's library both books were destroyed. And the real tragedy is that he hadn't finished colouring one.
Jonathan Hunt (1938–) New Zealand politician.
The Observer, 30 Aug 1981

10 Calumnies are answered best with silence.
Ben Jonson (1573–1637) English dramatist.
Volpone, II:2

11 They travel best in gangs, hanging around like clumps of bananas, thick skinned and yellow.
Neil Kinnock (1942–) British politician.
Referring to Tory critics
The Observer, 'Sayings of the Week', 22 Feb 1987

12 She only went to Venice because somebody told her she could walk down the middle of the street.
Neil Kinnock
Referring to Margaret Thatcher who attended a meeting in Venice just before the 1987 election
Speech, Leeds, 9 June 1987

13 When they circumcised Herbert Samuel they threw away the wrong bit.
David Lloyd George (1863–1945) British Liberal statesman.
Attrib. in *The Listener*, 7 Sept 1978

14 The answer is in the plural and they bounce.
Edwin Lutyens (1869–1944) British architect.
Attrib.

15 I have forgotten more law than you ever knew, but allow me to say, I have not forgotten much.
John Maynard (1602–90) English judge.
Replying to Judge Jeffreys' suggestion that he was so old he had forgotten the law

16 Thou whoreson zed! thou unnecessary letter!
William Shakespeare (1564–1616) English dramatist.
King Lear, II:2

17 You silly moo.
Johnny Speight (1920–) British television scriptwriter.
Till Death Do Us Part

18 Okie use' to mean you was from Oklahoma. Now it means you're scum. Don't mean nothing itself, it's the way they say it.
John Steinbeck (1902–68) US novelist.
The Grapes of Wrath, Ch. 18

19 I dunno. Maybe it's that tally-ho lads attitude. You know, there'll always be an England, all that Empire crap they dish out. But I never could cop Poms.
Jeff Thomson Australian cricketer.
Remark, Oct 1987

20 A triumph of the embalmer's art.
Gore Vidal (1925–) US novelist.
Referring to Ronald Reagan
The Observer, 26 Apr 1981

21 I have always said about Tony that he immatures with age.
Harold Wilson (1916–) British politician and prime minister.
Referring to Anthony Wedgwood Benn
The Chariot of Israel

22 If I had had to choose between him and a cockroach as a companion for a walking-tour, the cockroach would have had it by a short head.
P. G. Wodehouse (1881–1975) British humorous novelist.
My Man Jeeves, 'The Spot of Art'

□ **INTEGRITY** □

See also honesty, morality, principles, righteousness, self, sincerity

1 Be so true to thyself, as thou be not false to others.
Francis Bacon (1561–1626) English philosopher.
Essays, 'Of Wisdom for a Man's Self'

2 Caesar's wife must be above suspicion.
Julius Caesar (100–44 BC) Roman general and statesman.
Said in justification of his divorce from Pompeia, after she was unwittingly involved in a scandal
Lives, 'Julius Caesar' (Plutarch)

3 Integrity without knowledge is weak and useless, and knowledge without integrity is dangerous and dreadful.
Samuel Johnson (1709–84) British lexicographer.
Rasselas, Ch. 41

4 Neither a borrower nor a lender be;
For loan oft loses both itself and friend,
And borrowing dulls the edge of husbandry.
This above all: to thine own self be true,

And it must follow, as the night the day,
Thou canst not then be false to any man.
William Shakespeare (1564–1616) English dramatist.
Hamlet, I:3

☐ INTELLECT ☐

See also intelligence, mind, thinking

1 We should take care not to make the intellect our
god; it has, of course, powerful muscles, but no
personality.
Albert Einstein (1879–1955) German-born US physicist.
Out of My Later Life, 51

2 The voice of the intellect is a soft one, but it does
not rest till it has gained a hearing.
Sigmund Freud (1856–1939) Austrian psychoanalyst.
The Future of an Illusion

3 The highest intellects, like the tops of moun-
tains, are the first to catch and to reflect the dawn.
Lord Macaulay (1800–59) British historian.
Historical Essays Contributed to the 'Edinburgh Review', 'Sir James
Mackintosh'

4 The higher the voice the smaller the intellect.
Ernest Newman (1868–1959) British music critic.
Attrib.

5 Intellect is invisible to the man who has none.
Arthur Schopenhauer (1788–1860) German philosopher.
Aphorismen zur Lebensweisheit

☐ INTELLECTUALS ☐

See also academics

1 An intellectual is a man who doesn't know how to
park a bike.
Spiro Agnew (1918–) US politician.
Attrib.

2 To the man-in-the-street, who, I'm sorry to say
Is a keen observer of life,
The word Intellectual suggests straight away
A man who's untrue to his wife.
W. H. Auden (1907–73) British poet.
Note on Intellectuals

3 I've been called many things, but never an intel-
lectual.
Tallulah Bankhead (1903–68) US actress.
Tallulah, Ch. 15

4 An intellectual is someone whose mind watches
itself.
Albert Camus (1913–60) French existentialist writer.
Notebooks, 1935–42

5 Do you think it pleases a man when he looks into
a woman's eyes and sees a reflection of the British Museum Reading Room?
Muriel Spark (1918–) British novelist.
The Wit of Women (L. and M. Cowan)

☐ INTELLIGENCE ☐

See also intellect, knowledge, mind, perception, thinking, understanding, wisdom

1 The intelligent are to the intelligentsia what a
man is to a gent.
Stanley Baldwin (1867–1947) British statesman.
Attrib.

2 One wants to mutter deeply that apart from having two good legs I also have two good degrees
and it is just possible that I do know what I'm talking about.
Edwina Currie (1946–) British politician.
Remark, Nov 1986

3 A really intelligent man feels what other men
only know.
Baron de Montesquieu (1689–1755) French writer.
Essai sur les causes qui peuvent affecter les esprits et les caractères

4 The more intelligence one has the more people
one finds original. Commonplace people see no
difference between men.
Blaise Pascal (1623–62) French philosopher and
mathematician.
Pensées, I

5 Intelligence is quickness to apprehend as distinct from ability, which is capacity to act wisely
on the thing apprehended.
A. N. Whitehead (1861–1947) British philosopher.
Dialogues, 135

☐ INTERRUPTIONS ☐

1 As I was saying the other day.
Luis Ponce de Léon (1527–91) Spanish monk.
Said on resuming a lecture interrupted by five years' imprison-
ment

2 Mr Wordsworth is never interrupted.
Mary Wordsworth (1770–1859) Wife of William Wordsworth.
Rebuking John Keats for interrupting a long monologue by
William Wordsworth
Attrib.

☐ INTRIGUE ☐

1 Ay, now the plot thickens very much upon us.
Duke of Buckingham (1628–87) English politician.
The Rehearsal, III:1

2 Everybody was up to something, especially, of
course, those who were up to nothing.
Noël Coward (1899–1973) British dramatist.
Future Indefinite

☐ IRELAND ☐

See also Britain, Irish

1 Ulster will fight; Ulster will be right.
Lord Randolph Churchill (1849–95) British Conservative
politician.
Letter, 7 May 1886

2 By yesterday morning British troops were patrolling the streets of Belfast. I fear that once Catholics and Protestants get used to our presence they will hate us more than they hate each other.
Richard Crossman (1907–74) British politician.
Diaries, 17 Aug 1969

3 Thus you have a starving population, an absentee aristocracy, and an alien Church, and in addition the weakest executive in the world. That is the Irish Question.
Benjamin Disraeli (1804–81) British statesman.
Speech, House of Commons, 16 Feb 1844

4 I never met anyone in Ireland who understood the Irish question, except one Englishman who had only been there a week.
Keith Fraser (1867–1935) British politician.
Speech, House of Commons, May 1919

5 Ireland is the old sow that eats her farrow.
James Joyce (1882–1941) Irish novelist.
A Portrait of the Artist as a Young Man, Ch. 5

6 It is a symbol of Irish art. The cracked looking glass of a servant.
James Joyce
Ulysses

7 The problem with Ireland is that it's a country full of genius, but with absolutely no talent.
Hugh Leonard (1926–) Irish dramatist.
Said during an interview
The Times, Aug 1977

8 The English should give Ireland home rule – and reserve the motion picture rights.
Will Rogers (1879–1935) US actor and humorist.
Autobiography (published posthumously)

9 Before Irish Home Rule is conceded by the Imperial Parliament, England as the predominant member of the three kingdoms will have to be convinced of its justice and equity.
Lord Rosebery (1847–1929) British statesman.
Speech, House of Lords, 11 Mar 1894

10 The moment the very name of Ireland is mentioned, the English seem to bid adieu to common feeling, common prudence, and common sense, and to act with the barbarity of tyrants, and the fatuity of idiots.
Sydney Smith (1771–1845) British clergyman and essayist.
The Letters of Peter Plymley

☐ IRISH ☐

See also British, Ireland

1 Other people have a nationality. The Irish and the Jews have a psychosis.
Brendan Behan (1923–64) Irish playwright.
Richard's Cork Leg, I

2 Not in vain is Ireland pouring itself all over the earth...The Irish, with their glowing hearts and reverent credulity, are needed in this cold age of intellect and skepticism.
Lydia M. Child (1802–80) US abolitionist campaigner.
Letters from New York, Vol. I, No. 33, 8 Dec 1842

3 Irish Americans are about as Irish as Black Americans are African.
Bob Geldof (1952–) Irish rock musician.
The Observer, 'Sayings of the Week', 22 Jun 1986

4 The Irish are a fair people; – they never speak well of one another.
Samuel Johnson (1709–84) British lexicographer.
Life of Johnson (J. Boswell), Vol. II

5 The Irish don't know what they want and are prepared to fight to the death to get it.
Sidney Littlewood (1895–1967) President of the Law Society.
Speech, 13 Apr 1961

☐ IRREVOCABILITY ☐

1 The die is cast.
Julius Caesar (100–44 BC) Roman general and statesman.
Said on crossing the Rubicon (49 BC) at the start of his campaign against Pompey
Attrib.

2 The Gods themselves cannot recall their gifts.
Alfred, Lord Tennyson (1809–92) British poet.
Tithonus

J

☐JAMES☐
Henry

(1843–1916) US novelist, who spent much of his life in Europe (from 1876 in England). *Roderick Hudson* (1875), his first successful novel, was followed by *Washington Square* (1881), *The Bostonians* (1886), *The Turn of the Screw* (1898), *The Ambassadors* (1903), and several others.

QUOTATIONS ABOUT JAMES

1 Henry James has a mind so fine that no idea could violate it.
  T. S. Eliot (1888–1965) US-born British poet and dramatist. Attrib.

2 Henry James was one of the nicest old ladies I ever met.
  William Faulkner (1897–1962) US novelist. Attrib.

QUOTATIONS BY JAMES

3 Live all you can; it's a mistake not to. It doesn't so much matter what you do in particular, so long as you have your life. If you haven't had that what *have* you had?
  The Ambassadors, Bk. V, Ch. 2

4 Experience was to be taken as showing that one might get a five-pound note as one got a light for a cigarette, but one had to check the friendly impulse to ask for it in the same way.
  The Awkward Age

5 It takes a great deal of history to produce a little literature.
  Life of Nathaniel Hawthorne, Ch. 1

6 To kill a human being is, after all, the least injury you can do him.
  My Friend Bingham

7 What is character but the determination of incident? What is incident but the illustration of character?
  Partial Portraits, 'The Art of Fiction'

8 The superiority of one man's opinion over another's is never so great as when the opinion is about a woman.
  The Tragic Muse, Ch. 9

9 Summer afternoon – summer afternoon; to me those have always been the two most beautiful words in the English language.
  A Backward Glance (Edith Wharton), Ch. 10

10 So it has come at last, the distinguished thing.
  Referring to his own death.
  A Backward Glance (Edith Wharton), Ch. 14

☐JEALOUSY☐
See also envy

1 For the ear of jealousy heareth all things: and the noise of murmurings is not hid.
  Bible: Wisdom
  1.10

2 Jealousy is no more than feeling alone among smiling enemies.
  Elizabeth Bowen (1899–1973) Irish novelist.
  The House in Paris

3 O, beware, my lord, of jealousy;
  It is the green-ey'd monster which doth mock
  The meat it feeds on.
  William Shakespeare (1564–1616) English dramatist.
  Othello, III:3

☐JEWS☐
See also Nazism, prejudice, racism, religion

1 Other people have a nationality. The Irish and the Jews have a psychosis.
  Brendan Behan (1923–64) Irish playwright.
  Richard's Cork Leg, I

2 Now the Lord had said unto Abram, Get thee out of thy country, and from thy kindred, and from thy father's house, unto a land that I will shew thee:
  And I will make of thee a great nation, and I will bless thee, and make thy name great; and thou shalt be a blessing:
  And I will bless them that bless thee, and curse him that curseth thee: and in thee shall all families of the earth be blessed.
  Bible: Genesis
  12:1–3

3 How odd
  Of God
  To choose
  The Jews.
  William Norman Ewer (1885–1976) British writer.
  For a reply see Cecil BROWNE
  How Odd

4 But not so odd
  As those who choose
  A Jewish God,
  But spurn the Jews.
  Cecil Browne
  In reply to EWER (above)

5 It is extremely difficult for a Jew to be converted, for how can he bring himself to believe in the divinity of – another Jew?
  Heinrich Heine (1797–1856) German poet and writer.
  Attrib.

6 The very best that is in the Jewish blood: a faculty for pure disinterestedness, and warm, physically warm love, that seems to make the corpuscles of the blood glow.
D. H. Lawrence (1885–1930) British novelist.
Kangaroo, Ch. 6

7 Pessimism is a luxury that a Jew never can allow himself.
Golda Meir (1898–1978) Russian-born Israeli stateswoman.
The Observer, 'Sayings of the Year', 29 Dec 1974

8 There are not enough prisons and concentration camps in Palestine to hold all the Jews who are ready to defend their lives and property.
Golda Meir
Speech, 2 May 1940

9 A Jewish man with parents alive is a fifteen-year-old boy, and will remain a fifteen-year-old boy till they die.
Philip Roth (1933–) US novelist.
Portnoy's Complaint

10 I believe that the Jews have made a contribution to the human condition out of all proportion to their numbers: I believe them to be an immense people. Not only have they supplied the world with two leaders of the stature of Jesus Christ and Karl Marx, but they have even indulged in the luxury of following neither one nor the other.
Peter Ustinov (1921–) British actor.
Dear Me, Ch. 19

11 The law of dislike for the unlike will always prevail. And whereas the unlike is normally situated at a safe distance, the Jews bring the unlike into the heart of *every milieu*, and must there defend a frontier line as large as the world.
Israel Zangwill (1864–1926) British writer.
Speeches, Articles and Letters, 'The Jewish Race'

☐ JOHNSON ☐
Samuel

(1709–84) British lexicographer and writer. His *Dictionary of the English Language* appeared in 1755. The moral fable *Rasselas* (1759) was followed by *The Lives of the English Poets* (1781). His close friend James Boswell wrote his celebrated biography, *Boswell's Life of Johnson* (1791).

QUOTATIONS ABOUT JOHNSON

1 There is no arguing with Johnson, for when his pistol misses fire, he knocks you down with the butt of it.
Oliver Goldsmith (1728–74) Irish-born British writer.
Life of Johnson (J. Boswell)

QUOTATIONS BY JOHNSON

2 Every quotation contributes something to the stability or enlargement of the language.
Dictionary of the English Language

3 But these were the dreams of a poet doomed at last to wake a lexicographer.
Dictionary of the English Language

4 *Lexicographer.* A writer of dictionaries, a harmless drudge.
Dictionary of the English Language

5 When two Englishmen meet, their first talk is of the weather.
The Idler

6 We are perpetually moralists, but we are geometricians only by chance. Our intercourse with intellectual nature is necessary; our speculations upon matter are voluntary, and at leisure.
Lives of the English Poets, 'Milton'

7 Almost every man wastes part of his life in attempts to display qualities which he does not possess, and to gain applause which he cannot keep.
The Rambler

8 Human life is everywhere a state in which much is to be endured, and little to be enjoyed.
Rasselas, Ch. 11

9 Marriage has many pains, but celibacy has no pleasures.
Rasselas, Ch. 26

10 Integrity without knowledge is weak and useless, and knowledge without integrity is dangerous and dreadful.
Rasselas, Ch. 41

11 Madam, before you flatter a man so grossly to his face, you should consider whether or not your flattery is worth his having.
Diary and Letters (Mme D'Arblay), Vol. I, Ch. 2

12 It is very strange, and very melancholy, that the paucity of human pleasures should persuade us ever to call hunting one of them.
Johnsonian Miscellanies (ed. G. B. Hill), Vol. I

13 A man is in general better pleased when he has a good dinner upon his table, than when his wife talks Greek.
Johnsonian Miscellanies (ed. G. B. Hill), Vol. II

14 What is written without effort is in general read without pleasure.
Johnsonian Miscellanies (ed. G. B. Hill), Vol. II

15 Love is the wisdom of the fool and the folly of the wise.
Johnsonian Miscellanies (ed. G. B. Hill), Vol. II

16 It is incident to physicians, I am afraid, beyond all other men, to mistake subsequence for consequence.
Life of Johnson (J. Boswell), Vol. I

17 A fly, Sir, may sting a stately horse and make him wince; but one is but an insect, and the other is a horse still.
Referring to critics.
Life of Johnson (J. Boswell), Vol. I

18 If a man does not make new acquaintance as he advances through life, he will soon find himself left alone. A man, Sir, should keep his friendship in constant repair.
Life of Johnson (J. Boswell), Vol. I

19 But if he does really think that there is no distinction between virtue and vice, why, Sir, when he leaves our houses let us count our spoons.
Life of Johnson (J. Boswell), Vol. I

20 Why, Sir, most schemes of political improvement are very laughable things.
Life of Johnson (J. Boswell), Vol. II

21 It matters not how a man dies, but how he lives. The act of dying is not of importance, it lasts so short a time.
Life of Johnson (J. Boswell), Vol. II

22 I do not care to speak ill of any man behind his back, but I believe the gentleman is an *attorney*.
Life of Johnson (J. Boswell), Vol. II

23 Read over your compositions, and where ever you meet with a passage which you think is particularly fine, strike it out.
Recalling the advice of a college tutor.
Life of Johnson (J. Boswell), Vol. II

24 There are few ways in which a man can be more innocently employed than in getting money.
Life of Johnson (J. Boswell), Vol. II

25 Patriotism is the last refuge of a scoundrel.
Life of Johnson (J. Boswell), Vol. II

26 Knowledge is of two kinds. We know a subject ourselves, or we know where we can find information upon it.
Life of Johnson (J. Boswell), Vol. II

27 Fine clothes are good only as they supply the want of other means of procuring respect.
Life of Johnson (J. Boswell), Vol. II

28 If a madman were to come into this room with a stick in his hand, no doubt we should pity the state of his mind; but our primary consideration would be to take care of ourselves. We should knock him down first, and pity him afterwards.
Life of Johnson (J. Boswell), Vol. III

29 We would all be idle if we could.
Life of Johnson (J. Boswell), Vol. III

30 No man but a blockhead ever wrote, except for money.
Life of Johnson (J. Boswell), Vol. III

31 Depend upon it, Sir, when a man knows he is to be hanged in a fortnight, it concentrates his mind wonderfully.
Life of Johnson (J. Boswell), Vol. III

32 When a man is tired of London, he is tired of life; for there is in London all that life can afford.
Life of Johnson (J. Boswell), Vol. III

33 He who praises everybody praises nobody.
Life of Johnson (J. Boswell), Vol. III

34 Claret is the liquor for boys; port for men; but he who aspires to be a hero must drink brandy.
Life of Johnson (J. Boswell), Vol. III

35 They are forced plants, raised in a hot-bed; and they are poor plants; they are but cucumbers after all.
Referring to Gray's *Odes*.
Life of Johnson (J. Boswell), Vol. IV

36 There is a wicked inclination in most people to suppose an old man decayed in his intellects. If a young or middle-aged man, when leaving a company, does not recollect where he laid his hat, it is nothing; but if the same inattention is discovered in an old man, people will shrug up their shoulders, and say, 'His memory is going.'
Life of Johnson (J. Boswell), Vol. IV

37 As I know more of mankind I expect less of them, and am ready now to call a man *a good man*, upon easier terms than I was formerly.
Life of Johnson (J. Boswell), Vol. IV

38 Sir, I have found you an argument; but I am not obliged to find you an understanding.
Life of Johnson (J. Boswell), Vol. IV

39 Sir, I look upon every day to be lost, in which I do not make a new acquaintance.
Life of Johnson (J. Boswell), Vol. IV

40 I have, all my life long, been lying till noon; yet I tell all young men, and tell them with great sincerity, that nobody who does not rise early will ever do any good.
Tour to the Hebrides (J. Boswell)

41 I am always sorry when any language is lost, because languages are the pedigree of nations.
Tour to the Hebrides (J. Boswell)

42 Come, let me know what it is that makes a Scotch-man happy!

Ordering for himself a glass of whisky.

Tour to the Hebrides (J. Boswell)

□ JONSON □
Ben

(1573–1637) English dramatist and poet. His plays include *Volpone* (1606), *The Alchemist* (1610), and *Bartholomew Fair* (1614); he published two collections of verse.

1 Alas, all the castles I have, are built with air, thou know'st.

Eastward Ho, II:2

2 Ods me, I marvel what pleasure or felicity they have in taking their roguish tobacco. It is good for nothing but to choke a man, and fill him full of smoke and embers.

Every Man in His Humour, III:5

3 Talking and eloquence are not the same: to speak, and to speak well, are two things.

Timber, or Discoveries made upon Men and Matter

4 He was not of an age, but for all time!

To the Memory of William Shakespeare

□ JOURNALISM □

See also editors, newspapers

1 'Christianity, of course but why journalism?'

Arthur Balfour (1848–1930) British statesman.
In reply to Frank Harris's remark, '…all the faults of the age come from Christianity and journalism'
Autobiography (Margot Asquith), Ch. 10

2 Journalists say a thing that they know isn't true, in the hope that if they keep on saying it long enough it will be true.

Arnold Bennett (1867–1931) British novelist.
The Title, II

3 No news is good news; no journalists is even better.

Nicolas Bentley (1907–78) British cartoonist and writer.
Attrib.

4 Journalism is the only job that requires no degrees, no diplomas and no specialised knowledge of any kind.

Patrick Campbell (1913–80) British humorous writer and editor.
My Life and Easy Times

5 Journalism largely consists of saying 'Lord Jones is dead' to people who never knew Lord Jones was alive.

G. K. Chesterton (1874–1936) British writer.
Attrib.

6 Literature is the art of writing something that will be read twice; journalism what will be grasped at once.

Cyril Connolly (1903–74) British journalist.
Enemies of Promise, Ch. 3

7 I hesitate to say what the functions of the modern journalist may be; but I imagine that they do not exclude the intelligent anticipation of facts even before they occur.

Lord Curzon (1859–1925) British politician.
Speech, House of Commons, 29 Mar 1898

8 I am myself a gentleman of the Press, and I bear no other scutcheon.

Benjamin Disraeli (1804–81) British statesman.
Speech, House of Commons, 18 Feb 1863

9 On the whole I would not say that our Press is obscene. I would say that it trembles on the brink of obscenity.

Lord Longford (1905–   ) British politician and social reformer.
The Observer, 'Sayings of the Year', 1963

10 The gallery in which the reporters sit has become a fourth estate of the realm.

Lord Macaulay (1800–59) British historian.
Referring to the press gallery in the House of Commons
Historical Essays Contributed to the 'Edinburgh Review', 'Hallam's "Constitutional History"'

11 Once a newspaper touches a story, the facts are lost forever, even to the protagonists.

Norman Mailer (1923–   ) US writer.
The Presidential Papers

12 A good newspaper, I suppose, is a nation talking to itself.

Arthur Miller (1915–   ) US dramatist.
The Observer, 'Sayings of the Week', 26 Nov 1961

13 SIXTY HORSES WEDGED IN A CHIMNEY
The story to fit this sensational headline has not turned up yet.

J. B. Morton (1893–1979) British journalist.
The Best of Beachcomber, 'Mr Justice Cocklecarrot: Home Life'

14 Journalists belong in the gutter because that is where ruling classes throw their guilty secrets.

Gerald Priestland British broadcaster and writer.
The Times, 22 May 1988

15 Its primary office is the gathering of news. At the peril of its soul it must see that the supply is not tainted. Neither in what it gives, nor in what it does not give, nor in the mode of presentation, must the unclouded face of truth suffer wrong. Comment is free but facts are sacred.

C. P. Scott (1846–1932) British journalist.
Manchester Guardian, 6 May 1926

16 News is what a chap who doesn't care much about anything wants to read. And it's only news until he's read it. After that it's dead.
Evelyn Waugh (1903–66) British novelist.
Scoop Bk. 1, Ch. 5

17 Journalism – an ability to meet the challenge of filling the space.
Rebecca West (Cicely Isabel Fairfield; 1892–1983) British novelist and journalist.
The New York Herald Tribune, 22 April 1956

18 There is much to be said in favour of modern journalism. By giving us the opinions of the uneducated, it keeps us in touch with the ignorance of the community.
Oscar Wilde (1854–1900) Irish-born British dramatist.
The Critic as Artist, Pt. 2

19 You cannot hope to bribe or twist, thank God! the British journalist. But, seeing what the man will do unbribed, there's no occasion to.
Humbert Wolfe (1886–1940) British poet.
The Uncelestial City, Bk. I, 'Over the Fire'

☐ JUDGMENT ☐

1 Judge not, that ye be not judged.
Bible: Matthew
7:1

2 And why beholdest thou the mote that is in thy brother's eye, but considerest not the beam that is in thine own eye?
Bible: Matthew
7:3

3 And I saw a great white throne, and him that sat on it, from whose face the earth and the heaven fled away; and there was found no place for them. And I saw the dead, small and great, stand before God; and the books were opened: and another book was opened, which is the book of life: and the dead were judged out of those things which were written in the books, according to their works.
And the sea gave up the dead which were in it; and death and hell delivered up the dead which were in them: and they were judged every man according to their works.
Bible: Revelations
20:11–13

4 No man can justly censure or condemn another, because indeed no man truly knows another.
Thomas Browne (1605–82) British physician and writer.
Religio Medici, Pt. II

5 Your representative owes you, not his industry only, but his judgement; and he betrays instead of serving you if he sacrifices it to your opinion.
Edmund Burke (1729–97) British politician.
Speech to the electors of Bristol, 3 Nov 1774

6 You shall judge of a man by his foes as well as by his friends.
Joseph Conrad (Teodor Josef Konrad Korzeniowski; 1857–1924) Polish-born British novelist.
Lord Jim, Ch. 34

7 Force, if unassisted by judgement, collapses through its own mass.
Horace (Quintus Horatius Flaccus; 65–8 BC) Roman poet.
Odes, III

8 Everyone complains of his memory, but no one complains of his judgement.
Duc de la Rochefoucauld (1613–80) French writer.
Maximes, 89

☐ JUSTICE ☐

See also injustice, judgment, law, lawyers

1 The place of justice is a hallowed place.
Francis Bacon (1561–1626) English philosopher.
Essays, 'Of Judicature'

2 It is better that ten guilty persons escape than one innocent suffer.
William Blackstone (1723–80) British jurist.
Commentaries on the Laws of England, Bk. IV, Ch. 27

3 The rain it raineth on the just
And also on the unjust fella:
But chiefly on the just, because
The unjust steals the just's umbrella.
Charles Bowen (1835–94) British judge.
Sands of Time (Walter Sichel)

4 Let justice be done, though the world perish.
Ferdinand I (1503–64) Holy Roman Emperor.
Attrib.

5 Justice should not only be done, but should manifestly and undoubtedly be seen to be done.
Gordon Hewart (1870–1943) British lawyer and politician.
The Chief (R. Jackson)

6 Justice is the constant and perpetual wish to render to every one his due.
Justinian I (482–565 AD) Byzantine emperor.
Institutes, I

7 Justice is such a fine thing that we cannot pay too dearly for it.
Alain-René Lesage (1668–1747) French writer.
Crispin rival de son maître, IX

8 I'm arm'd with more than complete steel –
The justice of my quarrel.
Christopher Marlowe (1564–93) English dramatist.
Play also attributed to others
Lust's Dominion, IV:3

9 In England, Justice is open to all, like the Ritz hotel.
James Mathew (1830–1908) British judge.
Also attrib. to Lord Darling
Miscellany-at-Law (R. E. Megarry)

10 The love of justice in most men is simply the fear of suffering injustice.

Duc de la Rochefoucauld (1613–80) French writer.
Maximes, 78

11 Haste still pays haste, and leisure answers leisure;
Like doth quit like, and Measure still for Measure.

William Shakespeare (1564–1616) English dramatist.
Measure for Measure, V:1

12 This is a British murder inquiry and some degree of justice must be seen to be more or less done.

Tom Stoppard (1937–) Czech-born British dramatist.
Jumpers, II

13 Under a government which imprisons any unjustly, the true place for a just man is also a prison.

Henry David Thoreau (1817–62) US writer.
Civil Disobedience

K

KEATS
John

(1795–1821) British poet. Trained as a doctor, he devoted most of his short life to poetry. *Endymion* (1818) was attacked by the critics but he eventually established his reputation with *La Belle Dame Sans Merci* (1820), *Ode to a Nightingale* (1820), and other works. He died in Rome of tuberculosis.

QUOTATIONS ABOUT KEATS

1 I see a schoolboy when I think of him
With face and nose pressed to a sweetshop
window.
W. B. Yeats (1865–1939) Irish poet.
Attrib.

QUOTATIONS BY KEATS

2 A thing of beauty is a joy for ever:
Its loveliness increases; it will never
Pass into nothingness; but still will keep
A bower quiet for us, and a sleep
Full of sweet dreams, and health, and quiet
breathing.
Endymion, I

3 The poet and the dreamer are distinct,
Diverse, sheer opposite, antipodes.
The one pours out a balm upon the world,
The other vexes it.
The Fall of Hyperion, I

4 Ever let the fancy roam,
Pleasure never is at home.
Fancy, I

5 Love in a hut, with water and a crust,
Is – Love, forgive us! – cinders, ashes, dust;
Love in a palace is perhaps at last
More grievous torment than a hermit's fast.
Lamia, II

6 'Beauty is truth, truth beauty,' – that is all
Ye know on earth, and all ye need to know.
Ode on a Grecian Urn

7 O for a beaker full of the warm South,
Full of the true, the blushful Hippocrene,
With beaded bubbles winking at the brim,
And purple-stained mouth.
Ode to a Nightingale

8 O for a life of sensations rather than of thoughts!
Letter to Benjamin Bailey, 22 Nov 1817

9 There is an old saying 'well begun is half done' –
'tis a bad one. I would use instead – Not begun at
all until half done.
Letter, 1817

10 If poetry comes not as naturally as leaves to a
tree it had better not come at all.
Letter to John Taylor, 27 Feb 1818

11 Scenery is fine – but human nature is finer.
Letter to Benjamin Bailey, 13 Mar 1818

12 I do think better of womankind than to suppose
they care whether Mister John Keats five feet
high likes them or not.
Letter to Benjamin Bailey, 18 July 1818

13 Love is my religion – I could die for that.
Letter to Fanny Brawne, 13 Oct 1819

KILLING
See also assassination, death, murder, suicide

1 To save a man's life against his will is the same as
killing him.
Horace (Quintus Horatius Flaccus; 65–8 BC) Roman poet.
Ars Poetica

2 Killing
Is the ultimate simplification of life.
Hugh MacDiarmid (Christopher Murray Grieve; 1892–1978)
Scottish poet.
England's Double Knavery

3 ...there's no difference between one's killing and
making decisions that will send others to kill. It's
exactly the same thing, or even worse.
Golda Meir (1898–1978) Russian-born Israeli stateswoman.
L'Europeo (Oriana Fallaci)

4 Kill a man, and you are a murderer. Kill millions
of men, and you are a conqueror. Kill everyone,
and you are a god.
Jean Rostand (1894–1977) French biologist and writer.
Pensée d'un biologiste

5 Yet each man kills the thing he loves,
By each let this be heard,
Some do it with a bitter look,
Some with a flattering word.
The coward does it with a kiss,
The brave man with a sword!
Oscar Wilde (1854–1900) Irish-born British dramatist.
The Ballad of Reading Gaol, I:7

KINDNESS
See also charity, generosity

1 Recompense injury with justice, and recom-
pense kindness with kindness.
Confucius (K'ung Fu-tzu; 551–479 BC) Chinese philosopher.
Analects

2 Yet do I fear thy nature;
It is too full o' th' milk of human kindness
To catch the nearest way.
William Shakespeare (1564–1616) English dramatist.
Macbeth, I:5

3 This is a way to kill a wife with kindness.
William Shakespeare
The Taming of the Shrew, IV:1

4 That best portion of a good man's life,
His little, nameless, unremembered acts
Of kindness and of love.
William Wordsworth (1770–1850) British poet.
Lines composed a few miles above Tintern Abbey

□ KIPLING □
(Joseph) Rudyard

(1865–1936) Indian-born British writer and poet. His verse collection *Barrack Room Ballads and Other Verses* (1892) included the well-known poems 'If' and 'Gunga Din'. Other works were the *Jungle Books* (1894, 1895), *Kim* (1901), and the children's books *Just So Stories* (1902) and *Puck of Pook's Hill* (1906).

1 Oh, East is East, and West is West, and never the twain shall meet.
The Ballad of East and West

2 But the Devil whoops, as he whooped of old:
'It's clever, but is it art?'
The Conundrum of the Workshops

3 If you can keep your head when all about you
Are losing theirs and blaming it on you.
If

4 If you can talk with crowds and keep your virtue,
Or walk with Kings – nor lose the common touch,
If neither foes nor loving friends can hurt you,
If all men count with you, but none too much;
If you can fill the unforgiving minute
With sixty seconds' worth of distance run,
Yours is the Earth and everything that's in it,
And – which is more – you'll be a Man my son!
If

5 The silliest woman can manage a clever man; but it needs a very clever woman to manage a fool.
Plain Tales from the Hills, 'Three and – an Extra'

6 No one thinks of winter when the grass is green!
A St Helena Lullaby

7 It's Tommy this, an' Tommy that, an' 'Chuck him out, the brute!'
But it's 'Saviour of 'is country' when the guns begin to shoot.
Tommy

8 I've just read that I am dead. Don't forget to delete me from your list of subscribers.
Writing to a magazine that had mistakenly published an announcement of his death.
Anekdotenschatz (H. Hoffmeister)

9 A Soldier of the Great War Known unto God.
The words he selected to be inscribed on the headstones of the graves of unknown soldiers when he was literary adviser for the Imperial War Graves Commission, 1919.
Silent Cities (ed. Gavin Stamp)

10 Words are, of course, the most powerful drug used by mankind.
Speech, 14 Feb 1923

11 Power without responsibility – the prerogative of the harlot throughout the ages.
Better known for its subsequent use by BALDWIN.
Attrib.

□ KISSING □

1 What of soul was left, I wonder, when the kissing had to stop?
Robert Browning (1812–89) British poet.
A Toccata of Galuppi's

2 Being kissed by a man who didn't wax his moustache was – like eating an egg without salt.
Rudyard Kipling (1865–1936) Indian-born British writer.
A similar remark is attributed to the US poet Madison Julius Cawein (1865–1914)
Soldiers Three, 'The Gadsbys, Poor Dear Mamma'

3 A kiss without a moustache, they said then, is like an egg without salt; I will add to it: and it is like Good without Evil.
Jean-Paul Sartre (1905–80) French writer.
Words

□ KNOWLEDGE □
See also learning, self-knowledge, wisdom

1 *Nam et ipsa scientia potestas est.*
Knowledge is power.
Francis Bacon (1561–1626) English philosopher.
Religious Meditations, 'Of Heresies'

2 I have taken all knowledge to be my province.
Francis Bacon
Letter to Lord Burleigh, 1592

3 For in much wisdom is much grief: and he that increaseth knowledge increaseth sorrow.
Bible: Ecclesiastes
1:18

4 And the Lord God took the man, and put him into the garden of Eden to dress it and to keep it.
And the Lord God commanded the man, saying,
Of every tree of the garden thou mayest freely eat:
But of the tree of the knowledge of good and evil, thou shalt not eat of it: for in the day that thou eatest thereof thou shalt surely die.
Bible: Genesis
2:15–17

5 Knowledge dwells
In heads replete with thoughts of other men;
Wisdom in minds attentive to their own.
William Cowper (1731–1800) British poet.
The Task

6 A smattering of everything, and a knowledge of
nothing.
Charles Dickens (1812–70) British novelist.
Sketches by Boz, 'Tales', Ch. 3

7 It is the province of knowledge to speak and it is
the privilege of wisdom to listen.
Oliver Wendell Holmes (1809–94) US writer.
The Poet at the Breakfast Table, Ch. 10

8 Knowledge is proportionate to being. ...You
know in virtue of what you are.
Aldous Huxley (1894–1964) British novelist.
Time Must Have a Stop, Ch. 26

9 If a little knowledge is dangerous, where is the
man who has so much as to be out of danger?
T. H. Huxley (1825–95) British biologist.
On Elementary Instruction in Physiology

10 There was never an age in which useless knowl-
edge was more important than in our own.
Cyril Joad (1891–1953) British writer and broadcaster.
The Observer, 'Sayings of the Week', 30 Sept 1951

11 All knowledge is of itself of some value. There is
nothing so minute or inconsiderable, that I
would not rather know it than not.
Samuel Johnson (1709–84) British lexicographer.
Life of Johnson (J. Boswell)

12 Integrity without knowledge is weak and useless,
and knowledge without integrity is dangerous
and dreadful.
Samuel Johnson
Rasselas, Ch. 41

13 Knowledge is of two kinds. We know a subject
ourselves, or we know where we can find information upon it.
Samuel Johnson
Life of Johnson (J. Boswell), Vol. II

14 A study of history shows that civilizations that
abandon the quest for knowledge are doomed to
disintegration.
Bernard Lovell (1913–) British astronomer and writer.
The Observer, 'Sayings of the Week', 14 May 1972

15 Knowledge advances by steps, and not by leaps.
Lord Macaulay (1800–59) British historian.
Essays and Biographies, 'History'. *Edinburgh Review*

16 Our knowledge can only be finite, while our igno-
rance must necessarily be infinite.
Karl Popper (1902–) Austrian-born British philosopher.
Conjectures and Refutations

17 His had been an intellectual decision founded on
his conviction that if a little knowledge was a dangerous thing, a lot was lethal.
Tom Sharpe (1928–) British novelist.
Porterhouse Blue, Ch. 18

18 Beware you be not swallowed up in books! An
ounce of love is worth a pound of knowledge.
John Wesley (1703–91) British religious leader.
Life of Wesley (R. Southey), Ch. 16

L

☐ LA BRUYERE ☐
Jean de
(1645–96) French satirist. He served in the household of the Prince of Condé and wrote one book of lasting merit, *Les Caractères de Théophraste, avec les caractères ou les moeurs de ce siècle* (1688).

1 The majority of men devote the greater part of their lives to making their remaining years unhappy.
Les Caractères

2 There are only three events in a man's life; birth, life, and death; he is not conscious of being born, he dies in pain, and he forgets to live.
Les Caractères

3 Women run to extremes; they are either better or worse than men.
Les Caractères

4 One must laugh before one is happy, or one may die without ever laughing at all.
Les Caractères

5 If poverty is the mother of crime, stupidity is its father.
Les Caractères

6 To endeavour to forget anyone is a certain way of thinking of nothing else.
Les Caractères

7 The shortest and best way to make your fortune is to let people see clearly that it is in their interests to promote yours.
Les Caractères

☐ LAMB ☐
Charles
(1775–1834) British essayist. He is best remembered for his *Essays of Elia* (1822).

QUOTATIONS ABOUT LAMB

1 Charles Lamb, a clever fellow certainly, but full of villainous and abortive puns when he miscarries of every minute.
Thomas Moore (1779–1852) Irish poet.
Diary, 4 Apr 1823

QUOTATIONS BY LAMB

2 Man is a gaming animal. He must always be trying to get the better in something or other.
Essays of Elia, 'Mrs Battle's Opinions on Whist'

3 Boys are capital fellows in their own way, among their mates; but they are unwholesome companions for grown people.
Essays of Elia, 'The Old and the New Schoolmaster'

4 The human species, according to the best theory I can form of it, is composed of two distinct races, the men who borrow, and the men who lend.
Essays of Elia, 'The Two Races of Men'

5 Borrowers of books – those mutilators of collections, spoilers of the symmetry of shelves, and creators of odd volumes.
Essays of Elia, 'The Two Races of Men'

6 Newspapers always excite curiosity. No one ever lays one down without a feeling of disappointment.
Last Essays of Elia, 'Detached Thoughts on Books and Reading'

☐ LANGUAGE ☐
See also class, grammar, Goldwynisms, malapropisms, opera, pronunciation, speech, spoonerisms, style, words, writing

1 The Greeks Had a Word for It.
Zoë Akins (1886–1958) US dramatist.
Play title

2 Therefore is the name of it called Babel; because the Lord did there confound the language of all the earth: and from thence did the Lord scatter them abroad upon the face of all the earth.
Bible: Genesis
11:9

3 The cliché is dead poetry. English, being the language of an imaginative race, abounds in clichés, so that English literature is always in danger of being poisoned by its own secretions.
Gerald Brenan (Edward Fitzgerald Brenan; 1894–1987) British writer.
Thoughts in a Dry Season, 'Literature'

4 A silly remark can be made in Latin as well as in Spanish.
Miguel de Cervantes (1547–1616) Spanish novelist.
The Dialogue of the Dogs

5 Well, frankly, the problem as I see it at this moment in time is whether I should just lie down under all this hassle and let them walk all over me, or whether I should just say OK, I get the message, and do myself in.
I mean, let's face it, I'm in a no-win situation, and quite honestly, I'm so stuffed up to here with the whole stupid mess that I can tell you I've just got a good mind to take the easy way out. That's the bottom line. The only problem is, what happens if I find, when I've bumped myself off, there's some kind of...ah, you know, all that mystical stuff about when you die, you might find you're still – know what I mean?
Charles, Prince of Wales (1948–) Eldest son of Elizabeth II.
At the presentation of the Thomas Cranmer Schools Prize, 1989, suggesting a possible modern English version of Hamlet's soliloquy. The original version is:

To be, or not to be: that is the question:
Whether 'tis nobler in the mind to suffer
The slings and arrows of outrageous fortune,
Or to take arms against a sea of troubles,
And by opposing end them? To die: to sleep;
No more; and, by a sleep to say we end
The heartache and the thousand natural shocks
That flesh is heir to, 'tis a consummation
Devoutly to be wish'd. To die, to sleep;
To sleep: perchance to dream: aye, there's the rub;
For in that sleep of death what dreams may come
When we have shuffled off this mortal coil,
Must give us pause.

6 I speak Spanish to God, Italian to women, French to men, and German to my horse.

Charles V (1500–58) Holy Roman Emperor.
Attrib.

7 I don't hold with abroad and think that foreigners speak English when our backs are turned.

Quentin Crisp (?1910–) Model, publicist, and writer.
The Naked Civil Servant

8 Bring on the empty horses!

Michael Curtiz (1888–1962) Hungarian-born US film director. Said during the filming of *The Charge of the Light Brigade*. Curtiz, who was not noted for his command of the English language, meant 'riderless horses'. When people laughed at his order he became very angry, shouting, 'You think I know fuck-nothing, when I know fuck-all!' David Niven used the remark as the title of his second volume of autobiography about his experiences in the film industry
Bring on the Empty Horses (David Niven)

9 I have laboured to refine our language to grammatical purity, and to clear it from colloquial barbarisms, licentious idioms, and irregular combinations.

Samuel Johnson (1709–84) British lexicographer.
The Rambler

10 I am always sorry when any language is lost, because languages are the pedigree of nations.

Samuel Johnson
Tour to the Hebrides (J. Boswell)

11 I am not yet so lost in lexicography, as to forget that words are the daughters of earth, and that things are the sons of heaven. Language is only the instrument of science, and words are but the signs of ideas: I wish, however, that the instrument might be less apt to decay, and that signs might be permanent, like the things which they denote.

Samuel Johnson
Dictionary of the English Language

12 Language is a form of human reason and has its reasons which are unknown to man.

Claude Lévi-Strauss (1908–) French anthropologist.
The Savage Mind

13 If the English language had been properly organized...then there would be a word which meant both 'he' and 'she', and I could write, 'If John or Mary comes heesh will want to play tennis,' which would save a lot of trouble.

A. A. Milne (1882–1956) British writer.
The Christopher Robin Birthday Book

14 The great enemy of clear language is insincerity. When there is a gap between one's real and one's declared aims, one turns as it were instinctively to long words and exhausted idioms, like a cuttle-fish squirting out ink.

John Osborne (1929–) British dramatist.
Shooting an Elephant, 'Politics and the English Language'

15 I include 'pidgin-English'...even though I am referred to in that splendid language as 'Fella belong Mrs Queen'.

Prince Philip (1921–) The consort of Queen Elizabeth II.
Speech, English-Speaking Union Conference, Ottawa, 29 Oct 1958

16 Life is too short to learn German.

Richard Porson (1759–1808) British classicist.
Gryll Grange (T. L. Peacock), Ch. 3

17 If the men in the room would only think how they would feel graduating with a 'spinster of arts' degree they would see how important this is.

Gloria Steinem (1934–) US writer and feminist.
Referring to language reform.
Speech, Yale University, Sept 1981

18 Language grows out of life, out of its needs and experiences...*Language* and *knowledge* are indissolubly connected; they are interdependent. Good work in language presupposes and depends on a real knowledge of things.

Annie Sullivan (1866–1936) US teacher of the handicapped.
Speech, American Association to Promote the Teaching of Speech to the Deaf, July 1894

19 A foreign swear-word is practically inoffensive except to the person who has learnt it early in life and knows its social limits.

Paul Theroux (1941–) US-born writer.
Saint Jack, Ch. 12

20 We should constantly use the most common, little, easy words (so they are pure and proper) which our language affords.

John Wesley (1703–91) British religious leader.
Advice for preaching to 'plain people'
Attrib.

21 We dissect nature along lines laid down by our native language... Language is not simply a reporting device for experience but a defining framework for it.

Benjamin Lee Whorf (1897–1941) US linguist.
New Directions in the Study of Language (ed. Hoyer), 'Thinking in Primitive Communities'

☐ LAST WORDS ☐

Not always the actual last words said, but including remarks made when dying. Many are apocryphal, hence the fact that some people have more than one set of attributed 'last words'.
See also death, execution

1 A lot of people, on the verge of death, utter famous last words or stiffen into attitudes, as if the final stiffening in three days' time were not enough; they will have ceased to exist three days' hence, yet they still want to arouse admiration and adopt a pose and tell a lie with their last gasp.
Henry de Montherlant (1896–1972) French novelist.
Explicit Mysterium

SOME EXAMPLES

2 See in what peace a Christian can die.
Joseph Addison (1672–1719) British essayist.

3 *Ave Caesar, morituri te salutant.*
Hail Caesar; those who are about to die salute you.
Anonymous
Greeting to the Roman Emperor by gladiators

4 I am ready to die for my Lord, that in my blood the Church may obtain liberty and peace.
Thomas Becket (c. 1118–79) English churchman.
One version of his last words
Vita S. Thomae, Cantuariensis Archiepiscopi et Martyris (Edward Grim)

5 When Jesus therefore had received the vinegar, he said, It is finished: and he bowed his head, and gave up the ghost.
Bible: John
19:30

6 And when Jesus had cried with a loud voice, he said, Father, into thy hands I commend my spirit: and having said thus, he gave up the ghost.
Bible: Luke
23:46

7 Jesus, when he had cried again with a loud voice, yielded up the ghost.
And, behold, the veil of the temple was rent in twain from the top to the bottom; and the earth did quake, and the rocks rent;
And the graves were opened; and many bodies of the saints which slept arose.
Bible: Matthew
27:50–52

8 *Et tu, Brute?*
You too, Brutus?
Julius Caesar (100–44 BC) Roman general and statesman.

9 Let not poor Nelly starve.
Charles II (1630–85) King of England.
Referring to Nell Gwynne
Said on his death bed

10 Goodbye, my friends, I go on to glory.
Isadora Duncan (1878–1927) US dancer.
She was strangled when her long scarf became entangled in the wheel of a sports car
Attrib.

11 All my possessions for a moment of time.
Elizabeth I (1533–1603) Queen of England.

12 I have no pain, dear mother, now;
But oh! I am so dry:
Just moisten poor Jim's lips once more;
And, mother, do not cry!
Edward Farmer (1809–76) British writer.
A typical sentimental verse of the time
The Collier's Dying Child

13 I don't mind if my life goes in the service of the nation. If I die today every drop of my blood will invigorate the nation.
Indira Gandhi (1917–84) Indian stateswoman.
Said the night before she was assassinated by Sikh militants, 30 Oct 1984
The Sunday Times, 3 Dec 1989

14 Bugger Bognor.
George V (1865–1936) King of the United Kingdom.
His alleged last words, when his doctor promised him he would soon be well enough to visit Bognor Regis

15 How is the Empire?
George V
Last words
The Times, 21 Jan 1936

16 *Mehr Licht!*
More light!
Goethe (1749–1832) German poet and dramatist.
Attrib. last words. In fact he asked for the second shutter to be opened, to allow more light in

17 That is indeed very good. I shall have to repeat that on the Golden Floor!
A. E. Housman (1859–1936) British scholar and poet.
To his doctor, who had told him a joke just before he died
Attrib.

18 Why are you weeping? Did you imagine that I was immortal?
Louis XIV (1638–1715) French king.
Noticing as he lay on his deathbed that his attendants were crying
Louis XIV (V. Cronin)

19 I do not have to forgive my enemies, I have had them all shot.
Ramón Maria Narváez (1800–68) Spanish general and political leader.
Said on his deathbed, when asked by a priest if he forgave his enemies
Famous Last Words (B. Conrad)

20 Kiss me, Hardy.
Lord Nelson (1758–1805) British admiral.
Spoken to Sir Thomas Hardy, captain of the *Victory*, during the Battle of Trafalgar, 1805

21 I am just going outside and may be some time.
Captain Lawrence Oates (1880–1912) British soldier and
explorer.
Before leaving the tent and vanishing into the blizzard on the ill-
fated Antarctic expedition (1910–12). Oates was afraid that his
lameness would slow down the others
Journal (R. F. Scott), 17 Mar 1912

22 Die, my dear Doctor, that's the last thing I shall
do!
Lord Palmerston (1784–1865) British statesman.

23 I think I could eat one of Bellamy's veal pies.
William Pitt the Younger

24 Ring down the curtain, the farce is over.
François Rabelais

25 I have a long journey to take, and must bid the
company farewell.
Walter Raleigh (1554–1618) English explorer.
Sir Walter Raleigh (Edward Thompson), Ch. 26

26 Nonsense, they couldn't hit an elephant at this
distance
John Sedgwick (1813–64) US general.
In response to a suggestion that he should not show himself over
the parapet during the Battle of the Wilderness
Attrib.

27 Crito, we owe a cock to Aesculapius; please pay it
and don't let it pass.
Socrates (469–399 BC) Athenian philosopher.
Before his execution by drinking hemlock
Phaedo (Plato), 118

28 Dear me, I believe I am becoming a god. An
emperor ought at least to die on his feet.
Vespasian (9–79 AD) Roman emperor.
Lives of the Caesars (Suetonius)

☐LAUGHTER☐

See also happiness, humour

1 I said of laughter, It is mad: and of mirth, What
doeth it?
Bible: Ecclesiastes
2:2

2 But laughter is weakness, corruption, the foolish-
ness of our flesh.
Umberto Eco (1932–) Italian semiologist and writer.
The Name of the Rose

3 One must laugh before one is happy, or one may
die without ever laughing at all.
Jean de La Bruyère (1645–96) French satirist.
Les Caractères

4 Laugh, and the world laughs with you;
Weep, and you weep alone,
For the sad old earth must borrow its mirth,
But has trouble enough of its own.
Ella Wheeler Wilcox (1850–1919) US poet.
Solitude

☐LAW☐

See also crime, justice, lawyers

1 The good of the people is the chief law.
Cicero (106–43 BC) Roman orator and statesman.
De Legibus, III

2 The Law of England is a very strange one; it cannot compel anyone to tell the truth....But what
the Law can do is to give you seven years for not
telling the truth.
Lord Darling (1849–1936) British judge.
Lord Darling (D. Walker-Smith), Ch. 27

3 'If the law supposes that,' said Mr Bumble..., 'the
law is a ass – a idiot.'
Charles Dickens (1812–70) British novelist.
Oliver Twist, Ch. 51

4 There's no better way of exercising the imagination than the study of law. No poet ever interpreted nature as freely as a lawyer interprets
truth.
Jean Giraudoux (1882–1944) French dramatist.
Tiger at the Gates, I

5 Laws grind the poor, and rich men rule the law.
Oliver Goldsmith (1728–74) Irish-born British writer.
The Traveller

6 In university they don't tell you that the greater
part of the law is learning to tolerate fools.
Doris Lessing (1919–) British novelist.
Martha Quest, Pt. III, Ch. 2

7 No brilliance is needed in the law. Nothing but
common sense, and relatively clean finger nails.
John Mortimer (1923–) British lawyer and dramatist.
A Voyage Round My Father, I

8 Laws were made to be broken.
Christopher North (John Wilson; 1785–1854) Scottish writer.
Noctes Ambrosianae, 24 May 1830

9 Every law is a contract between the king and the
people and therefore to be kept.
John Selden (1584–1654) English historian.
Table Talk

10 Ignorance of the law excuses no man; not that all
men know the law, but because 'tis an excuse
every man will plead, and no man can tell how to
confute him.
John Selden
Table Talk

11 Still you keep o' th' windy side of the law.
William Shakespeare (1564–1616) English dramatist.
Twelfth Night, III:4

12 Laws are like spider's webs: if some poor weak
creature come up against them, it is caught; but a
bigger one can break through and get away.
Solon (6th century BC) Athenian statesman.
Lives of the Eminent Philosophers (Diogenes Laertius), I

☐LAWRENCE☐
D(avid) H(erbert)

(1885–1930) British novelist. The son of a coalminer, he earned his reputation with the autobiographical *Sons and Lovers* (1913). Subsequent novels include *Women in Love* (1921), *Kangaroo* (1923), and *Lady Chatterley's Lover* (1928).

QUOTATIONS ABOUT LAWRENCE

1   Interesting, but a type I could not get on with. Obsessed with self. Dead eyes and a red beard, long narrow face. A strange bird.
    John Galsworthy (1867–1933) British novelist.
    Life and Letters (edited by H. V. Marriot)

QUOTATIONS BY LAWRENCE

2   The English people on the whole are surely the *nicest* people in the world, and everyone makes everything so easy for everybody else, that there is almost nothing to resist at all.
    Dull London

3   The Romans and Greeks found everything human. Everything had a face, and a human voice. Men spoke, and their fountains piped an answer.
    Fantasia of the Unconscious, Ch. 4

4   The refined punishments of the spiritual mode are usually much more indecent and dangerous than a good smack.
    Fantasia of the Unconscious, Ch. 4

5   Morality which is based on ideas, or on an ideal, is an unmitigated evil.
    Fantasia of the Unconscious, Ch. 7

6   When Eve ate this particular apple, she became aware of her own womanhood, mentally. And mentally she began to experiment with it. She has been experimenting ever since. So has man. To the rage and horror of both of them.
    Fantasia of the Unconscious, Ch. 7

7   O pity the dead that are dead, but cannot make the journey, still they moan and beat against the silvery adamant walls of life's exclusive city.
    The Houseless Dead

8   How beastly the bourgeois is especially the male of the species.
    How beastly the bourgeois is

9   But tha mun dress thysen, an' go back to thy stately homes of England, how beautiful they stand. Time's up! Time's up for Sir John, an' for little Lady Jane! Put thy shimmy on, Lady Chatterley!
    Lady Chatterley's Lover, Ch. 15

10 The modern pantheist not only sees the god in everything, he takes photographs of it.
    St Mawr

11 There's nothing so artificial as sinning nowadays. I suppose it once was real.
    St Mawr

12 No absolute is going to make the lion lie down with the lamb unless the lamb is inside.
    The Later D. H. Lawrence

13 Pornography is the attempt to insult sex, to do dirt on it.
    Phoenix, 'Pornography and Obscenity'

14 It is no good casting out devils. They belong to us, we must accept them and be at peace with them.
    Phoenix, 'The Reality of Peace'

15 They are great parables, the novels, but false art. They are only parables. All the people are *fallen angels* – even the dirtiest scrubs. This I cannot stomach. People are not fallen angels, they are merely people.
    Referring to the novels of Dostoyevsky.
    Letter to J. Middleton Murray and Katherine Mansfield, 17 Feb 1916

16 The dead don't die. They look on and help.
    Letter

☐LAWYERS☐

See also law

1   Lawyers are the only persons in whom ignorance of the law is not punished.
    Jeremy Bentham (1748–1832) British philosopher.
    Attrib.

2   Woe unto you, lawyers! for ye have taken away the key of knowledge: ye entered not in yourselves, and them that were entering in ye hindered.
    Bible: Luke
    11:52

3   A client is fain to hire a lawyer to keep from the injury of other lawyers – as Christians that travel in Turkey are forced to hire Janissaries, to protect them from the insolencies of other Turks.
    Samuel Butler (1835–1902) British writer.
    Prose Observations

4   A lawyer with his briefcase can steal more than a hundred men with guns.
    Mario Puzo (1920–) US writer.
    The Godfather, Ch. 1

☐ LAZINESS ☐

See also bed, idleness

1 Happy is the man with a wife to tell him what to do and a secretary to do it.
Lord Mancroft (1917–87) British businessman and writer.
The Observer, 'Sayings of the Week', 18 Dec 1966

2 For one person who dreams of making fifty thousand pounds, a hundred people dream of being left fifty thousand pounds.
A. A. Milne (1882–1956) British writer.
If I May, 'The Future'

3 It is better to have loafed and lost than never to have loafed at all.
James Thurber (1894–1961) US humorist.
Fables for Our Time, 'The Courtship of Arthur and Al'

☐ LEADERSHIP ☐

See also guidance

1 The trouble in modern democracy is that men do not approach to leadership until they have lost the desire to lead anyone.
Lord Beveridge (1879–1963) British economist.
The Observer, 'Sayings of the Week', 15 Apr 1934

2 And he shall rule them with a rod of iron; as the vessels of a potter shall they be broken to shivers: even as I received of my Father.
Bible: Revelations
2:27

3 I believe in benevolent dictatorship provided I am the dictator.
Richard Branson (1950–) British entrepreneur.
Remark, Nov 1984

☐ LEARNING ☐

See also education, knowledge

1 What we have to learn to do, we learn by doing.
Aristotle (384–322 BC) Greek philosopher.
Nicomachean Ethics, Bk. II

2 Miss not the discourse of the elders: for they also learned of their fathers, and of them thou shalt learn understanding, and to give answer as need requireth.
Bible: Ecclesiasticus
8:9

3 Read, mark, learn and inwardly digest.
The Book of Common Prayer
Collect, 2nd Sunday in Advent

4 LIBOV ANDREEVNA. Are you still a student?
TROFIMOV. I expect I shall be a student to the end of my days.
Anton Chekhov (1860–1904) Russian dramatist.
The Cherry Orchard, I

5 ...that is what learning is. You suddenly understand something you've understood all your life, but in a new way.
Doris Lessing (1919–) British novelist.
The Four-Gated City

6 He intended, he said, to devote the rest of his life to learning the remaining twenty-two letters of the alphabet.
George Orwell (Eric Blair; 1903–50) British novelist.
Animal Farm, Ch. 9

7 For where is any author in the world
Teaches such beauty as a woman's eye?
Learning is but an adjunct to oneself.
William Shakespeare (1564–1616) English dramatist.
Love's Labour's Lost, IV:3

8 Some for renown, on scraps of learning dote,
And think they grow immortal as they quote.
Edward Young (1683–1765) British poet.
Love of Fame, I

☐ LEISURE ☐

See also idleness, merrymaking, pleasure, rest

1 The wisdom of a learned man cometh by opportunity of leisure: and he that hath little business shall become wise.
How can he get wisdom that holdeth the plough, and that glorieth in the goad, that driveth oxen, and is occupied in their labours, and whose talk is of bullocks?
Bible: Ecclesiasticus
38:24–25

2 Hey! Mr Tambourine Man, play a song for me.
I'm not sleepy and there is no place I'm going to.
Bob Dylan (Robert Allen Zimmerman; 1941–) US popular singer.
Mr Tambourine Man

3 If all the year were playing holidays, To sport would be as tedious as to work.
William Shakespeare (1564–1616) English dramatist.
Henry IV, Part One, I:2

☐ LETTER-WRITING ☐

1 ...a habit the pleasure of which increases with practise, but becomes more urksome with neglect.
Abigail Adams (1744–1818) US feminist.
Letter to her daughter, 8 May 1808

2 When he wrote a letter, he would put that which was most material in the postscript, as if it had been a by-matter.
Francis Bacon (1561–1626) English philosopher.
Essays, 'Of Cunning'

☐LEXICOGRAPHY☐

1 The responsibility of a dictionary is to record a language, not set its style.
Philip Babcock Gove (1902–72) US dictionary editor.
Letter to Life Magazine, 17 Nov 1961

2 *Dull.* 8. To make dictionaries is dull work.
Samuel Johnson (1709–84) British lexicographer.
Dictionary of the English Language

3 *Lexicographer.* A writer of dictionaries, a harmless drudge.
Samuel Johnson
Dictionary of the English Language

☐LIBERALISM☐

1 To be absolutely honest, what I feel really bad about is that I don't feel worse. There's the ineffectual liberal's problem in a nutshell.
Michael Frayn (1933–) British journalist and writer.
The Observer, 8 Aug 1965

2 When a liberal is abused, he says: Thank God they didn't beat me. When he is beaten, he thanks God they didn't kill him. When he is killed, he will thank God that his immortal soul has been delivered from its mortal clay.
Lenin (Vladimir Ilich Ulyanov, 1870–1924) Russian revolutionary leader.
Lenin heard this characterization at a meeting, and repeated it with approval
The Government's Falsification of the Duma and the Tasks of the Social-Democrats, 'Proletary', Dec 1906.

☐LIBERTY☐

1 It is not our frowning battlements…or the strength of our gallant and disciplined army. These are not our reliance against a resumption of tyranny in our fair land….Our defence is in the preservation of the spirit which prizes liberty as the heritage of all men, in all lands, everywhere.
Abraham Lincoln (1809–65) US statesman.
Speech, 11 Sept 1858

2 Liberty means responsibility. That is why most men dread it.
George Bernard Shaw (1856–1950) Irish dramatist and critic.

☐LIFE☐

See also afterlife, human condition, life and death, mortality, purpose, time, world-weariness

1 Before this strange disease of modern life, With its sick hurry, its divided aims.
Matthew Arnold (1822–88) British poet and critic.
The Scholar Gipsy

2 Remember that no man loses any other life than this which he now lives, nor lives any other than this which he now loses.
Marcus Aurelius (121–180 AD) Roman emperor.
Meditations, Bk. II, Ch. 14

3 The universe is transformation; our life is what our thoughts make it.
Marcus Aurelius
Meditations, Bk. IV, Ch. 3

4 The present life of men on earth, O king, as compared with the whole length of time which is unknowable to us, seems to me to be like this: as if, when you are sitting at dinner with your chiefs and ministers in wintertime,…one of the sparrows from outside flew very quickly through the hall; as if it came in one door and soon went out through another. In that actual time it is indoors it is not touched by the winter's storm; but yet the tiny period of calm is over in a moment, and having come out of the winter it soon returns to the winter and slips out of your sight. Man's life appears to be more or less like this; and of what may follow it, or what preceded it, we are absolutely ignorant.
St Bede (The Venerable Bede; c. 673–735 AD) English churchman and historian.
Ecclesiastical History of the English People, Bk. II, Ch. 13

5 Life is rather like a tin of sardines – we're all of us looking for the key.
Alan Bennett (1934–) British playwright.
Beyond the Fringe

6 At last awake
From life, that insane dream we take
For waking now.
Robert Browning (1812–89) British poet.
Easter-Day, XIV

7 Life is one long process of getting tired.
Samuel Butler (1835–1902) British writer.
Notebooks

8 Life is the art of drawing sufficient conclusions from insufficient premises.
Samuel Butler
Notebooks

9 Life is a tragedy when seen in close-up, but a comedy in long-shot.
Charlie Chaplin (Sir Charles Spencer C.; 1889–1977) British film actor.
In *The Guardian*, Obituary, 28 Dec 1977

10 Life is an incurable disease.
Abraham Cowley (1618–67) English poet.
To Dr Scarborough

11 People do not live nowadays – they get about ten percent out of life.
Isadora Duncan (1878–1927) US dancer.
This Quarter Autumn, 'Memoirs'

12 Life is just one damned thing after another.
Elbert Hubbard (1856–1915) US writer.
A Thousand and One Epigrams

13 Life isn't all beer and skittles.

Thomas Hughes (1822–96) British novelist.
Tom Brown's Schooldays, Pt. I, Ch. 2

14 Live all you can; it's a mistake not to. It doesn't so much matter what you do in particular, so long as you have your life. If you haven't had that what *have* you had?

Henry James (1843–1916) US novelist.
The Ambassadors, Bk. V, Ch. 2

15 Life is like a sewer. What you get out of it depends on what you put into it.

Tom Lehrer (1928–) US university teacher and songwriter.
We Will all Go together When We Go

16 Life is what happens to you while you're busy making other plans.

John Lennon (1940–80) British rock musician.
Beautiful Boy

17 And thou wilt give thyself relief, if thou doest every act of thy life as if it were the last.

Marcus Aurelius (121–180 AD) Roman emperor.
Meditations, Bk. II, Ch. 5

18 Life is as tedious as a twice-told tale
Vexing the dull ear of a drowsy man.

William Shakespeare (1564–1616) English dramatist.
King John, III:4

19 Tomorrow, and tomorrow, and tomorrow,
Creeps in this petty pace from day to day
To the last syllable of recorded time,
And all our yesterdays have lighted fools
The way to dusty death. Out, out, brief candle!
Life's but a walking shadow, a poor player,
That struts and frets his hour upon the stage,
And then is heard no more; it is a tale
Told by an idiot, full of sound and fury,
Signifying nothing.

William Shakespeare
Macbeth, V:5

20 Lift not the painted veil which those who live
Call life.

Percy Bysshe Shelley (1792–1822) British poet.
Lift not the Painted Veil

21 As our life is very short, so it is very miserable, and
therefore it is well it is short.

Jeremy Taylor (1613–67) English Anglican theologian.
The Rule and Exercise of Holy Dying, Ch. 1

22 A life that moves to gracious ends
Thro' troops of unrecording friends,
A deedful life, a silent voice.

Alfred, Lord Tennyson (1809–92) British poet.
To –, after reading a Life and Letters

23 Oh, isn't life a terrible thing, thank God?

Dylan Thomas (1914–53) Welsh poet.
Under Milk Wood

24 Never to have lived is best, ancient writers say;
Never to have drawn the breath of life,
never to have looked into the eye of day
The second best's a gay goodnight and quickly turn away.

W. B. Yeats (1865–1939) Irish poet.
Oedipus at Colonus

□LIFE AND DEATH□

See also death, life

1 Every moment dies a man,
Every moment one and one sixteenth is born.

Charles Babbage (1792–1871) British mathematician.
A parody of TENNYSON's *Vision of Sin*
Letter to Tennyson

2 I call heaven and earth to record this day against you, that I have set before you life and death, blessing and cursing: therefore choose life, that both thou and thy seed may live.

Bible: Deuteronomy
30:19

3 This world nis but a thurghfare ful of wo,
And we ben pilgrimes, passinge to and fro;
Deeth is an ende of every worldly sore.

Geoffrey Chaucer (c. 1342–1400) English poet.
The Canterbury Tales, 'The Knight's Tale'

4 Birth, and copulation, and death.
That's all the facts when you come to brass tacks.

T. S. Eliot (1888–1965) US-born British poet and dramatist.
Sweeney Agonistes, 'Fragment of an Agon'

5 I believe that the struggle against death, the unconditional and self-willed determination to live, is the motive power behind the lives and activities of all outstanding men.

Hermann Hesse (1877–1962) German novelist and poet.
Steppenwolf, 'Treatise on the Steppenwolf'

6 There are only three events in a man's life; birth, life, and death; he is not conscious of being born, he dies in pain, and he forgets to live.

Jean de La Bruyère (1645–96) French satirist.
Les Caractères

7 Many men would take the death-sentence without a whimper to escape the life-sentence which fate carries in her other hand.

T. E. Lawrence (1888–1935) British soldier and writer.
The Mint, Pt. I, Ch. 4

8 Life is a great surprise. I do not see why death should not be an even greater one.

Vladimir Nabokov (1899–1977) Russian-born US novelist.
Pale Fire, 'Commentary'

9 Every moment dies a man,
Every moment one is born.

Alfred, Lord Tennyson (1809–92) British poet.
For a parody, *see* BABBAGE
The Vision of Sin

☐LITERACY☐

See also reading, writing

1 The ratio of literacy to illiteracy is constant, but nowadays the illiterates can read and write.
Alberto Moravia (Alberto Pincherle; 1907–90) Italian novelist.
The Observer, 14 Oct 1979

2 To be a well-favoured man is the gift of fortune; but to write and read comes by nature.
William Shakespeare (1564–1616) English dramatist.
Much Ado About Nothing, III:3

☐LITERATURE☐

See also arts, books, criticism, fiction, novels, plays, poetry, poetry and prose, poets, prose, reading, theatre, writers, writing

1 Literature is the art of writing something that will be read twice; journalism what will be grasped at once.
Cyril Connolly (1903–74) British journalist.
Enemies of Promise, Ch. 3

2 The reading of all good books is like a conversation with the finest men of past centuries.
René Descartes (1596–1650) French philosopher.
Le Discours de la méthode

3 He knew everything about literature except how to enjoy it.
Joseph Heller (1923–) US novelist.
Catch-22, Ch. 8

4 The proper study of mankind is books.
Aldous Huxley (1894–1964) British novelist.
Chrome Yellow

5 Literature flourishes best when it is half a trade and half an art.
Dean Inge (1860–1954) British churchman.
The Victorian Age

6 It takes a great deal of history to produce a little literature.
Henry James (1843–1916) US novelist.
Life of Nathaniel Hawthorne, Ch. 1

7 Literature is mostly about having sex and not much about having children; life is the other way round.
David Lodge (1935–) British author.
The British Museum is Falling Down, Ch. 4

8 Literature and butterflies are the two sweetest passions known to man.
Vladimir Nabokov (1899–1977) Russian-born US novelist.
Radio Times, Oct 1962

9 Great Literature is simply language charged with meaning to the utmost possible degree.
Ezra Pound (1885–1972) US poet.
How to Read

10 Romanticism is the art of presenting people with the literary works which are capable of affording them the greatest possible pleasure, in the present state of their customs and beliefs. Classicism, on the other hand, presents them with the literature that gave the greatest possible pleasure to their great-grandfathers.
Stendhal (Henri Beyle; 1783–1842) French novelist.
Racine et Shakespeare, Ch. 3

11 Something that everybody wants to have read and nobody wants to read.
Mark Twain (Samuel Langhorne Clemens; 1835–1910) US writer.
Definition of a classic of literature
Speech at Nineteenth Century Club, New York, 20 Nov 1900

12 Literature is the orchestration of platitudes.
Thornton Wilder (1897–1975) US novelist and dramatist.
Time magazine

☐LOGIC☐

See also philosophy

1 'Contrariwise,' continued Tweedledee, 'if it was so, it might be; and if it were so, it would be: but as it isn't, it ain't. That's logic.'
Lewis Carroll (Charles Lutwidge Dodgson; 1832–98) British writer.
Through the Looking-Glass, Ch. 4

2 You can only find truth with logic if you have already found truth without it.
G. K. Chesterton (1874–1936) British writer.
The Man who was Orthodox

3 Logical consequences are the scarecrows of fools and the beacons of wise men.
T. H. Huxley (1825–95) British biologist.
Science and Culture, 'On the Hypothesis that Animals are Automata'

☐LONDON☐

See also England

1 Oranges and lemons,
Say the bells of St Clement's.
You owe me five farthings,
Say the bells of St Martin's.
When will you pay me?
Say the bells of Old Bailey.
When I grow rich,
Say the bells of Shoreditch.
When will that be?
Say the bells of Stepney.
I'm sure I don't know,
Says the great bell at Bow.
Here comes a candle to light you to bed,
Here comes a chopper to chop off your head.
Tommy Thumb's Pretty Song Book

2 Nobody is healthy in London, nobody can be.
Jane Austen (1775–1817) British novelist.
Emma, Ch. 12

3 London, that great cesspool into which all the
loungers of the Empire are irresistibly drained.
Arthur Conan Doyle (1856–1930) British writer.
A Study in Scarlet

4 I think the full tide of human existence is at
Charing-Cross.
Samuel Johnson (1709–84) British lexicographer.
Life of Johnson (J. Boswell), Vol. II

5 When a man is tired of London, he is tired of life;
for there is in London all that life can afford.
Samuel Johnson
Life of Johnson (J. Boswell), Vol. III

6 London, that great sea, whose ebb and flow
At once is deaf and loud, and on the shore
Vomits its wrecks, and still howls on for more.
Percy Bysshe Shelley (1792–1822) British poet.
Letter to Maria Gisborne, I

7 Hell is a city much like London –
A populous and smoky city.
Percy Bysshe Shelley
Peter Bell the Third

□ LONELINESS □

See also solitude

1 But who can count the beatings of the lonely
heart?
Susan Edmonstone Ferrier (1782–1854) Scottish novelist.
The Inheritance, Ch. 1

2 Pray that your loneliness may spur you into find-
ing something to live for, great enough to die for.
Dag Hammarskjöld (1905–61) Swedish diplomat.
Diaries, 1951

3 So lonely am I
My body is a floating weed
Severed at the roots
Were there water to entice me,
I would follow it, I think.
Ono no Komachi (834–880) Japanese poet.
Kokinshū, Anthology of Japanese Literature (ed. Donald Keene)

4 Waits at the window, wearing the face that she
keeps in a jar by the door
Who is it for? All the lonely people, where do
they all come from?
All the lonely people, where do they all belong?
John Lennon (1940–80) British rock musician.
Eleanor Rigby (with Paul McCartney)

5 My heart is a lonely hunter that hunts on a lonely
hill.
Fiona Macleod (William Sharp; 1856–1905) Scottish poet and
writer.
The Lonely Hunter

6 I grow lean
in loneliness,
like a water lily
gnawed by a beetle.
Kaccipe tu Nannakaiyar (3rd century) Indian poet.
Interior Landscape: Love Poems from a Classical Tamil Anthology
(ed. A. K. Tamanaujan)

7 To be alone is the fate of all great minds – a fate
deplored at times, but still always chosen as the
less grievous of two evils.
Arthur Schopenhauer (1788–1860) German philosopher.
Aphorismen zur Lebensweisheit

8 Loneliness and the feeling of being unwanted is
the most terrible poverty.
Mother Teresa (Agnes Gonxha Bojaxhui; 1910–)
Yugoslavian missionary in Calcutta.
Time, 'Saints Among Us', 29 Dec 1975

9 The wind blows out of the gates of the day,
The wind blows over the lonely of heart,
And the lonely of heart is withered away.
W. B. Yeats (1865–1939) Irish poet.
The Land of Heart's Desire

□ LONGEVITY □

See also age, life, old age

1 Aging seems to be the only available way to live a
long time.
Daniel-François-Esprit Auber (1782–1871) French
composer.
Dictionnaire Encyclopédique (E. Guérard)

2 Get your room full of good air, then shut up the
windows and keep it. It will keep for years. Anyway, don't keep using your lungs all the time. Let
them rest.
Stephen Leacock (1869–1944) English-born Canadian
economist and humorist.
Literary Lapses, 'How to Live to be 200'

3 If you live long enough, the venerability factor
creeps in; you get accused of things you never
did and praised for virtues you never had.
I. F. Stone (1907–) US writer and publisher.
Peter's Quotations (Laurence J. Peter)

□ LOSS □

See also defeat, mourning

1 'Tis better to have loved and lost than never to
have lost at all.
Samuel Butler (1835–1902) British writer.
The Way of All Flesh, Ch. 77

2 What's lost upon the roundabouts we pulls up on
the swings!
Patrick Reginald Chalmers (1872–1942) British banker and
novelist.
Green Days and Blue Days: Roundabouts and Swings

3 And much more am I sorrier for my good
knights' loss than for the loss of my fair queen;
for queens I might have enough, but such a

fellowship of good knights shall never be together in no company.

Thomas Malory (1400–71) English writer.
Morte d'Arthur, Bk. XX, Ch. 9

4 There is a ghost
That eats handkerchiefs;
It keeps you company
On all your travels.

Christian Morgenstern (1871–1914) German poet.
Der Gingganz, 'Gespenst'

5 Where have all the flowers gone?
Young girls picked them every one.

Pete Seeger (1919–) US folksinger and songwriter.
Where Have All the Flowers Gone?

6 To lose one parent, Mr Worthing, may be regarded as a misfortune; to lose both looks like carelessness.

Oscar Wilde (1854–1900) Irish-born British dramatist.
The Importance of Being Earnest, I

□ LOVE □

See also admiration, love and death, love and friendship, love and hate, love and marriage, lust, passion, sex

1 Greensleeves was all my joy,
Greensleeves was my delight,
Greensleeves was my heart of gold,
And who but Lady Greensleeves.

Anonymous
Greensleeves

2 Love is, above all, the gift of oneself.

Jean Anouilh (1910–87) French dramatist.
Ardèle

3 When it comes, will it come without warning
Just as I'm picking my nose?
Will it knock on my door in the morning,
Or tread in the bus on my toes?
Will it come like a change in the weather?
Will its greeting be courteous or rough?
Will it alter my life altogether?
O tell me the truth about love.

W. H. Auden (1907–73) British poet.
Twelve Songs, XII

4 Nuptial love maketh mankind; friendly love perfecteth it; but wanton love corrupteth and embaseth it.

Francis Bacon (1561–1626) English philosopher.
Essays, 'Of Love'

5 Love ceases to be a pleasure, when it ceases to be a secret.

Aphra Behn (1640–89) English novelist and dramatist.
The Lover's Watch, 'Four o'clock'

6 Beloved, let us love one another: for love is of God; and every one that loveth is born of God, and knoweth God.

He that loveth not knoweth not God; for God is love.

Bible: I John
4:7–8

7 There is no fear in love; but perfect love casteth out fear: because fear hath torment. He that feareth is not made perfect in love.

Bible: I John
4:18

8 Greater love hath no man than this, that a man lay down his life for his friends.

Bible: John
15:13

9 Jesus said unto him, Thou shalt love the Lord thy God with all thy heart, and with all thy soul, and with all thy mind.
This is the first and great commandment.
And the second is like unto it, Thou shalt love thy neighbour as thyself.
On these two commandments hang all the law and the prophets.

Bible: Matthew
22:37–40

10 Love seeketh not itself to please,
Nor for itself hath any care,
But for another gives its ease,
And builds a Heaven in Hell's despair.

William Blake (1757–1827) British poet.
Songs of Experience, 'The Clod and the Pebble'

11 Love seeketh only Self to please,
To bind another to its delight,
Joys in another's loss of ease,
And builds a Hell in Heaven's despite.

William Blake
Songs of Experience, 'The Clod and the Pebble'

12 Although love dwells in gorgeous palaces, and sumptuous apartments, more willingly than in miserable and desolate cottages, it cannot be denied but that he sometimes causes his power to be felt in the gloomy recesses of forests, among the most bleak and rugged mountains, and in the dreary caves of a desert...

Giovanni Boccaccio (1313–75) Italian writer and poet.
Decameron, 'Third Day'

13 I love thee with a love I seemed to lose
With my lost saints – I love thee with the breath,
Smiles, tears, of all my life! – and, if God choose,
I shall but love thee better after death.

Elizabeth Barrett Browning (1806–61) British poet.
Sonnets from the Portuguese, XLIII

14 Such ever was love's way; to rise, it stoops.

Robert Browning (1812–89) British poet.
A Death in the Desert

15 My love is like a red red rose
That's newly sprung in June:

My love is like the melodie
That's sweetly play'd in tune.
Robert Burns
A Red, Red Rose

16 God is Love – I dare say. But what a mischievous
devil Love is!
Samuel Butler (1835–1902) British writer.
Notebooks

17 Many a man has fallen in love with a girl in a light
so dim he would not have chosen a suit by it.
Maurice Chevalier (1888–1972) French singer and actor.
Attrib.

18 To the men and women who own men and
women
those of us meant to be lovers
we will not pardon you
for wasting our bodies and time
Leonard Cohen (1934–) Canadian poet.
The Energy of Slaves

19 See how love and murder will out.
William Congreve (1670–1729) British Restoration dramatist.
The Double Dealer, IV:6

20 Lord, what is a lover that it can give? Why one
makes lovers as fast as one pleases, and they live
as long as one pleases, and they die as soon as
one pleases: and then if one pleases one makes
more.
William Congreve
The Way of the World, II:4

21 Say what you will, 'tis better to be left than never
to have been loved.
William Congreve
The Way of the World, II:1

22 Love is a sickness full of woes,
All remedies refusing;
A plant that with most cutting grows,
Most barren with best using.
Why so?
More we enjoy it, more it dies;
If not enjoyed, it sighing cries,
Hey ho.
Samuel Daniel (c. 1562–1619) English poet and dramatist.
Hymen's Triumph, I

23 It has been said that love robs those who have it
of their wit, and gives it to those who have none.
Denis Diderot (1713–84) French writer.
Paradoxe sur le comédien

24 Come live with me, and be my love,
And we will some new pleasures prove
Of golden sands, and crystal brooks,
With silken lines, and silver hooks.
John Donne (1573–1631) English poet.
The Bait

25 I am two fools, I know,
For loving, and for saying so
In whining Poetry.
John Donne
The Triple Fool

26 All mankind love a lover.
Ralph Waldo Emerson (1803–82) US poet and essayist.
Essays, 'Love'

27 ...I don't want to live – I want to love first, and live
incidentally...
Zelda Fitzgerald (1900–48) US writer.
Letter to F. Scott Fitzgerald, 1919

28 *Plaisir d'amour ne dure qu'un moment,
Chagrin d'amour dure toute la vie.*
Love's pleasure lasts but a moment; love's
sorrow lasts all through life.
Jean-Pierre Claris de Florian (1755–94) French writer of
fables.
Celestine

29 She who has never loved has never lived.
John Gay (1685–1732) English poet and dramatist.
Captives

30 Love, love, love – all the wretched cant of it, masking egotism, lust, masochism, fantasy under a
mythology of sentimental postures, a welter of
self-induced miseries and joys, blinding and
masking the essential personalities in the frozen
gestures of courtship, in the kissing and the dat-
ing and the desire, the compliments and the quarrels which vivify its barrenness.
Germaine Greer (1939–) Australian-born British writer and
feminist.
The Female Eunuch

31 A lover without indiscretion is no lover at all.
Thomas Hardy (1840–1928) British novelist.
The Hand of Ethelberta, Ch. 20

32 'You must sit down,' says Love, 'and taste My
meat,'
So I did sit and eat.
George Herbert (1593–1633) English poet.
Love

33 My love she's but a lassie yet.
James Hogg (1770–1835) Scottish poet and writer.
Title of song

34 Love's like the measles – all the worse when it
comes late in life.
Douglas William Jerrold (1803–57) British dramatist.
Wit and Opinions of Douglas Jerrold, 'A Philanthropist'

35 Love is the wisdom of the fool and the folly of the
wise.
Samuel Johnson (1709–84) British lexicographer.
Johnsonian Miscellanies (ed. G. B. Hill), Vol. II

36 Drink to me only with thine eyes,
And I will pledge with mine;

Or leave a kiss but in the cup,
And I'll not look for wine.
The thirst that from the soul doth rise
Doth ask a drink divine;
But might I of Jove's nectar sup,
I would not change for thine.
I sent thee late a rosy wreath,
Not so much honouring thee,
As giving it a hope that there
It could not wither'd be.
Ben Jonson (1573–1637) English dramatist.
The Forest, IX, 'To Celia'

37 I'm not sure if a mental relation with a woman
doesn't make it impossible to love her. To know
the *mind* of a woman is to end in hating her. Love
means the pre-cognitive flow…it is the honest
state before the apple.
D. H. Lawrence (1885–1930) British novelist.
Letter to Dr Trigant Burrow, 3 Aug 1927

38 If there's anything that you want,
If there's anything I can do,
Just call on me,
And I'll send it along with love from me to you.
John Lennon (1940–80) British rock musician.
From Me to You (with Paul McCartney)

39 She loves you, yeh, yeh, yeh,
And with a love like that you know you should be
glad.
John Lennon
She Loves You (with Paul McCartney)

40 Two souls with but a single thought,
Two hearts that beat as one.
Maria Lovell (1803–77) British actress and dramatist.
Ingomar the Barbarian, II (transl. of Friedrich Halm)

41 Time was away and somewhere else,
There were two glasses and two chairs
And two people with one pulse.
Louis MacNeice (1907–63) Irish-born British poet.
Meeting Point

42 Come live with me, and be my love;
And we will all the pleasures prove
That hills and valleys, dales and fields,
Woods or steepy mountain yields.
Christopher Marlowe (1564–93) English dramatist.
The Passionate Shepherd to his Love

43 Love is based on a view of women that is impossible to those who have had any experience with
them.
H. L. Mencken (1880–1956) US journalist.

44 When a man is in love he endures more than at
other times; he submits to everything.
Friedrich Wilhelm Nietzsche (1844–1900) German
philosopher.
The Antichrist

45 By the time you swear you're his,
Shivering and sighing,
And he vows his passion is
Infinite, undying –
Lady, make a note of this:
One of you is lying.
Dorothy Parker (1893–1967) US writer.
Unfortunate Coincidence

46 Every love is the love before
In a duller dress.
Dorothy Parker
Death and Taxes

47 Love is like quicksilver in the hand. Leave the fin-
gers open and it stays. Clutch it, and it darts away.
Dorothy Parker
Attrib.

48 Let's Do It; Let's Fall in Love.
Cole Porter
Paris, song title

49 If all the world and love were young,
And truth in every shepherd's tongue,
These pretty pleasures might me move
To live with thee, and be thy love.
Walter Raleigh (1554–1618) English explorer.
Answer to Marlow

50 There are very few people who are not ashamed
of having been in love when they no longer love
each other.
Duc de la Rochefoucauld (1613–80) French writer.
Maximes, 71

51 Every little girl knows about love. It is only her
capacity to suffer because of it that increases.
Françoise Sagan (1935–   ) French writer.
Daily Express

52 True love's the gift which God has given
To man alone beneath the heaven.
Walter Scott (1771–1832) Scottish novelist.
The Lay of the Last Minstrel, V

53 Therefore love moderately: long love doth so;
Too swift arrives as tardy as too slow.
William Shakespeare (1564–1616) English dramatist.
Romeo and Juliet, II:6

54 There's beggary in the love that can be reckon'd.
William Shakespeare
Antony and Cleopatra, I:1

55 But love is blind, and lovers cannot see
The pretty follies that themselves commit.
William Shakespeare
The Merchant of Venice, II:6

56 For aught that I could ever read,
Could ever hear by tale or history,
The course of true love never did run smooth.
William Shakespeare
A Midsummer Night's Dream, I:1

57 Love looks not with the eyes, but with the mind;
And therefore is wing'd Cupid painted blind.
William Shakespeare
A Midsummer Night's Dream, I:1

58 Let me not to the marriage of true minds
Admit impediments. Love is not love
Which alters when it alteration finds,
Or bends with the remover to remove.
O, no! it is an ever-fixed mark,
That looks on tempests and is never shaken.
William Shakespeare
Sonnet 116

59 She never told her love,
But let concealment, like a worm i' th' bud,
Feed on her damask cheek. She pin'd in thought;
And with a green and yellow melancholy
She sat like Patience on a monument,
Smiling at grief.
William Shakespeare
Twelfth Night, II:4

60 Then must you speak
Of one that lov'd not wisely, but too well;
Of one not easily jealous, but, being wrought,
Perplexed in the extreme; of one whose hand,
Like the base Indian, threw a pearl away
Richer than all his tribe.
William Shakespeare
Othello, V:2

61 A woman despises a man for loving her, unless
she returns his love.
Elizabeth Drew Stoddard (1823–1902) US novelist and poet.
Two Men, Ch. 32

62 I hold it true, whate'er befall;
I feel it, when I sorrow most;
'Tis better to have loved and lost
Than never to have loved at all.
Alfred, Lord Tennyson (1809–92) British poet.
In Memoriam A.H.H., XXVII

63 Such a one do I remember, whom to look at was
to love.
Alfred, Lord Tennyson
Locksley Hall

64 O tell her, brief is life but love is long.
Alfred, Lord Tennyson
The Princess, IV

65 All, everything that I understand, I understand
only because I love.
Leo Tolstoy (1828–1910) Russian writer.
War and Peace, Bk. VII, Ch. 16

66 Those who have courage to love should have
courage to suffer.
Anthony Trollope (1815–82) British novelist.
The Bertrams, Ch. 27

67 Love conquers all things: let us too give in to
Love.
Virgil (Publius Vergilius Maro; 70–19 BC) Roman poet.
Eclogue, Bk. X

68 Beware you be not swallowed up in books! An
ounce of love is worth a pound of knowledge.
John Wesley (1703–91) British religious leader.
Life of Wesley (R. Southey), Ch. 16

69 I have found it impossible to carry the heavy burden of responsibility and to discharge my duties
as King as I would wish to do without the help
and support of the woman I love.
Duke of Windsor (1894–1972) King of the United Kingdom;
abdicated 1936.
Radio broadcast, 11 Dec 1936

70 There is a comfort in the strength of love;
'Twill make a thing endurable, which else
Would overset the brain, or break the heart.
William Wordsworth (1770–1850) British poet.
Michael, 448

71 Love fled
And paced upon the mountains overhead
And hid his face amid a crowd of stars.
W. B. Yeats (1865–1939) Irish poet.
When you are Old

72 A pity beyond all telling
Is hid in the heart of love.
W. B. Yeats
The Pity of Love

☐ LOVE AND DEATH ☐
See also death, love

1 For, Heaven be thanked, we live in such an age,
When no man dies for love, but on the stage.
John Dryden (1631–1700) British poet and dramatist.
Mithridates, Epilogue

2 How alike are the groans of love to those of the
dying.
Malcolm Lowry (1909–57) British novelist.
Under the Volcano, Ch. 12

3 'Tis said that some have died for love.
William Wordsworth (1770–1850) British poet.
'Tis Said that some have Died

☐ LOVE AND FRIENDSHIP ☐
See also friendship, love

1 Friendship is a disinterested commerce between
equals; love, an abject intercourse between
tyrants and slaves.
Oliver Goldsmith (1728–74) Irish-born British writer.
The Good-Natured Man, I

2 Friendship is constant in all other things
Save in the office and affairs of love.
William Shakespeare (1564–1616) English dramatist.
Much Ado About Nothing, II:1

☐LOVE AND HATE☐

See also hate, love

1 Now hatred is by far the longest pleasure;
Men love in haste, but they detest at leisure.
Lord Byron (1788–1824) British poet.
Don Juan, XIII

2 *Odi et amo.*
I hate and love.
Catullus (c. 84–c. 54 BC) Roman poet.
Carmina, LXXXV

3 Heaven has no rage like love to hatred turned,
Nor hell a fury like a woman scorned.
William Congreve (1670–1729) British Restoration dramatist.
The Mourning Bride, III

4 If one judges love by its visible effects, it looks
more like hatred than like friendship.
Duc de la Rochefoucauld (1613–80) French writer.
Maximes, 72

☐LOVE AND MARRIAGE☐

See also love, marriage

1 Love and marriage, love and marriage,
Go together like a horse and carriage.
Sammy Cahn (Samuel Cohen; 1913–) US songwriter.
Our Town, 'Love and Marriage'

2 ALMA. I rather suspect her of being in love with
him.
MARTIN. Her own husband? Monstrous! What a
selfish woman!
Jennie Jerome Churchill (1854–1921) US-born British
hostess and writer.
His Borrowed Plumes

3 Love is moral even without legal marriage, but
marriage is immoral without love.
Ellen Key (Karolina Sofia Key; 1849–1926) Swedish writer.
The Morality of Woman and Other Essays, 'The Morality of Woman'

4 Any one must see at a glance that if men and
women marry those whom they do not love, they
must love those whom they do not marry.
Harriet Martineau (1802–76) British writer.
Society in America, Vol. III, 'Marriage'

5 The amount of women in London who flirt with
their own husbands is perfectly scandalous. It
looks so bad. It is simply washing one's clean
linen in public.
Oscar Wilde (1854–1900) Irish-born British dramatist.
The Importance of Being Earnest, I

☐LOYALTY☐

See also betrayal, faithfulness, patriotism, support

1 And Ruth said, Intreat me not to leave thee, or to
return from following after thee: for whither thou
goest, I will go; and where thou lodgest, I will
lodge: thy people shall be my people, and thy
God my God:

Where thou diest, will I die, and there will I be
buried: the Lord do so to me, and more also, if
ought but death part thee and me.
Bible: Ruth
1:16–17

2 The State, in choosing men to serve it, takes no
notice of their opinions. If they be willing faithfully to serve it, that satisfies.
Oliver Cromwell (1599–1658) English soldier and statesman.
Said before the Battle of Marston Moor, 2 July 1644

3 Had I but served God as diligently as I have
served the king, he would not have given me
over in my gray hairs.
Cardinal Wolsey (1475–1530) English churchman.
Remark to Sir William Kingston
Negotiations of Thomas Wolsey (Cavendish)

☐LUCK☐

See also superstition

1 This is the temple of Providence where disciples
still hourly mark its ways and note the system of
its mysteries. Here is the one God whose worshippers prove their faith by their works and in
their destruction still trust in Him.
F. H. Bradley (1846–1924) British philosopher.
Referring to Monte Carlo
Aphorisms

2 Fortune, that favours fools.
Ben Jonson (1573–1637) English dramatist.
The Alchemist, Prologue

3 I am a great believer in luck, and I find the harder
I work the more I have of it.
Stephen Leacock (1869–1944) English-born Canadian
economist and humorist.
Literary Lapses

☐LUST☐

See also animalism, desire, love, sex

1 Licence my roving hands, and let them go,
Before, behind, between, above, below.
John Donne (1573–1631) English poet.
Elegies, 18, 'Love's Progress'

2 What is commonly called love, namely the desire
of satisfying a voracious appetite with a certain
quantity of delicate white human flesh.
Henry Fielding (1707–54) British novelist.
Tom Jones, Bk. VI, Ch. 1

3 Lolita, light of my life, fire of my loins. My sin, my
Soul.
Vladimir Nabokov (1899–1977) Russian-born US novelist.
Lolita

4 Th' expense of spirit in a waste of shame
Is lust in action; and till action, lust
Is perjur'd, murd'rous, bloody, full of blame,

Savage, extreme, rude, cruel, not to trust;
Enjoy'd no sooner but despised straight.
William Shakespeare (1564–1616) English dramatist.
Sonnet 129

5 Nonconformity and lust stalking hand in hand
through the country, wasting and ravaging.
Evelyn Waugh (1903–66) British novelist.
Decline and Fall, Pt. I, Ch. 5

☐ LUXURY ☐

See also extravagance, wealth

1 The saddest thing I can imagine is to get used to
luxury.
Charlie Chaplin (Sir Charles Spencer C.; 1889–1977) British
film actor.
My Autobiography

2 In the affluent society no useful distinction can
be made between luxuries and necessaries.
John Kenneth Galbraith (1908–) US economist.
The Affluent Society, Ch. 21

3 Give us the luxuries of life, and we will dispense
with its necessities.
John Lothrop Motley (1814–77) US historian and diplomat.
Also quoted by Frank Lloyd Wright
The Autocrat of the Breakfast Table (O. W. Holmes), Ch. 6

4 How many things I can do without!
Socrates (469–399 BC) Athenian philosopher.
Examining the range of goods on sale at a market
Lives of the Eminent Philosophers (Diogenes Laertius), II

☐ LYING ☐

See also deception, honesty, truth

1 It contains a misleading impression, not a lie. I
was being economical with the truth.
Robert Armstrong (1913–) British civil servant.
Giving evidence on behalf of the British Government in an Aus-
tralian court case, Nov 1986. Armstrong was, in fact, quoting
Edmund Burke (1729–97).

2 A lie can be half-way round the world before the
truth has got its boots on.
James Callaghan (1912–) British politician and prime
minister.
Speech, 1 Nov 1976

3 It cannot in the opinion of His Majesty's Government be classified as slavery in the extreme
acceptance of the word without some risk of terminological inexactitude.
Winston Churchill (1874–1965) British statesman.
Speech, House of Commons, 22 Feb 1906

4 The broad mass of a nation…will more easily fall
victim to a big lie than to a small one.
Adolf Hitler (1889–1945) German dictator.
Mein Kampf, Ch. 10

5 It is hard to believe that a man is telling the truth
when you know that you would lie if you were in
his place.
H. L. Mencken (1880–1956) US journalist.
Prejudices

6 He led a double life. Did that make him a liar? He
did not feel a liar. He was a man of two truths.
Iris Murdoch (1919–) Irish-born British novelist.
The Sacred and Profane Love Machine

7 He who does not need to lie is proud of not being
a liar.
Friedrich Wilhelm Nietzsche (1844–1900) German
philosopher.
Nachgelassene Fragmente

8 A lie is an abomination unto the Lord and a very
present help in trouble.
Adlai Stevenson (1900–65) US statesman.
Speech, Jan 1951

9 That a lie which is all a lie may be met and fought
with outright,
But a lie which is part a truth is a harder matter
to fight.
Alfred, Lord Tennyson (1809–92) British poet.
The Grandmother

M

□ MADNESS □

See also psychiatry, psychology

1 We all are born mad. Some remain so.
Samuel Beckett (1906–89) Irish novelist and dramatist.
Waiting for Godot, II

2 Those whom God wishes to destroy, he first makes mad.
Euripides (c. 480–406 BC) Greek dramatist.
Fragment

3 Show me a sane man and I will cure him for you.
Carl Gustav Jung (1875–1961) Swiss psychoanalyst.
The Observer, 19 July 1975

4 Every one is more or less mad on one point.
Rudyard Kipling (1865–1936) Indian-born British writer.
Plain Tales from the Hills, 'On the Strength of a Likeness'

5 A body seriously out of equilibrium, either with itself or with its environment, perishes outright. Not so a mind. Madness and suffering can set themselves no limit.
George Santayana (1863–1952) US philosopher.
The Life of Reason: Reason in Common Sense, 3

6 Though this be madness, yet there is method in't.
William Shakespeare (1564–1616) English dramatist.
Hamlet, II:2

7 Madness in great ones must not unwatch'd go.
William Shakespeare
Hamlet, III:1

8 When we remember that we are all mad, the mysteries disappear and life stands explained.
Mark Twain (Samuel Longhorne Clemens; 1835–1910) US writer.

9 Men will always be mad and those who think they can cure them are the maddest of all.
Voltaire (François-Marie Arouet; 1694–1778) French writer.
Letter, 1762

□ MAJORITY □

See also democracy, minority, public

1 The majority has the might – more's the pity – but it hasn't right…The minority is always right.
Henrik Ibsen (1828–1906) Norwegian dramatist.
An Enemy of the People, IV

2 The worst enemy of truth and freedom in our society is the compact majority. Yes, the damned, compact, liberal majority.
Henrik Ibsen
An Enemy of the People, IV

3 It is time for the great silent majority of Americans to stand up and be counted.
Richard Milhous Nixon (1913–) US president.
Election speech, Oct 1970

□ MALAPROPISMS □

Remarks of a type associated with Mrs Malaprop in Sheridan's play *The Rivals*.

1 Our watch, sir, have indeed comprehended two aspicious persons.
William Shakespeare (1564–1616) English dramatist.
Much Ado About Nothing, III:5

2 Comparisons are odorous.
William Shakespeare
Much Ado About Nothing, III:5

3 A progeny of learning.
Richard Brinsley Sheridan (1751–1816) British dramatist.
The Rivals, I

4 Illiterate him, I say, quite from your memory.
Richard Brinsley Sheridan
The Rivals, II

5 It gives me the hydrostatics to such a degree.
Richard Brinsley Sheridan
The Rivals, III

6 If I reprehend any thing in this world, it is the use of my oracular tongue, and a nice derangement of epitaphs!
Richard Brinsley Sheridan
The Rivals, III

□ MANKIND □

See also evolution, human condition, human nature, men, misanthropy, public, society, women

1 Either a beast or a god.
Aristotle (384–322 BC) Greek philosopher.
Politics, Bk. I

2 And God said, Let us make man in our image, after our likeness: and let them have dominion over the fish of the sea, and over the fowl of the air, and over the cattle, and over all the earth, and over every creeping thing that creepeth upon the earth.
So God created man in his own image, in the image of God created he him; male and female created he them.
And God blessed them, and God said unto them, Be fruitful, and multiply, and replenish the earth, and subdue it: and have dominion over the fish of the sea, and over the fowl of the air, and over every living thing that moveth upon the earth.
Bible: Genesis
1:26–28

3 For Mercy has a human heart,
Pity a human face,
And Love, the human form divine,
And Peace, the human dress.
William Blake (1757–1827) British poet.
Songs of Innocence, 'The Divine Image'

4 Man is a noble animal, splendid in ashes, and
pompous in the grave.
Thomas Browne (1605–82) English physician and writer.
Urn Burial, Ch. 5

5 Mankind is not a tribe of animals to which we
owe compassion. Mankind is a club to which we
owe our subscription.
G. K. Chesterton (1874–1936) British writer.
Daily News, 10 Apr 1906

6 The evolution of the human race will not be
accomplished in the ten thousand years of tame
animals, but in the million years of wild animals,
because man is and will always be a wild animal.
Charles Darwin (1887–1962) British life scientist.
The Next Ten Million Years, Ch. 4

7 On earth there is nothing great but man; in man
there is nothing great but mind.
William Hamilton (1788–1856) Scottish philosopher.
Lectures on Metaphysics

8 There are one hundred and ninety-three living
species of monkeys and apes. One hundred and
ninety-two of them are covered with hair. The
exception is a naked ape self-named *Homo
sapiens*.
Desmond Morris (1928–   ) British biologist and writer.
The Naked Ape, Introduction

9 Man, as he is, is not a genuine article. He is an
imitation of something, and a very bad imitation.
P. D. Ouspensky (1878–1947) Russian-born occultist.
The Psychology of Man's Possible Evolution, Ch. 2

10 I love mankind – it's people I can't stand.
Charles M. Schultz (1922–   ) US cartoonist.
Go Fly a Kite, Charlie Brown

11 After all, for mankind as a whole there are no
exports. We did not start developing by obtain-
ing foreign exchange from Mars or the moon.
Mankind is a closed society.
E. F. Schumacher (1911–77) German-born economist.
Small is Beautiful, A Study of Economics as if People Mattered,
Ch. 14

12 But man, proud man
Dress'd in a little brief authority,
Most ignorant of what he's most assur'd,
His glassy essence, like an angry ape,
Plays such fantastic tricks before high heaven
As makes the angels weep.
William Shakespeare (1564–1616) English dramatist.
Measure for Measure, II:2

13 What a piece of work is a man! How noble in reason! how infinite in faculties! in form and moving,
how express and admirable! in action, how like
an angel! in apprehension, how like a god! the
beauty of the world! the paragon of animals! And
yet, to me, what is this quintessence of dust?
Man delights not me – no, nor woman neither.
William Shakespeare
Hamlet, II:2

14 How beauteous mankind is! O brave new world
That has such people in't!
William Shakespeare
The Tempest, V:1

15 Man, unlike any other thing organic or inorganic
in the universe, grows beyond his work, walks up
the stairs of his concepts, emerges ahead of his
accomplishments.
John Steinbeck (1902–68) US novelist.
The Grapes of Wrath, Ch. 14

16 Glory to Man in the highest! for Man is the mas-
ter of things.
Algernon Charles Swinburne (1837–1909) British poet.
Hymn of Man

17 The highest wisdom has but one science – the
science of the whole – the science explaining the
whole creation and man's place in it.
Leo Tolstoy (1828–1910) Russian writer.
War and Peace, Bk.V, Ch. 2

18 We're all of us guinea pigs in the laboratory of
God. Humanity is just a work in progress.
Tennessee Williams (1911–83) US dramatist.
Camino Real, 12

19 If this belief from heaven be sent,
If such be Nature's holy plan,
Have I not reason to lament
What man has made of man?
William Wordsworth (1770–1850) British poet.
Lines written in Early Spring

☐ MANNERS ☐

See also courtesy, etiquette

1 Leave off first for manners' sake: and be not
unsatiable, lest thou offend.
Bible: Ecclesiasticus
31:17

2 To Americans English manners are far more
frightening than none at all.
Randall Jarrell (1914–65) US author.
Pictures from an Institution, Pt. I, Ch. 5

3 At one early, glittering dinner party at Buckingham Palace, the trembling hand of a nervous
waiter spilled a spoonful of decidedly hot soup
down my neck. How could I manage to ease his
mind and turn his embarrassed apologies into a
smile, except to put on a pretended frown and

say, without thinking: 'Never darken my Dior again!'

Beatrice Lillie (Constance Sylvia Munston, Lady Peel; 1898–1989) Canadian-born British actress.
Every Other Inch a Lady

4 On the Continent people have good food; in England people have good table manners.

George Mikes (1912–87) Hungarian-born British writer.
How to be an Alien

5 Manners are especially the need of the plain. The pretty can get away with anything.

Evelyn Waugh (1903–66) British novelist.
The Observer, 'Sayings of the Year,' 1962

6 Manners maketh man.

William of Wykeham (1324–1404) English churchman.
Motto of Winchester College and New College, Oxford

☐MAO TSE-TUNG☐

(1893–1976) Chinese communist leader. As chairman of the Communist Party, in 1949 he proclaimed the People's Republic of China and in 1966–68 launched the Cultural Revolution. He developed the form of communism known as Maoism.

QUOTATIONS ABOUT MAO TSE-TUNG

1 He dominated the room as I have never seen any person do except Charles de Gaulle.

Henry Kissinger (1923–) German-born US politician and diplomat.
Memoirs

QUOTATIONS BY MAO TSE-TUNG

2 'War is the continuation of politics'. In this sense war is politics and war itself is a political action.

Quotations from Chairman Mao Tse-Tung, Ch. 5

3 Every Communist must grasp the truth, 'Political power grows out of the barrel of a gun.'

Selected Works, Vol. II, 'Problems of War and Strategy', 6 Nov 1938

4 To read too many books is harmful.

The New Yorker, 7 Mar 1977

5 The atom bomb is a paper tiger which the United States reactionaries use to scare people.

Interview, Aug 1946

6 The government burns down whole cities while the people are forbidden to light lamps.

Attrib.

☐MARRIAGE☐

See also adultery, family, love and marriage, unfaithfulness

1 I had vaguely supposed that marriage in a registry office, while lacking both sanctity and style, was at least a swift, straightforward business. If not, then what was the use of it, even to the heathen? A few inquiries, however, showed it to be no such thing.

Richard Adams (1920–) British novelist.
The Girl in a Swing, Ch. 13

2 To marry a man out of pity is folly; and, if you think you are going to influence the kind of fellow who has 'never had a chance, poor devil,' you are profoundly mistaken. One can only influence the strong characters in life, not the weak; and it is the height of vanity to suppose that you can make an honest man of anyone.

Margot Asquith (1865–1945) The second wife of Herbert Asquith.
The Autobiography of Margot Asquith, Ch. 6

3 I married beneath me – all women do.

Nancy Astor (1879–1964) American-born British politician.
Dictionary of National Biography

4 Happiness in marriage is entirely a matter of chance.

Jane Austen (1775–1817) British novelist.
Pride and Prejudice, Ch. 6

5 Wives are young men's mistresses, companions for middle age, and old men's nurses.

Francis Bacon (1561–1626) English philosopher.
Essays, 'Of Marriage and Single Life'

6 He was reputed one of the wise men, that made answer to the question, when a man should marry? A young man not yet, an elder man not at all.

Francis Bacon
Essays, 'Of Marriage and Single Life'

7 It is easier to be a lover than a husband, for the same reason that it is more difficult to show a ready wit all day long than to produce an occasional *bon mot*.

Honoré de Balzac (1799–1850) French novelist.
Attrib.

8 The majority of husbands remind me of an orangutang trying to play the violin.

Honoré de Balzac
La Physiologie du mariage

9 Being a husband is a whole-time job. That is why so many husbands fail. They cannot give their entire attention to it.

Arnold Bennett (1867–1931) British novelist.
The Title, I

10 Husbands, love your wives, and be not bitter against them.

Bible: Colossians
3:19

11 Let the husband render unto the wife due benevolence: and likewise also the wife unto the husband.

Bible: I Corinthians
7:3

12 But if they cannot contain, let them marry: for it is better to marry than to burn.
Bible: I Corinthians
7:9

13 Wherefore they are no more twain, but one flesh. What therefore God hath joined together, let not man put asunder.
Bible: Matthew
19:6

14 *Marriage*, n. The state or condition of a community consisting of a master, a mistress and two slaves, making in all two.
Ambrose Bierce (1842–?1914) US writer and journalist.
The Devil's Dictionary

15 To have and to hold from this day forward, for better for worse, for richer for poorer, in sickness and in health, to love and to cherish, till death us do part.
The Book of Common Prayer
Solemnization of Matrimony

16 Marriage is distinctly and repeatedly excluded from heaven. Is this because it is thought likely to mar the general felicity?
Samuel Butler (1835–1902) British writer.
Notebooks

17 Wedlock – the deep, deep peace of the double bed after the hurly-burly of the chaise-longue.
Mrs Patrick Campbell (Beatrice Stella Tanner; 1865–1940) British actress.
Jennie (Ralph G. Martin), Vol. II

18 An archaeologist is the best husband any woman can have: the older she gets, the more interested he is in her.
Agatha Christie (1891–1976) British detective-story writer.
Attrib.

19 The most happy marriage I can picture or imagine to myself would be the union of a deaf man to a blind woman.
Samuel Taylor Coleridge (1772–1834) British poet.
Recollections (Allsop)

20 SHARPER: Thus grief still treads upon the heels of pleasure:
Marry'd in haste, we may repent at leisure.
SETTER: Some by experience find those words mis-plac'd:
At leisure marry'd, they repent in haste.
William Congreve (1670–1729) British Restoration dramatist.
The Old Bachelor, V:8

21 Marriage is a wonderful invention; but then again so is a bicycle repair kit.
Billy Connolly (1942–) British comedian.
The Authorized Version

22 Daisy, Daisy, give me your answer, do!
I'm half crazy, all for the love of you!
It won't be a stylish marriage,

I can't afford a carriage,
But you'll look sweet upon the seat
Of a bicycle made for two!
Harry Dacre (19th century) British songwriter.
Daisy Bell

23 If a man stays away from his wife for seven years, the law presumes the separation to have killed him; yet according to our daily experience, it might well prolong his life.
Lord Darling (1849–1936) British judge.
Scintillae Juris

24 Every woman should marry – and no man.
Benjamin Disraeli (1804–81) British statesman.
Lothair, Ch. 30

25 It destroys one's nerves to be amiable every day to the same human being.
Benjamin Disraeli
The Young Duke

26 Here lies my wife; here let her lie!
Now she's at rest, and so am I.
John Dryden (1631–1700) British poet and dramatist.
Epitaph Intended for Dryden's Wife

27 So that ends my first experience with matrimony, which I always thought a highly overrated performance.
Isadora Duncan (1878–1927) US dancer.
The New York Times, 1923

28 His designs were strictly honourable, as the phrase is; that is, to rob a lady of her fortune by way of marriage.
Henry Fielding (1707–54) British novelist.
Tom Jones, Bk. XI, Ch. 4

29 One fool at least in every married couple.
Henry Fielding
Amelia, Bk. IX, Ch. 4

30 Most marriages don't add two people together. They subtract one from the other.
Ian Fleming (1908–64) British journalist and author.
Diamonds are Forever

31 Husbands are like fires. They go out when unattended.
Zsa Zsa Gabor (1919–) Hungarian-born US film star.
Newsweek, 28 Mar 1960

32 Do you think your mother and I should have liv'd comfortably so long together, if ever we had been married?
John Gay (1685–1732) English poet and dramatist.
The Beggar's Opera

33 I...chose my wife, as she did her wedding gown, not for a fine glossy surface, but such qualities as would wear well.
Oliver Goldsmith
The Vicar of Wakefield, Preface

34 The critical period in matrimony is breakfast-time.
A. P. Herbert (1890–1971) British writer and politician.
Uncommon Law

35 Then be not coy, but use your time;
And while ye may, go marry:
For having lost but once your prime,
You may for ever tarry.
Robert Herrick (1591–1674) English poet.
Hesperides, 'To the Virgins, to Make Much of Time'

36 Marriage has many pains, but celibacy has no pleasures.
Samuel Johnson (1709–84) British lexicographer.
Rasselas, Ch. 26

37 Nothing is to me more distasteful than that entire complacency and satisfaction which beam in the countenances of a new-married couple.
Charles Lamb (1775–1834) British essayist.
Essays of Elia, 'A Bachelor's Complaint of Married People'

38 There was I, waiting at the church,
Waiting at the church, waiting at the church,
When I found he'd left me in the lurch,
Lor', how it did upset me!...
Can't get away to marry you today –
My wife won't let me.
Fred W. Leigh (19th century) British songwriter.
Waiting at the Church

39 I'm getting married in the morning!
Ding dong! the bells are gonna chime.
Pull out the stopper!
Let's have a whopper!
But get me to the church on time!
Alan Jay Lerner (1918–86) US songwriter.
My Fair Lady, II:3

40 When married people don't get on they can separate, but if they're not married it's impossible. It's a tie that only death can sever.
W. Somerset Maugham (1874–1965) British novelist.
The Circle, III

41 Marriage is like a cage; one sees the birds outside desperate to get in, and those inside equally desperate to get out.
Michel de Montaigne (1533–92) French essayist.
Essais, III

42 It has been said that a bride's attitude towards her betrothed can be summed up in three words: Aisle. Altar. Hymn.
Frank Muir (1920–) British writer and broadcaster.
Upon My Word! (Frank Muir and Dennis Norden), 'A Jug of Wine'

43 One doesn't have to get anywhere in a marriage. It's not a public conveyance.
Iris Murdoch (1919–) Irish-born British novelist.
A Severed Head

44 Writing is like getting married. One should never commit oneself until one is amazed at one's luck.
Iris Murdoch
The Black Prince, 'Bradley Pearson's Foreword'

45 It is now known...that men enter local politics solely as a result of being unhappily married.
Cyril Northcote Parkinson (1919–) British historian and writer.
Parkinson's Law, Ch. 10

46 Strange to say what delight we married people have to see these poor fools decoyed into our condition.
Samuel Pepys (1633–1703) English diarist.
Diary, 25 Dec 1665

47 When a man opens the car door for his wife, it's either a new car or a new wife.
Prince Philip (1921–) The consort of Queen Elizabeth II.
Remark, Mar 1988

48 It doesn't much signify whom one marries, for one is sure to find next morning that it was someone else.
Samuel Rogers (1763–1855) British poet.
Table Talk (ed. Alexander Dyce)

49 When you see what some girls marry, you realize how they must hate to work for a living.
Helen Rowland (1876–1950) US writer.
Reflections of a Bachelor Girl

50 The Western custom of one wife and hardly any mistresses.
Saki (Hector Hugh Munro; 1870–1916) British writer.
Reginald in Russia

51 It takes two to make a marriage a success and only one a failure.
Herbert Samuel (1870–1963) British Liberal statesman.
A Book of Quotations

52 For a light wife doth make a heavy husband.
William Shakespeare (1564–1616) English dramatist.
The Merchant of Venice, V:1

53 Many a good hanging prevents a bad marriage.
William Shakespeare
Twelfth Night, I:5

54 It is a woman's business to get married as soon as possible, and a man's to keep unmarried as long as he can.
George Bernard Shaw (1856–1950) Irish dramatist and critic.
Man and Superman, II

55 My definition of marriage:....it resembles a pair of shears, so joined that they cannot be separated; often moving in opposite directions, yet always punishing anyone who comes between them.
Sydney Smith (1771–1845) British clergyman and essayist.
Memoir (Lady Holland)

56 Marriage is like life in this – that it is a field of battle, and not a bed of roses.
Robert Louis Stevenson (1850–94) Scottish writer.
Virginibus Puerisque

57 What they do in heaven we are ignorant of; what they do *not* we are told expressly, that they neither marry, nor are given in marriage.
Jonathan Swift (1667–1745) Irish-born Anglican priest and writer.
Thoughts on Various Subjects

58 Remember, it is as easy to marry a rich woman as a poor woman.
William Makepeace Thackeray (1811–63) British novelist.
Pendennis, Ch. 28

59 This I set down as a positive truth. A woman with fair opportunities and without a positive hump, may marry whom she likes.
William Makepeace Thackeray
Vanity Fair, Ch. 4

60 Every night of her married life she has been late for school.
Dylan Thomas (1914–53) Welsh poet.
Under Milk Wood

61 Divorce? Never. But murder often!
Sybil Thorndike (1882–1976) British actress.
Replying to a query as to whether she had ever considered divorce during her long marriage to Sir Lewis Casson
Attrib.

62 Nearly all marriages, even happy ones, are mistakes: in the sense that almost certainly (in a more perfect world, or even with a little more care in this very imperfect one) both partners might have found more suitable mates. But the real soul-mate is the one you are actually married to.
J. R. R. Tolkien (1892–1973) British writer.
Letter to Michael Tolkien, 6–8 Mar 1941

63 Marriage is the only adventure open to the cowardly.
Voltaire (François-Marie Arouet; 1694–1778) French writer.
Thoughts of a Philosopher

64 Marriage is a great instatition, but I'm not ready for an institution, yet.
Mae West (1892–1980) US actress.

65 I think women are basically quite lazy. Marriage is still a woman's best investment, because she can con some man into supporting her for the rest of his life.
Alan Whicker (1925–) British television broadcaster and writer.
The Observer, 'Sayings of the Week', 10 Sept 1972

66 Of course, I do have a slight advantage over the rest of you. It helps in a pinch to be able to remind your bride that you gave up a throne for her.
Duke of Windsor (1894–1972) King of the United Kingdom; abdicated 1936.
Discussing the maintenance of happy marital relations
Attrib.

☐ MARTYRDOM ☐

See also execution

1 The king has been very good to me. He promoted me from a simple maid to be a marchioness. Then he raised me to be a queen. Now he will raise me to be a martyr.
Anne Boleyn (1507–36) Second wife of Henry VIII.
Notable Women in History (W. Abbot)

2 'Dying for an idea,' again, sounds well enough, but why not let the idea die instead of you?
Wyndham Lewis (1882–1957) British novelist.
The Art of Being Ruled, Pt. I, Ch. 1

3 And they blest him in their pain, that they were not left to Spain,
To the thumbscrew and the stake, for the glory of the Lord.
Alfred, Lord Tennyson (1809–92) British poet.
The Revenge, III

4 A thing is not necessarily true because a man dies for it.
Oscar Wilde (1854–1900) Irish-born British dramatist.
Oscariana

☐ MARXISM ☐

See also Communism, socialism

1 The workers have nothing to lose but their chains. They have a world to gain. Workers of the world, unite.
Karl Marx (1818–83) German philosopher and revolutionary.
The Communist Manifesto, 4

2 From each according to his abilities, to each according to his needs.
Karl Marx
Criticism of the Gotha Programme

3 The dictatorship of the proletariat.
Karl Marx
Attrib.

4 And what a prize we have to fight for: no less than the chance to banish from our land the dark divisive clouds of Marxist socialism.
Margaret Thatcher (1925–) British politician and prime minister.
Speech, Scottish Conservative Conference, 1983

□ MATERIALISM □

See also greed, money, wealth

1 Thinking to get at once all the gold that the goose could give, he killed it, and opened it only to find – nothing.
Aesop (6th century BC) Reputed Greek writer of fables.
Fables, 'The Goose with the Golden Eggs'

2 Jesus said unto him, If thou wilt be perfect, go and sell that thou hast, and give to the poor, and thou shalt have treasure in heaven: and come and follow me.
But when the young man heard that saying, he went away sorrowful: for he had great possessions.
Bible: Matthew
19:21–22

3 For gold in phisik is a cordial,
Therfore he lovede gold in special.
Geoffrey Chaucer (c. 1342–1400) English poet.
Referring to the doctor
The Canterbury Tales, Prologue

4 To be clever enough to get all that money, one must be stupid enough to want it.
G. K. Chesterton (1874–1936) British writer.
The Innocence of Father Brown

5 I never hated a man enough to give him diamonds back.
Zsa Zsa Gabor (1919–) Hungarian-born US film star.
The Observer, 'Sayings of the Week', 28 Aug 1957

6 The almighty dollar, that great object of universal devotion throughout our land, seems to have no genuine devotees in these peculiar villages.
Washington Irving (1783–1859) US writer.
Wolfert's Roost, 'The Creole Village'

7 Good morning to the day: and, next, my gold! –
Open the shrine, that I may see my saint.
Ben Jonson (1573–1637) English dramatist.
Volpone, I:1

8 Kissing your hand may make you feel very very good but a diamond and safire bracelet lasts forever.
Anita Loos (1891–1981) US novelist.
Gentlemen Prefer Blondes, Ch. 4

9 When an American heiress wants to buy a man, she at once crosses the Atlantic. The only really materialistic people I have ever met have been Europeans.
Mary McCarthy (1912–89) US novelist.
On the Contrary 1962

10 Diamonds Are A Girl's Best Friend.
Leo Robin (1899–1984) US songwriter.
Gentlemen Prefer Blondes, song title

11 Bell, book, and candle, shall not drive me back,
When gold and silver becks me to come on.
William Shakespeare (1564–1616) English dramatist.
King John, III:3

12 A gold rush is what happens when a line of chorus girls spot a man with a bank roll.
Mae West (1892–1980) US actress.
Klondike Annie, film 1936

□ MATHEMATICS □

See also numbers

1 As far as the laws of mathematics refer to reality, they are not certain, and as far as they are certain, they do not refer to reality.
Albert Einstein (1879–1955) German-born US physicist.
The Tao of Physics (F. Capra), Ch. 2

2 There is no 'royal road' to geometry.
Euclid (c. 300 BC) Greek mathematician.
Said to Ptolemy I when asked if there were an easier way to solve theorems
Comment on Euclid (Proclus)

3 MORIARTY. How are you at Mathematics?
HARRY SECOMBE. I speak it like a native.
Spike Milligan (1918–) British comic actor and author.
The Goon Show

4 Let no one ignorant of mathematics enter here.
Plato (429–347 BC) Greek philosopher.
Inscription written over the entrance to the Academy
Biographical Encyclopedia (I. Asimov)

5 The true spirit of delight, the exaltation, the sense of being more than Man, which is the touchstone of the highest excellence is to be found in mathematics as surely as in poetry.
Bertrand Russell (1872–1970) British philosopher.
Mysticism and Logic

6 Mathematics, rightly viewed, possesses not only truth by supreme beauty – a beauty cold and austere like that of sculpture.
Bertrand Russell
Mysticism and Logic

7 Pure mathematics consists entirely of assertions to the effect that, if such and such a proposition is true of *anything*, then such and such another proposition is true of that thing. It is essential not to discuss whether the first proposition is really true, and not to mention what the anything is, of which it is supposed to be true.
Bertrand Russell
Mysticism and Logic, Ch. 5

8 Numbers constitute the only universal language.
Nathaniel West (Nathan Weinstein; 1903–40) US novelist.
Miss Lonelyhearts

☐ MEANING ☐

See also purpose, words

1 'When *I* use a word,' Humpty Dumpty said in rather a scornful tone, 'it means just what I choose it to mean – neither more nor less.'
Lewis Carroll (Charles Lutwidge Dodgson; 1832–98) British writer.
Through the Looking-Glass, Ch. 6

2 Where in this small-talking world can I find
A longitude with no platitude?
Christopher Fry (1907–) British dramatist.
The Lady's Not for Burning, III

3 The least of things with a meaning is worth more in life than the greatest of things without it.
Carl Gustav Jung (1875–1961) Swiss psychoanalyst.
Modern Man in Search of a Soul

☐ MEDICINE ☐

See also disease, doctors, drugs, health and healthy living, illness, remedies

1 The prime goal is to alleviate suffering, and not to prolong life. And if your treatment does not alleviate suffering, but only prolongs life, that treatment should be stopped.
Christiaan Barnard (1922–) South African surgeon.

2 A miracle drug is any drug that will do what the label says it will do.
Eric Hodgins (1899–1971) US writer and editor.
Episode

3 The art of medicine is generally a question of time.
Ovid (Publius Ovidius Naso; 43 BC–17 AD) Roman poet.
Remedia Amoris

4 Not even medicine can master incurable diseases.
Seneca (c. 4 BC–65 AD) Roman author.
Epistulae ad Lucilium, XCIV

5 Formerly, when religion was strong and science weak, men mistook magic for medicine, now, when science is strong and religion weak, men mistake medicine for magic.
Thomas Szasz (1920–) US psychiatrist.
The Second Sin

6 The art of medicine consists of amusing the patient while Nature cures the disease.
Voltaire (François-Marie Arouet; 1694–1788) French writer.
Attrib.

☐ MEDIOCRITY ☐

See also inferiority

1 Only mediocrity can be trusted to be always at its best.
Max Beerbohm (1872–1956) British writer.
Conversations with Max (S.N. Behrman)

2 Mediocrity knows nothing higher than itself, but talent instantly recognizes genius.
Arthur Conan Doyle (1856–1930) British writer.
The Valley of Fear

3 Some men are born mediocre, some men achieve mediocrity, and some men have mediocrity thrust upon them. With Major Major it had been all three.
Joseph Heller (1923–) US novelist.
Catch-22, Ch. 9

4 It isn't evil that is ruining the earth, but mediocrity. The crime is not that Nero played while Rome burned, but that he played badly.
Ned Rorem (1923–) US composer and writer.
The Final Diary

5 Much of a muchness.
John Vanbrugh (1664–1726) English architect and dramatist.
The Provok'd Husband, I:1

☐ MELANCHOLY ☐

See also despair, sorrow

1 Nothing's so dainty sweet as lovely melancholy.
Francis Beaumont (1584–1616) English dramatist.
The Nice Valour, III:3

2 All my joys to this are folly,
Naught so sweet as Melancholy.
Robert Burton (1577–1640) English scholar and explorer.
Anatomy of Melancholy, Abstract

3 If there is a hell upon earth, it is to be found in a melancholy man's heart.
Robert Burton
Anatomy of Melancholy, Pt. I

4 Ay, in the very temple of delight
Veil'd Melancholy has her sovran shrine.
Though seen of none save him whose strenuous tongue
Can burst Joy's grape against his palate fine.
John Keats (1795–1821) British poet.
Ode on Melancholy

5 Wrapt in a pleasing fit of melancholy.
John Milton (1608–74) English poet.
Comus

☐ MEMORIALS ☐

See also epitaphs, memory, obituaries, reputation

1 When I am dead, and laid in grave,
And all my bones are rotten,
By this may I remembered be
When I should be forgotten.
Anonymous
On a girl's sampler, 1736

2 All your better deeds
Shall be in water writ, but this in marble.
Francis Beaumont (1584–1616) English dramatist.
The Nice Valour, V:3

3 They shall grow not old, as we that are left grow
old:
Age shall not weary them, nor the years con-
demn.
At the going down of the sun and in the morning
We will remember them.
Laurence Binyon (1869–1943) British poet.
Poems For the Fallen

4 John Brown's body lies a-mouldering in the
grave,
His soul is marching on!
Charles Sprague Hall (19th century) US songwriter.
The song commemorates the American hero who died in the
cause of abolishing slavery
John Brown's Body

5 In a larger sense we cannot dedicate, we cannot
consecrate, we cannot hallow this ground. The
brave men, living and dead, who struggled here,
have consecrated it far above our power to add or
detract. The world will little note, nor long
remember, what we say here, but it can never forget what they did here. It is for us, the living,
rather to be dedicated here to the unfinished
work which they who fought here have thus far
so nobly advanced. It is rather for us to be here
dedicated to the great task remaining before
us...that we here highly resolve that the dead
shall not have died in vain, that this nation, under
God, shall have a new birth of freedom; and that
government of the people, by the people, and for
the people, shall not perish from the earth.
Abraham Lincoln (1809–65) US statesman.
Report of Lincoln's address at the dedication (19 Nov 1863) of the
national cemetery on the site of the Battle of Gettysburg

6 In Flanders fields the poppies blow
Between the crosses, row on row,
That mark our place.
John McCrae (1872–1918) Canadian poet and doctor.
In Flanders Fields, 'Ypres Salient', 3 May 1915

7 Men's evil manners live in brass: their virtues
We write in water.
William Shakespeare (1564–1616) English dramatist.
Henry VIII, IV:2

8 Move Queen Anne? Most certainly not! Why it
might some day be suggested that *my* statue
should be moved, which I should much dislike.
Victoria (1819–1901) Queen of the United Kingdom.
Said at the time of her Diamond Jubilee (1897), when it was suggested that the statue of Queen Anne should be moved from outside St. Paul's
Men, Women and Things (Duke of Portland), Ch. 5

☐ MEMORY ☐
See also memorials, nostalgia, past

1 Memories are hunting horns whose sound dies
on the wind.
Guillaume Apollinaire (Wilhelm de Kostrowitzky;
1880–1918) Italian-born French poet.
Cors de Chasse

2 I have more memories than if I were a thousand
years old.
Charles Baudelaire (1821–67) French poet.
Spleen

3 Time whereof the memory of man runneth not
to the contrary.
William Blackstone (1723–80) British jurist.
Commentaries on the Laws of England, Bk. I, Ch. 18

4 To endeavour to forget anyone is a certain way of
thinking of nothing else.
Jean de La Bruyère (1645–96) French satirist.
Les Caractères

5 What a strange thing is memory, and hope; one
looks backward, the other forward. The one is of
today, the other is the Tomorrow. Memory is history recorded in our brain, memory is a painter,
it paints pictures of the past and of the day.
Grandma Moses (Anna Mary Robertson Moses; 1860–1961)
US primitive painter.
Grandma Moses, My Life's History (ed. Aotto Kallir), Ch. 1

6 The taste was that of the little crumb of madeleine which on Sunday mornings at Com-
bray..., when I used to say good-day to her in her
bedroom, my aunt Léonie used to give me, dip-
ping it first in her own cup of real or of lime-
flower tea.
Marcel Proust (1871–1922) French novelist.
À la recherche du temps perdu: Du côté de chez Swann

7 Thanks For the Memory.
Leo Robin (1899–1984) US songwriter.
Big Broadcast, song title

8 Better by far you should forget and smile
Than that you should remember and be sad.
Christina Rossetti (1830–74) British poet.
Remember

9 Old men forget; yet all shall be forgot,
But he'll remember, with advantages,
What feats he did that day.
William Shakespeare (1564–1616) English dramatist.
Henry V, IV:3

10 Music, when soft voices die,
Rose leaves, when the rose is dead,
Are heaped for the beloved's bed;
And so thy thoughts, when thou art gone,
Love itself shall slumber on.
Percy Bysshe Shelley (1792–1822) British poet.
To –

11 As a perfume doth remain
In the folds where it hath lain,
So the thought of you, remaining
Deeply folded in my brain,
Will not leave me: all things leave me:
You remain.
Arthur Symons (1865–1945) British poet.
Memory

□MEN□

See also mankind, marriage, sexes, women

1 A man's a man for a' that.
Robert Burns (1759–96) Scottish poet.
For a' that and a' that

2 It is men who face the biggest problems in the future, adjusting to their new and complicated role.
Anna Ford (1943–) British newscaster.
Remark, Jan 1981

3 All men are rapists and that's all they are. They rape us with their eyes, their laws and their codes.
Marilyn French (1929–) US novelist.
The Women's Room

4 Probably the only place where a man can feel really secure is in a maximum security prison, except for the imminent threat of release.
Germaine Greer (1939–) Australian-born British writer and feminist.
The Female Eunuch

5 How beastly the bourgeois is
especially the male of the species.
D. H. Lawrence (1885–1930) British novelist.
How beastly the bourgeois is

6 One realizes with horror, that the race of men is almost extinct in Europe. Only Christ-like heroes and woman-worshipping Don Juans, and rabid equality-mongrels.
D. H. Lawrence
Sea and Sardinia, Ch. 3

7 Why can't a woman be more like a man?
Men are so honest, so thoroughly square;
Eternally noble, historically fair.
Alan Jay Lerner (1918–86) US songwriter.
My Fair Lady, II:4

8 Sometimes I think if there was a third sex men wouldn't get so much as a glance from me.
Amanda Vail (Warren Miller; 1921–66) US writer.
Love Me Little, Ch. 6

9 A man in the house is worth two in the street.
Mae West (1892–1980) US actress.
Belle of the Nineties, film 1934

□MERCY□

1 I seem forsaken and alone,
I hear the lion roar;
And every door is shut but one,
And that is Mercy's door.
William Cowper (1731–1800) British poet.
Olney Hymns, 33

2 The quality of mercy is not strain'd;
It droppeth as the gentle rain from heaven
Upon the place beneath. It is twice blest;
It blesseth him that gives and him that takes.
William Shakespeare (1564–1616) English dramatist.
The Merchant of Venice, IV:1

□MERIT□

1 But many that are first shall be last; and the last shall be first.
Bible: Matthew
19:30

2 Use every man after his desert, and who shall scape whipping?
William Shakespeare (1564–1616) English dramatist.
Hamlet, II:2

3 I wasn't lucky. I deserved it.
Margaret Thatcher (1925–) British politician and prime minister.
Said after receiving school prize, aged nine
Attrib.

4 The Rise of the Meritocracy.
Michael Young (1915–) British political writer.
Book title

□MERRYMAKING□

See also parties, pleasure

1 There was a sound of revelry by night,
And Belgium's capital had gather'd then
Her Beauty and her Chivalry, and bright
The lamps shone o'er fair women and brave men.
Lord Byron (1788–1824) British poet.
Childe Harold's Pilgrimage, III

2 Dost thou think, because thou art virtuous, there shall be no more cakes and ale?
William Shakespeare (1564–1616) English dramatist.
Twelfth Night, II:3

3 You must wake and call me early, call me early, mother dear;
To-morrow 'ill be the happiest time of all the glad New-year;
Of all the glad New-year, mother, the maddest merriest day;
For I'm to be Queen o' the May, mother, I'm to be Queen o' the May.
Alfred, Lord Tennyson (1809–92) British poet.
The May Queen

□METAPHYSICS□

See also philosophy

1 A blind man in a dark room – looking for a black hat – which isn't there.
Lord Bowen (1835–94) British judge.
Characterization of a metaphysician
Attrib.

2 Metaphysics is the finding of bad reasons for what we believe upon instinct; but to find these reasons is no less an instinct.
F. H. Bradley (1846–1924) British philosopher.
Appearance and Reality, Preface

3 We used to think that if we knew one, we knew two, because one and one are two. We are finding that we must learn a great deal more about 'and'.
Arthur Eddington (1882–1944) British astronomer.
The Harvest of a Quiet Eye (A. L. Mackay)

4 Whither is fled the visionary gleam?
Where is it now, the glory and the dream?
Our birth is but a sleep and a forgetting:
The Soul that rises with us, our life's Star,
Hath had elsewhere its setting,
And cometh from afar;
Not in entire forgetfulness,
And not in utter nakedness,
But trailing clouds of glory do we come
From God, who is our home:
Heaven lies about us in our infancy!
Shades of the prison-house begin to close
Upon the growing boy.
William Wordsworth (1770–1850) British poet.
Ode. Intimations of Immortality, IV

☐ MILTON ☐
John
(1608–74) English poet. His poems include *L'Allegro* and *Il Penseroso* (1632) *and the great epics Paradise Lost* (1667) and *Paradise Regained* (1671).

1 Who kills man kills a reasonable creature, God's image; but he who destroys a good book kills reason itself, kills the image of God, as it were in the eye.
Areopagitica

2 Fame is the spur that the clear spirit doth raise...
Lycidas

3 Of Man's first disobedience, and the fruit
Of that forbidden tree, whose mortal taste
Brought death into the World, and all our woe...
Paradise Lost, Bk. I

4 Long is the way
And hard, that out of hell leads up to light.
Paradise Lost, Bk. II

☐ MIND ☐
See also intellect, intelligence, thinking

1 *Brain*, n. An apparatus with which we think that we think.
Ambrose Bierce (1842–?1914) US writer and journalist.
The Devil's Dictionary

2 The pendulum of the mind oscillates between sense and nonsense, not between right and wrong.
Carl Gustav Jung (1875–1961) Swiss psychoanalyst.
Memories, Dreams, Reflections, Ch. 5

3 A mind not to be changed by place or time.
The mind is its own place, and in itself
Can make a Heaven of Hell, a Hell of Heaven.
John Milton (1608–74) English poet.
Paradise Lost, Bk. I

4 That's the classical mind at work, runs fine inside but looks dingy on the surface.
Robert T. Pirsig (1928–) US writer.
Zen and the Art of Motorcycle Maintenance, Pt. III, Ch. 25

5 If it is for mind that we are seaching the brain, then we are supposing the brain to be much more than a telephone-exchange. We are supposing it a telephone-exchange along with the subscribers as well.
Charles Scott Sherrington (1857–1952) British physiologist.
Man on his Nature

6 When people will not weed their own minds, they are apt to be overrun with nettles.
Horace Walpole (1717–97) British writer.
Letter to Lady Ailesbury, 10 July 1779

☐ MINORITY ☐
See also majority

1 The majority has the might – more's the pity – but it hasn't right...The minority is always right.
Henrik Ibsen (1828–1906) Norwegian dramatist.
An Enemy of the People, IV

2 Minorities...are almost always in the right.
Sydney Smith (1771–1845) British clergyman and essayist.
The Smith of Smiths (H. Pearson), Ch. 9

☐ MISANTHROPY ☐
See also mankind

1 What though the spicy breezes
Blow soft o'er Ceylon's isle;
Though every prospect pleases,
And only man is vile...
Reginald Heber (1783–1826) British bishop and hymn writer.
From Greenland's Icy Mountains

2 I love mankind – it's people I can't stand.
Charles M. Schultz (1922–) US cartoonist.
Go Fly a Kite, Charlie Brown

3 Other people are quite dreadful. The only possible society is oneself.
Oscar Wilde (1854–1900) Irish-born British dramatist.
An Ideal Husband, III

☐MISFORTUNE☐

See also accidents, curses, sorrow, suffering

1 Prosperity doth best discover vice; but adversity doth best discover virtue.
Francis Bacon (1561–1626) English philosopher.
Essays, 'Of Adversity'

2 Calamities are of two kinds. Misfortune to ourselves and good fortune to others.
Ambrose Bierce (1842–?1914) US writer and journalist.
The Devil's Dictionary

3 Tragedie is to seyn a certeyn storie,
As olde bokes maken us memorie,
Of him that stood in greet prosperitee
And is y-fallen out of heigh degree
Into miserie, and endeth wrecchedly.
Geoffrey Chaucer (c. 1342–1400) English poet.
The Canterbury Tales, 'The Monk's Prologue'

4 A chapter of accidents.
Earl of Chesterfield (1694–1773) English statesman.
Letter to his son, 16 Feb 1753

5 Life is mostly froth and bubble;
Two things stand like stone,
Kindness in another's trouble,
Courage in your own.
Adam Lindsay Gordon (1833–70) Australian poet.
Ye Wearie Wayfarer, Fytte 8

6 There exist some evils so terrible and some misfortunes so horrible that we dare not think of them, whilst their very aspect makes us shudder; but if they happen to fall on us, we find ourselves stronger than we imagined, we grapple with our ill luck, and behave better than we expected we should.
Jean de La Bruyère (1645–96) French satirist.
Les Caractères

7 We are all strong enough to bear the misfortunes of others.
Duc de la Rochefoucauld (1613–80) French writer.
Maximes, 19

8 Misery acquaints a man with strange bedfellows.
William Shakespeare (1564–1616) English dramatist.
The Tempest, II:2

9 When sorrows come, they come not single spies,
But in battalions!
William Shakespeare
Hamlet, IV:5

☐MISOGYNY☐

See also women

1 I enjoy fucking my wife. She lets me do it any way I want. No Women's Liberation for her. Lots of male chauvinist pig.
Joseph Heller (1923–) US novelist.
Something Happened

2 I'd be equally as willing
For a dentist to be drilling
Than to ever let a woman in my life.
Alan Jay Lerner (1918–86) US songwriter.
My Fair Lady, I:2

3 Have you ever noticed how noisy women are? Have you? The way they kick the floor about, simply walking over it? Or have you watched them sitting at their dressing tables, dropping their weapons and banging down their bits of boxes and brushes and lipsticks?
John Osborne (1929–) British dramatist.
Look Back in Anger

4 Would you have me speak after my custom, as being a professed tyrant to their sex?
William Shakespeare (1564–1616) English dramatist.
Much Ado About Nothing, I:1

☐MISQUOTATIONS☐

1 Misquotations are the only quotations that are never misquoted.
Hesketh Pearson (1887–1964) British biographer.
Common Misquotations

2 A widely-read man never quotes accurately…Misquotation is the pride and privilege of the learned.
Hesketh Pearson
Common Misquotations

SOME EXAMPLES

3 That's one small step for man, one giant leap for mankind.
Neil Armstrong (1930–) US astronaut.
Said on stepping onto the moon. Often quoted as, 'small step for a man…' (which is probably what he intended)
Remark, 21 July 1969

4 I have seldom spoken with greater regret, for my lips are not yet unsealed. Were these troubles over I would make a case, and I guarantee that not a man would go into the Lobby against us.
Stanley Baldwin (1867–1947) British statesman.
Referring to the Abyssinian crisis; usually misquoted as 'My lips are sealed'
Speech, House of Commons, 10 Dec 1935

5 And behold joy and gladness, slaying oxen, and killing sheep, eating flesh, and drinking wine: let us eat and drink; for tomorrow we shall die.
Bible: Isaiah 22:13
A similar sentiment is expressed in Corinthians 15:32–33. Often misquoted as 'let us eat, drink, and be merry'

6 Then said Jesus unto him, Put up again thy sword into his place: for all they that take the sword shall perish with the sword.
Bible: Matthew 26:52
Often misquoted as 'They that live by the sword shall die by the sword'

7 Play it, Sam. Play 'As Time Goes By.'
Humphrey Bogart (1899–1957) US film star.
Often misquoted as 'Play it again, Sam'
Casablanca

8 You dirty double-crossing rat!
James Cagney (1899–1986) US actor.
Usually misquoted by impressionists as 'You dirty rat'
Blonde Crazy

9 I have nothing to offer but blood, toil, tears and sweat.
Winston Churchill (1874–1965) British statesman.
On becoming prime minister. Often misquoted as 'blood, sweat and tears'
Speech, House of Commons, 13 May 1940

10 I never said, 'I want to be alone.' I only said, 'I want to be *left* alone.' There is all the difference.
Greta Garbo (1905–90) Swedish-born US film star.
Garbo (John Bainbridge)

11 Take your hare when it is cased…
Hannah Glasse (18th century) English writer.
Often misquoted as, 'First catch your hare' and wrongly attributed to Mrs Beaton
The Art of Cookery Made Plain and Easy, Ch. 1

12 I am happy now that Charles calls on my bed-chamber less frequently than of old. As it is, I now endure but two calls a week and when I hear his steps outside my door I lie down on my bed, close my eyes, open my legs and think of England.
Lady Alice Hillingdon (1857–1940) Wife of 2nd Baron Hillingdon.
Often mistakenly attributed to Queen Victoria
Journal (1912)

13 Jerry Ford is so dumb that he can't fart and chew gum at the same time.
Lyndon B. Johnson (1908–73) US statesman.
Sometimes quoted as '…can't walk and chew gum'
A Ford, Not a Lincoln (R. Reeves), Ch. 1

14 Alae, poor Yorick! I knew him, Horatio: a fellow of infinite jest, of most excellent fancy.
William Shakespeare (1564–1616) English dramatist.
Often misquoted as 'I knew him well'
Hamlet, V:1

15 I always did like a man in uniform. And that one fits you grand. Why don't you come up sometime and see me?
Mae West (1892–1980) US actress.
Often misquoted as 'Come up and see me some time'
She Done Him Wrong, film 1933

☐MISTAKES☐

See also imperfection

1 It is worse than immoral, it's a mistake.
Dean Acheson (1893–1971) US lawyer and statesman.
Describing the Vietnam war
Quoted by Alistair Cooke in his radio programme *Letter from America*

2 The weak have one weapon: the errors of those who think they are strong.
Georges Bidault (1899–1983) French statesman.
The Observer, 1962

3 Erratum. In my article on the Price of Milk, 'Horses' should have read 'Cows' throughout.
J. B. Morton (1893–1979) British journalist.
The Best of Beachcomber

4 The man who makes no mistakes does not usually make anything.
Edward John Phelps (1822–1900) US lawyer and diplomat.
Speech, Mansion House, London, 24 Jan 1899

5 A man should never be ashamed to own he has been in the wrong, which is but saying, in other words, that he is wiser to-day than he was yesterday.
Alexander Pope (1688–1744) British poet.
Thoughts on Various Subjects

6 To err is human, to forgive, divine.
Alexander Pope
An Essay on Criticism

7 We often discover what *will* do, by finding out what will not do; and probably he who never made a mistake never made a discovery.
Samuel Smiles (1812–1904) British writer.
Self-Help, Ch. 11

8 Human blunders usually do more to shape history than human wickedness.
A. J. P. Taylor (1906–90) British historian.
The Origins of the Second World War, Ch. 10

9 If we had more time for discussion we should probably have made a great many more mistakes.
Leon Trotsky (Lev Davidovich Bronstein; 1879–1940) Russian revolutionary.
My Life

10 The physician can bury his mistakes, but the architect can only advise his client to plant vines.
Frank Lloyd Wright (1869–1959) US architect.
New York Times Magazine, 4 Oct 1953

☐MISTRUST☐

See also trust

1 While I see many hoof-marks going in, I see none coming out.
Aesop (6th century BC) Reputed Greek writer of fables.
Fables, 'The Lion, the Fox, and the Beasts'

2 The louder he talked of his honour, the faster we counted our spoons.
Ralph Waldo Emerson (1803–82) US poet and essayist.
Conduct of Life, 'Worship'

3 *Quis custodiet ipsos custodes?*
Who is to guard the guards themselves?
Juvenal (Decimus Junius Juvenalis; 60–130 AD) Roman satirist.
Satires, VI

4 Let me have men about me that are fat;
Sleek-headed men, and such as sleep o' nights.
Yon Cassius has a lean and hungry look;
He thinks too much. Such men are dangerous.
William Shakespeare (1564–1616) English dramatist.
Julius Caesar, I:2

5 An ally has to be watched just like an enemy.
Leon Trotsky (Lev Davidovich Bronstein; 1879–1940) Russian revolutionary.
Expansion and Coexistence (A. Ulam)

6 *Equo ne credite, Teucri.*
Quidquid id est timeo Danaos et dona ferentis.
Do not trust the horse, Trojans. Whatever it is, I fear the Greeks even when they bring gifts.
Virgil (Publius Vergilius Maro; 70–19 BC) Roman poet.
Aeneid, Bk. II

☐ MODERATION ☐

See also excess

1 By God, Mr Chairman, at this moment I stand astonished at my own moderation!
Clive of India (1725–74) British soldier and governor of Bengal.
Reply during Parliamentary Inquiry, 1773

2 Not too much zeal.
Talleyrand (Charles Maurice de Talleyrand-Périgord; 1754–1838) French politician.
Attrib.

3 Moderation is a fatal thing, Lady Hunstanton. Nothing succeeds like excess.
Oscar Wilde (1854–1900) Irish-born British dramatist.
A Woman of No Importance, III

☐ MODESTY ☐

1 She just wore
Enough for modesty – no more.
Robert Williams Buchanan (1841–1901) British poet and writer.
White Rose and Red, I

2 In some remote regions of Islam it is said, a woman caught unveiled by a stranger will raise her skirt to cover her face.
Raymond Mortimer (1895–1980) British literary critic and writer.
Colette

3 If you want people to think well of you, do not speak well of yourself.
Blaise Pascal (1623–62) French philosopher and mathematician.
Pensées, I

4 Be modest! It is the kind of pride least likely to offend.
Jules Renard (1894–1910) French writer.
Journal

5 Put off your shame with your clothes when you go in to your husband, and put it on again when you come out.
Theano (fl. c. 420s BC) Greek priestess.
Lives, Teachings, and Sayings of Famous Philosophers; Pythagoras, Bk VIII (Diogenes Laertius)

☐ MONARCHY ☐

See also royalty

1 The best reason why Monarchy is a strong government is that it is an intelligible government. The mass of mankind understand it, and they hardly anywhere in the world understand any other.
Walter Bagehot (1826–77) British economist and journalist.
The English Constitution, 'The Monarchy'

2 The Sovereign has, under a constitutional monarchy such as ours, three rights – the right to be consulted, the right to encourage, the right to warn.
Walter Bagehot
The English Constitution, 'The Monarchy'

3 That the king can do no wrong, is a necessary and fundamental principle of the English constitution.
William Blackstone (1723–80) British jurist.
Commentaries on the Laws of England, Bk. III, Ch. 17

4 The king never dies.
William Blackstone
Commentaries on the Laws of England, Bk. I, Ch. 7

5 There will soon ᴜe only five kings left – the Kings of England, Diamonds, Hearts, Spades and Clubs.
Farouk I (1920–65) The last king of Egypt.
Remark made to Lord Boyd-Orr

6 Kings govern by means of popular assemblies only when they cannot do without them.
Charles James Fox (1749–1806) British Whig politician.
Attrib.

7 A constitutional king must learn to stoop.
Leopold II (1835–1909) King of the Belgians.
Instructing Prince Albert, the heir apparent, to pick up some papers that had fallen onto the floor
The Mistress (Betty Kelen)

8 Every subject's duty is the King's; but every subject's soul is his own.
William Shakespeare (1564–1616) English dramatist.
Henry V, IV:1

9 Not all the water in the rough rude sea
Can wash the balm from an anointed king;

The breath of worldly men cannot depose
The deputy elected by the Lord.
William Shakespeare
Richard II, III:2

10 Uneasy lies the head that wears a crown.
William Shakespeare
Henry IV, Part Two, III:1

11 The king reigns, and the people govern themselves.
Louis Adolphe Thiers (1797–1877) French statesman and historian.
In an unsigned article attributed to Thiers
Le National, 20 Jan 1830

12 The monarchy is a labour-intensive industry.
Harold Wilson (1916–) British politician and prime minister.
The Observer, 13 Feb 1977

13 The king reigns, but does not govern.
Jan Zamoyski (1541–1605) Grand chancellor of Poland.
Speech, Polish Parliament, 1605

☐ MONEY ☐

See also bribery, economics, extravagance, greed, materialism, thrift, wealth

1 It does seem to be true that the more you get the more you spend. It is rather like being on a golden treadmill.
Charles Allsop (1940–) Commodities broker.
Remark, Dec 1988

2 Money is like muck, not good except it be spread.
Francis Bacon (1561–1626) English philosopher.
Essays, 'Of Seditions and Troubles'

3 Money, it turned out, was exactly like sex, you thought of nothing else if you didn't have it and thought of other things if you did.
James Baldwin (1924–87) US writer.
Nobody Knows My Name

4 A feast is made for laughter, and wine maketh merry: but money answereth all things.
Bible: Ecclesiastes
10:19

5 For the love of money is the root of all evil: which while some coveted after, they have erred from the faith, and pierced themselves through with many sorrows.
Bible: I Timothy
6:10

6 It is a kind of spiritual snobbery that makes people think that they can be happy without money.
Albert Camus (1913–60) French existentialist writer.
Notebooks, 1935–1942

7 Where large sums of money are concerned, it is advisable to trust nobody.
Agatha Christie (1891–1976) British detective-story writer.
Endless Night, Bk. II, Ch. 15

8 How pleasant it is to have money.
Arthur Hugh Clough (1819–61) British poet.
Dipsychus, Bk. I

9 It is only the poor who pay cash, and that not from virtue, but because they are refused credit.
Anatole France (Jacques Anatole François Thibault; 1844–1924) French writer.
A Cynic's Breviary (J. R. Solly)

10 If possible honestly, if not, somehow, make money.
Horace (Quintus Horatius Flaccus; 65–8 BC) Roman poet.
Epistles, I

11 There are few ways in which a man can be more innocently employed than in getting money.
Samuel Johnson (1709–84) British lexicographer.
Life of Johnson (J. Boswell), Vol. II

12 You don't seem to realize that a poor person who is unhappy is in a better position than a rich person who is unhappy. Because the poor person has hope. He thinks money would help.
Jean Kerr (1923–) US dramatist.
Poor Richard

13 For I don't care too much for money,
For money can't buy me love.
John Lennon (1940–80) British rock musician.
Can't Buy Me Love (with Paul McCartney)

14 The working classes are never embarrassed by money – only the absence of it.
Ken Livingstone (1945–) British Labour politician.
Speech, Sept 1987

15 Money can't buy friends, but you can get a better class of enemy.
Spike Milligan (1918–) British comic actor and author.
Puckoon, Ch. 6

16 Money is good for bribing yourself through the inconveniences of life.
Gottfried Reinhardt (1911–) Austrian film producer.
Picture, 'Looks Like We're Still in Business' (Lillian Ross)

17 My boy...always try to rub up against money, for if you rub up against money long enough, some of it may rub off on you.
Damon Runyon (1884–1946) US writer.
Furthermore, 'A Very Honourable Guy'

18 Put money in thy purse.
William Shakespeare (1564–1616) English dramatist.
Othello, I:3

19 Lack of money is the root of all evil.
George Bernard Shaw (1856–1950) Irish dramatist and critic.
Man and Superman, 'Maxims for Revolutionists.'

20 I think I could be a good woman if I had five thousand a year.
William Makepeace Thackeray (1811–63) British novelist.
Vanity Fair, Ch. 36

21 No one would have remembered the Good
Samaritan if he'd only had good intentions. He
had money as well.
Margaret Thatcher (1925–) British politician and prime
minister.
Television interview, 1980

22 The easiest way for your children to learn about
money is for you not to have any.
Katherine Whitehorn (1926–) British journalist.
How to Survive Children

23 You can be young without money but you can't
be old without it.
Tennessee Williams (1911–83) US dramatist.
Cat on a Hot Tin Roof, I

☐ MONTHS ☐

See also seasons

1 Thirty days hath September,
April, June, and November;
All the rest have thirty-one,
Excepting February alone,
And that has twenty-eight days clear
And twenty-nine in each leap year.
Anonymous
See also GRAFTON
Stevins Manuscript, c. 1555

2 There are twelve months in all the year,
As I hear many men say,
But the merriest month in all the year
Is the merry month of May.
Anonymous
Robin Hood and the Widow's Three Sons

3 And after April, when May follows,
And the whitethroat builds, and all the swallows!
Robert Browning (1812–89) British poet.
Home Thoughts from Abroad

4 Thirty days hath November,
April, June and September,
February hath twenty-eight alone,
And all the rest have thirty-one.
Richard Grafton (d. c. 1572) English chronicler and printer.
Abridgement of the Chronicles of England, Introduction

5 February, fill the dyke
With what thou dost like.
Thomas Tusser (1524–80) English farmer.
Five Hundred Points of Good Husbandry, 'February's Husbandry'

6 Sweet April showers
Do spring May flowers.
Thomas Tusser
Five Hundred Points of Good Husbandry, 'April's Husbandry'

☐ MOON ☐

See also astronomy, space, universe

1 I saw the new moon late yestreen
Wi' the auld moon in her arm;

And if we gang to sea master;
I fear we'll come to harm.
Anonymous
The 'new moon in the old moon's arms' is generally regarded as a
sign of bad weather
Sir Patrick Spens

2 The moving Moon went up the sky,
And no where did abide:
Softly she was going up,
And a star or two beside.
Samuel Taylor Coleridge (1772–1834) British poet.
The Rime of the Ancient Mariner, IV

3 who knows if the moon's
a balloon, coming out of a keen city
in the sky – filled with pretty people?
e. e. cummings (1894–1962) US poet.
Used for the title and epigraph of David Niven's first volume of
autobiography, *The Moon's a Balloon*, about his experiences in
the film industry

4 For years politicians have promised the moon,
I'm the first one to be able to deliver it.
Richard Milhous Nixon (1913–) US president.
Radio message to astronauts on the moon, 20 Jul 1969

5 Oh! shine on, shine on, harvest moon
Up in the sky.
I ain't had no lovin'
Since April, January, June or July.
Jack Norworth (1879–1959) US vaudeville comedian and
songwriter.
Shine On, Harvest Moon (song)

☐ MORALITY ☐

See also integrity, principles, righteousness

1 No morality can be founded on authority, even if
the authority were divine.
A. J. Ayer (1910–89) British philosopher.
Essay on Humanism

2 Morality's not practical. Morality's a gesture.
A complicated gesture learnt from books.
Robert Bolt (1924–) British playwright.
A Man for All Seasons

3 What is moral is what you feel good after, and
what is immoral is what you feel bad after.
Ernest Hemingway (1899–1961) US novelist.
Death in the Afternoon

4 Morality which is based on ideas, or on an ideal,
is an unmitigated evil.
D. H. Lawrence (1885–1930) British novelist.
Fantasia of the Unconscious, Ch. 7

5 We know no spectacle so ridiculous as the British public in one of its periodical fits of morality.
Lord Macaulay (1800–59) British historian.
Literary Essays Contributed to the 'Edinburgh Review', 'Moore's
'Life of Lord Byron''

6 Morality in Europe today is herd-morality.
Friedrich Wilhelm Nietzsche (1844–1900) German philosopher.
Jenseits von Gut und Böse

7 We have, in fact, two kinds of morality side by side; one which we preach but do not practise, and another which we practise but seldom preach.
Bertrand Russell (1872–1970) British philosopher.
Sceptical Essays

8 Without doubt the greatest injury…was done by basing morals on myth, for sooner or later myth is recognized for what it is, and disappears. Then morality loses the foundation on which it has been built.
Herbert Samuel (1870–1963) British Liberal statesman.
Romanes Lecture, 1947

9 The so-called new morality is too often the old immorality condoned.
Lord Shawcross (1902–) British Labour politician and lawyer.
The Observer, 17 Nov 1963

10 Moral indignation is in most cases 2 percent moral, 48 percent indignation and 50 percent envy.
Vittorio De Sica (1901–74) Italian film director.
The Observer, 1961

11 Victorian values…were the values when our country became great.
Margaret Thatcher (1925–) British politician and prime minister
Television interview, 1982

□MORTALITY□

See also death, human condition, immortality, life, life and death, time, transience

1 Mortality, behold and fear!
What a change of flesh is here!
Francis Beaumont (1584–1616) English dramatist.
On the Tombs in Westminster Abbey

2 That lyf so short, the craft so long to lerne,
Th' assay so hard, so sharp the conquerynge.
Geoffrey Chaucer (c. 1342–1400) English poet.
See also HIPPOCRATES
The Parliament of Fowls

3 What argufies pride and ambition?
Soon or late death will take us in tow:
Each bullet has got its commission,
And when our time's come we must go.
Charles Dibdin (1745–1814) British actor and dramatist.
Each Bullet has its Commission

4 All humane things are subject to decay,
And, when Fate summons, Monarchs must obey.
John Dryden (1631–1700) British poet and dramatist.
Mac Flecknoe

5 The boast of heraldry, the pomp of pow'r,
And all that beauty, all that wealth e'er gave,
Awaits alike th' inevitable hour,
The paths of glory lead but to the grave.
Thomas Gray (1716–71) British poet.
Elegy Written in a Country Churchyard

6 I expect to pass through this world but once; any good thing therefore that I can do, or any kindness that I can show to any fellow-creature, let me do it now; let me not defer or neglect it, for I shall not pass this way again.
Stephen Grellet (1773–1855) French-born US missionary.
Attrib
Treasure Trove (John o'London)

7 The life so short, the craft so long to learn.
Hippocrates (c. 460–c. 377 BC) Greek physician.
Describing medicine. It is often quoted in Latin as *Ars longa, vita brevis*, and interpreted as 'Art lasts, life is short'. *See also* CHAUCER
Aphorisms, I

8 *Inque brevi spatio mutantur saecla animantum
Et quasi cursores vitaï lampada tradunt.*
The generations of living things pass in a short time, and like runners hand on the torch of life.
Lucretius (Titus Lucretius Carus; c. 99–55 BC) Roman philosopher.
On the Nature of the Universe, II

9 Fear no more the heat o' th' sun
Nor the furious winter's rages;
Thou thy worldly task hast done,
Home art gone, and ta'en thy wages.
Golden lads and girls all must,
As chimney-sweepers, come to dust.
William Shakespeare (1564–1616) English dramatist.
Cymbeline, IV:2

10 Our revels now are ended. These our actors,
As I foretold you, were all spirits, and
Are melted into air, into thin air;
And, like the baseless fabric of this vision,
The cloud-capp'd towers, the gorgeous palaces,
The solemn temples, the great globe itself,
Yea, all which it inherit, shall dissolve,
And, like this insubstantial pageant faded,
Leave not a rack behind. We are such stuff
As dreams are made on; and our little life
Is rounded with a sleep.
William Shakespeare
The Tempest, IV:1

11 The woods decay, the woods decay and fall,
The vapours weep their burthen to the ground,
Man comes and tills the field and lies beneath,
And after many a summer dies the swan.
Alfred, Lord Tennyson (1809–92) British poet.
Tithonus

12 The clouds that gather round the setting sun
Do take a sober colouring from an eye
That hath kept watch o'er man's mortality.
William Wordsworth
Ode. Intimations of Immortality, XI

13 I am moved to pity, when I think of the brevity of human life, seeing that of all this host of men not one will still be alive in a hundred years' time.
Xerxes (d. 465 BC) King of Persia.
On surveying his army

14 That is no country for old men. The young
In one another's arms, birds in the trees
– Those dying generations – at their song,
The salmon-falls, the mackerel-crowded seas,
Fish, flesh, or fowl, commend all summer long
Whatever is begotten, born, and dies.
W. B. Yeats (1865–1939) Irish poet.
Sailing to Byzantium, I

□ MOTIVE □
See also purpose

1 Never ascribe to an opponent motives meaner than your own.
J. M. Barrie (1860–1937) British novelist and dramatist.
Speech, St Andrews, 3 May 1922

2 Because it is there.
George Mallory (1886–1924) British mountaineer.
Answer to the question 'Why do you want to climb Mt. Everest?'
George Mallory (D. Robertson)

3 Nobody ever did anything very foolish except from some strong principle.
Lord Melbourne (1779–1848) British statesman.
The Young Melbourne (Lord David Cecil)

□ MOUNTAINS □

1 Mountains interposed
Make enemies of nations, who had else,
Like kindred drops, been mingled into one.
William Cowper (1731–1800) British poet.
The Task

2 Mountains are the beginning and the end of all natural scenery.
John Ruskin (1819–1900) British art critic and writer.
Modern Painters, Vol. IV

3 They say that if the Swiss had designed these mountains they'd be rather flatter.
Paul Theroux (1941–) US-born writer.
Referring to the Alps
The Great Railway Bazaar, Ch. 28

□ MOURNING □
See also death, loss, regret, sorrow

1 We met…Dr Hall in such very deep mourning that either his mother, his wife, or himself must be dead.
Jane Austen (1775–1817) British novelist.
Letter to Cassandra Austen, 17 May 1799

2 With proud thanksgiving, a mother for her children,
England mourns for her dead across the sea.
Laurence Binyon (1869–1943) British poet.
In response to the slaughter of World War I
Poems For the Fallen

3 There's a one-eyed yellow idol to the north of Khatmandu,
There's a little marble cross below the town;
There's a broken-hearted woman tends the grave of Mad Carew
And the Yellow God forever gazes down.
J. Milton Hayes (1884–1940) British writer.
The Green Eye of the Yellow God

4 In a cavern, in a canyon,
Excavating for a mine
Dwelt a miner, Forty-niner,
And his daughter, Clementine.
Oh, my darling, Oh, my darling, Oh, my darling Clementine!
Thou art lost and gone for ever, dreadful sorry, Clementine.
Percy Montrose (19th century) US songwriter.
Clementine

5 She is far from the land where her young hero sleeps,
And lovers are round her, sighing:
But coldly she turns from their gaze, and weeps,
For her heart in his grave is lying.
Thomas Moore (1779–1852) Irish poet.
Irish Melodies, 'She is Far'

6 And my poor fool is hang'd! No, no, no life!
Why should a dog, a horse, a rat have life,
And thou no breath at all? Thou'lt come no more,
Never, never, never, never.
William Shakespeare (1564–1616) English dramatist.
King Lear, V:3

7 Alas, poor Yorick! I knew him, Horatio: a fellow of infinite jest, of most excellent fancy.
William Shakespeare
Hamlet, V:1

8 But I have that within which passes show –
these but the trappings and the suits of woe.
William Shakespeare
Hamlet, I:2

9 If thou didst ever hold me in thy heart,
Absent thee from felicity awhile,
And in this harsh world draw thy breath in pain,
To tell my story.
William Shakespeare
Hamlet, V:2

10 Home they brought her warrior dead.
She nor swoon'd, nor utter'd cry:
All her maidens, watching said,
'She must weep or she will die.'
Alfred, Lord Tennyson (1809–92) British poet.
The Princess, VI

☐ MURDER ☐

See also assassination, crime, killing

1 And the Lord said unto Cain, Where is Abel thy brother? And he said, I know not: Am I my brother's keeper?
And he said, What hast thou done? the voice of thy brother's blood crieth unto me from the ground.
Bible: Genesis
4:9–10

2 Mordre wol out, that see we day by day.
Geoffrey Chaucer (c. 1342–1400) English poet.
The Canterbury Tales, 'The Nun's Priest's Tale'

3 See how love and murder will out.
William Congreve (1670–1729) British Restoration dramatist.
The Double Dealer, IV:6

4 I made a remark a long time ago. I said I was very pleased that television was now showing murder stories, because it's bringing murder back into its rightful setting – in the home.
Alfred Hitchcock (1889–1980) British film director.
The Observer, 'Sayings of the Week', 17 Aug 1969

5 It takes two to make a murder. There are born victims, born to have their throats cut.
Aldous Huxley (1894–1964) British novelist.
Point Counter Point

6 Murder most foul, as in the best it is;
But this most foul, strange, and unnatural.
William Shakespeare (1564–1616) English dramatist.
Hamlet, I:5

7 Other sins only speak; murder shrieks out.
John Webster (1580–1625) English dramatist.
The Duchess of Malfi, IV:2

☐ MUSEUMS ☐

1 If there was a little room somewhere in the British Museum that contained only about twenty exhibits and good lighting, easy chairs, and a notice imploring you to smoke, I believe I should become a museum man.
J. B. Priestley (1894–1984) British novelist.
Self-Selected Essays, 'In the British Museum'

2 There is in the British Museum an enormous mind. Consider that Plato is there cheek by jowl with Aristotle; and Shakespeare with Marlowe. This great mind is hoarded beyond the power of any single mind to possess it.
Virginia Woolf (1882–1941) British novelist.
Jacob's Room, Ch. 9

☐ MUSIC ☐

See also criticism, musicians, opera, singing

1 Nothing is capable of being well set to music that is not nonsense.
Joseph Addison (1672–1719) British essayist.
The Spectator, 18

2 Brass bands are all very well in their place – outdoors and several miles away.
Thomas Beecham (1879–1961) British conductor.
Attrib.

3 The English may not like music – but they absolutely love the noise it makes.
Thomas Beecham
The Wit of Music (L. Ayre)

4 The sound of the harpsichord resembles that of a bird-cage played with toasting-forks.
Thomas Beecham
Attrib.

5 There are two golden rules for an orchestra: start together and finish together. The public doesn't give a damn what goes on in between.
Thomas Beecham
Beecham Stories (H. Atkins and A. Newman)

6 A musicologist is a man who can read music but can't hear it.
Thomas Beecham
Beecham Remembered (H. Procter-Gregg)

7 No one really understood music unless he was a scientist, her father had declared, and not just a scientist, either, oh, no, only the real ones, the theoreticians, whose language was mathematics.
Pearl Buck (1892–1973) US novelist.
The Goddess Abides, Pt. I

8 Music has charms to soothe a savage breast.
William Congreve (1670–1729) British Restoration dramatist.
The Mourning Bride, I

9 Strange how potent cheap music is.
Noël Coward (1899–1973) British dramatist.
Private Lives

10 Music is the arithmetic of sounds as optics is the geometry of light.
Claude Debussy (1862–1918) French composer.
Attrib.

11 Music was invented to confirm human loneliness.
Lawrence Durrell (1912–90) British novelist.
Clea

12 The hills are alive with the sound of music
With the songs they have sung
For a thousand years.
Oscar Hammerstein (1895–1960) US lyricist.
The Sound of Music, title song

13 I do not see any reason why the devil should have all the good tunes.
Rowland Hill (1744–1833) British clergyman.
Attrib.

14 Heard melodies are sweet, but those unheard
Are sweeter; therefore, ye soft pipes, play on.
John Keats (1795–1821) British poet.
Ode on a Grecian Urn

15 There's sure no passion in the human soul,
But finds its food in music.
George Lillo (1693–1739) English dramatist.
Fatal Curiosity, I:2

16 Music, Maestro, Please.
Herb Magidson (20th century) US songwriter.
Song title

17 Music creates order out of chaos; for rhythm imposes unanimity upon the divergent, melody imposes continuity upon the disjointed, and harmony imposes compatibility upon the incongruous.
Yehudi Menuhin (1916–) US-born British violinist.
The Sunday Times, 10 Oct 1976

18 The song that we hear with our ears is only the song that is sung in our hearts.
Ouida (Marie Louise de la Ramée; 1839–1908) British novelist.
Wisdom, Wit and Pathos, 'Ariadne'

19 Music and women I cannot but give way to, whatever my business is.
Samuel Pepys (1633–1703) English diarist.
Diary, 9 Mar 1666

20 The basic difference between classical music and jazz is that in the former the music is always greater than its performance – whereas the way jazz is performed is always more important than what is being played.
André Previn (1929–) German-born conductor.
An Encyclopedia of Quotations about Music (Nat Shapiro)

21 The sonatas of Mozart are unique; they are too easy for children, and too difficult for artists.
Artur Schnabel (1882–1951) Austrian concert pianist.
An Encyclopedia of Quotations about Music (Nat Shapiro)

22 I am never merry when I hear sweet music.
William Shakespeare (1564–1616) English dramatist.
The Merchant of Venice, V:1

23 The man that hath no music in himself,
Nor is not mov'd with concord of sweet sounds,
Is fit for treasons, stratagems, and spoils.
William Shakespeare
The Merchant of Venice, V:1

24 If music be the food of love, play on,
Give me excess of it, that, surfeiting,
The appetite may sicken and so die.
William Shakespeare
Twelfth Night, I:1

25 Jazz will endure just as long as people hear it through their feet instead of their brains.
John Philip Sousa (1854–1932) US composer, conductor, and writer.
Attrib.

26 Music that gentlier on the spirit lies,
Than tir'd eyelids upon tir'd eyes.
Alfred, Lord Tennyson (1809–92) British poet.
The Lotos-Eaters, 'Choric Song'

27 Oh I'm a martyr to music.
Dylan Thomas (1914–53) Welsh poet.
Under Milk Wood

☐ MUSICIANS ☐
See also critics, singers

1 Musicians don't retire; they stop when there's no more music in them.
Louis Armstrong (1900–71) US jazz trumpeter.
The Observer, 'Sayings of the Week', 21 Apr 1968

2 The public doesn't want a new music: the main thing it demands of a composer is that he be dead.
Arthur Honegger (1892–1955) French composer.
Attrib.

3 Of all musicians, flautists are most obviously the ones who know something we don't know.
Paul Jennings (1918–) British humorous writer.
The Jenguin Pennings, 'Flautists Flaunt Afflatus'

4 The conductor has the advantage of not seeing the audience.
André Kostalenetz (1903–80) Russian-born conductor.
Attrib.

5 A good composer does not imitate; he steals.
Igor Stravinsky (1882–1971) Russian-born composer.
Twentieth Century Music (Peter Yates)

☐ MYTHS ☐

1 Science must begin with myths, and with the criticism of myths.
Karl Popper (1902–) Austrian-born British philosopher.
British Philosophy in the Mid-Century (ed. C. A. Mace)

2 A myth is, of course, not a fairy story. It is the presentation of facts belonging to one category in the idioms appropriate to another. To explode a myth is accordingly not to deny the facts but to re-allocate them.
Gilbert Ryle (1900–76) British philosopher.
The Concept of Mind, Introduction

N

□NAKEDNESS□

1 Nakedness is uncomely as well in mind, as body.
Francis Bacon (1561–1626) English philosopher.
Essays, 'Of Simulation and Dissimulation'

2 No woman so naked as one you can see to be naked underneath her clothes.
Michael Frayn (1933–) British journalist and writer.
Constructions

3 JOURNALIST. Didn't you have anything on?
M. M. I had the radio on.
Marilyn Monroe (Norma-Jean Baker; 1926–62) US film star.
Attrib.

□NAMES□

1 A nickname is the heaviest stone that the devil can throw at a man.
William Hazlitt (1778–1830) British essayist.
Nicknames

2 No, Groucho is not my real name. I'm breaking it in for a friend.
Groucho Marx (Julius Marx; 1895–1977) US comedian.
Attrib.

3 What's in a name? That which we call a rose
By any other name would smell as sweet.
William Shakespeare (1564–1616) English dramatist.
Romeo and Juliet, II:2

□NASH□
Ogden
(1902–71) US poet. He wrote many books of satirical verse, including *I'm a Stranger Here Myself* (1938) and *Collected Verse* (1961).

1 The cow is of the bovine ilk;
One end is moo, the other, milk.
The Cow

2 A door is what a dog is perpetually on the wrong side of.
A Dog's Best Friend Is His Illiteracy

3 Home is heaven and orgies are vile
But you need an orgy, once in a while.
Home, 99.44/100% Sweet Home

4 Beneath this slab
John Brown is stowed.
He watched the ads
And not the road.
Lather as You Go

5 I think that I shall never see
A billboard lovely as a tree.
Perhaps unless the billboards fall,
I'll never see a tree at all.
Song of the Open Road

□NASTINESS□
See also cruelty, hurt

1 But are they all horrid, are you sure they are all horrid?
Jane Austen (1775–1817) British novelist.
Northanger Abbey, Ch. 6

2 I do not want people to be very agreeable, as it saves me the trouble of liking them a great deal.
Jane Austen
Letter, 24 Dec 1798

3 He was one of those born neither to obey nor to command, but to be evil to the commander and the obeyer alike. Perhaps there was nothing in life that he had much wanted to do, except to shoot rabbits and hit his father on the jaw, and both these things he had done.
John Masefield (1878–1967) British poet.
The Bird of Dawning

4 One of the worst things about life is not how nasty the nasty people are. You know that already. It is how nasty the nice people can be.
Anthony Powell (1905–) British novelist.
A Dance to the Music of Time: The Kindly Ones, Ch. 4

5 'I grant you that he's not two-faced,' I said. 'But what's the use of that when the one face he has got is so peculiarly unpleasant?'
C. P. Snow (1905–80) British novelist.
The Affair, Ch. 4

□NATIONALITY□
See also Americans, British

1 For he might have been a Roosian,
A French, or Turk, or Proosian,
Or perhaps Ital·ian!
But in spite of all temptations
To belong to other nations,
He remains an Englishman!
W. S. Gilbert (1836–1911) British dramatist.
HMS Pinafore, II

2 The Saxon is not like us Normans. His manners are not so polite.
But he never means anything serious till he talks about justice and right,
When he stands like an ox in the furrow with his sullen set eyes on your own,
And grumbles, 'This isn't fair dealing,' my son, leave the Saxon alone.
Rudyard Kipling (1865–1936) Indian-born British writer.
Norman and Saxon

3 Great artists have no country.
Alfred de Musset (1810–57) French dramatist and poet.
Lorenzaccio, I:5

4 I am not an Athenian or a Greek, but a citizen of the world.
Socrates (469–399 BC) Athenian philosopher.
Of Banishment (Plutarch)

5 Men of England! You wish to kill me because I am a Frenchman. Am I not punished enough in not being born an Englishman?
Voltaire (François-Marie Arouet; 1694–1778) French writer. Addressing an angry London mob who desired to hang him because he was a Frenchman
Attrib.

6 We are all American at puberty; we die French.
Evelyn Waugh (1903–66) British novelist.
Diaries, 'Irregular Notes', 18 July 1961

☐ NATIONS ☐
See also places

1 The day of small nations has long passed away. The day of Empires has come.
Joseph Chamberlain (1836–1914) British politician.
Speech, Birmingham, 12 May 1904

2 The nations which have put mankind and posterity most in their debt have been small states – Israel, Athens, Florence, Elizabethan England.
Dean Inge (1860–1954) British churchman.
Wit and Wisdom of Dean Inge (ed. Marchant)

3 This agglomeration which was called and which still calls itself the Holy Roman Empire was neither holy, nor Roman, nor an empire.
Voltaire (François-Marie Arouet; 1694–1778) French writer.
Essai sur les moeurs et l'esprit des nations, LXX

☐ NATURE ☐
See also animals, countryside, ecology, flowers, human nature, science

1 All things are artificial, for nature is the art of God.
Thomas Browne (1605–82) English physician and writer.
Religio Medici, Pt. I

2 There is a pleasure in the pathless woods,
There is a rapture on the lonely shore,
There is society, where none intrudes,
By the deep Sea, and music in its roar:
I love not Man the less, but Nature more.
Lord Byron (1788–1824) British poet.
Childe Harold's Pilgrimage, IV

3 Nature admits no lie.
Thomas Carlyle (1795–1881) Scottish historian and essayist.
Latter-Day Pamphlets, 5

4 Is ditchwater dull? Naturalists with microscopes have told me that it teems with quiet fun.
G. K. Chesterton (1874–1936) British writer.
The Spice of Life

5 All my life through, the new sights of Nature made me rejoice like a child.
Marie Curie (1867–1934) Polish chemist.
Pierre Curie

6 By viewing Nature, Nature's handmaid, art,
Makes mighty things from small beginnings grow.
John Dryden (1631–1700) British poet and dramatist.
Annus Mirabilis

7 All Nature wears one universal grin.
Henry Fielding (1707–54) British novelist.
Tom Thumb the Great, I:1

8 In nature there are neither rewards nor punishments – there are consequences.
Robert G. Ingersoll (1833–99) US lawyer and agnostic.
Lectures & Essays, 'Some Reasons Why'

9 Nature is very consonant and conformable with herself.
Isaac Newton (1642–1727) British scientist.
Opticks, Bk. III

10 Nature abhors a vacuum.
François Rabelais (1483–1553) French satirist.
Attrib.

11 Nature never did betray
The heart that loved her.
William Wordsworth (1770–1850) British poet.
Lines composed a few miles above Tintern Abbey

12 Come forth into the light of things,
Let Nature be your Teacher.
William Wordsworth
The Tables Turned

☐ NAVY ☐
See also boats, officers, sea, war

1 Don't talk to me about naval tradition. It's nothing but rum, sodomy, and the lash.
Winston Churchill (1874–1965) British statesman.
Former Naval Person (Sir Peter Gretton), Ch. 1

2 There were gentlemen and there were seamen in the navy of Charles the Second. But the seamen were not gentlemen; and the gentlemen were not seamen.
Lord Macaulay (1800–59) British historian.
History of England, Vol. I, Ch. 3

☐ NAZISM ☐
See also fascism, Germany, Hitler, Jews, World War II

1 I herewith commission you to carry out all preparations with regard to…a *total solution* of the Jewish question, in those territories of Europe which are under German influence.
Hermann Goering (1893–1946) German leader.
The Rise and Fall of the Third Reich (William Shirer)

2 *Kraft durch Freude.*
Strength through joy.
Robert Ley (1890–1945) German Nazi.
German Labour Front slogan

3 In Germany, the Nazis came for the Communists and I didn't speak up because I was not a Communist. Then they came for the Jews and I didn't speak up because I was not a Jew. Then they came for the trade unionists and I didn't speak up because I was not a trade unionist. Then they came for the Catholics and I was a Protestant so I didn't speak up. Then they came for me…By that time there was no one to speak up for anyone.
Martin Niemöller (1892–1984) German pastor.
Concise Dictionary of Religious Quotations (W. Neil)

□ NECESSITY □

1 Necessity is the plea for every infringement of human freedom. It is the argument of tyrants; it is the creed of slaves.
William Pitt the Younger (1759–1806) British statesman.
Speech, House of Commons, 18 Nov 1783

2 Teach thy necessity to reason thus:
There is no virtue like necessity.
William Shakespeare (1564–1616) English dramatist.
Richard II, I:3

3 Necessity knows no law.
Publilius Syrus (1st century BC) Roman dramatist.
Attrib.

□ NEGLECT □

1 A little neglect may breed mischief,…for want of a nail, the shoe was lost; for want of a shoe the horse was lost; and for want of a horse the rider was lost.
Benjamin Franklin (1706–90) US scientist and statesman.
Poor Richard's Almanack

2 The dust and silence of the upper shelf.
Lord Macaulay (1800–59) British historian.
Literary Essays Contributed to the 'Edinburgh Review', 'Milton'

□ NEIGHBOURS □

1 Thou shalt love thy neighbour as thy self.
Bible: Matthew
22:39

2 For it is your business, when the wall next door catches fire.
Horace (Quintus Horatius Flaccus; 65–8 BC) Roman poet.
Epistles, I

□ NEPOTISM □

1 I am against government by crony.
Harold L. Ickes (1874–1952) US Republican politician.
Comment on his resignation as Secretary of the Interior (1946) after a dispute with President Truman

2 I can't see that it's wrong to give him a little legal experience before he goes out to practice law.
John Fitzgerald Kennedy (1917–63) US statesman.
On being criticized for making his brother Robert attorney general
Nobody Said It Better (M. Ringo)

□ NEUROSIS □
See also psychiatry, psychology

1 Everything great in the world is done by neurotics; they alone founded our religions and created our masterpieces.
Marcel Proust (1871–1922) French novelist.
The Perpetual Pessimist (Sagittarius and George)

2 Neurosis is the way of avoiding non-being by avoiding being.
Paul Tillich (1886–1965) German-born US theologian.
The Courage to Be

□ NEWSPAPERS □
See also editors, journalism

1 Deleted by French censor.
James Gordon Bennett (1841–1918) US newspaper owner and editor.
Used to fill empty spaces in his papers during World War I when news was lacking
Americans in Paris (B. Morton)

2 Reading someone else's newspaper is like sleeping with someone else's wife. Nothing seems to be precisely in the right place, and when you find what you are looking for, it is not clear then how to respond to it.
Malcolm Bradbury (1932–) British academic and novelist.
Stepping Westward, Bk. I, Ch. 1

3 Well, there are only two posh papers on a Sunday – the one you're reading and this one.
John Osborne (1929–) British dramatist.
Look Back in Anger, I

4 News is what a chap who doesn't care much about anything wants to read. And it's only news until he's read it. After that it's dead.
Evelyn Waugh (1903–66) British novelist.
Scoop, Bk. I, Ch. 5

5 They were not so much published as carried screaming into the street.
H. G. Wells (1866–1946) British writer.
War In the Air

□ NIETZSCHE □
Friedrich Wilhelm
(1844–1900) German philosopher. His rejection of all religion and his glorification of the superman in *Thus Spake Zarathustra* (1883–92) influenced Nazi philosophy in Germany.

QUOTATIONS ABOUT NIETZSCHE

1 Nietzsche…was a confirmed Life Force worshipper. It was he who raked up the Superman, who is as old as Prometheus.
George Bernard Shaw (1856–1950) Irish dramatist and critic.
Man and Superman, Act 3

QUOTATIONS BY NIETZSCHE

2 When a man is in love he endures more than at other times; he submits to everything.
The Antichrist

3 God created woman. And boredom did indeed cease from that moment – but many other things ceased as well! Woman was God's *second* mistake.
The Antichrist

4 God is dead: but considering the state the species Man is in, there will perhaps be caves, for ages yet, in which his shadow will be shown.
Die Fröhliche Wissenschaft, Bk. III

5 Believe me! The secret of reaping the greatest fruitfulness and the greatest enjoyment from life is to *live dangerously!*
Die Fröhliche Wissenschaft, Bk. IV

6 The thought of suicide is a great source of comfort: with it a calm passage is to be made across many a bad night.
Jenseits von Gut und Böse

7 He who does not need to lie is proud of not being a liar.
Nachgelassene Fragmente

8 I teach you the Superman. Man is something that is to be surpassed.
Thus Spake Zarathustra

☐ NOBILITY ☐

See also aristocracy, honour

1 *Noblesse oblige.*
Nobility has its own obligations.
Duc de Lévis (1764–1830) French writer and soldier.
Maximes et Réflexions

2 This was the noblest Roman of them all.
All the conspirators save only he
Did that they did in envy of great Caesar.
William Shakespeare (1564–1616) English dramatist.
Julius Caesar, V:5

3 His life was gentle, and the elements
So mixed in him that Nature might stand up
And say to all the world, 'This was a man!'
William Shakespeare
Julius Caesar, V:5

☐ NONCOMMITMENT ☐

1 We know what happens to people who stay in the middle of the road. They get run over.
Aneurin Bevan (1897–1960) British Labour politician.
The Observer, 'Sayings of the Week', 9 Dec 1953

2 Let them eat the lie and swallow it with their bread. Whether the two were lovers or no, they'll have accounted to God for it by now. I have my own fish to fry.
Miguel de Cervantes (1547–1616) Spanish novelist.
Don Quixote, Pt. I, Ch. 25

☐ NONSENSE ☐

See also humour

1 If all the world were paper,
And all the sea were ink,
And all the trees were bread and cheese,
What should we do for drink?
Anonymous
If All the World were Paper

2 What happens to the hole when the cheese is gone?
Bertolt Brecht (1898–1956) German dramatist.
Mother Courage, VI

3 For the Snark *was* a Boojum, you see.
Lewis Carroll (Charles Lutwidge Dodgson; 1832–98) British writer.
The Hunting of the Snark

4 'Twas brillig, and the slithy toves
Did gyre and gimble in the wabe;
All mimsy were the borogoves,
And the mome raths outgrabe.
Lewis Carroll
Through the Looking-Glass, Ch. 1

5 'The time has come,' the Walrus said,
'To talk of many things:
Of shoes – and ships – and sealing-wax –
Of cabbages – and kings –
And why the sea is boiling hot –
And whether pigs have wings.'
Lewis Carroll
Through the Looking-Glass, Ch. 4

6 Lord Ronald said nothing; he flung himself from the room, flung himself upon his horse and rode madly off in all directions.
Stephen Leacock (1869–1944) English-born Canadian economist and humorist.
Nonsense Novels, 'Gertrude the Governess'

7 The Dong! – the Dong!
The wandering Dong through the forest goes!
The Dong! – the Dong!
The Dong with a luminous Nose!
Edward Lear (1812–88) British artist and writer.
The Dong with a Luminous Nose

8 Far and few, far and few,
Are the lands where the Jumblies live;
Their heads are green, and their hands are blue,
And they went to sea in a sieve.
Edward Lear
The Jumblies

9 He has many friends, laymen and clerical.
Old Foss is the name of his cat:
His body is perfectly spherical,
He weareth a runcible hat.
Edward Lear
Nonsense Songs, preface

10 The Owl and the Pussy-Cat went to sea
In a beautiful pea-green boat,
They took some honey, and plenty of money,
Wrapped up in a five-pound note.
Edward Lear
The Owl and the Pussy-Cat

11 As I was going up the stair
I met a man who wasn't there.
He wasn't there again to-day.
I wish, I wish he'd stay away.
Hughes Mearns (1875–1965) US writer.
The Psychoed

12 I'm walking backwards till Christmas.
Spike Milligan (1918–) British comic actor and author.
The Goon Show

□ NORMALITY □

1 She always says she dislikes the abnormal, it is
so obvious. She says the normal is so much more
simply complicated and interesting.
Gertrude Stein (1874–1946) US writer.
The Autobiography of Alice B. Toklas

2 My suit is pale yellow. My nationality is French,
and my normality has been often subject to
question.
Tennessee Williams (1911–83) US dramatist.
Camino Real, Block 4

□ NOSTALGIA □

See also homesickness, memory, past, regret

1 Nostalgia isn't what it used to be.
Anonymous
Graffito

2 Were we closer to the ground as children, or is
the grass emptier now?
Alan Bennett (1934–) British playwright.
Forty Years On

3 Stands the Church clock at ten to three?
And is there honey still for tea?
Rupert Brooke (1887–1915) British poet.
The Old Vicarage, Grantchester

4 Nothing recalls the past so potently as a smell.
Winston Churchill (1874–1965) British statesman.
My Early Life

5 What peaceful hours I once enjoyed!
How sweet their memory still!
But they have left an aching void
The world can never fill.
William Cowper (1731–1800) British poet.
Olney Hymns, 1

6 I have had playmates, I have had companions
In my days of childhood, in my joyful school-
days –
All, all are gone, the old familiar faces.
Charles Lamb (1775–1834) British essayist.
The Old Familiar Faces

7 For love that time was not as love is nowadays.
Thomas Malory (1400–71) English writer.
Morte d'Arthur, Bk. XX, Ch. 3

8 Oft in the stilly night,
Ere Slumber's chain has bound me,
Fond Memory brings the light
Of other days around me;
The smiles, the tears,
Of boyhood's years,
The words of love then spoken;
The eyes that shone,
Now dimmed and gone,
The cheerful hearts now broken!
Thomas Moore (1779–1852) Irish poet.
National Airs, 'Oft in the Stilly Night'

9 Before the war, and especially before the Boer
War, it was summer all the year round.
George Orwell (Eric Blair; 1903–50) British novelist.
Coming Up for Air, Pt. II, Ch. 1

10 Come to me in the silence of the night;
Come in the speaking silence of a dream;
Come with soft rounded cheeks and eyes as
bright
As sunlight on a stream;
Come back in tears,
O memory, hope, love of finished years.
Christina Rossetti (1830–74) British poet.
Echo

11 For now I see the true old times are dead,
When every morning brought a noble chance,
And every chance brought out a noble knight.
Alfred, Lord Tennyson (1809–92) British poet.
Idylls of the King, 'The Passing of Arthur'

12 Dear as remembered kisses after death,
And sweet as those by hopeless fancy feign'd
On lips that are for others: deep as love,
Deep as first love, and wild with all regret;
O Death in Life, the days that are no more.
Alfred, Lord Tennyson
The Princess, IV

13 And the stately ships go on
To their haven under the hill;
But O for the touch of a vanish'd hand,
And the sound of a voice that is still!
Alfred, Lord Tennyson
Break, Break, Break

14 Sweet childish days, that were as long
As twenty days are now.
William Wordsworth (1770–1850) British poet.
To a Butterfly, I've Watched you now

□ NOTHING □

1 Nothing can be created out of nothing.
Lucretius (Titus Lucretius Carus; c. 99–55 BC) Roman
philosopher.
On the Nature of the Universe, I

2 Nothing will come of nothing. Speak again.
William Shakespeare (1564–1616) English dramatist.
King Lear, I:1

□ NOVELS □

See also books, criticism, fiction, literature, writers, writing

1 A good novel tells us the truth about its hero; but
a bad novel tells us the truth about its author.
G. K. Chesterton (1874–1936) British writer.
Heretics, Ch. 15

2 Historians tell the story of the past, novelists the
story of the present.
Edmond de Goncourt (1822–96) French novelist.
Journal

3 I would sooner read a time-table or a catalogue
than nothing at all. They are much more enter-
taining than half the novels that are written.
W. Somerset Maugham (1874–1965) British novelist.
The Summing Up

4 People think that because a novel's invented, it
isn't true. Exactly the reverse is the case. Biography and memoirs can never be wholly true, since
they cannot include every conceivable circumstance of what happened. The novel can do that.
Anthony Powell (1905–) British novelist.
A Dance to the Music of Time: Hearing Secret Harmonies, Ch. 3

5 The detective novel is the art-for-art's-sake of
yawning Philistinism.
V. S. Pritchett (1900–) British short-story writer.
Books in General, 'The Roots of Detection'

6 It is the sexless novel that should be distin-
guished: the sex novel is now normal.
George Bernard Shaw (1856–1950) Irish dramatist and critic.
Table-Talk of G.B.S.

7 A novel is a mirror walking along a main road.
Stendhal (Henri Beyle; 1783–1842) French novelist.
Le Rouge et le noir, Ch. 49

8 A novel is a static thing that one moves through;
a play is a dynamic thing that moves past one.
Kenneth Tynan (1927–80) British theatre critic.
Curtains

9 The novel being dead, there is no point to writing
made-up stories. Look at the French who will not
and the Americans who cannot.
Gore Vidal (1925–) US novelist.
Myra Breckinridge, Ch. 2

□ NOVELTY □

See also conservatism, innovation, progress

1 There are three things which the public will
always clamour for, sooner or later: namely,
Novelty, novelty, novelty.
Thomas Hood (1799–1845) British poet.
Announcement of *Comic Annual*, 1836

2 There is always something new out of Africa.
Pliny the Elder (Gaius Plinius Secundus; 23–79 AD) Roman
scholar.
Natural History, VIII

3 If we do not find anything pleasant, at least we
shall find something new.
Voltaire (François-Marie Arouet; 1694–1778) French writer.
Candide, Ch. 17

□ NUCLEAR WEAPONS □

See also weapons

1 Now we are all sons of bitches.
Kenneth Bainbridge (1904–) US physicist.
After the first atomic test
The Decision to Drop the Bomb

2 The way to win an atomic war is to make certain
it never starts.
Omar Nelson Bradley (1893–1981) US general.
The Observer, 'Sayings of the Week', 20 Apr 1952

3 The Bomb brought peace but man alone can
keep that peace.
Winston Churchill (1874–1965) British statesman.
Speech, House of Commons, 16 Aug 1945

4 If only I had known, I should have become a
watchmaker.
Albert Einstein (1879–1955) German-born US physicist.
Reflecting on his role in the development of the atom bomb
New Statesman, 16 Apr 1965

5 We thus denounce the false and dangerous programme of the arms race, of the secret rivalry
between peoples for military superiority.
John Paul II (Karol Wojtyla; 1920–). Polish pope (1978–).
The Observer, 'Sayings of the Week', 19 Dec 1976

6 Hitherto man had to live with the idea of death as an individual; from now onward mankind will have to live with the idea of its death as a species.
Arthur Koestler (1905–83) Hungarian-born British writer.
Referring to the development of the atomic bomb
Peter's Quotations (Laurence J. Peter)

7 The statesmen of the world who boast and threaten that they have Doomsday weapons are far more dangerous, and far more estranged from 'reality', than many of the people on whom the label 'psychotic' is affixed.
R. D. Laing (1927–89) British psychiatrist.
The Divided Self, Preface

8 At first it was a giant column that soon took the shape of a supramundane mushroom.
William L. Laurence (1888–1977) US journalist.
Referring to the explosion of the first atomic bomb, over
Hiroshima, 6 Aug 1945
The New York Times, 26 Sept 1945

9 The atom bomb is a paper tiger which the United States reactionaries use to scare people.
Mao Tse-Tung (1893–1976) Chinese communist leader.
Interview, Aug 1946

10 As a military man who has given half a century of active service, I say in all sincerity that the nuclear arms race has no military purpose. Wars cannot be fought with nuclear weapons; their existence only adds to our perils because of the illusions which they have generated.
Louis Mountbatten of Burma (1900–79) British admiral and colonial administrator.
Speech, Strasbourg, 11 May 1979

11 We knew the world would not be the same.
J. Robert Oppenheimer (1904–67) US physicist.
After the first atomic test
The Decision to Drop the Bomb

12 There is no evil in the atom; only in men's souls.
Adlai Stevenson (1900–65) US statesman.
Speech, Hartford, Connecticut, 18 Sept 1952

□ NUMBERS □
See also mathematics, statistics

1 Round numbers are always false.
Samuel Johnson (1709–84) British lexicographer.
Life of Johnson (J. Boswell), Vol. III

2 No, I don't know his telephone number. But it was up in the high numbers.
John Maynard Keynes (1883–1946) British economist.
Attrib.

3 Oh, quite easy! The Septuagint minus the Apostles.
Arthur Woollgar Verrall (1851–1912) British classicist.
Reply to a person who thought the number 58 difficult to remember

O

☐ OBESITY ☐

See also food, greed

1 Outside every fat man there is an even fatter man trying to close in.
Kingsley Amis (1922–) British novelist.
See also CONNOLLY, ORWELL
One Fat Englishman, Ch. 3

2 Who's your fat friend?
'Beau' Brummel (George Bryan Brummell; 1778–1840) British dandy.
Referring to George, Prince of Wales
Reminiscences (Gronow)

3 Imprisoned in every fat man a thin one is wildly signalling to be let out.
Cyril Connolly (1903–74) British journalist.
See also AMIS, ORWELL
The Unquiet Grave

4 I'm fat, but I'm thin inside. Has it ever struck you that there's a thin man inside every fat man, just as they say there's a statue inside every block of stone?
George Orwell (Eric Blair; 1903–50) British novelist.
See also AMIS, CONNOLLY
Coming Up For Air, Pt. I, Ch. 3

5 My advice if you insist on slimming: Eat as much as you like – just don't swallow it.
Harry Secombe (1921–) Welsh singer, actor, and comedian.
Daily Herald, 5 Oct 1962

6 Falstaff sweats to death
And lards the lean earth as he walks along.
William Shakespeare (1564–1616) English dramatist.
Henry IV, Part One, II:2

7 I have more flesh than another man, and therefore more frailty.
William Shakespeare
Henry IV, Part One, III:3

8 She fitted into my biggest armchair as if it had been built round her by someone who knew they were wearing armchairs tight about the hips that season.
P. G. Wodehouse (1881–1975) British humorous novelist.
My Man Jeeves, 'Jeeves and the Unbidden Guest'

☐ OBITUARIES ☐

See also death, epitaphs, memorials

1 There's no such thing as bad publicity except your own obituary.
Brendan Behan (1923–64) Irish playwright.
My Brother Brendan (Dominic Behan)

2 I've just read that I am dead. Don't forget to delete me from your list of subscribers.
Rudyard Kipling (1865–1936) Indian-born British writer.
Writing to a magazine that had mistakenly published an announcement of his death
Anekdotenschatz (H. Hoffmeister)

3 In these days a man is nobody unless his biography is kept so far posted up that it may be ready for the national breakfast-table on the morning after his demise.
Anthony Trollope (1815–82) British novelist.
Doctor Thorne, Ch. 25

4 Reports of my death are greatly exaggerated.
Mark Twain (Samuel Langhorne Clemens; 1835–1910) US writer.
On learning that his obituary had been published
Cable to the Associated Press

☐ OBJECTIVITY ☐

See also perspective

1 Thus I live in the world rather as a Spectator of mankind, than as one of the species, by which means I have made myself a speculative statesman, soldier, merchant, and artisan, without ever meddling with any practical part of life.
Joseph Addison (1672–1719) British essayist.
The Spectator, 1

2 I am a camera with its shutter open, quite passive, recording, not thinking.
Christopher Isherwood (1904–86) British novelist.
Goodbye to Berlin

3 The man who sees both sides of a question is a man who sees absolutely nothing at all.
Oscar Wilde (1854–1900) Irish-born British dramatist.
The Critic as Artist, Pt. 2

☐ OBLIGATION ☐

See also duty

1 The debt which cancels all others.
Charles Caleb Colton (?1780–1832) British clergyman and writer.
Lacon, Vol. II

2 It is the nature of men to be bound by the benefits they confer as much as by those they receive.
Machiavelli (1469–1527) Italian statesman.
The Prince

☐ OBLIVION ☐

1 Many brave men lived before Agamemnon's time; but they are all, unmourned and unknown, covered by the long night, because they lack their sacred poet.
Horace (Quintus Horatius Flaccus; 65–8 BC) Roman poet.
Odes, IV

2 Annihilating all that's made
To a green thought in a green shade.
Andrew Marvell (1621–78) English poet.
The Garden

□ OBSESSIONS □

1 I have three phobias which, could I mute them,
would make my life as slick as a sonnet, but as
dull as ditch water: I hate to go to bed, I hate to
get up, and I hate to be alone.
Tallulah Bankhead (1903–68) US actress.
Tallulah, Ch. 1

2 *Papyromania* – compulsive accumulation of
papers...
Papyrophobia – abnormal desire for 'a clean
desk'.
Laurence J. Peter (1919–90) Canadian writer.
The Peter Principle, Glossary

□ OCCUPATIONS □

See also doctors, lawyers, police

1 Doctors bury their mistakes. Lawyers hang
them. But journalists put theirs on the front page.
Anonymous

2 The ugliest of trades have their moments of
pleasure. Now, if I were a grave-digger, or even a
hangman, there are some people I could work for
with a great deal of enjoyment.
Douglas William Jerrold (1803–57) British dramatist.
Wit and Opinions of Douglas Jerrold, 'Ugly Trades'

3 He did not know that a keeper is only a poacher
turned outside in, and a poacher a keeper turned
inside out.
Charles Kingsley (1819–75) British writer.
The Water Babies, Ch. 1

4 Under the spreading chestnut tree
The village smithy stands;
The smith, a mighty man is he,
With large and sinewy hands;
And the muscles of his brawny arms
Are strong as iron bands.
Henry Wadsworth Longfellow (1807–82) US poet.
The Village Blacksmith

5 No *man*, not even a doctor, ever gives any other
definition of what a nurse should be than this –
'devoted and obedient.' This definition would do
just as well for a porter. It might even do for a
horse. It would not do for a policeman.
Florence Nightingale (1820–1910) British nurse.
Notes on Nursing

6 A doctor who doesn't say too many foolish things
is a patient half-cured, just as a critic is a poet who
has stopped writing verse and a policeman a bur-
glar who has retired from practice.
Marcel Proust (1871–1922) French novelist.
À la recherche du temps perdu: Le Côté de Guermantes

7 Everybody hates house-agents because they
have everybody at a disadvantage. All other callings have a certain amount of give and take; the
house-agent simply takes.
H. G. Wells (1866–1946) British writer.
Kipps, Bk. III, Ch. 1

8 The best careers advice to give to the young is
'Find out what you like doing best and get some-
one to pay you for doing it.'
Katherine Whitehorn (1926–) British journalist.
The Observer, 1975

□ OFFICERS □

See also army, navy, soldiers, war

1 Any officer who shall behave in a scandalous
manner, unbecoming the character of an officer
and a gentleman shall...be cashiered.
Anonymous
The words 'conduct unbecoming the character of an officer' are a
direct quotation from the Naval Discipline Act (10 Aug 1860),
Article 24
Articles of War (1872), *Disgraceful Conduct*, 79

2 If Kitchener was not a great man, he was, at least,
a great poster.
Margot Asquith (1865–1945) The second wife of Herbert
Asquith.
Kitchener: Portrait of an Imperialist (Sir Philip Magnus), Ch. 14

3 In defeat unbeatable; in victory unbearable.
Winston Churchill (1874–1965) British statesman.
Referring to Viscount Montgomery
Ambrosia and Small Beer (E. Marsh), Ch. 5

4 War is too important to be left to the generals.
Georges Clemenceau (1841–1929) French statesman.
A similar remark is attributed to Talleyrand
Attrib.

5 Stick close to your desks and never go to sea,
And you all may be Rulers of the Queen's Navee!
W. S. Gilbert (1836–1911) British dramatist.
HMS Pinafore, I

6 LUDENDORFF: The English soldiers fight like lions.
HOFFMANN: True. But don't we know that they
are lions led by donkeys.
Max Hoffmann (1869–1927) German general.
Referring to the performance of the British army in World War I
The Donkeys (A. Clark)

7 The Nelson touch.
Lord Nelson (1758–1805) British admiral.
Diary, 9 Oct 1805

8 I didn't fire him because he was a dumb son of a
bitch, although he was, but that's not against the
law for generals. If it was, half to three-quarters
of them would be in gaol.
Harry S. Truman (1884–1972) US statesman.
Referring to General MacArthur
Plain Speaking (Merle Miller)

9 I don't know what effect these men will have on the enemy, but, by God, they frighten me.
Duke of Wellington (1769–1852) British general and statesman.
Referring to his generals
Attrib.

10 It is not the business of generals to shoot one another.
Duke of Wellington
Refusing an artillery officer permission to fire upon Napoleon himself during the Battle of Waterloo, 1815
Attrib.

11 I used to say of him that his presence on the field made the difference of forty thousand men.
Duke of Wellington
Referring to Napoleon
Notes of Conversations with the Duke of Wellington (Stanhope), 2 Nov 1831

☐OLD AGE☐
See also age, longevity

1 With the ancient is wisdom; and in length of days understanding.
Bible: Job
12:12

2 To be old is to be part of a huge and ordinary multitude…the reason why old age was venerated in the past was because it was extraordinary.
Ronald Blythe (1922–) British author.
The View in Winter

3 Old age takes away from us what we have inherited and gives us what we have earned.
Gerald Brenan (Edward Fitzgerald Brenan; 1894–1987) British writer.
Thoughts in a Dry Season, 'Life'

4 'You are old, Father William,' the young man said,
'And your hair has become very white;
And yet you incessantly stand on your head –
Do you think at your age, it is right?'
Lewis Carroll (Charles Lutwidge Dodgson; 1832–98) British writer.
See also Robert SOUTHEY
Alice's Adventures in Wonderland, Ch. 5

5 I prefer old age to the alternative.
Maurice Chevalier (1888–1972) French singer and actor.
Attrib.

6 Old-age, a second child, by Nature curs'd
With more and greater evils than the first,
Weak, sickly, full of pains; in ev'ry breath
Railing at life, and yet afraid of death.
Charles Churchill (1731–64) British poet.
Gotham, I

7 When a man fell into his anecdotage it was a sign for him to retire from the world.
Benjamin Disraeli (1804–81) British statesman.
Lothair, Ch. 28

8 I grow old…I grow old…
I shall wear the bottoms of my trousers rolled.
T. S. Eliot (1888–1965) US-born British poet and dramatist.
The Love Song of J. Alfred Prufrock

9 Old age brings along with its uglinesses the comfort that you will soon be out of it, – which ought to be a substantial relief to such discontented pendulums as we are.
Ralph Waldo Emerson (1803–82) US poet and essayist.
Journal

10 And now in age I bud again,
After so many deaths I live and write;
I once more smell the dew and rain,
And relish versing; O, my only Light,
It cannot be
That I am he
On whom Thy tempests fell all night.
George Herbert (1593–1633) English poet.
The Flower

11 There is a wicked inclination in most people to suppose an old man decayed in his intellects. If a young or middle-aged man, when leaving a company, does not recollect where he laid his hat, it is nothing; but if the same inattention is discovered in an old man, people will shrug up their shoulders, and say, 'His memory is going.'
Samuel Johnson (1709–84) British lexicographer.
Life of Johnson (J. Boswell), Vol. IV

12 Perhaps being old is having lighted rooms
Inside your head, and people in them, acting.
People you know, yet can't quite name.
Philip Larkin (1922–85) British poet.
The Old Fools

13 A 'Grand Old Man'. That means on our continent any one with snow white hair who has kept out of jail till eighty.
Stephen Leacock (1869–1944) English-born Canadian economist and humorist.
The Score and Ten

14 Old age is woman's hell.
Ninon de Lenclos (1620–1705) French courtesan.
Attrib.

15 From the earliest times the old have rubbed it into the young that they are wiser than they, and before the young had discovered what nonsense this was they were old too, and it profited them to carry on the imposture.
W. Somerset Maugham (1874–1965) British novelist.
Cakes and Ale, Ch. 9

16 Age only matters when one is ageing. Now that I have arrived at a great age, I might just as well be twenty.
Pablo Picasso (1881–1973) Spanish painter.
The Observer, Shouts and Murmurs, 'Picasso in Private' (John Richardson)

17 Growing old is like being increasingly penalized for a crime you haven't committed.
Anthony Powell (1905–) British novelist.
A Dance to the Music of Time: Temporary Kings, Ch. 1

18 Darling, I am growing old,
Silver threads among the gold.
Eben Rexford (1848–1916) British songwriter.
Silver Threads Among the Gold

19 Age seldom arrives smoothly or quickly. It's more often a succession of jerks.
Jean Rhys (1894–1979) Dominican-born British novelist.
The Observer, 'Sayings of the Week', 25 May 1975

20 As I grow older and older,
And totter towards the tomb,
I find that I care less and less
Who goes to bed with whom.
Dorothy L. Sayers (1893–1957) British writer.
That's Why I Never Read Modern Novels

21 Last scene of all,
That ends this strange eventful history,
Is second childishness and mere oblivion;
Sans teeth, sans eyes, sans taste, sans every thing.
William Shakespeare (1564–1616) English dramatist.
As You Like It, II:7

22 I have liv'd long enough.
My way of life
Is fall'n into the sear, the yellow leaf;
And that which should accompany old age,
As honour, love, obedience, troops of friends,
I must not look to have.
William Shakespeare
Macbeth, V:3

23 You are old, Father William, the young man cried,
The few locks which are left you are grey;
You are hale, Father William, a hearty old man,
Now tell me the reason, I pray.
Robert Southey (1774–1843) British poet.
See also Lewis CARROLL
The Old Man's Comforts, and how he Gained them

24 Being over seventy is like being engaged in a war. All our friends are going or gone and we survive amongst the dead and the dying as on a battlefield.
Muriel Spark (1918–) British novelist.
Memento Mori, Ch. 4

25 There are so few who can grow old with a good grace.
Richard Steele (1672–1729) Dublin-born British essayist.
The Spectator, 263

26 The greatest problem about old age is the fear that it may go on too long.
A. J. P. Taylor (1906–90) British historian.
Observer 'Sayings of the Week', 1 Nov 1981

27 Old age is the most unexpected of all the things that happen to a man.
Leon Trotsky (Lev Davidovich Bronstein; 1879–1940) Russian revolutionary.
Diary in Exile, 8 May 1935

28 The gods bestowed on Max the gift of perpetual old age.
Oscar Wilde (1854–1900) Irish-born British dramatist.
Referring to Max Beerbohm
Attrib.

29 The wiser mind
Mourns less for what age takes away
Than what it leaves behind.
William Wordsworth (1770–1850) British poet.
The Fountain

30 When you are old and gray and full of sleep,
And nodding by the fire, take down this book,
And slowly read, and dream of the soft look
Your eyes had once, and of their shadows deep…
W. B. Yeats (1865–1939) Irish poet.
When you are Old

☐ ONE-UPMANSHIP ☐

See also snobbery, superiority

1 Keeping up with the Joneses was a full-time job with my mother and father. It was not until many years later when I lived alone that I realized how much cheaper it was to drag the Joneses down to my level.
Quentin Crisp (?1910–) Model, publicist, and writer.
The Naked Civil Servant

2 *How to be one up* – how to make the other man feel that something has gone wrong, however slightly.
Stephen Potter (1900–69) British writer.
Lifemanship, Introduction

☐ OPERA ☐

See also music, singing

1 I do not mind what language an opera is sung in so long as it is a language I don't understand.
Edward Appleton (1892–1965) British physicist.
The Observer, 'Sayings of the Week,' 28 Aug 1955

2 No good opera plot can be sensible, for people do not sing when they are feeling sensible.
W. H. Auden (1907–73) British poet.
Time, 29 Dec 1961

3 The opera isn't over till the fat lady sings.
Dan Cook US journalist.
Washington Post, 13 June 1978

4 I sometimes wonder which would be nicer – an opera without an interval, or an interval without an opera.
Ernest Newman (1868–1959) British music critic.
Berlioz, Romantic and Classic, (ed. Peter Heyworth)

5 Tenors are noble, pure and heroic and get the soprano. But baritones are born villains in opera. Always the heavy and never the hero.
Leonard Warren (1911–60) US baritone singer.
The New York World Telegram, 13 Feb 1957

6 An unalterable and unquestioned law of the musical world required that the German text of French operas sung by Swedish artists should be translated into Italian for the clearer understanding of English speaking audiences.
Edith Wharton (1862–1937) US novelist.
The Age of Innocence, Bk. I, Ch. 1

☐OPINIONS☐
See also ideas

1 We must say that the same opinions have arisen among men in cycles, not once, twice, nor a few times, but infinitely often.
Aristotle (384–322 BC) Greek philosopher.
Meteorologica

2 They that approve a private opinion, call it opinion; but they that mislike it, heresy: and yet heresy signifies no more than private opinion.
Thomas Hobbes (1588–1679) English philosopher.
Leviathan, Pt. I, Ch. 11

3 The fact that an opinion has been widely held is no evidence whatever that it is not utterly absurd.
Bertrand Russell (1872–1970) British philosopher.
Attrib.

4 So many men, so many opinions.
Terence (Publius Terentius Afer; c. 190–159 BC) Roman poet.
Phormio

☐OPPORTUNITY☐
See also present

1 A wise man will make more opportunities than he finds.
Francis Bacon (1561–1626) English philosopher.
Essays, 'Of Ceremonies and Respects'

2 Opportunities are usually disguised as hard work, so most people don't recognise them.
Ann Landers (1918–) US journalist.
Attrib.

3 One can present people with opportunities. One cannot make them equal to them.
Rosamond Lehmann (1901–90) British novelist.
The Ballad and the Source

4 Equality of opportunity means equal opportunity to be unequal.
Iain Macleod (1913–70) British politician.
Way Of Life (John Boyd Carpenter)

5 Grab a chance and you won't be sorry for a might have been.
Arthur Ransome (1884–1967) British novelist.
We Didn't Mean to Go to Sea

6 There is a tide in the affairs of men
Which, taken at the flood, leads on to fortune;
Omitted, all the voyage of their life
Is bound in shallows and in miseries.
On such a full sea are we now afloat,
And we must take the current when it serves,
Or lose our ventures.
William Shakespeare (1564–1616) English dramatist.
Julius Caesar, IV:3

7 Why, then the world's mine oyster,
Which I with sword will open.
William Shakespeare
The Merry Wives of Windsor, II:2

☐OPPOSITES☐
See also conflict

1 The poet and the dreamer are distinct,
Diverse, sheer opposite, antipodes.
The one pours out a balm upon the world,
The other vexes it.
John Keats (1795–1821) British poet.
The Fall of Hyperion, I

2 Doublethink means the power of holding two contradictory beliefs in one's mind simultaneously, and accepting both of them.
George Orwell (Eric Blair; 1903–50) British novelist.
Nineteen Eighty-Four

3 The sublime and the ridiculous are often so nearly related that it is difficult to class them separately. One step above the sublime makes the ridiculous; and one step above the ridiculous makes the sublime again.
Thomas Paine (1737–1809) British writer.
The Age of Reason, Pt. 2

☐OPPOSITION☐
See also government, politics

1 It has been said that England invented the phrase, 'Her Majesty's Opposition'.
Walter Bagehot (1826–77) British economist and journalist.
See HOBHOUSE
The English Constitution, 'The Monarchy'

2 The duty of an opposition is to oppose.
Lord Randolph Churchill (1849–95) British Conservative politician.
Lord Randolph Churchill (W. S. Churchill)

3 When I invented the phrase 'His Majesty's Opposition' he paid me a compliment on the fortunate hit.
John Cam Hobhouse (1786–1869) British politician.
Speaking about Canning
Recollections of a Long Life, II, Ch. 12

4 ...I have spent many years of my life in opposition and I rather like the role.
Eleanor Roosevelt (1884–1962) US writer and lecturer.
Letter to Bernard Baruch, 18 Nov 1952

☐ OPPRESSION ☐

See also imprisonment, power politics, slavery, tyranny

1 When Israel was in Egypt land,
Let my people go,
Oppressed so hard they could not stand,
Let my people go.
Go down, Moses,
Way-down in Egypt land,
Tell old Pharaoh
To let my people go.
Anonymous
Negro spiritual

2 Christ in this country would quite likely have
been arrested under the Suppression of Com-
munism Act.
Joost de Blank (1908–68) Dutch-born British churchman.
Referring to South Africa
The Observer, 'Sayings of the Week', 27 Oct 1963

3 If you want a picture of the future, imagine a boot
stamping on a human face – for ever.
George Orwell (Eric Blair; 1903–50) British novelist.
Nineteen Eighty-Four

4 In the first days of the revolt you must kill: to
shoot down a European is to kill two birds with
one stone, to destroy an oppressor and the man
he oppresses at the same time: there remain a
dead man, and a free man.
Jean-Paul Sartre (1905–80) French writer.
The Wretched of the Earth (F. Fanon), Preface

☐ OPTIMISM ☐

See also hope

1 Are we downhearted? No!
Anonymous
A favourite expression of the British soldiers during World War I
Attrib.

2 What's the use of worrying?
It never was worth while,
So, pack up your troubles in your old kit-bag,
And smile, smile, smile.
George Asaf (George H. Powell; 1880–1951) US songwriter.
Pack up Your Troubles in Your Old Kit-bag

3 Let other pens dwell on guilt and misery.
Jane Austen (1775–1817) British novelist.
Mansfield Park, Ch. 48

4 *Future,* n. That period of time in which our affairs
prosper, our friends are true and our happiness is
assured.
Ambrose Bierce (1842–?1914) US writer and journalist.
The Devil's Dictionary

5 Don't you know each cloud contains
Pennies from Heaven?
Johnny Burke (1908–64) US songwriter.
Pennies from Heaven

6 The optimist proclaims we live in the best of all
possible worlds; and the pessimist fears this is
true.
James Cabell (1879–1958) US novelist and journalist.
The Silver Stallion

7 The worst is not
So long as we can say 'This is the worst'.
William Shakespeare (1564–1616) English dramatist.
King Lear, IV:1

8 The latest definition of an optimist is one who
fills up his crossword puzzle in ink.
Clement King Shorter (1857–1926) British journalist and
critic.
The Observer, 'Sayings of the Week', 22 Feb 1925

9 I am an optimist, unrepentant and militant. After
all, in order not to be a fool an optimist must
know how sad a place the world can be. It is only
the pessimist who finds this out anew every day.
Peter Ustinov (1921–) British actor.
Dear Me, Ch. 9

10 All is for the best in the best of possible worlds.
Voltaire (François-Marie Arouet; 1694–1778) French writer.
Candide, Ch. 30

☐ ORDER ☐

1 'Where shall I begin, please your Majesty?' he
asked.
'Begin at the beginning' the King said, gravely,
'and go on till you come to the end: then stop.'
Lewis Carroll (Charles Lutwidge Dodgson; 1832–98) British
writer.
Alice's Adventures in Wonderland, Ch. 11

2 Order is heaven's first law.
Alexander Pope (1688–1744) British poet.
An Essay on Man, IV

3 How sour sweet music is
When time is broke and no proportion kept!
So is it in the music of men's lives.
William Shakespeare
Richard II, V:5

4 A place for everything, and everything in its
place.
Samuel Smiles (1812–1904) British writer.
Thrift, Ch. 5

☐ ORIGINALITY ☐

See also imitation, innovation

1 An original writer is not one who imitates
nobody, but one whom nobody can imitate.
Vicomte de Chateaubriand (1768–1848) French diplomat
and writer.
Génie du Christianisme

2 A thought is often original, though you have uttered it a hundred times.
Oliver Wendell Holmes (1809–94) US writer.
The Autocrat of the Breakfast Table, Ch. 1

3 All good things which exist are the fruits of originality.
John Stuart Mill (1806–73) British philosopher.
On Liberty, Ch. 3

□ ORTHODOXY □

See also conformity

1 The difference between Orthodoxy or My-doxy and Heterodoxy or Thy-doxy.
Thomas Carlyle (1795–1881) Scottish historian and essayist.
A similar remark is attributed to the British churchman William Warburton (1698–1779)
History of the French Revolution, Pt. II, Bk. IV, Ch. 2

2 The word 'orthodoxy' not only no longer means being right; it practically means being wrong.
G. K. Chesterton (1874–1936) British writer.
Heretics, Ch. 1

□ ORWELL □
George

(Eric Blair; 1903–50) British novelist. His books include *The Road to Wigan Pier* (1937), *Animal Farm* (1945), and *Nineteen Eighty-Four* (1949).

QUOTATIONS ABOUT ORWELL

1 He could not blow his nose without moralising on the state of the handkerchief industry.
Cyril Connolly (1903–74) British journalist.
The Evening Colonnade

QUOTATIONS BY ORWELL

2 Man is the only creature that consumes without producing.
An allegory of the Marxist analysis of capitalism, with man representing the capitalist.
Animal Farm, Ch. 1

3 He was an embittered atheist (the sort of atheist who does not so much disbelieve in God as personally dislike Him).
Down and Out in Paris and London, Ch. 30

4 Probably the Battle of Waterloo *was* won on the playing-fields of Eton, but the opening battles of all subsequent wars have been lost there.
The Lion and the Unicorn, 'England, Your England'

5 A family with the wrong members in control – that, perhaps, is as near as one can come to describing England in a phrase.
The Lion and the Unicorn, 'The Ruling Class'

6 Who controls the past controls the future. Who controls the present controls the past.
Nineteen Eighty-Four

7 If you want a picture of the future, imagine a boot stamping on a human face – for ever.
Nineteen Eighty-Four

8 Doublethink means the power of holding two contradictory beliefs in one's mind simultaneously, and accepting both of them.
Nineteen Eighty-Four

9 It is brought home to you…that it is only because miners sweat their guts out that superior persons can remain superior.
The Road to Wigan Pier, Ch. 2

10 We may find in the long run that tinned food is a deadlier weapon than the machine-gun.
The Road to Wigan Pier, Ch. 6

11 As with the Christian religion, the worst advertisement for Socialism is its adherents.
The Road to Wigan Pier, Ch. 11

12 We have nothing to lose but our aitches.
Referring to the middle classes.
The Road to Wigan Pier, Ch. 13

13 The quickest way of ending a war is to lose it.
Second Thoughts on James Burnham

14 Serious sport has nothing to do with fair play. It is bound up with hatred, jealousy, boastfulness, disregard of all rules and sadistic pleasure in witnessing violence; in other words it is war minus the shooting.
The Sporting Spirit

15 Each generation imagines itself to be more intelligent than the one that went before it, and wiser than the one that comes after it.
Book Review

16 At 50, everyone has the face he deserves.
Last words in his manuscript notebook, 17 Apr 1949.

□ OSTENTATION □

1 That's it, baby, if you've got it, flaunt it.
Mel Brooks (Melvyn Kaminsky; 1926–) US film director.
The Producers

2 Wealth has never been a sufficient source of honour in itself. It must be advertised, and the normal medium is obtrusively expensive goods.
John Kenneth Galbraith (1908–) US economist.
The Affluent Society, Ch. 7

3 With the great part of rich people, the chief employment of riches consists in the parade of riches.
Adam Smith (1723–90) Scottish economist.
The Wealth of Nations

☐ OXFORD ☐

See also Cambridge, education, England

1 Home of lost causes, and forsaken beliefs, and unpopular names, and impossible loyalties!
Matthew Arnold (1822–88) British poet and critic.
Essays in Criticism, First Series, Preface

2 That sweet City with her dreaming spires She needs not June for beauty's heightening.
Matthew Arnold
Thyrsis

3 Oxford is on the whole more attractive than Cambridge to the ordinary visitor; and the traveller is therefore recommended to visit Cambridge first, or to omit it altogether if he cannot visit both.
Karl Baedeker (1801–59) German publisher.
Baedeker's Great Britain, 'From London to Oxford'

4 The King to Oxford sent a troop of horse, For Tories own no argument but force:
With equal skill to Cambridge books he sent, For Whigs admit no force but argument.
William Browne (1692–1774) English physician.
A reply to TRAPP
Literary Anecdotes (Nichols), Vol. III

5 The King, observing with judicious eyes The state of both his universities, To Oxford sent a troop of horse, and why? That learned body wanted loyalty; To Cambridge books, as very well discerning How much that loyal body wanted learning.
Joseph Trapp (1679–1747) English churchman and academic.
Written after George I donated the Bishop of Ely's library to Cambridge; for reply see BROWNE
Literary Anecdotes (Nichols), Vol. III

6 Oxford is, and always has been, full of cliques, full of factions, and full of a particular non-social snobbiness.
Mary Warnock (1924–) British philosopher and educationalist.
The Observer, 2 Nov 1980

P

☐PAINTING☐

See also art, artists

1 Buy old masters. They fetch a better price than old mistresses.
Lord Beaverbrook (1879–1964) British newspaper owner and politician.
Attrib.

2 *Painting, n.* The art of protecting flat surfaces from the weather and exposing them to the critic.
Ambrose Bierce (1842–?1914) US writer and journalist.
The Devil's Dictionary

3 Good painters imitate nature, bad ones spew it up.
Miguel de Cervantes (1547–1616) Spanish novelist.
El Licenciado Vidriera

4 A picture has been said to be something between a thing and a thought.
Samuel Palmer (1805–81) British landscape painter.
Life of Blake (Arthur Symons)

5 I paint objects as I think them, not as I see them.
Pablo Picasso (1881–1973) Spanish painter.
Attrib.

6 Painting is a blind man's profession. He paints not what he sees, but what he feels, what he tells himself about what he has seen.
Pablo Picasso
Journals (Jean Cocteau), 'Childhood'

7 I just keep painting till I feel like pinching. Then I know it's right.
Pierre Auguste Renoir (1841–1919) French impressionist painter.
Explaining how he achieved such lifelike flesh tones in his nudes
Attrib

8 My business is to paint not what I know, but what I see.
Joseph Turner (1775–1851) British painter.
Responding to a criticism of the fact that he had painted no port-holes on the ships in a view of Plymouth
Proust: The Early Years (G. Painter)

☐PANKHURST☐
Emmeline

(1858–1928) British suffragette. In 1889 she helped to found the Women's Franchise League which, in 1894, achieved the right for married women to vote in local elections. In 1903 she cofounded (with her daughter, Christabel) the Women's Social and Political Union (WSPU) whose aim was to keep alive the cause of women's suffrage.

QUOTATIONS ABOUT EMMELINE PANKHURST

1 What an extraordinary mixture of idealism and lunacy. Hasn't she the sense to see that the very worst method of campaigning for the franchise is

to try and intimidate or blackmail a man into giving her what he would gladly give her otherwise.
David Lloyd George (1863–1945) British Liberal statesman. *Lloyd George* (Richard Lloyd George)

2 She was as she instinctively knew, cast for a great role. She had a temperament akin to genius. She could have been a queen on the Stage or in the Salon.
Emmeline Pethwick-Lawrence (1867–1954) British suffragette.
My Part in a Changing World

QUOTATIONS BY EMMELINE PANKHURST

3 If civilisation is to advance at all in the future, it must be through the help of women, women freed of their political shackles, women with full power to work their will in society. It was rapidly becoming clear to my mind that men regarded women as a servant class in the community, and that women were going to remain in the servant class until they lifted themselves out of it.
My Own Story

4 Women had always fought for men, and for their children. Now they were ready to fight for their own human rights. Our militant movement was established.
My Own Story

5 I have no sense of guilt. I look upon myself as a prisoner of war. I am under no moral obligation to conform to, or in any way accept, the sentence imposed upon me.
Speech in court, Apr 1913.
The Fighting Pankhursts (David Mitchell)

6 We have taken this action, because as women...we realize that the condition of our sex is so deplorable that it is our duty even to break the law in order to call attention to the reasons why we do so.
Speech in court, 21 Oct 1908.
Shoulder to Shoulder (ed. Midge Mackenzie)

☐PARASITES☐

1 Many a man who thinks to found a home discovers that he has merely opened a tavern for his friends.
Norman Douglas (1868–1952) British novelist.
South Wind, Ch. 24

2 A free-loader is a confirmed guest. He is the man who is always willing to come to dinner.
Damon Runyon (1884–1946) US writer.
Short Takes, 'Free-Loading Ethics'

3 So, naturalist observe, a flea
Hath smaller fleas that on him prey,

And these have smaller fleas to bite 'em.
And so proceed *ad infinitum.*
Jonathan Swift (1667–1745) Irish-born Anglican priest and writer.
On Poetry

4 But was there ever dog that praised his fleas?
W. B. Yeats (1865–1939) Irish poet.
To a Poet, who would have me Praise certain Bad Poets, Imitators of His and Mine

☐ PARIS ☐

See also France

1 If you are lucky enough to have lived in Paris as a young man, then wherever you go for the rest of your life, it stays with you, for Paris is a moveable feast.
Ernest Hemingway (1899–1961) US novelist.
A Moveable Feast, Epigraph

2 Paris is worth a mass.
Henri IV (1553–1610) King of France.
Said on entering Paris (March 1594), having secured its submission to his authority by becoming a Roman Catholic
Attrib.

3 Is Paris burning?
Adolf Hitler (1889–1945) German dictator.
Referring to the liberation of Paris, 1944

4 As an artist, a man has no home in Europe save in Paris.
Friedrich Wilhelm Nietzsche (1844–1900) German philosopher.
Ecce Homo

☐ PARKER ☐
Dorothy (Rothschild)

(1893–1967) US writer and wit. Her New York circle in the 1920s included Ogden Nash and James Thurber. She is best known for her short stories, sketches, and poems; her books include *Not So Deep As a Well* (1936).

1 Razors pain you
Rivers are damp;
Acids stain you;
And drugs cause cramp.
Guns aren't lawful;
Nooses give;
Gas smells awful;
You might as well live.
Enough Rope, 'Resumé'

2 All I say is, nobody has any business to go around looking like a horse and behaving as if it were all right. You don't catch horses going around looking like people, do you?
Horsie

3 Why is it no one ever sent me yet
One perfect limousine, do you suppose?
Ah no, it's always just my luck to get
One perfect rose.
One Perfect Rose

4 By the time you swear you're his,
Shivering and sighing,
And he vows his passion is
Infinite, undying –
Lady, make a note of this:
One of you is lying.
Unfortunate Coincidence

5 If all the young ladies who attended the Yale promenade dance were laid end to end, no one would be the least surprised.
While Rome Burns (Alexander Woollcott)

6 This is not a novel to be tossed aside lightly. It should be thrown with great force.
Book review.
Wit's End (R. E. Dremman)

7 You can't teach an old dogma new tricks.
Wit's End (R. E. Drennan)

8 This is on me.
Suggesting words for tombstone.
You Might As Well Live (J. Keats), Pt. I, Ch. 5

9 How could they tell?
Reaction to news of the death of Calvin Coolidge, US President 1923–29; also attributed to H. L. Mencken.
You Might As Well Live (J. Keats)

10 You can lead a whore to culture but you can't make her think.
Speech to American Horticultural Society

11 You know, she speaks eighteen languages. And she can't say 'No' in any of them.
Speaking of an acquaintance.
Attrib.

12 Check enclosed.
Giving her version of the two most beautiful words in the English language.
Attrib.

☐ PARTIES ☐

See also society

1 The sooner every party breaks up the better.
Jane Austen (1775–1817) British novelist.
Emma, Ch. 25

2 And bring hither the fatted calf, and kill it; and let us eat, and be merry:
For this my son was dead, and is alive again; he was lost, and is found. And they began to be merry.
Bible: Luke
15:23–24

3 HE. Have you heard it's in the stars
Next July we collide with Mars?
SHE. Well, did you evah! What a swell party this is.
Cole Porter (1893–1964) US songwriter.
High Society 'Well, Did You Evah!'

4 'So like one's first parties' said Miss Runcible
'being sick with other people singing.'
Evelyn Waugh (1903–66) British novelist.
Vile Bodies

5 She had heard someone say something about an
Independent Labour Party, and was furious that
she had not been asked.
Evelyn Waugh
Vile Bodies

□PARTING□

See also departure, greetings, separation

1 There is a tavern in the town,
And there my dear love sits him down,
And drinks his wine 'mid laughter free,
And never, never thinks of me.
Fare thee well, for I must leave thee,
Do not let this parting grieve thee,
And remember that the best of friends must part.
Anonymous
There is a Tavern in the Town

2 Forty years on, when afar and asunder
Parted are those who are singing to-day.
E. E. Bowen (1836–1901) British writer.
Forty Years On (the Harrow school song)

3 Parting is all we know of heaven,
And all we need of hell.
Emily Dickinson (1830–86) US poet.
My Life Closed Twice Before its Close

4 Since there's no help, come let us kiss and part –
Nay, I have done, you get no more of me;
And I am glad, yea glad with all my heart
That thus so cleanly I myself can free.
Michael Drayton (1563–1631) English poet.
Sonnets, 61

5 It is seldom indeed that one parts on good terms,
because if one were on good terms one would
not part.
Marcel Proust (1871–1922) French novelist.
À la recherche du temps perdu: La Prisonnière

6 Good night, good night! Parting is such sweet
sorrow
That I shall say good night till it be morrow.
William Shakespeare (1564–1616) English dramatist.
Romeo and Juliet, II:2

7 Farewell! thou art too dear for my possessing,
And like enough thou know'st thy estimate:
The charter of thy worth gives thee releasing;
My bonds in thee are all determinate.
William Shakespeare
Sonnet 87

□PASSION□

See also emotion, love

1 The man who is master of his passions is
Reason's slave.
Cyril Connolly (1903–74) British journalist.
Turnstile One (ed. V. S. Pritchett)

2 A man who has not passed through the inferno of
his passions has never overcome them.
Carl Gustav Jung (1875–1961) Swiss psychoanalyst.
Memories, Dreams, Reflections, Ch. 9

3 For ever warm and still to be enjoy'd,
For ever panting and for ever young;
All breathing human passion far above,
That leaves a heart high-sorrowful and cloy'd,
A burning forehead, and a parching tongue.
John Keats (1795–1821) British poet.
Ode on a Grecian Urn

4 It is with our passions as it is with fire and water,
they are good servants, but bad masters.
Roger L'Estrange (1616–1704) English journalist and writer.
Aesop's Fables, 38

5 And hence one master-passion in the breast,
Like Aaron's serpent,
swallows up the rest.
Alexander Pope (1688–1744) British poet.
An Essay on Man, II

6 The ruling passion, be it what it will
The ruling passion conquers reason still.
Alexander Pope
Moral Essays, III

7 So I triumphed ere my passion, sweeping thro'
me, left me dry,
Left me with the palsied heart, and left me with
the jaundiced eye.
Alfred, Lord Tennyson (1809–92) British poet.
Locksley Hall

□PAST□

See also experience, future, history, memory, nostalgia, present,
regret, time

1 Even God cannot change the past.
Agathon (c. 446–401 BC) Athenian poet and playwright.
Nicomachean Ethics (Aristotle), VI

2 Study the past, if you would divine the future.
Confucius (K'ung Fu-tzu; 551–479 BC) Chinese philosopher.
Analects

3 The past is a foreign country: they do things
differently there.
L. P. Hartley (1895–1972) British novelist.
The Go-Between

4 Look back, and smile at perils past.
Walter Scott (1771–1832) Scottish novelist.
The Bridal of Triermain, Introduction

5 Keep off your thoughts from things that are past and done;
For thinking of the past wakes regret and pain.
Arthur Waley (1889–1966) British poet and translator.
Translation from the Chinese of Po-Chü-I
Resignation

☐ PATIENCE ☐

See also endurance, persistence

1 *Patience,* n. A minor form of despair, disguised as a virtue.
Ambrose Bierce (1842–?1914) US writer and journalist.
The Devil's Dictionary

2 Beware the Fury of a Patient Man.
John Dryden (1631–1700) British poet and dramatist.
Absalom and Achitophel, I

3 Patience and passage of time do more than strength and fury.
Jean de La Fontaine (1621–95) French poet.
Fables, II, 'Le Lion et le Rat'

4 It is very strange...that the years teach us patience; that the shorter our time, the greater our capacity for waiting.
Elizabeth Taylor (1912–75) British writer.
A Wreath of Roses, Ch. 10

☐ PATIENTS ☐

1 Keep a watch also on the faults of the patients, which often make them lie about the taking of things prescribed.
Hippocrates (c. 460–c. 377 BC) Greek physician.
Decorum, 14

2 The sick man is a parasite of society. In certain cases it is indecent to go on living. To continue to vegetate in a state of cowardly dependence upon doctors and special treatments, once the meaning of life, the right to life has been lost, ought to be regarded with the greatest contempt by society.
Friedrich Wilhelm Nietzsche (1844–1900) German philosopher.
The Twilight of the Idols, 'Skirmishes in a War with the Age'

☐ PATRIOTISM ☐

See also homesickness, loyalty, war

1 What pity is it
That we can die but once to serve our country!
Joseph Addison (1672–1719) British essayist.
Cato, IV:4

2 Speak for England.
Leopold Amery (1873–1955) British statesman.
Shouted to Arthur Greenwood, Labour Party spokesman, before he began to speak in a House of Commons debate immediately preceding the declaration of war, 2 Sept 1939

3 That this house will in no circumstances fight for its King and country.
Anonymous
Motion passed at the Oxford Union, 9 Feb 1933

4 'My country, right or wrong' is a thing that no patriot would think of saying, except in a desperate case. It is like saying 'My mother, drunk or sober.'
G. K. Chesterton (1874–1936) British writer.
The Defendant

5 Anyone who wants to carry on the war against the outsiders, come with me. I can't offer you either honours or wages; I offer you hunger, thirst, forced marches, battles and death. Anyone who loves his country, follow me.
Giuseppe Garibaldi (1807–82) Italian general and political leader.
Garibaldi (Guerzoni)

6 That kind of patriotism which consists in hating all other nations.
Elizabeth Gaskell (1810–65) British novelist.
Sylvia's Lovers, Ch. 1

7 I only regret that I have but one life to lose for my country.
Nathan Hale (1755–76) US revolutionary hero.
Speech before his execution, 22 Sept 1776

8 *Dulce et decorum est pro patria mori.*
It is a sweet and seemly thing to die for one's country.
Horace (Quintus Horatius Flaccus; 65–8 BC) Roman poet.
Odes, III

9 Patriotism is the last refuge of a scoundrel.
Samuel Johnson (1709–84) British lexicographer.
Life of Johnson (J. Boswell), Vol. II

10 Those who prate about Blimpish patriotism in the mode of Margaret Thatcher are also the ones who will take millions off the caring services of this country.
Neil Kinnock (1942–) British politician.
Speech, Labour Party Conference, Brighton, 1983

11 I would die for my country...but I would not let my country die for me.
Neil Kinnock
Speech on nuclear disarmament, 1987

12 The old Lie: *Dulce et decorum est
Pro patria mori.*
Wilfred Owen (1893–1918) British poet.
Dulce et decorum est

13 If I were an American, as I am an Englishman, while a foreign troop was landed in my country, I never would lay down my arms, – never – never – never!
William Pitt the Elder (1708–78) British statesman.
Speech, House of Lords, 18 Nov 1777

14 Patriots always talk of dying for their country
and never of killing for their country.
Bertrand Russell (1872–1970) British philosopher.
The Autobiography of Bertrand Russell

15 Not that I lov'd Caesar less, but that I lov'd Rome
more.
William Shakespeare (1564–1616) English dramatist.
Julius Caesar, III:2

16 True patriotism is of no party.
Tobias Smollett (1721–71) British novelist.
The Adventures of Sir Launcelote Greaves

17 Patriotism to the Soviet State is a revolutionary
duty, whereas patriotism to a bourgeois State is
treachery.
Leon Trotsky (Lev Davidovich Bronstein; 1879–1940) Russian
revolutionary.
Disputed Barricade (Fitzroy Maclean)

□PATRONAGE□
See also promotion

1 *Patron.* Commonly a wretch who supports with
insolence, and is paid with flattery.
Samuel Johnson (1709–84) British lexicographer.
Dictionary of the English Language

2 Is not a Patron, my Lord, one who looks with
unconcern on a man struggling for life in the
water, and, when he has reached ground, encum-
bers him with help? The notice which you have
been pleased to take of my labours, had it been
early, had been kind; but it has been delayed till I
am indifferent, and cannot enjoy it; till I am solitary, and cannot impart it; till I am known, and do
not want it.
Samuel Johnson
Letter to Lord Chesterfield, 7 Feb 1755
Life of Johnson (J. Boswell), Vol. I

□PEACE□
See also war and peace

1 There is no peace, saith the Lord, unto the
wicked.
Bible: Isaiah
48:22

2 Peace I leave with you, my peace I give unto you:
not as the world giveth, give I unto you. Let not
your heart be troubled, neither let it be afraid.
Bible: John
14:27

3 *Peace*, n. In international affairs, a period of
cheating between two periods of fighting.
Ambrose Bierce (1842–?1914) US writer and journalist.
The Devil's Dictionary

4 Give peace in our time, O Lord.
The Book of Common Prayer
Morning Prayer, Versicles

5 Don't tell me peace has broken out.
Bertolt Brecht (1898–1956) German dramatist.
Mother Courage, VIII

6 I believe it is peace for our time…peace with hon-
our.
Neville Chamberlain (1869–1940) British statesman.
Broadcast after Munich Agreement, 1 Oct 1938

7 Let us have peace.
Ulysses Simpson Grant (1822–85) US general.
On accepting nomination
Letter, 29 May 1868

8 Arms alone are not enough to keep the peace – it
must be kept by men.
John Fitzgerald Kennedy (1917–63) US statesman.
The Observer, 'Sayings of the Decade', 1962

9 The issues are the same. We wanted peace on
earth, love, and understanding between everyone around the world. We have learned that
change comes slowly.
Paul McCartney (1943–) British rock musician.
The Observer, 'Sayings of the Week', 7 June 1987

10 Nation shall speak peace unto nation.
Montague John Rendall (1862–1950) British schoolmaster.
Motto of BBC, 1927

11 We are the true peace movement.
Margaret Thatcher (1925–) British politician and prime
minister.
The Times, 1983

□PERCEPTION□

1 If the doors of perception were cleansed every-
thing would appear to man as it is, infinite.
William Blake (1757–1827) British poet.
The Marriage of Heaven and Hell, 'A Memorable Fancy'

2 Man's Desires are limited by his Perceptions;
none can desire what he has not perceived.
William Blake
There is no Natural Religion

□PERFECTION□
See also imperfection

1 The pursuit of perfection, then, is the pursuit of
sweetness and light…He who works for sweetness and light united, works to make reason and
the will of God prevail.
Matthew Arnold (1822–88) British poet and critic.
Culture and Anarchy, Ch. 1

2 What's come to perfection perishes.
Things learned on earth, we shall practise in
heaven.
Works done least rapidly, Art most cherishes.
Robert Browning (1812–89) British poet.
Old Pictures in Florence, XVII

3 You would attain to the divine perfection,
And yet not turn your back upon the world.
Henry Wadsworth Longfellow (1807–82) US poet.
Michael Angelo

4 Perfection has one grave defect; it is apt to be
dull.
W. Somerset Maugham (1874–1965) British novelist.
The Summing Up

5 Finality is death. Perfection is finality. Nothing is
perfect. There are lumps in it.
James Stephens (1882–1950) Irish novelist.
The Crock of Gold

□ PERSISTENCE □

See also determination, endurance, patience

1 And ye shall be hated of all men for my name's
sake: but he that endureth to the end shall be
saved.
Bible: Matthew
10:22

2 If at first you don't succeed,
Try, try again.
William Edward Hickson (1803–70) British educationalist.
Try and Try Again

3 You persisted for a certain number of years like a
stammer. You were a *stammer*, if you like, of
Space-Time.
Wyndham Lewis (1882–1957) British novelist.
The Human Age, 'The Childermass'

4 Constant dripping hollows out a stone.
Lucretius (Titus Lucretius Carus; c. 99–55 BC) Roman
philosopher.
On the Nature of the Universe, I

5 I am a kind of burr; I shall stick.
William Shakespeare (1564–1616) English dramatist.
Measure for Measure, IV:3

□ PERSPECTIVE □

See also objectivity

1 One sees great things from the valley; only small
things from the peak.
G. K. Chesterton (1874–1936) British writer.
The Hammer of God

2 Fleas know not whether they are upon the body
of a giant or upon one of ordinary size.
Walter Savage Landor (1775–1864) British poet and writer.
Imaginary Conversations, 'Southey and Porson'

□ PERSUASION □

1 They will conquer, but they will not convince.
Miguel de Unamuno y Jugo (1864–1936) Spanish writer.
Referring to the Franco rebels
Attrib.

2 For a priest to turn a man when he lies a-dying, is
just like one that has a long time solicited a
woman, and cannot obtain his end; at length
makes her drunk, and so lies with her.
John Selden (1584–1654) English historian.
Table Talk

□ PERVERSITY □

See also petulance, stubbornness

1 If it's heaven for climate, it's hell for company.
J. M. Barrie (1860–1937) British novelist and dramatist.
The Little Minister, Ch. 3

2 Let's find out what everyone is doing,
And then stop everyone from doing it.
A. P. Herbert (1890–1971) British writer and politician.
Let's Stop Somebody

3 I had never had a piece of toast
Particularly long and wide,
But fell upon the sanded floor,
And always on the buttered side.
James Payn (1830–98) British writer and editor.
Chambers's Journal, 2 Feb 1884

4 Adam was but human – this explains it all. He did
not want the apple for the apple's sake, he
wanted it only because it was forbidden.
Mark Twain (Samuel Langhorne Clemens; 1835–1910) US
writer.
Pudd'nhead Wilson's Calendar, Ch. 2

□ PESSIMISM □

1 More than any other time in history, mankind
faces a crossroads. One path leads to despair and
utter hopelessness. The other, to total extinction.
Let us pray we have the wisdom to choose
correctly.
Woody Allen (Allen Stewart Konigsberg; 1935–) US film
actor.
Side Effects 'My Speech to the Graduates'

2 Pessimism, when you get used to it, is just as
agreeable as optimism.
Arnold Bennett (1867–1931) British novelist.
Things that have Interested Me, 'The Slump in Pessimism'

3 Scratch a pessimist, and you find often a
defender of privilege.
Lord Beveridge (1879–1963) British economist.
The Observer, 'Sayings of the Week', 17 Dec 1943

4 The optimist proclaims we live in the best of all
possible worlds; and the pessimist fears this is
true.
James Cabell (1879–1958) US novelist and journalist.
The Silver Stallion

5 How many pessimists end up by desiring the
things they fear, in order to prove that they are
right.
Robert Mallet (1915–) French writer.
Apostilles

6 A pessimist is a man who looks both ways before crossing a one-way street.
Laurence J. Peter (1919–90) Canadian writer.
Peter's Quotations

□PETULANCE□

See also perversity, stubbornness

1 He has to learn that petulance is not sarcasm, and that insolence is not invective.
Benjamin Disraeli (1804–81) British statesman.
Said of Sir C. Wood
Speech, House of Commons, 16 Dec 1852

2 I am the emperor, and I want dumplings.
Ferdinand I (1793–1875) Emperor of Austria.
The Fall of the House of Habsburg (E. Crankshaw)

□PHILISTINISM□

See also arts, books, culture

1 For this class we have a designation which now has become pretty well known, and which we may as well still keep for them, the designation of Philistines.
Matthew Arnold (1822–88) British poet and critic.
Referring to the middle class
Culture and Anarchy, Ch. 3

2 The finest collection of frames I ever saw.
Humphry Davy (1778–1829) British chemist.
When asked what he thought of the Paris art galleries
Attrib.

3 When I hear anyone talk of Culture, I reach for my revolver.
Hermann Goering (1893–1946) German leader.
Attrib. to Goering but probably said by Hanns Johst

4 I've never been in there...but there are only three things to see, and I've seen colour reproductions of all of them.
Harold W. Ross (1892–1951) US journalist.
Referring to the Louvre
A Farewell to Arms (Ernest Hemingway)

□PHILOSOPHERS□

See also philosophy

1 All are lunatics, but he who can analyze his delusion is called a philosopher.
Ambrose Bierce (1842–?1914) US writer and journalist.
Epigrams

2 There is nothing so absurd but some philosopher has said it.
Cicero (106–43 BC) Roman orator and statesman.
De Divinatione, II

3 To a philosopher no circumstance, however trifling, is too minute.
Oliver Goldsmith (1728–74) Irish-born British writer.
The Citizen of the World

4 In the philosopher there is nothing whatever impersonal; and, above all, his morality bears decided and decisive testimony to *who he is* – that is to say, to the order of rank in which the innermost drives of his nature stand in relation to one another.
Friedrich Wilhelm Nietzsche (1844–1900) German philosopher.
Jenseits von Gut und Böse

5 Not to care for philosophy is to be a true philosopher.
Blaise Pascal (1623–62) French philosopher and mathematician.
Pensées, I

6 There are now-a-days professors of philosophy but not philosophers.
Henry David Thoreau (1817–62) US writer.
Walden, 'Economy'

□PHILOSOPHY□

See also logic, metaphysics, philosophers, thinking

1 The principles of logic and metaphysics are true simply because we never allow them to be anything else.
A. J. Ayer (1910–89) British philosopher.
Language, Truth and Logic

2 The formula 'Two and two make five' is not without its attractions.
Fedor Mikhailovich Dostoevsky (1821–81) Russian novelist.
Notes from the Underground

3 Do not all charms fly
At the mere touch of cold philosophy?
John Keats (1795–1821) British poet.
Lamia, II

4 Axioms in philosophy are not axioms until they are proved upon our pulses; we read fine things but never feel them to the full until we have gone the same steps as the author.
John Keats
Letter to J. H. Reynolds, 3 May 1818

5 There will be no end to the troubles of states, or indeed, my dear Glaucon, of humanity itself, till philosophers become kings in this world, or till those we now call kings and rulers really and truly become philosophers.
Plato (429–347 BC) Greek philosopher.
Republic, Bk. 5

6 We thought philosophy ought to be patient and unravel people's mental blocks. Trouble with doing that is, once you've unravelled them, their heads fall off.
Frederic Raphael (1931–) British author.
The Glittering Prizes: A Double Life, III:2

7 It is a great advantage for a system of philosophy to be substantially true.
George Santayana (1863–1952) US philosopher.
The Unknowable

8 Philosophy is the product of wonder.
A. N. Whitehead (1861–1947) British philosopher.
Nature and Life, Ch. 1

9 The history of Western philosophy is, after all, no more than a series of footnotes to Plato's philosophy.
A. N. Whitehead
Attrib.

10 Philosophy is not a theory but an activity.
Ludwig Wittgenstein (1889–1951) Austrian philosopher.
Tractatus Logico-Philosophicus, Ch. 4

☐ PHOTOGRAPHY ☐

1 Photography can never grow up if it imitates some other medium. It has to walk alone; it has to be itself.
Berenice Abbott (b. 1898) US photographer.
Infinity, 'It Has to Walk Alone'

2 Most things in life are moments of pleasure and a lifetime of embarrassment; photography is a moment of embarrassment and a lifetime of pleasure.
Tony Benn (1925–) British politician.
The Sunday Times, 31 Dec 1989

3 The camera cannot lie. But it can be an accessory to untruth.
Harold Evans (1928–) British journalist.
Pictures on a Page

4 I have for instance among my purchases...several original Mona Lisas and all painted (according to the Signature) by the great artist Kodak.
Spike Milligan (1918–) British comic actor and author.
A Dustbin of Milligan, 'Letters to Harry Secombe'

5 A photograph is not only an image (as a painting is an image), an interpretation of the real; it is also a trace, something directly stencilled off the real, like a footprint or a death mask.
Susan Sontag (1933–) US novelist and essayist.
On Photography

☐ PLACES ☐

See also Britain, Europe

1 The shortest way out of Manchester is notoriously a bottle of Gordon's gin.
William Bolitho (1890–1930) British writer.
Attrib.

2 India is a geographical term. It is no more a united nation than the Equator.
Winston Churchill (1874–1965) British statesman.
Speech, Royal Albert Hall, 18 Mar 1931

3 From Greenland's icy mountains,
From India's coral strand,
Where Afric's sunny fountains
Roll down their golden sand.
Reginald Heber (1783–1826) British bishop and hymn writer.
From Greenland's Icy Mountains

4 Dublin, though a place much worse than London, is not so bad as Iceland.
Samuel Johnson (1709–84) British lexicographer.
Letter to Mrs Christopher Smart
Life of Johnson (J. Boswell), Vol. IV

5 Asia is not going to be civilized after the methods of the West. There is too much Asia and she is too old.
Rudyard Kipling (1865–1936) Indian-born British writer.
Life's Handicap, 'The Man Who Was'

6 On the road to Mandalay
Where the flyin'-fishes play.
Rudyard Kipling
The Road to Mandalay

7 And all lying mysteriously within the Australian underdark, that peculiar, lost weary aloofness of Australia. There was the vast town of Sydney. And it didn't seem to be real, it seemed to be sprinkled on the surface of a darkness into which it never penetrated.
D. H. Lawrence (1885–1930) British novelist.
Kangaroo, Ch. 1

8 Jerusalem the golden,
With milk and honey blest,
Beneath thy contemplation
Sink heart and voice opprest.
John Mason Neale (1818–66) British churchman.
Jerusalem the Golden

9 Even the Hooligan was probably invented in China centuries before we thought of him.
Saki (Hector Hugh Munro; 1870–1916) British writer.
Reginald on House-Parties

10 Great God! this is an awful place.
Captain Robert Falcon Scott (1868–1912) British explorer.
Referring to the South Pole
Journal, 17 Jan 1912

11 I'm Charley's aunt from Brazil, where the nuts come from.
Brandon Thomas (1856–1914) British actor and dramatist.
Charley's Aunt, I

☐ PLATH ☐
Sylvia

(1932–63) US poet and novelist. Born in Boston, Massachusetts, she published her first poem at the age of eight. In 1960 she published her first book of poems, *The Colossus*, followed by a novel, *The Bell Jar* (1963). Posthumous publications include *Ariel* (1965), *Crossing the War* (1971), and *Winter Trees* (1971). Her *Collected Poems* (1981) won a Pulitzer prize.

1 Dying
is an art, like everything else.
I do it exceptionally well.
Lady Lazarus

2 The surgeon is quiet, he does not speak.
He has seen too much death, his hands are full
of it.
Winter Trees, 'The Courage of Shutting-Up'

3 I am no shadow
Though there is a shadow starting from my feet.
I am a wife.
The city waits and aches. The little grasses
Crack through stone, and they are green with
life.
Winter Trees, 'The Three Women'

□PLAYS□

See also acting, actors, criticism, literature, Shakespeare,
theatre, writers, writing

1 Depending upon shock tactics is easy, whereas
writing a good play is difficult. Pubic hair is no
substitute for wit.
J. B. Priestley (1894–1984) British novelist.
Outcries and Asides

2 My soul; sit thou a patient looker-on;
Judge not the play before the play is done:
Her plot hath many changes, every day
Speaks a new scene; the last act crowns the play.
Francis Quarles (1592–1644) English poet.
Epigram, Respice Finem

3 Rehearsing a play is making the word flesh.
Publishing a play is reversing the process.
Peter Shaffer (1926–) British dramatist.
Equus, Note

4 If it be true that good wine needs no bush, 'tis
true that a good play needs no epilogue.
William Shakespeare (1564–1616) English dramatist.
As You Like It, Epilogue

5 The play's the thing
Wherein I'll catch the conscience of the King.
William Shakespeare
Hamlet, II:2

6 A novel is a static thing that one moves through;
a play is a dynamic thing that moves past one.
Kenneth Tynan (1927–80) British theatre critic.
Curtains

7 The play was a great success, but the audience
was a disaster.
Oscar Wilde (1854–1900) Irish-born British dramatist.
Referring to a play that had recently failed
Attrib.

□PLEASURE□

See also debauchery, happiness, leisure, merrymaking

1 One half of the world cannot understand the
pleasures of the other.
Jane Austen (1775–1817) British novelist.
Emma, Ch. 9

2 Then I commended mirth, because a man hath
no better thing under the sun, than to eat, and to
drink, and to be merry: for that shall abide with
him of his labour the days of his life, which God
giveth him under the sun.
Bible: Ecclesiastes
8:15

3 Though sages may pour out their wisdom's
treasure,
There is no sterner moralist than Pleasure.
Lord Byron (1788–1824) British poet.
Don Juan, III

4 In Xanadu did Kubla Khan
A stately pleasure-dome decree:
Where Alph, the sacred river, ran
Through caverns measureless to man
Down to a sunless sea.
Samuel Taylor Coleridge (1772–1834) British poet.
Kubla Khan

5 It was a miracle of rare device,
A sunny pleasure-dome with caves of ice!
Samuel Taylor Coleridge
Kubla Khan

6 The art of pleasing consists in being pleased.
William Hazlitt (1778–1830) British essayist.
On Manner

7 Pleasure is very seldom found where it is sought;
our brightest blazes of gladness are commonly
kindled by unexpected sparks.
Samuel Johnson (1709–84) British lexicographer.
The Idler

8 No man is a hypocrite in his pleasures.
Samuel Johnson
Life of Johnson (J. Boswell), Vol. IV

9 Great lords have their pleasures, but the people
have fun.
Baron de Montesquieu (1689–1755) French writer.
Pensées diverses

10 I wish thee as much pleasure in the reading, as I
had in the writing.
Francis Quarles (1592–1644) English poet.
Emblems, 'To the Reader'

11 Pleasures are all alike simply considered in themselves…He that takes pleasure to hear sermons
enjoys himself as much as he that hears plays.
John Selden (1584–1654) English historian.
Table Talk

12 Pleasure is nothing else but the intermission of pain.
John Selden
Table Talk

13 This is the best moment of my life, since my Granny caught her tit in the mangle.
Daley Thompson (Francis Morgan T; 1958–) British decathlete.
On winning the decathlon at the Olympics
The Guardian, 1984

14 Everyone is dragged on by their favourite pleasure.
Virgil (Publius Vergilius Maro; 70–19 BC) Roman poet.
Eclogue, Bk. II

15 Pleasures newly found are sweet
When they lie about our feet.
William Wordsworth (1770–1850) British poet.
To the Small Celandine

☐ POETRY ☐

See also criticism, inspiration, literature, poetry and prose, poets

1 For this reason poetry is something more philosophical and more worthy of serious attention than history.
Aristotle (384–322 BC) Greek philosopher.
Poetics, Ch. 9

2 A criticism of life under the conditions fixed for such a criticism by the laws of poetic truth and poetic beauty.
Matthew Arnold (1822–88) British poet and critic.
Essays in Criticism, Second Series, 'The Study of Poetry'

3 I think it will be found that the grand style arises in poetry, when a noble nature, poetically gifted, treats with simplicity or with severity a serious subject.
Matthew Arnold
Closing words
On Translating Homer

4 The difference between genuine poetry and the poetry of Dryden, Pope, and all their school, is briefly this: their poetry is conceived and composed in their wits, genuine poetry is conceived and composed in the soul.
Matthew Arnold
Thomas Gray

5 Too many people in the modern world view poetry as a luxury, not a necessity like petrol. But to me it's the oil of life.
John Betjeman (1906–84) British poet.
The Observer, 'Sayings of the Year', 1974

6 Poetry is as much a part of the universe as mathematics and physics. It is not a cleverer device or recreation, unless the Eternal is clever.
Edmund Blunden (1896–1974) British poet.
Speech on his election as Professor of Poetry at Oxford University, 1966

7 For the godly poet must be chaste himself, but there is no need for his verses to be so.
Catullus (c. 84–c. 54 BC) Roman poet.
Carmina, XVI

8 Poetry is not a turning loose of emotion, but an escape from emotion; it is not the expression of personality, but an escape from personality.
T. S. Eliot (1888–1965) US-born British poet and dramatist.
Tradition and the Individual Talent

9 All one's inventions are true, you can be sure of that. Poetry is as exact a science as geometry.
Gustave Flaubert (1821–80) French novelist.
Letter to Louise Colet, 14 Aug 1853

10 We all write poems; it is simply that poets are the ones who write in words.
John Fowles (1926–) British novelist.
The French Lieutenant's Woman, Ch. 19

11 Even when poetry has a meaning, as it usually has, it may be inadvisable to draw it out…Perfect understanding will sometimes almost extinguish pleasure.
A. E. Housman (1859–1936) British scholar and poet.
The Name and Nature of Poetry

12 We hate poetry that has a palpable design upon us – and if we do not agree, seems to put its hand in its breeches pocket. Poetry should be great and unobtrusive, a thing which enters into one's soul, and does not startle or amaze it with itself, but with its subject.
John Keats (1795–1821) British poet.
Letter to J. H. Reynolds, 3 Feb 1818

13 If poetry comes not as naturally as leaves to a tree it had better not come at all.
John Keats
Letter to John Taylor, 27 Feb 1818

14 Perhaps no person can be a poet, or can even enjoy poetry, without a certain unsoundness of mind.
Lord Macaulay (1800–59) British historian.
Literary Essays Contributed to the 'Edinburgh Review', 'Milton'

15 Poetry is a comforting piece of fiction set to more or less lascivious music.
H. L. Mencken (1880–1956) US journalist.
Prejudices, 'The Poet and his Art'

16 Blest pair of Sirens, pledges of Heaven's joy, Sphere-born harmonious sisters, Voice and Verse.
John Milton (1608–74) English poet.
At a Solemn Music

17 …poetry, 'The Cinderella of the Arts.'
Harriet Monroe (1860–1936) US poet and editor.
Famous American Women (Hope Stoddard), 'Harriet Monroe'

18 What is poetry? The suggestion, by the imagination, of noble grounds for the noble emotions.
John Ruskin (1819–1900) British art critic and writer.
Modern Painters, Vol. III

19 The truest poetry is the most feigning.
William Shakespeare (1564–1616) English dramatist.
As You Like It, III:3

20 The poet's eye, in a fine frenzy rolling,
Doth glance from heaven to earth, from earth to heaven;
And as imagination bodies forth
The forms of things unknown, the poet's pen
Turns them to shapes, and gives to airy nothing
A local habitation and a name.
William Shakespeare
A Midsummer Night's Dream, V:1

21 The lunatic, the lover, and the poet,
Are of imagination all compact.
William Shakespeare
A Midsummer Night's Dream, V:1

22 Poetry is the record of the best and happiest moments of the happiest and best minds.
Percy Bysshe Shelley (1792–1822) British poet.
A Defence of Poetry

23 A man does not write poems about what he knows, but about what he does not know.
Robin Skelton (1925–) British academic.
Teach Yourself Poetry

24 These poems, with all their crudities, doubts, and confusions, are written for the love of Man and in praise of God, and I'd be a damn' fool if they weren't.
Dylan Thomas (1914–53) Welsh poet.
Collected Poems, Note

25 Poetry is the spontaneous overflow of powerful feelings: it takes its origin from emotion recollected in tranquillity.
William Wordsworth (1770–1850) British poet.
Lyrics Ballads, Preface

26 Out of the quarrel with others we make rhetoric; out of the quarrel with ourselves we make poetry.
W. B. Yeats (1865–1939) Irish poet.
Essay

□ POETRY AND PROSE □

See also poetry, prose

1 Poetry is not the proper antithesis to prose, but to science. Poetry is opposed to science, and prose to metre.
Samuel Taylor Coleridge (1772–1834) British poet.
Lectures and Notes of 1818, I

2 I wish our clever young poets would remember my homely definitions of prose and poetry; that is, prose = words in their best order; poetry = the best words in the best order.
Samuel Taylor Coleridge
Table Talk

3 Prose on certain occasions can bear a great deal of poetry: on the other hand, poetry sinks and swoons under a moderate weight of prose.
Walter Savage Landor (1775–1864) British poet and writer.
Imaginary Conversations, 'Archdeacon Hare and Walter Landor'

4 For to write good prose is an affair of good manners. It is, unlike verse, a civil art…. Poetry is baroque.
W. Somerset Maugham (1874–1965) British novelist.
The Summing Up

5 Poetry is to prose as dancing is to walking.
John Wain (1925–) British novelist and poet.
Talk, BBC radio, 13 Jan 1976

6 The poet gives us his essence, but prose takes the mould of the body and mind entire.
Virginia Woolf (1882–1941) British novelist.
The Captain's Death Bed, 'Reading'

□ POETS □

See also Chaucer, criticism, Milton, poetry, Shakespeare, writers

1 Poets and painters are outside the class system, or rather they constitute a special class of their own, like the circus people and the gipsies.
Gerald Brenan (Edward Fitzgerald Brenan; 1894–1987) British writer.
Thoughts in a Dry Season, 'Writing'

2 A poet without love were a physical and metaphysical impossibility.
Thomas Carlyle (1795–1881) Scottish historian and essayist.
Critical and Miscellaneous Essays, 'Burns'

3 A true poet does not bother to be poetical. Nor does a nursery gardener scent his roses.
Jean Cocteau (1889–1963) French poet and artist.
Professional Secrets

4 Immature poets imitate; mature poets steal.
T. S. Eliot (1888–1965) US-born British poet and dramatist.
Philip Massinger

5 To be a poet is a condition rather than a profession.
Robert Graves (1895–1985) British poet and novelist.
Horizon

6 Not gods, nor men, nor even booksellers have put up with poets' being second-rate.
Horace (Quintus Horatius Flaccus; 65–8 BC) Roman poet.
Ars Poetica

7 For ne'er
Was flattery lost on poet's ear:

A simple race! they waste their toil
For the vain tribute of a smile.
Walter Scott (1771–1832) Scottish novelist.
The Lay of the Last Minstrel, IV

8 There have been many most excellent poets that
have never versified, and now swarm many versi-
fiers that need never answer to the name of poets.
Philip Sidney (1554–86) English poet and courtier.
The Defence of Poesy

9 I hate the whole race…There is no believing a
word they say – your professional poets, I mean –
there never existed a more worthless set than
Byron and his friends for example.
Duke of Wellington (1769–1852) British general and
statesman.
Lady Salisbury's diary, 26 Oct 1833

□ POLICE □

1 When constabulary duty's to be done –
A policeman's lot is not a happy one.
W. S. Gilbert (1836–1911) British dramatist.
The Pirates of Penzance, II

2 The police are the only 24-hour social service in
the country.
Commander Alex Marnoch
Remark, Feb 1983

3 Policemen are numbered in case they get lost.
Spike Milligan (1918–) British comic actor and author.
The Last Goon Show of All

4 Reading isn't an occupation we encourage
among police officers. We try to keep the paper
work down to a minimum.
Joe Orton (1933–67) British dramatist.
Loot, II

5 One always has the air of someone who is lying
when one speaks to a policeman.
Charles-Louis Philippe (1874–1909) French novelist.
Les Chroniques du canard sauvage

□ POLITICIANS □

See also Churchill, compliments, government, Hitler, Houses of
Parliament, insults, politics

1 Politics and the fate of mankind are shaped by
men without ideas and without greatness. Men
who have greatness within them don't go in for
politics.
Albert Camus (1913–60) French existentialist writer.
Notebooks, 1935–42

2 For Politicians neither love nor hate.
John Dryden (1631–1700) British poet and dramatist.
Absalom and Achitophel, I

3 Since a politician never believes what he says, he
is surprised when others believe him.
Charles De Gaulle (1890–1970) French general and
statesman.
Attrib.

4 In order to become the master, the politician
poses as the servant.
Charles De Gaulle
Attrib.

5 I have come to the conclusion that politics are
too serious a matter to be left to the politicians.
Charles De Gaulle
Attrib.

6 Politicians are the same everywhere. They
promise to build bridges even where there are
no rivers.
Nikita Khrushchev (1894–1971) Soviet statesman.
Attrib., Oct 1960

7 Political renegades always start their career of
treachery as 'the best men of all parties' and end
up in the Tory knackery.
Neil Kinnock (1942–) British politician.
Speech, Welsh Labour Party Conference, 1985

8 The problem is that many MPs never see the
London that exists beyond the wine bars and
brothels of Westminster.
Ken Livingstone (1945–) British Labour politician.
The Times, 19 Feb 1987

9 A politician is a person with whose politics you
don't agree; if you agree with him he is a statesman.
David Lloyd George (1863–1945) British Liberal statesman.
Attrib.

10 When you're abroad you're a statesman: when
you're at home you're just a politician.
Harold Macmillan (1894–1986) British politician and prime
minister.
Speech, 1958

11 A statesman is a politician who places himself at
the service of the nation. A politician is a statesman who places the nation at his service.
Georges Pompidou (1911–74) French statesman.
The Observer, 'Sayings of the Year', 30 Dec 1973

12 Get thee glass eyes,
And, like a scurvy politician, seem
To see the things thou dost not.
William Shakespeare (1564–1616) English dramatist.
King Lear, IV:6

13 All politicians have vanity. Some wear it more
gently than others.
David Steel (1938–) British politician.
The Observer, 'Sayings of the Week', 14 July 1985

14 In politics, if you want anything said, ask a man; if you want anything done, ask a woman.
Margaret Thatcher (1925–) British politician and prime minister.
The Changing Anatomy of Britain (Anthony Sampson)

15 A politician is a man who understands government, and it takes a politician to run a government. A statesman is a politician who's been dead ten or fifteen years.
Harry S. Truman (1884–1972) US statesman.
New York World Telegram and Sun, 12 Apr 1958

16 Politicians can forgive almost anything in the way of abuse; they can forgive subversion, revolution, being contradicted, exposed as liars, even ridiculed, but they can never forgive being ignored.
Auberon Waugh (1939–) British novelist and critic.
The Observer, 11 Oct 1981

17 It is a pity, as my husband says, that more politicians are not bastards by birth instead of vocation.
Katherine Whitehorn (1926–) British journalist.
The Observer, 1964

□ POLITICS □

See also Communism, democracy, diplomacy, government, Houses of Parliament, monarchy, opposition, politicians, power politics, socialism

1 Politics, as a practice, whatever its professions, has always been the systematic organisation of hatreds.
Henry Brooks Adams (1838–1918) US historian.
The Education of Henry Adams

2 Man is by nature a political animal.
Aristotle (384–322 BC) Greek philosopher.
Politics, Bk. I

3 Politics is a blood sport.
Aneurin Bevan (1897–1960) British Labour politician.
My Life with Nye (Jennie Lee)

4 No attempt at ethical or social seduction can eradicate from my heart a deep burning hatred for the Tory Party…So far as I am concerned they are lower than vermin.
Aneurin Bevan
Speech, Manchester, 4 July 1949

5 Politics is not an exact science.
Bismarck (1815–98) German statesman.
Speech, Prussian Chamber, 18 Dec 1863

6 Politics is not a science…but an art.
Bismarck
Speech, Reichstag, 15 Mar 1884

7 You won't force South Africans to commit national suicide.
P. W. Botha (1916–) South African politician and president.
Speech, Aug 1986

8 Politics are usually the executive expression of human immaturity..
Vera Brittain (1893–1970) British writer and feminist.
The Rebel Passion

9 Party loyalty lowers the greatest of men to the petty level of the masses.
Jean de La Bruyère (1645–96) French satirist.
Les Caractères

10 Politics is the art of the possible.
R. A. Butler (1902–82) British Conservative politician. Often attrib. to Butler but used earlier by others, including Bismarck
The Art of the Possible, Epigraph

11 I am not made for politics because I am incapable of wishing for, or accepting the death of my adversary.
Albert Camus (1913–60) French existentialist writer.
The Rebel

12 What a genius the Labour Party has for cutting itself in half and letting the two parts writhe in public.
Cassandra (William Neil Cannon; 1910–67) Irish journalist.
The Daily Mirror

13 Labour is not fit to govern.
Winston Churchill (1874–1965) British statesman.
Election speech, 1920

14 The disastrous element in the Labour party is its intellectuals.
George Norman Clark (1890–1979) British historian.
A Man of the Thirties (A. L. Rowse)

15 We now are, as we always have been, decidedly and conscientiously attached to what is called the Tory, and which might with more propriety be called the Conservative, party.
John Wilson Croker (1780–1857) British Tory politician.
The first use of the term 'Conservative Party'
In *Quarterly Review*, Jan 1830

16 The Civil Service is profoundly deferential – 'Yes, Minister! No, Minister! If you wish it, Minister!'
Richard Crossman (1907–74) British politician.
Diaries, 22 Oct 1964

17 A Conservative government is an organized hypocrisy.
Benjamin Disraeli (1804–81) British statesman.
Speech, 17 Mar 1845

18 All terrorists, at the invitation of the Government, end up with drinks at the Dorchester.
Hugh Gaitskell (1906–63) British Labour politician.
Letter to *The Guardian*, 23 Aug 1977 (Dora Gaitskell)

19 There are some of us…who will fight, fight, fight, and fight again to save the party we love.
Hugh Gaitskell
After his policy for a nuclear deterrent had been defeated
Speech, Labour Party conference, Scarborough, 3 Oct 1960

20 There are times in politics when you must be on
the right side and lose.
John Kenneth Galbraith (1908–) US economist.
The Observer, 'Sayings of the Week', 11 Feb 1968

21 There is just one rule for politicians all over the
world. Don't say in Power what you say in Opposition: if you do you only have to carry out what the
other fellows have found impossible.
John Galsworthy (1867–1933) British novelist.
Maid in Waiting

22 I don't think that modesty is the oustanding char-
acteristic of contemporary politics, do you?
Edward Heath (1916–) British politician and prime minister.
Remark, Dec 1988

23 The essential thing is the formation of the political will of the nation: that is the starting point for
political action.
Adolf Hitler (1889–1945) German dictator.
Speech, Düsseldorf, 27 Jan 1932

24 A little rebellion, now and then, is a good thing,
and as necessary in the political world as storms
in the physical.
Thomas Jefferson (1743–1826) US statesman.

25 The politics of the left and centre of this country
are frozen in an out-of-date mould which is bad
for the political and economic health of Britain
and increasingly inhibiting for those who live
within the mould. Can it be broken?
Roy Jenkins (1920–) British politician.
Speech, 9 June 1980

26 If you're in politics and you can't tell when you
walk into a room who's for you and who's against
you, then you're in the wrong line of work.
Lyndon B. Johnson (1908–73) US statesman.
The Lyndon Johnson Story (B. Mooney)

27 Politics are now nothing more than a means of
rising in the world.
Samuel Johnson (1709–84) British lexicographer.
Life of Johnson (J. Boswell), Vol. II

28 The idea that there is a model Labour voter, a
blue-collar council house tenant who belongs to
a union and has 2.4 children, a five-year-old car
and a holiday in Blackpool, is patronizing and
politically immature.
Neil Kinnock (1942–) British politician.
Speech, 1986

29 Proportional Representation, I think, is funda-
mentally counter-democratic.
Neil Kinnock
Marxism Today, 1983

30 As usual the Liberals offer a mixture of sound
and original ideas. Unfortunately none of the
sound ideas is original and none of the original
ideas is sound.
Harold Macmillan (1894–1986) British politician and prime
minister.
Speech, 7 Mar 1961

31 There are three groups that no prime minister
should provoke: the Treasury, the Vatican, and
the National Union of Mineworkers.
Harold Macmillan
First used by Stanley Baldwin
Attrib.

32 In politics, as in grammar, one should be able to
tell the substantives from the adjectives. Hitler
was a substantive; Mussolini only an adjective.
Hitler was a nuisance. Mussolini was bloody.
Together a bloody nuisance.
Salvador de Madariaga y Rogo (1886–1978) Spanish
diplomat and writer.
Attrib.

33 Every intellectual attitude is latently political.
Thomas Mann (1875–1955) German novelist.
The Observer, 11 Aug 1974

34 We cannot change our policy now. After all, we
are not political whores.
Benito Mussolini (1883–1945) Italian dictator.
Hitler (Alan Bullock), Ch. 8

35 I still love you, but in politics there is no heart,
only head.
Napoleon I (Napoleon Bonaparte; 1769–1821) French
emperor.
Referring to his divorce, for reasons of state, from the Empress
Josephine (1809)
Bonaparte (C. Barnett)

36 In our time, political speech and writing are
largely the defence of the indefensible.
George Orwell (Eric Blair; 1903–50) British novelist.
Politics and the English Language

37 I used to say that politics was the second lowest
profession and I have come to know that it bears
a great similarity to the first.
Ronald Reagan (1911–) US politician and president.
The Observer, 13 May 1979

38 The more you read about politics, you got to
admit that each party is worse than the other.
Will Rogers (1879–1935) US actor and humorist.
Saturday Review, 'A Rogers Thesaurus', 25 Aug 1962

39 The collection of prejudices which is called political philosophy is useful provided that it is not
called philosophy.
Bertrand Russell (1872–1970) British philosopher.
The Observer, 'Sayings of the Year', 1962

40 History is past politics, and politics present
history.
John Robert Seeley (1834–95) British historian.
Quoting the historian E. A. Freeman
The Growth of British Policy

41 An independent is a guy who wants to take the politics out of politics.
Adlai Stevenson (1900–65) US statesman.
The Art Of Politics.

42 Politics is perhaps the only profession for which no preparation is thought necessary.
Robert Louis Stevenson (1850–94) Scottish writer.
Familiar Studies of Men and Books, 'Yoshida-Torajiro'

43 Socialists treat their servants with respect and then wonder why they vote Conservative.
Tom Stoppard (1937–) Czech-born British dramatist.
Lord Malquist and Mr Moon, Pt. V, Ch. 1

44 Any woman who understands the problems of running a home will be nearer to understanding the problems of running a country.
Margaret Thatcher (1925–) British politician and prime minister.
The Observer, 8 May 1979

45 I can trust my husband not to fall asleep on a public platform and he usually claps in the right places.
Margaret Thatcher
Observer, 20 Aug 1978

46 Britain is no longer in the politics of the pendulum, but of the ratchet.
Margaret Thatcher
Speech, Institute of Public Relations, 1977

47 Politics is the art of preventing people from taking part in affairs which properly concern them.
Paul Valéry (1871–1945) French poet and writer.
Tel quel

48 Any American who is prepared to run for President should automatically, by definition, be disqualified from ever doing so.
Gore Vidal (1925–) US novelist.
Attrib.

49 Politics come from man. Mercy, compassion and justice come from God.
Terry Waite (1939–) British churchman.
The Observer, 'Sayings of the Week', 13 Jan 1985

50 The Labour Party is going about the country stirring up apathy.
William Whitelaw (1918–) British politician.
Attrib.

51 A week is a long time in politics.
Harold Wilson (1916–) British politician and prime minister.
First said in 1965 or 1966, and repeated on several occasions
Attrib.

□POPE□
Alexander
(1688–1744) British poet. His witty and satirical poems include the mock-heroic *The Rape of the Lock* (1712), the mock epic *The Dunciad* (1728), and the philosophical *An Essay on Man* (1733).

QUOTATIONS ABOUT POPE

1 In Pope I cannot read a line,
But with a sigh I wish it mine;
When he can in one couplet fix
More sense than I can do in six:
It gives me such a jealous fit,
I cry, 'Pox take him and his wit!'
Jonathan Swift (1667–1745) Irish-born Anglican priest and writer.
On the Death of Dr. Swift

QUOTATIONS BY POPE

2 Ye gods! annihilate but space and time.
And make two lovers happy.
The Art of Sinking in Poetry, 11

3 The right divine of kings to govern wrong.
The Dunciad, IV

4 Yes; I am proud, I must be proud to see
Men not afraid of God, afraid of me.
Epilogue to the Satires, Dialogue II

5 Damn with faint praise, assent with civil leer,
And, without sneering, teach the rest to sneer.
Epistle to Dr. Arbuthnot

6 Nature, and Nature's laws lay hid in night:
God said, *Let Newton be!* and all was light.
Epitaphs, 'Intended for Sir Isaac Newton'

7 A little learning is a dangerous thing;
Drink deep, or taste not the Pierian spring:
There shallow draughts intoxicate the brain,
And drinking largely sobers us again.
An Essay on Criticism

8 Whoever thinks a faultless piece to see,
Thinks what ne'er was, nor is, nor e'er shall be.
An Essay on Criticism

9 True ease in writing comes from art, not chance,
As those move easiest who have learn'd to dance.
'Tis not enough no harshness gives offence,
The sound must seem an echo to the sense.
An Essay on Criticism

10 To err is human, to forgive, divine.
An Essay on Criticism

11 For fools rush in where angels fear to tread.
An Essay on Criticism

12 Hope springs eternal in the human breast;
Man never is, but always to be blest.
An Essay on Man, I

13 'Tis education forms the common mind,
Just as the twig is bent, the tree's inclined.
Moral Essays, I

14 See how the world its veterans rewards!
A youth of frolics, an old age of cards.
Moral Essays, II

15 Who shall decide when doctors disagree?
Moral Essays, III

16 A man should never be ashamed to own he has
been in the wrong, which is but saying, in other
words, that he is wiser to-day than he was yesterday.
Thoughts on Various Subjects

17 I never knew any man in my life who could not
bear another's misfortunes perfectly like a
Christian.
Thoughts on Various Subjects

18 I am His Highness' dog at Kew;
Pray tell me sir, whose dog are you?
On the collar of a dog given to Frederick, Prince of Wales

□ POP MUSIC □

1 Rock 'n' roll is part of a pest to undermine the morals of the youth of our nation. It... brings people
of both races together.
Anonymous
Statement by the North Alabama Citizens' Council in the 1950s

2 Roll Over Beethoven.
Chuck Berry (1931–) US rock-and-roll musician.
Song title.

3 Hail, hail rock 'n' roll'.
Deliver me from the days of old.
Chuck Berry
Hail, hail, rock 'n' roll

4 Strange how potent cheap music is.
Noël Coward (1899–1973) British dramatist.
Private Lives

5 I think popular music in this country is one of the
few things in the twentieth century that have
made giant strides in reverse.
Bing Crosby (Harry Lillis Crosby; 1904–77) US singer.
Interview in *This Week*

6 Rock Around the Clock.
Bill Haley and The Comets US rock-and-roll band.
Song title

7 We're more popular than Jesus Christ now. I
don't know which will go first, Rock and Roll or
Christianity.
John Lennon (1940–80) British rock musician.
The Beatles Illustrated Lyrics

8 Every popular song has at least one line or sentence that is perfectly clear – the line that fits the
music.
Ezra Pound (1885–1972) US poet and critic.
Attrib.

9 Rock journalism is people who can't write inter-
viewing people who can't talk for people who
can't read.
Frank Zappa (1940–) US rock musician.
Loose Talk (Linda Botts)

□ POPULARITY □
See also fame

1 Everybody hates me because I'm so universally
liked.
Peter De Vries (1910–) US novelist.
The Vale of Laughter, Pt. I

2 Popularity is a crime from the moment it is
sought; it is only a virtue where men have it
whether they will or no.
Lord Halifax (1633–95) English statesman.
Political, Moral and Miscellaneous Thoughts and Reflections

3 Popularity? It's glory's small change.
Victor Hugo (1802–85) French writer.
Ruy Blas, III

4 We're more popular than Jesus Christ now. I
don't know which will go first. Rock and roll or
Christianity.
John Lennon (1940–80) British rock musician.
The Beatles Illustrated Lyrics

□ PORNOGRAPHY □
See also censorship, prudery, sex

1 This is the kind of show that gives pornography a
bad name.
Clive Barnes (1927–) British-born theatre and ballet critic.
Reviewing *Oh, Calcutta!*
Attrib.

2 I don't think pornography is very harmful, but it
is terribly, terribly boring.
Noël Coward (1899–1973) British dramatist.
The Observer, 'Sayings of the Week', 24 Sept 1972

3 She is the pinup, the centerfold, the poster, the
postcard, the dirty picture, naked, half-dressed,
laid out, legs spread, breast or ass protruding.
She is the thing she is supposed to be: the thing
that makes him erect.
Andrea Dworkin (1946–) US writer and journalist.
Pornography: Men Possessing Women

4 Women, for centuries not having access to pornography and unable to bear looking... are astonished. Women do not believe that men believe
what pornography says about women. But they
do. From the worst to the best of them, they do.
Andrea Dworkin (1946–) US writer and journalist.
Pornography: Men Possessing Women

5 The fact remains that, no matter how disturbing
violent fantasies are, as long as they stay within
the world of pornography they are still only fantasies. The man masturbating in a theater showing

a snuff film is still only watching a movie, not actually raping and murdering.
Deirdre English (1948–) US writer and editor.
Mother Jones, Apr 1980

6 Pornography is the attempt to insult sex, to do dirt on it.
D. H. Lawrence (1885–1930) British novelist.
Phoenix, 'Pornography and Obscenity'

7 Its avowed purpose is to excite sexual desire, which, I should have thought, is unnecessary in the case of the young, inconvenient in the case of the middle aged, and unseemly in the old.
Malcolm Muggeridge (1903–90) British writer.
Tread Softly For You Tread On My Jokes, 1966

☐ POSSIBILITY ☐

1 The grand Perhaps!
Robert Browning (1812–89) British poet.
Bishop Blougram's Apology

2 Your If is the only peace-maker; much virtue is in If.
William Shakespeare (1564–1616) English dramatist.
As You Like It, V:4

☐ POSTERITY ☐

See also death, fame, future, immortality, reputation

1 Think of your forefathers! Think of your posterity!
John Quincy Adams (1767–1848) Sixth president of the USA.
Speech, Plymouth, Massachusetts, 22 Dec 1802

2 When a man is in doubt about this or that in his writing, it will often guide him if he asks himself how it will tell a hundred years hence.
Samuel Butler (1835–1902) British writer.
Notebooks

3 A writer's ambition should be to trade a hundred contemporary readers for ten readers in ten years' time and for one reader in a hundred years' time.
Arthur Koestler (1905–83) Hungarian-born British writer.
New York Times Book Review, 1 Apr 1951

4 Damn the age. I'll write for antiquity.
Charles Lamb (1775–1834) British essayist.
Referring to his lack of payment for the *Essays of Elia*
English Wits (L. Russell)

☐ POUND ☐
Ezra

(1885–1972) US poet and critic. His poetry includes *Hugh Selwyn Mauberly* (1920) and *The Pisan Cantos* (1925–69). His support for Mussolini led to his confinement in a US mental hospital (1946–58).

QUOTATIONS ABOUT POUND

1 I confess I am seldom interested in what he is saying, but only in the way he says it.
T. S. Eliot (1888–1965) US-born British poet and dramatist.
The Dial, 'Isolated superiority'

QUOTATIONS BY POUND

2 One of the pleasures of middle age is to *find out* that one WAS right, and that one was much righter than one knew at say 17 or 23.
ABC of Reading, Ch. 1

3 Literature is news that STAYS news.
ABC of Reading, Ch. 2

4 Any general statement is like a check drawn on a bank. Its value depends on what is there to meet it.
ABC of Reading, Ch. 2

☐ POVERTY ☐

See also hunger, poverty and wealth

1 To be poor and independent is very nearly an impossibility.
William Cobbett (1763–1835) British journalist and writer.
Advice to Young Men

2 Poverty, therefore, was comparative. One measured it by a sliding scale. One was always poor, in terms of those who were richer.
Margaret Drabble (1939–) British novelist.
The Radiant Way

3 There's no scandal like rags, nor any crime so shameful as poverty.
George Farquhar (1678–1707) Irish dramatist.
The Beaux' Stratagem, I:1

4 The very poor are unthinkable and only to be approached by the statistician and the poet.
E. M. Forster (1879–1970) British novelist.
Howards End

5 It is only the poor who are forbidden to beg.
Anatole France (Jacques Anatole François Thibault; 1844–1924) French writer.
Crainquebille

6 Let not Ambition mock their useful toil,
Their homely joys, and destiny obscure;
Nor Grandeur hear with a disdainful smile,
The short and simple annals of the poor.
Thomas Gray (1716–71) British poet.
Elegy Written in a Country Churchyard

7 People who are much too sensitive to demand of cripples that they run races ask of the poor that they get up and act just like everyone else in society.
Michael Harrington (1928–) US socialist and writer.
The Other America

8 I want there to be no peasant in my kingdom so poor that he is unable to have a chicken in his pot every Sunday.
Henri IV (1553–1610) King of France.
Hist. de Henry le Grand (Hardouin de Péréfixe)

9 Oh! God! that bread should be so dear,
And flesh and blood so cheap!
Thomas Hood (1799–1845) British poet.
The Song of the Shirt

10 Hard to train to accept being poor.
Horace (Quintus Horatius Flaccus; 65–8 BC) Roman poet.
Odes, I

11 It is easy enough to say that poverty is no crime.
No; if it were men wouldn't be ashamed of it. It is
a blunder, though, and is punished as such. A
poor man is despised the whole world over.
Jerome K. Jerome (1859–1927) British humorist.
Idle Thoughts of an Idle Fellow

12 Few, save the poor, feel for the poor.
Letitia Landon (1802–38) British poet and novelist.
The Poor

13 'The Workhouse' – always a word of shame, grey
shadow falling on the close of life, most feared by
the old (even when called The Infirmary);
abhorred more than debt, or prison, or beggary,
or even the stain of madness.
Laurie Lee (1914–) British novelist and poet.
Cider with Rosie

14 The poor don't know that their function in life is
to exercise our generosity.
Jean-Paul Sartre (1905–80) French writer.
Words

15 ...the poor are our brothers and sisters....people
in the world who need love, who need care, who
have to be wanted.
Mother Teresa (Agnes Gonxha Bojaxhui; 1910–)
Yugoslavian missionary in Calcutta.
Time, 'Saints Among Us', 29 Dec 1975

16 As for the virtuous poor, one can pity them, of
course, but one cannot possibly admire them.
Oscar Wilde (1854–1900) Irish-born British dramatist.
The Soul of Man under Socialism

17 But I, being poor, have only my dreams;
I have spread my dreams under your feet;
Tread softly because you tread on my dreams.
W. B. Yeats (1865–1939) Irish poet.
He Wishes for the Cloths of Heaven

□ POVERTY AND WEALTH □
See also money, poverty, wealth

1 She was poor but she was honest
Victim of a rich man's game.
First he loved her, then he left her,
And she lost her maiden name.
See her on the bridge at midnight,
Saying 'Farewell, blighted love.'
Then a scream, a splash and goodness,
What is she a-doin' of?
It's the same the whole world over,
It's the poor wot gets the blame,

It's the rich wot gets the gravy.
Ain't it all a bleedin' shame?
Anonymous
She was Poor but she was Honest

2 There was a certain rich man, which was clothed
in purple and fine linen, and fared sumptuously
every day:
And there was a certain beggar named Lazarus,
which was laid at his gate, full of sores,
And desiring to be fed with the crumbs which fell
from the rich man's table: moreover the dogs
came and licked his sores.
And it came to pass, that the beggar died, and
was carried by the angels into Abraham's bosom:
the rich man also died, and was buried;
And in hell he lift up his eyes, being in torments,
and seeth Abraham afar off, and Lazarus in his
bosom.
Bible: Luke
16:19–23

3 There are only two families in the world, my old
grandmother used to say, The *Haves* and the
Have-Nots.
Miguel de Cervantes (1547–1616) Spanish novelist.
Don Quixote, Pt. II, Ch. 20

4 Whereas it has long been known and declared
that the poor have no right to the property of the
rich, I wish it also to be known and declared that
the rich have no right to the property of the poor.
John Ruskin (1819–1900) British art critic and writer.
Unto this Last, Essay III

5 When the rich wage war it is the poor who die.
Jean-Paul Sartre (1905–80) French writer.
The Devil and the Good Lord

6 As long as men are men, a poor society cannot be
too poor to find a right order of life, nor a rich
society too rich to have need to seek it.
R. H. Tawney (1880–1962) British economist and historian.
The Acquisitive Society

□ POWER □
See also influence, leadership, responsibility

1 Power tends to corrupt, and absolute power corrupts absolutely. Great men are almost always
bad men...There is no worse heresy than that
the office sanctifies the holder of it.
Lord Acton (1834–1902) British historian.
Often misquoted as 'Power corrupts...'
Letter to Bishop Mandell Creighton, 5 Apr 1887

2 A friend in power is a friend lost.
Henry Brooks Adams (1838–1918) US historian.
The Education of Henry Adams

3 Nothing destroyeth authority so much as the
unequal and untimely interchange of power
pressed too far, and relaxed too much.
Francis Bacon (1561–1626) English philosopher.
Essays, 'Of Empire'

4 The greater the power, the more dangerous the abuse.
Edmund Burke (1729–97) British politician.
Speech, House of Commons, 7 Feb 1771

5 Men of power have not time to read; yet men who do not read are unfit for power.
Michael Foot (1913–) British Labour politician and journalist.
Debts Of Honour

6 It was a symptom of Britain's post-war condition that anyone given power before his hair turned white was called a whizz-kid.
Clive James (1939–) Writer and broadcaster, born in Australia.
Falling Towards England, Ch. 18

7 Power is the ultimate aphrodisiac.
Henry Kissinger (1923–) German-born US politician and diplomat.
The Guardian, 28 Nov 1976

8 It could never be a correct justification that, because the whites oppressed us yesterday when they had power, that the blacks must oppress them today because they have power.
Robert Mugabe (1925–) Zimbabwe politician and president.
Speech, Mar 1980

9 Who controls the past controls the future. Who controls the present controls the past.
George Orwell (Eric Blair; 1903–50) British novelist.
Nineteen Eighty-Four

10 Unlimited power is apt to corrupt the minds of those who possess it.
William Pitt the Elder (1708–78) British statesman.
See also Lord ACTON
Speech, House of Lords, 9 Jan 1770

11 You only have power over people so long as you don't take *everything* away from them. But when you've robbed a man of everything he's no longer in your power – he's free again.
Alexander Solzhenitsyn (1918–) Soviet novelist.
The First Circle, Ch. 17

12 Power corrupts, but lack of power corrupts absolutely.
Adlai Stevenson (1900–65) US statesman.
The Observer, Jan 1963

13 The balance of power.
Robert Walpole (1676–1745) British statesman.
Speech, House of Commons

14 The good old rule
Sufficeth them, the simple plan,
That they should take, who have the power,
And they should keep who can.
William Wordsworth (1770–1850) British poet.
Rob Roy's Grave

15 The wrong sort of people are always in power because they would not be in power if they were not the wrong sort of people.
Jon Wynne-Tyson (1924–) British humorous writer.
Times Literary Supplement

☐POWER POLITICS☐
See also force, oppression, violence, weapons

1 Guns will make us powerful; butter will only make us fat.
Hermann Goering (1893–1946) German leader.
Radio broadcast, 1936

2 A man may build himself a throne of bayonets, but he cannot sit on it.
Dean Inge (1860–1954) British churchman.
Wit and Wisdom of Dean Inge (ed. Marchant)

3 Every Communist must grasp the truth, 'Political power grows out of the barrel of a gun.'
Mao Tse-Tung (1893–1976) Chinese communist leader.
Selected Works, Vol II, 'Problems of War and Strategy', 6 Nov 1938

4 There is a homely adage which runs 'Speak softly and carry a big stick, you will go far'.
Theodore Roosevelt (1858–1919) US Republican president.
Speech, Minnesota State Fair, 2 Sept 1901

5 God is always on the side of the big battalions.
Vicomte de Turenne (1611–75) French marshal.
Attrib.

6 God is on the side not of the heavy battalions, but of the best shots.
Voltaire (François-Marie Arouet; 1694–1778) French writer.
Notebooks

☐PRAISE☐
See also admiration, compliments, flattery

1 Just as it is always said of slander that something always sticks when people boldly slander, so it might be said of self-praise (if it is not entirely shameful and ridiculous) that if we praise ourselves fearlessly, something will always stick.
Francis Bacon (1561–1626) English philosopher.
The Advancement of Learning

2 Let us now praise famous men, and our fathers that begat us.
Bible: Ecclesiasticus
44:1

3 The advantage of doing one's praising for oneself is that one can lay it on so thick and exactly in the right places.
Samuel Butler (1835–1902) British writer.
The Way of All Flesh, Ch. 34

4 Fondly we think we honour merit then,
When we but praise ourselves in other men.
Alexander Pope (1688–1744) British poet.
An Essay on Criticism

5 To refuse praise reveals a desire to be praised twice over.
Duc de la Rochefoucauld (1613–80) French writer.
Maximes, 149

□ **PRAYER** □

See also Christianity, faith, God, religion

1 But when ye pray, use not vain repetitions, as the heathen do: for they think that they shall be heard for their much speaking.
Be not ye therefore like unto them: for your Father knoweth what things ye have need of, before ye ask him.
After this manner therefore pray ye: Our Father which art in heaven, Hallowed be thy name.
Thy kingdom come. Thy will be done in earth, as it is in heaven.
Give us this day our daily bread.
And forgive us our debts, as we forgive our debtors.
And lead us not into temptation, but deliver us from evil: For thine is the kingdom, and the power, and the glory, for ever. Amen.
Bible: Matthew
6:7–13

2 To Mercy, Pity, Peace, and Love
All pray in their distress.
William Blake (1757–1827) British poet.
Songs of Innocence, 'The Divine Image'

3 When two or three are gathered together in thy Name thou wilt grant their requests.
The Book of Common Prayer
Morning Prayer, Prayer of St Chrysostom

4 A leap over the hedge is better than good men's prayers.
Miguel de Cervantes (1547–1616) Spanish novelist.
Don Quixote, Pt. I, Ch. 21

5 He prayeth well, who loveth well
Both man and bird and beast.
Samuel Taylor Coleridge (1772–1834) British poet.
The Rime of the Ancient Mariner, VII

6 He prayeth best, who loveth best
All things both great and small;
For the dear God who loveth us,
He made and loveth all.
Samuel Taylor Coleridge
The Rime of the Ancient Mariner, VII

7 Prayer makes the Christian's armour bright;
And Satan trembles when he sees
The weakest saint upon his knees.
William Cowper (1731–1800) British poet.
Olney Hymns, 29

8 Religion's in the heart, not in the knees.
Douglas William Jerrold (1803–57) British dramatist.
The Devil's Ducat, I.2

9 If thou shouldst never see my face again,
Pray for my soul. More things are wrought by prayer
Than this world dreams of.
Alfred, Lord Tennyson (1809–92) British poet.
Idylls of the King, 'The Passing of Arthur'

10 Whatever a man prays for, he prays for a miracle.
Every prayer reduces itself to this: 'Great God grant that twice two be not four.'
Ivan Turgenev (1818–83) Russian novelist.
Prayer

□ **PRECOCITY** □

See also children, youth

1 One of those men who reach such an acute limited excellence at twenty-one that everything afterward savours of anti-climax.
F. Scott Fitzgerald (1896–1940) US novelist.
The Great Gatsby, Ch. 1

2 Thank you, madam, the agony is abated.
Lord Macaulay (1800–59) British historian.
Replying, aged four, to a lady who asked if he had hurt himself
Life and Letters of Macaulay (Trevelyan), Ch. 1

□ **PREJUDICE** □

See also equality, feminism, Jews, objectivity, racism, religion

1 Mother is far too clever to understand anything she does not like.
Arnold Bennett (1867–1931) British novelist.
The Title

2 Common sense is the collection of prejudices acquired by age eighteen.
Albert Einstein (1879–1955) German-born US physicist.
Scientific American, Feb 1976

3 I do not intend to prejudge the past.
William Whitelaw (1918–) British politician.
Said on arriving in Ulster as Minister for Northern Ireland
The Times, 3 Dec 1973

4 No Jewish blood runs among my blood,
but I am as bitterly and hardly hated
by every anti-semite
as if I were a Jew. By this
I am a Russian.
Yevgeny Yevtushenko (1933–) Soviet poet.
Babi Yar

□ **PRESENT** □

See also future, opportunity, past, time

1 Happy the Man, and happy he alone,
He who can call today his own:
He who, secure within, can say,
Tomorrow do thy worst, for I have liv'd today.
John Dryden (1631–1700) British poet and dramatist.
Translation of Horace, III

2 Gather ye rosebuds while ye may,
Old time is still a-flying:

And this same flower that smiles today
Tomorrow will be dying.
Robert Herrick (1591–1674) English poet.
Hesperides, 'To the Virgins, to Make Much of Time'

3 *Carpe diem.*
Seize the day.
Horace (Quintus Horatius Flaccus; 65–8 BC) Roman poet.
Odes, I

4 Drop the question what tomorrow may bring,
and count as profit every day that Fate allows
you.
Horace
Odes, I

5 Believe each day that has dawned is your last.
Some hour to which you have not been looking
forward will prove lovely. As for me, if you want a
good laugh, you will come and find me fat and
sleek, in excellent condition, one of Epicurus'
herd of pigs.
Horace
Epistles, I

6 Redeem thy mis-spent time that's past;
Live this day, as if 'twere thy last.
Thomas Ken (1637–1711) English bishop.
A Morning Hymn

7 What is love? 'Tis not hereafter;
Present mirth hath present laughter;
What's to come is still unsure.
In delay there lies no plenty,
Then come kiss me, sweet and twenty;
Youth's a stuff will not endure.
William Shakespeare (1564–1616) English dramatist.
Twelfth Night, II:3

□ PRIDE □
See also conceit, egotism, self-respect

1 Pride goeth before destruction, and an haughty
spirit before a fall.
Bible: Proverbs
16:18

2 I know of no case where a man added to his
dignity by standing on it.
Winston Churchill (1874–1965) British politician.
Attrib.

3 We are not ashamed of what we have done,
because, when you have a great cause to fight
for, the moment of greatest humiliation is the
moment when the spirit is proudest.
Christabel Pankhurst (1880–1958) British suffragette.
Speech, Albert Hall, London, 19 Mar 1908

4 Of all the causes which conspire to blind
Man's erring judgment, and misguide the mind,
What the weak head with strongest bias rules,
Is Pride, the never-failing vice of fools.
Alexander Pope
An Essay on Criticism

5 There is false modesty, but there is no false pride.
Jules Renard (1894–1910) French writer.
Journal

□ PRINCIPLES □
See also integrity, morality

1 It is easier to fight for one's principles than to live
up to them.
Alfred Adler (1870–1937) Austrian psychiatrist.
Alfred Adler (P. Bottome)

2 If one sticks too rigidly to one's principles one
would hardly see anybody.
Agatha Christie (1891–1976) British detective-story writer.
Towards Zero, I

3 Whenever two good people argue over princi-
ples, they are both right.
Marie Ebner von Eschenbach (1830–1916) Austrian writer.
Aphorism

□ PRIVACY □

1 The house of every one is to him as his castle and
fortress.
Edward Coke (1552–1634) English lawyer and politician.
Semayne's Case

2 I never said, 'I want to be alone.' I only said, 'I
want to be *left* alone.' There is all the difference.
Greta Garbo (1905–90) Swedish-born US film star.
Garbo (John Bainbridge)

3 This is a free country, madam. We have a right to
share your privacy in a public place.
Peter Ustinov (1921–) British actor.
Romanoff and Juliet, I

□ PROCRASTINATION □

1 Give me chastity and continence, but not yet.
St Augustine of Hippo (354–430) Bishop of Hippo.
Confessions, Bk. VIII, Ch. 7

2 Procrastination is the thief of time.
Edward Young (1683–1765) British poet.
Night Thoughts

□ PROGRESS □
See also change, conservatism, improvement, innovation, novelty, technology

1 The people who live in the past must yield to the
people who live in the future. Otherwise the
world would begin to turn the other way round.
Arnold Bennett (1867–1931) British novelist.
Milestones

2 All progress is based upon a universal innate
desire on the part of every organism to live
beyond its income.
Samuel Butler (1835–1902) British writer.
Notebooks

3 As enunciated today, 'progress' is simply a comparative of which we have not settled the superlative.
G. K. Chesterton (1874–1936) British writer.
Heretics, Ch. 2

4 What we call progress is the exchange of one nuisance for another nuisance.
Havelock Ellis (1859–1939) British sexologist.
Attrib.

5 If I have seen further it is by standing on the shoulders of giants.
Isaac Newton (1642–1727) British scientist.
Letter to Robert Hooke, 5 Feb 1675

6 Man's 'progress' is but a gradual discovery that his questions have no meaning.
Antoine de Saint-Exupéry (1900–44) French novelist and aviator.
The Wisdom of the Sands

□ PROMISCUITY □

See also sex

1 I see – she's the original good time that was had by all.
Bette Davis (Ruth Elizabeth Davis; 1908–89) US film star.
Referring to a starlet of the time
The Filmgoer's Book of Quotes (Leslie Halliwell)

2 Lady Capricorn, he understood, was still keeping open bed.
Aldous Huxley (1894–1964) British novelist.
Antic Hay, Ch. 21

3 You were born with your legs apart. They'll send you to the grave in a Y-shaped coffin.
Joe Orton (1933–67) British dramatist.
What the Butler Saw, I

4 You know, she speaks eighteen languages. And she can't say 'No' in any of them.
Dorothy Parker (1893–1967) US writer.
Speaking of an acquaintance
Attrib.

5 I may be a prostitute, but I'm not promiscuous.
Barbra Streisand (1942–) US singer and film actress.
The Owl and the Pussycat

6 Prostitution is a blight on the human race…for if you men did not impose chastity on women as a necessary virtue while refusing to practise it yourselves, they would not be rejected by society for yielding to the sentiments of their hearts, nor would seduced, deceived and abandoned girls be forced into prostitution.
Flora Tristan (1803–44) French writer, feminist, and revolutionary socialist.
The London Journal of Flora Tristan

□ PROMISES □

1 Better is it that thou shouldest not vow, than that thou shouldest vow and not pay.
Bible: Ecclesiastes
5:5

2 The rule is, jam tomorrow and jam yesterday – but never jam today.
Lewis Carroll (Charles Lutwidge Dodgson; 1832–98) British writer.
Through the Looking-Glass, Ch. 5

3 A promise made is a debt unpaid.
Robert William Service (1874–1958) Canadian poet.
The Cremation of Sam McGee

4 Promises and pie-crust are made to be broken.
Jonathan Swift (1667–1745) Irish-born Anglican priest and writer.
Polite Conversation, Dialogue 1

□ PROMOTION □

See also patronage

1 Tired of knocking at Preferment's door.
Matthew Arnold (1822–88) British poet and critic.
The Scholar Gipsy

2 He had said he had known many kicked down stairs, but he never knew any kicked up stairs before.
Lord Halifax (1633–95) English statesman.
Original Memoirs (Burnet)

□ PROMPTNESS □

1 Punctuality is the politeness of kings.
Louis XVIII (1755–1824) French king.
Attrib.

2 He gives twice who gives promptly.
Publilius Syrus (1st century BC) Roman dramatist.
Attrib.

3 Punctuality is the virtue of the bored.
Evelyn Waugh (1903–66) British novelist.
Diaries, 'Irregular Notes', 26 Mar 1962

□ PRONUNCIATION □

See also class, language, speech, spelling

1 Everybody has a right to pronounce foreign names as he chooses.
Winston Churchill (1874–1965) British statesman.
The Observer, 'Sayings of the Week', 5 Aug 1951

2 They spell it Vinci and pronounce it Vinchy; foreigners always spell better than they pronounce.
Mark Twain (Samuel Langhorne Clemens; 1835–1910) US writer.
The Innocents Abroad, Ch. 19

□PROOF□

1 What is now proved was once only imagined.
William Blake (1757–1827) British poet.
The Marriage of Heaven and Hell, 'Proverbs of Hell'

2 If a man could pass through Paradise in a dream, and have a flower presented to him as a pledge that his soul had really been there, and if he found that flower in his hand when he awoke – Aye, and what then?
Samuel Taylor Coleridge (1772–1834) British poet.
Anima Poetae

3 Of course, before we *know* he is a saint, there will have to be miracles.
Graham Greene (1904–91) British novelist.
The Power and the Glory, Pt. IV

□PROPAGANDA□

1 Propaganda is that branch of the art of lying which consists in nearly deceiving your friends without quite deceiving your enemies.
F. M. Cornford (1886–1960) British poet.
New Statesman, 15 Sept 1978

2 The greater the lie, the greater the chance that it will be believed.
Adolf Hitler (1889–1945) German dictator.
Mein Kampf

□PROPHECY□

See also beginning, future

1 And there arose not a prophet since in Israel like unto Moses, whom the Lord knew face to face.
Bible: Deuteronomy
34:10

2 The lamps are going out over all Europe; we shall not see them lit again in our lifetime.
Lord Grey (1862–1933) British statesman.
Remark made on 3 Aug 1914, the eve of World War I

3 For not wanting to consent to the divorce, which then afterwards will be recognized as unworthy, the King of the islands will be forced to flee, and one put in his place who has no sign of kingship.
Nostradamus (1503–66) French astrologer.
Thought to refer to the abdication of Edward VIII
The Prophecies of Nostradamus, Century X, 22

4 The blood of the just will be demanded of London burnt by fire in three times twenty plus six. The ancient lady will fall from her high position, and many of the same denomination will be killed.
Nostradamus
Believed to refer to the Great Fire of London, 1666. The 'ancient lady' is interpreted as the Cathedral of St. Paul's, which was destroyed in the fire
The Prophecies of Nostradamus, Century II, 51

5 Beware the ides of March.
William Shakespeare (1564–1616) English dramatist.
Julius Caesar, I:2

6 Mr Turnbull had predicted evil consequences…and was now doing the best in his power to bring about the verification of his own prophecies.
Anthony Trollope (1815–82) British novelist.
Phineas Finn, Ch. 25

7 I see wars, horrible wars, and the Tiber foaming with
much blood.
Virgil (Publius Vergilius Maro; 70–19 BC) Roman poet.
Part of the Sibyl's prophecy to Aeneas, foretelling his difficulties in winning a home in Italy
Aeneid, Bk. VI

□PROSE□

See also books, criticism, fiction, literature, novels, poetry and prose, writing

1 Yet no one hears his own remarks as prose.
W. H. Auden (1907–73) British poet.
At a Party

2 Good heavens! I have been talking prose for over forty years without realizing it.
Molière (Jean Baptiste Poquelin; 1622–73) French dramatist.
Le Bourgeois Gentilhomme, II:4

□PROTESTANTISM□

See also Catholicism, Christianity, religion

1 The chief contribution of Protestantism to human thought is its massive proof that God is a bore.
H. L. Mencken (1880–1956) US journalist.
Notebooks, 'Minority Report'

2 Take heed of thinking. *The farther you go from the church of Rome, the nearer you are to God.*
Henry Wotton (1568–1639) English poet and diplomat.
Reliquiae Wottonianae (Izaak Walton)

□PROUST□
Marcel
(1871–1922) French novelist. His masterpiece was a series of partly autobiographical novels, *À la recherche du temps perdu* (1913–27), which give a detailed portrait of the life of his time.

QUOTATIONS ABOUT PROUST

1 Reading Proust is like bathing in someone else's dirty water.
Alexander Woollcott
Attrib.

QUOTATIONS BY PROUST

2 There can be no peace of mind in love, since the advantage one has secured is never anything but a fresh starting-point for further desires.
À la recherche du temps perdu: À l'ombre des jeunes filles en fleurs

3 As soon as one is unhappy one becomes moral.
À la recherche du temps perdu: À l'ombre des jeunes filles en fleurs

4 A PUSHING LADY. What are your views on love?
MME LEROI. Love? I make it constantly but I never talk about it.
À la recherche du temps perdu: Le Côté de Guermantes

5 It has been said that the highest praise of God consists in the denial of Him by the atheist, who finds creation so perfect that he can dispense with a creator.
À la recherche du temps perdu: Le Côté de Guermantes

6 I have a horror of sunsets, they're so romantic, so operatic.
À la recherche du temps perdu: Sodome et Gomorrhe

7 It is seldom indeed that one parts on good terms, because if one were on good terms one would not part.
À la recherche du temps perdu: La Prisonnière

8 One of those telegrams of which M. de Guermantes had wittily fixed the formula: 'Cannot come, lie follows'.
À la recherche du temps perdu: Le Temps retrouvé

9 Everything great in the world is done by neurotics; they alone founded our religions and created our masterpieces.
The Perpetual Pessimist (Sagittarius and George)

☐ PROVOCATION ☐

1 My wife hath something in her gizzard, that only waits an opportunity of being provoked to bring up.
Samuel Pepys (1633–1703) English diarist.
Diary, 17 June 1668

2 Ask you what provocation I have had? The strong antipathy of good to bad.
Alexander Pope (1688–1744) British poet.
Epilogue to the Satires, Dialogue II

☐ PRUDENCE ☐

See also caution, wisdom

1 It is always good
When a man has two irons in the fire.
Francis Beaumont (1584–1616) English dramatist.
The Faithful Friends, I:2

2 Put your trust in God, my boys, and keep your powder dry.
Valentine Blacker (1778–1823) British soldier.
Oliver Cromwell's Advice

3 Any girl who was a lady would not even think of having such a good time that she did not remember to hang on to her jewelry.
Anita Loos (1891–1981) US novelist.
Gentlemen Prefer Blondes, Ch. 4

4 Be nice to people on your way up because you'll meet 'em on your way down.
Wilson Mizner (1876–1933) US writer and wit.
Also attributed to Jimmy Durante
A Dictionary of Catch Phrases (Eric Partridge)

☐ PRUDERY ☐

See also censorship, pornography, puritanism

1 The perfect hostess will see to it that the works of male and female authors be properly separated on her bookshelves. Their proximity, unless they happen to be married, should not be tolerated.
Lady Gough
Etiquette

2 Would you allow your wife or your servant to read this book?
Mervyn Griffith-Jones (1909–78) British lawyer.
As counsel for the prosecution in the *Lady Chatterley's Lover* trial

3 Age will bring all things, and everyone knows, Madame, that twenty is no age to be a prude.
Molière (Jean Baptiste Poquelin; 1622–73) French dramatist.
Le Misanthrope, III:4

4 An orgy looks particularly alluring seen through the mists of righteous indignation.
Malcolm Muggeridge (1903–90) British writer.
The Most of Malcolm Muggeridge, 'Dolce Vita in a Cold Climate'

☐ PSYCHIATRY ☐

See also madness, neurosis, psychology

1 The psychic development of the individual is a short repetition of the course of development of the race.
Sigmund Freud (1856–1939) Austrian psychoanalyst.
Leonardo da Vinci

2 Anybody who goes to see a psychiatrist ought to have his head examined.
Samuel Goldwyn (Samuel Goldfish; 1882–1974) Polish-born US film producer.
Attrib.

3 If the nineteenth century was the age of the editorial chair, ours is the century of the psychiatrist's couch.
Marshall McLuhan (1911–81) Canadian sociologist.
Understanding Media, Introduction

4 A psychiatrist is a man who goes to the Folies-Bergère and looks at the audience.
Mervyn Stockwood (1913–) British churchman.
The Observer, 'Sayings of the Week', 15 Oct 1961

5 Psychiatrists classify a person as neurotic if he suffers from his problems in living, and a psychotic if he makes others suffer.
Thomas Szasz (1920–) US psychiatrist.
The Second Sin

6 A neurotic is the man who builds a castle in the air. A psychotic is the man who lives in it. And a psychiatrist is the man who collects the rent.
Lord Robert Webb-Johnstone (b. 1879)
Collected Papers

□PSYCHOLOGY□

See also mind, psychiatry

1 What progress we are making. In the Middle Ages they would have burned me. Now they are content with burning my books.
Sigmund Freud (1856–1939) Austrian psychoanalyst.
Referring to the public burning of his books in Berlin
Letter to Ernest Jones, 1933

2 I don't think the profession of historian fits a man for psychological analysis. In our work we have to deal only with simple feelings to which we give generic names such as Ambition and Interest.
Jean-Paul Sartre (1905–80) French writer.
Nausea

□PUBLIC□

See also class, majority

1 *Vox populi, vox dei.*
The voice of the people is the voice of God.
Alcuin (c. 735–804) English theologian.
Letter to Charlemagne

2 Our researchers into Public Opinion are content
That he held the proper opinions for the time of year;
When there was peace, he was for peace; when there was war, he went.
W. H. Auden (1907–73) British poet.
The Unknown Citizen

3 You cannot make a man by standing a sheep on its hind legs. But by standing a flock of sheep in that position you can make a crowd of men.
Max Beerbohm (1872–1956) British writer.
Zuleika Dobson, Ch. 9

4 The great Unwashed.
Henry Peter Brougham (1778–1868) Scottish lawyer and politician.
Attrib.

5 The public buys its opinions as it buys its meat, or takes in its milk, on the principle that it is cheaper to do this than to keep a cow. So it is, but the milk is more likely to be watered.
Samuel Butler (1835–1902) British writer.
Notebooks

6 The Public is an old woman. Let her maunder and mumble.
Thomas Carlyle (1795–1881) Scottish historian and essayist.
Journal, 1835

7 If by the people you understand the multitude, the *hoi polloi*, 'tis no matter what they think; they are sometimes in the right, sometimes in the wrong; their judgement is a mere lottery.
John Dryden (1631–1700) British poet and dramatist.
Essay of Dramatic Poesy

8 Ill fares the land, to hast'ning ills a prey,
Where wealth accumulates, and men decay;
Princes and lords may flourish, or may fade;
A breath can make them, as a breath has made;
But a bold peasantry, their country's pride,
When once destroy'd, can never be supplied.
Oliver Goldsmith (1728–74) Irish-born British writer.
The Deserted Village

9 There is not a more mean, stupid, dastardly, pitiful, selfish, spiteful, envious, ungrateful animal than the public. It is the greatest of cowards, for it is afraid of itself.
William Hazlitt (1778–1830) British essayist.
On Living to Oneself

10 Once the people begin to reason, all is lost.
Voltaire (François-Marie Arouet; 1694–1778) French writer.
Letter to Damilaville, 1 Apr 1766

11 The century on which we are entering – the century which will come out of this war – can be and must be the century of the common man.
Henry Wallace (1888–1965) US economist and politician.
Speech, 'The Price of Free World Victory', 8 May 1942

□PUBLIC HOUSES□

See also alcohol, drunkenness

1 A tavern chair is the throne of human felicity.
Samuel Johnson (1709–84) British lexicographer.
Johnsonian Miscellanies (ed. G. B. Hill), Vol. II

2 There is nothing which has yet been contrived by man, by which so much happiness is produced as by a good tavern or inn.
Samuel Johnson
Life of Johnson (J. Boswell), Vol. II

3 The hands of the clock have stayed still at half past eleven for fifty years. It is always opening time in the Sailors Arms.
Dylan Thomas (1914–53) Welsh poet.
Under Milk Wood

4 Come, Come, Come and have a drink with me
Down at the old 'Bull and Bush'.
Harry Tilzer (Albert von Tilzer; 1878–1956) British songwriter.
The Old Bull and Bush

□PUBLISHING□

See also books, editors

1 Publication is the male equivalent of childbirth.
Richard Acland (1906–) British politician and writer.
The Observer, 'Sayings of the Week', 19 May 1974

2 As repressed sadists are supposed to become
policemen or butchers so those with irrational
fear of life become publishers.
Cyril Connolly (1903–74) British journalist.
Enemies of Promise, Ch. 3

3 Let it be kept till the ninth year, the manuscript
put away at home: you may destroy whatever you
haven't published; once out, what you've said
can't be stopped.
Horace (Quintus Horatius Flaccus; 65–8 BC) Roman poet.
Ars Poetica

4 My own motto is publish and be sued.
Richard Ingrams (1937–) British editor.
Referring to his editorship of *Private Eye*
BBC radio broadcast, 4 May 1977

5 Publish and be damned!
Duke of Wellington (1769–1852) British general and
statesman.
On being offered the chance to avoid mention in the memoirs of
Harriette Wilson by giving her money
Attrib.

□ PUNISHMENT □

See also education, execution, imprisonment, retribution

1 When thou tillest the ground, it shall not hence-
forth yield unto thee her strength; a fugitive and
a vagabond shalt thou be in the earth.
And Cain said unto the Lord, My punishment is
greater than I can bear.
Bible: Genesis
4:12–13

2 Then the Lord rained upon Sodom and upon
Gomorrah brimstone and fire from the Lord out
of heaven.
Bible: Genesis
19:24

3 There is no peace, saith the Lord, unto the
wicked.
Bible: Isaiah
48:22

4 Love is a boy, by poets styl'd,
Then spare the rod, and spoil the child.
Samuel Butler (1612–80) English satirist.
Hudibras, Pt. II

5 Punishment is not for revenge, but to lessen
crime and reform the criminal.
Elizabeth Fry (1780–1845) British prison reformer.
Biography of Distinguished Women (Sarah Josepha Hale)

6 My object all sublime
I shall achieve in time –
To let the punishment fit the crime –
The punishment fit the crime.
W. S. Gilbert (1836–1911) British dramatist.
The Mikado, II

7 The billiard sharp whom any one catches,
His doom's extremely hard –
He's made to dwell –
In a dungeon cell
On a spot that's always barred.
And there he plays extravagant matches
In fitless finger-stalls
On a cloth untrue
With a twisted cue
And elliptical billiard balls.
W. S. Gilbert
The Mikado, II

8 Corporal punishment is as humiliating for him
who gives it as for him who receives it; it is inef-
fective besides. Neither shame nor physical pain
have any other effect than a hardening one…
Ellen Key (Karolina Sofia Key; 1849–1926) Swedish writer.
The Century of the Child, Ch. 8

9 The refined punishments of the spiritual mode
are usually much more indecent and dangerous
than a good smack.
D. H. Lawrence (1885–1930) British novelist.
Fantasia of the Unconscious, Ch. 4

□ PUNS □

See also humour

1 When I am dead, I hope it may be said:
'His sins were scarlet, but his books were read.'
Hilaire Belloc (1870–1953) French-born British poet.
Epigrams, 'On His Books'

2 VISITOR. Ah, Bottomley, sewing?
BOTTOMLEY. No, reaping.
Horatio William Bottomley (1860–1933) British newspaper
editor.
When found sewing mail bags
Horatio Bottomley (Julian Symons)

3 A man who could make so vile a pun would not
scruple to pick a pocket.
John Dennis (1657–1734) British critic and dramatist.
The Gentleman's Magazine, 1781

4 Any stigma will do to beat a dogma.
Philip Guedalla (1889–1944) British writer.
Attrib.

5 The love that loves a scarlet coat
Should be more uniform.
Thomas Hood (1799–1845) British poet.
Faithless Nelly Gray

6 Ben Battle was a soldier bold,
And used to war's alarms:
But a cannon-ball took off his legs,
So he laid down his arms!
Thomas Hood
Faithless Nelly Gray

7 You know it's hard to hear what a bearded man is saying. He can't speak above a whisker.
Herman J. Mankiewicz (1897–1953) US journalist and screenwriter.
Wit's End (R. E. Drennan)

8 What's a thousand dollars? Mere chicken feed. A poultry matter.
Groucho Marx (Julius Marx; 1895–1977) US comedian.
The Cocoanuts

9 It has been said that a bride's attitude towards her betrothed can be summed up in three words: Aisle. Altar. Hymn.
Frank Muir (1920–) British writer and broadcaster.
Upon My Word! (Frank Muir and Dennis Norden), 'A Jug of Wine'

10 You can lead a whore to culture but you can't make her think.
Dorothy Parker (1893–1967) US writer.
Speech to American Horticultural Society

11 You can't teach an old dogma new tricks.
Dorothy Parker
Wit's End (R. E. Drennan)

☐ PURITANISM ☐
See also prudery

1 A puritan's a person who pours righteous indignation into the wrong things.
G. K. Chesterton (1874–1936) British writer.
Attrib.

2 Puritanism – The haunting fear that someone, somewhere, may be happy.
H. L. Mencken (1880–1956) US journalist.
A Book of Burlesques

☐ PURITY ☐

1 I'm as pure as the driven slush.
Tallulah Bankhead (1903–68) US actress.
The Observer, 'Sayings of the Week', 24 Feb 1957

2 A simple maiden in her flower
Is worth a hundred coats-of-arms.
Alfred, Lord Tennyson (1809–92) British poet.
Lady Clara Vere de Vere, II

3 It is one of the superstitions of the human mind to have imagined that virginity could be a virtue.
Voltaire (François-Marie Arouet; 1694–1778) French writer.
Notebooks

4 I used to be Snow White…but I drifted.
Mae West (1892–1980) US actress.
The Wit and Wisdom of Mae West (ed. J. Weintraub)

☐ PURPOSE ☐
See also motive

1 The Answer to the Great Question Of…Life, the Universe and Everything…Is…Forty-two.
Douglas Adams (1952–) British writer.
The Hitch Hiker's Guide to the Galaxy, Ch. 27

2 Fortunately, in her kindness and patience, Nature has never put the fatal question as to the meaning of their lives into the mouths of most people. And where no one asks, no one needs to answer.
Carl Gustav Jung (1875–1961) Swiss psychoanalyst.
The Development of Personality

3 I go among the fields and catch a glimpse of a stoat or a fieldmouse peeping out of the withered grass – the creature hath a purpose and its eyes are bright with it. I go amongst the buildings of a city and I see a man hurrying along – to what? the Creature has a purpose and his eyes are bright with it.
John Keats (1795–1821) British poet.
Letter, 1819

4 Riddle of destiny, who can show
What thy short visit meant, or know
What thy errand here below?
Charles Lamb (1775–1834) British essayist.
On an Infant Dying as soon as Born

5 It should not merely be useful and ornamental; it should preach a high moral lesson.
Lytton Strachey (1880–1932) British writer.
Referring to Prince Albert's plans for the Great Exhibition
Queen Victoria, Ch. 4

Q

□ QUOTATIONS □

See also misquotations

1　It is a good thing for an uneducated man to read books of quotations.
Winston Churchill (1874–1965) British statesman.
My Early Life, Ch. 9

2　We prefer to believe that the absence of inverted commas guarantees the originality of a thought, whereas it may be merely that the utterer has forgotten its source.
Clifton Fadiman (1904–) US writer.
Any Number Can Play

3　Every quotation contributes something to the stability or enlargement of the language.
Samuel Johnson (1709–84) British lexicographer.
Dictionary of the English Language

4　To be amused at what you read – that is the great spring of happy quotation.
C. E. Montague (1867–1928) British editor and writer.
A Writer's Notes on his Trade

5　If with the literate I am
Impelled to try an epigram
I never seek to take the credit
We all assume that Oscar said it.
Dorothy Parker (1893–1967) US writer.
Oscar Wilde

6　The devil can cite Scripture for his purpose.
William Shakespeare (1564–1616) English dramatist.
The Merchant of Venice, I:3

7　It's better to be quotable than to be honest.
Tom Stoppard (1937–) Czech-born British dramatist.
The Guardian

8　In the dying world I come from quotation is a national vice. It used to be the classics, now it's lyric verse.
Evelyn Waugh (1903–66) British novelist.
The Loved One

9　The nicest thing about quotes is that they give us a nodding acquaintance with the originator which is often socially impressive.
Kenneth Williams (1926–88) British comic actor
Acid Drops

R

☐ RABBITS ☐

See also animals

1 The rabbit has a charming face;
Its private life is a disgrace.
Anonymous
The Rabbit

2 I shall tell you a tale of four little rabbits whose
names were Flopsy, Mopsy, Cottontail and Peter.
Beatrix Potter (1866–1943) British children's writer.
The Tale of Peter Rabbit

☐ RABELAIS ☐
François
(1483–1553) French humanist and satirist. He is best known for
his *Pantagruel* (1532) and *Gargantua* (1534), which are
renowned for their bawdiness.

QUOTATIONS ABOUT RABELAIS

1 Appetite comes with eating.
Gargantua, Bk. I, Ch. 5

2 In their rules there was only one clause: Do what
you will.
Referring to the fictional Abbey of Thélème.
Gargantua, Bk. I, Ch. 57

3 Man never found the deities so kindly
As to assure him that he'd live tomorrow.
Pantagruel, Bk. III, Ch. 2

4 Nature abhors a vacuum.
Attrib.

5 I owe much; I have nothing; the rest I leave to the
poor.
Last words.
Attrib.

☐ RACISM ☐

See also equality, freedom, human rights, Jews, oppression,
prejudice, slavery

1 The future is…black.
James Baldwin
The Observer, 'Sayings of the Week', 25 Aug 1963

2 People think we do not understand our black and
coloured countrymen. But there is a special relationship between us.
Elize Botha Wife of South African President, P. W. Botha.
Remark, May 1987

3 To like an individual because he's black is just as
insulting as to dislike him because he isn't white.
e. e. cummings (1894–1962) US poet.
Attrib.

4 I suffer from an incurable disease – colour blind-
ness.
Joost de Blank (1908–68) Dutch-born British churchman.
Attrib.

5 The so-called white races are really pinko-gray.
E. M. Forster (1879–1970) British novelist.
A Passage to India, Ch. 7

6 When the white man came we had the land and
they had the Bibles; now they have the land and
we have the Bibles.
Dan George (1899–1982) Canadian Indian chief.
Attrib.

7 All those who are not racially pure are mere
chaff.
Adolf Hitler (1889–1945) German dictator.
Mein Kampf, Ch. 2

8 A coloured man can tell, in five seconds dead,
whether a white man likes him or not. If the
white man *says* he does, he is instantly – and usually quite rightly – mistrusted.
Colin MacInnes (1914–76) British novelist.
England, Half English, 'A Short Guide for Jumbles'

9 The soil of our country [South Africa] is destined
to be the scene of the fiercest fight and the sharp-
est struggles to rid our continent of the last ves-
tiges of white minority rule.
Nelson Mandela (1918–) South African lawyer and
politician.
Said, June 1980

10 I have cherished the ideal of a democratic and
free society in which all persons live together in
harmony and with equal opportunites…if needs
be, it is an ideal for which I am prepared to die.
Nelson Mandela
Speech, 11 Feb 1990, after his release from prison. Mandela was
reiterating his words at his trial in 1964

11 One of the things that makes a Negro unpleasant
to white folk is the fact that he suffers from their
injustice. He is thus a standing rebuke to them.
H. L. Mencken (1880–1956) US journalist.
Notebooks, 'Minority Report'

12 He's really awfully fond of coloured people. Well,
he says himself, he wouldn't have white servants.
Dorothy Parker (1893–1967) US writer.
Arrangements in Black and White

13 He liked to patronise coloured people and
treated them as equals because he was quite
sure they were not.
Bertrand Russell (1872–1970) British philosopher.
The Autobiography of Bertrand Russell

14 We don't want apartheid liberalized. We want it dismantled. You can't improve something that is intrinsically evil.
Bishop Desmond Tutu (1931–) South African clergyman.
The Observer, 'Sayings of the Week', 10 Mar 1985

15 It seems that the British Government sees black people as expendable.
Bishop Desmond Tutu
Speech, June 1986

☐ READING ☐

See also books, criticism, fiction, literacy, literature, novels, writing

1 Reading maketh a full man; conference a ready man; and writing an exact man.
Francis Bacon (1561–1626) English philosopher.
Essays, 'Of Studies'

2 He has only half learned the art of reading who has not added to it the even more refined accomplishments of skipping and skimming.
Arthur Balfour (1848–1930) British statesman.
Mr. Balfour (E. T. Raymond)

3 I read, much of the night, and go south in the winter.
T. S. Eliot (1888–1965) US-born British poet and dramatist.
The Waste Land, 'The Burial of the Dead'

4 Reading is sometimes an ingenious device for avoiding thought.
Arthur Helps (1813–75) British historian.
Friends in Council

5 A man ought to read just as inclination leads him; for what he reads as a task will do him little good.
Samuel Johnson (1709–84) British lexicographer.
Life of Johnson (J. Boswell), Vol. I

6 I love to lose myself in other men's minds. When I am not walking, I am reading; I cannot sit and think. Books think for me.
Charles Lamb (1775–1834) British essayist.
Last Essays of Elia, 'Detached Thoughts on Books and Reading'

7 There are two motives for reading a book: one, that you enjoy it, the other that you can boast about it.
Bertrand Russell (1872–1970) British philosopher.
The Conquest of Happiness

8 People say that life is the thing, but I prefer reading.
Logan Pearsall Smith (1865–1946) US writer.
Afterthoughts, 'Myself'

9 Reading is to the mind what exercise is to the body.
Richard Steele (1672–1729) Dublin-born British essayist.
The Tatler, 147

10 I have led a life of business so long that I have lost my taste for reading, and now – what shall I do?
Horace Walpole (1717–97) British writer.
Thraliana (K. Balderston)

☐ REALISM ☐

1 Mr Lely, I desire you would use all your skill to paint my picture truly like me, and not flatter me at all; but remark all these roughnesses, pimples, warts, and everything as you see me, otherwise I will never pay a farthing for it.
Oliver Cromwell (1599–1658) English soldier and statesman.
The origin of the expression 'warts and all'
Anecdotes of Painting (Horace Walpole), Ch. 12

2 If at first you don't succeed, try, try again. Then quit. No use being a damn fool about it.
W. C. Fields (1880–1946) US actor.

☐ REALITY ☐

1 Human kind
Cannot bear very much reality.
T. S. Eliot (1888–1965) US-born British poet and dramatist.
Four Quartets, 'Burnt Norton'

2 I fancy, for myself, that they are rather out of touch with reality; by reality I mean shops like Selfridges, and motor buses, and the *Daily Express*.
T. E. Lawrence (1888–1935) British soldier and writer.
Referring to expatriate authors living in Paris, such as James Joyce
Letter to W. Hurley, 1 Apr 1929

3 If this were play'd upon a stage now, I could condemn it as an improbable fiction.
William Shakespeare (1564–1616) English dramatist.
Twelfth Night, III:4

☐ REASON ☐

See also motive

1 Reason is itself a matter of faith. It is an act of faith to assert that our thoughts have any relation to reality at all.
G. K. Chesterton (1874–1936) British writer.
Orthodoxy, Ch. 3

2 A man who does not lose his reason over certain things has none to lose.
Gotthold Ephraim Lessing (1729–81) German dramatist.
Emilia Galotti, IV:7

☐ REBELLION ☐

See also revolution

1 The defiance of established authority, religious and secular, social and political, as a world-wide phenomenon may well one day be accounted the outstanding event of the last decade.
Hannah Arendt (1906–75) German-born US philosopher and historian.
Crises of the Republic, 'Civil Disobedience'

2 When the People contend for their Liberty, they seldom get anything by their Victory but new masters.
Lord Halifax (1633–95) English statesman.
Political, Moral, and Miscellaneous Thoughts and Reflections

3 A little rebellion now and then is a good thing.
Thomas Jefferson (1743–1826) US statesman.
Letter to James Madison, 30 Jan 1787

4 Angry Young Man.
Leslie Paul (1905–85) British writer.
Book title

☐**REGRET**☐

See also apologies, memory, mourning, nostalgia, past, sorrow

1 One doesn't recognize in one's life the really important moments – not until it's too late.
Agatha Christie (1891–1976) British detective-story writer.
Endless Night, Bk. II, Ch. 14

2 Were it not better to forget
Than but remember and regret?
Letitia Landon (1802–38) British poet and novelist.
Despondency

3 We might have been – These are but common words,
And yet they make the sum of life's bewailing.
Letitia Landon
Three Extracts from the Diary of a Week

4 Make it a rule of life never to regret and never to look back. Regret is an appalling waste of energy; you can't build on it; it's only good for wallowing in.
Katherine Mansfield (1888–1923) New Zealand-born British writer.
Attrib.

5 Good-bye, I've barely said a word to you, it is always like that at parties, we never see the people, we never say the things we should like to say, but it is the same everywhere in this life. Let us hope that when we are dead things will be better arranged.
Marcel Proust (1871–1922) French novelist.
À la recherche du temps perdu: Sodome et Gomorrhe

6 But with the morning cool repentance came.
Walter Scott (1771–1832) Scottish novelist.
Rob Roy, Ch. 12

7 Things sweet to taste prove in digestion sour.
William Shakespeare (1564–1616) English dramatist.
Richard II, I:3

8 O, pardon me, thou bleeding piece of earth,
That I am meek and gentle with these butchers!
Thou art the ruins of the noblest man
That ever lived in the tide of times.
William Shakespeare
Julius Caesar, III:1

9 When to the sessions of sweet silent thought
I summon up remembrance of things past,
I sigh the lack of many a thing I sought,
And with old woes new wail my dear time's waste.
William Shakespeare
Sonnet 30

10 Had I but serv'd my God with half the zeal
I serv'd my King, he would not in mine age
Have left me naked to mine enemies.
William Shakespeare
Henry VIII, III:2

11 The bitterest tears shed over graves are for words left unsaid and deeds left undone.
Harriet Beecher Stowe (1811–96) US novelist.
Little Foxes, Ch. 3

12 Though nothing can bring back the hour
Of splendour in the grass, of glory in the flower;
We will grieve not, rather find
Strength in what remains behind…
William Wordsworth (1770–1850) British poet.
Ode. Intimations of Immortality, IX

☐**RELIGION**☐

See also atheism, belief, Bible, Catholicism, Christianity, Christmas, Church, damnation, devil, doomsday, faith, God, heaven, hell, Jews, martyrdom, prayer, Protestantism, Sunday

1 There is no salvation outside the church.
St Augustine of Hippo (354–430) Bishop of Hippo.
De Bapt., IV

2 The Jews and Arabs should sit down and settle their differences like good Christians.
Warren Austin (1877–1962) US politician and diplomat.
Attrib.

3 [INDIGESTION], n. A disease which the patient and his friends frequently mistake for deep religious conviction and concern for the salvation of mankind. As the simple Red Man of the western wild put it, with, it must be confessed, a certain force: 'Plenty well, no pray; big bellyache, heap God.'
Ambrose Bierce (1842–?1914) US writer and journalist.
The Devil's Dictionary

4 This Ariyan Eightfold Path, that is to say: Right view, right aim, right speech, right action, right living, right effort, right mindfulness, right contemplation.
Buddha (Gautama Siddhartha; c. 563–c. 483 BC) Indian religious teacher.
Some Sayings of the Buddha (F. L. Woodward)

5 Man is by his constitution a religious animal.
Edmund Burke (1729–97) British politician.
Reflections on the Revolution in France

6 One religion is as true as another.
Robert Burton (1577–1640) English scholar and explorer.
Anatomy of Melancholy, Pt. III

7 To be at all is to be religious more or less.
Samuel Butler (1835–1902) British writer.
Notebooks

8 The idea that only a male can represent Christ at the altar is a most serious heresy.
Dr George Carey (1935–) British churchman and Archbishop of Canterbury (1991–).
Reader's Digest, Apr 1991

9 Religion is by no means a proper subject of conversation in a mixed company.
Earl of Chesterfield (1694–1773) English statesman.
Letter to his godson

10 Men will wrangle for religion; write for it; fight for it; anything but – live for it.
Charles Caleb Colton (?1780–1832) British clergyman and writer.
Lacon, Vol. I

11 'Sensible men are all of the same religion.' 'And pray what is that?' inquired the prince. 'Sensible men never tell.'
Benjamin Disraeli (1804–81) British statesman.
Endymion, Bk. I, Ch. 81

12 Science without religion is lame, religion without science is blind.
Albert Einstein (1879–1955) German-born US physicist.
Out of My Later Years

13 The religions we call false were once true.
Ralph Waldo Emerson (1803–82) US poet and essayist.
Essays, 'Character'

14 Religion is an illusion and it derives its strength from the fact that it falls in with our instinctual desires.
Sigmund Freud (1856–1939) Austrian psychoanalyst.
New Introductory Lectures on Psychoanalysis, 'A Philosophy of Life'

15 Religion
Has made an honest woman of the supernatural,
And we won't have it kicking over the traces again.
Christopher Fry (1907–) British dramatist.
The Lady's Not for Burning, II

16 As I take my shoes from the shoemaker, and my coat from the tailor, so I take my religion from the priest.
Oliver Goldsmith (1728–74) Irish-born British writer.
Life of Johnson (J. Boswell)

17 Pray, good people, be civil. I am the Protestant whore.
Nell Gwyn (1650–87) English actress.
On being surrounded in her coach by an angry mob in Oxford at the time of the Popish Plot
Nell Gwyn (Bevan), Ch. 13

18 To become a popular religion, it is only necessary for a superstition to enslave a philosophy.
Dean Inge (1860–1954) British churchman.
Outspoken Essays

19 Many people believe that they are attracted by God, or by Nature, when they are only repelled by man.
Dean Inge
More Lay Thoughts of a Dean

20 Many people think they have religion when they are troubled with dyspepsia.
Robert G. Ingersoll (1833–99) US lawyer and agnostic.
Liberty of Man, Woman and Child, Section 3

21 The month of Ramadan shall ye fast, in which the Koran was sent down from heaven, a direction unto men, and declarations of direction, and the distinction between good and evil.
Koran
Ch. II

22 But I suppose even God was born
too late to trust the old religion –
all those setting out
that never left the ground,
beginning in wisdom, dying in doubt.
Robert Lowell (1917–77) US poet.
Tenth Muse

23 Religion…is the opium of the people.
Karl Marx (1818–83) German philosopher and revolutionary.
Criticism of the Hegelian Philosophy of Right, Introduction

24 Things have come to a pretty pass when religion is allowed to invade the sphere of private life.
Lord Melbourne (1779–1848) British statesman.
Attrib.

25 There is a very good saying that if triangles invented a god, they would make him three-sided.
Baron de Montesquieu (1689–1755) French writer.
Lettres persanes

26 There's no reason to bring religion into it. I think we ought to have as great a regard for religion as we can, so as to keep it out of as many things as possible.
Sean O'Casey (1884–1964) Irish dramatist.
The Plough and the Stars, I

27 Organized religion is making Christianity political rather than making politics Christian.
Laurens Van der Post (1906–) South African novelist.
The Observer, 'Sayings of the Week', 9 Nov 1986

28 Unlike Christianity, which preached a peace that it never achieved, Islam unashamedly came with a sword.
Steven Runciman (1903–) British academic and diplomat.
A History of the Crusades, 'The First Crusade'

29 Whenever a man talks loudly against religion, – always suspect that it is not his reason, but his passions which have got the better of his creed.
Laurence Sterne (1713–68) Irish-born British writer.
Tristram Shandy

30 Rock of ages, cleft for me,
Let me hide myself in Thee.
Augustus Montague Toplady (1740–78) British hymn writer.
Rock of Ages

31 Beware when you take on the Church of God. Others have tried and have bitten the dust.
Bishop Desmond Tutu (1931–) South African clergyman.
Speech, Apr 1987

32 Jesus loves me – this I know,
For the Bible tells me so.
Susan Warner (1819–85) US novelist.
The Love of Jesus

33 Our God, our help in ages past,
Our hope for years to come,
Our shelter from the stormy blast,
And our eternal home.
Isaac Watts
Our God, Our Help in Ages Past

34 I have noticed again and again since I have been in the Church that lay interest in ecclesiastical matters is often a prelude to insanity.
Evelyn Waugh (1903–66) British novelist.
Decline and Fall, Pt. I, Ch. 8

35 There is a species of person called a 'Modern Churchman' who draws the full salary of a beneficed clergyman and need not commit himself to any religious belief.
Evelyn Waugh
Decline and Fall, Pt. II, Ch. 4

36 Religion is love; in no case is it logic.
Beatrice Webb (1858–1943) British economist and writer.
My Apprenticeship, Ch. 2

37 Why do born-again people so often make you wish they'd never been born the first time?
Katherine Whitehorn (1926–) British journalist.
The Observer, 20 May 1979

38 'God knows how you Protestants can be expected to have any sense of direction,' she said. 'It's different with us, I haven't been to mass for years, I've got every mortal sin on my conscience, but I know when I'm doing wrong. I'm still a Catholic, it's there, nothing can take it away from me.' 'Of course, duckie,' said Jeremy... 'once a Catholic always a Catholic.'
Angus Wilson (1913–92) British novelist.
The Wrong Set

39 The Ethiopians say that their gods are snub-nosed and black, the Thracians that theirs have light blue eyes and red hair.
Xenophanes (c. 560–c. 478 BC) Greek poet and philosopher.
Fragment 15

40 No Jew was ever fool enough to turn Christian unless he was a clever man.
Israel Zangwill (1864–1926) British writer.
Children of the Ghetto, Ch. 1

☐ REMEDIES ☐

See also doctors, drugs, health and healthy living, illness, medicine

1 Cure the disease and kill the patient.
Francis Bacon (1561–1626) English philosopher.
Essays, 'Of Friendship'

2 The remedy is worse than the disease.
Francis Bacon
Essays, 'Of Seditions and Troubles'

3 And besought him that they might only touch the hem of his garment: and as many as touched were made perfectly whole.
Bible: Matthew
14:36

4 Well, now, there's a remedy for everything except death.
Miguel de Cervantes (1547–1616) Spanish novelist.
Don Quixote, Pt. II, Ch. 10

5 When a lot of remedies are suggested for a disease, that means it can't be cured.
Anton Chekhov (1860–1904) Russian dramatist.
The Cherry Orchard, II

6 Extreme remedies are most appropriate for extreme diseases.
Hippocrates (c. 460–c. 377 BC) Greek physician.
Aphorisms, I

7 As soon as he ceased to be mad he became merely stupid. There are maladies we must not seek to cure because they alone protect us from others that are more serious.
Marcel Proust (1871–1922) French novelist.
À la recherche du temps perdu: Le Côté de Guermantes

8 Our body is a machine for living. It is organized for that, it is its nature. Let life go on in it unhindered and let it defend itself, it will do more than if you paralyse it by encumbering it with remedies.
Leo Tolstoy (1828–1910) Russian writer.
War and Peace, Bk. X, Ch. 29

9 There is only one cure for grey hair. It was invented by a Frenchman. It is called the guillotine.
P. G. Wodehouse (1881–1975) British humorous novelist.
The Old Reliable

☐ RENUNCIATION ☐

See also dismissal

1 Renounce the devil and all his works.
The Book of Common Prayer
Publick Baptism of Infants

2 I'll break my staff,
Bury it certain fathoms in the earth,
And deeper than did ever plummet sound
I'll drown my book.
William Shakespeare (1564–1616) English dramatist.
The Tempest, V:1

☐ REPRESENTATION ☐

1 Taxation without representation is tyranny.
James Otis (1725–83) US political activist.
As 'No taxation without representation' this became the principal
slogan of the American Revolution
Attrib.

2 No annihilation without representation.
Arnold Toynbee (1889–1975) British historian.
Urging the need for a greater British influence in the UN 1947

☐ REPUBLIC ☐

See also democracy, State

1 Our object in the construction of the state is the
greatest happiness of the whole, and not that of
any one class.
Plato (429–347 BC) Greek philosopher.
Republic, Bk. 4

2 As there was no form of government common to
the peoples thus segregated, nor tie of language,
history, habit, or belief, they were called a Republic.
Evelyn Waugh (1903–66) British novelist.
Scoop, Bk. II, Ch. 1

☐ REPUTATION ☐

See also fame, posterity

1 I hold it as certain, that no man was ever written
out of reputation but by himself.
Richard Bentley (1662–1742) English academic.
The Works of Alexander Pope (W. Warburton), Vol. IV

2 Reputation is a bubble which bursts when a man
tries to blow it up for himself.
Emma Carleton
Attrib.

3 Until you've lost your reputation, you never real-
ize what a burden it was or what freedom really is.
Margaret Mitchell (1909–49) US novelist.
Gone with the Wind

4 Reputation, reputation, reputation! O, I have lost
my reputation! I have lost the immortal part of
myself, and what remains is bestial.
William Shakespeare (1564–1616) English dramatist.
Othello, II:3

5 Good name in man and woman, dear my lord,
Is the immediate jewel of their souls:
Who steals my purse steals trash; 'tis something,
nothing;
'Twas mine, 'tis his, and has been slave to thou-
sands;

But he that filches from me my good name
Robs me of that which not enriches him
And makes me poor indeed.
William Shakespeare
Othello, III:3

6 The purest treasure mortal times afford
Is spotless reputation; that away,
Men are but gilded loam or painted clay.
William Shakespeare
Richard II, I:1

7 I'm called away by particular business. But I
leave my character behind me.
Richard Brinsley Sheridan (1751–1816) British dramatist.
The School for Scandal, II

☐ RESEARCH ☐

1 Research! A mere excuse for idleness; it has
never achieved, and will never achieve any
results of the slightest value.
Benjamin Jowett (1817–93) British theologian.
Unforgotten Years (Logan Pearsall Smith)

2 The aim of research is the discovery of the equa-
tions which subsist between the elements of
phenomena.
Ernst Mach (1838–1916) Austrian physicist and philosopher.
Popular Scientific Lectures

3 The outcome of any serious research can only be
to make two questions grow where only one
grew before.
Thorstein Bunde Veblen (1857–1929) US social scientist.
The Place of Science in Modern Civilization

☐ RESPECT ☐

See also courtesy, self-respect

1 Let them hate, so long as they fear.
Lucius Accius (170–c. 85 BC) Roman tragic playwright.
Atreus, 'Seneca'

2 We owe respect to the living; to the dead we owe
only truth.
Voltaire (François-Marie Arouet; 1694–1778) French writer.
Oeuvres, 'Première lettre sur Oedipe'

☐ RESPECTABILITY ☐

1 Since when was genius found respectable?
Elizabeth Barrett Browning (1806–61) British poet.
Aurora Leigh, Bk. VI

2 Respectable means rich, and decent means poor.
I should die if I heard my family called decent.
Thomas Love Peacock (1785–1866) British novelist.
Crotchet Castle, Ch. 3

3 So live that you wouldn't be ashamed to sell the
family parrot to the town gossip.
Will Rogers (1879–1935) US actor and humorist.
Attrib.

☐RESPONSIBILITY☐

See also accusation

1 What the proprietorship of these papers is aiming at is power, and power without responsibility – the prerogative of the harlot through the ages.
Stanley Baldwin (1867–1947) British statesman.
Attacking the press barons Lords Rothermere and Beaverbrook.
It was first used by KIPLING. *See also* STOPPARD
Speech, election rally, 18 Mar 1931

2 Each man the architect of his own fate.
Appius Caecus (4th–3rd century BC) Roman statesman.
De Civitate (Sallust), Bk. I

3 Perhaps it is better to be irresponsible and right than to be responsible and wrong.
Winston Churchill
Party Political Broadcast, London, 26 Aug 1950

4 It matters not how strait the gate,
How charged with punishments the scroll,
I am the master of my fate:
I am the captain of my soul.
William Ernest Henley (1849–1903) British writer.
Echoes, IV, 'Invictus. In Mem. R.T.H.B.'

5 Power without responsibility – the prerogative of the harlot throughout the ages.
Rudyard Kipling (1865–1936) Indian-born British writer.
Better known for its subsequent use by BALDWIN
Attrib.

6 The salvation of mankind lies only in making everything the concern of all.
Alexander Solzhenitsyn (1918–) Soviet novelist.
Nobel Lecture, 1970

7 The House of Lords, an illusion to which I have never been able to subscribe – responsibility without power, the prerogative of the eunuch throughout the ages.
Tom Stoppard (1937–) Czech-born British dramatist.
See also BALDWIN
Lord Malquist and Mr Moon, Pt. VI, Ch. 1

8 For man is man and master of his fate.
Alfred, Lord Tennyson (1809–92) British poet.
Idylls of the King, 'The Marriage of Geraint'

9 The buck stops here.
Harry S. Truman (1884–1972) US statesman.
Sign kept on his desk during his term as president
Presidential Anecdotes (P. Boller)

☐REST☐

See also bed, idleness, leisure, sleep

1 Unarm, Eros; the long day's task is done,
And we must sleep.
William Shakespeare (1564–1616) English dramatist.
Antony and Cleopatra, IV:12

2 It is well to lie fallow for a while.
Martin Farquhar Tupper (1810–89) British writer.
Proverbial Philosophy, 'Of Recreation'

☐RESULTS☐

1 Ye shall know them by their fruits. Do men gather grapes of thorns, or figs of thistles? Even so every good tree bringeth forth good fruit; but a corrupt tree bringeth forth evil fruit. A good tree cannot bring forth evil fruit, neither can a corrupt tree bring forth good fruit. Every tree that bringeth not forth good fruit is hewn down, and cast into the fire. Wherefore by their fruits ye shall know them.
Bible: Matthew
7:16–20

2 Our love of what is beautiful does not lead to extravagance; our love of the things of the mind does not make us soft.
Pericles (c. 495–429 BC) Greek statesman.
Part of the funeral oration, 430 BC, for the dead of the first year of the Peloponnesian War
Attrib. in *Histories* Bk. II, Ch. 40 (Thucydides)

3 What dire offence from am'rous causes springs,
What mighty contests rise from trivial things.
Alexander Pope (1688–1744) British poet.
The Rape of the Lock, I

☐RETRIBUTION☐

See also punishment, revenge

1 *Nemo me impune lacessit.*
No one provokes me with impunity.
Anonymous
Motto of the Crown of Scotland

2 And if any mischief follow, then thou shalt give life for life,
Eye for eye, tooth for tooth, hand for hand, foot for foot,
Burning for burning, wound for wound, stripe for stripe.
Bible: Exodus
21:23–25

3 For they have sown the wind, and they shall reap the whirlwind: it hath no stalk: the bud shall yield no meal: if so be it yield, the strangers shall swallow it up.
Bible: Hosea
8:7

4 And if thy right eye offend thee, pluck it out, and cast it from thee: for it is profitable for thee that one of thy members should perish, and not that thy whole body should be cast into hell.
Bible: Matthew
5:29

5 For thou shalt heap coals of fire upon his head, and the Lord shall reward thee.
Bible: Proverbs
25:22

6 But men never violate the laws of God without
suffering the consequences, sooner or later.
Lydia M. Child (1802–80) US abolitionist campaigner.
The Freedmen's Book, 'Toussaint L'Ouverture'

□ RETURN □

1 Poor wandering one!
Though thou hast surely strayed,
Take heart of grace,
Thy steps retrace,
Poor wandering one!
W. S. Gilbert (1836–1911) British dramatist.
The Pirates of Penzance, I

2 Better lo'ed ye canna be,
Will ye no come back again?
Carolina Nairne (1766–1845) Scottish songwriter.
Referring to Bonnie Prince Charlie
Bonnie Charlie's now awa!

□ REVENGE □

See also retribution

1 Revenge is a kind of wild justice; which the more
man's nature runs to, the more ought law to
weed it out.
Francis Bacon (1561–1626) English philosopher.
Essays, 'Of Revenge'

2 A man that studieth revenge keeps his own
wounds green.
Francis Bacon
Essays, 'Of Revenge'

3 Perish the Universe, provided I have my revenge.
Cyrano de Bergerac (1619–55) French writer.
La Mort d'Agrippine, IV

4 And the Lord said unto him, Therefore whoso-
ever slayeth Cain, vengeance shall be taken on
him sevenfold. And the Lord set a mark upon
Cain, lest any finding him should kill him.
And Cain went out from the presence of the
Lord, and dwelt in the land of Nod, on the east of
Eden.
Bible: Genesis
4:15–16

5 No one delights more in vengeance than a
woman.
Juvenal (Decimus Junius Juvenalis; 60–130 AD) Roman satirist.
Satires, XIII

6 Revenge, at first though sweet,
Bitter ere long back on itself recoils.
John Milton (1608–74) English poet.
Paradise Lost, Bk. IX

□ REVOLUTION □

See also French Revolution, rebellion, Russian Revolution

1 Inferiors revolt in order that they may be equal
and equals that they may be superior. Such is the
state of mind which creates revolutions.
Aristotle (384–322 BC) Greek philosopher.
Politics, Bk. V

2 All modern revolutions have ended in a reinforce-
ment of the power of the State.
Albert Camus (1913–60) French existentialist writer.
The Rebel

3 Revolution is not the uprising against pre-
existing order, but the setting-up of a new order
contradictory to the traditional one.
José Ortega y Gasset (1883–1955) Spanish philosopher.
The Revolt of the Masses, Ch. 6

4 Revolutions are always verbose.
Leon Trotsky (Lev Davidovich Bronstein; 1879–1940) Russian
revolutionary.
History of the Russian Revolution, Pt. II, Ch. 12

5 Revolution by its very nature is sometimes compelled to take in more territory than it is capable
of holding. Retreats are possible – when there is
territory to retreat from.
Leon Trotsky
Diary in Exile, 15 Feb 1935

6 The word 'revolution' is a word for which you
kill, for which you die, for which you send the
labouring masses to their death, but which does
not possess any content.
Simone Weil (1909–43) French philosopher.
Oppression and Liberty, 'Reflections Concerning the Causes of
Liberty and Social Oppression'

7 We invented the Revolution
but we don't know how to run it.
Peter Weiss (1916–82) German novelist and dramatist.
Marat Sade, 15

□ RIDICULE □

See also satire

1 It often happens, that he who endeavours to ridicule other people, especially in things of a serious nature, becomes himself a jest, and
frequently to his great cost.
Giovanni Boccaccio (1313–75) Italian writer and poet.
Decameron, 'Second Day'

2 Ridicule often checks what is absurd, and fully as
often smothers that which is noble.
Walter Scott (1771–1832) Scottish novelist.
Quentin Durward

□ RIGHT □

1 A child becomes an adult when he realizes that
   he has a right not only to be right but also to be
   wrong.
   Thomas Szasz (1920–) US psychiatrist.
   The Second Sin

2 While I'd rather be right than president, at any
   time I'm ready to be both.
   Norman M. Thomas (1884–1968) US politician.
   Referring to his lack of success in presidential campaigns. The
   expression 'I'd rather be right than president' is also attributed to
   the US politician Henry Clay (1777–1852)
   Come to Judgment (A. Whitman)

3 Right is more precious than peace.
   Woodrow Wilson (1856–1925) US statesman.
   Radio Times, 10 Sept 1964

□ RIGHTEOUSNESS □

See also good, integrity, morality, virtue

1 The eternal *not ourselves* that makes for
   righteousness.
   Matthew Arnold (1822–88) British poet and critic.
   Literature and Dogma, Ch. 8

2 Righteous people terrify me…Virtue is its own
   punishment.
   Aneurin Bevan (1897–1960) British Labour politician.
   Aneurin Bevan 1897–1945 (Michael Foot)

3 Ye must leave righteous ways behind, not to
   speak of unrighteous ways.
   Buddha (Gautama Siddhartha; c. 563–c. 483 BC) Indian
   religious teacher.
   Some Sayings of the Buddha (F. L. Woodward)

□ RIVERS □

1 I have seen the Mississippi. That is muddy water.
   I have seen the St Lawrence. That is crystal
   water. But the Thames is liquid history.
   John Burns (1858–1943) British Labour politician.
   Attrib.

2 Ol' man river, dat ol' man river,
   He must know sumpin', but don't say nothin',
   He just keeps rollin', he keeps on rollin' along.
   Oscar Hammerstein (1895–1960) US lyricist.
   From the musical *Show Boat*
   Ol' Man River

3 *Die Wacht am Rhein.*
   The Watch on the Rhine.
   Max Schneckenburger (1819–49) German poet.
   Song title

4 I come from haunts of coot and hern,
   I make a sudden sally
   And sparkle out among the fern,
   To bicker down a valley.
   Alfred, Lord Tennyson (1809–92) British poet.
   The Brook

□ ROCHEFOUCAULD □
François, Duc de la
(1613–80) French writer. His literary circle included Mme de
Sévigné and the Comtesse de La Fayette. He is best known for his
Maximes, published in five editions between 1665 and 1678.

1 If we had no faults of our own, we would not take
   so much pleasure in noticing those of others.
   Maximes, 31

2 The love of justice in most men is simply the fear
   of suffering injustice.
   Maximes, 78

3 It is more shameful to distrust one's friends than
   to be deceived by them.
   Maximes, 84

4 Everyone complains of his memory, but no one
   complains of his judgement.
   Maximes, 89

5 One gives nothing so freely as advice.
   Maximes, 110

6 To refuse praise reveals a desire to be praised
   twice over.
   Maximes, 149

7 Hypocrisy is the homage paid by vice to virtue.
   Maximes, 218

8 The height of cleverness is to be able to conceal
   it.
   Maximes, 245

9 We only confess our little faults to persuade people that we have no large ones.
   Maximes, 327

10 The accent of one's birthplace lingers in the
   mind and in the heart as it does in one's speech.
   Maximes, 342

11 We seldom attribute common sense except to
   those who agree with us.
   Maximes, 347

12 Quarrels would not last so long if the fault were
   on only one side.
   Maximes, 496

□ ROYALTY □
See also monarchy

1 The King over the Water.
   Anonymous
   Jacobite toast

2 Speed, bonny boat, like a bird on the wing;
   'Onward', the sailors cry;

Carry the lad that's born to be king
Over the sea to Skye.
H. E. Boulton (1859–1935) Scottish songwriter.
Referring to Bonnie Prince Charlie
Skye Boat Song

3 Such grace had kings when the world begun!
Robert Browning (1812–89) British poet.
Pippa Passes, Pt. 1

4 Conquering kings their titles take.
John Chandler (1806–76) British clergyman and writer.
Poem title

5 The monarchy is the oldest profession in the world.
Charles, Prince of Wales (1948–) Eldest son of Elizabeth II.
Attrib.

6 I know I have the body of a weak and feeble woman, but I have the heart and stomach of a King, and of a King of England too.
Elizabeth I (1533–1603) Queen of England.
Speech at Tilbury on the approach of the Spanish Armada

7 I will make you shorter by a head.
Elizabeth I
Sayings of Queen Elizabeth (Chamberlin)

8 I should like to be a horse.
Elizabeth II (1926–) Queen of the United Kingdom.
When asked about her ambitions when a child
Attrib.

9 I think that everyone will conceed that – today of all days – I should begin by saying, 'My husband and I'.
Elizabeth II
On her silver-wedding
Speech, Guildhall, 1972

10 I'm prepared to take advice on leisure from Prince Philip. He's a world expert on leisure. He's been practising for most of his adult life.
Neil Kinnock (1942–) British politician.
Western Mail, 1981

11 I'm self-employed.
Prince Philip (1921–) The consort of Queen Elizabeth II.
Answering a query as to what nature of work he did
Attrib.

12 Not least among the qualities in a great King is a capacity to permit his ministers to serve him.
Cardinal Richelieu (1585–1642) French statesman.
Testament Politique, Maxims

13 Kings and such like are just as funny as politicians.
Theodore Roosevelt (1858–1919) US Republican president.
Mr Wilson's War (John Dos Passos), Ch. 1

14 Kings are earth's gods; in vice their law's their will.
William Shakespeare (1564–1616) English dramatist.
Pericles, I:1

15 For God's sake let us sit upon the ground
And tell sad stories of the death of kings:
How some have been depos'd, some slain in war,
Some haunted by the ghosts they have depos'd,
Some poison'd by their wives, some sleeping kill'd,
All murder'd – for within the hollow crown
That rounds the mortal temples of a king
Keeps Death his court.
William Shakespeare
Richard II, III:2

16 Authority forgets a dying king.
Alfred, Lord Tennyson (1809–92) British poet.
Idylls of the King, 'The Passing of Arthur'

17 We are not amused!
Victoria (1819–1901) Queen of the United Kingdom.
Attrib.

☐ RULES ☐

1 The exception proves the rule.
Proverb

2 Rules and models destroy genius and art.
William Hazlitt (1778–1830) British essayist.
On Taste

3 The golden rule is that there are no golden rules.
George Bernard Shaw (1856–1950) Irish dramatist and critic.
Man and Superman, 'Maxims for Revolutionists'

☐ RUSKIN ☐
John
(1819–1900) British art critic and writer on sociology and economics. His books include *Modern Painters* (1843–60), *The Seven Lamps of Architecture* (1849), and *Munera Pulveris* (1862).

QUOTATIONS ABOUT RUSKIN

1 I doubt that art needed Ruskin any more than a moving train needs one of its passengers to shove it.
Tom Stoppard (1937–) Czech-born British dramatist.
Times Literary Supplement, 3 June 1977

QUOTATIONS BY RUSKIN

2 No person who is not a great sculptor or painter can be an architect. If he is not a sculptor or painter, he can only be a *builder*.
Lectures on Architecture and Painting

3 Life without industry is guilt, and industry without art is brutality.
Lectures on Art, 3, 'The Relation of Art to Morals', 23 Feb 1870

4 Mountains are the beginning and the end of all natural scenery.
Modern Painters, Vol. IV

5 If a book is worth reading, it is worth buying.
Sesame and Lilies, 'Of Kings' Treasuries'

6 All books are divisible into two classes, the books of the hour, and the books of all time.
Sesame and Lilies, 'Of Kings' Treasuries'

7 How long most people would look at the best book before they would give the price of a large turbot for it!
Sesame and Lilies, 'Of Kings' Treasuries'

8 Remember that the most beautiful things in the world are the most useless, peacocks and lilies for instance.
The Stones of Venice, Vol. I, Ch. 2

9 No human being, however great, or powerful was ever so free as a fish.
The Two Paths, Lecture V

10 Whereas it has long been known and declared that the poor have no right to the property of the rich, I wish it also to be known and declared that the rich have no right to the property of the poor.
Unto this Last, Essay III

☐ RUSSELL ☐
Bertrand Arthur William, Earl
(1872–1970) British philosopher. His many books include *Principia Mathematica* (with A. N. Whitehead; 1910) and *Our Knowledge of the External World* (1914). He was an ardent pacifist and campaigner for nuclear disarmament.

QUOTATIONS ABOUT RUSSELL

1 In trying to recall his face I am able to see it only in profile – the sharp, narrow silhouette of an aggressive jester.
Arthur Koestler (1905–83) Hungarian-born British writer
Stranger on the Square

QUOTATIONS BY RUSSELL

2 Three passions, simple but overwhelmingly strong, have governed my life: the longing for love, the search for knowledge, and unbearable pity for the suffering of mankind.
The Autobiography of Bertrand Russell, Prologue

3 I was told that the Chinese said they would bury me by the Western Lake and build a shrine to my memory. I have some slight regret that this did not happen, as I might have become a god, which would have been very *chic* for an atheist.
The Autobiography of Bertrand Russell, Vol. II, Ch. 3

4 The megalomaniac differs from the narcissist by the fact that he wishes to be powerful rather than charming, and seeks to be feared rather than loved. To this type belong many lunatics and most of the great men of history.
The Conquest of Happiness

5 There are two motives for reading a book: one, that you enjoy it, the other that you can boast about it.
The Conquest of Happiness

6 Mathematics may be defined as the subject in which we never know what we are talking about, nor whether what we are saying is true.
Mysticism and Logic, Ch. 4

7 Pure mathematics consists entirely of assertions to the effect that, if such and such a proposition is true of *anything*, then such and such another proposition is true of that thing. It is essential not to discuss whether the first proposition is really true, and not to mention what the anything is, of which it is supposed to be true.
Mysticism and Logic, Ch. 5

8 Organic life, we are told, has developed gradually from the protozoon to the philosopher, and this development, we are assured, is indubitably an advance. Unfortunately it is the philosopher, not the protozoon, who gives us this assurance.
Mysticism and Logic, Ch. 6

9 Matter…a convenient formula for describing what happens where it isn't.
An Outline of Philosophy

10 We have, in fact, two kinds of morality side by side; one which we preach but do not practise, and another which we practise but seldom preach.
Sceptical Essays

11 Mathematics possesses not only truth, but supreme beauty – a beauty cold and austere, like that of sculpture.
The Study of Mathematics

12 People don't seem to realize that it takes time and effort and preparation to think. Statesmen are far too busy making speeches to think.
Kenneth Harris Talking To: 'Bertrand Russell' (Kenneth Harris)

13 There's a Bible on that shelf there. But I keep it next to Voltaire – poison and antidote.
Kenneth Harris Talking To: 'Bertrand Russell' (Kenneth Harris)

14 You may reasonably expect a man to walk a tightrope safely for ten minutes; it would be unreasonable to do so without accident for two hundred years.
On the subject of nuclear war between the USA and the USSR.
The Tightrope Men (D. Bagley)

15 Patriots always talk of dying for their country,
and never of killing for their country.
Attrib.

16 Of course not. After all, I may be wrong.
On being asked whether he would be prepared to die for his
beliefs.
Attrib.

□RUSSIA□

See also Cold War, oppression, Russian Revolution

1 I cannot forecast to you the action of Russia. It is
a riddle wrapped in a mystery inside an enigma.
Winston Churchill (1874–1965) British statesman.
Broadcast talk, 1 Oct 1939

2 Russia will certainly inherit the future. What we
already call the greatness of Russia is only her
pre-natal struggling.
D. H. Lawrence (1885–1930) British novelist.
Phoenix, Preface

3 Neither can you expect a revolution, because
there is no new baby in the womb of our society.
Russia is a collapse, not a revolution.
D. H. Lawrence
Phoenix, 'The Good Man'

4 From being a patriotic myth, the Russian people
have become an awful reality.
Leon Trotsky (Lev Davidovich Bronstein; 1879–1940) Russian
revolutionary.
History of the Russian Revolution, Pt. III, Ch. 7

5 'For a little light relief, how about halting the
work of the communist party?'...Mr Yeltsin lifted
his pen with a flourish. The clapping stopped:
'There, I've signed it.'
Boris Nikolayevich Yeltsin (1931–) Russian politician.
The Times, 24 Aug 1991

□RUSSIAN REVOLUTION□

See also revolution, Russia

1 Our hand will not tremble.
Joseph Stalin (J. Dzhugashvili; 1879–1953) Soviet statesman.
Reply to a telegram from Lenin at the start of the Red Terror
(1918) urging him to be merciless against the Bolsheviks'
enemies

2 The 23rd of February was International
Woman's Day...It had not occurred to anyone
that it might become the first day of the
revolution.
Leon Trotsky (Lev Davidovich Bronstein; 1879–1940) Russian
revolutionary.
History of the Russian Revolution, Pt. I, Ch. 7

3 The revolution does not choose its paths: it made
its first steps towards victory under the belly of a
Cossack's horse.
Leon Trotsky
History of the Russian Revolution, Pt. I, Ch. 7

□RUTHLESSNESS□

1 3RD FISHERMAN. Master, I marvel how the fishes
live in the sea.
1ST FISHERMAN. Why, as men do a-land – the great
ones eat up the little ones.
William Shakespeare (1564–1616) English dramatist.
Pericles, II:1

2 The world continues to offer glittering prizes to
those who have stout hearts and sharp swords.
F. E. Smith (1872–1930) British lawyer and politician.
Speech, Glasgow University, 7 Nov 1923

3 It is not enough to succeed. Others must fail.
Gore Vidal (1925–) US novelist.
Antipanegyric for Tom Driberg (G. Irvine)

S

□SAKI□

(Hector Hugh Munro; 1870–1916) British writer. He is best-known for his collections of humorous short stories, including *Reginald* (1904), *The Chronicles of Clovis* (1911), and *Beasts and Super-Beasts* (1914).

1 By insisting on having your bottle pointing to the north when the cork is being drawn, and calling the waiter Max, you may induce an impression on your guests which hours of laboured boasting might be powerless to achieve. For this purpose, however, the guests must be chosen as carefully as the wine.
The Chaplet

2 Addresses are given to us to conceal our where-abouts.
Cross Currents

3 'I believe I take precedence,' he said coldly; 'you are merely the club Bore: I am the club Liar.'
A Defensive Diamond

4 The people of Crete unfortunately make more history than they can consume locally.
The Jesting of Arlington Stringham

5 To say that anything was a quotation was an excellent method, in Eleanor's eyes, for with-drawing it from discussion.
The Jesting of Arlington Stringham

6 All decent people live beyond their incomes nowadays, and those who aren't respectable live beyond other people's. A few gifted individuals manage to do both.
The Match-Maker

7 His socks compelled one's attention without losing one's respect.
Ministers of Grace

8 The young have aspirations that never come to pass, the old have reminiscences of what never happened.
Reginald at the Carlton

9 There may have been disillusionments in the lives of the medieval saints, but they would scarcely have been better pleased if they could have foreseen that their names would be associated nowadays chiefly with racehorses and the cheaper clarets.
Reginald at the Carlton

10 But, good gracious, you've got to educate him first.
You can't expect a boy to be vicious till he's been to a good school.
Reginald in Russia

11 People may say what they like about the decay of Christianity; the religious system that produced green Chartreuse can never really die.
Reginald on Christmas Presents

12 Even the Hooligan was probably invented in China centuries before we thought of him.
Reginald on House-Parties

13 Every reformation must have its victims. You can't expect the fatted calf to share the enthusi-asm of the angels over the prodigal's return.
Reginald on the Academy

14 I think she must have been very strictly brought up, she's so desperately anxious to do the wrong thing correctly.
Reginald on Worries

15 I always say beauty is only sin deep.
Reginald's Choir Treat

□SARCASM□

1 Sarcasm I now see to be, in general, the language of the devil.
Thomas Carlyle (1795–1881) Scottish historian and essayist. *Sartor Resartus*, Bk. II, Ch. 4

2 If you don't want to use the army, I should like to borrow it for a while. Yours respectfully,
A. Lincoln.
Abraham Lincoln (1809–65) US statesman.
Letter to General George B. McClellan, whose lack of activity during the US Civil War irritated Lincoln

□SARTRE□
Jean-Paul

(1905–80) French philosopher, dramatist, and novelist. The prin-cipal exponent of existentialism, he wrote a number of books on this subject, including *Critique de la raison dialectique* (1960). His novels include the trilogy *The Roads to Freedom* (1945–49), and *The Respectable Prostitute* (1946) is the best known of his plays.

1 I hate victims who respect their executioners.
Altona

2 Man is condemned to be free.
Existentialism is a Humanism

3 My thought is *me*: that is why I can't stop. I exist by what I think...and I can't prevent myself from thinking.
Nausea

4 I know perfectly well that I don't want to do any-thing; to do something is to create existence – and there's quite enough existence as it is.
Nausea

5 She believed in nothing; only her scepticism kept her from being an atheist.
Words

6 There is no such thing as psychological. Let us say that one can improve the biography of the person.
The Divided Self (R. D. Laing), Ch. 8

□SATIRE□

See also ridicule, sarcasm

1 It's hard not to write satire.
Juvenal (Decimus Junius Juvenalis; 60–130 AD) Roman satirist.
Satires, I

2 Satire should, like a polished razor keen,
Wound with a touch that's scarcely felt or seen.
Lady Mary Wortley Montagu (1689–1762) English writer.
To the Imitator of the First Satire of Horace, Bk. II

3 Satire is a sort of glass, wherein beholders do generally discover everybody's face but their own.
Jonathan Swift (1667–1745) Irish-born Anglican priest and writer.
The Battle of the Books, 'Preface'

□SATISFACTION□

See also contentment

1 Youth will be served, every dog has his day, and mine has been a fine one.
George Henry Borrow (1803–81) British writer.
Lavengro, Ch. 92

2 The reward of a thing well done is to have done it.
Ralph Waldo Emerson (1803–82) US poet and essayist.
Essays, 'New England Reformers'

□SAYINGS□

See also quotations

1 A platitude is simply a truth repeated till people get tired of hearing it.
Stanley Baldwin (1867–1947) British statesman.
Attrib.

2 A new maxim is often a brilliant error.
Chrétien Guillaume de Lamoignonde Malesherbes (1721–94) French statesman.
Pensées et maximes

3 A proverb is one man's wit and all men's wisdom.
Lord John Russell (1792–1878) British statesman.
Attrib.

4 A truism is on that account none the less true.
Herbert Samuel (1870–1963) British Liberal statesman.
A Book of Quotations

□SCEPTICISM□

See also doubt, proof

1 We don't believe in rheumatism and true love until after the first attack.
Marie Ebner von Eschenbach (1830–1916) Austrian writer.
Aphorism

2 I am too much of a sceptic to deny the possibility of anything.
T. H. Huxley (1825–95) British biologist.
Letter to Herbert Spencer, 22 Mar 1886

3 The temerity to believe in nothing.
Ivan Turgenev (1818–83) Russian novelist.
Fathers and Sons, Ch. 14

□SCHOPENHAUER□
Arthur
(1788–1860) German philosopher. His books include *Die Welt als Wille und Vorstellung* (1819) and *Die Beiden Grundprobleme der Ethik* (1841).

1 To be alone is the fate of all great minds – a fate deplored at times, but still always chosen as the less grievous of two evils.
Aphorismen zur Lebensweisheit

2 Intellect is invisible to the man who has none.
Aphorismen zur Lebensweisheit

3 Every parting gives a foretaste of death; every coming together again a foretaste of the resurrection.
Gedanken über vielerlei Gegenstände, XXVI

4 To expect a man to retain everything that he has ever read is like expecting him to carry about in his body everything that he has ever eaten.
Parerga and Paralipomena

5 After your death you will be what you were before your birth.
Parerga and Paralipomena

□SCIENCE□

See also discovery, mathematics, Nature, progress, research, scientists, technology

1 That is the essence of science: ask an impertinent question, and you are on the way to the pertinent answer.
Jacob Bronowski (1908–74) British scientist and writer.
The Ascent of Man, Ch. 4

2 Physics becomes in those years the greatest collective work of science – no, more than that, the great collective work of art of the twentieth century.
Jacob Bronowski
Referring to the period around the turn of the century marked by the elucidation of atomic structure and the development of the quantum theory
The Ascent of Man, Ch. 10

3 When a distinguished but elderly scientist states that something is possible, he is almost certainly right. When he states that something is impossible, he is very probably wrong.

Arthur C. Clarke (1917–) British science-fiction writer.
Profiles of the Future

4 We have discovered the secret of life!

Francis Crick (1916–) British biophysicist.
Excitedly bursting into a Cambridge pub with James Watson to celebrate the fact that they had unravelled the structure of DNA
The Double Helix (J. D. Watson)

5 After all, science is essentially international, and it is only through lack of the historical sense that national qualities have been attributed to it.

Marie Curie (1867–1934) Polish chemist.
Memorandum, 'Intellectual Co-operation'

6 When you are courting a nice girl an hour seems like a second. When you sit on a red-hot cinder a second seems like an hour. That's relativity.

Albert Einstein (1879–1955) German-born US physicist.
News Chronicle, 14 Mar 1949

7 The whole of science is nothing more than a refinement of everyday thinking.

Albert Einstein
Out of My Later Years

8 Science without religion is lame, religion without science is blind.

Albert Einstein
Out of My Later Years

9 God does not play dice.

Albert Einstein
Einstein's objection to the quantum theory, in which physical events can only be known in terms of probabilities. It is sometimes quoted as 'God does not play dice with the Universe'
Albert Einstein, Creator and Rebel (B. Hoffman), Ch. 10

10 Science has 'explained' nothing; the more we know the more fantastic the world becomes and the profounder the surrounding darkness.

Aldous Huxley (1894–1964) British novelist.
Views Of Holland

11 Science is nothing but trained and organized common sense, differing from the latter only as a veteran may differ from a raw recruit: and its methods differ from those of common sense only as far as the guardsman's cut and thrust differ from the manner in which a savage wields his club.

T. H. Huxley (1825–95) British biologist.
Collected Essays, 'The Method of Zadig'

12 The great tragedy of Science – the slaying of a beautiful hypothesis by an ugly fact.

T. H. Huxley
Collected Essays, 'Biogenesis and Abiogenesis'

13 Reason, Observation, and Experience – the Holy Trinity of Science.

Robert G. Ingersoll (1833–99) US lawyer and agnostic.
The Gods

14 Science should leave off making pronouncements: the river of knowledge has too often turned back on itself.

James Jeans (1877–1946) British scientist.
The Mysterious Universe, Ch. 5

15 We have genuflected before the god of science only to find that it has given us the atomic bomb, producing fears and anxieties that science can never mitigate.

Martin Luther King (1929–68) US Black civil-rights leader.
Strength through Love, Ch. 13

16 Scientific discovery is a private event, and the delight that accompanies it, or the despair of finding it illusory does not travel.

Peter Medawar (1915–87) British immunologist.
Hypothesis and Imagination

17 *Laboratorium est oratorium*. The place where we do our scientific work is a place of prayer.

Joseph Needham (1900–) British biochemist.
The Harvest of a Quiet Eye (A. L. Mackay)

18 Do you really believe that the sciences would ever have originated and grown if the way had not been prepared by magicians, alchemists, astrologers and witches whose promises and pretensions first had to create a thirst, a hunger, a taste for *hidden* and *forbidden* powers? Indeed, infinitely more had to be *promised* than could ever be fulfilled in order that anything at all might be fulfilled in the realms of knowledge.

Friedrich Wilhelm Nietzsche (1844–1900) German philosopher.
The Gay Science

19 There are no such things as applied sciences, only applications of science.

Louis Pasteur (1822–95) French scientist.
Address, 11 Sept 1872

20 Traditional scientific method has always been at the very *best*, 20-20 hindsight. It's good for seeing where you've been.

Robert T. Pirsig (1928–) US writer.
Zen and the Art of Motorcycle Maintenance, Pt. III, Ch. 24

21 Science is built up of facts, as a house is built of stones; but an accumulation of facts is no more a science than a heap of stones is a house.

Henri Poincaré (1854–1912) French scientist.
Science and Hypothesis, Ch. 9

22 Should we force science down the throats of those that have no taste for it? Is it our duty to drag them kicking and screaming into the twenty-first century? I am afraid that it is.

George Porter (1920–) British chemist.
Speech, Sept 1986

23 Science without conscience is the death of the soul.

François Rabelais (1483–1553) French satirist.

24 The simplest schoolboy is now familiar with truths for which Archimedes would have sacrificed his life.

Ernest Renan (1823–92) French philosopher and theologian.
Souvenirs d'enfance et de jeunesse

25 If all the arts aspire to the condition of music, all the sciences aspire to the condition of mathematics.

George Santayana (1863–1952) US philosopher.
The Observer, 'Sayings of the Week', 4 Mar 1928

26 People must understand that science is inherently neither a potential for good nor for evil. It is a potential to be harnessed by man to do his bidding.

Glenn T. Seaborg (1912–) US physicist.
Associated Press interview with Alton Blakeslee, 29 Sept 1964

27 A science which hesitates to forget its founders is lost.

A. N. Whitehead (1861–1947) British philosopher.
Attrib.

□ SCIENCE FICTION □

1 Far out in the uncharted backwaters of the unfashionable end of the Western Spiral arm of the Galaxy lies a small unregarded yellow sun. Orbiting this at a distance of roughly ninety-two million miles is an utterly insignificant little blue green planet whose ape-descended life forms are so amazingly primitive that they still think digital watches are a pretty neat idea.

Douglas Adams (1952–) British writer.
The Hitch Hiker's Guide to the Galaxy, Introduction

2 Science fiction is the search for a definition of mankind and his status in the universe which will stand in our advanced but confused state of knowledge (science), and is characteristically cast in the Gothic or post-Gothic mode.

Brian Aldiss (1925–) British science-fiction writer.
Trillion Year Spree, Ch. 1

□ SCIENTISTS □

See also science

1 When I find myself in the company of scientists, I feel like a shabby curate who has strayed by mistake into a drawing-room full of dukes.

W. H. Auden (1907–73) British poet.
The Dyer's Hand

2 The true men of action in our time, those who transform the world, are not the politicians and statesmen, but the scientists. Unfortunately, poetry cannot celebrate them, because their

deeds are concerned with things, not persons and are, therefore, speechless.

W. H. Auden
The Dyer's Hand

3 If you want to find out anything from the theoretical physicists about the methods they use, I advise you to stick closely to one principle: Don't listen to their words fix your attention on their deeds.

Albert Einstein (1879–1955) German-born US physicist.
The World As I See It

4 The physicists have known sin; and this is a knowledge which they cannot lose.

J. Robert Oppenheimer (1904–67) US physicist.
Lecture, Massachusetts Institute of Technology, 25 Nov 1947

5 He doubted the existence of the Deity but accepted Carnot's cycle, and he had read Shakespeare and found him weak in chemistry.

H. G. Wells (1866–1946) British writer.
Short Stories, 'The Lord of the Dynamos'

□ SCOTLAND □

See also Britain, Scots

1 O ye'll tak' the high road, and I'll tak' the low road,
And I'll be in Scotland afore ye,
But me and my true love will never meet again,
On the bonnie, bonnie banks o' Loch Lomon'.

Anonymous
The Bonnie Banks o' Loch Lomon'

2 *Oats.* A grain, which in England is generally given to horses, but in Scotland supports the people.

Samuel Johnson (1709–84) British lexicographer.
Dictionary of the English Language

3 Seeing Scotland, Madam, is only seeing a worse England.

Samuel Johnson
Life of Johnson (J. Boswell), Vol. III

4 Roamin' in the gloamin',
By the bonny banks of Clyde.

Harry Lauder (Hugh MacLennon; 1870–1950) Scottish music-hall artist.
Song

5 That knuckle-end of England – that land of Calvin, oat-cakes, and sulphur.

Sydney Smith (1771–1845) British clergyman and essayist.
Memoir (Lady Holland)

□ SCOTS □

See also British, Scotland

1 You've forgotten the grandest moral attribute of a Scotsman, Maggie, that he'll do nothing which might damage his career.

J. M. Barrie (1860–1937) British novelist and dramatist.
What Every Woman Knows, II

2 There are few more impressive sights in the world than a Scotsman on the make.
J. M. Barrie
What Every Woman Knows, II

3 A Scotchman must be a very sturdy moralist who does not love Scotland better than truth.
Samuel Johnson (1709–84) British lexicographer.
Journey to the Western Islands of Scotland, 'Col'

4 In all my travels I never met with any one Scotchman but what was a man of sense. I believe everybody of that country that has any, leaves it as fast as they can.
Francis Lockier (1667–1740) English writer.
Anecdotes (Joseph Spence)

5 Join a Highland regiment, me boy. The kilt is an unrivalled garment for fornication and diarrhoea.
John Masters (1914–83) British writer
Bugles and a Tiger

6 It is never difficult to distinguish between a Scotsman with a grievance and a ray of sunshine.
P. G. Wodehouse (1881–1975) British humorous novelist.
Wodehouse at Work to the End (Richard Usborne), Ch. 8

□ SCOTT □
Sir Walter
(1771–1832) Scottish novelist. Originally a lawyer, he turned to writing for a living after the success of his narrative poem, *The Lay of the Last Minstrel* (1805). *Waverley* (1814) was the first of many successful historical novels, including *Rob Roy* (1817), *The Heart of Midlothian* (1818), *The Bride of Lammermoor* (1818), *Ivanhoe* (1819) and *The Talisman* (1825).

QUOTATIONS ABOUT SCOTT

1 Sir Walter Scott, when all is said and done, is an inspired butler.
William Hazlitt (1778–1830) British essayist.
Mrs Siddons

QUOTATIONS BY SCOTT

2 Look back, and smile at perils past.
The Bridal of Triermain, Introduction

3 O Caledonia! stern and wild,
Meet nurse for a poetic child!
Land of brown heath and shaggy wood,
Land of the mountain and the flood,
Land of my sires! what mortal hand
Can e'er untie the filial band
That knits me to thy rugged strand!
The Lay of the Last Minstrel, VI

4 His morning walk was beneath the elms in the churchyard; 'for death,' he said, 'had been his next-door neighbour for so many years, that he had no apology for dropping the acquaintance.'
The Legend of Montrose, Introduction

5 So faithful in love, and so dauntless in war,
There never was knight like the young Lochinvar.
Marmion, V

6 The stubborn spear-men still made good
Their dark impenetrable wood,
Each stepping where his comrade stood,
The instant that he fell.
Marmion, VI

7 Ridicule often checks what is absurd, and fully as often smothers that which is noble.
Quentin Durward

8 See yon pale stripling! when a boy,
A mother's pride, a father's joy!
Rokeby, III

9 No, this right hand shall work it all off.
Refusing offers of help following his bankruptcy in 1826.
Century of Anecdote (J. Timbs)

□ SEA □
See also boats, Navy, seaside

1 The sea is calm to-night,
The tide is full, the moon lies fair
Upon the Straits.
Matthew Arnold (1822–88) British poet and critic.
Dover Beach

2 For all at last return to the sea – to Oceanus, the ocean river, like the ever-flowing stream of time, the beginning and the end.
Rachel Carson (1907–64) US biologist.
The closing words of the book
The Sea Around Us

3 The voice of the sea speaks to the soul. The touch of the sea is sensuous, enfolding the body in its soft, close embrace.
Kate Chopin (1851–1904) US writer.
The Awakening, Ch. 6

4 The snotgreen sea. The scrotumtightening sea.
James Joyce (1882–1941) Irish novelist.
Ulysses

5 I must down to the seas again, to the lonely sea and the sky,
And all I ask is a tall ship and a star to steer her by,
And the wheel's kick and the wind's song and the white sail's shaking,
And a grey mist on the sea's face and a grey dawn breaking.
John Masefield (1878–1967) British poet.
Often quoted using 'sea' rather than 'seas', and 'I must go down' rather than 'I must down'
Sea Fever

6 A life on the ocean wave,
A home on the rolling deep.
Epes Sargent (1813–80) US writer and dramatist.
A Life on the Ocean Wave

7 O hear us when we cry to Thee
For those in peril on the sea.
William Whiting (1825–78) British hymn writer.
Eternal Father Strong to Save

8 The sea! the sea!
Xenophon (430–354 BC) Greek historian.
Anabasis, IV:7

□ **SEASIDE** □
See also sea

1 The Walrus and the Carpenter
Were walking close at hand;
They wept like anything to see
Such quantities of sand:
'If this were only cleared away,'
They said, 'it *would* be grand!'
Lewis Carroll (Charles Lutwidge Dodgson; 1832–98) British writer.
Through the Looking-Glass, Ch. 4

2 It is the drawback of all sea-side places that half the landscape is unavailable for purposes of human locomotion, being covered by useless water.
Norman Douglas (1868–1952) British novelist.
Alone, 'Mentone'

3 I do Like to be Beside the Seaside.
John A. Glover-Kind (19th century) US songwriter.
Song title

□ **SEASONS** □
See also months

1 Sumer is icumen in,
Lhude sing cuccu!
Groweth sed, and bloweth med,
And springth the wude nu.
Anonymous
Cuckoo Song

2 Many human beings say that they enjoy the winter, but what they really enjoy is feeling proof against it.
Richard Adams (1920–) British novelist.
Watership Down, Ch. 50

3 All the live murmur of a summer's day.
Matthew Arnold (1882–88) British poet and critic.
The Scholar Gipsy

4 Summer afternoon – summer afternoon; to me those have always been the two most beautiful words in the English language.
Henry James (1843–1916) US novelist.
A Backward Glance (Edith Wharton), Ch. 10

5 St Agnes Eve – Ah, bitter chill it was!
The owl, for all his feathers, was a-cold;
The hare limp'd trembling through the frozen grass,
And silent was the flock in woolly fold.
John Keats (1795–1821) British poet.
The Eve of Saint Agnes, I

6 Four seasons fill the measure of the year;
There are four seasons in the mind of men.
John Keats
Four Seasons

7 Where are the songs of Spring? Ay, where are they?
John Keats
To Autumn

8 Season of mists and mellow fruitfulness,
Close bosom-friend of the maturing sun;
Conspiring with him how to load and bless
With fruit the vines that round the thatch-eaves run.
John Keats
To Autumn

9 No one thinks of winter when the grass is green!
Rudyard Kipling (1865–1936) Indian-born British writer.
A St Helena Lullaby

10 Russia has two generals in whom she can confide – Generals Janvier and Février.
Nicholas I (1796–1855) Tsar of Russia.
Referring to the Russian winter. Nicholas himself succumbed to a February cold in 1855 – the subject of the famous *Punch* Cartoon, 'General Février turned traitor', 10 Mar 1855
Attrib.

11 Winter is icummen in,
Lhude sing Goddamm,
Raineth drop and staineth slop
And how the wind doth ramm!
Sing: Goddamm.
Ezra Pound (1885–1972) US poet.
Ancient Music

12 In the bleak mid-winter
Frosty wind made moan,
Earth stood hard as iron,
Water like a stone;
Snow had fallen, snow on snow,
Snow on snow,
In the bleak mid-winter,
Long ago.
Christina Rossetti (1830–74) British poet.
Mid-Winter

13 The country habit has me by the heart,
For he's bewitched for ever who has seen,
Not with his eyes but with his vision, Spring
Flow down the woods and stipple leaves with sun.
Vita Sackville-West (Victoria Sackville-West; 1892–1962) British poet and novelist.
The Land, 'Winter'

14 If Winter comes, can Spring be far behind?
Percy Bysshe Shelley (1792–1822) British poet.
Ode to the West Wind

15 When the hounds of spring are on winter's traces,
The mother of months in meadow or plain
Fills the shadows and windy places
With lisp of leaves and ripple of rain...
Algernon Charles Swinburne (1837–1909) British poet.
Atalanta in Calydon

16 In the Spring a young man's fancy lightly turns to
thoughts of love.
Alfred, Lord Tennyson (1809–92) British poet.
Locksley Hall

17 It is a winter's tale
That the snow blind twilight ferries over the lakes
And floating fields from the farm in the cup of the
vales.
Dylan Thomas (1914–53) Welsh poet.
A Winter's Tale

18 The comic almanacs give us dreadful pictures of
January and February; but, in truth, the months
which should be made to look gloomy in England are March and April. Let no man boast himself that he has got through the perils of winter
till at least the seventh of May.
Anthony Trollope (1815–82) British novelist.
Doctor Thorne, Ch. 47

☐ SECRECY ☐
See also gossip

1 If thou hast heard a word, let it die with thee; and
be bold, it will not burst thee.
Bible: Ecclesiasticus
19:10

2 Stolen waters are sweet, and bread eaten in
secret is pleasant.
Bible: Proverbs
9:17

3 Mum's the word.
George Colman, the Younger (1762–1836) British
dramatist.
The Battle of Hexham, II:1

4 O fie miss, you must not kiss and tell.
William Congreve (1670–1729) British Restoration dramatist.
Love for Love, II:10

5 Three may keep a secret, if two of them are dead.
Benjamin Franklin (1706–90) US scientist and statesman.
Poor Richard's Almanack

☐ SELF ☐
See also self-confidence, etc.

1 Lord, deliver me from myself.
Thomas Browne (1605–82) English physician and writer.
Religio Medici, Pt. II

2 I have always disliked myself at any given
moment; the total of such moments is my life.
Cyril Connolly (1903–74) British journalist.
Enemies of Promise, Ch. 18

3 But I do nothing upon myself, and yet I am mine
own Executioner.
John Donne (1573–1631) English poet.
Devotions, 12

4 Whenever I look inside myself I am afraid.
Cyril Joad (1891–1953) British writer and broadcaster.
The Observer, 'Sayings of the Week', 8 Nov 1942

5 All censure of a man's self is oblique praise. It is
in order to shew how much he can spare.
Samuel Johnson (1709–84) British lexicographer.
Life of Johnson (J. Boswell), Vol. III

6 One should examine oneself for a very long time
before thinking of condemning others.
Molière (Jean Baptiste Poquelin, 1622–73) French dramatist.
Le Misanthrope, III:4

7 Self-love seems so often unrequited.
Anthony Powell (1905–) British novelist.
The Acceptance World

8 Do not love your neighbour as yourself. If you
are on good terms with yourself it is an impertinence; if on bad, an injury.
George Bernard Shaw (1856–1950) Irish dramatist and critic.
Man and Superman, 'Maxims for Revolutionists'

9 The unexamined life is not worth living.
Socrates (469–399 BC) Athenian philosopher.
Apology (Plato)

☐ SELF-CONFIDENCE ☐
See also shyness

1 Those who believe that they are exclusively in
the right are generally those who achieve something.
Aldous Huxley (1894–1964) British novelist.
Proper Studies

2 I can honestly say that I was never affected by
the question of the success of an undertaking. If I
felt it was the right thing to do, I was for it regardless of the possible outcome.
Golda Meir (1898–1978) Russian-born Israeli stateswoman.
Golda Meir: Woman with a Cause (Marie Syrkin)

3 'Tis an ill cook that cannot lick his own fingers.
William Shakespeare (1564–1616) English dramatist.
Romeo and Juliet, IV:2

4 I am certain that we will win the election with a
good majority. Not that I am ever over-confident.
Margaret Thatcher (1925–) British politician and prime
minister.
Evening Standard, 1987

□ SELF-CONTROL □

1 He that is slow to anger is better than the mighty;
and he that ruleth his spirit than he that taketh a
city.
Bible: Proverbs
16:32

2 The highest possible stage in moral culture is
when we recognize that we ought to control our
thoughts.
Charles Darwin (1809–82) British life scientist.
Descent of Man, Ch. 4

3 If you can keep your head when all about you
Are losing theirs and blaming it on you.
Rudyard Kipling (1865–1936) Indian-born British writer.
If

4 He that would govern others, first should be
The master of himself.
Philip Massinger (1583–1640) English dramatist.
The Bondman, I

□ SELF-DENIAL □

See also abstinence, selflessness

1 Self-denial is not a virtue; it is only the effect of
prudence on rascality.
George Bernard Shaw (1856–1950) Irish dramatist and critic.
Man and Superman, 'Maxims for Revolutionists'

2 Thy need is yet greater than mine.
Philip Sidney (1554–86) English poet and courtier.
Giving his own water bottle to a humble wounded soldier after he
had himself been wounded
Attrib.

□ SELF-INTEREST □

See also selfishness

1 The land self-interest groans from shore to shore,
For fear that plenty should attain the poor.
Lord Byron (1788–1824) British poet.
The Age of Bronze, XIV

2 The least pain in our little finger gives us more
concern and uneasiness than the destruction of
millions of our fellow-beings.
William Hazlitt (1778–1830) British essayist.
American Literature, 'Dr Channing'

3 Self-interest speaks all sorts of tongues, and
plays all sorts of roles, even that of disinterestedness.
Duc de la Rochefoucauld (1613–80) French writer.
Maximes, 39

□ SELFISHNESS □

See also egotism, self-interest

1 I have been a selfish being all my life, in practice,
though not in principle.
Jane Austen (1775–1817) British novelist.
Pride and Prejudice, Ch. 58

2 It's 'Damn you, Jack – I'm all right!' with you
chaps.
David Bone (1874–1959) British sea captain and writer.
The Brassbounder, Ch. 3

□ SELF-KNOWLEDGE □

1 Resolve to be thyself: and know, that he
Who finds himself, loses his misery.
Matthew Arnold (1822–88) British poet and critic.
Self-Dependence

2 We confess our bad qualities to others out of fear
of appearing naive or ridiculous by not being
aware of them.
Gerald Brenan (Edward Fitzgerald Brenan; 1894–1987)
British writer.
Thoughts in a Dry Season

3 Know then thyself, presume not God to scan,
The proper study of Mankind is Man.
Alexander Pope (1688–1744) British poet.
An Essay on Man, II

4 That true self-love and social are the same;
That virtue only makes our bliss below;
And all our knowledge is, ourselves to know.
Alexander Pope
An Essay on Man, IV

□ SELFLESSNESS □

See also charity, self-denial

1 The way to get things done is not to mind who
gets the credit of doing them.
Benjamin Jowett (1817–93) British theologian.
Attrib.

2 To give and not to count the cost;
To fight and not to heed the wounds;
To toil and not to seek for rest;
To labour and not ask for any reward
Save that of knowing that we do Thy will.
St Ignatius Loyola (1491–1556) Spanish priest.
Prayer for Generosity

□ SELF-MADE MEN □

1 He was a self-made man who owed his lack of
success to nobody.
Joseph Heller (1923–) US novelist.
Catch-22, Ch. 3

2 A self-made man is one who believes in luck and
sends his son to Oxford.
Christina Stead (1902–83) Australian novelist.
House of All Nations, 'Credo'

□ SELF-PRESERVATION □

See also survival

1 He that fights and runs away
May live to fight another day.
Anonymous
Musarum Deliciae

2 This animal is very bad; when attacked it defends itself.
Anonymous
La Ménagerie (P. K. Théodore), 1828

3 If a madman were to come into this room with a stick in his hand, no doubt we should pity the state of his mind; but our primary consideration would be to take care of ourselves. We should knock him down first, and pity him afterwards.
Samuel Johnson (1709–84) British lexicographer.
Life of Johnson (J. Boswell), Vol. III

4 The better part of valour is discretion; in the which better part I have saved my life.
William Shakespeare (1564–1616) English dramatist.
Henry IV, Part One, V:4

5 Greater love hath no man than this, that he lay down his friends for his life.
Jeremy Thorpe (1929–) British politician.
After Macmillan's 1962 Cabinet reshuffle
The Pendulum Years (Bernard Levin), Ch. 12

6 Scheherazade is the classical example of a woman saving her head by using it.
Esme Wynne-Tyson (1898–) British writer.
Attrib.

□ SELF-RELIANCE □

See also independence

1 The gods help them that help themselves.
Aesop (6th century BC) Reputed Greek writer of fables.
Fables, 'Hercules and the Waggoner'

2 The greatest thing in the world is to know how to be self-sufficient.
Michel de Montaigne (1533–92) French essayist.
Essais, I

3 Our remedies oft in ourselves do lie,
Which we ascribe to heaven.
William Shakespeare (1564–1616) English dramatist.
All's Well that Ends Well, I:1

□ SELF-RESPECT □

See also pride, respect

1 It is better to die on your feet than to live on your knees.
Dolores Ibarruri (1895–1989) Spanish politician.
Speech, Paris, 1936

2 And, above all things, never think that you're not good enough yourself. A man should never think that. My belief is that in life people will take you very much at your own reckoning.
Anthony Trollope (1815–82) British novelist.
The Small House at Allington, Ch. 32

3 When people do not respect us we are sharply offended; yet deep down in his heart no man much respects himself.
Mark Twain (Samuel Langhorne Clemens; 1835–1910) US writer.
Notebooks

□ SENSATION □

1 O for a life of sensations rather than of thoughts!
John Keats (1795–1821) British poet.
Letter to Benjamin Bailey, 22 Nov 1817

2 'The story is like the wind', the Bushman prisoner said. 'It comes from a far off place, and we feel it.'
Laurens Van der Post (1906–) South African novelist.
A Story Like the Wind

□ SENTIMENTALITY □

See also emotion

1 They had been corrupted by money, and he had been corrupted by sentiment. Sentiment was the more dangerous, because you couldn't name its price. A man open to bribes was to be relied upon below a certain figure, but sentiment might uncoil in the heart at a name, a photograph, even a smell remembered.
Graham Greene (1904–91) British novelist.
The Heart of the Matter

2 Sentimentality is a superstructure covering brutality.
Carl Gustav Jung (1875–1961) Swiss psychoanalyst.
Reflections

3 She likes stories that make her cry – I think we all do, it's so nice to feel sad when you've nothing particular to be sad about.
Annie Sullivan (1866–1936) US teacher of the handicapped.
Referring to Helen Keller
Letter, 12 Dec 1887

□ SEPARATION □

See also absence, parting

1 If I should meet thee
After long years,
How should I greet thee? –
With silence and tears.
Lord Byron (1788–1824) British poet.
When we two parted

2 Absence from whom we love is worse than death.
William Cowper (1731–1800) British poet.
'Hope, like the Short-lived Ray'

3 As it will be the right of all, so it will be the duty of some, definitely to prepare for a separation, amicably if they can, violently if they must.
Josiah Quincy (1772–1864) US statesman.
Abridgement of Debates of Congress, Vol. IV, 14 Jan 1811

4 Every parting gives a foretaste of death; every coming together again a foretaste of the resurrection.

Arthur Schopenhauer (1788–1860) German philosopher.
Gedanken über vielerlei Gegenstände, XXVI

□ SERIOUSNESS □

1 Though this may be play to you, 'tis death to us.

Roger L'Estrange (1616–1704) English journalist and writer.
Aesop's Fables, 398

2 You must not think me necessarily foolish because I am facetious, nor will I consider you necessarily wise because you are grave.

Sydney Smith (1771–1845) British clergyman and essayist.
Letter to Bishop Blomfield

□ SERMONS □

See also brevity, speeches, verbosity

1 They are written as if sin were to be taken out of man like Eve out of Adam – by putting him to sleep.

Sydney Smith (1771–1845) British clergyman and essayist.
Referring to boring sermons
Anecdotes of the Clergy (J. Larwood)

2 I never quite forgave Mahaffy for getting himself suspended from preaching in the College Chapel. Ever since his sermons were discontinued, I suffer from insomnia in church.

George Tyrrell (1861–1909) Irish Catholic theologian.
As I Was Going Down Sackville Street (Oliver St John Gogarty), Ch. 25

□ SERVICE □

1 His lord said unto him, Well done, thou good and faithful servant: thou hast been faithful over a few things, I will make thee ruler over many things: enter thou into the joy of thy lord.

Bible: Matthew
25:21

2 God doth not need
Either man's work or his own gifts. Who best
Bear his mild yoke, they serve him best: his state
Is kingly; thousands at his bidding speed,
And post o'er land and ocean without rest;
They also serve who only stand and wait.

John Milton (1608–74) English poet.
Sonnet: 'On his Blindness'

3 Small service is true service, while it lasts.

William Wordsworth (1770–1850) British poet.
To a Child, Written in her Album

□ SERVILITY □

See also flattery, humility

1 I am well aware that I am the 'umblest person going....My mother is likewise a very 'umble person. We live in a numble abode.

Charles Dickens (1812–70) British novelist.
Said by Uriah Heep
David Copperfield, Ch. 16

2 A pious man is one who would be an atheist if the king were.

Jean de La Bruyère (1645–96) French satirist.
Les Caractères

3 Wit that can creep, and pride that licks the dust.

Alexander Pope (1688–1744) British poet.
Epistle to Dr. Arbuthnot

4 Whenever he met a great man he grovelled before him, and my-lorded him as only a freeborn Briton can do.

William Makepeace Thackeray (1811–63) British novelist.
Vanity Fair, Ch. 13

□ SEX □

See also abstinence, adultery, animalism, contraception, debauchery, lust, pornography, promiscuity, prudery, purity, sexes

1 Is sex dirty? Only if it's done right.

Woody Allen (Allen Stewart Konigsberg; 1935–) US film actor.
All You've Ever Wanted to Know About Sex

2 It was the most fun I ever had without laughing.

Woody Allen
Annie Hall

3 Don't knock it, it's sex with someone you love.

Woody Allen
Referring to masturbation
Annie Hall

4 It is called in our schools 'beastliness', and this is about the best name for it...should it become a habit it quickly destroys both health and spirits; he becomes feeble in body and mind, and often ends in a lunatic asylum.

Robert Baden-Powell (1857–1941) British soldier and founder of the Boy Scouts.
Referring to masturbation
Scouting for Boys

5 Money, it turned out, was exactly like sex, you thought of nothing else if you didn't have it and thought of other things if you did.

James Baldwin (1924–87) US writer.
Nobody Knows My Name

6 If God had meant us to have group sex, I guess he'd have given us all more organs.

Malcolm Bradbury (1932–) British academic and novelist.
Who Do You Think You Are?, 'A Very Hospitable Person'

7 SIECUS was founded in 1964, when one in two marriages was warped by sexual problems. Sex had to be brought out of the Victorian closet – freed from the guilt and fear, bigotry and misconceptions which shrouded it, if America was to recover from its deep-rooted sexual trouble.
Mary Calderone (1904–) US physician and sex educator.
SIECUS is an acronym for Sex Information and Education Council of the United States.
SIECUS Fund-raising Letter, 1979

8 It doesn't matter what you do in the bedroom as long as you don't do it in the street and frighten the horses.
Mrs Patrick Campbell (Beatrice Stella Tanner; 1865–1940) British actress.
The Duchess of Jermyn Street (Daphne Fielding), Ch. 2

9 I'll wager you that in 10 years it will be fashionable again to be a virgin.
Barbara Cartland (1902–) British romantic novelist.
The Observer, 'Sayings of the Week', 20 June 1976

10 I said 10 years ago that in 10 years time it would be smart to be a virgin. Now everyone is back to virgins again.
Barbara Cartland
The Observer, 'Sayings of the Week', 12 July 1987

11 She gave me a smile I could feel in my hip pocket.
Raymond Chandler (1888–1959) US novelist.
Farewell, My Lovely, Ch. 18

12 No more about sex, it's too boring.
Lawrence Durrell (1912–90) British novelist.
Tunc

13 He in a few minutes ravished this fair creature, or at least would have ravished her, if she had not, by a timely compliance, prevented him.
Henry Fielding (1707–54) British novelist.
Jonathan Wild, Bk. III, Ch. 7

14 Older women are best because they always think they may be doing it for the last time.
Ian Fleming (1908–64) British journalist and author.
Life of Ian Fleming (John Pearson)

15 But did thee feel the earth move?
Ernest Hemingway (1899–1961) US novelist.
For Whom the Bell Tolls, Ch. 13

16 People will insist...on treating the *mons Veneris* as though it were Mount Everest.
Aldous Huxley (1894–1964) British novelist.
Eyeless in Gaza, Ch. 30

17 'Bed,' as the Italian proverb succinctly puts it, 'is the poor man's opera.'
Aldous Huxley
Heaven and Hell

18 Sexual intercourse began
In nineteen sixty-three
(Which was rather late for me) –

Between the end of the *Chatterley* ban
And the Beatles' first LP.
Philip Larkin (1922–85) British poet.
High Windows, 'Annus Mirabilis'

19 When Eve ate this particular apple, she became aware of her own womanhood, mentally. And mentally she began to experiment with it. She has been experimenting ever since. So has man. To the rage and horror of both of them.
D. H. Lawrence (1885–1930) British novelist.
Fantasia of the Unconscious, Ch. 7

20 No sex without responsibility.
Lord Longford (1905–) British politician and social reformer.
The Observer, 'Sayings of the Week', 3 May 1954

21 The Duke returned from the wars today and did pleasure me in his top-boots.
Sarah, Duchess of Marlborough (1660–1744) Wife of John Churchill, 1st Duke of Marlborough.
Attributed to her in various forms, a more ambitious version goes '...pleasure me three times in his top-boots'

22 If sex is such a natural phenomenon, how come there are so many books on how to?
Bette Midler (1944–) US actress and comedienne.

23 The daughter-in-law of Pythagoras said that a woman who goes to bed with a man ought to lay aside her modesty with her skirt, and put it on again with her petticoat.
Michel de Montaigne (1533–92) French essayist.
Essais, I

24 The orgasm has replaced the Cross as the focus of longing and the image of fulfilment.
Malcolm Muggeridge (1903–90) British writer.
The Most of Malcolm Muggeridge, 'Down with Sex'

25 It has to be admitted that we English have sex on the brain, which is a very unsatisfactory place to have it.
Malcolm Muggeridge
The Observer, 'Sayings of the Decade', 1964

26 Love is not the dying moan of a distant violin – it's the triumphant twang of a bedspring.
S. J. Perelman (1904–79) US humorous writer.
Quotations for Speakers and Writers (A. Andrews)

27 The Christian view of sex is that it is, indeed, a form of holy communion.
John Robinson (1919–83) Bishop of Woolwich.
Giving evidence in the prosecution of Penguin Books for publishing *Lady Chatterley's Lover*

28 Sex is something I really don't understand too hot. You never know *where* the hell you are. I keep making up these sex rules for myself, and then I break them right away.
J. D. Salinger (1919–) US novelist.
The Catcher in the Rye, Ch. 9

29 Girls are taught from childhood that any exhibition of sexual feeling is unwomanly and intolerable; they also learn from an early age that if a woman makes a mistake it is upon her and upon her alone that social punishment will descend.
Mary Scharlieb (1845–1930) British gynaecological surgeon.
The Seven Ages of Woman

30 Is it not strange that desire should so many years outlive performance?
William Shakespeare (1564–1616) English dramatist.
Henry IV, Part Two, II:4

31 Lechery, lechery! Still wars and lechery! Nothing else holds fashion.
William Shakespeare
Troilus and Cressida, V:2

32 I do not believe that the normal man's sex needs are stronger than the normal woman's. The *average* man's undoubtedly are, owing to the utterly false repression of the woman's and the utterly unnatural stimulation of the man's which have been current for so long.
Marie Stopes (1880–1958) British birth-control campaigner.
Letter, 17 Dec 1918

33 Masturbation: the primary sexual activity of mankind. In the nineteenth century it was a disease; in the twentieth, it's a cure.
Thomas Szasz (1920–) US psychiatrist.
The Second Sin

34 Traditionally, sex has been a very private, secretive activity. Herein perhaps lies its powerful force for uniting people in a strong bond. As we make sex less secretive, we may rob it of its power to hold men and women together.
Thomas Szasz
The Second Sin

35 Sex is the biggest nothing of all time.
Andy Warhol (Andrew Warhola; 1926–87) US pop artist.
Halliwell's Filmgoer's and Video Viewer's Companion

36 All this fuss about sleeping together. For physical pleasure I'd sooner go to my dentist any day.
Evelyn Waugh (1903–66) British novelist.
Vile Bodies, Ch. 6

37 When women go wrong, men go right after them.
Mae West (1892–1980) US actress.
The Wit and Wisdom of Mae West (ed. J. Weintraub)

38 It's not the men in my life that count; it's the life in my men.
Mae West
Attrib.

□SEXES□

See also feminism, marriage, men, sex, woman's role, women

1 And the man said, The woman whom thou gavest to be with me, she gave me of the tree, and I did eat.

And the Lord God said unto the woman, What is this that thou hast done? And the woman said, The serpent beguiled me, and I did eat.
And the Lord God said unto the serpent, Because thou hast done this, thou art cursed above all cattle, and above every beast of the field; upon thy belly shalt thou go, and dust shalt thou eat all the days of thy life:
And I will put enmity between thee and the woman, and between thy seed and her seed; it shall bruise thy head, and thou shalt bruise his heel.
Unto the woman he said, I will greatly multiply thy sorrow and thy conception; in sorrow thou shalt bring forth children; and thy desire shall be to thy husband, and he shall rule over thee.
And unto Adam he said, Because thou hast hearkened unto the voice of thy wife, and has eaten of the tree, of which I commanded thee, saying, Thou shalt not eat of it: cursed is the ground for thy sake; in sorrow shalt thou eat of it all the days of thy life.
Bible: Genesis
3:12–17

2 Mr. Darwin…has failed to hold definitely before his mind the principle that the difference of sex, whatever it may consist in, must itself be subject to natural selection and to evolution.
Antoinette Brown Blackwell (1825–1921) US feminist writer.
The Sexes Throughout Nature

3 Man's love is of man's life a thing apart,
'Tis woman's whole existence.
Lord Byron (1788–1824) British poet.
Don Juan, I

4 There is more difference within the sexes than between them.
Ivy Compton-Burnett (1892–1969) British novelist.
Mother and Son

5 In the sex-war thoughtlessness is the weapon of the male, vindictiveness of the female.
Cyril Connolly (1903–74) British journalist.
The Unquiet Grave

6 The reason that husbands and wives do not understand each other is because they belong to different sexes.
Dorothy Dix (Elizabeth Meriwether Gilmer; 1861–1951) US journalist and writer.
News item

7 I don't think men and women were meant to live together. They are totally different animals.
Diana Dors (1931–84) British actress.
Remark, May 1988

8 Man has his will, – but woman has her way.
Oliver Wendell Holmes (1809–94) US writer.
The Autocrat of the Breakfast Table, Prologue

9 For men must work, and women must weep,
And there's little to earn, and many to keep,
Though the harbour bar be moaning.
Charles Kingsley (1819–75) British writer.
The Three Fishers

10 The seldom female in a world of males!
Ruth Pitter (1897–) British poet.
The Kitten's Eclogue, IV

11 I often want to cry. That is the only advantage
women have over men – at least they can cry.
Jean Rhys (1894–1979) Dominican-born British novelist.
Good Morning, Midnight, Pt. II

12 Woman's virtue is man's greatest invention.
Cornelia Otis Skinner (1901–79) US stage actress.
Attrib.

13 Man is the hunter; woman is his game:
The sleek and shining creatures of the chase,
We hunt them for the beauty of their skins.
Alfred, Lord Tennyson (1809–92) British poet.
The Princess, V

14 Man for the field and woman for the hearth:
Man for the sword and woman for the needle she:
Man with the head and woman with the heart:
Man to command and woman to obey;
All else confusion.
Alfred, Lord Tennyson
The Princess, V

15 The War between Men and Women.
James Thurber (1894–1961) US humorist.
Title of a series of cartoons

16 All women become like their mothers. That is
their tragedy. No man does. That's his.
Oscar Wilde (1854–1900) Irish-born British dramatist.
The Importance of Being Earnest, I

17 Why are women…so much more interesting to
men than men are to women?
Virginia Woolf (1882–1941) British novelist.
A Room of One's Own

□ SHAKESPEARE □
William
(1564–1616) English dramatist and poet, universally acknowledged to be the greatest English writer of historical plays, comedies, and tragedies. His sonnets have love and friendship as their themes.

QUOTATIONS ABOUT SHAKESPEARE

1 Others abide our question, Thou art free,
We ask and ask: Thou smilest and art still,
Out-topping knowledge.
Matthew Arnold (1822–88) British poet and critic.
Shakespeare

2 When he killed a calf he would do it in a high
style, and make a speech.
John Aubrey (1626–1697) English antiquary.
Brief Lives, 'William Shakespeare'

3 Our myriad-minded Shakespeare.
Samuel Taylor Coleridge (1772–1834) British poet.
Biographia Literaria, Ch. 15

4 I have tried lately to read Shakespeare, and
found it so intolerably dull that it nauseated me.
Charles Darwin (1809–82) British life scientist.
Autobiography

5 We can say of Shakespeare, that never has a man
turned so little knowledge to such great account.
T. S. Eliot (1888–1965) US-born British poet and dramatist.
The Classics and the Man of Letters (lecture)

6 The remarkable thing about Shakespeare is that
he is really very good – in spite of all the people
who say he is very good.
Robert Graves (1895–1985) British poet and novelist.
The Observer, 'Sayings of the Week', 6 Dec 1964

7 Shakespeare never had six lines together without a fault. Perhaps you may find seven, but this
does not refute my general assertion.
Samuel Johnson (1709–84) British lexicographer.
Life of Johnson (J. Boswell), Vol. II

8 Sweet Swan of Avon!
Ben Jonson
To the Memory of William Shakespeare

9 Shakespeare – the nearest thing in incarnation to
the eye of God.
Laurence Olivier (1907–89) British actor.
Kenneth Harris Talking To, 'Sir Laurence Olivier'

10 A man can be forgiven a lot if he can quote Shakespeare in an economic crisis.
Prince Philip (1921–) The consort of Queen Elizabeth II.
Attrib.

QUOTATIONS BY SHAKESPEARE

11 Our remedies oft in ourselves do lie,
Which we ascribe to heaven.
All's Well that Ends Well, I:1

12 Th' inaudible and noiseless foot of Time.
All's Well that Ends Well, V:3

13 My salad days,
When I was green in judgment, cold in blood,
To say as I said then!
Antony and Cleopatra, I:5

14 The barge she sat in, like a burnish'd throne,
Burn'd on the water. The poop was beaten gold;
Purple the sails, and so perfumed that
The winds were love-sick with them; the oars
were silver,
Which to the tune of flutes kept stroke and made
The water which they beat to follow faster,
As amorous of their strokes. For her own person,
It beggar'd all description.
Antony and Cleopatra, II:2

15 I will praise any man that will praise me.
Antony and Cleopatra, II:6

16 I had rather bear with you than bear you.
As You Like It, II:4

17 If thou rememb'rest not the slightest folly
That ever love did make thee run into,
Thou hast not lov'd.
As You Like It, II:4

18 All the world's a stage,
And all the men and women merely players;
They have their exits and their entrances;
And one man in his time plays many parts,
His acts being seven ages.
As You Like It, II:7

19 Last scene of all,
That ends this strange eventful history,
Is second childishness and mere oblivion;
Sans teeth, sans eyes, sans taste, sans every thing.
As You Like It, II:7

20 He that wants money, means, and content, is without three good friends.
As You Like It, III:2

21 Do you not know I am a woman? When I think, I must speak.
As You Like It, III:2

22 I do desire we may be better strangers.
As You Like It, III:2

23 Men have died from time to time, and worms have eaten them, but not for love.
As You Like It, IV:1

24 Your If is the only peace-maker; much virtue in If.
As You Like It, V:4

25 Fear no more the heat o' th' sun
Nor the furious winter's rages;
Thou thy worldly task hast done,
Home art gone, and ta'en thy wages.
Golden lads and girls all must,
As chimney-sweepers, come to dust.
Cymbeline, IV:2

26 A little more than kin, and less than kind.
Hamlet, I:2

27 But I have that within which passes show –
these but the trappings and the suits of woe.
Hamlet, I:2

28 Do not, as some ungracious pastors do,
Show me the steep and thorny way to heaven,
Whiles, like a puff'd and reckless libertine,

Himself the primrose path of dalliance treads
And recks not his own rede.
Hamlet, I:3

29 Neither a borrower nor a lender be;
For loan oft loses both itself and friend,
And borrowing dulls the edge of husbandry.
This above all: to thine own self be true,
And it must follow, as the night the day,
Thou canst not then be false to any man.
Hamlet, I:3

30 But to my mind, though I am native here
And to the manner born, it is a custom
More honour'd in the breach than the observance.
Hamlet, I:4

31 There are more things in heaven and earth, Horatio,
Than are dreamt of in your philosophy.
Hamlet, I:5

32 Brevity is the soul of wit.
Hamlet, II:2

33 Though this be madness, yet there is method in't.
Hamlet, II:2

34 There is nothing either good or bad, but thinking makes it so.
Hamlet, II:2

35 What a piece of work is a man! How noble in reason! how infinite in faculties! in form and moving, how express and admirable! in action, how like an angel! in apprehension, how like a god! the beauty of the world! the paragon of animals! And yet, to me, what is this quintessence of dust? Man delights not me – no, nor woman neither.
Hamlet, II:2

36 To be, or not to be – that is the question;
Whether 'tis nobler in the mind to suffer
The slings and arrows of outrageous fortune,
Or to take arms against a sea of troubles,
And by opposing end them? To die, to sleep –
No more; and by a sleep to say we end
The heart-ache and the thousand natural shocks
That flesh is heir to, 'tis a consummation
Devoutly to be wish'd. To die, to sleep;
To sleep, perchance to dream. Ay, there's the rub;
For in that sleep of death what dreams may come,
When we have shuffled off this mortal coil,
Must give us pause.
Hamlet, III:1

37 Suit the action to the word, the word to the action; with this special observance, that you o'erstep not the modesty of nature.
Hamlet, III:2

38 The lady doth protest too much, methinks.
Hamlet, III:2

39 When sorrows come, they come not single spies,
But in battalions!
Hamlet, IV:5

40 Alas, poor Yorick! I knew him, Horatio: a fellow
of infinite jest, of most excellent fancy.
Hamlet, V:1

41 There's a divinity that shapes our ends,
Rough-hew them how we will.
Hamlet, V:2

42 Honour pricks me on. Yea, but how if honour
prick me off when I come on? How then? Can
honour set to a leg? No. Or an arm? No. Or take
away the grief of a wound? No. Honour hath no
skill in surgery, then? No. What is honour? A
word. What is in that word? Honour. What is that
honour? Air.
Henry IV, Part One, V:1

43 The better part of valour is discretion; in the
which better part I have saved my life.
Henry IV, Part One, V:4

44 Uneasy lies the head that wears a crown.
Henry IV, Part Two, III:1

45 Once more unto the breach, dear friends, once
more;
Or close the wall up with our English dead.
Henry V, III:1

46 Men of few words are the best men.
Henry V, III:2

47 I think the King is but a man as I am: the violet
smells to him as it doth to me.
Henry V, IV:1

48 Every subject's duty is the King's; but every
subject's soul is his own.
Henry V, IV:1

49 Old men forget; yet all shall be forgot,
But he'll remember, with advantages,
What feats he did that day.
Henry V, IV:3

50 I would not be a queen
For all the world.
Henry VIII, II:3

51 Had I but serv'd my God with half the zeal
I serv'd my King, he would not in mine age
Have left me naked to mine enemies.
Henry VIII, III:2

52 Men's evil manners live in brass: their virtues
We write in water.
Henry VIII, IV:2

53 Let me have men about me that are fat;
Sleek-headed men, and such as sleep o' nights.
Yond Cassius has a lean and hungry look;
He thinks too much. Such men are dangerous.
Julius Caesar, I:2

54 Cowards die many times before their deaths:
The valiant never taste of death but once.
Julius Caesar, II:2

55 *Et tu, Brute?*
Julius Caesar, III:1

56 Cry 'Havoc!' and let slip the dogs of war.
Julius Caesar, III:1

57 Not that I lov'd Caesar less, but that I lov'd Rome
more.
Julius Caesar, III:2

58 Friends, Romans, countrymen, lend me your
ears
I come to bury Caesar, not to praise him.
The evil that men do lives after them;
The good is oft interred with their bones.
Julius Caesar, III:2

59 There is a tide in the affairs of men
Which, taken at the flood, leads on to fortune;
Omitted, all the voyage of their life
Is bound in shallows and in miseries.
On such a full sea are we now afloat,
And we must take the current when it serves,
Or lose our ventures.
Julius Caesar, IV:3

60 Bell, book, and candle, shall not drive me back,
When gold and silver becks me to come on.
King John, III:3

61 This is the excellent foppery of the world, that,
when we are sick in fortune, often the surfeits of
our own behaviour, we make guilty of our disasters the sun, the moon, and stars.
King Lear, I:2

62 O, let me not be mad, not mad, sweet heaven!
Keep me in temper; I would not be mad!
King Lear, I:5

63 I am a man
More sinn'd against than sinning.
King Lear, III:2

64 Out vile jelly!
Where is thy lustre now?
Spoken by Cornwall as he puts out Gloucester's remaining eye.
King Lear, III:7

65 As flies to wanton boys are we to th' gods –
They kill us for their sport.
King Lear, IV:1

66 When we are born, we cry that we are come
To this great stage of fools.
King Lear, IV:6

67 When icicles hang by the wall,
And Dick the shepherd blows his nail,
And Tom bears logs into the hall,
And milk comes frozen home in pail,
When blood is nipp'd, and ways be foul,
Then nightly sings the staring owl:
'Tu-who;
Tu-whit, Tu-who' – A merry note,
While greasy Joan doth keel the pot.
Love's Labour's Lost, V:2

68 So foul and fair a day I have not seen.
Macbeth, I:3

69 Yet do I fear thy nature;
It is too full o' th' milk of human kindness
To catch the nearest way.
Macbeth, I:5

70 If it were done when 'tis done, then 'twere well
It were done quickly.
Macbeth, I:7

71 I have no spur
To prick the sides of my intent, but only
Vaulting ambition, which o'er-leaps itself,
And falls on th' other.
Macbeth, I:7

72 It provokes the desire, but it takes away the performance. Therefore much drink may be said to be an equivocator with lechery.
Macbeth, II:3

73 Stand not upon the order of your going,
But go at once.
Macbeth, III:4

74 Out, damned spot! out, I say!
Macbeth, V:1

75 Here's the smell of the blood still. All the perfumes of Arabia will not sweeten this little hand.
Macbeth, V:1

76 Tomorrow, and tomorrow, and tomorrow,
Creeps in this petty pace from day to day
To the last syllable of recorded time,
And all our yesterdays have lighted fools
The way to dusty death. Out, out, brief candle!
Life's but a walking shadow, a poor player,
That struts and frets his hour upon the stage,
And then is heard no more; it is a tale

Told by an idiot, full of sound and fury,
Signifying nothing.
Macbeth, V:5

77 The miserable have no other medicine
But only hope.
Measure for Measure, III:1

78 Haste still pays haste, and leisure answers leisure;
Like doth quit like, and Measure still for Measure.
Measure for Measure, V:1

79 It is a wise father that knows his own child.
The Merchant of Venice, II:2

80 But love is blind, and lovers cannot see
The pretty follies that themselves commit.
The Merchant of Venice, II:6

81 Hath not a Jew eyes? Hath not a Jew hands, organs, dimensions, senses, affections, passions, fed with the same food, hurt with the same weapons, subject to the same diseases, healed by the same means, warmed and cooled by the same winter and summer, as a Christian is? If you prick us, do we not bleed? If you tickle us, do we not laugh? If you poison us, do we not die? And if you wrong us, shall we not revenge?
The Merchant of Venice, III:1

82 The quality of mercy is not strain'd;
It droppeth as the gentle rain from heaven
Upon the place beneath. It is twice blest;
It blesseth him that gives and him that takes.
The Merchant of Venice, IV:1

83 Why, then the world's mine oyster,
Which I with sword will open.
The Merry Wives of Windsor, II:2

84 For aught that I could ever read,
Could ever hear by tale or history,
The course of true love never did run smooth.
A Midsummer Night's Dream, I:1

85 Love looks not with the eyes, but with the mind;
And therefore is wing'd Cupid painted blind.
A Midsummer Night's Dream, I:1

86 I thank God I am as honest as any man living that is an old man and no honester than I.
Much Ado About Nothing, III:5

87 Comparisons are odorous.
Much Ado About Nothing, III:5

88 For there was never yet philosopher
That could endure the toothache patiently.
Much Ado About Nothing, V:1

89 To mourn a mischief that is past and gone
Is the next way to draw new mischief on.
Othello, I:3

90 Good name in man and woman, dear my lord,
Is the immediate jewel of their souls:
Who steals my purse steals trash; 'tis something, nothing;
'Twas mine, 'tis his, and has been slave to thousands;
But he that filches from me my good name
Robs me of that which not enriches him
And makes me poor indeed.
Othello, III:3

91 O, beware, my lord, of jealousy;
It is the green-ey'd monster which doth mock
The meat it feeds on.
Othello, III:3

92 Farewell the neighing steed and the shrill trump,
The spirit-stirring drum, th'ear piercing fife,
The royal banner, and all quality,
Pride, pomp, and circumstance, of glorious war!
Othello, III:3

93 Put out the light, and then put out the light.
If I quench thee, thou flaming minister,
I can again thy former light restore,
Should I repent me; but once put out thy light,
Thou cunning'st pattern of excelling nature,
I know not where is that Promethean heat
That can thy light relume.
Othello, V:2

94 Then must you speak
Of one that lov'd not wisely, but too well;
Of one not easily jealous, but, being wrought,
Perplexed in the extreme; of one whose hand,
Like the base Indian, threw a pearl away
Richer than all his tribe.
Othello, V:2

95 Crabbed age and youth cannot live together:
Youth is full of pleasure, age is full of care;
Youth like summer morn, age like winter weather;
Youth like summer brave, age like winter bare.
The Passionate Pilgrim, XII

96 3RD FISHERMAN. Master, I marvel how the fishes live in the sea.
1ST FISHERMAN. Why, as men do a-land – the great ones eat up the little ones.
Pericles, II:1

97 This royal throne of kings, this sceptred isle,
This earth of majesty, this seat of Mars,
This other Eden, demi-paradise,
This fortress built by Nature for herself
Against infection and the hand of war,
This happy breed of men, this little world,
This precious stone set in the silver sea,
Which serves it in the office of a wall,
Or as a moat defensive to a house,
Against the envy of less happier lands;
This blessed plot, this earth, this realm, this England,
This nurse, this teeming womb of royal kings,
Fear'd by their breed, and famous by their birth.
Richard II, II:1

98 For God's sake let us sit upon the ground
And tell sad stories of the death of kings:
How some have been depos'd, some slain in war,
Some haunted by the ghosts they have depos'd,
Some poison'd by their wives, some sleeping kill'd,
All murder'd – for within the hollow crown
That rounds the mortal temples of a king
Keeps Death his court.
Richard II, III:2

99 Now is the winter of our discontent
Made glorious summer by this sun of York.
Richard III, I:1

100 A horse! a horse! my kingdom for a horse.
Richard III, V:4

101 O Romeo, Romeo! wherefore art thou Romeo?
Romeo and Juliet, II:2

102 What's in a name? That which we call a rose
By any other name would smell as sweet.
Romeo and Juliet, II:2

103 O, swear not by the moon, th' inconstant moon,
That monthly changes in her circled orb,
Lest that thy love prove likewise variable.
Romeo and Juliet, II:2

104 Good night, good night! Parting is such sweet sorrow
That I shall say good night till it be morrow.
Romeo and Juliet, II:2

105 A plague o' both your houses!
They have made worms' meat of me.
Romeo and Juliet, III:1

106 Shall I compare thee to a summer's day?
Thou art more lovely and more temperate.
Rough winds do shake the darling buds of May,
And summer's lease hath all too short a date.
Sonnet 18

107 A woman's face, with Nature's own hand painted,
Hast thou, the Master Mistress of my passion.
Sonnet 20

108 Like as the waves make towards the pebbled
shore,
So do our minutes hasten to their end.
Sonnet 60

109 For sweetest things turn sourest by their deeds:
Lilies that fester smell far worse than weeds.
Sonnet 94

110 My mistress' eyes are nothing like the sun;
Coral is far more red than her lips' red.
Sonnet 130

111 This is a way to kill a wife with kindness.
The Taming of the Shrew, IV:1

112 Our purses shall be proud, our garments poor;
For 'tis the mind that makes the body rich;
And as the sun breaks through the darkest
clouds,
So honour peereth in the meanest habit.
The Taming of the Shrew, IV:3

113 Full fathom five thy father lies;
Of his bones are coral made;
Those are pearls that were his eyes;
Nothing of him that doth fade
But doth suffer a sea-change
Into something rich and strange.
The Tempest, I:2

114 How beauteous mankind is! O brave new world
That has such people in't!
The Tempest, V:1

115 To be wise and love
Exceeds man's might.
Troilus and Cressida, III:2

116 Lechery, lechery! Still wars and lechery!
Nothing else holds fashion.
Troilus and Cressida, V:2

117 If music be the food of love, play on,
Give me excess of it, that, surfeiting,
The appetite may sicken and so die.
Twelfth Night, I:1

118 She never told her love,
But let concealment, like a worm i' th' bud,
Feed on her damask cheek. She pin'd in
thought;
And with a green and yellow melancholy
She sat like Patience on a monument,
Smiling at grief.
Twelfth Night, II:4

119 Some are born great, some achieve greatness,
and some have greatness thrust upon 'em.
Twelfth Night, II:5

120 Love sought is good, but given unsought is
better.
Twelfth Night, III:1

121 Who is Silvia? What is she,
That all our swains commend her?
Holy, fair, and wise is she.
The Two Gentlemen of Verona, IV:2

122 What's gone and what's past help
Should be past grief.
The Winter's Tale, III:2

123 I would there were no age between ten and
three and twenty, or that youth would sleep out
the rest; for there is nothing in the between but
getting wenches with child, wronging the
ancientry, stealing, fighting.
The Winter's Tale, III:3

124 Though I am not naturally honest, I am so sometimes by chance.
The Winter's Tale, IV:3

□ SHAW □
George Bernard
(1856–1950) Irish dramatist and critic. His plays, with their long
prefaces, established him as the leading British playwright of his
time. Included among his prose works are *The Intelligent
Woman's Guide to Socialism and Capitalism* (1928) and *The Black
Girl in Search of God* (1932).

QUOTATIONS ABOUT SHAW

1 Shaw's works make me admire the magnificent
tolerance and broadmindedness of the English.
James Joyce (1882–1941) Irish novelist.
The Wild Geese (Gerald Griffin)

QUOTATIONS BY SHAW

2 Whether you think Jesus was God or not, you
must admit that he was a first-rate political
economist.
Androcles and the Lion, Preface, 'Jesus as Economist'

3 When a stupid man is doing something he is
ashamed of, he always declares that it is his duty.
Caesar and Cleopatra, III

4 A man of great common sense and good taste, –
meaning thereby a man without originality or
moral courage.
Referring to Julius Caesar.
Caesar and Cleopatra, Notes

5 The British soldier can stand up to anything
except the British War Office.
The Devil's Disciple, II

6 My way of joking is to tell the truth. It's the funni-
est joke in the world.
John Bull's Other Island, II

7 Nobody can say a word against Greek: it stamps a man at once as an educated gentleman.
Major Barbara, I

8 Alcohol is a very necessary article...It enables Parliament to do things at eleven at night that no sane person would do at eleven in the morning.
Major Barbara, II

9 He knows nothing; and he thinks he knows everything. That points clearly to a political career.
Major Barbara, III

10 Give women the vote, and in five years there will be a crushing tax on bachelors.
Man and Superman, Preface

11 A lifetime of happiness: no man alive could bear it: it would be hell on earth.
Man and Superman, I

12 Very nice sort of place, Oxford, I should think, for people that like that sort of place.
Man and Superman, II

13 There are two tragedies in life. One is to lose your heart's desire. The other is to gain it.
Man and Superman, IV

14 In heaven an angel is nobody in particular.
Man and Superman, 'Maxims for Revolutionists'

15 Do not love your neighbour as yourself. If you are on good terms with yourself it is an impertinence; if on bad, an injury.
Man and Superman, 'Maxims for Revolutionists'

16 If you strike a child, take care that you strike it in anger, even at the risk of maiming it for life. A blow in cold blood neither can nor should be forgiven.
Man and Superman, 'Maxims for Revolutionists'

17 The golden rule is that there are no golden rules.
Man and Superman, 'Maxims for Revolutionists'

18 He who can, does. He who cannot, teaches.
Man and Superman, 'Maxims for Revolutionists'

19 The secret of being miserable is to have leisure to bother about whether you are happy or not.
Misalliance, Preface

20 The English have no respect for their language, and will not teach their children to speak it...It is impossible for an Englishman to open his mouth, without making some other Englishman despise him.
Pygmalion, Preface

21 Assassination is the extreme form of censorship.
The Shewing-Up of Blanco Posnet, 'The Limits of Toleration'

22 Well, sir, you never can tell. That's a principle in life with me, sir, if you'll excuse my having such a thing, sir.
You Never Can Tell, II

23 I've been offered titles, but I think they get one into disreputable company.
Gossip (A. Barrow)

24 The trouble, Mr Goldwyn is that you are only interested in art and I am only interested in money.
Turning down Goldwyn's offer to buy the screen rights of his plays.
The Movie Moguls (Philip French), Ch. 4

25 I quite agree with you, sir, but what can two do against so many?
Responding to a solitary hiss heard amongst the applause at the first performance of *Arms and the Man* in 1894.
Oxford Book of Literary Anecdotes

26 Certainly, there is nothing else here to enjoy.
Said at a party when his hostess asked him whether he was enjoying himself.
Pass the Port (Oxfam)

27 Far too good to waste on children.
Reflecting upon youth.
10,000 Jokes, Toasts, and Stories (L. Copeland)

28 Better never than late.
Responding to an offer by a producer to present one of Shaw's plays, having earlier rejected it.
The Unimportance of Being Oscar (Oscar Levant)

29 If all economists were laid end to end, they would not reach a conclusion.
Attrib.

☐ SHELLEY ☐
Percy Bysshe
(1792–1822) British poet. Most of his poetry was written in Italy, including *Prometheus Unbound* (1818–19), *Adonais* (1821), and much lyrical poetry.

QUOTATIONS ABOUT SHELLEY

1 In his poetry as well as in his life Shelley was indeed 'a beautiful and ineffectual angel', beating in the void his luminous wings in vain.
Matthew Arnold (1822–88) British poet and critic.
Literature and Drama, 'Shelley'

2 Poor Shelley always was, and is, a kind of ghastly object; colourless, pallid, tuneless, without health or warmth or vigour.
Thomas Carlyle (1795–1881) Scottish historian and essayist.
Reminiscences

QUOTATIONS BY SHELLEY

3 He hath awakened from the dream of life –
'Tis we, who lost in stormy visions, keep
With phantoms an unprofitable strife,

And in mad trance, strike with our spirit's knife
Invulnerable nothings.
Adonais, XXXIX

4 I am the daughter of Earth and Water,
And the nursling of the Sky;
I pass through the pores of the ocean and shores;
I change, but I cannot die,
For after the rain when with never a stain
The pavilion of Heaven is bare,
And the winds and sunbeams with their convex
gleams
Build up the blue dome of air,
I silently laugh at my own cenotaph,
And out of the caverns of rain,
Like a child from the womb, like a ghost from the
tomb,
I arise and unbuild it again.
The Cloud

5 Poetry is the record of the best and happiest
moments of the happiest and best minds.
A Defence of Poetry

6 Life may change, but it may fly not;
Hope may vanish, but can die not;
Truth be veiled, but still it burneth;
Love repulsed, – but it returneth!
Hellas, I

7 London, that great sea, whose ebb and flow
At once is deaf and loud, and on the shore
Vomits its wrecks, and still howls on for more.
Letter to Maria Gisborne, I

8 If Winter comes, can Spring be far behind?
Ode to the West Wind

9 'My name is Ozymandias, king of kings:
Look on my works, ye Mighty, and despair!'
Ozymandias

10 Sometimes
The Devil is a gentleman.
Peter Bell the Third

□ SHERIDAN □
Richard Brinsley
(1751–1816) British dramatist. His best-known comedies are *The Rivals* (1775) and *School for Scandal* (1777). He was manager of the Drury Lane Theatre and a Whig MP (1780–1812).

QUOTATIONS ABOUT SHERIDAN

1 Good at a fight, but better at a play
God-like in giving, but the devil to pay.
Lord Byron (1788–1824) British poet.
On a Cast of Sheridan's Hand

QUOTATIONS BY SHERIDAN

2 If it is abuse – why one is always sure to hear of it
from one damned good-natured friend or other!
The Critic, I

3 It gives me the hydrostatics to such a degree.
The Rivals, III

4 He is the very pine-apple of politeness!
The Rivals, III

5 If I reprehend any thing in this world, it is the use
of my oracular tongue, and a nice derangement
of epitaphs!
The Rivals, III

6 You had no taste when you married me.
The School for Scandal, I

7 I'm called away by particular business. But I
leave my character behind me.
The School for Scandal, II

8 Well, then, my stomach must just digest in its
waistcoat.
On being warned that his drinking would destroy the coat of his
stomach.
The Fine Art of Political Wit (L. Harris)

9 What His Royal Highness most particularly
prides himself upon, is the excellent harvest.
Lampooning George IV's habit of taking credit for everything
good in England.
The Fine Art of Political Wit (L. Harris)

10 A man may surely be allowed to take a glass of
wine by his own fireside.
As he sat in a coffeehouse watching his Drury Lane Theatre burn
down.
Memoirs of the Life of the Rt. Hon. Richard Brinsley Sheridan
(T. Moore)

11 Won't you come into the garden? I would like my
roses to see you.
Said to a young lady.
Attrib. in The Perfect Hostess

12 It is not my interest to pay the principal, nor my
principle to pay the interest.
To his tailor when he requested the payment of a debt, or of the
interest on it at least.
Attrib.

13 The Right Honourable gentleman is indebted to
his memory for his jests, and to his imagination
for his facts.
Replying to a speech in the House of Commons.
Attrib.

14 Mr. Speaker, I said the honorable member was a
liar it is true and I am sorry for it. The honourable member may place the punctuation where
he pleases.
On being asked to apologize for calling a fellow MP a liar.
Attrib.

□SHYNESS□

See also self-confidence

1 A timid question will always receive a confident answer.
Lord Darling (1849–1936) British judge.
Scintillae Juris

2 Shyness is just egotism out of its depth.
Penelope Keith British actress.
Remark, July 1988

3 Had we but world enough, and time,
This coyness, lady, were no crime,
Andrew Marvell (1621–78) English poet.
To His Coy Mistress

4 Shyness is *common*....Self-consciousness it was always called when I was young, and that is what it is. To imagine that it shows a sense of modesty is absurd. *Modesty*. Why, I have never known a *truly* modest person to be the least bit shy.
Elizabeth Taylor (1912–75) British writer.
The Bush, 'You'll Enjoy It When You Get There'

□SIGNATURES□

1 There, I guess King George will be able to read that.
John Hancock (1737–93) US revolutionary.
Referring to his signature, written in a bold hand, on the US Declaration of Independence
The American Treasury (C. Fadiman)

2 The hand that signed the treaty bred a fever,
And famine grew, and locusts came;
Great is the hand that holds dominion over
Man by a scribbled name.
Dylan Thomas (1914–53) Welsh poet.
The Hand that Signed the Paper

□SILENCE□

See also speech

1 When you have nothing to say, say nothing.
Charles Caleb Colton (?1780–1832) British clergyman and writer.
Lacon, Vol. I

2 Silence is as full of potential wisdom and wit as the unhewn marble of great sculpture.
Aldous Huxley (1894–1964) British novelist.
Point Counter Point

3 Thou still unravish'd bride of quietness,
Thou foster-child of silence and slow time,
John Keats (1795–1821) British poet.
Ode on a Grecian Urn

4 Silence is the best tactic for him who distrusts himself.
Duc de la Rochefoucauld (1613–80) French writer.
Maximes, 79

5 Silence is the perfectest herald of joy: I were but little happy if I could say how much.
William Shakespeare (1564–1616) English dramatist.
Much Ado About Nothing, II:1

6 Silence is the most perfect expression of scorn.
George Bernard Shaw (1856–1950) Irish dramatist and critic.
Back to Methuselah

7 The cruellest lies are often told in silence.
Robert Louis Stevenson (1850–94) Scottish writer.
Virginibus Puerisque

8 Whereof one cannot speak, thereon one must remain silent.
Ludwig Wittgenstein (1889–1951) Austrian philosopher.
Tractatus Logico-Philosophicus, Ch. 7

□SIMPLICITY□

1 'Excellent!' I cried. 'Elementary,' said he.
Arthur Conan Doyle (1856–1930) British writer.
Watson talking to Sherlock Holmes; Holmes's reply is often misquoted as 'Elementary my dear Watson'
The Crooked Man

2 The ability to simplify means to eliminate the unnecessary so that the necessary may speak.
Hans Hofmann (1880–1966) German-born US painter.
Search for the Real

3 O holy simplicity!
John Huss (Jan Hus; c. 1369–1415) Bohemian religious reformer.
On noticing a peasant adding a faggot to the pile at his execution
Apophthegmata (Zincgreff-Weidner), Pt. III

4 A child of five would understand this. Send somebody to fetch a child of five.
Groucho Marx (Julius Marx; 1895–1977) US comedian.
Duck Soup

5 Our life is frittered away by detail...Simplify, simplify.
Henry David Thoreau (1817–62) US writer.
Walden, 'Where I lived, and What I Lived For'

□SIN□

See also evil, vice

1 Old sins cast long shadows.
Proverb

2 All sin tends to be addictive, and the terminal point of addiction is what is called damnation.
W. H. Auden (1907–73) British poet.
A Certain World

3 So when they continued asking him, he lifted up himself, and said unto them, He that is without sin among you, let him first cast a stone at her.
Bible: John
8:7

4 If we say that we have no sin, we deceive ourselves, and the truth is not in us.
If we confess our sins, he is faithful and just to
forgive us our sins, and to cleanse us from all
unrighteousness.
Bible: I John
1:8–9

5 But if ye will not do so, behold, ye have sinned
against the Lord: and be sure your sin will find
you out.
Bible: Numbers
32:23

6 We have left undone those things which we
ought to have done; and we have done those
things we ought not to have done.
The Book of Common Prayer
Morning Prayer, General Confession

7 A private sin is not so prejudicial in the world as a
public indecency.
Miguel de Cervantes (1547–1616) Spanish novelist.
Don Quixote, Pt. II, Ch. 22

8 It is my belief, Watson, founded upon my experience, that the lowest and vilest alleys of London
do not present a more dreadful record of sin than
does the smiling and beautiful countryside.
Arthur Conan Doyle (1856–1930) British writer.
Copper Beeches

9 Sin brought death, and death will disappear with
the disappearance of sin.
Mary Baker Eddy (1821–1910) US religious leader.
Science and Health, with Key to the Scriptures

10 There's nothing so artificial as sinning nowa-
days. I suppose it once was real.
D. H. Lawrence (1885–1930) British novelist.
St Mawr

11 The only people who should really sin
Are the people who can sin with a grin.
Ogden Nash (1902–71) US poet.
I'm a Stranger Here Myself

□ SINCERITY □
See also frankness, honesty, integrity

1 What comes from the heart, goes to the heart.
Samuel Taylor Coleridge (1772–1834) British poet.
Table Talk

2 Some of the worst men in the world are sincere
and the more sincere they are the worse they are.
Lord Hailsham (1907–) British Conservative politician.
The Observer, 'Sayings of the Week', 7 Jan 1968

3 A little sincerity is a dangerous thing, and a great
deal of it is absolutely fatal.
Oscar Wilde (1854–1900) Irish-born British dramatist.
The Critic as Artist, Pt. 2

□ SINGERS □
See also musicians, singing

1 Swans sing before they die – 'twere no bad thing,
Did certain persons die before they sing.
Samuel Taylor Coleridge (1772–1834) British poet.
Epigram on a Volunteer Singer

2 A wandering minstrel I –
A thing of shreds and patches,
Of ballads, songs and snatches,
And dreamy lullaby!
W. S. Gilbert (1836–1911) British dramatist.
The Mikado, I

□ SINGING □
See also music, opera, singers

1 You know whatta you do when you shit? Singing,
it's the same thing, only up!
Enrico Caruso (1873–1921) Italian tenor.
Whose Little Boy Are You? (H. Brown)

2 I have a song to sing O!
Sing me your song, O!
W. S. Gilbert (1836–1911) British dramatist.
The Yeoman of the Guard, I

□ SLAVERY □
See also imprisonment, oppression, racism

1 The future is the only kind of property that the
masters willingly concede to slaves.
Albert Camus (1913–60) French existentialist writer.
The Rebel

2 There they are cutting each other's throats,
because one half of them prefer hiring their
servants for life, and the other by the hour.
Thomas Carlyle (1795–1881) Scottish historian and essayist.
Referring to the American Civil War
Attrib.

3 The whole commerce between master and slave
is a perpetual exercise of the most boisterous passions, the most unremitting despotism on the
one part, and degrading submissions on the
other.
Thomas Jefferson (1743–1826) US statesman.
Notes on the State of Virginia

□ SLEEP □
See also bed, dreams

1 Now I lay me down to sleep,
I pray the Lord my soul to keep.
If I should die before I wake,
I pray the Lord my soul to take.
Anonymous
New England Primer, 1781

2 Rock-a-bye baby on the tree top,
When the wind blows the cradle will rock,

When the bough bends the cradle will fall,
Down comes the baby, cradle and all.
Charles Dupee Blake (1846–1903) British writer of nursery rhymes.
Attrib.

3 Laugh and the world laughs with you; snore and you sleep alone.
Anthony Burgess (John Burgess Wilson; 1917–) British novelist.
Inside Mr. Enderby

4 Golden slumbers kiss your eyes,
Smiles awake you when you rise.
Thomas Dekker (c. 1572–1632) English dramatist.
Patient Grissil, IV:2

5 He's a wicked man that comes after children when they won't go to bed and throws handfuls of sand in their eyes.
Ernst Hoffmann (1776–1822) German composer.
The Sandman

6 The amount of sleep required by the average person is about five minutes more.
Max Kauffmann
Attrib.

7 Sleep that knits up the ravell'd sleave of care,
The death of each day's life, sore labour's bath,
Balm of hurt minds, great nature's second course,
Chief nourisher in life's feast.
William Shakespeare (1564–1616) English dramatist.
Macbeth, II:2

8 Sleep, Death's twin-brother, knows not Death,
Nor can I dream of thee as dead.
Alfred, Lord Tennyson (1809–92) British poet.
In Memoriam A.H.H., LXVIII

9 It was the time when first sleep begins for weary mortals and by the gift of the gods creeps over them
most welcomely.
Virgil (Publius Vergilius Maro; 70–19 BC) Roman poet.
Aeneid, Bk. II

10 I believe the greatest asset a head of state can have is the ability to get a good night's sleep.
Harold Wilson (1916–) British politician and prime minister.
The World Tonight, BBC Radio, 16 Apr 1975

11 Dear God! the very houses seem asleep;
And all that mighty heart is lying still!
William Wordsworth (1770–1850) British poet.
Sonnets, 'Composed upon Westminster Bridge'

□SMALLNESS□
See also triviality

1 The Microbe is so very small
You cannot make him out at all.
Hilaire Belloc (1870–1953) French-born British poet.
More Beasts for Worse Children, 'The Microbe'

2 Small is beautiful.
E. F. Schumacher (1911–77) German-born economist.
Title of book

□SMITH□
Sydney
(1771–1845) British clergyman, essayist, and wit. He helped to found the *Edinburgh Review* (1802), and published many of his sermons, essays, speeches, and letters.

1 The moment the very name of Ireland is mentioned, the English seem to bid adieu to common feeling, common prudence, and common sense, and to act with the barbarity of tyrants, and the fatuity of idiots.
The Letters of Peter Plymley

2 Heat, madam! It was so dreadful that I found there was nothing for it but to take off my flesh and sit in my bones.
Discussing the hot weather with a lady acquaintance.
Lives of the Wits (H. Pearson)

3 What you don't know would make a great book.
Memoir (Lady Holland)

4 He has occasional flashes of silence, that make his conversation perfectly delightful.
Referring to Lord Macaulay.
Memoir (Lady Holland)

5 Minorities…are almost always in the right.
The Smith of Smiths (H. Pearson), Ch. 9

6 I look upon Switzerland as an inferior sort of Scotland.
Letter to Lord Holland, 1815

7 He who drinks a tumbler of London water has literally in his stomach more animated beings than there are men, women and children on the face of the globe.
Letter

8 No furniture so charming as books.
Memoir (Lady Holland)

9 He rose by gravity; I sank by levity.
Comparing his career with that of his brother, Robert Percy Smith.
Attrib.

□SMOKING□
See also abstinence

1 Certainly not – if you don't object if I'm sick.
Thomas Beecham (1879–1961) British conductor.
When asked whether he minded if someone smoked in a non-smoking compartment
Attrib.

2 Tobacco, divine, rare, superexcellent tobacco, which goes far beyond all their panaceas, potable

gold, and philosopher's stones, a sovereign remedy to all diseases.
Robert Burton (1577–1640) English scholar and explorer.
Anatomy of Melancholy

3 It is quite a three-pipe problem.
Arthur Conan Doyle (1856–1930) British writer.
The Red-Headed League

4 What a blessing this smoking is! perhaps the greatest that we owe to the discovery of America.
Arthur Helps (1813–75) British historian.
Friends in Council

5 A custom loathsome to the eye, hateful to the nose, harmful to the brain, dangerous to the lungs, and in the black, stinking fume thereof, nearest resembling the horrible Stygian smoke of the pit that is bottomless.
James I (1566–1625) King of England.
A Counterblast to Tobacco

6 Neither do thou lust after that tawney weed tobacco.
Ben Jonson (1573–1637) English dramatist.
Bartholomew Fair, II:6

7 Ods me, I marvel what pleasure or felicity they have in taking their roguish tobacco. It is good for nothing but to choke a man, and fill him full of smoke and embers.
Ben Jonson
Every Man in His Humour, III:5

8 This very night I am going to leave off tobacco! Surely there must be some other world in which this unconquerable purpose shall be realized. The soul hath not her generous aspirings implanted in her in vain.
Charles Lamb (1775–1834) British essayist.
Letter to Thomas Manning, 26 Dec 1815

9 The very act of smoking a cigarette is, for many, a major source of Displacement Activities…They are stress-smokers, not drug-smokers, and in that capacity at least, smoking can play a valuable role in a society full of minute-by-minute tensions and pressures. It is so much more than a question of inhaling smoke.
Desmond Morris (1928–) British biologist.
Manwatching, 'Displacement Activities'

10 This vice brings in one hundred million francs in taxes every year. I will certainly forbid it at once – as soon as you can name a virtue that brings in as much revenue.
Napoleon III (1808–73) French emperor.
Reply when asked to ban smoking
Anehdotenschatz (H. Hoffmeister)

11 We shall not refuse tobacco the credit of being sometimes medical, when used temperately, though an acknowledged poison.
Jesse Torrey (1787–1834)
The Moral Instructor, Pt. IV

12 When I was young, I kissed my first woman, and smoked my first cigarette on the same day. Believe me, never since have I wasted any more time on tobacco.
Arturo Toscanini (1867–1957) Italian conductor.
Attrib.

13 There are people who strictly deprive themselves of each and every eatable, drinkable and smokable which has in any way acquired a shady reputation. They pay this price for health. And health is all they get for it.
Mark Twain (Samuel Langhorne Clemens; 1835–1910) US writer.

14 I've done it a hundred times!
Mark Twain
Referring to giving up smoking
Attrib.

15 Tobacco drieth the brain, dimmeth the sight, vitiateth the smell, hurteth the stomach, destroyeth the concoction, disturbeth the humors and spirits, corrupteth the breath, induceth a trembling of the limbs, exsiccateth the windpipe, lungs, and liver, annoyeth the milt, scorcheth the heart, and causeth the blood to be adjusted.
Tobias Venner (1577–1660)
Via Recta ad Vitam Longam

☐ SNOBBERY ☐

See also aristocracy, class, one-upmanship

1 In our way we were both snobs, and no snob welcomes another who has risen with him.
Cecil Beaton (1904–80) British photographer.
Referring to Evelyn Waugh
Attrib.

2 And this is good old Boston,
The home of the bean and the cod,
Where the Lowells talk only to Cabots,
And the Cabots talk only to God.
John Collins Bossidy (1860–1928) US writer.
Toast at Holy Cross Alumni dinner, 1910

3 His hatred of snobs was a derivative of his snobbishness, but made the simpletons (in other words, everyone) believe that he was immune from snobbishness.
Marcel Proust (1871–1922) French novelist.
À la recherche du temps perdu: Le Côté de Guermantes

4 He who meanly admires mean things is a Snob.
William Makepeace Thackeray (1811–63) British novelist.
The Book of Snobs, Ch. 2

5 It is impossible, in our condition of society, not to be sometimes a Snob.
William Makepeace Thackeray
The Book of Snobs, Ch. 3

6 Never speak disrespectfully of Society,
Algernon. Only people who can't get into it do
that.
Oscar Wilde (1854–1900) Irish-born British dramatist.
The Importance of Being Earnest, III

□ SOCIALISM □

See also Communism, Marxism

1 Why is it always the intelligent people who are
socialists?
Alan Bennett (1934–) British playwright.
Forty Years On

2 The people's flag is deepest red;
It shrouded oft our martyred dead,
And ere their limbs grew stiff and cold,
Their heart's blood dyed its every fold.
Then raise the scarlet standard high!
Within its shade we'll live or die.
Tho' cowards flinch and traitors sneer,
We'll keep the red flag flying here.
James Connell (1852–1929) British socialist.
Traditionally sung at the close of annual conferences of the
British Labour Party
The Red Flag, in *Songs that made History* (H. E. Piggot), Ch. 6

3 Socialism can only arrive by bicycle.
José Antonio Viera Gallo (1943–) Chilean politician.
Energy and Equity (Ivan Illich)

4 Compassion is not a sloppy, sentimental feeling
for people who are underprivileged or sick…it is
an absolutely practical belief that, regardless of a
person's background, ability or ability to pay, he
should be provided with the best that society has
to offer.
Neil Kinnock (1942–) British politician.
Maiden speech, House of Commons, 1970

5 It is inconceivable that we could transform this
society without a major extension of public
ownership.
Neil Kinnock
Marxism Today, 1983

6 Under socialism *all* will govern in turn and will
soon become accustomed to no one governing.
Lenin (Vladimir Ilich Ulyanov; 1870–1924) Russian
revolutionary leader.
The State and Revolution, Ch. 6

7 As with the Christian religion, the worst adver-
tisement for Socialism is its adherents.
George Orwell (Eric Blair; 1903–50) British novelist.
The Road to Wigan Pier, Ch. 11

8 To the ordinary working man, the sort you
would meet in any pub on Saturday night, Socialism does not mean much more than better wages
and shorter hours and nobody bossing you
about.
George Orwell
The Road to Wigan Pier, Ch. 11

9 State socialism is totally alien to the British
character.
Margaret Thatcher (1925–) British politician and prime
minister.
The Times, 1983

□ SOCIETY □

See also mankind

1 Man was formed for society.
William Blackstone (1723–80) British jurist.
Commentaries on the Laws of England, Introduction

2 No man is an Island, entire of itself; every man is
a piece of the Continent, a part of the main.
John Donne (1573–1631) English poet.
Devotions, 17

3 Our civilization…has not yet fully recovered
from the shock of its birth – the transition from
the tribal or 'closed society', with its submission
to magical forces, to the 'open society' which sets
free the critical powers of man.
Karl Popper (1902–) Austrian-born British philosopher.
The Open Society and Its Enemies

4 Society is no comfort
To one not sociable.
William Shakespeare (1564–1616) English dramatist.
Cymbeline, IV:2

5 Man is a social animal.
Benedict Spinoza (Baruch de Spinoza; 1632–77) Dutch
philosopher.
Ethics

6 There is no such thing as Society. There are individual men and women, and there are families.
Margaret Thatcher (1925–) British politician and prime
minister.
Woman's Own, 31 Oct 1987

□ SOLDIERS □

See also army, officers, war

1 It's Tommy this, an' Tommy that, an' 'Chuck him
out, the brute!'
But it's 'Saviour of 'is country' when the guns
begin to shoot.
Rudyard Kipling (1865–1936) Indian-born British writer.
Tommy

2 They're changing guard at Buckingham Palace
Christopher Robin went down with Alice.
Alice is marrying one of the guard.
'A soldier's life is terrible hard,'
Says Alice.
A. A. Milne (1882–1956) British writer.
When We Were Very Young, 'Buckingham Palace'

3 Soldiers are citizens of death's grey land,
Drawing no dividend from time's tomorrows.
Siegfried Sassoon (1886–1967) British poet.
Dreamers

4 I never expect a soldier to think.
George Bernard Shaw
The Devil's Disciple, III

5 They're overpaid, overfed, oversexed and over here.
Tommy Trinder (1909–89) British entertainer.
Referring to the G.I.s
Attrib.

□ SOLITUDE □

See also loneliness

1 Whosoever is delighted in solitude is either a wild beast or a god.
Francis Bacon (1561–1626) English philosopher.
Essays, 'Of Friendship'

2 Alone, alone, all, all alone,
Alone on a wide wide sea!
And never a saint took pity on
My soul in agony.
Samuel Taylor Coleridge (1772–1834) British poet.
The Rime of the Ancient Mariner, IV

3 Oh for a lodge in some vast wilderness,
Some boundless contiguity of shade,
Where rumour of oppression and deceit,
Of unsuccessful or successful war,
Might never reach me more!
William Cowper (1731–1800) British poet.
The Task

4 I want to be alone.
Greta Garbo (1905–90) Swedish-born US film star.
Words spoken by Garbo in the film *Grand Hotel*, and associated with her for the rest of her career.

5 Far from the madding crowd's ignoble strife,
Their sober wishes never learn'd to stray;
Along the cool sequester'd vale of life
They kept the noiseless tenor of their way.
Thomas Gray (1716–71) British poet.
Elegy Written in a Country Churchyard

6 One of the pleasantest things in the world is going on a journey; but I like to go by myself.
William Hazlitt (1778–1830) British essayist.
On Going a Journey

7 It is a fine thing to be out on the hills alone. A man can hardly be a beast or a fool alone on a great mountain.
Francis Kilvert (1840–79) British diarist and clergyman.
Diary, 29 May 1871

8 In solitude
What happiness? who can enjoy alone,
Or, all enjoying, what contentment find?
John Milton (1608–74) English poet.
Paradise Lost, Bk. VIII

9 A man must keep a little back shop where he can be himself without reserve. In solitude alone can he know true freedom.
Michel de Montaigne (1533–92) French essayist.
Essais, I

10 I never found the companion that was so companionable as solitude.
Henry David Thoreau (1817–62) US writer.
Walden, 'Solitude'

□ SORROW □

See also despair, melancholy, mourning, regret

1 Do you hear the children weeping, O my brothers,
Ere the sorrow comes with years?
Elizabeth Barrett Browning (1806–61) British poet.
The Cry of the Children

2 One often calms one's grief by recounting it.
Pierre Corneille (1606–84) French dramatist.
Polyeucte, I:3

3 There is no greater sorrow than to recall a time of happiness when in misery.
Dante (1265–1321) Italian poet.
Divine Comedy, Inferno, V

4 *Adieu tristesse*
Bonjour tristesse
Tu es inscrite dans les lignes du plafond.
Farewell sadness
Good day sadness
You are written in the lines of the ceiling.
Paul Éluard (Eugène Grindel; 1895–1952) French surrealist poet.
La Vie immédiate

5 A moment of time may make us unhappy for ever.
John Gay (1685–1732) English poet and dramatist.
The Beggar's Opera

6 They say my verse is sad: no wonder;
Its narrow measure spans
Tears of eternity, and sorrow,
Not mine, but man's.
A. E. Housman (1859–1936) British scholar and poet.
Last Poems, 'Fancy's Knell'

7 Art thou weary, art thou languid,
Art thou sore distressed?
John Mason Neale (1818–66) British churchman.
Art thou Weary?

8 Sorrow is tranquillity remembered in emotion.
Dorothy Parker (1893–1967) US writer.
Sentiment

9 It is such a secret place, the land of tears.
Antoine de Saint-Exupéry (1900–44) French novelist and aviator.
The Little Prince, Ch. 7

10 If you have tears, prepare to shed them now.
William Shakespeare (1564–1616) English dramatist.
Julius Caesar, III:2

11 Down, thou climbing sorrow,
Thy element's below.
William Shakespeare
King Lear, II:4

12 'Tis held that sorrow makes us wise.
Alfred, Lord Tennyson (1809–92) British poet.
In Memoriam A.H.H., CXIII

□ SOUL □

1 We cannot kindle when we will
The fire which in the heart resides,
The spirit bloweth and is still,
In mystery our soul abides.
Matthew Arnold (1822–88) British poet and critic.
Morality

2 And see all sights from pole to pole,
And glance, and nod, and bustle by;
And never once possess our soul
Before we die.
Matthew Arnold
A Southern Night

3 Man has no Body distinct from his Soul; for that
called Body is a portion of Soul discerned by the
five Senses, the chief inlets of Soul in this age.
William Blake (1757–1827) British poet.
The Marriage of Heaven and Hell, 'The Voice of the Devil'

4 Leave the flesh to the fate it was fit for! the spirit
be thine!
Robert Browning (1812–89) British poet.
Saul, XIII

5 The dark night of the soul.
St John of the Cross (Juan de Yepes y Alvarez; 1542–91)
Spanish churchman and poet.
English translation of *Noche obscura del alma*, the title of a poem

6 And looks commercing with the skies,
Thy rapt soul sitting in thine eyes.
John Milton (1608–74) English poet.
Il Penseroso

7 Fair seed-time had my soul, and I grew up
Fostered alike by beauty and by fear.
William Wordsworth (1770–1850) British poet.
The Prelude, I

□ SPACE □

See also astronomy, discovery, exploration, moon, science,
stars, sun, technology, universe

1 That's one small step for man, one giant leap for
mankind.
Neil Armstrong (1930–) US astronaut.
Said on stepping onto the moon. Often quoted as, 'small step for a
man...' (which is probably what he intended)
Remark, 21 July 1969

2 Outer space is no place for a person of breeding.
Violet Bonham Carter (1887–1969) British politician.
The New Yorker

3 I am a passenger on the spaceship, Earth.
Richard Buckminster Fuller (1895–1983) US architect and
inventor.
Operating Manual for Spaceship Earth

4 Space isn't remote at all. It's only an hour's drive
away if your car could go straight upwards.
Fred Hoyle (1915–) British astronomer.
The Observer, 9 Sept 1979

5 Space is almost infinite. As a matter of fact we
think it *is* infinite.
Dan Quayle (James Danforth Q.; 1946–) US statesman.
The Sunday Times, 31 Dec 1989

□ SPECULATION □

1 While to deny the existence of an unseen kingdom is bad, to pretend that we know more about
it than its bare existence is no better.
Samuel Butler (1835–1902) British writer.
Erewhon, Ch. 15

2 If the world were good for nothing else, it is a fine
subject for speculation.
William Hazlitt (1778–1830) British essayist.
Characteristics

3 I think the primary notion back of most gambling is the excitement of it. While gamblers naturally want to win, the majority of them derive
pleasure even if they lose. The desire to win,
rather than the excitement involved, seems to
me the compelling force behind speculation.
Joseph Kennedy (1888–1969) US businessman.
The Kennedys, Ch. 2 (Peter Collier and David Horowitz)

□ SPEECH □

See also silence, speeches, verbosity, words

1 Let your speech be alway with grace, seasoned
with salt, that ye may know how ye ought to
answer every man.
Bible: Colossians
4:6

2 Let thy speech be short, comprehending much
in few words; be as one that knoweth and yet
holdeth his tongue.
Bible: Ecclesiasticus
32:8

3 To know how to say what others only know how
to think is what makes men poets or sages; and
to dare to say what others only dare to think
makes men martyrs or reformers – or both.
Elizabeth Charles (1828–96) British writer.
Chronicle of the Schönberg-Cotta Family

4 Most men make little use of their speech than to give evidence against their own understanding.
Lord Halifax (1633–95) English statesman.
Political, Moral, and Miscellaneous Thoughts and Reflections

5 The most precious things in speech are pauses.
Ralph Richardson (1902–83) British actor.
Attrib.

6 But words once spoke can never be recall'd.
Earl of Roscommon (1633–85) Irish-born English poet.
Art of Poetry

7 Speech was given to man to disguise his thoughts.
Talleyrand (Charles Maurice de Talleyrand-Périgord; 1754–1838) French politician.
Attrib.

□ SPEECHES □

See also brevity, sermons, verbosity

1 I take the view, and always have done, that if you cannot say what you have to say in twenty minutes, you should go away and write a book about it.
Lord Brabazon of Tara (1910–74) British businessman and Conservative politician.
Attrib.

2 An after-dinner speech should be like a lady's dress – long enough to cover the subject and short enough to be interesting.
R. A. Butler (1902–82) British Conservative politician.
Remark made at an Anglo-Jewish dinner

3 For I have neither wit, nor words, nor worth,
Action, nor utterance, nor the power of speech,
To stir men's blood; I only speak right on.
William Shakespeare (1564–1616) English dramatist.
Julius Caesar, III:2

□ SPELLING □

See also language, pronunciation, words, writing

1 Put it down a we, my lord, put it down a we!
Charles Dickens (1812–70) British novelist.
Pickwick Papers, Ch. 34

2 They spell it Vinci and pronounce it Vinchy; foreigners always spell better than they pronounce.
Mark Twain (Samuel Langhorne Clemens; 1835–1910) US writer.
The Innocents Abroad, Ch. 19

□ SPONTANEITY □

See also impetuosity

1 Spontaneity is only a term for man's ignorance of the gods.
Samuel Butler (1835–1902) British writer.
Erewhon, Ch. 25

2 Away with all ideals. Let each individual act spontaneously from the for ever incalculable prompt-

ing of the creative wellhead within him. There is no universal law.
D. H. Lawrence (1885–1930) British novelist.
Phoenix, Preface to 'All Things are Possible' by Leo Shostov

□ SPOONERISMS □

Sayings associated with the Oxford clergyman and academic William Archibald Spooner (1844–1930).

1 I remember your name perfectly, but I just can't think of your face.

2 Let us drink to the queer old Dean.

3 Sir, you have tasted two whole worms; you have hissed all my mystery lectures and have been caught fighting a liar in the quad; you will leave Oxford by the town drain.

□ SPORT AND GAMES □

See also cricket, fishing, football, golf, horses, hunting

1 Follow up! Follow up! Follow up! Follow up! Follow up!
Till the field ring again and again,
With the tramp of the twenty-two men,
Follow up!
E. E. Bowen (1836–1901) British writer.
Forty Years On (the Harrow school song)

2 There is plenty of time to win this game, and to thrash the Spaniards too.
Francis Drake (1540–96) British navigator and admiral.
Referring to the sighting of the Armada during a game of bowls, 20 July 1588
Attrib.

3 Exercise is bunk. If you are healthy, you don't need it: if you are sick, you shouldn't take it.
Henry Ford (1863–1947) US car manufacturer.
Attrib.

4 I am sorry I have not learned to play at cards. It is very useful in life: it generates kindness and consolidates society.
Samuel Johnson (1709–84) British lexicographer.
Tour to the Hebrides (J. Boswell)

5 Man is a gaming animal. He must always be trying to get the better in something or other.
Charles Lamb (1775–1834) British essayist.
Essays of Elia, 'Mrs Battle's Opinions on Whist'

6 O, he flies through the air with the greatest of ease,
This daring young man on the flying trapeze.
George Leybourne (?–1884) British songwriter.
The Man on the Flying Trapeze

7 Serious sport has nothing to do with fair play. It is bound up with hatred, jealousy, boastfulness, disregard of all rules and sadistic pleasure in

witnessing violence; in other words it is war minus the shooting.
George Orwell (Eric Blair; 1903–50) British novelist.
The Sporting Spirit

8 Gamesmanship or The Art of Winning Games Without Actually Cheating.
Stephen Potter (1900–69) British writer.
Book title

9 I wanted a play that would paint the full face of sensuality, rebellion and revivalism. In South Wales these three phenomena have played second fiddle only to the Rugby Union which is a distillation of all three.
Gwyn Thomas (1913–81) British writer.
Jackie the Jumper (Introduction), 'Plays and Players' 19 Jan 1963

☐ STARS ☐

See also astronomy, moon, space, sun, universe

1 ...things called Stars appeared, which robbed men of their souls and left them unreasoning brutes, so that they destroyed the civilization they themselves had built up.
Isaac Asimov (1920–) US science-fiction writer.
On the fictional world of Lagash night comes once every 2049 years
Nightfall

2 And God made two great lights: the greater light to rule the day, and the lesser light to rule the night: he made the stars also.
Bible: Genesis
1:16

3 Bright star, would I were steadfast as thou art.
John Keats (1795–1821) British poet.
Bright Star

4 Twinkle, twinkle, little star,
How I wonder what you are!
Up above the world so high,
Like a diamond in the sky!
Jane Taylor (1783–1824) British writer.
Rhymes for the Nursery (with Ann Taylor), 'The Star'

5 Stars lay like yellow pollen
That from a flower has fallen;
And single stars I saw
Crossing themselves in awe;
Some stars in sudden fear
Fell like a falling tear.
Andrew John Young (1885–1971) Scottish poet.
The Stars

☐ STATE ☐

See also democracy, government, republic

1 So long as the state exists there is no freedom. When there is freedom there will be no state.
Lenin (Vladimir Ilich Ulyanov; 1870–1924) Russian revolutionary leader.
The State and Revolution, Ch. 5

2 In a free society the state does not administer the affairs of men. It administers justice among men who conduct their own affairs.
Walter Lippman (1889–1974) US editor and writer.
An Enquiry into the Principles of a Good Society

3 The worth of a State in the long run is the worth of the individuals composing it.
John Stuart Mill (1806–73) British philosopher.
On Liberty, Ch. 5

4 The state is an instrument in the hands of the ruling class for suppressing the resistance of its class enemies.
Joseph Stalin (J. Dzhugashvili; 1879–1953) Soviet statesman.
Stalin's Kampf (ed. M. R. Werner)

☐ STATELY HOMES ☐

See also architecture, aristocracy, houses

1 Now Spring, sweet laxative of Georgian strains,
Quickens the ink in literary veins,
The Stately Homes of England ope their doors
To piping Nancy-boys and Crashing Bores.
Roy Campbell (1901–57) South African poet.
The Georgiad

2 The Stately Homes of England
How beautiful they stand,
To prove the upper classes
Have still the upper hand.
Noël Coward (1899–1973) British dramatist.
Operette, 'The Stately Homes of England'

3 And though the Van Dycks have to go
And we pawn the Bechstein grand,
We'll stand by the Stately Homes of England.
Noël Coward
Operette, The Stately Homes of England

4 The stately homes of England,
How beautiful they stand!
Amidst their tall ancestral trees,
O'er all the pleasant land.
Felicia Dorothea Hemans (1793–1835) British poet.
The Homes of England

☐ STATISTICS ☐

1 There are three kinds of lies: lies, damned lies and statistics.
Benjamin Disraeli (1804–81) British statesman.
Autobiography (Mark Twain)

2 You cannot feed the hungry on statistics.
David Lloyd George (1863–1945) British Liberal statesman.
Advocating Tariff Reform
Speech, 1904

3 Statistics will prove anything, even the truth.
Noël Moynihan (1916–) British doctor and writer.
Attrib.

4 I am one of the unpraised, unrewarded millions without whom Statistics would be a bankrupt

science. It is we who are born, who marry, who die, in constant ratios.
Logan Pearsall Smith (1865–1946) US writer.
Trivia

5 A single death is a tragedy; a million is a statistic.
Joseph Stalin (J. Dzhugashvili; 1879–1953) Soviet statesman.
Attrib.

☐STEVENSON☐
Robert Louis
(1850–94) Scottish writer. His books include *Treasure Island* (1883), *Kidnapped* (1886), and *The Strange Case of Dr Jekyll and Mr Hyde* (1886).

QUOTATIONS ABOUT STEVENSON

1 Stevenson seemed to pick the right word up on the point of his pen, like a man playing spillikins.
G. K. Chesterton (1874–1936) British writer.
The Victorian Age in Literature

QUOTATIONS BY STEVENSON

2 If your morals make you dreary, depend upon it, they are wrong.
Across the Plains

3 Politics is perhaps the only profession for which no preparation is thought necessary.
Familiar Studies of Men and Books, 'Yoshida-Torajiro'

4 Vanity dies hard; in some obstinate cases it outlives the man.
Prince Otto

5 Wealth I ask not; hope nor love,
Nor a friend to know me;
All I seek, the heaven above
And the road below me.
Songs of Travel, 'The Vagabond'

6 Many's the long night I've dreamed of cheese – toasted, mostly.
Treasure Island, Ch. 15

7 Under the wide and starry sky
Dig the grave and let me lie.
Glad did I live and gladly die,
– And I laid me down with a will.
This is the verse you grave for me:
'Here he lies where he longed to be;
Home is the sailor, home from sea,
And the hunter home from the hill.'
Underwoods, Bk. I, 'Requiem'

8 Man is a creature who lives not upon bread alone, but principally by catchwords; and the little rift between the sexes is astonishingly widened by simply teaching one set of catchwords to the girls and another to the boys.
Virginibus Puerisque

9 The cruellest lies are often told in silence.
Virginibus Puerisque

10 Books are good enough in their own way, but they are a mighty bloodless substitute for life.
Virginibus Puerisque

11 Lastly (and this is, perhaps, the golden rule), no woman should marry a teetotaller, or a man who does not smoke.
Virginibus Puerisque

12 Marriage is a step so grave and decisive that it attracts light-headed, variable men by its very awfulness.
Virginibus Puerisque

13 In marriage, a man becomes slack and selfish and undergoes a fatty degeneration of his moral being.
Virginibus Puerisque

14 To travel hopefully is a better thing than to arrive, and the true success is to labour.
Virginibus Puerisque

15 It's deadly commonplace, but, after all, the commonplaces are the great poetic truths.
Weir of Hermiston, Ch. 6

☐STRIKES☐
See also industrial relations

1 Not a penny off the pay; not a minute on the day.
A. J. Cook (1885–1931) British trade-union leader.
Slogan used in the miners' strike, 1926

2 There is no right to strike against the public safety by anybody, anywhere, any time.
Calvin Coolidge (1872–1933) US president.
Referring to the Boston police strike
Remark, 14 Sept 1919

3 The trouble with employers is that they only like ballots so long as you lose them.
Jimmy Knapp (1940–) General Secretary of the National Union of Railwaymen.
Referring to British Rail's decision to go to court following a ballot solidly in favour of strike action
The Guardian, 1989

4 People are now discovering the price of insubordination and insurrection. And boy, are we going to make it stick!
Ian MacGregor (1912–) British businessman.
Referring to the miners' strike
Sunday Telegraph, 10 Mar 1985

5 Another fact of life that will not have escaped you is that, in this country, the twenty-four-hour strike is like the twenty-four-hour flu. You have to reckon on it lasting at least five days.
Frank Muir (1920–) British writer and broadcaster.
You Can't Have Your Kayak and Heat It (Frank Muir and Dennis Norden), 'Great Expectations'

☐STUBBORNNESS☐

See also determination, inflexibility, petulance

1 Obstinate people can be divided into the opinionated, the ignorant, and the boorish.
Aristotle (384–322 BC) Greek philosopher.
Nicomachean Ethics, Bk. VII

2 'Tis known by the name of perseverance in a good cause, – and of obstinacy in a bad one.
Laurence Sterne (1713–68) Irish born British writer.
Tristram Shandy

☐STUPIDITY☐

See also foolishness, ignorance

1 His mind is open; yes, it is so open that nothing is retained; ideas simply pass through him.
F. H. Bradley (1846–1924) British philosopher.
Attrib.

2 Jerry Ford is so dumb that he can't fart and chew gum at the same time.
Lyndon B. Johnson (1908–73) US statesman.
Sometimes quoted as '…can't walk and chew gum'
A Ford, Not a Lincoln (R. Reeves), Ch. 1

3 You've got the brain of a four-year-old boy, and I bet he was glad to get rid of it.
Groucho Marx (Julius Marx; 1895–1977) US comedian.
Horse Feathers

4 Music-hall songs provide the dull with wit, just as proverbs provide them with wisdom.
W. Somerset Maugham (1874–1965) British novelist.
A Writer's Notebook

5 Stupidity does not consist in being without ideas. Such stupidity would be the sweet, blissful stupidity of animals, molluscs and the gods. Human Stupidity consists in having lots of ideas, but stupid ones.
Henry de Montherlant (1896–1972) French novelist.
Notebooks

6 I've examined your son's head, Mr Glum, and there's nothing there.
Frank Muir (1920–) British writer and broadcaster.
Take It from Here (Frank Muir and Dennis Norden), 1957

7 Against stupidity the gods themselves struggle in vain.
Friedrich von Schiller (1759–1805) German dramatist.
Die Jungfrau von Orleans, III:6

8 There is no sin except stupidity.
Oscar Wilde (1854–1900) Irish-born British dramatist.
The Critic as Artist, Pt. 2

☐STYLE☐

1 Style is the man himself.
Comte de Buffon (1707–88) French naturalist.
Discours sur le style

2 Style, like sheer silk, too often hides eczema.
Albert Camus (1913–60) French existentialist writer.
The Fall

3 All styles are good except the tiresome sort.
Voltaire (François-Marie Arouet; 1694–1778) French writer.
L'Enfant prodigue, Preface

4 In matters of grave importance, style, not sincerity, is the vital thing.
Oscar Wilde (1854–1900) Irish-born British dramatist.
The Importance of Being Earnest, III

☐SUBURBIA☐

1 I come from suburbia, Dan, personally, I don't ever want to go back. It's the one place in the world that's further away than anywhere else.
Frederic Raphael (1931–) British author.
The Glittering Prizes: A Sex Life, I:3

2 She was more than ever proud of the position of the bungalow, so almost in the country.
Angus Wilson (1913–91) British novelist.
A Bit Off the Map, 'A Flat Country Christmas'

☐SUCCESS☐

See also achievement, failure, victory

1 One's religion is whatever he is most interested in, and yours is Success.
J. M. Barrie (1860–1937) British novelist and dramatist.
The Twelve-Pound Look

2 Success is counted sweetest
By those who ne'er succeed.
Emily Dickinson (1830–86) US poet.
Success is Counted Sweetest

3 Sweet Smell of Success.
Ernest Lehman (1920–) US screenwriter.
Novel and film title

4 As is the case in all branches of art, success depends in a very large measure upon individual initiative and exertion, and cannot be achieved except by dint of hard work.
Anna Pavlova (1881–1931) Russian ballet dancer.
Pavlova: A Biography (ed. A. H. Franks), 'Pages of My Life'

5 To succeed in the world, we do everything we can to appear successful.
Duc de la Rochefoucauld (1613–80) French writer.
Maximes, 50

6 The only place where success comes before work is a dictionary.
Vidal Sassoon (1928–) British hair stylist.
Quoting one of his teachers in a BBC radio broadcast

7 The world continues to offer glittering prizes to those who have stout hearts and sharp swords.
F. E. Smith (1872–1930) British lawyer and politician.
Speech, Glasgow University, 7 Nov 1923

8 There are no gains without pains.
Adlai Stevenson (1900–65) US statesman.
Speech, Chicago, 26 July 1952

□ SUFFERING □

1 One does not love a place the less for having suffered in it unless it has all been suffering, nothing but suffering.
Jane Austen (1775–1817) British novelist.
Persuasion, Ch. 20

2 Once drinking deep of that divinest anguish,
How could I seek the empty world again?
Emily Brontë (1818–48) British novelist.
Remembrance

3 If suffer we must, let's suffer on the heights.
Victor Hugo (1802–85) French writer.
Contemplations, 'Les Malheureux'

4 Rather suffer than die is man's motto.
Jean de La Fontaine (1621–95) French poet.
Fables, I, 'La Mort et le Bûcheron'

5 A man who fears suffering is already suffering from what he fears.
Michel de Montaigne (1533–92) French essayist.
Essais, III

6 Thou art a soul in bliss; but I am bound
Upon a wheel of fire, that mine own tears
Do scald like molten lead.
William Shakespeare (1564–1616) English dramatist.
King Lear, IV:7

7 I know, by sad experience, with what difficulty a mind, weakened by long and uninterrupted suffering, admits hope, much less assurance.
Sarah Siddons (1755–1831) English actress.
Letter to Mrs. FitzHugh, 14 July 1801

□ SUICIDE □

See also death

1 If you must commit suicide…always contrive to do it as decorously as possible; the decencies, whether of life or of death, should never be lost sight of.
George Borrow (1803–81) British writer.
Lavengro, Ch. 23

2 Suicide is the worst form of murder, because it leaves no opportunity for repentance.
John Churton Collins (1848–1908)
Life and Memoirs of John Churton Collins (L. C. Collins),
Appendix VII

3 The thought of suicide is a great source of comfort: with it a calm passage is to be made across many a bad night.
Friedrich Wilhelm Nietzsche (1844–1900) German philosopher.
Jenseits von Gut und Böse

4 Razors pain you
Rivers are damp;
Acids stain you;
And drugs cause cramp.
Guns aren't lawful;
Nooses give;
Gas smells awful;
You might as well live.
Dorothy Parker (1893–1967) US writer.
Enough Rope, 'Resumé'

5 It is against the law to commit suicide in this man's town … although what the law can do to a guy who commits suicide I am never able to figure out.
Damon Runyon (1884–1946) US writer.
Guys and Dolls

6 Dost thou not see my baby at my breast
That sucks the nurse asleep?
William Shakespeare (1564–1616) English dramatist.
Holding the asp to her breast
Antony and Cleopatra, V:2

7 To be, or not to be – that is the question;
Whether 'tis nobler in the mind to suffer
The slings and arrows of outrageous fortune,
Or to take arms against a sea of troubles,
And by opposing end them? To die, to sleep –
No more; and by a sleep to say we end
The heart-ache and the thousand natural shocks
That flesh is heir to, 'tis a consummation
Devoutly to be wish'd. To die, to sleep;
To sleep, perchance to dream. Ay, there's the rub;
For in that sleep of death what dreams may come,
When we have shuffled off this mortal coil,
Must give us pause.
William Shakespeare
Hamlet, III:1

8 Never murder a man who is committing suicide.
Woodrow Wilson (1856–1925) US statesman.
Mr Wilson's War (John Dos Passos), Pt. II, Ch. 10

□ SUITABILITY □

1 In seed time learn, in harvest teach, in winter enjoy.
William Blake (1757–1827) British poet.
The Marriage of Heaven and Hell, 'Proverbs of Hell'

2 Today I dressed to meet my father's eyes; yesterday it was for my husband's.
Julia (39 BC–14 AD) Daughter of Augustus.
On being complimented by her father, the emperor Augustus, on her choice of a more modest dress than the one she had worn the previous day
Saturnalia (Macrobius)

□ SUMMONS □

1 Whistle and she'll come to you.
Francis Beaumont (1584–1616) English dramatist.
Wit Without Money, IV:4

2 Mr Watson, come here; I want you.
Alexander Graham Bell (1847–1922) Scottish scientist.
The first telephone conversation, 10 Mar 1876, in Boston
Attrib.

3 Dauntless the slug-horn to my lips I set,
And blew. *Childe Roland to the Dark Tower came.*
Robert Browning (1812–89) British poet.
Childe Roland to the Dark Tower Came, XXXIV

□SUN□

See also weather

1 The Sun came up upon the left,
Out of the sea came he!
And he shone bright, and on the right
Went down into the sea.
Samuel Taylor Coleridge (1772–1834) British poet.
The Rime of the Ancient Mariner, I

2 Busy old fool, unruly Sun,
Why dost thou thus,
Through windows and through curtains call on
us?
John Donne (1573–1631) English poet.
The Sun Rising

□SUNDAY□

1 And on the seventh day God ended his work
which he had made; and he rested on the seventh day from all his work which he had made.
Bible: Genesis
2:2

2 And he said unto them, The sabbath was made
for man, and not man for the sabbath: Therefore
the Son of man is Lord also of the sabbath.
Bible: Mark
2:27–28

3 The feeling of Sunday is the same everywhere,
heavy, melancholy, standing still. Like when they
say, 'As it was in the beginning, is now, and ever
shall be, world without end.'
Jean Rhys (1894–1979) Dominican-born British novelist.
Voyage in the Dark, Ch. 4

□SUPERIORITY□

See also equality, excellence, one-upmanship, snobbery

1 The superior man is satisfied and composed; the
mean man is always full of distress.
Confucius (K'ung Fu-tzu; 551–479 BC) Chinese philosopher.
Analects

2 The superior man is distressed by his want of
ability.
Confucius
Analects

3 Though I've belted you an' flayed you,
By the livin' Gawd that made you,
You're a better man than I am, Gunga Din!
Rudyard Kipling (1865–1936) Indian-born British writer.
Gunga Din

4 Above the vulgar flight of common souls.
Arthur Murphy (1727–1805) Irish dramatist, writer, and actor.
Zenobia, V

5 I teach you the Superman. Man is something
that is to be surpassed.
Friedrich Wilhelm Nietzsche (1844–1900) German
philosopher.
Thus Spake Zarathustra

6 It is brought home to you…that it is only because
miners sweat their guts out that superior persons
can remain superior.
George Orwell (Eric Blair; 1903–50) British novelist.
The Road to Wigan Pier, Ch. 2

□SUPERNATURAL□

See also fairies

1 From ghoulies and ghosties and long-leggety
beasties
And things that go bump in the night,
Good Lord, deliver us!
Anonymous
Cornish prayer

2 Thou shalt not suffer a witch to live.
Bible: Exodus
22:18

3 For my part, I have ever believed, and do now
know, that there are witches.
Thomas Browne (1605–82) English physician and writer.
Religio Medici, Pt. I

4 This time it vanished quite slowly, beginning
with the end of the tail, and ending with the grin,
which remained some time after the rest of it had
gone.
Lewis Carroll (Charles Lutwidge Dodgson; 1832–98) British
writer.
Describing the Cheshire Cat
Alice's Adventures in Wonderland, Ch. 6

5 Religion
Has made an honest woman of the supernatural,
And we won't have it kicking over the traces
again.
Christopher Fry (1907–) British dramatist.
The Lady's Not for Burning, II

6 'La belle Dame sans Merci
Hath thee in thrall!'
John Keats (1795–1821) British poet.
La Belle Dame Sans Merci

7 That old black magic has me in its spell.
Johnny Mercer (1909–76) US lyricist and composer.
That Old Black Magic

8 Once upon a midnight dreary, while I pondered,
weak and weary,
Over many a quaint and curious volume of forgotten lore,
While I nodded, nearly napping, suddenly there
came a tapping,
As of some one gently rapping, rapping at my
chamber door.
Edgar Allan Poe (1809–49) US poet and writer.
The Raven

9 There are more things in heaven and earth,
Horatio,
Than are dreamt of in your philosophy.
William Shakespeare (1564–1616) English dramatist.
Hamlet, I:5

10 This supernatural soliciting
Cannot be ill; cannot be good.
William Shakespeare
Macbeth, I:3

11 His eyes flamed red with devilish passion; the
great nostrils of the white aquiline nose opened
wide and quivered at the edges; and the white
sharp teeth, behind the full lips of the blood-
dripping mouth, champed together like those
of a wild beast.
Bram Stoker (1847–1912) Irish novelist.
Referring to Count Dracula
Dracula, Ch. 21

□ SUPERSTITION □

See also luck

1 Of course I don't believe in it. But I understand
that it brings you luck whether you believe in it
or not.
Niels Bohr (1885–1962) Danish physicist.
When asked why he had a horseshoe on his wall
Attrib.

2 Superstition is the religion of feeble minds.
Edmund Burke (1729–97) British politician.
Reflections on the Revolution in France

3 Superstition is the poetry of life.
Goethe (1749–1832) German poet and dramatist.
Sprüche in Prosa, III

4 They say there is divinity in odd numbers, either
in nativity, chance, or death.
William Shakespeare (1564–1616) English dramatist.
The Merry Wives of Windsor, V:1

5 Superstition sets the whole world in flames;
philosophy quenches them.
Voltaire (François-Marie Arouet; 1694–1778) French writer.
Dictionnaire philosophique, 'Superstition'

□ SUPPORT □

See also loyalty

1 Either back us or sack us.
James Callaghan (1912–) British politician and prime
minister.
Speech, Labour Party Conference, Brighton, 5 Oct 1977

2 While I cannot be regarded as a pillar, I must be
regarded as a buttress of the church, because I
support it from the outside.
Lord Melbourne
Attrib.

3 Ladies and gentleman, it takes more than one to
make a ballet.
Ninette de Valois (Edris Stannus; 1898–) British ballet
dancer and choreographer.
New Yorker

□ SURVIVAL □

See also evolution, self-preservation

1 The perpetual struggle for room and food.
Thomas Robert Malthus (1766–1834) British clergyman and
economist.
Essays on the Principle of Population

2 The thing-in-itself, the will-to-live, exists whole
and undivided in every being, even in the tiniest;
it is present as completely as in all that ever were,
are, and will be, taken together.
Arthur Schopenhauer (1788–1860) German philosopher.
Parerga and Paralipomena

3 This is the Law of the Yukon, that only the strong
shall thrive;
That surely the weak shall perish, and only the
Fit survive.
Robert William Service (1874–1958) Canadian poet.
The Law of the Yukon

□ SWIFT □
Jonathan
(1667–1745) Irish-born Anglican priest who became a poet and
satirist in London. He is remembered for his *Journal to Stella*
(1710–13) and *A Tale of A Tub* (1704), but best of all for *Gulliver's
Travels* (1726), written after his return to Dublin as dean of St
Patrick's.

QUOTATIONS ABOUT SWIFT

1 He delivered Ireland from plunder and oppression; and showed that wit, confederated with
truth, had such force as authority was unable to
resist.
Samuel Johnson (1709–84) British lexicographer.
Attrib.

2 A monster gibbering, shrieking and gnashing
imprecations against mankind.
William Makepeace Thackeray (1811–63) British novelist.
Attrib.

3 Satire is a sort of glass, wherein beholders do generally discover everybody's face but their own.
The Battle of the Books, 'Preface'

4 'Tis an old maxim in the schools,
That flattery's the food of fools;
Yet now and then your men of wit
Will condescend to take a bit.
Cadenus and Vanessa

5 I have heard of a man who had a mind to sell his house, and therefore carried a piece of brick in his pocket, which he shewed as a pattern to encourage purchasers.
The Drapier's Letters, 2 (4 Aug 1724)

6 I cannot but conclude the bulk of your natives to be the most pernicious race of little odious vermin that nature ever suffered to crawl upon the surface of the earth.
Referring to the English.
Gulliver's Travels, 'Voyage to Brobdingnag', Ch. 6

7 So, naturalist observe, a flea
Hath smaller fleas that on him prey,
And these have smaller fleas to bite 'em.
And so proceed *ad infinitum*.
On Poetry

8 Promises and pie-crust are made to be broken.
Polite Conversation, Dialogue 1

9 I never saw, heard, nor read, that the clergy were beloved in any nation where Christianity was the religion of the country. Nothing can render them popular, but some degree of persecution.
Thoughts on Religion

10 Laws are like cobwebs, which may catch small flies, but let wasps and hornets break through.
Similar remarks have been made by others.
A Tritical Essay upon the Faculties of the Mind

11 For God's sake, madam, don't say that in England for if you do, they will surely tax it.
Responding to Lady Carteret's admiration for the quality of the air in Ireland.
Lives of the Wits (H. Pearson)

12 Ah, a German and a genius! a prodigy, admit him!
Learning of the arrival of Handel; Swift's last words.
Attrib.

☐ SWITZERLAND ☐
See also Europe

1 Since both its national products, snow and chocolate, melt, the cuckoo clock was invented solely in order to give tourists something solid to remember it by.
Alan Coren (1938–) British humorist and writer.
The Sanity Inspector, 'And Though They Do Their Best'

2 They say that if the Swiss had designed these mountains they'd be rather flatter.
Paul Theroux (1941–) US-born writer.
Referring to the Alps
The Great Railway Bazaar, Ch. 28

3 In Italy for thirty years under the Borgias they had warfare, terror, murder, bloodshed – they produced Michelangelo, Leonardo da Vinci and the Renaissance. In Switzerland they had brotherly love, five hundred years of democracy and peace, and what did they produce…? The cuckoo clock.
Orson Welles (1915–85) US film actor.
The Third Man

☐ SYMPATHY ☐
See also comfort

1 Sympathy – for all these people, for being foreigners – lay over the gathering like a woolly blanket; and no one was enjoying it at all.
Malcolm Bradbury (1932–) British academic and novelist.
Eating People is Wrong, Ch. 2

2 To be sympathetic without discrimination is so very debilitating.
Ronald Firbank (1886–1926) British novelist.
Vainglory

3 To show pity is felt as a sign of contempt because one has clearly ceased to be an object of *fear* as soon as one is pitied.
Friedrich Wilhelm Nietzsche (1844–1900) German philosopher.
The Wanderer and His Shadow

☐ SZASZ ☐
Thomas
(1920–) US psychiatrist and writer. His writings include *Pain and Pleasure* (1957) and *The Second Sin* (1974).

1 Men are rewarded and punished not for what they do, but rather for how their acts are defined. This is why men are more interested in better justifying themselves than in better behaving themselves.
The Second Sin

2 Traditionally, sex has been a very private, secretive activity. Herein perhaps lies its powerful force for uniting people in a strong bond. As we make sex less secretive, we may rob it of its power to hold men and women together.
The Second Sin

3 Formerly, when religion was strong and science weak, men mistook magic for medicine, now, when science is strong and religion weak, men mistake medicine for magic.

The Second Sin

4 Happiness is an imaginary condition, formerly often attributed by the living to the dead, now usually attributed by adults to children, and by children to adults.

The Second Sin

5 Psychiatrists classify a person as neurotic if he suffers from his problems in living, and a psychotic if he makes others suffer.

The Second Sin

6 Masturbation: the primary sexual activity of mankind. In the nineteenth century it was a disease; in the twentieth, it's a cure.

The Second Sin

☐ T ☐

☐ TACT ☐
See also diplomacy

1 Social tact is making your company feel at home,
even though you wish they were.
Anonymous

2 One shouldn't talk of halters in the hanged man's
house.
Miguel de Cervantes (1547–1616) Spanish novelist.
Don Quixote, Pt. I, Ch. 25

3 Tact consists in knowing how far we may go too
far.
Jean Cocteau (1889–1963) French poet and artist.
In *Treasury of Humorous Quotations*

☐ TALENT ☐
See also genius, talent and genius

1 Whom the gods wish to destroy they first call
promising.
Cyril Connolly (1903–74) British journalist.
Enemies of Promise, Ch. 3

2 Talent develops in quiet places, character in the
full current of human life.
Goethe (1749–1832) German poet and dramatist.
Torquato Tasso, I

3 There is no substitute for talent. Industry and all
the virtues are of no avail.
Aldous Huxley (1894–1964) British novelist.
Point Counter Point

4 It's not enough to be Hungarian, you must have
talent too.
Alexander Korda (Sandor Kellner; 1893–1956)
Hungarian-born British film director.
Alexander Korda (K. Kulik)

5 Let our children grow tall, and some taller than
others if they have it in them to do so.
Margaret Thatcher (1925–) British politician and prime
minister.
Speech, US tour, 1975

☐ TALENT AND GENIUS ☐
See also genius, talent

1 It takes people a long time to learn the difference
between talent and genius, especially ambitious
young men and women.
Louisa May Alcott (1832–88) US novelist.
Little Women, Pt. II

2 Mediocrity knows nothing higher than itself, but
talent instantly recognizes genius.
Arthur Conan Doyle (1856–1930) British writer.
The Valley of Fear

3 Genius does what it must, and Talent does what
it can.
Owen Meredith (Robert Bulwer-Lytton, 1st Earl of Lytton;
1831–91) British statesman and poet.
Last Words of a Sensitive Second-rate Poet

☐ TASTE ☐
See also individuality

1 Good taste is better than bad taste, but bad taste
is better than no taste.
Arnold Bennett (1867–1931) British novelist.
The Observer, 'Sayings of the Week', 24 Aug 1930

2 Taste is the feminine of genius.
Edward Fitzgerald (1809–83) British poet.
Letter to J. R. Lowell, Oct 1877

3 What is food to one man is bitter poison to others.
Lucretius (Titus Lucretius Carus; c. 99–55 BC) Roman
philosopher.
On the Nature of the Universe, IV

☐ TAXATION ☐

1 They can't collect legal taxes from illegal money.
Al Capone (1899–1947) Italian-born US gangster.
Objecting to the US Bureau of Internal Revenue claiming large
sums in unpaid back tax
Capone (J. Kobler)

2 The hardest thing in the world to understand is
income tax.
Albert Einstein (1879–1955) German-born US physicist.
Attrib.

3 In this world nothing is certain but death and
taxes.
Benjamin Franklin (1706–90) US scientist and statesman.
Letter to Jean-Baptiste Leroy, 13 Nov 1789

4 *Excise.* A hateful tax levied upon commodities.
Samuel Johnson (1709–84) British lexicographer.
Dictionary of the English Language

5 The avoidance of taxes is the only pursuit that
still carries any reward.
John Maynard Keynes (1883–1946) British economist.
Attrib.

6 The taxpayer is someone who works for the fed-
eral government but doesn't have to take a civil
service examination.
Ronald Reagan (1911–) US politician and president.
Attrib.

☐ TECHNOLOGY ☐
See also progress, science

1 Give me a firm place to stand, and I will move the
earth.
Archimedes (c. 287–212 BC) Greek mathematician.
On the Lever

2 Any sufficiently advanced technology is indistinguishable from magic.
Arthur C. Clarke (1917–) British science-fiction writer.
The Lost Worlds of 2001

3 One machine can do the work of fifty ordinary men. No machine can do the work of one extraordinary man.
Elbert Hubbard (1856–1915) US writer.
Roycroft Dictionary and Book of Epigrams

4 It was difficult to decide whether the system that produced the kettle was a miracle of human ingenuity and co-operation or a colossal waste of resources, human and natural. Would we all be better off boiling our water in a pot hung over an open fire? Or was it the facility to do such things at the touch of a button that freed men, and more particularly women, from servile labour and made it possible for them to become literary critics?
David Lodge (1935–) British author.
Nice Work, V

5 For tribal man space was the uncontrollable mystery. For technological man it is time that occupies the same role.
Marshall McLuhan
The Mechanical Bride, 'Magic that Changes Mood'

6 The machine threatens all achievement.
Rainer Maria Rilke (1875–1926) Austrian poet.
Die Sonette an Orpheus, II, 10

7 I see no reason to suppose that these machines will ever force themselves into general use.
Duke of Wellington (1769–1852) British general and statesman.
Referring to steam locomotives
Geoffrey Madan's Notebooks (J. Gere)

☐ TEETH ☐

1 Certain people are born with natural false teeth.
Robert Robinson (1927–) British writer and broadcaster.
BBC radio programme, *Stop the Week*, 1977

2 Adam and Eve had many advantages, but the principal one was that they escaped teething.
Mark Twain (Samuel Langhorne Clemens; 1835–1910) US writer.
The Tragedy of Pudd'nhead Wilson, Ch. 4

3 To lose a lover or even a husband or two during the course of one's life can be vexing. But to lose one's teeth is a catastrophe.
Hugh Wheeler (1912–87) British-born US writer.
A Little Night Music

☐ TELEGRAMS ☐

1 To hell with you. Offensive letter follows.
Anonymous
Telegram to Sir Alec Douglas-Home

2 Winston's back.
Anonymous
Signal to all ships of the Royal Navy from the Admiralty when Churchill was reappointed First Sea Lord, 3 Sept 1939

3 Streets full of water. Please advise.
Robert Benchley (1889–1945) US humorist.
Telegram sent to his editor on arriving in Venice
Attrib.

4 'Old Cary Grant fine. How you?'
Cary Grant (Archibald Leach; 1904–86) British-born US film star.
Replying to a telegram sent to his agent inquiring: 'How old Cary Grant?'
The Filmgoer's Book of Quotes (Leslie Halliwell)

5 ?
Victor Hugo (1802–85) French writer.
The entire contents of a telegram sent to his publishers asking how *Les Misérables* was selling the reply was '!'
The Literary Life (R. Hendrickson)

6 Have strong suspicions that Crippen London cellar murderer and accomplice are amongst saloon passengers moustache taken off growing beard accomplice dressed as boy voice manner and build undoubtedly a girl both travelling as Mr and Master Robinson.
Captain Kendall
This was the first time a wireless telegraphy message from a ship at sea led to the arrest of criminals
Telegram to Scotland Yard, 22 July 1910

7 We have finished the job, what shall we do with the tools?
Haile Selassie (1892–1975) Emperor of Ethiopia.
Telegram sent to Winston Churchill, mimicking his 'Give us the tools, and we will finish the job'
Ambrosia and Small Beer, Ch. 4 (Edward Marsh)

8 Reports of my death are greatly exaggerated.
Mark Twain (Samuel Langhorne Clemens; 1835–1910) US writer.
On learning that his obituary had been published
Cable to the Associated Press

9 Nurse unupblown.
Evelyn Waugh (1903–66) British novelist.
Cable sent after he had failed, while a journalist serving in Ethiopia, to substantiate a rumour that an English nurse had been blown up in an Italian air raid
Our Marvelous Native Tongue (R. Claiborne)

☐ TELEVISION ☐

1 Television is more interesting than people. If it were not, we should have people standing in the corners of our rooms.
Alan Coren (1938–) British humorist and writer.
In *The Times*

2 If any reader of this book is in the grip of some habit of which he is deeply ashamed, I advise him not to give way to it in secret but to do it on television. No-one will pass him with averted gaze on the other side of the street. People will

cross the road at the risk of losing their own lives in order to say 'We saw you on the telly'.
Quentin Crisp (?1910–) Model, publicist, and writer.
How to Become a Virgin

3 Let's face it, there are no plain women on television.
Anna Ford (1943–) British newscaster.
Observer, 23 Sept 1979

4 Television is an invention that permits you to be entertained in your living room by people you wouldn't have in your home.
David Frost (1939–) British television personality.
Attrib., CBS television, 1971

□ TEMPTATION □

1 I am not over-fond of resisting temptation.
William Beckford (1759–1844) British writer.
Vathek

2 Blessed is the man that endureth temptation: for when he is tried, he shall receive the crown of life, which the Lord hath promised to them that love him.
Bible: James
1:12

3 Not all that tempts your wand'ring eyes And heedless hearts, is lawful prize; Nor all, that glisters, gold.
Thomas Gray (1716–71) British poet.
Ode on the Death of a Favourite Cat

4 I can resist everything except temptation.
Oscar Wilde (1854–1900) Irish-born British dramatist.
Lady Windermere's Fan, I

5 The only way to get rid of a temptation is to yield to it.
Oscar Wilde
Repeating a similar sentiment expressed by Clementina Stirling Graham (1782–1877)
The Picture of Dorian Gray, Ch. 2

□ TENNYSON □
Alfred, Baron
(1809–92) British poet. He established his reputation with *Morte d'Arthur* (1842). Of his many other works, *In Memoriam* (1850), *The Charge of the Light Brigade* (1854), *Maud* (1855), and *The Idylls of the King* (1859) are outstanding. He became poet laureate in 1850.

QUOTATIONS ABOUT TENNYSON

1 Alfred is always carrying a bit of chaos round with him, and turning it into cosmos.
Thomas Carlyle (1795–1881) Scottish historian and essayist.

2 Tennyson was not Tennysonian.
Henry James (1843–1916) US novelist.
The Middle Years

QUOTATIONS BY TENNYSON

3 And the stately ships go on To their haven under the hill; But O for the touch of a vanish'd hand, And the sound of a voice that is still!
Break, Break, Break

4 For men may come and men may go But I go on for ever.
The Brook

5 'Forward the Light Brigade!' Was there a man dismay'd? Not tho' the soldier knew Some one had blunder'd: Their's not to make reply, Their's not to reason why, Their's but to do and die: Into the valley of Death Rode the six hundred.
The Charge of the Light Brigade

6 Come not, when I am dead, To drop thy foolish tears upon my grave, To trample round my fallen head, And vex the unhappy dust thou wouldst not save.
Come Not, When I Am Dead

7 Half light, half shade, She stood, a sight to make an old man young.
The Gardener's Daughter

8 His honour rooted in dishonour stood, And faith unfaithful kept him falsely true.
Idylls of the King, 'Lancelot and Elaine'

9 For man is man and master of his fate.
Idylls of the King, 'The Marriage of Geraint'

10 For words, like Nature, half reveal And half conceal the Soul within.
In Memoriam A.H.H., V

11 I hold it true, whate'er befall; I feel it, when I sorrow most; 'Tis better to have loved and lost Than never to have loved at all.
In Memoriam A.H.H., XXVII

12 Sleep, Death's twin-brother, knows not Death, Nor can I dream of thee as dead.
In Memoriam A.H.H., LXVIII

13 So many worlds, so much to do, So little done, such things to be.
In Memoriam A.H.H., LXXIII

14 'Tis held that sorrow makes us wise.
In Memoriam A.H.H., CXIII

15 A simple maiden in her flower
Is worth a hundred coats-of-arms.
Lady Clara Vere de Vere, II

16 Kind hearts are more than coronets,
And simple faith than Norman blood.
Lady Clara Vere de Vere, VI

17 On either side the river lie
Long fields of barley and of rye,
That clothe the wold and meet the sky;
And thro' the field the road runs by
To many-tower'd Camelot.
The Lady of Shalott, Pt. I

18 'The curse is come upon me,' cried
The Lady of Shalott.
The Lady of Shalott, Pt. III

19 In the Spring a young man's fancy lightly turns to
thoughts of love.
Locksley Hall

20 So I triumphed ere my passion, sweeping thro'
me, left me dry,
Left me with the palsied heart, and left me with
the jaundiced eye.
Locksley Hall

21 Music that gentlier on the spirit lies,
Than tir'd eyelids upon tir'd eyes.
The Lotos-Eaters, 'Choric Song'

22 Come into the garden, Maud,
For the black bat, night, has flown,
Come into the garden, Maud,
I am here at the gate alone.
Maud, I

23 But the churchmen fain would kill their church,
As the churches have kill'd their Christ.
Maud, V

24 O tell her, brief is life but love is long.
The Princess, IV

25 Man is the hunter; woman is his game:
The sleek and shining creatures of the chase,
We hunt them for the beauty of their skins.
The Princess, V

26 Home they brought her warrior dead.
She nor swoon'd, nor utter'd cry:
All her maidens, watching said,
'She must weep or she will die.'
The Princess, VI

27 Battering the gates of heaven with storms of
prayer.
St Simeon Stylites

28 The Gods themselves cannot recall their gifts.
Tithonus

29 A still small voice spake unto me,
'Thou art so full of misery,
Were it not better not to be?'
The Two Voices

30 We are not now that strength which in old days
Moved earth and heaven; that which we are, we
are;
One equal temper of heroic hearts,
Made weak by time and fate, but strong in will
To strive, to seek, to find, and not to yield.
Ulysses

31 Every moment dies a man,
Every moment one is born.
The Vision of Sin

☐ THATCHER ☐
Margaret

(1925–) British politician, prime minister since 1979. Trained
as a chemist and a barrister, she became a Conservative MP in
1959 and minister of education and science (1970–74).

QUOTATIONS ABOUT THATCHER

1 Mrs Thatcher is a woman of common views but
uncommon abilities.
Julian Critchley (1930–) British Conservative politician.
The Times, Profile: Margaret Thatcher

2 She approaches the problems of our country
with all the one-dimensional sublety of a comic-
strip.
Denis Healey (1917–) British Labour politician.
Speech, House of Commons, 22 May 1979

QUOTATIONS BY THATCHER

3 I'm not hard – I'm frightfully soft. But I will not be
hounded.
Daily Mail, 1972

4 I love argument, I love debate. I don't expect anyone just to sit there and agree with me, that's not
their job.
The Times, 1980

5 If a woman like Eva Peron with no ideals can get
that far, think how far I can go with all the ideals
that I have.
The Sunday Times, 1980

6 U-turn if you want to. The lady's not for turning.
Speech, Conservative Conference, 1980

7 Pennies do not come from heaven. They have to
be earned here on earth.
Sunday Telegraph, 1982

8 I am painted as the greatest little dictator, which
is ridiculous – you always take some consulta-
tions.
The Times, 1983

9 Young people ought not to be idle. It is very bad for them.
The Times, 1984

10 I don't mind how much my ministers talk – as long as they do what I say.
The Times, 1987

☐ THEATRE ☐

See also acting, actors, criticism, literature, plays, Shakespeare

1 It's one of the tragic ironies of the theatre that only one man in it can count on steady work – the night watchman.
Tallulah Bankhead (1903–68) US actress.
Tallulah, Ch. 1

2 Tragedy is if I cut my finger. Comedy is if I walk into an open sewer and die.
Mel Brooks (Melvyn Kaminsky; 1926–) US film director.
New Yorker, 30 Oct 1978

3 You know, I go to the theatre to be entertained…I don't want to see plays about rape, sodomy and drug addiction…I can get all that at home.
Peter Cook (1937–) British writer and entertainer.
The Observer, caption to cartoon, 8 July 1962

4 Don't put your daughter on the stage, Mrs Worthington.
Noël Coward (1899–1973) British dramatist.
Title of song

5 Farce is the essential theatre. Farce refined becomes high comedy: farce brutalized becomes tragedy.
Gordon Craig (1872–1966) British actor.
The Story of my Days, Index

6 We participate in a tragedy; at a comedy we only look.
Aldous Huxley (1894–1964) British novelist.
The Devils of Loudon, Ch. 11

7 I depict men as they ought to be, but Euripides portrays them as they are.
Sophocles (c. 496–406 BC) Greek dramatist.
Poetics (Aristotle)

☐ THEFT ☐

See also crime

1 The fault is great in man or woman
Who steals a goose from off a common;
But what can plead that man's excuse
Who steals a common from a goose?
Anonymous
The Tickler Magazine, 1 Feb 1821

2 Prisoner, God has given you good abilities, instead of which you go about the country stealing ducks.
William Arabin (1773–1841) British judge.
Arabinesque at Law (Sir R. Megarry)

3 Stolen sweets are best.
Colley Cibber (1671–1757) British actor and dramatist.
The Rival Fools, I

4 Stolen sweets are always sweeter,
Stolen kisses much completer,
Stolen looks are nice in chapels,
Stolen, stolen, be your apples.
Hunt Leigh (1784–1859) British poet.
Song of Fairies Robbing an Orchard

☐ THEORY ☐

See also ideas

1 A thing may look specious in theory, and yet be ruinous in practice; a thing may look evil in theory, and yet be in practice excellent.
Edmund Burke (1729–97) British politician.
Impeachment of Warren Hastings, 19 Feb 1788

2 A theory can be proved by experiment; but no path leads from experiment to the birth of a theory.
Albert Einstein (1879–1955) German-born US physicist.
The Sunday Times, 18 July 1976

3 Dear friend, theory is all grey,
And the golden tree of life is green.
Goethe (1749–1832) German poet and dramatist.
Faust, Pt. I

☐ THINKING ☐

See also intellect, intelligence, mind, philosophy

1 *Cogito, ergo sum.*
I think, therefore I am.
René Descartes (1596–1650) French philosopher.
Le Discours de la méthode

2 The most fluent talkers or most plausible reasoners are not always the justest thinkers.
William Hazlitt (1778–1830) British essayist.
On Prejudice

3 Most of one's life…is one prolonged effort to prevent oneself thinking.
Aldous Huxley (1894–1964) British novelist.
Mortal Coils, 'Green Tunnels'

4 Many people would sooner die than think. In fact they do.
Bertrand Russell (1872–1970) British philosopher.
Thinking About Thinking (A. Flew)

5 There is nothing either good or bad, but thinking makes it so.
William Shakespeare (1564–1616) English dramatist.
Hamlet, II:2

6 Thinking is to me the greatest fatigue in the world.
John Vanbrugh (1664–1726) English architect and dramatist.
The Relapse, II:1

7 Great thoughts come from the heart.
Marquis de Vauvenargues (1715–47) French soldier and writer.
Réflexions et maximes

8 In order to draw a limit to thinking, we should have to be able to think both sides of this limit.
Ludwig Wittgenstein (1889–1951) Austrian philosopher.
Tractatus Logico-Philosophicus, Preface

☐ THOMAS ☐
Dylan
(1914–53) Welsh poet. His collections include *18 Poems* (1934) and *Deaths and Entrances* (1946). His radio play *Under Milk Wood* (1954) is also well known. His early death resulted from alcoholism.

QUOTATIONS ABOUT THOMAS

1 The first time I saw Dylan Thomas I felt as if Rubens had suddenly taken it into his head to paint a youthful Silenus.
Edith Sitwell (1887–1964) British poet and writer.
Taken Care of: An Autobiography

2 He was a detestable man. Men pressed money on him, and women their bodies. Dylan took both with equal contempt. His great pleasure was to humiliate people.
A. J. P. Taylor (1906–90) British historian.
Autobiography

QUOTATIONS BY THOMAS

3 I, born of flesh and ghost, was neither A ghost nor man, but mortal ghost. And I was struck down by death's feather.
Before I knocked

4 Do not go gentle into that good night, Old age should burn and rave at close of day; Rage, rage, against the dying of the light.
Do not go gentle into that good night

5 The hand that signed the treaty bred a fever, And famine grew, and locusts came; Great is the hand that holds dominion over Man by a scribbled name.
The hand that signed the paper

6 And the wild boys innocent as strawberries.
The hunchback in the park

7 After the first death, there is no other.
A Refusal to Mourn the Death, by Fire, of a Child in London

8 This bread I break was once the oat, This wine upon a foreign tree Plunged in its fruit;

Man in the day or wind at night Laid the crops low, broke the grape's joy.
This bread I break

9 MR PRITCHARD. I must dust the blinds and then I must raise them.
MRS OGMORE-PRITCHARD. And before you let the sun in, mind it wipes its shoes.
Under Milk Wood

10 Sleeping as quiet as death, side by wrinkled side, toothless, salt and brown, like two old kippers in a box.
Under Milk Wood

11 The hands of the clock have stayed still at half past eleven for fifty years. It is always opening time in the Sailors Arms.
Under Milk Wood

12 Chasing the naughty couples down the grass-green gooseberried double bed of the wood.
Under Milk Wood

13 Oh, isn't life a terrible thing, thank God?
Under Milk Wood

14 ...his nicotine eggyellow weeping walrus Victorian moustache worn thick and long in memory of Doctor Crippen.
Under Milk Wood

15 Portraits of famous bards and preachers, all fur and wool from the squint to the kneecaps.
Under Milk Wood

16 The land of my fathers. My fathers can have it.
Referring to Wales.
Dylan Thomas (John Ackerman)

17 Somebody's boring me, I think it's me.
Remark made after he had been talking continuously for some time.
Four Absentees (Rayner Heppenstall)

☐ THREATS ☐

1 Violet Elizabeth dried her tears. She saw that they were useless and she did not believe in wasting her effects. 'All right,' she said calmly, 'I'll thcream then. I'll thcream, an' thcream, an' thcream till I'm thick.'
Richmal Crompton (Richmal Crompton Lamburn; 1890–1969) British writer.
Violet Elizabeth Bott, a character in the *William* books, had both a lisp and an exceptional ability to get her own way
Just William

2 After I die, I shall return to earth as a gatekeeper of a bordello and I won't let any of you – not a one of you – enter!
Arturo Toscanini (1867–1957) Italian conductor.
Rebuking an incompetent orchestra
The Maestro: The Life of Arturo Toscanini (Howard Taubman)

□THRIFT□

See also extravagance, money

1 I knew once a very covetous, sordid fellow, who used to say, 'Take care of the pence, for the pounds will take care of themselves.'
Earl of Chesterfield (1694–1773) English statesman.
Possibly referring to William Lowndes
Letter to his son, 6 Nov 1747

2 …we owe something to extravagance, for thrift and adventure seldom go hand in hand.
Jennie Jerome Churchill (1854–1921) US-born British hostess and writer.
Pearson's, 'Extravagance'

3 Thrift has nearly killed her on several occasions, through the agency of old sausages, slow-punctured tyres, rusty blades.
Margaret Drabble (1939–) British novelist.
The Radiant Way

4 Everybody is always in favour of general economy and particular expenditure.
Anthony Eden (1897–1977) British statesman.
The Observer, 'Sayings of the Week', 17 June 1956

5 Economy is going without something you do want in case you should, some day, want something you probably won't want.
Anthony Hope (Sir Anthony Hope Hawkins; 1863–1933) British novelist.
The Dolly Dialogues

□THURBER□
James

(1894–1961) US writer, humorist, and cartoonist. A contributor to the New Yorker, he published a number of collected writings, including The Thurber Carnival (1945).

QUOTATIONS ABOUT THURBER

1 A tall, thin, spectacled man with the face of a harassed rat.
Russell Maloney
Saturday Review, 'Tilley the Toiler'

QUOTATIONS BY THURBER

2 I was seized by the stern hand of Compulsion, that dark, unseasonable Urge that impels women to clean house in the middle of the night.
Alarms and Diversions, 'There's a Time for Flags'

3 It is better to have loafed and lost than never to have loafed at all.
Fables for Our Time, 'The Courtship of Arthur and Al'

4 You can fool too many of the people too much of the time.
Fables for Our Time, 'The Owl Who Was God'

5 Early to rise and early to bed makes a male healthy and wealthy and dead.
Fables for Our Time, 'The Shrike and the Chipmunks'

6 Her own mother lived the latter years of her life in the horrible suspicion that electricity was dripping invisibly all over the house.
My Life and Hard Times, Ch. 2

7 A man should not insult his wife publicly, at parties. He should insult her in the privacy of the home.
Thurber Country

8 Well, if I called the wrong number, why did you answer the phone?
Cartoon caption

9 Surely you don't mean by unartificial insemination!
On being accosted at a party by a drunk woman who claimed she would like to have a baby by him.
Attrib.

10 God bless…God damn.
His last words.
Attrib.

□TIME□

See also eternity, future, life, past, present, transience

1 Except Time all other things are created. Time is the creator; and Time has no limit, neither top nor bottom.
The Persian Rivayat

2 To choose time is to save time.
Francis Bacon (1561–1626) English philosopher.
Essays, 'Of Dispatch'

3 Time is a great teacher, but unfortunately it kills all its pupils.
Hector Berlioz (1803–69) French composer.
Almanach des lettres françaises

4 To every thing there is a season, and a time to every purpose under the heaven:
A time to be born, and a time to die; a time to plant, and a time to pluck up that which is planted;
A time to kill, and a time to heal; a time to break down, and a time to build up;
A time to weep, and a time to laugh; a time to mourn, and a time to dance;
A time to cast away stones, and a time to gather stones together; a time to embrace, and a time to refrain from embracing;
A time to get, and a time to lose; a time to keep, and a time to cast away;
A time to rend, and a time to sew; a time to keep silence, and a time to speak;
A time to love, and a time to hate; a time of war, and a time of peace.
Bible: Ecclesiastes
3:1–8

5 Men talk of killing time, while time quietly kills them.
Dion Boucicault (Dionysius Lardner Boursiquot; 1820–90) Irish-born US actor and dramatist.
London Assurance, II:1

6 Dost thou love life? Then do not squander time, for that's the stuff life is made of.
Benjamin Franklin (1706–90) US scientist and statesman.
Poor Richard's Almanack

7 You must remember this;
A kiss is just a kiss,
A sigh is just a sigh –
The fundamental things apply
As time goes by.
Herman Hupfeld (20th century) US songwriter.
From the film *Casablanca*
As Time Goes By

8 O aching time! O moments big as years!
John Keats (1795–1821) British poet.
Hyperion, I

9 The Future is something which everyone reaches at the rate of sixty minutes an hour, whatever he does, whoever he is.
C. S. Lewis (1898–1963) British academic and writer.
The Screwtape Letters

10 The man is killing time – there's nothing else.
Robert Lowell (1917–77) US poet.
The Drinker

11 A physician can sometimes parry the scythe of death, but has no power over the sand in the hourglass.
Hester Lynch Piozzi (Mrs. Henry Thrale; 1741–1821) British writer.
Letter to Fanny Burney, 22 Nov 1781

12 They do that to pass the time, nothing more. But Time is too large, it refuses to let itself be filled up.
Jean-Paul Sartre (1905–80) French writer.
Nausea

13 Come what come may,
Time and the hour runs through the roughest day.
William Shakespeare (1564–1616) English dramatist.
Macbeth, I:3

14 Th' inaudible and noiseless foot of Time.
William Shakespeare
All's Well that Ends Well, V:3

15 Like as the waves make towards the pebbled shore,
So do our minutes hasten to their end.
William Shakespeare
Sonnet 60

16 In reality, *killing time*
Is only the name for another of the multifarious ways
By which Time kills us.
Osbert Sitwell (1892–1969) British writer.
Milordo Inglese

17 Time is but the stream I go a-fishing in.
Henry David Thoreau (1817–62) US writer.
Walden, 'Where I Lived, and What I Lived For'

18 As if you could kill time without injuring eternity.
Henry David Thoreau
Walden, 'Economy'

19 But meanwhile it is flying, irretrievable time is flying.
Virgil (Publius Vergilius Maro; 70–19 BC) Roman poet.
Georgics, Bk. III

20 Time flies, death urges, knells call, heaven invites,
Hell threatens.
Edward Young (1683–1765) British poet.
Night Thoughts

□ TITLES □

See also aristocracy, courtesy, honour, nobility

1 Pooh-Bah (Lord High Everything Else)
W. S. Gilbert (1836–1911) British dramatist.
The Mikado, Dramatis Personae

2 I like the Garter; there is no damned merit in it.
Lord Melbourne (1779–1848) British statesman.
Lord Melbourne (H. Dunckley), 'On the Order of the Garter'

3 Call me madame.
Francis Perkins (1882–1965) US social worker and politician.
Deciding the term of address she would prefer when made the first woman to hold a cabinet office in the USA
Familiar Quotations (J. Bartlett)

4 Members rise from CMG (known sometimes in Whitehall as 'Call me God') to the KCMG ('Kindly Call me God') to…The GCMG ('God Calls me God').
Anthony Sampson (1926–   ) British writer and journalist.
Anatomy of Britain, Ch. 18

5 Titles distinguish the mediocre, embarrass the superior, and are disgraced by the inferior.
George Bernard Shaw (1856–1950) Irish dramatist and critic.
Man and Superman, 'Maxims for Revolutionists'

□ TOLERANCE □

1 There is, however, a limit at which forbearance ceases to be a virtue.
Edmund Burke (1729–97) British politician.
Observations on a Publication, 'The Present State of the Nation'

2 It is flattering some men to endure them.
Lord Halifax (1633–95) English statesman.
Political, Moral and Miscellaneous Thoughts and Reflections

3 If you cannot mould yourself as you would wish,
how can you expect other people to be entirely to
your liking?
Thomas à Kempis (Thomas Hemmerken; c. 1380–1471)
German monk.
The Imitation of Christ, I

4 So long as a man rides his hobby-horse peace-
ably and quietly along the king's highway, and
neither compels you or me to get up behind him,
– pray, Sir, what have either you or I to do with it?
Laurence Sterne (1713–68) Irish-born British writer.
Tristram Shandy

□TRANSIENCE□

See also life, mortality, time

1 Time is like a river made up of the events which
happen, and its current is strong; no sooner does
anything appear than it is swept away, and
another comes in its place, and will be swept
away too.
Marcus Aurelius (121–180 AD) Roman emperor.
Meditations, Bk. IV, Ch. 43

2 Faith, Sir, we are here to-day, and gone tomorrow.
Aphra Behn (1640–89) English novelist and dramatist.
The Lucky Chance, IV

3 Vanity of vanities, saith the Preacher, vanity of
vanities; all is vanity.
What profit hath a man of all his labour which he
taketh under the sun?
One generation passeth away, and another generation cometh: but the earth abideth for ever.
Bible: Ecclesiastes
1:2–4

4 Whatsoever thy hand findeth to do, do it with thy
might; for there is no work, nor device, nor
knowledge, nor wisdom, in the grave, whither
thou goest.
Bible: Ecclesiastes
9:10

5 And behold joy and gladness, slaying oxen, and
killing sheep, eating flesh, and drinking wine: let
us eat and drink; for tomorrow we shall die.
Bible: Isaiah
A similar sentiment is expressed in Corinthians 15:32–33
22:13

6 Heaven and earth shall pass away, but my words
shall not pass away.
Bible: Matthew
24:35

7 They are not long, the days of wine and roses.
Ernest Dowson (1867–1900) British lyric poet.
Vitae Summa Brevis Spem Nos Vetat Incohare Longam

8 The Worldly Hope men set their Hearts upon
Turns Ashes – or it prospers; and anon,

Like Snow upon the Desert's dusty face,
Lighting a little Hour or two – is gone.
Edward Fitzgerald (1809–83) British poet.
The Rubáiyát of Omar Khayyám, XIV

9 Fair daffodils, we weep to see
You haste away so soon:
As yet the early-rising sun
Has not attain'd his noon.
Stay, stay,
Until the hasting day
Has run
But to the even-song;
And, having pray'd together, we
Will go with you along.
We have short time to stay, as you,
We have as short a Spring;
As quick a growth to meet decay,
As you or any thing.
Robert Herrick (1591–1674) English poet.
Hesperides, 'To Daffodils'

10 Not to hope for things to last for ever, is what the
year teaches and even the hour which snatches a
nice day away.
Horace (Quintus Horatius Flaccus; 65–8 BC) Roman poet.
Odes, IV

11 Ships that pass in the night, and speak each
other in passing;
Only a signal shown and a distant voice in the
darkness;
So on the ocean of life we pass and speak one
another,
Only a look and a voice; then darkness again and
a silence.
Henry Wadsworth Longfellow (1807–82) US poet.
Tales of a Wayside Inn, 'The Theologian's Tale. Elizabeth'

□TRANSLATION□

1 Translations (like wives) are seldom faithful if
they are in the least attractive.
Roy Campbell (1901–57) South African poet.
Poetry Review

2 Poetry is what gets lost in translation.
Robert Frost (1875–1963) US poet.
Attrib

3 Humour is the first of the gifts to perish in a
foreign tongue.
Virginia Woolf (1882–1941) British novelist.
The Common Reader

□TRAVEL□

See also boats, flying

1 Travel, in the younger sort, is a part of education;
in the elder, a part of experience.
Francis Bacon (1561–1626) English philosopher.
Essays, 'Of Travel'

2 The only way to be sure of catching a train is to miss the one before it.
G. K. Chesterton (1874–1936) British writer.
Vacances à tous prix, 'Le Supplice de l'heure' (P. Daninos)

3 Travelling is almost like talking with men of other centuries.
René Descartes (1596–1650) French philosopher.
Le Discours de la méthode

4 How does it feel
To be without a home
Like a complete unknown
Like a rolling stone?
Bob Dylan (Robert Allen Zimmerman; 1941–) US popular singer.
Like a Rolling Stone

5 One of the pleasantest things in the world is going on a journey; but I like to go by myself.
William Hazlitt (1778–1830) British essayist.
On Going a Journey

6 A man who has not been in Italy, is always conscious of an inferiority, from his not having seen what it is expected a man should see. The grand object of travelling is to see the shores of the Mediterranean.
Samuel Johnson (1709–84) British lexicographer.
Life of Johnson (J. Boswell), Vol. III

7 Much have I travell'd in the realms of gold,
And many goodly states and kingdoms seen.
John Keats (1795–1821) British poet.
On first looking into Chapman's Homer

8 Mr Stephenson having taken me on the bench of the engine with him, we started at about ten miles an hour. You cannot imagine how strange it seemed to be journeying on thus, without any visible cause of progressing other than that magical machine, with its flying white breath, and rhythmical unwearying pace.
Fanny Kemble (1809–93) British actress and writer.
Record of a Girlhood

9 Like Brighton pier, all right as far as it goes, but inadequate for getting to France.
Neil Kinnock (1942–) British politician.
Speech, House of Commons, 1981

10 The great and recurrent question about abroad is, is it worth getting there?
Rose Macaulay (1889–1958) British writer.
Attrib.

11 Whenever I prepare for a journey I prepare as though for death. Should I never return, all is in order. This is what life has taught me.
Katherine Mansfield (1888–1923) New-Zealand-born British writer.
The Journal of Katherine Mansfield, 1922

12 *Rush hour:* that hour when traffic is almost at a standstill.
J. B. Morton (1893–1979) British journalist.
Morton's Folly

13 Travel is the most private of pleasures. There is no greater bore than the travel bore. We do not in the least want to hear what he has seen in Hong-Kong.
Vita Sackville-West (Victoria Sackville-West; 1892–1962) British poet and novelist.
Passenger to Tehran, Ch. 1

14 A man should know something of his own country, too, before he goes abroad.
Laurence Sterne (1713–68) Irish-born British writer.
Tristram Shandy

15 Wealth I ask not; hope nor love,
Nor a friend to know me;
All I seek, the heaven above
And the road below me.
Robert Louis Stevenson (1850–94) Scottish writer.
Songs of Travel, 'The Vagabond'

16 For my part, I travel not to go anywhere, but to go. I travel for travel's sake. The great affair is to move.
Robert Louis Stevenson
Travels with a Donkey, 'Cheylard and Luc'

17 Travel is glamorous only in retrospect.
Paul Theroux (1941–) US-born writer.
The Observer, 'Sayings of the Week', 7 Oct 1979

☐ **TREASON** ☐
See also betrayal

1 Please to remember the Fifth of November,
Gunpowder Treason and Plot.
We know no reason why gunpowder treason
Should ever be forgot.
Anonymous
Traditional

2 During his Office, Treason was no Crime.
The Sons of Belial had a Glorious Time.
John Dryden (1631–1700) British poet and dramatist.
Absalom and Achitophel, I

3 Treason doth never prosper: what's the reason?
For if it prosper, none dare call it treason.
John Harington (1561–1612) English writer.
Epigrams, 'Of Treason'

4 Caesar had his Brutus – Charles the First, his Cromwell – and George the Third – ('Treason,' cried the Speaker)...*may profit by their example*.
If *this* be treason, make the most of it.
Patrick Henry (1736–99) US statesman.
Speech, Virginia Convention, May 1765

5 To betray, you must first belong. I never
belonged.
Kim Philby (1912–88) British double-agent who defected to
the Soviet Union (1963).
Sunday Times, 17 Dec 1967

☐ **TREES** ☐

See also countryside, Nature

1 And the Lord God took the man, and put him into
the garden of Eden to dress it and to keep it.
And the Lord God commanded the man, saying,
Of every tree of the garden thou mayest freely
eat:
But of the tree of the knowledge of good and evil,
thou shalt not eat of it: for in the day that thou eatest thereof thou shalt surely die.
Bible: Genesis
2:15–17

2 O leave this barren spot to me!
Spare, woodman, spare the beechen tree.
Thomas Campbell (1777–1844) British poet.
The Beech-Tree's Petition

3 The poplars are felled, farewell to the shade,
And the whispering sound of the cool colonnade!
William Cowper (1731–1800) British poet.
The Poplar Field

4 As when, upon a trancèd summer-night,
Those green-rob'd senators of mighty woods,
Tall oaks, branch-charmèd by the earnest stars,
Dream, and so dream all night without a stir.
John Keats (1795–1821) British poet.
Hyperion, I

5 I think that I shall never see
A poem lovely as a tree.
Alfred Joyce Kilmer (1886–1918) US poet.
Trees

6 Woodman, spare that tree!
Touch not a single bough!
In youth it sheltered me,
And I'll protect it now.
George Pope Morris (1802–64) US journalist.
Woodman, Spare That Tree

7 I think that I shall never see
A billboard lovely as a tree.
Perhaps unless the billboards fall,
I'll never see a tree at all.
Ogden Nash (1902–71) US poet.
Song of the Open Road

☐ **TRIVIALITY** ☐

See also insignificance

1 Nothing matters very much, and very few things
matter at all.
Arthur Balfour (1848–1930) British statesman.
Attrib.

2 A Storm in a Teacup.
W. B. Bernard (1807–75) British dramatist.
Play title

3 Little things affect little minds.
Benjamin Disraeli (1804–81) British statesman.
Sybil, Bk. III, Ch. 2

4 It has long been an axiom of mine that the little
things are infinitely the most important.
Arthur Conan Doyle (1856–1930) British writer.
A Case of Identity

5 Little minds are interested in the extraordinary;
great minds in the commonplace.
Elbert Hubbard (1856–1915) US writer.
Roycroft Dictionary and Book of Epigrams

6 It's deadly commonplace, but, after all, the
commonplaces are the great poetic truths.
Robert Louis Stevenson (1850–94) Scottish writer.
Weir of Hermiston, Ch. 6

☐ **TROLLOPE** ☐
Anthony
(1815–82) British novelist. He established his reputation with the
Barsetshire series of novels, including *The Warden* (1855) and
Barchester Towers (1857). Later books include *Phineas Finn*
(1869).

QUOTATIONS ABOUT TROLLOPE

1 He has a gross and repulsive face but appears
bon enfant when you talk to him. But he is the
dullest Briton of them all.
Henry James (1843–1916) US novelist.
Letter to his family, 1 Nov 1875

QUOTATIONS BY TROLLOPE

2 He must have known me had he seen me as he
was wont to see me, for he was in the habit of flogging me constantly. Perhaps he did not recognize
me by my face.
Autobiography, Ch. 1

3 No man thinks there is much ado about nothing
when the ado is about himself.
The Bertrams, Ch. 27

4 The comic almanacs give us dreadful pictures of
January and February; but, in truth, the months
which should be made to look gloomy in England are March and April. Let no man boast himself that he has got through the perils of winter
till at least the seventh of May.
Doctor Thorne, Ch. 47

5 As for conceit, what man will do any good who is
not conceited? Nobody holds a good opinion of a
man who has a low opinion of himself.
Orley Farm, Ch. 22

6 Mr Turnbull had predicted evil consequences...and was now doing the best in his

power to bring about the verification of his own prophecies.
Phineas Finn, Ch. 25

7 I doubt whether any girl would be satisfied with her lover's mind if she knew the whole of it.
The Small House at Allington, Ch. 4

8 And, above all things, never think that you're not good enough yourself. A man should never think that. My belief is that in life people will take you very much at your own reckoning.
The Small House at Allington, Ch. 32

□ TRUST □
See also faith, mistrust

1 Trust ye not in a friend, put ye not confidence in a guide: keep the doors of thy mouth from her that lieth in thy bosom.
Bible: Micah
7:5

2 We are inclined to believe those whom we do not know because they have never deceived us.
Samuel Johnson (1709–84) British lexicographer.
The Idler

3 Never trust a husband too far, nor a bachelor too near.
Helen Rowland (1876–1950) US writer.
The Rubaiyat of a Bachelor

□ TRUTH □
See also facts, frankness, honesty, lying, sincerity

1 The truth that makes men free is for the most part the truth which men prefer not to hear.
Herbert Sebastian Agar (1897–1980) US writer.
A Time for Greatness

2 Truth sits upon the lips of dying men.
Matthew Arnold (1822–88) British poet and critic.
Sohrab and Rustum

3 I tore myself away from the safe comfort of certainities through my love for truth; and truth rewarded me.
Simone de Beauvoir (1908–86) French writer and feminist.
All Said and Done

4 And ye shall know the truth, and the truth shall make you free.
Bible: John
8:32

5 A truth that's told with bad intent
Beats all the lies you can invent.
William Blake (1757–1827) British poet.
Auguries of Innocence

6 Agree to a short armistice with truth.
Lord Byron (1788–1824) British poet.
Don Juan, III

7 'Tis strange – but true; for truth is always strange;
Stranger than fiction: if it could be told,
How much would novels gain by the exchange!
Lord Byron
Don Juan, XIV

8 Much truth is spoken, that more may be concealed.
Lord Darling (1849–1936) British judge.
Scintillae Juris

9 Perjury is often bold and open. It is truth that is shamefaced – as, indeed, in many cases is no more than decent.
Lord Darling
Scintillae Juris

10 It is an old maxim of mine that when you have excluded the impossible, whatever remains, however improbable, must be the truth.
Arthur Conan Doyle (1856–1930) British writer.
The Beryl Coronet

11 Ethical axioms are found and tested not very differently from the axioms of science. Truth is what stands the test of experience.
Albert Einstein (1879–1955) German-born US physicist.
Out of My Later Years

12 Truth, like a torch, the more it's shook it shines.
William Hamilton (1788–1856) Scottish philosopher.
Discussions on Philosophy, title page

13 True and False are attributes of speech, not of things. And where speech is not, there is neither Truth nor Falsehood.
Thomas Hobbes (1588–1679) English philosopher.
Leviathan, Pt. I, Ch. 4

14 'Beauty is truth, truth beauty,' – that is all
Ye know on earth, and all ye need to know.
John Keats (1795–1821) British poet.
Ode on a Grecian Urn

15 It is one thing to show a man that he is in an error, and another to put him in possession of truth.
John Locke (1632–1704) English philosopher.
An Essay Concerning Human Understanding, Bk. IV, Ch. 7

16 It is hard to believe that a man is telling the truth when you know that you would lie if you were in his place.
Henry Louis Mencken (1880–1956) US journalist.

17 Truth has no special time of its own. Its hour is now – always.
Albert Schweitzer (1875–1965) French Protestant theologian, philosopher, physician, and musician.
Out of My Life and Thought

18 Truth telling is not compatible with the defence of the realm.
George Bernard Shaw (1856–1950) Irish dramatist and critic.
Heartbreak House

19 It takes two to speak the truth – one to speak, and another to hear.
Henry David Thoreau (1817–62) US writer.
A Week on the Concord and Merrimack Rivers

20 There are no whole truths; all truths are half-truths. It is trying to treat them as whole truths that plays the devil.
A. N. Whitehead (1861–1947) British philosopher.
Dialogues, 16

21 I believe that in the end the truth will conquer.
John Wycliffe (1329–84) English religious reformer.
Said to John of Gaunt, Duke of Lancaster, 1381
Short History of the English People (J. R. Green)

☐ TWAIN ☐
Mark
(Samuel Langhorne Clemens; 1835–1910) US writer. A steam-boat pilot, he wrote a novel, *The Adventures of Huckleberry Finn* (1884), which established his reputation as a writer.

QUOTATIONS ABOUT TWAIN

1 The average American loves his family. If he has any love left over for some other person, he generally selects Mark Twain.
Thomas Edison (1847–1931) US inventor.
Attrib.

2 Mark Twain and I are in the same position. We have to put things in such a way as to make people, who would otherwise hang us, believe that we are joking.
George Bernard Shaw (1856–1950) Irish dramatist and critic.
Attrib.

QUOTATIONS BY TWAIN

3 There was things which he stretched, but mainly he told the truth.
The Adventures of Huckleberry Finn, Ch. 1

4 There are three kinds of lies: lies, damned lies, and statistics.
Autobiography

5 It takes your enemy and your friend, working together, to hurt you to the heart; the one to slander you and the other to get the news to you.
Following the Equator

6 It is by the goodness of God that in our country we have those three unspeakably precious things: freedom of speech, freedom of conscience, and the prudence never to practice either of them.
Following the Equator, heading of Ch. 20

7 Man is the only animal that blushes. Or needs to.
Following the Equator, heading of Ch. 27

8 I must have a prodigious quantity of mind; it takes me as much as a week, sometimes, to make it up.
The Innocents Abroad, Ch. 7

9 The radical invents the views. When he has worn them out, the conservative adopts them.
Notebooks

10 Familiarity breeds contempt – and children.
Notebooks

11 Good breeding consists in concealing how much we think of ourselves and how little we think of other persons.
Notebooks

12 Something that everybody wants to have read and nobody wants to read.
Definition of a classic of literature.
Speech at Nineteenth Century Club, New York, 20 Nov 1900

13 Reports of my death are greatly exaggerated.
On learning that his obituary had been published.
Cable to the Associated Press

14 Scarce, sir. Mighty scarce.
Responding to the question 'In a world without women what would men become?'.
Attrib.

15 I've done it a hundred times!
Referring to giving up smoking.
Attrib.

☐ TYRANNY ☐
See also authoritarianism, oppression

1 Nature has left this tincture in the blood,
That all men would be tyrants if they could.
Daniel Defoe (1660–1731) British journalist and writer.
The Kentish Petition, Addenda

2 'Twixt kings and tyrants there's this difference known;
Kings seek their subjects' good: tyrants their own.
Robert Herrick (1591–1674) English poet.
Hesperides, 'Kings and Tyrants'

3 ...whenever kingship approaches tyranny it is near its end, for by this it becomes ripe for division, change of dynasty, or total destruction, especially in a temperate climate...where men are habitually, morally and naturally free.
Nicholas of Oresme (c. 1320–82) Chaplain to Charles V of France.
De Moneta

4 Where laws end, tyranny begins.
William Pitt the Elder (1708–78) British statesman.
Speech, House of Lords, referring to the Wilkes case, 9 Jan 1770

U

□ UNDERSTANDING □

See also intelligence, wisdom

1 And come hither, and I shall light a candle of understanding in thine heart, which shall not be put out, till the things be performed which thou shalt begin to write.
Bible: II Esdras
14:25

2 It is good to know what a man is, and also what the world takes him for. But you do not understand him until you have learnt how he understands himself.
F. H. Bradley (1846–1924) British philosopher.
Aphorisms

3 The people may be made to follow a course of action, but they may not be made to understand it.
Confucius (K'ung Fu-tzu; 551–479 BC) Chinese philosopher.
Analects

4 Even when poetry has a meaning, as it usually has, it may be inadvisable to draw it out...Perfect understanding will sometimes almost extinguish pleasure.
A. E. Housman (1859–1936) British scholar and poet.
The Name and Nature of Poetry

5 Thought must be divided against itself before it can come to any knowledge of itself.
Aldous Huxley (1894–1964) British novelist.
Do What You Will

6 I have striven not to laugh at human actions, not to weep at them, nor to hate them, but to understand them.
Benedict Spinoza (Baruch de Spinoza; 1632–77) Dutch philosopher.
Tractatus Theologico-Politicus, Ch. 1

7 All, everything that I understand, I understand only because I love.
Leo Tolstoy (1828–1910) Russian writer.
War and Peace, Bk. VII, Ch. 16

□ UNEMPLOYMENT □

See also idleness, work

1 My father did not wait around...he got on his bike and went out looking for work.
Norman Tebbitt (1931–) British Conservative politician.
Speech, Conservative Party conference, 1981

2 It's a recession when your neighbour loses his job; it's a depression when you lose your own.
Harry S. Truman (1884–1972) US statesman.
The Observer, 'Sayings of the Week', 6 Apr 1958

□ UNFAITHFULNESS □

See also adultery

1 But I kissed her little sister,
And forgot my Clementine.
Percy Montrose (19th century) US songwriter.
Clementine

2 O, swear not by the moon, th' inconstant moon,
That monthly changes in her circled orb,
Lest that thy love prove likewise variable.
William Shakespeare (1564–1616) English dramatist.
Romeo and Juliet, II:2

3 His honour rooted in dishonour stood,
And faith unfaithful kept him falsely true.
Alfred, Lord Tennyson (1809–92) British poet.
Idylls of the King, 'Lancelot and Elaine'

4 Why should marriage bring only tears?
All I wanted was a man
With a single heart,
And we would stay together
As our hair turned white,
Not somebody always after wriggling fish
With his big bamboo rod.
Chuo Wên-chün (?179–117 BC) Chinese poet.
Orchid Boat, Women Poets of China (Kenneth Rexroth and Ling Chung)

□ UNITY □

1 That typically English characteristic for which there is no English name – *esprit de corps*.
Frank Ezra Adcock (1886–1968) British classicist.
Presidential address

2 And if one prevail against him, two shall withstand him; and a threefold cord is not quickly broken.
Bible: Ecclesiastes
4:12

3 And the whole earth was of one language, and of one speech.
Bible: Genesis
11:1

4 All for one, and one for all.
Alexandre Dumas, père (1802–70) French novelist and dramatist.
The Three Musketeers

5 We must indeed all hang together, or most assuredly, we shall all hang separately.
Benjamin Franklin (1706–90) US scientist and statesman.
Remark on signing the Declaration of Independence, 4 July 1776

6 No human relation gives one possession in another – every two souls are absolutely different. In friendship or in love, the two side by side

raise hands together to find what one cannot
reach alone.
Kahil Gibran (1833–1931) Lebanese mystic and poet.
Beloved Prophet (ed. Virginia Hilu)

7 Everyone has observed how much more dogs
are animated when they hunt in a pack, than
when they pursue their game apart. We might,
perhaps, be at a loss to explain this phenomenon,
if we had not experience of a similar in ourselves.
David Hume (1711–76) Scottish philosopher.
A Treatise of Human Nature

□ UNIVERSE

1 Had I been present at the Creation, I would have
given some useful hints for the better ordering of
the universe.
Alfonso the Wise (c. 1221–84) King of Castile and Léon.
Referring to the complicated Ptolemaic model of the universe.
Often quoted as, 'Had I been consulted I would have recom-
mended something simpler'
Attrib.

2 The visible universe was an illusion or, more precisely, a sophism. Mirrors and fatherhood are
abominable because they multiply it and extend
it.
Jorge Luis Borges (1899–1986) Argentinian writer.
Ficciones, 'Tlön, Uqbar, Orbis Tertius'

3 The cosmos is about the smallest hole that a man
can hide his head in.
G. K. Chesterton (1874–1936) British writer.
Orthodoxy, Ch. 1

4 The universe is not hostile, nor yet is it friendly. It
is simply indifferent.
John Haynes Holmes (1879–1964) US clergyman.
A Sensible Man's View of Religion

5 The universe begins to look more like a great
thought than like a great machine.
James Jeans (1877–1946) British scientist.
The Mysterious Universe

V

☐VENICE☐

See also Europe

1 Streets full of water. Please advise.
   Robert Benchley (1889–1945) US humorist.
   Telegram sent to his editor on arriving in Venice
   Attrib.

2 Venice, the eldest Child of Liberty.
   She was a maiden City, bright and free.
   William Wordsworth (1770–1850) British poet.
   Venice, a republic since the Middle Ages, was conquered by
   Napoleon in 1797 and absorbed into his Kingdom of Italy in 1805
   Sonnets, 'Once did she hold'

3 Once did she hold the gorgeous east in fee;
   And was the safeguard of the west.
   William Wordsworth
   Sonnets, 'Once did she hold'

☐VERBOSITY☐

See also brevity, sermons, speech, speeches, writing

1 There was a young man of Japan
   Whose limericks never would scan;
   When they said it was so,
   He replied, 'Yes, I know,
   But I always try to get as many words into the
   last line as ever I possibly can.'
   Anonymous

2 But far more numerous was the Herd of such,
   Who think too little, and who talk too much.
   John Dryden (1631–1700) British poet and dramatist.
   Absalom and Achitophel, I

3 Nothing is more despicable than a professional
   talker who uses his words as a quack uses his
   remedies.
   François Fénelon (1651–1715) French writer and prelate.
   Letter to M. Dacier

4 Words are like leaves; and where they most
   abound,
   Much fruit of sense beneath is rarely found.
   Alexander Pope (1688–1744) British poet.
   An Essay on Criticism

☐VICE☐

See also crime, evil, sin, virtue and vice

1 We make ourselves a ladder out of our vices if we
   trample the vices themselves underfoot.
   St Augustine of Hippo (354–430) Bishop of Hippo.
   Sermons, Bk. III, 'De Ascensione'

2 Often the fear of one evil leads us into a worse.
   Nicolas Boileau (1636–1711) French writer.
   L'Art poétique, I

3 Vice is its own reward.
   Quentin Crisp (?1910–) Model, publicist, and writer.
   The Naked Civil Servant

4 Whenever I'm caught between two evils, I take
   the one I've never tried.
   Mae West (1892–1980) US actress.
   Attrib.

5 Never support two weaknesses at the same time.
   It's your combination sinners – your lecherous
   liars and your miserly drunkards – who dishon-
   our the vices and bring them into bad repute.
   Thornton Wilder (1897–1975) US novelist and dramatist.
   The Matchmaker, III

☐VICTORY☐

See also war

1 *Veni, vidi, vici.*
   I came, I saw, I conquered.
   Julius Caesar (100–44 BC) Roman general and statesman.
   The Twelve Caesars (Suetonius)

2 Victory at all costs, victory in spite of all terror,
   victory however long and hard the road may be;
   for without victory there is no survival.
   Winston Churchill (1874–1965) British statesman.
   Speech, House of Commons, 13 May 1940

3 We triumph without glory when we conquer
   without danger.
   Pierre Corneille (1606–84) French dramatist.
   Le Cid, II:2

4 The most important thing in the Olympic Games
   is not winning but taking part…The essential
   thing in life is not conquering but fighting well.
   Pierre de Coubertin (1863–1937) French educator and
   sportsman.
   Speech, Banquet to Officials of Olympic Games, London,
   24 July 1908

5 Winning isn't everything, but wanting to win is.
   Vince Lombardi (1913–70) US football coach.

6 Who overcomes
   By force, hath overcome but half his foe.
   John Milton (1608–74) English poet.
   Paradise Lost, Bk. I

7 See, the conquering hero comes!
   Sound the trumpets, beat the drums!
   Thomas Morell (1703–84) British classicist.
   The libretto for Handel's oratorio
   Joshua, Pt. III

8 I came; I saw; God conquered.
   John III Sobieski (1624–96) King of Poland.
   Announcing his victory over the Turks at Vienna to the pope
   (paraphrasing Caesar's 'veni, vidi, vici')
   Attrib.

9 The next greatest misfortune to losing a battle is to gain such a victory as this.
Duke of Wellington (1769–1852) British general and statesman.
Recollections (S. Rogers)

10 I always say that, next to a battle lost, the greatest misery is a battle gained.
Duke of Wellington
Diary (Frances, Lady Shelley)

□VIOLENCE□
See also cruelty, force

1 A bit of shooting takes your mind off your troubles – it makes you forget the cost of living.
Brendan Behan (1923–64) Irish playwright.
The Hostage

2 So soon as the man overtook me, he was but a word and a blow.
John Bunyan (1628–88) English writer.
The Pilgrim's Progress, Pt. I

3 Two lovely black eyes,
Oh, what a surprise!
Only for telling a man he was wrong.
Two lovely black eyes!
Charles Coborn (1852–1945) US songwriter.
Two Lovely Black Eyes

4 It's possible to disagree with someone about the ethics of non-violence without wanting to kick his face in.
Christopher Hampton (1946–   ) British writer and dramatist.
Treats, Sc. 4

□VIRGIL□
(Publius Vergilius Maro; 70–19 BC) Roman poet. His *Eclogues* (42–37 BC) were followed by the *Georgics* (36–29 BC), works that expressed his pastoral and agricultural interests. His national epic in 12 books, the *Aeneid*, led to his veneration by subsequent generations.

QUOTATIONS ABOUT VIRGIL

1 Thou art my master and my author, thou art he from whom alone I took the style whose beauty has done me honour.
Dante (1265–1321) Italian poet.
Divine Comedy, 'Inferno', I

2 Virgil's great judgement appears in putting things together, and in his picking gold out of the dunghills of old Roman writers.
Alexander Pope (1688–1744) British poet.
Observations, Anecdotes and Characters (Rev. Joseph Spence)

QUOTATIONS BY VIRGIL

3 I sing of arms and the man who first from the shores of Troy came destined an exile to Italy and the Lavinian beaches, much buffeted he on land and on the deep by force of the gods because of fierce Juno's never-forgetting anger.
Referring to Aeneas.
Aeneid, Bk. I

4 Maybe one day we shall be glad to remember even these hardships
Aeneid, Bk. I

5 *Equo ne credite, Teucri.*
Quidquid id est timeo Danaos et dona ferentis.
Do not trust the horse, Trojans. Whatever it is, I fear the Greeks even when they bring gifts.
Aeneid, Bk. II

6 It was the time when first sleep begins for weary mortals and by the gift of the gods creeps over them most welcomely.
Aeneid, Bk. II

7 Woman is always fickle and changing.
Aeneid, Bk. IV

8 The way down to Hell is easy.
Aeneid, Bk. VI

9 I see wars, horrible wars, and the Tiber foaming with much blood.
Part of the Sibyl's prophecy to Aeneas, foretelling his difficulties in winning a home in Italy.
Aeneid, Bk. VI

10 Fear lent wings to his feet.
Aeneid, Bk. VIII

11 Love conquers all things: let us too give in to Love.
Eclogue, Bk. X

12 But meanwhile it is flying, irretrievable time is flying.
Georgics, Bk. III

□VIRTUE□
See also good, morality, purity, righteousness, virtue and vice

1 Unhappy as the event must be for Lydia, we may draw from it this useful lesson: that loss of virtue in a female is irretrievable; that one false step involves her in endless ruin; that her reputation is no less brittle than it is beautiful; and that she cannot be too much guarded in her behavior towards the undeserving of the other sex.
Jane Austen (1775–1817) British novelist.
Pride and Prejudice, Ch. 47

2 Virtue is like a rich stone, best plain set.
Francis Bacon (1561–1626) English philosopher.
Essays, 'Of Beauty'

3 As in nature things move violently to their place and calmly in their place, so virtue in ambition is violent, in authority settled and calm.
Francis Bacon
Essays, 'Of Great Place'

4 Finally, brethren, whatsoever things are true, whatsoever things are honest, whatsoever things are just, whatsoever things are pure, whatsoever things are lovely, whatsoever things are of good report; if there be any virtue; and if there be any praise, think on these things.
Bible: Philippians
4:8

5 Virtue consisted in avoiding scandal and venereal disease.
Robert Cecil (1913–) British writer.
Life in Edwardian England

6 To be able to practise five things everywhere under heaven constitutes perfect virtue...gravity, generosity of soul, sincerity, earnestness, and kindness.
Confucius (K'ung Fu-tzu; 551–479 BC) Chinese philosopher.
Analects

7 How next to impossible is the exercise of virtue! It requires a constant watchfulness, constant guard.
William Golding (1911–) British novelist.
Rites of Passage, 'Colley's Letter'

8 The greatest offence against virtue is to speak ill of it.
William Hazlitt (1778–1830) British essayist.
On Cant and Hypocrisy

9 To be discontented with the divine discontent, and to be ashamed with the noble shame, is the very germ and first upgrowth of all virtue.
Charles Kingsley
Health and Education

10 Most men admire
Virtue, who follow not her lore.
John Milton (1608–74) English poet.
Paradise Regained, Bk. I

11 Woman's virtue is man's greatest invention.
Cornelia Otis Skinner (1901–79) US stage actress.
Attrib.

☐ VIRTUE AND VICE ☐

See also good and evil, vice, virtue

1 Our virtues and vices couple with one another, and get children that resemble both their parents.
Lord Halifax (1633–95) English statesman.
Political, Moral and Miscellaneous Thoughts and Reflections

2 Most usually our virtues are only vices in disguise.
Duc de la Rochefoucauld (1613–80) French writer.
Maximes, added to the 4th edition

☐ VOLTAIRE ☐

(François-Marie Arouet; 1694–1778) French writer and philosopher. A fearless campaigner against injustice, he was imprisoned in the Bastille, exiled to England, Germany, and Switzerland, and later became a hero of French culture. His works include *Lettres philosophiques* (1734), the fable *Candide* (1759), and the *Dictionnaire philosophique* (1764).

QUOTATIONS ABOUT VOLTAIRE

1 When he talked our language he was animated with the soul of a Briton. He had bold flights. He had humour. He had an extravagance.
James Boswell (1740–95) Scottish lawyer and writer.
Boswell on the Grand Tour (ed. by F. A. Pottle)

2 I was born much too soon, but I do not regret it; I have seen Voltaire.
Frederick the Great (1712–86) King of Prussia.
Attrib.

QUOTATIONS BY VOLTAIRE

3 If we do not find anything pleasant, at least we shall find something new.
Candide, Ch. 17

4 *Dans ce pay-ci, il est bon de tuer de temps en temps un amiral pour encourager les autres.*
In this country it is good to kill an admiral from time to time, to encourage the others.
Referring to England: Admiral Byng was executed for failing to defeat the French at Minorca (1757).
Candide, Ch. 23

5 All is for the best in the best of possible worlds.
Candide, Ch. 30

6 'That is well said,' replied Candide, 'but we must cultivate our garden.'
Candide, Ch. 30

7 Work banishes those three great evils, boredom, vice, and poverty.
Candide, Ch. 30

8 ...use thought only to justify their injustices, and speech only to conceal their thoughts.
Referring to men.
Dialogue, 'Le Chapon et la poularde'

9 The best is the enemy of the good.
Dictionnaire philosophique, 'Art dramatique'

10 If God did not exist, it would be necessary to invent Him.
Épitres, 'À l'auteur du livre des trois Imposteurs'

11 The secret of the arts is to correct nature.
Épitres, 'À M. de Verrière'

12 This agglomeration which was called and which still calls itself the Holy Roman Empire was neither holy, nor Roman, nor an empire.
Essai sur les moeurs et l'esprit des nations, LXX

13 All our ancient history, as one of our wits remarked, is no more than accepted fiction.
Jeannot et Colin

14 All styles are good except the tiresome sort.
L'Enfant prodigue, Preface

15 If God made us in His image, we have certainly returned the compliment.
Le Sottisier

16 It is one of the superstitions of the human mind to have imagined that virginity could be a virtue.
Notebooks

17 Governments need to have both shepherds and butchers.
Notebooks

18 God is on the side not of the heavy battalions, but of the best shots.
Notebooks

19 We owe respect to the living; to the dead we owe only truth.
Oeuvres, 'Première lettre sur Oedipe'

20 Faith consists in believing when it is beyond the power of reason to believe. It is not enough that a thing be possible for it to be believed.
Questions sur l'encyclopédie

21 Marriage is the only adventure open to the cowardly.
Thoughts of a Philosopher

22 There are two things for which animals are to be envied: they know nothing of future evils, or of what people say about them.
Letter, 1739

23 Men will always be mad and those who think they can cure them are the maddest of all.
Letter, 1762

24 The great consolation in life is to say what one thinks.
Letter, 1765

25 I am not like a lady at the court of Versailles, who said: 'What a dreadful pity that the bother at the tower of Babel should have got language all mixed up, but for that, everyone would always have spoken French.
French was the dominant language in the educated circles of 18th-century Europe.
Letter to Catherine the Great, Empress of Russia, 26 May 1767

26 The man who leaves money to charity in his will is only giving away what no longer belongs to him.
Letter, 1769

27 I think it must be so, for I have been drinking it for sixty-five years and I am not dead yet.
On learning that coffee was considered a slow poison.
Attrib.

28 He was a great patriot, a humanitarian, a loyal friend – provided, of course, that he really is dead.
Giving a funeral oration.
Attrib.

29 Once: a philosopher; twice: a pervert!
Turning down an invitation to an orgy, having attended one the previous night for the first time.
Attrib.

30 I disapprove of what you say, but I will defend to the death your right to say it.
Attrib.

☐ VULGARITY ☐
See also humour

1 The aristocratic pleasure of displeasing is not the only delight that bad taste can yield. One can love a certain kind of vulgarity for its own sake.
Aldous Huxley (1894–1964) British novelist.
Vulgarity in Literature, Ch. 4

2 It is disgusting to pick your teeth. What is vulgar is to use a gold toothpick.
Louis Kronenberger (1904–80) US writer and literary critic.
The Cat and the Horse

3 With our James vulgarity begins at home, and should be allowed to stay there.
Oscar Wilde (1854–1900) Irish-born British dramatist.
Referring to the artist James Whistler
Letter to the *World*

W

☐WALES☐

See also Britain, Welsh

1 The thing I value about Wales and Welsh background is that it has always been a genuinely more classless society than many people present England as being.
Geoffrey Howe (1926–) British politician.
The Observer, 'Sayings of the Week', 9 Nov 1986

2 The land of my fathers. My fathers can have it.
Dylan Thomas (1914–53) Welsh poet.
Referring to Wales
Dylan Thomas (John Ackerman)

3 Make me content
With some sweetness
From Wales
Whose nightingales
Have no wings.
Edward Thomas (1878–1917) British poet.
Words

4 We can trace almost all the disasters of English history to the influence of Wales.
Evelyn Waugh (1903–66) British novelist.
Decline and Fall, Pt. I, Ch. 8

☐WAR☐

See also army, Cold War, defeat, navy, nuclear weapons, officers, patriotism, soldiers, victory, war and peace, weapons, World War II

1 And we are here as on a darkling plain
Swept with confused alarms of struggle and flight,
Where ignorant armies clash by night.
Matthew Arnold (1822–88) British poet and critic.
Dover Beach

2 The only defence is in offence, which means that you have to kill more women and children more quickly than the enemy if you want to save yourselves.
Stanley Baldwin (1867–1947) British statesman.
Speech, Nov 1932

3 I think it is well also for the man in the street to realise that there is no power on earth that can protect him from being bombed. Whatever people may tell him, the bomber will always get through, and it is very easy to understand that, if you realise the area of space.
Stanley Baldwin
Speech, House of Commons, 10 Nov 1932

4 It takes twenty years or more of peace to make a man, it takes only twenty seconds of war to destroy him.
Baudouin I (1930–) King of Belgium.
Addressing US Congress, 12 May 1959

5 I have never understood this liking for war. It panders to instincts already catered for within the scope of any respectable domestic establishment.
Alan Bennett (1934–) British playwright.
Forty Years On, I

6 And ye shall hear of wars and rumours of wars: see that ye be not troubled: for all these things must come to pass, but the end is not yet.
For nation shall rise against nation, and kingdom against kingdom: and there shall be famines, and pestilences, and earthquakes, in divers places.
All these are the beginning of sorrows.
Bible: Matthew
24:6–8

7 Then said Jesus unto him, Put up again thy sword into his place: for all they that take the sword shall perish with the sword.
Bible: Matthew
26:52

8 *C'est magnifique, mais ce n'est pas la guerre.*
It is magnificent, but it is not war.
Pierre Bosquet (1810–61) French marshal.
Referring to the Charge of the Light Brigade at the Battle of Balaclava, 25 Oct 1854
Attrib.

9 War is like love, it always finds a way.
Bertolt Brecht
Mother Courage, VI

10 If I should die, think only this of me:
That there's some corner of a foreign field
That is forever England.
Rupert Brooke (1887–1915) British poet.
The Soldier

11 War knows no power. Safe shall be my going,
Secretly armed against all death's endeavour;
Safe though all safety's lost; safe where men fall;
And if these poor limbs die, safest of all.
Rupert Brooke
Safety

12 War, war is still the cry, 'War even to the knife!'
Lord Byron (1788–1824) British poet.
Childe Harold's Pilgrimage, I

13 In war, whichever side may call itself the victor, there are no winners, but all are losers.
Neville Chamberlain (1869–1940) British statesman.
Speech, Kettering, 3 July 1938

14 Wars, conflict, it's all business. One murder makes a villain. Millions a hero. Numbers sanctify.
Charlie Chaplin (Sir Charles Spencer C.; 1889–1977) British film actor.
Monsieur Verdoux

15 I said that the world must be made safe for at least fifty years. If it was only for fifteen to twenty years then we should have betrayed our soldiers.
Winston Churchill (1874–1965) British statesman.
Closing the Ring, Ch. 20

16 No one can guarantee success in war, but only deserve it.
Winston Churchill
Their Finest Hour

17 War is the continuation of politics by other means.
Karl von Clausewitz (1780–1831) Prussian general.
The usual misquotation of 'War is nothing but a continuation of politics with the admixture of other means'
Vom Kriege

18 There is plenty of time to win this game, and to thrash the Spaniards too.
Francis Drake (1540–96) British navigator and admiral.
Referring to the sighting of the Armada during a game of bowls, 20 July 1588
Attrib.

19 I have singed the Spanish king's beard.
Francis Drake
Referring to the raid on Cadiz harbour, 1587
Attrib.

20 We are not at war with Egypt. We are in an armed conflict.
Anthony Eden (1897–1977) British statesman.
Speech, House of Commons, 4 Nov 1956

21 I got there fustest with the mostest.
Nathan Bedford Forrest (1821–77) Confederate general.
Popular misquotation of his explanation of his success in capturing Murfreesboro; his actual words were, 'I just took the short cut and got there first with the most men'
A Civil War Treasury (B. Botkin)

22 I have many times asked myself whether there can be more potent advocates of peace upon earth through the years to come than this massed multitude of silent witnesses to the desolation of war.
George V (1865–1936) King of the United Kingdom.
Referring to the massed World War I graves in Flanders, 1922
Silent Cities (ed. Gavin Stamp)

23 In starting and waging a war it is not right that matters, but victory.
Adolf Hitler (1889–1945) German dictator.
The Rise and Fall of the Third Reich (W. L. Shirer), Ch. 16

24 Older men declare war. But it is youth that must fight and die.
Herbert Clark Hoover (1874–1964) US statesman.
Speech, Republican National Convention, Chicago, 27 June 1944

25 East and west on fields forgotten
Bleach the bones of comrades slain,
Lovely lads and dead and rotten;
None that go return again.
A. E. Housman (1859–1936) British scholar and poet.
A Shropshire Lad, 'The Welsh Marches'

26 The first casualty when war comes is truth.
Hiram Warren Johnson (1866–1945) US politician.
Speech, U.S. Senate, 1917

27 Formerly, a nation that broke the peace did not trouble to try and prove to the world that it was done solely from higher motives…*Now war has a bad conscience*. Now every nation assures us that it is bleeding for a human cause, the fate of which hangs in the balance of its victory…. No nation dares to admit the guilt of blood before the world.
Ellen Key (Karolina Sofia Key; 1849–1926) Swedish writer.
War, Peace, and the Future, Preface

28 Everything, everything in war is barbaric…But the worst barbarity of war is that it forces men collectively to commit acts against which individually they would revolt with their whole being.
Ellen Key
War, Peace, and the Future, Ch. 6

29 Our scientific power has outrun our spiritual power. We have guided missiles and misguided men.
Martin Luther King (1929–68) US Black civil-rights leader.
Strength to Love

30 The conventional army loses if it does not win. The guerrilla wins if he does not lose.
Henry Kissinger (1923–) German-born US politician and diplomat.
Foreign Affairs, XIII (Jan 1969), 'The Vietnam Negotiations'

31 The most persistent sound which reverberates through men's history is the beating of war drums.
Arthur Koestler (1905–83) Hungarian-born British writer.
Janus: A Summing Up, Prologue

32 We have all lost the war. All Europe.
D. H. Lawrence (1885–1930) British novelist.
The Ladybird, 'The Ladybird'

33 It is well that war is so terrible; else we would grow too fond of it.
Robert E. Lee (1807–70) US general.
Speaking to another general during the battle of Fredericksburg
The American Treasury (C. Fadiman)

34 'War is the continuation of politics'. In this sense war is politics and war itself is a political action.
Mao Tse-Tung (1893–1976) Chinese communist leader.
See also CLAUSEWITZ
Quotations from Chairman Mao Tse-Tung, Ch. 5

35 We are advocates of the abolition of war, we do not want war; but war can only be abolished

through war, and in order to get rid of the gun it is necessary to take up the gun.
Mao Tse-Tung
Quotations from Chairman Mao Tse-Tung, Ch. 5

36 Television brought the brutality of war into the comfort of the living room. Vietnam was lost in the living rooms of America – not on the battle-fields of Vietnam.
Marshall McLuhan (1911–81) Canadian sociologist.
Montreal *Gazette*, 16 May 1975

37 War is the national industry of Prussia.
Comte de Mirabeau (1749–91) French statesman.
Attrib.

38 War hath no fury like a non-combatant.
C. E. Montague (1867–1928) British editor and writer.
Disenchantment, Ch. 15

39 An empire founded by war has to maintain itself by war.
Baron de Montesquieu (1689–1755) French writer.
Considérations sur les causes de la grandeur et de la décadence des romains, Ch. 8

40 The Minstrel Boy to the war has gone,
In the ranks of death you'll find him;
His father's sword he has girded on,
And his wild harp slung behind him.
Thomas Moore (1779–1852) Irish poet.
Irish Melodies, 'The Minstrel Boy'

41 The sand of the desert is sodden red, –
Red with the wreck of a square that broke; –
The gatling's jammed and the colonel dead,
And the regiment blind with the dust and smoke.
The river of death has brimmed its banks
And England's far and honour a name.
But the voice of a schoolboy rallies the ranks:
'Play up! play up! and play the game!'
Henry John Newbolt (1862–1938) British poet.
Vitaï Lampada

42 The quickest way of ending a war is to lose it.
George Orwell (Eric Blair; 1903–50) British novelist.
Second Thoughts on James Burnham

43 War should belong to the tragic past, to history: it should find no place on humanity's agenda for the future.
John Paul II (Karol Wojtyla; 1920–) Polish pope (1978–).
Speech, 1982

44 Don't fire until you see the whites of their eyes.
William Prescott (1726–95) US revolutionary soldier.
Command given at the Battle of Bunker Hill

45 War is, after all, the universal perversion. We are all tainted: if we cannot experience our perversion at first hand we spend our time reading war stories, the pornography of war; or seeing war films, the blue films of war; or titillating our senses with the imagination of great deeds, the masturbation of war.
John Rae (1931–) British schoolmaster and writer.
The Custard Boys, Ch. 6

46 As a woman I can't go to war, and I refuse to send anyone else.
Jeannette Rankin (1880–1973) US suffragette, pacifist, and politician.
Jeannette Rankin: First Lady in Congress, Prologue

47 In a civil war, a general must know – and I'm afraid it's a thing rather of instinct than of prac-tice – he must know exactly when to move over to the other side.
Henry Reed (1914–86) British poet and dramatist.
Not a Drum was Heard: The War Memoirs of General Gland

48 And the various holds and rolls and throws and breakfalls
Somehow or other I always seemed to put
In the wrong place. And as for war, my wars
Were global from the start.
Henry Reed
A Map of Verona, 'Lessons of the War', III

49 All Quiet on the Western Front.
Erich Maria Remarque (1898–1970) German novelist.
Title of novel

50 All wars are planned by old men
In council rooms apart.
Grantland Rice (1880–1954) US sportswriter.
Two Sides of War

51 More than an end to war, we want an end to the beginnings of all wars.
Franklin D. Roosevelt (1882–1945) US Democratic president.
Speech broadcast on the day after his death (13 Apr 1945)

52 War is not an adventure. It is a disease. It is like typhus.
Antoine de Saint-Exupéry (1900–44) French novelist and aviator.
Flight to Arras

53 Sometime they'll give a war and nobody will come.
Carl Sandburg (1878–1967) US author and poet.
The People, Yes

54 And when the war is done and youth stone dead
I'd toddle safely home and die – in bed.
Siegfried Sassoon (1886–1967) British poet.
Base Details

55 'Good morning; good morning!' the general said
When we met him last week on our way to the line.
Now the soldiers he smiled at are most of 'em dead,
And we're cursing his staff for incompetent swine.
Siegfried Sassoon
The General

56 All wars are popular for the first thirty days.
Arthur Schlesinger Jnr (1917–) US historian, educator, and author.
Attrib.

57 Everyone is always talking about our defense effort in terms of defending women and children, but no one ever asks the women and children what they think.
Patricia Schroeder (1940–) US politician, lawyer, and educator.
American Political Women

58 When we, the Workers, all demand: 'What are we fighting for?...
Then, then we'll end that stupid crime, that devil's madness – War.
Robert William Service (1874–1958) Canadian poet.
Michael

59 Cry 'Havoc!' and let slip the dogs of war.
William Shakespeare (1564–1616) English dramatist.
Julius Caesar, III:1

60 Farewell the neighing steed and the shrill trump,
The spirit-stirring drum, th'ear piercing fife,
The royal banner, and all quality,
Pride, pomp, and circumstance, of glorious war!
William Shakespeare
Othello, III:3

61 I am tired and sick of war. Its glory is all moonshine...War is hell.
General William Sherman (1820–91) US general.
Attrib. in address, Michigan Military Academy, 19 June 1879

62 That's what you are. That's what you all are. All of you young people who served in the war. You are a lost generation.
Gertrude Stein (1874–1946) US writer.
A Moveable Feast (E. Hemingway)

63 War is capitalism with the gloves off.
Tom Stoppard (1937–) Czech-born British dramatist.
Travesties

64 The guerrilla fights the war of the flea, and his military enemy suffers the dog's disadvantages: too much to defend; too small, ubiquitous, and agile an enemy to come to grips with.
Robert Taber (20th century) US writer.
The War of the Flea, Ch. 2

65 They make a wilderness and call it peace.
Tacitus (c. 55–c. 120 AD) Roman historian.
Agricola, 30

66 The military don't start wars. The politicians start wars.
William Westmorland (1914–) US army officer.
Attrib.

67 As long as war is regarded as wicked, it will always have its fascination. When it is looked upon as vulgar, it will cease to be popular.
Oscar Wilde (1854–1900) Irish-born British dramatist.
The Critic as Artist, Pt. 2

68 You will be home before the leaves have fallen from the trees.
Wilhelm II (1859–1941) King of Prussia and Emperor of Germany.
Said to troops leaving for the Front, Aug 1914
August 1914 (Barbara Tuchman), Ch. 9

69 There is such a thing as a man being too proud to fight.
Woodrow Wilson (1856–1925) US statesman.
Address to foreign-born citizens, 10 May 1915

70 The war we have just been through, though it was shot through with terror, is not to be compared with the war we would have to face next time.
Woodrow Wilson
Mr Wilson's War (John Dos Passos), Pt. V, Ch. 22

71 Once lead this people into war and they'll forget there ever was such a thing as tolerance.
Woodrow Wilson
Mr Wilson's War (John Dos Passos), Pt. III, Ch. 2

□ WAR AND PEACE □

See also peace, war

1 Since wars begin in the minds of men, it is in the minds of men that the defences of peace must be constructed.
Anonymous
Constitution of UNESCO

2 And he shall judge among the nations, and shall rebuke many people: and they shall beat their swords into plowshares, and their spears into pruning-hooks: nation shall not lift up sword against nation, neither shall they learn war any more.
Bible: Isaiah
2:4

3 In war, resolution; in defeat, defiance; in victory, magnanimity; in peace, goodwill.
Winston Churchill (1874–1965) British statesman.
Epigram used by Sir Edward Marsh after World War II; used as 'a moral of the work' in Churchill's book
The Second World War

4 Those who can win a war well can rarely make a good peace and those who could make a good peace would never have won the war.
Winston Churchill
My Early Life, Ch. 26

5 There never was a good war or a bad peace.
Benjamin Franklin (1706–90) US scientist and statesman.
Letter to Josiah Quincy, 11 Sept 1783

6 The war ended, the explosions stopped.
The men surrendered their weapons
And hung around limply.
Peace took them all prisoner.
Ted Hughes (1930–) British poet.
Selected Poems 1957–1981, 'A Motorbike'

7 Peace hath her victories
No less renowned than war.
John Milton (1608–74) English poet.
Sonnet: 'To the Lord General Cromwell, May 1652'

8 Let him who desires peace, prepare for war.
Vegetius (Flavius Vegetius Renatus; 4th century AD) Roman writer.
Epitoma Rei Militaris, 3, 'Prologue'

9 When you're at war you think about a better life;
when you're at peace you think about a more
comfortable one.
Thornton Wilder (1897–1975) US novelist and dramatist.
The Skin of Our Teeth, III

□WATER□

See also drinks

1 Water, water, every where,
And all the boards did shrink;
Water, water, every where,
Nor any drop to drink.
Samuel Taylor Coleridge (1772–1834) British poet.
The Rime of the Ancient Mariner, II

2 Instead of drinking Coca Colas, turn on the tap
and drink what the good Lord gave us.
Edwina Currie (1946–) British politician.
Speech, Nov 1988

3 The biggest waste of water in the country by far.
You spend half a pint and flush two gallons.
Prince Philip (1921–) The consort of Queen Elizabeth II.
Speech, 1965

4 Human beings were invented by water as a
device for transporting itself from one place to
another.
Tom Robbins (1936–) US novelist.
Another Roadside Attraction

5 He who drinks a tumbler of London water has literally in his stomach more animated beings than
there are men, women and children on the face
of the globe.
Sydney Smith (1771–1845) British clergyman and essayist.
Letter

□WAUGH□
Evelyn

(1903–66) British novelist. He established his reputation with
Decline and Fall (1928) and *Vile Bodies* (1930). Later books, after
his conversion to Catholicism, include *Brideshead Revisited*
(1945) and the war trilogy *Sword of Honour* (1952–61).

QUOTATIONS ABOUT WAUGH

1 Mr. Waugh, I always feel, is an antique in search
of a period, a snob in search of a class, perhaps
even a mystic in search of a beatific vision.
Malcolm Muggeridge (1903–90) British writer.
The Most of Malcolm Muggeridge

QUOTATIONS BY WAUGH

2 I expect you'll be becoming a schoolmaster sir.
That's what most of the gentlemen does sir, that
gets sent down for indecent behaviour.
Decline and Fall, Prelude

3 We class schools you see, into four grades: Lead-
ing School, First-rate School, Good School, and
School.
Decline and Fall, Pt. I, Ch. 1

4 Very hard for a man with a wig to keep order.
Decline and Fall, Pt. I, Ch. 3

5 Meanwhile you will write an essay on 'self-
indulgence'. There will be a prize of half a crown
for the longest essay, irrespective of any possible
merit.
Decline and Fall, Pt. I, Ch. 5

6 I can't quite explain it, but I don't believe one can
ever be unhappy for long provided one does just
exactly what one wants to and when one wants to.
Decline and Fall, Pt. I, Ch. 5

7 For generations the British bourgeoisie have
spoken of themselves as gentlemen, and by that
they meant, among other things, a self-
respecting scorn of irregular perquisites. It is the
quality that distinguishes the gentleman from
both the artist and the aristocrat.
Decline and Fall, Pt. I, Ch. 6

8 There aren't many left like him nowadays, what
with education and whisky the price it is.
Decline and Fall, Pt. I, Ch. 7

9 I have noticed again and again since I have been
in the Church that lay interest in ecclesiastical
matters is often a prelude to insanity.
Decline and Fall, Pt. I, Ch. 8

10 I have often observed in women of her type a ten-
dency to regard all athletics as inferior forms of
fox-hunting.
Decline and Fall, Pt. I, Ch. 10

11 I came to the conclusion many years ago that
almost all crime is due to the repressed desire for
aesthetic expression.
Decline and Fall, Pt. III, Ch. 1

12 Anyone who has been to an English public school will always feel comparatively at home in prison.
Decline and Fall, Pt. III, Ch. 4

13 Punctuality is the virtue of the bored.
Diaries, 'Irregular Notes', 26 Mar 1962

14 You never find an Englishman among the under-dogs – except in England of course.
The Loved One

15 Enclosing every thin man, there's a fat man demanding elbow-room.
Similar sentiments have been expressed by others. *See* AMIS; CONNOLLY; ORWELL.
Officers and Gentlemen, Interlude

16 'I will not stand for being called a woman in my own house,' she said.
Scoop, Bk. I, Ch. 5

17 Other nations use 'force'; we Britons alone use 'Might'.
Scoop, Bk. II, Ch. 5

18 Particularly against books the Home Secretary is. If we can't stamp out literature in the country, we can at least stop it being brought in from out-side.
Vile Bodies, Ch. 2

19 All this fuss about sleeping together. For physi-cal pleasure I'd sooner go to my dentist any day.
Vile Bodies, Ch. 6

20 Lady Peabury was in the morning room reading a novel; early training gave a guilty spice to this recreation, for she had been brought up to believe that to read a novel before luncheon was one of the gravest sins it was possible for a gentlewoman to commit.
Work Suspended, 'An Englishman's Home'

21 Manners are especially the need of the plain. The pretty can get away with anything.
The Observer, 'Sayings of the Year,' 1962

22 No writer before the middle of the 19th century wrote about the working classes other than as grotesque or as pastoral decoration. Then when they were given the vote certain writers started to suck up to them.
Interview.
Paris Review, 1963

23 Nurse unupblown.
Cable sent after he had failed, while a journalist serving in Ethio-pia, to substantiate a rumor that an English nurse had been blown up in an Italian air raid.
Our Marvelous Native Tongue (R. Claiborne)

24 Like German opera, too long and too loud.
Giving his opinions of warfare after the Battle of Crete, 1941.
Attrib.

□ **WEAKNESS** □

See also imperfection, yielding

1 Oh, your precious 'lame ducks'!
John Galsworthy (1867–1933) British novelist.
The Man of Property, Pt. II, Ch. 12

2 Frailty, thy name is woman!
William Shakespeare (1564–1616) English dramatist.
Hamlet, I:2

□ **WEALTH** □

See also capitalism, extravagance, materialism, money, ostenta-tion, poverty and wealth

1 For the Lord thy God bringeth thee into a good land, a land of brooks of water, of fountains and depths that spring out of valleys and hills;
A land of wheat, and barley, and vines, and fig trees, and pomegranates; a land of oil olive, and honey;
A land wherein thou shalt eat bread without scarceness, thou shalt not lack any thing in it; a land whose stones are iron, and out of whose hills thou mayest dig brass.
When thou hast eaten and art full, then thou shalt bless the Lord thy God for the good land which he hath given thee.
Bible: Deuteronomy
8:7–10

2 For what shall it profit a man, if he shall gain the whole world, and lose his own soul? Or what shall a man give in exchange for his soul?
Bible: Mark
8:36–37

3 Then said Jesus unto his disciples, Verily I say unto you, That a rich man shall hardly enter into the kingdom of heaven.
And again I say unto you, It is easier for a camel to go through the eye of a needle, than for a rich man to enter into the kingdom of God.
Bible: Matthew
19:23–24

4 The rich are the scum of the earth in every country.
G. K. Chesterton (1874–1936) British writer.
The Flying Inn

5 Poor Little Rich Girl.
Noël Coward (1899–1973) British dramatist.
Title of song

6 Riches have wings, and grandeur is a dream.
William Cowper (1731–1800) British poet.
The Task

7 Wealth is not without its advantages, and the case to the contrary, although it has often been made, has never proved widely persuasive.
John Kenneth Galbraith (1908–) US economist.
The Affluent Society, Ch. 1

8 The meek shall inherit the earth but not the mineral rights.
J. Paul Getty (1892–1976) US oil magnate.
Attrib.

9 As I walk along the Bois Bou-long,
With an independent air,
You can hear the girls declare,
'He must be a millionaire',
You can hear them sigh and wish to die,
You can see them wink the other eye
At the man who broke the Bank at Monte Carlo.
Fred Gilbert (1850–1903) British songwriter.
The Bois de Boulogne was a fashionable recreational area on the outskirts of Paris
The Man who Broke the Bank at Monte Carlo (song)

10 And, as their wealth increaseth, so inclose
Infinite riches in a little room.
Christopher Marlowe (1564–93) English dramatist.
The Jew of Malta, I:1

11 God shows his contempt for wealth by the kind of person he selects to receive it.
Austin O'Malley (1858–1932) US writer.

12 Who Wants to Be a Millionaire? I don't.
Cole Porter (1893–1964) US songwriter.
Who Wants to be a Millionaire?, title song

13 With the great part of rich people, the chief employment of riches consists in the parade of riches.
Adam Smith (1723–90) Scottish economist.
The Wealth of Nations

14 It is the wretchedness of being rich that you have to live with rich people.
Logan Pearsall Smith (1865–1946) US writer.
Afterthoughts, 'In the World'

15 One can never be too thin or too rich.
Duchess of Windsor (Wallis Warfield Simpson; 1896–1986)
The wife of the Duke of Windsor (formerly Edward VIII).
Attrib.

☐ WEAPONS ☐

See also nuclear weapons, power politics, war

1 If you carry this resolution and follow out all its implications and do not run away from it, you will send a Foreign Secretary, whoever he may be, naked into the conference chamber.
Aneurin Bevan (1897–1960) British Labour politician.
Referring to unilateral disarmament
Speech, Labour Party Conference, 2 Oct 1957

2 Arms control so easily becomes an incantation rather than policy.
Richard Perle US politician.
Remark, Mar 1987

3 Though loaded firearms were strictly forbidden at St Trinian's to all but Sixth-Formers…one or two of them carried automatics acquired in the holidays, generally the gift of some indulgent relative.
Ronald Searle (1920–) British cartoonist.
The Terror of St Trinian's, Ch. 3

4 But bombs *are* unbelievable until they actually fall.
Patrick White (1912–90) British-born Australian novelist.
Riders in the Chariot, I:4

☐ WEATHER ☐

See also sun

1 This is a London particular…A fog, miss.
Charles Dickens (1812–70) British novelist.
Bleak House, Ch. 3

2 I'm singing in the rain, just singing in the rain;
What a wonderful feeling, I'm happy again.
Arthur Freed (1894–1973) US film producer and songwriter.
From the musical, *Hollywood Revue of 1929*
Singing in the Rain

3 This is the weather the cuckoo likes,
And so do I;
When showers betumble the chestnut spikes,
And nestlings fly:
And the little brown nightingale bills his best,
And they sit outside at 'The Travellers' Rest'.
Thomas Hardy (1840–1928) British novelist.
Weathers

4 This is the weather the shepherd shuns,
And so do I.
Thomas Hardy
Weathers

5 When two Englishmen meet, their first talk is of the weather.
Samuel Johnson (1709–84) British lexicographer.
The Idler

6 Who has seen the wind?
Neither you nor I:
But when the trees bow down their heads,
The wind is passing by.
Christina Rossetti (1830–74) British poet.
Who Has Seen the Wind?

7 Blow, winds, and crack your cheeks; rage, blow.
You cataracts and hurricanoes, spout
Till you have drench'd our steeples, drown'd the cocks.
William Shakespeare (1564–1616) English dramatist.
King Lear, III:2

8 Rumble thy bellyful. Spit, fire; spout rain.
Nor rain, wind, thunder, fire, are my daughters
I tax not you, you elements, with unkindness.
William Shakespeare
King Lear, III:2

9 Poor naked wretches, wheresoe'er you are,
That bide the pelting of this pitiless storm,
How shall your houseless heads and unfed sides,
Your loop'd and window'd raggedness, defend
you
From seasons such as these?
William Shakespeare
King Lear, III:4

10 So foul and fair a day I have not seen.
William Shakespeare
Macbeth, I:3

11 I wield the flail of the lashing hail,
And whiten the green plains under,
And then again I dissolve it in rain,
And laugh as I pass in thunder.
Percy Bysshe Shelley (1792–1822) British poet.
The Cloud

12 O Wild West Wind, thou breath of Autumn's
being,
Thou, from whose unseen presence the leaves
dead
Are driven, like ghosts from an enchanter fleeing,
Yellow, and black, and pale, and hectic red,
Pestilence-stricken multitudes.
Percy Bysshe Shelley
Ode to the West Wind

13 Willows whiten, aspens quiver,
Little breezes dusk and shiver.
Alfred, Lord Tennyson (1809–92) British poet.
The Lady of Shalott, Pt. I

☐ WELLINGTON ☐
Arthur Wellesley, Duke of
(1769–1852) British general and statesman. He defeated the
French in the Peninsular War and Napoleon at Waterloo. Known
as the 'Iron Duke', he became Tory prime minister (1828–30).
Under Peel he served as foreign secretary (1834–35).

QUOTATIONS ABOUT WELLINGTON

1 The Duke of Wellington has exhausted nature
and exhausted glory. His career was one
unclouded longest day.
The Times, Obituary, 16 Sept 1852

QUOTATIONS BY WELLINGTON

2 It all depends upon that article there.
Indicating a passing infantryman when asked if he would be able
to defeat Napoleon.
The Age of Elegance (A. Bryant)

3 Yes, and they went down very well too.
Replying to the observation that the French cavalry had come up
very well during the Battle of Waterloo.
The Age of Elegance (A. Bryant)

4 I see no reason to suppose that these machines
will ever force themselves into general use.
Referring to steam locomotives.
Geoffrey Madan's Notebooks (J. Gere)

5 I hate the whole race...There is no believing a
word they say – your professional poets, I mean –
there never existed a more worthless set than
Byron and his friends for example.
Lady Salisbury's diary, 26 Oct 1833

6 I used to say of him that his presence on the field
made the difference of forty thousand men.
Referring to Napoleon.
Notes of Conversations with the Duke of Wellington (Stanhope),
2 Nov 1831

7 The next greatest misfortune to losing a battle is
to gain such a victory as this.
Recollections (S. Rogers)

8 I don't know what effect these men will have on
the enemy, but, by God, they frighten me.
Referring to his generals.
Attrib.

9 It is not the business of generals to shoot one
another.
Refusing an artillery officer permission to fire upon Napoleon
himself during the Battle of Waterloo, 1815.
Attrib.

10 Up, Guards, and at 'em.
Order given at the battle of Waterloo, 18 June 1815.
Attrib.

11 The battle of Waterloo was won on the playing
fields of Eton.
Attrib.

12 Yes, about ten minutes.
Responding to a vicar's query as to whether there was anything
he would like his forthcoming sermon to be about.
Attrib.

13 Very well, then I shall not take off my boots.
Responding to the news, as he was going to bed, that the ship in
which he was travelling seemed about to sink.
Attrib.

14 Ours is composed of the scum of the earth.
Of the British army.
Remark, 4 Nov 1831

15 Publish and be damned!
On being offered the chance to avoid mention in the memoirs of
Harriette Wilson by giving her money.
Attrib.

16 Don't quote Latin; say what you have to say, and then sit down.

Advice to a new Member of Parliament.
Attrib.

☐WELLS☐
H(erbert) G(eorge)

(1866–1946) British writer. After studying science, he won a literary reputation with *The Time Machine* (1895) and *Kipps* (1905). His other books included *An Outline of History* (1920) and *The Shape of Things to Come* (1933).

QUOTATIONS ABOUT WELLS

1 Whatever Wells writes is not only alive, but kicking.

Henry James (1843–1916) US novelist.
Attrib.

QUOTATIONS BY WELLS

2 The cat is the offspring of a cat and the dog of a dog, but butlers and lady's maids do not reproduce their kind. They have other duties.

Bealby, Pt I, Ch. 1

3 The army ages men sooner than the law and philosophy; it exposes them more freely to germs, which undermine and destroy, and it shelters them more completely from thought, which stimulates and preserves.

Bealby, Pt. VIII, Ch. 1

4 He had one peculiar weakness; he had faced death in many forms but he had never faced a dentist. The thought of dentists gave him just the same sick horror as the thought of Socialism.

Bealby, Pt. VIII, Ch. 1

5 In the Country of the Blind the One-eyed Man is King.

The Country of the Blind

6 Arson, after all, is an artificial crime…A large number of houses deserve to be burnt.

The History of Mr Polly, Pt. X, Ch. 1

7 Everybody hates house-agents because they have everybody at a disadvantage. All other callings have a certain amount of give and take; the house-agent simply takes.

Kipps, Bk. III, Ch. 1

8 Cynicism is humour in ill-health.

Short Stories, 'The Last Trump'

9 Bricklayers kick their wives to death, and dukes betray theirs; but it is among the small clerks and shopkeepers nowadays that it comes most often to the cutting of throats.

Short Stories, 'The Purple Pileus'

10 If Max gets to Heaven he won't last long. He will be chucked out for trying to pull of a merger between Heaven and Hell…after having secured a controlling interest in key subsidiary companies in both places, of course.

Referring to Lord Beaverbrook.
Beaverbrook (A. J. P. Taylor)

☐WELSH☐

See also British, Wales

1 There are still parts of Wales where the only concession to gaiety is a striped shroud.

Gwyn Thomas (1913–81) British writer.
Punch, 18 June 1958

2 …an impotent people,
Sick with inbreeding,
Worrying the carcase of an old song.

R. S. Thomas (1913–) Welsh poet.
Welsh Landscape

3 'The Welsh,' said the Doctor, 'are the only nation in the world that has produced no graphic or plastic art, no architecture, no drama. They just sing,' he said with disgust, sing and blow down wind instruments of plated silver.'

Evelyn Waugh (1903–66) British novelist.
Decline and Fall, Pt. I, Ch. 8

☐WEST☐
Mae

(1892–1980) US actress, sex symbol, and comedienne. She made her reputation in the theater with *Diamond Lil* (1928). Her films included *She Done Him Wrong* (1933) and *I'm No Angel* (1933).

QUOTATIONS ABOUT WEST

1 In a non-permissive age, she made remarkable inroads against the taboos of her day, and did so without even lowering her neckline.

Leslie Halliwell
The Filmgoer's Book of Quotes

2 She stole everything but the cameras.

George Raft (1895–1980) US actor.
Attrib.

QUOTATIONS BY WEST

3 A man in the house is worth two in the street.

Belle of the Nineties, film 1934

4 – My goodness those diamonds are lovely!
Goodness had nothing whatever to do with it.

Used in 1959 as the title of the first volume of her autobiography.
Diamond Lil, film 1932

5 Beulah, peel me a grape.

I'm No Angel, film 1933

6 A gold rush is what happens when a line of chorus girls spot a man with a bank roll.

Klondike Annie, film 1936

7 I always did like a man in uniform. And that one fits you grand. Why don't you come up sometime and see me?

Often misquoted as 'Come up and see me some time'.
She Done Him Wrong, film 1933

8 You can say what you like about long dresses, but they cover a multitude of shins.
Peel Me a Grape (J. Weintraub)

9 It is better to be looked over than overlooked.
The Wit and Wisdom of Mae West (ed. J. Weintraub)

10 I used to be Snow White...but I drifted.
The Wit and Wisdom of Mae West (ed. J. Weintraub)

11 When women go wrong, men go right after them.
The Wit and Wisdom of Mae West (ed. J. Weintraub)

12 I'm glad you like my Catherine. I like her too. She ruled thirty million people and had three thousand lovers. I do the best I can in two hours.
After her performance in *Catherine the Great*.
Speech from the stage

13 Everything.
When asked what she wanted to be remembered for.
Attrib.

14 When I'm good I'm very good, but when I'm bad I'm better.
Attrib.

15 Whenever I'm caught between two evils, I take the one I've never tried.
Attrib.

□ **WHISTLER** □
James Abbott McNeill
(1834–1903) US painter. Living mostly in Europe, he established his reputation with *The Artist's Mother* and *Nocturne in Blue and Gold*. He was also the author of *The Gentle Art of Making Enemies* (1890).

QUOTATIONS ABOUT WHISTLER

1 That he is indeed one of the very greatest masters of painting, is my opinion. And I may add that in this opinion Mr. Whistler himself entirely concurs.
Oscar Wilde (1854–1900) Irish-born British dramatist.
Pall Mall Gazette, 21 Feb 1885

QUOTATIONS BY WHISTLER

2 I am not arguing with you – I am telling you.
The Gentle Art of Making Enemies

3 Nature is usually wrong.
The Gentle Art of Making Enemies

4 No, no, Oscar, you forget. When you and I are together we never talk about anything except me.
Cable replying to Oscar Wilde's message: 'When you and I are together we never talk about anything except ourselves'.
The Gentle Art of Making Enemies

5 No, I ask it for the knowledge of a lifetime.
Replying to the taunt, during the Ruskin trial, that he was asking a fee of 200 guineas for two days' painting.
Lives of the Wits (H. Pearson)

6 Isn't it? I know in my case I would grow intolerably conceited.
Replying to the pointed observation that it was as well that we do not not see ourselves as others see us.
The Man Whistler (H. Pearson)

7 A LADY. I only know of two painters in the world: yourself and Velasquez.
WHISTLER. Why drag in Velasquez?
Whistler Stories (D. Seitz)

8 A LADY. This landscape reminds me of your work.
WHISTLER. Yes madam, Nature is creeping up.
Whistler Stories (D. Seitz)

□ **WHISTLING** □
See also fear

1 The schoolboy, with his satchel in his hand, Whistling aloud to bear his courage up.
Robert Blair (1699–1746) Scottish poet.
The Grave

2 I Whistle a Happy Tune.
Oscar Hammerstein (1895–1960) US lyricist.
From the musical *The King and I*
Song title

□ **WILDE** □
Oscar Fingal O'Flahertie Wills
(1856–1900) Irish-born British poet and dramatist. His comedies *Lady Windermere's Fan* (1892), *An Ideal Husband* (1895), and *The Importance of Being Earnest* (1895) made him a leading figure in London society. However he was ruined by a trial (1895) arising from his homosexual relationships, especially with Lord Alfred Douglas. During his imprisonment he wrote *De Profundis* (1905) and the *The Ballad of Reading Gaol* (1898).

QUOTATIONS ABOUT WILDE

1 From the beginning Wilde performed his life and continued to do so even after fate had taken the plot out of his hands.
W. H. Auden (1907–73) British poet.
Forewords and Afterwords

2 If with the literate I am
Impelled to try an epigram
I never seek to take the credit
We all assume that Oscar said it.
Dorothy Parker (1893–1967) US writer.
Attrib.

QUOTATIONS BY WILDE

3 Yet each man kills the thing he loves,
By each let this be heard,
Some do it with a bitter look,
Some with a flattering word.
The coward does it with a kiss,
The brave man with a sword!
The Ballad of Reading Gaol, I:7

4 Something was dead in each of us,
And what was dead was Hope.
The Ballad of Reading Gaol, III:31

5 As long as war is regarded as wicked, it will
always have its fascination. When it is looked
upon as vulgar, it will cease to be popular.
The Critic as Artist, Pt. 2

6 The man who sees both sides of a question is a
man who sees absolutely nothing at all.
The Critic as Artist, Pt. 2

7 A little sincerity is a dangerous thing, and a great
deal of it is absolutely fatal.
The Critic as Artist, Pt. 2

8 Ah! don't say you agree with me. When people
agree with me I always feel that I must be wrong.
The Critic as Artist, Pt. 2

9 There is much to be said in favour of modern
journalism. By giving us the opinions of the
uneducated, it keeps us in touch with the ignorance of the community.
The Critic as Artist, Pt. 2

10 Art never expresses anything but itself.
The Decay of Lying

11 To love oneself is the beginning of a lifelong
romance.
An Ideal Husband, III

12 All women become like their mothers. That is
their tragedy. No man does. That's his.
The Importance of Being Earnest, I

13 The amount of women in London who flirt with
their own husbands is perfectly scandalous. It
looks so bad. It is simply washing one's clean
linen in public.
The Importance of Being Earnest, I

14 The old-fashioned respect for the young is fast
dying out.
The Importance of Being Earnest, I

15 To lose one parent, Mr Worthing, may be
regarded as a misfortune; to lose both looks like
carelessness.
The Importance of Being Earnest, I

16 I hope you have not been leading a double life,
pretending to be wicked and being really good all
the time. That would be hypocrisy.
The Importance of Being Earnest, II

17 I never travel without my diary. One should
always have something sensational to read in the
train.
The Importance of Being Earnest, II

18 No woman should ever be quite accurate about
her age. It looks so calculating.
The Importance of Being Earnest, III

19 This suspense is terrible. I hope it will last.
The Importance of Being Earnest, III

20 It is a terrible thing for a man to find out suddenly
that all his life he has been speaking nothing but
the truth.
The Importance of Being Earnest, III

21 Please do not shoot the pianist. He is doing his
best.
Impressions of America, 'Leadville'

22 I can resist everything except temptation.
Lady Windermere's Fan, I

23 We are all in the gutter, but some of us are looking at the stars.
Lady Windermere's Fan, III

24 There is nothing in the whole world so unbecoming to a woman as a Nonconformist conscience.
Lady Windermere's Fan, III

25 A man who knows the price of everything and
the value of nothing.
A cynic.
Lady Windermere's Fan, III

26 There is only one thing in the world worse than
being talked about, and that is not being talked
about.
The Picture of Dorian Gray, Ch. 1

27 The only way to get rid of a temptation is to yield
to it.
The Picture of Dorian Gray, Ch. 2

28 A cigarette is the perfect type of a perfect pleas-
ure. It is exquisite, and it leaves one unsatisfied.
What more can one want?
The Picture of Dorian Gray, Ch. 6

29 Democracy means simply the bludgeoning of
the people by the people for the people.
See LINCOLN.
The Soul of Man under Socialism

...ty years of romance makes a woman look
...e a ruin; but twenty years of marriage make
her something like a public building.
A Woman of No Importance, I

31 MRS ALLONBY. They say, Lady Hunstanton, that
when good Americans die they go to Paris.
LADY HUNSTANTON. Indeed? And when bad Ameri-
cans die, where do they go to?
LORD ILLINGWORTH. Oh, they go to America.
See APPLETON, THOMAS GOLD.
A Woman of No Importance, I

32 The English country gentleman galloping after
a fox – the unspeakable in full pursuit of the
uneatable.
A Woman of No Importance, I

33 LORD ILLINGWORTH. The Book of Life begins with
a man and a woman in a garden.
MRS ALLONBY. It ends with Revelations.
A Woman of No Importance, I

34 Moderation is a fatal thing, Lady Hunstanton.
Nothing succeeds like excess.
A Woman of No Importance, III

35 One would have to have a heart of stone to read
the death of Little Nell without laughing.
Lecturing upon Dickens.
Lives of the Wits (H. Pearson)

36 The man who can dominate a London dinner-
table can dominate the world.
Attrib. by R. Aldington in his edition of Wilde

37 The play was a great success, but the audience
was a disaster.
Referring to a play that had recently failed.
Attrib.

38 It requires one to assume such indecent pos-
tures.
Explaining why he did not play cricket.
Attrib.

39 If this is the way Queen Victoria treats her prisoners, she doesn't deserve to have any.
Complaining at having to wait in the rain for transport to take him
to prison.
Attrib.

40 Grief has turned her fair.
Referring to the fact that a recently bereaved lady friend had dyed
her hair blonde.
Attrib.

41 Work is the curse of the drinking classes.
Attrib.

42 Nothing, except my genius.
Replying to a US customs official on being asked if he had anything to declare.

43 Either that wall paper goes, or I do.
Last words, as he lay dying in a drab Paris bedroom.
Time, 16 Jan 1984

□ **WILLIAMS** □
Tennessee
(1911–83) US dramatist. He established his reputation with *The
Glass Menagerie* (1945). Subsequent successes include *A Streetcar Named Desire* (1947) and *Cat on a Hot Tin Roof* (1955).

1 My suit is pale yellow. My nationality is French,
and my normality has been often subject to
question.
Camino Real, Block 4

2 You can be young without money but you can't
be old without it.
Cat on a Hot Tin Roof, I

3 I have always depended on the kindness of
strangers.
A Streetcar Named Desire, II:3

4 If people behaved in the way nations do they
would all be put in straitjackets.
BBC interview

5 He was meddling too much in my private life.
Explaining why he had given up visiting his psychoanalyst.
Attrib.

□ **WISDOM** □
See also intelligence, knowledge, prudence, wisdom and
foolishness

1 For in much wisdom is much grief: and he that
increaseth knowledge increaseth sorrow.
Bible: Ecclesiastes
1:18

2 The words of wise men are heard in quiet more
than the cry of him that ruleth among fools.
Bible: Ecclesiastes
9:17

3 No mention shall be made of coral, or of pearls:
for the price of wisdom is above rubies.
Bible: Job
28:18

4 Wisdom is the principal thing; therefore get wisdom: and with all thy getting get understanding.
Bible: Proverbs
4:7

5 Wisdom reacheth from one end to another
mightily: and sweetly doth she order all things.
Bible: Wisdom
8:1

6 Does the Eagle know what is in the pit
Or wilt thou go ask the Mole?

Can Wisdom be put in a silver rod,
Or love in a golden bowl?
William Blake (1757–1827) British poet.
The Book of Thel, 'Thel's Motto'

7 I care not whether a man is Good or Evil; all that I care
Is whether he is a Wise Man or a Fool. Go! put off Holiness,
And put on Intellect.
William Blake
Jerusalem

8 A sadder and a wiser man,
He rose the morrow morn.
Samuel Taylor Coleridge (1772–1834) British poet.
The Rime of the Ancient Mariner, VII

9 Knowledge dwells
In heads replete with thoughts of other men;
Wisdom in minds attentive to their own.
William Cowper (1731–1800) British poet.
The Task

10 Knowledge can be communicated but not wisdom.
Hermann Hesse (1877–1962) German novelist and poet.
Siddhartha

11 It is the province of knowledge to speak and it is the privilege of wisdom to listen.
Oliver Wendell Holmes (1809–94) US writer.
The Poet at the Breakfast Table, Ch. 10

12 It is never wise to try to appear to be more clever than you are. It is sometimes wise to appear slightly less so.
William Whitelaw (1918–) British politician.
The Observer, 'Sayings of the Year', 1975

□ WISDOM AND FOOLISHNESS □

1 Then I saw that wisdom excelleth folly, as far as light excelleth darkness.
The wise man's eyes are in his head; but the fool walketh in darkness: and I myself perceived also that one event happeneth to them all.
Bible: Ecclesiastes
2:13–14

2 For ye suffer fools gladly, seeing ye yourselves are wise.
Bible: II Corinthians
11:19

3 Many have been the wise speeches of fools, though not so many as the foolish speeches of wise men.
Thomas Fuller (1608–61) English historian.
The Holy State and the Profane State

□ WODEHOUSE □
Sir P(elham) G(renville)

(1881–1975) British humorous novelist. His books feature the 1920s upper-class bachelor Bertie Wooster and his manservant Jeeves. He lived abroad, becoming a US citizen in 1955.

QUOTATIONS ABOUT WODEHOUSE

1 English Literature's performing flea.
Sean O'Casey (1884–1964) Irish dramatist.
Attrib.

QUOTATIONS BY WODEHOUSE

2 All the unhappy marriages come from the husbands having brains. What good are brains to a man? They only unsettle him.
The Adventures of Sally

3 Big chap with a small moustache and the sort of eye that can open an oyster at sixty paces.
The Code of the Woosters

4 It was my Uncle George who discovered that alcohol was a food well in advance of modern medical thought.
The Inimitable Jeeves, Ch. 16

5 It is a good rule in life never to apologize. The right sort of people do not want apologies, and the wrong sort take a mean advantage of them.
The Man Upstairs

6 I don't owe a penny to a single soul – not counting tradesmen, of course.
My Man Jeeves, 'Jeeves and the Hard-Boiled Egg'

7 She fitted into my biggest armchair as if it had been built round her by someone who knew they were wearing armchairs tight about the hips that season.
My Man Jeeves, 'Jeeves and the Unbidden Guest'

8 There is only one cure for grey hair. It was invented by a Frenchman. It is called the guillotine.
The Old Reliable

9 The Right Hon. was a tubby little chap who looked as if he had been poured into his clothes and had forgotten to say 'When!'
Very Good Jeeves!, 'Jeeves and the Impending Doom'

10 Unlike the male codfish which, suddenly finding itself the parent of three million five hundred thousand little codfish, cheerfully resolves to love them all, the British aristocracy is apt to look with a somewhat jaundiced eye on its younger sons.
Wodehouse at Work to the End (Richard Usborne), Ch. 5

11 It is never difficult to distinguish between a Scotsman with a grievance and a ray of sunshine.
Wodehouse at Work to the End (Richard Usborne), Ch. 8

☐ WOLLSTONECRAFT ☐
Mary

(1759–97) British writer. A passionate advocate of social and educational equality for women her first work was *Thoughts on the Education of Daughters* (1787). In 1792 her most celebrated pamphlet, *A Vindication of the Rights of Woman*, was published.

QUOTATIONS ABOUT WOLLSTONECRAFT

1 In all probability had she been married well in early life, she had then been a happy woman and universally respected.
   Monthly Visitor, Feb 1798

QUOTATIONS BY WOLLSTONECRAFT

2 The *divine right* of husbands, like the divine right of kings, may, it is hoped, in this enlightened age, be contested without danger.
   A Vindication of the Rights of Woman, Ch. 3

3 I do not wish them to have power over men; but over themselves.
   Referring to women.
   A Vindication of the Rights of Woman, Ch. 4

☐ WOMAN'S ROLE ☐

See also feminism, housework, marriage, women, sexes

1 Conventionality has indeed curtailed feminine force by hindering healthful and varied activity.
   Antoinette Brown Blackwell (1825–1921) US feminist, writer, and minister.
   The Sexes Throughout Nature

2 Whoever rightly considers the order of things may plainly see the whole race of woman-kind is by nature, custom, and the laws, made subject to man, to be governed according to his discretion: therefore it is the duty of every one of us that desires to have ease, comfort, and repose, with those men to whom we belong, to be humble, patient, and obedient, as well as chaste...
   Giovanni Boccaccio (1313–75) Italian writer and poet.
   Decameron, 'Ninth Day'

3 A man is in general better pleased when he has a good dinner upon his table, than when his wife talks Greek.
   Samuel Johnson (1709–84) British lexicographer.
   Johnsonian Miscellanies (ed. G. B. Hill), Vol. II

4 Women exist in the main solely for the propagation of the species.
   Arthur Schopenhauer (1788–1860) German philosopher.

☐ WOMEN ☐

See also feminism, men, sexes, woman's role

1 Old-fashioned ways which no longer apply to changed conditions are a snare in which the feet of women have always become readily entangled.
   Jane Addams (1860–1935) US social worker.
   In *Newer Ideals of Peace*, 'Utilization of Women in City Government'

2 ...girls are so queer you never know what they mean. They say No when they mean Yes, and drive a man out of his wits for the fun of it...
   Louisa May Alcott (1832–88) US novelist.
   Little Women, Pt. II

3 Next to being married, a girl likes to be crossed in love a little now and then.
   Jane Austen (1775–1817) British novelist.
   Pride and Prejudice, Ch. 24

4 A woman, especially if she have the misfortune of knowing anything, should conceal it as well as she can.
   Jane Austen
   Northanger Abbey, Ch. 14

5 A lady's imagination is very rapid; it jumps from admiration to love, from love to matrimony in a moment.
   Jane Austen
   Pride and Prejudice, Ch. 6

6 One is not born a woman, one becomes one.
   Simone de Beauvoir (1908–86) French writer.
   Le Deuxième Sexe (trans. The Second Sex)

7 You will find that the woman who is really kind to dogs is always one who has failed to inspire sympathy in men.
   Max Beerbohm (1872–1956) British writer.
   Zuleika Dobson, Ch. 6

8 And the Lord God caused a deep sleep to fall upon Adam, and he slept: and he took one of his ribs, and closed up the flesh instead thereof;
   And the rib, which the Lord God had taken from man, made he a woman, and brought her unto the man.
   And Adam said, This is now bone of my bones, and flesh of my flesh: she shall be called Woman, because she was taken out of Man.
   Therefore shall a man leave his father and his mother, and shall cleave unto his wife: and they shall be one flesh.
   And they were both naked, the man and his wife, and were not ashamed.
   Bible: Genesis
   2:21–25

9 Who can find a virtuous woman? for her price is far above rubies.
   The heart of her husband doth safely trust in her, so that he shall have no need of spoil.
   She will do him good and not evil all the days of her life.
   Bible: Proverbs
   31:10–12

10 Brigands demand your money or your life; women require both.
   Samuel Butler (1612–80) English satirist.
   Attrib.

11 I thought it would appear
That there had been a lady in the case.
Lord Byron (1788–1824) British poet.
Don Juan, V

12 Do you know why God withheld the sense of
humour from women?
That we may love you instead of laughing at you.
Mrs Patrick Campbell (1865–1940) British actress.
To a man
The Life of Mrs Pat (M. Peters)

13 Women are much more like each other than
men: they have, in truth, but two passions, vanity
and love; these are their universal characteristics.
Earl of Chesterfield (1694–1773) English statesman.
Letter to his son, 19 Dec 1749

14 How lucky we are that women defend themselves so poorly! We should, otherwise, be no
more to them than timid slaves.
Pierre Choderlos de Laclos (1741–1803) French novelist.
Les Liaisons Dangereuses, Letter 4

15 Women never have young minds. They are born
three thousand years old.
Shelagh Delaney (1939–) British dramatist.
A Taste of Honey, I:1

16 It is only the women whose eyes have been
washed clear with tears who get the broad vision
that makes them little sisters to all the world.
Dorothy Dix (Elizabeth Meriwether Gilmer; 1861–1951) US
journalist and writer.
Dorothy Dix, Her Book, Introduction

17 She takes just like a woman, yes, she does
She makes love just like a woman, yes, she does
And she aches just like a woman
But she breaks just like a little girl.
Bob Dylan (Robert Allen Zimmerman; 1941–) US popular
singer.
Just Like a Woman

18 I should like to know what is the proper function
of women, if it is not to make reasons for husbands to stay at home, and still stronger reasons
for bachelors to go out.
George Eliot (Mary Ann Evans; 1819–80) British novelist.
The Mill on the Floss, Ch. 6

19 The great question…which I have not been able
to answer, despite my thirty years of research
into the feminine soul, is 'What does a woman
want?'
Sigmund Freud (1856–1939) Austrian psychoanalyst.
Psychiatry in American Life (Charles Rolo)

20 Fighting is essentially a masculine idea; a
woman's weapon is her tongue.
Hermione Gingold (1897–1987) British actress.
Attrib.

21 I know you do not make the laws but I also know
that you are the wives and mothers, the sisters
and daughters of those who do…
Angelina Grimké (1805–79) US writer and reformer.
The Anti-Slavery Examiner (Sep 1836), 'Appeal to the Christian
Women of the South'

22 No one delights more in vengeance than a
woman.
Juvenal (Decimus Junius Juvenalis; 60–130 AD) Roman satirist.
Satires, XIII

23 When the Himalayan peasant meets the he-bear
in his pride,
He shouts to scare the monster, who will often
turn aside.
But the she-bear thus accosted rends the peasant
tooth and nail
For the female of the species is more deadly than
the male.
Rudyard Kipling (1865–1936) Indian-born British writer.
The Female of the Species

24 Women run to extremes; they are either better
or worse than men.
Jean de La Bruyère (1645–96) French satirist.
Les Caractères

25 Women do not find it difficult nowadays to
behave like men; but they often find it extremely
difficult to behave like gentlemen.
Compton Mackenzie (1883–1972) British writer.
On Moral Courage

26 The Professor of Gynaecology began his course
of lectures as follows: Gentlemen, woman is an
animal that micturates once a day, defecates
once a week, menstruates once a month,
parturates once a year and copulates whenever
she has the opportunity.
W. Somerset Maugham (1874–1965) British novelist.
A Writer's Notebook

27 A woman will always sacrifice herself if you give
her the opportunity. It is her favourite form of
self-indulgence.
W. Somerset Maugham
The Circle, III

28 Because women can do nothing except love,
they've given it a ridiculous importance.
W. Somerset Maugham
The Moon and Sixpence, Ch. 41

29 Treat a whore like a lady and a lady like a whore.
Wilson Mizner (1876–1933) US writer and wit.
The Legendary Mizners (Alva Johnston)

30 Women would rather be right than reasonable.
Ogden Nash (1902–71) US poet.
Frailty, Thy Name Is a Misnomer

31 When a woman becomes a scholar there is usually something wrong with her sexual organs.
Friedrich Wilhelm Nietzsche (1844–1900) German
philosopher.
Bartlett's Unfamiliar Quotations (Leonard Louis Levinson)

32 If women didn't exist, all the money in the world
would have no meaning.
Aristotle Onassis (1906–75) Greek businessman.
Attrib.

33 Whether a pretty woman grants or withholds her
favours, she always likes to be asked for them.
Ovid (Publius Ovidius Naso; 43 BC–17 AD) Roman poet.
Ars Amatoria

34 I don't think a prostitute is more moral than a
wife, but they are doing the same thing.
Prince Philip (1921–) The consort of Queen Elizabeth II.
Remark, Dec 1988

35 There are two kinds of women – goddesses and
doormats.
Pablo Picasso (1881–1973) Spanish painter.
Attrib.

36 Most women have no characters at all.
Alexander Pope (1688–1744) British poet.
Moral Essays, II

37 Frailty, thy name is woman!
William Shakespeare (1564–1616) English dramatist.
Hamlet, I:2

38 I have no other but a woman's reason:
I think him so, because I think him so.
William Shakespeare
The Two Gentlemen of Verona, I:2

39 Womanhood is the great fact in her life; wifehood
and motherhood are but incidental relations.
Elizabeth Stanton (1815–1902) US suffragette.
History of Woman Suffrage (with Susan B. Anthony and Mathilda
Gage), Vol. I

40 Now, we are becoming the men we wanted to
marry.
Gloria Steinem (1934–) US writer.
Ms, July 1982

41 I've got a woman's ability to stick to a job and get
on with it when everyone else walks off and
leaves it.
Margaret Thatcher (1925–) British politician and prime
minister.
The Observer, 'Sayings of the Week', 16 Feb 1975

42 It is a great glory in a woman to show no more
weakness than is natural to her sex, and not be
talked of, either for good or evil by men.
Thucydides (c. 460–c. 400 BC) Greek historian and general.
History of the Peloponnesian War, Bk. II, Ch. 45

43 With many women I doubt whether there be any
more effectual way of touching their hearts than

ill-using them and then confessing it. If you wish
to get the sweetest fragrance from the herb at
your feet, tread on it and bruise it.
Anthony Trollope (1815–82) British novelist.
Miss Mackenzie, Ch. 10

44 Woman is unrivaled as a wet nurse.
Mark Twain (Samuel Langhorne Clemens; 1835–1910) US
writer.
Attrib.

45 Woman is always fickle and changing.
Virgil (Publius Vergilius Maro; 70–19 BC) Roman poet.
Aeneid, Bk. IV

46 The question of the rights of women to hold secular office is a quite separate matter and should
not in any way be connected to or paralleled with
the question of women's ordination.
Cardinal Willebrands (1909–) Dutch ecclesiastic.
Remark, June 1986

47 I would venture to guess that Anon, who wrote so
many poems without signing them, was often a
woman.
Virginia Woolf (1882–1941) British novelist.
A Room of One's Own

48 Women have served all these centuries as looking-glasses possessing the magic and delicious
power of reflecting the figure of man at twice its
natural size.
Virginia Woolf
A Room of One's Own

☐ WONDER ☐
See also admiration, curiosity

1 Two things fill the mind with ever new and
increasing wonder and awe, the more often and
the more seriously reflection concentrates upon
them: the starry heaven above me and the moral
law within me.
Immanuel Kant (1724–1804) German philosopher.
Critique of Practical Reason, Conclusion

2 Philosophy is the product of wonder.
A. N. Whitehead (1861–1947) British philosopher.
Nature and Life, Ch. 1

☐ WOOLF ☐
Virginia
(born Stephen; 1882–1941) British novelist and critic. Her novel
Jacob's Room (1922) established her reputation as an innovative
novelist – a reputation which was secured by her major novels,
Mrs Dalloway (1925), *To the Lighthouse* (1927), and *The Waves*
(1931). Her interest in feminism is acknowledged in *A Room of
One's Own* (1929) and its sequel, *Three Guineas* (1938).

1 I do not believe that she wrote one word of fiction
which does not put out boundaries a little way;
one book which does not break new ground and
form part of the total experiment.
Susan Hill (1942–) British novelist and playwright. *Daily
Telegraph* 5 May 1974

2 I enjoyed talking to her, but thought *nothing* of her writing. I considered her 'a beautiful little knitter'.
Edith Sitwell (1887–1964) British poet and writer. Letter to G. Singleton

QUOTATIONS BY WOOLF

3 If you do not tell the truth about yourself you cannot tell it about other people.
The Moment and Other Essays

4 The older one grows the more one likes indecency.
Monday or Tuesday

5 When one reads of a witch being ducked, of a woman possessed by devils, of a wise woman selling herbs, or even of a very remarkable man who had a mother, then I think we are on the track of a lost novelist, a suppressed poet, of some mute and inglorious Jane Austen, some Emilty Drontë who dashed her brains out on the moor or mopped and mowed about the highways crazed with the torture her gift had put her to. Indeed I would venture that Anon, who wrote so many poems without signing them, was a woman.
A Room of One's Own

6 Dearest, I feel certain that I am going mad again: I feel we cant go through another of those terrible times. And I shant recover this time. I begin to hear voices, and cant concentrate. So I am doing what seems the best thing to do…If anybody could have saved me it would have been you. Everything has gone from me but the certainty of your goodness. I cant go on spoiling your life any longer.
I dont think two people could have been happier than we have been.
Suicide note to her husband, ?18 Mar 1941

□WORDS□

See also language, speech, verbosity

1 In the beginning was the Word, and the Word was with God, and the Word was God.
Bible: – John
1:1

2 Oaths are but words, and words but wind.
Samuel Butler (1612–80) English satirist.
Hudibras, Pt. II

3 Be not the slave of Words.
Thomas Carlyle (1795–1881) Scottish historian and essayist.
Sartor Resartus, Bk. I, Ch. 8

4 We must have a better word than 'prefabricated'. Why not 'ready-made'?
Winston Churchill (1874–1965) British statesman.
Closing the Ring, Appendix C

5 It was in the barbarous, gothic times when words had a meaning; in those days, writers expressed thoughts.
Anatole France (Jacques Anatole François Thibault; 1844–1924) French writer.
The Literary Life, 'M. Charles Morice'

6 Thanks to words, we have been able to rise above the brutes; and thanks to words, we have often sunk to the level of the demons.
Aldous Huxley (1894 1964) British novelist.
Adonis and the Alphabet

7 Words are, of course, the most powerful drug used by mankind.
Rudyard Kipling (1865–1936) Indian-born British writer.
Speech, 14 Feb 1923

8 Words are men's daughters, but God's sons are things.
Samuel Madden (1686–1765) Irish writer.
Boulter's Monument

9 I am a Bear of Very Little Brain, and long words Bother me.
A. A. Milne (1882–1956) British writer.
Winnie-the-Pooh, Ch. 4

10 There is a Southern proverb, – fine words butter no parsnips.
Walter Scott (1771–1832) Scottish novelist.
The Legend of Montrose, Ch. 3

11 Man does not live by words alone, despite the fact that sometimes he has to eat them.
Adlai Stevenson (1900–65) US statesman.
Attrib.

12 For words, like Nature, half reveal
And half conceal the Soul within.
Alfred, Lord Tennyson (1809–92) British poet.
In Memoriam A.H.H., V

□WORDSWORTH□
William

(1770–1850) British poet. His reputation was based on his *Lyrical Ballads* (1798), written with Samuel Taylor Coleridge. After settling in the Lake District with his wife and sister he produced *The Prelude*, a verse autobiography published posthumously, and much other verse.

QUOTATIONS ABOUT WORDSWORTH

1 Time may restore us in his course
Goethe's sage mind and Byron's force:
But where will Europe's latter hour
Again find Wordsworth's healing power?
Matthew Arnold (1822–88) British poet and critic.
Memorial Verses 2

2 Wordsworth went to the Lakes, but he never was a lake poet. He found in stones the sermons he had already put there.
Oscar Wilde (1854–1900) Irish-born British dramatist.
The Decay of Lying

QUOTATIONS BY WORDSWORTH

3 Strongest minds
Are often those of whom the noisy world
Hears least.
The Excursion

4 The good die first,
And they whose hearts are dry as summer dust
Burn to the socket.
The Excursion

5 I wandered lonely as a cloud
That floats on high o'er vales and hills,
When all at once I saw a crowd,
A host, of golden daffodils.
I Wandered Lonely as a Cloud

6 For oft, when on my couch I lie
In vacant or in pensive mood,
They flash upon that inward eye
Which is the bliss of solitude.
I Wandered Lonely as a Cloud

7 That best portion of a good man's life,
His little, nameless, unremembered acts
Of kindness and of love.
Lines composed a few miles above Tintern Abbey

8 Nature never did betray
The heart that loved her.
Lines composed a few miles above Tintern Abbey

9 If this belief from heaven be sent,
If such be Nature's holy plan,
Have I not reason to lament
What man has made of man?
Lines written in Early Spring

10 Poetry is the spontaneous overflow of powerful
feelings: it takes its origin from emotion recollected in tranquillity.
Lyrics Ballads, Preface

11 Every great and original writer, in proportion as
he is great and original, must himself create the
taste by which he is to be relished.
Lyrical Ballads, Preface

12 Why art thou silent! Is thy love a plant
Of such weak fibre that the treacherous air
Of absence withers what was once so fair?
Miscellaneous Sonnets, III

13 My heart leaps up when I behold
A rainbow in the sky:
So was it when my life began;
So is it now I am a man;
So be it when I shall grow old,
Or let me die!
The Child is Father of the Man;

And I could wish my days to be
Bound each to each by natural piety.
My Heart Leaps Up

14 The clouds that gather round the setting sun
Do take a sober colouring from an eye
That hath kept watch o'er man's mortality.
Ode. Intimations of Immortality, XI

15 Bliss was it in that dawn to be alive,
But to be young was very heaven!
Referring to the French Revolution.
The Prelude, XI

16 There is
One great society alone on earth:
The noble living and the noble dead.
The Prelude, XI

17 She dwelt among the untrodden ways
Beside the springs of Dove,
A maid whom there were none to praise
And very few to love...
She Dwelt Among the Untrodden Ways

18 Dear God! the very houses seem asleep;
And all that mighty heart is lying still!
Sonnets, 'Composed upon Westminster Bridge'

19 Thy soul was like a star, and dwelt apart.
Sonnets, 'Milton! thou shouldst'

20 Strange fits of passion have I known:
And I will dare to tell,
But in the lover's ear alone,
What once to me befell.
Strange Fits of Passion

21 One impulse from a vernal wood
May teach you more of man,
Of moral evil and of good,
Than all the sages can.
The Tables Turned

22 'Tis said that some have died for love.
'Tis Said that some have Died

23 Thrice welcome, darling of the spring!
Even yet thou art to me
No bird, but an invisible thing,
A voice, a mystery.
To the Cuckoo

24 Thou unassuming common-place
Of Nature.
To the Daisy

25 Pleasures newly found are sweet
When they lie about our feet.
To the Small Celandine

☐WORK☐

See also effort, unemployment

1 Whatsoever thy hand findeth to do, do it with thy might; for there is no work, nor device, nor knowledge, nor wisdom, in the grave, whither thou goest.
Bible: Ecclesiastes
9:10

2 There is dignity in work only when it is work freely accepted.
Albert Camus (1913–60) French existentialist writer.
Notebooks, 1935–42

3 Work is the grand cure of all the maladies and miseries that ever beset mankind.
Thomas Carlyle (1795–1881) Scottish historian and essayist.
Speech, Edinburgh, 2 Apr 1886

4 When work is a pleasure, life is a joy! When work is a duty, life is slavery.
Maxim Gorky (Aleksei Maksimovich Peshkov; 1868–1936) Russian writer.
The Lower Depths

5 Horny-handed sons of toil.
Denis Kearney (1847–1907) US Labor leader.
Speech, San Francisco, c. 1878

6 It's been a hard day's night.
John Lennon (1940–80) British rock musician.
A Hard Day's Night (with Paul McCartney)

7 Work expands so as to fill the time available for its completion.
Cyril Northcote Parkinson
Parkinson's Law, Ch. 1

8 Work is necessary for man. Man invented the alarm clock.
Pablo Picasso (1881–1973) Spanish painter.
Attrib.

9 One of the symptoms of approaching nervous breakdown is the belief that one's work is terribly important. If I were a medical man, I should prescribe a holiday to any patient who considered his work important.
Bertrand Russell (1872–1970) British philosopher.
The Autobiography of Bertrand Russell, Vol. II, Ch. 5

10 The only place where success comes before work is a dictionary.
Vidal Sassoon (1928–) British hair stylist.
Quoting one of his teachers in a BBC radio broadcast

11 Pennies do not come from heaven. They have to be earned here on earth.
Margaret Thatcher (1925–) British politician and prime minister.
Sunday Telegraph, 1982

12 Work banishes those three great evils, boredom, vice, and poverty.
Voltaire (François-Marie Arouet; 1694–1778) French writer.
Candide, Ch. 30

☐WORLD WAR I☐

1 Belgium put the kibosh on the Kaiser,
Europe took a stick and made him sore;
And if Turkey makes a stand
She'll get ghurka'd and japanned,
And it won't be Hoch the Kaiser any more.
Anonymous
Song of World War I

2 Six million young men lie in premature graves, and four old men sit in Paris partitioning the earth.
Anonymous
New York Nation, 1919

3 The battlefield is fearful. One is overcome by a peculiar sour, heavy and penetrating smell of corpses....The legs of an Englishman, still encased in puttees, stick out of a trench, the corpse being built into the parapet; a soldier hangs his rifle on them.
Rudolph Binding
A Fatalist At War

4 What did you do in the Great War, Daddy?
British Recruiting Poster

5 My centre is giving way, my right is in retreat; situation excellent. I shall attack.
Marshal Foch (1851–1929) French soldier.
Message sent during the second battle of the Marne, 1918
Biography of Foch (Aston), Ch. 13

6 Every position must be held to the last man: there must be no retirement. With our backs to the wall, and believing in the justice of our cause, each one of us must fight on to the end.
Douglas Haig (1861–1928) British general.
Order to the British Army, 12 Apr 1918

7 This war, like the next war, is a war to end war.
David Lloyd George (1863–1945) British Liberal statesman.

8 We travelled miles of trenches to reach the point we occupy. Some of the places we passed were liquid mud up to our knees. The town we passed through was an absolute ruin, not a house that is not blown to bits. I never saw the like of it, not a soul anywhere. I can't describe the look it has. It made me shiver – wooden crosses on the roadside and in places in the town marking the heroes' death – what devastation – a day of judgement more like. Man builds and then builds machines to destroy, well he seems to have made a better job of destroying this town.
Peter McGregor (1871–1916) Private soldier.
Letter to his wife, 21 June 1916

9 What passing-bells for these who die as cattle?
Only the monstrous anger of the guns,
Only the stuttering rifles' rapid rattle
Can patter out their hasty orisons.
Wilfred Owen (1893–1918) British poet.
Anthem for Doomed Youth

10 Man, it seemed, had been created to jab the life
out of Germans.
Siegfried Sassoon (1886–1967) British poet.
Memoirs of an Infantry Officer, Pt. I, Ch. 1

11 ...The lecturer's voice still battered on my brain.
'The bullet and the bayonet are brother and sis-
ter.' 'If you don't kill him, he'll kill you.' 'Stick him
between the eyes, in the throat, in the chest.'
'Don't waste good steel. Six inches are enough.
What's the use of a foot of steel sticking out at the
back of a man's neck? Three inches will do for
him; when he coughs, go and look for another.'
Siegfried Sassoon
Memoirs of an Infantry Officer

12 On St Paul's steps I watched a recruiting meeting
for some time. There was a tremendous crowd
round and a soldier who looked like a Colonial
was letting out for all he was worth. He had a
number of men in uniform with him and every little while stopped and pointed his finger at some
man in the crowd and shouted 'Why haven't you
joined?' Of course everyone looked at the victim
who felt called upon to make an excuse if he
could, and one of the assistants pushed through
the crowd to tackle the one singled out.
Robert Saunders Headmaster.
Letter to his son, 31 May 1915

13 We drove the Boche across the Rhine,
The Kaiser from his throne.
Oh, Lafayette, we've paid our debt,
For Christ's sake, send us home.
US Army song

14 You will be home before the leaves have fallen
from the trees.
Wilhelm II (1859–1941) King of Prussia and Emperor of
Germany.
Said to troops leaving for the Front, Aug 1914
August 1914 (Barbara Tuchman), Ch. 9

15 It is my Royal and Imperial Command that
you...exterminate first the treacherous English,
and...walk over General French's contemptible
little Army.
Wilhelm II
Referring to the British Expeditionary Force; veterans of this
force became known as 'Old Contemptibles'
The Times, 1 Oct 1914

16 There is a price which is too great to pay for
peace, and that price can be put into one word.
One cannot pay the price of self-respect.
Woodrow Wilson (1856–1925) US statesman.
Speech, Des Moines, Iowa, 1 Feb 1916

□**WORLD WAR II**□

See also Churchill, Germany, Hitler, Nazism, war

1 Hitler has missed the bus.
Neville Chamberlain (1869–1940) British statesman.
Speech, House of Commons, 4 Apr 1940

2 We have sustained a defeat without a war.
Winston Churchill (1874–1965)
Speech, House of Commons, 5 Oct 1938

3 We shall not flag or fail. We shall fight in France,
we shall fight on the seas and oceans, we shall
fight with growing confidence and growing
strength in the air, we shall defend our island,
whatever the cost may be, we shall fight on the
beaches, we shall fight on the landing grounds,
we shall fight in the fields and in the streets, we
shall fight in the hills; we shall never surrender.
Winston Churchill
Speech, House of Commons, 4 June 1940

4 Let us therefore brace ourselves to our duties,
and so bear ourselves that, if the British Empire
and its Commonwealth last for a thousand years,
men will still say: 'This was their finest hour'.
Winston Churchill
Referring to the forthcoming Battle of Britain
Speech, House of Commons, 18 June 1940

5 The battle of Britain is about to begin.
Winston Churchill
Speech, House of Commons, 18 June 1940

6 Never in the field of human conflict was so much
owed by so many to so few.
Winston Churchill
Referring to the Battle of Britain pilots
Speech, House of Commons, 20 Aug 1940

7 Give us the tools, and we will finish the job.
Winston Churchill
Referring to Lend-lease, which was being legislated in the USA
Radio broadcast, 9 Feb 1941

8 You do your worst, and we will do our best.
Winston Churchill
Addressed to Hitler
Speech, 14 July 1941

9 Do not let us speak of darker days; let us rather
speak of sterner days. These are not dark days:
these are great days – the greatest days our country has ever lived.
Winston Churchill
Address, Harrow School, 29 Oct 1941

10 When I warned them that Britain would fight on
alone whatever they did, their Generals told their
Prime Minister and his divided Cabinet: 'In three
weeks England will have her neck wrung like a
chicken.' Some chicken! Some neck!
Winston Churchill
Referring to the French Government
Speech, Canadian Parliament, 30 Dec 1941

11 This is not the end. It is not even the beginning of the end. But it is, perhaps, the end of the beginning.
Winston Churchill
Referring to the Battle of Egypt
Speech, Mansion House, 10 Nov 1942

12 Wars are not won by evacuations.
Winston Churchill
Referring to Dunkirk
Their Finest Hour

13 Before Alamein we never had a victory. After Alamein we never had a defeat.
Winston Churchill
The Hinge of Fate, Ch. 33

14 Now we can look the East End in the face.
Elizabeth the Queen Mother (1900–   ) The widow of King George VI.
Surveying the damage caused to Buckingham Palace by a bomb during the Blitz in World War II
Attrib.

15 The little ships, the unforgotten Homeric catalogue of *Mary Jane* and *Peggy IV*, of *Folkestone Belle*, *Boy Billy*, and *Ethel Maud*, of *Lady Haig* and *Skylark*…the little ships of England brought the Army home.
Philip Guedalla (1889–1944) British writer.
Referring to the evacuation of Dunkirk
Mr Churchill

16 When Barbarossa commences, the world will hold its breath and make no comment.
Adolf Hitler (1889–1945) German dictator.
Referring to the planned invasion of the USSR, Operation Barbarossa, which began on 22 June 1941
Attrib.

17 If we are going in without the help of Russia we are walking into a trap.
David Lloyd George (1863–1945) British Liberal statesman.
Speech, House of Commons, 3 Apr 1939

18 Dear Ike, Today I spat in the Seine.
General George Patton (1885–1945) US general.
Message sent to Eisenhower reporting his crossing of the Seine in World War II
The American Treasury (C. Fadiman)

19 Our great-grandchildren, when they learn how we began this war by snatching glory out of defeat…may also learn how the little holiday steamers made an excursion to hell and came back glorious.
J. B. Priestley (1894–1984) British novelist.
Referring to the British Expeditionary Force's evacuation from Dunkirk
Broadcast, 5 June 1940

20 Defeat of Germany means the defeat of Japan, probably without firing a shot or losing a life.
Franklin D. Roosevelt (1882–1945) US Democratic president.
The Hinge of Fate (Winston S. Churchill), Ch. 25

21 We have finished the job, what shall we do with the tools?
Haile Selassie (1892–1975) Emperor of Ethiopia.
Telegram sent to Winston Churchill, mimicking his 'Give us the tools, and we will finish the job'
Ambrosia and Small Beer, Ch. 4 (Edward Marsh)

□ WORLD-WEARINESS □

1 Bankrupt of Life, yet Prodigal of Ease.
John Dryden (1631–1700) British poet and dramatist.
Absalom and Achitophel, I

2 Death is a delightful hiding-place for weary men.
Herodotus (c. 484–c. 424 BC) Greek historian.
Histories, VII, 46

3 Stop the World, I Want to Get Off.
Anthony Newley (1931–   ) British actor, composer, singer, and comedian.
With Leslie Bricusse
Title of musical

4 How weary, stale, flat, and unprofitable,
Seem to me all the uses of this world!
William Shakespeare (1564–1616) English dramatist.
Hamlet, I:2

5 I gin to be aweary of the sun,
And wish th' estate o' th' world were now undone.
William Shakespeare
Macbeth, V:5

6 Death is not the greatest of ills; it is worse to want to die, and not be able to.
Sophocles (c. 496–406 BC) Greek dramatist.
Electra, 1007

□ WORRY □
See also misfortune

1 Behold the fowls of the air: for they sow not, neither do they reap, nor gather into barns; yet your heavenly Father feedeth them. Are ye not much better than they?
Which of you by taking thought can add one cubit unto his stature?
And why take ye thought for raiment? Consider the lilies of the field, how they grow; they toil not, neither do they spin:
And yet I say unto you, That even Solomon in all his glory was not arrayed like one of these.
Wherefore, if God so clothe the grass of the field, which today is, and tomorrow is cast into the oven, shall he not much more clothe you, O ye of little faith?
Therefore take no thought, saying, What shall we eat? or, What shall we drink? or, Wherewithal shall we be clothed?
Bible: Matthew
6:26–31

2 But seek ye first the kingdom of God, and his righteousness; and all these things shall be added unto you.

Take therefore no thought for the morrow: for
the morrow shall take thought for the things of
itself. Sufficient unto the day is the evil thereof.
Bible: Matthew
6:33–34

3 Before the cherry orchard was sold everybody
was worried and upset, but as soon as it was all
settled finally and once for all, everybody calmed
down, and felt quite cheerful.
Anton Chekhov (1860–1904) Russian dramatist.
The Cherry Orchard, IV

4 When I look back on all these worries I remember the story of the old man who said on his
deathbed that he had had a lot of trouble in his
life, most of which had never happened.
Winston Churchill (1874–1965) British statesman.
Their Finest Hour

5 Care
Sat on his faded cheek.
John Milton (1608–74) English poet.
Paradise Lost, Bk. I

6 Worrying is the most natural and spontaneous of
all human functions. It is time to acknowledge
this, perhaps even to learn to do it better.
Lewis Thomas (1913–) US pathologist.
More Notes of a Biology Watcher, 'The Medusa and the Snail'

□ WRITERS □

See also Chaucer, criticism, Dickens, Milton, poets,
Shakespeare, writing

1 Times have changed since a certain author was
executed for murdering his publisher. They say
that when the author was on the scaffold he said
goodbye to the minister and to the reporters, and
then he saw some publishers sitting in the front
row below, and to them he did not say goodbye.
He said instead, 'I'll see you later.'
J. M. Barrie (1860–1937) British novelist and dramatist.
Speech, New York, 5 Nov 1896

2 The idea that it is necessary to go to a university
in order to become a successful writer, or even a
man or woman of letters (which is by no means
the same thing), is one of those phantasies that
surround authorship.
Vera Brittain (1893–1970) British writer and feminist.
On Being an Author, Ch. 2

3 Literary men are…a perpetual priesthood.
Thomas Carlyle (1795–1881) Scottish historian and essayist.
Critical and Miscellaneous Essays, 'The State of German
Literature'

4 I believe the souls of five hundred Sir Isaac New-
tons would go to the making up of a Shakespeare
or a Milton.
Samuel Taylor Coleridge (1772–1834) British poet.
Letter to Thomas Poole, 23 Mar 1801

5 A great writer creates a world of his own and his
readers are proud to live in it. A lesser writer may
entice them in for a moment, but soon he will
watch them filing out.
Cyril Connolly (1903–74) British journalist.
Enemies of Promise, Ch. 1

6 Authors are easy to get on with – if you're fond of
children.
Michael Joseph (1897–1958) British publisher.
The Observer, 1949

7 One man is as good as another until he has writ-
ten a book.
Benjamin Jowett (1817–93) British theologian.
Letters of B. Jowett (Abbott and Campbell)

8 Our principal writers have nearly all been fortu-
nate in escaping regular education.
Hugh MacDiarmid (Christopher Murray Grieve; 1892–1978)
Scottish poet.
The Observer, 'Sayings of the Week', 29 Mar 1953

9 I think that if a third of all the novelists and
maybe two-thirds of all the poets now writing
dropped dead suddenly, the loss to literature
would not be great.
Charles Osborne (1927–) Author, critic, and Director of
Arts Council.
Remark, Nov 1985

10 A list of authors who have made themselves
most beloved and therefore, most comfortable
financially, shows that it is our national joy to mistake for the first-rate, the fecund rate.
Dorothy Parker (1893–1967) US writer.
Wit's End (R. E. Drennan)

11 Everybody writes a book too many.
Mordecai Richler (1931–) Canadian novelist.
The Observer, 'Sayings of the Week', 9 Jan 1985

12 Among the many problems which beset the nov-
elist, not the least weighty is the choice of the
moment at which to begin his novel.
Vita Sackville-West (Victoria Sackville-West; 1892–1962)
British poet and novelist.
The Edwardians, Ch. 1

13 When I was a little boy they called me a liar but
now that I am a grown up they call me a writer.
Isaac Bashevis Singer (1904–91) US novelist and short-story
writer.
Remark, July 1983

14 No regime has ever loved great writers, only
minor ones.
Alexander Solzhenitsyn (1918–) Soviet novelist.
The First Circle, Ch. 57

15 It is a sad feature of modern life that only women
for the most part have time to write novels, and
they seldom have much to write about.
Auberon Waugh (1939–) British novelist and critic.
Remark, June 1981

16 Literature is strewn with the wreckage of men who have minded beyond reason the opinions of others.
Virginia Woolf (1882–1941) British novelist.
A Room of One's Own

□WRITING□

See also books, criticism, fiction, inspiration, letter-writing, literacy, literature, novels, plays, poetry, poetry and prose, prose, reading, style, writers

1 Beneath the rule of men entirely great,
The pen is mightier than the sword.
Edward Bulwer-Lytton (1803–73) British novelist and politician.
Richelieu, II:2

2 From this it is clear how much more cruel the pen is than the sword.
Robert Burton (1577–1640) English scholar and explorer.
Anatomy of Melancholy, Pt. I

3 Better to write for yourself and have no public, than write for the public and have no self.
Cyril Connolly (1903–74) British journalist.
Turnstile One (ed. V. S. Pritchett)

4 No tears in the writer, no tears in the reader.
Robert Frost (1875–1963) US poet.
Collected Poems, Preface

5 You must write for children in the same way as you do for adults, only better.
Maxim Gorky (Aleksei Maksimovich Peshkov; 1868–1936) Russian writer.
Attrib.

6 You will have written exceptionally well if, by skilful arrangement of your words, you have made an ordinary one seem original.
Horace (Quintus Horatius Flaccus; 65–8 BC) Roman poet.
Ars Poetica

7 A bad book is as much a labour to write as a good one; it comes as sincerely from the author's soul.
Aldous Huxley (1894–1964) British novelist.
Point Counter Point

8 What is written without effort is in general read without pleasure.
Samuel Johnson (1709–84) British lexicographer.
Johnsonian Miscellanies (ed. G. B. Hill), Vol. II

9 Read over your compositions, and where ever you meet with a passage which you think is particularly fine, strike it out.
Samuel Johnson
Recalling the advice of a college tutor
Life of Johnson (J. Boswell), Vol. II

10 No man but a blockhead ever wrote, except for money.
Samuel Johnson
Life of Johnson (J. Boswell), Vol. III

11 Many suffer from the incurable disease of writing, and it becomes chronic in their sick minds.
Juvenal (Decimus Junius Juvenalis; 60–130 AD) Roman satirist.
Satires, VII

12 When once the itch of literature comes over a man, nothing can cure it but the scratching of a pen.
Samuel Lover (1797–1868) Irish novelist.
Handy Andy, Ch. 36

13 There is an impression abroad that everyone has it in him to write one book; but if by this is implied a good book the impression is false.
W. Somerset Maugham (1874–1965) British novelist.
The Summing Up

14 If you steal from one author, it's plagiarism; if you steal from many, it's research.
Wilson Mizner (1876–1933) US writer and wit.
The Legendary Mizners (Alva Johnston)

15 Writing is like getting married. One should never commit oneself until one is amazed at one's luck.
Iris Murdoch (1919–) Irish-born British novelist.
The Black Prince, 'Bradley Pearson's Foreword'

16 True ease in writing comes from art, not chance,
As those move easiest who have learn'd to dance.
'Tis not enough no harshness gives offence,
The sound must seem an echo to the sense.
Alexander Pope (1688–1744) British poet.
An Essay on Criticism

17 The profession of letters is, after all, the only one in which one can make no money without being ridiculous.
Jules Renard (1894–1910) French writer.
Journal

18 Whatever sentence will bear to be read twice, we may be sure was thought twice.
Henry David Thoreau (1817–62) US writer.
Journal, 1842

19 Not that the story need be long, but it will take a long while to make it short.
Henry David Thoreau
Letter, 16 Nov 1867

20 Three hours a day will produce as much as a man ought to write.
Anthony Trollope (1815–82) British novelist.
Autobiography, Ch. 15

21 Every great and original writer, in proportion as he is great and original, must himself create the taste by which he is to be relished.
William Wordsworth (1770–1850) British poet.
Lyrical Ballads, Preface

Y

☐ YEATS ☐
W(illiam) B(utler)

(1865–1939) Irish poet and dramatist. His verse collections include *The Tower* (1928) and *The Winding Stair* (1929). With Lady Gregory, he founded the Abbey Theatre in Dublin, for which he wrote many plays.

QUOTATIONS ABOUT YEATS

1 Yeats is not a man of this world; and when you hurl an enormous, smashing chunk of it at him, he dodges it, small blame to him.
George Bernard Shaw (1856–1950) Irish dramatist and critic.
Letter to Sean O'Casey

QUOTATIONS BY YEATS

2 When I think of all the books I have read, and of the wise words I have heard spoken, and of the anxiety I have given to parents and grand-parents, and of the hopes that I have had, all life weighed in the scales of my own life seems to me preparation for something that never happens.
Autobiography

3 Wine comes in at the mouth
And love comes in at the eye;
That's all we shall know for truth
Before we grow old and die.
A Drinking Song

4 Out of the quarrel with others we make rhetoric; out of the quarrel with ourselves we make poetry.
Essay

5 Nor law, nor duty bade me fight,
Nor public men, nor cheering crowds,
A lonely impulse of delight
Drove to this tumult in the clouds;
I balanced all, brought all to mind,
The years to come seemed waste of breath,
A waste of breath the years behind
In balance with this life, this death.
An Irish Airman Foresees his Death

6 I will arise and go now, and go to Innisfree,
And a small cabin build there, of clay and wattles made;
Nine bean rows will I have there, a hive for the honey bee,
And live alone in the bee-loud glade.
The Lake Isle of Innisfree

7 I shudder and I sigh to think
That even Cicero
And many-minded Homer were
Mad as the mist and snow.
Mad as the Mist and Snow

8 Never to have lived is best, ancient writers say;
Never to have drawn the breath of life,
never to have looked into the eye of day

The second best's a gay goodnight and quickly turn away.
Oedipus at Colonus

9 Where, where but here have Pride and Truth,
That long to give themselves for wage,
To shake their wicked sides at youth
Restraining reckless middle age?
On hearing that the Students of our New University have joined the Agitation against Immoral Literature

10 Things fall apart; the centre cannot hold;
Mere anarchy is loosed upon the world,
The blood-dimmed tide is loosed, and every-where
The ceremony of innocence is drowned;
The best lack all conviction, while the worst
Are full of passionate intensity.
The Second Coming

11 But was there ever dog that praised his fleas?
To a Poet, who would have me Praise certain Bad Poets, Imitators of His and Mine

12 When you are old and gray and full of sleep,
And nodding by the fire, take down this book,
And slowly read, and dream of the soft look
Your eyes had once, and of their shadows deep...
When you are Old

13 But I, being poor, have only my dreams;
I have spread my dreams under your feet;
Tread softly because you tread on my dreams.
He Wishes for the Cloths of Heaven

14 It's not a writer's business to hold opinions.
Speaking to playwright, Denis Johnston.
The Guardian, 5 May 1977

☐ YIELDING ☐

See also determination, weakness

1 The concessions of the weak are the concessions of fear.
Edmund Burke (1729–97) British politician.
Speech on Conciliation with America (House of Commons, 22 Mar 1775)

2 He that complies against his will,
Is of his own opinion still.
Samuel Butler (1612–80) English satirist.
Hudibras, Pt. III

☐ YOUTH ☐

See also age, children

1 Better is a poor and a wise child than an old and foolish king, who will no more be admonished.
Bible: Ecclesiastes
4:13

2 It is good for a man that he bear the yoke in his youth.
Bible: Lamentations
3:27

3 Youth is something very new: twenty years ago no one mentioned it.
Coco Chanel (1883–1971) French dress designer.
Coco Chanel, Her Life, Her Secrets (Marcel Haedrich)

4 The young always have the same problem – how to rebel and conform at the same time. They have now solved this by defying their parents and copying one another.
Quentin Crisp (?1910–   ) Model, publicist, and writer.
The Naked Civil Servant

5 *Les enfants terribles.*
The embarrassing young.
Paul Gavarni (1801–66) French illustrator.
Title of a series of prints

6 Young men make great mistakes in life; for one thing, they idealize love too much.
Benjamin Jowett (1817–93) British theologian.
Letters of B. Jowett (Abbott and Campbell)

7 Youth is a malady of which one becomes cured a little every day.
Benito Mussolini (1883–1945) Italian dictator.
Said on his 50th birthday

8 My salad days,
When I was green in judgment, cold in blood,
To say as I said then!
William Shakespeare (1564–1616) English dramatist.
Antony and Cleopatra, I:5

9 I would there were no age between ten and three and twenty, or that youth would sleep out the rest; for there is nothing in the between but getting wenches with child, wronging the ancientry, stealing, fighting.
William Shakespeare
The Winter's Tale, III:3

10 Live as long as you may, the first twenty years are the longest half of your life.
Robert Southey (1774–1843) British poet.
The Doctor, Ch. 130

KEYWORD INDEX

angry A. Young Man REBELLION, 4
The man who gets a....in the right way...is commended ANGER, 1
anguish drinking deep of that divinest a. BRONTË, 3; SUFFERING, 4
animal information vegetable, a. and mineral GILBERT, 3
Man is a gaming a. LAMB, 2; SPORT AND GAMES, 5
man is and will always be a wild a. MANKIND, 6
Man is an intellectual a. HAZLITT, 3
Man is a noble a. MANKIND, 4
man is...a religious a. BURKE, 6; RELIGION, 5
Man is a social a. SOCIETY, 5
Man is by nature a political a. POLITICS, 2
This a. is very bad SELF-PRESERVATION, 2
true to your a. instincts ANIMALISM, 2
Whenever you observe an a. closely ANIMALS, 2
animality its own a. either objectionable or funny HUMOUR, 11
animals All a. are equal EQUALITY, 14
all a. were created...for the use of man ANIMALS, 4
A. are such agreeable friends ANIMALS, 3
a....know nothing...of what people say about them ANIMALS, 5; VOLTAIRE , 22
differs in no respect from the ovules of other a. EVOLUTION, 2
I could...live with a. MANKIND, 6
paragon of a. MANKIND, 13; SHAKESPEARE, 35
some a. are more equal than others EQUALITY, 14
There are two things for which a. are...envied ANIMALS, 5; VOLTAIRE , 22
Wild a. never kill for sport HUNTING, 2
Anna great A.! whom three realms obey DRINKS, 4
annals short and simple a. of the poor POVERTY, 6
Anne Move Queen A.? Most certainly not MEMORIALS, 8
annihilating A. all that's made OBLIVION, 2
annihilation No a. REPRESENTATION, 2
annual A. income twenty pounds DICKENS, 4; ECONOMICS, 3
anon I would...guess that A....was often a woman WOOLF, 5; WOMEN, 47
another A. year! – a. deadly blow DEFEAT, 6
He who would do good to a. BLAKE, 10
Life is just one damned thing after a. LIFE, 12
No man can...condemn a. JUDGMENT, 4
answer a. a fool according to his folly FOOLISHNESS, 2
A. to the Great Question PURPOSE, 1
A timid question will...receive a confident a. SHYNESS, 1
give a. as need requireth LEARNING, 2
more than the wisest man can a. EXAMINATIONS, 1
The a....is blowin' in the wind FREEDOM, 6
where no one asks, no one needs to a. PURPOSE, 2
anticipation the intelligent a. of facts JOURNALISM, 7
anti-clerical it makes me uncomfortable a. things BELLOC, 10
anti-climax everything afterward savours of a. PRECOCITY, 1
antidote the a. to desire DESIRE, 4
antipathy strong a. of good to bad PROVOCATION, 2
antiquity Damn the age. I'll write for a. POSTERITY, 4
anti-semite An American is either a Jew, or an a. AMERICANS, 6
hated /by every a. /as if I were a Jew PREJUDICE, 4
anxious a. to do the wrong thing correctly ETIQUETTE, 3; SAKI, 14
anyone a. here whom I have not insulted INSULTS, 3
apartheid We don't want a. liberalized RACISM, 14
apathy going about the country stirring up a. POLITICS, 50
sheer a. and boredom DISCOVERY, 3
ape having an a. for his grandfather EVOLUTION, 6
the a. from which he is descended EVOLUTION, 7
The exception is a naked a. MANKIND, 8
ape-like The a. virtues without which CONNOLLY, 2
aphrodisiac Fame is a powerful a. FAME, 4
Power is the ultimate a. POWER, 7
apologize a good rule in life never to a. APOLOGIES, 3; WODEHOUSE, 8
Apostles The Septuagint minus the A. NUMBERS, 3
apparatus Brain, n. An a. with which we think MIND, 1
apparel a. oft proclaims the man CLOTHES, 8
appeal The whole of art is an a. to a reality ARTS, 2
appear Things are...what they a. to be APPEARANCES, 8
appearance secret of a successful a. APPEARANCE, 15
appearances A. are not...a clue to the truth APPEARANCES, 2
Keep up a. APPEARANCES, 3
shallow people...do not judge by a. APPEARANCES, 12
appeaser An a. is one who feeds a crocodile DIPLOMACY, 4
appetite A. comes with eating RABELAIS, 1
a. may sicken and so die MUSIC, 24; SHAKESPEARE, 117
the desire of satisfying a voracious a. LUST, 2
apple want the a. for the a.'s sake PERVERSITY, 4
When Eve ate this particular a. LAWRENCE, 6; SEX, 19

applications only a. of science SCIENCE, 19
applied no such things as a. sciences SCIENCE, 19
appreciation total dependence on the a. of others CHARM, 1
apprehend Intelligence is quickness to a. INTELLIGENCE, 5
approve They that a....call it opinion OPINIONS, 2
April And after A. when May follows MONTHS, 3
months...gloomy in England are March and A. SEASONS, 18; TROLLOPE, 4
Now that A.'s there ENGLAND, 4
Sweet A. showers MONTHS, 6
Arabia All the perfumes of A. SHAKESPEARE, 75
Arabs The Jews and A. should...settle their differences GOLDWYNISMS, 26; RELIGION, 1
arch All experience is an a. EXPERIENCE, 9
archaeologist An a. is the best husband MARRIAGE, 18
archbishop the sign of an a. is a double-cross CLERGY, 2
arches Underneath the a. DREAMS, 5
Archimedes The...schoolboy is now familiar with truths for which A. SCIENCE, 24
architect Each man the a. of his own fate RESPONSIBILITY, 2
not a great sculptor or painter can be an a. ARCHITECTURE, 5
the a. can only advise MISTAKES, 10
who is not a great sculptor or painter can be an a. RUSKIN, 2
architecture A. in general is frozen music ARCHITECTURE, 7
Fashion is a. FASHION, 1
What has happened to a....that the only passers-by who can contemplate it ARCHITECTURE, 4
ardua Per a. ad astra AMBITION, 1
arguing I am not a. with you WHISTLER, 2
argument I have found you an a. JOHNSON, 38
I love a., I love debate ARGUMENTS, 7; THATCHER, 4
to get the best of an a. ARGUMENTS, 1
work of art must start an a. ART, 19
arguments beware of long a. and long beards BREVITY, 4
Arian In three sips the A. frustrate DRINKS, 1
aristocracy an absentee a. IRELAND, 3
An a. in a republic is like a chicken ARISTOCRACY, 9
a....government by the badly educated ARISTOCRACY, 5; CHESTERTON, 21
a. to what is decent CLASS, 8
displeased with it...call it oligarchy GOVERNMENT, 8
If human beings could be propagated...a. would be...sound ARISTOCRACY, 7
Unlike the male codfish the British a. is ARISTOCRACY, 12; WODEHOUSE, 10
aristocrat the quality that distinguishes the gentleman from both the artist and the a. WAUGH, 7
aristocratic to distinguish...the a. class from the Philistines ARNOLD, 4; CLASS, 2
arithmetic different branches of A. CARROLL, 7
Music is the a. of sounds MUSIC, 10
armchair She fitted into my biggest a. OBESITY, 8; WODEHOUSE, 7
arm'd a. with more than complete steel JUSTICE, 8
Armenteers A mademoiselle from A. FRANCE, 7
armies ignorant a. clash by night WAR, 1
not a....but flocks of sheep CERVANTES, 4
armistice a short a. with truth TRUTH, 6
armour Conceit is the finest a. CONCEIT, 5
Prayer makes the Christian's a. bright PRAYER, 7
arms A. control so easily becomes an incantation WEAPONS, 2
Anger supplies the a. ANGER, 6
I never would lay down my a. PATRIOTISM, 13
I sing of a. and the man ENDURANCE, 12; VIRGIL, 3
It is always opening time in the Sailors A. PUBLIC HOUSES, 3; THOMAS, 11
So he laid down his a. PUNS, 6
army An a. is a nation within a nation ARMY, 3
An a. marches on its stomach FOOD, 19
If you don't want to use the a., I should like to borrow it SARCASM, 2
little ships of England brought the A. home BOATS, 6; WORLD WAR II, 15
The a. ages men sooner than the law ARMY, 5; WELLS, 3
The conventional a. loses if it does not win WAR, 30
Arnold A. is a dandy Isaiah ARNOLD, 2
arrested Christ...would quite likely have been a. OPPRESSION, 2
arrive To travel hopefully is...better...than to a. STEVENSON, 14
arrow Every a....feels the attraction of earth AMBITION, 6
arson A., after all, is an artificial crime WELLS, 6
art All A. is quite useless ART, 20
A. and religion first; then philosophy IMPORTANCE, 2
a. constantly aspires towards...music ART, 12
A. for a.'s sake ART, 3

B. girls don't have the time — DIARIES, 2
b. taste is better than no taste — BENNETT, 6; TASTE, 1
never was a b. peace — WAR AND PEACE, 5
nothing either good or b. — SHAKESPEARE, 34; THINKING, 5
resolved to do something b. — DECISION, 2
so much b. in the best of us — GOOD AND EVIL, 1
strong antipathy of good to b. — PROVOCATION, 2
the b. die late — GOOD AND EVIL, 2
the name of…obstinacy in a b. one — STUBBORNNESS, 2
what I feel really b. about — LIBERALISM, 1
when I'm b. I'm better — WEST, 14
Bailey When will you pay me? /Say the bells of Old B. — LONDON, 1
balance The b, of power — POWER, 13
balanced Food is an important part of a b. diet — FOOD, 13
ballet it takes more than one to make a b. — SUPPORT, 3
balloon the moon's /a b. — MOON, 5
ballot The b. is stronger than the bullet — DEMOCRACY, 4
ballots employers…only like b. so long as you lose them — STRIKES, 3
balm wash the b. from an anointed king — MONARCHY, 9
bananas hanging around like clumps of b. — INSULTS, 11
bands Brass b. are all very well in their place — MUSIC, 2
banes Here lie Willie Michie's b. — BURNS, 6
bang Not with a b. but a whimper — ELIOT, 5; ENDING, 1
banish to b….the clouds of Marxist socialism — MARXISM, 4
bank the man who broke the B. at Monte Carlo — WEALTH, 9
bankrupt B. of Life — DRYDEN, 4; WORLD-WEARINESS, 1
banned any book should be b. — CENSORSHIP, 3
banner A b. with the strange device, /Excelsior — AMBITION, 5
bar an olfactory b. — FAMILIARITY, 3
though hell should b. the way — DETERMINATION, 1
Barbarians society distributes itself into B., Philistines, and Populace — AMERICA, 1
barbarity the…b. of war…forces men…to commit acts — WAR, 28
the English seem…to act with the b. of tyrants — IRELAND, 10; SMITH, 1
bards Portraits of famous b. and preachers — THOMAS, 15
bargains rule for b. — BUSINESS, 1; DICKENS, 7
barge The b. she sat in, like a burnish'd throne — SHAKESPEARE, 14
baritones b. are born villains in opera — OPERA, 5
bark to hear the watch-dog's honest b. — DOGS, 3
barrage chemical b. has been hurled against the fabric of life — ECOLOGY, 1
barrel out of the b. of a gun — MAO TSE-TUNG, 3; POWER POLITICS, 3
barrenness quarrels which vivify its b. — LOVE, 30
barricade At some disputed b. — DEATH, 50
bars Nor iron b. a cage — IMPRISONMENT, 8
barter All government…is founded on compromise and b. — BURKE, 8; COMPROMISE, 2
base It takes a certain courage…to be truly b. — EVIL, 2
based All progress is b. — EXTRAVAGANCE, 2; PROGRESS, 2
basing b. morals on myth — MORALITY, 1
basket Have you ever taken anything out of the clothes b. — CLEANNESS, 1
bastard Because I am a b. — HEMINGWAY, 4
bastards It is a pity…that more politicians are not b. — POLITICIANS, 17
bat black b., night, has flown — TENNYSON, 22
bath B….once a week to avoid being a public menace — CLEANNESS, 1
bathroom fierce and revolutionary in a b. — AMERICANS, 4
battalions God is always on the side of the big b. — POWER POLITICS, 5
God is on the side not of the heavy b. — POWER POLITICS, 6; VOLTAIRE, 18
battering B. the gates of heaven — TENNYSON, 27
battle greatest misery is a b. gained — VICTORY, 10
march into b. together with the men — COURAGE, 1
next greatest misfortune to losing a b. — VICTORY, 9; WELLINGTON, 3
The b. of Britain — CHURCHILL, 23; WORLD WAR II, 5
battlefield b. is fearful — WORLD WAR I, 3
we survive amongst the dead and the dying as on a b. — OLD AGE, 24
battlements Fate sits on these dark b. — DESTINY, 5
Battle of Waterloo the B. was won on the playing-fields of Eton — ORWELL, 4
bayonet bullet and the b. are brother and sister — WORLD WAR I, 11
bayonets A man may build…a throne of b. — POWER POLITICS, 2
be To b., or not to b. — LANGUAGE, 5; SHAKESPEARE, 36; SUICIDE, 1
beaches we shall fight on the b. — CHURCHILL, 22; WORLD WAR II, 4
beacons Logical consequences are the scarecrows of fools and the b. of wise men — LOGIC, 3
beaker a b. full of the warm South — ALCOHOL, 20; KEATS, 7
Beale Miss Buss and Miss B. /Cupid's darts do not reach — INSENSITIVITY, 1
bean The home of the b. and the cod — SNOBBERY, 2
bear a B. of Very Little Brain — WORDS, 9

any man…who could not b. another's misfortunes…like a Christian — POPE, 17
authority be a stubborn b. — BRIBERY, 3
Human kind cannot b. — ELIOT, 4; REALITY, 1
I had rather b. with you than b. you — SHAKESPEARE, 16
beard singed the Spanish king's b. — WAR, 19
bearded hard to hear what a b. man is saying — PUNS, 7
He reaps the b. grain at a breath — DEATH, 40
beards beware of long arguments and long b. — BREVITY, 4
men wore their b., like they wear their neckties — APPEARANCE, 9
beast b. of the earth — ANIMALS, 1; CREATION, 4
Dialect words – those terrible marks of the b. — CLASS, 7
Either a b. or a god — MANKIND, 1
hardly be a b. or a fool alone on a great mountain — SOLITUDE, 7
the mark…of the b. — DEVIL, 3
beastie Wee, sleekit, cow'rin', tim'rous b. — BURNS, 11
beastliness It is called in our schools b.' — SEX, 4
beat make the b. keep time with short steps — FUNERALS, 1
Two hearts that b. as one — LOVE, 40
beaten I was b. up by Quakers — ALLEN, 4
beatings b. of the lonely heart — LONELINESS, 1
beautiful light, shade, and perspective…make it b. — BEAUTY, 8
most b. things…are the most useless — BEAUTY, 17; RUSKIN, 8
Our love of what is b. does not lead to extravagance — RESULTS, 2
summer afternoon…two most b. words — SEASONS, 4
The good is the b. — GOOD, 4
beauty A thing of b. is a joy for ever — BEAUTY, 12; KEATS, 2
B. and the lust for learning — BEAUTY, 3
b. being the best of all we know — BEAUTY, 5
B. in distress — BEAUTY, 6; BURKE, 5
B. in things exists in the mind which contemplates them — BEAUTY, 10
B. is altogether in the eye of the beholder — BEAUTY, 11
b. is only sin deep — BEAUTY, 18; SAKI, 15
B. is truth, truth b. — KEATS, 4
B. itself doth of itself persuade /The eyes of men — BEAUTY, 19
B. stands /In the admiration…of weak minds — BEAUTY, 15
Exuberance is B. — BEAUTY, 4
Fostered alike by b. and by fear — SOUL, 7
her b. made /The bright world dim — BEAUTY, 20
Love built on b. — BEAUTY, 9; DONNE, 7
love permanence more than…b. — BRITISH, 1
Mathematics possesses…b. — RUSSELL, 11
perceive real b. in a person…older — BEAUTY, 1
She walks in b. — BEAUTY, 7
Teaches such b. as a woman's eye — LEARNING, 7
the laws of poetic truth and poetic b. — POETRY, 2
the overwhelming b. of endurance — HEROISM, 3
There is no excellent b. — BEAUTY, 2
this generation…found England a land of b. — ECOLOGY, 3
because B. it is there — MOTIVE, 2
Becket Thomas B. — ASSASSINATION, 3
becoming b. the men we wanted to marry — WOMEN, 40
I believe I am b. a god — LAST WORDS, 28
Sunburn is very b. — APPEARANCE, 6
bed and die – in b. — WAR, 54
And so to b. — BED, 3
B….is the poor man's opera — SEX, 17
Each within our narrow b. — DEATH, 16
Here comes a candle to light you to b. — LONDON, 1
Lady Capricorn,…was…keeping open b. — PROMISCUITY, 2
Never go to b. mad — ANGER, 3
nicer to stay in b. — BED, 2
The b. be blest — BLESSING, 1
Wedlock – the…deep peace of the double b. after the…chaise-longue — MARRIAGE, 17
Who goes to b. with whom — OLD AGE, 20
woman who goes to b. with a man — SEX, 23
bedfellows Misery acquaints…strange b. — MISFORTUNE, 8
bedroom meeting in a darkened b. in a Brussels hotel — EUROPE, 5
beds Minds like b. always made up — INFLEXIBILITY, 3
bedspring the triumphant twang of a b. — SEX, 26
beechen spare the b. tree — TREES, 2
beer Life isn't all b. and skittles — LIFE, 13
Beerbohm Max B. — OLD AGE, 28
Beethoven Roll Over B. — POP MUSIC, 5
beg only the poor…are forbidden to b. — POVERTY, 5
beggar'd b. all description — SHAKESPEARE, 14
beggary b. in the love that can be reckon'd — LOVE, 54
no vice but b. — HYPOCRISY, 8
begin B. at the beginning — CARROLL, 8; ORDER, 1
beginning As it was in the b. — ETERNITY, 2

b. of fairies FAIRIES, 2
end of the b. WORLD WAR II, 11
I like a film to have a b., a middle and an end CINEMA, 1
in the b. God CREATION, 1
in the b. was the word WORDS, 1
beginnings end to the b. of all wars WAR, 51
mighty things from small b. DRYDEN, 11; NATURE, 6
begins my family b. with me ANCESTRY, 2
begotten Whatever is b., born, and dies MORTALITY, 14
begun There is an old saying 'well b. is half done' KEATS, 9
behaving men are more interested in…justifying themselves than in…b. SZASZ, 1
behaviour The quality of moral b. varies HUXLEY, 10
behind In the dusk, with a light b. her AGE, 22
behold b. it was a dream DREAMS, 2
beholder Beauty is…in the eye of the b. BEAUTY, 11
being Knowledge is proportionate to b. KNOWLEDGE, 8
To kill a human b. JAMES, 1
Belfast British troops were patrolling the streets of B. IRELAND, 2
belief *Action will furnish b.* BELIEF, 2
believe a verb meaning 'to b. falsely' BELIEF, 5
b. in the life to come AFTERLIFE, 1
B. it or not BELIEF, 3
don't b. in…true love until after the first attack SCEPTICISM, 1
I b. because it is impossible BELIEF, 4
I b. I am becoming a god LAST WORDS, 28
I don't b. in fairies FAIRIES, 1
inclined to b. those whom we do not know TRUST, 2
it brings you luck whether you b….or not SUPERSTITION, 1
believes politician never b. what he says POLITICIANS, 3
bell B., book, and candle MATERIALISM, 11; SHAKESPEARE, 60
for whom the b. tolls DEATH, 21; DONNE, 6
Bellamy I could eat one of B.'s veal pies LAST WORDS, 23
belle La b. Dame sans Merci SUPERNATURAL, 6
bells The b. of hell go ting-a-ling-a-ling DEATH, 3
With silver b. and cockle shells GARDENS, 1
belly Every man with a b. full of the classics CLASSICS, 6
to banish hunger by rubbing the b. HUNGER, 2
upon thy b. shalt thou go SEXES, 1
victory under the b. of a Cossack's horse RUSSIAN REVOLUTION, 3
bellyful Rumble thy b. WEATHER, 8
belong betray, you must first b. TREASON, 5
below Down and away b. DEPARTURE, 1
What thy errand here b. PURPOSE, 1
Ben Battle B. was a soldier bold PUNS, 6
benefactors gratitude to most b. is the same as…for dentists INGRATITUDE, 2
benefits It is the nature of men to be bound by the b. they confer OBLIGATION, 2
benevolence husband render unto the wife due b. MARRIAGE, 11
Bennett B. – a sort of pig in clover BENNETT, 1
berth Things hitherto undone should be given…a wide b. BEERBOHM, 7
best all that's b. of dark and bright BEAUTY, 7
as in the b. it is MURDER, 4
beauty being the b. of all we know BEAUTY, 5
b. of life is but intoxication BYRON, 8; DRUNKENNESS, 6
b. that is known and thought in the world CRITICISM, 1
b. words in the b. order COLERIDGE, 15; POETRY AND PROSE, 2
Culture, the acquainting ourselves with the b. ARNOLD, 10; CULTURE, 1
For home is b. HOME, 4
His worst is better than any other person's b. HAZLITT, 1
It was the b. of times DICKENS, 18; FRENCH REVOLUTION, 1
look at the b. book…price of a turbot… BOOKS, 25; RUSKIN, 7
Men of few words are the b. BREVITY, 6; SHAKESPEARE, 46
Stolen sweets are b. THEFT, 4
The b. is the enemy of the good EXCELLENCE, 3; VOLTAIRE, 9
The b. lack all conviction YEATS, 1
the b. of possible worlds OPTIMISM, 10; VOLTAIRE, 5
the shortest works are always the b. BREVITY, 2
we live in the b. of all possible worlds OPTIMISM, 6; PESSIMISM, 4
we will do our b. WORLD WAR II, 8
bestial what remains is b. REPUTATION, 4
Bethlehem O little town of B. CHRISTMAS, 8
betimes to be up b. BED, 4
betray b., you must first belong TREASON, 5
Nature never did b. NATURE, 11; WORDSWORTH, 7
betraying if I had to choose between b. my country and b. my friend BETRAYAL, 2
betrothed a bride's attitude towards her b. MARRIAGE, 42; PUNS, 9
better a far, far, b. thing EXECUTION, 4

always…trying to get the b. LAMB, 2; SPORT AND GAMES, 5
b. is he…who hath not seen the evil work…under the sun EVIL, 3
b. strangers SHAKESPEARE, 22
b. to have loved and lost LOVE, 62; TENNYSON, 11
b. to marry than to burn GOD, 3
for b. for worse MARRIAGE, 12
I've got to admit it's getting b. MARRIAGE, 15
nae b. than he should be IMPROVEMENT, 2
something b. than our brains to depend upon BURNS, 5
the old is b. ARISTOCRACY, 4
when I'm bad I'm b. AGE, 6; ALCOHOL, 5
You're a b. man than I am, Gunga Din WEST, 14
Beulah B., peel me a grape SUPERIORITY, 3
bewailing the sum of life's b. WEST, 5
beware all should cry, B. REGRET, 3
B. of the artist who's an intellectual CAUTION, 1
B. of the dog FITZGERALD, 5
B. of the man who does not return your blow DOGS, 1
bewildered I was b. once FORGIVENESS, 6
Bewitched, Bothered and B. CONFUSION, 1
bewitched B., Bothered and Bewildered CONFUSION, 3
beyond All decent people live b. their incomes nowadays EXTRAVAGANCE, 3; SAKI, 6
Bible B. and Church have been the greatest stumbling block FEMINISM, 17
have used the B. as if it was a constable's handbook BIBLE, 4
searching through the B. for loopholes BIBLE, 3
that book is the B. ARNOLD, 12; BIBLE, 1
The B. is literature BIBLE, 8
the B. tells me so RELIGION, 32
The English B. BIBLE, 5
There's a B. on that shelf there BIBLE, 7; RUSSELL, 13
Bibles they have the land and we have the B. RACISM, 6
bicycle a b. made for two MARRIAGE, 22
Socialism can only arrive by b. SOCIALISM, 3
big A b. man has no time FITZGERALD, 6
A government…b. enough to give you all you want GOVERNMENT, 7
B. Brother is watching you AUTHORITARIANISM, 5
he was too b. for them CONCEIT, 2
The b. print giveth and the fine print taketh away BUSINESS, 11
bike he got on his b. UNEMPLOYMENT, 1
billboard A b. lovely as a tree NASH, 5; TREES, 7
billiard The b. sharp whom any one catches PUNISHMENT, 7
biographies History is the essence of…b. BIOGRAPHY, 2; CARLYLE, 5; HISTORY, 1
biography a man is nobody unless his b. OBITUARIES, 3
history…the b. of great men GREATNESS, 4
how difficult it is to write b. BIOGRAPHY, 4
no history; only b. BIOGRAPHY, 3
bird A strange b. LAWRENCE, 1
bird-cage a b. played with toasting-forks MUSIC, 4
birds no b. sing ILLNESS, 6
birth B., and copulation, and death ELIOT, 8; LIFE AND DEATH, 4
B. may be a matter of a moment BIRTH, 5
From b. to age eighteen, a girl needs good parents AGE, 43
no credentials…not even…a certificate of b. ARISTOCRACY, 7
The history of man for the nine months preceding his b. BIRTH, 3
what you were before your b. AFTERLIFE, 7; SCHOPENHAUER, 5
birthday A diplomat…always remembers a woman's b. AGE, 21
birthplace accent of one's b. lingers HOMESICKNESS, 2; ROCHEFOUCAULD, 10
bishop a b….must be blameless CLERGY, 1
blonde to make a b. kick a hole CHANDLER, 1
How can a b. marry CLERGY, 6
Make him a b., and you will silence him CHESTERFIELD, 13
the symbol of a b. is a crook CLERGY, 2
bit The dog,…/Went mad and b. the man GOLDSMITH, 7
bitches Now we are all sons of b. NUCLEAR WEAPONS, 1
bite b. the hand that fed them BURKE, 12; INGRATITUDE, 1
black Any colour, so long as it's b. CHOICE, 1
British Government sees b. people as expendable RACISM, 15
looking for a b. hat METAPHYSICS, 1
People think we do not understand our b….countrymen RACISM, 2
That old b. magic SUPERNATURAL, 7
The Ethiopians say that their gods are…b. RELIGION, 39
The future is…b. RACISM, 3
To like an individual because he's b. RACISM, 3
Two lovely b. eyes VIOLENCE, 3
Blake William B.'s insanity was worth BLAKE, 1
blank Where were you fellows when the paper was b. EDITORS, 1

Pain – has an Element of B.   DICKINSON, 3
bleak In the b. mid-winter   SEASONS, 12
bleed If you prick us, do we not b.   EQUALITY, 17; SHAKESPEARE, 81
blemish Christianity…the one immortal b. of mankind
    CHRISTIANITY, 20
bless God b. us, every one   BLESSING, 4
blessed B. are the meek   HUMILITY, 1
   b. is the man that endureth temptation   TEMPTATION, 2
   B. is the man who expects nothing   EXPECTATION, 2
blessing a b. that money cannot buy   HEALTH AND HEALTHY LIVING, 9
blest It is twice b.   MERCY, 2; SHAKESPEARE, 82
   The bed be b.   BLESSING, 1
   they b him in their pain   MARTYRDOM, 3
blight Prostitution is a b. on the human race   PROMISCUITY, 5
blind A b. man in a dark room   METAPHYSICS, 1
   all the discomforts that will accompany my being b.   BLINDNESS, 5
   Country of the B.   WELLS, 5
   love is b.   LOVE, 55; SHAKESPEARE, 80
   Painting is a b. man's profession   PAINTING, 6
   union of a deaf man to a b. woman   MARRIAGE, 19
   wing'd Cupid painted b.   LOVE, 57; SHAKESPEARE, 85
blindness the…world was stumbling…in social b.   BLINDNESS, 1
bliss B. was it in that dawn to be alive
    FRENCH REVOLUTION, 3; WORDSWORTH, 14
   where ignorance is b., /'Tis folly to be wise   IGNORANCE, 1
block there's a statue inside every b. of stone   OBESITY, 4
blockhead No man but a b. ever wrote   JOHNSON, 30; WRITING, 10
blocks philosophy ought to…unravel people's mental b.
    PHILOSOPHY, 6
blonde A b. to make a bishop kick a hole   CHANDLER, 1
blondes Gentlemen always seem to remember b.   APPEARANCE, 12
blood b., toil, tears and sweat   EFFORT, 1
   critics…desire our b., not our pain   CRITICS, 10
   his b. be on us   GUILT, 2
   humble and meek are thirsting for b.   HUMILITY, 4
   If I die today every drop of my b.   LAST WORDS, 13
   rather have b. on my hands   COMMITMENT, 2
   the b. that she has spilt   COWPER, 2
   the old savage England, whose last b. flows still   ENGLAND, 11
   thy brother's b. crieth unto me   MURDER, 1
   without shedding of b. is no remission   EXECUTION, 1
   your b. of your lives will I require   CRIME, 1
bloodiness The sink is the great symbol of the b. of family life
    FAMILY, 15
bloody All the faces…seem to be b. Poms   ENGLISH, 4
bloom lilac is in b.   FLOWERS, 2
blow A b. in cold blood   SHAW, 16
   Another year! – another deadly b.   DEFEAT, 6
   Beware of the man who does not return your b.   FORGIVENESS, 6
   B., b., thou winter wind   INGRATITUDE, 3
   B., winds, and crack your cheeks   WEATHER, 7
   but a word and a b.   VIOLENCE, 2
bludgeoning the b. of the people   DEMOCRACY, 8; WILDE, 29
blue that little tent of b.   IMPRISONMENT, 5
blunder poverty…is a b.   POVERTY, 11
   Youth is a b.   AGE, 13; DISRAELI, 3
blunders b. usually do more to shape history than…wickedness
    MISTAKES, 8
blush a b. to the cheek of a young person   EMBARRASSMENT, 1
   b. to find it fame   GOOD, 5
blushes Man is the only animal that b.   EMBARRASSMENT, 2; TWAIN, 7
boat a beautiful pea-green b.   NONSENSE, 10
boating Jolly b. weather   BOATS, 3
boats messing about in b.   BOATS, 5
Boche drove the B. across the Rhine   WORLD WAR I, 13
bodies many b. of the saints which slept arose   LAST WORDS, 7
   our dead b. must tell the tale   ENDURANCE, 7
   well-developed b., fairly developed minds   EDUCATION, 8
   women's b. are softer than men's, so their understanding is
   sharper   CHRISTINE DE PISAN, 2
body A b. seriously out of equilibrium   MADNESS, 5
   b. of a weak and feeble woman   ELIZABETH I, 7; ROYALTY, 6
   fear made manifest on the b.   DISEASE, 12
   Man has no B. distinct from his Soul   SOUL, 3
   mind that makes the b. rich   APPEARANCES, 11; SHAKESPEARE, 112
   Our b. is a machine for living   REMEDIES, 8
Bognor Bugger B.   LAST WORDS, 14
boiler The United States is like a gigantic b.   AMERICA, 10
boldness B., and again boldness   COURAGE, 3
bomb god of science…has given us the atomic b.   SCIENCE, 15

bombed no power on earth that can protect him from being b.
    WAR, 3
bombs b. are unbelievable until they…fall   WEAPONS, 4
   Come, friendly b., and fall on Slough   BETJEMAN, 6
bon to produce an occasional *b. mot*   MARRIAGE, 7
Bonaparte The three-o'-clock in the morning courage, which B.
thought was the rarest   COURAGE, 15
bones Bleach the b. of comrades slain   WAR, 25
   Heat, madam!…to take off my flesh and sit in my b.   SMITH, 2
   Of his b. are coral made   SHAKESPEARE, 113
bonjour B. tristesse   SORROW, 4
bonny good heart will help…a b. face   BRONTË, 4
bonum Summum b.   GOOD, 1
Boojum Snark was a B.   NONSENSE, 3
book A b. may be amusing   BOOKS, 13
   A b.'s a b., although there's nothing in't   BYRON, 15; BYRON, 15
   A good b. is the best of friends   BOOKS, 27
   A good b. is the precious life-blood   BOOKS, 18
   any b. should be banned   CENSORSHIP, 3
   Bell, b., and candle   MATERIALISM, 11; SHAKESPEARE, 60
   b. is not harmless…consciously offended   BOOKS, 10
   do not throw this b. about   BELLOC, 2
   Everybody writes a b. too many   WRITERS, 1
   go away and write a b. about it   SPEECHES, 1
   Go, litel b.   BOOKS, 6
   he who destroys a good b., kills reason   BOOKS, 17
   I do not believe that she wrote…one b. which does not break new
   ground   WOOLF, 1
   If a b. is worth reading   BOOKS, 23; RUSKIN, 5
   I'll drown my b.   RENUNCIATION, 2
   moral or an immoral b.   BOOKS, 29
   that everyone has it in him to write one b.   WRITING, 13
   The number one b….was written by a committee   BIBLE, 6
   There are two motives for reading a b.   READING, 7; RUSSELL, 5
   unprintable b. that is readable   BOOKS, 20
   What is the use of a b.   BOOKS, 5; CARROLL, 1
   What you don't know would make a great b.   SMITH, 3
   Would you allow your wife…to read this b.   PRUDERY, 2
books against b. the Home Secretary is   WAUGH, 18
   All b. are divisible into two classes   BOOKS, 24; RUSKIN, 6
   An author who speaks about his own b.   EGOTISM, 3
   be not swallowed up in b.   KNOWLEDGE, 18; LOVE, 68
   between a man of sense and his b.   BOOKS, 7; CHESTERFIELD, 9
   B. are a load of crap   BOOKS, 14
   B. are…a mighty bloodless substitute for life
    BOOKS, 26; STEVENSON, 10
   B. are made…like pyramids   BOOKS, 11
   B. are well written, or badly written   BOOKS, 12
   b. by which the printers have lost   BOOKS, 8
   B. cannot always please   BOOKS, 28
   b. cannot be killed by fire   BOOKS, 9
   B., I don't know what you see in them   READING, 6
   B….propose to *instruct* or to *amuse*   BOOKS, 15
   B. think for me   BORROWING, 3; LAMB, 5
   b….written by people who don't understand them   BOOKS, 22
   Borrowers of b.   DAMNATION, 2
   but b. never die   BELLOC, 6; PUNS, 1
   come not, Lucifer! /I'll burn my b.   CHANDLER, 3
   His b. were read   MORALITY, 2
   If my b. had been any worse   SMITH, 8
   Morality's a gesture…learnt from b.   BOOKS, 3
   No furniture so charming as b.   CRITICISM, 11
   of making many b. there is no end   HUXLEY, 7; LITERATURE, 4
   Prolonged…reviewing of b. involves constantly *inventing* reactions   BOOKS, 2
   proper study of mankind is b.   AUDEN, 7; BOOKS, 1
   Some b. are to be tasted   BOOKS, 24; RUSKIN, 6
   Some b. are undeservedly forgotten   BOOKS, 19
   the b. of the hour
   The b. one reads in childhood…create in one's mind a…false map
    LITERATURE, 2
   The reading of all good b.   MAO TSE-TUNG, 4
   To read too many b.   BOOKS, 22
   We all know that b. burn   CENSORSHIP, 1
   Whenever b. are burned   YEATS, 2
   When I think of all the b. I have read
booksellers nor even b. have put up with poets' being second-rate
    HORACE, 3; POETS, 6
boorish the opinionated, the ignorant, and the b.   STUBBORNNESS, 1
boot imagine a b. stamping on a human face   OPPRESSION, 3; ORWELL, 7
boots before the truth has got its b. on   LYING, 2

If ever he went to school without any b. CONCEIT, 2
Very well, then I shall not take off my b. WELLINGTON, 13
bordello After I die, I shall return to earth as a gatekeeper of a b.
THREATS, 2
bore A b. is a man who BORES, 3
A healthy male adult b. BORES, 5
B., n. A person who talks BORES, 1
Is not life...too short...to b. ourselves BOREDOM, 5
no greater b. than the travel b. TRAVEL, 13
proof that God is a b. PROTESTANTISM, 1
you are...the club B.: I am the club Liar SAKI, 3
bored aged diplomats to be b. DIPLOMACY, 1
Bores and B. BORES, 2
I wanted to be b. to death BOREDOM, 1
Punctuality is the virtue of the b. PROMPTNESS, 3; WAUGH, 13
When you're b. with yourself BOREDOM, 6
boredom sheer apathy and b. DISCOVERY, 3
The effect of b. on a large scale BOREDOM, 4
three great evils, b., vice, and poverty VOLTAIRE , 7; WORK, 12
bores the B. and Bored BORES, 2
boring curiously b. about...happiness HUXLEY, 11
Somebody's b. me, I think it's me BORES, 4; THOMAS, 17
you ought to be ashamed of...being b. BOREDOM, 2
born a silly little mouse will be b. DISAPPOINTMENT, 3
a time to be b., and a time to die TIME, 4
B. under one law HUMAN CONDITION, 4
Every moment one is b. LIFE AND DEATH, 9; TENNYSON, 16
he is not conscious of being b. LA BRUYERE, 2; LIFE AND DEATH, 6
I was b. old AGE, 41
joy that a man is b. into the world BIRTH, 1
Man was b. free FREEDOM, 22
natural to die as to be b. DEATH, 8
One is not b. a woman BEAUVOIR, 2; WOMEN, 6
one of woman b. BIRTH, 6
powerless to be b. ARNOLD, 9
Some are b. great GREATNESS, 7; SHAKESPEARE, 119
Some men are b. mediocre MEDIOCRITY, 3
to have been b. BIRTH, 2
to the manner b. SHAKESPEARE, 30
We are all b. mad MADNESS, 1
Whatever is begotten, b., and dies MORTALITY, 14
born-again b. people...make you wish RELIGION, 37
borrow If you don't want to use the army, I should like to b. it
SARCASM, 2
men who b. BORROWING, 2; LAMB, 4
borrower Neither a b. nor a lender be
BORROWING, 4; INTEGRITY, 4; SHAKESPEARE, 29
borrowers B. of books BORROWING, 3; LAMB, 5
borrowing be not made a beggar by banqueting upon b.
BORROWING, 1
b. dulls the edge of husbandry
BORROWING, 4; INTEGRITY, 4; SHAKESPEARE, 29
bosom Abraham's b. POVERTY AND WEALTH, 2
Boston this is good old B. SNOBBERY, 2
both said on b. sides ADDISON, 5
bother long words B. me WORDS, 9
bothered Bewitched, B. and Bewildered CONFUSION, 3
bottinney b. means a knowledge of plants DICKENS, 10
bottle Yo-ho-ho, and a b. of rum ALCOHOL, 32
bottles It is with...people as with...b. CHARACTER, 5
the English have hot-water b. ENGLISH, 12
bough Loaf of Bread beneath the B. CONTENTMENT, 2
bouillabaisse B. is only good because cooked by the French
FOOD, 8
Boulogne There was an old man of B. INNUENDO, 1
bourgeois B.,...is an epithet CLASS, 3
How beastly the b. is LAWRENCE, 8; MEN, 5
bourgeoisie the British b. have spoken of themselves as gentlemen
WAUGH, 7
bourn from whose b. /No traveller returns AFTERLIFE, 3
bovine The cow is of the b. ilk NASH, 1
Bow B., b., ye lower middle classes CLASS, 5
Says the great bell at B. LONDON, 1
bowl love in a golden b. WISDOM, 6
bow-wow Daddy wouldn't buy me a b. DOGS, 7
boy every b. and every gal /That's born into the world alive
GILBERT, 4
Love is a b. BUTLER 3; INDULGENCE, 1; PUNISHMENT, 4
rarely...one can see in a little b. the promise of a man CHILDREN, 8
Shades of the prison-house begin to close /Upon the growing b.
METAPHYSICS, 4

The b. stood on the burning deck COURAGE, 5
When I was a little b. they called me a liar WRITERS, 13
boyhood The smiles, the tears, /Of b.'s years NOSTALGIA, 8
boys As flies to wanton b. SHAKESPEARE, 65
B. are capital fellows in their own way LAMB, 3
Claret is the liquor for b. ALCOHOL, 17; JOHNSON, 34
bracelet diamond and safire b. lasts forever MATERIALISM, 8
brain a Bear of Very Little B. WORDS, 9
B., n. An apparatus with which we think MIND, 1
If it is for mind that we are seaching the b. MIND, 5
Let schoolmasters puzzle their b. ALCOHOL, 14; GOLDSMITH, 11
Tobacco drieth the b. SMOKING, 15
we are supposing the b....more than a telephone-exchange MIND, 5
You've got the b. of a four-year-old boy STUPIDITY, 3
brains something better than our b. to depend upon ARISTOCRACY, 4
What good are b. to a man WODEHOUSE, 2
braking British civil service...effective b. mechanism
BUREAUCRACY, 8
brass B. bands are all very well in their place MUSIC, 2
Men's evil manners live in b. MEMORIALS, 7; SHAKESPEARE, 52
sounding b. CHARITY, 4
brave b. new world...such people in't MANKIND, 14; SHAKESPEARE, 114
Fortune favours the b. COURAGE, 14
land of the free, and the home of the b. AMERICA, 14
Many b. men...before Agamemnon's time OBLIVION, 1
the B. deserves the Fair DRYDEN, 9
we could never learn to be b....if there were only joy ENDURANCE, 5
Brazil B., where the nuts come from PLACES, 11
breach a custom more honour'd in the b. SHAKESPEARE, 30
Once more unto the b. COURAGE, 11; SHAKESPEARE, 45
bread b. eaten in secret is pleasant SECRECY, 1
Loaf of B. beneath the Bough CONTENTMENT, 2
that b. should be so dear POVERTY, 9
This b. I break was once the oat THOMAS, 8
breakdown One of the symptoms of approaching nervous b.
WORK, 9
breakfast she must not reheat his sins for b. FORGIVENESS, 4
breakfast-table ready for the national b. OBITUARIES, 3
breakfast-time critical period in matrimony is b. MARRIAGE, 34
breast charms to soothe a savage b. CONGREVE, 6; MUSIC, 8
my baby at my b. SUICIDE, 6
breast-feeding atheism, b., circumcision INDULGENCE, 2
breasts they add weight to the b. FOOD, 7
breath blow hot and cold with the same b. INDECISION, 1
Can starved urn.../Back to its mansion call the fleeting b. DEATH, 27
He reaps the bearded grain at a b. DEATH, 40
in this harsh world draw thy b. in pain MOURNING, 9
The years to come seemed waste of b. FLYING, 4; YEATS, 15
world will hold its b. WORLD WAR II, 16
breathed God...b. into his nostrils GARDENS, 3
breed happy b. of men ENGLAND, 20; SHAKESPEARE, 97
breeding Good b. consists in concealing how...we think of ourselves
TWAIN, 11
who are formed by a different b. DISRAELI, 7
breeze The fair b. blew EXPLORATION, 1
breezes spicy b. /Blow soft o'er Ceylon's isle MISANTHROPY, 1
brevity B. is the soul of lingerie BREVITY, 3; CLOTHES, 2
B. is the soul of wit BREVITY, 5; SHAKESPEARE, 32
bribe The man who offers a b. BRIBERY, 2
You cannot hope to b. or twist JOURNALISM, 19
bribing Money is good for b. yourself MONEY, 16
brick carried a...b. in his pocket SWIFT, 5
he found it b. IMPROVEMENT, 1
bricklayers B. kick their wives to death WELLS, 9
bride a b.'s attitude towards her betrothed MARRIAGE, 42; PUNS, 9
It helps...to remind your b. that you gave up a throne for her
MARRIAGE, 66
unravish'd b. of quietness SILENCE, 3
bridge Beautiful Railway B. of the Silv'ry Tay DISASTER, 3
I am not going to speak to the man on the b. DEPARTURE, 3
Like a b. over troubled water COMFORT, 2
over the B. of Sighs into eternity DEATH, 38
brief I strive to be b., and I become obscure HORACE, 2
Out, out, b. candle LIFE, 19; SHAKESPEARE, 76
briefcase lawyer with his b. can steal LAWYERS, 4
brigands B. demand your money WOMEN, 10
bright her beauty made /The b. world dim BEAUTY, 20
the creature hath a purpose and its eyes are b. with it PURPOSE, 3
Tiger! burning b. BLAKE, 20
Brighton Like B. pier...inadequate for getting to France TRAVEL, 9
brilliance No b. is needed in the law LAW, 7

brilliant b. men...will come to a bad end — GREATNESS, 1
brillig Twas b., and the slithy toves — NONSENSE, 4
brimstone b. and fire — PUNISHMENT, 2
bring thou knowest not what a day may b. forth — FUTURE, 3
Britain a time when B. had a savage culture — CIVILIZATION, 2
  battle of B. is about to begin — CHURCHILL, 23; WORLD WAR II, 5
  B....Fabian Society writ large — BRITAIN, 4
  B. is no longer in the politics of the pendulum — POLITICS, 46
  B. is not...easily rocked by revolution — BRITAIN, 4
  When B. first, at heaven's command — BRITAIN, 7
Britannia Rule, B., rule the waves — BRITAIN, 7
British but we are B. – thank God — HOMOSEXUALITY, 8
  socialism...alien to the B. character — SOCIALISM, 9
  The B., being brought up on team games — HOUSES OF PARLIAMENT, 1
  The B. love permanence — BRITISH, 1
  the magnificent fair play of the B. criminal law — DOYLE, 5
  when a B. Prime Minister sneezed — BRITAIN, 6
British Empire 'Can't' will be the epitaph of the B. — BRITISH EMPIRE, 3
  liquidation of the B. — BRITISH EMPIRE, 2
British Museum a little room somewhere in the B. that — MUSEUMS, 1
  a reflection of the B. Reading Room — INTELLECTUALS, 5
  There is in the B., an enormous mind — MUSEUMS, 2
Briton as only a free-born B. can do — SERVILITY, 4
  he was animated with the soul of a B. — VOLTAIRE, 1
  the dullest B. of them all — TROLLOPE, 1
Britons B. never will be slaves — BRITAIN, 7
broad She's the B. and I'm the High — ACADEMICS, 5
broken He liked the sound of b. glass — ARISTOCRACY, 2
  Laws were made to be b. — LAW, 8
  peace has to be out — PEACE, 5
brothels b. with bricks of Religion — BLAKE, 14
brother am I my b.'s keeper — MURDER, 1
  Big B. is watching you — AUTHORITARIANISM, 5
brotherhood Freedom! Equality! B. — HUMAN RIGHTS, 2
brotherly let b. love continue — HOSPITALITY, 2
brothers B. all /In honour — HONOUR, 5
  the poor are our b. and sisters — POVERTY, 15
brought never b. to min' — BURNS, 3; FRIENDSHIP, 3
Browning B. used words — BROWNING, 1
Brown's John B. body — MEMORIALS, 4
bruise it shall b. thy head — SEXES, 1
  sweetest fragrance from the herb...tread on it and b. it — WOMEN, 43
bruised it is often a comfort to...be b. in a new place — CHANGE, 9
Brussels meeting in a darkened bedroom in a B. hotel — EUROPE, 5
brutality industry without art is b. — ART, 15; RUSKIN, 2
  Sentimentality is a superstructure covering b. — SENTIMENTALITY, 2
brute I never saw a b. I hated so — BROWNING, 6
brutes Thanks to words, we have been able to rise above the b. — HUXLEY, 3; WORDS, 6
Brutus Caesar had his B. – Charles the First, his Cromwell — TREASON, 4
bubble Life is mostly froth and b. — MISFORTUNE, 5
bubbles With beaded b. winking at the brim — ALCOHOL, 20; KEATS, 7
buck The b. stops here — RESPONSIBILITY, 8
Buckingham changing guard at B. Palace — SOLDIERS, 1
bud And now in age I b. again — OLD AGE, 10
budget b. is a method of worrying — ECONOMICS, 1
buds Gather the flowers, but spare the b. — FLOWERS, 5
  the darling b. of May — COMPLIMENTS, 3; SHAKESPEARE, 106
buffalo give me a home where the b. roam — HOMESICKNESS, 1
bugger B. Bognor — LAST WORDS, 14
build let us think that we b. for ever — ARCHITECTURE, 2
  The *end* is to b. well — ARCHITECTURE, 9
builder he can only be a *b.* — ARCHITECTURE, 5; RUSKIN, 2
building human organism needs...good b. material — HEALTH AND HEALTHY LIVING, 4
  twenty years of marriage make her...like a public b. — WILDE, 30
  Well b. hath three Conditions — ARCHITECTURE, 1
buildings I go amongst the b. of a city — PURPOSE, 3
  Luftwaffe –...knocked down our b. — ARCHITECTURE, 1
built till we have b. Jerusalem — ENGLAND, 5
bull Down at the old 'B. and Bush' — PUBLIC HOUSES, 4
bullet ballot is stronger than the b. — DEMOCRACY, 4
  b. and the bayonet are brother and sister — WORLD WAR I, 11
  Each b. has got its commission — MORTALITY, 1
  Every b. has its billet — DESTINY, 3
bulrushes dam...the Nile with b. — FREEDOM, 1
bump And things that go b. in the night — SUPERNATURAL, 1
bums art and literature are left to a lot of shabby b. — AMERICA, 16

bungalow proud of the position of the b.,...in the country — SUBURBIA, 2
bunk History is more or less b. — HISTORY, 7
Burgundy a Naïve Domestic B. — ALCOHOL, 34
Burke B. was a damned wrong-headed fellow — BURKE, 1
burn better to marry than to b. — MARRIAGE, 12
  come not, Lucifer! /I'll b. my books — DAMNATION, 2
burned every government...should have its old speeches b. — GOVERNMENT, 13
  Whenever books are b. — CENSORSHIP, 1
burning The boy stood on the b. deck — COURAGE, 1
  The spirit b. but unbent — BYRON, 6; DETERMINATION, 3
  To keep a lamp b. — CHARITY, 11
burnings B. of people — ART, 14
burr kind of b.; I shall stick — PERSISTENCE, 5
bury I come to b. Caesar, not to praise him — EVIL, 11; SHAKESPEARE, 58
bus Hitler has missed the b. — WORLD WAR II, 1
business A b. that makes nothing but money — BUSINESS, 3
  All b. sagacity reduces itself...to...sabotage — BUSINESS, 12
  a successful b. — BUSINESS, 2
  a woman's b. to get married — MARRIAGE, 54
  B. as usual — BRITISH, 2; CHURCHILL, 18
  B. underlies everything in our national life — BUSINESS, 14
  dinner lubricates b. — BUSINESS, 9
  everybody's b. is nobody's b. — GOSSIP, 2
  friendship founded on b. — BUSINESS, 8
  If everybody minded their own b. — CURIOSITY, 2
  I have led a life of b. so long that I have lost my taste for reading — READING, 10
  it is...our b. to lose innocence — INNOCENCE, 4
  That's the true b. precept — BUSINESS, 1; DICKENS, 7
  The b. of America is b. — AMERICA, 8
  To b. that we love we rise betime — ENTHUSIASM, 4
businessmen My message to the b. of this country — ILLNESS, 1
Buss Miss B. and Miss Beale /Cupid's darts do not feel — INSENSITIVITY, 1
bust It's a funny thing about that b. — AGE, 39
butchers Governments need to have both shepherds and b. — GOVERNMENT, 14; VOLTAIRE, 17
butlers b. and lady's maids do not reproduce their kind — WELLS, 2
butter b. will only make us fat — POWER POLITICS, 1
  fine words b. no parsnips — WORDS, 10
buttered a piece of toast...fell...always/ on the b. side — PERVERSITY, 3
butterflies Literature and b. are the two sweetest passions — LITERATURE, 8
butterfly Happiness is like a b. — HAPPINESS, 6
buttock B. fetishism is comparatively rare — GREER, 3
button facility to do such things at the touch of a b. — TECHNOLOGY, 4
buttress a b. of the church — SUPPORT, 2
buy American heiress wants to b. a man — MATERIALISM, 9
Byron A more worthless set than B. — POETS, 9; WELLINGTON, 5
  When B.'s eyes were shut in death — BYRON, 1
cabbages c. and kings — CARROLL, 10; NONSENSE, 5
  The c. are coming now — BETJEMAN, 2
cabs busy driving c. and cutting hair — GOVERNMENT, 4
Caesar *Ave C., morituri te salutant* — LAST WORDS, 2
  C.! dost thou lie so low — DEATH, 52
  C. had his Brutus – Charles the First, his Cromwell — TREASON, 4
  I come to bury C. — EVIL, 11; SHAKESPEARE, 58
  Not that I lov'd C. less — PATRIOTISM, 15; SHAKESPEARE, 57
  Rose...where some buried C. bled — FLOWERS, 3
Caesar's C. wife must be above suspicion — INTEGRITY, 2
cage Marriage is like a c. — MARRIAGE, 41
  Nor iron bars a c. — IMPRISONMENT, 3
  robin redbreast in a c. — IMPRISONMENT, 1
caged We think c. birds sing, when indeed they cry — IMPRISONMENT, 4
Cain the Lord set a mark upon C. — REVENGE, 4
cake Let them eat c. — HUNGER, 6
cakes no more c. and ale — MERRYMAKING, 2
calamities C. are of two kinds — MISFORTUNE, 2
Caledonia C.! stern and wild — SCOTT, 3
calf killed a c....in a high style — SHAKESPEARE, 2
  the fatted c. — PARTIES, 2
calm sea is c. to-night — SEA, 1
calumnies C. are answered best — INSULTS, 10
Calvary the place, which is called C. — EXECUTION, 2
Calvin land of C., oat-cakes, and sulphur — SCOTLAND, 5
Calvinist maniacal C. and coddled poet — COWPER, 1
Cambridge C. people rarely smile — CAMBRIDGE, 2

Oxford is on the whole more attractive than C.

CAMBRIDGE, 1; OXFORD, 3

To C. books
CAMBRIDGE, 5; OXFORD, 3
With equal skill to C. books he sent
CAMBRIDGE, 3; OXFORD, 4
came I c.; I saw; God conquered
VICTORY, 8
I c., I saw, I conquered
VICTORY, 1
camel easier for a c. to go through the eye of a needle
WEALTH, 3
Camelot many-tower'd C.
TENNYSON, 17
To look down to C.
CURSES, 4
camera I am a c.
OBJECTIVITY, 2
The c. cannot lie. But...
PHOTOGRAPHY, 3
cameras everything but the c.
WEST, 2
can Talent does what it c.
TALENT AND GENIUS, 3
cancel to c. half a Line
DESTINY, 4
cancels debt which c. all others
OBLIGATION, 1
cancer chronic diseases more destructive to life than c.
DISEASE, 15
candid save me, from the c. friend
FRANKNESS, 1
candidates C. should not attempt more than six
BELLOC, 12
candle a c. of understanding
UNDERSTANDING, 1
Bell, book, and c.
MATERIALISM, 11; SHAKESPEARE, 60
little c. throws his beams
GOOD, 6
Out, out, brief c.
LIFE, 19; SHAKESPEARE, 76
we shall this day light such a c./, by God's grace, in England as I
trust shall never be put out.
EXECUTION, 7
canem Cave c.
DOGS, 1
canker killing as the c. to the rose
CORRUPTION, 3
cannibal Better sleep with a sober c. than a drunken Christian
DRUNKENNESS, 9
cannon-ball c. took off his legs
PUNS, 6
canoe every man paddle his own c.
INDEPENDENCE, 2
cant love – all the wretched c. of it
LOVE, 30
'C.' will be the epitaph of the British Empire
BRITISH EMPIRE, 3
capable c. of being well set to music
MUSIC, 1
capital Boys are c. fellows in their own way
LAMB, 3
capitalism c....: the process whereby American girls turn into
American women
CAPITALISM, 2
I am going to fight c.
CAPITALISM, 8
militarism...is one of the chief bulwarks of c.
CAPITALISM, 4
unacceptable face of c.
CAPITALISM, 1
We cannot remove the evils of c.
CAPITALISM, 5
capitalist C. production begets...its own negation
CAPITALISM, 7
Capricorn Lady C.,...was...keeping open bed
PROMISCUITY, 2
captain I am the c. of my soul
RESPONSIBILITY, 4
captive Beauty stands...Led c.
BEAUTY, 15
carbuncle Like a c. on the face of an old and valued friend
ARCHITECTURE, 2
cards an old age of c.
POPE, 14
I have not learned to play at c.
SPORT AND GAMES, 4
care age is full of c.
AGE, 37; SHAKESPEARE, 95
C. /Sat on his faded cheek
WORRY, 5
People who are always taking c. of their health are like misers
HYPOCHONDRIA, 1
pleasures are their only c.
EXPLOITATION, 2
Sleep that knits up the ravell'd sleave of c.
SLEEP, 7
so vain...c. for the opinion of those we don't c. for
CONCEIT, 4
take c. of the minutes
CHESTERFIELD, 7
Take c. of the pence
CHESTERFIELD, 6; THRIFT, 1
what is past my help is past my c.
INDIFFERENCE, 1
career nothing which might damage his c.
SCOTS, 1
careers The best c. advice to give to the young
OCCUPATIONS, 8
careless first fine c. rapture
BROWNING, 9
carelessness To lose one parent,...a misfortune; to lose both
looks like c.
LOSS, 6; WILDE, 15
cargo With a c. of ivory
BOATS, 7
With a c. of Tyne coal
BOATS, 8
caring take millions off the c. services
PATRIOTISM, 10
Carlyle C. is a poet
CARLYLE, 2
carpe C. diem
HORACE, 10; PRESENT, 3
carpenter Walrus and the C.
SEASIDE, 2
carpet only men in rags.../Mistake themselves for c. bags
ETIQUETTE, 1
carriage Go together like a horse and c.
LOVE AND MARRIAGE, 4
Cary Grant Old C. fine
TELEGRAMS, 4
case there had been a lady in the c.
WOMEN, 11
cash only the poor who pay c.
MONEY, 9
Cassius C. has a lean and hungry look
MISTRUST, 4; SHAKESPEARE, 53
cast he that is without sin...let him first c. a stone
SIN, 3
pale c. of thought
CONSCIENCE, 4
The die is c.
IRREVOCABILITY, 1
caste measure the social c. of a person
CLASS, 1
casteth perfect love c. out fear
FEAR, 3; LOVE, 7

casting It is no good c. out devils
LAWRENCE, 14
castle A c. called Doubting Castle
DESPAIR, 1
A neurotic is the man who builds a c. in the air
PSYCHIATRY, 6
The house of every one is to him as his c.
PRIVACY, 1
castles Pale Death kicks his way...into...the c. of kings
HORACE, 8; EQUALITY, 19
the c. I have, are built with air
JONSON, 1
casualty The first c. when war comes
WAR, 26
cat a C. of such deceitfulness
CATS, 2; ELIOT, 6
c. is a diagram and pattern of subtle air
CATS, 4
Had Tiberius been a c.
ARNOLD, 13; CATS, 1
The C., the Rat, and Lovell our dog
INSULTS, 5
When I play with my c.
CATS, 5
catastrophe to lose one's teeth is a c.
TEETH, 3
catchwords Man is a creature who lives...by c.
STEVENSON, 8
Catherine I'm glad you like my C.
WEST, 12
Catholic I am a C.....I go to Mass every day
BELLOC, 11
I'm still a C.
CATHOLICISM, 6
once a C. always a C.
RELIGION, 38
quite lawful for a C. woman to avoid pregnancy by...mathematics
CONTRACEPTION, 5
Catholics C. and Communists have committed great crimes
COMMITMENT, 2
cats what c. most appreciate...is...entertainment value
CATS, 3
cattle Actors should be treated like c.
ACTORS, 5
these who die as c.
WORLD WAR I, 9
cause the name of perseverance in a good c.
STUBBORNNESS, 2
causes Home of lost c.
ARNOLD, 7; OXFORD, 1
they should declare the c. which impel them to...separation
INDEPENDENCE, 1
cavaliero a perfect c.
HEROISM, 2
cave C. canem
DOGS, 1
caverns Through c. measureless to man
COLERIDGE, 6; PLEASURE, 4
caves be c....in which his shadow will be shown
NIETZSCHE, 5
sunny pleasure-dome with c. of ice
COLERIDGE, 7; PLEASURE, 5
cease I will not c. from mental fight
ENGLAND, 1
ceases forbearance c. to be a virtue
BURKE, 3; TOLERANCE, 1
celebrity A c....works hard...to become known
FAME, 1
celerity C. is never more admir'd
IMPETUOSITY, 2
censor Deleted by French c.
NEWSPAPERS, 1
censorship Assassination...the extreme form of c.
ASSASSINATION, 4; SHAW, 21
C....depraving and corrupting
CENSORSHIP, 2
censure All c. of a man's self
SELF, 5
centre I love being at the c. of things
COMMITMENT, 3
My c. is giving way
WORLD WAR I, 5
the c. cannot hold
YEATS, 10
century The c. on which we are entering...must be the c. of the
common man
PUBLIC, 11
the twentieth c. will be...the c. of Fascism
FASCISM, 1
certain I am c. that we will win the election with a good majority
SELF-CONFIDENCE, 4
nothing is c. but death and taxes
TAXATION, 3
certainties begin with c.
CERTAINTY, 1; DOUBT, 1
Cervantes C. laughed chivalry out of fashion
CERVANTES (SAAVEDRA), 1
cesspit people swirling about in a human c.
AIDS, 1
cesspool London, that great c.
DOYLE, 8; LONDON, 3
Ceylon spicy breezes /Blow soft o'er C.'s isle
MISANTHROPY, 1
chaff An editor...separates the wheat from the c.
EDITORS, 1
not racially pure are mere c.
RACISM, 7
chain the flesh to feel the c.
IMPRISONMENT, 2
chains Man...everywhere he is in c.
FREEDOM, 22
nothing to lose but their c.
MARXISM, 1
chair Give Dayrolles a c.
CHESTERFIELD, 14
the nineteenth century was the age of the editorial c.
PSYCHIATRY, 3
chaise-longue Wedlock – the...deep peace of the double bed after
the...c.
MARRIAGE, 17
chalices In old time we had treen c. and golden priests
CLERGY, 4
chamber rapping at my c. door
SUPERNATURAL, 8
chambermaid a man would be as happy in the arms of a c.
IMAGINATION, 3
chamois springing from blonde to blonde like the c. of the Alps
AMERICANS, 10
champagne like a glass of c. that has stood
HOUSES OF PARLIAMENT, 2
water flowed like c.
ABSTINENCE, 4
chance every c. brought out a noble knight
NOSTALGIA, 1
Grab a c.
OPPORTUNITY, 5
change c. is the very essence of life
CHANGE, 6
I c., but I cannot die
SHELLEY, 4

No Jew was ever fool enough to turn C.   RELIGION, 40
Onward, C. soldiers   CHRISTIANITY, 2
The C. religion...cannot be believed by any reasonable person
without one   CHRISTIANITY, 16
The C. religion not only was at first attended with miracles
    CHRISTIANITY, 16
Christianity C. accepted as given a metaphysical system
    CHRISTIANITY, 17
'C.,...but why journalism   CHRISTIANITY, 1; JOURNALISM, 1
C. has done a great deal for love   CHRISTIANITY, 12
C. has made of death a terror   CHRISTIANITY, 21
C. is part of the Common Law of England   CHRISTIANITY, 13
C. is the most materialistic of all great religions   CHRISTIANITY, 22
C....says that they are all fools   CHESTERTON, 9
C. the one great curse   CHRISTIANITY, 20
C....the one immortal blemish of mankind   CHRISTIANITY, 20
decay of C.   ALCOHOL, 28; SAKI, 11
local cult called C.   CHRISTIANITY, 15
Rock and roll or C.   POPULARITY, 4
Christians C. awake, salute the happy morn   CHRISTMAS, 9
Onward, C., onward go   ENDURANCE, 13
settle their differences like good C.   GOLDWYNISMS, 26; RELIGION, 3
Christ-like C. heroes and woman-worshipping Don Juans   MEN, 6
Christmas C. should fall out in the Middle of Winter   CHRISTMAS, 1
For C. comes but once a year   CHRISTMAS, 14
I'm walking backwards till C.   NONSENSE, 12
Let them know it's C.   CHARITY, 3
perceive C. through its wrapping   CHRISTMAS, 15
'Twas the night before C.   CHRISTMAS, 11
Christopher C. Robin went down with Alice   SOLDIERS, 2
church Beware when you take on the C. of God   RELIGION, 31
Bible and C. have been the greatest stumbling block   FEMINISM, 17
But get me to the c. on time   MARRIAGE, 39
The C. exists   CHURCH, 3
The farther you go from the c. of Rome   PROTESTANTISM, 2
There is no salvation outside the c.   RELIGION, 1
There was I, waiting at the c.   MARRIAGE, 38
an alien C.   IRELAND, 3
churches c. have kill'd their Christ   TENNYSON, 23
churchman a species of person called a 'Modern C.'   RELIGION, 35
Cicero C...Homer were /Mad as the mist and snow   YEATS, 7
cider c. and tinned salmon   FOOD, 23
cigarette A c. is...a perfect pleasure   WILDE, 28
I kissed my first woman, and smoked my first c.   SMOKING, 12
Cinderella A sort of literary C.   BRONTË, 1
poetry, 'The C. of the Arts.'   POETRY, 17
cinema c. is truth twenty-four times a second   CINEMA, 2
circumcised When they c. Herbert Samuel   INSULTS, 13
circumcision atheism, breast-feeding, c.   INDULGENCE, 2
circumlocution C. Office   BUREAUCRACY, 3
circumstance Pride, pomp, and c.   SHAKESPEARE, 92; WAR, 60
To a philosopher no c...is too minute   PHILOSOPHERS, 3
cities The government burns down whole c.   INJUSTICE, 6; MAO TSE-TUNG, 6
citizen a c. of the world   COURTESY, 1; NATIONALITY, 1
city every man in the c. wants a farm   ENVY, 3
first c. Cain   GARDENS, 4
hiring taxis to scuttle around a c.   INCOMPETENCE, 2
I go amongst the buildings of a c.   PURPOSE, 3
the c. of perspiring dreams   CAMBRIDGE, 4
civil In a c. war, a general must know   WAR, 47
civilisation Disinterested intellectual curiosity...life blood of...c.
    CURIOSITY, 5
If c. is to advance...it must be through...women   PANKHURST, 3
civilization C. is a method of living   CIVILIZATION, 1
C. is...equal respect for all men   CIVILIZATION, 1
It is so stupid of modern c.   DEVIL, 6
little in c. to appeal to a Yeti   CIVILIZATION, 3
The degree of a nation's c.   CIVILIZATION, 6
without the usual interval of c.   AMERICA, 6
civil service British c....effective braking mechanism
    BUREAUCRACY, 1
C. is profoundly deferential   POLITICS, 16
clapped c. the glass to his sightless eye   BLINDNESS, 4
claret C. is the liquor for boys   ALCOHOL, 17; JOHNSON, 34
class an...young Englishman of our upper c.
    ARISTOCRACY, 1; ARNOLD, 3
a special machine for the suppression of one c. by another
    CAPITALISM, 6
Every c. is unfit to govern   GOVERNMENT, 1
for one c. to appreciate the wrongs of another   CLASS, 18

For this c. we have...the designation of Philistines   PHILISTINISM, 1
Like many of the upper c.   ARISTOCRACY, 2
Poets and painters are outside the c. system   ARTISTS, 1
Poets and painters...constitute a special c.   POETS, 1
The constitution...first and second c. citizens   CLASS, 21
The history of all...society is the history of c. struggles   CLASS, 13
The one c. you do not belong to   CLASS, 14
The state is an instrument...of the ruling c.   STATE, 4
classes back the masses against the c.   CLASS, 6
I'm not interested in c.   CLASS, 11
responsible and the irresponsible c.   CLASS, 9
classical That's the ç. mind at work   MIND, 4
The basic difference between c. music and jazz   MUSIC, 20
classicism C.,...the literature that gave...pleasure to their great-grandfathers   LITERATURE, 10
classics Every man with a belly full of the c.   CLASSICS, 4
The c. are only primitive literature   CLASSICS, 5
clean Bath...once a day to be passably c.   CLEANNESS, 1
hard to be funny when you have to be c.   HUMOUR, 18
clearing-house the C. of the World   ECONOMICS, 2
cleft Rock of ages, c. for me   RELIGION, 30
Clementine Dwelt a miner, Forty-niner, /And his daughter, C.
    MOURNING, 4
clenched You cannot shake hands with a c. fist   INFLEXIBILITY, 1
Cleopatra Had C.'s nose been shorter   APPEARANCE, 14
clergy c. are men   CLERGY, 3
I never saw...the c. were beloved in any nation   CLERGY, 7; SWIFT, 9
clergyman c. whose mendicity is only equalled by their mendacity   CLERGY, 8
good enough to be a c.   CLERGY, 5
clerk diplomatic history is...what one c. said to another c.
    HISTORY, 14
C. ther was of Oxenford also   CHAUCER, 3
clever It's c., but is it art   ART, 7; KIPLING, 2
never wise to try to appear...more c.   WISDOM, 12
no use trying to be c.   ACADEMICS, 3
To be c. enough to get...money, one must be stupid
    CHESTERTON, 12; MATERIALISM, 4
cleverness height of c. is...to conceal it   ROCHEFOUCAULD, 8
cliché The c. is dead poetry   LANGUAGE, 1
climate common where the c.'s sultry   ADULTERY, 1; BYRON, 7
If it's heaven for c.   PERVERSITY, 1
clock Stands the Church c. at ten to three   NOSTALGIA, 3
Rock Around the C.   POP MUSIC, 6
cloke knyf under the c.   CHAUCER, 5; HYPOCRISY, 2
Clootie Satan, Nick, or C.   BURNS, 2; DEVIL, 4
close a breathless hush in the C. tonight   CRICKET, 3
closed Mankind is a c. society   MANKIND, 11
the transition from the...'c. society',...to the 'open society'
    SOCIETY, 3
close-up Life is a tragedy...in c.   LIFE, 9
clothes After that you just take the girl's c. off   ALCOHOL, 9
Fine c. are good   CLOTHES, 6; JOHNSON, 27
hanging the baby on the c. line to dry   INNOVATION, 2
Have you ever taken anything out of the c. basket   CLEANNESS, 3
if it be our c. alone which fit us for society   CLOTHES, 3
No woman so naked as...underneath her c.   NAKEDNESS, 2
Put off your shame with your c.   MODESTY, 5
wrapped him in swaddling c.   CHRISTMAS, 2
cloud I wandered lonely as a c.   FLOWERS, 9; WORDSWORTH, 4
clouds But trailing c. of glory   METAPHYSICS, 4
c. that gather round the setting sun   MORTALITY, 12; WORDSWORTH, 13
clover Bennett – a sort of pig in c.   BENNETT, 1
clown I remain just one thing...and that is a c.   HUMOUR, 4
club Mankind is a c.   MANKIND, 5
the best c. in London   DICKENS, 13
Clyde the bonny banks of C.   SCOTLAND, 4
CMG Members rise from C.   TITLES, 3
coals heap c. of fire upon his head   RETRIBUTION, 5
coaster Dirty British c.   BOATS, 8
cobwebs Laws are like c.   SWIFT, 10
coca colas Instead of drinking C.   WATER, 2
cocaine C. isn't habit-forming   ADDICTION, 1
cock He was like a c.   ELIOT, 2
we owe a c. to Aesculapius   LAST WORDS, 27
cockroach to choose between him and a c. as a companion
    INSULTS, 22
cod The home of the bean and the c.   SNOBBERY, 2
codfish Unlike the male c....the British aristocracy is
    ARISTOCRACY, 12; WODEHOUSE, 10
coffee C. which makes the politician wise   DRINKS, 3

cogito *C., ergo sum* THINKING, 1
coil shuffled off this mortal c. SHAKESPEARE, 36; SUICIDE, 7
cold blow hot and c. with the same breath INDECISION, 1
C. Pastoral ETERNITY, 3
I beg c. comfort COMFORT, 1
The Irish…are needed in this c. age IRISH, 2
we are…in the midst of a c. war COLD WAR, 1
coldly c. she turns from their gaze, and weeps MOURNING, 5
Coliseum While stands the C., Rome shall stand BYRON, 5
collapse Russia is a c., not a revolution RUSSIA, 3
collapses Force…c. through its own mass JUDGMENT, 7
collections those mutilators of c. BORROWING, 3; LAMB, 5
collective the greatest c. work of science SCIENCE, 2
college I am Master of this c. ACADEMICS, 2
Like so many ageing c. people ACADEMICS, 4
colonel The gatling's jammed and the c. dead WAR, 41
colonnade whispering sound of the cool c. TREES, 3
colour an incurable disease – c. blindness RACISM, 4
Any c., so long as it's black CHOICE, 1
come 'Cannot c., lie follows' PROUST, 8
C. what c. may TIME, 13
Mr Watson, c. here; I want you SUMMONS, 2
Thou'lt c. no more MOURNING, 6
Whistle and she'll c. to you SUMMONS, 1
Why don't you c. up sometime MISQUOTATIONS, 15; WEST, 7
Will ye no c. back again RETURN, 2
comedian A c. can only last HUMOUR, 15
comedies c. are ended by a marriage BYRON, 9
comedy at a c. we only look HUXLEY, 8; THEATRE, 6
C. is if I walk into an open sewer and die THEATRE, 2
C., we may say, is society HUMOUR, 14
Farce refined becomes high c. THEATRE, 5
Life is…a c. in long-shot LIFE, 9
comfort carrion c., Despair, not feast on thee DESPAIR, 2
From ignorance our c. flows IGNORANCE, 4
I beg cold c. COMFORT, 1
thought of suicide is a great…c. NIETZSCHE, 8; SUICIDE, 3
Two loves I have, of c. and despair CONFLICT, 4
comic first c. genius…in Downing Street DISRAELI, 1
comic-strip all the one-dimensional subtlety of a c. THATCHER, 8
coming C. through the rye BURNS, 4
he…c. after me is preferred before me CHRISTIANITY, 4
command mortals to c. success ADDISON, 2
one of those born neither to obey nor to c. NASTINESS, 3
commas absence of inverted c. guarantees…originality QUOTATIONS, 2
commend into thy hands I c. my spirit LAST WORDS, 6
commended The man who gets angry…in the right way…is c. ANGER, 1
commendeth obliquely c. himself CRITICISM, 4
comment C. is free but facts are sacred JOURNALISM, 15
commerce Friendship is a disinterested c. between equals GOLDSMITH, 10; LOVE AND FRIENDSHIP, 1
honour sinks where c. long prevails BUSINESS, 6
commercing looks c. with the skies SOUL, 6
commission A Royal C. is a broody hen BUREAUCRACY, 4
Each bullet has got its c. MORTALITY, 5
committee A c. is a cul-de-sac BUREAUCRACY, 2
The number one book…was written by a c. BIBLE, 6
commodity C., Firmness, and Delight ARCHITECTURE, 9
common C. sense is the collection of prejudices EINSTEIN, 5; PREJUDICE, 2
good thing, to make it too c. ENGLAND, 21
He nothing c. did or mean EXECUTION, 8
lose the c. touch IDEALISM, 1; KIPLING, 4
Mrs Thatcher is a woman of c. views THATCHER, 1
seldom attribute c. sense AGREEMENT, 2; ROCHEFOUCAULD, 11
the happiness of the c. man GOVERNMENT, 3
'Tis education forms the c. mind EDUCATION, 22; POPE, 13
trained and organized c. sense SCIENCE, 11
common-looking The Lord prefers c. people APPEARANCE, 10
commonplace nothing so unnatural as the c. DOYLE, 3
unassuming c. /Of Nature WORDSWORTH, 23
commonplaces c. are the great poetic truths STEVENSON, 15; TRIVIALITY, 6
Commonwealth a C. of Nations BRITISH EMPIRE, 5
communism arrested under the Suppression of C. Act OPPRESSION, 2
C. continued to haunt Europe as a spectre COMMUNISM, 5
C. is like prohibition COMMUNISM, 3
C. is Soviet power plus the electrification COMMUNISM, 2

For us in Russia c. is a dead dog COMMUNISM, 4
communist Every c. has a fascist frown FASCISM, 3
communists Catholics and C. have committed great crimes COMMITMENT, 2
In Germany, the Nazis came for the C. NAZISM, 3
community journalism…keeps us in touch with the ignorance of the c. JOURNALISM, 18; WILDE, 9
Marriage…a c….making in all two MARRIAGE, 14
the c. of Europe EUROPE, 4
compact the damned, c., liberal majority MAJORITY, 2
companion to choose between him and a cockroach as a c. INSULTS, 22
companionable so c. as solitude SOLITUDE, 10
companions Boys…are unwholesome c. for grown people LAMB, 3
c. for middle age MARRIAGE, 5
company better to be alone than in bad c. FRIENDS, 10
find myself in the c. of scientists SCIENTISTS, 1
I've been offered titles,…get one into disreputable c. SHAW, 23
Take the tone of the c. CONFORMITY, 2
Tell me what c. thou keepest CERVANTES, 11; FRIENDS, 3
comparative progress is simply a c. PROGRESS, 3
compare c. thee to a summer's day COMPLIMENTS, 3; SHAKESPEARE, 106
Learn, c., collect the facts EDUCATION, 21
compared The war we have just been through,…is not to be c. WAR, 70
comparisons C. are odorous MALAPROPISMS, 2; SHAKESPEARE, 87
compass my heart shall be /The faithful c. FAITHFULNESS, 4
compassion But a certain Samaritan…had c. on him CHARITY, 5
competition happiest conversation where there is no c. CONVERSATION, 2
complacency c. and satisfaction…in…a new-married couple MARRIAGE, 37
complain one hardly knows to whom to c. COMPLAINTS, 2
complaints The imaginary c. of indestructible old ladies HYPOCHONDRIA, 2
complex Wherever an inferiority c. exists, there is…reason INFERIORITY, 1
compliance by a timely c. SEX, 13
compliment returned the c. GOD, 34; VOLTAIRE, 13
composer A good c. does not imitate MUSICIANS, 5
comprehended c. two auspicious persons MALAPROPISMS, 1
compromise All government…is founded on c. and barter BURKE, 8; COMPROMISE, 2
C. used to mean that half a loaf CHESTERTON, 19; COMPROMISE, 3
compulsion seized by the stern hand of C. THURBER, 2
computers so many c….use them in the search for love CRITICISM, 17
comrade stepping where his c. stood COURAGE, 9; SCOTT, 6
comrades Bleach the bones of c. slain WAR, 25
conceal Addresses…c. our whereabouts SAKI, 2
height of cleverness is…to c. it ROCHEFOUCAULD, 8
speech only to c. their thoughts VOLTAIRE, 8
concealed Much truth is spoken,…more…c. TRUTH, 8
concealing Good breeding consists in c. how…we think of ourselves TWAIN, 11
concealment c., like a worm i' th' bud LOVE, 59; SHAKESPEARE, 118
conceit C. is the finest armour CONCEIT, 5
conceited I would grow intolerably c. WHISTLER, 6
what man will do any good who is not c. TROLLOPE, 5
concepts walks up the stairs of his c. MANKIND, 15
concessions The c. of the weak are the c. of fear YIELDING, 1
conclusions Life is the art of drawing…c. LIFE, 8
concord toleration produced…religious c. GIBBON, 4
condemn No man can justly censure or c. another JUDGMENT, 4
condemned If God were suddenly c. to live the life HUMAN CONDITION, 2
Man is c. to be free FREEDOM, 24; SARTRE, 2
condemning One should examine oneself…before…c. others SELF, 6
condition fools decoyed into our c. MARRIAGE, 46
The c. of man…is a c. of war HUMAN CONDITION, 5
the c. of our sex is so deplorable that it is our duty…to break the law PANKHURST, 6
the Jews have made a contribution to the human c. JEWS, 10
To be a poet is a c. POETS, 5
wearisome c. of humanity HUMAN CONDITION, 4
conditioned Americans have been c. to respect newness AMERICANS, 8
condoms rarely wear c. AIDS, 5

coughing keeping people from c.   ACTING, 6
council The grotesque chaos of a Labour c.   INCOMPETENCE, 2
counsel sometimes c. take – and sometimes Tea   DRINKS, 4
count To give and not to c. the cost   SELFLESSNESS, 2
countenance the Lord lift up his c. upon thee   BLESSING, 4
counter-democratic Proportional Representation…is fundamentally c.   POLITICS, 29
counties see the coloured c.   COUNTRYSIDE, 4
countries preferreth all c. before his own   DISCONTENT, 5
country a c. diversion   CONGREVE, 10
a c. of young men   AMERICA, 9
A man should know something of his own c.   TRAVEL, 14
an honest man sent to lie abroad for…his c.   DIPLOMACY, 11
Anyone who loves his c., follow me   PATRIOTISM, 6
c. from whose bourn no traveller returns   AFTERLIFE, 8
God made the c.   COUNTRYSIDE, 1; COWPER, 9
Great artists have no c.   NATIONALITY, 3
I have but one life to lose for my c.   PATRIOTISM, 7
I would die for my c.   PATRIOTISM, 11
loathe the c.   CONGREVE, 10
My c., right or wrong   PATRIOTISM, 4
Patriots…talk of dying for their c.   RUSSELL, 15
proud of the position of the bungalow,…in the c.   SUBURBIA, 2
That is no c. for old men   MORTALITY, 14
The idiot who praises…every c. but his own   DISCONTENT, 2
The past is a foreign c.   PAST, 3
The soil of our c.   RACISM, 9
The undiscover'd c.   AFTERLIFE, 8
This c.…belongs to the people who inhabit it   DEMOCRACY, 5
to leave his c. as good as he had found it   DUTY, 1
understanding the problems of running a c.   POLITICS, 44
we can die but once to serve our c.   ADDISON, 4; PATRIOTISM, 1
When I am in the c. I wish to vegetate   COUNTRYSIDE, 3
countryside a more dreadful record of sin than…c.   DOYLE, 4; SIN, 8
courage be strong and of a good c.   GOD, 5
C. is the price…for granting peace   COURAGE, 4
c. to love…courage to suffer   LOVE, 66
good deal of physical c. to ride a horse   HORSES, 4
In c. and honor   ANTHONY, 1
tale…of…c. of my companions   ENDURANCE, 7
three o'clock in the morning c.   COURAGE, 15
Whistling aloud to bear his c. up   WHISTLING, 1
course c. of true love never did run smooth   LOVE, 56; SHAKESPEARE, 84
courteous If a man be…c. to strangers   COURTESY, 1
courtesy C. is not dead   COURTESY, 2
courting When you are a c. a nice girl   SCIENCE, 6
covet thou shalt not c.   GOD, 6
cow The c. is of the bovine ilk   NASH, 1
till the c. comes home   ETERNITY, 1
coward better to be the widow of a hero than the wife of a c.   COURAGE, 1
Conscience is a c.   GOLDSMITH, 13
No c. soul is mine   BRONTË, 2
None but a c.…has never known fear   COWARDICE, 1
The c. does it with a kiss   KILLING, 5; WILDE, 3
cowardly Marriage is the only adventure open to the c.   MARRIAGE, 63; VOLTAIRE, 21
cowards C. die many times   COWARDICE, 3; SHAKESPEARE, 54
Thus conscience does make c. of us all   CONSCIENCE, 2
cows 'Horses' should have read 'C.'   MISTAKES, 3
coyness This c., lady, were no crime   SHYNESS, 3
compassion C. is not a sloppy, sentimental feeling   SOCIALISM, 4
cracked The c. looking glass of a servant   IRELAND, 5
cradle The hand that rocks the c.   INFLUENCE, 4
cradles bit the babies in the c.   BROWNING, 12
craft the c. so long to lerne   MORTALITY, 2
The life so short, the c. so long to learn   MORTALITY, 7
craftsmanship Skill without imagination is c.   ART, 17
cranny We seek…In every c. but the right   COWPER, 8
crap Books are a load of c.   BOOKS, 14
crazy going to go c., living this epidemic every minute   DISEASE, 13
created God c.…the earth   CREATION, 1
we cannot be c. for this sort of suffering   AFTERLIFE, 5
creation Had I been present at the C.   UNIVERSE, 1
creator Man…hasn't been a c., only a destroyer   ECOLOGY, 1
creature the c. hath a purpose and its eyes are bright with it   PURPOSE, 3
Who kills a man kills a reasonable c.   BOOKS, 17
credentials no c.…not even…a certificate of birth   ARISTOCRACY, 8

credit The way to get things done is not to mind who gets the c.   SELFLESSNESS, 1
creed got the better of his c.   RELIGION, 29
creeds Vain are the thousand c.   BELIEF, 1
creep Wit that can c.   SERVILITY, 3
Crete The people of C.…make more history   SAKI, 4
cricket c. as organised loafing   CRICKET, 5
c. is the greatest thing that God ever created   CRICKET, 4
I do love c. – it's so very English   CRICKET, 1
If the French noblesse had been capable of playing c. with their peasants   ARISTOCRACY, 11; CRICKET, 6
It's not in support of c.   GOLF, 1
crieth thy brother's blood c. unto me   MURDER, 1
crime all c. is due to the repressed desire for aesthetic expression   WAUGH, 11
Arson, after all, is an artificial c.   WELLS, 6
C., like virtue, has its degrees   CRIME, 3
If poverty is the mother of c., stupidity is its father   CRIME, 2; LA BRUYERE, 5
man's greatest c.   BIRTH, 2
no…c. so shameful as poverty   POVERTY, 3
The punishment fit the c.   PUNISHMENT, 6
This coyness, lady, were no c.   SHYNESS, 3
Treason was no C.   TREASON, 2
crimes Catholics and Communists have committed great c.   COMMITMENT, 2
history…a tableau of c. and misfortunes   HISTORY, 16
Oh liberty!…What c. are committed in thy name   EXECUTION, 12; FREEDOM, 21
Crippen strong suspicions that C. London cellar murderer   TELEGRAMS, 6
crisp Deep and c. and even   CHRISTMAS, 12
critic A c. is a man who   CRITICS, 13
A good c.…narrates the adventures of his mind   CRITICS, 4
A good drama c. is   CRITICS, 14
c. spits on what is done   CRITICS, 7
Nor in the c. let the man be lost   CRITICS, 11
the function of the c.   CRITICS, 1
critical c. judgement is so exquisite   CRITICS, 5
nothing if not c.   CRITICISM, 15
criticism A great deal of contemporary c.   CHESTERTON, 1; CRITICISM, 5
As far as c. is concerned   CRITICISM, 16
my own definition of c.   CRITICISM, 1
People ask you for c.   CRITICISM, 10
The Stealthy School of C.   CRITICISM, 14
criticize don't c. /What you can't understand   CHANGE, 5; DYLAN, 4
criticizing The pleasure of c.   CRITICISM, 9
critics Asking a working writer…about c.   CRITICS, 2
c. all are ready made   CRITICS, 2
C. are more malicious about poetry   CRITICS, 8
c.…desire our blood, not our pain   CRITICS, 10
The greater part of c. are parasites   CRITICS, 12
crocodile An appeaser is one who feeds a c.   DIPLOMACY, 4
Cromwell Caesar had his Brutus – Charles the First, his C.   TREASON, 4
crony government by c.   NEPOTISM, 1
crook the symbol of a bishop is a c.   CLERGY, 2
crooked the c. timber of humanity   HUMAN NATURE, 8
crop watering the last year's c.   ELIOT, 1
crops Man…/Laid the c. low   THOMAS, 8
cross no c., no crown   ENDURANCE, 6
The orgasm has replaced the C.   SEX, 24
When I survey the wondrous C.   HUMILITY, 6
crossed a girl likes to be c. in love a little now and then   WOMEN, 3
crosses wooden c. on the roadside   WORLD WAR I, 8
crossroads mankind faces a c.   PESSIMISM, 1
crossword an optimist…fills up his c. puzzle in ink   OPTIMISM, 8
crow sun had risen to hear him c.   ELIOT, 2
crowd And hid his face amid a c. of stars   LOVE, 71
Far from the madding c.   SOLITUDE, 5
crowds If you can talk with c. and keep your virtue   IDEALISM, 1; KIPLING, 4
crown no cross, no c.   ENDURANCE, 6
the c. of life   TEMPTATION, 2
Uneasy lies the head that wears a c.   MONARCHY, 10; SHAKESPEARE, 44
within the hollow c.   ROYALTY, 15; SHAKESPEARE, 98
crucible America is God's C.   AMERICA, 23
crucify Diseases c. the soul of man   DISEASE, 7
Do you want to c. the boy   GOLDWYNISMS, 28
cruel A c. story runs on wheels   CRUELTY, 4
C., but composed and bland   ARNOLD, 13; CATS, 1

cruelty Fear is the parent of c.   CRUELTY, 2
crumbs c. which fell from the rich man's table
    POVERTY AND WEALTH, 2
cry I often want to c.   SEXES, 11
  mother, do not c.   LAST WORDS, 12
  She likes stories that make her c.   SENTIMENTALITY, 3
  the c. of him that ruleth among fools   WISDOM, 2
  the only advantage women have over men –...they can c.   SEXES, 11
  We think caged birds sing, when indeed they c.   IMPRISONMENT, 4
  when we c. to Thee   SEA, 7
cuckoo the c. clock was invented...to give tourists something solid   SWITZERLAND, 1
  This is the weather the c. likes   WEATHER, 3
cucumbers they are but c. after all   JOHNSON, 35
cul-de-sac A committee is a c.   BUREAUCRACY, 2
cult local c. called Christianity   CHRISTIANITY, 15
cultivate c. our garden   VOLTAIRE, 6
culture C. is the passion for sweetness and light   CULTURE, 2
  C., the acquainting ourselves with the best   ARNOLD, 10; CULTURE, 1
  two half-cultures do not make a c.   HALF MEASURES, 1
  When I hear anyone talk of C.   PHILISTINISM, 3
  You can lead a whore to c.   PARKER, 10; PUNS, 10
cup tak a c. o' kindness yet   FRIENDSHIP, 4
Cupid wing'd C. painted blind   LOVE, 57; SHAKESPEARE, 85
curates abundant shower of c.   BRONTË, 5
cur'd C....of my disease   DOCTORS, 5
cure C. the disease   DISEASE, 4; REMEDIES, 1
  Show me a sane man and I will c. him for you   MADNESS, 3
  the c. for admiring the House of Lords   HOUSES OF PARLIAMENT, 3
  There are maladies we must not seek to c.   REMEDIES, 7
  Work is the grand c.   WORK, 3
cured the only disease you don't look forward to being c. of   DEATH, 41
curfew The C. tolls the knell of parting day   DAY, 4
curiosity C. will conquer fear   CURIOSITY, 4
  Disinterested intellectual c....life blood of...civilisation   CURIOSITY, 5
curious Be not c. in unnecessary matters   CURIOSITY, 1
  'That was the c. incident,' remarked...Holmes   DOYLE, 5
curiouser C. and curiouser   CONFUSION, 2
curse A c. is on her if she stay   CURSES, 4
  Christianity the one great c.   CHRISTIANITY, 20
  The c. is come upon me   CURSES, 3; TENNYSON, 18
  Work is the c. of the drinking classes   WILDE, 41
cursed thou art c. above all cattle   SEXES, 1
curses C....always come home to roost   CURSES, 2
curtain An iron c.   CHURCHILL, 30; COLD WAR, 2
  iron c.   CHURCHILL, 30
  Ring down the c.   LAST WORDS, 24
custodiet Quis c. ipsos /custodes   MISTRUST, 3
custom A c. loathsome to the eye, hateful to the nose   SMOKING, 5
  C. calls me to't   CUSTOM, 3
  c. /More honour'd in the breach than the observance   SHAKESPEARE, 30
  c. stale /Her infinite variety   ADMIRATION, 5
  C., then, is the great guide of human life   CUSTOM, 2
customer The c. is always right   BUSINESS, 10
cut c. to the heart   ANGER, 2
  the human pack is shuffled and c.   EDUCATION, 15
cuts he that c. off twenty years of life   DEATH, 51
cutting busy driving cabs and c. hair   GOVERNMENT, 4
cycles the same opinions have arisen among men in c.   OPINIONS, 1
cymbal a tinkling c.   CHARITY, 4
Cynara faithful to thee, C.   FAITHFULNESS, 3
cynic c. is a man who   CYNICISM, 4
cynicism C. is an unpleasant way of saying the truth   CYNICISM, 1
  C. is humour in ill-health   CYNICISM, 4; WELLS, 8
dad They fuck you up, your mum and d.   FAMILY, 11
Daddy D. wouldn't buy me a bow-wow   DOGS, 7
daffodils Fair d., we weep to see   TRANSIENCE, 9
  host, of golden d.   FLOWERS, 9; WORDSWORTH, 4
  I never saw d. so beautiful   FLOWERS, 8
dainty Nothing's so d. sweet   MELANCHOLY, 1
Daisy D., give me your answer, do   MARRIAGE, 22
dalliance primrose path of d.   EXAMPLE, 5; SHAKESPEARE, 28
damage nothing which might d. his career   SCOTS, 1
dame La belle D. sans Merci   SUPERNATURAL, 6
damn D. the age. I'll write for antiquity   POSTERITY, 1
  D. with faint praise   CRITICISM, 13; POPE, 5
  D. you, England. You're rotting   ENGLAND, 17
  The public doesn't give a d.   MUSIC, 3
damnation the terminal point of addiction is...d.   AUDEN, 4; SIN, 2

damned d. good-natured friend   SHERIDAN, 2
  d. if you do – And...damned if you don't   DAMNATION, 1
  Life is just one d. thing after another   LIFE, 12
  Publish and be d.   PUBLISHING, 5; WELLINGTON, 15
damner He is your only good d.   HAZLITT, 1
Danaos timeo D. et dona ferentis   MISTRUST, 6; VIRGIL, 5
dandy Arnold is a d. Isaiah   ARNOLD, 2
  d....lies in acting well   EXCELLENCE, 2
  development of industry has created many new sources of d.   DISEASE, 22
  I realized there was a measure of d.   DANGER, 3
  Oft in d., oft in woe   ENDURANCE, 13
  the only real d. that exists is man himself   HUMAN NATURE, 7
  when we conquer without d.   VICTORY, 3
dangerous A little learning is a d. thing   POPE, 7
  He thinks too much. Such men are d.   MISTRUST, 4; SHAKESPEARE, 53
  If a little knowledge is d., where is the man...out of danger   KNOWLEDGE, 9
  if a little knowledge was a d. thing   KNOWLEDGE, 17
  more d. the abuse   BURKE, 15; POWER, 4
  What is d. about the tranquilliser   DRUGS, 5
dangerously live d.   DANGER, 4; NIETZSCHE, 5
dangers D. by being despised   DANGER, 2
daring d. to excel   EXCELLENCE, 2
dark A blind man in a d. room   METAPHYSICS, 1
  children fear...the d.   DEATH, 7
  O d., d., d., amid the blaze of noon   BLINDNESS, 3
  slow, sure doom falls pitiless and d.   HUMAN CONDITION, 7
  The d. night of the soul   SOUL, 5
  we are for the d.   ENDING, 3
darken 'Never d. my Dior again   MANNERS, 3
  never d. my towels again   DISMISSAL, 3
darkling as on a d. plain   WAR, 1
  D. I listen   DEATH, 34
darkly through a glass, d.   CHARITY, 4
darkness Before us pass'd the door of D.   DEATH, 15
  d. was upon the face of the deep   CREATION, 1
  men loved d....because their deeds were evil   EVIL, 5
  The d. falls at Thy behest   DAY, 3
darling Thrice welcome, d. of the spring   WORDSWORTH, 22
daughter as is the mother, so is her d.   FAMILY, 4
  d. of Earth and Water   SHELLEY, 4
  Don't put your d. on the stage   COWARD, 8; THEATRE, 4
  Dwelt a miner, Forty-niner, /And his d., Clementine   MOURNING, 4
daughters Words are men's d.   WORDS, 8
dauntless faithful in love,...d. in war   SCOTT, 5
David's Once in royal D. city   CHRISTMAS, 2
dawn a grey d. breaking   SEA, 5
  Bliss was it in that d. to be alive   FRENCH REVOLUTION, 3; WORDSWORTH, 14
dawned each day that has d. is your last   PRESENT, 5
day As I was saying the other d.   INTERRUPTIONS, 1
  compare thee to a summer's d.   COMPLIMENTS, 3; SHAKESPEARE, 106
  count as profit every d. that Fate allows you   PRESENT, 4
  Drop...what tomorrow may bring...count as profit every d. that Fate allows you   HORACE, 9
  each d. is like a year   IMPRISONMENT, 6
  each d. that has dawned is your last   PRESENT, 5
  every dog has his d.   SATISFACTION, 1
  from this d. forward   MARRIAGE, 15
  God called the light D.   CREATION, 1
  Good morning to the d.: and, next, my gold   MATERIALISM, 7
  I look upon every d. to be lost   JOHNSON, 39
  in the d. of judgement   DEATH, 14
  It takes place every d.   DOOMSDAY, 3
  Live this d., as...thy last   PRESENT, 6
  long d.'s task is done   REST, 1
  Now the d. is over   DAY, 1
  Seize the d.   HORACE, 10; PRESENT, 4
  So foul and fair a d.   SHAKESPEARE, 68; WEATHER, 10
  Stay, stay, /Until the hasting d. /Has run   TRANSIENCE, 4
  Sweet d., so cool, so calm   DAY, 5
  The bright d. is done   ENDING, 3
  The d. begins to droop   DAY, 2
  the twenty-four hour d.   BEERBOHM, 5
  thou knowest not what a d. may bring forth   FUTURE, 3
  Without all hope of d.   BLINDNESS, 3
Dayrolles Give D. a chair   CHESTERFIELD, 14
days D. and moments quickly flying   DEATH, 16
  d. of wine and roses   TRANSIENCE, 7

deeds better d. shall be in water writ — MEMORIALS, 2
The bitterest tears...are for words...unsaid and d....undone
— REGRET, 11
deep beauty is only sin d. — BEAUTY, 18; SAKI, 15
D. and crisp and even — CHRISTMAS, 12
deeper d. than did ever plummet sound — RENUNCIATION, 2
deeth D. is an ende of every worldly sore — LIFE AND DEATH, 3
defeat a d. without a war — WORLD WAR II, 2
D. of Germany means — WORLD WAR II, 20
every victory turns into a d. — BEAUVOIR, 3; DISILLUSION, 2
In d. unbeatable — OFFICERS, 3
defeated man can be destroyed...not d. — DEFEAT, 3; HEMINGWAY, 3
defect Chief D. of Henry King — BELLOC, 3
defence The only d. is in offence — WAR, 2
Truth telling is not compatible with the d. of the realm — TRUTH, 18
defend I disapprove of what you say, but I will d. to the death your
right to say it — FREEDOM, 27; VOLTAIRE, 30
defense d. effort in terms of defending women — WAR, 57
deferential Civil Service is profoundly d. — POLITICS, 16
deferred long d. and often wished for — BRONTË, 2
defiance in defeat, a — CHURCHILL, 12; WAR AND PEACE, 3
The d. of established authority — REBELLION, 1
defining Language is...a d. framework — LANGUAGE, 21
definition Science fiction is the search for a d. of mankind
— SCIENCE FICTION, 2
defying by d. their parents and copying one another — YOUTH, 4
degeneration fatty d. of his moral being — STEVENSON, 13
degradation a...sense of intellectual d. after an interview with a
doctor — DOCTORS, 3
degree d. of delight — BURKE, 4
degrees Crime, like virtue, has its d. — CRIME, 3
deid Gey few, and they're a' d. — INDIVIDUALITY, 1
deities the d. so kindly — DESTINY, 8; RABELAIS, 3
deity doubted the existence of the D. — SCIENTISTS, 5
to distinguish between the D. and the Drains — GOD, 31
deleted D. by French censor — NEWSPAPERS, 1
deliberates woman that d. is lost — ADDISON, 3
deliberation D. is the work of many men — ACTION, 3
delicacy the talent of flattering with d. — FLATTERY, 1
delicate Young ladies are d. plants — HEALTH AND HEALTHY LIVING, 1
delight a degree of d. — BURKE, 4
Commodity, Firmness, and D. — ARCHITECTURE, 9
go to't with d. — ENTHUSIASM, 4
Studies serve for d. — EDUCATION, 2
The leaping light for your d. discovers — DISCOVERY, 2
very temple of d. — MELANCHOLY, 4
delighted Whosoever is d. in solitude — SOLITUDE, 1
delightful make his conversation perfectly d. — SMITH, 4
delights Man d. not me — MANKIND, 13; SHAKESPEARE, 35
deliver d. me from myself — SELF, 1
delusion he who can analyze his d. is called a philosopher
— PHILOSOPHERS, 1
delusive Decades have a d. edge — CLASSIFICATION, 2
demands the populace cannot exact their d.
— HOUSES OF PARLIAMENT, 11
democracy D....government by the uneducated
— ARISTOCRACY, 5; CHESTERTON, 21
D. is only an experiment in government — DEMOCRACY, 3
D. passes into despotism — DEMOCRACY, 7
extreme d. or absolute oligarchy...will come — GOVERNMENT, 2
grieved under a d., call it *anarchy* — GOVERNMENT, 8
In Switzerland they had...five hundred years of d. and peace
— SWITZERLAND, 3
Man's capacity for evil makes d. necessary — DEMOCRACY, 6
world...made safe for d. — DEMOCRACY, 9
democratic the ideal of a d. and free society — RACISM, 10
demons thanks to words, we have often sunk to the level of the d.
— HUXLEY, 3
denial the highest praise of God consists in the d. of Him
— ATHEISM, 5; PROUST, 5
Denmark rotten in the state of D. — CORRUPTION, 6
denounce We thus d....the arms race — NUCLEAR WEAPONS, 5
dentist fuss about sleeping together...sooner go to my d.
— SEX, 36; WAUGH, 10
dentists gratitude to most benefactors is the same as...for d.
— INGRATITUDE, 2
The thought of d. gave him just the same sick horror — WELLS, 4
deny let him d. himself — CHRISTIANITY, 10
Those who d. freedom — FREEDOM, 15
depart D.,...and let us have done with you — DISMISSAL, 1
depends It all d. upon that article there — WELLINGTON, 2

depraved No one...suddenly became d. — DEBAUCHERY, 2
depression Recession...a neighbour loses...d....you lose
— ECONOMICS, 10
derangement a nice d. of epitaphs — MALAPROPISMS, 6; SHERIDAN, 5
derision Ambition, Distraction, Uglification, and D.. — CARROLL, 7
description beggar'd all d. — SHAKESPEARE, 14
desert The sand of the d. is sodden red — WAR, 41
Use every man after his d. — MERIT, 2
deserts D. of vast eternity — AGE, 26
deserved I wasn't lucky. I d. it — MERIT, 3
deserves At 50, everyone has the face he d. — AGE, 20; ORWELL, 16
the government it d. — GOVERNMENT, 9
desire antidote to d. — DESIRE, 4
a universal innate d. — EXTRAVAGANCE, 2; PROGRESS, 2
d. is got without content — CONTENTMENT, 5
D. is the very essence of man — DESIRE, 7
d. should so many years outlive performance — SEX, 30
d. to be praised twice over — PRAISE, 5; ROCHEFOUCAULD, 6
It provokes the d. — ALCOHOL, 30; SHAKESPEARE, 72
nothing like d. for preventing the thing one says — DESIRE, 5
to have few things to d. — FEAR, 1
to lose your heart's d. — DESIRE, 6; SHAW, 13
The D. of Man being Infinite — INFINITY, 1
Those who restrain D. — DESIRE, 1
desires than nurse unacted d. — BLAKE, 15; DESIRE, 2
Man's D. are limited by his Perceptions
— BLAKE, 25; DESIRE, 3; PERCEPTION, 2
desiring pessimists end up by d. the things they fear — PESSIMISM, 5
desks Stick...to your d. and never go to sea — GILBERT, 2; OFFICERS, 5
despair carrion comfort, D., not feast on thee — DESPAIR, 2
Don't, not even over...d. — DESPAIR, 4
Patience, n. A minor form of d. — PATIENCE, 1
desperation lives of quiet d. — DESPAIR, 4
despise some other Englishman d. him — ENGLISH, 16; SHAW, 20
despised A poor man is d. the whole world over — POVERTY, 11
despises A woman d. a man for loving her — LOVE, 61
despotism Democracy passes into d. — DEMOCRACY, 7
extreme democracy or absolute oligarchy or d. will come
— GOVERNMENT, 2
France was a long d. — CARLYLE, 9; FRANCE, 2
destiny I were walking with d. — DESTINY, 1
Riddle of d. — PURPOSE, 2
destroy Man...builds machines to d. — WORLD WAR I, 8
whom God wishes to d. — MADNESS, 1
Whom the gods wish to d. — TALENT, 1
destroy'd a bold peasantry,.../When once d. — GOLDSMITH, 5; PUBLIC, 8
destroyed man can be d....not defeated — DEFEAT, 3; HEMINGWAY, 3
destroyer Man...hasn't been a creator, only a d. — ECOLOGY, 3
destroying simplifying something by d. nearly everything
— CHESTERTON, 2
destroys he who d. a good book, kills reason — BOOKS, 17
destruction one purpose....d. of Hitler — HITLER, 2
detail life is frittered away by d. — SIMPLICITY, 5
detective The d. novel is — NOVELS, 5
detest they d. at leisure — BYRON, 14; LOVE AND HATE, 1
detested D. sport — HUNTING, 1
Deutschland D., D. *über alles* — GERMANY, 1
device A banner with the strange d., /Excelsior — AMBITION, 5
devil Abashed the d....felt how awful goodness is — GOOD, 3
D. always builds a chapel there — DEVIL, 5
d. can cite Scripture — QUOTATIONS, 6
given up believing in the d. — DEVIL, 6
God-like in giving, but the d. to pay — SHERIDAN, 1
I do not see...why the d. should have all the good tunes — MUSIC, 13
nickname is the heaviest stone that the d. can throw — NAMES, 1
Renounce the d. — RENUNCIATION, 1
Sarcasm...the language of the d. — SARCASM, 1
The D. is a gentleman — DEVIL, 7; SHELLEY, 10
the d. played at chess with me — EXPLOITATION, 1
devilish eyes flamed red with d. passion — SUPERNATURAL, 14
devils It is no good casting out d. — LAWRENCE, 14
devotion The almighty dollar...object of universal d. — MATERIALISM, 6
diagram cat is a d. and pattern of subtle air — CATS, 4
dialect D. words – those terrible marks of the beast — CLASS, 7
diamond D.! D. — ACCIDENTS, 1
diamonds D. Are — MATERIALISM, 10
My goodness those d. are lovely — GOOD, 8; WEST, 4
to give him d. back — MATERIALISM, 8
diaries Let d, therefore — DIARIES, 1
Only good girls keep d. — DIARIES, 2
diary I never travel without my d. — WILDE, 17

To write a d....returning to one's own vomit — DIARIES, 3
What is a d. as a rule — DIARIES, 4
dictation God wrote it. I merely did his d. — INSPIRATION, 3
dictator and finally a single d. substitutes himself — COMMUNISM, 6
I am painted as the greatest little d. — THATCHER, 8
I believe in benevolent dictatorship provided I am the d. — LEADERSHIP, 3
dictators D. ride to and fro upon tigers — AUTHORITARIANISM, 3
dictatorship D. of the proletariat — MARXISM, 3
dictionaries To make a d. is dull work — LEXICOGRAPHY, 2
dictionary The responsibility of a d. — LEXICOGRAPHY, 1
die better to d. on your feet than to live on your knees — SELF-RESPECT, 1
but to do and d. — TENNYSON, 5
D....the last thing I shall do — LAST WORDS, 22
either do, or d. — ACTION, 2
I am ready to d. for my Lord — LAST WORDS, 4
I d. a Christian — EXECUTION, 3
I d. because I do not d. — DEATH, 31
If I d. today every drop of my blood — LAST WORDS, 13
If I should d. — WAR, 10
in what peace a Christian can d. — ADDISON, 7; LAST WORDS, 2
It is natural to d. — DEATH, 8
it is worse to want to d. — WORLD-WEARINESS, 6
it is youth that must fight and d. — WAR, 24
I would d. for my country — PATRIOTISM, 11
live for ever or d. in the attempt — IMMORTALITY, 3
man can d. but once — DEATH, 55
Many people would sooner d. than think — THINKING, 4
No young man believes he shall ever d. — HAZLITT, 8; IMMORTALITY, 2
one may d. without ever laughing — LA BRUYERE, 4; LAUGHTER, 3
Rather suffer than d. — SUFFERING, 4
save your world you asked this man to d. — AUDEN, 8
The dead don't d. — LAWRENCE, 16
The d. is cast — IRREVOCABILITY, 1
the only decent thing...is to d. at once — REQUESTS, 1
those who are about to d. salute you — LAST WORDS, 3
To d. will be an awfully big adventure — DEATH, 9
we can d. but once to serve our country — ADDISON, 4; PATRIOTISM, 1
we must live as though...never going to d. — ACHIEVEMENT, 6
when good Americans d. they go to Paris — AMERICANS, 9; WILDE, 31
died dog it was that d. — GOLDSMITH, 8
I d....of my physician — DOCTORS, 3
Men have d. from time to time — SHAKESPEARE, 23
'Tis said that some have d. for love — LOVE AND DEATH, 3; WORDSWORTH, 21
diem Carpe d. — HORACE, 10; PRESENT, 3
dies a young person...marries or d., is sure to be kindly spoken of — AUSTEN, 6; HUMAN NATURE, 1
because a man d. for it — MARTYRDOM, 4
Every moment d. a man — LIFE AND DEATH, 1
he d. in pain — LA BRUYERE, 2; LIFE AND DEATH, 6
He that d. pays all debts — DEATH, 53
It matters not how a man d. — DEATH, 32; JOHNSON, 21
king never d. — MONARCHY, 4
One d. only once — DEATH, 43
Whatever is begotten, born, and d. — MORTALITY, 14
diet Food is an important part of a balanced d. — FOOD, 13
The right d. directs sexual energy into the parts that matter — FOOD, 6
dieting Unnecessary d. — APPEARANCE, 3
diets I feel about airplanes the way I feel about d. — FLYING, 2
difference made the d. of forty thousand men — OFFICERS, 11; WELLINGTON, 6
more d. within the sexes than between them — SEXES, 4
the d. of sex, if there is any — ANTHONY, 3
differences The Jews and Arabs should...settle their d. — GOLDWYNISMS, 26; RELIGION, 2
difficult It is d. to be humble — HUMILITY, 3
It is very d. to get up resentment — BITTERNESS, 2
never let them persuade you that things are too d. — DETERMINATION, 1
difficulty A d. for every solution — BUREAUCRACY, 5
digest mark, learn and inwardly d. — LEARNING, 2
Well, then, my stomach must just d. in its waistcoat — SHERIDAN, 8
digestion Things sweet to taste prove in d. sour — REGRET, 7
digital still think d. watches are a pretty neat idea — SCIENCE FICTION, 1
dignity human beings are born free...d. and rights — HUMAN RIGHTS, 1
man added to his d. by standing on it — PRIDE, 2
Official d....in inverse ratio to...importance — HUXLEY, 5
diligently Had I...served God as d. as I have served the king — LOYALTY, 3

dim my lamp burns low and d. — ENVY, 1
dimensions sickness enlarges the d. of a man's self — ILLNESS, 7
dimmed The eyes that shone, /Now d. and gone — NOSTALGIA, 8
dined More d. against than dining — FOOD, 2
dinky Hinky, d., par-lee-voo — FRANCE, 7
dinner A d. lubricates business — BUSINESS, 9
A man is...better pleased when he has a good d. upon his table — JOHNSON, 13; WOMAN'S ROLE, 3
dinner-table dominate a London d. — WILDE, 36
Dior 'Never darken my D. again — MANNERS, 3
diplomacy All d. is a continuation of war — DIPLOMACY, 7
diplomat A d....always remembers a woman's birthday — AGE, 21
d. these days is nothing but a head-waiter — DIPLOMACY, 9
diplomatic d. history is...what one clerk said to another clerk — HISTORY, 12
diplomats aged d. to be bored — DIPLOMACY, 1
direction 'God knows how you Protestants...have any sense of d. — CATHOLICISM, 6
directions rode madly off in all d. — NONSENSE, 6
director Theatre d.: a person — ACTING, 1
dirt After the first four years the d. doesn't get any worse — HOUSEWORK, 3
dirty Is sex d. — ALLEN, 1; SEX, 1
disadvantage d. of merely counting votes — DEMOCRACY, 3
disagree Who shall decide when doctors d. — DOCTORS, 4; POPE, 15
disapprove I d. of what you say, but I will defend to the death your right to say it — FREEDOM, 27; VOLTAIRE, 30
disaster the audience was a d. — PLAYS, 7; WILDE, 37
disasters trace...the d. of English history to...Wales — WALES, 4
disbelief willing suspension of d. — COLERIDGE, 3
disciples d....mark its ways and note...its mysteries — LUCK, 1
discomforts all the d. that will accompany my being blind — BLINDNESS, 5
discommendeth He who d. others — CRITICISM, 4
discontent lent /To youth and age...– d. — ARNOLD, 18; DISCONTENT, 1
To be discontented with the divine d. — VIRTUE, 9
winter of our d. — SHAKESPEARE, 99
discontents the family...source of all our d. — FAMILY, 12
discovered We have d. the secret of life — SCIENCE, 4
discovery D. consists of seeing what everybody has seen — DISCOVERY, 4
he who never made a mistake never made a d. — MISTAKES, 7
Scientific d. is a private event — SCIENCE, 16
discretion better part of valour is d. — SELF-PRESERVATION, 4; SHAKESPEARE, 43
the years of d. — AGE, 8
discussion more time for d....more mistakes — MISTAKES, 9
disdains He d. all things above his reach — DISCONTENT, 5
disease amusing the patient while Nature cures the d. — MEDICINE, 6
an incurable d. – colour blindness — RACISM, 4
Cur'd...of my d. — DOCTORS, 5
Cure the d. — REMEDIES, 1
Decay and d. are often beautiful — DISEASE, 23
D. is...of the place — DISEASE, 20
dread d. which so prepares its victim...for death — DISEASE, 10
Life is an incurable d. — DISEASE, 9; LIFE, 10
only so you don't look forward to being cured of — DISEASE, 14
remedies...suggested for a d. — REMEDIES, 5
remedy is worse than the d. — REMEDIES, 2
strange d. of modern life — ARNOLD, 14; DISEASE, 3; LIFE, 1
the incurable d. of writing — WRITING, 15
the only d. you don't look forward to being cured of — DEATH, 41
diseases D. are the tax — DISEASE, 18
d....no less natural than the instincts which preserve him. — DISEASE, 19
Extreme remedies...for extreme d. — REMEDIES, 6
Hungry Joe collected lists of fatal d. — ILLNESS, 4
disgracefully The world is d. managed — COMPLAINTS, 2
disguise virtues are...vices in d. — VIRTUE AND VICE, 2
dishonour honour rooted in d. — TENNYSON, 8; UNFAITHFULNESS, 3
disillusionments d. in the lives of the medieval saints — DECLINE, 4; SAKI, 9
disinterested D. intellectual curiosity...life blood of...civilisation — CURIOSITY, 5
dislike that my statue should be moved, which I should much d. — MEMORIALS, 8
The law of d. for the unlike — JEWS, 11
disliked I have always d. myself — CONNOLLY, 5; SELF, 2
Disney D. the most significant figure...since Leonardo — ART, 8
Disraeli D....never quite in earnest — DISRAELI, 2

disreputable I've been offered titles,…get one into d. company SHAW, 23
disrespectfully Never speak d. of Society SNOBBERY, 6
distance The d. doesn't matter BEGINNING, 2
distinguished So it has come at last, the d. thing JAMES, 10
When a d. but elderly scientist states SCIENCE, 3
distraction Ambition, D., Uglification, and Derision.' CARROLL, 7
distress All pray in their d. BLAKE, 24; PRAYER, 2
the mean man is always full of d. SUPERIORITY, 1
distrust shameful to d. one's friends FRIENDS, 4; ROCHEFOUCAULD, 3
distrusts him who d. himself SILENCE, 4
disturb What isn't part of ourselves doesn't d. us HATE, 2
disturbances think of diseases as isolated in. in a healthy body DISEASE, 1
ditchwater Is d. dull CHESTERTON, 18; NATURE, 4
diversion 'tis a country d. CONGREVE, 10
divided Obstinate people can be d. into STUBBORNNESS, 1
Thought must be d. against itself UNDERSTANDING, 5
divine attain to the d. perfection PERFECTION, 3
The d. *right* of husbands WOLLSTONECRAFT, 2
The right d. of kings to govern wrong POPE, 3
To be discontented with the d. discontent VIRTUE, 9
To err is human, to forgive, d. FORGIVENESS, 5; MISTAKES, 6; POPE, 10
divinity a d. that shapes our ends DESTINY, 10; SHAKESPEARE, 41
d. in odd numbers SUPERSTITION, 4
divorce D.? Never. But murder often MARRIAGE, 61
not wanting to consent to the d. PROPHECY, 3
do D. as you would be done by CHESTERFIELD, 5
D. other men BUSINESS, 1; DICKENS, 7
d. what the mob d. DICKENS, 14
either d., or die ACTION, 2
for they know not what they d. FORGIVENESS, 1
people who d. things EFFORT, 3
so much to d., /So little done ACTION, 5; TENNYSON, 13
they would d. you BUSINESS, 1; DICKENS, 7
to d. something is to create existence EXISTENCE, 5; SARTRE, 4
doctor A d.…is a patient half-cured OCCUPATIONS, 6
a…sense of intellectual degradation after an interview with a d. DOCTORS, 3
Imperative drugging…no longer…the chief function of the d. DRUGS, 7
The d. found,…/Her last disorder mortal GOLDSMITH, 6
doctors Who shall decide when d. disagree DOCTORS, 4; POPE, 15
doctrines What makes all d. plain BUTLER, 5
dog A door is what a d. is…on the wrong side of NASH, 2
America is a large, friendly d. AMERICA, 20
Beware of the d. DOGS, 1
d. that praised his fleas PARASITES, 4; YEATS, 11
every d. has his day SATISFACTION, 1
I am His Highness' d. at Kew POPE, 18
If a d. jumps…but if a cat CATS, 6
passers-by who can contemplate it…are those…with a white stick and a d. ARCHITECTURE, 4
The d. it was that died GOLDSMITH, 8
The d.,…/Went mad and bit the man GOLDSMITH, 7
The great pleasure of a d. DOGS, 2
The world regards such a person as…an unmuzzled d. CLASSIFICATION, 1
whose d. are you POPE, 18
dogma Any stigma…to beat a d. PUNS, 4
You can't teach an old d. CONSERVATISM, 4; PARKER, 7; PUNS, 11
dogmas these d. or goals are in doubt FANATICISM, 3
dogs Anybody who hates children and d. CHILDREN, 9; DOGS, 4
how much more d. are animated when they hunt in a pack UNITY, 7
I loathe people who keep d. DOGS, 6
let slip the d. of war SHAKESPEARE, 56; WAR, 59
like asking a lamp-post…about d. CRITICS, 6
Mad and Englishmen COWARD, 9
Rats…fought the d. BROWNING, 12
woman who is…kind to d. WOMEN, 7
doing Anything that is worth d. BEERBOHM, 7
Find out what you like d. best and get someone to pay you for d. it OCCUPATIONS, 8
we learn by d. LEARNING, 4
Whatever is worth d. CHESTERFIELD, 3; EXCELLENCE, 1
doings All our d. without charity CHARITY, 6
dollar The almighty d.…object of universal devotion MATERIALISM, 6
dollars What's a thousand d. PUNS, 8
dominate d. the world WILDE, 36
dominated He d. the room MAO TSE-TUNG, 1
dona *timeo Danaos et d. ferentis* MISTRUST, 6; VIRGIL, 5

done bright day is d. ENDING, 3
Do as you would be d. by CHESTERFIELD, 5
d. those things we ought not SIN, 6
If it were d. when 'tis d. HASTE, 5; SHAKESPEARE, 70
Justice should…be seen to be d. JUSTICE, 5
Let justice be d. JUSTICE, 4
long day's task is d. REST, 1
One never notices what has been d. ACHIEVEMENT, 2; CURIE, 6
so little d. ACTION, 5; TENNYSON, 13
The way to get things d. is not to mind who gets the credit SELFLESSNESS, 1
thy worldly task hast d. MORTALITY, 9; SHAKESPEARE, 25
What you do not want d. to yourself EXAMPLE, 2
Dong The D. with a luminous Nose NONSENSE, 7
Don Juans Christ-like heroes and woman-worshipping D. MEN, 6
donkeys lions led by d. OFFICERS, 1
Don Quixote the only absolutely original creation…is D. FICTION, 3
Doodle Yankee D. came to town AMERICA, 3
doom purpose of God and the d. assigned DESTINY, 12
slow, sure d. falls pitiless and dark HUMAN CONDITION, 7
door A d. is what a dog is…on the wrong side of NASH, 2
no d. to slam BEAUTY, 21
sweetest thing that ever grew /Beside a human d. ADMIRATION, 8
doors the d. of perception were cleansed BLAKE, 13; PERCEPTION, 1
Dorchester All terrorists…end up with drinks at the D. POLITICS, 18
double bed down the grassgreen gooseberried d. THOMAS, 12
double-crossing You dirty d. rat MISQUOTATIONS, 8
double-entendre But the horrible d. INNUENDO, 1
doublethink D. means the power of holding two contradictory beliefs OPPOSITES, 2; ORWELL, 8
doubt all my mind is clouded with a d. AFTERLIFE, 9
Humility is only d. BLAKE, 8; HUMILITY, 2
No…shadow of d. CERTAINTY, 2
O thou of little faith, wherefore didst thou d. DOUBT, 2
these dogmas or goals are in d. FANATICISM, 3
Through the night of d. and sorrow ENDURANCE, 2
When a man is in d. about…his writing POSTERITY, 2
doubting castle called D. Castle DESPAIR, 1
doubts end in d. CERTAINTY, 1; DOUBT, 1
douche the rattling of a thousand d. bags CHILDREN, 14
dower forfeited their ancient English d. DECLINE, 7
down put it d. a we SPELLING, 1
Yes, and they went d. very well too WELLINGTON, 3
downhearted Are we d.? No OPTIMISM, 1
drain you will leave Oxford by the town d. SPOONERISMS, 2
drains to distinguish between the Deity and the D. GOD, 31
drama A good d. critic is CRITICS, 14
draught O, for a d. of vintage ALCOHOL, 19
drawbacks One of the d. of Fame FAME, 6
dreadful d. is the check IMPRISONMENT, 2
Other people are quite d. MISANTHROPY, 3
some have called thee /Mighty and d. DEATH, 20; DONNE, 8
dream All men d.: but not equally DREAMS, 6
awakened from the d. of life SHELLEY, 3
behold it was a d. DREAMS, 2
Happiness is no vague d. HAPPINESS, 11
I have a d. EQUALITY, 13
The young men's vision, and the old men's d. DREAMS, 3
To sleep, perchance to d. SHAKESPEARE, 34; SUICIDE, 7
warned of God in a d. CHRISTMAS, 7
Where is it now, the glory and the d. METAPHYSICS, 2
dreamer The poet and the d. are distinct KEATS, 3; OPPOSITES, 1
dreamers the d. of the day are dangerous men DREAMS, 6
dreaming City with her d. spires OXFORD, 1
dreams do we not live in d. DREAMS, 7
dream our d. away DREAMS, 5
D. and predictions DREAMS, 1
Fanatics have their d. FANATICISM, 2
For one person who d. of making fifty thousand pounds LAZINESS, 2
I, being poor, have only my d. POVERTY, 17; YEATS, 13
spread my d. under your feet DREAMS, 8
Than this world d. of PRAYER, 3
the city of perspiring d. CAMBRIDGE, 4
We are such stuff /As d. are made on MORTALITY, 10
what d. may come SHAKESPEARE, 34; SUICIDE, 7
d. of in your philosophy SHAKESPEARE, 31; SUPERNATURAL, 4
dreary If your morals make you d. STEVENSON, 2
Once upon a midnight d. SUPERNATURAL, 8
dress I have no d. except the one I wear CURIE, 5
put on a d. of guilt GUILT, 1
Those who make their d.…themselves CLOTHES, 5; HAZLITT, 1

For God's sake, madam, don't say that in E. for…they will surely
tax it SWIFT, 11
go back to thy stately homes of E. LAWRENCE, 9
in E. people have good table manners MANNERS, 4
In E. there is only silence or scandal ENGLAND, 14
little ships of E. brought the Army home BOATS, 6; WORLD WAR II, 15
Living in E.,…must be like being married to a stupid…wife
 ENGLAND, 9
Oh, to be in E. ENGLAND, 4
Speak for E. PATRIOTISM, 2
Stately Homes of E. ARISTOCRACY, 6; COWARD, 6; STATELY HOMES, 2
that is forever E. WAR, 10
the Kings of E., Diamonds, Hearts, Spades and Clubs MONARCHY, 5
The Law of E. is a very strange one LAW, 2
the old savage E., whose last blood flows still ENGLAND, 11
There'll always be an E. ENGLAND, 18
The stately homes of E. STATELY HOMES, 4
this generation…found E. a land of beauty ECOLOGY, 3
this realm, this E. ENGLAND, 20; SHAKESPEARE, 97
When people say E. ENGLAND, 15
England's For E. the one land ENGLAND, 3
English E. people…are surely the *nicest* people in the world
 LAWRENCE, 2
E. soldiers fight like lions OFFICERS, 6
E.…the language of an imaginative race LANGUAGE, 3
forfeited their ancient E. dower DECLINE, 7
I do love cricket – it's so very E. CRICKET, 1
If the E. language had been properly organized LANGUAGE, 13
our E. nation, if they have a good thing, to make it too common
 ENGLAND, 21
part of E. middle-class education is devoted to the training of ser-
vants EDUCATION, 34
The E.…are rather a foul-mouthed nation ENGLISH, 8
the E. have hot-water bottles ENGLISH, 12
The E. have no respect for their language ENGLISH, 16; SHAW, 20
The E. may not like music MUSIC, 3
This is the sort of E. CHURCHILL, 16; GRAMMAR, 3
To Americans E. manners are…frightening MANNERS, 2
two most beautiful words in the E. language JAMES, 9
typically E. characteristic ENGLISH, 1; UNITY, 1
Englishman Am I not punished enough in not being born an E.
 NATIONALITY, 5
An E.…forms an orderly queue of one ENGLISH, 11
An E.'s way of speaking CLASS, 10
an…young E. of our upper class ARISTOCRACY, 1; ARNOLD, 3
E.…is afraid to feel EDUCATION, 7
E. never enjoys himself except for a noble purpose ENGLISH, 9
If I were an American, as I am an E. PATRIOTISM, 13
in spite of all temptations…He remains an E. NATIONALITY, 1
it takes a great deal to produce ennui in an E. ENGLISH, 6
never find an E. among the underdogs WAUGH, 14
Remember that you are an E. ENGLISH, 15
some other E. despise him ENGLISH, 16; SHAW, 20
tale…which would have stirred…E. ENDURANCE, 3
You may be the most liberal Liberal E. CLASS, 9
Englishman's an E. heaven-born privilege of doing as he likes
 ARNOLD, 5
Englishmen Mad dogs and E. COWARD, 9
to create Frenchmen in the image of E. CHURCHILL, 28
to see the absurd nature of E. ENGLISH, 14
When two E. meet, their first talk is of the weather
 ENGLISH, 10; JOHNSON, 5; WEATHER, 5
enigma a riddle wrapped in a mystery inside an e.
 CHURCHILL, 20; RUSSIA, 1
enjoy Certainly, there is nothing else here to e. SHAW, 26
He knew everything about literature except how to e. it
 LITERATURE, 3
Since God has given us the papacy…e. it CATHOLICISM, 4
enjoyment capacity for e. so vast HEMINGWAY, 1
enlightened In this e. age WOLLSTONECRAFT, 2
ennui it takes a great deal to produce e. in an Englishman
 ENGLISH, 6
entente *La cordiale e.* DIPLOMACY, 8
entertained Television…permits you to be e. in your living room
 TELEVISION, 1
entertainment what cats most appreciate…is…e. value CATS, 3
enthusiasm Nothing great was ever achieved without e.
 ENTHUSIASM, 2
Nothing is so contagious as e. ENTHUSIASM, 1
envied There are two things for which animals are…e.
 ANIMALS, 5; VOLTAIRE, 22

environment President Robbins was so well adjusted to his e.
 ADAPTABILITY, 3
environmental Population growth…e. damage CONSERVATION, 2
envy 2 percent moral, 48 percent indignation and 50 percent e.
 MORALITY, 10
e. is a kind of praise ENVY, 4
The dullard's e. of brilliant men GREATNESS, 1
Epicurus one of E.' herd of pigs PRESENT, 5
epidemic going to go crazy, living this e. every minute DISEASE, 13
epidemics E. have often been more influential than statesman
 DISEASE, 11
epigrams long despotism tempered by e. CARLYLE, 9; FRANCE, 2
epilogue good play needs no e. PLAYS, 4
epitaph 'Can't' will be the e. of the British Empire BRITISH EMPIRE, 3
epitaphs a nice derangement of e. MALAPROPISMS, 6; SHERIDAN, 5
epithet *Bourgeois*,…is an e. CLASS, 8
epoch From today…there begins a new e. in the history of the
world BEGINNING, 3
equal All animals are e. EQUALITY, 14
all men are created e. EQUALITY, 13; HUMAN RIGHTS, 3
All shall e. be CLASS, 4
Inferiors revolt…that they may be e. REVOLUTION, 1
some animals are more e. than others EQUALITY, 14
That all men are e. is a proposition HUXLEY, 15
equality E.…is the thing EQUALITY, 15
E. may perhaps be a right, but no…fact EQUALITY, 1
e.…with our superiors EQUALITY, 3
Freedom! E.! Brotherhood HUMAN RIGHTS, 2
There never will be…e.…until women…make laws ANTHONY, 2
equally Pale Death kicks his way e. EQUALITY, 19; HORACE, 8
That all who are happy, are e. happy HAPPINESS, 4
equanimity an e. bordering on indifference GILBERT, 9
ergo *Cogito, e. sum* THINKING, 1
Eros Unarm, E. REST, 1
err The Most may e. as grosly DRYDEN, 6
To e. is human, to forgive, divine FORGIVENESS, 5; MISTAKES, 6; POPE, 10
errand What thy e. here below PURPOSE, 4
error A new maxim is often a brilliant e. SAYINGS, 2
show a man that he is in an e. TRUTH, 15
errors E., like Straws, upon the surface flow DRYDEN, 10
few e. they have ever avoided CHURCHILL, 29
the e. of those who think they are strong MISTAKES, 2
escape Gluttony is an emotional e. GREED, 2
escaping fortunate in e. regular education WRITERS, 8
esprit English characteristic…e. *de corps* ENGLISH, 1; UNITY, 1
essence change is the very e. of life CHANGE, 6
Desire is the very e. of man DESIRE, 7
The poet gives us his e. POETRY AND PROSE, 6
estate a fourth e. of the realm JOURNALISM, 10
e. o' th' world were now undone WORLD-WEARINESS, 5
eternal Hope springs e. in the human breast HOPE, 4; POPE, 12
The e. *not ourselves* that makes for righteousness RIGHTEOUSNESS, 1
We feel…we are e. IMMORTALITY, 4
eternity Deserts of vast e. AGE, 26
E. in an hour BLAKE, 7
E.'s a terrible thought ETERNITY, 4
He has made his impress on e. HYPATIA, 3
over the Bridge of Sighs into e. DEATH, 38
Tears of e. and sorrow SORROW, 5
without injuring e. TIME, 18
Ethiopians The E. say that their gods are…black RELIGION, 39
Eton the playing fields of E. EDUCATION, 33; ORWELL, 4; WELLINGTON, 11
eunuch prerogative of the e. RESPONSIBILITY, 7
Eureka E. DISCOVERY, 1
Euripides E. portrays them as they are THEATRE, 7
Europe Communism continued to haunt E. as a spectre
 COMMUNISM, 5
E. is the unfinished negative AMERICA, 17
glory of E. is extinguished EUROPE, 1
In Western E. there are now only small countries EUROPE, 3
lamps are going out over all E. PROPHECY, 2
That E.'s nothin' on earth EUROPE, 6
the community of E. EUROPE, 4
the race of men is almost extinct in E. MEN, 6
This going into E. EUROPE, 5
United States of E. CHURCHILL, 31; EUROPE, 2
European to shoot down a E. is to kill two birds with one stone
 OPPRESSION, 4
Europeans only really materialistic people…E. MATERIALISM, 9
Eva If a woman like E. Peron with no ideals IDEALISM, 4; THATCHER 5
evacuations Wars are not won by e. CHURCHILL, 13; WORLD WAR II, 12

evah Well, did you e.! What a swell party — PARTIES, 3
Eve When E. ate this particular apple — LAWRENCE, 6; SEX, 19
even Deep and crisp and e. — CHRISTMAS, 12
evening Soup of the e. — FOOD, 5
event greatest e....that ever happened — FRENCH REVOLUTION, 2
events There are only three e. in a man's life — LA BRUYERE, 2; LIFE AND DEATH, 6
When in the course of human e., it becomes necessary — INDEPENDENCE, 1
Everest treating the *mons Veneris* as...Mount E. — SEX, 16
every God bless us, e. one — BLESSING, 4
everybody E. is always in favour of general economy — THRIFT, 4
E. was up to something — COWARD, 5; INTRIGUE, 2
everyman E., I will go with thee, and be thy guide — GUIDANCE, 1
everyone e. against e. — HUMAN CONDITION, 5
stop e. from doing it — PERVERSITY, 2
everything A place for e. — ORDER, 4
destroying nearly e. — CHESTERTON, 2
e. in its place — ORDER, 4
E. is funny — HUMOUR, 16
e. that lives is holy — BLAKE, 3
making e. the concern of all — RESPONSIBILITY, 6
evidence E. of life after death — HOUSES OF PARLIAMENT, 9
Most men...give e. against their own understanding — SPEECH, 4
evil a thing may look e. in theory — THEORY, 1
belief in a supernatural source of e. — EVIL, 6
better is he...who hath not seen the e. work...under the sun — EVIL, 3
deliver us from e. — PRAYER, 1
E., be thou my Good — EVIL, 9
E. be to him who evil thinks — EVIL, 1
E. comes at leisure — DISEASE, 8
e. is wrought by want of thought — EVIL, 7
e. men and seducers — EVIL, 4
Government,...is but a necessary e. — GOVERNMENT, 11
He who passively accepts e. — EVIL, 8
know all the e. he does — EVIL, 10
love of money is the root of all e. — MONEY, 5
Man's capacity for e. makes democracy necessary — DEMOCRACY, 6
men loved darkness...because their deeds were e. — EVIL, 5
Men's e. manners live in brass — MEMORIALS, 7; SHAKESPEARE, 52
No man is justified in doing e. — EXPEDIENCY, 4
science is...neither a potential for good nor for e. — SCIENCE, 26
The e. that men do lives after them — EVIL, 11; SHAKESPEARE, 58
the fear of one e. — VICE, 2
There is no e. in the atom — NUCLEAR WEAPONS, 12
we are the origin of all coming e. — HUMAN NATURE, 7
evils death...the least of all e. — DEATH, 5
He...must expect new e. — INNOVATION, 1
There exist some e. so terrible...that we dare not think of them — MISFORTUNE, 6
We cannot remove the e. of capitalism — CAPITALISM, 5
Whenever I'm caught between two e. — VICE, 4; WEST, 15
Work banishes those three great e. — VOLTAIRE, 7; WORK, 12
evolution e. of the human race — MANKIND, 5
sex...must itself be subject...to e. — SEXES, 2
exact Politics is not an e. science — POLITICS, 5
exaggerated Reports of my death are greatly e. — OBITUARIES, 4; TWAIN, 13
examine One should e. oneself...before...condemning others — SELF, 6
example E. is the school of mankind — EXAMPLE, 1
George the Third.......*may profit by their e.* — TREASON, 4
exasperating that the afterlife will be any less e. — AFTERLIFE, 3; COWARD, 3
excel daring to e. — EXCELLENCE, 2
excellence acute limited e. at twenty-one — PRECOCITY, 1
excellences e. carried to an excess — COLERIDGE, 9
excelsior A banner with the strange device, /E. — AMBITION, 5
exception The e. proves the rule — RULES, 1
excess excellences carried to an e. — COLERIDGE, 9
e. is most exhilarating — EXCESS, 2
Give me e. of it — MUSIC, 24; SHAKESPEARE, 117
In charity there is no e. — CHARITY, 2
Nothing succeeds like e. — EXCESS, 8; MODERATION, 3; WILDE, 34
The road of e. — BLAKE, 16; EXCESS, 3
'Tis not the drinking...but the e. — EXCESS, 5
exchange conversation must be an e. of thought — CONVERSATION, 4
excluded when you have e. the impossible — DOYLE, 1; TRUTH, 10
executed certain author was e. for murdering his publisher — WRITERS, 1
execution some are daily led to e. — EXECUTION, 9

executioner I am mine own E. — DONNE, 4; SELF, 3
executioners victims who respect their e. — SARTRE, 1
executive the e. expression of human immaturity — POLITICS, 8
exercise E. is bunk — SPORT AND GAMES, 3
exertion success depends...upon individual initiative and e. — EFFORT, 4; SUCCESS, 4
exhausted Our agenda is now e. — AGREEMENT, 3
exist Facts do not cease to e. — FACTS, 1; HUXLEY, 17
I e. by what I think — SARTRE, 3
If God did not e. — GOD, 33; VOLTAIRE, 10
liberty cannot long e. — CORRUPTION, 1
existence A God who let us prove his e. — GOD, 10
disregard for the necessities of e. — CIVILIZATION, 6
doubted the e. of the Deity — SCIENTISTS, 5
Let us contemplate e. — EXISTENCE, 2
mere e. is swollen to a horror — IDEALISM, 2
the sole purpose of human e. is to kindle a light — EXISTENCE, 3
to deny the e. of an unseen kingdom is bad — SPECULATION, 1
to do something is to create e. — EXISTENCE, 5; SARTRE, 4
exits They have their e. and their entrances — HUMAN CONDITION, 8; SHAKESPEARE, 18
expect people e. me to neigh, grind my teeth — HORSES, 1
you e. other people to be...to your liking — TOLERANCE, 3
expectations the difference between our talents and our e. — DISAPPOINTMENT, 1
expects Blessed is the man who e. nothing — EXPECTATION, 2
England e. every man will do his duty — DUTY, 3
expediency the most useful thing about a principle...sacrificed to e. — EXPEDIENCY, 3
expendable British Government sees black people as e. — RACISM, 15
expenditure annual e. nineteen nineteen six — DICKENS, 4; ECONOMICS, 3
in favour of...particular e. — THRIFT, 4
expense flatterers live at the e. of those who listen — FLATTERY, 3
who /Would be at the e. of two — GOD, 12
experience All e. is an arch — EXPERIENCE, 9
E. is a good teacher — EXPERIENCE, 1
E. isn't interesting — EXPERIENCE, 3
I can't see that it's wrong to give him a little legal e. — NEPOTISM, 2
Language is not simply a reporting device for e. — LANGUAGE, 21
moment's insight...worth a life's e. — EXPERIENCE, 7
my e. of life has been drawn from life itself — BEERBOHM, 10; EXPERIENCE, 2
Reason, Observation, and E. — SCIENCE, 13
the light which e. gives — COLERIDGE, 10; EXPERIENCE, 4
experiences the child should be allowed to meet the real e. of life — CHILDREN, 12
experiment A theory can be proved by e. — EINSTEIN, 6; THEORY, 2
existence remains a...lamentable e. — HAPPINESS, 12
no path leads from e. to...theory — EINSTEIN, 6; THEORY, 2
expert An e....has made all the mistakes...in a very narrow field — EXPERTS, 1
An e....knows some of the worst mistakes that can be made — EXPERTS, 2
Prince Philip...a world e. on leisure — ROYALTY, 10
explanations less hideous than e. — EXPLANATIONS, 1
export I integrate the current e. drive — BETJEMAN, 4
exposes A man who e. himself when he is intoxicated — DRUNKENNESS, 8
expression the executive e. of human immaturity — POLITICS, 8
exquisite It is e., and it leaves one unsatisfied — WILDE, 28
extinct a convention which says you must not make species e. — CONSERVATION, 6
the Tasmanians...are now e. — ADULTERY, 5
extinguished glory of Europe is e. — EUROPE, 1
extraordinary Little minds are interested in the e. — TRIVIALITY, 5
extravagance e....thrift and adventure — THRIFT, 2
Our love of what is beautiful does not lead to e. — RESULTS, 2
extreme E. remedies...for e. diseases — REMEDIES, 6
extremism e. in the defence of liberty is no vice — EXCESS, 4
exuberance E. is Beauty — BEAUTY, 4
ex-wife no fury like an e. searching for a new lover — CONNOLLY, 8
eye A custom loathsome to the e., hateful to the nose — SMOKING, 5
a sober colouring from an e. — MORTALITY, 12; WORDSWORTH, 13
clapped the glass to his sightless e. — BLINDNESS, 4
e. for e. — RETRIBUTION, 2
He had but one e. — DICKENS, 2
his keener e. /The axe's edge did try — EXECUTION, 8
man who looks you...in the e....hiding something — INSINCERITY, 1
such beauty as a woman's e. — LEARNING, 2
There is a road from the e. to the heart — CHESTERTON, 3; EMOTION, 1

Nothing else holds f.   SEX, 31; SHAKESPEARE, 116
fashionable an idea...to be f. is ominous   FASHION, 5
fashions F....only induced epidemics   FASHION, 6
fast US has to move very f.   AMERICA, 13
faster Will you walk a little f.   HASTE, 1
fat butter will only make us f.   POWER POLITICS, 1
  Enclosing every thin man, there's a f. man   APPEARANCE, 17; WAUGH, 15
  in every f. man a thin one   OBESITY, 3
  Let me have men about me that are f.   MISTRUST, 4; SHAKESPEARE, 53
  Outside every f. man...an even fatter man   OBESITY, 1
  The opera isn't over till the f. lady sings   OPERA, 3
  there's a thin man inside every f. man   OBESITY, 4
  Who's your f. friend   OBESITY, 2
  you will come and find me f. and sleek   PRESENT, 5
fatal Nature has never put the f. question as to the meaning of their lives   PURPOSE, 2
fate count as profit every day that F. allows you   PRESENT, 4
  Drop...what tomorrow may bring...count as profit every day that F. allows you   HORACE, 9
  Each man the architect of his own f.   RESPONSIBILITY, 2
  F. has not been kind to Mrs Browning   BROWNING, 1
  F. sits on these dark battlements   DESTINY, 9
  hostages given to f.   FAMILY, 13
  Leave the flesh to the f. it was fit for   SOUL, 4
  master of his f.   RESPONSIBILITY, 8; TENNYSON, 9
  the life-sentence which f. carries   LIFE AND DEATH, 7
  the master of my f.   RESPONSIBILITY, 4
  when F. summons   MORTALITY, 4
father a wise f. that knows his own child   FAMILY, 19; SHAKESPEARE, 79
  except to shoot rabbits and hit his f. on the jaw   NASTINESS, 3
  Full fathom five thy f. lies   SHAKESPEARE, 113
  God is...an exalted f.   GOD, 17
  If poverty is the mother of crime, stupidity is its f.   CRIME, 2; LA BRUYERE, 5
  in my F.'s house are many mansions   HEAVEN, 3
  left me by my F.   EXECUTION, 3
  No man is responsible for his f.   FAMILY, 21
  our F.   PRAYER, 1
  The Child is F. of the Man   AGE, 45; WORDSWORTH, 12
  the F. of lights   GIFTS, 1
  Today I dressed to meet my f.'s eyes   SUITABILITY, 4
  You are old, F. William   OLD AGE, 23
fatherhood Mirrors and f. are abominable   UNIVERSE, 2
fathers atone for the sins of your f.   HORACE, 13; INJUSTICE, 4
  Come mothers and f./Throughout the land   CHANGE, 5; DYLAN, 4
  f., provoke not your children   FAMILY, 3
  land of my f.   THOMAS, 16; WALES, 2
fathom Full f. five thy father lies   SHAKESPEARE, 113
fatted the f. calf   PARTIES, 2
fatter But the valley sheep are f.   GREED, 3
fatty f. degeneration of his moral being   STEVENSON, 13
fatuity the English seem...to act with...the f. of idiots   IRELAND, 10; SMITH, 1
fault Shakespeare never had six lines together without a f.   SHAKESPEARE, 7
  the f. were on only one side   ARGUMENTS, 5; ROCHEFOUCAULD, 12
faultless Whoever thinks a f. piece to see   POPE, 8
faults Don't tell your friends their social f.   ADVICE, 5
  f., do not fear to abandon them   IMPERFECTION, 2
  If we had no f. of our own   IMPERFECTION, 6; ROCHEFOUCAULD, 1
  only confess our little f.   IMPERFECTION, 5; ROCHEFOUCAULD, 9
  When you have f.   IMPERFECTION, 2
favour accepts a smaller as a f.   INJUSTICE, 2
favoured play-actors...they're a f. race   ACTORS, 3
favours Whether a pretty woman grants or withholds her f.   WOMEN, 33
fear concessions of f.   YIELDING, 1
  Curiosity will conquer f.   CURIOSITY, 4
  do I f. thy nature   KINDNESS, 2; SHAKESPEARE, 69
  F. has many eyes   CERVANTES, 5; FEAR, 4
  f. in a handful of dust   ELIOT, 9
  F. is the parent of cruelty   CRUELTY, 2
  F. lent wings to his feet   FEAR, 7; VIRGIL, 10
  f. made manifest on the body   DISEASE, 12
  F. no more the heat o' th' sun   MORTALITY, 9; SHAKESPEARE, 25
  fools rush in where angels f. to tread   HASTE, 4; POPE, 11
  Fostered alike by beauty and by f.   SOUL, 7
  freedom from f.   HUMAN RIGHTS, 4
  have...many things to f.   FEAR, 1
  He who pretends to look on death without f. lies   DEATH, 49
  Men f. death   DEATH, 7

None but a coward...has never known f.   COWARDICE, 1
one has...ceased to be an object of f. as soon as one is pitied   SYMPATHY, 2
  only thing we have to f. is f. itself   FEAR, 6
  perfect love casteth out f.   FEAR, 3; LOVE, 7
  Perhaps your f. in passing judgement   COURAGE, 2
  pessimists end up by desiring the things they f.   PESSIMISM, 5
  the f. of one evil   VICE, 2
fearful facing f. odds   COURAGE, 8
  thy f. symmetry   BLAKE, 20
fears A man who f. suffering   SUFFERING, 5
  man f....only the stroke of death   DEATH, 6
feast Paris is a moveable f.   HEMINGWAY, 2; PARIS, 1
February dreadful pictures of January and F.   TROLLOPE, 4
  F., fill the dyke   MONTHS, 2
fecund to mistake for the first-rate, the f. rate   WRITERS, 2
fed bite the hand that f. them   BURKE, 12; INGRATITUDE, 1
fee hold the gorgeous east in f.   VENICE, 3
feed F. the World   CHARITY, 3
  You cannot f. the hungry on statistics   STATISTICS, 2
feel Englishman...is afraid to f.   EDUCATION, 7
  what I f. really bad about   LIBERALISM, 1
feeling A man is as old as he's f.   AGE, 12
  Compassion is not a sloppy, sentimental f.   SOCIALISM, 4
feelings a talent for describing the involvements and f. and characters   AUSTEN, 2
  First f. are always the most natural   FIRST IMPRESSIONS, 1
feels A really intelligent man f. what other men...know   INTELLIGENCE, 3
feet An emperor ought at least to die on his f.   LAST WORDS, 28
  better to die on your f. than to live on your knees   SELF-RESPECT, 1
  Fear lent wings to his f.   FEAR, 7; VIRGIL, 10
  those f. in ancient time   ENGLAND, 1
feigning truest poetry is the most f.   POETRY, 19
felicity likely to mar the general f.   MARRIAGE, 16
fell crumbs which f. from the rich man's table   POVERTY AND WEALTH, 2
  men f. out   BUTLER, 1
felled The poplars are f.   TREES, 3
fellow f. of infinite jest   MOURNING, 7; SHAKESPEARE, 40
  fellows Boys are capital f. in their own way   LAMB, 3
fellowship such a f. of good knights shall never be together   LOSS, 3
female male and f. created he them   CREATION, 5; MANKIND, 2
  the f. of the species is more deadly than the male   WOMEN, 23
  The seldom f.   SEXES, 10
  works of male and f. authors be properly separated   PRUDERY, 1
feminine Taste is the f. of genius   TASTE, 2
fetishism Buttock f. is comparatively rare   GREER, 3
fettered so f. fast we are   BROWNING, 3; FREEDOM, 1
fever hand that signed the treaty bred a f.   SIGNATURES, 2; THOMAS, 5
Février Generals Janvier and F.   SEASONS, 10
few err as grosly as the F.   DRYDEN, 6
  How f. of his friends' houses   ILLNESS, 5
  owed by so many to so f.   CHURCHILL, 24; WORLD WAR II, 6
fickle Woman is always f. and changing   VIRGIL, 7; WOMEN, 45
fiction ancient history,...is no more than accepted f.   HISTORY, 15; VOLTAIRE, 13
  an improbable f.   REALITY, 3
  Children should acquire...heroes and villains from f.   AUDEN, 3; HISTORY, 2
  Poetry is a comforting piece of f.   POETRY, 15
  Science f. is no more written for scientists   FICTION, 1
  Stranger than f.   TRUTH, 7
field Man for the f. and woman for the hearth   SEXES, 14
  shepherds abiding in the f.   CHRISTMAS, 6
  some corner of a foreign f.   WAR, 10
  What though the f. be lost   DETERMINATION, 4
fields East and west on f. forgotten   WAR, 25
  Now there are f. where Troy once was   DECLINE, 3
fiend a frightful f. /Doth close behind him tread   COLERIDGE, 13; FEAR, 5
fifteen F. men on the dead man's chest   ALCOHOL, 3
  f. minutes everybody will be famous   FAME, 13
fifty For one person who dreams of making f. thousand pounds   LAZINESS, 2
  'You'll know when you're f.   AGE, 35
fight a great cause to f. for   PRIDE, 1
  easier to f. for one's principles   PRINCIPLES, 1
  f., f., f., and f. again   POLITICS, 19
  F. the good fight with all thy might   CHRISTIANITY, 6
  I will not cease from mental f.   ENGLAND, 1

The wisest f. in Christendom — FOOLISHNESS, 4
Wise Man or a F. — BLAKE, 11; WISDOM, 7
You can f. too many of the people — DECEPTION, 4; THURBER, 4
foolish anything very f. — MOTIVE, 3
If you are f. enough to be contented, don't show it — COMPLAINTS, 3
No man was more f....pen in his hand — GOLDSMITH, 1
You must not think me...f. because I am facetious — SERIOUSNESS, 2
foolishness Mix a little f. with your serious plans — FOOLISHNESS, 5; HORACE, 16
fools Christianity...says that they are all f. — CHESTERTON, 9
flattery's the food of f. — SWIFT, 4
f. decoyed into our condition — MARRIAGE, 46
f. rush in where angels fear to tread — HASTE, 4; POPE, 11
Fortune, that favours f. — LUCK, 2
I am two f. — LOVE, 25
Is Pride, the never-failing vice of f. — PRIDE, 4
Many have been the wise speeches of f. — WISDOM AND FOOLISHNESS, 3
suffer f. gladly — WISDOM AND FOOLISHNESS, 2
the greater part of the law is learning to tolerate f. — LAW, 6
this great stage of f. — HUMAN CONDITION, 9; SHAKESPEARE, 66
what f. these mortals be — FOOLISHNESS, 7
world is made up...of f. and knaves — FOOLISHNESS, 3
foot noiseless f. of Time — SHAKESPEARE, 12; TIME, 14
football F....is a species of fighting — FOOTBALL, 2
F. isn't a matter of life and death — FOOTBALL, 3
Professional f. is no longer a game — FOOTBALL, 1
footeball F....causeth fighting — FOOTBALL, 4
foothold a f. when he returns from flight — BLAKE, 2
footprints F. on the sands of time — ACTION, 1
footsteps home his f. he hath turn'd — HOMESICKNESS, 3
foppery excellent f. of the world — SHAKESPEARE, 61
forbearance f. ceases to be a virtue — BURKE, 3; TOLERANCE, 1
forbidden he wanted it only because it was f. — PERVERSITY, 4
we're f. to know – what end the gods have in store — DESTINY, 6
force as base as to use f. — HYPATIA, 4
f. alone is but *temporary* — BURKE, 9; FORCE, 2
F., if unassisted by judgement, collapses — JUDGMENT, 7
F. is not a remedy — FORCE, 1
Other nations use 'f.'; we Britons...use 'Might' — BRITISH, 5; WAUGH, 17
Who overcomes /By f. — VICTORY, 6
Ford Jerry F. is so dumb — STUPIDITY, 2
The time of our F. — HUXLEY, 6
forefathers Think of your f. — POSTERITY, 1
forehead A burning f., and a parching tongue — PASSION, 3
foreign pronounce f. names as he chooses — CHURCHILL, 15; PRONUNCIATION, 1
wandering on a f. strand — HOMESICKNESS, 3
foreigners f. speak English when our backs are turned — LANGUAGE, 7
f....spell better than they pronounce — PRONUNCIATION, 2; SPELLING, 2
Sympathy...for being f. — SYMPATHY, 1
foreparents His f. came to America — EQUALITY, 11
forests the f. of the night — BLAKE, 20
foretaste Every parting gives a f. of death — SCHOPENHAUER, 3; SEPARATION, 4
forever That is f. England — WAR, 10
forget Better by far you should f. and smile — MEMORY, 8
Old men f. — MEMORY, 9; SHAKESPEARE, 49
To endeavour to f. anyone — LA BRUYERE, 6; MEMORY, 4
Were it not better to f. — REGRET, 2
forgetful conscious of being decrepit and f. — BELLOC, 1
forgive do not have to f. my enemies — LAST WORDS, 19
Father, f. them — FORGIVENESS, 1
how oft shall...I f. him — FORGIVENESS, 2
To err is human, to f., divine — FORGIVENESS, 5; MISTAKES, 6; POPE, 10
forgiven Once a woman has f. her man — FORGIVENESS, 4
forgot auld acquaintance be f. — BURNS, 3; FRIENDSHIP, 3
I have f. my part — FAILURE, 3
forgotten I have f. more than you ever knew — INSULTS, 15
Nobody is f. when it is convenient to remember him — DISRAELI, 17
what has been learnt has been f. — EDUCATION, 29
forlorn The British postgraduate student is a lonely f. soul — EDUCATION, 15
formed not f. by nature to bear — ENDURANCE, 1
formidable Examinations are f. — EXAMINATIONS, 1
forms from outward f. to win — APPEARANCES, 4
formula Matter...a convenient f. — RUSSELL, 9
fortress f. built by Nature — ENGLAND, 20; SHAKESPEARE, 97
fortune f. favours the brave — COURAGE, 14
F., that favours fools — LUCK, 2
hostages to f. — FAMILY, 1

slings and arrows of outrageous f. — SHAKESPEARE, 36; SUICIDE, 7
to make your f....let people see...it is in their interests to promote yours — LA BRUYERE, 7
fortunes f. sharp adversitee — CHAUCER, 6
share in the good f. of the mighty — INJUSTICE, 1
forty F. years on — PARTING, 2
I am just turning f. — AGE, 25
I have been talking prose for over f. years — PROSE, 2
Life begins at f. — AGE, 42
look young till f. — AGE, 14
made the difference of f. thousand men — OFFICERS, 11; WELLINGTON, 6
forty-niner Dwelt a miner, F., /And his daughter, Clementine — MOURNING, 2
forty-three She may very well pass for f. — AGE, 22
foster-child f. of silence and slow time — SILENCE, 3
fought better to have f. and lost — DEFEAT, 1
foul Murder most f. — MURDER, 6
So f. and fair a day — SHAKESPEARE, 68; WEATHER, 10
foul-mouthed English...are rather a f. nation — ENGLISH, 8
found he f. it brick — IMPROVEMENT, 1
I have f. it — DISCOVERY, 1
Pleasure is...seldom f. where it is sought — PLEASURE, 7
Suppose it had been someone else who f. you like this — ADULTERY, 6
fountains their f. piped an answer — LAWRENCE, 3
four f. essential human freedoms — HUMAN RIGHTS, 10
Great God grant that twice two be not f. — PRAYER, 10
fourth a f. estate of the realm — JOURNALISM, 10
four-year-old You've got the brain of a f. boy — STUPIDITY, 3
fox a f. from his lair — HUNTING, 3
fox-hunting athletics as inferior forms of f. — WAUGH, 10
fraction Only a residual f. is thought — BUREAUCRACY, 6
fragrant a thousand f. posies — FLOWERS, 1
frailty F., thy name is woman — WEAKNESS, 2; WOMEN, 37
more flesh...more f. — OBESITY, 7
frames The finest collection of f. — PHILISTINISM, 2
framework Language is...a defining f. — LANGUAGE, 21
France Fair stood the wind for F. — BOATS, 4
F. is a country where the money falls apart — FRANCE, 9
F. was a long despotism — CARLYLE, 9; FRANCE, 2
Had we gone the way of F. — ECOLOGY, 6
Like Brighton pier,...inadequate for getting to F. — TRAVEL, 9
frankincense gold, and f., and myrrh — CHRISTMAS, 7
fraternité *Liberté! Égalité! F.* — HUMAN RIGHTS, 2
frauds pious f. of friendship — FRIENDSHIP, 7
free All human beings are born f. — HUMAN RIGHTS, 1
F. Will and Predestination — CHURCHILL, 8; DESTINY, 2
In a f. society the state...administers justice among men — STATE, 2
land of the f., and the home of the brave — AMERICA, 14
Man is condemned to be f. — FREEDOM, 24; SARTRE, 2
Man was born f. — FREEDOM, 22
No human being,...was ever so f. as a fish — FREEDOM, 23; RUSKIN, 2
none the less f. than you were — ADAPTABILITY, 1
So f. we seem — BROWNING, 3; FREEDOM, 1
the truth shall make you f. — TRUTH, 4
Thou art f. — SHAKESPEARE, 1
truth that makes men f. — TRUTH, 1
We have to believe in f. will — CHOICE, 3; GOLDWYNISMS, 30
woman was a f. agent — EQUALITY, 6
freedom fit to use their f. — FREEDOM, 16
F.! Equality! Brotherhood — HUMAN RIGHTS, 3
F. is an indivisible word — HUMAN RIGHTS, 5
f. of speech, of conscience, and the prudence never to practise...them — FREEDOM, 26; TWAIN, 6
If f. were not so economically efficient — ECONOMICS, 4
In solitude alone can he know true f. — SOLITUDE, 9
Necessity is the plea for every infringement of human f. — NECESSITY, 1
None can love f. heartily, but good men — FREEDOM, 18
So long as the state exists there is no f. — STATE, 1
The worst enemy of truth and f. — MAJORITY, 2
Those who deny f. to others — FREEDOM, 15
Until you've lost your reputation, you never realize...what f. really is — REPUTATION, 3
what is F. — FREEDOM, 4
You took my f. away a long time ago — FREEDOM, 25
freedoms four essential human f. — HUMAN RIGHTS, 4
free-loader A f. is a confirmed guest — PARASITES, 2
freely nothing so f. as advice — ADVICE, 4; ROCHEFOUCAULD, 5
freemasonry a kind of bitter f. — BEERBOHM, 2
free-will believe in f. We've got no choice — HUMAN CONDITION, 10
French Bouillabaisse is only good because cooked by the F. — FOOD, 8

everyone would always have spoken F. — VOLTAIRE , 25
F. governments more selfish than most — GOVERNMENT, 5
I speak...Italian to women, F. to men — LANGUAGE, 6
My suit is pale yellow. My nationality is F. — NORMALITY, 2; WILLIAMS, 1
something fishy about the F. — COWARD, 4
The F. are wiser than they seem — APPEARANCES, 2
The F. will only be united under the threat of danger — FRANCE, 3
the German text of F. operas — OPERA, 6
Frenchman F. must be always talking — FRANCE, 4
Frenchmen to create F. in the image of Englishmen — CHURCHILL, 28
frenzy poet's eye, in a fine f. rolling — POETRY, 20
Freudian the F., it is a very low, Central European sort of humour — HUMOUR, 9
friend A f. in power — POWER, 2
A f. should bear his f.'s infirmities — FRIENDS, 9
a good f., but bad acquaintance — FRIENDS, 2
a new f. is as new wine — FRIENDS, 1
damned good-natured f. — SHERIDAN, 2
F....masterpiece of Nature — FRIENDS, 6
f., wherefore art thou come — BETRAYAL, 1
He makes no f. — ENEMIES, 1
It takes your enemy and your f...., to hurt you — TWAIN, 5
no f. like a sister — FAMILY, 18
save me, from the candid f. — FRANKNESS, 1
trust ye not in a f. — TRUST, 1
friendly so large, /So f., and so rich — AMERICA, 2
friends Animals are such agreeable f. — ANIMALS, 3
F., Romans, countrymen — EVIL, 11; SHAKESPEARE, 58
guessed you were f. — FRIENDSHIP, 2
Have no f. not equal — FRIENDS, 4
How few of his f.' houses — ILLNESS, 5
How to Win F. — INFLUENCE, 1
lay down his f. for his life — SELF-PRESERVATION, 5
Money can't buy f. — MONEY, 15
not so much our f.' help that helps us — FRIENDSHIP, 6
Once more unto the breach, dear f. — COURAGE, 11; SHAKESPEARE, 45
our f. are true and our happiness — OPTIMISM, 4
shameful to distrust one's f. — FRIENDS, 8; ROCHEFOUCAULD, 3
that a man lay down his life for his f. — LOVE, 8
the best of f. must part — PARTING, 1
troops of unrecording f. — LIFE, 22
with a little help from my f. — FRIENDS, 7
without three good f. — SHAKESPEARE, 20
you choose your f. — FAMILY, 6; FRIEND, 5
friendship A man, Sir, should keep his f. in constant repair — JOHNSON, 18
F. is a disinterested commerce between equals — GOLDSMITH, 10; LOVE AND FRIENDSHIP, 1
F. is constant in all other things — LOVE AND FRIENDSHIP, 2
F. is unnecessary — FRIENDSHIP, 9
love...looks more like hatred than like f. — LOVE AND HATE, 4
Most f. is feigning — INSINCERITY, 3
The dupe of f., and the fool of love — BITTERNESS, 1
To like...the same things, that is...true f. — FRIENDSHIP, 11
true bond of f. — FRIENDSHIP, 10
frighten by God, they f. me — OFFICERS, 9; WELLINGTON, 8
f. the horses — SEX, 8
frittered life is f. away by detail — SIMPLICITY, 5
frivolity gay without f. — FUTURE, 1
frontier We stand today on the edge of a new f. — BEGINNING, 5
froth Life is mostly f. and bubble — MISFORTUNE, 5
frozen politics...of this country are f. — POLITICS, 25
fruit every good tree bringeth forth good f. — RESULTS, 1
Ignorance is like a delicate exotic f. — IGNORANCE, 6
fruitful be f. and multiply — CREATION, 5; MANKIND, 2
The command 'Be f. and multiply — CONTRACEPTION, 4
fruitfulness secret of reaping the greatest f...from life — DANGER, 4; NIETZSCHE, 5
fruits by their f. ye shall know them — RESULTS, 1
frustrate In three sips...Arian f. — DRINKS, 1
fuck They f. you up, your mum and dad — FAMILY, 11
fugitive a f. and a vagabond — PUNISHMENT, 1
full of new wine — DRUNKENNESS, 4
Reading maketh a f. man — READING, 1
fun the most f. I ever had without laughing — ALLEN, 2; SEX, 2
the people have f. — PLEASURE, 9
Work is much more f. than f. — COWARD, 11; COWARD, 11
you feel as if a human being sitting inside were making f. of you — ANIMALS, 2
function f. of the critic — CRITICS, 1

funerals If you don't go to other men's f. — FUNERALS, 3
funny Everything is f. — HUMOUR, 16
hard to be f. when you have to be clean — HUMOUR, 18
its own animality either objectionable or f. — HUMOUR, 11
Kings...are just as f. — ROYALTY, 13
fury full of sound and f. — LIFE, 19; SHAKESPEARE, 76
hell a f. like a woman scorned — CONGREVE, 7; LOVE AND HATE, 3
no f. like an ex-wife searching for a new lover — CONNOLLY, 8
strength and f. — PATIENCE, 3
the F. of a Patient Man — DRYDEN, 7; PATIENCE, 2
fustest I got there f. with the mostest — WAR, 21
futile f. argument as to the relative superiority of men and women — EQUALITY, 5
future F., n. That period of time in which — OPTIMISM, 4
If you want a picture of the f. — OPPRESSION, 3; ORWELL, 7
if you would divine the f. — PAST, 2
I have a vision of the f. — FUTURE, 2
I mean a F. Life — AFTERLIFE, 2
people who live in the f. — BENNETT, 2; PROGRESS, 1
The f. is...black — RACISM, 1
The f. is made of the same stuff — FUTURE, 5
The f. is the only kind of property — SLAVERY, 1
Who controls the past controls the f. — ORWELL, 6; POWER, 9
gaiety the only concession to g. — WELSH, 1
gain richest f. I count but loss — HUMILITY, 6
gained learning hath g. most — BOOKS, 12
gains no g. without pains — SUCCESS, 8
gallant a loyal, a g., a generous, an ingenious, and good-temper'd people — FRANCE, 8
gallantry What men call g. — ADULTERY, 1; BYRON, 7
gambling primary notion back of most g. is the excitement — SPECULATION, 3
game He no play-a da g. — CONTRACEPTION, 3
It's more than a g. It's an institution — CRICKET, 2
Play up! play up! and play the g. — WAR, 41
win this g. and thrash the Spaniards — SPORT AND GAMES, 2; WAR, 18
woman is his g. — SEXES, 13; TENNYSON, 25
games The most important thing in the Olympic G. — VICTORY, 4
gamesmanship G. Or The Art of Winning Games — SPORT AND GAMES, 8
gaming Man is a g. animal — LAMB, 2; SPORT AND GAMES, 5
garden A g. is a lovesome thing — GARDENS, 11
Come into the g., Maud — TENNYSON, 22
cultivate our g. — VOLTAIRE, 6
God Almighty first planted a g. — GARDENS, 2
God the first g. made — GARDENS, 6
the g. of Eden — KNOWLEDGE, 4; TREES, 1
There are fairies at the bottom of our g. — FAIRIES, 3
gardener Every time I talk to...my g., I'm convinced of the opposite — HAPPINESS, 9
Nor does a...g. scent his roses — POETS, 3
garter I like the G. — TITLES, 2
gate I am here at the g. alone — TENNYSON, 22
I said to the man who stood at the g. of the year — FAITH, 6
matters not how strait the g. — RESPONSIBILITY, 4
the g. of heaven — HEAVEN, 2
gatekeeper After I die, I shall return to earth as a g. of a bordello — THREATS, 2
gates Battering the g. of heaven — TENNYSON, 27
the g. of the day — LONELINESS, 2
gather G. the flowers... — FLOWERS, 5
G. ye rosebuds while ye may — PRESENT, 2
gathered two or three are g. together — PRAYER, 3
where two or three are g. together — CHURCH, 2
gatling The g.'s jammed and the colonel dead — WAR, 41
Gaul G. is divided into three — FRANCE, 1
gave God...g. his only begotten Son — CHRISTIANITY, 6
gay g. without frivolity — FUTURE, 1
Gaza Eyeless in G. — BLINDNESS, 2
general In a civil war, a g. must know — WAR, 47
generalizations All g. are dangerous — GENERALIZATIONS, 2
generalize To g. is to be an idiot — BLAKE, 26; GENERALIZATIONS, 1
generals It is not the business of g. to shoot one another — OFFICERS, 10; WELLINGTON, 9
that's not against the law for g. — OFFICERS, 8
to be left to the g. — OFFICERS, 4
generation Each g. imagines itself...more intelligent — AGE, 31; ORWELL, 15
You are a lost g. — WAR, 62
generations g....pass in a short time — MORTALITY, 8

generosity The poor…their function…is to exercise our g.
POVERTY, 14

generous a loyal, a gallant, a g., an ingenious, and good-temper'd people
FRANCE, 8

genius a country full of g., but with absolutely no talent
IRELAND, 7

a German and a g.
SWIFT, 12

G. does what it must
TALENT AND GENIUS, 3

G. is one per cent inspiration
GENIUS, 1

Nothing, except my g.
WILDE, 42

Only an organizing g.
INCOMPETENCE, 1

Rules and models destroy g. and art
RULES, 2

She had a temperament akin to g.
PANKHURST, 2

Since when was g….respectable
BROWNING, 2; RESPECTABILITY, 1

talent instantly recognizes g.
DOYLE, 9; MEDIOCRITY, 2; TALENT AND GENIUS, 2

Taste is the feminine of g.
TASTE, 2

the difference between talent and g.
TALENT AND GENIUS, 1

the most remarkable and seductive g.
BEERBOHM, 2

true g. is a mind of large general powers
GENIUS, 3

True g. walks along a line
GENIUS, 2; GOLDSMITH, 3

When a true g. appears
GENIUS, 4

gen'l'm'n as the g. said to the fi' pun' note
DICKENS, 15

gent what a man is to a g.
INTELLIGENCE, 1

gentil verray parfit g. knight
CHIVALRY, 4

gentleman a g….never inflicts pain
CHIVALRY, 6

A g….wouldn't hit a woman with his hat on
CHIVALRY, 1

g……robbing the poor
CLASS, 17

The Devil is a g.
DEVIL, 7; SHELLEY, 10

the g. is an *attorney*
JOHNSON, 22

gentlemanly secondly, g. conduct
EDUCATION, 1

gentlemen extremely difficult to behave like g.
WOMEN, 25

Good-morning, g. both
INSULTS, 6

Scholars and g.
HONOUR, 5

the British bourgeoisie have spoken of themselves as g.
WAUGH, 7

There were g. and…seamen in the navy of Charles the Second
NAVY, 2

the seamen were not g.
NAVY, 2

G….remember blondes
APPEARANCE, 12

gentlewoman gravest sins it was possible for a g. to commit
WAUGH, 20

geographical India is a g. term
PLACES, 2

geography G. is about Maps
BIOGRAPHY, 1

geometrical Population,…increases in a g. ratio
ECONOMICS, 7

geometricians we are g. only by chance
JOHNSON, 6

geometry Poetry is as exact a science as g.
POETRY, 9

There is no 'royal road' to g.
MATHEMATICS, 2

George G. the Third……*may profit by their example*
TREASON, 4

King G. will be able to read that
SIGNATURES, 1

German A g. and a genius
SWIFT, 12

I speak…G. to my horse
LANGUAGE, 6

Life is too short to learn G.
LANGUAGE, 16

Only peace/ will emanate from G. soil
GERMANY, 2

the G. text of French operas
OPERA, 6

Germans created to jab the life out of us
WORLD WAR I, 10

Germany Defeat of G. means
WORLD WAR II, 20

G., G. before all else
GERMANY, 1

G. will be…a world power
GERMANY, 2

In G., the Nazis came for the Communists
NAZISM, 3

ghost I, born of flesh and g.
DEATH, 62; THOMAS, 3

There is a g. /That eats handkerchiefs
LOSS, 4

yielded up the g.
LAST WORDS, 7

The Papacy is not other than the G. of the deceased Roman Empire
CATHOLICISM, 2

ghoulies From g. and ghosties and long-leggety beasties
SUPERNATURAL, 1

giant Fleas…upon the body of a g.
PERSPECTIVE, 2

owner whereof was G. Despair
DESPAIR, 1

giants it is by standing on the shoulders of g.
PROGRESS, 5

not g. but windmills
CERVANTES, 3; DELUSION, 2

Gibbon G. is an ugly, affected, disgusting fellow
GIBBON, 1

gift True love's the g. which God has given /To man alone
LOVE, 52

worth more than the g.
GIFTS, 3

gifts God's g. put man's best g.
BROWNING, 4; GOD, 11

I fear the Greeks even when they bring g.
MISTRUST, 6; VIRGIL, 5

The Gods themselves cannot recall their g.
IRREVOCABILITY, 2; TENNYSON, 28

gild To g. refined gold
EXCESS, 7

gin No man is genuinely happy, married, who has to drink worse g.
ALCOHOL, 23

The shortest way out of Manchester is…g.
PLACES, 1

girded Pavilioned in splendour, and g. with praise
GOD, 18

girl Every little g. knows about love
LOVE, 51

From birth to age eighteen, a g. needs good parents
AGE, 43

Give me a g. at an impressionable age
IMPRESSIONABILITY, 2

one can…see in a little g. the threat of a woman
CHILDREN, 8

girls g. are so queer
WOMEN, 2

g….say No when they mean Yes
WOMEN, 2

g. who wear glasses
APPEARANCE, 13

the…rift between the sexes is…widened by…teaching…to the g.
STEVENSON, 8

Treaties are like roses and young g.
DIPLOMACY, 6

When you see what some g. marry
MARRIAGE, 49

give freely ye have received, freely g.
GENEROSITY, 2; GIFTS, 2

g. me liberty or g. me death
FREEDOM, 9

G. me your tired,…/Your huddled masses
AMERICA, 15

my peace I g. unto you
PEACE, 2

To g. and not to count the cost
SELFLESSNESS, 2

given I wish that God had not g. me what I prayed for
DISAPPOINTMENT, 5

gives He g. twice who g. promptly
PROMPTNESS, 2

giving The manner of g.
GIFTS, 3

gizzard My wife hath something in her g.
PROVOCATION, 1

glad She had /A heart…too soon made g.
BROWNING, 10; IMPRESSIONABILITY, 1

with a love like that you know you should be g.
LOVE, 39

gladsome Let us with a g. mind /Praise the Lord
GOD, 26

Gladstone Mr G. read Homer for fun
CHURCHILL, 7; CLASSICS, 2

glamorous g. only in retrospect
TRAVEL, 17

glass He liked the sound of broken g.
ARISTOCRACY, 2

Satire is a sort of g.
SATIRE, 3; SWIFT, 3

through a g., darkly
CHARITY, 4

glasses girls who wear g.
APPEARANCE, 13

glimpse I…catch a g. of a stoat
PURPOSE, 3

glisters Nor all that g. gold
TEMPTATION, 3

glittering The world continues to offer g. prizes
RUTHLESSNESS, 2; SUCCESS, 7

gloamin' Roamin' in the g.
SCOTLAND, 4

global my wars /Were g.
WAR, 38

globe the great g. itself
MORTALITY, 10

globule I can trace my ancestry back to a…g.
ANCESTRY, 1

gloire *Le jour de g. est arrivé*
FRANCE, 5

gloria *Sic transit g. mundi*
GLORY, 2

glorious G. things of thee are spoken
HEAVEN, 7

Happy and g.
BRITAIN, 3

glory Another g. awaits us in heaven
HEAVEN, 8

But trailing clouds of g.
METAPHYSICS, 4

greatest g. is not in never falling
ACHIEVEMENT, 1

I go on to g.
LAST WORDS, 10

It is a great g. in a woman
WOMEN, 42

Land of Hope and G.
BRITAIN, 2

Mine eyes have seen the g. of the coming of the Lord
GOD, 21

paths of g. lead but to the grave
MORTALITY, 5

Popularity?…g.'s small change
POPULARITY, 3

the g. of Europe is extinguished for ever
EUROPE, 1

the Son of man coming…with power and great g.
DOOMSDAY, 1

To the greater g. of God
CATHOLICISM, 1

Where is it now, the g. and the dream
METAPHYSICS, 4

glow make the corpuscles of the blood g.
JEWS, 6

Glum I've examined your son's head, Mr G.
STUPIDITY, 6

gluttony G. is an emotional escape
GREED, 2

go In the name of God, g.!
DISMISSAL, 1

I shall be the last to g. out
COURAGE, 1

not to g. anywhere, but to g.
TRAVEL, 16

whither thou goest, I will g.
LOYALTY, 1

god Either a beast or a g.
MANKIND, 1

either a wild beast or a g.
SOLITUDE, 1

I believe I am becoming a g.
LAST WORDS, 28

if triangles invented a g., they would make him three-sided
RELIGION, 25

Kill everyone, and you are a g.
KILLING, 4

Act of G….*something which no reasonable man could have expected*
DISASTER, 2

A G. who let us prove his existence
GOD, 10

a kind of Providence will…end…the acts of G.
DISASTER, 1

A man with G.
GOD, 23

America is G.'s Crucible
AMERICA, 23

an absolute faith that all things are possible to G.
FAITH, 5

An honest G.
GOD, 22

better to have no opinion of G.
GOD, 3

charged with the grandeur of G.
GOD, 20

cricket is the greatest thing that G. ever created
CRICKET, 4

effect Whose cause is G.
COWPER, 11

Even G. cannot change the past — PAST, 1
even G. was born /too late — RELIGION, 22
Every man thinks G. is on his side — GOD, 2
final proof of G.'s omnipotence — GOD, 14
for which…the good G. prepare me — BLINDNESS, 5
G. as a working hypothesis — GOD, 9
G. bless…G. damn — THURBER, 10
'G. bless us every one!' — BLESSING, 4
G. could cause us considerable embarrassment — DISCOVERY, 3
G. does not play dice — EINSTEIN, 3; SCIENCE, 9
G. erects a house of prayer — DEVIL, 5
G.…first planted a garden — GARDENS, 2
G. is always on the side of the big battalions — POWER POLITICS, 5
G. is dead — NIETZSCHE, 4
G. is nothing more than an exalted father — GOD, 17
G. is on the side not of the heavy battalions, but of the best shots — POWER POLITICS, 6; VOLTAIRE, 18
G. is really only another artist — GOD, 28
G. is subtle but he is not malicious — GOD, 16
G. is the immemorial refuge of the incompetent — GOD, 25
G. made the country — COUNTRYSIDE, 1; COWPER, 9
G. said, *Let Newton be* — POPE, 6
G. save our gracious King — BRITAIN, 3
G.'s gifts put man's best gifts — BROWNING, 4; GOD, 11
G. should go before such villains — GOD, 29
G.'s in His heaven — BROWNING, 14
G. the first garden made — GARDENS, 6
G. will grant an end to these too — ENDURANCE, 10
Great G. grant that twice two be not four — PRAYER, 10
Had I but serv'd my G. with half the zeal /I serv'd my King — REGRET, 10; SHAKESPEARE, 51
Had I…served G. as diligently as I have served the king — LOYALTY, 3
have one G. only — GOD, 12
her conception of G. was certainly not orthodox — GOD, 31
Holy, holy, holy, Lord G. Almighty — GOD, 19
I did not write it. G. wrote it — INSPIRATION, 3
If G. did not exist — GOD, 33; VOLTAIRE, 10
If G. made us in His image — GOD, 34; VOLTAIRE, 15
If G. were suddenly condemned to live the life — HUMAN CONDITION, 2
Know then thyself, presume not G. to scan — SELF-KNOWLEDGE, 3
Many people believe that they are attracted by G. — RELIGION, 19
May G. deny you peace — GLORY, 1
nature is the art of G. — NATURE, 1
none deny there is a G. — ATHEISM, 2
One on G.'s side is a majority — GOD, 27
Our G., our help in ages past — RELIGION, 33
poems…for the love of Man and in praise of G. — POETRY, 24
proof that G. is a bore — PROTESTANTISM, 1
put your hand into the hand of G. — FAITH, 6
Since G. has given us the papacy…enjoy it — CATHOLICISM, 4
that G. is interested only…in religion — GOD, 32
The Act of G. designation — ACCIDENTS, 1
the dear G. who loveth us — PRAYER, 6
the highest praise of G. consists in the denial of Him — ATHEISM, 5; PROUST, 5
the nearer you are to G. — PROTESTANTISM, 2
the one G. whose worshippers…still trust in Him — LUCK, 1
There once was a man who said 'G. — EXISTENCE, 4
The true G.,…God of ideas — INSPIRATION, 4
we come /From G., who is our home — METAPHYSICS, 4
we owe G. a death — DEATH, 55
What G. does, He does well — GOD, 24
What sort of G. are we portraying — GOD, 15
whom G. wishes to destroy — MADNESS, 2
godlike patient endurance is g. — ENDURANCE, 4
gods Against stupidity the g.…struggle in vain — STUPIDITY, 7
by force of the g. — ENDURANCE, 12; VIRGIL, 3
G. help them — SELF-RELIANCE, 1
Kings are earth's g. — ROYALTY, 14
leave the rest to the G. — DUTY, 2
Live with the g. — CONTENTMENT, 1
man's ignorance of the g. — SPONTANEITY, 1
no other g. before me — GOD, 6
The Ethiopians say that their g. are…black — RELIGION, 39
The G. themselves cannot recall their gifts — IRREVOCABILITY, 2; TENNYSON, 28
we're forbidden to know – what end the g. have in store — DESTINY, 6
Whom the g. love — DEATH, 42
Whom the g. wish to destroy — TALENT, 1
going I am just g. outside — LAST WORDS, 21
Men must endure /Their g. hence — ENDURANCE, 8

Stand not upon the order of your g. — DISMISSAL, 5; SHAKESPEARE, 73
gold A g. rush is what happens when — MATERIALISM, 12
all the g. that the goose could give — MATERIALISM, 1
For g. in phisik is a cordial — MATERIALISM, 3
gild refined g. — EXCESS, 7
Good morning to the day: and next my g. — MATERIALISM, 7
Nor all that glisters g. — TEMPTATION, 3
Silver threads among the g. — OLD AGE, 18
To a shower of g. — BRIBERY, 1
travell'd in the realms of g. — TRAVEL, 7
golden G. slumbers kiss your eyes — SLEEP, 4
In old time we had treen chalices and g. priests — CLERGY, 4
Jerusalem the g. — PLACES, 8
perhaps, the g. rule — ABSTINENCE, 10; STEVENSON, 11
repeat that on the G. Floor — LAST WORDS, 17
there are no g. rules — RULES, 3; SHAW, 17
gold rush A g. is what happens when — WEST, 6
Goldwyn knew where you were with G. — GOLDWYNISMS, 1
golf an earnest protest against g. — GOLF, 1
G.…a form of moral effort — GOLF, 2
Gomorrah Sodom and…G. — PUNISHMENT, 2
good a g. friend, but bad acquaintance — BYRON, 10
A g. novel tells us the truth — CHESTERTON, 10; NOVELS, 1
All g. writing — FITZGERALD, 8
being really g. all the time — HYPOCRISY, 10; WILDE, 16
Do g. by stealth — GOOD, 5
Evil, be thou my G. — EVIL, 9
Far too g. to waste on children — SHAW, 27
General G. is the plea of the scoundrel — BLAKE, 10
God saw that it was g. — CREATION, 2
g. in business…kind of art — BUSINESS, 13
G. isn't the word — GILBERT, 10
g. shepherd giveth his life for the sheep — CHRISTIANITY, 8
G. things, when short, are twice as good — BREVITY, 1
g. tidings of great joy — CHRISTMAS, 6
greatest g. — GOOD, 1
happiness makes them g. — GOOD, 2
He who would do g. to another — BLAKE, 10
If…'feeling g.' could decide, drunkenness would be — DRUNKENNESS, 7
It is g. to know what a man is — UNDERSTANDING, 2
It is seldom…one parts on g. terms — PARTING, 5; PROUST, 7
never was a g. war — WAR AND PEACE, 5
Nothing can harm a g. man — GOOD, 7
nothing either g. or bad — SHAKESPEARE, 34; THINKING, 5
One man is as g. as another — WRITERS, 7
Only g. girls keep diaries — DIARIES, 2
science is…neither a potential for g. nor for evil — SCIENCE, 26
strong antipathy of g. to bad — PROVOCATION, 2
suppose the people g. — CORRUPTION, 5
The g. die early — GOOD AND EVIL, 2
The g. die first — WORDSWORTH, 3
The g. is oft interred with their bones — EVIL, 11; SHAKESPEARE, 10
The g. is the beautiful — GOOD, 4
The g. of the people — LAW, 1
The king has been very g. to me — MARTYRDOM, 1
the name of perseverance in a g. cause — STUBBORNNESS, 2
There is so much g. in the worst of us — GOOD AND EVIL, 1
those who go about doing g. — CHARITY, 9
thou g. and faithful servant — SERVICE, 1
to write g. prose is an affair of g. manners — POETRY AND PROSE, 4
Whenever two g. people argue over principles — PRINCIPLES, 3
When I'm g. I'm very g. — WEST, 14
Why care for grammar as long as we are g. — GRAMMAR, 5
goodness And felt how awful g. is — GOOD, 3
G. does not…make men happy — GOOD, 3
My g. those diamonds are lovely — GOOD, 8; WEST, 4
the certainty of your g. — WOOLF, 6
goods isn't a bad bit of g., the Queen — COMPLIMENTS, 1
good-temper'd a loyal, a gallant, a generous, an ingenious, and g. people — FRANCE, 8
goodwill in peace, g. — CHURCHILL, 12; WAR AND PEACE, 3
goose all the gold that the g. could give — MATERIALISM, 1
gorgeous hold the g. east in fee — VENICE, 3
gossips No one g. about…secret virtues — GOSSIP, 1
gout G…physician's name for — DISEASE, 6
govern Every class is unfit to g. — GOVERNMENT, 1
Grammar, which can g. even kings — GRAMMAR, 4
He that would g. others — SELF-CONTROL, 4
king reigns, but does not g. — MONARCHY, 13
Kings g. by…assemblies only when — MONARCHY, 6
Labour is not fit to g. — CHURCHILL, 19; POLITICS, 13

Under socialism *all* will g. SOCIALISM, 6
governing become accustomed to no one g. SOCIALISM, 6
government A g....big enough to give you all you want GOVERNMENT, 7
a g. organization could do it that quickly BUREAUCRACY, 1
All g....is founded on compromise and barter BURKE, 8; COMPROMISE, 2
Democracy is only an experiment in g. DEMOCRACY, 3
every g....should have its old speeches burned GOVERNMENT, 13
g. by crony NEPOTISM, 1
G....is but a necessary evil GOVERNMENT, 11
g. of the people, by the people, and for the people MEMORIALS, 8
Monarchy is a strong g. MONARCHY, 1
no man believes, that want of g., is any new kind of g. GOVERNMENT, 8
people's g. GOVERNMENT, 16
The g. burns down whole cities INJUSTICE, 6; MAO TSE-TUNG, 6
the g. it deserves GOVERNMENT, 9
there was no form of g. common to the peoples REPUBLIC, 2
the things which g. does...social progress GOVERNMENT, 15
The worst g. is the most moral GOVERNMENT, 10
governments all G. are selfish GOVERNMENT, 5
G. need to have both shepherds and butchers GOVERNMENT, 14; VOLTAIRE, 17
Gower moral G. BOOKS, 6
grace Such g. had kings ROYALTY, 3
gracious A life that moves to g. ends LIFE, 22
graduating g. with a 'spinster of arts' degree LANGUAGE, 17
grain A g., which in England is generally given to horses SCOTLAND, 2
He reaps the bearded g. at a breath DEATH, 40
grammar down to posterity talking bad g. DISRAELI, 10
G., which can govern even kings GRAMMAR, 4
Why care for g. as long as we are good GRAMMAR, 5
grammatical I have laboured to refine our language to g. purity LANGUAGE, 9
grand A 'G. Old Man' OLD AGE, 13
The g. Perhaps POSSIBILITY, 1
the g. style arises in poetry POETRY, 3
grandeur g. is a dream WEALTH, 6
g. of God GOD, 20
grandfather having an ape for his g. EVOLUTION, 6
granny G. caught her tit in the mangle PLEASURE, 13
granted human beings have an...infinite capacity for taking things for g. HUXLEY, 18
grape Beulah, peel me a g. WEST, 5
grapes I am sure the g. are sour ENVY, 2
trampling out the vintage where the g. of wrath GOD, 21
grasp man's reach should exceed his g. AMBITION, 2; BROWNING, 4
grassgreen It is the g. gooseberried double bed THOMAS, 12
gratifying It is quite g. to feel guilty GUILT, 1
grave a-mouldering in the g. MEMORIALS, 4
And digs my g. at each remove DEATH, 28
Dig the g. and let me lie DEATH, 60; STEVENSON, 7
her heart in his g. is lying MOURNING, 5
I may dread /The g. as little DEATH, 36
I shall soon be laid in the quiet g. DEATH, 35
Marriage is a step so g. and decisive STEVENSON, 12
no work, nor device, nor knowledge...in the g. TRANSIENCE, 4; WORK, 1
O g., where is thy victory DEATH, 12
O g.! where is thy victory DEATH, 48
paths of glory lead but to the g. MORTALITY, 5
grave-digger if I were a g., or...a hangman OCCUPATIONS, 2
graven any g. image GOD, 6
graves Six million young men lie in premature g. WORLD WAR I, 2
The bitterest tears shed over g. REGRET, 11
graveyards G....people associate them with death DEATH, 10
gravity He rose by g.; I sank by levity SMITH, 9
gray When you are old and g. OLD AGE, 30; YEATS, 12
great All my shows are g. GOLDWYNISMS, 27
All things both g. and small PRAYER, 6
Everything g. in the world is done by neurotics NEUROSIS, 1; PROUST, 9
everything that is g....done by youth DISRAELI, 4
G. men are but life-sized BEERBOHM, 4
g. men have not commonly been g. scholars GREATNESS, 5
History is full of ignominious getaways by the g. COWARDICE, 2
No g. man lives in vain GREATNESS, 4
On earth there is nothing g. but man MANKIND, 7
Some are born g. GREATNESS, 7; SHAKESPEARE, 119

the g. ones eat up the little ones RUTHLESSNESS, 1; SHAKESPEARE, 96
greater g. love hath no man LOVE, 8
The g. the power BURKE, 15; POWER, 4
They need is yet g. than mine SELF-DENIAL, 2
greatest the g. deeds require a certain insensitivity INSENSITIVITY, 2
The g. happiness of the g. number HAPPINESS, 1
the g. of these is charity CHARITY, 4
great-grandfathers Classicism,...the literature that gave...pleasure to their g. LITERATURE, 10
greatness Men who have g....don't go in for politics POLITICIANS, 1
some have g. thrust upon 'em GREATNESS, 7; SHAKESPEARE, 119
Great War A Soldier of the G. KIPLING, 9
Greece Athens holds sway over all G. INFLUENCE, 3
Greek I...impress upon you the study of G. literature CLASSICS, 3
Nobody can say a word against G. SHAW, 7
Greeks G. Had a Word LANGUAGE, 1
I fear the G. even when they bring gifts MISTRUST, 6; VIRGIL, 3
The Romans and G. found everything human LAWRENCE, 3
To the G. the Muse gave native wit CLASSICS, 4
which came first, the G. or the Romans DISRAELI, 19
green a g. thought in a g. shade OBLIVION, 2
I was g. in judgment SHAKESPEARE, 13; YOUTH, 8
religious system that produced g. Chartreuse ALCOHOL, 28; SAKI, 11
tree of life is g. THEORY, 3
G. grow the rashes O BURNS, 7
G. politics is not about being far left CONSERVATION, 4
green-ey'd jealousy...g. monster JEALOUSY, 3; SHAKESPEARE, 91
Greenland From G.'s icy mountains PLACES, 4
green-rob'd g. senators of mighty woods TREES, 4
Greensleeves G. was all my joy LOVE, 1
greenwood Under the g. tree COUNTRYSIDE, 5
grey theory is all g. THEORY, 3
There is only one cure for g. hair....the guillotine REMEDIES, 9; WODEHOUSE, 8
grief calms one's g. by recounting it SORROW, 2
G. has turned her fair WILDE, 40
in much wisdom is much g. KNOWLEDGE, 3; WISDOM, 1
Should be past g. SHAKESPEARE, 122
The heart which g. hath cankered ALCOHOL, 8
grill be careful not to look like a mixed g. APPEARANCE, 6
grin All Nature wears one universal g. NATURE, 7
ending with the g., which remained some time CARROLL, 3; SUPERNATURAL, 4
groans How alike are the g. of love to those of the dying LOVE AND DEATH, 2
Groucho had Marx been G. instead of Karl HUMOUR, 2
No, G. is not my real name NAMES, 2
group A g. of closely related persons FAMILY, 14
grovelled Whenever he met a great man he g. SERVILITY, 4
groves And seek for truth in the g. of Academe EDUCATION, 10
grow Green g. the rashes O BURNS, 7
make two questions g. where only one RESEARCH, 3
They shall g. not old MEMORIALS, 3
growing G. old is like being increasingly penalized OLD AGE, 17
grown Boys...are unwholesome companions for g. people LAMB, 3
grows Nothing g. well in the shade GREATNESS, 3
growth as short a Spring; /As quick a g. to meet decay TRANSIENCE, 3
grub it is poor g., poor pay, and easy work ENGLAND, 12
grumbling the muttering grew to a g. BROWNING, 13
gruntled far from feeling g. DISCONTENT, 6
guarantee No one can g. success in war WAR, 16
guards Who is to guard the g. themselves MISTRUST, 3
Up, G., and at 'em WELLINGTON, 10
guerre *ce n'est pas la g.* WAR, 3
guerrilla The g. fights the war of the flea WAR, 64
The g. wins if he does not lose WAR, 30
guest A free-loader is a confirmed g. PARASITES, 2
guests the g. must be chosen as carefully as the wine ALCOHOL, 29; SAKI, 9
guide Custom, then, is the great g. of human life CUSTOM, 2
Everyman, I will go with thee, and be thy g. GUIDANCE, 1
guiding little onward lend thy g. hand GUIDANCE, 2
guillotine There is only one cure for grey hair....the g. REMEDIES, 9; WODEHOUSE, 8
guilt I have no sense of g. PANKHURST, 5
Let other pens dwell on g. and misery OPTIMISM, 3
Life without industry is g. ART, 15; RUSKIN, 3
put on a dress of g. GUILT, 4
guilty It is quite gratifying to feel g. GUILT, 1

ten g. persons escape than one innocent suffer	JUSTICE, 2
gum can't fart and chew g. at the same time	MISQUOTATIONS, 13
gun it is necessary to take up the g.	WAR, 35
we have got /The Maxim G., and they have not	BELLOC, 8
Gunga Din You're a better man than I am, G.	SUPERIORITY, 3
gunpowder G., Printing, and the Protestant Religion	
	CARLYLE, 7; CIVILIZATION, 5
guns But it's 'Saviour of 'is country' when the g.	
	KIPLING, 7; SOLDIERS, 1
G. will make us powerful	POWER POLITICS, 1
gutless W. H. Auden, a sort of g. Kipling	AUDEN, 2
gutter We are all in the g.	WILDE, 23
habit a h. the pleasure of which increases with practise	
	LETTER-WRITING, 1
honour peereth in the meanest h.	APPEARANCES, 11; SHAKESPEARE, 112
some h. of which he is deeply ashamed	TELEVISION, 2
habitation to airy nothing /A local h.	POETRY, 20
habits Cultivate only the h.	HABIT, 3
Curious things, h.	HABIT, 1
h. that carry them far apart	HABIT, 2
hail h. and farewell	GREETINGS, 1
H., h. rock'n'roll	POP MUSIC, 3
the flail of the lashing h.	WEATHER, 11
hair busy driving cabs and cutting h.	GOVERNMENT, 4
if a woman have long h.	APPEARANCE, 2
half And when they were only h. way up	ARMY, 1
h. a loaf is better than a whole	CHESTERTON, 19; COMPROMISE, 1
longest h. of your life	YOUTH, 10
One h....cannot understand...the other	AUSTEN, 3; PLEASURE, 1
There is an old saying 'well begun is h. done'	KEATS, 9
half-developed the working-class which, raw and h.	ARNOLD, 5
half-wits a wit out of two h.	FOOLISHNESS, 6
hall one of the sparrows...flew...through the h.	LIFE, 4
We met...Dr H. in such very deep mourning	
	AUSTEN, 18; MOURNING, 1
hallowed The place of justice is a h. place	JUSTICE, 1
halters talk of h. in the hanged man's house	TACT, 2
hamburger British h. thus symbolised...failure to provide its ordi-	
nary people with food	FOOD, 11
hammer Art is not a mirror...but a h.	ART, 9
hand bite the h. that fed them	BURKE, 12; INGRATITUDE, 1
educate with the head instead of with the h.	EDUCATION, 14
h. that signed the treaty bred a fever	SIGNATURES, 2; THOMAS, 5
little onward lend thy guiding h.	GUIDANCE, 2
No, this right h. shall work it all off	SCOTT, 9
Our h. will not tremble	RUSSIAN REVOLUTION, 1
put your h. into the h. of God	FAITH, 6
sweeten this little h.	SHAKESPEARE, 75
touch his weaknesses with a delicate h.	IMPERFECTION, 4
handbook have used the Bible as if it was a constable's h.	BIBLE, 4
handicraft Art is not a h.	ART, 18
handkerchiefs There is a ghost /That eats h.	LOSS, 4
hands don't raise your h. because I am also nearsighted	AUDEN, 14
into thy h. I commend my spirit	LAST WORDS, 6
Licence my roving h.	LUST, 1
Pilate...washed his h.	GUILT, 2
You cannot shake h. with a clenched fist	INFLEXIBILITY, 1
handsome not as h. as...his poetry	ARNOLD, 11
hang I will find something...to h. him	EXECUTION, 11
We must indeed all h. together	UNITY, 5
hanged Men are not h. for stealing	EXAMPLE, 3
talk of halters in the h. man's house	TACT, 2
to be h. for nonsense	DRYDEN, 8
when a man knows he is to be h. in a fortnight	
	EXECUTION, 5; JOHNSON, 31
hanging h. prevents a bad marriage	MARRIAGE, 53
H. and wiving goes by destiny	DESTINY, 11
hangman if I were a grave-digger, or...a h.	OCCUPATIONS, 7
happen poetry makes nothing h.	AUDEN, 10
happened most of which had never h.	WORRY, 4
happening h. to somebody else	HUMOUR, 16
happens I just don't want to be there when it h.	ALLEN, 6
life...seems to me preparation for something that never h.	YEATS, 3
happiest h. time of all the glad New-year	MERRYMAKING, 3
Poetry is the record of the best and h. moments	
	POETRY, 22; SHELLEY, 5
happiness A lifetime of h....hell on earth	HAPPINESS, 14; SHAW, 11
curiously boring about...h.	HUXLEY, 11
greatest h. of the greatest number	HAPPINESS, 1
h. fails, existence remains...experiment	HAPPINESS, 12
H. in marriage	AUSTEN, 12; MARRIAGE, 4

H. is a mystery like religion	HAPPINESS, 2
H. is an imaginary condition	HAPPINESS, 15; SZASZ, 4
H. is like a butterfly	HAPPINESS, 6
H. is no laughing matter	HAPPINESS, 16
h. is not an ideal of reason	HAPPINESS, 5
H. is not best achieved	HAPPINESS, 8
H. is no vague dream	HAPPINESS, 11
H. is the only sanction of life	HAPPINESS, 12
h. makes them good	GOOD, 2
H.? That's nothing more than health	HAPPINESS, 13
In solitude /What h.	SOLITUDE, 8
I thought that success spelled h.	HAPPINESS, 6
life, liberty, and the pursuit of h.	HUMAN RIGHTS, 3
nothing...by which so much h. is produced as by a good tavern	
	PUBLIC HOUSES, 2
our friends are true and our h.	OPTIMISM, 4
recall a time of h. when in misery	SORROW, 3
result h.	DICKENS, 4; ECONOMICS, 1
the greatest h. for the greatest numbers	HAPPINESS, 3
the greatest h. of the whole	REPUBLIC, 1
the h. of the common man	GOVERNMENT, 3
Who never knew the price of h.	HAPPINESS, 17
you take away his h.	DELUSION, 3
happy a h. woman and universally respected	WOLLSTONECRAFT, 1
be h. later on, but it's much harder	BEAUVOIR, 4
Few people can be h. unless they hate	HATE, 3
Goodness does not...make men h.	GOOD, 2
h. families resemble each other	FAMILY, 20
H. the hare at morning	AUDEN, 5
H. the Man	DRYDEN, 14; PRESENT, 1
I've had a h. life	HAZLITT, 13
I were but little h.	SILENCE, 5
laugh before one is h.	LA BRUYÈRE, 4; LAUGHTER, 3
Let us all be h., and live within our means	BORROWING, 5
One is h. as a result of one's own efforts	HAPPINESS, 11
policeman's lot is not a h. one	GILBERT, 7; POLICE, 1
Puritanism – The haunting fear that someone...may be h.	
	PURITANISM, 2
That all who are h., are equally h.	HAPPINESS, 4
To make men h.	ADMIRATION, 4
what it is that makes a Scotchman h.	ALCOHOL, 18; JOHNSON, 42
hard H. and high to the stars	AMBITION, 1
I'm not h. – I'm frightfully soft	THATCHER, 3
It's been a h. day's night	WORK, 6
hardness without h. will be sage	FUTURE, 1
hardships we shall be glad to remember even these h.	
	ENDURANCE, 11; VIRGIL, 4
Hardy Kiss me, H.	LAST WORDS, 20
hare First catch your h.'	MISQUOTATIONS, 11
Happy the h. at morning	AUDEN, 5
Take your h. when it is cased...	FOOD, 10
harlot the prerogative of the h. through the ages	RESPONSIBILITY, 1
harm No people do so much h.	CHARITY, 9
harmony h. imposes compatibility upon the incongruous	MUSIC, 17
harp his wild h. slung behind him	WAR, 40
harps To touch their h. of gold	CHRISTMAS, 13
harpsichord The sound of the h.	MUSIC, 4
harsh in this h. world	MOURNING, 9
harvest His Royal Highness...prides himself upon...the excellent	
h.	SHERIDAN, 9
In seed time learn, in h. teach	SUITABILITY, 1
haste Men love in h.	BYRON, 14; LOVE AND HATE, 1
You h. away	TRANSIENCE, 9
Hastings ancestors on either side of the Battle of H.	ANCESTRY, 3
hat A gentleman...wouldn't hit a woman with his h. on	CHIVALRY, 1
looking for a black h.	METAPHYSICS, 1
hatched count their chickens ere they're h.	BUTLER, 2
hatchet I did it with my little h.	HONESTY, 5
hate Few...can be happy unless they h.	HATE, 3
If you h. a person, you h....yourself	HATE, 2
I h. and love	LOVE AND HATE, 1
I h. the whole race...your professional poets	POETS, 9; WELLINGTON, 5
Let them h.	RESPECT, 1
not to weep at them, nor to h. them	UNDERSTANDING, 4
scarcely h. any one that we know	HATE, 1; HAZLITT, 7
to h. the man you have hurt	HUMAN NATURE, 11
hated h. /by every anti-semite /as if I were a Jew	PREJUDICE, 1
h. of all men for my name's sake	PERSISTENCE, 1
I never h. a man enough	MATERIALISM, 5
I never saw a brute I h. so	BROWNING, 6
hates Anybody who h. children and dogs	CHILDREN, 9; DOGS, 4

Everybody h. house-agents OCCUPATIONS, 7; WELLS, 7
Everybody h. me POPULARITY, 1
hating patriotism which consists in h. all other nations PATRIOTISM, 6
hatred a deep burning h. for the Tory Party POLITICS, 4
An intellectual h. HATE, 4
h. is...the longest pleasure BYRON, 14; LOVE AND HATE, 1
love...looks more like h. than like friendship LOVE AND HATE, 4
hatter 'Not the same thing a bit!' said the H. CARROLL, 4
have To h. and to hold MARRIAGE, 15
haves H. and the Have-nots CERVANTES, 9; POVERTY AND WEALTH, 3
havoc h. of the German bombs ARCHITECTURE, 8
head educate with the h. instead of with the hand EDUCATION, 14
God be in my h., /And in my understanding GOD, 1
Here comes a chopper to chop off your h. LONDON, 1
If you can keep your h. KIPLING, 3; SELF-CONTROL, 3
in politics there is no heart, only h. POLITICS, 35
it shall bruise thy h. SEXES, 1
ought to have his h. examined PSYCHIATRY, 2
Scheherazade...a woman saving her h. SELF-PRESERVATION, 6
shorter by a h. ELIZABETH I, 6; ROYALTY, 7
the greatest asset a h. of state can have SLEEP, 10
Uneasy lies the h. that wears a crown MONARCHY, 10; SHAKESPEARE, 44
you incessantly stand on your h. CARROLL, 2; OLD AGE, 4
headmasters H. have powers CHURCHILL, 6
head-waiter diplomat...is nothing but a h. DIPLOMACY, 9
heal I will h. me of my grievous wound AFTERLIFE, 9
physician, h. thyself DOCTORS, 2
health h. is the second blessing HEALTH AND HEALTHY LIVING, 9
h. is all they get for it SMOKING, 13
h. is his most valuable possession HEALTH AND HEALTHY LIVING, 5
in sickness and in h. MARRIAGE, 15
Look to your h. HEALTH AND HEALTHY LIVING, 9
Only do always in h. what you have often promised to do when you are sick ILLNESS, 8
selling them in h. food shops FOOD, 18
selling them in h. food shops HEALTH AND HEALTHY LIVING, 5
They pay this price for h. SMOKING, 13
healthful hindering h. and varied activity WOMAN'S ROLE, 1
healthy h. and wealthy and dead BED, 5; THURBER, 5
He that goes to bed thirsty rises h. ALCOHOL, 15
Nobody is h. in London AUSTEN, 4; LONDON, 2
think of diseases as isolated disturbances in a h. body DISEASE, 1
hear any of you at the back who do not h. me AUDEN, 14
ear begins to h. IMPRISONMENT, 2
one is always sure to h. of it SHERIDAN, 2
truth which men prefer not to h. TRUTH, 1
heart Absence makes the h. grow fonder ABSENCE, 1
beatings of the lonely h. LONELINESS, 1
by want of thought, as well as want of h. EVIL, 2
cut to the h. ANGER, 2
Death took him by the h. DEATH, 45
God be in my h., /And in my thinking GOD, 1
good h. will help...a bonny face BRONTË, 3
Great thoughts come from the h. THINKING, 7
h. and stomach of a King ELIZABETH I, 7; ROYALTY, 7
holiness of the h.'s affections IMAGINATION, 4
If thou didst ever hold me in thy h. MOURNING, 9
in politics there is no h., only head POLITICS, 35
let not your h. be troubled PEACE, 2
lonely of h. is withered away LONELINESS, 4
look in thy h. and write INSPIRATION, 2
Mother is the dead h. of the family GREER, 2
My h. is a lonely hunter LONELINESS, 5
my h. shall be /The faithful compass FAITHFULNESS, 4
My h.'s in the Highlands BURNS, 2
She had /A h....too soon made glad BROWNING, 10; IMPRESSIONABILITY, 1
strings...in the human h. DICKENS, 2
that mighty h. is lying still SLEEP, 11; WORDSWORTH, 17
The fire which in the h. resides SOUL, 1
The h. that loved her NATURE, 11; WORDSWORTH, 7
The intellect is always fooled by the h. EMOTION, 2
There is a road from the eye to the h. CHESTERTON, 3; EMOTION, 1
the waters of the h. /Push in their tides EMOTION, 3
The way to a man's h. is through his stomach FOOD, 3
to lose your h.'s desire DESIRE, 6; SHAW, 13
What comes from the h. COLERIDGE, 16; SINCERITY, 1
with the palsied h. PASSION, 7; TENNYSON, 20
hearth Man for the field and woman for the h. SEXES, 14
hearts glittering prizes to those who have stout h. SUCCESS, 7
Kind h. are more than coronets ARISTOCRACY, 10; TENNYSON, 16

One equal temper of heroic h. DETERMINATION, 6; TENNYSON, 30
The Queen of H. FOOD, 4
the song that is sung in our h. MUSIC, 18
The Worldly Hope men set their H. upon TRANSIENCE, 8
those who have stout h. and sharp swords RUTHLESSNESS, 2
Two h. that beat as one LOVE, 40
well-developed bodies, fairly developed minds, and undeveloped h. EDUCATION, 8
heat can't stand the h., get out of the kitchen ENDURANCE, 9
H., madam!...to take off my flesh and sit in my bones SMITH, 2
heaven a H. in Hell's despair BLAKE, 18; LOVE, 10
all H. in a rage IMPRISONMENT, 1
All place shall be hell that is not h. DOOMSDAY, 1
Another glory awaits us in h. HEAVEN, 8
from whose face the earth and the h. fled JUDGMENT, 3
God created the h. CREATION, 1
h. and earth shall pass away TRANSIENCE, 8
H. in a wild flower BLAKE, 7
H....is a place so inane, so dull HEAVEN, 9
Home is h. DEBAUCHERY, 4; NASH, 3
If it's h. for climate PERVERSITY, 1
If Max gets to H. WELLS, 10
If this belief from h. be sent MANKIND, 19; WORDSWORTH, 1
In h. an angel is nobody in particular IMPORTANCE, 1; SHAW, 14
make a H. of Hell, a Hell of H. MIND, 3
man is as H. made him CERVANTES, 7
Marriage is...excluded from h. MARRIAGE, 16
more things in h. and earth SHAKESPEARE, 31; SUPERNATURAL, 3
no invention came more easily to man than H. HEAVEN, 5
Order is h.'s first law ORDER, 2
Parting is all we know of h. DICKINSON, 2; PARTING, 3
Pennies do not come from h. THATCHER, 7; WORK, 11
Pennies from H. OPTIMISM, 5
so much of earth...of h. IMPETUOSITY, 1
steep and thorny way to h. EXAMPLE, 5; SHAKESPEARE, 28
there was war in h. DEVIL, 3
the starry h. above me WONDER, 1
to be young was very h. FRENCH REVOLUTION, 3; WORDSWORTH, 14
what's a h. for AMBITION, 2; BROWNING, 4
What they do in h. MARRIAGE, 5
heavenward A homely face...aided many women h. APPEARANCE, 1
heavier O you who have borne even h. things ENDURANCE, 10
heaviest nickname is the h. stone that the devil can throw NAMES, 1
heav'n h. on earth HEAVEN, 6
hedge A leap over the h. PRAYER, 4
heed To fight and not to h. the wounds SELFLESSNESS, 2
heesh If John or Mary comes h. will want to play LANGUAGE, 13
heights If suffer we must, let's suffer on the h. SUFFERING, 3
heiress American h. wants to buy a man MATERIALISM, 9
hell a H. in Heaven's despite BLAKE, 19; LOVE, 11
A lifetime of happiness...h. on earth HAPPINESS, 14; SHAW, 11
All place shall be h. that is not heaven DOOMSDAY, 4
all we need of h. DICKINSON, 2; PARTING, 3
h. a fury like a woman scorned CONGREVE, 7; LOVE AND HATE, 3
H. is a city much like London LONDON, 7
h. upon earth...in a melancholy man's heart MELANCHOLY, 3
make a Heaven of H., a H. of Heaven MIND, 3
Old age is woman's h. OLD AGE, 14
out of h. leads up to light HELL, 3
Raises from H. a human soul BLAKE, 4; HELL, 1
the h. of horses ENGLAND, 8
the little holiday steamers made an excursion to h. WORLD WAR II, 19
though h. should bar the way DETERMINATION, 5
To h. with you TELEGRAMS, 1
Ugly h., gape not DAMNATION, 2
War is h. WAR, 61
way down to H. is easy HELL, 4; VIRGIL, 8
help gods h. them that h. themselves SELF-RELIANCE, 1
going in without the h. of Russia WORLD WAR II, 17
not so much our friends' h. that helps us FRIENDSHIP, 6
Since there's no h. PARTING, 1
The dead...look on and h. LAWRENCE, 16
of too many physicians DOCTORS, 1
what is past my h. is past my care INDIFFERENCE, 1
with a little h. from my friends FRIENDS, 7
helps not so much our friends' help that h. us FRIENDSHIP, 6
hem only touch the h. of his garment REMEDIES, 1
hen a broody h. sitting on a china egg BUREAUCRACY, 4
herb sweetest fragrance from the h....tread on it and bruise it WOMEN, 43
herbs nature runs either to h., or to weeds HUMAN NATURE, 2

hunt how much more dogs are animated when they h. in a pack
UNITY, 7
hunter Man is the h. SEXES, 13; TENNYSON, 25
My heart is a lonely h. LONELINESS, 5
hunting Memories are h. horns MEMORY, 1
hurricanes You cataracts and h. WEATHER, 7
hurry So who's in a h. ALCOHOL, 2
hurrying I see a man h. along – to what PURPOSE, 3
hurt it h. too much to laugh DISAPPOINTMENT, 6
It takes your enemy and your friend…, to h. you TWAIN, 5
Those have most power to h. HURT, 1
wish to h. CRUELTY, 1
husband An archaeologist is the best h. MARRIAGE, 18
Being a h. is a whole-time job BENNETT, 4; MARRIAGE, 9
easier to be a lover than a h. MARRIAGE, 7
happened unawares to look at her h. AUSTEN, 16
h. render unto the wife due benevolence MARRIAGE, 11
in love with…Her own h. LOVE AND MARRIAGE, 2
light wife doth make a heavy h. MARRIAGE, 52
My h. and I' ROYALTY, 9
Never trust a h. too far TRUST, 3
trust my h. not to fall asleep POLITICS, 45
husbandry borrowing dulls the edge of h.
BORROWING, 4; INTEGRITY, 4; SHAKESPEARE, 29
husbands flirt with their own h. LOVE AND MARRIAGE, 5; WILDE, 13
h. and wives…belong to different sexes SEXES, 6
H. are like fires MARRIAGE, 31
h., love your wives MARRIAGE, 10
h. remind me of an orangutang MARRIAGE, 8
h. to stay at home ELIOT, 4; WOMEN, 18
The *divine right* of h. WOLLSTONECRAFT, 2
hush a breathless h. in the Close tonight CRICKET, 3
hut Love in a h. KEATS, 5
Huxley Mr. H.…perpetrate thirty bad novels HUXLEY, 1
hyacinth every H. the Garden wears FLOWERS, 3
hydrostatics It gives me the h. MALAPROPISMS, 5; SHERIDAN, 3
hymn Aisle. Altar. H. MARRIAGE, 42; PUNS, 9
hypocrisy an organized h. DISRAELI, 12; POLITICS, 17
H.…is a whole-time job HYPOCRISY, 5
H. is the homage paid by vice to virtue
HYPOCRISY, 7; ROCHEFOUCAULD, 7
H. is the most…nerve-racking vice HYPOCRISY, 5
neither man nor angel can discern /H. HYPOCRISY, 6
That would be h. HYPOCRISY, 10; WILDE, 16
hypocrite No man is a h. In his pleasures PLEASURE, 8
see…into a h. CHESTERTON, 8; HYPOCRISY, 3
hypocritical Man…learns by being h. HYPOCRISY, 4
hypodermic man who cannot work without his h. needle DRUGS, 2
hypothesis the slaying of a beautiful h. by an ugly fact SCIENCE, 12
ice skating over thin i. HASTE, 2
iced three parts i. over AGE, 1; ARNOLD, 19
icicles When i. hang by the wall SHAKESPEARE, 67
icumen Sumer is i. in SEASONS, 1
idea An i. isn't responsible for the people IDEAS, 4
constant repetition…in imprinting an i. HITLER, 6
Dying for an i. MARTYRDOM, 2
I think it would be a good i. CIVILIZATION, 4
no stand can be made against invasion by an i. IDEAS, 1
the i. of death as an individual NUCLEAR WEAPONS, 6
ideal the i. American AMERICANS, 2
idealism an extraordinary mixture of i. and lunacy PANKHURST, 1
idealist An i.…, on noticing that a rose smells better than a cabbage IDEALISM, 3
people call me an i. AMERICA, 21
ideals Away with all i. SPONTANEITY, 2
think how far I can go with all the i. that I have
IDEALISM, 4; THATCHER, 5
ideas down which i. are lured and…strangled BUREAUCRACY, 2
Human Stupidity consists in having lots of i. STUPIDITY, 5
i. simply pass through him STUPIDITY, 1
Many i. grow better when transplanted into another mind IDEAS, 2
Morality which is based on i. LAWRENCE, 5; MORALITY, 4
The true God,…God of i. INSPIRATION, 4
ides Beware the i. of March PROPHECY, 5
idiot An inspired i. GOLDSMITH, 2
tale told by an i. LIFE, 19; SHAKESPEARE, 76
The i. who praises…every country but his own DISCONTENT, 2
To generalize is to be an i. BLAKE, 26; GENERALIZATIONS, 1
idiots the English seem…to act with…the fatuity of i.
IRELAND, 10; SMITH, 1
idle As i. as a painted ship BOATS, 2; COLERIDGE, 11

Satan finds…mischief…/For i. hands IDLENESS, 6
We would all be i. IDLENESS, 4; JOHNSON, 29
Young people ought not to be i. IDLENESS, 5; THATCHER, 9
idleness Research! A mere excuse for i. RESEARCH, 1
I…the refuge of weak minds CHESTERFIELD, 10; IDLENESS, 1
idling It is impossible to enjoy i. IDLENESS, 2
idol one-eyed yellow i. to the north of Khatmandu MOURNING, 3
idolatry There is no i. in the Mass CATHOLICISM, 3
if I, you can keep your head KIPLING, 3; SELF-CONTROL, 3
much virtue in 'I. POSSIBILITY, 2; SHAKESPEARE, 24
ignominious History is full of i. getaways by the great COWARDICE, 2
ignorance From i. our comfort flows IGNORANCE, 4
I. is like a delicate exotic fruit IGNORANCE, 6
I. of the law excuses LAW, 10
journalism…keeps us in touch with the i. of the community
JOURNALISM, 18; WILDE, 9
Lawyers are the only persons in whom i.…is not punished
LAWYERS, 1
man's i. of the gods SPONTANEITY, 1
no sin but i. IGNORANCE, 3
Somebody else's i. is bliss IGNORANCE, 5
where i. is bliss, /'Tis folly to be wise IGNORANCE, 1
ignorant Let no one i. of mathematics enter here MATHEMATICS, 4
The i. man always adores IGNORANCE, 2
the opinionated, the i., and the boorish STUBBORNNESS, 1
To confess that you are totally I. about the Horse HORSES, 5
what may follow it, or what preceded it, we are absolutely i. LIFE, 4
ill Cannot be i.; cannot be good SUPERNATURAL, 10
human i. does not dawn seem…an alternative HUMAN CONDITION, 12
If…someone is speaking i. of you CRITICISM, 6
woman colour'd i. CONFLICT, 2
illegal collect legal taxes from i. money TAXATION, 1
ill-health Cynicism is humour in i. CYNICISM, 4; WELLS, 8
illiteracy The ratio of literacy to i. LITERACY, 1
illiterate I. him…from your memory MALAPROPISMS, 4
illogical Faith…an i. belief in…the improbable FAITH, 7
ills sharp remedy…for all i. EXECUTION, 10
illusion Religion is an i. RELIGION, 14
The House of Lords, an i. HOUSES OF PARLIAMENT, 10; RESPONSIBILITY, 1
visible universe was an i. UNIVERSE, 2
image any graven i. GOD, 8
A photograph is not only an i. PHOTOGRAPHY, 5
If God made us in His i. GOD, 34; VOLTAIRE, 15
make man in our own i. CREATION, 5; MANKIND, 2
imaginary Happiness is an i. condition HAPPINESS, 15; SZASZ, 4
imagination A lady's i. is very rapid AUSTEN, 11; WOMEN, 5
Art is ruled…by the i. IMAGINATION, 1
I. and fiction…three quarters of our real life IMAGINATION, 5
I.!…I put it first years ago ACTING, 7
I. without skill gives us modern art ART, 17
indebted to his…i. for his facts SHERIDAN, 13
no i. and…no compassion IMAGINATION, 2
not an ideal of reason but of i. HAPPINESS, 5
of i. all compact POETRY, 21
truth of i. IMAGINATION, 4
imagined What is now proved was…i. PROOF, 1
imagining How reconcile this world…with…my i. BLINDNESS, 1
imitate A good composer does not i. MUSICIANS, 5
An original writer is…one whom nobody can i. ORIGINALITY, 1
never failed to i. CHILDREN, 1
people…usually i. each other IMITATION, 2
imitates Photography can never grow up if it i. PHOTOGRAPHY, 1
imitation Man…is an i. MANKIND, 9
I. is the sincerest form of flattery IMITATION, 1
Immanuel call his name I. CHRISTIANITY, 3
immaturity the executive expression of human i. POLITICS, 8
immoral moral or an i. book BOOKS, 29
worse than i. MISTAKES, 1
immorality the most rigid code of i. ENGLISH, 2
immortal I have lost the i. part REPUTATION, 4
make me i. with a kiss BEAUTY, 14
Why are you weeping? Did you imagine that I was i. LAST WORDS, 18
immortality I…want to achieve i.…through not dying
ALLEN, 2; IMMORTALITY, 1
just ourselves /And I. DEATH, 19; DICKINSON, 1
imperfection i. itself may have its…perfect state IMPERFECTION, 3
impersonal in the philosopher there is nothing whatever i.
PHILOSOPHERS, 4
impertinent ask an i. question SCIENCE, 1
impetuous such i. blood IMPETUOSITY, 3
importance Official dignity…in inverse ratio to…i. HUXLEY, 5

important One doesn't recognize...the really i. moments...until it's too late — REGRET, 1
the little things are infinitely the most i. — TRIVIALITY, 4
imposed wish to be i. on, and then are — EXPLOITATION, 2
impossibility a physical and metaphysical i. — CARLYLE, 3; POETS, 2
impossible complete sorrow is as i. — EMOTION, 4
I believe because it is i. — BELIEF, 4
something is i., he is...wrong — SCIENCE, 3
when you have excluded the i. — DOYLE, 1; TRUTH, 10
impotent an i. people, /Sick with inbreeding — WELSH, 2
impressionable Give me a girl at an i. age — IMPRESSIONABILITY, 2
impressions i....lasting as...an oar upon the water — INSIGNIFICANCE, 1
improbable an i. fiction — REALITY, 3
Faith...an illogical belief in...the i. — FAITH, 7
whatever remains, however i., must be the truth — DOYLE, 1; TRUTH, 10
impromptu preparing...i. speeches — CHURCHILL, 3
impropriety I. is the soul of wit — HUMOUR, 12
improvement most schemes of political i. are very laughable — JOHNSON, 20
impulse the i. of the moment — FLATTERY, 1
the need to talk is a primary i. — CERVANTES, 6
impulses Mistrust first i. — FIRST IMPRESSIONS, 3
inadequate Like Brighton pier,...i. for getting to France — TRAVEL, 9
inbreeding an impotent people, /Sick with i. — WELSH, 2
inches They that die by famine die by i. — HUNGER, 3
incident What is i. but the illustration of character — CHARACTER, 4; JAMES, 7
inclination A man ought to read just as i. leads him — READING, 5
income Annual i. twenty pounds — DICKENS, 4; ECONOMICS, 3
hardest thing .to understand is i. tax — TAXATION, 2
live beyond its i. — EXTRAVAGANCE, 2; PROGRESS, 2
incomes people live beyond their i. — EXTRAVAGANCE, 2; SAKI, 6
incomparable The I. Max — BEERBOHM, 1
incompetence Work...by those employees who have not yet reached...i. — INCOMPETENCE, 4
incompetent God is the immemorial refuge of the i. — GOD, 25
i. swine — WAR, 55
inconstancy Man with that i. was born — BEHN, 3
inconvenience Change is not made without i. — CHANGE, 8
inconvenient i. to be poor — COWPER, 3
incorruptible the dead shall be raised i. — DEATH, 12
incurable Not even medicine can master i. diseases — MEDICINE, 4
the i. disease of writing — WRITING, 11
indecency prejudicial...as a public i. — CERVANTES (SAAVEDRA), 10; SIN, 7
The older one grows the more one likes i. — WOOLF, 4
indecent It requires one to assume such i. postures — WILDE, 38
much more i...than a good smack — LAWRENCE, 4; PUNISHMENT, 9
sent down for i. behaviour — WAUGH, 2
indecision Nothing is so exhausting as i. — INDECISION, 2
indefatigable i. and unsavoury engine of pollution — DOGS, 5
indefensible political speech and writing are largely the defence of the i. — POLITICS, 36
independent an I. Labour Party — PARTIES, 5
An i....wants to take the politics out of politics — POLITICS, 41
to become fully i. — FAMILY, 8
To be poor and i. — POVERTY, 1
India From I.'s coral strand — PLACES, 3
I. is a geographical term — PLACES, 2
Indian base I., threw a pearl away — LOVE, 60; SHAKESPEARE, 94
indictment an i. against an whole people — ACCUSATION, 1
indifference and cold i. came — INDIFFERENCE, 3
equanimity bordering on i. — GILBERT, 9
Nothing is so fatal to religion as i. — BURKE, 14; INDIFFERENCE, 2
indignation Moral i. is in most cases 2 percent moral — MORALITY, 10
puritan pours righteous i. — CHESTERTON, 24; PURITANISM, 1
the mists of righteous i. — PRUDERY, 4
indiscretion lover without i. — LOVE, 31
indispensables She was one of those i. — HUXLEY, 13; INSIGNIFICANCE, 2
indistinguishable in America the successful writer or picture-painter is i. from any other decent business man — AMERICA, 16
individual i. men and women — SOCIETY, 6
the idea of death as an i. — NUCLEAR WEAPONS, 6
The liberty of the i. must be thus far limited — FREEDOM, 17
The psychic development of the i. — PSYCHIATRY, 1
individualism American system of rugged i. — AMERICA, 12
Art is the most intense mode of i. — ART, 21
individuality England is the paradise of i. — ENGLAND, 19
Industrial I. relations are like sexual relations — INDUSTRIAL RELATIONS, 2

industry development of i. has created many new sources of danger — DISEASE, 22
Life without i. is guilt — ART, 15; RUSKIN, 3
national i. of Prussia — WAR, 37
inebriated i. with...his own verbosity — DISRAELI, 15
inexactitude terminological i. — LYING, 3
infallible an i. sign of the second-rate — INFERIORITY, 2
The only i. criterion of wisdom — BURKE, 2
We are none of us i. — IMPERFECTION, 8
infancy Heaven lies about us in our i. — METAPHYSICS, 4
infant Sooner murder an i. in its cradle — BLAKE, 15; DESIRE, 2
infanticide as indefensible as i. — CENSORSHIP, 3
inferior No one can make you feel i. without your consent — INFERIORITY, 3
Switzerland...an i. sort of Scotland — SMITH, 6
inferiority minds so impatient of i. — GRATITUDE, 1
Wherever an i. complex exists, there is...reason — INFERIORITY, 1
inferiors I. revolt in order that they may be equal — REVOLUTION, 1
inferno A man who has not passed through the i. of his passions — PASSION, 2
infinite The Desire of Man being I. — INFINITY, 1
infinitive When I split an i. — CHANDLER, 4; GRAMMAR, 2
infinity I cannot help it;...i. torments me — INFINITY, 2
I. in the palm of your hand — BLAKE, 7
infirmities friend should bear his friend's i. — FRIENDS, 9
infirmity last i. of noble mind — FAME, 7
inflation a little i. is like being a little pregnant — ECONOMICS, 2
influence How to...I. People — INFLUENCE, 1
infortune The worst kinde of i. is this — CHAUCER, 6
infringement Necessity is the plea for every i. of human freedom — NECESSITY, 1
ingenious a loyal, a gallant, a generous, an i., and good-temper'd people — FRANCE, 8
ingratitude I hate i. more in a man — INGRATITUDE, 5
I., thou marble-hearted fiend — INGRATITUDE, 4
man's i. — INGRATITUDE, 3
inherit Russia will certainly i. the future — RUSSIA, 2
inhumanity Man's i. to man — BURNS, 8; CRUELTY, 2
initiative success depends...upon individual i. and exertion — EFFORT, 4; SUCCESS, 4
injury An i. is much sooner forgotten — CHESTERFIELD, 4; INSULTS, 4
Recompense i. with justice — KINDNESS, 1
injustice fear of suffering i. — JUSTICE, 10; ROCHEFOUCAULD, 2
threatened with a great i. — INJUSTICE, 2
injustices thought only to justify their i. — VOLTAIRE, 8
ink an optimist...fills up his crossword puzzle in i. — OPTIMISM, 8
inn no room for them in the i. — CHRISTMAS, 5
inner Conscience is the i. voice — CONSCIENCE, 3
Innisfree I will arise and...go to I. — YEATS, 6
innocence it is...our business to lose i. — INNOCENCE, 4
my i. begins to weigh me down — INNOCENCE, 2
Ralph wept for the end of i. — INNOCENCE, 2
innocent ten guilty persons escape than one i. suffer — JUSTICE, 2
innocently i. employed than in getting money — JOHNSON, 24; MONEY, 11
innovator time is the greatest i. — INNOVATION, 1
inquiry The world is but a school of i. — CURIOSITY, 3
insanity lay interest in ecclesiastical matters...often a prelude to i. — RELIGION, 34; WAUGH, 9
William Blake's i. was worth — BLAKE, 1
inscrutable Dumb, i. and grand — ARNOLD, 13; CATS, 1
insect the Egyptians worshipped an i. — DISRAELI, 16
insemination Surely you don't mean by unartificial i. — THURBER, 9
insensitiveness the greatest deeds require a certain i. — INSENSITIVITY, 2
inside attention to the i....contempt for the outside — BOOKS, 7; CHESTERFIELD, 9
insight moment's i....worth a life's experience — EXPERIENCE, 7
insignificant utterly i. little blue green planet — SCIENCE FICTION, 1
insincerity great enemy of clear language is i. — LANGUAGE, 14
insolence a wretch who supports with i. — PATRONAGE, 1
i. is not invective — DISRAELI, 13; PETULANCE, 1
inspiration Genius is one per cent i. — GENIUS, 1
instincts diseases...no less natural than the i. which preserve him. — DISEASE, 19
institution Any i. which does not suppose the people good — CORRUPTION, 5
more than a game. It's an i. — CRICKET, 2
institutions working of great i. — BUREAUCRACY, 6
instrument there you sit with that magnificent i. between your legs — INCOMPETENCE, 5

The state is an i....of the ruling class | STATE, 4
insubordination price of i. and insurrection | STRIKES, 4
insult A man should not i. his wife publicly | THURBER, 7
sooner forgotten than an i. | CHESTERFIELD, 4; INSULTS, 4
insulted anyone here whom I have not i. | INSULTS, 3
insured you cannot be i. for the accidents...most likely to happen | ACCIDENTS, 1
insurrection price of insubordination and i. | STRIKES, 4
integrate I i. the current export drive | BETJEMAN, 6
Integrity I. without knowledge is weak | INTEGRITY, 3; JOHNSON, 10; KNOWLEDGE, 10
intellect a road...that does not go through the i. | CHESTERTON, 3; EMOTION, 1
i. is...fooled by the heart | EMOTION, 2
I. is invisible | INTELLECT, 5; SCHOPENHAUER, 2
put on I. | BLAKE, 11; WISDOM, 7
take care not to make the i. our god | INTELLECT, 1
The voice of the i. is a soft one | INTELLECT, 3
intellects highest i., like the tops of mountains | INTELLECT, 3
There is a wicked inclination...to suppose an old man decayed in his i. | JOHNSON, 36; OLD AGE, 11
intellectual an i....mind watches itself | INTELLECTUALS, 4
artist who's an i | FITZGERALD, 5
Beware of the artist who's an i. | ARTISTS, 2
Every i. attitude is latently political | POLITICS, 33
i....doesn't know how to park a bike | INTELLECTUALS, 1
I've been called many things, but never an i. | INTELLECTUALS, 5
Man is an i. animal | HAZLITT, 3
The word I. suggests | AUDEN, 11; INTELLECTUALS, 3
thirdly, i. ability | EDUCATION, 1
intelligence I. is quickness to apprehend | INTELLIGENCE, 5
i. is the great polluter | ENVIRONMENT, 3
The more i....the more...one finds original | INTELLIGENCE, 1
You ask whether woman possesses any natural i. | CHRISTINE DE PISAN, 2
intelligent A really i. man feels what other men...know | INTELLIGENCE, 3
Each generation imagines itself...more i. | AGE, 31; ORWELL, 15
i. people...are socialists | SOCIALISM, 1
stupid are cocksure...i. full of doubt | DOUBT, 4
The i. are to the intelligentsia | INTELLIGENCE, 1
intelligentsia intelligent are to the i. | INTELLIGENCE, 1
intended i. to give you some advice | ADVICE, 2
intensity excellence of every art is its i. | ARTS, 1
intent A truth that's told with bad i. | TRUTH, 5
prick the sides of my i. | AMBITION, 8; SHAKESPEARE, 71
intercourse Sexual i. began /In nineteen sixty-three | SEX, 18
interest It is not my i. to pay the principal, nor my principle to pay the i. | SHERIDAN, 12
interested seldom i. in what he is saying | POUND, 1
intermission Pleasure is...i. of pain | PLEASURE, 12
international science is essentially i. | CURIE, 3; SCIENCE, 5
I. Woman's Day | RUSSIAN REVOLUTION, 2
interpreter The soul fortunately, has an i. | BRONTË, 3
interrupted Mr Wordsworth is never i. | INTERRUPTIONS, 1
interval an opera without an i., or an i. without an opera | OPERA, 4
intolerable I would grow i. conceited | WHISTLER, 6
intoxicated A man who exposes himself when he is i. | DRUNKENNESS, 4
intoxication best of life is...i. | BYRON, 8; DRUNKENNESS, 4
intrudes society, where none i. | NATURE, 7
invade when religion is allowed to i....private life | RELIGION, 24
invasion no stand can be made against i. by an idea | IDEAS, 1
invective insolence is not i. | DISRAELI, 13; PETULANCE, 1
invent it would be necessary to i. Him | GOD, 33; VOLTAIRE, 10
inventing Prolonged...reviewing of books involves constantly i. reactions | CRITICISM, 11
invention own greatest i. | COWARD, 1
Woman's virtue is man's greatest i. | SEXES, 12; VIRTUE, 11
inventions All one's i. are true | POETRY, 8
investment To bear many children is considered...an i. | CHILDREN, 10
inviolable the i. shade | HOPE, 1
invisible the only evil that walks /I. | HYPOCRISY, 6
invisibly electricity was dripping i. | THURBER, 8
invite We i. people like that to tea | BETJEMAN, 3
involvements a talent for describing the i. and feelings and characters | AUSTEN, 2
inward They flash upon that i. eye | WORDSWORTH, 7
inwards he looked i., and found her | DRYDEN, 12
Ireland English should give I. home rule | IRELAND, 8

He delivered I. from plunder | SWIFT, 1
I never met anyone in I. who understood the Irish question | IRELAND, 4
L is the old sow | IRELAND, 5
Now I. has her madness | AUDEN, 10
The moment...I. is mentioned | IRELAND, 10; SMITH, 1
The problem with I. | IRELAND, 7
Irish as I. as Black Americans | IRISH, 3
That is the I. Question | IRELAND, 3
The I. and the Jews have a psychosis | IRISH, 1; JEWS, 1
The I. are a fair people | IRISH, 4
The I.,...are needed in this cold age | IRISH, 2
The I. don't know what they want | IRISH, 5
iron An i. curtain | CHURCHILL, 30; COLD WAR, 2
muscles.../Are strong as i. bands | OCCUPATIONS, 4
rule them with a rod of i. | LEADERSHIP, 2
the i. enter into his soul | BITTERNESS, 3
irons two i. in the fire | PRUDENCE, 1
irrelevant the most i. thing in nature | FAMILY, 10
irresponsible better to be i. and right | CHURCHILL, 32; RESPONSIBILITY, 3
irretrievable loss of virtue in a female is i. | VIRTUE, 1
Isaiah Arnold is a dandy I. | ARNOLD, 2
Ishmaelites I....will not publicly eat human flesh uncooked in Lent | CANNIBALISM, 2
Islam In some remote regions of I. | MODESTY, 2
I. unashamedly came with a sword | RELIGION, 28
island No man is an I. | DONNE, 5; SOCIETY, 2
isle this sceptred i. | ENGLAND, 20; SHAKESPEARE, 97
Israel When I. was in Egypt land | OPPRESSION, 1
Italian I speak...I. to women, French to men | LANGUAGE, 6
Italy A man who has not been in I. | TRAVEL, 6
itch the i. of literature | WRITING, 12
itself Love seeketh not i. to please | BLAKE, 18; LOVE, 10
ivy The holly and the I. | CHRISTMAS, 4
Jack Damn you, J. – I'm all right | SELFISHNESS, 2
jackals J. piss at their foot | BOOKS, 11
jam The rule is, j. tomorrow and j. yesterday | CARROLL, 11; PROMISES, 2
James Henry J. has a mind so fine | JAMES, 1
Henry J. was one of the nicest old ladies | JAMES, 2
Jane Time's up for Sir John, an' for little Lady J. | LAWRENCE, 9
Jane Eyre J. strikes us as a personage...from the head of a man | BRONTË, 1
January dreadful pictures of J. and February | TROLLOPE, 4
Janvier Generals J. and Février | SEASONS, 10
Japan There was a young man of J. | VERBOSITY, 1
jaundiced with the j. eye | PASSION, 7, TENNYSON, 20
jaw-jaw To j. is better than to war-war | CHURCHILL, 33; DIPLOMACY, 3
jazz J....people hear it through their feet | MUSIC, 25
The basic difference between classical music and j. | MUSIC, 20
jealous a j. God | GOD, 6
Art is a j. mistress | ART, 4
jealousy J....feeling alone among smiling enemies | JEALOUSY, 2
of j.; /It is the green-ey'd monster | JEALOUSY, 3; SHAKESPEARE, 91
the ear of j. heareth all things | JEALOUSY, 1
jeering laughing and j. at everything...strange | ENGLISH, 14
jelly Out vile j. | SHAKESPEARE, 64
Jerusalem J. the golden | PLACES, 8
Till we have built J. | ENGLAND, 1
jest a fellow of infinite j. | MOURNING, 7; SHAKESPEARE, 40
A j.'s prosperity lies in the ear | HUMOUR, 17
Jesus Gentle J. | HUMILITY, 7
J. loves me – this I know | RELIGION, 32
J. was...a first-rate political economist | SHAW, 2
We're more popular than J. Christ now | POP MUSIC, 7
jeunesse Si j. savait | AGE, 18
Jew An American is either a J., or an anti-Semite | AMERICANS, 6
difficult for a J. to be converted | JEWS, 5
hated /by every anti-semite /as if I were a J. | PREJUDICE, 4
Hath not a J. eyes | EQUALITY, 17; SHAKESPEARE, 81
I'm not really a J.; just J.-ish | HALF MEASURES, 2
No J. was ever fool enough to turn Christian | RELIGION, 40
Pessimism is a luxury that a J. never can allow himself | JEWS, 7
jewelry she did not remember...her j. | PRUDENCE, 3
Jewish A J. man with parents alive | JEWS, 9
a total solution of the J. question | NAZISM, 1
best that is in the J. blood | JEWS, 6
I'm not really a Jew; just J. | HALF MEASURES, 2
Jews But spurn the J. | JEWS, 4
not enough prisons...in Palestine to hold all the J. | JEWS, 8
The Irish and the J. have a psychosis | IRISH, 1; JEWS, 1

The J. and Arabs should…settle their differences
GOLDWYNISMS, 26; RELIGION, 2
the J. bring the unlike into the heart of *every milieu* JEWS, 11
the J. have made a contribution to the human condition JEWS, 10
To choose /The J. JEWS, 3
Joan greasy J. doth keel the pot SHAKESPEARE, 67
job Being a husband is a whole-time j. BENNETT, 4; MARRIAGE, 9
If two men on the same j. agree AGREEMENT, 5
We have finished the j. TELEGRAMS, 7; WORLD WAR II, 21
we will finish the j. CHURCHILL, 25; WORLD WAR II, 7
woman's ability to stick to a j. WOMEN, 41
Joe Hungry J. collected lists of fatal diseases ILLNESS, 4
John Beneath this slab /J. Brown is stowed NASH, 4
D'ye ken J. Peel HUNTING, 3
J. Brown's body MEMORIALS, 4
Matthew, Mark, Luke and J. BLESSING, 1
Time's up for Sir J., an' for little Lady Jane LAWRENCE, 9
Johnson There is no arguing with J. JOHNSON, 1
joined what…God hath j. together MARRIAGE, 13
Why haven't you j. WORLD WAR I, 12
joke a j. with a double meaning HUMOUR, 1
good deed to forget a poor j. HUMOUR, 3
Housekeeping ain't no j. HOUSEWORK, 1
The coarse j. proclaims HUMOUR, 11
jokes A different taste in j. is a…strain on the affections ELIOT, 3
A j. a very serious thing HUMOUR, 5
joking My way of j. is to tell the truth SHAW, 6
Joneses drag the J. down to my level ONE-UPMANSHIP, 1
journalism Christianity,…but why j. CHRISTIANITY, 1; JOURNALISM, 1
J. is the only job that requires no degrees JOURNALISM, 4
j.…..keeps us in touch with the ignorance of the community
JOURNALISM, 18; WILDE, 9
J. largely consists of saying 'Lord Jones is dead' JOURNALISM, 5
J.…the challenge of filling…space JOURNALISM, 17
j. what will be grasped at once
CONNOLLY, 3; JOURNALISM, 6; LITERATURE, 1
Rock j. is people who can't write POP MUSIC, 9
journalist the functions of the modern j. JOURNALISM, 7
to bribe or twist…the British j. JOURNALISM, 19
journalists j. put theirs on the front page OCCUPATIONS, 1
J. say a thing that they know isn't true BENNETT, 5; JOURNALISM, 2
journey I prepare for a j.…as though for death TRAVEL, 11
long j.…must bid the company farewell LAST WORDS, 25
One of the pleasantest things in the world is going on a j.
SOLITUDE, 6; TRAVEL, 5
journeying You cannot imagine how strange it seemed to be j.
TRAVEL, 3
Jowett First come I; my name is J. ACADEMICS, 2
joy a father's j. SCOTT, 8
A thing of beauty is a j. for ever BEAUTY, 12; KEATS, 2
Silence is the perfectest herald of j. SILENCE, 1
Strength through j. NAZISM, 2
we could never learn to be brave…if there were only j.
ENDURANCE, 3
joys j. of parents are secret FAMILY, 2
judge j. not, that ye be not judged JUDGMENT, 1
j. of a man by his foes JUDGMENT, 6
shallow people…do not j. by appearances APPEARANCES, 12
judged they were j. every man according to their works
JUDGMENT, 3
why is my liberty j. of another man's conscience CONSCIENCE, 1
judgement day of j. DEATH, 14
Don't wait for the Last J. DOOMSDAY, 3
Force, if unassisted by j., collapses JUDGMENT, 7
let my will replace reasoned j. AUTHORITARIANISM, 4
no one complains of his j. JUDGMENT, 8; ROCHEFOUCAULD, 4
Perhaps your fear in passing j. COURAGE, 2
Your representative owes you…his j. JUDGMENT, 5
judgment 'Tis the Last J.'s fire DOOMSDAY, 2
Jumblies far and few, /Are the lands where the J. live NONSENSE, 8
Juno fierce J.'s never-forgetting anger VIRGIL, 3
J.'s never-forgetting anger ENDURANCE, 12
just it raineth on the j. JUSTICE, 3
rain on the j. and on the unjust ENEMIES, 1
justice In a free society the state…administers j. among men
STATE, 2
J. is open to all JUSTICE, 5
J. is such a fine thing JUSTICE, 7
J. is the means by which established injustices are sanctioned
INJUSTICE, 3
J. is the…perpetual wish JUSTICE, 6

j. must be seen to be more or less done JUSTICE, 12
J. should not only be done JUSTICE, 5
Let j. be done JUSTICE, 4
moderation in the pursuit of j. is no virtue EXCESS, 4
Recompense injury with j. KINDNESS, 1
Revenge is a kind of wild j. REVENGE, 1
The j. of my quarrel JUSTICE, 8
The love of j. in most men JUSTICE, 10; ROCHEFOUCAULD, 2
The place of j. is a hallowed place JUSTICE, 1
justified No man is j. in doing evil EXPEDIENCY, 4
justify thought only to j. their injustices VOLTAIRE , 8
justifying men are more interested in…j. themselves than
in…behaving SZASZ, 1
Kaiser Belgium put the kibosh on the K. WORLD WAR I, 1
Karl had Marx been Groucho instead of K. HUMOUR, 2
Keats Mister John K. five feet high ADMIRATION, 2; KEATS, 12
keen out of a k. city /in the sky MOON, 3
Satire should, like a polished razor k. SATIRE, 2
keep if they k. on saying it…it will be true BENNETT, 5; JOURNALISM, 2
K. up appearances APPEARANCES, 3
they should k. who can POWER, 14
keeper am I my brother's k. MURDER, 1
a poacher a k. turned inside out OCCUPATIONS, 3
Kew I am His Highness' dog at K. POPE, 18
key lawyers…have taken away the k. of knowledge LAWYERS, 2
keys the k. of the kingdom of heaven CHURCH, 1
Khatmandu one-eyed yellow idol to the north of K. MOURNING, 3
kibosh Belgium put the k. on the Kaiser WORLD WAR I, 1
kick k. you out, but…never let you down EDUCATION, 32
kicked he had known many k. down stairs PROMOTION, 2
kiddies k. have crumpled the serviettes BETJEMAN, 5
kidnapped my parents finally realize that I'm k. EXPEDIENCY, 1
kids Cleaning your house while your k. are still growing
HOUSEWORK, 1
nice thing about having relatives' k. CHILDREN, 15
kill a man can't step up and k. a woman CHIVALRY, 2
churchmen fain would k. their church TENNYSON, 23
good to k. an admiral VOLTAIRE , 4
He would k. Himself HUMAN CONDITION, 2
K. a man, and you are a murderer KILLING, 4
k. a wife with kindness KINDNESS, 3; SHAKESPEARE, 111
K. everyone, and you are a god KILLING, 4
k. the patient REMEDIES, 1
k. us for their sport SHAKESPEARE, 65
The word 'revolution' is a word for which you k. REVOLUTION, 2
thou shalt not k. GOD, 6
To k. a human being JAMES, 6
When you have to k. a man DIPLOMACY, 5
killing k. for their country RUSSELL, 15
K. /is the ultimate KILLING, 2
k. time /is only…another of the multifarious ways /By which Time
kills us TIME, 16
no difference between…k. and making decisions that…kill
KILLING, 3
The man is k. time TIME, 10
To save a man's life against his will is…k. him HORACE, 4; KILLING, 1
kills Time is a great teacher, but…k. all its pupils TIME, 3
time quietly k. them TIME, 5
Who k. a man k. a reasonable creature BOOKS, 17; BOOKS, 17
Yet each man k. the thing he loves KILLING, 5; WILDE, 8
kilt The k. is an unrivalled garment for fornication SCOTS, 5
kin more than k., and less than kind SHAKESPEARE, 26
kind charity suffereth long, and is k. CHARITY, 4
more than kin, and less than k. SHAKESPEARE, 26
try to be k. ACADEMICS, 3
kindle the sole purpose of human existence is to k. a light
EXISTENCE, 3
kindly a young person…marries or dies, is sure to be k. spoken of
AUSTEN, 6; HUMAN NATURE, 1
the deities so k. DESTINY, 8; RABELAIS, 3
kindness a cup o' k. yet FRIENDSHIP, 4
full o' th' milk of human k. KINDNESS, 3; SHAKESPEARE, 69
kill a wife with k. KINDNESS, 3; SHAKESPEARE, 111
recompense k. with k. KINDNESS, 1
set a high value on spontaneous k. FRIENDSHIP, 8
the k. of strangers WILLIAMS, 3
unremembered acts /Of k. and of love KINDNESS, 4; WORDSWORTH, 6
kindred Like k. drops, been mingled COWPER, 12; MOUNTAINS, 1
king A constitutional k. must learn to stoop MONARCHY, 7
a k. may make a nobleman CHIVALRY, 4
an atheist if the k. were SERVILITY, 2

Authority forgets a dying k. ROYALTY, 16
better…a poor and a wise child than an old and foolish k. YOUTH, 1
Every subject's duty is the K.'s MONARCHY, 8; SHAKESPEARE, 48
God save our Gracious K. BRITAIN, 3
half the zeal I serv'd my K. REGRET, 10; SHAKESPEARE, 51
heart and stomach of a K. ELIZABETH I, 7; ROYALTY, 6
I think the k. is but a man EQUALITY, 16; SHAKESPEARE, 47
k. reigns, but does not govern MONARCHY, 13
the k. can do no wrong MONARCHY, 3
The k. has been very good to me MARTYRDOM, 1
The k. never dies MONARCHY, 4
The K. over the Water ROYALTY, 1
The k. reigns, and the people govern themselves MONARCHY, 11
The present life of men on earth, O k. LIFE, 4
this house will in no circumstances fight for its K. and country PATRIOTISM, 3
wash the balm from an anointed k. MONARCHY, 9
kingdom my k. for a horse HORSES, 6; SHAKESPEARE, 100
No k. has…had as many…wars as the k. of Christ CHRISTIANITY, 19
the k. of God is not in word, but in power GOD, 8
kings Conquering k. their titles take ROYALTY, 4
Grammar, which can govern even k. GRAMMAR, 4
K. are earth's gods ROYALTY, 14
K.…are just as funny ROYALTY, 13
K. are naturally lovers of low company BURKE, 10
K. govern by…assemblies only when MONARCHY, 6
Or walk with K. IDEALISM, 1; KIPLING, 4
Pale Death kicks his way…into…the castles of k. EQUALITY, 19
sad stories of the death of k. ROYALTY, 15; SHAKESPEARE, 98
Such grace had k. ROYALTY, 3
teeming womb of royal k. ENGLAND, 20; SHAKESPEARE, 97
the K. of England, Diamonds, Hearts, Spades and Clubs MONARCHY, 5
This royal throne of k. ENGLAND, 20; SHAKESPEARE, 97
till philosophers become k. PHILOSOPHY, 5
'Twixt k. and tyrants there's this difference TYRANNY, 2
kingship k. approaches tyranny it is near its end TYRANNY, 3
Kipling W. H. Auden, a sort of gutless K. AUDEN, 1
kippers like two old k. in a box THOMAS, 10
kiss A k. without a moustache KISSING, 3
come let us k. and part PARTING, 4
K. me, Hardy LAST WORDS, 20
make me immortal with a k. BEAUTY, 14
The coward does it with a k. KILLING, 5; WILDE, 1
Then come k. me, sweet and twenty PRESENT, 7
you must not k. and tell CONGREVE, 4; SECRECY, 4
You must remember this; /A k. is just a k. TIME, 7
kissed Being k. by a man who didn't wax his moustache KISSING, 2
hail, master; and k. him BETRAYAL, 1
I k. her little sister UNFAITHFULNESS, 1
kisses remembered k. after death NOSTALGIA, 12
Stolen sweets are always sweeter, /Stolen k. much completer THEFT, 1
kissing K. don't last FOOD, 16
when the k. had to stop BROWNING, 16; KISSING, 1
kit-bag pack up your troubles in your old k. OPTIMISM, 2
kitchen can't stand the heat, get out of the k. ENDURANCE, 9
Kitchener If K. was not a great man, he was…a great poster OFFICERS, 2
knaves world is made up…of fools and k. FOOLISHNESS, 3
knew I k. him, Horatio MOURNING, 7; SHAKESPEARE, 40
much righter than one k. at say 17 or 23 AGE, 32; POUND, 2
knife it keeps them on the k. FOOD, 1
War even to the k. WAR, 12
knight a verray parfit gentil k. CHIVALRY, 4
every chance brought out a noble k. NOSTALGIA, 11
what can all thee, k. at arms ILLNESS, 6
knights sorrier for my good k.' loss than for…my fair queen LOSS, 3
knitter a beautiful little k. WOOLF, 2
knock Don't k. it ALLEN, 3; SEX, 3
k. him down first, and pity him afterwards JOHNSON, 28; SELF-PRESERVATION, 3
know all /Ye k. on earth BEAUTY, 13; KEATS, 6; TRUTH, 14
A really intelligent man feels what other men…k. INTELLIGENCE, 3
flautists are most obviously the ones who k. something we don't k. MUSICIANS, 1
for they k. not what they do FORGIVENESS, 1
I k. what I like BEERBOHM, 12
K. then thyself, presume not God to scan SELF-KNOWLEDGE, 7
Mad, bad, and dangerous to k. BYRON, 2
scarcely hate any one that we k. HATE, 1; HAZLITT, 7

To k. how to say what others only…think SPEECH, 3
What you don't k. would make a great book SMITH, 3
You k.…what you are KNOWLEDGE, 8
knowing A woman, especially if she have the misfortune of k. anything AUSTEN, 8; WOMEN, 1
knowledge a k. of nothing DICKENS, 17; KNOWLEDGE, 6
All k. is of itself of some value KNOWLEDGE, 11
all k. to be my province KNOWLEDGE, 2
all our k. is, ourselves to know SELF-KNOWLEDGE, 4
an age in which useless k. KNOWLEDGE, 10
an intimate k. of its ugly side DISILLUSION, 1
civilizations…abandon the quest for k. KNOWLEDGE, 14
If a k. is dangerous, where is the man…out of danger KNOWLEDGE, 9
if a little k. was a dangerous thing KNOWLEDGE, 17
if education is…a mere transmission of k. EDUCATION, 19
Integrity without k. is weak INTEGRITY, 3; JOHNSON, 10; KNOWLEDGE, 12
K. advances by steps KNOWLEDGE, 15
K. can be communicated but not wisdom WISDOM, 10
K. dwells /In heads replete COWPER, 14; KNOWLEDGE, 5; WISDOM, 9
K. is of two kinds JOHNSON, 26; KNOWLEDGE, 13
K. is proportionate to being KNOWLEDGE, 8
K. itself is power KNOWLEDGE, 1
lawyers…have taken away the key of k. LAWYERS, 2
let him receive the new k. HEAVEN, 4
never has a man turned so little k. to such great account SHAKESPEARE, 5
No, I ask it for the k. of a lifetime WHISTLER, 5
Our k. can only be finite KNOWLEDGE, 16
Out-topping k. SHAKESPEARE, 1
province of K. to speak KNOWLEDGE, 7; WISDOM, 11
the river of k. has too often turned back on itself SCIENCE, 14
the search for k. RUSSELL, 2
the tree of the k. of good and evil GARDENS, 3
What I don't know isn't k. ACADEMICS, 2
worth a pound of k. KNOWLEDGE, 18; LOVE, 68
knows he thinks he k. everything SHAW, 9
knuckle-end k. of England SCOTLAND, 5
knyf The smyler with the k. CHAUCER, 5; HYPOCRISY, 2
Kodak painted…by the great artist K. PHOTOGRAPHY, 4
Kubla In Xanadu did K. Khan COLERIDGE, 6; PLEASURE, 4
laboratorium L. est oratorium SCIENCE, 17
laboratory We're all of us guinea pigs in the l. of God MANKIND, 18
Labour an Independent L. Party PARTIES, 5
disastrous element in the L. party POLITICS, 14
genius the L. Party has for cutting itself in half POLITICS, 12
L. is not fit to govern CHURCHILL, 19; POLITICS, 13
model L. voter POLITICS, 28
The grotesque chaos of a L. council – a L. council INCOMPETENCE, 2
labour To l. and not ask for any reward SELFLESSNESS, 2
labours Children sweeten l. CHILDREN, 2
lack l. of power corrupts absolutely POWER, 12
own up to a l. of humour HUMOUR, 6
ladder behold a l. set up on earth HEAVEN, 1
We make ourselves a l. out of our vices VICE, 1
ladies Young l. are delicate plants HEALTH AND HEALTHY LIVING, 1
lady l. doth protest too much EXCESS, 6; SHAKESPEARE, 38
l. of a certain age AGE, 11; BYRON, 13
Put thy shimmy on, L. Chatterley LAWRENCE, 9
The L.'s not for turning INFLEXIBILITY, 2; THATCHER, 6
there had been a l. in the case WOMEN, 11
Treat a whore like a l. WOMEN, 29
laid all the young ladies who attended the Yale promenade dance were l. end to end PARKER, 5
laissez L. faire FREEDOM, 7; FREEDOM, 20
lake sedge is wither'd from the l. ILLNESS, 6
Lamb Charles L., a clever fellow certainly LAMB, 1
lamb Did he who made the L. make thee BLAKE, 21; CREATION, 6
Little L., who made thee CREATION, 7
Pipe a song about a L. BLAKE, 23
the L. of God CHRISTIANITY, 5
to make the lion lie down with the l. LAWRENCE, 12
lambs We're poor little l. DEBAUCHERY, 3
lame your precious 'l. ducks' WEAKNESS, 1
lament reason to l. /What man has made of man MANKIND, 19; WORDSWORTH, 8
lamp my l. burns low and dim ENVY, 1
To keep a l. burning CHARITY, 11
lampada vitai l. MORTALITY, 8
lamp-post like asking a l…about dogs CRITICS, 6
lamps l. are going out all over Europe PROPHECY, 2

the people are forbidden to light l.   INJUSTICE, 6; MAO TSE-TUNG, 6
land England's green and pleasant l.   ENGLAND, 1
For England's the one l.   ENGLAND, 3
L. of Hope and Glory   BRITAIN, 2
the l. grows poorer and uglier every day   ECOLOGY, 2
The l. of my fathers   THOMAS, 16; WALES, 2
they have the l. and we have the Bibles   RACISM, 6
Unhappy the l. that has no heroes   HEROISM, 2
landlord Come l., fill the flowing bowl   DRUNKENNESS, 1
lands l. where the Jumblies live   NONSENSE, 8
landscape half the l. is...covered by useless water   SEASIDE, 2
When will the l. tire the view   COUNTRYSIDE, 2
language Babel; because the Lord did there confound the l.   LANGUAGE, 2
I have laboured to refine our l. to grammatical purity   LANGUAGE, 9
L. grows out of life   LANGUAGE, 18
L. is a form of human reason   LANGUAGE, 12
L. is not simply a reporting device for experience   LANGUAGE, 21
L. is only the instrument of science   LANGUAGE, 11
Literature is simply l. charged with meaning   LITERATURE, 9
The English have no respect for their l.   ENGLISH, 16; SHAW, 20
the tower of Babel should have got l. all mixed up   VOLTAIRE, 25
the whole earth was of one l.   UNITY, 3
what l. an opera is sung in   OPERA, 1
languages l. are the pedigree of nations   JOHNSON, 41; LANGUAGE, 10
she speaks eighteen l. And she can't say 'No' in any of them   PARKER, 11; PROMISCUITY, 4
lards And l. the lean earth as he walks   OBESITY, 6
lascivious Poetry...set to more or less l. music   POETRY, 15
lash rum, sodomy, and the l.   CHURCHILL, 14; NAVY, 1
last as if it were the l.   LIFE, 17
Die...the l. thing I shall do   LAST WORDS, 22
Don't wait for the L. Judgement   DOOMSDAY, 3
each day that has dawned is your l.   PRESENT, 5
'Fan vaulting'...belongs to the 'L-supper-carved-on-a-peach-stone'   ARCHITECTURE, 3
hoping that it will eat him l.   DIPLOMACY, 4
I hope it will l.   WILDE, 19
I shall be the l. to go out   COURAGE, 1
l. act crowns the play   PLAYS, 2
the l. shall be first   MERIT, 1
there is no l. or first   EQUALITY, 4
'Tis the L. Judgment's fire   DOOMSDAY, 2
late Better never than l.   SHAW, 28
One doesn't recognize...the really important moments...until it's too l.   REGRET, 1
Latin A silly remark can be made in L.   CERVANTES (SAAVEDRA), 2; LANGUAGE, 4
Don't quote L.   WELLINGTON, 16
laugh L., and the world laughs with you   LAUGHTER, 4
l. before one is happy   LA BRUYERE, 4; LAUGHTER, 3
not to l. at human actions   UNDERSTANDING, 6
laughable most schemes of political improvement are very l.   JOHNSON, 20
laughed No man who has once...l.   CARLYLE, 10
When the first baby l.   FAIRIES, 2
laughing Happiness is no l. matter   HAPPINESS, 16
l. and jeering at everything...strange   ENGLISH, 14
One cannot be always l. at a man   AUSTEN, 13
one may die without ever l.   LA BRUYERE, 4; LAUGHTER, 3
read the death of Little Nell without l.   DICKENS, 1; WILDE, 35
the most fun I ever had without l.   ALLEN, 2; SEX, 2
laughter I said of l., it is mad   LAUGHTER, 1
l. is weakness   LAUGHTER, 2
present l.   PRESENT, 7
laurels The l. all are cut   ENDING, 2
law Born under one l.   HUMAN CONDITION, 4
Every l. is a contract   LAW, 9
Ignorance of the l.   LAW, 10
I have forgotten more l. than you ever knew   INSULTS, 15
No brilliance is needed in the l.   LAW, 7
Nor l., nor duty bade me fight   FLYING, 4; YEATS, 5
Order is heaven's first l.   ORDER, 2
Prisons are built with stones of L.   BLAKE, 14
rich men rule the l.   GOLDSMITH, 12; LAW, 5
The army ages men sooner than the l.   ARMY, 5; WELLS, 3
the condition of our sex is so deplorable that it is our duty...to break the l.   PANKHURST, 6
the greater part of the l. is learning to tolerate fools   LAW, 6
The L. of England is a very strange one   LAW, 2
the L. of the Yukon   SURVIVAL, 3

the l. is a ass   DICKENS, 12; LAW, 3
The l. of dislike for the unlike   JEWS, 11
the magnificent fair play of the British criminal l.   DOYLE, 5
The majestic egalitarianism of the l.   EQUALITY, 8
the moral l.   WONDER, 1
There is no universal l.   SPONTANEITY, 2
th' windy side of the l.   LAW, 11
laws I know not whether L. be right   IMPRISONMENT, 6
L. are like cobwebs   SWIFT, 10
L. are like spider's webs   LAW, 12
L. grind the poor   GOLDSMITH, 12; LAW, 5
L. were made to be broken   LAW, 8
the l. of poetic truth and poetic beauty   POETRY, 2
There never will be...equality until women...make l.   ANTHONY, 2
Where l. end, tyranny begins   TYRANNY, 5
not governed by the same l. ..../'the rich and the poor.'   DISRAELI, 7
you do not make the l. but...are the wives...of those who do   WOMEN, 21
lawyer A client is fain to hire a l. to keep from...other lawyers   LAWYERS, 3
l. with his briefcase can steal   LAWYERS, 4
No poet ever interpreted nature...as a l. interprets truth   LAW, 4
lawyers L. are the only persons...ignorance...not punished   LAWYERS, 1
woe unto you, l.   LAWYERS, 2
laxative sweet l. of Georgian strains   STATELY HOMES, 1
lay I never would l. down my arms   PATRIOTISM, 13
Lazarus L....laid at his gate, full of sores   POVERTY AND WEALTH, 2
L. was not /Questioned about after-lives   DEATH, 30
lazy There are no ugly women, only l. ones   BEAUTY, 16
leadership men do not approach to l.   LEADERSHIP, 1
leap A l. over the hedge   PRAYER, 4
one giant l. for mankind   SPACE, 1
learn L., compare, collect the facts   EDUCATION, 21
The life so short, the craft so long to l.   MORTALITY, 7
we could never l. to be brave...if there were only joy   ENDURANCE, 3
What we have to l. to do   LEARNING, 1
learned He was naturally l.   DRYDEN, 12
I am...of the opinion with the l.   AGREEMENT, 1
Misquotation is the pride and privilege of the l.   MISQUOTATIONS, 2
people...never have l. anything from history   EXPERIENCE, 6
the l. roast an egg   FOOD, 20
learning A little l. is a dangerous thing   POPE, 7
A progeny of l.   MALAPROPISMS, 1
beauty and the lust for l.   BEAUTY, 3
L. hath gained most   BOOKS, 12
L. is but an adjunct   LEARNING, 7
learnt what has been l. has been forgotten   EDUCATION, 29
least death...the l. of all evils   DEATH, 5
Strongest minds /...the noisy world /Hears l.   WORDSWORTH, 2
leave Fare thee well, for I must l. thee   PARTING, 1
If you l. a thing alone you l. it to a torrent of change   CONSERVATISM, 1
to l. his country as good as he had found it   DUTY, 1
leaves before the l. have fallen   WAR, 68
before the l. have fallen from the trees   WORLD WAR I, 14
If poetry comes not...as l. to a tree   KEATS, 10; POETRY, 13
Words are like l.   VERBOSITY, 4
leaving became him like the l. it   DEATH, 54
She's l. home   DEPARTURE, 6
lecher small gilded fly does l.   ANIMALISM, 4
lechery drink...an equivocator with l.   ALCOHOL, 28; SHAKESPEARE, 72
Still wars and l.   SEX, 31; SHAKESPEARE, 116
led l. by the nose with gold   BRIBERY, 3
left And we are l., or shall be l., alone   DEFEAT, 6
better to be l. than never to have been loved   CONGREVE, 9; LOVE, 21
not l. to Spain   MARTYRDOM, 3
legal collect l. taxes from illegal money   TAXATION, 1
legs apart from having two good l.   INTELLIGENCE, 2
cannon-ball took off his l.   PUNS, 6
there you sit with that magnificent instrument between your l.   INCOMPETENCE, 5
You were born with your l. apart   PROMISCUITY, 3
Leicester Square Good-bye Piccadilly, Farewell L.   HOMESICKNESS, 5
leisure Evil comes at l.   DISEASE, 3
Men...detest at l.   BYRON, 14; LOVE AND HATE, 1
Prince Philip...a world expert on l.   ROYALTY, 10
The secret of being miserable is to have l.   SHAW, 19
wisdom...cometh by opportunity of l.   LEISURE, 1

The prime goal is to alleviate suffering, and not to prolong l.
MEDICINE, 1
There are only three events in a man's l.
LA BRUYERE, 2; LIFE AND DEATH, 6
therefore choose l. LIFE AND DEATH, 2
the stuff l. is made of TIME, 6
the tree of l. GARDENS, 3
the veil which those who live call l. DEATH, 56
they get about ten percent out of l. LIFE, 11
Three passions...have governed my l. RUSSELL, 2
To save a man's l. against his will is...killing him
HORACE, 4; KILLING, 1
total of such moments is my l. CONNOLLY, 5; SELF, 2
veil which those who live /Call l. LIFE, 20
We have discovered the secret of l. SCIENCE, 4
We see into the l. of things DEATH, 66
when religion is allowed to invade...private l. RELIGION, 24
While there is l. HOPE, 2
life-blood A good book is the precious l. BOOKS, 18
life-lie Take the l. away from the average man DELUSION, 1
life-sized Great men are but l. BEERBOHM, 4
lifetime No, I ask it for the knowledge of a l. WHISTLER, 5
light Culture is the passion for sweetness and l. CULTURE, 2
Fond Memory brings the l. /Of other days NOSTALGIA, 6
Give me a l. that I may tread safely into the unknown FAITH, 6
I am the l. of the world CHRISTIANITY, 7
let there be l. CREATION, 1
l. a candle of understanding UNDERSTANDING, 1
L. breaks where no sun shines EMOTION, 3
Lolita, l. of my life LUST, 3
one might get a five-pound note as one got a l. for a cigarette
GENEROSITY, 3; JAMES, 4
Put out the l. SHAKESPEARE, 93
The leaping l. for your delight discovers DISCOVERY, 2
the l. that led astray BURNS, 13; DELUSION, 1
we shall this day l. such a candle...as I trust shall never be put out.
EXECUTION, 7
wisdom excelleth folly, as...l. excelleth darkness
WISDOM AND FOOLISHNESS, 1
Light Brigade 'Forward the L.!' TENNYSON, 5
light-headed l., variable men STEVENSON, 12
lighthouse sitivation at the l. DICKENS, 16
lightning beheld Satan as l. fall from heaven DEVIL, 1
lights God made two great l. CREATION, 3; STARS, 2
the Father of l. GIFTS, 1
like I know what I l. BEERBOHM, 12
I shall not look upon his l. ADMIRATION, 6
L. doth quit like JUSTICE, 11; SHAKESPEARE, 78
To l...the same things, that is...true friendship FRIENDSHIP, 11
liked I'm so universally l. POPULARITY, 1
liking it saves me the trouble of l. them AUSTEN, 17; NASTINESS, 2
this l. for war WAR, 5
you expect other people to be...to your l. TOLERANCE, 3
lilac the l. is in bloom FLOWERS, 2
lilies consider the l. of the field WORRY, 1
L. that fester CORRUPTION, 7; SHAKESPEARE, 109
lily paint the l. EXCESS, 1
limb perils...of wind and l. FAITHFULNESS, 2
limericks Whose l. never would scan VERBOSITY, 1
limit In order to draw a l. to thinking THINKING, 8
limited Liberty too must be l. BURKE, 43; FREEDOM, 2
limousine One perfect l. PARKER, 3
line cancel half a l. DESTINY, 4
l. that fits the music POP MUSIC, 8
True genius walks along a l. GENIUS, 2; GOLDSMITH, 3
linen washing one's clean l. in public LOVE AND MARRIAGE, 1; WILDE, 13
lines give me six l...by the most honest man EXECUTION, 11
Pray to God and say the l. ACTING, 3
lingerie Brevity is the soul of l. BREVITY, 3; CLOTHES, 1
lion I hear the l. roar MERCY, 1
The nation had the l.'s heart CHURCHILL, 34
to make the l. lie down with the lamb LAWRENCE, 2
lions English soldiers fight like l. OFFICERS, 6
l. led by donkeys OFFICERS, 6
lips l. that touch liquor must never touch mine ABSTINENCE, 11
liquidation of the British Empire BRITISH EMPIRE, 2
liquor If...Orientals...drank a l. ALCOHOL, 7
lips that touch l. must never touch mine ABSTINENCE, 11
liquors alcoholic l. have been used by the...best races ALCOHOL, 27
listen privilege of wisdom to l. KNOWLEDGE, 7; WISDOM, 11
literacy The ratio of l. to illiteracy LITERACY, 1

literary A sort of l. Cinderella BRONTË, 1
L. men are...a perpetual priesthood WRITERS, 3
literature All that is l. seeks to communicate power BOOKS, 9
Emily Brontë remains the sphinx of l. BRONTË, 1
great deal of history to produce a little l.
HISTORY, 10; JAMES, 5; LITERATURE, 1
He knew everything about l. except how to enjoy it LITERATURE, 3
If we can't stamp out l. WAUGH, 18
I...impress upon you the study of Greek l. CLASSICS, 3
itch of l. WRITING, 12
L. and butterflies are the two sweetest passions LITERATURE, 4
L. flourishes best LITERATURE, 5
L. is mostly about having sex LITERATURE, 7
L. is news POUND, 5
L. is simply language charged with meaning LITERATURE, 9
L. is strewn with the wreckage of men WRITERS, 1
L. is the orchestration of platitudes LITERATURE, 12
L....poisoned by its own secretions LANGUAGE, 1
L....something that will be read twice
CONNOLLY, 3; JOURNALISM, 6; LITERATURE, 1
The Bible is l. BIBLE, 8
litmus Like a piece of l. paper HUXLEY, 1
little l. girls...slamming doors BELLOC, 1
L. things affect little minds TRIVIALITY, 3
read the death of L. Nell without laughing DICKENS, 1; WILDE, 35
the l. things are infinitely the most important TRIVIALITY, 4
live anything but l. for it RELIGION, 10
better to die on your feet than to l. on your knees SELF-RESPECT, 1
Come l. with me DONNE, 3; LOVE, 24; LOVE, 42
eat to l., not l. to eat FOOD, 17
he forgets to l. LA BRUYERE, 2; LIFE AND DEATH, 6
Houses are built to l. in HOUSES, 1
If God were suddenly condemned to l. the life HUMAN CONDITION, 2
If you l. long enough, the venerability factor creeps in LONGEVITY, 3
in Rome, l. as the Romans CONFORMITY, 1
I want to love first, and l. incidentally LOVE, 27
L. all you can; it's a mistake not to JAMES, 3; LIFE, 14
l. beyond his income EXTRAVAGANCE, 2; PROGRESS, 2
l. dangerously DANGER, 4; NIETZSCHE, 5
l. for ever or die in the attempt IMMORTALITY, 3
L. that thou mayest desire to l. again AFTERLIFE, 6
L. this day, as...thy last PRESENT, 6
l. to fight another day SELF-PRESERVATION, 1
L. with the gods CONTENTMENT, 1
People do not l. nowadays LIFE, 11
people l. beyond their incomes EXTRAVAGANCE, 3; SAKI, 6
self-willed determination to l. LIFE AND DEATH, 5
Teach me to l. DEATH, 36
than to l. up to them PRINCIPLES, 1
there shall no man see me, and l. GOD, 7
To l. with thee, and be thy love LOVE, 49
we l. but to make sport AUSTEN, 14
we must l. as though...never going to die ACHIEVEMENT, 6
You might as well l. PARKER, 1; SUICIDE, 4
lived Never to have l. is best LIFE, 24; YEATS, 8
no man...hath l. better than I ACHIEVEMENT, 4
She...has never l. LOVE, 29
livelihood slave for l. ENVY, 1
lives of quiet desperation DESPAIR, 4
men devote the greater part of their l. LA BRUYERE, 2
no man loses any other life than...he now l. LIFE, 2
living A house is a machine for l. in HOUSES, 2
Civilization is a method of l. CIVILIZATION, 1
History is...the wrong way of l. HISTORY, 6
It does not then concern either the l. or the dead DEATH, 23
let the earth bring forth the l. creature ANIMALS, 1; CREATION, 4
L. frugally,...he died early ABSTINENCE, 1
l. need charity CHARITY, 1
no one has yet found a way to drink for a l. ALCOHOL, 21
Television...permits you to be entertained in your l. room
TELEVISION, 4
The noble l. and the noble dead WORDSWORTH, 15
Vietnam was lost in the l. rooms of America WAR, 36
We owe respect to the l. RESPECT, 2; VOLTAIRE, 19
Livingstone Dr L., I presume GREETINGS, 1
loaf half a l. is better than a whole l. CHESTERTON, 19; COMPROMISE, 3
loafed It is better to have l. and lost LAZINESS, 3; THURBER, 3
loathe I l. the country CONGREVE, 10
lodge a l. in some vast wilderness SOLITUDE, 3
log-cabin L. to White House ACHIEVEMENT, 8
logic That's l. LOGIC, 1

L. seeketh only Self to please   BLAKE, 19; LOVE, 11
L.'s like the measles   LOVE, 34
L. sought is good   SHAKESPEARE, 120
L.'s pleasure lasts but a moment   LOVE, 28
l. that loves a scarlet coat /Should be more uniform   PUNS, 5
L….the gift of oneself   LOVE, 2
L., the human form divine   MANKIND, 3
l. the Lord thy God with all thy heart   LOVE, 9
l. thy neighbour as thyself   LOVE, 9
l. until after the first attack   SCEPTICISM, 1
l….was not as l. is nowadays   NOSTALGIA, 7
l. your enemies   ENEMIES, 1
Many a man has fallen in l. with a girl   LOVE, 17
Men l. in haste   BYRON, 14; LOVE AND HATE, 1
My l. and I would lie   COUNTRYSIDE, 4
My l. is like a red red rose   BURNS, 10; LOVE, 15
My l. she's but a lassie yet   LOVE, 33
no man dies for L., but on the stage   DRYDEN, 13; LOVE AND DEATH, 1
Nuptial l. maketh mankind   LOVE, 4
office and affairs of l.   LOVE AND FRIENDSHIP, 2
One can l….vulgarity   VULGARITY, 1
O tell me the truth about l.   AUDEN, 12; LOVE, 3
Our L. of what is beautiful does not lead to extravagance   RESULTS, 2
perfect l. casteth out fear   FEAR, 3; LOVE, 7
poet without l.   CARLYLE, 3; POETS, 2
Religion is l.   RELIGION, 36
Saying 'Farewell, blighted l.'   POVERTY AND WEALTH, 1
She makes l. just like a woman   WOMEN, 17
She never told her l.   LOVE, 59; SHAKESPEARE, 118
so many computers…use them in the search for l.   CRITICISM, 17
Such ever was l.'s way   LOVE, 14
The dupe of friendship, and the fool of l.   BITTERNESS, 1
The l. of life is necessary to…any undertaking   ENTHUSIASM, 3
the L. that dare not speak its name   HOMOSEXUALITY, 3
the most intense l. on the mother's side   FAMILY, 8
There can be no peace of mind in l.   PROUST, 3
Those have most power to hurt us that we l.   HURT, 1
'Tis said that some have died for l.   LOVE AND DEATH, 3; WORDSWORTH, 21
To be wise and l.   SHAKESPEARE, 115
To business that we l. we rise betime   ENTHUSIASM, 4
To live with thee, and be thy l.   LOVE, 49
to l. and to cherish   MARRIAGE, 15
To L. oneself is the beginning of a lifelong romance   WILDE, 11
True l.'s the gift which God has given /To man alone   LOVE, 52
vanity and l….universal characteristics   CHESTERFIELD, 11; WOMEN, 13
War is like l.   WAR, 9
what a mischievous devil L. is   LOVE, 16
What are your views on l.   PROUST, 3
What is commonly called l.   LUST, 2
What is l.? 'Tis not hereafter   PRESENT, 7
When a man is in l. he endures more   LOVE, 44; NIETZSCHE, 2
whom to look at was to l.   LOVE, 63
with a l. like that you know you should be glad   LOVE, 39
with l. from me to you   LOVE, 38
worms have eaten them, but not for l.   SHAKESPEARE, 23
loved better to be left than never to have been l.   CONGREVE, 9; LOVE, 21
better to have l. and lost   LOSS, 1
L., to have thought, to have done   ARNOLD, 6
She who has never l. has never lived   LOVE, 29
'Tis better to have l. and lost   LOVE, 62; TENNYSON, 16
Who ever l., that l. not at first sight   FIRST IMPRESSIONS, 2
lovely Some hour to which you have not been looking forward will prove l.   PRESENT, 5
lover All mankind love a l.   LOVE, 26
A l. without indiscretion is no l.   LOVE, 31
an ex-wife searching for a new l.   CONNOLLY, 2
easier to be a l. than a husband   MARRIAGE, 2
lunatic, the l., and the poet   POETRY, 21
satisfied with her l.'s mind   TROLLOPE, 7
lovers l. cannot see /The pretty follies   LOVE, 55; SHAKESPEARE, 80
l. fled away into the storm   DEPARTURE, 5
make two l. happy   POPE, 2
one makes l. as fast as one pleases   LOVE, 20
those of us meant to be l.   LOVE, 18
loves Anyone who l. his country, follow me   PATRIOTISM, 5
I have reigned with l.   ELIZABETH I, 3
Two l. I have, of comfort and despair   CONFLICT, 5
lovesome garden is a l. thing   GARDENS, 4
loveth God l. a cheerful giver   GENEROSITY, 1

He prayeth best who l. best   PRAYER, 6
loving A woman despises a man for l. her   LOVE, 61
most l. mere folly   INSINCERITY, 1
low Caesar! dost thou lie so l.   DEATH, 52
I'll tak' the l. road   SCOTLAND, 1
Kings are naturally lovers of l. company   BURKE, 10
my lamp burns l. and dim   ENVY, 1
lower The l. one's vitality   ART, 2
lower-middle No one ever describes himself as belonging to the l. class   CLASS, 14
loyal a l….and good-temper'd people   FRANCE, 8
loyalty Party l. lowers the greatest of men   POLITICS, 2
luck A self-made man…believes in l.   SELF-MADE MEN, 2
it brings you l. whether you believe…or not   SUPERSTITION, 1
l.,…the harder I work the more I have   LUCK, 3
l. to give the roar   CHURCHILL, 34
lucky I wasn't l.. I deserved it   MERIT, 3
luminous Dong with a l. Nose   NONSENSE, 7
lunacy an extraordinary mixture of idealism and l.   PANKHURST, 1
lunatic L., the lover, and the poet   POETRY, 21
lunatics All are l.   PHILOSOPHERS, 1
luncheon to read a novel before l. was one of the gravest sins   WAUGH, 20
lungs don't keep using your l.   LONGEVITY, 2
lured down which ideas are l. and…strangled   BUREAUCRACY, 2
lust l. in action   LUST, 4
Nonconformity and l. stalking hand in hand   LUST, 5
luxuries Give us the l. of life   LUXURY, 3
luxury Every l….atheism, breast-feeding, circumcision   INDULGENCE, 2
The saddest thing…to get used to l.   LUXURY, 2
lyf That l. so short   MORTALITY, 2
lying One of you is l.   LOVE, 45; PARKER, 4
the air of someone who is l….to a policeman   POLICE, 5
macaroni And called it M.   AMERICA, 3
Macavity there's no one like M.   CATS, 2; ELIOT, 6
machine One m. can do the work of fifty ordinary men   TECHNOLOGY, 3
Our body is a m. for living   REMEDIES, 8
that magical m., with its flying white breath   TRAVEL, 3
The m. threatens   TECHNOLOGY, 6
machines I see no reason to suppose that these m. will ever force themselves into general use   WELLINGTON, 4
- no reason…these m. will ever force themselves into general use   TECHNOLOGY, 7
machine tools I would like to suggest we…make him sit on a crate of m.   ECONOMICS, 9
mad Cicero /And…Homer were /M. as the mist and snow   YEATS, 7
Every one is more or less m. on one point   MADNESS, 4
he ceased to be m. he became merely stupid   REMEDIES, 7
he first makes m.   MADNESS, 2
I am going m. again   WOOLF, 6
I said of laughter, it is m.   LAUGHTER, 1
let me not be m.   SHAKESPEARE, 62
M., bad, and dangerous to know   BYRON, 1
Men will always be m.   MADNESS, 9; VOLTAIRE, 23
Never go to bed m.   ANGER, 3
The dog,…/Went m. and bit the man   GOLDSMITH, 2
We all are born m.   MADNESS, 1
When we remember that we are all m.   MADNESS, 8
Madam M. I may not call you   ELIZABETH I, 4
madame Call me m.   TITLES, 3
maddest those who think they can cure them are the m.   MADNESS, 9; VOLTAIRE, 23
made Annihilating all that's m.   OBLIVION, 2
Little Lamb, who m. thee   CREATION, 7
madeleine The taste was that of the little crumb of m.   MEMORY, 6
mademoiselle A m. from Armenteers   FRANCE, 7
madman If a m. were to come into this room   JOHNSON, 28; SELF-PRESERVATION, 5
The m….has lost everything except his reason   CHESTERTON, 15
madness devil's m. – War   WAR, 58
Great Wits…to M. near alli'd   DRYDEN, 3
M. and suffering can set themselves no limit   MADNESS, 5
M. in great ones   MADNESS, 7
Now Ireland has her m.   AUDEN, 10
Maestro Music, M., Please   MUSIC, 16
magic men mistook m. for medicine   MEDICINE, 5
That old black m.   SUPERNATURAL, 7

manger In a m. for His bed — CHRISTMAS, 2
laid him in a m. — CHRISTMAS, 5
mangle Granny caught her tit in the m. — PLEASURE, 13
manhood m. a struggle — AGE, 13; DISRAELI, 3
mankind a decent respect to the opinions of m. — INDEPENDENCE, 1
As I know more of m. — EXPECTATION, 1; JOHNSON, 37
giant leap for m. — SPACE, 1
Ideal m. would abolish death — IDEALISM, 2
I love m. — MANKIND, 10; MISANTHROPY, 2
m. faces a crossroads — PESSIMISM, 1
M. is a closed society — MANKIND, 11
M. is a club — MANKIND, 5
M. is not a tribe of animals — MANKIND, 5
proper study of m. is books — HUXLEY, 7; LITERATURE, 4
Spectator of m. — OBJECTIVITY, 1
The nations which have put m....most in their debt — NATIONS, 2
The proper study of M. is Man — SELF-KNOWLEDGE, 3
truly m.'s war of liberation — HUNGER, 3
manners In England people have good table m. — MANNERS, 4
leave off first for m.' sake — MANNERS, 1
M. are...the need of the plain — MANNERS, 5; WAUGH, 21
M. maketh man — MANNERS, 6
the m. of a Marquis — GILBERT, 8
To Americans English m. are...frightening — MANNERS, 2
Tom Jones...picture of human m. — GIBBON, 3
to write good prose is an affair of good m. — POETRY AND PROSE, 4
mansion Back to its m. call the fleeting breath — DEATH, 27
mansions in my Father's house are many m. — HEAVEN, 3
manure The tree of liberty must be refreshed... It is its natural m. — FREEDOM, 11
many I quite agree with you, sir, but what can two do against so m. — SHAW, 25
so much owed by so m. — CHURCHILL, 24; WORLD WAR II, 6
map The books one reads in childhood...create in one's mind a...false m. — BOOKS, 19
maps Geography is about M. — BIOGRAPHY, 1
mar likely to m. the general felicity — MARRIAGE, 16
marble he...left it m. — IMPROVEMENT, 1
march Beware the ides of M. — PROPHECY, 5
m. into battle together with the men — COURAGE, 7
M., whan God first maked man — CREATION, 8
months...gloomy in England are M. and April — SEASONS, 18; TROLLOPE, 4
marched He m. them up to the top of the hill — ARMY, 1
March Hare 'you should say what you mean,' the M. went on — CARROLL, 4
mark an ever-fixed m. — LOVE, 58
If you would hit the m. — AMBITION, 6
the Lord set a m. upon Cain — REVENGE, 4
the m....of the beast — DEVIL, 3
Marquis the manners of a M. — GILBERT, 8
marriage comedies are ended by a m. — BYRON, 9
hanging prevents a bad m. — MARRIAGE, 53
Happiness in m. — AUSTEN, 12; MARRIAGE, 4
In no country...are the m. laws so iniquitous as in England — ENGLAND, 13
It takes two to make a m. — MARRIAGE, 51
love and m. — LOVE AND MARRIAGE, 1
Love is moral even without...m. — LOVE AND MARRIAGE, 3
M....a community...making in all two — MARRIAGE, 14
M....a woman's best investment — MARRIAGE, 65
M. has many pains — JOHNSON, 9; MARRIAGE, 36
m. in a registry office — MARRIAGE, 1
m....not a public conveyance — MARRIAGE, 43
M. is a great instition — MARRIAGE, 64
M. is a step so grave and decisive — STEVENSON, 12
M. is a wonderful invention — MARRIAGE, 22
M. is...excluded from heaven — MARRIAGE, 16
M. is like a cage — MARRIAGE, 41
M. is like life in this — MARRIAGE, 56
M. is the only adventure open to the cowardly — MARRIAGE, 63; VOLTAIRE, 21
m. of true minds — LOVE, 58
m....resembles a pair of shears — MARRIAGE, 55
rob a lady of her fortune by way of m. — MARRIAGE, 28
they neither marry, nor are given in m. — MARRIAGE, 58
twenty years of m. make her...like a public building — WILDE, 30
Why should m. bring only tears — UNFAITHFULNESS, 4
marriages m. don't add two people together — MARRIAGE, 30
Nearly all m....are mistakes — MARRIAGE, 62
married a woman's business to get m. — MARRIAGE, 54

complacency and satisfaction...in...a new-m. couple — MARRIAGE, 37
don't sleep with m. men — ADULTERY, 4
if ever we had been m. — MARRIAGE, 32
I m. beneath me — MARRIAGE, 3
I'm getting m. in the morning — MARRIAGE, 39
Living in England...like being m. to a stupid wife — ENGLAND, 9
No man is genuinely happy, m., who has to drink worse gin — ALCOHOL, 23
no taste when you m. me — SHERIDAN, 6
Reader, I m. him — BRONTË, 4
that Albert m. beneath him — COWARD, 13
what delight we m. people have to see — MARRIAGE, 46
When m. people don't get on — MARRIAGE, 40
Writing is like getting m. — MARRIAGE, 44; WRITING, 15
marries a young person...m. or dies...kindly spoken of — AUSTEN, 6; HUMAN NATURE, 1
doesn't much signify whom one m. — MARRIAGE, 48
marry as easy to m. a rich woman as a poor woman — MARRIAGE, 58
A woman...may m. whom she likes — MARRIAGE, 59
better to m. than to burn — MARRIAGE, 12
Every woman should m. — MARRIAGE, 24
if men and women m. those whom they do not love — LOVE AND MARRIAGE, 4
no woman should m. a teetotaller — ABSTINENCE, 10; STEVENSON, 11
To m. a man out of pity is folly — MARRIAGE, 2
when a man should m. — MARRIAGE, 6
When you see what some girls m. — MARRIAGE, 49
while ye may, go m. — MARRIAGE, 35
marry'd M. in haste — CONGREVE, 8; MARRIAGE, 20
Mars seat of M. — ENGLAND, 20; SHAKESPEARE, 97
martyr a m. to music — MUSIC, 2
Now he will raise me to be a m. — MARTYRDOM, 1
martyrdom M. is the test — FREEDOM, 12
Marx had M. been Groucho instead of Karl — HUMOUR, 2
M. is a case in point — ILLNESS, 2
Marxist to banish...M. socialism — MARXISM, 4
Mary M., M., quite contrary — GARDENS, 1
masculine Fighting is essentially a m. idea — WOMEN, 20
mass I am a Catholic....I go to M. every day — BELLOC, 11
Paris is worth a m. — PARIS, 2
There is no idolatry in the M. — CATHOLICISM, 3
masses Give me your tired,.../Your huddled m. — AMERICA, 15
I will back the m. against the classes — CLASS, 6
master commerce between m. and slave is...exercise of...boisterous passions — SLAVERY, 3
Man is the m. of things — MANKIND, 16
m. of himself — SELF-CONTROL, 4
Not bound to swear allegiance to any m. — FREEDOM, 10
the m. of my fate — RESPONSIBILITY, 4
the M. Mistress of my passion — SHAKESPEARE, 107
Thou art my m. and my author — VIRGIL, 1
masterpiece the m. of Nature — FRIENDS, 6
masters an ambitious man has as many m. as...may be useful — AMBITION, 4
Buy old m. — PAINTING, 1
good servants, but bad m. — PASSION, 4
people are the m. — BURKE, 11
that the m. willingly concede to slaves — SLAVERY, 1
masturbation m. of war — WAR, 45
M.: the primary sexual activity — SEX, 33; SZASZ, 6
material that which was most m. in the postscript — LETTER-WRITING, 2
materialistic Christianity is the most m. of all great religions — CHRISTIANITY, 22
only really m. people...Europeans — MATERIALISM, 9
mates moves, and m., and slays — DESTINY, 3
mathematics Angling may be said to be...like the m. — FISHING, 3
As far as the laws of m. refer to reality — EINSTEIN, 7; MATHEMATICS, 1
How are you at M. — MATHEMATICS, 3
Let no one ignorant of m. enter here — MATHEMATICS, 4
M. may be defined as the subject — RUSSELL, 6
M....possesses...supreme beauty — MATHEMATICS, 6; RUSSELL, 11
Pure m. consists entirely of assertions — MATHEMATICS, 7
quite lawful for a Catholic woman to avoid pregnancy by...m. — CONTRACEPTION, 5
spirit of delight...in m. — MATHEMATICS, 5
mating Only in the m. season — ANIMALISM, 3
matrimony critical period in m. is breakfast-time — MARRIAGE, 34
it jumps from...love to m. — AUSTEN, 11; WOMEN, 5
m., which I always thought a highly overrated performance — MARRIAGE, 27
matter M....a convenient formula — RUSSELL, 9

matters Nothing m. very much — TRIVIALITY, 1
Matthew M., Mark, Luke and John — BLESSING, 1
maturing Do you think my mind is m. late — AGE, 29
maturity m. is only a short break in adolescence — AGE, 19
Maud Come into the garden, M. — TENNYSON, 22
maunder m. and mumble — PUBLIC, 6
Max If M. gets to Heaven — WELLS, 10
The Incomparable M. — BEERBOHM, 1
maxim A new m. is often a brilliant error — SAYINGS, 2
we have got /The M. Gun, and they have not — BELLOC, 1
May And after April, when M. follows — MONTHS, 3
darling buds of M. — COMPLIMENTS, 3; SHAKESPEARE, 106
Do spring M. flowers — MONTHS, 6
got through the perils of winter till at least the seventh of M. — TROLLOPE, 4
I'm to be Queen o' the M. — MERRYMAKING, 3
the merry month of M. — MONTHS, 2
maze Life is a m. in which we take the wrong turning — CONNOLLY, 6
me My thought is m. — SARTRE, 3
on m. — PARKER, 8
When you and I are together we never talk about anything except m. — WHISTLER, 4
mean He nothing common did or m. — EXECUTION, 1
He who meanly admires m. things is a Snob — SNOBBERY, 4
'it means just what I choose it to m. — CARROLL, 12; MEANING, 1
'you should say what you m.,' the March Hare went on — CARROLL, 4
meaner A patronizing disposition…has its m. side — CHARACTER, 1
motives m. than your own — MOTIVE, 1
meanest the m….deeds require spirit and talent — INSENSITIVITY, 2
meaning Even when poetry has a m. — HOUSMAN, 3; POETRY, 11; UNDERSTANDING, 4
Literature is simply language charged with m. — LITERATURE, 9
Nature has never put the fatal question as to the m. of their lives — PURPOSE, 2
The least of things with a m. is worth more…than the greatest — MEANING, 2
means Let us all be happy, and live within our m. — BORROWING, 5
m. just what I choose it to mean — CARROLL, 12; MEANING, 1
We are living beyond our m. — ECOLOGY, 4
measles Love's like the m. — LOVE, 34
measure M. still for M. — JUSTICE, 11; SHAKESPEARE, 78
Shrunk to this little m. — DEATH, 52
measureless caverns m. to man — COLERIDGE, 6; PLEASURE, 4
meat man loves the m. in his youth — AGE, 36
Some hae m., and canna eat — FOOD, 3
The public buys its opinions as it buys its m. — PUBLIC, 5
meddling He was m. too much in my private life — WILLIAMS, 5
medical We shall not refuse tobacco the credit of being…m. — SMOKING, 11
medicine art of m. consists of — DISEASE, 24
men mistook magic for m. — MEDICINE, 5
miserable have no other m. — SHAKESPEARE, 77
The art of m. is generally a question of time — MEDICINE, 13
when religion was strong and science weak, men mistook magic for m. — SZASZ, 3
medieval disillusionments in the lives of the m. saints — DECLINE, 4
medieval saints disillusionments in the lives of the m. — SAKI, 9
mediocre Some men are born m. — MEDIOCRITY, 3
Titles distinguish the m. — TITLES, 5
mediocrity It isn't evil…but m. — MEDIOCRITY, 4
m….always at its best — MEDIOCRITY, 1
M. knows nothing higher — DOYLE, 9; MEDIOCRITY, 2; TALENT AND GENIUS, 2
meek Blessed are the m. — HUMILITY, 1
humble and m. are thirsting for blood — HUMILITY, 4
m. and mild — HUMILITY, 7
The m….not the mineral rights — WEALTH, 8
meet never the twain shall m. — KIPLING, 1
Two may talk…yet never really m. — FRIENDSHIP, 5
We only part to m. again — FAITHFULNESS, 4
meeting My life's been a m., Dad — BUREAUCRACY, 7
megalomaniac m….seeks to be feared — RUSSELL, 4
melancholy a pleasing fit of m. — MELANCHOLY, 1
hell upon earth…in a m. man's heart — MELANCHOLY, 3
M. has her sovran shrine — MELANCHOLY, 4
so sweet as M. — MELANCHOLY, 2
mellows A tart temper never m. with age — CHARACTER, 3
melodies Heard m. are sweet — MUSIC, 14
melody m. imposes continuity upon the disjointed — MUSIC, 17
melting the races of Europe are m. — AMERICA, 23
melting-pot America is…the great M. — AMERICA, 23

members family with the wrong m. in control – that, perhaps, is as near as one can come to describing England in a phrase. — ENGLAND, 16
même plus c'est la m. chose — CONSTANCY, 2
memories M. are hunting horns — MEMORY, 1
memory Everyone complains of his m. — JUDGMENT, 8; ROCHEFOUCAULD, 4
Fond M. brings the light /Of other days — NOSTALGIA, 8
His m. is going — JOHNSON, 36; OLD AGE, 11
How sweet their m. still — NOSTALGIA, 5
Illiterate him…from your m. — MALAPROPISMS, 4
m. is a painter — MEMORY, 5
O m., hope, love of finished years — NOSTALGIA, 10
Time whereof the m. of man — MEMORY, 3
What a strange thing is m., and hope — MEMORY, 5
men all m. are created equal — HUMAN RIGHTS, 3
all m. would be tyrants — TYRANNY, 1
becoming the m. we wanted to marry — WOMEN, 40
depict m. as they ought to be — THEATRE, 7
don't sleep with married m. — ADULTERY, 4
England…purgatory of m. — ENGLAND, 8
give place to better m. — DISMISSAL, 2
Great m. are almost always bad m…. — POWER, 1
great m. have not commonly been great scholars — GREATNESS, 5
happy breed of m. — ENGLAND, 20; SHAKESPEARE, 97
I don't think m. and women were meant to live together — SEXES, 7
It is m. who face the biggest problems — MEN, 2
It's not the m. in my life that count — SEX, 38
Many m. would take the death-sentence — LIFE AND DEATH, 7
m. about me that are fat — MISTRUST, 4; SHAKESPEARE, 53
M. are but children of a larger growth — AGE, 15
M. are not hanged for stealing horses — EXAMPLE, 3
m….capable of every wickedness — EVIL, 6
m. devote the greater part of their lives — LA BRUYÈRE, 1
M. fear death — DEATH, 7
M. of few words are the best men — BREVITY, 6; SHAKESPEARE, 46
M.'s natures are alike — HABIT, 2
M. will always be mad — MADNESS, 9; VOLTAIRE, , 23
M. will confess — HUMOUR, 6
Most m. admire /Virtue — VIRTUE, 10
power over m. — WOLLSTONECRAFT, 3
rich m. rule the law — GOLDSMITH, 12; LAW, 5
schemes o' mice an' m. — BURNS, 12; DISAPPOINTMENT, 2
So many m., so many opinions — OPINIONS, 4
Such m. are dangerous — MISTRUST, 4; SHAKESPEARE, 53
That all m. are equal — HUXLEY, 15
The mass of m. lead lives — DESPAIR, 4
the m. who borrow, and the m. who lend — BORROWING, 2; LAMB, 4; LAMB, 1
the only advantage women have over m. –…they can cry — SEXES, 11
the race of m. is almost extinct in Europe — MEN, 6
the tongues of m. and of angels — CHARITY, 4
The War between M. and Women — SEXES, 15
tide in the affairs of m. — OPPORTUNITY, 6; SHAKESPEARE, 59
To famous m. all the earth is a sepulchre — FAME, 11
when m. and mountains meet — BLAKE, 9; GREATNESS, 2
Why are women…so much more interesting to m. — SEXES, 17
Women…are either better or worse than m. — LA BRUYÈRE, 3; WOMEN, 24
Women had always fought for m. — PANKHURST, 4
mendacity clergyman whose mendicity is only equalled by their m. — CLERGY, 8
mental philosophy ought to…unravel people's m. blocks — PHILOSOPHY, 6
merci La belle Dame sans M. — SUPERNATURAL, 6
mercies For his m. ay endure — GOD, 26
mercy And that is M.'s door — MERCY, 1
For M. has a human heart — MANKIND, 3
quality of m. is not strain'd — MERCY, 2; SHAKESPEARE, 82
To M., Pity, Peace, and Love — BLAKE, 24; PRAYER, 2
merit no damned m. in it — TITLES, 2
meritocracy The Rise of the M. — MERIT, 4
merry For tonight we'll m., m. be — DRUNKENNESS, 1
I am never m. when I hear sweet music — MUSIC, 22
I commended mirth…to eat…to drink, and to be m. — PLEASURE, 2
messing m. about in boats — BOATS, 5
met I m. a man who wasn't there — NONSENSE, 11
metaphor all m. is poetry — CHESTERTON, 4
metaphysical a physical and m. impossibility — CARLYLE, 3
a physical and m. impossibility — POETS, 2
metaphysics M. is the finding of bad reasons — METAPHYSICS, 2
method madness, yet there is m. in't — MADNESS, 6; SHAKESPEARE, 33

Traditional scientific m. has always been SCIENCE, 20
You know my m. DOYLE, 2
metre Poetry is opposed to science,...prose to m.
POETRY AND PROSE, 1
mice schemes o' m. an' men BURNS, 12; DISAPPOINTMENT, 2
microbe The M. is so very small BELLOC, 9; SMALLNESS, 1
mid-day go out in the m. sun COWARD, 9
middle Bow, bow, ye lower m. classes CLASS, 5
I like a film to have a beginning, a m. and an end CINEMA, 1
One of the pleasures of m. age is to *find out* that one WAS right
AGE, 32
people who stay in the m. of the road
COMPROMISE, 1; NONCOMMITMENT, 1
middle age One of the pleasures of m. is to *find out* that one WAS
right POUND, 2
middle-class part of English m. education is devoted to the train-
ing of servants EDUCATION, 34
midnight It came upon the m. clear CHRISTMAS, 13
Not to be abed after m. BED, 4
Once upon a m. dreary SUPERNATURAL, 8
See her on the bridge at m. POVERTY AND WEALTH, 1
To cease upon the m. with no pain DEATH, 34
mid-winter In the bleak m. SEASONS, 12
might Fight the good fight with all thy m. CHRISTIANITY, 18
Other nations use 'force'; we Britons...use 'M.' WAUGH, 17
The majority has the m. MAJORITY, 1; MINORITY, 1
We m. have been REGRET, 3
Might-have-been Look in my face; my name is M.
DISAPPOINTMENT, 4
mightier pen is m. than the sword WRITING, 1
mighty Another m. empire overthrown DEFEAT, 6
share in the good fortunes of the m. INJUSTICE, 1
militant I am an optimist, unrepentant and m. OPTIMISM, 9
militarism m....is one of the chief bulwarks of capitalism
CAPITALISM, 4
milk drunk the m. of Paradise CAUTION, 1
too full o' th' m. of human kindness KINDNESS, 2; SHAKESPEARE, 69
million Son, here's a m. dollars ADVICE, 3
millionaire He must be a m. WEALTH, 9
Who Wants to Be a M. WEALTH, 12
millions can't. m. off the caring services PATRIOTISM, 10
unrewarded m. without whom Statistics would be a bankrupt science STATISTICS, 2
Milton Malt does more than M. can ALCOHOL, 16; HOUSMAN, 5
M.! thou shouldst be living at this hour DECLINE, 7
the making up of a Shakespeare or a M. COLERIDGE, 17; WRITERS, 4
mimsy All m. were the borogoves NONSENSE, 4
min' never brought to m. BURNS, 3; FRIENDSHIP, 3
mince dined on m., and slices of quince FOOD, 12
mind A good critic...narrates the adventures of his m. CRITICS, 4
A short neck denotes a good m. APPEARANCE, 2
Beauty in things exists in the m. which contemplates them
BEAUTY, 10
Do you think my m. is maturing late AGE, 29
If it is for m. that we are seaching the brain MIND, 5
it's all in the m. ILLNESS, 9
making things plain to uninstructed people was...best means of
clearing...one's own m. EDUCATION, 12
Many ideas grow better when transplanted into another m. IDEAS, 2
m. that makes the body rich APPEARANCES, 11; SHAKESPEARE, 112
No m. is thoroughly well organized HUMOUR, 7
our love...of the m. does not make us soft RESULTS, 2
prodigious quantity of m. INDECISION, 3; TWAIN, 8
Reading is to the m. READING, 2
someone whose m. watches itself INTELLECTUALS, 4
spirit... of a sound m. FEAR, 2
That's the classical m. at work MIND, 4
The m....Can make a Heaven of Hell MIND, 3
The m. is its own place MIND, 3
The pendulum of the m. oscillates between sense and nonsense
MIND, 2
There is in the British Museum an enormous m. MUSEUMS, 2
'Tis education forms the common m. EDUCATION, 22; POPE, 13
to change your m. ADAPTABILITY, 1
To know the *m.* of a woman LOVE, 37
true genius is a m. of large general powers GENIUS, 3
what difficulty a m....admits hope SUFFERING, 7
minded If everybody m. their own business CURIOSITY, 4
minds All things can corrupt perverted m. CORRUPTION, 4
Little m. are interested in the extraordinary TRIVIALITY, 5
marriage of true m. LOVE, 58

M. are not ever craving BOOKS, 8
M. like beds always made up INFLEXIBILITY, 5
m. so impatient of inferiority GRATITUDE, 1
Strongest m. /...the noisy world /Hears least WORDSWORTH, 2
Superstition is the religion of feeble m. BURKE, 7; SUPERSTITION, 2
To be alone is the fate of all great m.
GREATNESS, 6; LONELINESS, 7; SCHOPENHAUER, 1
well-developed bodies, fairly developed m. EDUCATION, 8
When people will not weed their own m. MIND, 6
miner Dwelt a m., Forty-niner, /And his daughter, Clementine
MOURNING, 1
miners it is only because m. sweat their guts out
ORWELL, 7; SUPERIORITY, 6
the Vatican, the Treasury and the m. DIPLOMACY, 2
mingled Like kindred drops, been m. COWPER, 12; MOUNTAINS, 1
ministers I don't mind how much my m. talk
AUTHORITARIANISM, 6; THATCHER, 10
minorities M....are almost always in the right MINORITY, 2; SMITH, 5
minority The m. is always right MAJORITY, 1; MINORITY, 1
minstrel A wandering m. I SINGERS, 2
The M. Boy WAR, 40
minute M. Particulars BLAKE, 10
not a m. on the day STRIKES, 1
To a philosopher no circumstance,...is too m. PHILOSOPHERS, 3
minutes at the rate of sixty m. an hour TIME, 9
some of them are about ten m. long DYLAN, 5
take care of the m. CHESTERFIELD, 7
Yes, about ten m. WELLINGTON, 12
miracle a m. of rare device COLERIDGE, 7; PLEASURE, 5
man prays...for a m. PRAYER, 10
miracles before we *know* he is a saint, there will have to be m.
PROOF, 3
The Christian religion not only was at first attended with m.
CHRISTIANITY, 16
mirror A novel is a m. NOVELS, 7
Art is not a m....but a hammer ART, 9
Look not in my eyes, for fear /They m. true the sight I see
HOUSMAN, 4
mirrors M. and fatherhood are abominable UNIVERSE, 2
mirth I commended m....to eat...to drink, and to be merry
PLEASURE, 2
mischief Satan finds...m..../For idle hands IDLENESS, 6
thou little knowest the m. done ACCIDENTS, 3
To mourn a m. that is past SHAKESPEARE, 89
mischievous what a m. devil Love is LOVE, 16
miserable make only two people m. CARLYLE, 1
m. have no other medicine SHAKESPEARE, 77
The secret of being m. is to have leisure SHAW, 19
miserie y-fallen out of heigh degree. Into m. MISFORTUNE, 3
miseries all the maladies and m. WORK, 3
misery greatest m. is a battle gained VICTORY, 10
he /Who finds himself, loses his m. ARNOLD, 15; SELF-KNOWLEDGE, 1
Let other pens dwell on guilt and m. OPTIMISM, 3
M. acquaints a man with strange bedfellows MISFORTUNE, 8
'Thou art so full of m. TENNYSON, 29
misfortune next greatest m. to losing a battle
VICTORY, 9; WELLINGTON, 7
misfortunes any man...not bear another's m....like a Christian
POPE, 17
history...a tableau of crimes and m. HISTORY, 16
history...the register of the...m. of mankind HISTORY, 9
strong enough to bear the m. of others MISFORTUNE, 7
the real m. and pains of others BURKE, 4
misguided We have guided missiles and m. men WAR, 29
misquotation M. is the pride and privilege of the learned
MISQUOTATIONS, 2
misquotations M. are...never misquoted MISQUOTATIONS, 1
miss Cicero /And...the one before it CHESTERTON, 23; TRAVEL, 2
missiles We have guided m. and misguided men WAR, 29
mist Cicero /And...Homer were /Mad as the m. and snow YEATS, 1
mistake he who never made a m. never made a discovery
MISTAKES, 7
Live all you can; it's a m. not to JAMES, 3; LIFE, 14
Woman was God's *second* m. NIETZSCHE, 3
mistakes An expert...knows... the worst m. that can be made
EXPERTS, 2
Nearly all marriages...are m. MARRIAGE, 62
The man who makes no m. MISTAKES, 4
Young men make great m. in life YOUTH, 6
mistress Art is a jealous m. ART, 1
m. I am ashamed to call you ELIZABETH I, 4

M. interposed /Make enemies of nations COWPER, 12; MOUNTAINS, 1
M....the beginning and the end of all natural scenery
MOUNTAINS, 2; RUSKIN, 3
M. will heave in childbirth DISAPPOINTMENT, 3
Two voices...one is of the sea, /One of the m. FREEDOM, 28
when men and m. meet BLAKE, 9; GREATNESS, 2
mourn countless thousands m. BURNS, 8; CRUELTY, 2
it is chiefly our own deaths that we m. for FUNERALS, 2
To m. a mischief that is past SHAKESPEARE, 89
mourning tedium is the very basis of m. BOREDOM, 3
We met...Dr Hall in such very deep m. AUSTEN, 18; MOURNING, 1
mouse a silly little m. will be born DISAPPOINTMENT, 3
moustache A kiss without a m. KISSING, 3
Being kissed by a man who didn't wax his m. KISSING, 4
his nicotine eggyellow weeping walrus Victorian m. THOMAS, 14
mouth God be in my m., /And in my speaking GOD, 1
mouth-brothels Great restaurants are...nothing but m. FOOD, 22
move But did thee feel the earth m. SEX, 15
I will m. the earth TECHNOLOGY, 1
The great affair is to m. TRAVEL, 16
movement We are the true peace m. PEACE, 11
moves m., and mates, and slays DESTINY, 3
Yet it m. ASTRONOMY, 2
moving In home-sickness you must keep m. HOMESICKNESS, 4
m. Moon went up the sky MOON, 7
The M. Finger writes DESTINY, 4
Mozart The sonatas of M. are unique MUSIC, 31
much m....said on both sides ADDISON, 5
so m. owed by so many to so few CHURCHILL, 24; WORLD WAR II, 6
muchness Much of a m. MEDIOCRITY, 5
muck Money is like m. MONEY, 2
muesli Many children are suffering from m.-belt malnutrition
FOOD, 14
multiply be fruitful and m. CREATION, 5; MANKIND, 2
multitude long dresses,...cover a m. of shins CLOTHES, 10; WEST, 8
this massed m. of silent witnesses to...war WAR, 22
mum M.'s the word SECRECY, 3
They fuck you up, your m. and dad FAMILY, 11
mumble maunder and m. PUBLIC, 6
mundi Sic transit gloria m. GLORY, 2
murder Divorce? Never. But m. often MARRIAGE, 61
love and m. will out CONGREVE, 3; LOVE, 19; MURDER, 3
m. back into its rightful setting – in the home MURDER, 4
M. most foul MURDER, 5
m. shrieks out MURDER, 7
Never m. a man who is committing suicide SUICIDE, 8
Sooner m. an infant in its cradle BLAKE, 15; DESIRE, 2
murderer Kill a man, and you are a m. KILLING, 4
murderous at Yuletide men are the more m. CHRISTMAS, 10
Muse To the Greeks the M. gave native wit CLASSICS, 4
mushroom a supramundane m. NUCLEAR WEAPONS, 1
Fame is sometimes like unto a...m. FAME, 3
to stuff a m. HOUSEWORK, 2
music a martyr to m. MUSIC, 27
Architecture...is frozen m. ARCHITECTURE, 7
art constantly aspires towards...m. ART, 12
capable of being well set to m. MUSIC, 1
food in m. MUSIC, 15
how potent cheap m. is COWARD, 7; MUSIC, 9
How sour sweet m. is ORDER, 3
If all the arts aspire to the condition of m. SCIENCE, 25
If m. be the food of love MUSIC, 24; SHAKESPEARE, 117
line that fits the m. POP MUSIC, 8
man that hath no m. in himself MUSIC, 23
M. and women I cannot but give way to MUSIC, 19
M. begins to atrophy ARTS, 3
M....confirm human loneliness MUSIC, 11
M. creates order out of chaos MUSIC, 10
M. has charms to soothe CONGREVE, 6; MUSIC, 8
M. is the arithmetic of sounds MUSIC, 10
M., Maestro, Please MUSIC, 16
M. that gentlier on the spirit lies MUSIC, 26; TENNYSON, 21
M., when soft voices die MEMORY, 10
never merry when I hear sweet m. MUSIC, 22
Poetry...set to more or less lascivious m. POETRY, 15
popular m....made giant strides in reverse POP MUSIC, 5
potent cheap m. is POP MUSIC, 9
public doesn't want a new m. MUSICIANS, 2
The English may not like m. MUSIC, 12
The hills are alive with the sound of m. MUSIC, 12
thy chosen m., Liberty FREEDOM, 28

music-hall M. songs provide the dull with wit STUPIDITY, 4
musicians M. don't retire MUSICIANS, 1
musicologist A m....can read music but can't hear it MUSIC, 6
Mussolini Hitler was a nuisance. M. was bloody POLITICS, 32
must Genius does what it m. TALENT AND GENIUS, 4
muttering the m. grew to a grumbling BROWNING, 13
myriad-minded m. Shakespeare SHAKESPEARE, 3
myself deliver me from m. SELF, 1
I have always disliked m. CONNOLLY, 5; SELF, 2
I like to go by m. SOLITUDE, 6; TRAVEL, 5
I've over-educated m. COWARD, 10
mysteries disciples...mark its ways and note...its m. LUCK, 1
mysterious God moves in a m. way COWPER, 6; GOD, 13
mystery a riddle wrapped in a m. inside an enigma
CHURCHILL, 20; RUSSIA, 1
Happiness is a m. like religion HAPPINESS, 2
in m. our soul abides SOUL, 1
myth A m. is, of course, not a fairy story MYTHS, 2
basing morals on m. MORALITY, 8
myths Science must begin with m. MYTHS, 1
naive the n. forgive FORGIVENESS, 7
naked m. into the conference chamber WEAPONS, 1
No woman so n. as...underneath her clothes NAKEDNESS, 2
Poor n. wretches WEATHER, 9
The exception is a n. ape MANKIND, 8
they were both n. WOMEN, 8
nakedness N. is uncomely NAKEDNESS, 1
name Good n. in man and woman REPUTATION, 5; SHAKESPEARE, 90
I remember your n. perfectly SPOONERISMS, 1
local habitation and a n. POETRY, 20
No, Groucho is not my real n. NAMES, 2
Oh liberty!...What crimes are committed in thy n.
EXECUTION, 12; FREEDOM, 21
People you know, yet can't quite n. OLD AGE, 12
rose by any other n. NAMES, 3; SHAKESPEARE, 102
thou shalt not take the n. of...God in vain GOD, 6
two or three...gathered together in my n. CHURCH, 2
What's in a n. NAMES, 3; SHAKESPEARE, 102
Napoleon N. OFFICERS, 11; WELLINGTON, 6
narcissist megalomaniac differs from the n. RUSSELL, 4
narcotics Two great European n. DRUGS, 6
nasty how n. the nice people can be NASTINESS, 1
nation An army is a n. within a n. ARMY, 3
A n. is not in danger ECONOMICS, 8
a n. of amateurs BRITISH, 4
England is a n. of shopkeepers ENGLISH, 13
I will make of thee a great n. JEWS, 2
n....fall victim to a big lie HITLER, 2; LYING, 4
n. had the lion's heart CHURCHILL, 34
n. shall not lift up sword against n. WAR AND PEACE, 2
n. shall rise against n. WAR, 6
No n. is fit to sit in judgement DIPLOMACY, 10
No n. was ever ruined by trade BUSINESS, 4
N. shall speak peace PEACE, 10
Teddy Bear to the N. BETJEMAN, 1
nationality My n. is French NORMALITY, 2
My suit is pale yellow. My n. is French WILLIAMS, 1
Other people have a n. IRISH, 1; JEWS, 1
nations Commonwealth of N. BRITISH EMPIRE, 5
If people behaved in the way n. do GOVERNMENT, 17; WILLIAMS, 4
languages are the pedigree of n. JOHNSON, 41; LANGUAGE, 10
The day of small n. has long passed away NATIONS, 1
The n. which have put mankind and posterity most in their debt
NATIONS, 2
native my own, my n. land HOMESICKNESS, 3
to appear considerable in his n. place FAME, 5
natural First feelings are always the most n. FIRST IMPRESSIONS, 1
It is n. to die DEATH, 8
n. false teeth TEETH, 1
N. Selection EVOLUTION, 4
You ask whether woman possesses any n. intelligence
CHRISTINE DE PISAN, 1
naturally Though I am not n. honest HONESTY, 4; SHAKESPEARE, 124
nature All N. wears one universal grin NATURE, 1
a noble n.,...treats...a serious subject POETRY, 3
but N. more NATURE, 2
Consistency is contrary to n. CONSTANCY, 1; HUXLEY, 3
drive out n. with a pitchfork HORACE, 7; HUMAN NATURE, 4
fortress built by N. ENGLAND, 20; SHAKESPEARE, 97
Friend...masterpiece of N. FRIENDS, 6
Human n. is so well disposed AUSTEN, 6; HUMAN NATURE, 1

oversexed They're overpaid, overfed, o. and over here SOLDIERS, 5
overthrown Another mighty empire o. DEFEAT, 6
ovule Man is developed from an o. EVOLUTION, 2
ovules differs in no respect from the o. of other animals
EVOLUTION, 2
owe I don't o. a penny to a single soul WODEHOUSE, 6
owed so much o. by so many to so few CHURCHILL, 24; WORLD WAR II, 6
owes A nation is not in danger...because it o. itself money
ECONOMICS, 8
owl The O. and the Pussy-Cat went to sea NONSENSE, 10
own mine o. Executioner DONNE, 4; SELF, 3
ownership its source of power: o. CAPITALISM, 5
transform this society without...extension of public o. SOCIALISM, 5
own-goal Aids pandemic is a classic o. AIDS, 2
ox When he stands like an o. in the furrow NATIONALITY, 2
Oxenford Clerk...of O. CHAUCER, 3
Oxford nice sort of place, O. SHAW, 12
O. is on the whole more attractive than Cambridge
CAMBRIDGE, 1; OXFORD, 3
The King to O. sent a troop of horse CAMBRIDGE, 3; OXFORD, 4
To O. sent a troop of horse CAMBRIDGE, 5; OXFORD, 5
To the University of O. I acknowledge no obligation GIBBON, 2
You will hear more good things on...a stagecoach from London to
O. HAZLITT, 5
you will leave O. by the town drain SPOONERISMS, 3
oyster the sort of eye that can open an o. at sixty paces
WODEHOUSE, 3
world's mine o. OPPORTUNITY, 7; SHAKESPEARE, 83
pace this petty p. from day to day LIFE, 19; SHAKESPEARE, 76
pack how much more dogs are animated when they hunt in a p.
UNITY, 7
the human p. is shuffled and cut EDUCATION, 15
paddle every man p. his own canoe INDEPENDENCE, 2
pageant insubstantial p. faded MORTALITY, 10
pain a gentleman...never inflicts p. CHIVALRY, 6
critics...desire our blood, not our p. CRITICS, 10
I have no p., dear mother, now LAST WORDS, 12
momentary intoxication with p. CRUELTY, 1
Neither shame nor physical p. have any...effect PUNISHMENT, 8
owes its pleasures to another's p. HUNTING, 1
P. – has an Element of Blank DICKINSON, 3
Pleasure is...intermission of p. PLEASURE, 12
The least p. in our little finger HAZLITT, 2; SELF-INTEREST, 2
they blest him in their p. MARTYRDOM, 3
what p. it was to drown DROWNING, 1
paint I p. objects as I think them PAINTING, 5
My business is to p....what I see PAINTING, 8
to p. the lily EXCESS, 5
painted As idle as a p. ship BOATS, 2; COLERIDGE, 11
I am p. as the greatest little dictator THATCHER, 8
Most women are not so young as they are p. BEERBOHM, 6
p....by the great artist Kodak PHOTOGRAPHY, 4
painter A p. should not paint what he sees ARTISTS, 5
memory is a p. MEMORY, 5
who is not a great sculptor or p. can be an architect
ARCHITECTURE, 5; RUSKIN, 2
painters Good p. imitate nature PAINTING, 3
P. and poets...licence to dare anything HORACE, 1
Poets and p. are outside the class system ARTISTS, 1; POETS, 1
painting a great difference between p. a face APPEARANCE, 2
I just keep p. till I feel like pinching. Then I know it's right
PAINTING, 2
one of the very greatest masters of p. WHISTLER, 1
P. is a blind man's profession PAINTING, 6
P....protecting flat surfaces from the weather PAINTING, 1
palace Love in a p. KEATS, 5
palaces Mid pleasures and p. though we may roam HOME, 3
pale a p. horse DEATH, 13
Palestine not enough prisons...in P. to hold all the Jews JEWS, 3
Palladium Liberty of the press is the P. of...rights FREEDOM, 13
palsied with the p. heart PASSION, 7; TENNYSON, 20
pantheist The modern p. not only LAWRENCE, 10
papacy Since God has given us the p....enjoy it CATHOLICISM, 4
The P. is not other than the Ghost of the deceased Roman Empire
CATHOLICISM, 2
paper The atom bomb is a p. tiger
MAO TSE-TUNG, 5; NUCLEAR WEAPONS, 9
Where were you fellows when the p. was blank EDITORS, 1
papers only two posh p. on a Sunday NEWSPAPERS, 3
Papyromania P. – compulsive accumulation OBSESSIONS, 2
Papyrophobia P. – abnormal desire OBSESSIONS, 2

parables great p.,..., but false art LAWRENCE, 15
parade the chief employment of riches consists in the p. of riches
OSTENTATION, 3; WEALTH, 13
paradise A p. for a sect FANATICISM, 2
England is the p. of individuality ENGLAND, 19
England is the p. of women ENGLAND, 8
drunk the milk of P. CAUTION, 1
If a man could pass through P. PROOF, 2
Wilderness is P. enow CONTENTMENT, 2
paragon the p. of animals MANKIND, 13; SHAKESPEARE, 35
paralyse p. it by encumbering it with remedies REMEDIES, 8
paranoid Even a p. can have enemies ENEMIES, 2
parasite The sick man is a p. of society PATIENTS, 2
pardon God may p. you, but I never can ELIZABETH I, 5
parent To lose one p.,...a misfortune; to lose both looks like carelessness LOSS, 6; WILDE, 15
parents A Jewish man with p. alive JEWS, 9
by defying their p. and copying one another YOUTH, 4
Don't hold your p. up to contempt FAMILY, 22
From birth to age eighteen, a girl needs good p. AGE, 43
joys of p. are secret FAMILY, 2
necessary precautions to avoid having p. FAMILY, 5
P....a disappointment to their children FAMILY, 17
P. learn a lot from their children CHILDREN, 16
what p. were created for FAMILY, 16
Paris Good Americans, when they die, go to P. AMERICANS, 1
Is P. burning PARIS, 3
no home...save in P. PARIS, 4
P. is worth a mass PARIS, 2
when good Americans die they go to P. AMERICANS, 9; WILDE, 31
par-lee-voo Hinky, dinky, p. FRANCE, 7
parliament build your House of P. upon the river
HOUSES OF PARLIAMENT, 11
P. is the longest running farce GOVERNMENT, 12
parliaments England...mother of p. ENGLAND, 2
parrot to sell the family p. RESPECTABILITY, 3
parsnips fine words butter no p. WORDS, 10
part I have forgot my p. FAILURE, 3
let us kiss and p. PARTING, 4
till death us do p. MARRIAGE, 15
We only p. to meet again FAITHFULNESS, 4
particular a London p....A fog WEATHER, 1
did nothing in p. GILBERT, 5; HOUSES OF PARLIAMENT, 5
particulars Minute P. BLAKE, 10
parties it is always like that at p. REGRET, 5
parting Every p. gives a foretaste of death
SCHOPENHAUER, 3; SEPARATION, 4
P. is all we know of heaven DICKINSON, 2; PARTING, 3
P. is such sweet sorrow PARTING, 6; SHAKESPEARE, 104
partly Man p. is AMBITION, 1
parts It is seldom...one p. on good terms PARTING, 5; PROUST, 7
one man in his time plays many p.
HUMAN CONDITION, 8; SHAKESPEARE, 18
part-time p. nihilist COMMITMENT, 1
party soft drink at a p. ABSTINENCE, 2
The sooner every p. breaks up the better PARTIES, 1
Well, did you evah! What a swell p. PARTIES, 3
party's I always voted at my p. call GILBERT, 1
pass ideas simply p. through him STUPIDITY, 1
I shall not p. this way again MORTALITY, 6
p. for forty-three AGE, 22
passage calm p....across many a bad night NIETZSCHE, 6; SUICIDE, 3
Patience and p. of time PATIENCE, 3
passes Men seldom make p. APPEARANCE, 13
passion All breathing human p. far above PASSION, 3
Culture is the p. for sweetness and light CULTURE, 2
Master Mistress of my p. SHAKESPEARE, 107
one master-p.../swallows up the rest PASSION, 5
p. and party blind our eyes COLERIDGE, 10; EXPERIENCE, 4
p. in the human soul MUSIC, 15
So I triumphed ere my p. PASSION, 7; TENNYSON, 20
Strange fits of p. WORDSWORTH, 4
The p. and the life, whose fountains are within APPEARANCES, 4
The ruling p. conquers reason still PASSION, 6
passions A man who has not passed through the inferno of his p.
PASSION, 2
It is with our p. as it is with fire and water PASSION, 4
Literature and butterflies are the two sweetest p. LITERATURE, 4
not his reason, but his p. RELIGION, 29
The man who is master of his p. CONNOLLY, 10; PASSION, 1

Three p., simple but overwhelmingly strong, have governed my
life   RUSSELL, 12
past Even God cannot change the p.   PAST, 1
Historians tell the story of the p.   NOVELS, 2
I do not...prejudge the p.   PREJUDICE, 3
Keep off your thoughts from things that are p.   PAST, 5
Nothing recalls the p. so potently as a smell   NOSTALGIA, 4
people who live in the p.   BENNETT, 2; PROGRESS, 1
remembrance of things p.   REGRET, 9
something...absurd about the p.   BEERBOHM, 3
Study the p.   PAST, 2
The only thing I regret about my p. life   AGE, 3
The p. is a foreign country   PAST, 3
Those who cannot remember the p.   HISTORY, 13
Time present and time p.   ELIOT, 3
to know nothing but the present, or nothing but the p.
    CONSERVATISM, 2
what is p. my help is p. my care   INDIFFERENCE, 1
what's p. help /Should be p. grief   SHAKESPEARE, 122
Who controls the p. controls the future   ORWELL, 6; POWER, 9
pastoral Cold P.   ETERNITY, 3
pastures fresh woods, and p. new   CHANGE, 12
patches thing of shreds and p.   SINGERS, 2
path the primrose p. of dalliance   EXAMPLE, 5; SHAKESPEARE, 28
patience like P. on a monument   LOVE, 59; SHAKESPEARE, 118
P. and passage of time   PATIENCE, 3
P., n. A minor form of despair   PATIENCE, 1
the years teach us p.   PATIENCE, 4
patient A doctor...is a p. half-cured   OCCUPATIONS, 6
amusing the p. while Nature cures the disease   MEDICINE, 1
Fury of a P. Man   DRYDEN, 7; PATIENCE, 2
[INDIGESTION], n. A disease which the p.   RELIGION, 3
kill the p.   REMEDIES, 1
p. endurance is godlike   ENDURANCE, 4
patients the faults of the p.   PATIENTS, 1
patrie Allons, enfants, de la p.   FRANCE, 5
patriot A good historian...is a p.   HISTORIANS, 1
He was a great p....provided...that he really is dead
    ADMIRATION, 7; VOLTAIRE , 28
patriotism Blimpish p. in the mode of Margaret Thatcher
    PATRIOTISM, 10
p. which consists in hating all other nations   PATRIOTISM, 6
P....is a revolutionary duty   PATRIOTISM, 17
P. is the last refuge   JOHNSON, 25; PATRIOTISM, 9
P....looking out for yourself while   AMERICA, 7
True p. is of no party   PATRIOTISM, 16
patriots P. always talk of dying for their country
    PATRIOTISM, 14; RUSSELL, 15
patron Is not a P., my Lord, one who looks with unconcern
    PATRONAGE, 2
patronise He liked to p. coloured people   RACISM, 13
patronizing A p. disposition...has its meaner side   CHARACTER, 1
The idea that there is a model Labour voter,...is p.   POLITICS, 28
pattern p. of excelling nature   SHAKESPEARE, 93
paucity p. of human pleasures   HUNTING, 4; JOHNSON, 12
pavilion The p. of Heaven is bare   SHELLEY, 4
pavilioned P. in splendour, and girded with praise   GOD, 18
pay better...not vow, than vow and not p.
    PROMISES, 1
get someone to p. you for doing it   OCCUPATIONS, 8
it is poor grub, poor p., and easy work   ENGLAND, 12
Not a penny off the p.   STRIKES, 1
we cannot p. too dearly for it   JUSTICE, 7
peace Arms alone are not enough to keep the p.   PEACE, 8
Courage is the price...for granting p.   COURAGE, 4
He accepted p. as if he had been defeated   WELLINGTON, 1
In Switzerland they had brotherly love...and p.   SWITZERLAND, 1
in what p. a Christian can die   ADDISON, 7; LAST WORDS, 2
it is in the minds of men that the defences of p. must be constructed   WAR AND PEACE, 1
Let him who desires p., prepare for war   WAR AND PEACE, 8
Let us have p.   PEACE, 7
make a wilderness and call it p.   WAR, 65
May God deny you p.   GLORY, 1
my p. I give unto you   PEACE, 2
Nation shall speak p.   PEACE, 10
never was a good war or a bad p.   WAR AND PEACE, 5
no p....unto the wicked   PEACE, 1; PUNISHMENT, 3
Only p./ will emanate from German soil   GERMANY, 2
P....a period of cheating   PEACE, 6
p. for our time   PEACE, 4
p. has broken out   PEACE, 5

P. hath her victories   WAR AND PEACE, 7
p. I hope with honour   DISRAELI, 15
p. in our time   PEACE, 4
P., the human dress   MANKIND, 3
P. took them all prisoner   WAR AND PEACE, 6
p. with honour   PEACE, 6
price which is too great to pay for p.   WORLD WAR I, 16
The Bomb brought p. but man alone   NUCLEAR WEAPONS, 3
There can be no p. of mind in love   PROUST, 2
They made p. between us   ENEMIES, 3
those who could make a good p.   CHURCHILL, 10; WAR AND PEACE, 4
We are the true p. movement   PEACE, 11
We wanted p. on earth   PEACE, 9
When there was p., he was for p.   AUDEN, 13; PUBLIC, 2
peach 'Fan vaulting'...belongs to the 'Last-supper-carved-on-a-p.-
stone'   ARCHITECTURE, 3
peak One sees...only small things from the p.
    CHESTERTON, 6; PERSPECTIVE, 1
pearl base Indian, threw a p. away   LOVE, 60; SHAKESPEARE, 94
pearls He who would search for P.   DRYDEN, 10
p. before swine   FOOLISHNESS, 1
p. that were his eyes   SHAKESPEARE, 113
peas I always eat p. with honey   FOOD, 1
peasant hard-handed Scottish p.   BURNS, 1
peasantry a bold p.,.../When once destroy'd   GOLDSMITH, 5; PUBLIC, 8
peasants If the French noblesse had been capable of playing
cricket with their p.   ARISTOCRACY, 11; CRICKET, 6
peculiar a tense and p. family, the Oedipuses
    BEERBOHM 13; CLASSICS, 1
the p. situation of the human male   BEAUVOIR, 1
pedigree languages are the p. of nations   JOHNSON, 41; LANGUAGE, 10
Peel D'ye ken John P.   HUNTING, 3
peers Fears, prejudices, misconceptions – those are the p.
    HOUSES OF PARLIAMENT, 6
pen how much more cruel the p.   WRITING, 2
nothing can cure it but the scratching of a p.   WRITING, 12
p. is mightier than the sword   WRITING, 1
pence Take care of the p.   CHESTERFIELD, 6; THRIFT, 1
pendulum politics of the p., but of the ratchet   POLITICS, 46
The p. of the mind oscillates between sense and nonsense   MIND, 2
penetrable most things are p.   BRIBERY, 1
pennies P. do not come from heaven   THATCHER, 7; WORK, 11
P. from Heaven   OPTIMISM, 5
penny I don't owe a p. to a single soul   WODEHOUSE, 6
Not a p. off the pay   STRIKES, 1
pens Let other p. dwell on guilt and misery   OPTIMISM, 3
people a loyal, a gallant, a generous, an ingenious, and good-
temper'd p.   FRANCE, 8
Be nice to p. on your way up   PRUDENCE, 4
Boys...are unwholesome companions for grown p.   LAMB, 3
good of the p.   LAW, 1
government of the p. by the p.   MEMORIALS, 6
If p. behaved in the way nations do   GOVERNMENT, 17; WILLIAMS, 4
indictment against an whole p.   ACCUSATION, 1
It is with...p. as with...bottles   CHARACTER, 5
Most of the p....will be children   FUNERALS, 1
Once the p. begin to reason   PUBLIC, 10
p....are attracted by God   RELIGION, 19
P. are either charming or tedious   CHARM, 3
P. are not fallen angels   LAWRENCE, 15
p. are the masters   BURKE, 11
p. may be made to follow a course of action   UNDERSTANDING, 3
p.'s government   GOVERNMENT, 16
p. standing in the corners of our rooms   TELEVISION, 1
p....usually imitate each other   IMITATION, 2
p. who do things   EFFORT, 3
p. who stay in the middle of the road   NONCOMMITMENT, 1
P. will cross the road...to say 'We saw you on the telly'   TELEVISION, 2
Religion...is the opium of the p.   RELIGION, 23
the bludgeoning of the p.   DEMOCRACY, 8; WILDE, 29
The Lord prefers common-looking p.   APPEARANCE, 10
the p. are forbidden to light lamps   INJUSTICE, 6; MAO TSE-TUNG, 6
The p.'s flag is deepest red   SOCIALISM, 2
This country...belongs to the p. who inhabit it   DEMOCRACY, 5
thy p. shall be my p.   LOYALTY, 1
two p. with one pulse   LOVE, 41
we are not a small p.   BRITAIN, 5
When...it becomes necessary for one p. to dissolve...political
bonds   INDEPENDENCE, 1
When the P. contend for their Liberty   REBELLION, 1
You can fool too many of the p.   DECEPTION, 4; THURBER, 4

perception doors of p. were cleansed — BLAKE, 13; PERCEPTION, 1
perceptions Man's Desires are limited by his P. — BLAKE, 25; DESIRE, 3; PERCEPTION, 2
perfect A cigarette is...a p. pleasure — WILDE, 28
p. love casteth out fear — FEAR, 3; LOVE, 7
perfection attain to the divine p. — PERFECTION, 3
Finality is death. P. is finality — PERFECTION, 5
P. has one grave defect — PERFECTION, 4
The pursuit of p. — PERFECTION, 1
performance desire should...outlive p. — SEX, 30
it takes away the p. — ALCOHOL, 30; SHAKESPEARE, 72
perfume As a p. doth remain — MEMORY, 11
perfumes All the p. of Arabia — SHAKESPEARE, 75
perhaps The grand P. — POSSIBILITY, 1
peril For those in p. on the sea — SEA, 7
perils all p. and dangers of this night — DANGER, 1
smile at p. past — PAST, 4; SCOTT, 2
periods Decades...are not...really p. at all — CLASSIFICATION, 2
perish P. the Universe — REVENGE, 3
they that take the sword shall p. with the sword — WAR, 7
though the world p. — JUSTICE, 4
weak shall p. — SURVIVAL, 3
perjury P....is truth that is shamefaced — TRUTH, 9
permanence love p. more than...beauty — BRITISH, 1
pernicious the most p. race — SWIFT, 6
Peron If a woman like Eva P. with no ideals — IDEALISM, 4
perpetual gift of p. old age — OLD AGE, 28
Literary men are...a p. priesthood — WRITERS, 3
perseverance the name of p. in a good cause — STUBBORNNESS, 2
persistent The most p. sound...through men's history — WAR, 31
person My idea of an agreeable p. — DISRAELI, 6
the only thing that can exist is an uninterested p. — CHESTERTON, 7
The world regards such a p. as...an unmuzzled dog — CLASSIFICATION, 1
to the cheek of a young p. — EMBARRASSMENT, 1
personality Simply a radio p. — CHURCHILL, 4
persons God is no respecter of p. — GOD, 4
persuade Beauty...doth...p. the eyes of men — BEAUTY, 19
perversion that melancholy sexual p. known as continence — ABSTINENCE, 6
War is...universal p. — WAR, 45
pervert Once: a philosopher; twice: a p. — DEBAUCHERY, 5; VOLTAIRE, 29
p. climbs into the minds — CRUELTY, 1
pessimism P. is a luxury that a Jew never can allow himself — JEWS, 7
P.,...is just as agreeable as optimism — BENNETT, 3; PESSIMISM, 2
pessimist A p. is a man who — PESSIMISM, 6
Scratch a p. — PESSIMISM, 3
the p. fears this is true — OPTIMISM, 6; PESSIMISM, 4
pessimists p. end up by desiring the things they fear — PESSIMISM, 5
Peter thou art P. — CHURCH, 1
Peter Pan He was once Slightly in P. — COWARD, 2
petticoat lay aside...modesty...and put it on again with her p. — SEX, 23
petulance p. is not sarcasm — DISRAELI, 13; PETULANCE, 1
Pharisees Now is the time of P. — DESTINY, 7
Philip Prince P....a world expert on leisure — ROYALTY, 10
Philistines For this class we have...the designation of P. — PHILISTINISM, 1
society distributes itself into Barbarians, P., and Populace — AMERICA, 1
to distinguish...the aristocratic class from the P. — ARNOLD, 4; CLASS, 2
philosopher he who can analyze his delusion is called a p. — PHILOSOPHERS, 1
In the p. there is nothing whatever impersonal — PHILOSOPHERS, 4
never yet p. /That could endure the toothache — SHAKESPEARE, 88
Once: a p.; twice: a pervert — DEBAUCHERY, 5; VOLTAIRE, 29
Organic life...has developed...from the protozoon to the p. — RUSSELL, 8
some p. has said it — PHILOSOPHERS, 2
To a p. no circumstance,...is too minute — PHILOSOPHERS, 3
philosophers now-a-days professors of philosophy but not p. — PHILOSOPHERS, 6
till p. become kings — PHILOSOPHY, 5
philosophy a great advantage for...p. to be...true — PHILOSOPHY, 7
Art and religion first; then p. — IMPORTANCE, 2
Axioms in p. are not axioms — PHILOSOPHY, 4
collection of prejudices which is called political p. — POLITICS, 39
dreamt of in your p. — SHAKESPEARE, 31; SUPERNATURAL, 9
History is p....by examples — HISTORY, 5
mere touch of cold p. — PHILOSOPHY, 3
necessary for a superstition to enslave a p. — RELIGION, 18

Not to care for p. — PHILOSOPHERS, 5
now-a-days professors of p. but not philosophers — PHILOSOPHERS, 6
P. is not a theory — PHILOSOPHY, 10
P. is the product of wonder — PHILOSOPHY, 8; WONDER, 2
p. ought to...unravel people's mental blocks — PHILOSOPHY, 6
Western p. is,...a series of footnotes to Plato's p. — PHILOSOPHY, 9
phobias I have three p. which...would make my life as slick as a sonnet — OBSESSIONS, 1
photograph A p. is not only an image — PHOTOGRAPHY, 5
photography p. is a...lifetime of pleasure — PHOTOGRAPHY, 2
P. can never grow up if it imitates — PHOTOGRAPHY, 1
P. is truth — CINEMA, 2
physic Take p., pomp — HUMILITY, 5
physical a p. and metaphysical impossibility — CARLYLE, 3; POETS, 2
women possess but one class of p. organs — HEALTH AND HEALTHY LIVING, 7
physician A p. can sometimes parry the scythe of death — TIME, 11
died last night of my p. — DISEASE, 17
I died...of my p. — DOCTORS, 5
p., heal thyself — DOCTORS, 2
The p. can bury his mistakes — MISTAKES, 10
the p. cutteth off a long disease — DEATH, 11
physicians the help of too many p. — DOCTORS, 1
physicists have known sin — SCIENTISTS, 4
to find out anything from the theoretical p. — SCIENTISTS, 3
pianist do not shoot the p. — WILDE, 21
Picardy Roses are flowering in P. — COMPLIMENTS, 5
Picasso Nothing divides them like P. — ART, 10
Piccadilly Good-bye P., Farewell Leicester Square — HOMESICKNESS, 5
pickle weaned on a p. — APPEARANCE, 11
picnic futile to attempt a p. in Eden — INNOCENCE, 4
picture If you want a p. of the future — OPPRESSION, 3; ORWELL, 1
pictures book...without p. — BOOKS, 5; CARROLL, 1
dearth of bad p. — GOLDWYNISMS, 24
pidgin-English I include 'p.' — LANGUAGE, 15
piece What a p. of work is a man — MANKIND, 13; SHAKESPEARE, 35
pie-crust Promises and p. are made to be broken — PROMISES, 4; SWIFT, 8
pier Like Brighton P. — TRAVEL, 9
Pierian Drink deep, or taste not the P. spring — POPE, 7
pies I could eat one of Bellamy's veal p. — LAST WORDS, 23
pig Bennett – a sort of p. in clover — BENNETT, 1
pigs And whether p. have wings — CARROLL, 10; NONSENSE, 5
one of Epicurus' herd of p. — PRESENT, 5
Pilate P....washed his hands — GUILT, 2
rather have blood on my hands...P. — COMMITMENT, 2
pilgrims strangers and p. on the earth — FAITH, 2
pinching I just keep painting till I feel like p.. Then I know it's right — PAINTING, 7
pine-apple p. of politeness — SHERIDAN, 4
pinko-gray white races are...p. — RACISM, 5
pint You spend half a p. and flush two gallons — WATER, 3
pin-up p., the centerfold, the poster — PORNOGRAPHY, 2
pious A p. man...would be an atheist — SERVILITY, 2
p. frauds of friendship — FRIENDSHIP, 7
piped their fountains p. an answer — LAWRENCE, 3
piping P. down the valleys wild — BLAKE, 22
pitchfork drive out nature with a p....she'll be constantly running back — HORACE, 7; HUMAN NATURE, 6
pitied one has....ceased to be an object of *fear* as soon as one is p. — SYMPATHY, 2
pitiless slow, sure doom falls p. and dark — HUMAN CONDITION, 7
pity A p. beyond all telling — LOVE, 72
knock him down first, and p. him afterwards — JOHNSON, 28; SELF-PRESERVATION, 3
P. a human face — MANKIND, 3
p. for the suffering of mankind — RUSSELL, 2
To marry a man out of p. is folly — MARRIAGE, 2
To show p. is felt as a sign of contempt — SYMPATHY, 2
place A p. for everything — ORDER, 4
everything in its p. — ORDER, 4
firm p. to stand — TECHNOLOGY, 1
give p. to better men — DISMISSAL, 2
Home is the p. where — HOME, 1
I go to prepare a p. for you — HEAVEN, 3
there's no p. like home — HOME, 3
this is an awful p. — PLACES, 10
Upon the p. beneath — MERCY, 2; SHAKESPEARE, 82
plagiarism steal from one author, it's p. — WRITING, 14
plague A p. o' both your houses — CURSES, 1; SHAKESPEARE, 105

The p. of logic and metaphysics are true — PHILOSOPHY, 1
Whenever two good people argue over p. — PRINCIPLES, 3
whoever is moved...is conscious of a continued miracle...which
subverts all the p. of his understanding — CHRISTIANITY, 16
print pleasant, sure, to see one's name in p. — BYRON, 15
The big p. giveth and the fine p. taketh away — BUSINESS, 11
printers those books by which the p. have lost — BOOKS, 12
printing Gunpowder, P., and the Protestant Religion
— CARLYLE, 7; CIVILIZATION, 3
prison Anyone who has been to...public school...at home in p.
— WAUGH, 12
Stone walls do not a p. make — IMPRISONMENT, 3
The world...is but a large p. — EXECUTION, 3
prisoner Peace took them all p. — WAR AND PEACE, 6
P., God has given you good abilities — THEFT, 2
prisoners If this is the way Queen Victoria treats her p. — WILDE, 39
prisons not enough p....in Palestine to hold all the Jews — JEWS, 8
P. are built with stones of Law — BLAKE, 14
privacy a right to share your p. in a public place — PRIVACY, 3
private He was meddling too much in my p. life — WILLIAMS, 5
Scientific discovery is a p. event — SCIENCE, 16
sex has been a very p., secretive activity — SEX, 34; SZASZ, 2
Travel is the most p. of pleasures — TRAVEL, 13
when religion is allowed to invade...p. life — RELIGION, 24
privilege a defender of p. — PESSIMISM, 3
an Englishman's heaven-born p. of doing as he likes — ARNOLD, 5
prize Not all that tempts your wand'ring eyes...is lawful p.
— TEMPTATION, 3
prizes The world continues to offer glittering p. — RUTHLESSNESS, 2
P.R.O partly a liaison man and partly P. — BETJEMAN, 4
problem ineffectual liberal's p. — LIBERALISM, 1
the p. as I see it — LANGUAGE, 5
problems Among the many p....the choice of the moment...to
begin his novel — WRITERS, 12
procession A torchlight p. — ALCOHOL, 25
prodigal P. of Ease — DRYDEN, 4; WORLD-WEARINESS, 1
producing Man...consumes without p. — ORWELL, 2
production Capitalist p. begets...its own negation — CAPITALISM, 7
profession Politics is...the only p. — POLITICS, 42; STEVENSON, 3
The price...for pursuing any p. — DISILLUSION, 1
professor A p. is one who talks in someone else's sleep
— ACADEMICS, 1; AUDEN, 15
professors now-a-days p. of philosophy but not philosophers
— PHILOSOPHERS, 6
profit Count as p. every day that Fate allows you
— HORACE, 9; PRESENT, 4
No p. grows where is no pleasure — EDUCATION, 26
progeny A p. of learning — MALAPROPISMS, 3
progress All p. is based — EXTRAVAGANCE, 2; PROGRESS, 2
Man's 'p.' is but a gradual discovery — PROGRESS, 6
P....depends on retentiveness — HISTORY, 13
'p.' is simply a comparative — PROGRESS, 3
the things which government does...social p. — GOVERNMENT, 15
What p....In the Middle Ages — PSYCHOLOGY, 1
What we call p. is — PROGRESS, 4
progression Without Contraries is no p. — BLAKE, 12; CONFLICT, 1
prohibition Communism is like p. — COMMUNISM, 3
proletariat The dictatorship of the p. — MARXISM, 3
promiscuous prostitute, but I'm not p. — PROMISCUITY, 4
promise A p. made is a debt unpaid — PROMISES, 1
rarely...one can see in a little boy the p. of a man — CHILDREN, 8
promised Only do...in health what...p. to do when you are sick
— ILLNESS, 8
promises young man of p. — CHURCHILL, 1
P. and pie-crust are made to be broken — PROMISES, 4; SWIFT, 8
promptly He gives twice who gives p. — PROMPTNESS, 2
pronounce foreigners...spell better than they p.
— PRONUNCIATION, 2; SPELLING, 2
p. foreign names as he chooses — CHURCHILL, 15; PRONUNCIATION, 1
spell it Vinci and p. it Vinchy — PRONUNCIATION, 2; SPELLING, 2
pronouncements Science should leave off making p. — SCIENCE, 14
propaganda P....consists in nearly deceiving your friends
— PROPAGANDA, 1
propagated If human beings could be p....aristocracy would
be...sound — ARISTOCRACY, 7
propagation Women exist...solely for the p. of the species
— WOMAN'S ROLE, 4
proper The p. study of Mankind is Man — SELF-KNOWLEDGE, 3
property poor have no right to the p. of the rich
— POVERTY AND WEALTH, 4; RUSKIN, 10
P. has its duties — CAPITALISM, 1

P. is theft — CAPITALISM, 9
The future is the only kind of p. — SLAVERY, 1
prophecies bring about the verification of his own p.
— PROPHECY, 6; TROLLOPE, 6
prophet A historian is a p. in reverse — HISTORIANS, 5
a p. is not without honour — HONOUR, 1
there arose not a p....like unto Moses — PROPHECY, 1
proportion strangeness in the p. — BEAUTY, 2
Proportional Representation P....fundamentally counter-
democratic — POLITICS, 29
prose I have been talking p. for over forty years — PROSE, 2
no one hears his own remarks as p. — PROSE, 1
P....can bear a great deal of poetry — POETRY AND PROSE, 1
Poetry is opposed to science,...p. to metre — POETRY AND PROSE, 4
Poetry is to p. — POETRY AND PROSE, 5
poetry sinks and swoons under...p. — POETRY AND PROSE, 3
p. = words in their best order — COLERIDGE, 15; POETRY AND PROSE, 2
to write good p. is an affair of good manners — POETRY AND PROSE, 4
prosper Treason doth never p. — TREASON, 3
prospentee A man to have ben in p. — CHAUCER, 6
him that stood in greet p. — MISFORTUNE, 2
prosperity P. doth best discover vice — MISFORTUNE, 1
prostitute I don't think a p. is more moral — WOMEN, 34
p., but I'm not promiscuous — PROMISCUITY, 4
prostitution P. is a blight on the human race — PROMISCUITY, 5
protest lady doth p. too much — EXCESS, 6; SHAKESPEARE, 38
Protestant Gunpowder, Printing, and the P. Religion
— CARLYLE, 7; CIVILIZATION, 3
I am the P. whore — RELIGION, 17
Protestantism The chief contribution of P. to human thought
— PROTESTANTISM, 1
Protestants 'God knows how you P....have any sense of direction
— CATHOLICISM, 6
protozoon Organic life...has developed...from the p. to the philosopher — RUSSELL, 8
proud Death be not p. — DEATH, 20; DONNE, 8
He who does not need to lie is p. — LYING, 7; NIETZSCHE, 7
no guarantee...you will not be p. of the feat — HUMILITY, 3
p. me no prouds — GRATITUDE, 2
too p. to fight — WAR, 69
Yes; I am p. — POPE, 4
proudest moment of greatest humiliation...when the spirit is p.
— PRIDE, 3
Proust Reading P. is like bathing in...dirty water — PROUST, 1
prove p. anything by figures — CARLYLE, 4
proved p. upon our pulses — PHILOSOPHY, 4
What is now p. was...imagined — PROOF, 1
proverb no p. to you till your life has illustrated it — EXPERIENCE, 8
p. is one man's wit and all men's wisdom — SAYINGS, 3
proverbs p. provide them with wisdom — STUPIDITY, 4
Providence A kind of P. will...end...the acts of God — DISASTER, 1
that P. dictates with the assurance of a sleepwalker
— DESTINY, 5; HITLER, 10
This is the temple of P. — LUCK, 1
province all knowledge to be my p. — KNOWLEDGE, 2
provincialism rather be taken in adultery than...p. — HUXLEY, 4
provoke p. not your children — FAMILY, 3
provoked an opportunity of being p. — PROVOCATION, 1
provokes No one p. me with impunity — RETRIBUTION, 1
prude twenty is no age to be a p. — PRUDERY, 3
prudence freedom of speech...and the p. never to practise
— FREEDOM, 26; TWAIN, 6
psychiatrist And a p. is the man who collects the rent — PSYCHIATRY, 6
Anybody who goes to see a p. — PSYCHIATRY, 2
A p. is a man who goes to the Folies-Bergère — PSYCHIATRY, 4
the century of the p.'s couch — PSYCHIATRY, 3
psychiatrists P. classify a person as neurotic — PSYCHIATRY, 5; SZASZ, 5
psychic p. development of the individual — PSYCHIATRY, 1
psychological historian fits a man for p. analysis — PSYCHOLOGY, 2
There is no such thing as p. — CHARACTER, 6; SARTRE, 6
psychotic A p. is the man who lives in it — PSYCHIATRY, 6
Psychiatrists classify a person as...p. — PSYCHIATRY, 5; SZASZ, 5
puberty We are all American at p. — NATIONALITY, 6
public a more mean, stupid...ungrateful animal than the p.
— HAZLITT, 9; PUBLIC, 9
Anyone who has been to...p. school will...feel...at home in prison
— WAUGH, 12
a right to share your privacy in a p. place — PRIVACY, 3
more...ungrateful animal than the p. — HAZLITT, 9
strike against p. safety — STRIKES, 2
The p. buys its opinions as it buys its meat — PUBLIC, 5

The p. doesn't give a damn — MUSIC, 5
The P. is an old woman — PUBLIC, 6
three things...the p. will always clamour for — NOVELTY, 1
transform this society without a major extension of p. ownership — SOCIALISM, 5
twenty years of marriage make her...like a p. building — WILDE, 30
publicity no such thing as bad p. — OBITUARIES, 1
publicly explained p. the writings of Plato — HYPATIA, 1
public school enjoy a p. — CONNOLLY, 2
the p. system all over — EDUCATION, 32
publish P. and be damned — PUBLISHING, 5; WELLINGTON, 15
p. and be sued — PUBLISHING, 4
published not so much p. as carried screaming — NEWSPAPERS, 5
you may destroy whatever you haven't p. — PUBLISHING, 3
publisher certain author was executed for murdering his p. — WRITERS, 2
publishers those with irrational fear of life become p. — CONNOLLY, 4; PUBLISHING, 2
pulse two people with one p. — LOVE, 41
pulses proved upon our p. — PHILOSOPHY, 4
pun A man who could make so vile a p. — PUNS, 3
punctuality P. is the politeness of kings — PROMPTNESS, 1
P. is the virtue of the bored — PROMPTNESS, 3; WAUGH, 10
punished Am I not p. enough in not being born an Englishman — NATIONALITY, 5
Men are rewarded and p. not for what they do — SZASZ, 1
punishing p. anyone who comes between them — MARRIAGE, 55
punishment Corporal p. is...humiliating for him who gives it — PUNISHMENT, 8
let the p. fit the crime — PUNISHMENT, 6
P. is not for revenge — PUNISHMENT, 5
Virtue is its own p. — RIGHTEOUSNESS, 2
punishments In nature there are neither rewards nor p. — NATURE, 8
pupils Time is a great teacher, but...kills all its p. — TIME, 3
purchasers a pattern to encourage p. — SWIFT, 5
pure All those who are not racially p. — HITLER, 5
p. as the driven slush — PURITY, 1
P. mathematics consists entirely of assertions — RUSSELL, 7
purgatory the p. of men — ENGLAND, 8
puritan A p.'s a person who pours righteous indignation — CHESTERTON, 24; PURITANISM, 1
Puritanism P. – The haunting fear that someone...may be happy — PURITANISM, 2
purity I have laboured to refine our language to grammatical p. — LANGUAGE, 9
purple-stained And p. mouth — ALCOHOL, 20; KEATS, 7
purpose p. of God and the doom assigned — DESTINY, 12
the creature hath a p. and its eyes are bright with it — PURPOSE, 3
purse Put money in thy p. — MONEY, 18
put I p. away childish things — CHARITY, 4
pyramids Books are made...like p. — BOOKS, 11
quack uses his words as a q. uses his remedies — VERBOSITY, 3
quad I am always about in the Q. — EXISTENCE, 1
no one about in the Q. — EXISTENCE, 4
Quakers I was beaten up by Q. — ALLEN, 4
qualifications actor...q., including no money — ACTORS, 6
qualities Almost every man...q. which he does not possess — JOHNSON, 7
q....necessary for success upon the stage — ACTING, 7
quantity a prodigious q. of mind — INDECISION, 3; TWAIN, 8
quarrel a q. in the streets is...to be hated — ARGUMENTS, 3
It takes...one to make a q. — ARGUMENTS, 2
Out of the q....we make rhetoric — POETRY, 26; YEATS, 4
q....energies displayed in it are fine — ARGUMENTS, 3
The justice of my q. — JUSTICE, 8
quarrels q. which vivify its barrenness — LOVE, 30
Q. would not last — ARGUMENTS, 5; ROCHEFOUCAULD, 2
queen 'Fella belong Mrs Q.' — LANGUAGE, 15
isn't a bad bit of goods, the Q. — COMPLIMENTS, 1
I would not be a q. /For all the world — SHAKESPEARE, 50
Move Q. Anne? Most certainly not — MEMORIALS, 8
sorrier for my good knights' loss than for...my fair q. — LOSS, 3
The Q. of Hearts — FOOD, 4
queens for q. I might have enough — LOSS, 3
Queen Victoria If this is the way Q. treats her prisoners — WILDE, 39
queer girls are so q. — WOMEN, 2
the q. old Dean — SPOONERISMS, 2
question Answer to the Great Q. — PURPOSE, 1
A timid q. will...receive a confident answer — SHYNESS, 1
man who sees both sides of a q. — OBJECTIVITY, 3; WILDE, 6

Nature has never put the fatal q. as to the meaning of their lives — PURPOSE, 2
q....which I have not been able to answer — WOMEN, 19
That is the Irish Q. — IRELAND, 3
that is the q. — SHAKESPEARE, 36; SUICIDE, 7
To be, or not to be: that is the q. — LANGUAGE, 5
questioning Q. is not the mode of conversation — CONVERSATION, 1
questions make two q. grow where only one — RESEARCH, 3
queue An Englishman...forms an orderly q. of one — ENGLISH, 11
quiet Anythin' for a q. life — DICKENS, 16
quietness unravish'd bride of q. — SILENCE, 3
quince dined on mince, and slices of q. — FOOD, 12
quintessence this q. of dust — MANKIND, 13; SHAKESPEARE, 35
quotable It's better to be q. than...honest — QUOTATIONS, 7
quotation Every q. contributes something — JOHNSON, 2; QUOTATIONS, 6
the great spring of happy q. — QUOTATIONS, 4
To say that anything was a q. — SAKI, 5
quotations good thing...to read books of q. — CHURCHILL, 9; QUOTATIONS, 1
It needs no dictionary of q. — BEERBOHM, 8
quote can q. Shakespeare in an economic crisis — SHAKESPEARE, 10
quotes q....give us a nodding acquaintance with the originator — QUOTATIONS, 8
rabbit The r. has a charming face — RABBITS, 1
rabbits a tale of four little r. — RABBITS, 2
except to shoot r. and hit his father on the jaw — NASTINESS, 3
race Slow and steady wins the r. — HASTE, 3
races human species...composed of two distinct r. — BORROWING, 2; LAMB, 4
the r. of Europe are melting — AMERICA, 23
racially not r. pure are mere chaff — RACISM, 7
those who are not r. pure — HITLER, 5
rack Leave not a r. behind — MORTALITY, 10
radical The r. invents the views....the conservative adopts them — CONSERVATISM, 5; TWAIN, 9
radio I had the r. on — NAKEDNESS, 1
Simply a r. personality — CHURCHILL, 4
radioactive The Irish Sea is naturally r. — ECOLOGY, 5
rage all Heaven in a r. — IMPRISONMENT, 1
R., r., against the dying of the light — THOMAS, 4
rags no scandal like r. — POVERTY, 3
only men in r..../Mistake themselves for carpet bags — ETIQUETTE, 2
railing R. at life, and yet afraid of death — OLD AGE, 6
raiment they parted his r., and cast lots — FORGIVENESS, 1
rain droppeth as the gentle r. — MERCY, 2; SHAKESPEARE, 82
falls not hail, or r., or any snow — AFTERLIFE, 9
singing in the r. — WEATHER, 2
raineth it r. on the just — JUSTICE, 3
rainy when it is not r. — BYRON, 4
raise My God shall r. me up — FAITH, 8
Now he will r. me to be a martyr — MARTYRDOM, 1
rake lene...as is a r. — HORSES, 2
Ralph R. wept for the end of innocence — INNOCENCE, 5
Ramadan month of R. shall ye fast — RELIGION, 21
rapists All men are r. — MEN, 3
rapping r. at my chamber door — SUPERNATURAL, 8
rapture a r. on the lonely shore — NATURE, 2
The first fine careless r. — BROWNING, 9
rare as r. things will, it vanished — BROWNING, 11
rat with the face of a harassed r. — THURBER, 2
ratchet politics of the pendulum, but of the r. — POLITICS, 46
rationalized Happiness...should never be r. — HAPPINESS, 2
rats R.! /They fought the dogs — BROWNING, 12
ravages What do the r. of time not injure — HORACE, 14
ravished He...r. this fair creature — SEX, 13
raw the working-class which, r. and half-developed — ARNOLD, 5
razor Satire should, like a polished r. keen — SATIRE, 2
razors R. pain you — PARKER, 1; SUICIDE, 4
reach a man's r. should exceed his grasp — AMBITION, 2; BROWNING, 4
read A man ought to r. just as inclination leads him — READING, 5
books....criticized and r. by people who don't understand them — BOOKS, 15
everybody wants to have r. — LITERATURE, 11; TWAIN, 12
His books were r. — BELLOC, 6; PUNS, 1
I've just r. that I am dead — KIPLING, 8; OBITUARIES, 2
King George will be able to r. that — SIGNATURES, 1
Men of power have not time to r. — POWER, 5
only news until he's r. it — JOURNALISM, 16
R., mark, learn and inwardly digest — LEARNING, 3
sooner r. a time-table...than nothing — NOVELS, 3
When I want to r. a novel — DISRAELI, 20

I'd rather be r. than president — RIGHT, 2
Liberty is the r. to do everything — FREEDOM, 19
Minorities...are almost always in the r. — MINORITY, 2; SMITH, 5
no r. to strike against public safety — STRIKES, 2
No, this r. hand shall work it all off — SCOTT, 9
One of the pleasures of middle age is to *find out* that one WAS r. — AGE, 32; POUND, 2
'orthodoxy'...no longer means being r. — ORTHODOXY, 2
R. is more precious — RIGHT, 3
r. mindfulness, r. contemplation — RELIGION, 4
r. of all...duty of some — SEPARATION, 3
something is possible, he is...r. — SCIENCE, 3
The customer is always r. — BUSINESS, 10
The *divine* r. of husbands — WOLLSTONECRAFT, 2
The man who gets angry...in the r. way...is commended — ANGER, 1
The minority is always r. — MAJORITY, 1; MINORITY, 1
The r. divine of kings to govern wrong — POPE, 3
the r. to be consulted,...to encourage,...to warn — MONARCHY, 2
Those who believe that they are exclusively in the r. — HUXLEY, 16; SELF-CONFIDENCE, 1
Ulster will be r. — IRELAND, 1
Women would rather be r. than reasonable — WOMEN, 30
righteous leave r. ways behind — RIGHTEOUSNESS, 3
righteousness The eternal *not ourselves* that makes for r. — RIGHTEOUSNESS, 1
righter much r. than one knew at say 17 or 23 — AGE, 32; POUND, 2
rights human beings are born free...dignity and r. — HUMAN RIGHTS, 1
Men their r. and nothing more — ANTHONY, 4
The Sovereign has, under a constitutional monarchy...three r. — MONARCHY, 2
women their r. and nothing less — ANTHONY, 4
ring R. down the curtain — LAST WORDS, 24
ripeness R. is all — ENDURANCE, 8
ripp'd mother's womb untimely r. — BIRTH, 6
rise Early to r. and early to bed — BED, 5; THURBER, 5
nobody who does not r. early — JOHNSON, 40
Thanks to words, we have been able to r. above the brutes — HUXLEY, 3; WORDS, 6
Ritz like the R. hotel — JUSTICE, 9
river build your House of Parliament upon the r. — HOUSES OF PARLIAMENT, 11
Fame is like a r. — FAME, 2
Ol' man r. — RIVERS, 2
On either side the r. lie — TENNYSON, 17
On the breast of the r. of Time — ARNOLD, 8
the r. of knowledge has too often turned back on itself — SCIENCE, 14
road All I seek...the r. below me — STEVENSON, 5; TRAVEL, 15
a r....that does not go through the intellect — CHESTERTON, 3; EMOTION, 1
He watched the ads /And not the r. — NASH, 4
On the r. to Mandalay — PLACES, 9
people who stay in the middle of the r. — COMPROMISE, 1
tell us of the R. — DEATH, 25
There is a r. from the eye to the heart — CHESTERTON, 3; EMOTION, 1
the rolling English r. — CHESTERTON, 17
roads How many r. must a man walk down — DYLAN, 1; EXPERIENCE, 5
Two r. diverged — CHOICE, 2
roam Mid pleasures and palaces though we may r. — HOME, 3
roamin' R. in the gloamin' — SCOTLAND, 4
roar luck to give the r. — CHURCHILL, 2
roast the learned r. an egg — FOOD, 20
robbed We was r. — INJUSTICE, 5
when you've r. a man of everything — POWER, 11
Robbins President R. was so well adjusted to his environment — ADAPTABILITY, 3
robes R. and furr'd gowns hide all — APPEARANCES, 10
robin A r. redbreast in a cage — IMPRISONMENT, 1
rock R. and roll or Christianity — POPULARITY, 4
R. Around the Clock — POP MUSIC, 6
R. journalism is people who can't write — POP MUSIC, 9
R. of ages, cleft for me — RELIGION, 30
upon this r. I will build my church — CHURCH, 1
rock'n'roll R. is part of a pest — POP MUSIC, 1
rocks The hand that r. the cradle — INFLUENCE, 4
rod he that spareth his r. hateth his son — CHILDREN, 6
rule them with a r. of iron — LEADERSHIP, 2
spare the r. — BUTLER, 3; INDULGENCE, 1; PUNISHMENT, 4
rode and r. madly off in all directions — NONSENSE, 6
Roland *Childe R. to the Dark Tower came* — SUMMONS, 2
roll our soul /Had *felt* him like the thunder's r. — BYRON, 1
rolled bottoms of my trousers r. — OLD AGE, 8

rolling Like a r. stone — DYLAN, 2; TRAVEL, 4
The r. English drunkard — CHESTERTON, 17
Roma R. *locuta est* — AUTHORITARIANISM, 1
Roman noblest R. of them all — NOBILITY, 2
the Holy R. Empire was neither holy, nor R., nor an empire — NATIONS, 3; VOLTAIRE, 12
The Papacy is not other than the Ghost of the deceased R. Empire — CATHOLICISM, 2
romance The r. of *Tom Jones* — GIBBON, 4
Twenty years of r. makes a woman look like a ruin — WILDE, 30
Romans Friends, R., countrymen, lend me your ears — EVIL, 11; SHAKESPEARE, 58
The R. and Greeks found everything human — LAWRENCE, 3
which came first, the Greeks or the R. — DISRAELI, 19
Romanticism R. is...presenting people with the literary works...affording...the greatest...pleasure — LITERATURE, 10
Rome I lov'd R. more — PATRIOTISM, 15; SHAKESPEARE, 57
R. has spoken; the case is concluded — AUTHORITARIANISM, 1
R. shall perish — COWPER, 2
The farther you go from the church of R. — PROTESTANTISM, 2
When in R. — CONFORMITY, 1
when R. falls – the World — BYRON, 5
Romeo R.! wherefore art thou R. — SHAKESPEARE, 101
room before my little r. — FLOWERS, 2
Infinite riches in a little r. — WEALTH, 10
no r. for them in the inn — CHRISTMAS, 5
The perpetual struggle for r. and food — SURVIVAL, 1
rooms being old is having lighted r. — OLD AGE, 12
roost Curses...always come home to r. — CURSES, 1
root love of money is the r. of all evil — MONEY, 2
rose a r. /By any other name — NAMES, 3; SHAKESPEARE, 102
killing as the canker to the r. — CORRUPTION, 3
One perfect r. — PARKER, 3
R....where some buried Caesar bled — FLOWERS, 3
the last r. of summer — FLOWERS, 6
rosebuds Gather ye r. while ye may — PRESENT, 2
roses a wreath of r. — FLOWERS, 1
days of wine and r. — TRANSIENCE, 7
I will make thee beds of r. — FLOWERS, 4
I would like my r. to see you — COMPLIMENTS, 4; SHERIDAN, 11
Nor does a...gardener scent his r. — POETS, 3
not a bed of r. — MARRIAGE, 56
R. are flowering in Picardy — COMPLIMENTS, 5
Treaties are like r. and young girls — DIPLOMACY, 1
rotten r. in the state of Denmark — CORRUPTION, 6
rotting Damn you, England. You're r. — ENGLAND, 17
rough-hew R. them how we will — DESTINY, 10; SHAKESPEARE, 41
roundabouts What's lost upon the r. — LOSS, 2
royal A R. Commission is a broody hen — BUREAUCRACY, 4
Once in r. David's city — CHRISTMAS, 2
rub there's the r. — SHAKESPEARE, 38; SUICIDE, 7
try to r. up against money — MONEY, 17
rubies her price is far above r. — WOMEN, 9
the price of wisdom is above r. — WISDOM, 3
Rugby R. Union which is a distillation — SPORT AND GAMES, 9
ruin Twenty years of romance makes a woman look like a r. — WILDE, 30
rule a good r. in life never to apologize — WODEHOUSE, 5
English should give Ireland home r. — IRELAND, 8
Irish Home R. is conceded — IRELAND, 9
R. all England under a hog — INSULTS, 5
r. them with a rod of iron — LEADERSHIP, 2
rulers R. of the Queen's Navee — GILBERT, 2; OFFICERS, 5
rules R. and models destroy genius and art — RULES, 2
the hand that r. the world — INFLUENCE, 4
there are no golden r. — RULES, 3; SHAW, 17
two golden r. for an orchestra — MUSIC, 5
ruleth the cry of him that r. among fools — WISDOM, 2
ruling The state is an instrument...of the r. class — STATE, 4
rum r., sodomy, and the lash — CHURCHILL, 24; NAVY, 1
Yo-ho-ho, and a bottle of r. — ALCOHOL, 32
rumble R. thy bellyful — WEATHER, 8
rumour Where r. of oppression and deceit — SOLITUDE, 3
runcible ate with a r. spoon — FOOD, 12
He weareth a r. hat — NONSENSE, 9
runners like r. hand on the torch of life — MORTALITY, 8
running drive out nature with a pitchfork...she'll be constantly r. back — HUMAN NATURE, 6
running back drive out nature with a pitchfork...she'll be constantly r. — HORACE, 7
rush R. *hour*: that hour when — TRAVEL, 12

seventh God...rested on the s. day	SUNDAY, 1
seventy Being over s. is like being engaged in a war	OLD AGE, 24
sever a tie that only death can s.	MARRIAGE, 40
sewage piped growing volumes of s. into the sea	ENVIRONMENT, 1
sex As we make s. less secretive, we may rob it of its power	SEX, 34; SZASZ, 2
Christian view of s.	SEX, 27
Continental people have s. life	ENGLISH, 12
farmyard world of s.	ANIMALISM, 1
If s. is such a natural phenomenon	SEX, 22
if there was a third s.	MEN, 8
in the schoolroom...does the difference of s....need to be forgotten	ANTHONY, 3
In the s.-war thoughtlessness is the weapon of the male	CONNOLLY, 7, SEXES, 3
Is s. dirty	ALLEN, 1; SEX, 1
it's s. with someone you love	ALLEN, 3; SEX, 3
Literature is mostly about having s.	LITERATURE, 7
meant us to have group s.	SEX, 6
Money, it turned out, was exactly like s.	MONEY, 3; SEX, 5
no more weakness than is natural to her s.	WOMEN, 42
normal man's s. needs are stronger	SEX, 32
No s. without responsibility	SEX, 20
Pornography is the attempt to insult	LAWRENCE, 13; PORNOGRAPHY, 6
professed tyrant to their s.	MISOGYNY, 4
S. had to be brought out of the Victorian closet	SEX, 7
s. has been a very private, secretive activity	SEX, 34; SZASZ, 2
S. is something I really don't understand	SEX, 28
S. Is the biggest nothing	SEX, 35
s....must itself be subject...to evolution	SEXES, 2
the condition of our s. is so deplorable that it is our duty...to break the law	PANKHURST, 6
the difference of s., if there is any	ANTHONY, 3
the s. novel is now normal	NOVELS, 6
we English have s. on the brain	SEX, 25
sexes husbands and wives...belong to different s.	SEXES, 6
more difference within the s. than between them	SEXES, 4
the...rift between the s. is...widened by...teaching...to the girls	STEVENSON, 6
sexual avowed purpose is to excite s. desire	PORNOGRAPHY, 7
Industrial relations are like s. relations	INDUSTRIAL RELATIONS, 2
Lesbianism Is not a matter of s. preference	HOMOSEXUALITY, 6
Masturbation: the primary s. activity	SZASZ, 6
shade a green thought in a green s.	OBLIVION, 2
inviolable s.	HOPE, 1
Nothing grows well in the s.	GREATNESS, 3
shadow he caves...in which his s. will be shown	NIETZSCHE, 4
I am no s....I am a wife	PLATH, 3
lose the substance by grasping at the s.	GREED, 1
Your s. at morning	ELIOT, 9
Shakespeare myriad-minded S.	SHAKESPEARE, 3
S. is...really very good	SHAKESPEARE, 6
S. never had six lines together without a fault	SHAKESPEARE, 4
S. – the nearest thing	SHAKESPEARE, 1
the making up of a S. or a Milton	COLERIDGE, 17; WRITERS, 4
tried lately to read S.	SHAKESPEARE, 4
We can say of S.	SHAKESPEARE, 5
shame expense of spirit in a waste of s.	LUST, 4
Neither s. nor physical pain have any...effect	PUNISHMENT, 8
Put off your s. with your clothes	MODESTY, 5
shamefaced Perjury...is truth that is s.	TRUTH, 9
share s. in the good fortunes of the mighty	INJUSTICE, 1
sharp those who have stout hearts and s. swords	RUTHLESSNESS, 2
sharper women's bodies are softer than men's, so their understanding is s.	CHRISTINE DE PISAN, 2
Shaw S.'s works make me	SHAW, 1
shears marriage...resembles a pair of s.	MARRIAGE, 55
shedding without s. of blood is no remission	EXECUTION, 1
sheep good shepherd giveth his life for the s.	CHRISTIANITY, 8
make a man by standing as s.	BEERBOHM, 11; PUBLIC, 3
not armies...but flocks of s.	CERVANTES, 4
savaged by a dead s.	INSULTS, 8
s.'s clothing	DECEPTION, 1
The mountain s. are sweeter	GREED, 3
the wolf in the s.'s clothing	APPEARANCES, 1
useless for the s. to pass resolutions in favour of vegetarianism	ARGUMENTS, 2
shelf The dust and silence of the upper s.	NEGLECT, 2
Shelley Poor S....a kind of ghastly object	SHELLEY, 2
shells With silver bells and cockle s.	GARDENS, 1
shelter Our s. from the stormy blast	RELIGION, 33

shepherd I am the good s.	CHRISTIANITY, 8
This is the weather the s. shuns	WEATHER, 4
shepherds Governments needs to have both s. and butchers	GOVERNMENT, 14; VOLTAIRE, 17
s. abiding in the field	CHRISTMAS, 6
shimmy Put thy s. on, Lady Chatterley	LAWRENCE, 9
shine s. on, s. on, harvest moon	MOON, 5
shins long dresses,...cover a multitude of s.	CLOTHES, 10; WEST, 8
ship A whale s. was my Yale College	EDUCATION, 18
The s. follows Soviet custom	CLASS, 19
ships I spied three s. come sailing by	CHRISTMAS, 3
little s. of England brought the Army home	BOATS, 6; WORLD WAR II, 15
S. that pass in the night	TRANSIENCE, 11
something wrong with our bloody s.	BOATS, 1
stately s. go on	NOSTALGIA, 13; TENNYSON, 3
the face that launch'd a thousand s.	BEAUTY, 14
shit People will swim through s.	GREED, 5
the sun shining ten days a year and s. in the streets	ENGLAND, 10
when you s.? Singing, it's the same thing	SINGING, 1
shocked how to be amused rather than s.	AGE, 10
shocks /That flesh is heir to	SHAKESPEARE, 36; SUICIDE, 7
shoemaker I take my shoes from the s.	RELIGION, 16
shoes before you let the sun in, mind it wipes its s.	CLEANNESS, 2; THOMAS, 9
I take my s. from the shoemaker	RELIGION, 16
s. and ships and sealing wax	CARROLL, 10; NONSENSE, 5
shoot do not s. the pianist	WILDE, 21
except to s. rabbits and hit his father on the jaw	NASTINESS, 3
It is not the business of generals to s. one another	OFFICERS, 10; WELLINGTON, 9
shooting A bit of s. takes your mind off	VIOLENCE, 1
war minus the s.	ORWELL, 14; SPORT AND GAMES, 7
shop A man must keep a little back s.	SOLITUDE, 9
shopkeepers England is a nation of s.	ENGLISH, 13
shore adieu! my native s.	DEPARTURE, 4
waves make towards the pebbled s.	SHAKESPEARE, 108; TIME, 15
Shoreditch When I grow rich, /Say the bells of S.	LONDON, 1
short Good things, when s., are twice as good	BREVITY, 1
Is not life...too s....to bore ourselves	BOREDOM, 5
it will take a long while to make it s.	WRITING, 19
make the beat keep time with s. steps	FUNERALS, 1
s. and simple annals of the poor	POVERTY, 6
We have s. time to stay, as you	TRANSIENCE, 9
shortage a s. of coal and fish...at the same time	INCOMPETENCE, 1
shorter s. by a head	ELIZABETH I, 6; ROYALTY, 7
shortest the s. works are always the best	BREVITY, 2
shot had them all s.	LAST WORDS, 19
shots God is on the side not of the heavy battalions, but of the best s.	VOLTAIRE, 18
God is on the side...of the best s.	POWER POLITICS, 6
They really are bad s.	ASSASSINATION, 1
should nae better than he s. be	BURNS, 5
shoulders it is by standing on the s. of giants	PROGRESS, 5
shout S. with the largest	DICKENS, 14
show I have that within which passes s.	MOURNING, 8; SHAKESPEARE, 27
showers Sweet April s.	MONTHS, 6
shows All my s. are great	GOLDWYNISMS, 27
shreds A thing of s. and patches	SINGERS, 2
shrine Melancholy has her...s.	MELANCHOLY, 4
shrink all the boards did s.	COLERIDGE, 12; WATER, 1
shuffled s. off this mortal coil	SHAKESPEARE, 36; SUICIDE, 7
the human pack is s. and cut	EDUCATION, 15
shyness S. is common	SHYNESS, 4
S. is just egotism out of its depth	SHYNESS, 2
sick being s. with other people singing	PARTIES, 4
if you don't object if I'm s.	SMOKING, 1
The prayer that...heals the s.	FAITH, 5
The s. man is a parasite of society	PATIENTS, 2
sickness in s. and in health	MARRIAGE, 15
Love is a s.	LOVE, 22
s. enlarges the dimensions of a man's self	ILLNESS, 7
s. need not be a part of life	HEALTH AND HEALTHY LIVING, 3
side A door is what a dog is...on the wrong s. of	NASH, 2
sides Do not...write on both s. of the paper	EXAMINATIONS, 4
said on both s.	ADDISON, 5
Sighs over the Bridge of S. into eternity	DEATH, 38
sight s. to make an old man young	TENNYSON, 4
we walk by faith, not by s.	FAITH, 3
Who ever loved, that loved not at first s.	FIRST IMPRESSIONS, 4
sightless clapped the glass to his s. eye	BLINDNESS, 4

sights And see all s. from pole to pole ARNOLD, 17; SOUL, 2
few more impressive s. in the world SCOTS, 2
signifying S. nothing LIFE, 19; SHAKESPEARE, 76
silence Come to me in the s. of the night NOSTALGIA, 10
foster-child of s. and slow time SILENCE, 3
In England there is only s. or scandal ENGLAND, 14
Make him a bishop, and you will s. him CHESTERFIELD, 13
occasional flashes of s. SMITH, 4
S. is as full of potential wisdom SILENCE, 2
S. is the best tactic SILENCE, 4
S. is the perfectest herald of joy SILENCE, 5
S. is the…perfect expression of scorn SILENCE, 6
Sorrow and s. are strong ENDURANCE, 4
The cruellest lies are…told in s. SILENCE, 7; STEVENSON, 9
The dust and s. of the upper shelf NEGLECT, 2
With s. and tears BYRON, 16; SEPARATION, 1
silent burst /Into that s. sea EXPLORATION, 1
the great s. majority MAJORITY, 3
thereon one must remain s. SILENCE, 3
Silenus Dylan Thomas…a youthful S. THOMAS, 1
silk s., too often hides eczema STYLE, 2
silly A s. remark can be made in Latin CERVANTES, 2; LANGUAGE, 4
it's lovely to be s. at the right moment FOOLISHNESS, 5; HORACE, 16
silver S. threads among the gold OLD AGE, 18
silvery the s. adamant walls of life's exclusive city DEATH, 39; LAWRENCE, 7
Silvia Who is S.? What is she SHAKESPEARE, 121
simple A s. race POETS, 7
short and s. annals of the poor POVERTY, 6
simplicity O holy s. SIMPLICITY, 3
simplify ability to s. means SIMPLICITY, 2
S., simplify SIMPLICITY, 5
simplifying s. something by destroying nearly everything CHESTERTON, 2
sin All s. tends to be addictive AUDEN, 4; SIN, 2
a more dreadful record of s. than…countryside DOYLE, 4; SIN, 8
A private s. is not so prejudicial CERVANTES, 10; SIN, 7
beauty is only s. deep BEAUTY, 18; SAKI, 15
he that is without s.…let him first cast a stone SIN, 3
if we say that we have no s., we deceive SIN, 4
no s. but to be rich HYPOCRISY, 8
no s. except stupidity STUPIDITY, 8
people who can s. with a grin SIN, 11
S. brought death DEATH, 22; SIN, 9
They are written as if s. were to be taken out…by…sleep SERMONS, 1
which taketh away the s. of the world CHRISTIANITY, 5
your s. will find you out SIN, 5
sincere Some of the worst men in the world are s. SINCERITY, 2
sincerest imitation…s. of flattery IMITATION, 1
sincerity A little s. is a dangerous thing SINCERITY, 3; WILDE, 7
style, not s., is the vital thing STYLE, 4
sinews Anger is one of the s. of the soul ANGER, 4
sing Did certain persons die before they s. COLERIDGE, 4; SINGERS, 1
The Welsh…just s. WELSH, 3
singed s. the Spanish king's beard WAR, 19
singing s. in the rain WEATHER, 2
when you shit? S., it's the same thing SINGING, 1
single a s. man in possession of a good fortune must be in want of a wife AUSTEN, 10
sink The s. is the great symbol of the bloodiness of family life FAMILY, 15
sinn'd More s. against than sinning INJUSTICE, 7; SHAKESPEARE, 63
sinners It's your combination s.…who dishonour the vices VICE, 5
sinning nothing so artificial as s. nowadays LAWRENCE, 11; SIN, 10
sins atone for the s. of your fathers HORACE, 13; INJUSTICE, 4
gravest s. it was possible for a gentlewoman to commit WAUGH, 20
His s. were scarlet BELLOC, 6; PUNS, 1
One of the unpardonable s.,…, is…to go about unlabelled CLASSIFICATION, 1
she must not reheat his s. for breakfast FORGIVENESS, 4
to read a novel before luncheon was one of the gravest s. WAUGH, 20
Sirens Blest pair of S. POETRY, 16
sister I kissed her little s. UNFAITHFULNESS, 1
no friend like a s. FAMILY, 18
sisters little s. to all the world WOMEN, 16
sit say what you have to say, and then s. down WELLINGTON, 16
So I did s. and eat LOVE, 32
sitting s. down round you HOUSES OF PARLIAMENT, 11
six Candidates should not attempt more than s. BELLOC, 12
sixty at the rate of s. minutes an hour TIME, 9

s. horses wedged in a /chimney JOURNALISM, 13
sixty-five I have been drinking it for s. years and I am not dead yet VOLTAIRE, 27
sixty-three Sexual intercourse began /In nineteen s. SEX, 18
skating s. over thin ice HASTE, 2
skies looks commercing with the s. SOUL, 6
skill S. without imagination is craftsmanship ART, 17
skins beauty of their s. SEXES, 13; TENNYSON, 25
skirt a woman…ought to lay aside…modesty with her s. SEX, 23
skittles Life isn't all beer and s. LIFE, 13
sky Which prisoners call the s. IMPRISONMENT, 5
Skye Over the sea to S. ROYALTY, 2
slack a man becomes s. and selfish STEVENSON, 13
slam no door to s. BEAUTY, 21
slamming doors little girls…s. BELLOC, 4
slander it is always said of s. that something always sticks PRAISE, 1
slang All s. is metaphor CHESTERTON, 4
slave Be not the s. of Words WORDS, 3
came to America in s. ships EQUALITY, 11
commerce between master and s. is…exercise of…boisterous passions SLAVERY, 3
man…is Reason's s. CONNOLLY, 10; PASSION, 1
s. for livelihood ENVY, 1
slaves love, an…intercourse between tyrants and s. GOLDSMITH, 10; LOVE AND FRIENDSHIP, 1
Practical men,…are usually the s. of some defunct economist INFLUENCE, 2
S. cannot breathe in England COWPER, 13
that the masters willingly concede to s. SLAVERY, 1
slaying the s. of a beautiful hypothesis by an ugly fact SCIENCE, 12
slays moves, and mates, and s. DESTINY, 3
sleave ravell'd s. of care SLEEP, 7
sleek you will come and find me fat and s. PRESENT, 5
sleep amount of s. required SLEEP, 6
A professor is one who talks in someone else's s. ACADEMICS, 1; AUDEN, 15
Better s. with a sober cannibal than a drunken Christian DRUNKENNESS, 9
Every time you s. with a boy AIDS, 4; ILLNESS, 3
Now I lay me down to s. SLEEP, 1
Our birth is but a s. METAPHYSICS, 4
our little life /Is rounded with a s. MORTALITY, 10
s. begins for weary /mortals SLEEP, 9; VIRGIL, 6
S.…knows not Death SLEEP, 8; TENNYSON, 12
S. that knits up the ravell'd sleave SLEEP, 7
They are written as if sin were to be taken out…by…s. SERMONS, 1
To s., perchance to dream SHAKESPEARE, 36; SUICIDE, 7
we must s. REST, 1
youth would s. out the rest SHAKESPEARE, 123; YOUTH, 9
sleeping fuss about s. together…sooner go to my dentist SEX, 36; WAUGH, 10
S. as quiet as death THOMAS, 10
sleeps eats, s. and watches the television GREER, 2
She s. alone at last EPITAPHS, 1
sleepwalker that Providence dictates with the assurance of a s. DESTINY, 5; HITLER, 10
slick I have three phobias which…would make my life as s. as a sonnet OBSESSIONS, 1
slings s. and arrows of outrageous fortune SHAKESPEARE, 36; SUICIDE, 7
slogan democracy is just a s. DEMOCRACY, 2
Slough Come, friendly bombs, and fall on S. BETJEMAN, 6
slow S. and steady wins the race HASTE, 3
too swift arrives as tardy as too s. LOVE, 53
slug-horn the s. to my lips I set SUMMONS, 3
slumber A s. did my spirit seal IMMORTALITY, 5
Love itself shall s. on MEMORY, 10
Oft in the stilly night, /Ere S.'s chain NOSTALGIA, 8
slumbers Golden s. kiss your eyes SLEEP, 4
slush pure as the driven s. PURITY, 1
smack much more indecent…than a good s. LAWRENCE, 4; PUNISHMENT, 9
small In Western Europe there are now only s. countries EUROPE, 3
Microbe is so very s. BELLOC, 9; SMALLNESS, 1
Popularity?…glory's s. change POPULARITY, 3
smaller accepts a s. as a favour INJUSTICE, 2
these have s. fleas to bite 'em PARASITES, 3; SWIFT, 7
small-talking Where in this s. world MEANING, 2
smattering A s. of everything DICKENS, 17; KNOWLEDGE, 6
smell rose…would s. as sweet NAMES, 3; SHAKESPEARE, 102
Sweet S. of Success SUCCESS, 3

smile a s. I could feel in my hip pocket CHANDLER, 2; SEX, 11
Cambridge people rarely s. CAMBRIDGE, 2
s. at perils past PAST, 4; SCOTT, 2
s., s., s. OPTIMISM, 2
the vain tribute of a s. POETS, 7
smiled the soldiers he s. at WAR, 55
smiles She is Venus when she s. COMPLIMENTS, 2
The s., the tears, /Of boyhood's years NOSTALGIA, 8
smith The s., a mighty man is he OCCUPATIONS, 4
smoke Don't screw around, and don't s.
　　HEALTH AND HEALTHY LIVING, 2
no woman should marry...a man who does not s.
　　ABSTINENCE, 10; STEVENSON, 1
resembling the horrible Stygian s. of the pit SMOKING, 5
smoking resolve to give up s., drinking and loving ARSTINENCE, 8
s. can play a valuable role in a society SMOKING, 9
s. cigars and...drinking of alcohol before, after, and if need be dur-
　　ing all meals CHURCHILL, 11
What a blessing this s. is SMOKING, 4
smooth course of true love never did run s.
　　LOVE, 56; SHAKESPEARE, 84
smyler The s. with the knyf CHAUCER, 5; HYPOCRISY, 2
snail said a whiting to a s. HASTE, 1
s.'s on the thorn BROWNING, 14
snare a s. in which the feet of women have always become readily
entangled WOMEN, 1
Snark For the S. was a Boojum NONSENSE, 3
sneezed when a British Prime Minister s. BRITAIN, 6
snob He who meanly admires...is a S. SNOBBERY, 4
impossible, in our condition of society, not to be sometimes a S.
　　SNOBBERY, 5
no s. welcomes another SNOBBERY, 1
snobbish Don't be s., we seek to abolish CLASS, 12
snobs His hatred of s. SNOBBERY, 3
snore s. and you sleep alone SLEEP, 3
snotgreen The s. sea SEA, 4
snow both its national products, s. and chocolate, melt
　　SWITZERLAND, 1
I used to be S. White PURITY, 4
Snow White I used to be S. WEST, 10
soap S. and education...are more deadly EDUCATION, 31
sober a s. colouring from an eye MORTALITY, 12; WORDSWORTH, 13
Better sleep with a s. cannibal than a drunken Christian
　　DRUNKENNESS, 9
he that will go to bed s. ALCOHOL, 13
My mother, drunk or s. PATRIOTISM, 4
Tomorrow we'll be s. DRUNKENNESS, 1
sociable Society is no comfort to one not s. SOCIETY, 4
social Man is a s. animal SOCIETY, 5
the things which government does...s. progress GOVERNMENT, 15
the...world was stumbling...in s. blindness BLINDNESS, 1
true self-love and s. are the same SELF-KNOWLEDGE, 4
socialism s...alien to the British character SOCIALISM, 9
S. can only arrive by bicycle SOCIALISM, 3
S. with a human face COMMUNISM, 1
the worst advertisement for S. is its adherents
　　ORWELL, 11; SOCIALISM, 7
to banish the dark divisive clouds of Marxist s. MARXISM, 4
To the ordinary working man,...S. SOCIALISM, 8
Under s. all will govern SOCIALISM, 6
socialists intelligent people...are s. SOCIALISM, 1
S. treat their servants with respect POLITICS, 43
society a poor s. cannot be too poor POVERTY AND WEALTH, 6
Comedy, we may say, is s. HUMOUR, 14
if it be our clothes alone which fit us for s. CLOTHES, 3
impossible, in our condition of s., not to be sometimes a Snob
　　SNOBBERY, 5
Mankind is a closed s. MANKIND, 11
Man was formed for s. SOCIETY, 1
Never speak disrespectfully of S. SNOBBERY, 6
no new baby in the womb of our s. RUSSIA, 3
only possible s. is oneself MISANTHROPY, 3
S. goes on and on and on IDEAS, 3
S. is no comfort /To one not sociable SOCIETY, 4
S. is now one polish'd horde BORES, 2
s., where none intrudes NATURE, 2
The history of all...s. is the history of class struggles CLASS, 13
the ideal of a democratic and free s. RACISM, 10
There are two classes in good s. CLASS, 16
The sick man is a parasite of s. PATIENTS, 2
the transition from the...'closed s.',...to the 'open s.' SOCIETY, 3

transform this s. without a major extension of public ownership
　　SOCIALISM, 5
socks His s. compelled one's attention SAKI, 7
sod off I don't want you here – now s. INSULTS, 1
Sodom S. and...Gomorrah PUNISHMENT, 2
the men of S. were wicked HOMOSEXUALITY, 1
sodomy rum, s., and the lash CHURCHILL, 14; NAVY, 1
soft I'm not hard – I'm frightfully s. THATCHER, 3
our love...of the mind does not make us s. RESULTS, 2
softer women's bodies are s. than men's, so their understanding is
sharper CHRISTINE DE PISAN, 2
soldier A S. of the Great War KIPLING, 9
Ben Battle was a s. bold PUNS, 6
I never expect a s. to think SOLDIERS, 4
soldiers English s. fight like lions OFFICERS, 6
S. are citizens of death's grey land SOLDIERS, 3
soliciting supernatural s. SUPERNATURAL, 10
solitude In s. alone can he know true freedom SOLITUDE, 9
In s. /What happiness SOLITUDE, 8
so companionable as s. SOLITUDE, 10
the bliss of s. WORDSWORTH, 5
Whosoever is delighted in s. SOLITUDE, 1
solution A difficulty for every s. BUREAUCRACY, 5
total s. of the Jewish question NAZISM, 1
sombrero sunbonnet as well as the s. EQUALITY, 7
some I...may be s. time LAST WORDS, 21
You can fool s. of the people all the time DECEPTION, 2
somebody s. may be looking CONSCIENCE, 3
someone like sleeping with s. else's wife NEWSPAPERS, 2
something Everybody was up to s. COWARD, 5; INTRIGUE, 2
sometime .... Why don't you come up s. and see me WEST, 7
somewhere 'Tis always morning s. BEGINNING, 4
son I've examined your s.'s head, Mr Glum STUPIDITY, 6
the S. of man coming...with power DOOMSDAY, 1
sonatas The s. of Mozart are unique MUSIC, 21
song I have a s. to sing O SINGING, 1
the s. that is sung in our hearts MUSIC, 18
songs Where are the s. of Spring SEASONS, 7
sonnet I have three phobias which...would make my life as slick
as a s. OBSESSIONS, 1
son-of-a-bitch The poor s. FITZGERALD, 2
sons I have a wife, I have s. FAMILY, 13
Now we are all s. of bitches NUCLEAR WEAPONS, 1
S. of Belial had a Glorious Time TREASON, 2
sores Lazarus...laid at his gate, full of s. POVERTY AND WEALTH, 2
sorrow Down, thou climbing s. SORROW, 11
in s. thou shalt bring forth children SEXES, 1
Much in s., oft in woe ENDURANCE, 13
Parting is such sweet s. PARTING, 6; SHAKESPEARE, 104
Pure and complete s. is as impossible EMOTION, 4
S. and silence are strong ENDURANCE, 4
S. is tranquillity remembered in emotion SORROW, 8
s. makes us wise SORROW, 12; TENNYSON, 14
Tears of eternity and s. SORROW, 6
There is no greater s. SORROW, 3
Through the night of doubt and s. ENDURANCE, 2
sorrows When s. come, they come not single spies
　　MISFORTUNE, 9; SHAKESPEARE, 39
sort that like that s. of place SHAW, 12
sought Love s. is good SHAKESPEARE, 120
Pleasure is...seldom found where it is s. PLEASURE, 7
soul And never once possess our s. ARNOLD, 17; SOUL, 2
Anger is one of the sinews of the s. ANGER, 4
Artists are not engineers of the s. ART, 6
become a living s. DEATH, 66
education is a leading out of what is...in the pupil's s. EDUCATION, 30
Education is...the s. of a society CHESTERTON, 22; EDUCATION, 5
Fair seed-time had my s. SOUL, 7
His s. is marching on MEMORIALS, 4
his s. is satisfied with what is assigned to him CONTENTMENT, 1
I am the captain of my s. RESPONSIBILITY, 4
Impropriety is the s. of wit HUMOUR, 12
In mystery our s. abides SOUL, 1
I pray the Lord my s. to keep SLEEP, 1
Man has no Body distinct from his S. SOUL, 3
My s. in agony SOLITUDE, 2
No coward s. is mine BRONTË, 2
passion in the human s. MUSIC, 15
Raises from Hell a human s. BLAKE, 4; HELL, 1
real dark night of the s. FITZGERALD, 3

The British postgraduate student is a lonely forlorn s.
EDUCATION, 15

The dark night of the s. SOUL, 5
the...essence of a human s. BOOKS, 4
the eyes are the windows of the s. BEERBOHM, 3
the iron enter into his s. BITTERNESS, 3
The s. fortunately, has an interpreter BRONTË, 3
The s. hath not her generous aspirings SMOKING, 8
The S. that rises with us, our life's Star METAPHYSICS, 4
The voice of the sea speaks to the s. SEA, 3
Thy rapt s. sitting in thine eyes SOUL, 6
Thy s. was like a star, and dwelt apart WORDSWORTH, 18
souls Above the vulgar flight of common s. SUPERIORITY, 4
Stars...robbed men of their s. STARS, 1
the s. of five hundred...Newtons COLERIDGE, 17; WRITERS, 4
The s. of women are so small BUTLER, 6
Two s. dwell, alas! in my breast CONFLICT, 3
Two s. with but a single thought LOVE, 40
sound full of s. and fury LIFE, 19; SHAKESPEARE, 76
Liberals offer a mixture of s. and original ideas POLITICS, 30
The hills are alive with the s. of music MUSIC, 12
The most persistent s....through men's history WAR, 31
The s. must seem an echo to the sense POPE, 9; WRITING, 16
the trumpet shall s. DEATH, 12
whispering s. of the cool colonnade TREES, 3
sounding s. brass CHARITY, 4
sounds Music is the arithmetic of s. MUSIC, 10
the s. will take care of themselves CARROLL, 6
soup concludes that it will...make better s. IDEALISM, 2
S. of the evening, beautiful S. FOOD, 5
sour How s. sweet music is ORDER, 3
I am sure the grapes are s. ENVY, 2
sourest sweetest things turn s. CORRUPTION, 7; SHAKESPEARE, 109
south beaker full of the warm S. ALCOHOL, 20; KEATS, 7
go s. in the winter READING, 3
South Africans You won't force S. POLITICS, 1
Sovereign The S. has, under a constitutional monarchy...three rights MONARCHY, 2
Soviet Communism is S. power plus the electrification COMMUNISM, 2
The ship follows S. custom CLASS, 19
sow Ireland is the old s. IRELAND, 5
soya workers' flats in fields of s. beans FUTURE, 2
space annihilate but s. and time POPE, 2
In the United States there is more s. AMERICA, 19
Outer s. is no place SPACE, 2
S. is almost infinite SPACE, 5
S. isn't remote at all SPACE, 4
spaceship passenger on the s., Earth SPACE, 3
Spain not left to S. MARTYRDOM, 3
Spaniards the S. seem wiser than they are APPEARANCES, 2
time to win this game, and to thrash the S. SPORT AND GAMES, 2; WAR, 18
Spanish I speak S. to God LANGUAGE, 4
singed the S. king's beard WAR, 19
spare s. the rod BUTLER, 3; INDULGENCE, 1; PUNISHMENT, 4
Woodman, s. that tree TREES, 6
spareth he that s. his rod hateth his son CHILDREN, 2
sparrows one of the s....flew...through the hall LIFE, 4
spat Today I s. in the Seine WORLD WAR II, 18
speak I didn't s. up NAZISM, 3
I truly am right on SPEECHES, 2
province of knowledge to s. KNOWLEDGE, 7; WISDOM, 11
some...s....before they think IMPETUOSITY, 1
S. softly and carry a big stick POWER POLITICS, 4
When I think, I must s. SHAKESPEARE, 21
Whereof one cannot s. SILENCE, 8
speaking An Englishman's way of s. CLASS, 10
specialist S. – A man who knows more and more about less and less EXPERTS, 3
species the idea of its death as a s. NUCLEAR WEAPONS, 6
Women exist...solely for the propagation of the s. WOMAN'S ROLE, 4
spectator a S. of mankind OBJECTIVITY, 1
spectre Communism continued to haunt Europe as a s. COMMUNISM, 5
speculation If the world were good for...s. SPECULATION, 2
speech An after-dinner s. should be like a lady's dress SPEECHES, 2
freedom of s. and expression HUMAN RIGHTS, 4
freedom of s., freedom of conscience, and the prudence never to practise...them FREEDOM, 26; TWAIN, 6
let thy s. be short SPEECH, 2

perfect plainness of s....perfect nobleness ARNOLD, 12; BIBLE, 1
s. only to conceal their thoughts VOLTAIRE, 8
s....seasoned with salt SPEECH, 1
S. was given to man to disguise his thoughts SPEECH, 7
The most precious things in s. SPEECH, 5
The true use of s. GOLDSMITH, 9
the whole earth was...of one s. UNITY, 3
True and False are attributes of s., not of things TRUTH, 12
speeches every government...should have its old s. burned GOVERNMENT, 13
Many have been the wise s. of fools WISDOM AND FOOLISHNESS, 3
Statesmen are far too busy making s. RUSSELL, 12
speechless The Times is s. CHURCHILL, 17
speed safety is in our s. HASTE, 2
spell s. it Vinci and pronounce it Vinchy PRONUNCIATION, 2; SPELLING, 2
spendest whatsoever thou s. more...I will repay CHARITY, 5
spending Riches are for s. EXTRAVAGANCE, 1
spent Nought's had, all's s. CONTENTMENT, 3
sphinx Variety's the very s. of life CHANGE, 3; COWPER, 10
spice Emily Brontë remains the s. of literature BRONTË, 1
spies sorrows...come not single s. MISFORTUNE, 9; SHAKESPEARE, 39
spilt the blood that she has s. COWPER, 2
spinster graduating with a 's. of arts' degree LANGUAGE, 17
spires City with her dreaming g. OXFORD, 2
spirit and an haughty s. before a fall PRIDE, 1
Give me the s. APPEARANCES, 2
history of the human s. ARNOLD, 10; CULTURE, 1
into thy hands I commend my s. LAST WORDS, 6
Music that gentlier on the s. lies MUSIC, 26; TENNYSON, 21
my s. found outlet in the air FLYING, 1
s.... of a sound mind FEAR, 2
the meanest...deeds require s. and talent INSENSITIVITY, 2
The s. burning but unbent BYRON, 6; DETERMINATION, 3
the s....is willing IMPERFECTION, 1
the S. of God moved upon...the waters CREATION, 1
Th' expense of s. in a waste of shame LUST, 3
spit I am not going to s. on the deck DEPARTURE, 3
spleen S. can subsist on any kind of food ANGER, 5
splendour Pavilioned in s., and girded with praise GOD, 18
split when I s. an infinitive...it stays s. CHANDLER, 4; CHANDLER, 4; GRAMMAR, 2
spoil s. the child BUTLER, 3; INDULGENCE, 1; PUNISHMENT, 4
spontaneous set a high value on s. kindness FRIENDSHIP, 8
Worrying is the most natural and s. of...functions WORRY, 6
spoons let us count our s. JOHNSON, 19
the faster we counted our s. MISTRUST, 2
sport kill us for their s. SHAKESPEARE, 65
Serious s. has nothing to do with fair play ORWELL, 14; SPORT AND GAMES, 7
s. would be as tedious as to work LEISURE, 3
to make s. for our neighbours AUSTEN, 11
spot Out, damned s. GUILT, 5; SHAKESPEARE, 74
spotless s. reputation REPUTATION, 6
spots or the leopard his s. CHANGE, 1
spreading Under the s. chestnut tree OCCUPATIONS, 4
spring as short a S.; /As quick a growth to meet decay TRANSIENCE, 9
can S. be far behind SEASONS, 14; SHELLEY, 8
Drink deep, or taste not the Pierian s. POPE, 7
hounds of s. are on winter's traces SEASONS, 15
In the S. a young man's fancy SEASONS, 16; TENNYSON, 19
lived light in the s. ARNOLD, 6
S....stipple leaves with sun SEASONS, 13
The year's at the s. BROWNING, 14
Thrice welcome, darling of the s. WORDSWORTH, 22
Where are the songs of S. SEASONS, 7
springboard reality as a s. into space BLAKE, 2
spur Fame is the s. FAME, 7
squire Bless the s. and his relations CLASS, 3
staff I'll break my s. RENUNCIATION, 2
stage All the world's a s. HUMAN CONDITION, 8; SHAKESPEARE, 48
Don't put your daughter on the s. COWARD, 8; THEATRE, 4
If this were play'd upon a s. REALITY, 3
no man dies for love, but on the s. DRYDEN, 13; LOVE AND DEATH, 1
qualities...necessary for success upon the s. ACTING, 7
this great s. of fools HUMAN CONDITION, 9; SHAKESPEARE, 66
stagecoach You will hear more good things on...a s. from London to Oxford HAZLITT, 5
stair As I was going up the s. NONSENSE, 11
stairs he had known many kicked down s. PROMOTION, 6

strings 'There are s.', said Mr Tappertit, 'in the human heart' DICKENS, 2
stripling yon pale s. SCOTT, 8
strive I s. to be brief, and I become obscure HORACE, 2
men should s. to learn HUMAN CONDITION, 11
To s., to seek, to find, and not to yield DETERMINATION, 6; TENNYSON, 30
strives s. to touch the stars AMBITION, 9
stroke man fears…only the s. of death DEATH, 6
strong be s. and of a good courage GOD, 5
disarm the s. and arm the weak INJUSTICE, 3
how sublime…/To suffer and be s. ENDURANCE, 5
Sorrow and silence are s. ENDURANCE, 4
s. enough to bear the misfortunes of others MISFORTUNE, 7
the errors of those who think they are s. MISTAKES, 2
the s. shall thrive SURVIVAL, 3
the wall is s. IMPRISONMENT, 6
woe unto them that…follow s. drink ALCOHOL, 3
stronger normal man's sex needs are s. SEX, 32
strongest S. minds /…the noisy world /Hears least WORDSWORTH, 2
struggle manhood a s. AGE, 13; DISRAELI, 3
The perpetual s. for room and food SURVIVAL, 1
struggles The history of all…society is the history of class s. CLASS, 13
struggling the greatness of Russia is only her pre-natal s. RUSSIA, 2
struts player that s. and frets LIFE, 19; SHAKESPEARE, 76
stubborn s. spear-men COURAGE, 9; SCOTT, 6
student a s. to the end of my days LEARNING, 4
studies s. serve for delight EDUCATION, 2
study much s. is a weariness of the flesh BOOKS, 3
s. what you most affect EDUCATION, 26
The proper s. of Mankind is Man SELF-KNOWLEDGE, 3
the result of previous s. FLATTERY, 1
stuff Ambition should be made of sterner s. AMBITION, 7
such s. as dreams are made on MORTALITY, 10
The future is made of the same s. FUTURE, 5
to s. a mushroom HOUSEWORK, 2
stumbling the…world was s.…in social blindness BLINDNESS, 1
stumbling block Bible and Church have been the greatest s. FEMINISM, 17
stupid he ceased to be mad he became merely s. REMEDIES, 7
Living in England,…must be like being married to a s.…wife ENGLAND, 9
s. are cocksure…intelligent full of doubt DOUBT, 4
The s. neither forgive FORGIVENESS, 7
To be clever enough to get…money, one must be s. CHESTERTON, 12; MATERIALISM, 4
stupidity Against s. the gods…struggle in vain STUPIDITY, 7
Human S. consists in having lots of ideas STUPIDITY, 5
If poverty is the mother of crime, s. is its father CRIME, 2; LA BRUYERE, 5
no sin except s. STUPIDITY, 2
Stygian resembling the horrible S. smoke of the pit SMOKING, 5
style s. is the man himself STYLE, 1
s., not sincerity, is the vital thing STYLE, 4
s.…often hides eczema STYLE, 2
the grand s. arises in poetry POETRY, 3
styles All s. are good except the tiresome sort STYLE, 3; VOLTAIRE, 14
subject a noble nature,…treats…a serious s. POETRY, 3
Every s.'s duty is the King's MONARCHY, 8; SHAKESPEARE, 48
Her Majesty is not a s. DISRAELI, 18
sublime a step from the s. to the ridiculous DECLINE, 2
how s.…/To suffer and be strong ENDURANCE, 5
The s. and the ridiculous OPPOSITES, 3
subsequence It is incident to physicians…to mistake s. for consequence JOHNSON, 16
substance faith is the s. of things hoped for FAITH, 1
lose the s. by grasping at the shadow GREED, 1
substantives tell the s. from the adjectives POLITICS, 32
substitute no s. for talent HUXLEY, 14; TALENT, 3
substitutes and finally a single dictator s. himself COMMUNISM, 6
subtle Time, the s. thief of youth AGE, 28
suburbia I come from s. SUBURBIA, 1
subverts a continued miracle in his own person, which s. all the principles of his understanding CHRISTIANITY, 16
succeed don't s., try, try again. Then quit REALISM, 2
If at first you don't s. PERSISTENCE, 2
If they s., they fail HOMOSEXUALITY, 2
It is not enough to s. RUTHLESSNESS, 3
Never having been able to s. in the world ENVY, 6

those who ne'er s. DICKINSON, 4; SUCCESS, 2
success a self-made man who owed his lack of s. to nobody SELF-MADE MEN, 1
I thought that s. spelled happiness HAPPINESS, 6
I was never affected by the question of the s. SELF-CONFIDENCE, 2
no s. like failure DYLAN, 3; FAILURE, 1
not in mortals to command s. ADDISON, 2
only place where s. comes before work SUCCESS, 6; WORK, 10
religion…yours is S. SUCCESS, 3
s.…by dint of hard work EFFORT, 4; SUCCESS, 4
s. depends…upon individual initiative and exertion EFFORT, 4; SUCCESS, 4
S. is counted sweetest DICKINSON, 4; SUCCESS, 2
Sweet Smell of S. SUCCESS, 3
two to make a marriage a s. MARRIAGE, 51
successful we do everything we can to appear s. SUCCESS, 5
sucks s. the nurse asleep SUICIDE, 6
suddenly No one…s. became depraved DEBAUCHERY, 2
sued publish and be s. PUBLISHING, 4
suffer courage to love…courage to s. LOVE, 66
how sublime…/To s. and be strong ENDURANCE, 5
If s. we must, let's s. on the heights SUFFERING, 4
Rather s. than die SUFFERING, 4
s. fools gladly WISDOM AND FOOLISHNESS, 2
suffered love a place the less for having s. AUSTEN, 9; SUFFERING, 1
suffering A man who fears s. SUFFERING, 5
Madness and s. can set themselves no limit MADNESS, 5
pity for the s. of mankind RUSSELL, 2
The prime goal is to alleviate s., and not to prolong life MEDICINE, 1
we cannot be created for this sort of s. AFTERLIFE, 5
sufficient s. unto the day is the evil thereof WORRY, 2
suicide If you must commit s. SUICIDE, 1
Never murder a man who is committing s. SUICIDE, 8
s. in this man's town SUICIDE, 5
S. is the worst form of murder SUICIDE, 2
thought of s. is a great…comfort NIETZSCHE, 6; SUICIDE, 3
suit in a light so dim he would not have chosen a s. by it LOVE, 17
My s. is pale yellow. My nationality is French NORMALITY, 2; WILLIAMS, 1
sulphur land of Calvin, oat-cakes, and s. SCOTLAND, 5
sultry common where the climate's s. ADULTERY, 1; BYRON, 7
sum Cogito, ergo s. THINKING, 1
sumer S. is icumen in SEASONS, 1
summer after many a s. dies the swan MORTALITY, 11
All on a s. day FOOD, 7
Before the war…it was s. all the year round NOSTALGIA, 5
Made glorious s. SHAKESPEARE, 99
murmur of a s.'s day SEASONS, 3
s. afternoon…two most beautiful words SEASONS, 4
S. afternoon – s. afternoon JAMES, 9
the last rose of s. FLOWERS, 6
summons when Fate s. MORTALITY, 4
summum S. bonum GOOD, 1
sun aweary of the s. WORLD-WEARINESS, 5
before you let the s. in, mind it wipes its shoes CLEANLINESS, 2; THOMAS, 9
better is he…who hath not seen the evil work…under the s. EVIL, 3
Busy old fool, unruly S. SUN, 2
Fear no more the heat o' th' s. MORTALITY, 9; SHAKESPEARE, 25
go out in the mid-day s. COWARD, 9
Light breaks where no s. shines EMOTION, 3
nothing like the s. SHAKESPEARE, 110
on which the s. never sets BRITISH EMPIRE, 4
Spring…stipple leaves with s. SEASONS, 13
s. had risen to hear him crow ELIOT, 2
S. remains fixed in the centre ASTRONOMY, 1
The S. came up upon the left SUN, 1
the s. shining ten days a year and shit in the streets ENGLAND, 10
this s. of York SHAKESPEARE, 99
To have enjoy'd the s. ARNOLD, 5
sunbonnet s. as well as the sombrero EQUALITY, 7
sunburn S. is very becoming APPEARANCE, 6
Sunday A Christian…feels /Repentance on a S. HYPOCRISY, 11
only two posh papers on a S. NEWSPAPERS, 3
The feeling of S. is the same everywhere SUNDAY, 3
sunk thanks to words, we have often s. to the level of the demons HUXLEY, 3; WORDS, 6
sunless Down to a s. sea COLERIDGE, 6; PLEASURE, 1
sunset s. breezes shiver BOATS, 6
sunsets I have a horror of s. PROUST, 6
superfluous that controversy is either s. or hopeless ARGUMENTS, 4

I u. only because I love   LOVE, 65; UNDERSTANDING, 7
not to weep at them, nor to hate them, but to u. them
   UNDERSTANDING, 6
people...may not be made to u.   UNDERSTANDING, 3
When men u. what each other mean   ARGUMENTS, 4
Wot do they u.   DISCONTENT, 4
You suddenly u. something...in a new way   LEARNING, 5
understanding a candle of u.   UNDERSTANDING, 1
Donne's verses...pass all u.   DONNE, 2
Most men...give evidence against their own u.   SPEECH, 4
u. will...extinguish pleasure
   HOUSMAN, 3; POETRY, 11; UNDERSTANDING, 4
We need more u. of human nature   HUMAN NATURE, 7
women's bodies are softer than men's, so their u. is sharper
   CHRISTINE DE PISAN, 2
undertaking The love of life is necessary to...any u.   ENTHUSIASM, 3
undone estate o' th' world were now u.   WORLD-WEARINESS, 1
left u. those things   SIN, 6
Things hitherto u. should be given...a wide berth   BEERBOHM, 1
uneasy U. lies the head that wears a crown
   MONARCHY, 10; SHAKESPEARE, 44
uneatable the unspeakable in full pursuit of the u.
   HUNTING, 5; WILDE, 32
uneducated Democracy...government by the u.
   ARISTOCRACY, 5; CHESTERTON, 21
unequal Men are made by nature u.   EQUALITY, 9
unexamined The u. life   SELF, 9
unexpected Old age is the most u.   OLD AGE, 27
unfaithful better to be u.   FAITHFULNESS, 1
unfortunates one of those u. to whom death is   EXPLANATIONS, 1
unhappy A moment of time may make us u. for ever   SORROW, 5
don't believe one can ever be u. for long   WAUGH, 6
each u. family is u. in its own way   FAMILY, 20
making their remaining years u.   LA BRUYERE, 1
one is u. one becomes moral   PROUST, 3
U. the land that has no heroes   HEROISM, 2
uniform love that loves a scarlet coat /Should be more u.   PUNS, 5
uniformity let use be preferred before u.   HOUSES, 1
uninstructed making things plain to u. people was...best means of
clearing...one's own mind   EDUCATION, 12
uninteresting no...u. subject   CHESTERTON, 2
unite Workers of the world, u.   MARXISM, 1
United States In the U. there is more space   AMERICA, 19
The U.,...are twenty years in advance of this country   AMERICA, 11
The U. has to move very fast   AMERICA, 10
The U. is like a gigantic boiler   AMERICA, 10
The U....six hours behind...   AMERICA, 1
U. of Europe   CHURCHILL, 31; EUROPE, 2
universal There is no u. law   SPONTANEITY, 2
universally a happy woman and u. respected   WOLLSTONECRAFT, 1
universe Perish the U.   REVENGE, 3
the better ordering of the u.   UNIVERSE, 1
The u. is not hostile   UNIVERSE, 4
The u. is transformation   LIFE, 3
The u....more like a great thought   UNIVERSE, 5
The visible u. was an illusion   UNIVERSE, 2
universities The King, observing...the state of both his u.
   CAMBRIDGE, 5; OXFORD, 5
U. are the cathedrals of the modern age   EDUCATION, 16
university it is necessary to go to a u....to become a successful
writer   WRITERS, 2
unjust The u. steals the just's umbrella   JUSTICE, 3
unkind Thou art not so u.   INGRATITUDE, 3
unkindness Like not you, you elements, with u.   WEATHER, 8
unknown Give me a light that I may tread safely into the u.   FAITH, 6
I travelled among u. men   HOMESICKNESS, 6
unmourned and u.   OBLIVION, 1
unlabelled One of the unpardonable sins...is...to go about u.
   CLASSIFICATION, 1
unlike the Jews bring the u. into the heart of *every milieu*   JEWS, 11
The law of dislike for the u.   JEWS, 11
unmarried to keep u.   MARRIAGE, 54
unmuzzled The world regards such a person as...an u. dog
   CLASSIFICATION, 1
unnatural so u. as the commonplace   DOYLE, 3
unobtrusive Poetry should be great and u.   POETRY, 12
unpaid A promise made is a debt u.   PROMISES, 3
unpardonable One of the u. sins...is...to go about unlabelled
   CLASSIFICATION, 1
unpleasant Cynicism is an u. way of saying the truth   CYNICISM, 1
unprofitable How weary, stale, flat, and u.   WORLD-WEARINESS, 4

unrecording troops of u. friends   LIFE, 22
unremembered u. acts /Of kindness and of love
   KINDNESS, 4; WORDSWORTH, 6
unsaid The bitterest tears...are for words...u. and deeds...undone
   REGRET, 11
unsatisfied It is exquisite, and it leaves one u.   WILDE, 28
unsavoury indefatigable and u. engine of pollution   DOGS, 5
unseen to deny the existence of an u. kingdom is bad
   SPECULATION, 1
unsoundness no person can be a poet...without...u. of mind
   POETRY, 14
unspeakable the u. in full pursuit of the uneatable
   HUNTING, 5; WILDE, 32
untravelled Gleams that u. world   EXPERIENCE, 9
untruth The camera...an accessory to u.   PHOTOGRAPHY, 3
unupblown Nurse u.   WAUGH, 2
unused left over from last year u.   ADVICE, 2
unwashed The great U.   PUBLIC, 4
unwholesome Boys...are u. companions for grown people   LAMB, 3
unwomanly sexual feeling is u. and intolerable   SEX, 29
up *How to be one* u.   ONE-UPMANSHIP, 2
u. with which I will not put   CHURCHILL, 16; GRAMMAR, 3
upper Like many of the u. class   ARISTOCRACY, 2
the u. classes /Have still the u. hand
   ARISTOCRACY, 6; COWARD, 6; STATELY HOMES, 2
urn Can storied u...../Back to its mansion call the fleeting breath
   DEATH, 27
use I see no reason to suppose that these machines will ever force
themselves into general u.   WELLINGTON, 4
let u. be preferred before uniformity   HOUSES, 1
no reason...these machines will ever force themselves into general
u.   TECHNOLOGY, 7
what is the u. of a book   BOOKS, 5; CARROLL, 1
useful not merely...u. and ornamental   PURPOSE, 5
the most u. thing about a principle...sacrificed to expediency
   EXPEDIENCY, 3
useless All Art is quite u.   ART, 20
most beautiful things...are the most u.   BEAUTY, 17; RUSKIN, 8
uses all the u. of this world   WORLD-WEARINESS, 4
usual Business as u.   BRITISH, 2; CHURCHILL, 18
U-turn U. if you want to   INFLEXIBILITY, 2; THATCHER, 6
vacant In v. or in pensive mood   WORDSWORTH, 5
vacation a change of nuisances is as good as a v.   CHANGE, 10
vagabond A fugitive and a v.   PUNISHMENT, 1
vaguery For V. in the Field   INCOMPETENCE, 2
vain generous aspirings implanted in her in v.   SMOKING, 8
thou shalt not take the name of...God in v.   GOD, 6
V. are the thousand creeds   BELIEF, 1
vale *ave atque* u.   GREETINGS, 1
valet No man is a hero to his v.   FAMILIARITY, 1
valiant the level of the most v. of men   COURAGE, 10
v. never taste of death but once   COWARDICE, 3; SHAKESPEARE, 54
valid If...'feeling good' could decide, drunkenness would
be...supremely v.   DRUNKENNESS, 7
valley One sees great things from the v.
   CHESTERTON, 6; PERSPECTIVE, 1
valleys Piping down the v. wild   BLAKE, 1
valour The better part of v. is discretion
   SELF-PRESERVATION, 4; SHAKESPEARE, 43
value All knowledge is of itself of some v.   KNOWLEDGE, 11
Friendship...has no survival v.   FRIENDSHIP, 9
the price of everything and the v. of nothing   CYNICISM, 5; WILDE, 25
values Victorian v....were the v. when our country   MORALITY, 11
vanished as rare things will, it v.   BROWNING, 11
vanity v. and love...universal characteristics
   CHESTERFIELD, 11; WOMEN, 13
V. dies hard   CONCEIT, 7; STEVENSON, 4
v. of vanities   TRANSIENCE, 2
V. plays lurid tricks   CONCEIT, 3
variable light-headed, v. men   STEVENSON, 2
varies quality of moral behaviour v.   HUXLEY, 10
variety custom stale her infinite v.   ADMIRATION, 5
V.'s the very spice of life   CHANGE, 3; COWPER, 10
vasectomy V. means not ever having to say you're sorry
   CONTRACEPTION, 1
Vatican the V., the Treasury and the miners   DIPLOMACY, 2
vaulting 'Fan v.'...belongs to the 'Last-supper-carved-on-a-peach-
stone'   ARCHITECTURE, 1
veal I could eat one of Bellamy's v. pies   LAST WORDS, 23
vegetables you must talk to your v.   GARDENS, 5

I were w. with destiny — DESTINY, 1
When I am not w., I am reading — READING, 6
walks She w. in beauty — BEAUTY, 7
wall it is your business, when the w. next door catches fire — NEIGHBOURS, 2
With our backs to the w. — WORLD WAR I, 6
wall paper Either that w. goes, or I do — WILDE, 43
walls Stone w. do not a prison make — IMPRISONMENT, 3
Walrus The W. and the Carpenter — SEASIDE, 1
wandered I w. lonely as a cloud — FLOWERS, 9; WORDSWORTH, 4
wanderer A w. is man from his birth — ARNOLD, 8
wandering Poor w. one — RETURN, 1
w. minstrel I — SINGERS, 2
want be without some of the things you w. — HAPPINESS, 10
Economy is going without something you do w. — THRIFT, 5
evil is wrought by w. of thought — EVIL, 7
for w. of a nail — NEGLECT, 1
freedom from w. — HUMAN RIGHTS, 4
I w. to be alone. — MISQUOTATIONS, 10
What does a woman w. — WOMEN, 19
war All diplomacy is a continuation of w. — DIPLOMACY, 7
An empire founded by w. — WAR, 39
As a woman I can't go to w. — WAR, 46
As long as w. is regarded as wicked — WAR, 67; WILDE, 5
Before the w....it was summer all the year round — NOSTALGIA, 9
Being over seventy is like being engaged in a w. — OLD AGE, 24
defeat without a w. — WORLD WAR II, 2
do in the Great W., Daddy — WORLD WAR I, 4
him who desires peace, prepare for w. — WAR AND PEACE, 8
In a civil w., a general must know — WAR, 47
In starting and waging a w. it is not right that matters, but victory — HITLER, 8; WAR, 23
In w....there are no winners — WAR, 13
is a w. to end w. — WORLD WAR I, 7
It is well that w. is so terrible;... — WAR, 33
lead this people into w. and they'll forget...tolerance — WAR, 71
let slip the dogs of w. — SHAKESPEARE, 56; WAR, 59
never was a good w. — WAR AND PEACE, 5
No one can guarantee success in w. — WAR, 16
Now w. has a bad conscience — WAR, 27
Older men declare w. — WAR, 24
only twenty seconds of w. to destroy him — WAR, 4
Television brought the brutality of w. — WAR, 36
that devil's madness – W. — WAR, 58
the...barbarity of w....forces men...to commit acts — WAR, 28
The first casualty when w. comes — WAR, 26
The quickest way of ending a w. — ORWELL, 13; WAR, 42
there was w. in heaven — DEVIL, 2
The W. between Men and Women — SEXES, 15
The w. we have just been through,...is not to be compared — WAR, 70
they'll give a w. and nobody will come — WAR, 53
this liking for w. — WAR, 5
this massed multitude of silent witnesses to...w. — WAR, 22
Those who can win a w. well — CHURCHILL, 10; WAR AND PEACE, 4
w. can only be abolished through w. — WAR, 35
w. ended, the explosions stopped — WAR AND PEACE, 6
W. even to the knife — WAR, 12
W. hath no fury like a non-combatant — WAR, 38
W. is, after all, the universal perversion — WAR, 45
W. is capitalism — WAR, 63
W. is hell — WAR, 61
W. is like love — WAR, 9
W. is not an adventure — WAR, 52
W. is the continuation of politics — MAO TSE-TUNG, 2; WAR, 17; WAR, 34
W. is too important — OFFICERS, 4
W. knows no power — WAR, 11
w. minus the shooting — ORWELL, 14; SPORT AND GAMES, 7
W. should belong to the tragic past — WAR, 43
we are...in the midst of a cold w. — COLD WAR, 1
We are not at w. with Egypt — WAR, 20
We have all lost the w. — WAR, 32
when there was w., he went — AUDEN, 12; PUBLIC, 2
When the rich wage w. — POVERTY AND WEALTH, 5
when they learn how we began this w. — WORLD WAR II, 19
When you're at w. you think about a better life — WAR AND PEACE, 7
Ware And I should dine at W. — COWPER, 5
warn the right to be consulted,...to encourage,...to w. — MONARCHY, 2
warning will it come without w. /Just as I'm picking my nose — AUDEN, 12; LOVE, 3
War Office except the British W. — SHAW, 5
wars All w. are planned by old men — WAR, 50

All w. are popular for the first thirty days — WAR, 56
end to the beginnings of all w. — WAR, 51
military don't start w. — WAR, 66
my w. /Were global — WAR, 48
No kingdom has...had as many...w. as the kingdom of Christ — CHRISTIANITY, 19
Still w. and lechery — SEX, 31; SHAKESPEARE, 116
W. are not won by evacuations — CHURCHILL, 13; WORLD WAR II, 12
W. cannot be fought with nuclear weapons — NUCLEAR WEAPONS, 10
W., conflict, it's all business — WAR, 14
w., horrible w. — PROPHECY, 7; VIRGIL, 9
warts pimples, w., and everything as you see me — REALISM, 1
war-war To jaw-jaw is better than to w. — CHURCHILL, 33; DIPLOMACY, 3
washed Pilate...w. his hands — GUILT, 2
washing painting a face and not w. — APPEARANCE, 7
wasps w. and hornets break through — SWIFT, 10
waste biggest w. of water in the country — CONSERVATION, 5
Far too good to w. on children — SHAW, 27
The years to come seemed w. of breath — FLYING, 4; YEATS, 5
wasting she did not believe in w. her effects — THREATS, 1
watch keeping w. over their flock by night — CHRISTMAS, 6
The W. on the Rhine — RIVERS, 3
w. and pray — IMPERFECTION, 1
watch-dog to hear the w.'s honest bark — DOGS, 3
watchmaker I should have become a w. — EINSTEIN, 4; NUCLEAR WEAPONS, 4
watchman only one...can count on steady work – the night w. — THEATRE, 1
water better deeds /Shall be in w. writ — MEMORIALS, 2
biggest waste of w. in the country — WATER, 3
half the landscape is...covered by useless w. — SEASIDE, 2
He who drinks a tumbler of London w. — SMITH, 7; WATER, 5
Human beings were invented by w. — WATER, 4
impressions...lasting as...an oar upon the w. — INSIGNIFICANCE, 1
It is with our passions as it is with fire and w. — PASSION, 4
Like a bridge over troubled w. — COMFORT, 2
Streets full of w. — TELEGRAMS, 3; VENICE, 1
virtues we write in w. — MEMORIALS, 7; SHAKESPEARE, 52
w. flowed like champagne — ABSTINENCE, 4
w. still keeps falling over — CHURCHILL, 5
W., w., every where — COLERIDGE, 12; WATER, 1
watering a-w. the last year's crop — ELIOT, 1
Waterloo Every man meets his W. — DEFEAT, 5
waters dreadful noise of w. in my ears — DROWNING, 1
stolen w. are sweet — SECRECY, 2
the Spirit of God moved upon...the w. — CREATION, 1
the w. of the heart /Push in their tides — EMOTION, 3
Watson Mr W., come here: I want you — SUMMONS, 2
Waugh Mr W....an antique in search of a period — WAUGH, 1
waves the w. make towards the pebbled shore — SHAKESPEARE, 108; TIME, 15
way catch the nearest w. — KINDNESS, 2; SHAKESPEARE, 69
I am the w., the truth, and the life — CHRISTIANITY, 9
plowman homeward plods his weary w. — DAY, 4
The w. to dusty death — LIFE, 19; SHAKESPEARE, 76
though hell should bar the w. — DETERMINATION, 5
w. of all flesh — DEATH, 17; HUMAN NATURE, 10
woman has her w. — SEXES, 8
ways She dwelt among the untrodden w. — WORDSWORTH, 16
we put it down a w. — SPELLING, 1
weak Beauty stands /In the admiration...of w. minds — BEAUTY, 15
concessions of the w. — YIELDING, 1
disarm the strong and arm the w. — INJUSTICE, 3
Idleness...the refuge of w. minds — CHESTERFIELD, 10; IDLENESS, 1
Is thy love a plant /Of such w. fibre — ABSENCE, 3; WORDSWORTH, 11
surely the w. shall perish — SURVIVAL, 3
The w. have one weapon — MISTAKES, 2
w., diffusive, weltering, ineffectual man — COLERIDGE, 1
weakness no more w. than is natural to her sex — WOMEN, 42
weaknesses I have got lots of human w. — IMPERFECTION, 7
Never support two w. — VICE, 5
touch his w. with a delicate hand — IMPERFECTION, 4
wealth God shows his contempt for w. — WEALTH, 11
when the nation depended on agriculture for its w. — ECONOMICS, 9
Where w. and freedom reign, contentment fails — BUSINESS, 6
W. has never been a sufficient source of honour — OSTENTATION, 2
W. I ask not — STEVENSON, 5; TRAVEL, 15
W. is like sea-water — GREED, 4
W. is not without its advantages — WEALTH, 7
wealthy Where some people are very w. and others have nothing — GOVERNMENT, 2

will-power no such thing as a great talent without great w.
      DETERMINATION, 2
will-to-live The thing-in-itself, the w., exists...in every being
      SURVIVAL, 2
win I am certain that we will w. the election with a good majority
      SELF-CONFIDENCE, 4
The conventional army loses if it does not w.
      WAR, 30
Those who can w. a war well
      CHURCHILL, 10; WAR AND PEACE, 4
wind Blow, blow, thou winter w.
      INGRATITUDE, 3
of w. and limb
      FAITHFULNESS, 2
O Wild West W.
      WEATHER, 12
The answer...is blowin' in the w.
      FREEDOM, 6
The story is like the w.
      SENSATION, 2
what w. is to fire
      ABSENCE, 2
wherever the w. takes me I travel as a visitor
      FREEDOM, 10
Who has seen the w.
      WEATHER, 4
words but w.
      BUTLER, 4; WORDS, 2
windmills not giants but w.
      CERVANTES, 3; DELUSION, 2
wine A Flask of W.
      CONTENTMENT, 2
A man may surely be allowed to take a glass of w. by his own fire-side
      SHERIDAN, 10
And drink of my Algerian w.
      INSULTS, 2
days of w. and roses
      TRANSIENCE, 7
drinks his w. 'mid laughter free
      PARTING, 1
full of new w.
      DRUNKENNESS, 4
good w. needs no bush
      PLAYS, 4
look not thou upon the w. when it is red
      ALCOHOL, 6
MPs never see the London that exists beyond the w. bars
      POLITICIANS, 8
no man...having drunk old w. straightway desireth new
      AGE, 6; ALCOHOL, 5
the guests must be chosen as carefully as the w.
      ALCOHOL, 29; SAKI, 1
the w. is in, the wit is out
      DRUNKENNESS, 3
This w. upon a foreign tree
      THOMAS, 8
Truth comes out in w.
      ALCOHOL, 26
use a little w. for thy stomach's sake
      ALCOHOL, 4
W. comes in at the mouth
      YEATS, 3
w. is a mocker
      DRUNKENNESS, 5
winged Time's w. chariot
      AGE, 26
wings Fear lent w. to his feet
      FEAR, 7; VIRGIL, 10
whether pigs have w.
      CARROLL, 10; NONSENSE, 5
winners In war...there are no w.
      WAR, 13
winning not w. but taking part
      VICTORY, 4
W. isn't everything, but wanting to win is
      VICTORY, 5
Winston The first time you meet W.
      CHURCHILL, 2
W.'s back
      TELEGRAMS, 2
winter got through the perils of w. till at least the seventh of May
      TROLLOPE, 4
human beings say that they enjoy the w.
      SEASONS, 2
It is a w.'s tale
      SEASONS, 17
No one thinks of w.
      KIPLING, 6; SEASONS, 9
the furious w.'s rages
      MORTALITY, 9; SHAKESPEARE, 25
W. is icummen in
      SEASONS, 11
w. of our discontent
      SHAKESPEARE, 99
wisdom in much w. is much grief
      KNOWLEDGE, 3; WISDOM, 1
Knowledge can be communicated but not w.
      WISDOM, 10
Love is the w. of the fool
      JOHNSON, 15; LOVE, 35
privilege of w. to listen
      KNOWLEDGE, 7; WISDOM, 11
proverb is one man's wit and all men's w.
      SAYINGS, 3
proverbs provide them with w.
      STUPIDITY, 4
Silence is...full of potential w.
      SILENCE, 2
The highest w. has but one science
      MANKIND, 17
The only infallible criterion of w.
      BURKE, 2
the palace of W.
      BLAKE, 16; EXCESS, 3
the price of w. is above rubies
      WISDOM, 3
therefore get w.
      WISDOM, 4
W. be put in a silver rod
      WISDOM, 6
w....cometh by opportunity of leisure
      LEISURE, 1
w. excelleth folly, as...light excelleth darkness
      WISDOM AND FOOLISHNESS, 1
W. in minds attentive
      COWPER, 14; KNOWLEDGE, 5; WISDOM, 9
w....sweetly doth...order all things
      WISDOM, 5
with the ancient is w.
      OLD AGE, 1
wise A w. man will make more opportunities
      OPPORTUNITY, 1
Coffee which makes the politician w.
      DRINKS, 3
Many have been the w. speeches of fools
      WISDOM AND FOOLISHNESS, 3
more of the fool than of the w.
      HUMAN NATURE, 3
No man...so w. as Thurlow looked
      APPEARANCES, 6
sorrow makes us w.
      SORROW, 12; TENNYSON, 14
The only wretched are the w.
      IGNORANCE, 4

the w. forgive
      FORGIVENESS, 7
To be w. and love
      SHAKESPEARE, 115
where ignorance is bliss, /'Tis folly to be w.
      IGNORANCE, 1
wisely lov'd not w., but too well
      LOVE, 60; SHAKESPEARE, 94
wiser Be w. than other people
      CHESTERFIELD, 2
sadder and a w. man
      COLERIDGE, 14; WISDOM, 8
The French are w. than they seem
      APPEARANCES, 2
the old have rubbed it into the young that they are w.
      OLD AGE, 15
w. to-day than...yesterday
      MISTAKES, 5; POPE, 16
wish Conscience is...rejection of a...w.
      CONSCIENCE, 2
Justice is the...perpetual w.
      JUSTICE, 6
most...w. they were the only one alive
      EGOTISM, 1
The w. to hurt
      CRUELTY, 1
The w. to spread those opinions that we hold
      ENGLISH, 3
wished consummation devoutly to be w.
      SHAKESPEARE, 36; SUICIDE, 7
long deferred and often w. for
      BRONTË, 2
wit a w. out of two half-wits
      FOOLISHNESS, 6
Brevity is the soul of w.
      BREVITY, 5; SHAKESPEARE, 32
His foe was folly and his weapon w.
      HUMOUR, 10
I have neither w., nor words, nor worth
      SPEECHES, 3
Impropriety is the soul of w.
      HUMOUR, 12
love robs those who have it of their w.
      LOVE, 23
Music-hall songs provide the dull with w.
      STUPIDITY, 4
proverb is one man's w. and all men's wisdom
      SAYINGS, 3
To the Greeks the Muse gave native w.
      CLASSICS, 4
True w. is nature to advantage dress'd
      HUMOUR, 13
wine is in, the w. is out
      DRUNKENNESS, 3
W. that can creep
      SERVILITY, 3
witch thou shalt not suffer a w. to live
      SUPERNATURAL, 2
witches I have ever believed,...that there are w.
      SUPERNATURAL, 1
wither Age cannot w. her
      ADMIRATION, 5
withered lonely of heart is w. away
      LONELINESS, 9
within that w. which passes show
      MOURNING, 8; SHAKESPEARE, 27
when the fight begins w. himself
      CONFLICT, 2
without I can do w.
      LUXURY, 4
witness thou shalt not bear false w.
      GOD, 6
witnesses this massed multitude of silent w. to...war
      WAR, 22
wits their poetry is conceived and composed in their w.
      POETRY, 4
Great W....to Madness near alli'd
      DRYDEN, 3
witty stumbling on something w.
      AUSTEN, 13
wives Bricklayers kick their w. to death
      WELLS, 3
husbands and w....belong to different sexes
      SEXES, 6
husbands, love your w.
      MARRIAGE, 10
Translations (like w.) are seldom faithful
      TRANSLATION, 1
W. are young men's mistresses
      MARRIAGE, 5
you do not make the laws but...are the w....of those v .io do
      WOMEN, 21
wiving Hanging and w. goes by destiny
      DESTINY, 11
woe Much in sorrow, oft in w.
      ENDURANCE, 13
suits of w.
      MOURNING, 8; SHAKESPEARE, 24
w. to him that is alone when he falleth
      FRIE..DSHIP, 1
W. to the vanquished
      DEFEAT, 4
w. unto them that...follow strong drink
      ALCOHOL, 3
wolf the w. in the sheep's clothing
      APPEARANCES, 1
woman A diplomat...always remembers a w.'s birthday
      AGE, 21
A man is only as old as the w.
      AGE, 27
Any w. who understands the problems of running a home
      POLITICS, 44
a w....ought to lay aside...modesty with her skirt
      SEX, 23
a w.'s reason
      WOMEN, 38
A w. will always sacrifice herself
      WOMEN, 27
body of a weak and feeble w.
      ELIZABETH I, 7; ROYALTY, 6
Christ-like heroes and w.-worshipping Don Juans
      MEN, 6
educate a w. you educate a family
      EDUCATION, 17
Every w. is infallibly to be gained
      FLATTERY, 2
Every w. should marry
      MARRIAGE, 24
Frailty, thy name is w.
      WEAKNESS, 2; WOMEN, 37
good w. if I had five thousand
      MONEY, 20
hell a fury like a w. scorned
      CONGREVE, 7; LOVE AND HATE, 3
I am a w.? When I think, I must speak
      SHAKESPEARE, 21
if a w. have long hair
      APPEARANCE, 2
If a w. like Eva Peron with no ideals
      IDEALISM, 4; THATCHER, 5
International W.'s Day
      RUSSIAN REVOLUTION, 2
It is a great glory in a w.
      WOMEN, 42
I would...guess that Anon...was often a w.
      WOMEN, 47; WOOLF, 5
Man for the field and w. for the hearth
      SEXES, 14
Man to command and w. to obey
      SEXES, 14
Man with the head and w. with the heart
      SEXES, 14
No one delights more in vengeance than a w.
      REVENGE, 5; WOMEN, 22
nor w. neither
      MANKIND, 13; SHAKESPEARE, 35
No w. should ever be quite accurate about her age
      WILDE, 18

No w. so naked as…underneath her clothes	NAKEDNESS, 2
Old age is w.'s hell	OLD AGE, 14
one can…see in a little girl the threat of a w.	CHILDREN, 2
One is not born a w.	BEAUVOIR, 2; WOMEN, 6
one of w. born	BIRTH, 6
She makes love just like a w.	WOMEN, 17
such beauty as a w.'s eye	LEARNING, 7
Than to ever let a w. in my life	MISOGYNY, 2
the help and support of the w. I love	LOVE, 69
the rib…made he a w.	WOMEN, 8
The w. that deliberates is lost	ADDISON, 3
the w. who is really kind to dogs	WOMEN, 7
The w. who outranks us all	ANTHONY, 1
To know the *mind* of a w.	LOVE, 37
Twenty years of romance makes a w. look like a ruin	WILDE, 30
What does a w. want	WOMEN, 19
When a w. becomes a scholar	WOMEN, 31
who can find a virtuous w.	WOMEN, 9
Why can't a w. be more like a man	MEN, 7
will not stand…being called a w. in my own house	WAUGH, 16
w. as old as she looks	AGE, 12
w. has her way	SEXES, 8
W. is always fickle and changing	VIRGIL, 7; WOMEN, 45
w. is an animal that	WOMEN, 26
w. is his game	SEXES, 13; TENNYSON, 25
W. is unrivaled as a wet nurse	WOMEN, 44
w….knowing anything	AUSTEN, 8; WOMEN, 4
W.'s virtue is man's greatest invention	SEXES, 12; VIRTUE, 11
w.'s weapon is her tongue	WOMEN, 20
w.'s whole existence	SEXES, 3
W. was God's *second* mistake	NIETZSCHE, 3
womanhood W. is the great fact in her life	WOMEN, 39
womankind Honour to W.	CHRISTINE DE PISAN, 2
whole race of w. is…made subject to man	WOMAN'S ROLE, 2
womb mother's w. /Untimely ripp'd	BIRTH, 6
no new baby in the w. of our society	RUSSIA, 3
teeming w. of royal kings	ENGLAND, 20; SHAKESPEARE, 97
women A homely face…aided many w. heavenward	APPEARANCE, 1
all w. do	MARRIAGE, 3
a snare in which the feet of w. have always become readily entangled	WOMEN, 1
Because w. can do nothing except love	WOMEN, 28
defense effort in terms of defending w.	WAR, 57
Give w. the vote	SHAW, 10
God withheld the sense of humour from w.	WOMEN, 12
I don't think men and w. were meant to live together	SEXES, 7
If civilisation is to advance…it must be through…w.	PANKHURST, 3
If w. didn't exist,…money…no meaning	WOMEN, 32
It is a sad feature…that only w….have time to write novels	WRITERS, 15
Most w. have no characters	WOMEN, 36
Most w. set out to try to change a man	CHANGE, 4
Music and w. I cannot but give way to	MUSIC, 19
Older w. are best	SEX, 14
proper function of w.	ELIOT, 4; WOMEN, 18
souls of w. are so small	BUTLER, 6
the only advantage w. have over men –…they can cry	SEXES, 11
The question of the rights of w.	WOMEN, 46
There are two kinds of w.	WOMEN, 35
There never will be…equality until w….make laws	ANTHONY, 2
The War between Men and W.	SEXES, 15
the w. whose eyes have been washed…with tears	WOMEN, 16
tide in the affairs of w.	BYRON, 12
Whatever w. do, they must do it twice as well	EQUALITY, 18
When w. go wrong	SEX, 37; WEST, 11
Why are w…so much more interesting to men	SEXES, 17
Why need…w. know so much	BROWNING, 5
W….are either better or worse than men	LA BRUYERE, 3; WOMEN, 24
W. are much more like each other	CHESTERFIELD, 11; WOMEN, 13
w. become like their mothers	SEXES, 16; WILDE, 12
W. cannot be part of the Institute of France	CURIE, 1
w. defend themselves so poorly	WOMEN, 14
W. exist…solely for the propagation of the species	WOMAN'S ROLE, 4
W. had always fought for men	PANKHURST, 4
W. have served…as looking-glasses	WOMEN, 48
w….ill-using them and then confessing it	WOMEN, 43
W. never have young minds	WOMEN, 15
w….not so young as…painted	BEERBOHM, 6
w. require both	WOMEN, 10
w. their rights and nothing less	ANTHONY, 4
W. who love the same man	BEERBOHM, 9

W. would rather be right than reasonable	WOMEN, 30
womman worthy w. al hir lyve	CHAUCER, 4
wonder Many a man has been a w. to the world	ADMIRATION, 3
Philosophy is the product of w.	PHILOSOPHY, 8; WONDER, 2
the common w. of all men	INDIVIDUALITY, 1
wonders His w. to perform	COWPER, 6; GOD, 13
wondrous When I survey the w. Cross	HUMILITY, 6
wont seen me as he was w. to see me	TROLLOPE, 2
woodman w. spare the beechen tree	TREES, 2
W., spare that tree	TREES, 6
woods fresh w., and pastures new	CHANGE, 12
the w. decay and fall	MORTALITY, 11
We'll to the w. no more	ENDING, 2
word better w. than prefabricated	WORDS, 4
but a w. and a blow	VIOLENCE, 2
Good isn't the w.	GILBERT, 10
Greeks had a W. for It	LANGUAGE, 1
in the beginning was the w.	WORDS, 1
Rehearsing a play is making the w. flesh	PLAYS, 3
the kingdom of God is not in w., but in power	GOD, 8
What is honour? A w.	HONOUR, 4; SHAKESPEARE, 42
when *I* use a w.	CARROLL, 12; MEANING, 1
words Be not the slave of W.	WORDS, 3
beet w. in the best order	COLERIDGE, 15; POETRY AND PROSE, 2
by skilful arrangement of your w.	WRITING, 6
fine w. butter no parsnips	WORDS, 10
For w., like Nature, half reveal	TENNYSON, 10; WORDS, 12
I always try to get as many w.	VERBOSITY, 1
It wasn't the w. /That frightened the birds	INNUENDO, 1
Man does not live by w. alone	WORDS, 11
Men of few w. are the best	BREVITY, 6; SHAKESPEARE, 46
neither wit, nor w., nor worth	SPEECHES, 1
thanks to w., we have often sunk to the level of the demons	HUXLEY, 3; WORDS, 6
the barbarous, gothic times when w. had a meaning	WORDS, 5
uses his w. as a quack uses his remedies	VERBOSITY, 3
use the most common,…w.	LANGUAGE, 20
W. are like leaves	VERBOSITY, 4
W. are men's daughters	WORDS, 8
w. are the daughters of earth	LANGUAGE, 11
W. are…the most powerful drug	KIPLING, 10; WORDS, 7
w. but wind	BUTLER, 4; WORDS, 2
w. left unsaid and deeds left undone	REGRET, 11
w. once spoke…never be recall'd	SPEECH, 6
Wordsworth Mr W. is never interrupted	INTERRUPTIONS, 2
W.'s healing power	ARNOLD, 11; WORDSWORTH, 1
W. went to the Lakes	WORDSWORTH, 1
wore w. enough for modesty	MODESTY, 1
work dignity in w.	WORK, 2
For men must w., and women must weep	SEXES, 9
I like w.; it fascinates me	IDLENESS, 3
it is poor grub, poor pay, and easy w.	ENGLAND, 12
No, this right hand shall w. it all off	SCOTT, 9
no w., nor device, nor knowledge…in the grave	TRANSIENCE, 4; WORK, 1
only place where success comes before w.	SUCCESS, 6; WORK, 10
success…by dint of hard w.	EFFORT, 4; SUCCESS, 4
the world's w.,…is done by men who do not feel…well	ILLNESS, 2
they must hate to w. for a living	MARRIAGE, 49
To sport would be as tedious as to w.	LEISURE, 3
When w. is a pleasure	WORK, 4
W. banishes those three great evils	VOLTAIRE, 7; WORK, 12
W….by those employees who have not yet reached…incompetence	INCOMPETENCE, 4
W. expands so as to fill the time	WORK, 7
W. is much more fun than fun	COWARD, 11
W. is necessary for man	WORK, 8
W. is the curse of the drinking classes	WILDE, 41
W. is the grand cure	WORK, 3
workers hiring taxis…handing out redundancy notices…w.	INCOMPETENCE, 2
W. of the world, unite	MARXISM, 1
workhouse 'The W.' – always a word of shame	POVERTY, 13
working God as a w. hypothesis	GOD, 9
No writer before the…19th century wrote about the w. classes	CLASS, 20; WAUGH, 22
To the ordinary w. man,…Socialism	SOCIALISM, 1
working-class the w. which, raw and half-developed	ARNOLD, 5
works all his w.	RENUNCIATION, 1
faith, if it hath not w., is dead	FAITH, 4
they were judged every man according to their w.	JUDGMENT, 3

W. done least rapidly — PERFECTION, 2
workshop England...the w. of the world — ENGLAND, 7
world a citizen of the w. — NATIONALITY, 4
A great writer creates a w. of his own — WRITERS, 5
All's right with the w. — BROWNING, 14
all the uses of this w. — WORLD-WEARINESS, 4
All the w.'s a stage — HUMAN CONDITION, 8; SHAKESPEARE, 18
A man travels the w. over — HOME, 2
as good be out of the w. — FASHION, 2
a W. in a grain of sand — BLAKE, 7
brave new w. /That has such people in't — MANKIND, 14; SHAKESPEARE, 114
citizen of the w. — COURTESY, 1
dominate the w. — WILDE, 36
excellent foppery of the w. — SHAKESPEARE, 61
Feed the W. — CHARITY, 3
Germany will be...a w. power — GERMANY, 2
God so loved the w. — CHRISTIANITY, 6
good deed in a naughty w. — GOOD, 6
Had we but w. enough, and time — SHYNESS, 3
he could not avoid making Him set the w. in motion — CREATION, 10
I am the light of the w. — CHRISTIANITY, 7
I called the New W. into existence — AMERICA, 5
If all the w. were paper — NONSENSE, 1
If the w. were good for...speculation — SPECULATION, 2
in this harsh w. — MOURNING, 9
I...pass through this w. but once — MORTALITY, 6
It's the same the whole w. over — POVERTY AND WEALTH, 1
joy that a man is born into the w. — BIRTH, 1
little sisters to all the w. — WOMEN, 16
Many a man has been a wonder to the w. — ADMIRATION, 3
Never having been able to succeed in the w. — ENVY, 6
One w. at a time — AFTERLIFE, 10
queen for all the w. — SHAKESPEARE, 50
Stop the W., I Want to Get Off — WORLD-WEARINESS, 3
Superstition sets the whole w. in flames — SUPERSTITION, 5
the hand that rules the w. — INFLUENCE, 4
The w....is but a large prison — EXECUTION, 9
The w. is but a school of inquiry — CURIOSITY, 3
The w. is disgracefully managed — COMPLAINTS, 3
The w. is made up for the most part of fools — FOOLISHNESS, 3
the w. must be made safe for...fifty years — WAR, 15
the w.'s mine oyster — OPPORTUNITY, 7; SHAKESPEARE, 83
the w. would not be the same — NUCLEAR WEAPONS, 1
they only saved the w. — BELLOC, 5; HEROISM, 1
This is the way the w. ends — ELIOT, 5; ENDING, 1
this little w. — ENGLAND, 20; SHAKESPEARE, 97
This w. nis but a thurghfare — LIFE AND DEATH, 3
though the w. perish — JUSTICE, 4
turn your back upon the w. — PERFECTION, 3
When all the w. dissolves — DOOMSDAY, 4
where in this small-talking w. — MEANING, 2
which taketh away the sin of the w. — CHRISTIANITY, 5
w. is a beautiful place — HUMAN CONDITION, 3
w. is charged with the grandeur of God — GOD, 20
w....made safe for democracy — DEMOCRACY, 9
w. without end — ETERNITY, 2
Yeats is not a man of this w. — YEATS, 1
worldly The W. Hope men set their Hearts upon — TRANSIENCE, 8
worlds best of possible w. — OPTIMISM, 10; VOLTAIRE, 5
So many w. — ACTION, 5; TENNYSON, 13
Wandering between two w. — ARNOLD, 9
we live in the best of all possible w. — OPTIMISM, 6; PESSIMISM, 4
worm a w. at one end and a fool at the other — FISHING, 2
The cut w. — FORGIVENESS, 3
worms Sir, you have tasted two whole w. — SPOONERISMS, 3
w. have eaten them, but not for love — SHAKESPEARE, 23
worrying W. is the most natural and spontaneous of...functions — WORRY, 4
worse Dublin, though...much w. than London — PLACES, 4
for better for w. — MARRIAGE, 15
If my books had been any w. — CHANDLER, 3
worship freedom...to w. — HUMAN RIGHTS, 4
No one can w. God...on an empty stomach — BUSINESS, 14
O w. the King — GOD, 18
worshippers the one God whose w....still trust in Him — LUCK, 1
worst His w. is better than any other person's best — HAZLITT, 4
it was the w. of times — DICKENS, 18; FRENCH REVOLUTION, 1
They...like to be told the w. — BRITISH, 3
we can say 'This is the w.' — OPTIMISM, 7
w. kinde of infortune — CHAUCER, 6

You do your w. — WORLD WAR II, 8
worth A man's w. something — CONFLICT, 2
Paris is w. a mass — PARIS, 2
The w. of a State — STATE, 3
Whatever is w. doing — CHESTERFIELD, 3; EXCELLENCE, 1
worthless a more w. set than Byron — POETS, 9; WELLINGTON, 5
Our parents' age...has produced us, more w. still — HORACE, 14
wound W. with a touch — SATIRE, 2
wounds To fight and not to heed the w. — SELFLESSNESS, 2
wrapped w. him in swaddling clothes — CHRISTMAS, 5
wrapping perceive Christmas through its w. — CHRISTMAS, 15
wrath trampling out the vintage where the grapes of w. — GOD, 21
wreckage Literature is strewn with the w. of men — WRITERS, 16
wren The w. goes to't — ANIMALISM, 4
wretch a w. who supports with insolence — PATRONAGE, 1
wretched love – all the w. cant of it — LOVE, 30
The only w. are the wise — IGNORANCE, 4
wretches feel what w. feel — HUMILITY, 5
Poor naked w. — WEATHER, 9
write as much as a man ought to w. — WRITING, 20
Better to w. for yourself — CONNOLLY, 9; WRITING, 3
Do not on any account attempt to w. on both sides — EXAMINATIONS, 2
look in thy heart and w. — INSPIRATION, 2
Rock journalism is people who can't w. — POP MUSIC, 9
w. and read comes by nature — LITERACY, 2
w. for children...as you do for adults — WRITING, 5
writer A great w. creates a world of his own — WRITERS, 5
Asking a working w....about critics — CRITICS, 6
A w.'s ambition should be — POSTERITY, 2
Every great and original w. — WORDSWORTH, 10; WRITING, 21
it is necessary to go to a university...to become a successful w. — WRITERS, 2
not a w.'s business to hold opinions — YEATS, 14
No tears in the w. — WRITING, 4
successful w....is indistinguishable — AMERICA, 14
writers As w. become more numerous — GOLDSMITH, 4
No regime has ever loved great w. — WRITERS, 14
writes Moving Finger w. — DESTINY, 4
writhing Reeling and W. — CARROLL, 7
writing All good w. is swimming under water — FITZGERALD, 8
as I had in the w. — PLEASURE, 10
the incurable disease of w. — WRITING, 11
the worst..., is w. about w. — CRITICISM, 2
True ease in w. comes from art — POPE, 9; WRITING, 16
When a man is in doubt about...his w. — POSTERITY, 2
w. an exact man — READING, 1
W. is like getting married — MARRIAGE, 44; WRITING, 15
written Books are well w., or badly w. — BOOKS, 29
books...w. by people who don't understand them — BOOKS, 17
w. or thought, it can be filmed — CINEMA, 5
wrong A door is what a dog is...on the w. side of — NASH, 2
A man should...own he has been in the w. — MISTAKES, 5; POPE, 16
anxious to do the w. thing correctly — ETIQUETTE, 3; SAKI, 14
History is...the w. way of living — HISTORY, 6
Of course not...I may be w. — RUSSELL, 16
orthodoxy...practically means being w. — CHESTERTON, 6; ORTHODOXY, 2
responsible and w. — RESPONSIBILITY, 3
right deed for the w. reason — ELIOT, 7
something is impossible, he is...w. — SCIENCE, 1
something w. with our bloody ships — BOATS, 1
The right divine of kings to govern w. — POPE, 3
the unclouded face of truth suffer w. — JOURNALISM, 15
When women go w. — SEX, 37; WEST, 11
wrongs for one class to appreciate the w. of another — CLASS, 18
Xanadu In X. did Kubla Khan — COLERIDGE, 6; PLEASURE, 4
yacht I had to sink my y. to make my guests go home — FITZGERALD, 4
Yale all the young ladies who attended the Y. promenade dance were laid end to end — PARKER, 5
A whale ship was my Y. College — EDUCATION, 18
Yankee Y. Doodle came to town — AMERICA, 3
yarn web of our life is of a mingled y. — GOOD AND EVIL, 2
year all the y. were playing holidays — LEISURE, 3
Another y.! – another deadly blow — DEFEAT, 6
each day is like a y. — IMPRISONMENT, 6
I said to the man who stood at the gate of the y. — FAITH, 2
Let it be kept till the ninth y. — PUBLISHING, 3
Not to hope for things to last for ever, is what the y. teaches — HORACE, 15; TRANSIENCE, 10
two months of every y. — BYRON, 4
y.'s at the spring — BROWNING, 14

⬛NAMES INDEX⬛

Bible: II Corinthians FAITH, 3; GENEROSITY, 1; WISDOM AND FOOLISHNESS, 2

Bible: Deuteronomy GOD, 5; LIFE AND DEATH, 2; PROPHECY, 1; WEALTH, 1

Bible: Ecclesiastes BOOKS, 3; EVIL, 3; FRIEND-SHIP, 1; KNOWLEDGE, 3; LAUGHTER, 1; MONEY, 4; PLEASURE, 2; PROMISES, 1; TIME, 4; TRANSIENCE, 3, 4; UNITY, 2; WISDOM, 1, 2; WISDOM AND FOOLISHNESS, 1; WORK, 1; YOUTH, 1

Bible: Ecclesiasticus AGE, 5; BORROWING, 1; CURIOSITY, 1; DEATH, 11; FRIENDS, 1; LEARNING, 2; LEISURE, 1; MANNERS, 1; PRAISE, 2; SECRECY, 1; SPEECH, 2

Bible: II Esdras UNDERSTANDING, 1

Bible: Exodus GOD, 6, 7; RETRIBUTION, 2; SUPERNATURAL, 2

Bible: Ezekiel FAMILY, 4

Bible: Genesis ANIMALS, 1; CREATION, 1, 2, 3, 4, 5; CRIME, 1; GARDENS, 3; HEAVEN, 1, 2; HOMOSEXUALITY, 4; JEWS, 2; KNOWLEDGE, 4; LANGUAGE, 2; MANKIND, 2; MURDER, 1; PUNISHMENT, 1, 2; REVENGE, 4; SEXES, 1; STARS, 2; SUNDAY, 1; TREES, 1; UNITY, 3; WOMEN, 8

Bible: Hebrews EXECUTION, 1; FAITH, 1, 2; HOSPITALITY, 2

Bible: Hosea RETRIBUTION, 3

Bible: Isaiah ALCOHOL, 3; CHRISTIANITY, 3; PEACE, 1; PUNISHMENT, 3; TRANSIENCE, 5; WAR AND PEACE, 2

Bible: James FAITH, 4; GIFTS, 1; TEMPTATION, 2

Bible: Jeremiah CHANGE, 1

Bible: Job HUMAN CONDITION, 1; OLD AGE, 1; WISDOM, 3

Bible: John BIRTH, 1; CHRISTIANITY, 4, 5, 6, 7, 8, 9; EVIL, 5; FEAR, 3; HEAVEN, 3; LAST WORDS, 5; LOVE, 6, 7, 8; PEACE, 2; SIN, 3, 4; TRUTH, 4; WORDS, 1

Bible: Lamentations YOUTH, 2

Bible: Luke AGE, 6; ALCOHOL, 5; CHARITY, 5; CHRISTMAS, 5, 6; DEVIL, 1; DOCTORS, 2; EXECUTION, 2; FORGIVENESS, 1; LAST WORDS, 6; LAWYERS, 2; PARTIES, 2; POVERTY AND WEALTH, 2

Bible: Mark CHILDREN, 4; SUNDAY, 2; WEALTH, 2

Bible: Matthew BETRAYAL, 1; CHILDREN, 5; CHRISTIANITY, 10; CHRISTMAS, 7; CHURCH, 1, 2; CRITICISM, 3; DECEPTION, 1; DOOMSDAY, 1; DOUBT, 2; ENEMIES, 1; FOOLISHNESS, 1; FORGIVENESS, 2; GENEROSITY, 2; GIFTS, 2; GUILT, 2; HONOUR, 1; HUMILITY, 1; HYPOCRISY, 1; IMPERFECTION, 1; JUDGMENT, 1, 2; LAST WORDS, 7; LOVE, 9; MARRIAGE, 13; MATERIALISM, 2; MERIT, 1; NEIGHBOURS, 1; PERSISTENCE, 1; PRAYER, 1; REMEDIES, 3; RESULTS, 1; RETRIBUTION, 4; SERVICE, 1; TRANSIENCE, 6; WAR, 6, 7; WEALTH, 3; WORRY, 2

Bible: Micah TRUST, 1

Bible: Numbers BLESSING, 3; SIN, 5

Bible: Philippians VIRTUE, 4

Bible: Proverbs ALCOHOL, 6; CHILDREN, 6; DRUNKENNESS, 5; FOOLISHNESS, 2; FUTURE, 3; PRIDE, 1; RETRIBUTION, 5; SECRECY, 2; SELF-CONTROL, 1; WISDOM, 4; WOMEN, 9

Bible: Revelations DEATH, 13; DEVIL, 2, 3; JUDGMENT, 3; LEADERSHIP, 2

Bible: Ruth LOYALTY, 1

Bible: I Timothy ALCOHOL, 4; CLERGY, 1; MONEY, 5

Bible: II Timothy EVIL, 4; FEAR, 2

Bible: Wisdom JEALOUSY, 1; WISDOM, 5

Bidault, Georges MISTAKES, 2

Bierce, Ambrose BORES, 1; DEBAUCHERY, 1; DISEASE, 6; EGOTISM, 2; FUTURE, 4; MARRIAGE, 14; MIND, 1; MISFORTUNE, 2; OPTIMISM, 4; PAINTING, 2; PATIENCE, 1; PEACE, 3; PHILOSOPHERS, 1; RELIGION, 3

Binding, Rudolph WORLD WAR I, 3

Binyon, Laurence MEMORIALS, 1; MOURNING, 2

Bismarck CHILDREN, 7; POLITICS, 5, 6

Blacker, Valentine PRUDENCE, 2

Blackstone, William JUSTICE, 2; MEMORY, 3; MONARCHY, 3, 4; SOCIETY, 1

Blackwell, Antoinette Brown SEXES, 2; WOMAN'S ROLE, 1

Blair, Robert WHISTLING, 1

Blake, Charles Dupee SLEEP, 2

Blake, William BEAUTY, 4; CONFLICT, 1; CREATION, 6, 7; DESIRE, 1, 2, 3; DOUBT, 3; ENGLAND, 1; EXCESS, 3; FORGIVENESS, 3; GENERALIZATIONS, 1; GREATNESS, 2; HELL, 1; HUMILITY, 2; IMPRISONMENT, 1; INFINITY, 1; LOVE, 10, 11; MANKIND, 3; PERCEPTION, 1, 2; PRAYER, 2; PROOF, 1; SOUL, 3; SUITABILITY, 1; TRUTH, 5; WISDOM, 6, 7

Blank, Joost de OPPRESSION, 2; RACISM, 4

Blunden, Edmund POETRY, 6

Blythe, Ronald AGE, 7; OLD AGE, 2

Boccaccio, Giovanni LOVE, 12; RIDICULE, 1; WOMAN'S ROLE, 2

Bogart, Humphrey MISQUOTATIONS, 7

Bohr, Niels EXPERTS, 1; SUPERSTITION, 1

Boileau, Nicolas ADMIRATION, 1; VICE, 2

Boleyn, Anne MARTYRDOM, 1

Bolitho, William PLACES, 1

Bolt, Robert ARISTOCRACY, 3; MORALITY, 2

Bone, David SELFISHNESS, 2

Bonhoeffer, Dietrich GOD, 9, 10

Bono, Edward de DISAPPOINTMENT, 1

Book of Common Prayer, The AGE, 8; CHARITY, 6; DANGER, 1; DEATH, 14; ETERNITY, 2; LEARNING, 3; MARRIAGE, 15; PEACE, 4; PRAYER, 3; RENUNCIATION, 1; SIN, 6

Boone, Daniel CONFUSION, 1

Borges, Jorge Luis UNIVERSE, 2

Borrow, George SATISFACTION, 1; SUICIDE, 1

Bosquet, Pierre WAR, 8

Bossidy, John Collins SNOBBERY, 2

Boswell, James GIBBON, 1; VOLTAIRE, 1

Botha, Elize RACISM, 2

Botha, P. W. POLITICS, 7

Bottomley, Horatio William PUNS, 2

Boucicault, Dion TIME, 5

Boulton, H. E. ROYALTY, 1

Bowen, Charles JUSTICE, 3

Bowen, E. E. PARTING, 2; SPORT AND GAMES, 1

Bowen, Elizabeth EXPERIENCE, 3; INNOCENCE, 4; JEALOUSY, 2

Bowen, Lord METAPHYSICS, 1

Bowra, Maurice FOOD, 2

Bracken, Brendan HUMOUR, 3

Bracken, Peg APPEARANCE, 3

Bradbury, Malcolm ENGLISH, 2; FRIENDSHIP, 2; NEWSPAPERS, 2; SEX, 6; SYMPATHY, 1

Bradley, F. H. LUCK, 1; METAPHYSICS, 2; STUPIDITY, 1; UNDERSTANDING, 2

Bradley, Omar Nelson NUCLEAR WEAPONS, 1

Brahms, Johannes INSULTS, 3

Brancusi, Constantin GREATNESS, 3

Brando, Marlon ACTORS, 1

Branson, Richard LEADERSHIP, 3

Braude, Jacob M. ENVY, 3

Brecht, Bertolt HEROISM, 2; INJUSTICE, 1; NONSENSE, 2; PEACE, 5; WAR, 9

Brenan, Gerald ARTISTS, 1; FUNERALS, 2; LANGUAGE, 3; OLD AGE, 3; POETS, 1; SELF-KNOWLEDGE, 2

Bridges, Robert BEAUTY, 5; DAY, 2

Bright, John ENGLAND, 2; FORCE, 1

Brittain, Vera POLITICS, 8; WRITERS, 2

Bronowski, Jacob CRUELTY, 1; SCIENCE, 1, 2

Brontë, Anne

Brontë, Charlotte

Brontë, Emily BELIEF, 1; IMPRISONMENT, 2; SUFFERING, 2

Brooke, Rupert CAMBRIDGE, 2; ENGLAND, 3; FLOWERS, 2; NOSTALGIA, 3; WAR, 10, 11

Brooks, Mel OSTENTATION, 1; THEATRE, 2

Brooks, Phillips CHRISTMAS, 8

Brougham, Henry Peter PUBLIC, 4

Brown, Thomas Edward GARDENS, 4

Browne, Cecil JEWS, 4

Browne, Thomas CHARITY, 7; CRITICISM, 4; EXPLOITATION, 1; INDIVIDUALITY, 3; JUDGMENT, 4; MANKIND, 4; NATURE, 1; SELF, 1; SUPERNATURAL, 3

Browne, William CAMBRIDGE, 3; OXFORD, 4

Browning, Elizabeth Barrett GOD, 11; LOVE, 13; RESPECTABILITY, 1; SORROW, 1

Browning, Robert AGE, 9; AMBITION, 2, 3; CHRISTIANITY, 11; CONFLICT, 2; DEATH, 15; DOOMSDAY, 2; DRINKS, 1; ENGLAND, 4; EQUALITY, 4; FREEDOM, 1; HEAVEN, 4; IMPRESSIONABILITY, 1; KISSING, 1; LIFE, 6; LOVE, 14; MONTHS, 3; PERFECTION, 2; POSSIBILITY, 1; ROYALTY, 3; SOUL, 4; SUMMONS, 3

Brummel, 'Beau' OBESITY, 2

Bruno, Giordano COURAGE, 2

Bruyère, Jean de La ALCOHOL, 7; AMBITION, 4; CRIME, 2; CRITICISM, 9; IMPETUOSITY, 1; LAUGHTER, 3; LIFE AND DEATH, 6; MEMORY, 4; MISFORTUNE, 6; POLITICS, 9; SERVILITY, 2; WOMEN, 24

Buchanan, Robert Williams MODESTY, 1

Buck, Pearl AGE, 10; MUSIC, 7

Buckingham, Duke of FOOLISHNESS, 3; INTRIGUE, 1

Buddha RELIGION, 4; RIGHTEOUSNESS, 3

Buffon, Comte de STYLE, 1

Bullock, Alan HITLER, 1

Bulmer-Thomas, Ivor CONCEIT, 2

Bulwer-Lytton, Edward ENTHUSIASM, 1; WRITING, 1

Bunyan, John DESPAIR, 1; DREAMS, 2; VIOLENCE, 2

Burgess, Anthony CLEANNESS, 1; FITZGERALD, 1; SLEEP, 3

Burke, Edmund ACCUSATION, 1; BEAUTY, 6; CHIVALRY, 3; COMPROMISE, 2; CORRUPTION, 1; DANGER, 2; EUROPE, 1; EXAMPLE, 1; FORCE, 2; FREEDOM, 2; HONOUR, 2; INDIFFERENCE, 2; INGRATITUDE, 1; JUDGMENT, 5; POWER, 4; RELIGION, 5; SUPERSTITION, 2; THEORY, 1; TOLERANCE, 1; YIELDING, 1

Burke, Johnny OPTIMISM, 5

Burney, Fanny INNOCENCE, 1

Burns, George GOVERNMENT, 4

Burns, John RIVERS, 1

Burns, Robert CRUELTY, 2; DELUSION, 1; DEVIL, 4; DISAPPOINTMENT, 2; FOOD, 3; FRIENDSHIP, 3, 4; LOVE, 15; MEN, 1

Burton, Richard ACTORS, 2

Burton, Robert DISEASE, 7; MELANCHOLY, 2, 3; RELIGION, 6; SMOKING, 2; WRITING, 2

Bussy-Rabutin ABSENCE, 2

Butler, Joseph AFTERLIFE, 2

Butler, R. A. POLITICS, 10; SPEECHES, 2

Butler, Samuel BEQUESTS, 1; CARLYLE, 1; DOGS, 2; ENGLISH, 3; EXTRAVAGANCE, 2; FAITHFULNESS, 2; INDULGENCE, 1; LAWYERS, 3; LIFE, 7, 8; LOSS, 1; LOVE, 16; MARRIAGE, 16; POSTERITY, 2; PRAISE, 3; PROGRESS, 2; PUBLIC, 5; PUNISHMENT, 4; RELIGION, 7; SPECULATION, 1; SPONTANEITY, 1; WOMEN, 10; WORDS, 2; YIELDING, 2

Butz, Earl CONTRACEPTION, 3

Byrom, John CHRISTMAS, 9

Byron, Lord ADULTERY, 1; AGE, 11; BEAUTY, 7; BORES, 2; CHAUCER, 1; COWPER, 1; CRITICS, 2; DEPARTURE, 4; DETERMINATION, 3; DOGS, 3; DRUNKENNESS, 6; FEMINISM, 2; FRIENDS, 2; HEROISM, 2; LOVE AND HATE, 1; MERRYMAKING, 1; NATURE, 2; PLEASURE, 3; SELF-INTEREST, 1; SEPARATION, 1; SEXES, 3; SHERIDAN, 1; TRUTH, 6, 7; WAR, 12; WOMEN, 11

Cabell, James DRINKS, 2; OPTIMISM, 6; PESSIMISM, 4

Caecus, Appius RESPONSIBILITY, 2

Caesar, Julius FRANCE, 1; INTEGRITY, 2; IRREVOCABILITY, 1; LAST WORDS, 8; VICTORY, 1

Cagney, James MISQUOTATIONS, 8

Cahn, Sammy LOVE AND MARRIAGE, 1

Calderone, Mary SEX, 7

Callaghan, James LYING, 2; SUPPORT, 1